Fodor's 2000

P9-ECV-892

Mexico

Fodor's Travel Publications, Inc. • New York, Toronto, London, Sydney, Auckland

www.fodors.com/mexico

CONTENTS

MAPS

Circled letters in text correspond to letters on the photographs. For more information on the sights pictured, turn to the indicated page number Ⓐ▷ on each photograph.

DESTINATION MEXICO

It could happen while you're climbing the Pyramid of the Magician at the magnificent Maya ruins of Uxmal in the Yucatán, descending into the formidable Barrancas del Cobre (Copper Canyon), strolling through the shady plaza of a colonial Heartland town in the heat and torpor of siesta time, lolling on the beach in glittering Acapulco, snorkeling off Quintana Roo in the waters of the Caribbean, or gawking at the variety of chiles in Oaxaca's Central de Abastos market. And you won't be in Mexico too long before it does happen—you realize that what makes this country so alluring is its diversity. Mexico is a blend—of peoples, of cultures, of landscapes, of worlds new and old, of the legacies of the vanquished and the conqueror—and the mix is so enchanting that you'll hardly even notice that you're falling under its spell.

MEXICO CITY
AND SIDE TRIPS

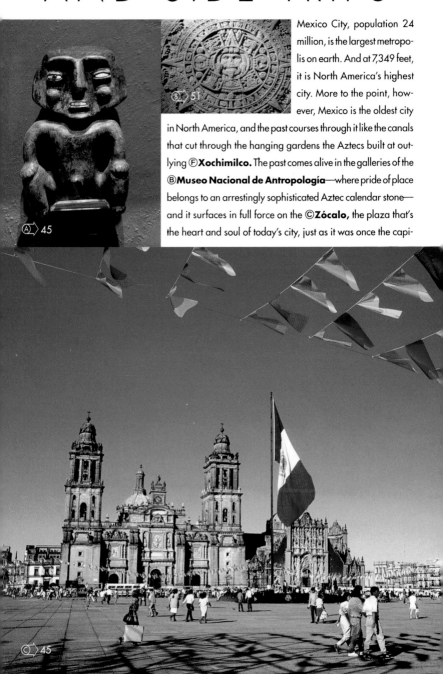

Ⓐ▷45

Ⓑ▷51

Mexico City, population 24 million, is the largest metropolis on earth. And at 7,349 feet, it is North America's highest city. More to the point, however, Mexico is the oldest city in North America, and the past courses through it like the canals that cut through the hanging gardens the Aztecs built at outlying Ⓕ**Xochimilco.** The past comes alive in the galleries of the Ⓑ**Museo Nacional de Antropología**—where pride of place belongs to an arrestingly sophisticated Aztec calendar stone— and it surfaces in full force on the Ⓒ**Zócalo,** the plaza that's the heart and soul of today's city, just as it was once the capi-

Ⓒ▷45

tal of the Aztec empire, Tenochtitlán. A stroll through this square takes you past the 16th-century Catedral Metropolitana, Latin America's oldest and largest cathedral, to the ruined Ⓐ**Templo Mayor,** the ceremonial Aztec center of human sacrifice. An adjacent museum displays the treasures unearthed during its excavation. Southeast of the city the gilded carvings in Ⓓ**Iglesia de Santo Domingo,** one of 224 churches the Spanish built in the valley of Puebla, hover over the faithful as if to promise a glittering life after death. Looming above the city and the Valley of Mexico, the rumbling 17,887-foot volcano

Ⓔ**Popocatépetl** is a constant reminder of forces mightier than any civilization, past or present, and an opportunity to hike off last night's rich chicken mole dinner beneath the crater, so long as you don't pass the 12,000-foot danger point.

BAJA

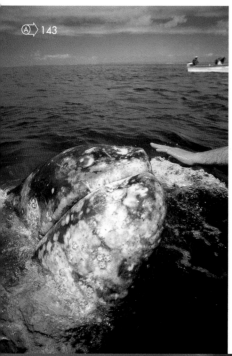

Ⓐ 143

Lively border traffic colors the culture of the upper reaches of Baja Norte, the half of the peninsula attached to the state of California, where Tijuana keeps right on living up to its raucous and rowdy reputation. Down the coast Rosarita and Puerto Nuevo open their doors for weekending Californians; likewise Ⓓ**Ensenada,** which also has a busy fishing port and fish market to show for it. But you can't say you've really experienced the 1,000-mile-long finger of land that is Baja California until you head south, off the beaten path. Here, in some of the most beautiful terrain on earth, quiet

Ⓑ 160

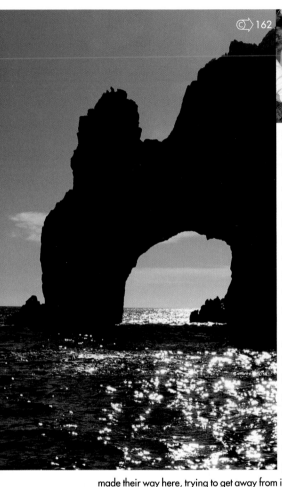

162
125

fishing villages and pristine beaches punctuate two coastlines. On the Sea of Cortés you can dip your paddles into protected Bahía Concepción—or on the Pacific coast, off Ⓐ**San Ignacio,** pull up within petting distance of migrating gray whales. Inland, boulder-strewn wastes are dotted with cacti, mountain peaks soar to 10,000 feet, and the high sierra yields its wonders as you hike through Parque Nacional San Pedro Martir. Galleries near Mision San Javier display ancient paintings left by Baja's earliest inhabitants. In their wake, explorers, missionaries, pirates, and movie stars have made their way here, trying to get away from it all. The silhouettes of golfers, anglers, and sun seekers stand out in today's crowds, which flock to the elegant hostelries of that still wonderfully natural area at Baja California's tip known as Los Cabos. And with secluded coves like Playa de Amor and a spectacular land's end at Ⓒ**El Arco,** it's no wonder that newlyweds are among the Los Cabos pilgrims—the hacienda-style Ⓑ**Palmilla** even has its own adobe wedding chapel.

SONORA

Ⓐ▷189

Imagine Arizona a hundred years ago, when cowboys drove cattle across wide open ranges and lined up along the bars of saloons to sing *rancheras,* ballads right out of the storybooks of the Old West. Then add a coastline— a fringe of beach washed by a balmy turquoise sea—and you've conjured up Sonora, Mexico's northernmost state. South of Nogales, a some-times-rowdy border town, relatively unspoiled coastal towns like Bahía Kino and Guaymas keep company with quiet, undiscovered seaside ⒷⒸ**San Carlos,** for exam-ple. And arid coffee-colored hills tumble into the Sea of

Ⓑ▷187

Cortés in a profusion of creosote bushes, saguaro, and organ-pipe cacti. Off-shore, dolphins, pelicans, sea lions, and migrating whales thrive—as do swim-mers, snorkelers, sea kayakers, and enthusiasts of just about every other aquatic stripe. Inland, Father Eusebio Francisco Kino's missions pop-ulate towns like Magdalena and San Ignacio, and deserts give way to stands of cotton-woods and evergreens rising into the foothills of the Sierra Madre. Their hidden treasures include Ⓐ**Alamos,** a former silver-mining center that is one of Mexico's loveliest and best-preserved colonial towns.

Ⓒ▷187

The high desert of the Sierra Madre gives way to high drama when it plunges into the four gorges known as the Barrancas del Cobre—the Copper Canyon—a mile deep, a mile wide, and four times the size of the Grand Canyon. Most people see it from the Chihuahua al Pacífico railroad on its run between Los

COPPER CANYON

Mochis and Chihuahua City. From whistle stops like the one at ©**Divisadero,** you'll see how this difficult terrain has pushed its resident Tarahumara Indians to master extraordinary skills—like superlong-distance running. Tarahumara ancestors left marks all around the Paquimé Ruins at Ⓐ**Casas Grandes.** Of the priests who worked among the tribes, creating missions like the one at Ⓑ**Cusárare,** Father Miguel Hidalgo began preaching Mexican independence in 1810. A hundred years later General Pancho Villa launched Mexico's civil war from his home in lively Chihuahua City.

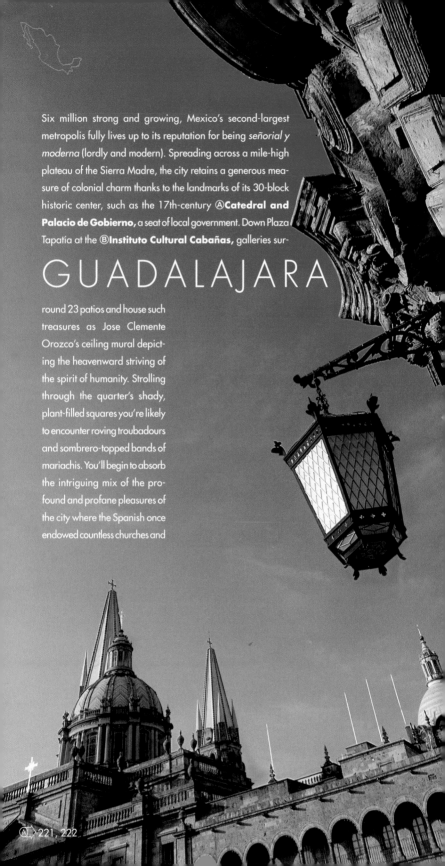

Six million strong and growing, Mexico's second-largest metropolis fully lives up to its reputation for being *señorial y moderna* (lordly and modern). Spreading across a mile-high plateau of the Sierra Madre, the city retains a generous measure of colonial charm thanks to the landmarks of its 30-block historic center, such as the 17th-century Ⓐ**Catedral and Palacio de Gobierno,** a seat of local government. Down Plaza Tapatía at the Ⓑ**Instituto Cultural Cabañas,** galleries sur-

GUADALAJARA

round 23 patios and house such treasures as Jose Clemente Orozco's ceiling mural depicting the heavenward striving of the spirit of humanity. Strolling through the quarter's shady, plant-filled squares you're likely to encounter roving troubadours and sombrero-topped bands of mariachis. You'll begin to absorb the intriguing mix of the profound and profane pleasures of the city where the Spanish once endowed countless churches and

monuments with vast sums—
and invented such traditional
Mexican mainstays as *el jarabe
tapatío* (the hat dance) and
charreadas (rodeos), in which
cowboys still compete weekly.
In the Ⓓ**Mercado Libertad,**
one of Latin America's largest
enclosed markets, with its
thousand-odd stalls, you can
haggle with local vendors
for a piece of fruit or a gold
watch. Locally made handicrafts are the reward for a

Ⓑ⟩221

Ⓒ⟩235

trip across the cactus-studded
plains surrounding Guadalajara. In Tlaquepaque and
nearby Ⓒ**Tonalá** thousands
of artisans fashion artful ceramics and glassware, from
the baroque to the whimsical
and contemporary. It's all sold
in outdoor markets, studios in old adobe houses, and shops along
pedestrian malls and plazas. The dusty cobblestone streets of
these towns and their air of old-time Mexico make a refreshing antidote to Guadalajara's urban bustle. Nearby at Tequila
you can drink at the source of Mexico's famous firewater.

Ⓓ⟩232

In this fertile swath of farm country, traditions cling as tenaciously as the prickly pear and other cacti that spring from the rolling landscape. On Ⓑ**Lake Pátzcuaro,** Purépecha Indians fish and ply their canoes as they have for hundreds of years. Even in

THE HEARTLAND

Ⓐ▷ 281

mountainous San Miguel de Allende, known for its substantial English-speaking community, local women still gather at the public *lavandería* for laundry and gossip. These connections with the past keep the Heartland's turbulent history alive, as do a wealth of monuments, museums, and landmarks. In Ⓐ**Querétaro,** handsome mansions bespeak civic pride that stems in no small measure from the city's status as an eyewitness to history—it was here that Mexico's short-term Emperor Maximilian was executed and the Mexican constitution signed. In Ⓒ**Guanajuato,** musicians

Ⓑ▷ 298

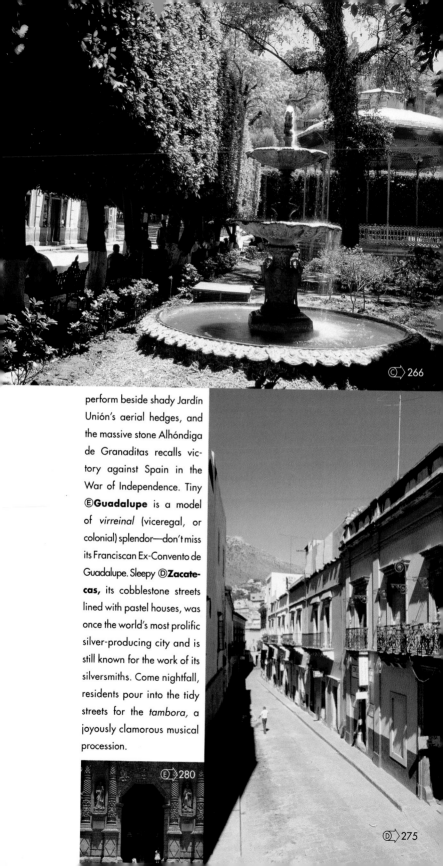

perform beside shady Jardín Unión's aerial hedges, and the massive stone Alhóndiga de Granaditas recalls victory against Spain in the War of Independence. Tiny ⒠**Guadalupe** is a model of *virreinal* (viceregal, or colonial) splendor—don't miss its Franciscan Ex-Convento de Guadalupe. Sleepy ⒟**Zacatecas,** its cobblestone streets lined with pastel houses, was once the world's most prolific silver-producing city and is still known for the work of its silversmiths. Come nightfall, residents pour into the tidy streets for the *tambora,* a joyously clamorous musical procession.

Ⓒ▷266

Ⓔ▷280

Ⓓ▷275

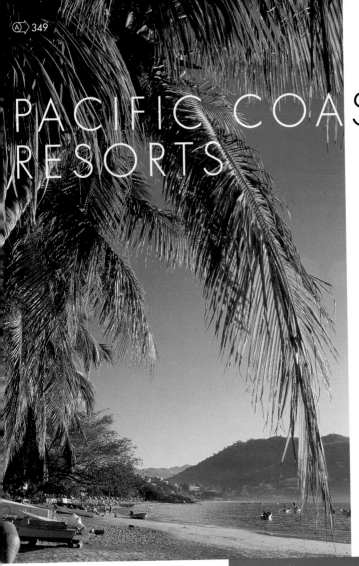

Ⓐ 349

PACIFIC COAST RESORTS

Ⓑ 309

People call it the Mexican Riviera and Gold Coast, but the most apt way to refer to this jungle-backed coastline might just be Tropical Paradise. Historical landmarks like the colonial church of Nuestra Señora de Guadalupe in the once-sleepy fishing village—now glittering resort—of Ⓒ**Puerto Vallarta** are few and far between. But the 900 miles of cove-scalloped white strands edging the Pacific provide more-than-ample diversion for sun worshippers and water-sports lovers, from angling in Ⓑ**Mazatlán,** to snorkeling off the white- or black-sand beaches of Manzanillo, to simply feeling sand between your toes in low-key Ⓐ**Zihuatanejo** or its glitzy neighbor, Ixtapa.

Ⓒ 323

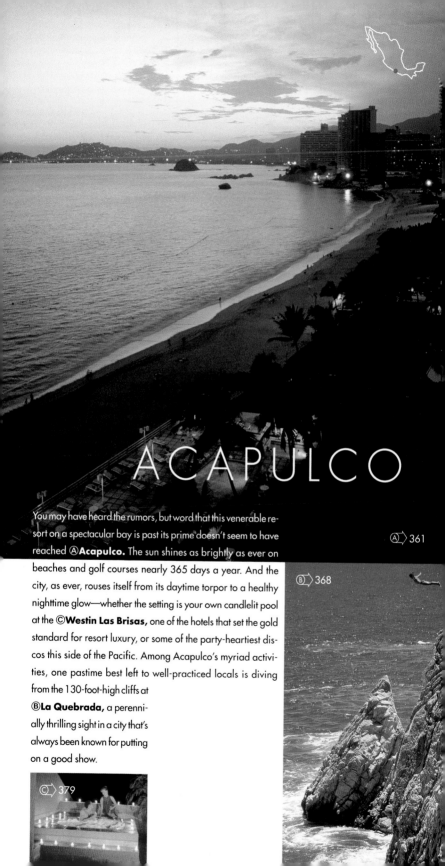

ACAPULCO

You may have heard the rumors, but word that this venerable resort on a spectacular bay is past its prime doesn't seem to have reached Ⓐ**Acapulco.** The sun shines as brightly as ever on beaches and golf courses nearly 365 days a year. And the city, as ever, rouses itself from its daytime torpor to a healthy nighttime glow—whether the setting is your own candlelit pool at the ©**Westin Las Brisas,** one of the hotels that set the gold standard for resort luxury, or some of the party-heartiest discos this side of the Pacific. Among Acapulco's myriad activities, one pastime best left to well-practiced locals is diving from the 130-foot-high cliffs at Ⓑ**La Quebrada,** a perennially thrilling sight in a city that's always been known for putting on a good show.

Ⓐ⟩ 361

Ⓑ⟩ 368

©⟩ 379

OAXACA

Ⓐ▷412

Ⓑ▷405

Surfers and beach lovers know Oaxaca for its more than 300 miles of lush coastline, washed by the warm Pacific. Zicatela, pounded by the so-called Mexican Pipeline, is one of the world's top surfing beaches. But the prime appeal of Oaxaca state and its eponymous colonial capital is the old and the older. Brilliantly ornamented Baroque monuments from the Spanish conquest, including the colorfully tile-domed Ⓑ**Catedral Metropolitana de Oaxaca**, pass almost for new, when magnificent remnants of civilizations long past are so near at hand. Mountaintop Ⓐ**Monte Albán,** with its still-intact ball court, temples, and observatory, was already a thriving city of 40,000 more than 2,500 years ago. A full millennium of civilization passed before the original Zapotec people were surpassed by the Mixtec, who turned the site into a rich necropolis that has yielded some of North America's greatest archaeological treasures. Today the descendants of both peoples enrich life in Oaxaca City. Festivals are lavish and intense, none more so than the macabre celebrations leading up to the Ⓒ**Día de Muertos** (Day of the Dead/All Souls' Day). Elegantly singsong native languages lend a distinctly musical note to the commotion in Saturday's Central de Abastos, Mexico's largest Indian market. Here and elsewhere, vendors sell everything from herbs and chiles to baskets, rugs, tin toys, and *huipiles* (embroidered tunics). After dark, strings of lights deck the 19th-century Ⓓ**Palacio de Gobierno** for no special reason. Every turn of a corner is likely to deliver a dose of local color that will etch itself into your memory.

Ⓒ▷ 403

Ⓓ▷ 406

19

These less-developed southern states are at the heart of Maya and Lacandon Indian country and are for most people a gateway to Guatemala. But if you linger here you'll discover what is arguably Mexico's most authentic culture, in

CHIAPAS AND TABASCO

Ⓐ 451

Ⓑ 447

colonial San Cristóbal de las Casas and traditional villages around it such as Ⓑ**San Juan Chamula,** whose daily life turns on centuries-old rituals. Make your way from the city through jungles and sinuous mountainscapes to verdant Ⓐ**Sumidero Canyon,** a 4,000-foot-deep near-vertical gash carved by the Grijalva River. In all of Mexico there is nothing like the mesmerizing power of the 2,000-year-old Maya city of Ⓒ**Palenque** rising out of the lush forests, echoing in its stone-capped tower and temples the spirit of the surrounding hills.

Ⓒ 453

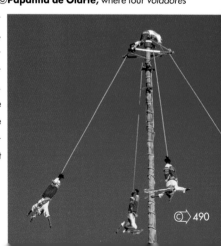

If you were to work your way south from the Texas border, from souvenir-choked Nuevo Laredo through the mountain city of Saltillo and low-profile coastal Tampico, you'd get a taste of Mexico as heady as the brew from the coffee beans harvested in the tropical highlands outside the raffish city of Ⓐ**Veracruz.** In the antique city itself the diverse citizenry takes to the streets for entertainment and exuberant self-expression: trios slap away at tiny guitars and portable harps, singers belt out that famed local song, *La Bamba*, and, most alluring of all, evening strollers pause in the Ⓑ**Plaza des Armas** for a little *danzón*—the sensuous, once-scandalous dance brought to Mexico by 19th-century Cubans. Elegance of movement is an aerial affair in colonial Ⓒ**Papantla de Olarte,** where four *voladores* (fliers) enact the ancient Totonac Indian calendrical cycle, diving backwards while tethered to an 82-foot pole and circling it upside down 52 times. The sublime Pyramid of the Niches at El Tajín, nearby, is the architectural flower of the ancient Indian civilizations that once dominated the coast.

Ⓐ▷ 476

Ⓑ▷ 483

Ⓒ▷ 490

YUCATAN

Ⓐ 584

Beaches and ruins, beaches and ruins, beaches and ruins: Mexico's most-visited region will reward you with an embarrassment of both riches, sometimes simultaneously— on Ⓒ**Playa Chacmool** in Cancún, the Chichén Maya rain god Chac looks as much like a beach-goer as he does like the sacrificial altar he once was. Ⓓ**Tulum** may well be the most satisfying spot in the Yucatán (in spite of the crowds). Here, alongside the Caribbean, the local limestone of the temples has mellowed

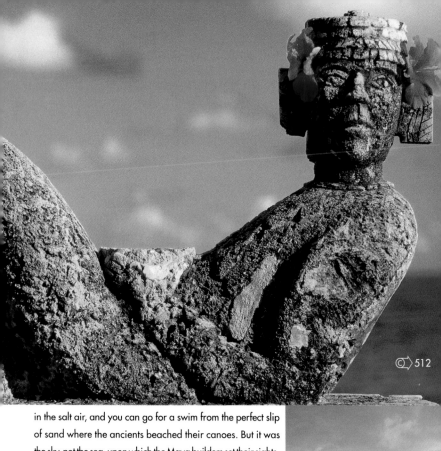

Ⓒ 512

in the salt air, and you can go for a swim from the perfect slip of sand where the ancients beached their canoes. But it was the sky, not the sea, upon which the Maya builders set their sights, and in their displays of might they erected monumental temple-pyramids to soar above their now-deserted cities. The enormous Ⓐ**Chichén Itzá,** which once dominated the Yucatán, is populated with hundreds of structures. Elegant, refined Uxmal is exceptional in another way—for the grace of its pyramids, courtyards, and relief carvings. And along the Puuc Route, satellite cities like Kabah, Sayil, and Labná help color the picture of one of the Americas' most intriguing civilizations. These cities once hummed with activity, but today many are

quiet: at Ⓑ**Cobá,** the lonely silence is broken only by the shrieks of spider monkeys from the encroaching jungle. And Ⓔ**Cenote Xkeken,** the swimmable, skylit sinkhole near colonial Valladolid, is as eerily mysterious as ever.

Ⓓ 568

Ⓔ 587

YUCATAN

(F) 534

Ruins of Maya civilizations may beckon, remnants of Spanish colonialism, like quirky Mérida and fortified Campeche and the formidable ⓖ**Convento de San Antonio de Padua** at Izamal, may cry out to be explored, but let's face it—the reason you're thinking about the Yucatán is its irresistible mix of sun, sand, and sea. On much of the Quintana Roo coast between Cancún and Akumal, luxury hotel strips like those at Playa del Carmen preside over balmy, crystalline waters and unbroken beaches as white as alabaster. The world's fifth-largest barrier reef lies just off the island of Cozumel, luring divers and snorkelers, and nature reserves farther south at Sian Ka'an and Boca Paila and north at Parque Natural Río Lagartos attract migrating flamingoes, herons, and other birds, as well as their binocular-toting admirers. To the west, along the shores of the Golfo de México, temperatures hover appealingly at 80 degrees, and the sun shines 240-plus days a year—even more than on the Caribbean—and you'll find relaxed coastal villages like ①**Celestún.** The epicenter of the peninsula, where your every whim can be satisfied both by day and by night, is ⓗ**Cancún,** hacked out of the jungle three decades ago and purpose-built for pleasure. The let-the-good-

ⓖ 583

ⓗ 515

times-roll attitude of Mexico's top resort is so entrenched that even roadside art aims to amuse. For a bit more quiet— and more beach life than nightlife—tiny fish-shaped Ⓕ**Isla Mujeres** is just the thing, a mere half-hour by boat across the bay from Cancún. Or head down the coast to laid-back Paamul for great beachcombing, the midsummer hatching of sea turtles, and a lagoon that's ideal for snorkeling. Whatever your passion, you'll find a place to pursue it under the Yucatán sun—and you don't have to set your sights any farther than that point out there where the blue-green sea meets the cloudless sky.

GREAT ITINERARIES

CHIHUAHUA

Chihuahua

Guaymas

Cuauhtémoc

Basaseachi Falls · 73 km

128 km

Divisadero · Creel

San Ignacio

140 km · Bacajipare

Mulege · Cerocahui

104 km

BAJA CALIFORNIA SUR

240 km

Loreto

Mision San Javier

La Poza · 120 km

Los Mochis

San Carlos/ Bahía Magdalena

234 km

1

La Paz

183 km

195 km · 9

1

San José del Cabo/ Costa Azul

33 km · Playa Palmilla

Cabo San Lucas

Playa Solmar

Ⓐ ➪ 154

Canyons and Coasts

8 to 12 days

Natural wonders never cease in northern and western Mexico. From the heart-stopping views and hikes into the Barrancas del Cobre—the Copper Canyon—to Baja Sur's inland deserts, its annual migrations of whales, and the beaches of Los Cabos, opportunities for adventure and relaxation are everywhere.

3 to 5 days. Riding the Ferrocarril Chihuahua al Pacífico rail line from west to east affords the best views of the Copper Canyon. So start off in Los Mochis and make the mountain village of Cerocahui your first stop. From here, views of Urique Canyon are superb, and the cave paintings at the Cueva de las Cruces are worth a

detour. Then head up the line to Divisadero, *the* place for sunset views, horseback trips to the Tarahumara Indian village of Bacajipare in the canyon, and the most luxurious lodgings on the way to Chihuahua City. Farther on, outside of Creel, the 806-foot Basaseachi Falls are one of North America's highest cascades. If a dose of urban life feels like the appropriate tonic after taking in the canyons, spend the night in Chihuahua before catching a plane for La Paz in Baja Sur.
☞ *Chapter 5*

5 to 7 days. Vast as it is, Baja is all about choices—whale-watching in Bahía Magdalena, sea-kayaking or fishing off Loreto, hiking among arid mountain ranges from Mision San Javier, windsurfing off the East Cape, diving and snorkeling or golf in Ⓐ Los Cabos—pick two or three and be sure to give yourself time to relax on the beaches of Costa Azul, Playa Palmilla, or Playa Solmar at the southern tip of the peninsula. Bahía Magdalena and Loreto are west and north of La Paz and the East Cape and Los Cabos are to the south, so figure travel time between them into the mix.
☞ *Baja California Sur in Chapter 3*

By Public Transportation
Distances here demand a fair amount of air travel: first from Mexico City to Los Mochis, then from Chihuahua to La Paz—which flies you over the canyons you just saw from cliff's edge—then from Los Cabos home. The rail trip from Los Mochis to Chihuahua is a 15-hour proposition straight through, but it's best to stop at towns along the way and reboard later in the day or the next day, or even the next. From La Paz, tour companies will take you to Bahía Magdalena to see whales. To get to Loreto (3 hrs north of La Paz), the East Cape (1 hr south), and Los Cabos (2 hrs south), renting a car will allow you to explore quieter coastal stretches on your own. Buses also run throughout Baja Sur.

Colonial Mexico

7 to 10 days

Remarkably well-preserved, these colonial cities are full of atmospheric haciendas and richly decorated cathedrals—along with intriguing juxtapositions of the colonial and the Indian that are classic Mexico.

QUERÉTARO

1 day. This Heartland city has been called the cradle of independence, and Querétaro's most beautiful area is the restored Plaza de la Independencia, filled with grand mansions once belonging to titled friends of the Crown. Amble around the square and a few of the surrounding streets to see the Baroque ⒷState Museum of Art, the Casa de la Marquesa, the Palacio del Gobierno del Estado, the Jardín de la Corregidora, and 16th-century hermitages turned into museums. Then head for San Miguel de famed Allende for the night.
☞ *Querétaro in Chapter 7*

SAN MIGUEL DE ALLENDE

1 to 2 days. You can cover most of what you'll want to see around the pretty town plaza in half a day. Serving as a cultural hub of the region, this friendly city is full of bookstores, art galleries, and coffee shops where you'll run into some of the American expatriates. San Miguel's historic inns are perfect for soaking up more local ambiance. Take time to visit churches—the Gothic Revival San Miguel de Archangel, the churrigueresque Iglesia de San Francisco, and the unique Oratorio de San Felipe Neri, built by Indians. The Casa de Ignacio Allende museum is the birthplace of the revered revolutionary hero. Consider a side trip to the picturesque village of Dolores Hidalgo and the Casa Hidalgo, home of the insurgent priest whose cry for independence from Spain started the

1810 war. If you're here for an extended stay, you might enroll in one of the town's art or language institutes.
☞ *San Miguel de Allende in Chapter 7*

GUANAJUATO

2 to 3 days. Splendid buildings rising above labyrinthine streets give Guanajuato its medieval appearance. Make your way to the main square and the impressive Teatro Juárez, headquarters of the annual Cervantes Festival (October), which draws noted international artists. El Museo Casa Diego Rivera, birthplace of the famed muralist, and the hulking Alhóndiga de Granaditas fortress are nearby. On day two, visit the Basílica Colegiata de Nuestra Señora de Guanajuato and La Valenciana churches—the former for its 8th-century statue of the Virgin, the latter for its elaborately carved pink facade and gilded altars. Don't miss the Mansion del Conde de Rul, owned by the richest colonial mine owners of the district, or a concert by an *estudiantina* (student) group dressed in old Spanish capes and caps.
☞ *Guanajuato in Chapter 8*

SAN CRISTÓBAL DE LAS CASAS

1 to 2 days. San Cristóbal in the southern state of Chiapas is a walking city, and on foot you can encounter the same mix of colonial and native cultures—from the iconic ochre-colored *catedral* to the *mercado municipal* bustling with Lacandon Maya merchants—that exists between the city itself

Ⓑ 284

and the surrounding Indian villages. One of them, San Juan Chamula, is known for its colorfully trimmed white stucco church, named for John the Baptist. Here a devout syncretism of traditional Maya rituals and the Catholicism that the Spanish brought to the New World makes for a fascinating snapshot of Mexico.
☞ *San Cristóbal de las Casas in Chapter 11*

MÉRIDA

2 days. No city in Mexico comes close to Mérida's quirky self-confidence and its almost Continental flair. At the same time the jaunty metropolis is just as Maya as San Cristóbal. Urbane streets like Paseo de Montejo—styled late in the 19th century like Paris' Champs-Elysées—are offset by the chiles-to-crafts *mercado* (market). And the catedral, built with stone from a Maya temple, contains a dark-skinned Christ that aims to reconcile people of Maya and Spanish descent. In that spirit, Mérida is at once the largest city on the Yucatán peninsula and, at heart, a typical Yucatecan town unafraid to welcome you into its midst.
☞ *Mérida in Chapter 13*

By Public Transportation
The easiest way to get to and between the Heartland cities of Querétaro, San Miguel, and Guanajuato is by luxury bus. From Mexico City the bus from the Observatorio or Northern bus terminals to Querétaro takes about two hours. From Querétaro it's another two hours to San Miguel, and Dolores Hidalgo is 45 minutes from San Miguel. Return to San Miguel for the 2½-hour ride to Guanajuato. Nearby León's airport has flights to Mexico (1 hr), from which you can fly to Tuxtla Gutiérrez (2 hrs), an hour west of San Cristóbal by bus. Then fly out of Tuxtla straight to Mérida (1 hr).

Léon
100 km Dolores Hidalgo
Guanajuato   **San Miguel de Allende**
53 km
Querétaro
220 km
HIDALGO
Tula
Teotihuacán
Mexico City
Cuernavaca   Puebla

GUANAJUATO

La Cocina Mexicana

8 to 11 days

Considering the poor representation that Mexican food gets in the United States, savoring the true flavors of Mexico can only deepen your appreciation of the country and its culture. By necessity—Mexico is a vast country—this gastronomic tour is limited to a few cities, but keep in mind that every region has its own excellent cuisine.

☞ *For descriptions of the foods mentioned below, see the La Cocina Mexicana box in the dining section of Chapter 1*

© 93

advantage of the city's variety of restaurants—from quaint fondas to colonial mansions and elegant old haciendas.
☞ *Dining in Chapter 1*

PUEBLA

2 days. From Mexico City, make your way out to colonial convents like the Convento de Santa Rosa, where nuns invented the city's most famous dishes—mole and *chiles en nogadas*. Then tuck into the food itself in restaurants in Puebla's historic district, most of which are lavishly decorated with *talavera* tile, for which Puebla is famous. Visit the Calle de los Dulces (Sweets Street), filled with shops selling the nuns' fruit, coconut, and sweet-potato candies. And don't miss sampling the town's fruit wines.
☞ *Puebla in Chapter 2*

VERACRUZ

2 to 3 days. The transit from inland Puebla to coastal Veracruz will take you to the source of a dish that appears on menus throughout Mexico—*huachinango á la veracruzana* (red snapper covered in tomatoes, onions, olives, and herbs)—and the home of that notorious chile, Jalapa's *jalapeño*. In

MEXICO CITY

2 to 4 days. Mexico City chefs turn out everything from colonial to *cocina Mexicana moderna* (modern Mexican cuisine) to pre-Hispanic dishes like chilied maguey worms for their *chilango* (Mexico City) clientele. Many restaurants focus on some regional cuisine, which means that you'll find the best of Veracruz seafood, Yucatecan *pibil*, Tampico *carne asada*, and Chihuahua *carnitas* within the confines of the capital. And five-star hotels often invite regional chefs to oversee gastronomic festivals in their on-site restaurants. Take

Mexican *altura*, fuels a café society in Veracruz—look for Gran Café del Portal, a local stronghold of *cafe lechero* (coffee with hot milk).
☞ *The State of Veracruz in Chapter 12*

OAXACA CITY

2 days. Several native cultures merge in exotic Oaxaca City, where you can feast on the seven types of mole the city is known for, or taste its sweet and salty tamales. Try one of the traditional fondas under the *portales* (arcades) in the main square. You'll also find *quesillo*, Oaxaca's special cheese, as well as table chocolate and giant *totopos* (baked tortillas) in regional dishes and piled in heaps at the local mercado, an essential stop for its symphony of colors and smells. Mountaintop Monte Albán, where archaeologists found royal tombs full of splendid gold jewelry, makes an easy day trip from the city.
☞ *Oaxaca City in Chapter 10*

By Public Transportation
The best way to get from Mexico City to Puebla is by luxury bus (2 hrs), from the TAPO terminal or the international airport. The bus from Puebla over the mountains and into Veracruz City takes four hours. From Veracruz to Oaxaca it's best to fly: back to Mexico (1½ hrs), then on to Oaxaca (2 hrs).

Veracruz City seafood is a way of life, and you can expect stunning sea bass, prawns, and lobster and dishes like crab *salpicón*—finely chopped with onion, cilantro, and lime. Coffee grown in the highlands around Jalapa, the famous

Léon

100 km Dolores Hidalgo

Guanajuato

San Miguel de Allende
53 km

Querétaro

VERACRUZ

HIDALGO

220 km Tula 53 km **Teotihuacán**

Jalapa

TLAXCALA

Mexico City
133 km

MEXICO

Cuernavaca

Puebla 150 km Córdoba

PUEBLA Orizaba 151 km **Veracruz**

88 km

124 km

Tuxtepec

Monte Albán 218 km **Oaxaca City**

OAXACA

Puerto Escondido Tehuantepec

Puerto Angel

PACIFIC OCEAN

The Lost Cities of Ancient Mexico
9 to 11 days

Once inhabited by numerous pre-Columbian cultures, Mexico has one of the world's most impressive collections of archaeological sites. The Maya are the standout. Their monumental cities are at their finest on the Yucatán peninsula and in jungle-clad Tabasco and mountainous Chiapas.

TEOTIHUACÁN

1 day. For the 14th- to 16th-century Aztecs, this was the birthplace of the gods. At its 8th-century peak Teotihuacán hummed with as many as 250,000 people, its massive, spellbinding ©pyramids rising above their city as symbols of the ordered lives that they lived in the ancient Valley of Mexico. Just an hour outside of Mexico City by bus, these ruins of a people who to this day remain nameless are an essential first site.
☞ *Teotihuacán in Chapter 2*

VILLAHERMOSA

2 to 3 days. The banana and oil capital of Mexico, Villahermosa is a rough midpoint between ancient sites and ancient cultures. Head for the Parque Museo La Venta, with its enormous Olmec stone heads, for an in-depth look at the mother culture that preceded the Maya by several centuries. Later in the day, swing north out of town to Comalcalco, a Maya site with giant stucco masks and the only known brick temples in the Maya world. Save the best for last and make your way to Palenque in Chiapas the next day. With a classicism akin to Greek architecture, this site exudes an ethereal beauty that is nothing short of bewitching. It's also the first site in the Americas where the tomb of a pre-Hispanic ruler was discovered in a burial chamber within a pyramid.
☞ *Villahermosa, Comalcalco, and Palenque in Chapter 11*

MÉRIDA

6 or 7 days. A capital city of the Yucatán, Mérida is a perfect base for getting out to the ruins in the surrounding countryside. Here in the most Maya of all Yucatecan cities, take in the Museum of Anthropology for a preview of Maya art, and walk around the lively main square to see its colonial mansions, cathedral, and small churches set in shady plazas. On your second day, head to Chichén Itzá, an extensive site built by two different Maya empires. Climb to the top of the Temple of the Warriors for a glimpse of its famous Chacmool and a bird's-eye view of the site. Later in the afternoon you might visit the Cave of Balamcanchén, with its ceremonial artifacts, and the Maya village of Izamal, on the way back to Mérida. Spend all of day three at beautiful Uxmal, the sterling example of the graceful Puuc architectural style. Optional overnights are possible at hotels near Chichén Itzá and Uxmal, which has an evening sound-and-light show. If time permits, you can spend a day at the smaller Puuc ruins of Kabah, Sayil, and Labná. Consider planning your trip around a local Maya festival to see the intriguing blend of pre-Hispanic beliefs and Catholic rituals.
☞ *The State of Yucatán in Chapter 13*

By Public Transportation
In Villahermosa you can take a cab to the Parque Museo La Venta but need to book an excursion to Comalcalco. Buses are unreliable. To get to Palenque you can catch a luxury bus from the ADO terminal; the trip takes about 2½ hours. There are also full-day excursions to Palenque from Villahermosa. From Tuxtla Gutiérrez there is a one-hour flight to Mérida. You can take day trips to the major Yucatán sites from Mérida. Second-class buses do run to Chichén Itzá and Uxmal from Mérida's main bus terminal, but they have no air-conditioning and are a bit uncomfortable.

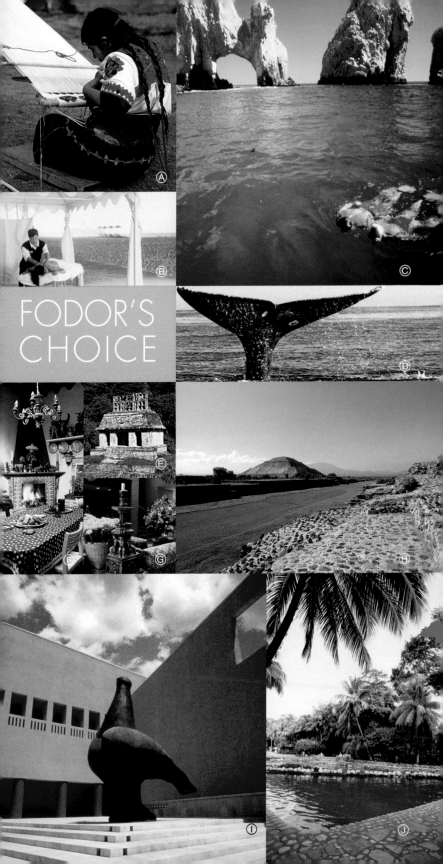

FODOR'S
CHOICE

Even with so many special places in Mexico, Fodor's writers and editors have their favorites. Here are a few that stand out.

ARCHAEOLOGICAL SITES

El Tajín. The Pyramid of the Niches rises out of the jungle like the fantasy of a lost world. ☞ p 489

Ⓔ **Palenque.** Nestled in a rain forest in Chiapas, these Maya ruins have a magical quality, perhaps because of their intimacy. The most magnificent royal tomb in the Maya empire was uncovered here. ☞ p 453

Ⓗ **Teotihuacán.** Predating the Aztecs and believed by them to be the birthplace of the gods, this pyramid complex outside Mexico City was one of the largest cities in the ancient world. ☞ p 93

BEACHES

Ⓒ **Playa de Amor, Cabo San Lucas.** From this secluded cove at the very tip of Baja California you can see the Sea of Cortés on one side, the Pacific Ocean on the other. ☞ p 162

Playa Norte (Playa Cocoteros), Isla Mujeres. This beach on sleepy Isla Mujeres is ideal for water sports and lounging under grass-roofed *palapas*. ☞ p 537

Zicatela, Oaxaca Coast. A long stretch of cream-color sand, Zicatela is one of the top 10 surfing beaches in the world. ☞ p 417

SPECIAL MOMENTS

A *calesa* (horse-drawn carriage) ride through Mérida. Discover Old World graciousness by trotting slowly through the wide streets and French-style neighborhoods of Yucatán's capital. ☞ p 575

Don Porfirio's Bar, Querétaro. After a day of exploring, stop in at the bar of the Casa de la Marquesa hotel for a drink, and to drink in the Old World elegance of this 18th-century house. ☞ p 282

Ⓓ **Whale-watching, Baja.** Go out on a boat for the best views of the great gray mammals, who pass through Scammon's and San Ignacio lagoons en route from Alaska each winter. ☞ p 141

MUSEUMS

① **Museo de Arte Contemporaneo, Monterrey.** The best of postmodern Latin American art is gathered at this gallery. A chic coffeehouse attracts the city's intellectuals. ☞ p 500

Museo de Frida Kahlo, Mexico City. The former home of the now-fashionable Kahlo is filled with her disturbing, surrealistic paintings and those of friends such as Klee and Duchamp. ☞ p 58

Museo Na-Bolom, San Cristóbal de las Casas. Franz and Gertrude Blom lived in a lovely, rambling home surrounded by gardens. Their former residence contains displays reflecting their extensive archaeological, ethnological, and ecological interests. ☞ p 437

SHOPPING

Ⓐ **Casa de las Artesanías and Sna Jolobil, San Cristóbal de las Casas.** Stop here for some of Mexico's most striking Indian weavings, hand-embroidered blouses and tunics, multicolored *fajas* (sashes), and beribboned hats. ☞ p 443

Old Town, Puerto Vallarta. Few Mexican cities have a collection of native crafts, among them clothing and household goods, as representative as that of Puerto Vallarta. ☞ p 324

Zona Rosa, Mexico City. Antiques, crafts, and the latest fashions are abundant in this tony neighborhood. ☞ p 80

FLAVORS

Cicero Centenario, Mexico City. The setting, in a restored 17th-century mansion, is superb, and the menu is enticing, featuring inventive versions of authentic Colonial dishes. $$$ ☞ p 65

La Choza, Cozumel. Mexican entrées are super-fresh at this friendly, family-run place, and the tortillas are baked on the premises. $$ ☞ p 549

La Estancia de los Tecajetes, Jalapa. Local *cocina Mexicana* doesn't get much better than the enchiladas or *crepa consentida*—chicken crepes doused with a poblano-and-cheese sauce—served here. $$ ☞ p 486

COMFORTS

Ⓑ **Las Ventanas al Paraíso, Cabo San Lucas.** This waterside architectural wonder is the last word in earthy elegance—and reason enough to hop on the next plane to the southern tip of the Baja Peninsula. $$$$ ☞ p 160

Ⓖ **Quinta Real, Guadalajara.** Colonial architecture and Spanish-style furnishings distinguish this luxury hotel in a quiet residential neighborhood. $$$$ ☞ p 226

Ⓕ **La Casa de Espiritus Alegres, Guanajuato.** This renovated hacienda is a folkart paradise filled with whimsical treasures from every state in Mexico. $$$$ ☞ p 271

Ⓙ **Chan Kah, Palenque.** A resident monkey is among the charms of this jungle retreat near the Maya ruins; accommodations are in comfortable bungalows. $$ ☞ p 458

AFTER HOURS

Fantasy and Enigma discos, Acapulco. Two standouts in a city where Saturday-night fever still rages, Fantasy attracts an older crowd, and Enigma's great light-and-sound show comes with dropdead views of Acapulco Bay. ☞ p 384

Gran Café del Portal, Veracruz. People-watch into the wee hours over a cup of *café con leche* at this renowned coffeehouse. ☞ p 480

Plaza de los Mariachis, Guadalajara. A personal serenade might be expensive, but the price of a beer will let you listen in on heartrending songs in the city where they originated. ☞ p 223

1   MEXICO CITY

Two volcanoes and a pyramid complex
flank Mexico's capital, once the center of
Aztec civilization and now the country's
cosmopolitan business, art, and culinary
hub. From the Alameda, a leafy center of
activity since Aztec times, to the Zona Rosa,
a chic shopping neighborhood, Mexico
City offers endless options to urban
adventurers. Day trips might include the
legendary pyramids of Teotihuacán, colonial
Puebla, where mole sauce and Talavera tiles
originated, or the floating gardens of
Xochimilco.

By Frank Shiell

Updated by
Paige Bierma
and Martha
Brant

MEXICO CITY is a city of superlatives. It is both the oldest (675 years) and the highest (7,556 ft) metropolis on the North American continent. And with nearly 24 million inhabitants, it is the most populous city in the world. It is Mexico's cultural, political, and financial core—on the verge of the 21st century but clinging to its deeply entrenched Aztec heritage.

As the gargantuan pyramids of Teotihuacán attest—the name is Aztec, meaning "the place where one becomes a god"—the area around Mexico City was occupied from early times by a great civilization, probably Nahuatl in origin. The founding of the Aztec capital nearby did not occur until more than 600 years after Teotihuacán was abandoned, around 750. As the story goes, the nomadic Aztecs were searching for a promised land in which to settle. Their prophecies said they would recognize the spot when they encountered an eagle, perched on a prickly pear cactus, holding a snake in its beak. In 1325, the disputed date given for the founding of the city of Tenochtitlán, the Aztecs discovered this eagle in the valley of Mexico. They built Tenochtitlán on what was then an island in shallow Lake Texcoco and connected it to lakeshore satellite towns by a network of *calzadas* (canals and causeways, now freeways). Even then it was the largest city in the Western hemisphere and, according to historians, one of the three largest cities on earth. When he first laid eyes on Tenochtitlán in the 16th century, Spanish conquistador Hernán Cortés was dazzled by the glistening metropolis, which reminded him of Venice.

A combination of factors made the conquest possible. The superstitious Aztec emperor Moctezuma II believed the white, bearded Cortés on horseback to be the mighty plumed serpent-god Quetzalcóatl, who, according to a tragically ironic prophesy, was supposed to arrive from the east in the year 1519 to rule the land. Moctezuma therefore welcomed the foreigner with gifts of gold and palatial accommodations.

But in return, Cortés initiated the bloody massacre of Tenochtitlán, which lasted almost two years. Joining forces with him was a massive army of Indian "allies," gathered from other settlements like Cholula and Tlaxcala, who were fed up with the Aztec empire's domination and with paying tribute, especially sending warriors and maidens to be sacrificed. With the strength of their numbers and the European tactical advantages of brigantines built to cross the lake, imported horses, firearms, armor, and, inadvertently, smallpox and the common cold, Cortés succeeded in devastating Tenochtitlán. Only two centuries after it was founded, the young Aztec capital lay in ruins, about half of its population dead from battle, starvation, and contagious European diseases against which they had no immunity.

Cortés began building the capital of what he patriotically dubbed New Spain, the Spanish empire's colony that would spread north to cover what is now the United States southwest, and south to Panama. *Mexico* comes from the word *Mexica* (pronounced *meh*-shee-ka), which is the Aztec name for themselves. Aztec is the Spaniards' name for the Mexica. At the site of the demolished Aztec ceremonial center—now the 10-acre Zócalo—Cortés started building a church (the precursor of the gigantic Metropolitan Cathedral), mansions, and government buildings. He utilized the slave labor—and artistry—of the vanquished native Mexicans. On top of the ruins of their city, and using rubble from it, they were forced to build what became the most European-style city in North America. But instead of having the random layout of contemporary medieval European cities, it followed the sophisticated grid pattern of the Aztecs. The Spaniards also drained and filled in Lake Texcoco, preferring wheels and horses (which they introduced to Mexico) over canals and canoes for transport. The land-filled lake bed turned out to be a soggy support for the immense buildings that have been slowly sinking into it ever since they were built. For much of the construction material the Spaniards quarried the local porous, volcanic pink stone called *tezontle*, which forms the thick walls of many historic buildings downtown.

During the colonial period the city grew, and the Franciscans and Dominicans converted the Aztecs to Christianity. In 1571 the Spaniards established the Inquisition in New Spain and burned heretics at its palace headquarters, which still stands in Plaza de Santo Domingo.

It took more than 200 years for Mexicans to successfully rise up against Spain. The historic downtown street 16 de Septiembre commemorates the "declaration" of the War of Independence. On that date in 1810, Father Miguel Hidalgo rang a church bell and cried out his history-making *grito* (shout): "Viva Ferdinand VII [king of Spain at the time]! Death to bad government!" Some historians conclude that Hidalgo's call to arms in the name of the Spanish monarch was just a facade to start an independence movement, which Hidalgo successfully accomplished. That "liberty bell," which now hangs above the main entrance to the National Palace, is rung on every eve of September 16 by the president of the republic, who then shouts a revised version of the patriot's cry: "Viva Mexico! Viva Mexico! Viva Mexico!"

Now, flying in or out of Mexico City, you'll get an aerial view of the remaining part of Lake Texcoco on the eastern outskirts of the city. At night the expanse of city lights abruptly ends at a black void that appears to be an ocean. In daylight you can also see the sprawling flatness of the 1,482-square-km (572-square-mi) *Meseta de Anáhuac* (Valley of Mexico), completely surrounded by mountains. On its south side, two usually snowcapped volcanoes, Popocatépetl and Iztaccíhuatl, are both well over 17,000 ft high. Over decades, many thought the twin volcanoes were extinct, but Popocatépetl has recently awakened—it began spewing smoke, ash, and even some lava in 1994 and has remained active on and off since then.

Unfortunately, the single most widely known fact about Mexico City is that its air is polluted. So you might picture the city, its streets packed with vehicles, wrapped daily in a cloak of black smog. In reality, in spite of the capital's serious pollution problem, it also has some of the clearest, bluest skies anywhere, especially in spring and summer. At 7,556 ft, it often has mild daytime weather perfect for sight-seeing and cool evenings comfortable for sleeping. Mornings can be glorious—chilly and bright with the promise of the warming sun.

If Mexico City's smog brings Los Angeles to mind, so might the fault line that runs through the valley. In 1957 a major earthquake took a tragic toll, and scars are still visible from the devastating 1985 earthquake—8.1 on the Richter scale. The government reported 10,000 deaths, but the word around town put the toll at 50,000.

Growing nonstop, Mexico City covers a 1,480-square-km (570-square-mi) area of the valley. The city is surrounded on three sides by the state of Mexico and bordered on the south by the state of Morelos. Glossy magazine ads usually tout Mexico's paradisiacal beach resorts and ancient ruins, but cosmopolitan, historic Mexico City is a vital destination in itself—more foreign and fascinating than many major capitals on faraway continents.

Pleasures and Pastimes

Dining

Mexico City has been a culinary capital ever since the time of Moctezuma. Chronicles tell of the extravagant daily banquets prepared for the slender Aztec emperor by his palace chefs. More than 300 different dishes were served for every meal—vast assortments of meat and fowl seasoned in dozens of ways; limitless fruit, vegetables, and herbs; freshwater fish; and fresh seafood that was rushed to Tenochtitlán from both seacoasts by sprinting relay runners.

Until the 15th century, Europeans had never seen indigenous Mexican edibles such as corn, chilies of all varieties, tomatoes, potatoes, pumpkin, squash, avocado, turkey, cacao (chocolate), and vanilla. In turn, the colonization brought European gastronomic influence and ingredients—wheat, onions, garlic, olives, citrus fruit, cattle, sheep, goats, chickens, domesticated pigs (and lard for frying)—and ended up broadening the already complex pre-Hispanic cuisine into one of the most multifaceted and exquisite in the world: traditional Mexican.

Today's cosmopolitan Mexico City is a gastronomic melting pot with some 15,000 restaurants. You'll find everything from simple family-style eateries to five-star world-class restaurants. And international restaurants serve foods from around the world—although Spanish and French haute-cuisine are dominant.

In the past decade a renaissance of Mexican cooking has brought about a new wave known as *cocina mexicana moderna* (modern Mexican cuisine), which many Mexico City restaurants serve. Emphasis is on presentation, the delicate tastes of traditional regional dishes gleaned from colonial cookbooks, and ancient indigenous cooking techniques like steaming and baking, which used a lot less fat, as there were no pigs for lard. Also, items such as crunchy fried grasshoppers and cooked *maguey* (cactus) worms now grace the menus of the best restaurants in town.

Lodging

As might be expected of a megalopolis, Mexico City has more than 25,000 hotel rooms—enough to accommodate every taste and budget. You can lodge in the quaint or the colonial, the smoked-glass-and-steel high-rise, or the elegant replica of an Italianate palace.

Museums

Mexico City is the cultural as well as political capital of the country, as evidenced by its 80-plus museums—some of the finest in Latin America. In buildings of architectural merit, you can see the sweeping murals of native sons like Diego Rivera, Clemente Orozco, and Juan O'Gorman; the gripping surrealism of Frida Kahlo; stunning pre-Hispanic ceremonial pieces; and outstanding collections of religious art.

Nightlife and the Arts

Mexico City is the cultural capital of Latin America and, with the exception of Río de Janiero, has the liveliest nightlife of the region. There's something for every taste, from opera and symphonies to a renowned folklore ballet and a lively square where *mariachi* (musicians) play. You'll also find discos and offbeat places where salsa and *danzón* (Cuban dance music) are headliners.

Shopping

Native crafts and specialties from all over Mexico are available in the capital, as are designer clothes. You'll also find modern art by some of the best contemporary painters, many of whom are making a name for themselves in the United States. And of course Mexican goods are a far better deal here than they are in overseas outlets.

Sports and the Outdoors

Latin sports like the *fiesta brava* (bullfighting)— brought to Mexico by the conquistadores—have enjoyed popularity for more than four centuries in the capital, which attracts the country's best athletes. And though the roots of soccer ("fútbol") are probably English, a weekend afternoon game at Mexico City's giant Estadio Azteca leaves no question that this is the sport Mexicans are craziest about. Adventure travel agencies have also sprouted up in Mexico City recently to offer great weekend getaways like white-water rafting in nearby Veracruz. Tennis, golf, running—even rowing a boat in a park—are other outdoor pursuits to engage in while in town.

EXPLORING MEXICO CITY

Most of Mexico City is aligned on two major intersecting thoroughfares: Paseo de la Reforma and Avenida Insurgentes—at 34 km (21 mi), the longest avenue in the city. Administratively, Mexico City is divided into 16 *delegaciones* (districts) and about 400 *colonias* (neighborhoods), each with street names fitting a given theme, such as river, philosopher, doctor, or revolutionary hero. The same street can change names as it goes through different colonias. Hence, most street addresses include their colonia. And, unless you're going to an obvious place, it is important to tell your taxi driver the name of the colonia.

The principal sights of Mexico City fall into three areas. Allow a full day to cover each thoroughly, though you could race through them in four or five hours apiece. You can cover the first two areas—the Zócalo and Alameda Central, and Zona Rosa and Bosque de Chapultepec (Chapultepec Park)—on foot. Getting around Coyoacán and San Angel in southern Mexico City will require a taxi ride or two.

Numbers in the text correspond to numbers in the margin and on the Zócalo and Alameda Central; Zona Rosa, Bosque de Chapultepec, and Colonia Condesa; and San Angel and Coyoacán maps.

Great Itineraries

You can spend a month in Mexico City and just begin to grasp the tip of its iceberg of sights, sounds, and tastes. For stays shorter than this, here are some highlights.

IF YOU HAVE 3 DAYS

Start with the **Zócalo** ① with its exotic ruins, museums, and public buildings; then stroll to the **Palacio de Bellas Artes** ⑮ and surroundings—don't forget a stop at the **Casa de los Azulejos** ⑬ for a Mexican lunch—and end the day at **Alameda Central** ⑱. Day 2, head for the **Museo Nacional de Antropología** ㉖ in the morning and the **Zona Rosa** in the afternoon, when it starts to come alive. Visit the **Mercado Insurgentes** (☞ Shopping, *below*) for some fun shopping, or any other of the stores on our list. Consider an evening in the pleasant **Colonia Condesa** for dinner; it is one of the city's up-and-coming neighborhoods. Day 3, go to **Bosque de Chapultepec** ㉑ to stroll the green pathways past the rowing lake and visit the **Castillo de Chapultepec** ㉒, the **Museo de Arte Moderno** ㉔, **Museo Rufino Tamayo** ㉕, and, of course, the **Zoológico** ㉗ to see the pandas. Visit downtown's **Plaza Garibaldi** (☞ Nightlife, *below*) on your last night in town for a rousing mariachi send-off. If the Classic period site of **Teotihuacán** intrigues you, however, you could spend the third day there (☞ Chapter 2).

IF YOU HAVE 5 DAYS

Follow the itinerary of the first three days (☞ *above*); on Day 4 spend your time in **San Angel**—start with the Bazar Sábado if your plans bring

Mexico City Orientation *(Boxes Refer to Detail Maps)*

San Angel and Coyoacán

Mexico City Subways

you here on a Saturday—and in **Coyoacán** with its lovely casa-museums, especially **Museo de Frida Kahlo** �37 and **Museo de Leon Trotsky** �38. On Day 5 take an excursion to the **Basílica of the Virgin of Guadalupe,** Latin America's holiest shrine, and the pyramids of **Teotihuacán,** where a powerful regime held sway over the region more than a millennium before the arrival of the Spanish. Climb at least one pyramid, visit the museum, and head back to Mexico City.

IF YOU HAVE 10 DAYS

Follow the five-day option and add a visit to the resort town of **Cuernavaca,** about an hour's drive southeast of Mexico City (☞ Chapter 2). Spend the day in its museums and browsing on its pretty main square, then overnight at one of the town's converted mansions. On Day 7 head back to Mexico City by Highway 95 and stop in **Xochimilco,** where you can ride through the floating gardens on a gondola-like boat and view an outstanding private collection of works by Diego Rivera and Frida Kahlo at the Dolores Olmedo Patino Museum. On Day 8 drive to the ancient Toltec ruins at **Tula** and continue to the village of **Tepotzotlán,** which has a beautiful Jesuit church. The next day, head to **Puebla** for a couple hours' tour, including the main square and the fine Amparo Museum, then pop over to the nearby town of **Cholula,** once a sacred ceremonial site. Climb to the top of the church built over a pyramid, and return to Puebla for the night. En route back to Mexico City on the last day, drive to **Cacaxtla** to see some of the best-preserved Mesoamerican murals in Mexico.

The Zócalo and Alameda Central

This area is all about history: the Zócalo, its surrounding Centro Histórico, and Alameda Park were the heart of both the Aztec and Spanish cities. Many of the streets in downtown Mexico City have been converted into pedestrian-only thoroughfares, adding to the ease of strolling here.

A Good Walk

An excellent point of departure for any tour of the city's center is the **Zócalo** ①, the heart and soul of old downtown. From here, you can literally see the layers of history in the buildings around you. On the north side of this huge square you'll see the tilting **Catedral Metropolitana** ② and adjacent to it the comparatively small 18th-century Sagrario Chapel, even more angled than the cathedral. The **Templo Mayor** ③, ruins from the Aztec capital, is northeast of the cathedral, across the pedestrian plaza. If you're interested in modern art, walk south about half a block from the Templo Mayor to the end of Calle Seminario, then go two blocks east on Calle Moneda to Academia to find the **Museo José Luis Cuevas** ④. Take Moneda back (west) to the Zócalo. The first building you'll see on your left is the massive **Palacio Nacional** ⑤, covering two city blocks. Walk south past the palacio to the corner and turn right, crossing the street to get to the section of the Zócalo occupied by the 1722 **Ayuntamiento** ⑥. Recross the street and walk northwest through the open square to Calle Cinco de Mayo and the National Pawn Shop in the **Monte de Piedad** ⑦. Three-and-a-half blocks north is the historic **Plaza de Santo Domingo** ⑧. Walk one block east along Calle Republica de Cuba and one block south to get to Calle Justo Sierra and the **Conjunto de San Ildefonso** ⑨, now an art gallery. Turn west and follow Calle Justo Sierra three blocks—it will change into Calle Donceles—to Calle República de Chile, then turn left (south) a block to Calle Tacuba. Turn right and walk one block to have scrumptious lunch at the **Café de Tacuba** (☞ Dining, *below*) on the right side of the street. Or, you can continue east on Tacuba

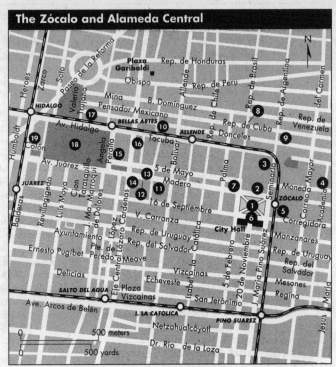

The Zócalo and Alameda Central

one and a half blocks to the **Museo Nacional de Arte** ⑩ in the colonial Plaza Manuel Tolsa.

From Calle Tacuba, head two short blocks south to Calle Madero, one of the city's most architecturally varied streets. On the south side of Madero, between Bolivar and Gante, is the 1780 Baroque **Palacio de Iturbide** ⑪. Continue along on the south side of Madero; less than a block west of the palacio you'll come to the **Iglesia de San Francisco** ⑫, with its beautifully painted walls. The stunning tilework of the **Casa de los Azulejos** ⑬ will draw your eye across Calle Madero.

The ultimate goals of the remainder of this walk are an antiques museum and a Diego Rivera mural museum. From Calle Madero, walk less than half a block west to Eje Central Lázaro Cárdenas, a wide four-lane avenue. At the corner and on your left, you can't miss the 1950s-style skyscraper, the **Torre Latinoamericana** ⑭, which has one of the best aerial views of the city. Cross the avenue and turn right (north) to explore the beautiful **Palacio de Bellas Artes** ⑮ opera house, the long side of which skirts Lázaro Cárdenas (its entrance is on Juárez). The turn-of-the-last-century post office building of **Dirección General de Correos** ⑯ is up Lázaro Cárdenas another 150 ft across from Bellas Artes.

Pass the post office to Calle Tacuba and cross Lázaro Cárdenas one last time, where Calle Tacuba turns into Avenida Hidalgo. One block west, you'll come to the antique-filled **Museo Franz Mayer** ⑰. Across Avenida Hidalgo is the north end of the leafy park, **Alameda Central** ⑱. At its south end, on Avenida Juárez, **FONART** is a government-owned handicrafts store (☞ Shopping, *below*). To get to the **Museo Mural Diego Rivera** ⑲, take Juárez west to Calle Balderas, about three and a half blocks from FONART. Turn right and walk a short block to Calle Colón.

TIMING

The Zócalo area will be quietest on Sunday, when bureaucrats have their day of rest. But Alameda Park will be jumping with children and their parents enjoying a Sunday outing. The park will be particularly festive during Christmas, when dozens of "Santas" will appear with plastic reindeer to take wish lists from long lines of children. While Mexicans do celebrate on Dec. 25, the traditional Mexican Christmas kicks in on January 5, the eve of the Day of the Three Kings, and the Three Wise Men of biblical lore replace the Santas in the Alameda. Gorgeous Christmas paintings-in-lights deck the Zócalo from end to end and stream up Calle Madero past the Alameda Park to Paseo de la Reforma beyond the museums in Bosque de Chapultepec.

During the daytime, the downtown area is filled with people and vibrant with activity. As in any big city, watch out for pickpockets, especially on crowded buses and subways, and avoid dark, deserted streets at night.

The streets in the walking tour are fairly close to one another and can be covered in half a day. The National Palace, Templo Mayor and its museum, and Franz Mayer Museum are worth an hour each of your time; you can cover the Palace of Fine Arts in a half hour.

Sights to See

THE ZÓCALO

⑥ Ayuntamiento (City Hall). The two buildings of Mexico's city hall stand on the south side of the Zócalo. Colonial tiles of the arms of Cortés and other conquistadores decorate the one on the west. Originally built in 1532, it was destroyed by fire in 1692 and rebuilt in 1722. In 1935 the Distrito Federal needed more office space, and to maintain the architectural integrity of the Zócalo, the "matching" structure across the street (20 de Noviembre) was built. In 1997, for the first time in 70 years, Mexico City residents were allowed to elect their own mayor (the post had previously been appointed by the president). Thus did the city's first leftist mayor, Cuauhtémoc Cárdenas—son of Mexico's populist president Lázaro Cárdenas—take over the reins in these buildings from 1997–2000.

② Catedral Metropolitana (Metropolitan Cathedral). Construction on this oldest and largest cathedral in Latin America began in 1573 on the north side of the Zócalo and continued intermittently throughout the next three centuries. The result is a medley of Baroque and neoclassical touches. Inside are four identical domes, their airiness grounded by rows of supportive columns. There are five altars and 14 chapels, mostly in the fussy churrigueresque style, an ornate Baroque style named for Spanish architect José Churriguera (d. 1725). Like most Mexican churches, the cathedral itself is all but overwhelmed by the innumerable paintings, altarpieces, and statues—in graphic color—of Christ and the saints. Over the centuries, this cathedral has sunk noticeably into the spongy subsoil. Its list is evident when it is viewed from across the square, and engineering projects to stabilize the structure are constantly under way.

⑦ Monte de Piedad (Mountain of Pity). Now housing the National Pawn Shop—which sells jewelry, antiques, and other goods not reclaimed by their owners—this structure was built to help the poor in the late 18th century. It's on the northwest corner of the Zócalo, on what was once the site of an Aztec palace. ☯ Mon.–Sat. about 10–7.

④ Museo José Luis Cuevas. One of the newest museums downtown, installed in a refurbished ex-convent, it has a superb collection of contemporary art, as well as work by Mexico's enfant terrible, José Luis Cuevas, who is one of the country's best contemporary artists. Don't miss the sensational *La Giganta* (The Giantess), Cuevas's 8-ton bronze sculpture in the central patio. Up-and-coming Latin American artists appear in temporary exhibits throughout the year. ⊠ *Academia 13,* ☎ *5/542–8959.* ⊡ *50¢.* ⊙ *Tues.–Sun. 10–5:30.*

★ ❺ **Palacio Nacional** (National Palace). This grand government building was initiated by Cortés on the site of Moctezuma's home and remodeled by the viceroys. Its current form dates from 1693, although a third floor was added in 1926. Now the seat of government, it has always served as a public-function site. In fact, during colonial times, the first bullfight in New Spain took place in the inner courtyard.

Diego Rivera's sweeping, epic murals on the second floor of the main courtyard have the power to mesmerize. For more than 16 years (1929–45), he and his assistants mounted scaffolds day and night, perfecting techniques adapted from Renaissance Italian frescoes. The result, nearly 1,200 square ft of vividly painted wall space, is grandiosely entitled *Epic of the Mexican People in Their Struggle for Freedom and Independence.* The larger-than-life paintings represent two millennia of Mexican history, filtered through Rivera's imagination. He painted pre-Hispanic times in innocent, almost sugary scenes of Tenochtitlán. Only a few vignettes—a lascivious woman baring her leg in the marketplace, a man offering a human arm for sale, and the carnage of warriors—acknowledge the darker aspects of ancient life. As you walk around the floor, you'll pass images of the savagery of the conquest and the hypocrisy of the Spanish priests, the noble independence movement, and the bloody revolution. Marx appears amid scenes of class struggle, toiling workers, industrialization (which Rivera idealized), bourgeois decadence, and nuclear holocaust. These are among Rivera's finest—and most accessible and likely most visited—paintings. The palace also houses two minor museums—dealing with 19th-century president Benito Juárez and the Mexican Congress. And the liberty bell rung by Padre Hidalgo to proclaim independence in 1810 hangs high on the central facade. It chimes every eve of September 16, while from the balcony below the president repeats *el grito,* the historic shout of independence to throngs of *chilangos* (Mexico City residents) below. Usually the people demand that the chief executive continue shouting until he loses his voice. ⊠ *East side of the Zócalo.* ⊡ *Free (you will be asked to leave an I.D. at the front desk).* ⊙ *Daily 9–5.*

❽ **Plaza de Santo Domingo** (Santo Domingo Plaza). The Aztec emperor Cuauhtémoc built a palace here, where heretics were later burned at the stake in the Spanish Inquisition. The plaza was the intellectual hub of the city during the colonial era. Today, its most colorful feature is the **Portal de los Evangelistas** (Portal of the Evangelists), filled with scribes at old-fashioned typewriters who are most likely composing letters for love-stricken swains. This age-old custom, which originated when quill pens were in vogue, has successfully launched quite a few of Cupid's arrows. The gloomy-looking **Palace of the Inquisition,** founded by the Catholic Church in 1571 (50 years after the conquest) and closed by government decree in 1820, is catercorner to the lively portal. It was a medical school for many years and now serves as a museum portraying the history of both the Inquisition and medicine. The 18th-century Baroque **Santo Domingo church** slightly north of the portal is all that remains of the first Dominican convent in New Spain. The convent building was demolished in 1861 under the Reform laws that forced clerics to turn over all religious buildings not used for worship to the government. Today, you can still see white-robed Dominican nuns visiting the church. ⊠ *Between República de Cuba, República de Brasil, República de Venezuela, and Palma.*

❸ Templo Mayor (Great Temple). The ruins of the ancient hub of the Aztec empire were unearthed accidentally in 1978 by telephone repairmen and have since been turned into a vast and historically significant archaeological site and museum. At this temple, dedicated to the Aztec cult of death, captives from rival tribes—as many as 10,000 at a time—were sacrificed to the bloodthirsty god of war, Huitzilopochtli. Seven rows of leering stone skulls adorn one side of the structure.

The adjacent **Museo del Templo Mayor** contains 3,000 pieces unearthed from the site and from other ruins in central Mexico; they include ceramic warriors, stone carvings and knives, skulls of sacrificial victims, a rare gold ingot, models and scale reproductions, and a room on the destruction of Tenochtitlán by the Spaniards. The centerpiece is an 8-ton disk discovered at the Templo Mayor. It depicts the moon goddess Coyolxauhqui, who, according to myth, was decapitated and dismembered by her brother Huitzilopochtli for trying to persuade her 400 other brothers to murder their mother. ⊠ *Seminario 8, at República de Guatemala (entrance on plaza, near Catedral),* ☎ *5/542–4784, 5/ 542–4785, or 5/542–4786.* ☑ *$2.* ⊙ *Tues.–Sun. 9–5. Call 1 wk ahead to schedule free English-language tours by museum staff, or hire a freelance guide outside the museum.*

❶ Zócalo (formal name: Plaza de la Constitución). Mexico City's historic plaza and the buildings around it were built by the Spaniards, using Indian slave labor. This enormous paved square, the largest in the Western Hemisphere, occupies the site of the ceremonial center of Tenochtitlán, the capital of the Aztec empire, which once comprised 78 buildings. Throughout the 16th, 17th, and 18th centuries, the Spaniards and their descendants constructed elaborate churches and convents, elegant mansions, and stately public edifices, many of which have long since been converted to other uses. There is an air of Old Europe in this part of the city, which, in its entirety (the Centro Histórico), is a national monument that has been undergoing major refurbishing. At press time, much had already been accomplished and even more was under way. Imposing buildings are constructed with the pink volcanic tezontle stone and the quarry stones that the Spaniards recycled from the rubble of the Aztec temples they razed. Throngs of small shops, eateries, cantinas, street vendors, and women in native Indian dress contribute to an inimitably Mexican flavor and exuberance.

Zócalo literally means "pedestal" or "base": in the mid-19th century an independence monument was planned for the square, but it was never built. The term stuck, however, and now the word "zócalo" is applied to the main plazas of most Mexican cities. Mexico City's Zócalo (because it's the original, it is always capitalized) is used for government rallies, protest marches, sit-ins, and festive events. It is the focal point for Independence Day celebrations on the eve of September 16 and is spectacularly festooned during the Christmas season. Flag-raising and -lowering ceremonies take place here in the early morning and late afternoon. ⊠ *Bounded on the south by 16 de Septiembre, north by Cinco de Mayo, east by Piño Suarez, and west by Monte de Piedad.*

ALAMEDA CENTRAL

⑱ Alameda Central (Alameda Park). This has been one of the capital's oases of greenery and centers of activity since Aztec times, when the Indians held their *tianguis* (market) on the site. In the early days of the Viceroyalty, the Inquisition burned its victims at the stake here. Later, national leaders, from 18th-century viceroys to Emperor Maximilian and President Porfirio Díaz, clearly envisioned the park as a symbol of civic pride and prosperity: over the centuries, it has been endowed with fountains, railings, a Moorish kiosk imported from Paris, and ash, willow, and poplar trees. Its most conspicuous man-made structure is the semicircular, white marble **Hemiciclo a Benito Juárez** (monument to Juárez) on the Avenida Juárez side of the park. It is a fine place for strolling, relaxing, and listening to live music on Sundays and holidays.

⓭ **Casa de los Azulejos** (House of Tiles). Built as the palace of the counts of the Valle de Orizaba, an aristocratic family from the early period of Spanish rule, this 17th-century masterpiece acquired its name from the tilework installed by a later descendant, a ne'er-do-well scion who married a rich woman. In addition to its well-preserved white, blue, and yellow tiles, the facade also has iron grillwork balconies and gray stonework. One of the prettiest Baroque structures in the country, it is currently occupied by Sanborns, a chain store–restaurant. The dazzling interior, which includes a Moorish patio, a monumental staircase, and a mural by Orozco, is worth seeing. If you have plenty of time— service is slow—this is a good place to stop for breakfast, lunch, or dinner. ⊠ *Calle Madero 4 (at Callejón de la Condesa)*, ☎ *5/512–9820 ext. 103.* ⊙ *Daily 7 AM–1 AM.*

❾ **Conjunto de San Idelfonso** (San Idelfonso Complex). This colonial building with lovely patios started out as a Jesuit school for the sons of wealthy Mexicans in the 18th century, then took life as a medical college, and finally became a public preparatory school. After a complete renovation, it reopened in 1992 with the "Splendors of Mexico: 30 Centuries of Art" and has been showcasing outstanding traveling Mexican exhibits ever since. The interior contains extraordinary works by the big three of mural painting—Diego Rivera, David Alfaro Siqueiros, and Clemente Orozco. ⊠ *Justo Sierra 16, almost at corner of República de Argentina, 2 blocks north of Zócalo,* ☎ *5/789–2505.* ⊠ *$2; free Tues.* ⊙ *Tues.–Sun. 10–5:30.*

⓰ **Dirección General de Correos** (General Post Office). Mexico City's main post-office building is a fine example of Renaissance revival architecture. Constructed of cream-color sandstone in 1908, it epitomizes the grand imitations of European architecture common in Mexico during the Porfiriato—the rather long dictatorship of Porfirio Díaz (1876–1911). The upstairs **Museo del Palacio Postal** exhibits the postal history of Mexico. ⊠ *Calle Tacuba and Eje Central Lázaro Cárdenas,* ☎ *5/510–2999 for museum.* ⊠ *Free.* ⊙ *Museum weekdays 9–5, weekends 10–2; post office weekdays 8 AM–10 PM, Sat. 8–8.*

⓬ **Iglesia de San Francisco.** Supposedly the site of Moctezuma's zoo, and certifiably built on the site of Mexico's first convent (1524), this iglesia's current 18th-century French Gothic incarnation is one of the newest buildings on the street. The paintings on the inside walls are beautiful. ⊠ *Calles Madero and 16 de Septiembre.* ☎ *5/518–4698.* ⊙ *Daily 7 AM–8:30 PM.*

⓱ **Museo Franz Mayer.** Opened in 1986 in the 16th-century Hospital de San Juan de Dios, this museum has exhibits that include 16th- and 17th-century antiques, such as wooden chests inlaid with ivory, tortoiseshell, and ebony; tapestries, paintings, and lacquerware; rococo clocks, glassware, and architectural ornamentation; and an unusually large assortment of Talavera ceramics and tiles. Plaques explain in detail the production history of the *azulejos* (tiles)—a technique that was carried from Mesopotamia and Egypt to the Persians, Arabs, and Spaniards, who brought it to Mexico. The museum also has an impressive collection of more than 700 different editions of Cervantes's *Don Quixote.* The old hospital building is faithfully restored, with pieces of the original frescoes peeking through. Classical music plays in the background. ⊠ *Av. Hidalgo 45 at Plaza Santa Veracruz,* ☎ *5/518–2267.* ⊠ *$1.50;*

free Tues. ⊙ *Tues.–Sun. 10–5. Call 1 day ahead for an English-speaking guide.*

⑲ **Museo Mural Diego Rivera.** Diego Rivera's controversial mural, *Sunday Afternoon Dream in the Alameda Park,* was originally painted on a lobby wall of the Hotel Del Prado in 1947–48. Its controversy grew out of Rivera's Marxist inscription, "God does not exist," which the artist later replaced with the bland "Conference of San Juan de Letrán" to placate Mexico's dominant Catholic population. The 1985 earthquake destroyed the hotel but not the gentle and poetic mural. This museum was built across the street from the hotel to house the work. ⊠ *Calles Balderas and Colón,* ☎ *5/510–2329.* ⌑ *$1; free Sun.* ⊙ *Tues.–Sun. 10–6.*

⑩ **Museo Nacional de Arte** (National Art Museum). This neoclassical building, built during the Porfiriato and turned into a museum in 1982, contains a superb collection from nearly every school of Mexican art, with a concentration on Mexico's artistic development from 1810 to 1950. Works include Diego Rivera's portrait of Adolfo Best Maugard, José María Velasco's *Vista del Valle de México desde el Cerro de Santa Isabel* (View of the Valley of Mexico from the Hill of Santa Isabel), and Ramón Cano Manilla's *El Globo* (The Balloon). *El Caballito,* a statue of Spain's Carlos V on horseback, stands out front. ⊠ *Calle Tacuba 8,* ☎ *5/512–3224.* ⌑ *$2; free Sun.* ⊙ *Tues.–Sun. 10–5:30.*

★ ⑮ **Palacio de Bellas Artes** (Fine Arts Palace). Construction on this colossal white-marble opera house was begun in 1904 by Porfirio Díaz, who wanted to add yet another ornamental building to his accomplishments. He was ousted seven years later after winning yet another rigged election. He died in 1915, and the building wasn't finished until 1934. Today the theater serves as a handsome venue for international and national artists, including such groups as the Ballet Folklórico de México (☞ *Dance, below*). The palace is indeed renowned for its architecture, the work of Italian Adamo Boari, who also designed the post office; it includes an art-nouveau facade trimmed in pre-Hispanic motifs. Inside are a Tiffany stained-glass curtain depicting the two volcanoes outside Mexico City and paintings by several celebrated Mexican artists, including Rufino Tamayo and Mexico's trio of muralists: Rivera, Orozco, and Siqueiros. It was here that Rivera reconstructed his mural *Man at the Crossroads,* which was commissioned for and then torn down from Rockefeller Center in New York City because of its political message (epitomized by the face of Lenin). Temporary art exhibits are also held at the palace museum. ⊠ *Eje Central Lázaro Cárdenas and Av. Juárez,* ☎ *5/512–3633.* ⌑ *$2; museum free Sun. (no charge to look at the building and gift shops inside).* ⊙ *Tues.–Sun. 10–8.*

OFF THE
BEATEN PATH

TLATELOLCO – At Avenida Reforma's northern end, about 2 km (1 mi) north of the Palacio de Bellas Artes, the area known as Tlatelolco (pronounced tla-tel-ohl-coh) was the domain of Cuauhtémoc (pronounced kwa-oo-teh-muck)—the last Aztec emperor before the conquest—and the sister city of Tenochtitlán. In modern times its name makes residents shudder, because it was here that several hundred protesting students were massacred by the Mexican army in 1968. In addition, the 1985 earthquake destroyed several high-rise apartments in Tlatelolco, killing hundreds. The center of Tlatelolco is the **Plaza de las Tres Culturas,** so named because Mexico's three cultural eras—pre-Hispanic, colonial, and modern—are represented on the plaza in the form of the small ruins of a pre-Hispanic ceremonial center (visible from the roadway); the Iglesia de Santiago Tlatelolco (1609) and Colegio de la Santa Cruz de Tlatelolco (1535–36); and the ultracontemporary Ministry of Foreign Affairs (1970). The church contains the baptismal font of Juan Diego, the Indian to whom the Virgin of Guadalupe appeared in 1531. The Colegio (college), founded by the Franciscans after the conquest, was once attended by the sons of the Aztec nobility. ⊠ *Plaza is bounded on north by Manuel González, on west by Av. San Juan de Letrán Norte, and on east by Paseo de la Reforma, between Glorieta de Peralvillo and Glorieta Cuitláhuac.*

⑪ **Palacio de Iturbide** (Emperor Iturbide's Palace). Built in 1780, this handsome baroque structure—note the imposing door and its carved-stone trimmings—became the residence of Iturbide in 1822. One of the heroes of the independence movement, the misguided Iturbide proclaimed himself emperor of a country that had thrown off the imperial yoke of the Hapsburgs only a year before. His own empire, needless to say, was short-lived. Now his home is owned by Banamex (Banco Nacional de México) and sponsors cultural exhibits in the atrium. ⊠ *Calle Madero 17,* ☎ *5/518–2187.* ☞ *Free.* ☉ *Inner atrium daily 10–7.*

⑭ **Torre Latinoamericana** (Latin American Tower). Touted as the tallest building in the capital before the Hotel de Mexico was built in the 1980s, this 47-story skyscraper was completed in 1956, and on clear days the observation deck and café on the top floors afford fine views of the city. The oxymoronic **Fantastic World of the Sea,** a sky-high aquarium, miraculously transported small sharks and crocodiles to the 38th floor. ⊠ *Calle Madero and Eje Central Lázaro Cárdenas,* ☎ *Observation deck 5/521–0844; aquarium 5/521–7455.* ☞ *Deck $2.60; aquarium $1.80.* ☉ *Deck daily 9:30 AM–10:30 PM; aquarium daily 10 AM–10 PM.*

Zona Rosa, Bosque de Chapultepec, and Colonia Condesa

Bosque de Chapultepec (Chapultepec Park), originally called Cerro de Chapultepec, is the largest park in the city, a great green refuge from gray urban living. Housing five-plus world-class museums, a castle, a lake, an amusement park, and the Mexican president's official residence, Chapultepec is a saving grace for visitors and locals. If you pick only one of these museums to visit, make it the Museo Nacional de Antropología—you won't find the likes of its exhibits anywhere else.

The Zona Rosa, once a cultural center of Mexico City, is now a first stop for shopping, where shops, hotels, travel agencies, and restaurants line the avenues. Nearby Colonia Condesa is the newcomer on foreigners' itineraries. This tranquil neighborhood is filled with casual cafés and the city's hottest new eateries.

A Good Walk

Emperor Maximilian built the Paseo de la Reforma in 1865, modeling it after the Champs-Elysées in Paris. Its purpose was to connect the Palacio Nacional (☞ The Zócalo and Alameda Central, *above*) with his residence, the Castillo de Chapultepec. At the northern end of Reforma are Tlatelolco (☞ The Zócalo and Alameda Central, *above*), the Lagunilla Market, and Plaza Garibaldi, where the mariachis gather. To the south, Reforma wends its leisurely way west into the wealthy neighborhoods of Lomas de Chapultepec, where most of the houses and estates are behind stone walls.

Two areas of particular interest along Reforma are the Zona Rosa and Bosque de Chapultepec. Start your exploration of the Zona Rosa sections at the junction of Reforma, Avenida Juárez, and Bucareli, just west of the Alameda Central. Along the stretch of Reforma west of this intersection are a number of statues erected at the request of Porfirio Díaz to honor illustrious men, including Simón Bolívar, Columbus, Pasteur, and Cuauhtémoc. The best known, the **Monumento a la Independencia** ⑳, also known as The Angel, marks the western edge of the Zona Rosa. To get the best of the area's sights, walk along Hamburgo, Londres, and Copenhague streets—like others in the Zona, named for Continental cities. There is a crafts market, Mercado Zona Rosa, on Londres.

Four blocks southwest of the Zona Rosa, at Avenida Chapultepec, you'll come to the main entrance of **Bosque de Chapultepec** ㉑, or Chapultepec Park. Uphill from the entrance is the **Castillo de Chapultepec** ㉒ and its National History Museum. Heading downhill again after leaving the Castillo, you'll go past the much smaller, also historical, **Museo del Caracol** ㉓. North of the Castillo on the near side of Paseo de la Reforma is the **Museo de Arte Moderno** ㉔. Almost directly across Paseo de la Reforma on its south side and west of Calle Gandhi, you'll see the **Museo Rufino Tamayo** ㉕, in which you'll find Tamayo's works as well as those of other modern artists. West of the Museo Tamayo on the same side of Reforma is the **Museo Nacional de Antropología** ㉖, with its superb collections of Mesoamerican art and artifacts. Cross Reforma again and you'll come to the entrance to the **Zoológico** ㉗.

Southeast of Bosque de Chapultepec, **Colonia Condesa** ㉘ is a tree-lined neighborhood, whose meandering streets make for pleasant strolling, especially in spring when jacaranda blossoms color the colonia. From the Bosque de Chapultepec, take a *pesero* (minibus) from beside the Chapultepec metro or a five-minute taxi ride to Calle Michoacán. On foot it is a 15- to 20-minute walk up Calle Veracruz going away from the park. Turn right on Avenida Mazatlán, then left onto Calle Michoacán.

TIMING

You can easily spend an hour each at Bosque de Chapultepec's museums (☞ Sights to See, *below*), with the exception of the National Museum of Anthropology, which is gigantic compared to its sister cultural centers. You can have a quick go-through in two hours, but to really appreciate the fine exhibits, anywhere from a half-day to two full days would be more appropriate. Tuesday to Saturday are good days to visit the museums and stroll around the park. On Sunday and Mexican holidays, when museum entry is free, the park and museums are packed with families with lots of small children. Adding Colonia Condesa to the end of a day of museum visits will make for a delightful evening.

Sights to See
BOSQUE DE CHAPULTEPEC

㉑ **Bosque de Chapultepec** ("The Woods of Chapultepec," or Chapultepec Park). This 1,600-acre green space, divided into three sections, draws families on weekend outings, cyclists, and joggers. And its museums—including the Museo Nacional de Antropología—are among the finest in Mexico. This is one of the oldest parts of Mexico City, having been inhabited by the Mexica (Aztec) tribe as early as the 13th century. The Mexica poet-king Nezahualcoyotl had his palace here and ordered construction of the aqueduct that brought water to Tenochtitlán. Ahuehuete trees (Moctezuma cypress) still stand from that era, when the woods were used as hunting preserves.

At the park's principal entrance, one block west of the Chapultepec metro station, the **Monumento a los Niños Héroes** (Monument to the Boy Heroes) consists of six marble columns adorned with eaglets. In the monument are supposedly buried the six young cadets who wrapped themselves in the Mexican flag then jumped to their deaths from the ramparts during the U.S. invasion of 1847. That war may not take up

Zona Rosa, Bosque de Chapultepec, and Condesa

much space in U.S. textbooks, but to Mexicans it is still a troubling symbol of their neighbor's aggressive dominance: the war cost Mexico almost half of its national territory—the present states of Texas, California, Arizona, New Mexico, and Nevada.

Other sights in the first section of Bosque de Chapultepec include three small boating lakes, a botanical garden, and the Casa del Lago cultural center, which hosts free plays, cultural events, and live music on weekends. **Los Pinos,** the residential palace of the president of Mexico, is on a small highway called Avenida Constituyentes, which cuts through the park. This is heavily guarded and cannot be visited.

The less-crowded second and third sections of Bosque de Chapultepec contain a fancy restaurant; **La Feria de Chapultepec** (☞ *below*); **El Papalote** (☞ *below*); the national cemetery; and the **Lienzo Charro** (Mexican rodeos) held on Sunday afternoons.

★ ㉒ **Castillo de Chapultepec** (Chapultepec Castle). On Cerro del Chapulín (Grasshopper Hill), the Castillo has borne witness to all the turbulence and grandeur of Mexican history. In its earliest permutations, it was a Mexica palace, where the Indians made one of their last stands against the Spaniards. Later it was a Spanish hermitage, gunpowder plant, and military college. Emperor Maximilian used the castle, parts of which date from 1783, as his residence, and his example was followed by various presidents from 1872 to 1940, when Lázaro Cárdenas decreed that it be turned into the **Museo Nacional de Historia** (National History Museum).

Displays on the museum's ground floor cover Mexican history from the conquest to the revolution. The bathroom, bedroom, tea salon, and gardens were used by Maximilian and his wife, Carlotta, during the 19th century. The ground floor also contains works by 20th-century muralists O'Gorman, Orozco, and Siqueiros, while the upper floor is devoted to temporary exhibits, Porfirio Díaz's malachite vases, and religious art. A 30-cent shuttle bus runs between this museum and the Museo del Caracol (☞ *below*). ⊠ *Section 1 of Bosque de Chapultepec,* ☎ *5/553–6224.* ⊡ *$2; free Sun.* ☉ *Tues.–Sun. 9–5.*

☽ **La Feria de Chapultepec.** This children's amusement park has various games and more than 50 rides, including a truly hair-raising haunted house and a *montaña rusa*—"Russian mountain," or roller coaster. ⊠ *Section 2 of Bosque de Chapultepec,* ☎ *5/230–2112.* ⊡ *$6.50 day pass includes all rides.* ☉ *Tues.–Fri. 11–7, weekends 10–9.*

☽ **El Papalote, Museo del Niño** (The Butterfly, Children's Museum). Five theme sections compose this excellent interactive museum: *Our World*; *The Human Body*; the pun-intended *Con-Sciencia,* with exhibits relating to both consciousness and science; *Communication,* which focuses on topics ranging from language to computers; and *Expression,* which includes art, music, theater, and literature. There are also workshops, an IMAX theater, store, and restaurant. ⊠ *Av. Constituyentes 268, Section 2 of Bosque de Chapultepec,* ☎ *5/237–1781.* ⊡ *$3.50.* ☉ *Weekdays 9–1 and 2–6; weekends 10–2 and 3–7.*

★ ㉔ **Museo de Arte Moderno** (Museum of Modern Art). Exhibits here focus on Mexican artists. Two rooms are devoted to plastic arts from the 1930s to the 1960s; a third focuses on the past 20 years; and a fourth room and annex house temporary exhibits of contemporary Mexican painting, lithography, sculpture, and photography. ⊠ *Reforma and Gandhi, Section 1 of Bosque de Chapultepec,* ☎ *5/553–6313.* ⊡ *$1.50; free Sun.* ☉ *Tues.–Sun. 10–5:30.*

☽ ㉓ **Museo del Caracol.** Officially, it's the Galeria de la Lucha del Pueblo Mexicano por su Libertad, but most people refer to it by the more fanciful name "Museum of the Snail," because of its spiral shape. The gallery concentrates on the 400 years from the establishment of the Viceroyalty to the Constitution of 1917, using dioramas and light-and-sound displays that children can appreciate. ⊠ *Section 1 of Bosque de Chapultepec, on the ramp up to the Castillo,* ☎ *5/553–6285.* ⊡ *$1.60.* ☉ *Daily 10–5:30.*

★ ㉖ **Museo Nacional de Antropología** (National Museum of Anthropology). This is the greatest museum in the country—and arguably one of the finest archaeological museums anywhere. Even its architectural design, by Pedro Ramírez Vázquez, is distinguished. The museum is arranged on two floors, surrounded by salons, with each displaying artifacts from a particular geographic region and/or culture. The collection is so extensive—covering some 100,000 square ft—that you could easily spend a full day here, and that in itself might be barely adequate. Labels and explanations are in Spanish, but you can reserve an English-speaking tour guide by calling the museum 15 days in advance, or hire an unofficial bilingual guide outside the museum for about $10. The museum has English audio guides for rent for $3, and English-language guidebooks are available in the bookshop.

A good place to start is in the Orientation Room, where a film is shown in Spanish nearly every hour on the hour during the week and every two hours on the weekends. The film traces the course of Mexican prehistory and the pre-Hispanic cultures of Mesoamerica. The 12 ground floor rooms treat pre-Hispanic cultures by region—such as Sala Teotihuacána, Sala Tolteca, Sala Oaxaca (Zapotec and Mixtec peoples), Sala Maya (Maya groups from many areas, including Guatemala), and so on. The famous Aztec calendar stone, the original *Piedra del Sol* (Stone of the Sun) is found in Room 7, the Sala Mexica, which describes Aztec life. A copy of the Aztec ruler Moctezuma's feathered headdress is displayed nearby in the same salon—strangely, the original headdress is in Vienna. An original stela from Tula, near Mexico City, massive Olmec heads from Veracruz, and vivid reproductions of Maya murals in a reconstructed temple are just some of the other highlights. The magnificent tomb of the 8th-century Maya ruler Pacal, which was discovered in the ruins of Palenque, is another must to explore (Sala Maya). The perfectly preserved skeletal remains lie in state in an immense stone chamber, and the stairwell walls leading to it are beautifully decorated with bas-relief scenes of the underworld. Pacal's jade death mask is also on display nearby. The Maya section was updated in 1996 to include pieces from digs in remote places like Calakmul in Campeche and Tonina and Yaxchílan in Chiapas. Otherwise the ground floor is filled with everything from the early remnants of nomadic societies to the statuary, jewelry, weapons, figurines, and pottery that evoke the brilliant, quirky, and frequently bloodthirsty civilizations that peopled Mesoamerica for the 3,000 years that preceded the Spanish invasion.

The nine rooms on the upper floor contain faithful ethnographic displays of current indigenous peoples, using maps, photographs, household objects, folk art, clothing, and religious articles. When leaving the museum take a rest and watch the famous *Voladores de Papantla* (flyers of Papantla) as they swing by their feet down an incredibly high maypole-like structure. ⊠ *Paseo de la Reforma at Calle Gandhi, Section 1 of Bosque de Chapultepec,* ☎ *5/286–2923; 5/553–6381 for a guide.* ⊡ *$2; free Sun.* ⊙ *Tues.–Sun. 9–7.*

★ ㉕ **Museo Rufino Tamayo** (Rufino Tamayo Museum). Within its modernist shell, this sleek museum contains the paintings of the noted Mexican muralist, works from his private collection, and pieces by contemporary artists from around the world in temporary exhibits. The majority of paintings are by Tamayo; those from his collection, which demonstrate his unerring eye for great art, include a Picasso and a few scattered works by Joan Miró, René Magritte, Francis Bacon, and Henry Moore. ⊠ *Av. Reforma west of Gandhi, Section 1 of Bosque de Chapultepec,* ☎ *5/286–6519.* ⊡ *$1.85.* ⊙ *Tues.–Sun. 10–6.*

↺ **Ripley's Museo de lo Increíble** (Museum of the Incredible) and the **Museo de Cera de la Ciudad de Mexico** (Mexico City Wax Museum). Fun for children of all ages, the Ripley's museum has 14 exhibit rooms chockablock with believe-it-or-not items, while in the wax museum Placido Domingo and Mexican politicians come to life. ⊠ *Londres 4 (east of Zona Rosa),* ☎ *5/546–3784.* ⊡ *$3 each museum or $4 for both.* ⊙ *Weekdays 11–7, weekends 10–7.*

↺ ㉗ **Zoológico.** In the early 16th century, Mexico City's zoo housed a small private collection of animals belonging to Moctezuma II; it became quasi-public when he allowed favored subjects to visit it. The current zoo opened on this site in the 1920s and has the usual suspects as well as some superstar pandas. A gift from China, the original pair—Pepe and Ying Ying—produced the world's first panda baby born in captivity (much to competitive China's chagrin). The zoo also produced the first spectacled bears in captivity in 1998, the same year officials added the Moctezuma Aviary, where parrots, toucans, herons, and pelicans fly freely. The zoo is surrounded by a miniature train depot, botanical gardens, and lakes where you can go rowing. You'll see the entrance on Reforma, across the street from the Museum of Anthropology. ⊠ *Section 1 of Bosque de Chapultepec,* ☎ *5/553–6263 or 5/256–4104.* ⊡ *Free; Spanish audio guide, $2.* ⊙ *Tues.–Sun. 9:30–4:15.*

COLONIA CONDESA

28 **Colonia Condesa.** Colonia Condesa sprang up in the early 1900s around the city's elite, who quickly abandoned it in the '40s for other more fashionable areas, leaving decaying mansions and parks behind. Today, the neighborhood is getting new life and renovation from an influx of new residents, mostly young artists, entrepreneurs, and foreigners. Restaurants have sprung up everywhere in the colonia, quickly making Condesa a new center for cuisine.

Condesa doesn't have much in the way of museums or monuments, but it is the perfect place to break from a hectic day of sight-seeing—just sit back in one of the neighborhood's relaxed sidewalk cafés and watch Mexico go by. And with a new restaurant opening nearly every week, it is the place to come for dinner. The main drag is Avenida Michoacán, from which restaurants radiate out in every direction. Avenida México loops the main park in the area, Parque México, and Avenida Amsterdam makes another loop around the area. The park area used to be a racetrack, which explains the looping roads.

There is also an abundance of hip and trendy clothing shops in the area. The most famous are on Michoacán: **Soho,** for example, is a clothing and music store whose name refers to the often-made comparison of Condesa to New York's Soho in the 1950s; the trendy **La Esquina** clothing store down the street is similar. On Nuevo Leon, another great shop to browse through is **El Péndulo** (✉ 115 Nuevo Leon, ☎ 5/286–9493), a sort of cultural center. It has a large selection of Spanish books and an international collection of CDs, and the restaurant here has a great breakfast menu, with classical guitarists playing on Sunday mornings. El Péndulo often hosts other performers—jazz, classical, folk, or unplugged rock bands—on weekends.

Farther east on Michoacán, you can always head to the Parque México for a picnic or a stroll. There are also two great movie theaters along Avenida Tamaulipas: turn northwest to get to the **Plaza Condesa** (☎ 5/286–4973) at the Parque España, or turn southwest down Tamaulipas to arrive at the **Bella Epoca** (☎ 5/515–1550). Both show a variety of Hollywood, Mexican, and foreign films; the Plaza Condesa has waiters who serve popcorn and drinks during the flick.

ZONA ROSA

For years the Zona Rosa has been a favorite part of the city because of its plethora of restaurants, cafés, art and antiques galleries, hotels, discos, and shops. With the mushrooming of fast-food places and some tacky bars and stores, the Zona—as it is affectionately called—has lost some of its former gloss, but nonetheless still draws the faithful. Most of the buildings in the Zona Rosa are on a very human scale, at two or three stories high: they were originally private homes built in the 1920s for the wealthy. All the streets are wistfully named after European cities; some, such as Genova, are garden-lined pedestrian malls accented with contemporary bronze statuary.

To enjoy the Zona Rosa, just walk the lengths of Hamburgo and Londres and some of the side streets, especially Copenhague—a veritable restaurant row. The large crafts market on Londres is officially Mercado Insurgentes, though most people call it either Mercado Zona Rosa or Mercado Londres. Just opposite the market's Londres entrance is Plaza del Angel, a small upscale shopping mall, the halls of which are crowded by antiques vendors on weekends.

20 **Monumento a la Independencia** (Independence Monument). A Corinthian column topped by a gold-covered angel is the city's most beautiful monument, built to celebrate the 100th anniversary of Mexico's War of Independence. Beneath the pedestal lie the remains of the principal heroes of the independence movement; an eternal flame burns in their honor. ⊠ *Traffic circle between Calle Río Tiber, Paseo de la Reforma, and Calle Florencia, 1 block west of U.S. embassy.*

San Angel and Coyoacán

Originally separate colonial towns, San Angel and Coyoacán were both absorbed by the ever-growing capital. In the process they've managed to retain their original pueblo charm and tranquility.

San Angel is a little colonial enclave of cobblestone streets, stone walls, pastel houses, and gardens drenched in bougainvillea. It became a haven for wealthy Spaniards during the Viceroyalty period, around the time of the construction of the **Ex-Convento del Carmen** (☞ *below*). The elite were drawn to the area because of its rivers, pleasant climate, and rural ambience, and proceeded to build haciendas and mansions that, for many, were country homes. Like neighboring Coyoacán, San Angel was just a suburb of Mexico City until the government decided to incorporate it into the capital.

Coyoacán means "Place of the Coyotes." According to local legend, a coyote used to bring chickens to a friar who had saved the coyote from being strangled by a snake. Coyoacán was founded by Toltecs in the 10th century and later settled by the Aztecs, or Mexica. Bernal Díaz Castillo, a Spanish chronicler, wrote that there were 6,000 houses at the time of the conquest. Cortés set up headquarters in Coyoacán during his siege of Tenochtitlán and at one point considered making it his capital. He changed his mind for political reasons, but many of the Spanish buildings left from the two-year period during which Mexico City was built still stand.

Coyoacán has had many illustrious residents from Mexico's rich and intellectual elite, including Miguel de la Madrid, president of Mexico from 1982 to 1988; Orozco, the muralist; Gabriel Figueroa, cinematographer for Luis Buñuel and John Huston; the film star Dolores del Río; film director El Indio Fernández; and writers Carlos Monsiváis, Elena Poniatowska, and Jorge Ibargüengoitia. It is also the neighborhood where Leon Trotsky in exile met his violent death. Although superficially it resembles San Angel, Coyoacán has a more animated street life. Most of the houses and other buildings honor the traditions of colonial Mexican architecture, and the neighborhood is well kept by residents, many of whose families have lived here for generations.

A Good Tour

To explore the southern part of the city—which until 50 years ago comprised separate pueblos—take a taxi or pesero down Avenida Insurgentes and get off at Avenida La Paz. On the east side of Insurgentes is the bizarre **Monumento al General Alvaro Obregón** ㉙. Cross Insurgentes on Avenida La Paz, and take the southern fork off Avenida La Paz (Calle Madero) until you come to San Angel's center, **Plaza San Jacinto** ㉚. Stroll to the **Casa del Risco** ㉛ on the north side of the plaza and, if it's a Saturday, head for the **Bazar Sábado** (☞ Shopping, *below*) on the north end. Return to Avenida Revolución and Plaza del Carmen, which lies at the corner of Calle Monasterio. Inside is the colonial **Ex-Convento del Carmen** ㉜, interesting as an example of sacred architecture and for its religious artifacts. Now take Avenida Revolución one long block north to see the modern Mexican and European works of **Museo Alvar y Carmen T. de Carrillo Gil** ㉝.

The next part of the tour goes to Coyoacán, which extends east of Avenida Insurgentes about 1 km (½ mi) from San Angel. Consider tak-

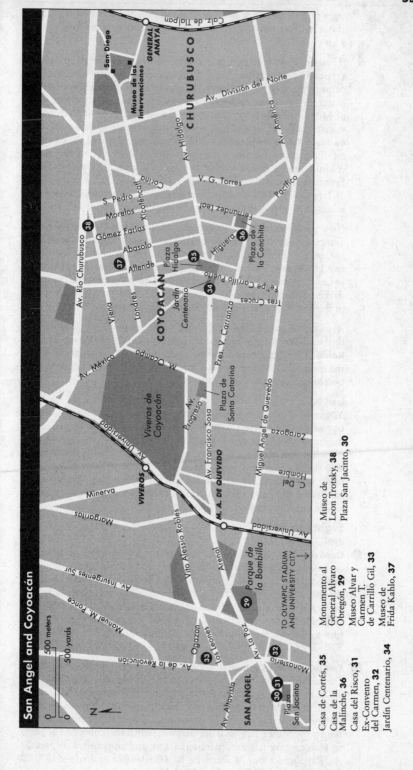

San Angel and Coyoacán

Casa de Cortés, **35**

Casa de la
Malinche, **36**

Casa del Risco, **31**

Ex-Convento
del Carmen, **32**

Jardín Centenario, **34**

Monumento al
General Alvaro
Obregón, **29**

Museo Alvar y
Carmen T.
de Carrillo Gil, **33**

Museo de
Frida Kahlo, **37**

Museo de
Leon Trotsky, **38**

Plaza San Jacinto, **30**

ing a taxi to the Plaza de Santa Catarina on Avenida Francisco Sosa, about halfway into the center of Coyoacán, because the tour involves a lot of walking.

If you decide to hoof it, make your way to the corner of Avenidas Universidad and Francisco Sosa. Head east on Francisco Sosa until you come to the pretty 16th-century Iglesia de Santa Catarina, which dominates the tiny **Plaza de Santa Catarina.** The plaza also contains a bust of Mexican historian Francisco Sosa, who lived here and wrote passionately about Coyoacán. Across the street from the plaza is the **Casa de Jesús Reyes Heroles** (No. 202); the former home of the ex-minister of education is a fine example of 20th-century architecture on the colonial model. It's now used as a cultural center. Continue east on Francisco Sosa and you'll pass Casa de Diego de Ordaz at the corner of Tres Cruces. This *mudéjar* (Spanish-Arabic) structure, adorned with inlaid mortar, was the home of a former captain in Cortés's army.

Now you're standing at the entrance of the **Jardín Centenario** ㉞. The Templo de San Juan Bautista and the picturesque **Casa de Cortés** ㉟ sit in the small Plaza Hidalgo adjacent to and north of the Jardín. Walk two blocks southeast of Plaza Hidalgo on Calle Higuera to the corner of Calle Vallarta, where you'll find the **Casa de la Malinche** ㊱. The house, darkened with age, faces an attractive park called Plaza de la Conchita, in the center of which lies an 18th-century church.

Return to Plaza Hidalgo and walk five blocks north on Calle Allende to the corner of Calle Londres and the house-turned- **Museo de Frida Kahlo** ㊲. It is linked historically—or should we say romantically—with the fortresslike **Museo de Leon Trotsky** ㊳, east of it on Londres, then two long blocks north on Morelos.

TIMING

You're likely to want to linger in these elegant and beautiful sections of town, especially in Coyoacán. The Frida Kahlo and Leon Trotsky museums give intense, intimate looks at the lives of two famous people who were friends and lovers, and who breathed their personalities into the places where they lived. Allow at least an hour at each. The other museums are much smaller and merit less time. Weekends are liveliest at the Plaza Hidalgo and its neighboring Jardín Centenario, where street life explodes into a fiesta.

Sights to See

SAN ANGEL

㉛ **Casa del Risco** (Risco House). This 1681 mansion is one of the prettiest houses facing the Plaza de San Jacinto. A huge free-form sculpture—exploding with colorful porcelain, tiles, shells, and mosaics—covers the entire eastern wall of its patio. Although it's not ranked among the city's top museums, the **Museo de la Casa del Risco** houses a splendid collection of 14th- to 18th-century European and colonial Mexican paintings as well as period furnishings. ⊠ *Plaza de San Jacinto 15,* ☎ *5/616-2711.* ☜ *Free.* ☉ *Tues.–Sun. 10–5.*

㉜ **Ex-Convento del Carmen** (Carmelite Convent and Church). Erected by Carmelite friars with the help of an Indian chieftain between 1615 and 1628, this cloister, with its tile-covered domes, fountains, and gardens, is one of the most interesting examples of colonial religious architecture in this part of the city. The church still operates, but the convent is now the **Museo Regional del Carmen,** with a fine collection of 16th- to 18th-century religious paintings, icons, and mummified corpses. ⊠ *Av. Revolución 4 at Monasterio,* ☎ *5/550–4896 or 5/616–1177.* ☜ *$1.60; free Sun.* ☉ *Tues.–Sun. 10–4:45.*

㉙ **Monumento al General Alvaro Obregón.** This somber gray granite monument marks the spot where reformer and national hero Obregón was gunned down by a religious zealot in a restaurant in 1928, soon before he was to begin his second term as president. ⊠ *Parque de la Bombilla, east of Av. La Paz at Av. Insurgentes.*

㉝ **Museo Alvar y Carmen T. de Carrillo Gil.** This private collection contains early murals by Orozco, Rivera, and Siqueiros; works by modern European artists such as Klee and Picasso; and temporary expositions of young Mexican artists. ⊠ *Av. Revolución 1608 at Desierto de los Leones,* ☏ *5/550–3983.* ⊡ *$1.* ☉ *Tues.–Sun. 10–6.*

★ ㉚ **Plaza San Jacinto.** This cozy plaza with a grisly history is the center of San Angel. In 1847 about 50 Irish soldiers of St. Patrick's Battalion, who had sided with the Mexicans in the Mexican-American War, had their foreheads branded here with the letter *D*—for deserter—and were then hanged by the Americans. These men had been enticed to swim the Rio Grande, deserting the ranks of U.S. General Zachary Taylor, by pleas to the historic and religious ties between Spain and Ireland. As settlers in Mexican Texas, they felt their allegiance lay with Catholic Mexico, and they were among the bravest fighters in the war. They met their end when the American flag flew over Castillo de Chapultepec (☞ *above*) after the death of the *niños héroes*. A memorial plaque (located on a building on the plaza's west side) lists their names and expresses Mexico's gratitude for their help in the "unjust North American invasion." Each September a ceremony is conducted here in honor of the Irish heroes. Off to one side of the plaza, the excellent handicrafts market, **Bazar Sábado,** is held on Saturday (☞ *Shopping, below*). ⊠ *Between Miramon, Cda. Santisima, Dr. Galvez, and Madero.*

COYOACÁN

㉟ **Casa de Cortés** (Cortés House). The place where the Aztec emperor Cuauhtémoc was held prisoner by the conquistador Cortés is reputed to have been rebuilt in the 18th century from the stones of his original house by one of Cortés's descendants; the municipal government now has offices here. Dominating the little square on which it sits, this was almost the city's first city hall, but Cortés decided to rebuild Tenochtitlán instead. The two-story, deep-red house, with its wide arches and tiled patio, is gorgeous. The house is not open to the public, but there is a tourist information booth in the front room staffed by friendly employees eager to tell you about Coyoacán. ⊠ *Plaza Hidalgo between Calles Carillo Puerto and Caballo Calco.*

㊱ **Casa de la Malinche.** One of the most powerful symbols of the conquest is located in Coyoacán but, significantly perhaps, is not even marked. It's the somber-looking, fortresslike residence of Malinche, Cortés's Indian mistress and interpreter, whom the Spaniards called Doña María and the Indians called Malintzín. Malinche aided the conquest by enabling Cortés to communicate with the Nahuatl-speaking tribes he met en route to Tenochtitlán. Today she is a much-reviled Mexican symbol of a traitorous xenophile—hence the term *malinchista,* used to describe a Mexican who prefers things foreign. The legends say that Cortés's wife died in this house, poisoned by the conquistador. ⊠ *2 blocks east of Plaza Hidalgo on Calle Higuera at Vallarta.*

㉞ **Jardín Centenario** (Centenary Gardens). Small fairs, amateur musical performances, poetry readings, and palm readings are frequent occurrences in this large park surrounded by outdoor cafés. At the far end of the Jardín you'll see **Templo San Juan Bautista,** one of the first churches to be built in New Spain. It was completed in 1582, and its door has a baroque arch. ⊠ *Between Calles Centenario, Hidalgo, and Caballo Calco.*

★ ㊲ **Museo de Frida Kahlo.** The house where the painter Frida Kahlo was born (in 1907)—and lived with Diego Rivera almost continuously from 1929 until her death in 1954—is fascinating. Kahlo has become a cult figure, not only because of her paintings—55 of 143 being self-portraits—but also because of her bohemian lifestyle and flamboyant individualism. As a child Kahlo was crippled by polio, and several years later she was impaled on a tramway rail. She had countless operations, including the amputation of a leg; was addicted to painkillers; had affairs with Leon Trotsky and several women; and married Rivera twice. Kahlo's astounding vitality and originality are reflected in this house, from the giant papier-mâché skeletons outside and the painted tin *retablos* (ex-votos) on the staircase to the gloriously decorated kitchen and the bric-a-brac in her bedroom. Even if you know nothing about Kahlo, a visit to the museum—filled with letters, diaries, clothes, and paintings by Kahlo and other great moderns, including Klee and Duchamp—will leave you with a strong, visceral impression of this pivotal feminist artist. ⊠ *Londres 247, at Allende,* ☎ *5/554–5999.* ⊡ *$1.* ۞ *Tues.–Sun. 10–5:45.*

㊳ **Museo de Leon Trotsky.** Resembling an anonymous and forbidding fortress, with turrets for armed guards, this is where Leon Trotsky lived and was murdered. It is difficult to believe that it's the final resting place for the ashes of one of the most important figures of the Russian Revolution, but that only adds to the allure of the house, which is owned by Trotsky's grandson.

This is a modest, austere dwelling. Anyone taller than 5 ft must stoop to pass through doorways to Trotsky's bedroom—with bullet holes still in the walls from the first assassination attempt, in which the muralist Siqueiros was implicated—his wife's study, the dining room, and the study where the Mexican communist Ramón Mercader finally drove an ice pick into Trotsky's head. On his desk, cluttered with writing paraphernalia and an article he was revising in Russian, the calendar is open to that fateful day, August 20, 1940. The volunteers will tell you how Trotsky's teeth left a permanent scar on Mercader's hand, how he clung to life for 26 hours, what his last words were, and how his death was sponsored by the United States (others would say Stalin). Not all of the volunteers, however, speak English. ⊠ *Río Churubusco 410,* ☎ *5/658–8732.* ⊡ *$1.* ۞ *Tues.–Sun. 10–5.*

㋡ **Nuevo Reino Aventura.** This 100-acre theme park on the southern edge of the city comprises six "villages": Mexican, French, Swiss, Polynesian, American, and Children's World. Shows include performances by trained dolphins. The most famous of the playful swimmers was an orca whale named Keiko, star of the film *Free Willy*, who was sent to an aquarium in Oregon to recover his health before he was released into his native Icelandic waters in 1998. The park added a Virtual Reality room recently as well as a new ride, El Latigo (The Whip). ⊠ *Southwest of Coyoacán on Carretera Picacho a Ajusco at Km 1.5 on road,* ☎ *5/645–5434 or 5/654–6232.* ⊡ *$12.50 includes entrance and all rides.* ۞ *Tues.–Thurs. 10–6, Fri.–Sun. 10–7.*

DINING

Mexico City mealtime hours are 7–11 AM for breakfast (*desayuno*), 2–5 PM for lunch (*comida*), and 9 PM–midnight for dinner (*cena*). At deluxe restaurants, dress is generally formal (jacket and tie), and reservations are almost always required; see reviews for details. (Even if a

LA COCINA MEXICANA

TO ENTERTAIN THE notion that Mexican food is little more than tacos, enchiladas, and burritos—or Tex-Mex or Taco Bell—would be culinary blasphemy to native gastronomes. Regional cooking is the heart and soul of Mexico, multiplied by the republic's 32 states and the provinces within them. Fresh ingredients abound, recipes are passed down through generations (think Like Water for Chocolate), and preparation requires much patience and loving care. With the staples—rice, beans, chilies, and tortillas—chefs are turning out ever more sophisticated variations on national dishes. But in terms of the Mexican chef's arsenal of ingredients, they're only the beginning.

Maize was sacred to the Indians, who have innumerable ways of preparing cornmeal—from faithful tortillas and tamales (cornmeal wrapped in banana leaves or corn husks) to tostadas (lightly fried, open tortillas topped with meat, lettuce, and the like) and tacos (tortillas briefly heated, filled, and wrapped into slim cylinders). *Pozole* (giant corn kernels) are most often served in corn-and-pork-based soups. The sweet, corn-based drink *atole,* similar in consistency to hot chocolate, is a favorite breakfast or before-bed treat.

You'll find seafood not just on the coasts but also in the lake regions around Guadalajara and in the state of Michoacán. *Huachinango* (sea bass), abalone, crab, and swordfish are all popular. And ceviche—raw *mariscos* (fish and shellfish) marinated in lime juice then topped with chile, onions, and cilantro (fresh coriander leaves)—is almost a national dish; just make sure it's fresh. Shrimp, lobster, and oysters can be huge and succulent; bear in mind the folk adage and eat oysters only in months with names that contain the letter *r.* Likewise avoid raw shellfish wherever cholera or water pollution might be a risk.

Mexicans love beef, pork, and *barbacoa* (barbecued lamb) with a variety of sauces. The complex, spicy *mole*—its ingredients can number more than 100, among them many kinds of chilies, and in one mole cocoa—is one of Mexico's proudest culinary inventions. It is usually served over chicken or lamb. Chicken is often roasted, served in sauces like mole, or tucked in enchiladas, tacos, or burritos.

Fresh fruits and vegetables are another Mexican pleasure. Jicama, papaya, mamey, avocado, mango, guayaba, peanuts, squash, and tomatoes are just some of the produce native to Mexico. (All fresh produce should be washed in water with a commercial disinfectant—bacteria exist in Mexico that your stomach might not be happy with.)

Other Mexican specialties are less common abroad: *antojitos* or *botanas* (appetizers), *chilaquiles* (breakfast dishes made with tortilla strips scrambled with chili, tomatoes, onions, cream, and cheese), and *chiles en nogada* (a large poblano chili stuffed with beef or cheese, raisins, onion, olives, and almonds and topped with a creamy walnut sauce and pomegranate seeds). Soups are hearty—particularly pozole, *sopa azteca* (avocado and tortilla in a broth), and *sopa de flor de calabaza* (squash-flower soup).

The astonishing assortment of breads, sweets, beers, wines (which are fast improving), and cactus-based liquors goes on and on. Freshly squeezed fruit juices and fruit shakes (*licuados*) are safe to drink—if ordered in a restaurant with hygienic practices—and taste heavenly. And coffee ranges from Americano to organic varieties to *café de olla,* which is laced with spices and served in a coarse clay mug.

deluxe restaurant doesn't *require* a jacket and tie, men are likely to feel out-of-place if not well dressed.) If you're short on time, there are American-style coffee shops (VIPS, Denny's, Shirley's, and Sanborns) all over the city; some are open 24 hours.

Colonia Polanco is an attractive, upscale neighborhood on the edge of Chapultepec Park that has some of the best and most expensive dining (and Lodging, ☞ *below*) in the city. Zona Rosa restaurants get filled pretty quickly on Saturday nights, especially the Saturday coinciding with most people's *quincena* (payday), which falls on the 1st and 15th of each month.

CATEGORY	COST*
$$$$	over $40
$$$	$25–$40
$$	$15–$25
$	under $15

per person for a three-course meal, excluding drinks and service

Argentine

$$$ ✕ **Cambalache.** Before entering this ever-busy beef lover's dream, you can see the chefs preparing their thick cuts in the window. If you come with a few people, try the Super Lomo Cambalache, a steak big enough for three to four people. If you're not in the mood for beef, there are also several chicken dishes on the menu such as the Don Ignacio: a boneless chicken breast served in a mushroom sauce with pineapple and fresh sweet peppers. Vegetables *do* come with menu items, and potatoes, particularly the soufflé, are a specialty. ⊠ *Arquímedes 85, Col. Polanco,* ☎ *5/280–2080 or 5/280–2957. AE, MC, V.*

$$$ ✕ **Rincon Argentino.** This most talked about Argentine restaurant in the city is known as much for its decor as for its exquisitely prepared cuts of beef. The interior is like the outdoors, with the ceiling painted into a sky, the bar covered by a thatched roof, and the dining areas turned into a stone-and-wood lodge—you might as well be in some Patagonian village. The focus here is beef—such as *lomo mignon,* filet mignon served with bacon and a rich mushroom sauce, or a tender, thick, and juicy *bife de chorizo* (chorizo steak). Most Argentines prefer their beef *cocida* (well-done), but you can have it any way you like. ⊠ *Presidente Masaryk 177, Col. Polanco,* ☎ *5/531–8617 or 5/254–8775. AE, DC, MC, V.*

$ ✕ **Fonda Garufa.** Its tables spilling out onto a Condesa sidewalk, this is a perfect place for a relaxed meal after a day of sight-seeing. Filet mignon, served with mushrooms and watercress, is especially delicious. There is also an extensive list of innovative pastas. A favorite with regulars is fettuccine Hindú: half a chicken breast bathed in a yogurt sauce laced with cilantro, ginger, onion, and of touch of chili, served over fresh fettuccine. ⊠ *Michoacán 93, Col. Condesa,* ☎ *5/286–8295. AE, V. Closed Sun.*

French

$$$$ ✕ **Fouquet's de Paris.** Located in the Camino Real hotel, this branch
  ★   of the renowned Parisian restaurant is an elegant haven of peace and tranquility. The best pâtés in Mexico and tender, juicy lamb chops are part of the diverse and stylish menu. Desserts are in a class of their own: sorbets, such as the delicately flavored passion fruit, are outstanding, and the cakes, mousses, and pastries are light and delicious. Month-long gastronomic festivals are held here throughout the year, and each October or November, chefs from the original Fouquet's in Paris take

over the kitchen. ⊠ *Hotel Camino Real, Mariano Escobedo 700, Col. Polanco,* ☎ *5/203–2121. Reservations essential. Jacket and tie. AE, DC, MC, V. Closed Sun. No lunch Sat.*

$$$ ✕ **Champs Elysées.** On the corner of Amberes and Reforma, com-
★ manding a superb view of the Independence Monument, is one of the bastions of haute cuisine in Mexico City. The variety of sauces served with both meat and fish dishes is impressive—hollandaise over sea bass or red snapper takes top honors. Regulars find either the roast duck (carved at your table) or the pepper steak hard to resist. The cheese board is particularly generous. ⊠ *Paseo de la Reforma 316 (at Estocolmo), Zona Rosa,* ☎ *5/525–7259. AE, DC, MC, V. Closed Sun.*

$ ✕ **El Buen Comer.** One of the more original Polanco eating spots, El Buen Comer (Eating Well) consists of not more than 20 tables in the covered garage of a private house. The entrance is discreet and easily missed, and the atmosphere inside is that of a large, private lunch party. The emphasis is on French cuisine from Lyon. House specialties include an endive salad with a cream-and-nut vinaigrette served with scallops. The fondues and pâtés are excellent. A favorite main course of habitués is quiche Lorraine, and the quiche royale with shrimp is a must for seafood lovers. Whole steaks can be served to order with fine herbs, pepper, or shallots. Desserts include mango or chocolate mousse or raspberries smothered in cream. El Buen Comer makes a great stop after shopping in Polanco. ⊠ *Edgar Allan Poe 50, Col. Polanco,* ☎ *5/282–0325. Reservations essential. AE, DC, MC, V. Closed Sun. No dinner.*

Greek

$ ✕ **Agapi Mu (My Love).** This 16-table Greek bistro tucked in a con-verted Colonia Condesa home with a Greek flag out front and snug rooms inside attracts its share of actors, singers, and artists. Come for authentic Greek food in a casual, intimate setting and rambunctious Greek song and dance on Thursday through Saturday nights. The menu includes *paputsáka* (stuffed eggplant), *kalamárea* (fried squid Greek style), *dalmádes* (stuffed grape leaves), plus daily specials such as lamb fricassee. Wash it all down with a Hungarian Sangre de Toro wine, and finish it off with a smooth, sweet Greek coffee. ⊠ *Alfonso Reyes 96, Col. Condesa,* ☎ *5/286–1384. AE. Closed Sun.*

International

$$$$ ✕ **Estoril.** From their exquisitely furnished 1930s town house in fash-
★ ionable Colonia Polanco, Rosa Martin serves French cuisine with a Mex-ican flair. *Perejil frito* (fried parsley) is a popular starter, and main dishes offer some unusual combinations: giant prawns in Chablis or curry sauce, and sea bass in fresh coriander sauce. If you have a sweet tooth, try either the delicious tart Tatin—an upside-down apple tart with caramel—or the homemade sorbets. ⊠ *Alejandro Dumas 24, Col. Polanco,* ☎ *5/280–9828. Jacket and tie. AE, DC, MC, V. Closed Sun.*

$$$$ ✕ **Hacienda de los Morales.** This Mexican institution, set in a former hacienda that dates back to the 16th century, is grandly colonial in style, with dark wood beams and huge terra-cotta expanses. The menu com-bines international and Mexican cuisines with imaginative variations on both. Walnut soup, served either hot or cold, is a delicate and un-usual specialty. Fish is seemingly unlimited, ranging from sea bass *marinière* (in a white-wine sauce) to a mixed seafood gratin. The char-coal-broiled grain-fed chicken has a distinct flavor, and the paillard is always of the highest quality. Live mariachi music completes the atmo-sphere. ⊠ *Vázquez de Mella 525, Col. Chapultepec Morales,* ☎ *5/281–4554 or 5/281–4703. AE, DC, MC, V.*

Les Célébrités, **8**
Los Almendros, **11, 25**
Los Arroces, **15**
Los Girasoles, **34**
Los Irabien, **31**
Maxim's de Paris, **7**
Meson El Cid, **33**
Rincon Argentino, **10**

San Angel Inn, **29**
Suntory, **28**
Tezka, **23**

$$$$ ✕ **Les Célébrités.** In addition to its superb French fare, this elegant hotel
★   restaurant also serves good Mexican food. When the Nikko México
       opened in 1987, chef Joël Robouchon, one of the creators of nouvelle
       cuisine in France, came to Mexico to set up this restaurant off the hotel
       lobby. With him came a menu that features such one-of-a-kind entrées
       as medallions of lobster in guayaba sauce or smoked salmon with spinach
       crepes; for dessert you might find pomegranate or prickly pear sher-
       bet. ⊠ *Nikko México, Campos Elíseos 204, Col. Polanco,* ☎ *5/280–*
       1111. Reservations essential. Jacket and tie. AE, DC, MC, V. Closed
       Sat. No lunch Sun.

$$$$ ✕ **Maxim's de Paris.** Under the auspices of the original Parisian
       Maxim's, this spacious but intimate Art Deco restaurant sits under a
       stained-glass ceiling and serves classic Gallic cuisine spiced up with the
       best of Mexican ingredients. Among the offerings are tongue in a del-
       icate vermouth sauce and abalone dressed in zesty chipotle chilies. Some
       of the pastry chef's irresistible desserts are mouthwatering Grand
       Marnier or hazelnut soufflés and extra-rich chocolate *turrón* (Spanish
       nougat). The wine cellar is nonpareil, and the service impeccable. ⊠
       Hotel Presidente Inter-Continental México, Campos Elíseos 218, Col.
       Polanco, ☎ *5/327–7700. Reservations essential. Jacket and tie. AE,*
       DC, MC, V. Closed Sun. No lunch Sat.

$$$ ✕ **Bellini.** While its great turntable slowly revolves on the 45th floor
       of the World Trade Center, executives from surrounding offices pack
       Bellini at lunch. At night it turns romantic, and the view of the city by
       lamplight is fantastic. The majority of the dishes here aren't in fact Ital-
       ian but Mexican and international. The house special is a lobster of
       your choosing from a tank brought tableside, which is prepared to your
       taste. Other favorites are filet mignon and homemade pastas prepared
       with classic Italian sauces. Finish with a flambéed dessert, such as straw-
       berries jubilee or crêpes suzette. After dinner, work off the extra calo-
       ries at the disco one floor above the restaurant. ⊠ *Av. de las Naciones*
       1, World Trade Center Tower, Col. Napoles, 10 mins by car south of
       Zona Rosa, ☎ *5/628–8305. Jacket and tie. AE, DC, MC, V.*

$$–$$$ ✕ **Bellinghausen.** This is one of the most pleasant lunch spots in the
       Zona Rosa; it's only open until 7 PM. The partially covered hacienda-
       style courtyard at the back, set off by an ivy-laden wall, is a magnet
       midday for executives and tourists. A veritable army of waiters scur-
       ries back and forth serving such tried-and-true favorites as *sopa de hon-*
       gos (mushroom soup) and *filete chemita* (broiled steak with mashed
       potatoes). The *higaditos de pollo* (chicken livers) with a side order of
       sautéed spinach is another winning dish. Other specials include *cabrito*
       (baby goat), roast lamb, and Spanish paella; fish and seafood are also
       superb. ⊠ *Londres 95, Zona Rosa,* ☎ *5/525–8738 or 5/207–4978.*
       AE, DC, MC, V. No dinner.

$ ✕ **Los Arroces.** The name means "rices," and rice is exactly what
       you'll get at this trendy spot in Colonia Condesa—50 different rices
       from around the world in soups, salads, and main dishes—everywhere
       but desserts. There's *pastel de arroz,* for example—white Mexican rice
       prepared with *rajas* (green pepper strips), *flor de calabaza* (squash flower),
       corn, and bacon—and Maya rice—served with squid, chopped red onion,
       sour oranges, and beans—and Spanish paella with rice from Valencia.
       There are a few noteworthy nonrice dishes like chicken with raspberry
       mole and blue-corn tortilla quesadillas stuffed with cheese, spinach,
       and chili. ⊠ *Michoacán 126,* ☎ *5/286–4287. AE, MC, V.*

Italian

$–$$ ✕ **La Lanterna.** The Petterino family has run this two-story restaurant
       for more than 20 years. The downstairs has the rustic feel of a north-

ern Italian trattoria, with the cramped seating adding to the intimacy. Upstairs is more spacious. All pastas are made on the premises; the Bolognese sauce, in particular, is a local favorite. Raw artichoke salad, *conejo al Salmi* (rabbit in a wine sauce), *filete al burro nero* (steak in black butter), or *saltimbocca à la Romana* (veal and ham in Marsala sauce), are all worthy dishes. ✉ *Paseo de la Reforma 458, Col. Juárez,* ☎ *5/207–9969. Reservations not accepted. MC, V. Closed Sun.*

Japanese

$$$ ✕ **Suntory.** This Suntory branch transports you to Japan by way of a Zen dry garden at the entryway and a dense green garden that follows. In this enchanted world you are not absolved of the difficulty of choice. Will it be the teppanyaki room to watch your fresh meat or fish prepared with a variety of vegetables—or if your protein cravings can no longer be ignored, perhaps the sushi bar—or maybe you'll end up in the shabu-shabu room, with its wafer-thin sashimi and a copper pot of steaming vegetable broth in which elegant slices of beef are cooked? Prices are high, but the ingredients are of the best quality. ✉ *Torres Adalid 14, Col. del Valle,* ☎ *5/536–9432;* ✉ *Montes Urales 535, Lomas Chapultepec,* ☎ *5/202–4711. AE, DC, MC, V. No dinner Sun.*

Mexican

$$$ ✕ **Cicero Centenario.** This thoroughly Mexican restaurant occupies a
★   restored 17th-century mansion in the heart of the historic downtown. Elegant colonial antiques are strikingly posed against folk art and pastel walls, and the bar has an outstanding collection of tin ex-votos and other religious memorabilia. The enticing menu includes excellent versions of authentic colonial dishes such as *pollo en pipián verde* (chicken in green-pumpkin-seed sauce). Try the *chicharrón* (crispy pork rind) - guacamole appetizer, but be sure to leave room for desserts such as rose-petal ice cream. An ebullient street-level cantina has drinks, *botanas* (appetizers), and afternoon serenades by a folk trio. ✉ *República de Cuba 79,* ☎ *5/521–1949 or 5/521–2934. Reservations essential. AE, DC, MC, V. No dinner Sun.*

$$$ ✕ **San Angel Inn.** In the south of the city, this magnificent old hacienda
★   and ex-convent, with elegant grounds and immaculately tended gardens, is both a joy to the eye and an inspiration to the palate. Dark mahogany furniture, crisp white table linens, and beautiful blue-and-white Talavera place settings strike a note of restrained opulence. Many dishes are to be recommended, especially the classic *huitlacoche* (corn-fungus) served in crepes, as well as *sopa de tortilla* (tortilla soup). The *puntas de filete* (sirloin tips) are liberally laced with chili, and the *huachinango* (sea bass) is offered in a variety of ways. Desserts—from light and crunchy meringues to pastries bulging with cream—can be rich to the point of surfeit. ✉ *Calle Diego Rivera 50 at Altavista, Col. San Angel,* ☎ *5/616–0537, 5/616–2222 or 5/616–1402. Jacket required. AE, DC, MC, V.*

$$ ✕ **El Arroyo.** This dining complex, complete with its own bullring, is a famous attraction in itself. Located at the south end of town near the beginning of the highway to Cuernavaca, it was founded more than 50 years ago by the Arroyo family and is now run by jovial Jesús ("Chucho") Arroyo. His loyal following includes celebrities, dignitaries, and bullfighters, along with local families, groups, and tourists: more than 2,600 people can dine simultaneously in a labyrinth of 11 picturesque dining areas. Typical Mexican specialties—roast baby lamb wrapped in maguey leaves, chicken mole, a dozen types of tacos, and much more—are prepared in open kitchens. There's mariachi music and the full gamut of Mexican drinks, including *pulque,* a classic alcoholic Maya bever-

age made from cactus. The small bullring is the forum for *novilleros,* or young bullfighters just beginning their careers, during the season (from about April through October). Breakfast starts at 8 AM and lunch is served until 8 PM. ⊠ *Insurgentes Sur 4003, Col. Tlalpán,* ☎ *5/573–4344. AE, DC, MC, V. No dinner.*

$$ ✕ **El Tajín.** Named after the enchanting Pyramid of the Niches in Veracruz, this eatery serves the innovative Mexican cooking that has taken the metropolis by storm. El Tajín adds zest and style to many well-known dishes. Dazzling main dishes include soft-shell crab accented by sesame seeds and a tad of chipotle chili. This lovely restaurant is hidden behind the functional facade of the Veracruz Cultural Center in Colonia Coyoacán. Ancient Huastecan faces grinning from a splashing fountain add a bit of levity to the dining experience. ⊠ *Miguel Angel de Queveda 687 in Coyoacán,* ☎ *5/659–4447 or 5/659–5759. AE, DC, MC, V. No dinner.*

$$ ✕ **Fonda del Recuerdo.** A popular family restaurant, the *fonda* (inn)
★ also has a solid reputation among tourists. Every day from 2 to 10, five marimba groups from Veracruz provide festive music. The place made its name with its fish and seafood platters from the gulf state of Veracruz, and the house special is huachinango *à la Veracruzano* (a whole red snapper in a succulent tomato, chopped onion, and olive sauce, mildly spiced). Sharing its fame is the *torito,* a potent drink made from tequila and exotic tropical fruit juices. Meat from the kitchen's own *parillas* (grills) is always first-rate. Portions are huge, but if you have room for dessert, try *crepas de cajeta al tequila* (milk-caramel crepes with tequila). ⊠ *Bahía de las Palmas 39, Col. Anzures,* ☎ *5/260–7339 or 5/260–1292. AE, DC, MC, V.*

$$ ✕ **Fonda Don Chón.** This simple family-style restaurant, deep in downtown, is famed for its indigenous Mexican dishes. A knowledge of zoology, Spanish, and Nahuatl helps in making sense of a menu that takes in a gamut of ingredients—no processed foods among them—from throughout the republic. *Escamoles de hormiga* (red-ant roe), 97% protein, is known as the "caviar of Mexico" for both its deliciousness and its costliness. Among the exotic entrées are armadillo in sesame mole sauce, iguana soup, and snake (boa or rattle) steak. More traditional specialties include *mixiote de carnero* (barbecued lamb in maguey leaves). The coconut cake is excellent, and live music adds to the atmosphere. ⊠ *Misionarios 213 near La Merced market, Col. Centro,* ☎ *5/522–2160. Reservations not accepted. AE, MC, V. No dinner Sun.*

$$ ✕ **Fonda El Refugio.** Since it opened in 1954, this Zona Rosa restaurant in a converted two-story town house has served the best dishes from each major region of the country—such as Guerrero, Michoacán, Sonora, and Veracruz. Atmosphere is casual but elegant in the intimate colonial-decor dining rooms (the one downstairs is the prettiest). Along with a varied regular menu, there is a daily selection of appetizers and entrées; you might find a mole made with pumpkin seeds or *albóndigas en chile chipotle* (meatballs in chipotle chili sauce). Try the refreshing *aguas* (fresh-fruit and seed juices) with your meal and the *café de olla* (cinnamon-flavored coffee sweetened with brown sugar) after dessert. ⊠ *Liverpool 166, Zona Rosa,* ☎ *5/207–2732 or 5/525–8128. AE, DC, MC, V. No dinner Sun.*

$$ ✕ **Isadora.** Some of Mexico City's most inventive cooking takes place in this converted private house in Polanco. The three smallish dining rooms have a 1920s feel and are uncharacteristically ascetic—pale walls dabbed with minimal modern-artistic flourishes. The management sponsors "cooking festivals," and every three months the kitchen produces dishes from a different country. The basic menu changes six times a year, and over that same period it will include three Mexican food fests. The set menu features duck pâté and excellent seafood pasta, with juicy prawns, shellfish, and squid. Ice creams, meringues, and chocolate cake for dessert benefit from the addition of the chef's delicate, pale green mint sauce. ⊠ *Moliere 50, Col. Polanco,* ☎ 5/280–1586. *Jacket and tie. AE, DC, MC, V. Closed Sun.*

$$ ✕ La Tecla. ★ This see-and-be-seen newcomer is a welcome addition to Mexico City's growing nueva Mexicana scene. Named after an old-fashioned type-setting key, the restaurant's Polanco location and a newsprint collage set a hip tone. The artsy Roma locale has copped a bit of an attitude toward those who don't reserve, but the food is worth a little cheekiness. The appetizers are especially intriguing, including squash flowers stuffed with goat cheese in a chipotle chili sauce and a spicy crab-stuffed chili relleno. The house special beef dish, *filete La Tecla,* shows a flair for sauces, in this case combining roquefort with huitlacoche. Best of all, the prices are still unpretentious. ⊠ *Col. Polanco: Moliere 56; Col. Roma: 186A Durango,* ☎ *Polanco: 5/282–0010; Roma: 5/525–4920. AE, MC, V. No dinner Sun.*

$$ ✕ Los Almendros. If you can't make it to the Yucatán, at least try the peninsula's unusual and lively food at one of this restaurant's two locations. If the spacious, cool white interior and bubbling fountain don't transport you to the balmy coast, then the habanero chilies, red onions, and other native Yucatecan ingredients will. Traditional dishes, like a refreshing lime soup or *frijol con puerco* (pieces of tender pork with black beans), share the menu with impossible-to-pronounce Maya cuisine. Especially worth trying is the *pescado tikinxic*—white fish in a mild red marinade of achiote chilies and bitter orange. This is a good place to sample a wide array of fine tequila, served with sliced jicama and a tangy tomato juice chaser called sangrita. ⊠ *Col. Polanco: Campos Eliseos 164; Col. Guadalupe: Insurgentes Sur 1759,* ☎ *Polanco: 5/531–6646; Guadalupe: 5/663–5151. AE, MC, V. No dinner Sun.*

$$ ✕ Los Girasoles. This downtown spot is owned by two prominent Mexico City society columnists. Los Girasoles (sunflowers) is on a lovely old square in a restored three-story colonial home and serves nueva Mexicana cuisine—light, tasty, and innovative. Traditional Mexican bean soup is dressed up with noodles and a pinch of chili. Meat, fish, and seafood dishes are blended with exotic herbs and spices. There are also pre-Hispanic delicacies such as *escamoles* (ant roe), *gusanos de maguey* (chilied worms), and *chapulines* (crispy fried grasshoppers). The desserts pay homage to local produce with such creations as *guanabana*- and *zapote*-fruit mousses. One of the nicest places for dining is the covered terrace outdoors on the street level. A branch of the restaurant has opened in Miami. ⊠ *Plaza Manuel Tolsa on Xicoténcatl 1,* ☎ *5/510–0630 or 5/510–3281. AE, MC, V. No dinner Sun.*

$$ ✕ Los Irabien. This beautiful dining area filled with plants and the owner's impressive art collection is a worthwhile stop for foodies and culture vultures. Chef Arturo Fuentes turns out nueva Mexicana and traditional Mexican dishes. His *ensalada Irabien* triumphs as a mixture of smoked salmon, abalone, prawn, quail eggs, and watercress. One outstanding entrée is nopal cactus stuffed with fish fillet in garlic. You'll also find less exotic dishes. Los Irabien is one of the city's breakfast spots par excellence—tempting you with *huevos de codorniz huitzilopochtli*—quail eggs with tortilla on the treasured corn delicacy in a squash-blossom sauce. ⊠ *Av. de la Paz 45, Col. San Angel,* ☎ *5/616–0014. Jacket and tie. AE, DC, MC, V. No dinner Sun.*

$ ✕ Café de Tacuba. An essential breakfast, lunch, dinner, or snack stop downtown, this Mexican classic has been charming all comers since it opened in 1912 in a section of an old convent. In the rear dining room, huge 18th-century oil paintings depict the historic invention of *mole poblano,* a complex sauce including a variety of chilies and chocolate, created by the nuns in the Santa Rosa Convent of Puebla. Along with

mole poblano, look for delicious tamales made fresh every morning—
Oaxaca style with black mole and wrapped in banana leaf, or a fluffy
Mexico City version. There are also pastries galore. ⌧ *Tacuba 28, Col.
Centro,* ☎ *5/518–4950. Reservations not accepted. AE, DC, MC, V.
No dinner Sun.*

$ ✕ **Hosteria de Santo Domingo.** This genteel institution near downtown's
Plaza Santo Domingo has been serving *authentico* colonial dishes for
more than a century in an atmospheric turn-of-the-century town house.
Feast on tried-and-true favorites such as stuffed cactus paddles, thou-
sand-flower soup, pot roast, and a stunning array of quesadillas filled
with meat or the delicious *flor de calabaza* (pumpkin flower). Among
what may be the best homemade Mexican desserts in town are the com-
forting flan, *arroz con leche* (rice pudding), and the rich milk-based
natilla (another type of pudding). The place is open for breakfast and
always full at lunch. Get there early to avoid standing in line. ⌧ *Belisario Dominguez 72, Col. Centro,* ☎ *5/510–1434 or 5/526–5276. AE,
DC, MC, V. No dinner Sun.*

$ ✕ **Las Cazuelas.** Traditional Mexican cooking at its best is the word
★ at one of the most famous of the capital's fondas. The large dining area
is brightened by hand-painted chairs from Michoacán and by the crisp
green-and-white table linen. Ideal Mexican appetizers to share are
ranchero de carnitas (pork morsels in red sauce). The tortilla soup, with
its dash of *chili pasilla* and bits of cheese, makes another excellent starter.
Main courses center on various moles or the piquant sesame-flavored
pipián sauce with pork or chicken. Finish with a café de olla and a domestic brandy. ⌧ *San Antonio 143 at Illinois, Col. Napoles,* ☎ *5/563–
4118. Reservations not accepted. AE, MC, V. No dinner. Closed Sun.*

Spanish

$$ ✕ **El Parador de Manolo.** A two-story period house was remodeled into
this Spanish restaurant in fashionable Polanco. The Bar Porrón on the
ground floor serves a variety of Spanish tapas, including an excellent
prawn mix in a spicy sauce, and after 9, the bar has live music and fla-
menco. In the brasserie-style dining room upstairs, choose from a
Spanish menu or from the list of the chef's recommendations. Specially
cured Serrano ham is possibly the best in the city; *calamares fritos* (fried
squid) and *crepas de flor de calabaza al gratin* (squash-blossom crepes)
are other fine starters. Fish dishes make the most appealing main
courses, although the chateaubriand Parador for two (in a black corn-
fungus sauce) is truly original. Desserts are less notable. Wines are on
display downstairs, as are the fresh fish of the day. ⌧ *Presidente
Masarik 433, Col. Polanco,* ☎ *5/281–2357 or 5/281–5762. AE, DC,
MC, V. No dinner Sun.*

$$ ✕ **Meson El Cid.** This meson (tavern) exudes an atmosphere of Old Spain.
During the week, classic dishes like paella, spring lamb, suckling baby
pig, and Cornish hens with truffles keep customers happy, but on Saturday night this place really comes into its own with a medieval ban-
quet. The fun unfolds with a procession of costumed waiters carrying
huge trays of steaming hot viands. A caged cat—the grandson of the
first feline to play this role, the waiters will tell you—heads the parade
as in olden days, when a king's food was tested for poisoning by let-
ting a cat nose around in it first, cats being keen enough not to touch
the stuff if it had been tampered with. Entertainment is provided by a
student singing group dressed in medieval Spanish capes and hats. ⌧
Humboldt 61, Col. Centro, ☎ *5/521–1940, 5/521–8881, or 5/512–
7629. AE, DC, MC, V. No dinner Sun.*

$$ ✕ **Tezka.** This Zona Rosa restaurant is Mexico's first and only with
nueva cocina Basque created by famous Basque chef Arzac, who trans-

posed many of his best dishes to Mexico from his restaurant in San Sebastíen, Spain. It's always packed with a Spanish clientele. Feast on baked fish in parsley sauce and sweet garlic cream, or pheasant prepared with dates, pine nuts, and apple puree. Arzac disdains appetizers, which he believes ruin appreciation of entrées, and you will find no starters here. There *are* tempting and original desserts, like cheese tart with blueberries and clotted English cream plus pears in toffee sauce. There's a decent list of Spanish wines such as Cune, Vina Ardanza, and Reserva 904. ⊠ *Amberes 78 and Liverpool in the Royal Hotel,* ☎ *5/228–9918. AE, DC, MC, V. Closed Sun.*

Vegetarian

$ ✕ **El Jug.** To duck the madding crowd, head for this small, tidy retreat near the Zona Rosa. You'll enjoy delicious vegetarian fare to the accompaniment of soothing New Age music. Heaping salads, homemade soups, and entrées like *chiles rellenos* (stuffed green peppers) come with chunks of whole-grain bread. You can choose the filling daily *comida corrida* (fixed-price menu) or order à la carte. After lunch, you might want to browse through the store on the premises and absorb the vibes of crystals, incense holders, aromatherapy pillows, and the like. ⊠ *Puebla 326-A (entrance on Calle Cozumel), Col. Roma,* ☎ *5/553–3872. Reservations not accepted. No credit cards. No dinner. Closed Sun.*

$ ✕ **Las Fuentes.** About three blocks north of the U.S. Embassy on Calle Río Tiber, Las Fuentes is run by Philipe Culbert, a lifelong vegetarian who ascribes to the time-honored dietary dictates of ancient Persia in balancing his menu. A sample meal might be tacos stuffed with carrots and potatoes accompanied by apple salad and followed by whole-grain cookies made with honey. Don't be put off by the sterile Formica tables—like those who pack the place at lunchtime, come for the food rather than the ambience. ⊠ *Río Panuco 27, at Río Tiber, Col. Cuauhtémoc,* ☎ *5/525–0843. MC, V.*

LODGING

Though the city is huge and spread out, most hotels are within a relatively manageable group of neighborhoods. Stylish Colonia Polanco and Bosque de Chapultepec are on the west side of the city. Paseo de la Reforma runs from Chapultepec, northeast through "midtown," and intersects with Avenida Juárez at the beginning of the downtown area. Juárez becomes Avenida Madero, which continues east to the downtown historic district and its very core, the Zócalo. The Zona Rosa, replete with boutiques, cafés, restaurants, and nightspots, is just south of Reforma in the western midtown area.

Huge numbers of business travelers tend to fill up deluxe hotels during the week; some major hotels discount their weekend rates. You can expect hotels in the $$$ and $$$$ categories to have purified water, air-conditioning, cable TV, radio, minibars, and extended (often 24-hour) room service.

CATEGORY	COST*
$$$$	over $160
$$$	$90–$160
$$	$40–$90
$	under $40

All prices are for a standard double room, excluding service charge and 15% sales tax. There is an additional 2% room tax.

Colonia Polanco and Bosque de Chapultepec

$$$$ 🏨 **Camino Real.** Immense and super luxurious—about the size of the Teoti-
★   huacán's Pyramid of the Sun—this sleek, minimalist, bright pink and yellow, 8-acre city-within-a-city attracts everyone from heads of state and
celebrities to holiday travelers. Impressive works of art embellishing the
endless corridors and lounges include Rufino Tamayo's mural of *Man
Facing Infinity* and a Calder sculpture. The fifth-floor executive level has
100 extra-large guest rooms with special amenities. Fouquet's de Paris
restaurant (☞ Dining, *above*) holds culinary events, and the airy Azulejos serves Mexican fare and has Sunday buffet brunches. A nightclub
hosts top Latin American artists who perform Thursday–Saturday starting at 11 PM; there's dancing after the show. ✉ *Mariano Escobedo 700,
11590,* ☎ *5/203–2121 or 800/722–6466,* 🅵🅰🆇 *5/250–6897 or 5/250–6723.
673 rooms, 36 suites. 3 restaurants, 4 bars, pool, 4 tennis courts, health
club, nightclub, business services. AE, DC, MC, V.*

$$$$ 🏨 **Casa Vieja.** This classically elegant and sumptuously decorated
Colonia Polanco mansion is the dream-come-true of a local businessman who took his love of things Mexican and expressed it in his all-
suites (one and two bedrooms) hotel. Tastefully selected folk art,
handsomely hand-carved furniture, and gilded wall trimmings complement patios and splashing fountains. Lively Mexican colors are a
light-hearted touch in the suites, all of which are different—some have
four-poster beds, for example. All have a full kitchen, fax machine, CD
player, hot tub, and huge picture window overlooking an inside garden. The hotel's Mexican restaurant is named after its huge floor-to-
ceiling *Tree of Life* sculpture. Breakfast is included in the rates. ✉
Eugenio Sue 45, Col. Polanco, 11560, ☎ *5/282–0067,* 🅵🅰🆇 *5/281–
3780. 10 suites. Restaurant, bar, concierge, free parking. AE, MC, V.*

$$$$ 🏨 **J. W. Marriott.** In posh Colonia Polanco, this hotel was designed as
a boutique property with personalized service and small, clubby public areas; nothing overwhelms here. Rooms are done with plenty of wood
and warm colors but are otherwise unremarkable in decor. Each has a
work desk with an outlet for a personal computer and modem. The hotel
has the best-equipped business center in the city, open 24 hours. Executive floors come with extra amenities. The pretty Thai House restaurant is also on site. ✉ *Andrés Bello, no. 29, and Campos Eliseos, Col.
Polanco, 11560,* ☎ *5/282–8888 or 800/228–9290,* 🅵🅰🆇 *5/282–8811. 312
rooms. 3 restaurants, bar, coffee shop, pool, exercise room, business services, meeting rooms, travel services, car rental. AE, DC, MC, V.*

$$$$ 🏨 **Presidente Inter-Continental México.** This 42-story Inter-Continental, adjacent to Bosque de Chapultepec and Colonia Polanco, has a dramatic five-story lobby—a hollow pyramid of balconies—with music
performed daily at the lively lobby bar. Rooms are spacious, and all
have work areas. On clear days, the top two floors have views of the
nearby snowcapped volcanoes, Popocatépetl and Iztaccíhuatl. There
are a number of smart stores and six eateries on the premises, including branches of Maxim's de Paris (☞ Dining, *above*) and the Palm,
and Alfredo Di Roma. ✉ *Campos Elíseos 218, 11560,* ☎ *5/327–
7700 or 01/800/327–0200,* 🅵🅰🆇 *5/327–7730. 627 rooms, 32 suites. 6
restaurants, coffee shop, lobby lounge, exercise room, baby-sitting, parking (fee). AE, DC, MC, V.*

$$$ 🏨 **Nikko México.** Part of the Japanese Nikko chain, this glistening, 42-
floor high-rise occupies a prime Polanco position: adjacent to Bosque
de Chapultepec, just a five-minute walk from the Anthropology Mu-
seum. Standard rooms are a little claustrophobic; executive floors have
better rooms and extra facilities. Three top restaurants excel in their
gastronomic specialties: Les Célébrités (French) (☞ Dining, *above*), Tep-
pan Grill (Japanese), and El Jardín (international). The elegant, cozy

Mexico City Lodging

Aristos, **15**
Calinda Geneve, **12**
Camino Real, **5**
Casa Vieja, **1**
Catedral, **23**
Crowne Plaza
Reforma 1, **21**

Fiesta Americana
Reforma, **20**
Four Seasons
Mexico City, **8**
Galería Plaza, **9**
Gran Hotel de la
Ciudad de
México, **25**
Hotel de Cortés, **22**

Imperial, **20**
J.W. Marriott, **2**
Krystal Rosa, **11**
La Casona, **6**
Majestic, **24**
Marco Polo, **13**
Maria Cristina, **16**

María Isabel
Sheraton, **14**
Marquis Reforma, **7**
Marriott
Aeropuerto, **26**
Misión Park Plaza
México, **17**
Nikko México, **4**

Plaza Florencia, **10**
Presidente
Inter-Continental
México, **3**
Sevilla Palace, **18**

Shelty's Pub is also a big hit with locals and serves a fancy high tea on weekdays (5–7). ⊠ *Campos Elíseos 204, 11560,* ☎ *5/280–1111; 800/ 64–5687 in the U.S.,* FAX *5/280–9191. 724 rooms, 24 suites. 4 restaurants, 2 bars, indoor pool, 4 tennis courts, health club, jogging, dance club, meeting rooms, travel services, car rental. AE, DC, MC, V.*

Zona Rosa

$$$$ ★ Galería Plaza. Part of the Westin Hotel deluxe chain, this ultramodern property is conveniently located on a quiet street in elegant Zona Rosa, ideal for shopping, enjoying the nightlife, and dining out. Standard rooms are relatively small, but service and facilities are faultless. Rooms on the executive floor, where a special concierge desk provides personalized service and easy checkout, are larger. Other advantages include voice mail in all rooms, a heated rooftop pool with sundeck, a secure underground parking lot, and a 24-hour restaurant, which has a popular buffet breakfast. ⊠ *Hamburgo 195 at Varsovia, 06600,* ☎ *5/208–0370 or 800/228–3000,* FAX *5/207–5867. 420 rooms, 19 suites. 3 restaurants, lobby lounge, room service, pool, exercise room, concierge, travel services, parking (fee). AE, DC, MC, V.*

$$$ Calinda Geneve. A Quality Inn, referred to locally as El Génova, this five-story 1906 hotel is fitted with traditional colonial-style carved wood chairs and tables in the pleasant lobby, and guest rooms are smallish but comfortable. The hotel's attraction as a gathering place has always been the Salón Jardín, a striking Belle Epoque gallery with a profusion of plants and a high stained-glass ceiling. It's a popular place for meals and cocktails. The hotel's informal street-front Café Jardín serves until 11 PM, and a branch of Sanborns, which sells sundries and has a restaurant, opens off the lobby. There is also a gym on site. ⊠ *Londres 130, 06600,* ☎ *5/211–0071 or 800/228–5151,* FAX *5/ 208–7422. 320 rooms. Restaurant, bar, café, room service, exercise room, coin laundry. AE, DC, MC, V.*

$$$ Krystal Rosa. Part of the Mexican Krystal Hotel chain, this superbly run high-rise hotel is in the heart of Zona Rosa and has an excellent view of the city from the rooftop pool terrace. There is a stylish lobby cocktail lounge, a bar with local entertainers, and a restaurant, Kamakura, that serves excellent Japanese cuisine. Three club floors have VIP check-in and service, complimentary Continental buffet breakfast, and rooms with extra amenities. ⊠ *Liverpool 155, 06600,* ☎ *5/228– 9928. 267 rooms, 35 suites. 2 restaurants, 2 bars, pool, concierge, parking (fee). AE, DC, MC, V.*

$$$ La Casona. This elegant, understated turn-of-the-last-century mansion, registered as an artistic monument by Mexico's Institute of Fine Arts, was turned into a charming 30-room hotel in 1996. Filled with sunny patios and sitting rooms, the hotel is finely decorated with antiques, expensive rugs, hardwood floors, and accessories in the spirit of the days of the *Porfiriato* (presidency of Porfirio Díaz) when the house was built. No two rooms are alike, but all have hair dryers, fluffy bathrobes and slippers, and good-sized bathtubs. Room service orders are discreetly delivered through a tiny two-way cupboard near the door. There's a small restaurant that serves old-style country cooking. The two-story hotel building, with its demure salmon facade, looks out on a tree-lined street in Colonia Roma about a 10-minute walk south of the Zona Rosa, in easy reach of museums, restaurants, and Reforma Avenue. ⊠ *Durango 280, at Cozumel,* ☎ *5/286–3001 or 800/223–5652,* FAX *5/211–0871. 30 rooms. Restaurant, bar, exercise room. AE, DC, MC, V.*

$$$ ★ Marco Polo. Ultramodern and intimate, the central Zona Rosa all-suites Marco Polo has the amenities and outstanding personalized service often associated with a small European hotel. All rooms have climate control, cable TV, FM radio, minibar, and kitchenette; some suites have hot tubs. North-facing top-floor rooms have excellent views of Paseo de la Reforma—the four penthouse suites have terraces—and the U.S. Embassy is close by. In the street-level Bistro de Marco Polo, you can listen to sophisticated jazz at lunch, over cocktails, and at dinner. ☒ *Amberes 27, 06600,* ☎ *5/207–1893,* FAX *5/533–3727. 60 suites. Restaurant, bar, business services. AE, DC, MC, V.*

$$$ ⊞ **Plaza Florencia.** This modern hotel is on a busy avenue that borders the Zona Rosa. The lobby's heavy furniture and dark colors make it feel more like a lodge, in which guests relax after a day of exploring. Rooms are well furnished in hotel-modern style—cheerfully decorated, and soundproofed against the location's heavy traffic noise; higher floors have views of the Angel monument. Some large family suites are available. All rooms have air-conditioning, heat, a color TV, and a phone. ☒ *Florencia 61, 06600,* ☎ *5/211–0064,* FAX *5/511–1542. 130 rooms, 10 suites. Restaurant, bar, coffee shop. AE, DC, MC, V.*

$$ ⊞ **Aristos.** This 15-story, Zona Rosa–fringe hotel is on bustling Paseo de la Reforma in front of the U.S. Embassy, near the Mexican Stock Exchange. Rooms are well supplied with all the amenities and are attractively decorated in shades of peach and mauve, with brass and wood accents. The business center has a bilingual staff and a message service. ☒ *Paseo de la Reforma 276, 06600,* ☎ *5/211–0112,* FAX *5/514– 3543. 298 rooms, 29 suites. 3 restaurants, 2 bars, beauty salon, sauna, exercise room, travel services, parking (fee). AE, DC, MC, V.*

$$ ⊞ **Misión Park Plaza México.** A part of the Misión chain, this very comfortable hotel is well placed for shopping and sight-seeing. Mirrors, good light, and like-new bathrooms make the rooms more pleasant, and all have air-conditioning and color TV with U.S. channels. Staff is friendly and accommodating, and breakfast is included in room rates. ☒ *Nápoles 62, 06600,* ☎ *5/533–0535,* FAX *5/533–1589. 50 rooms. Coffee shop, lobby lounge, exercise room, meeting room. AE, MC, V.*

Midtown and along the Reforma

$$$$ ⊞ **Four Seasons Mexico City.** This is—perhaps by definition—one of the most luxurious hotels in the capital. Surrounding a traditional courtyard with a fountain, the eight-story building was modeled after the 18th-century Iturbide Palace downtown. Huge bowls of fresh flowers and lovely European furnishings fill the spacious marble lobby. Geared for business travelers, rooms have modem ports and all of the amenities you'd expect at a Four Seasons hotel. There's also a boardroom on the premises and a business center with computer and cellular phone rentals. Dining and drinking areas have highly original names: El Restaurant (for breakfast, lunch, and dinner), El Bar, El Café, and El Lounge. ☒ *Paseo de la Reforma 500, 06600,* ☎ *5/230–1818 or 800/ 332–3442,* FAX *5/230–1808. 200 rooms, 40 suites. 2 restaurants, 2 bars, pool, exercise room, health club. AE, DC, MC, V.*

$$$$ ⊞ **María Isabel Sheraton.** Don Antenor Patiño, the Bolivian "Tin King," inaugurated this Mexico City classic in 1969 and named it after his granddaughter, socialite Isabel Goldsmith. The entire hotel has been remodeled, but the glistening brown marble and Art Deco details in the lobby and other public areas remain. All guest and public rooms are impeccably maintained; penthouse suites in the 22-story tower section are extra-spacious and exceptionally luxurious. The location—across from the Angel and the Zona Rosa, with Sanborns next door and the U.S. Embassy a half block away—is prime. ☒ *Paseo de la Reforma 325, 06500,* ☎ *5/ 207–3933 or 800/334–8484,* FAX *5/207–0684. 681 rooms, 74 suites. 3 restaurants, bar, room service, pool, massage, sauna, health club, concierge floor. AE, DC, MC, V.*

$$$$ ⊞ **Marquis Reforma.** Opened in 1991, this plush privately owned
★ hotel is within walking distance of the Zona Rosa. It has a striking pink
stone and curved glass facade, and its seventh-floor suites afford pic-
ture-perfect views of the castillo in Chapultepec. The elegant lobby is
fitted in a classically European style, with paintings, sculpture, and palatial furniture. Guest-room furniture and decor are Art Deco–inspired.
The award-winning La Jolla restaurant serves international cuisine. The
fully staffed corporate center has state-of-the-art computer services, and
guest-room phones feature a second plug for computers with fax
modem. The health club has hard-to-find holistic, stress-busting massages. ⊠ *Paseo de la Reforma 465, 06500,* ☎ *5/211–3600 or 800/525–
4800,* FAX *5/211–5561. 133 rooms, 84 suites. 2 restaurants, bar, exercise room, business services, meeting room. AE, DC, MC, V.*

$$$ ⊞ **Crowne Plaza Reforma 1.** Perched at the junction of Reforma,
Juárez, and Bucareli—convenient to downtown, the Zona Rosa, and
the Stock Exchange—this flashy 22-story smoked-glass behemoth
looks quite spectacular in its otherwise nondescript surroundings. It
touts the ultimate in high-tech amenities for business travelers: a stock
market indicator, computers, cellular phones, and secretarial, transla-
tion, messenger, and shipping services. Executive rooms have PC and
fax-modem outlets and three telephone lines. Public areas include a cof-
fee bar with 20 different java concoctions, an oyster-and-jazz bar, and
a French restaurant. The hotel also has limousine rental, a pharmacy,
and boutiques. ⊠ *Reforma 1, Col. Tabacalera, 06030,* ☎ *5/128–5000
or 800/227–6963,* FAX *5/128–5050. 424 rooms, 30 suites. 2 restaurants,
2 bars, room service, beauty salon, shops, business services, travel ser-
vices, car rental. AE, DC, MC, V.*

$$$ ⊞ **Fiesta Americana Reforma.** This immense hotel is well organized
for business travelers and large groups. It has an ample selection of
bars, restaurants, and entertainment, including a popular nightclub,
the Barbarella. There isn't much Mexican atmosphere, but there's
something to say for being able to get a good tan on the sundeck, work
out in the gym, listen to live Mexican music in the lobby bar, and choose
from three restaurants on site. ⊠ *Paseo de la Reforma 80, 06600,* ☎
5/705–1515 or 800/343–7821, FAX *5/705–1313. 610 rooms. 3 restaurants, 2 bars, exercise room. AE, DC, MC, V.*

$$ ⊞ **Imperial.** Opened in 1990, the Imperial occupies a stately turn-of-
the-century European-style building right on the Reforma alongside
the Columbus Monument. Quiet elegance and personal service are
keynotes of this privately owned property. The hotel's Restaurant
Gaudí has an understated, tony atmosphere and serves Continental cui-
sine with some Spanish selections. All rooms have safes. ⊠ *Paseo de
la Reforma 64, 06600,* ☎ *5/705–4911,* FAX *5/703–3122. 50 rooms, 10
junior suites, 5 master suites. Restaurant, bar, café, business services,
meeting rooms, travel services. AE, DC, MC, V.*

$$ ⊞ **Sevilla Palace.** This glistening modern showplace has five panoramic
elevators for its 23 floors, a covered rooftop pool with hot tub, a health
club, restaurants, a top-floor supper club with entertainment, a terraced
rooftop lounge with a city view, and convention halls with capacities
of up to 1,000. It's well located near the Columbus traffic circle and
attracts lots of tourists from Spain. ⊠ *Paseo de la Reforma 105, 06030,*
☎ *5/705–2800 or 800/732–9488,* FAX *5/703–1521. 413 rooms. 2 restaurants, 3 bars, pool, health club, nightclub, meeting rooms. AE, MC, V.*

$ ⊞ **María Cristina.** Full of old-world charm, this Spanish colonial–style
★ gem is a Mexico City classic. Impeccably maintained since it was built
in 1937 (it was last refurbished in January 1995), the peach-color building surrounds a delightful garden courtyard, which is the setting for its
El Retiro bar. Three tastefully decorated apartment-style master suites,
complete with hot tubs, were added in the early '90s. All rooms have

safes. Located in a quiet residential setting near Sullivan Park, the hotel is just a block from the Paseo de la Reforma and close to the Zona Rosa. ⊠ *Río Lerma 31, 06500,* ☎ *5/566–9688,* FAX *5/566–9194. 140 rooms, 8 suites. Bar, room service, beauty salon, travel services. DC, MC, V.*

Downtown

$$ ⚕ **Gran Hotel de la Ciudad de México.** Ensconced in what was formerly a 19th-century department store, this more traditional hotel has contemporary rooms with all the amenities. Its central location—adjacent to the Zócalo and near the Templo Mayor—makes it a good choice for local sight-seeing. Its distinctive Belle Epoque lobby—with a striking stained-glass Tiffany dome, chandeliers, gilded birdcages, and 19th-century wrought-iron elevators—are worth a visit in their own right. The fourth-floor Mirador breakfast restaurant overlooks the Zócalo. The Del Centro restaurant-bar run by Delmónicos is one of Mexico City's best—a great place to stop for a drink while exploring nearby. The hotel has been undergoing a long-term, gradual refurbishing; be sure to request a renovated room that does not look out onto a brick wall. ⊠ *16 de Septiembre 82, 06000,* ☎ *5/510–4040,* FAX *5/512–6772. 125 rooms. 2 restaurants, bar, concierge, travel services, parking (fee). AE, DC, MC, V.*

$$ ⚕ **Hotel de Cortés.** This delightful small hotel, managed by Best Western, is housed in a 1780 colonial building that was designated a national monument. Colonial-decor rooms are small and simply furnished; they open onto an enclosed central courtyard. Two comfortable soundproof suites overlook Alameda Park across the busy street. A restaurant also looks onto the park, and a friendly bar opens to the tree-shaded central courtyard and fountain, a lovely setting for tea or cocktails. The Franz Mayer Museum is just a block away, and it's an easy walk to Bellas Artes. Loyal guests make reservations many months in advance. ⊠ *Av. Hidalgo 85, 06000,* ☎ *5/518–2184 or 800/334–7234,* FAX *5/512–1863. 19 rooms, 10 suites. Restaurant, bar. AE, DC, MC, V.*

$$ ⚕ **Majestic.** The atmospheric, colonial-style Majestic, built in 1937, is a Best Western, perfectly located if you're interested in exploring the historic downtown: on the Zócalo at the corner of Madero. It's also perfect for viewing the Independence Day (September 16) celebrations, which draw hundreds of thousands of people to this square, and many people reserve a room a year in advance of the festivities. Rooms are decorated in the style of the 1940s and have air-conditioning and king-size beds, remote-control color TVs, and minibars. Although the front units have balconies and a charming view of the plaza, they can be noisy with car traffic until about 11 at night. Service is efficient and courteous. The seventh-floor La Terraza dining room and terrace—which serve international and Mexican specialties—have marvelous panoramas of the entire Zócalo. The Sunday buffet (1–5 PM) features live Mexican music. The fun El Campanario piano bar welcomes anyone who wants to make his first singing debut, and has become a favorite with locals. ⊠ *Madero 73, 06000,* ☎ *5/521–8600 or 800/528–1234,* FAX *5/512–6262. 85 rooms. Restaurant, bar, coffee shop, travel services. AE, DC, MC, V.*

$ ⚕ **Catedral.** In the heart of historic downtown, this refurbished older
★ hotel is a bargain, with many of the amenities of the more upscale hotels at less than half the price. Public areas sparkle with marble and glass. Guest rooms are done in a cheerful contemporary fashion, and all have color TVs (local channels only) and phones. You can get one with a view of the namesake Catedral, but keep in mind that its bells chime every 15 minutes late into the night. Service is friendly, the hotel restaurant is excellent, and the El Retiro bar attracts a largely Mexican clientele to hear live Latin music. ⊠ *Donceles 95, 06000,* ☎ *5/512–8581,* FAX *5/*

512–4344. 116 rooms. Bar, coffee shop, room service, nightclub, laundry service and dry cleaning, travel services. AE, MC, V.

Airport

$$$ 🏨 **Marriott Aeropuerto.** This deluxe hotel is sleek and modern but still manages to be comfortable. Just over a short covered footbridge from the airport terminal, it is convenient if you arrive late or have an early morning flight. For this convenience you pay a price. There is a pool on the eighth floor. Discounted corporate rates are available. ⊠ *Benito Juárez International Airport, 15520,* ☎ *5/230–0505 or 800/228–9290,* FAX *5/230–0555. 600 rooms, 8 suites. Restaurant, bar, coffee shop, pool, sauna, health club, meeting rooms, car rental, free parking. AE, DC, MC, V.*

NIGHTLIFE AND THE ARTS

Good places to check for current events are the Friday editions of *The News* and *The Mexico City Times,* both daily English-language newspapers, and *Tiempo Libre,* a weekly magazine listing activities and events in Spanish. All are available at newsstands.

Summer citywide cultural festivals with free music, dance, and theater performances by local groups take place in July and August. A three-week spring cultural festival with international headliners takes place in the Historic Center between March and April. Check with the Mexico City Tourist Office (☞ Visitor Information *in* Mexico City A to Z, *below*) for dates and details.

The Arts

Dance

The world-renowned **Ballet Folklórico de México,** directed by Amalia Hernández, presents stylized Mexican regional folk dances and is one of the most popular shows in Mexico. Performances Wednesday at 8:30 PM and Sunday at 9:30 AM and 8:30 PM are at the beautiful Palacio de Bellas Artes (Palace of Fine Arts; ⊠ Avenida Juárez at Eje Central Lázaro Cárdenas)—it's a treat to see its Tiffany glass curtain lowered. Call the **Palace of Fine Arts** box office (☎ 5/512–3633) or **Ticketmaster** (☎ 5/325–9000) for information on prices and for reservations. Hotels and travel agencies can also secure tickets.

Not to be confused with the above is the **Ballet Folklórico Nacional de México,** directed and choreographed by Silvia Lozano. The company performs authentic regional folk dances at the National Dance Theater (☎ 5/280–8771) behind the National Auditorium during the renovation of the Teatro de la Ciudad, their usual auditorium. Performances are sporadically scheduled.

The **National Dance Theater,** (*above*) and the **Miguel Covarrubias Hall** (⊠ Av. Insurgentes Sur 3000, Ciudad Universitaria at the National Autonomous University of Mexico [UNAM], ☎ 5/622–7051 at the university's dance department) frequently sponsor modern-dance performances.

Music

The primary venue for classical music is the **Palace of Fine Arts** (⊠ Av. Juárez and Eje Central Lázaro Cárdenas, ☎ 5/512–3633), which has a main auditorium and the smaller Manuel Ponce concert hall. The National Opera has two seasons at the Palace: January–March and August–October. The National Symphony Orchestra stages classical and modern pieces at the palace in the spring and fall.

The top concert hall, often touted as the best in Latin America, is **Ollin Yolitzli** (✉ Periférico Sur 1541, ☎ 5/606–7573), which hosts the Mexico City Philharmonic several times a year. The National Autonomous University of Mexico's Philharmonic orchestra performs at **Nezahualcoyotl Hall** (✉ Av. Insurgentes Sur 3000, Ciudad Universitaria at the UNAM, ☎ 5/622–7112).

For music stars like Alanis Morissette, Luis Miguel, the Rolling Stones, and Juan Gabriel check newspapers for attractions at the following halls: **Auditorio Nacional** (✉ Reforma 50 across the street from the Nikko Hotel, ☎ 5/280–9234 or 5/280–9979), **Teatro Metropolitano** (✉ Independencia 90, downtown, ☎ 5/510–1035 or 5/510–1045), **Palacio de los Deportes** (✉ Av. Río Churubusco and Calle Añil, ☎ 5/237–9999, ext. 4264), and **Hard Rock Cafe** (✉ Reforma and Campos Elíseos, Col. Condesa, ☎ 5/327–7171).

Theater

You might find some English-language plays by checking listings in *The News*. However, if you understand Spanish (or are content to watch), you'll be able to enjoy a wider range of theatrical entertainment in Mexico City, including recent Broadway hits. Prices are reasonable compared with those for stage productions of similar caliber in the United States. Though Mexico City has no central theater district, most theaters are within a 15- to 30-minute taxi ride from the major hotels. The top venues include **Hidalgo** (✉ Av. Hidalgo 23 at Lázaro Cárdenas, ☎ 5/521–5859), **Silvia Pinal** (✉ Yucatán 160 at Coahuila, Col. Roma, ☎ 5/264–1172), **Insurgentes** (✉ Av. Insurgentes Sur 1587, ☎ 5/598–6894), and **Virginia Fabregas** (✉ Velasquez de León 29, ☎ 5/592–2142). Theater tickets are available through **Ticketmaster** (☎ 5/325–9000).

Nightlife

Night is the key word to understanding the timing of going out in Mexico City. People generally have cocktails at 7 or 8 PM, take in dinner and a show at 10 or 11, head to discos at midnight, then find a spot for a nightcap somewhere around 3 AM. The easiest way to do this if you don't speak Spanish is on a nightlife tour (☞ Guided Tours *in* Mexico City A to Z, *below*). If you set off on your own you should have no trouble getting around, but for personal safety absolutely avoid taking taxis off the street—take official hotel taxis or call a sitio taxi (☞ Getting Around *in* Mexico City A to Z, *below*).

Niza and Florencia streets in the Zona Rosa are practically lined with nightclubs, bars, and discos that are especially lively on Friday and Saturday nights. Big hotels have both bars and places to dance or be entertained, and they are frequented by locals. Outside of the Zona Rosa, Paseo de la Reforma and Insurgentes Sur have the greatest concentration of nightspots. Mexico City has something for everyone in the way of night entertainment, but remember that the capital's high altitude makes liquor extremely potent, even jolting. Imported booze is very expensive, so you may want to stick with what the Mexicans order: tequila, rum, and *cerveza* (beer).

Dancing

Dance emporiums in the capital run the gamut from cheek-to-cheek romantic to throbbing strobe lights and ear-splitting music. Most places have a cover charge, but it is rarely more than $10.

To really experience the nightlife Mexico has to offer it's imperative to visit a dance club. **Bar León** (✉ Republica de Brasil 5, Col. Centro, ☎ 5/510–2979) is a traditional salsa bar with great live music and a kitschy feel. **Salon Los Ángeles** (⊠ Lerdo 206, Col. Guerrero, ☎ 5/ 597–5181) takes you back in time to the 1930s, with decor straight out of a movie. The grand, open dance floor swings to the rhythms of danzón and salsa. When renowned musicians like Celia Cruz come to town this is where they perform. Another Colonia Guerrero danzón spot is the popular **Salon México** (⊠ 2 DO. Callejon San Juan de Dios 25, ☎ 5/518–0931). **Meneo** (⊠ Nueva York 315, Col. Napoles, just off Insurgentes Sur, ☎ 5/523–9448) is a modern dance hall for live salsa and merengue with two dance floors. One of the capital's best-kept secrets is **Mama Rumba** (⊠ Querétaro 230 at Medillín, Col. Roma, ☎ 5/564–6920), a 10-minute cab ride from the Zona Rosa. A nondescript Cuban restaurant during the day, it turns on the hot salsa, danzón, cha-cha-cha, and conga beat Thursday, Friday, and Saturday nights, when the top-rate Cuban house band takes the stand. Both Bar León and Mama Rumba are great if you aren't an expert dancer because the tiny dance floors are so packed no one will notice mistakes. Reservations Thursday through Saturday nights are definitely encouraged by the management of these last two clubs.

If Latin music isn't your thing, two of the hippest discos in the city stand next to each other in the center. The **Pervert Lounge** (⊠ Uruguay 70.5, Col. Centro, ☎ 5/518–0976) and **Club 69** (⊠ Uruguay 69.5, Col. Centro, ☎ 5/518–0976) are, despite the slightly lewd names, swank, upscale places where the young and beautiful come to see and be seen while shaking their exposed belly buttons on the dance floor.

Bars

Nice bars to sit and have a few drinks in are hard to come by in Mexico City. Often they are either too noisy or too seedy. Bars are usually open Tuesday–Saturday 8–3 and generally don't charge a cover. **La Nueva Ópera** (⊠ Cinco de Mayo 10, downtown, ☎ 5/512–8959) is the exception: it is one of the city's finest cantinas, and it's brought in top personalities since it opened in 1870. The bar provides a relaxing atmosphere, Mexican appetizers and entrées, and an expansive drink list. Don't forget to have your waiter point out the bullet hole allegedly left in the ceiling by Mexican revolutionary hero Pancho Villa. **Bar Milán** (⊠ Milán 18, Col. Juárez, ☎ 5/592–0031) is a very casual, unpretentious favorite among locals. Upon entering you need to change pesos into *milagros* (miracles), which are notes necessary to buy drinks throughout the night. The catch is not to forget to change them back for pesos before last call. The music tends to be the latest alternative grooves, Latin rock, and '80s singers like Diana Ross. Make sure to check out the amazing cactus sculpture covering the wall behind the main bar. **Bar Mata** (⊠ Filomeno Mata 11, at Cinco de Mayo, ☎ 5/ 518–0237) is on the fourth and fifth floors of a colonial building near Bellas Artes in the centro. The atmosphere is conducive to dancing and mingling, especially in the rooftop (fifth floor) bar, which has great views of the night-lit city and is a place to escape from the cigarette smoke. If a hotel bar is what you're after, go to **Del Centro** at the Gran Hotel (⊠ 16 de Septiembre 82, ☎ 5/510–4040).

Dinner Shows

The liveliest shows are in clubs downtown and in the Zona Rosa. The new **Feria de México** (⊠ Reforma 28 at Balderas, across from the Crowne Plaza Reforma hotel, ☎ 5/535–1065) is the newest venue for enjoying traditional Mexican music and dance over dinner. Show times at this rustic dinner club are 3:30, 6:30, and 10:30 PM daily. The show is free and even includes a free *cerveza* (beer), but you pay for your meal (varied Mexican-American fare) à la carte. At **Focolare** (⊠ Hamburgo 87 at Río Niza, ☎ 5/207–8257), you can watch a cock fight, mariachi singers, and traditional folk dancers Thursday through Saturday nights. The show costs $6.50; Mexican dinner and drinks are separate. At the **Hotel de Cortés** (✉ Hidalgo 85, downtown, ☎ 5/518–2184) you can take in the strains of marimba and mariachi players as well as watch traditional dancers in the hotel's beautiful outdoor patio. The show goes on Friday nights only and for $15.50 includes a full meal.

Hotel Bars

The following hotel lobby bars are all good bets for a sophisticated crowd and more mellow music, from about 7 PM to 1 AM daily: **María Isabel Sheraton** (✉ Reforma 325, ☎ 5/207–3933), **Presidente Inter-Continental México** (✉ Campos Elíseos 218, Col. Polanco, ☎ 5/327–7700), **Camino Real** (✉ Mariano Escobedo 700, Chapultepec, ☎ 5/203–2121), and **Galería Plaza** (✉ Hamburgo 195, Zona Rosa, ☎ 5/208–0370).

Mariachi Music

The traditional last stop for nocturnal Mexicans is **Plaza Garibaldi** (✉ East of Eje Central Lázaro Cárdenas, between República de Honduras and República de Perú), where exuberant mariachis gather to unwind after evening performances—by performing even more. There are roving mariachis, as well as norteño (country-style) music and white-clad jarocho bands (Veracruz-style), peddling songs in the outdoor plaza, where you can also buy beer and shots of tequila. Well-to-do Mexicans park themselves inside one of the cantinas or clubs surrounding the plaza and belt out their favorite songs with the hired musicians.

The better cantinas are **Guadalajara de Noche** (☎ 5/526–5521) and **Tenampa** (☎ 5/526–6176). Choose a cantina and order a tequila; the musicians will be around shortly offering to serenade you (a song costs about $4). Mexicans typically buy songs by the dozen, so the bar is rarely without the wailing mariachis for more than 10 minutes. These places stay open Sunday through Thursday until 4 AM, and even later on Friday and Saturday. Note: The square was spruced up in the early '90s to rid it of its seedy image, but things can still get a bit raucous late at night.

Arrange for transportation from Plaza Garibaldi. Or call a travel agency (☞ Guided Tours *in* Mexico City A to Z, *below*), drive your car and park in the well-lighted ramp below the plaza, or call a sitio taxi (☞ Getting Around *in* Mexico City A to Z, *below*).

OUTDOOR ACTIVITIES AND SPORTS

Adventure Sports

A number of adventure travel agencies have sprouted up to entice both tourists and natives out of the smog and chaos of Mexico City for a weekend of white-water rafting, rappelling, or biking. One of the best is **México Verde Expeditions** (✉ Homero 526, Interior 801, Col. Polanco, ☎ 5/255–4400 or 5/255–4465), whose guides speak English and lead tours weekly to the pristine areas of nearby states like Veracruz and Morelos. Call a week in advance to make reservations and bring a sleeping bag and sunblock. The small **Planeta Expeditions** (✉ Amatlán 51-C at Montes de Oca, ☎ 5/211–9020) runs out of a café in trendy Colonia Condesa. They have journeys to climb the Iztaccíhuatl volcano, as well as rafting and rock climbing. Three-day trips cost from $100 to $150.

Bullfighting

The main season is the dry season, around November through March, when celebrated *matadores* appear at **Plaza México** (✉ Calle Agusto

Rodín and Holbein, Col. Ciudad de los Deportes, ☎ 5/563–3959), the world's largest bullring, which seats 40,000. Gray Line Tours offers bullfight tour packages (☞ Guided Tours *in* Mexico City A to Z, *below*); or tickets, which range from about $2 to $25, can be purchased at hotel travel desks or at the bullring's ticket booths Thursday–Sunday 9 AM to 1 PM and 3–7 PM. The ring is located next to the Ciudad de Deportes sports complex, and the show goes on at 4:00 PM.

Golf

All golf courses are private in Mexico City, but you can play if you are the guest of a member. If you stay at the Camino Real hotel, you can have the hotel arrange admittance to the **Bella Vista Golf Club** (☎ 5/360–3501), off the Querétaro Highway. Greens fees Tuesday through Friday are $85; weekends, $125.

Soccer

Fútbol is the sport that Mexicans are most passionate about, which is evident in the size of their soccer stadium, **Estadio Azteca** (✉ Calzada de Tlalpan 3465), the second largest in Latin America. The World Cup Finals were held here in 1970 and 1986. You can buy tickets outside of the stadium in the south of the city on the same day of any minor game. For more important games, buy tickets a week in advance. The Pumas, a popular university-sponsored team, play at **Estadio Olímpica** (✉ Avenida Insurgentes Sur at Universidad Nacional Autónoma de México).

Tennis

Tennis clubs are private in Mexico, so if you want to play, consider staying at a hotel (☞ Lodging, *above*) that has courts on site.

Water Sports

The best place for swimming is your hotel pool. If you're desperate to row a boat, however, you can rent one in the lakes of Bosque de Chapultepec, near the Zoológico.

SHOPPING

The finest, most concentrated shopping area is the **Zona Rosa,** a 29-square-block area bounded by Reforma on the north, Niza on the east, Avenida Chapultepec on the south, and Varsovia on the west. The neighborhood is chock-full of boutiques, jewelry stores, leather-goods shops, antiques stores, and art galleries, as well as dozens of great little restaurants and coffee shops. Day or night, the Zona Rosa is always lively.

Polanco, a choice residential neighborhood along the northeast perimeter of Bosque de Chapultepec, has blossomed into a more upscale shopping area with exclusive stores and boutiques. Many are in malls like the huge ultramodern **Plaza Polanco** (✉ Jaime Balmes 11), the new upscale **Plaza Moliere** (✉ Moliere between Calles Horacio and Homero), and the **Plaza Masarik** (✉ Presidente Masarik and Anatole France).

There are hundreds of shops with more modest trappings and better prices spread out along the length of Avenida Insurgentes, as well as along Avenida Juárez and in the old downtown area.

Department Stores, Malls, and Shopping Arcades

The major department-store **chains** are **Liverpool** (✉ Av. Insurgentes Sur 1310, Mariano Escobedo 425, and in the Plaza Satélite and Perisur shopping centers), **Suburbia** (✉ Horacio 203, Sonora 180, Av. Insurgentes Sur 1235, and also in Plaza Satélite and Perisur), and **El Palacio de Hierro** (✉ Calles Durango and Salamanca in Col. Condesa and in the Plaza Moliere in Col. Polanco), which is noted for items by well-known designers at prices now on par with those found in the United States. **Santa Fe** mall is the largest in Latin America, with 285 stores, a movie theater, and several restaurants. It's in the elegant Santa Fe district, which in recent years has become the favored office real estate property in the city. To get here, take the Periférico Expressway south to the exit marked CENTRO SANTA FE. The posh and pricey shopping mall **Perisur** is also on the southern edge of the city near where the Periférico Expressway meets Avenida Insurgentes. Department stores are generally open Monday, Tuesday, Thursday, and Friday from 10 to 7, and on Wednesday and Saturday from 10 to 8.

Sanborns is a chain of mini-department stores with some 65 branches in Mexico City. The most convenient are at Madero 4 (its original store in the House of Tiles, downtown); several along Paseo de Reforma (including one at the Angel monument and another four blocks west of the Diana Fountain); and in the Zona Rosa (one at the corner of Niza and Hamburgo and another at Londres 130 in the Hotel Calinda Geneve). They carry quality ceramics and crafts (and can ship anywhere), and most have restaurants or coffee shops, a pharmacy, ATMs, and periodical and book departments with English-language publications.

Plaza La Rosa, a modern shopping arcade (⊠ Between Amberes and Génova in Zona Rosa), has 72 prestigious shops and boutiques including Aldo Conti and Diesel. It spans the depth of the block between Londres and Hamburgo, with entrances on both streets.

Bazar del Centro (⊠ Downtown, at Isabel la Católica 30, just below Madero) is a restored, late-17th-century nòble mansion built around a garden courtyard that houses several chic boutiques and prestigious jewelers such as **Aplijsa** (☎ 5/521–1923), known for its fine gold, silver, pearls, and gemstones, and **Ginza** (☎ 5/518–6453), which has Japanese pearls, including the prized cultured variety. Other shops sell Taxco silver, Tonalá stoneware, and Mexican tequilas and liqueurs. This complex is elegant and also has a congenial bar.

Portales de los Mercaderes (Merchants' Arcade; ⊠ Extending the length of the west side of the zócalo between Avs. Madero and 16 de Septiembre) has attracted merchants since 1524. It is lined with jewelry shops selling gold (often by the gram) and authentic Taxco silver at prices lower than those in Taxco itself, where the overhead is higher. In the middle of the arcade is **Tardán** (⊠ Plaza de la Constitución 7, ☎ 5/512–2459), an unusual shop specializing in fashionable men's hats of every shape and style.

Markets

A "must"—even for browsers—is a visit to the **Bazar Sábado** (Saturday Bazaar) at Plaza San Jacinto in the southern San Angel district. It's been selling unique handicrafts at excellent prices for more than three decades. Outside, vendors sell embroidered clothing, leather goods, wooden masks, beads, *amates* (bark paintings), and trinkets. Inside the bazaar building, a renovated two-story colonial mansion, are the better-quality—and higher-priced—goods, including *alebrijes* (painted wooden animals from Oaxaca), glassware, pottery, jewelry, and papier-mâché flowers. There is an indoor restaurant as well. Market and restaurant are open 10–7.

Sundays between 10 and 4, more than 100 artists exhibit and sell their painting and sculpture at the **Jardín del Arte** (Garden of Art) in Parque Sullivan, just northeast of the Reforma–Insurgentes intersection.

Along the west side of the park, a colorful weekend mercado with scores of food stands is also worth a visit.

The **Mercado Insurgentes** (also called **Mercado Zona Rosa**) is an entire block deep, with entrances on both Londres and Liverpool (✉ Between Florencia and Amberes). This is a typical neighborhood public market with one big difference: most of the stalls (222 of them) sell crafts. You can find all kinds of handmade items—including serapes and ponchos, baskets, pottery, silver, pewter, fossils, and onyx, as well as regional Mexican dresses and costumes.

Also in the Zona Rosa, the pink neocolonial Plaza del Angel (✉ Londres 161) has a **Centro de Antigüedades** (antiques center) with several fine shops. On Saturday, together with other freelance vendors, the dealers set up a flea market in the arcades and patios. On Sunday, bibliophiles join the antiques vendors here to sell, peruse, and buy collectors' books and periodicals.

The Zócalo and Alameda Park areas have interesting markets for browsing and buying handicrafts and curios; polite bargaining is customary. The biggest is the **Centro Artesanal Buenavista** (✉ Aldama 187, by Buenavista Train Station, about 1½ km (1 mi) northwest of downtown). **La Lagunilla** market (✉ Libertad, between República de Chile and Calle Allende) attracts antiques hunters who know how to determine authenticity, as well as coin collectors. The best day is Sunday, when flea-market stands are set up outside, with everything from collectibles to interesting knickknacks to junk. This market is known affectionately as the Thieves' Market: local lore says you can buy back on Sunday what was stolen from your home on Saturday. Within the colonial walls of **La Ciudadela** market (✉ Balderas and Ayuntamiento, about 4 blocks south of Av. Juárez), more than 300 artisans' stalls display a variety of good handicrafts from all over the country, at better prices than you can find at the rest of the markets.

Specialty Shops

Antiques

Antigüedades Coloniart (✉ Estocolmo 37, Zona Rosa, ☎ 5/514–4799) has good-quality antique paintings, furniture, and sculpture. The store is open weekdays 10–3 and 4–7, and Saturday 10–2. **Antigüedades Imperio** (✉ Hamburgo 149, Zona Rosa, ☎ 5/525–5798) specializes in 19th-century European furniture, paintings, glass, and vases. They are open weekdays 11:30–2 and 4–7, and Saturday 11:30–3.

Art

The **Juan Martín Gallery** (✉ Dickens 33-B, Col. Polanco, ☎ 5/280–0277) is an avant-garde studio. The store and gallery of the renowned **Sergio Bustamante** (✉ Nikko México hotel, Campos Elíseos 204, Col. Polanco, ☎ 5/282–2638 and Amberes 13, Zona Rosa, ☎ 5/525–9059) displays and sells the artist's wild sculpture, jewelry, and interior-design pieces. The **Oscar Roman Gallery** (✉ Julio Verne 14, Col. Polanco, ☎ 5/282–0436) is packed with work by good Mexican painters with a contemporary edge. The **Nina Menocal de Rocha Gallery** (✉ Zacatecas 93, Col. Roma, ☎ 5/564–7209) specializes in up-and-coming Cuban painters. **Misrachi** (✉ Presidente Masarik 523, Col. Polanco, ☎ 5/280–2967), a veteran among galleries, promotes well-known Mexican and international artists.

Candy

Celaya (✉ Cinco de Mayo 39, ☎ 5/521–1787), in the downtown historic section, is a decades-old haven for those with a sweet tooth. It specializes in candied pineapple, papaya, guava, and other exotic fruit, almond-paste, candied walnut rolls, and *cajeta,* a typical Mexican dessert of thick caramelized milk.

Clothing

The Spanish designer store **Zara** (⊠ Londres 102, Zona Rosa, ☎ 5/ 525–1516; ⊠ Presidente Masarik 332 at Tennyson, Col. Polanco, ☎ 5/280–1529; and in the ⊠ Plaza Moliere, Col. Polanco, ☎ 5/280–7572) has sleek women's fashions in cotton, linen, and wool. **Guess** (⊠ Amberes 17, Zona Rosa, ☎ 5/207–2891) sells chic denim sportswear.

Designer Items

Cartier (⊠ Amberes 9, Zona Rosa, ☎ 5/207–6109; ⊠ Presidente Masarik 438, Col. Polanco, ☎ 5/281–5528) sells genuine designer jewelry and clothes, under the auspices of the French Cartier. **Gucci** (⊠ Hamburgo 136, Zona Rosa, ☎ 5/207–9997) has no connection with the European store of the same name; nevertheless, it has a fine selection of shoes, gloves, and handbags.

Jewelry

The owner of **Los Castillo** (⊠ Amberes 41, Zona Rosa, ☎ 5/511–8396) developed a unique method of melding silver, copper, and brass and is considered by many to be Taxco's top silversmith. Taxco silver of exceptional style is sold at **Arte en Plata** (⊠ Londres 162-A, Zona Rosa, ☎ 5/511–1422), with many designs inspired by pre-Columbian art. **Pelletier** (⊠ Torcuato Caso 237, Col. Polanco, ☎ 5/250–8600) sells fine jewelry and watches. **Tane** (⊠ Amberes 70, Zona Rosa, ☎ 5/511–9429; ⊠ Presidente Masarik 460, Col. Polanco, ☎ 5/281–4775; ⊠ Santa Catarina 207, Col. San Angel Inn, ☎ 5/616–0165 and other locations) is a treasure trove of perhaps the best silver work in Mexico—jewelry, flatware, candelabra, museum-quality reproductions of archaeological finds, and bold new designs by young Mexican silversmiths.

Leather

For leather goods you have a couple of choices in Mexico City. **Aries** (⊠ Florencia 14, Zona Rosa, ☎ 5/533–2509) is Mexico's finest purveyor of leather goods, with a superb selection of bags and accessories for men and women; prices are high. **Gaitán** (⊠ Calle Saraseté 95-B at Tetracini, Col. Peralvillo downtown, ☎ 5/759-3393) carries an extensive array of leather coats, luggage, golf bags, and saddles. **Antil** (⊠ Florencia 22, Zona Rosa, ☎ 5/525–1573) also specializes in high-quality leather goods.

Mexican Crafts

Browse for folk art, sculpture, and furniture in the gallery **Artesanos de México** (⊠ Londres 117, Zona Rosa, ☎ 5/514–7455). Handwoven wool rugs, tapestries, and fabrics with original and unusual designs can be found at **Tamacani** (⊠ Varsovia 51, Zona Rosa, ☎ 5/207-3720). **Arte Popular en Miniatura** (⊠ Hamburgo 85, ☎ 5/525–8145) is a tiny shop filled with tiny things, from dollhouse furniture and lead soldiers to miniature Nativity scenes. **Flamma** (⊠ Hamburgo 167, Zona Rosa, ☎ 5/511–8499 or 5/511–0266) is a town house that sells beautiful handmade candles. **Galerís del Arcángel** (⊠ Estocolmo 40, Zona Rosa, ☎ 5/511–6303) is an exquisite crafts and furniture shop tucked away in the Zona Rosa. It specializes in carved wood furniture from Patzcuaro, Michoacán (brought to life by brightly painted sunflowers, calla lilies, and suns) as well as wooden angel wall decorations, pottery, and paintings.

Under the auspices of the National Council for Culture and Arts, **FONART** (National Fund for Promoting Handicrafts) operates four stores in Mexico City and others around the country. Prices are fixed (and high), but the diverse, top-quality folk art and hand-crafted furnishings from all over Mexico represent the best artisans. The most convenient locations are at ⊠ 115 Carranza, Col. Coyoacán (☏ 5/554–6270), and at ⊠ Juárez 89 (☏ 5/521–0171), downtown just west of Alameda Park. Major sales at near wholesale prices are held at the main store-warehouse (⊠ Av. Patriotismo 691, Col. Mixcoac, ☏ 5/5563–4060) year-round.

Feders (⊠ Bufon 25 in Col. Nueva Anzures, ☏ 5/260–2958 factory; ⊠ Bazar Sábado, Plaza San Jacinto 11, San Angel, booth, ☏ no phone) has great handblown glass, Tiffany-style lamps, and artistic wrought iron.

MEXICO CITY A TO Z

Arriving and Departing

By Bus
Greyhound (☏ 5/592–3766 in Mexico; 800/231–2222 in the U.S.) buses make connections to major U.S. border cities, from which Mexican bus lines depart throughout the day. Reserved seating is available on first-class coaches, which are comfortable but not nearly as plush as the intercity buses. If you plan stopovers en route, make sure in advance that your ticket is written up accordingly. In Mexico, platform announcements are in Spanish only.

Within Mexico, buses are becoming the most popular way to travel: you can board ultramodern, superdeluxe motor coaches that show U.S. movies and serve soft drinks and coffee. **ETN** (Enlaces Terrestres Nacionales, ☏ 5/577–6529, 5/271–1262, or 5/567–9634) serves cities to the west and northwest, such as Guadalajara, Morelia, Querétaro, Guanajuato, San Miguel de Allende, and Toluca. **ADO** (☏ 5/785–9659; 5/133–2444; 91–800/7–02–80 within Mexico) buses depart southeast to such places as Puebla, Oaxaca, Veracruz, Mérida, and Cancún. Reserved-seat tickets can be purchased at Mexico City travel agencies.

Various other classes of intercity bus tickets can be purchased at virtually any travel agency in the city; there are an especially large number in the Zona Rosa. Buses depart from four outlying stations (*terminales de autobuses*), where tickets can also be purchased: **Central de Autobuses del Norte,** going north (⊠ Av. Cién Metros 4907, ☏ 5/587–1552); **Central de Autobuses del Sur,** going south (⊠ Taxqueña 1320, ☏ 5/689–9745); **Central de Autobuses del Oriente,** known as TAPO, going east (⊠ Ignacio Zaragoza 200, ☏ 5/762–5977); and **Terminal de Autobuses del Poniente,** going west (⊠ Río Tacubaya and Sur 122, ☏ 5/271–4519).

By Car
Major arteries into Mexico City include Highway 57 to the north, which starts at Laredo, Texas, and goes through Monterrey and Querétaro. Highway 95 comes in from Cuernavaca to the south, and Highway 190D from Puebla to the east. Highway 15 via Toluca and Valle de Bravo is the main western route.

By Plane
THE AIRLINES
All flights lead to Mexico City. **Mexicana** (☏ 5/448–0990) has scheduled service from Chicago, Denver, Los Angeles, Miami, New York, San Antonio, San Francisco, and San Jose. It has direct or connecting service at 30 locations throughout the country. **Aeroméxico** (☏ 5/133–4000) serves Mexico City daily from Dallas, Houston, Los Angeles, Miami, Orlando, New Orleans, Atlanta, New York, Ontario (California), Phoenix, San Antonio, San Diego, and Tucson (as well as Tijuana). Aeroméxico serves some 35 cities within Mexico. **Aerolitoral,**

a subsidiary of Aeroméxico based in Monterrey, serves north-central cities as well as San Antonio, El Paso, and McAllen, Texas, via Monterrey from Mexico City. **Taesa** (☎ 5/227–0700), a fast-growing Mexican airline, has direct flights (but not nonstop) to Mexico City from Chicago and Oakland; directs and nonstops from Tijuana; and nonstops from Laredo, Texas.

North American carriers serving Mexico City include **Air Canada, Alaska, American, America West, Canadian, Continental, Delta, Northwest, Trans World Airlines, United,** and **US Airways. Air France** flies nonstop between Houston and Mexico City.

THE AIRPORT

The newest wing of Mexico City's *Aeropuerto Internacional Benito Juárez* is a high-tech, state-of-the-art elongation of the east end of the existing airport. It is occupied by American, Delta, and United airlines, as well as by all the major car-rental agencies; four banks and seven currency exchanges (*casas de cambio*); Cirrus and Plus ATMs that disburse pesos to Visa and MasterCard holders; places to rent cellular phones; and a food court, pharmacy, bookstore, and pricey shops. A multilevel parking garage for 2,500 cars has also been added (short-term parking: about $1.50 per hr).

Porters and free carts are available in the baggage-retrieval areas. Banks and currency exchanges rotate their schedules to provide around-the-clock service. Though dollar bills (not coins!) are acceptable at the airport, you'll get the best exchange rate by changing dollars at the currency offices here. You can also use your ATM card to take pesos directly out of your U.S. account in ATMs (called *cajero automático* locally) here and throughout the city—and you'll get an even better exchange rate. Just remember that your home bank will charge $3 or more for the transaction. The Mexico City Tourist Office, Mexican Ministry of Tourism (SECTUR), and the Hotel Association have stands in the arrival areas that can provide information and find visitors a room for the night.

BETWEEN THE AIRPORT AND CENTER CITY

If you're taking a taxi, be sure to purchase your ticket at one of the official airport taxi counters marked **Transportación Terrestre** (ground transportation), located in the baggage carousel areas as well as in the concourse area and curbside; avoid *pirata* (taxi drivers offering their services). Government-controlled fares are based on which colonia you are going to and are usually about $7 (per car, not per person) to most hotels. A 10% tip is customary for airport drivers if they help with baggage. All major car-rental agencies have booths at both arrival areas, but renting a car is not recommended unless you are heading out of town or know Mexico City *very* well.

By Train

The train system in Mexico is currently in the process of being privatized and is badly in need of refurbishing. At press time, there was direct service on only one route from the U.S. border to Mexico City—the line from Ciudad Juárez (across the border from El Paso). We don't recommend train travel at this time, but if you're determined to go by rail, you can get up-to-date information about schedules and prices in the United States from **Mexico by Train** (☎ FAX 210/725–3659 or ☎ 800/321–1699).

Getting Around

By Bus

The Mexico City bus system is used by millions of commuters daily because it's cheap and goes everywhere. Buses are packed during rush hours, so as in all big cities, you should be wary of pickpockets. One of the principal bus routes runs along Paseo de la Reforma, Avenida Juárez, and Calle Madero. This west–east route connects Bosque de Chapultepec with the Zócalo. A southbound bus also may be taken along Avenida Insurgentes Sur to San Angel and University City, or northbound along Avenida Insurgentes Norte to the Guadalupe Basilica. Mexico City Tourism offices provide free bus-route maps. The price was raised at the end of 1996 from 1 to a maximum 3.50 pesos (depending on how far you're going)—still a bargain, especially for foreigners.

By Car

Millions of intrepid drivers brave Mexico City's streets every day and survive, but for out-of-towners the experience can be frazzling. One-way streets are confusing, rush-hour traffic is nightmarish, and parking places can be hard to come by. Police tow trucks haul away illegally parked vehicles, and the owner is heavily fined. As in any large city, getting your car back here is a byzantine process. **LOCATEL** (☎ 5/658–1111) is an efficient 24-hour service for tracing vehicles that are towed, stolen, or lost (in case you forgot where you parked). There's a chance an operator on duty may speak English, but the service is primarily in Spanish. Visitors can hire a chauffeur for their cars through a hotel concierge or travel service such as American Express.

Also keep in mind that the strictly enforced law **Hoy No Circula** (Today My Car Can't Circulate) applies to all private vehicles, including your own. One of several efforts to reduce smog and traffic congestion, this law prohibits every privately owned vehicle (including out-of-state, foreign, and even rental cars) from being used on one designated weekday. During emergency smog-alerts, which usually occur in December and January, cars are prohibited from circulating on two days of the week. Cars in violation are inevitably impounded by the police. Expect a hefty fine as well.

The weekday you can't drive is specified by the last number or letter of the license plate: on a non-emergency week, 1-2 are prohibited on Monday; 3-4 on Tuesday; 5-6 on Wednesday; 7-8 on Thursday; and 9-0 on Friday. For further information, contact the Mexican Government Tourism Office nearest you, and by all means plan your schedule accordingly.

By Pesero

Originally six-passenger sedans, then vans, and now minibuses, peseros operate on a number of fixed routes and charge a flat rate (a peso once upon a time, hence the name). Peseros offer a good alternative to buses and taxis; however, be prepared for a jolting ride because many drivers like to turn their buses into bucking broncos. Likely routes for tourists are along the city's major west–east axis (Bosque de Chapultepec–Reforma–Avenida Juárez–Zócalo) and north–south along Insurgentes, between the Guadalupe Basilica and San Angel–University City. Peseros pick up passengers at bus stops and outside almost all metro stations these days. Just stand on the curb, check the route sign on the oncoming pesero's windshield, and hold out your hand. Tell the driver where to stop, or press the button by the back door. If it's really crowded and you can't reach the back door in time, just bang on the ceiling and yell, "Baja," which means "Getting off" in Spanish. Base fares are 1.50 pesos with the price going up to 3 according to how far you travel. Exact change is appreciated by drivers.

By Subway

Transporting 5 million passengers daily, Mexico City's metro is one of the world's best, busiest, safest, and cheapest transportation systems—

1.50 pesos. The impeccably clean marble-and-onyx stations are brightly lit, and modern French-designed trains run quietly on rubber tires. Some stations, such as Insurgentes, are shopping centers. Even if you don't take a ride, visit the Zócalo station, which has large models of central Mexico City during three historic periods. Many stations have temporary cultural displays ranging from archaeological treasures to modern art; the Pino Suárez station has a small Aztec pyramid inside, a surprise discovery during construction.

There are 10 intersecting metro lines covering more than 160 km (100 mi). It's a bit confusing: The number 8 had been previously assigned to a line whose construction was canceled because it would have destroyed unearthed Aztec ruins. Line 9 was subsequently built. Now number 8 designates the newest (10th) line. The ninth line was A, and plans to build Line B have been been announced. In 1996 the government pledged $2 million to build 29 km (18 mi) of subway. Segments of Lines 1 and 2 cover most points of interest to foreigners, including the Zona Rosa, Bellas Artes, and the Centro Histórico. At the southern edge of the city, the Tasqueña station (Line 2) connects with the electric train (*tren eléctrico*) that continues south to Xochimilco. To the southeast, the *Tren Ligero* from the Pantitlán station (Lines 1, 5, and 9) heads east to Chalco in the state of Mexico. The various lines also serve all four bus stations, the Buenavista train station, and the airport; however, only light baggage is allowed on board during rush hours. User-friendly, color-coded maps are sometimes available free at metro-station information desks (if there's an attendant) and Mexico City tourism offices, and color-keyed signs and maps are posted all around.

Trains run frequently (about two minutes apart) and are least crowded at night and between 10 AM and 4 PM. To reduce incidences of harassment during crowded rush hours, regulations (not strictly enforced) require men to ride separate cars from women and children. Hours vary somewhat according to the line, but service is essentially from 5 AM to 1 AM weekdays; 6 AM to 2 AM Saturdays; 7 AM to 1 AM Sundays and holidays.

By Taxi

The Mexico City variety comes in several colors, types, and sizes. Unmarked *turismo* sedans with hooded meters are usually stationed outside major hotels and in tourist areas; however, they are uneconomical for short trips. Their drivers are almost always English-speaking guides and can be hired for sight-seeing on a daily or hourly basis (always negotiate the price in advance). *Sitio* (stationed) taxis operate out of stands, take radio calls, and are authorized to charge a small premium. Among these, **Servi-Taxis** (☎ 5/271–2560) and **Taxi-Mex** (☎ 5/538–0912 and 5/538–0573), which accepts American Express, offer 24-hour service.

Serious dangers to your safety come from unscrupulous cab drivers who are preying on tourists, robbing and assaulting them or forcing them to withdraw money from ATMs. **Take only registered hotel taxis or have a hotel concierge call a sitio cab—do not hail taxis on the street under any circumstances.** Be sure to establish the fare in advance.

Taxi drivers are authorized to charge 10% more at night, usually after 10 PM. Taking a taxi in Mexico City is extremely inexpensive and tips are not expected unless you have luggage—then 10% is sufficient.

Contacts and Resources

Consulates and Embassies

The **U.S. Embassy** (✉ Paseo de la Reforma 305, ☎ 5/209–9100) is open weekdays 9–2 and 3–5, but is closed for American and Mexican holidays; however, there's always a duty officer to take emergency calls on holidays and after closing hours. The embassy keeps a list of English-speaking local doctors on hand if you need to consult one. The **Canadian Embassy** (⊠ Schiller 529, ☎ 5/724–7900) is open weekdays 9–1 and 2–5 and is closed for Canadian and Mexican holidays. The **British Embassy** (⊠ Río Lerma 71, ☎ 5/207–2449) is open weekdays 8:30–3:30.

Emergencies

Dial ☎ 060 or 080 for **police, Red Cross, ambulance, fire,** or other emergency situations. If you are not able to reach an English-speaking operator, call the SECTUR hot line (☞ Visitor Information, *below*). For missing persons or cars call **LOCATEL** (☎ 5/658–1111).

HOSPITAL

American British Cowdray Hospital (⊠ Calle Sur 136–116, corner of Observatorio, Col. las Américas, ☎ 5/230–8161 for emergencies; 5/230–8000 switchboard).

English-Language Bookstores and Publications

The best place for English-language and foreign-language newspapers and magazines is **Casa de la Prensa,** which has two locations in the Zona Rosa (⊠ Florencia 57; ⊠ Hamburgo 141). **Sanborns** (☞ Shopping, *above*) carries a limited number of U.S. newspapers but an ample supply of magazines, paperbacks, and guidebooks. The **American Book Store** (⊠ Calle Madero 25) has even more extensive selections. Two daily English-language newspapers, *The News* and *The Mexico City Times,* are available at hotels and at newsstands in the tourist areas; they provide a summary of what is happening in Mexico and the rest of the world with cultural and entertainment listings and daily stock-market reports. Remember that most U.S. or foreign-published publications are about double the price you'd pay for them at home.

The **Benjamin Franklin Library** is actually a part of the U.S. Embassy instituted to create greater understanding and cultural exchange between the United States and Mexico. The library has a substantial collection of English novels, a good reference section, and many U.S. periodicals. You must fill out an application, be at least 20 years old, and have a Mexican resident sign it in order to check out books, but anyone can browse through the stacks. ⊠ Londres 16, Zona Rosa, ☎ 5/209–9100, ext. 3500 or 3510. ☉ *Mon. and Fri. 3–7:30, Tues.–Thurs. 10–3.*

Guided Tours

Except for the Tren Turístico, the tours described below can be booked. through the agents listed in the Travel Agencies section (☞ *below*).

ORIENTATION

The basic city tour ($30) lasts four hours and takes in the Zócalo, Palacio Nacional, Catedral Metropolitana, and Bosque de Chapultepec. A four-hour pyramid tour costs around $36 and covers the Basílica de Nuestra Señora de Guadalupe and the major ruins at Teotihuacán.

A good way to see the historic downtown—if you know some Spanish—is on **Tren Turístico's** (☎ 5/512–1012 or 5/512–1013) charming replicas of 20-passenger trolleys from the 1920s. The 50-minute narrated tour ($2.50) includes the Zócalo, Colegio de San Idelfonso, Plaza de Santo Domingo, Plaza Manuel Tolsá (location of the Palacio de Minería and Museo Nacional de Arte), Plaza de la Santa Veracruz (Museo Franz Mayer), and the Palacio de Iturbide. Trolleys depart hourly from 10 to 5 from the train's offices in front of Alameda Park (⊠ Av. Juárez 66 at Revillagigedo).

SPECIAL-INTEREST

Travel agencies offer various city tours. The most popular ones seem to fall in the following general categories:

Cultural: The seven-hour tour ($66) is run on Sunday mornings only and usually includes a performance of the folkloric dances at the Palacio de Bellas Artes, a gondola ride in the canals of Xochimilco's floating gardens, and a visit to the modern campus of the National University.

Bullfighting: On Sunday only are trips to the bullring with a guide who will explain the finer points of this spectacle. This four-hour afternoon tour ($35) can usually be combined with the Ballet Folklórico–Xochimilco trip ($85).

Nightlife: These tours are among the most popular tours of Mexico City. The best are scheduled to last five hours and include transfers by private car rather than bus; dinner at an elegant restaurant (frequently Bellini on top of the World Trade Center or at the Del Lago); a drink and a show at the Plaza Garibaldi, where mariachis play; and a nightcap at Gitanerías, which features Spanish flamenco performances. Nightlife tours begin at $56.

Travel Agencies

Gray Line Tours (⊠ Londres 166, ☎ 5/208–1163), **American Express** (⊠ Paseo de la Reforma 234, ☎ 5/326–2831), and **Mexico Travel Advisors (MTA)** (⊠ Génova 30, ☎ 5/525–7520 and 5/525–7534) .

Visitor Information

The **Mexico City Tourist Office** (Departamento de Turismo del Distrito Federal, or DDF) maintains information booths at both the international and domestic arrival areas at the airport. In town visit the city's tourism module at Amberes 54, at the corner of Londres in the Zona Rosa. This office also provides information by phone with its **INFOTUR** service (☎ 5/525–9380) from 9 to 8 daily. Multilingual operators are available and have access to an extensive data bank.

The **Secretariat of Tourism** (SECTUR) operates a 24-hour multilingual hot line that provides information on both Mexico City and the entire country (☎ 5/250–0123, 5/250–0493, 5/250–0027, 5/250–0589, 5/250–0151, 5/250–0292, or 5/250–0741). If lines are busy, keep trying. Outside Mexico City, call toll-free (☎ 91–800/9–03–92; 800/482–9832 from the U.S.) to reach the **SECTUR Tourist Information Center** at Presidente Masarik 172 (in Col. Polanco), open weekdays 8–8.

2 SIDE TRIPS FROM MEXICO CITY

If the pace—or smog—of the megalopolis begins to run you down, just an hour or two outside of Mexico City lies a plethora of towns and archaeological sites guaranteed to make you feel that you've turned back the clock on the concrete jungle. Take a deep breath of fresh air while you hike up one of the twin volcanoes or water ski at Valle de Bravo, relax in the bougainvillea-scented town of Cuernavaca, or take in the spectacular pyramids at Teotihuacán.

ALTHOUGH THE URBAN lifestyle in Mexico city is steeped in American culture, you'll be pleasantly surprised to find that just a short drive or bus ride can place you in a traditional small town church, in the middle of a gorgeous national park, or on top of breathtaking ancient ruins. Quaint towns like Cholula or Tepoztlán give a taste of what life might have been like in Mexico City before its population began exploding with industrial growth in the 1960s and '70s. Cholula is famous for its friendly townsfolk and colonial churches. Tepoztlán has a curious cultural mix of its indigenous community and the New Age proselytes drawn by the town's pyramid. Just an hour north of the city, the famous Teotihuacán ruins have larger and more historically significant pyramids, as do the former Toltec capital of Tula and the splendid ruins at Cacaxtla and Xochitécatl to the southeast.

By Frank Shiell

Updated by
Paige Bierma

Two nearby state capitals, the medium-sized cities of Cuernavaca and Puebla, are windows on the diversity of Mexican life. Cuernavaca's flower power and springlike climate have made this culturally hip city a favorite weekend getaway for *chilangos* (Mexico City residents), as well as a center for Spanish-language schools that draw people from around the world. Puebla, on the other hand, is a conservative city, surrounded by important agricultural valleys and populated with an abundance of churches, chapels, ex-convents, and monasteries.

NORTH OF MEXICO CITY

Hugging the roads to the north of Mexico City are several of the country's most celebrated pre-Columbian and colonial monuments. The Basílica de Guadalupe, a church dedicated to Mexico's patron saint, and the pyramids of Teotihuacán make an easy day tour, as does the combination of the ex-convent (now a magnificent museum of the viceregal period) at Tepotzotlán and the ruins at Tula, also to the north but in a slightly different direction.

There are no tourist offices in the area, but a good English-language guidebook to Teotihuacán is sold at the site.

La Villa de Guadalupe

"La Villa"—the local moniker of the site of the two Basilicas of the Virgin of Guadalupe—is Mexico's holiest shrine. Its importance derives from the miracle that the devout believe transpired here on December 12, 1531, when an Indian named Juan Diego received from the Virgin a cloak permanently imprinted with her image so he could prove to the priests that he had indeed had a holy vision. On that date each year millions of pilgrims arrive, many crawling on their knees for the last few hundred yards, praying for cures and other divine favors. The **Antigua Basílica** (Old Basilica) dates from 1536; various additions have been made since then. The altar was executed by sculptor Manuel Tolsá. The basilica now houses a museum of ex-votos (hand-painted tin retablos) and popular religious art, painting, sculpture, and decorative and applied arts from the 15th to the 18th century.

Because the structure of the Antigua Basílica had weakened over the years and the building was no longer large enough or safe enough to accommodate all the worshipers, Pedro Ramírez Vázquez, the architect responsible for Mexico City's splendid National Museum of Anthropology, was commissioned to design a new shrine. In this case, alas, the architect's inspiration failed him: the **Nueva Basílica** is a grotesque

Side Trips from Mexico City

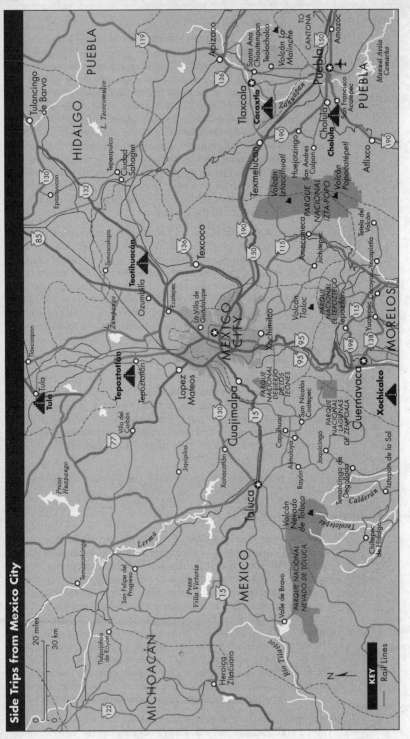

and most unspiritual mass of steel, wood, resinous fibers, and polyethylene. The famous cloak is enshrined in its own altar and can be viewed from a moving sidewalk that passes below it.

Teotihuacán

 This meso-American Giza is one of the most powerful sites in Mexico—based on its size and scale, there's no doubting Teotihuacán's (*teh*-oh-tee-wa-*can*) monumental place in history. It was likely a small town already by 100 BC; four centuries later it had reached its zenith. At the time of its decline in the 8th century, it was one of the largest cities in the world, with possibly as many as 250,000 people. The sacred metropolis lay in the midst of rich obsidian mines, which provided the means for its rise as a major regional trading power and center for the arts—its influence on Maya pottery stretched as far away as Tikal in present-day Guatemala. The glasslike obsidian is still being fashioned into animal figures, which are sold in market stalls on the site. Just who lived here isn't exactly clear—even the original name of the city is lost. It is believed that water shortages and crises caused by local deforestation contributed to Teotihuacán's downfall. It was set on fire and destroyed by raiders around AD 650. Centuries later, the Aztecs arrived in the Valley of Mexico. Because the memory of the grandeur of this city survived the passage of time, these new settlers named the site Teotihuacán, which meant "place where the gods were born." It was here, the Aztecs believed, that the gods created the universe.

The awesome **Pirámide del Sol** (Pyramid of the Sun), with a base as broad as that of the pyramid of Cheops in Egypt, is off the center of Teotihuacán's main axis. Estimated to have been built between AD 100 and AD 250, it is the site's oldest structure. Its planes and angles were precisely built in relation to the movement of the sun—marking the equinoxes, for example—and the Pleiades constellation. The 242 steps of the 215-ft pyramid face west, the cardinal point where it was believed that the sun was transformed into a jaguar in order to pass nightly through the darkness of death.

The most impressive sight in Teotihuacán is the 4-km-long (2½-mi-long) **Calzada de los Muertos** (Avenue of the Dead), the main axis of the ancient city along which six major structures lie. The Aztecs gave the avenue this name because of the stepped platforms lining it, which they mistook for tombs. The graceful 126-ft-high **Pirámide de la Luna** (Pyramid of the Moon) dominates the northern end of the avenue, and the compact, square **Ciudadela** (Citadel) flanks the opposite end. More than 4,000 one-story dwellings constructed of adobe and stone and occupied by artisans, warriors, and tradesmen once surrounded the avenue. On the west side of the spacious plaza facing the Pyramid of the Moon are the **Palacio del Quetzalpápalotl** (Palace of the Plumed Butterfly), **Templo de las Conchas Emplumados** (Temple of Plumed Conch Shells), and **Palacio de los Jaguares** (Palace of Jaguars), which is where the priests resided. The palaces are best known for the spectacular bird and jaguar murals in their winding underground chambers.

The Ciudadela, with its **Templo de Quetzalcóatl** (Temple of the Plumed Serpent) and **Tlaloc** (Rain God), shows off the plastic arts of the time with its brawny toothed serpent heads jutting out of the temple facade. Quetzalcóatl and Tlaloc together represent the fusion of earth and sky.

Climbing one pyramid is probably enough for most people. The Pyramid of the Sun is the taller by 89 ft, and affords a spectacular view of the entire area. Wear comfortable clothes (especially shoes) and bring sunscreen or a visored hat when you visit.

Many of the artifacts uncovered at Teotihuacán are on display at the Museum of Anthropology in Mexico City. The **on-site museum,** opened in 1994 near the Pyramid of the Sun, contains fabulous pieces from the archaeological zone—like the stone sculpture of Tlaloc, the goggle-eyed god of rain; black and green obsidian arrowheads; and simulated burial sites of exalted personages of the empire, their skeletons arranged as they were when discovered.

Seeing the ruins will take two to four hours, depending on how smitten you are by the place—or when your tour bus leaves. ☎ 595/60052 or 595/60276. 🖼 $2; free Sun. ☉ Site and on-site museum daily 8–6.

Many tour buses to the ruins stop briefly in **San Agustín Acolmán** to see the outstanding plateresque (an ornate 16th-century Spanish-style) church and ex-convent, now a museum. The original Augustinian church (1539) is noteworthy for its vaulted roof and pointed towers. The ornate cloister and plateresque facade, set off with candelabra-like columns, were added a century later by the monks.

Dining and Lodging

$$ ✕⊞ **Villa Arqueológica.** If you'd like to overnight at the pyramids, this Club Med stands across the road from the fenced-off site and has snug rooms and a huge garden and patio restaurant-bar surrounding a pool and tennis court. This is the only hotel that has permission to be in the area. ⊠ Villa Arqueológica Teotihuacán, San Juan de Teotihuacán, Mexico, C.P. 55800, ☎ Teotihuacán: 595/60909; Mexico City: 5/203–3086; 800/258–2633 in the U.S. 40 rooms. Restaurant, pool, tennis court. AE, MC, V.

Tepotzotlán

The **Jesuit church** and **school of San Francisco Javier** at Tepotzotlán (pronounced teh-po-tzot-*lan*) rank among the masterpieces of Mexican churrigueresque architecture. The unmitigated Baroque facade of the church (1682) is the first thing to catch the eye, but inside and out, every square inch has been worked over, like an overdressed Christmas tree. Note especially the gilded, mirrored Chapel of the Virgin of Loreto.

In pre-Hispanic times, the village was an important stop along the salt route—salt was used as money—between Toluca and Texcoco (near Teotihuacán) and had a prestigious school of dance and the plastic arts. When Cortés arrived, he brutally massacred the whole town on the pretense of asking for help for his wounded soldiers. In 1580, four Jesuit priests arrived, learned the native language, and turned the village into a center of evangelization by setting up a school for the young nobles of the conquered nation. The church, of course, was built with Indian slave labor, but as a concession to the slaves, many of the angels decorating the chambers have been painted with dark-skinned indigenous faces. This is probably the only church in Mexico where you will find such paintings. There's also a museum of religious art in the complex. There are two notable restaurants for taking a light snack or lunch after viewing the Jesuit complex. One is the museum's coffee shop and the other is **Casa Mago,** directly across the square from the church. Casa Mago's owners will proudly recount how Elizabeth Taylor dropped in in 1963 to have a beer.

This village is also famous for its traditional Christmas *pastorela,* a charming and humorous morality play that has been taking place for more than 30 years, telling the story of the birth of Jesus Christ. Staged every year from December 16 to 23 in the patio of the church at night, the cast includes a few professionals and loads of extras from the town who portray shepherds, angels, and, of course, the Devil. Tickets are

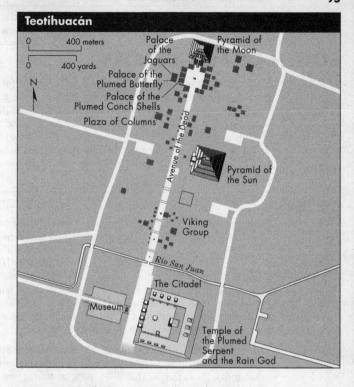

Teotihuacán

0 — 400 meters
0 — 400 yards

N

Palace of the Jaguars
Pyramid of the Moon
Palace of the Plumed Butterfly
Palace of the Plumed Conch Shells
Plaza of Columns
Avenue of the Dead
Pyramid of the Sun
Viking Group
Río San Juan
The Citadel
Museum
Temple of the Plumed Serpent and the Rain God

available through **Ticketmaster** (☎ 5/325–9000 in Mexico City; or the church's offices in Tepotzotlán at 5/876–0243).

Tula

Tula, capital of the Toltecs—whose name for it was Tollán—was founded around AD 1000 and abandoned two centuries later. Quetzalcóatl was born in Tula and became its priest-king. Under his rule, the Toltecs reached the pinnacle of their civilization, with art, science, and philosophy flourishing. According to myth, Quetzalcóatl went into exile in Yucatán but vowed to return—on a date (1519) that unfortunately coincided with the arrival of Hernán Cortés, whom the Aztecs therefore fatefully welcomed. Visible from afar, Tula's 15-ft **warrior statues** (*atlantes*), rather than the ruins themselves, make the show. These basalt figures tower over Pyramid B, their strong geometrics looking vaguely totemic. Crocodiles, jaguars, coyotes, and eagles are also depicted in the carvings and represent the various warrior orders of the Toltecs. ✉ *$2; free Sun.* ☉ *Tues.–Sun. 9:30–4:30.*

North of Mexico City A to Z

Getting There

To get to **La Villa de Guadalupe** by car, take Paseo de la Reforma Norte until it forks into Calzada de Guadalupe, which leads directly to the shrine. Or take the No. 3 (red) metro line from downtown to the Basílica stop (the station symbol is the virgin's image). Buses run every 20 minutes between 7 AM and 3 PM from the Central de Autobuses del Norte to **Teotihuacán,** and the trip takes about one hour. Tour companies also offer combination visits to the two sights.

To get to **Tepotzotlán** from Mexico City, follow Periférico Norte. After 41 km (25 mi), you'll come to the exit for Tepotzotlán. **Tula** is about

8 km (5 mi) north of Tepotzotlán. Buses to Tula/Tepotzotlán leave Mexico City every 20 minutes, also from the Central de Autobuses del Norte.

SOUTH OF MEXICO CITY

Xochimilco (pronounced kso-chee-*meel*-co) is famous for its floating gardens, where you can ride in gondola-like boats and get a fleeting sense of a pre-Hispanic Mexico City. Beyond Xochimilco, in the neighboring state of Morelos, Cuernavaca is a weekend retreat for wealthy *chilangos* (residents of Mexico City) and foreigners. From Cuernavaca we suggest a detour to the town of Tepoztlán, which has a 16th-century Dominican convent, a lively Sunday market, its own little pyramid, and plenty of New Age devotees.

Xochimilco

When the first nomadic settlers arrived in the Valley of Mexico, they found an enormous lake. As the years went by and their population grew, the land was not sufficient to satisfy their agricultural needs. They solved the problem by devising a system of *chinampas* (floating gardens), rectangular structures something like barges, which they filled with reeds, branches, and mud. They planted them with willows, whose roots anchored the floating gardens to the lake bed, making a labyrinth of small islands and canals on which they carried the flowers and produce grown on the chinampas to market.

Today Xochimilco is the only place in Mexico where the gardens still exist. Go on a Saturday, when the *tianguis* (market) is most active, or on a Sunday. (Note that Xochimilco is popular among families on Sunday.) On weekdays the place is practically deserted, so it loses much of its charm. Hire a *trajinera* (flower-painted launch); an arch over each spells out its name in flowers. As you sail through the canals, you'll pass mariachis and women selling tacos from other trajineras.

★ People also flock to Xochimilco for the **Museo Dolores Olmedo Patino,** which holds the largest private collection of works by flamboyant muralist Diego Rivera. It was put together by Olmedo, his lifelong model, patron, and onetime mistress (which she denies). The lavish display of nearly 140 pieces from his cubist, post-cubist, and mural periods hangs in a magnificent 18th-century hacienda with beautiful gardens. The museum also has works by Rivera's legal wife, Frida Kahlo, and his common-law wife, Angelina Beloff. ✉ *Av. México 5843,* ☎ *5/555–1016.* 🎫 *$1.* ☉ *Tues.–Sun. 10–6.*

Cuernavaca

The climate in Cuernavaca, a trifling 85 km (53 mi) from Mexico City, changes dramatically to lush and semitropical as the altitude descends almost 2,500 ft. In fact, it was this balmy springlike temperature that first attracted the rich and famous to what has become a resort: Hernán Cortés built the first summer place—read palace—here in the 16th century. There are spectacular restaurants and hotels, in addition to the beautiful Borda Gardens and Diego Rivera murals in the Palacio de Cortés. An overnight stay is recommended.

Cuernavaca is built on a series of small hills whose streets intertwine at a maddening pace. If you're not used to driving in San Francisco, say, it's better to get around by cab, especially on weekends, when the number of cars swells to disproportionate numbers.

Most sights are concentrated around the central **Plaza de Armas,** which is surrounded by crafts shops, sidewalk cafés, and government buildings. The square itself is filled with vendors from neighboring villages. Throughout the week they hawk local arts and crafts; on weekends, one side of the square is taken over by stalls in which you'll find silver and gold jewelry and leather goods from elsewhere in the country. **Jardín Juárez** (Juárez Gardens), a smaller square across the street from Plaza de Armas, puts on free band concerts Thursday evenings at 6 under its colonial arcade. Either of these two squares is the perfect place for whiling away a pleasant afternoon after a visit to the tourist sights. After dark, the hip spot is the **Plazuela del Zacate** (corner of Galeana and Fray Bartolomé de Las Casas, two blocks from the Plaza de Armas), where sidewalk cafés and bars open every night and young people gather around the plaza.

The **Palacio de Cortés** (Cortés's palace-cum-fortress) houses the **Museo de Cuauhnáhuac**—Cuauhnáhuac being the native name for Cuernavaca—which focuses on Mexican history before and after the conquest. Diego Rivera painted some of his finest murals on the palace's top floor in 1930–32. Like those of Mexico City's National Palace, they dramatize the history and the horrors of the conquest, colonialism, and the revolution. Former U.S. Ambassador to Mexico Dwight Morrow commissioned Rivera to paint the murals for $30,000. ✉ *Juárez and Hidalgo,* ☎ *73/12–81–71.* ✆ *$1.60; free Sun.* ☉ *Tues.–Sun. 10–5.*

The beautiful, spacious **Jardín Borda** (Borda Gardens) is the most visited sight in Cuernavaca. The jardín was designed in the late 18th century by a member of the Borda family—rich miners of French extraction—for one of his relatives; Maximilian and Carlotta visited the gardens frequently. Here Maximilian had a dalliance with the gardener's wife, La India Bonita, who was immortalized in a portrait by a noted painter of the time. In this century novelist Malcolm Lowry turned the gardens into a sinister symbol in *Under the Volcano.* ✉ *Av. Morelos, No. 103 at Hidalgo, 3 blocks west of Palacio de Cortés,* ☎ *73/12–92–37.* ✆ *Less than $1; free Sun.* ☉ *Tues.–Sun. 10-5:30.*

The **Catedral de la Asunción,** an eclectic structure begun in 1529 by Hernán Cortés, is noteworthy for the skull and crossbones over its main entrance and its 17th-century Japanese wall paintings. It's also famous for mariachi masses Sunday mornings. Paintings inside the **Palacio Municipal,** diagonally opposite the cathedral, depict pre-Hispanic city life. ✉ *Hidalgo and Av. Morelos opposite Borda gardens.*

Also near the main square is the **Robert Brady Museum,** a delightful restored colonial mansion housing a diverse collection of art and artifacts assembled by the late Brady, an artist, antiquarian, and decorator from Fort Dodge, Iowa. You can see ceramics, antique furniture, sculptures, paintings, and tapestries all beautifully arranged in rooms painted with bright Mexican colors. ✉ *Netzahuacóyotl 4, between Hidalgo and Abasolo,* ☎ *73/18–85–54.* ✆ *$2.* ☉ *Tues.–Sun. 10–6.*

The small ruins of **Xochicalco** ("place of flowers") include a pyramid and ball court. Showing Maya, Toltec, and Zapotec influences, the ancient fortified city reached its peak between AD 700 and 900. A solar-powered museum has six rooms of artifacts, including beautiful sculptures of Xochicalco deities found on site. The museum has a café, bookstore, and gift shop. ✉ *23 mi southwest of Cuernavaca (take Hwy. 95D south; look for sign for turnoff).* ✆ *$2; free Sun.* ☉ *Tues.–Sun. 10–5.*

Dining and Lodging

If you've missed getting invited to one of the wealthy weekender's mansions set in the hills on the edge of town, not to worry: there are a number of remarkable hotels and restaurants with equally remarkable gardens—several of them in restored colonial mansions and even haciendas—where you can get a taste of life behind the high stone walls. Many people come here to do just that, and many Cuernavaca hostelries that began as restaurants added on rooms to satisfy clients who felt too relaxed to drive back to Mexico City after their elaborate meals.

$ ✕ **La Strada.** For a change from Mexican food, come to this old-timer to enjoy a good Italian meal on a colonial candlelit patio. You can't go wrong with the fish dishes, pizzas (ask for the pizza menu), or the house beef specialty, *filete de Estrada,* served with homemade pasta. A guitarist plays Wednesday and Friday nights and the chef whips up weekend specials each Friday. ⊠ *Salazar 3, around corner from Palace of Cortés,* ☎ 73/18–60–85. AE, MC, V.

$ ✕ **Vienes.** Founded by an Austrian several generations ago, this Austro-Hungarian restaurant—which has grown up with the town—serves excellent Wiener schnitzel and goulash and irresistible pastries like Sacher torte and apple strudel. ⊠ *Lerdo de Tejada 302, at Comonfort, 1 block west of main square,* ☎ 73/14–34–04. AE, MC, V.

$$$ ✕🏨 **Las Mañanitas.** Opened 41 years ago by an American expat, rooms and suites here are exquisitely decorated with traditional Mexican fireplaces, hand-carved bedsteads, hand-painted tiles in the bathrooms, and gilded handicrafts. Mexico City residents drive an hour on weekends just to dine at the restaurant, with its spectacular dining open-air terraces and garden inhabited by flamingos, peacocks, and African cranes. Portions are ample, as with the tried-and-true favorite Mexican Plate—enchilada, chile relleno, *carne asada* (thinly sliced oven-grilled beef), and tamale, served with side dishes of guacamole and refried beans. Don't miss the black bottom (chocolate) pie. ⊠ *Ricardo Linares 107, Cuernavaca 62000,* ☎ 73/14–14–66, 𝖥𝖠𝖷 73/18–36–72. 1 room, 22 suites. Restaurant, bar, pool. AE.

$$$ 🏨 **Camino Real Sumiya.** The romantic hideaway, built by Woolworth heiress Barbara Hutton, was converted into a restaurant after she died. In 1993 new owners took over and turned it into a posh hotel. It's set amid formal Japanese gardens (including a contemplative rock garden) and contains an original Kabuki theater brought over from Kyoto. A concierge takes care of every need. The rooms, which are equipped with modern furniture, two queen-size beds, and color satellite TVs, are set in the far part of the garden for privacy. Nonguests dine in the restaurant. ⊠ *Morelos, 62550, about 15 mins south of town at Interior del Fraccionamiento Sumiya, Col. José Parres, Juitepec (take Civac exit on Acapulco Hwy.),* ☎ 73/20–91–99 or 800/722–6466, 𝖥𝖠𝖷 73/20–91–42. 163 rooms. 2 restaurants, bar, coffee shop, pool, 7 tennis courts, travel services. AE, DC, MC, V.

$$ 🏨 **Clarion Cuernavaca Racquet Club.** This posh tennis club–turned–hotel is less expensive than most lodgings, and its appeal is in its beautiful gardens and spacious two-room suites equipped with romantic fireplaces. Families converge here on weekends. The restaurant admits nonguests. ⊠ *Francisco Villa 100, Rancho de Cortés, Cuernavaca 62120,* ☎ 73/11–24–00 or 800/228–5151, 𝖥𝖠𝖷 73/17–54–83. 52 suites. Restaurant, bar, pool, 9 tennis courts. AE, DC, MC, V.

$–$$ 🏨 **Hacienda de Cortés.** This old hacienda dates from the 16th century and *did* belong to the conquistador. Rooms are decorated in traditional Mexican furnishings; they have lovely patios and gardens that will beckon you outdoors. There's a TV room off the lobby for addicts, but there are no in-room TVs. ⊠ *Plaza Kennedy 90, Col. Atlacomulco, Morelos 62250,* ☎ 73/15–88–44, 𝖥𝖠𝖷 73/15–00–35. 22 rooms. Restaurant, bar, pool. MC, V.

$–$$ 🏨 **Hotel Jacarandas.** Another former hacienda close to the downtown area, this hotel has the open, luxurious feel of an old-time Cuernavaca ranch. Huge laurel and fruit trees, jacarandas (of course), and poinsettias fill out the hotel's 98,000 square ft of terraced gardens, as do two pools, two tennis courts, and herb and vegetable gardens the hotel restaurant uses for its salads and herbal teas. This is a popular spot among Mexico City families. The rooms are simple with TVs but no cable. ⊠ *Cuauhtémoc 33, Col. Chapultepec, Cuernavaca 62450,* ☎ *73/15–77–77,* ☒ *73/15–78–88. 80 rooms, 6 suites. Restaurant, bar, 2 pools, 2 tennis courts, squash court. AE, DC, MC, V.*

Tepoztlán

 Some say Tepoztlán, surrounded by beautiful sandstone monoliths that throw off a russet glow at sunset, is a magical place—Mexico's answer to Sedona, Arizona. It attracts practitioners of hatha yoga, meditation, crystal healing, herbal cures, astrology, and native sorcery. This town of 13,000, with a village atmosphere and cobblestone streets, is primarily known for its tiny **Tepozteco pyramid,** probably of Aztec origin, perched on top of a hill; hundreds of people come each weekend to climb it. Other things of interest include the lively **Sunday market,** with its fruits, vegetables, and handicrafts, and the **dances** held during the pre-Lenten Carnival, when celebrants don bright masks depicting birds, animals, and Christian figures. Anthropologists Robert Redfield and Oscar Lewis both did fieldwork here in the 1950s. Tepoztlán's landmark is the multibuttressed 1559 **Templo y Ex-Convento de la Natividad de la Virgen María** (Temple and Ex-Convent of the Birth of the Virgin Mary), its fine paneled doors adorned with Indian motifs. Yearly on September 8, the faithful assemble here to celebrate the birth of the Virgin Mary, the town's patron saint. The date also commemorates the baptism of the legendary ruler Tepoztecatl, for whom the pyramid is named.

Tepoztlán drew national attention in September 1995, when townspeople stormed city hall and took government officials hostage to protest the proposed building of a mega–golf resort on their revered Tepozteco terrain. They eventually ousted the mayor and town police and continued protesting until the developers abandoned the project. In 1997 they finally elected a member of the Party of the Democratic Revolution, but for more than a year they governed themselves.

Lodging

At the **Posada del Tepozteco** (Calle del Paraíso 3, Tepoztlán, ☎ 73/95–00–10, $$–$$$), two pools, a tennis court, and terraced gardens spilling over with bougainvillea perched above the downtown area provide great views of both the village and the pyramid. The tranquil hotel has 18 rooms, most with Jacuzzi.

South of Mexico City A to Z

Getting There

To get to **Xochimilco** by car, take Periférico Sur to the extension of División del Norte. Xochimilco is 21 km (13 mi) from the Zócalo in Mexico City; the trip should take between 45 minutes and 1 hour, depending on traffic. If Xochimilco is your final stop, you are probably best off taking a taxi. By public transportation, take metro line No. 2 to Taxqueña and then any bus marked Xochimilco.

To continue south by car, return to Periférico Sur, turn left (south) on Viaducto Tlalpán, and watch for signs to **Cuernavaca** in about a half hour. The *cuota* (toll road, Rte. 95D), costs about $6 but is much faster than the *carretera libre* (free road, Rte. 95). On Route 95D, it will take you about 1½ hours to cover 85 km (53 mi).

Tepoztlán is 26 km (16 mi) east of Cuernavaca via Route 95D. Buses also run every 20 minutes.

Visitor Information

The **Morelos State Tourist Office** (⊠ Morelos Sur 187, ☎ 73/14–38–72) in Cuernavaca is located in Colonia Las Palmas; it's open weekdays 8 AM–3 PM and 6–9, weekends 9–2.

SOUTHEAST OF MEXICO CITY

Well-preserved colonial Puebla was once the center of the Spanish tile industry. Nearby Cholula is a sacred spot in ancient Mexico and home to an important pyramid and scores of churches. You can detour along the way to see the volcanoes, Popocatépetl (pronounced poh-poh-kah-*teh*-pettle) and Iztaccíhuatl (pronounced eesh-tah-*see*-wattle). On your return to the capital, leave time—an entire day would be best—to visit the city of Tlaxcala, with its rare church and former convent, and an amazing archaeological site nearby.

The Volcanoes

Leaving Mexico City, you can view **Popocatépetl and Iztaccíhuatl** to the south—if the smog is not too thick. "Popo," 17,887 ft high, last erupted in 1802, but rumblings and bubblings in late 1994 were sufficiently strong to cause nearby villages to be evacuated temporarily. It continued to burp and belch and spew large clouds of smoke and ash over the following years—and even a bit of lava in 1998—though most seismologists found little cause for alarm. In any case, Popo is currently off-limits for climbing beyond the 12,000-ft point. Check with the U.S. State Department for the latest developments if you plan to climb Izta—a feat for serious mountaineers. The Parque Nacional, a verdant pine forest, makes a good spot for a picnic.

The legend states that Popocatépetl, an Aztec warrior, had been sent by the emperor—father of his beloved Iztaccíhuatl—to bring back the head of a feared enemy in order to win Iztaccíhuatl's hand. He returned triumphantly only to find that Iztaccíhuatl had killed herself, believing him dead. The grief-stricken Popo laid out her body on a small knoll and lit an eternal torch that he watches over, kneeling. Each of the four peaks composing the volcano is named for a different part of her body, and its silhouette conjures up its nickname, "Sleeping Woman."

Lodging

At the 12,000-ft marker on Popo, there's a park shelter with spartan dormitory accommodations (cement slab beds), but it will only open when and if climbers are again allowed to scale Popo. You'll pay a few dollars a night here, and you must bring your own sleeping bag. You can drive here from the main highway, but this is the end of the road; if you want to go higher, you'll have to hoof it.

For lodging in town, try the venerable **Los Volcanes** (⊠ Blvd. Los Volcanes, Popo Park, ☎ 597/60294), at the foot of the volcano, which has 38 rustic rooms, all with potbellied stoves.

Adventure Sports

If you're itching to climb Izta, the small **Planeta Expeditions** (⊠ Amatlán 51-C at Montes de Oca, ☎ 5/211–9020) runs out of a café in trendy Colonia Condesa in Mexico City. Three-day trips cost $150.

Cholula

The town fathers claim that Cholula has 365 church cupolas, one for every day in the year. Alas, the 37 churches in Cholula are mostly in poor condition. But 6½ km (4 mi) south of town, **San Francisco Acatepec** has one of the two most stunning, well-preserved churches in the country. Covered with Puebla tiles, it's been called the most ornate rococo Poblano facade in Mexico. Equally unusual is **Santa María Tonantzintla**'s church interior, on the way to Cholula. Its polychrome wood-and-stucco carvings—inset columns, altarpieces, and the main archway—are the essence of churrigueresque. Set off by ornate gold-leaf figures of plant forms, angels, and saints, the carvings were done by native craftsmen.

 Closer to town, the **Gran Pirámide** (Great Pyramid) was the centerpiece of Toltec and then Aztec religious centers. It consists of seven superimposed structures connected by tunnels and stairways. The Spaniards, as they often did, built a chapel to **Nuestra Señora de los Remedios** (Our Lady of the Remedies) on top of it. Behind the pyramid is a vast 43-acre temple complex, once dedicated to Quetzalcóatl. ☑ *About $2, includes museum; free Fri.* ☉ *Daily 10–5; museum 10–6.*

Puebla

Maize was first cultivated in the Tehuacán Valley. Later, the region was a crossroads for many ancient Mesoamerican cultures, including the Olmecs and Totonacs. The young Spanish colony Puebla had the first glass factory, the first textile mill, and the second hospital. The battle of May 5, 1862—resulting in a short-lived victory against French invaders—took place just north of town. The national holiday, Cinco de Mayo, is celebrated yearly on that date in its honor, and the battle is reenacted.

Puebla today retains a strong conservative religious element and was one of the cities chosen by Pope John Paul II to visit during his 1978 Mexican tour. Overrun with religious structures, this city probably has more ex-convents and monasteries, chapels, and churches per square mile than anywhere else in the country. In fact, the valley of Puebla, which includes Cholula, was said to have 224 churches and 10 convents and monasteries in its heyday. The city is full of idiosyncratic Baroque structures built with red bricks, gray stone, white stucco, and the beautiful Talavera tiles produced from local clay.

Don't miss the **cathedral,** partially financed by Puebla's most famous son, Bishop Juan de Palafox y Mendoza—who donated his personal fortune to build its famous tower, the second-largest church tower in the country. Palafox was the illegitimate son of a Spanish nobleman who grew up poor but inherited his father's wealth upon his death. Onyx, marble, and gold adorn the cathedral's high altar, designed by Mexico's most illustrious colonial architect, Manuel Tolsá. The facade itself is gray and cheerless. ☒ *Calle 2 Sur, south of the Zócalo.*

In addition, the **Iglesia de Santo Domingo** (Santo Domingo Church; ☒ Av. Cinco de Mayo at Av. 4 Poniente) is especially famous for its Rosary Chapel, where almost every centimeter of the walls, ceilings, and altar is covered with gilded carvings and sculpture. The **Museo Amparo** (☒ Calle 2 Sur at Av. 9 Oriente, ☑ $2; free Mon. ☉ Daily 10–6), filled with the private collection of Precolumbian and colonial art of Mexican banker and philanthropist Manuel Espinoza Yglesias, is one of the most beautiful in Mexico. Puebla is one of the few cities in Mexico declared a Patrimony of Humanities site by the United Nations because of the splendor of its colonial architecture.

The **Uriarte Talavera** pottery factory was founded in 1824 and is one of the few authentic Talavera workshops left today. To be authentic, the pieces must be hand-painted in intricate designs with natural dyes derived from minerals, which is why only five colors are used: blue, black, yellow, green, and a reddish pink. There is a shop on site, and free tours of the factory run Monday through Saturday on the hour from 10 AM to 1 PM. ✉ *4 Poniente 911, between 9 and 11 Norte,* ☎ *22/32–15–98.* ⊙ *Mon.–Sat. 9–6:30, Sun. 11–6.*

The colonial **Ex-Convento de Santa Rosa,** now a museum of native crafts, contains the intricately tiled kitchen where Puebla's renowned mole sauce was believed to have been invented by the nuns as a surprise for their demanding gourmet bishop. ✉ *Av. 14 Poniente between Calles 3 and 5 Norte.* ⊑ *4 pesos.*

Puebla is also famous for *camote,* a popular candy made from sweet potatoes and fruit. **La Calle de las Dulces** (Sweets Street) is lined with shops competing to sell a wide variety of freshly made camote.

Dining and Lodging

Puebla is noted for its cuisine—some consider it to be the best in the country. Two of Mexico's most popular dishes were created here to celebrate special occasions: *mole,* a sauce made with as many as 100 ingredients, the best-known mole being one with bitter chocolate. The other local specialty, believed to have been initiated by the town's nuns, is *chiles en nogada,* a green poblano chili filled with ground meats, fruits, and nuts, then covered with a sauce of chopped walnuts and cream, and topped with red pomegranate seeds; the colors represent the red, green, and white of the Mexican flag.

Las Bodegas del Molino is set in a 16th-century hacienda at the edge of town (✉ Molino de San José del Puente, ☎ 22/49–03–99); this restaurant is truly remarkable, both for its setting and its cuisine. A traditional favorite is **Fonda Santa Clara** (✉ 307 Calle 3 Poniente, ☎ 22/42–26–59), a few blocks from the Zócalo. The most talked-about restaurant in town is **La Guadalupana** (✉ 5 Oriente 605, at the Plazuela de los Sapos [Plaza of the Frogs], ☎ 22/42–48–86), in a homey colonial building, which features typical Poblano dishes.

Worthy hotels in Puebla include the following. In a converted 16th-century convent, the deluxe 83-room **Camino Real** (✉ 7 Poniente 105, ☎ 22/29–09–09 or 22/29–09–10; 800/722–6466 in the U.S., 🆁🅰🆇 22/32–92–51) has gilded antique furnishings, luminous restored fresco murals, and an exceptionally warm and professional staff. The 9-room **Meson Sacristia de la Compania** (✉ 6 Sur, No. 304, at Callejón de los Sapos, ☎ 22/32–45–13) is a reconditioned 200-year-old town house in which every room is outfitted with priceless antiques that you can purchase right out of your room. The 192-room **El Meson del Angel** (✉ Hermanos Serdan 807, ☎ 22/24–30–00) is at the entrance to the city. The quaint 47-room **Royalty** on the main square (☎ 22/42–47–40) is small, well maintained, and considerably less expensive.

Cantona

 Puebla state is home to the fascinating Cantona—opened to the public in 1995—which has 24 ball courts where a precursor to soccer was played. It's built into a hillock that looks like a massive military fortress from afar. Larger than Teotihuacán (its archenemy) outside Mexico City, it supposedly reached its pinnacle after AD 600, and we can judge its importance from the fact that around 500 cobblestone streets and lanes crisscross its 13-square-km (5-square-mi) area. ✉ *107 km (66 mi) northeast of Puebla: take Hwy. 150 to Hwy. 129; turn off Hwy. 129 at Oriental. In rainy season (Aug.–Oct.), you can only navigate it with 4-wheel drive.* ⊑ *$2.* ⊙ *Tues.–Sun. 9–5.*

Tlaxcala

The warriors of the state of Tlaxcala (pronounced tlas-*ca*-la) played a pivotal role in the Spanish conquest by aligning themselves with Cortés against the army of their enemy Aztecs, thus swelling the military ranks of the conqueror by 5,000 men. The state capital, seat of the ancient nation with the same name, will interest both archaeology buffs and church lovers. A former Franciscan church, now called the **Catedral de Nuestro Señora de la Asunción** (Our Lady of the Assumption Cathedral), with its adjoining **monastery** (1537–40), stands atop a hill one block from the handsome main square. This was the first permanent Catholic edifice in the New World. The most unusual feature of the church is its wooden ceiling beams, carved and gilded with gold studs after the Moorish fashion. There are only three churches of this kind in Mexico. (Moorish, or mudéjar, architecture appeared in Mexico only during the very early years after the conquest, when the Moorish occupation was still recent enough to influence Spain with Arabic architectural styles.) The austere monastery, now a museum of history, displays 16th- and 18th-century religious paintings and a small collection of pre-Columbian pieces. A beautiful outdoor **chapel** near the monastery has notable Moorish and Gothic traces.

The **Palacio de Gobierno** (Government Palace), which occupies the north side of the Zócalo, was built in about 1550. Inside are vivid epic murals of Tlaxcala before the conquest, painted in the 1960s by local artist Desiderio Hernández Xochitiotzin.

About 1 km (½ mi) west of Tlaxcala is the large, ornate **Basilica of Our Lady of Ocotlán.** The legend of the Virgin dates from 1541, when, during a severe epidemic, she appeared to a poor Indian and told him to take the water from a stream, which had miraculously appeared, to his people to cure them. The villagers recovered. The Virgin then asked for the Franciscan monks from a nearby monastery. When they arrived in her forest, they were blinded by the raging flames of a fire that didn't harm the trees. They returned the next day with an axe to cut open one particular pine (*ocotlán*) tree that had caught their attention. When they split it open, they discovered the wooden image of the Virgin, which they installed in the present basilica. Many miracles have been attributed to the Virgin since then. Noteworthy sights of the church here are the churrigueresque white-plaster facade, which conjures up images of a wedding cake; the two white Poblano towers adorned with the apostles; and, inside, the brilliantly painted and gilded **Camarín de la Virgen** (the Virgin's Dressing Room) with figures on each of its eight sides portraying the history of the Lady of Ocotlán.

Cacaxtla

 The archaeological site at Cacaxtla, accidentally discovered in 1975 by a peasant working the land, contains a breathtaking series of **murals** (AD 650–700) depicting scenes of a fierce battle between Maya and Central Mexican warriors. It is considered a major breakthrough in tracing the immigration and trade patterns of pre-Hispanic Mexico. The site was settled around 2000 BC by the Olmeca-Xicalancas, a transition culture between the Olmecs and the peoples of central Mexico, researchers say. It reached its height between AD 600 and 900 and was abandoned by 1000. The vividly portrayed battle scenes with life-size figures show warriors in lofty bird headdresses and plumage being vanquished by victors wearing jaguar skins and wielding spears, obsidian knives, and lances. The murals—painted on the walls of a series of palaces built one on top of another—are protected under a huge roof. The site is some 19 km (12 mi) southwest of Tlaxcala. Give yourself at least three hours to see both Cacaxtla and Xochitécatl (☞ *below*). 🎟 *$2 includes admission to Xochitécatl.* ⊘ *Tues.–Sun. 10–5.*

Xochitécatl

Whereas Cantona in neighboring Puebla is all military ambience (☞ *above*), little Xochitécatl is decidedly soft and feminine, having been dedicated to a bevy of important goddesses. Four Classic period **pyramids** are built on a hill that affords a spectacular view of the valleys of Tlaxcala and Puebla. A small on-site **museum** has a good collection of sculpted stone heads and pregnant women. ⊠ *Less than 1½ km (1 mi) north of Cacaxtla.* 🎟 *Free with Cacaxtla ticket.* ⊘ *Tues.– Sun. 10–5.*

Southeast of Mexico City A to Z

Getting There
From Mexico City, head east toward the airport and turn onto Calzada Zaragoza, the last wide boulevard before arriving at the airport; it becomes the Puebla Highway at the tollbooth. Route 150D is the toll road straight to **Puebla**; Route 190 is the scenic free road (the trip on the former takes about 1½ hours, on the latter approximately three hours). To go directly to **Cholula,** take the exit at San Martín Texmelucan and follow the signs. From Puebla, Cholula is 8 km (5 mi) west. To stop at the **volcanoes,** take the free road 33 km (20 mi) to Chalco. From there it is 4 km (2½ mi) to the Amecameca-Chalco sign, from which you continue 22 km (13½ mi) on Route 115 to Amecameca. You'll need to go to Puebla to get to **Tlaxcala**; from there, take Highway 119 north.

Visitor Information
Puebla Tourist Office (⊠ 5 Oriente 3, ☎ 22/46–20–44); open daily 9–8.

WEST OF MEXICO CITY

A good day-trip west of Mexico City would take you to Toluca, renowned for its Friday market. For a longer stay, stop over in Valle de Bravo, a lovely lakeside village popular with vacationing chilangos; it's often called Mexico's Switzerland because of its green, hilly setting. We suggest nipping into Parque Nacional Desierto de los Leones— a forested national park whose centerpiece is an intriguing Carmelite monastery—and making a detour from Toluca for a picnic at Parque Nacional Nevado de Toluca.

Parque Nacional Desierto de los Leones

Several walking trails crisscross this 5,000-acre national park's pine forest. Its focal point is the ruined 17th-century **ex-monastery of the Carmelites,** isolated amid an abundance of greenery. The park played a significant role in the War of Independence: in late October of 1810, at a spot called **Las Cruces,** Father Hidalgo's troops trounced the Spaniards but resolved not to go on to attack Mexico City, an error that cost the insurgents 10 more years of fighting.

Toluca

The capital of the state of Mexico, Toluca is an industrial town. Once famous only for its Friday market, Toluca now has much more to offer. Indians still come in from the surrounding villages on Friday to sell their produce and handicrafts at the huge municipal market, but it's hard to find any indigenous goods among the radios and CDs from

Asia and the denim jackets and jeans from the United States. For local crafts, your best bet is the **Casa de Artesanías** on Paseo Tolloca.

Three sights not to miss are the **Jardín Botánico Cosmovitral** (Cosmovitral Botanical Garden), in a remodeled, turn-of-the-century Art Nouveau structure that once housed the public market; the **Iglesia de la Santa Veracruz,** which displays a rare black Christ; and the **Museo de Artes Populares** in the Centro Cultural.

Parque Nacional Nevado de Toluca

At 15,090 ft, the Nevado de Toluca, a now-extinct volcano, is Mexico's fourth-tallest mountain; on clear days its crater affords wonderful views of the valley. You can hire a guide at the entrance to go with your car to the top of the crater and lead you down to its sandy floor, which surrounds two lakes. Self-guided hiking trails are plentiful.

Valle de Bravo

In colonial Valle de Bravo, white stucco houses are trimmed with wrought-iron balconies and red-tile roofs, and red-potted succulents clutter the doorways. A hilly town that rises from the shores of Lake Avandaro and is surrounded by pines and mountains, Valle was founded in 1530 but has no historical monuments to speak of other than the town church. It does, however, have plenty of diversions: boating, water-skiing, and swimming in the lake and its waterfalls, and the more sociable pleasures of the Sunday market, where exceptional pottery is the draw. Although Valle and its suburb of Avandaro are enclaves for artists and the wealthy, locals like to keep a low profile.

Lodging

For a weekend stay, head for the posh **Avandaro Golf & Spa Resort** (✉ Vega del Río, Fraccionamiento Avandaro, Valle de Bravo, 52100, ☎ 726/6–03–66 in Mexico; 800/223–6510 in the U.S., FAX 726/6–09–05), a former country club. All 74 rooms have romantic fireplaces. In addition to its 18-hole golf course, the resort has one of the best high-tech spas in Mexico, equipped with hot tubs and offering massage, facials, body toning, and aerobics classes.

West of Mexico City A to Z

Getting There

By car from Mexico City, follow Paseo de la Reforma all the way west. It eventually merges with the Carretera Libre at Toluca, and after 20 km (12 mi), you'll see signs for the turnoff to the **Parque Nacional Desierto de los Leones;** it's another 10 km (6 mi) to the park. To go straight to **Toluca,** take the toll highway (expensive, but worth it); alternatively, buses depart Terminal Poniente every 20 minutes. To reach **Parque Nacional Nevado de Toluca,** make a 44-km (27-mi) detour south of Toluca on Route 130. There are two choices for getting to **Valle de Bravo:** the winding, scenic route, which you pick up 3 km (2 mi) west of Zincantepec, or Route 15. The former takes twice as much time but is worth it for the unspoiled mountain scenery.

Visitor Information

Mexico State Tourist Office (✉ Urawa 100, Gate 110, Toluca, ☎ 72/19–51–90 or 72/19–61–58) is open weekdays 9–6.

3 BAJA CALIFORNIA

Separated from mainland Mexico by the Sea of Cortés, the Baja California peninsula stretches 1,625 km (1,000 mi) from Tijuana to Los Cabos. The desert landscape harbors isolated fishing retreats, Prohibition-era gambling palaces, state-of-the-art golf courses, and one of the busiest international borders in the world. Adventurers delight in kayaking alongside migrating gray whales, diving with hammerhead sharks, and hiking to hidden cave paintings.

By Maribeth
Mellin

BAJA (MEANING LOWER) CALIFORNIA is a moon-
scaped finger of land dipping southward from the
international boundary that divides California and
Mexico. Separated from the Mexican mainland by the 240-km-wide
(150-mi-wide) Sea of Cortés—also called the Gulf of California—Baja
extends about 1,625 km (1,000 mi) into the Pacific. Both Baja California and the Gulf of California are part of Mexico.

Although only 21 km (13 mi) across at one point and 193 km (120
mi) at its widest, Baja has one of the most varied and beautiful ter-
rains on the planet. The peninsula's two coasts are separated by great
mountain ranges, with one peak soaring more than 10,000 ft high.
Countless bays and coves with pristine beaches indent both shores, and
islands big and small—many inhabited only by sea lions—dot the
3,364 km (2,000 mi) of coastline. You'll find stretches of desert as empty
as the Sahara where only cacti thrive, and in contrast, you'll see cultivated farmlands and vineyards.

Varied, too, is the demographic makeup of Baja. The border strip of
northern Baja is densely populated. Tijuana, Mexico's fourth-largest
city, is home to more than 2 million people, making it more populous
than the entire remainder of the peninsula. La Paz, with about 170,000
residents, is the only city of any size south of Ensenada. The two
towns at Los Cabos (The Capes) have yet to reach city status.

Baja is divided politically into two states—Baja California (also
called Baja Norte, meaning North Baja) and Baja California Sur
(South)—at the 25th parallel, about 710 km (440 mi) south of the
border. Near the tip of the peninsula, a monument marks the spot
where the Tropic of Cancer crosses the Transpeninsular Highway (Mexico Highway 1).

Native Baja Californians will tell you in no uncertain terms that they
live in the first California, discovered by pirates, missionaries, and explorers long before the California of the United States. Most Baja travelers have that same sense of adventure, and the peninsula has become
a cult destination. Long before the rich and famous stumbled upon the
resorts of mainland Mexico, they found Baja. Back in the days of Prohibition, when Hollywood was new, the movie crowd learned the joy
of having an international border so near. John Steinbeck brought attention to La Paz when he made it a setting for his novella *The Pearl*.
Erle Stanley Gardner took a break from writing to battle marlin off
Los Cabos. Bing Crosby is said to have put up some of the money for
the first resort hotel in San José del Cabo, when the only way to get
there was aboard a yacht or private plane.

Today you'll fly in on commercial jets and check into thoroughly modern hotels. The rich and famous still find Baja, particularly the southern tip, an ideal escape, and you can see them in secluded hotels along
the Los Cabos Corridor. But Baja is no longer the exclusive turf of adventurers and the owners of private yachts and planes. Caravans of
motor homes and pickups occasionally clog the Transpeninsular Highway, and flights into Loreto, La Paz, and Los Cabos are often packed
with regular folks on their first forays into Mexico. Baja's resort towns
have become mainstream, but you can still find adventure and sublime
solitude at the peninsula's hidden beaches and bays.

Pleasures and Pastimes

Dining

Baja's cuisine highlights food from the sea. Fresh fish, lobster, shrimp, and abalone are particularly good. In both states, scores of restaurants and kitchens serve great, authentically Mexican seafood dishes. Beef and pork are also excellent, both grilled and marinated. Imported steak, lamb, duck, and quail are popular in upscale places. And although very few restaurants serve regional Mexican cuisine, plenty of spots throughout the peninsula combine U.S. and Mexican flavors in tacos, burritos, burgers, and pizza.

Two dishes originated in Baja and have become standard fare in southern California. Lobster Puerto Nuevo–style (shellfish grilled or boiled in oil and served with beans, rice, and tortillas) comes from the fishing settlement of the same name near Tijuana. Fish tacos (chunks of deep-fried fish wrapped with condiments in a corn tortilla) are said to have originated in the northern Baja town of San Felipe. Mexico's best domestic wines are nurtured in the vineyards and wineries in the Santo Tomás and Guadalupe valleys outside Ensenada, and one of the country's most popular beers, Tecate, comes from the northern Baja town of the same name.

Restaurants as a rule are low-key, except in Tijuana, Ensenada, and Los Cabos, where dining options range from *taquerías* (taco stands) to upscale Continental dining rooms. Dress is accordingly casual at nearly all Baja restaurants, and reservations are not required unless otherwise noted. Moderate prices prevail even in city restaurants—except in Los Cabos, where prices and menu items reflect a distinct California influence. Some places add a 15% service charge to the bill.

CATEGORY	COST*
$$$	over $20
$$	$10–$20
$	under $10

per person for a three-course meal, excluding drinks and service

Fishing

Sportfishing is one of Baja's greatest attractions. The fishing is best in the south, with large fishing fleets in Loreto, La Paz, and Los Cabos. Though the summer months bring the most fish, anglers are sure to catch something year-round. Fishing from Ensenada and San Quintín is best in the summer and early fall.

Golf

With championship-level courses in Tijuana, Rosarito, and Ensenada, Baja is growing in popularity among golfers. Los Cabos is experiencing a particular boom; several excellent courses have opened in the past few years.

Kayaking

Both the Pacific Ocean and the Sea of Cortés have isolated bays and coves ideal for kayaking. Some hotels and outfitters in Ensenada, Loreto, La Paz, and Los Cabos offer kayak rentals and excursions, and some U.S. companies offer kayaking trips to the Sea of Cortés.

Lodging

Baja lodging is mostly low-key—except world-class Los Cabos. Until the 1980s, its hotels were mostly fishing lodges where die-hard sportsmen took refuge. Now Los Cabos draws golfers to deluxe hotels that front championship courses. Rates are much higher here than in the rest of Baja, where you can find great deals at small, one-of-a-kind hostelries.

Reservations are a must on holiday weekends for most of Baja's coastal towns; some hotels require a minimum two-night stay for a confirmed reservation. Several hotels in Baja have toll-free numbers that connect directly to the hotel; though the operator may answer in Spanish, there is usually someone who speaks English in the reservations office. Many hotels have fax numbers (a good way to confirm reservations), though you may have to ask them to turn on the fax machine when you call. A few of the out-of-the-way and budget-priced hotels do not accept credit cards; some of the more lavish places add a 10%–20% service charge to your bill. Most properties also raise their rates for the December–April high season. Rates here are based on high-season standards. Expect to pay 25% less during the off-season. Many hotels offer midweek discounts of 30%–50% off the weekend rates; always ask about special promotions.

Several agencies in the United States book reservations at Baja hotels, condos, and time-share resorts, which may actually cost less than hotel rooms if you are traveling with a group of four or more (☞ Contacts and Resources *in* Baja Norte A to Z, *below*).

CATEGORY	COST*
$$$$	over $160
$$$	$90–$160
$$	$40–$90
$	under $40

All prices are for a standard double room, excluding service charge and 12%–17% hotel occupancy tax.

Whale-Watching

Gray whales migrate to the Pacific coast of Baja from January through March. Whale-watching expeditions are available in Ensenada, Guerrero Negro, Loreto, La Paz, and Los Cabos.

Exploring Baja California

The Baja Peninsula is made up of two Mexican states: Baja California, which begins at the U.S. border, and Baja California Sur.

The northern half of the peninsula contains the largest cities and highest population. Tijuana, Tecate, and Mexicali—the peninsula's border cities—are U.S. suburbs in a sense. San Felipe, the northernmost town on the Sea of Cortés, is a popular weekend escape for Arizonans and southern Californians. Similarly, Rosarito and Ensenada, on Baja's northern Pacific coast, are practically extensions of the southern California coast, offering an experience both familiar and foreign. South of Ensenada the natural side of Baja begins to appear in desolate mountain ranges and fields of cacti and boulders.

Baja California Sur is more remote, in spite of its strong American influences. The most populated areas lie on the Sea of Cortés coast. The Pacific side is more popular with migrating gray whales, who travel by the thousands every winter from the Bering Strait to isolated coves and lagoons along this coast. For those few months, people come from around the world to Guerrero Negro and a few bays and lagoons farther south. Loreto, on the Sea of Cortés, is beloved by sportfishers who find seclusion in this small, largely undiscovered town. La Paz is capital of Baja California Sur, the region's major port, and a busy center of commerce and government. Los Cabos, made up of the two towns of Cabo San Lucas and San José del Cabo, has become one of the fastest-growing resort areas in Mexico. Despite all the development and steep prices, it remains a mysteriously natural hideaway.

Numbers in the text correspond to numbers in the margin and on the Tijuana, Ensenada, La Paz, Los Cabos Coast, San José del Cabo, and Cabo San Lucas maps.

Great Itineraries

Baja aficionados will tell you that you haven't really explored the peninsula unless you've driven its entire length, stopping at small towns and secluded beaches along the way. That's a major journey, requiring at least 10 days of travel time. If you plan to drive the peninsula certain precautions are in order. You must have Mexican auto insurance, available by the day, for the length of your drive. Always carry water, and make sure your vehicle is in good condition. Keep your gas tank at least half full at all times—some remote gas stations may be out of gas just when you need it. For the most part, the Transpeninsular Highway is well maintained, though you may come across areas marred by potholes or gravel and rocks.

Even if you don't have 10 days you can still see plenty of the peninsula's attractions by focusing on the area around where you enter Baja. A full week would allow a quick rush through the peninsula or a more leisurely exploration of northern Baja or Baja Sur. If you have five days, you can see the most interesting towns in one of the states and still be able to linger a bit. With three days you're best off staying within the immediate vicinity of your entry point.

IF YOU HAVE 3 DAYS

In northern Baja, you can explore Tijuana, Rosarito, and Ensenada. Start in **Tijuana** ①–⑫ at the **Centro Cultural,** then stroll down **Avenida Revolución.** Head south before nightfall to a hotel in **Rosarito** or **Puerto Nuevo.** Tour **Ensenada** ⑬–㉓ the next day, taking in the **Fish Market** ⑭, the **Riviera del Pacífico** ⑱, and the shops on **Avenida López Mateos** ⑲. Take the third day in Rosarito.

In Baja Sur, you're best off staying in **Los Cabos,** allowing time for golf, sportfishing, and snorkeling at **Bahía Santa Maria** or **Bahía Chileno.**

IF YOU HAVE 5 DAYS

You can do a thorough tour of northern Baja, starting with a full day and overnight in **Tijuana** ①–⑫. From there head to the small town of **Tecate,** then on to **Mexicali** and **San Felipe.** Overnight in San Felipe; then spend Day 3 checking out the beaches before driving the backcountry to **Ensenada** ⑬–㉓. Devote Day 4 to exploring **La Bufadora** and downtown Ensenada; then head up the coast for a lobster feast at **Puerto Nuevo.** On Day 5 head back to Tijuana and the border.

If you'd rather tour Baja Sur, begin in **Los Cabos,** spending the night there and starting out early the next day for **La Paz.** Spend Day 2 exploring downtown La Paz, making sure to see the **malecón** ㉔, or boardwalk, and the **Plaza Constitución** ㉗. On Day 3, head up the coast to the small mission town of **Loreto.** Spend Days 4 and 5 making your way back to Los Cabos at a leisurely pace, stopping to explore the desert and coast along the way.

IF YOU HAVE 7 DAYS

If you want to cover a lot of distance, and spend much of your time in the car, you could technically make the long drive down the entire peninsula in a week, especially if you arrange to begin your tour in the north and drop off your car in the south. Start in **Tijuana** ①–⑫ on Day 1, touring the **Centro Cultural** and **Avenida Revolución.** Head south before nightfall to a hotel in **Rosarito** or **Puerto Nuevo.** On Day 2, move on to **Ensenada** ⑬–㉓ for a brief tour of the city; then head south to **San Quintín** and **Guerrero Negro.** If you're traveling between January and March, arrange for a whale-watching tour for the next day and spend Nights 2 and 3 in Guerrero Negro. If not, overnight in Guerrero Negro and then move on for a full day's trip to **Mulege** on the Sea of Cortés. The drive between the two coasts, through stark desert scenery, is one of the most beautiful and desolate in Baja. Spend Night 3 or 4 in Mulege, allowing plenty of relaxation time after the long drive. Move on to **Loreto,** stopping off for a swim at **Bahía Concepción,** and spend the next night there. If you didn't stay in Guerrero Negro for whale-watching, spend an extra night in Loreto and arrange a boat tour of the Sea of Cortés. Devote Day 6 to the drive to **La Paz,** spending the evening strolling the waterfront malecón. On Day 7, continue on to **Los Cabos.**

When to Tour Baja

Baja's climate is extreme, thanks to its desert locale. Temperatures are less drastic in the north—Tijuana, Ensenada, and Rosarito's are similar to those in southern California. Mexicali, on the other hand, gets extremely hot in the summer months. Northern Baja's resort cities are very crowded on holiday weekends, and advance reservations are a must. Tijuana's attractions are rarely overcrowded, and you should be able to tour them easily at any time of day.

Baja Sur's winters are mild, but not warm; Loreto, La Paz, and Los Cabos can get downright chilly in the evening. Sportfishing aficionados prefer the summer months: though the temperatures are high, the fish are abundant. Loreto and La Paz tend to be crowded only on holiday weekends, but Los Cabos is crowded through much of the year, except at the height of the summer heat.

BAJA CALIFORNIA (NORTH)

The most densely populated area of the Baja California peninsula, the state of Baja California begins at the U.S. border and extends 699 km (433 mi) to the border with Baja California Sur. Tijuana, just 29 km (18 mi) south of San Diego, is Baja's largest city; in fact, with a population that has now surpassed 2 million, it is the fourth-largest city in Mexico. Tijuana's promoters like to call it "the most visited city in the world," and certainly the border crossing to Tijuana is the busiest in the United States.

By comparison, the state's capital, Mexicali, has a population of only 800,000 residents. Though it also sits on the U.S. border, Mexicali attracts few tourists. Tecate, located between Tijuana and Mexicali, is a typical village whose main claim to fame is the Tecate brewery, where one of Mexico's most popular beers originates. Those travelers who do pass through Tecate and Mexicali are usually en route to San Felipe, the northernmost town on the Sea of Cortés.

On Baja's Pacific coast, travelers stream down the Transpeninsular Highway (Highway 1) to Rosarito and Ensenada. These beach communities are like Mexican suburbs of southern California, where English is spoken as freely as Spanish and the dollar is as readily accepted as the peso. Between Baja's towns, the landscape is unlike any other, with cacti growing beside the sea, and stark mountains and plateaus rising against clear blue skies.

Highway 3 runs east from Ensenada to San Felipe through the foothills of the Sierra Pedro San Martir. The same highway runs north from Ensenada to Tecate through the Guadalupe Valley, where you'll find many of the area's vineyards and wineries. If you are traveling south, Ensenada is the last major city you'll see for hundreds of miles on Mex-

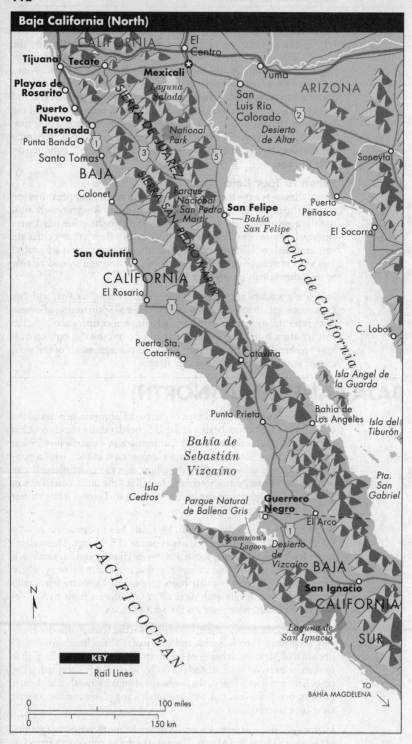

Baja California (North)

CALIFORNIA

El Centro

Tijuana
Tecate
Mexicali
Yuma
ARIZONA

Playas de Rosarito

Laguna Salada

San Luis Rio Colorado

Puerto Nuevo

SIERRA DE JUAREZ

Desierto de Altar

Ensenada

Punta Banda

National Park

Santo Tomas

Sonoyta

BAJA

Colonet

SIERRA SAN PEDRO MARTIR

Parque Nacional San Pedro Martir

San Felipe

Bahía San Felipe

Puerto Peñasco

El Socorro

San Quintin

Golfo de California

CALIFORNIA

El Rosario

C. Lobos

Puerto Sta. Catarina

Cataviña

Isla Angel de la Guarda

Punta Prieta

Bahía de Los Angeles

Isla del Tiburón

Bahía de Sebastián Vizcaíno

Isla Cedros

Pta. San Gabriel

Parque Natural de Ballena Gris

Guerrero Negro

El Arco

Scammon's Lagoon

Desierto de Vizcaíno

BAJA

San Ignacio

CALIFORNIA

Laguna de San Ignacio

SUR

PACIFIC OCEAN

N

KEY

—— Rail Lines

0   100 miles
0   150 km

TO BAHÍA MAGDALENA

ico Highway 1. San Quintín, 184 km (115 mi) south of Ensenada, is an agricultural community said to be the windiest spot in Baja. Sportfishing is particularly good here, and tourism fluctuates with the reports of successful catches. Farther south are turnoffs for a dirt road to San Felipe and a paved road to Bahía de los Angeles, a formerly remote bay beloved by fishermen and naturalists.

At the end of the northern section of Baja, 595 km (370 mi) from Ensenada, stands a steel monument in the form of an eagle, 138 ft high. It marks the border between the states of Baja California and Baja California Sur, and the time changes from Pacific to Mountain as you cross that 28th parallel. Guerrero Negro, Baja Sur's northernmost town, with hotels and gas stations, is 2 km (1 mi) south.

Tijuana

29 km (18 mi) south of San Diego.

Tijuana is the only part of Mexico many people see, and it gives a distorted view of the country's many cultures. Before the city became a gigantic recreation center for southern Californians, it was a ranch populated by a few hundred Mexicans. In 1911 a group of Americans invaded the area and attempted to set up an independent republic; they were quickly driven out by Mexican soldiers. When Prohibition hit the United States in the 1920s and the Agua Caliente Racetrack and Casino opened (1929), Tijuana boomed. Americans seeking alcohol, gambling, and more fun than they could find back home flocked across the border, spending freely and fueling the region's growth. Tijuana became the entry port for what some termed a "sinful, steamy playground" frequented by Hollywood stars and the idle rich.

Then Prohibition was repealed, Mexico outlawed gambling, and Tijuana's fortunes declined. Though the flow of travelers from the north slowed to a trickle for a while, Tijuana still captivated those in search of the sort of fun that was illegal or just frowned upon at home. The ever-growing numbers of servicemen stationed in San Diego kept Tijuana's sordid reputation alive, while southern Californians continued to cross the border to explore the foreign culture and landscape. Drivers heading into Baja's wilderness passed through downtown Tijuana, stopping along Avenida Revolución and its side streets for supplies and souvenirs.

When the toll highway to Ensenada was finished in 1967, travelers bypassed the city and tourism dropped again. But Tijuana began attracting residents from throughout Latin America. The city's population mushroomed from a mere 300,000 in 1970 to more than 2 million today. The city has spread into canyons and dry riverbeds, over hillsides, and onto ocean cliffs. As the government struggles to keep up with the growth and demand for services, thousands live without electricity, running water, or adequate housing in squatters' villages along the border. Crime is now a significant problem in Tijuana. The fall of the peso caused many Mexicans from the interior to move to the border in search of work at all levels of industry. Poverty is vast and petty crime is on the rise. Moreover, the area has become headquarters for serious drug cartels, and violent crime—reaching the highest levels of law enforcement and business—is booming. You're unlikely to witness a shooting or some other frightening situation, but be mindful of your surroundings and guard your belongings.

City leaders, realizing that tourism creates jobs and bolsters Tijuana's fragile economy, are working hard to attract visitors. Avenida Revolución, the main street that was once lined with brothels and bars, now has a lineup of shopping arcades and pseudo-Mexican restaurants and bars that cater to (often rowdy) tourists. The city has an international airport; a fine cultural center that presents professional music, dance, and theater groups from throughout the world; and deluxe high-rise hotels. The demand for high-end accommodations has increased with the growth of *maquiladoras* (foreign manufacturing plants). Casual tourists tend to visit for the day or one night. Although it's no longer considered just a bawdy border town, the city remains best known as a place for an intense, somewhat exotic daylong adventure.

Tijuana's tourist attractions have remained much the same throughout the century. The impressive El Palacio Frontón (Jai Alai Palace), where betting is allowed, draws crowds of cheering fans to its fast-paced matches. Some of Mexico's greatest bullfighters appear at the oceanfront and downtown bullrings, and there are an extraordinary number of places in town that provide good food and drink.

And then, of course, there's shopping. From the moment you cross the border, people will approach you or call out and insist that you look at their wares. If you drive, workers will run out from auto-body shops to place bids on new paint or upholstery for your car. All along Avenida Revolución and its side streets, shops sell everything from tequila to Tiffany-style lamps. Serious shoppers can spend a full day searching and bargaining for their items of choice. If you intend to buy food in Mexico, get the U.S. customs list of articles that are illegal to bring back so that your purchases won't be confiscated.

❶ At the **San Ysidro Border Crossing,** locals and tourists jostle each other along the pedestrian walkway through the Viva Tijuana dining and shopping center and into the center of town. Artisans' stands line the walkway and adjoining streets, offering a quick overview of the wares to be found all over town.

❷ An unusual perspective on Mexico's culture can be found at **Mexitlán,** a fascinating combination of museum and entertainment–shopping center. Designed by architect Pedro Ramírez Vásquez, the complex has scale models of all the major architectural and cultural landmarks throughout Mexico; unfortunately, the place has not been well maintained and has lost its festive air. ⊠ *Av. Ocampo between Calles 2 and 3,* ☎ *66/ 38–41–65.* ⌷ *$2.50.* ☉ *Wed.–Sun. 9–5.*

❸ Tijuana's main tourism zone has long been the raffish **Avenida Revolución,** lined with a cacophonous array of shops and restaurants, all catering to uninhibited tourists. Shopkeepers call out from their doorways, offering low prices for an odd assortment of garish souvenirs. Many shopping arcades open onto Avenida Revolución; inside the front doors are mazes of stands with low-priced pottery and other crafts.

❹ The magnificent Moorish-style **El Palacio Frontón** (Jai Alai Palace) is an exciting place to watch and bet on fast-paced jai alai games. Next door, at a large branch of the Caliente Race Book, bettors wager on horse races and sports events broadcast from California via satellite TV (☞ Outdoor Activities and Sports, *below*).

❺ Most of Baja's legendary wineries are located in the Ensenada region, but Tijuana now has a branch of the **L.A. Cetto Winery.** You can tour the bottling plant, sample the wine, and spend as long as you like in the gift and wine shop. ⊠ *Cañon Johnson 8151, at Av. Constitución,* ☎ *66/85–30–31 or 66/85–16–44.* ⌷ *$1 for tour, $2 for tour and wine tasting.* ☉ *Tues.–Sun. 10–5.*

❻ **Mundo Divertido** is a popular family attraction in the Río zone. The amusement park includes a miniature golf course, batting cages, an ex-

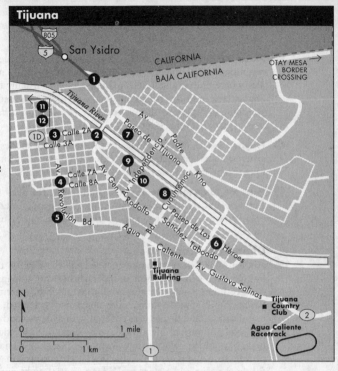

citing roller coaster, and a video-game parlor with more than 130 games. The park has a food court with hot dogs and burgers along with tacos and corn on the cob. Admission is free, and the rides cost just a few pesos. ⊠ *Paseo de los Héroes at Calle Velasco,* ☎ *66/34–32–13 or 66/34–32–14.* ☉ *Weekdays noon–9, weekends 11–10.*

❼ The **Pueblo Amigo** entertainment center was built to resemble a colonial Mexican village, with stuccoed buildings painted soft yellow, blue, and rose and tree-lined pathways leading to a gazebo with a brick dome. The complex includes the fanciest hotel near downtown, several restaurants and clubs, a huge grocery store, and a large branch of the Caliente Race Book, where gambling on televised races and sporting events is legal. ⊠ *Paseo Tijuana between Puente Mexico and Av. Independencia.*

❽ The **Río Tijuana** area—as the section that runs along Avenida Paseo de los Héroes parallel to the dry Tia Juana River is called—is one of the city's main thoroughfares, with large statues of historical figures, including one of Abraham Lincoln, in the center of the *glorietas* (traffic circles). With its impressive **Centro Cultural** (☞ *below*), several shopping complexes, fine restaurants, and fashionable discos, this part of town rivals Avenida Revolución for tourists' and locals' attention. ⊠ *Between Blvd. Agua Caliente and border.*

❾ The **Centro Cultural** (Cultural Center) was designed by architects Manuel Rosen and Pedro Ramírez Vásquez, who also created Mexico City's famous Museum of Anthropology. The center's exhibits of Mexican history are a good introduction for those visitors whose first taste of Mexico is at the border. The Omnimax Theater, with its curving 180-degree screen, shows films on a rotating schedule, often coinciding with temporary exhibits. Usually one English-language film is shown daily. Temporary exhibits on art and culture change frequently. The center's bookstore has an excellent selection of Mexican history, culture, and arts in both Spanish and English. ⊠ *Paseo de los Héroes and Av. Independencia,* ☎ *66/84–11–11 or 66/84–11–25.* ▣ *Museum $2, museum and Omnimax Theater $3.50.* ☉ *Daily 9–8.*

⑩ **Plaza Río Tijuana,** the area's largest shopping complex, has good restaurants, department stores, hundreds of shops, and a multiplex theater where at least one English-language film is usually being shown. Shade trees and flowers line the long, wide sidewalks leading from the shopping complex to the Cultural Center. ⊠ *Paseo de los Héroes across from Cultural Center.*

⑪ **Playas Tijuana,** along the oceanfront, is a mix of modest and expensive residential neighborhoods, with a few restaurants and hotels. The long, isolated beaches are visited mostly by residents.

⑫ **Plaza de Toros Monumental,** the "Bullring by the Sea" (☞ Outdoor Activities and Sports, *below*), sits at the northwest corner of the beach area, right by the border. The bullring is occasionally used for summer concerts as well.

Dining and Lodging

$$$ ✕ **Cien Años.** Mexican haute cuisine is all the rage on the mainland but has been slow to appear in Baja. This gracious Spanish colonial–style restaurant has met the need with aplomb, offering *crepas de huilacoche* (a mushroomlike corn delicacy), beet salad, shrimp with nopal cactus, and tender beef covered with avocado and cheese. Each dish has an unusual blend of flavors—tamarind, Mexican oregano, mango, poblano chilies—that elevates the taste of even common appetizers such as *queso fundido* (melted cheese wrapped in tortillas). The soothing decor and service make for a special night out. ⊠ *Av. José María 1407, in the Zona Río,* ☎ *66/34–30–39. MC, V.*

$$ ✕ **El Faro de Mazatlán.** Fresh fish simply prepared is the hallmark of one of Tijuana's best seafood restaurants. This is the place to try ceviche, abalone, squid, and lobster without spending a fortune. Meals start with a savory soup and crusty rolls. The dining room, frequented by professionals from nearby offices, is a peaceful spot for a long, leisurely lunch. Appetizers and soup are included in the price of the meal. ⊠ *Blvd. Sanchez Taboada 9542,* ☎ *66/84–88–82. MC, V.*

$$ ✕ **La Fonda de Roberto.** Roberto's is by far the best restaurant in Tijuana for traditional cuisine from the many culinary regions of Mexico. Try the *chiles en nogada* (chilies stuffed with raisins and meat and topped with cream and pomegranate seeds), meats with spicy *achiote* (a blend of seasonings) sauce, and many varieties of mole. Portions are small, so order liberally and share samples of many dishes. ⊠ *La Siesta Motel, Old Ensenada Hwy. (also called Calle 16 de Septiembre) near Blvd. Agua Caliente,* ☎ *No phone. MC, V.*

$$ ✕ **La Taberna Española.** The mainstay of Plaza Fiesta's multiethnic cafés, this Spanish tapas bar attracts a youthful, sophisticated crowd. The tapa menu is printed only in Spanish, but with a bit of imagination you should be able to select a representative sampling, such as octopus in its own ink, spicy sausages, Spanish tortilla with potatoes and eggs, and fava beans. Inside the café, it's smoky, fragrant, and invariably crowded; outdoor tables have better people-watching. ⊠ *Plaza Fiesta, Paseo de los Héroes 10001,* ☎ *66/84–75–62. No credit cards.*

$ ✕ **Carnitas Uruapan.** You'll need to take a cab to this large, noisy restaurant, where patrons mingle at long wood tables, toasting one another with chilled *cervezas* (beer). The main attraction here is *carnitas* (marinated pork roasted over an open pit), sold by weight and served with homemade tortillas, salsa, cilantro, guacamole, and onions. ⊠ *Blvd. Díaz Ordaz 550,* ☎ *66/81–61–81;* ⊠ *Paseo de los Héroes at Av. Rodríguez,* ☎ *No phone. No credit cards.*

$ ✗ **La Especial.** At the foot of the stairs leading to an underground shop-
★ ping arcade, this place serves up home-style Mexican cooking at low
prices. The gruff, efficient waiters, decked out in black slacks and
vests, shuttle platters of *carne asada* (grilled strips of marinated meat),
enchiladas, and burritos, all with a distinctive flavor found nowhere
but in this busy, cavernous basement dining room. ⊠ *Av. Revolución
718,* ☎ *66/85–66–54. No credit cards.*

$ ✗ **Señor Frog's.** Heaping plates of barbecued chicken and ribs and buck-
ets of ice-cold bottles of cerveza are the mainstay at this fun and festive formula eatery, one of many in the Carlos Anderson chain. The
loud music and laughter make for a raucous atmosphere, and the food
is consistently good. ⊠ *In Pueblo Amigo Center, Paseo Tijuana,* ☎
66/82–49–64. AE, MC, V.

$$$ ▥ **Camino Real.** Elegant and fashionable, this branch of one of Mex-
ico's best hotel chains opened in 1996 near the Centro Cultural—an
ideal spot for walking to most attractions. Rooms are plushly deco-
rated in browns and gold and have in-room fax lines and direct-dial
phones. The hotel's Fouquet's de Paris restaurant specializes in French
haute cuisine, and has a garden café. Azulejos is less formal. ⊠ *Paseo
de los Héroes 10305, 22320,* ☎ *66/33–40–00; 800/722–6466 in the
U.S.,* ℻ *66/33–40–01. 235 rooms, 15 suites. 2 restaurants, 2 bars, room
service, laundry service. AE, MC, V.*

$$$ ▥ **Grand Hotel.** The mirrored towers of the hotel and a high-rise of-
fice building are Tijuana's most ostentatious landmarks. The hotel's
atrium restaurant is a favorite lunch and Sunday brunch spot. The rooms
used to be the nicest in town, but new hotels have upped the standards.
Still, it's a good spot for golfers, business travelers, and anyone looking for moderately priced luxury. ⊠ *Blvd. Agua Caliente 4558, 22420,*
☎ *66/81–70–00; 01–800/02–66–007 in Mexico; 800/472–6385 in
the U.S.,* ℻ *66/81–70–16. 422 rooms. Restaurant, pool, 2 tennis
courts, exercise room, nightclub, travel services. AE, MC, V.*

$$ ▥ **Lucerna.** Once one of the most charming hotels in Tijuana, the
Lucerna is now showing its age. Still, the lovely gardens, large swim-
ming pool surrounded by palms, touches of tile work, and folk art lend
Mexican character to the hotel. ⊠ *Paseo de los Héroes 10902, and
Av. Rodríguez, 22320,* ☎ *66/64–70–00 or 01–800/02–66–300; 800/
582–3762 in the U.S.,* ℻ *66/34–24–00. 147 rooms, 28 suites. Restau-
rant, coffee shop, pool, nightclub, travel services. MC, V.*

$$ ▥ **Otay Bugambilias.** Proximity to the Tijuana airport and the Otay
Mesa manufacturing plants makes this modest hotel a great find. The
pink three-story building has motel-like rooms; suites have kitchenettes. The hotel offers free transportation to and from the Tijuana
airport. ⊠ *Blvd. Industrial at Carretera Aeropuerto, 22450,* ☎ *66/23–
76–00 or 91/800–66–426; 800/472–1153 in the U.S. 132 rooms, 9 suites.
Restaurant, bar, pool, exercise room. AE, MC, V.*

$ ▥ **Holiday Inn Vita Spa Agua Caliente.** It's hard to resist this quirky
hotel, despite its odd location. Set between two major boulevards on
a landscaped island, the building stands beside the underground thermal water spring that fed the pools at the 1920s-era Agua Caliente Spa.
Today's rooms are not as luxurious as in the past, though they're perfectly modern and sufficiently comfortable. But the true star of the property is the Vita Spa, with individual and couples' hot tubs fed from the
hot, healing springs. Facials, massage, soothing mud wraps, and a
cozy relaxation room make the spa a perfect weekend retreat. The on-
site Cafe La Faraona is good enough to attract the ladies who lunch
from nearby wealthy neighborhoods. ⊠ *Paseo de los Héroes 18818,
Zona Río 22450,* ☎ *66/34–69–01; 800/465–4329 (for reservations)
or 888/848–2928 (for the hotel),* ℻ *66/34–69–12. 122 rooms, 5 suites.
Restaurant, pool, spa. AE, MC, V.*

$ ⊞ **La Villa de Zaragoza.** This brown stucco motel is such a success that the management keeps adding rooms—the newest have kitchenettes, and all offer air-conditioning and cable TV. The location, near the Jai Alai Palace and one block from Revolución, is ideal. The neighborhood can be noisy, however, and it's best to choose a room at the back. The guarded parking lot is a major plus, though you won't need a car if you stay here. The motel is used by tour groups, so book ahead for holidays and weekends. Discounts are available for extended stays. ⊠ *Av. Madero 1120, 22000,* ☎ *66/85–18–32,* FAX *66/85–18–37. 66 rooms. Restaurant, parking. MC, V.*

Nightlife and the Arts

Tijuana has toned down its Sin City image, though there are still plenty of raucous bars on Avenida Revolución. Locals, however, prefer the classier nightclubs in the Zona Río.

The **Hard Rock Cafe** (⊠ Av. Revolución 520, between Calles 1 and 2, ☎ 66/85–02–06) has the same menu and decor as other branches of the ubiquitous London club. This one, too, is popular with families and singles. **Como Que No** (⊠ Av. Sanchez Taboada 95, ☎ 66/84–27–91) is popular with the sophisticated disco set, while the adjacent **Dime Que Si** (☎ 66/84–27–91) is a romantic piano bar. **Baby Rock** (⊠ Calle Diego Rivera 1482, Zona Río, ☎ 66/34–24–04), an offshoot of a popular Acapulco disco, attracts a young, hip crowd. **Rodeo la Media Noche** (⊠ Av. Paseo Tijuana at Pueblo Amigo, Zona Río, ☎ 66/82–49–67) has three levels of dance floors with a musical combination of recorded disco, live norteño bands, and romantic ballads. The scene includes a live indoor rodeo on weekend nights. Tijuana's discos usually have strict dress codes—no T-shirts, jeans, or sandals allowed.

Outdoor Activities and Sports

BULLFIGHTING

Bullfights feature skilled matadors from throughout Mexico and Spain. They are held at **El Toreo de Tijuana** (⊠ Av. Agua Caliente outside downtown, ☎ 66/85–22–10) Sunday at 4, May through October. In July and August you can also see fights at the **Plaza de Toros Monumental** (⊠ Playas Tijuana area, Ensenada Hwy., ☎ 66/85–22–10) Sunday at 4. Admission to bullfights varies, depending on the fame of the matador and the location of your seat.

GOLF

The **Tijuana Country Club** (⊠ Blvd. Agua Caliente, east of downtown, ☎ 66/81–78–55) is open to Grand Hotel guests, but other hotels can set up golf for their guests, too. You can rent clubs, electric and hand carts, and caddies for the 18-hole course.

GREYHOUND RACES

At the **Hipódromo de Agua Caliente,** horse racing was phased out in 1993, but greyhounds race nightly at 7:45 and weekend afternoons at 2. Wagering on horse races broadcast via satellite is also available. ⊠ *Blvd. Agua Caliente at Salinas,* ☎ *66/81–78–11; 619/231–1910 in San Diego, CA; or 800/745–2252.*

JAI ALAI

This ancient Basque sport, in some ways similar to handball but using a large, scooped-out paddle called a *frontón,* is played in the Moorish-style **El Palacio Frontón,** or Jai Alai Palace. Matinee games start at noon on Monday and Friday; night games start at 8 from Tuesday through Saturday. General admission is $5; box seats in the Concha Club are $5. ⊠ *Av. Revolución and Calle 8,* ☎ *66/38–43–08.*

Shopping

The Avenida Revolución shopping area spreads down Calle 1 to the pedestrian walkway leading from the border. Begin by checking out the stands along the border-crossing walkway, comparing prices as you travel toward Avenida Revolución. You may find that the best bargains are closer to the border; you can pick up your piñatas and serapes on your way out of town. The traditional shopping strip is Avenida Revolución, between Calles 1 and 8; it's lined with shops and arcades that display a wide range of crafts and curios. Bargaining is expected on the streets and in the arcades, but not in the finer shops.

The shops in **Plaza Revolución** (⊠ Calle 1 and Avenida Revolución) sell quality crafts. **Bazar de Mexico** (⊠ Av. Revolución at Calle 7, ☎ 66/86–52–80) is a huge complex of shops and stalls carrying the full gamut of Tijuana treasures. The **Mexicoach Termina** (⊠ Av. Revolución between Calle 6 and 7, ☎ 66/85–14–70) is a similar one-stop center more like a modern mall. **La Piel** (⊠ Av. Revolución between Calles 4 and 5, ☎ 66/87–23–98) offers dependable quality in its leather jackets, backpacks, and luggage. **Ralph Lauren Polo Outlet** (⊠ Viva Tijuana Center, ☎ 66/88–76–98) is a licensed outlet for the designer's sportswear.

Sanborns (⊠ Av. Revolución at Calle 8, ☎ 66/88–14–62) has beautiful crafts from throughout Mexico, an excellent bakery, and chocolates from Mexico City. **Sara's** (⊠ Av. Revolución at Calle 4, ☎ 66/88–29–32), one of the best department stores in Tijuana, sells imported perfumes and fine clothing. For the finest folk-art store, **Tolan** (⊠ Av. Revolución between Calles 7 and 8, ☎ 66/88–36–37), carries everything from antique, carved wooden doors to tiny, ceramic miniature village scenes.

MARKET

The **Mercado Hidalgo** (⊠ Av. Independencia at Av. Sanchez Taboada, 2 blocks south of Paseo de los Héroes) is Tijuana's municipal market, with rows of fresh produce, grains, herbs, some souvenirs, and the best selection of piñatas in Baja.

SHOPPING CENTERS

Plaza Fiesta, on Paseo de los Héroes across from Plaza Río Tijuana, has a collection of boutiques, jewelry stores, and stained-glass shops. You can find great buys on fashionable clothing and shoes at **Plaza Río Tijuana** on Paseo de los Héroes. **Pueblo Amigo,** also on Paseo de los Héroes, has a few small folk-art shops and Ley, a gourmet grocery that sells salad by the pint and hard-to-find Mexican delicacies such as fresh mole sauce and pickled carrots and cauliflower.

Rosarito

29 km (18 mi) south of Tijuana.

This one-time small seaside community had virtually no tourist trade. It was part of the municipality of Tijuana, an overlooked suburb on the way to the port city of Ensenada. But as the roads improved—and particularly after the completion of Baja's Transpeninsular Highway in 1973—Rosarito began to flower. In 1995 it became its own municipality, with a separate government from that of Tijuana. Rosarito's population, about 110,000, is growing steadily. In 1996 Rosarito attracted considerable attention when 20th Century Fox built a permanent movie-production studio on the coastline south of town. The mega-success *Titanic* was shot here in 1996 and 1997, and the municipality is now experiencing a boom from the sudden influx of tourists and businesspeople. Future filming at the studio is much anticipated. A Titanic museum opened on the site after the filming, but its hours are erratic and it may be closed if other filming is in progress. Ask at the gatehouse for information.

Rosarito's main street, alternately known as the Old Ensenada Highway and Boulevard Benito Juárez, reflects the unrestrained growth and speculation that have both helped and harmed the city. The street is packed with restaurants, bars, and shops in a jarring juxtaposition of building styles, with some of the largest developments halted midway for lack of investors. As a result, the city has lost much of its charm; some find it downright ugly.

It nevertheless remains a relaxing place to visit—if you're here on a weekday when there are few tourists in town. Southern Californians have practically made Rosarito a weekend suburb, and the crowd is far from subdued. Surfers, swimmers, and sunbathers come here to enjoy the beach, one of the longest in northern Baja: it's an uninterrupted stretch of sand from the power plant at the far north end of town to below the Rosarito Beach Hotel, about 8 km (5 mi) south. Horseback riding, jogging, and strolling are popular along this strand. Whales pass not far from shore on their winter migration; dolphins and sea lions sun on rocks jutting out from the sea.

Rosarito has always attracted a varied group, and these days it's made up of prosperous young Californians building villas in vacation developments, retired Americans and Canadians homesteading in gated communities and trailer parks, and an abundance of young adults seeking cheap food and drink and an escape from supervision. It sometimes seems that spring break is a year-round event here, and families with small children might be offended by the rowdy behavior and general lack of courtesy. The local police do their best to control the revelers, but weekend nights can be outrageously noisy. If you're here to relax in peace, choose a hotel room far from any bars or restaurants.

Hedonism and health get equal billing in Rosarito. Seafood is a favorite here, especially lobster, shrimp, and abalone, and visiting Americans act as if they've been dry for months—margaritas and beer are the favored thirst quenchers. People throw off their inhibitions, at least to the degree permitted by local constables. A typical Rosarito day might begin with a breakfast of eggs, refried beans, and tortillas, followed by a few hours of horseback riding on the beach. Lying in the sun or browsing in shops takes care of midday. Siestas are imperative and are usually followed by more shopping, strolling, or sunbathing before dinner, dancing, and sleep.

Rosarito has few historic or cultural attractions, beaches and bars being the main draws. Sightseeing consists of strolling along the beach or down **Boulevard Benito Juárez,** which runs parallel to it. An immense PEMEX gasoline installation and electric plant anchor the northern end of Boulevard Juárez, which then runs along a collection of shopping arcades, restaurants, and motels.

Dining and Lodging

$$ ✕ **Calafia.** Though not in Rosarito proper, this unusual restaurant and trailer park are worth a visit (it's a 10-minute car or cab ride south). The owners have added a historic element to their property by filling the public spaces with photos and artifacts from Baja's early days. But most visitors are drawn to the tables that are scattered on small terraces down the cliffside to the crashing sea. The food is standard Mexican fare, but it all tastes great when combined with the fresh salt air and sea breezes. Calafia has an outdoor dance floor at the base of the cliffs, where live bands sometimes perform. The complex has a few rooms

for rent as well. ⊠ *Km 35.5 Old Ensenada Hwy.,* ☎ *661/2–15–81; 800/225–2342 in the U.S.,* FAX *661/2–15–80. MC, V.*

$$ ✕ **El Nido.** A dark, wood-paneled restaurant with leather booths and a large central fireplace, this is one of the oldest eateries in Rosarito. Diners unimpressed with newer, fancier places come here for mesquite-grilled steaks and for grilled quail from the owner's farm in the Baja wine country. ⊠ *Blvd. Juárez 67,* ☎ *661/2–14–30. MC, V.*

$$ ✕ **El Patio.** Designed like a colonial-style café amid the bustle of the Festival Plaza complex, this tasteful restaurant is the best spot for a calm, authentically Mexican meal. Umbrellas cover tables set within soft blue and purple walls, and the aromas of chilies, mole, and grilled meats spark the appetite. The menu shuns tacos and burgers in favor of savory grilled quail, shrimp crepes, and chicken with poblano sauce. The bar is peaceful as well—a good spot to quaff a cerveza or margarita away from the streetside crowds. ⊠ *Blvd. Juárez in the Festival Plaza,* ☎ *661/2–29–50. MC, V.*

$$ ✕ **La Leña.** The cornerstone restaurant of the Quinta Plaza shopping
★ center, La Leña is spacious and impeccably clean, with the tables spread far enough apart for privacy. Try any of the beef dishes, especially the tender carne asada with tortillas and guacamole. ⊠ *Quinta Plaza,* ☎ *661/2–08–26. MC, V.*

$ ✕ **La Flor de Michoacán.** Carnitas Michoacán-style, served with home-made tortillas, guacamole, and salsa, are the house specialty at this Rosarito landmark, established in 1950. The tacos, *tortas* (sandwiches), and tostadas are great. The surroundings are simple but clean. Takeout is available. ⊠ *Blvd. Juárez 291,* ☎ *661/2–18–58. No credit cards. Closed Wed.*

$ ✕ **La Taberna Española.** This branch of Tijuana's favorite tapas bar draws people from the more raucous bars across the boulevard to its rustic rooms designed for people-watching and conversation. Octopus, eel, olives, and paella all redolent with garlic are served in the two-story dining room and on the rooftop terrace. ⊠ *Blvd. Juárez across from Festival Plaza,* ☎ *661/2–19–82. MC, V.*

$$$ ⬚ **Marriott Real Del Mar Residence Inn.** Golfers and escapists relish
★ their privacy at this cliffside all-suites hotel with faraway views of the sea north of Rosarito. The standard accommodations have living rooms with vaulted brick ceilings, fireplaces, kitchens, and two double beds. Larger units come with one or two bedrooms. Greens fees at the on-site golf course are included in packages. The hotel, 19 km (12 mi) south of downtown Tijuana and 10 km (6 mi) north of Rosarito Beach, is completely removed from the action. Though not immediately connected with the hotel, a nearby branch of Tijuana's Pedrin's restaurant serves good seafood meals and Mexican dishes. A full spa opened in 1998 on the property. ⊠ *Km 19.5 Ensenada toll road, 22710,* ☎ *66/31–36–70; 800/331–3131 in the U.S.,* FAX *66/31–36–77. 75 suites. Restaurant, bar, snack bar, pool, spa, 18-hole golf course, exercise room. AE, MC, V.*

$$$ ⬚ **Rosarito Beach Hotel.** This Prohibition-era charmer—Rosarito's centerpiece—has huge ballrooms, tiled public rest rooms, and a glassed-in pool deck overlooking a long beach. Rooms are less impressive. Those in the tower have air-conditioning; some units in the original building have fans only and are very run-down. Rooms near the pools, playground, and side lawn, where live bands play on summer afternoons, are noisy. Reduced midweek rates and special packages are often available. A refurbished 1930s mansion next door hosts the Casa Playa Spa, with massage, beauty treatments, exercise equipment, saunas, and hot tubs. A French restaurant, Chabert's, is also housed in the mansion and is open nightly in high season, Friday through Sunday nights off-season. ⊠ *Blvd. Juárez, south end of town, 22710,* ☎ *661/2–01–44 or*

661/2–11–26; 800/343–8582 in Mexico and the U.S., ₣₳ₓ 661/2–11–25. In the U.S.: ⊠ Box 430145, San Diego, CA 22710. 186 rooms, 61 suites, 28 2-bedroom suites. 3 restaurants, bar, 2 pools, spa, tennis court, exercise room, beach, playground. MC, V.

$$ ⛁ **Festival Plaza.** Designed with unrestrained fun in mind, Festival Plaza is geared toward a youthful crowd. The motel-like rooms are in an eight-story building with a facade resembling a roller coaster. The casitas (in the $$$ range) close to the beach are the quietest accommodations and have small hot tubs, separate living rooms with foldout couches, and private garages, but no kitchen facilities. The hotel also operates a complex of 13 villas just south of Rosarito; these have full kitchens. Within the hotel complex are several bars and good restaurants—try the traditional Mexican dishes at El Patio—and the central courtyard serves as a concert stage, children's playground, and party headquarters. Discounted room rates are often available, especially in winter. ⊠ Blvd. Juárez 11, 22710, ☎ 661/2–08–42 or 661/2–29–50; 800/453–8606 in the U.S., ₣₳ₓ 661/2–01–24. 108 rooms, 5 penthouse suites, 7 casitas, 13 villas. 3 restaurants, 4 bars, pool, dance club. AE, MC, V.

$$ ⛁ **Los Pelicanos Hotel.** One of the few hotels on the beach, the Pelicanos is a favorite with Americans and Canadians who stay for weeks on end in winter. The best rooms have oceanfront balconies, though the others—with white walls, light-wood furnishings, and large bathrooms—are nice as well. The lack of a pool is a drawback, but the sea is just a few steps away. The second-story restaurant and bar, popular sunset-watching spots, tend to attract an older, more subdued clientele feasting on steak and lobster. ⊠ Calle Cedros 115, at Calle Ebano, 22710, ☎ 661/2–04–45, ₣₳ₓ 661/2–17–57. In the U.S.: ⊠ Box 433871, San Ysidro, CA 92143. 39 rooms. Restaurant, bar. AE, MC, V.

$ ⛁ **Brisas del Mar.** A modern motel (built in 1992), the Brisas del Mar is especially good for families, since the large pastel rooms comfortably accommodate four persons. A few of the suites on the second story have hot tubs and views of the ocean; all have air-conditioning and TV. The motel is located on the inland side of Boulevard Juárez, and traffic noise can be a problem. ⊠ Blvd. Juárez 22, 22710, ☎ ₣₳ₓ 661/2–25–47. In the U.S., ⊠ Box 18903, Coronado, CA 92178–9003. 69 rooms, 2 junior suites. Bar, coffee shop, pool. AE, MC, V.

Nightlife and the Arts

Rosarito's many restaurants keep customers entertained with live music, piano bars, or folklórico (folk music and dance) shows. The bar scene is also active. Drinking-and-driving laws are stiff—the police will fine you no matter how little you've had. If you plan to drink, take a cab or assign a designated driver.

There's a lot going on at night at the **Rosarito Beach Hotel** (⊠ Blvd. Juárez, ☎ 661/2–01–44): live music at the ocean-view **Beachcomber Bar** and **Hugo's**; a Mexican Fiesta on Friday nights; and occasional live bands and dances in the cavernous ballroom. **Papas and Beer** (⊠ Blvd. Juárez near Rosarito Beach Hotel, ☎ 661/2–02–44 or 661/2–04-44) draws a young, energetic crowd. The **Festival Plaza** (⊠ Blvd. Juárez 11, ☎ 661/2–08–42) has become party central for Rosarito's younger crowd and presents live concerts on the hotel's courtyard stage most weekends. In the hotel complex are **El Museo Cantina Tequila** (☎ 661/2–29–50)—locals call it the Rattlesnake Bar—dedicated to the art of imbibing tequila and stocked with more than 130 brands of the fiery drink, and **Rock & Roll Taco**—as its name suggests, a taco stand and boisterous bar all in one. **Rene's Sports Bar** (☎ 661/2–74–84) draws a somewhat quieter, older crowd; the restaurant isn't great, but a few pool tables, TVs broadcasting sporting events, and a convivial gaggle of gringos make the bar a great hangout.

Outdoor Activities and Sports

GOLF

The **Real del Mar Golf Club** (⊠ 18 km [11 mi] south of the border on Ensenada toll road, ☎ 66/31–34–01) has 18 holes overlooking the ocean. Golf packages are available at some Rosarito Beach hotels.

HORSEBACK RIDING

You can hire horses at the north and south ends of Juárez and on the beach south of the Rosarito Beach Hotel for $10 per hour. If you're a dedicated equestrian, ask about tours into the countryside, which can be arranged with the individual owners.

SURFING

The waves are particularly good at **Popotla,** Km 33; **Calafía,** Km 35.5; and **Costa Baja,** Km 36, on the Old Ensenada Highway. **Tony's Surf Shop** (⊠ Blvd. Juárez 312, ☎ 661/2–11–92) sells and rents surfing gear.

Shopping

Shopping is far better in Rosarito than in most Baja cities, especially for pottery, wood furniture, and high-end household items favored by condo-owners in nearby expat clusters. Curio stands and open-air artisans' markets line Boulevard Juárez both north and south of town. Major hotels have shopping arcades with restaurants, taco stands, and some decent crafts stores.

Interios del Rio Casa del Arte y La Madera (⊠ Quinta del Mar Plaza, ☎ 661/2–13–00) has an irresistible selection of Mexican folk art with a fish and sea theme, and creatively painted furnishings. **Casa la Carreta** (⊠ Km 29 Old Ensenada Hwy., ☎ 661/2–05–02), one of Rosarito's best furniture shops, keeps expanding and is worth a visit just to see the wood-carvers shaping elaborate desks, dining tables, and armoires. **Don Quijote Furniture** (⊠ Blvd. Juárez s/n, across from La Quinta Plaza, ☎ No phone) is another great outlet for custom furnishings and wrought iron. **The Cuban Cigar Shop** (⊠ Blvd. Juárez s/n, near the Rosarito Beach Hotel, ☎ No phone) is run by a Cubana who visits her homeland monthly, bringing back the requisite cigars along with art work, photos, and other Cuban novelties. **Pancho's Curios** (⊠ Blvd. Juárez, ☎ No phone) has a hodepodge of blown glass, wrought iron, patio furniture, wooden masks, and pottery in the front yard and interior shop.

Casa Torres (⊠ Rosarito Beach Hotel Shopping Center, ☎ 661/2–10–08) carries a wide array of imported perfumes. **Margarita's** (⊠ Rosarito Beach Hotel Shopping Center, ☎ No phone) has a great selection of Guatemalan textiles and clothing. The shelves of **Taxco Curios** (⊠ Quinta del Mar Plaza, ☎ 661/2–18–77) are filled with handblown glassware. **Apisa** (⊠ Quinta del Mar Plaza, ☎ 661/2–01–25) sells state-of-the-art furnishings and iron sculpture from Guadalajara.

The **Calimax** grocery store on Boulevard Juárez is a good place to stock up on necessities.

Puerto Nuevo (Newport)

Km 44 Old Ensenada Hwy., 12 km (7½ mi) south of Rosarito.

Not so many years ago, the only way you could tell you'd reached this fishing community at Km 44 on the old highway from Rosarito was by the huge painting of a 7UP bottle on the side of a building. You'd drive down the rutted dirt road to a row of restaurants where you were served the classic Newport meal: grilled lobster, refried beans, rice, homemade tortillas, butter, salsa, and lime. The meal became a legend, and now at least 30 restaurants in the same area have the identical menu. An artisans' market sits at the entrance to the restaurant row; other stands selling pottery, serapes, and T-shirts line the nearby highway. Several hotels have opened in the area, making Puerto Nuevo a self-contained destination where you can party all day and night and not have to drive to hotels in Rosarito or Ensenada. Several longtime favorite small inns and restaurants line the road south of Puerto Nuevo to Ensenada.

Dining and Lodging

Don't expect there to be much variety in the food at any of the Puerto Nuevo restaurants: people come here for the classic lobster meal, and they're not about to be disappointed. Some places have full bars; others serve only wine and beer. **Ortega's,** with four branches in Newport and two in Rosarito, is the most crowded; **Ponderosa** is smaller and quieter and is run by a gracious family; **Costa Brava** is the most elegant, with tablecloths and an ocean view; and **La Casa de la Langosta** serves grilled fish along with lobster and shrimp. Lobsters in most places are priced as small, medium, and large—medium is about $15. Some of the lobster served in Newport comes from local waters during lobster season (October through March), though the supply can hardly keep up with the demand and most of the lobster is imported. There is some concern that the waters close to shore have become polluted, but the fishermen say they trap the lobsters 1½ km (1 mi) or so offshore, where the waters are safe. Most places are open for lunch and dinner on a first-come, first-served basis. Some take credit cards.

$$ ✕🏨 **La Fonda.** A longtime favorite with beachgoers, La Fonda has a
★ few well-worn rooms decorated with carved-wood furniture, old bullfighting posters, and folk art; most have great views of the ocean. There are no phones or televisions, just the sound of the surf and miles of empty beach to keep you entertained. At the restaurant you can sit on an outdoor patio and sip potent margaritas served with fresh lobster, grilled steaks, prime rib, suckling pig, and traditional Mexican dishes. The Saturday and Sunday brunch is a feast well worth a few hours of your time. The bar is packed on weekend nights, and the patrons boisterous. If you plan on getting any sleep, ask for a room as close to the sounds of the surf as possible. ✉ *Km 59 Old Ensenada Hwy., 22710,* ☎ *66/28–73–52 or 66/28–73–53. In the U.S.:* ✉ *Box 430268, San Ysidro, CA 92143. 26 rooms. Restaurant, bar, beach. MC, V at restaurant; no credit cards at hotel.*

$$$$ 🏨 **Sierra Plaza Bajamar.** On the grounds of the Bajamar golf resort, about halfway between Rosarito and Ensenada, the hacienda-style hotel surrounds a central courtyard. Rooms have hand-carved furnishings and French doors leading to landscaped patios. Staying here can be peaceful except when golfers neglect to remove their shoes and clump around the brick hallways like herds of goats. Maintenance has been a problem, and some rooms need renovation. Private condos (some for rent) edge the golf course and the cliffs overlooking the ocean. The rooms are being refurbished in early 1999. ✉ *Km 77.5 Old Ensenada Hwy., Ensenada 22800,* ☎ *615/5–01–51 or 619/299–1112; 800/225–2418 in the U.S.,* 𝖥𝖠𝖷 *615/5–01–50. 81 rooms. Restaurant, bar, pool, 18-hole golf course, 2 tennis courts. AE, MC, V.*

$$ 🏨 **Castillos Del Mar.** One of the few places with direct access to the beach, this small hotel has 34 rooms with basic amenities. Older and slightly run-down, Castillos is clean, fun, and inexpensive by local standards. Some rooms have terraces overlooking the beach. The bar gets hopping evenings, with live music most nights. ✉ *Km 36.5 Old Ensenada Hwy., 22712,* ☎ *661/2–10–88. Restaurant, bar, pool. 34 rooms. No credit cards.*

$$ 🏨 **Las Rocas.** This white hotel with blue-tile domes is still the prettiest in the area, but it is beginning to look its age. The building is terraced up a hillside, giving all the rooms ocean views, but the accommodations are not otherwise equal. The least expensive ones are small, with dripping faucets and worn furnishings. The most expensive are much larger and have fireplaces and microwaves. The pool and whirlpool seem to spill over the cliffs into the ocean. A full spa has massage, facials, wraps, and other treatments. ✉ *Km 37 Old Ensenada Hwy., 22710,* ☎ FAX *661/2–21–40. In the U.S.:* ✉ *Box 8851, Chula Vista, CA 91912,* ☎ *619/425–2682; 800/733–6394 outside CA. 74 rooms and suites. Restaurant, bar, hot tub, spa, beach. AE, MC, V.*

$$ 🏨 **New Port Beach Hotel.** The closest accommodations to the lobster restaurants are in this sand-color complex with ocean views. Rooms don't have air-conditioning, but they do have heaters for chilly winter nights, along with cable TV, small balconies, and simple blue-gray and white furnishings. The hotel has dance bands in the upstairs lounge, marimba music on weekends in the lobby bar, and classical music on Sunday. ✉ *Km 45 Old Ensenada Hwy., 22712,* ☎ *661/4–11–66; 800/ 582–1018,* FAX *661/4–11–74. 147 rooms. Restaurant, bar, pool, 2 tennis courts, exercise room. MC, V.*

Outdoor Activities and Sports

GOLF

Bajamar (✉ Km 77.5 Old Ensenada Hwy., ☎ 615/5–01–51; 615/5–01–61 for tee times), a 1976 course revamped and reopened in late 1993, has 18 holes of challenging championship golf on the cliffs above the ocean and another nine holes near the beach.

En Route   Vast vistas of pounding surf and solitary cliffs are interspersed with one-of-a-kind hotels and restaurants along the coastline between Rosarito and Ensenada. The paved highway (Mexico Route 1) between the two cities often cuts a path between low mountains and high oceanside cliffs. Exits lead to rural roads, oceanfront campgrounds, and an ever-increasing number of resort communities. The small fishing communities of **San Miguel** and **El Sauzal** sit off the highway to the north of Ensenada, and you can see the **Coronado Islands** clearly off the coast.

Ensenada

104 km (65 mi) south of Tijuana, 75 km (47 mi) south of Rosarito.

In 1542 Juan Rodríguez Cabrillo first discovered the seaport that Sebastián Vizcaino named Ensenada-Bahía de Todos Santos (All Saints' Bay) in 1602. Since then the town has drawn a steady stream of "discoverers" and developers. First ranchers made their homes on large spreads along the coast and up into the mountains. Gold miners followed, turning the area into a boomtown during the late 1800s. After the mines were depleted, the area settled back into a pastoral state for a while, but the harbor gradually grew into a major port for shipping agricultural goods from the surrounding ranches and farms. Now, with a population of some 300,000, it is one of Mexico's largest seaports and has a thriving fishing fleet and fish-processing industry. The smell of fish from the canneries lining the north and south sides of the city can be overpowering at times.

There are no beaches in Ensenada proper, but beaches north and south of town are satisfactory for swimming, sunning, surfing, and camping. On summer and holiday weekends the population swells, but the town rarely gets overly crowded. Whereas the hotels and resorts along the coast, especially around Rosarito, attract the bulk of the weekend escapists, Ensenada tends to draw those who want to explore a more traditional Mexican city.

In a concerted effort to attract vacationers, conventioneers, and business travelers, the waterfront area has been razed and rebuilt, with taco stands replaced by shopping centers, hotels, and the massive Plaza Marina, a large shopping complex with few tenants. Several strip malls have opened in town, but many of the storefronts remain empty. Cruise ships occasionally anchor in the port, bringing day-trippers for shopping and dining.

Ensenada, the third-largest city in Baja, hugs the harbor of Bahía de Todos Santos. As Alternate Highway 1 leads into town from the north, it becomes Boulevard Costero, running past shipyards filled with massive freighters.

⑬ Parque Revolución (Revolution Park) is the most traditional plaza in Ensenada, with a bandstand, playground, and plenty of benches in the shade. The plaza takes on a festive feeling on Saturday and Sunday evenings, when neighbors congregate on the benches and children chase seagulls down the pathways. ⊠ *Av. Juárez at Av. Obregón.*

The main street along the waterfront is Boulevard Costero. At its **⑭** northernmost point, there is an indoor-outdoor **Fish Market,** where row after row of counters displays piles of shrimp, tuna, dorado, marlin, snapper, and dozens of other species of fish caught off Baja's coasts. Outside, stands sell grilled or smoked fish, seafood cocktails, and fish tacos. Browsers can pick up some standard souvenirs, eat well for very little money, and take some great photographs. The original fish taco stands line the dirt path to the fish market. If your stomach is on the delicate side, try the fish tacos at the cleaner, quieter **Plaza de Mariscos** in the shadow of the giant beige **Plaza de Marina** that blocks the view of the traditional fish market from the street.

⑮ Fishing and whale-watching boats depart from the **Sportfishing Pier** (⊠ Blvd. Costero at Av. Alvarado). *See* Outdoor Activities and Sports, *below,* for fishing and whale-watching information.

⑯ Plaza Cívica (⊠ Blvd. Costero at Av. Riveroll) is a block-long concrete park with sculptures of Mexican heroes Benito Juárez, Miguel Hidalgo, and Venustiano Carranza.

⑰ South of the Plaza Cívica is the **Centro Artesenal de Ensenada** shopping center, which formerly benefited from the traffic of a nearby, now defunct cruise ship pier. Ships now dock amid the repair yards at the north end of the port. Because taxis and tour buses carry passengers straight from the port to Ensenada's main attractions, the center has lost many of its tenants.

⑱ The **Riviera del Pacífico,** officially called the Centro Social, Cívico y Cultural de Ensenada (Social, Civic and Cultural Center of Ensenada), is a rambling, white, hacienda-style mansion built in the 1920s with money raised on both sides of the border. An enormous gambling palace, hotel, restaurant, and bar, the glamorous Riviera was frequented by wealthy U.S. citizens and Mexicans, particularly during Prohibition. When gambling was outlawed in Mexico and Prohibition ended in the United States, the palace lost its raison d'être. You can tour some of the elegant ballrooms and halls, which host occasional art shows and civic events. Many of the rooms are locked; check at the main office to see if there is someone available to show you around. The gardens alone are worth visiting, and the building now houses the **Museo de Historia de Ensenada**, a museum on Baja's history. ⊠ *Blvd. Costero and Av. Riviera,* ☎ *Riviera 61/76–43–10; 61/76–05–94 museum.* ⊞ *Building and gardens free, museum $1.* ☉ *Tues.–Sun. 9–5.*

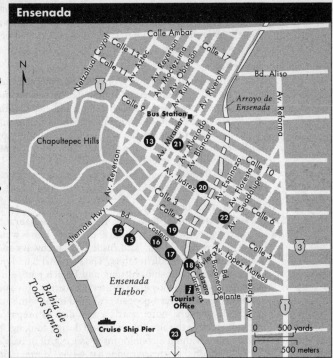

Ensenada

(19) Ensenada's traditional tourist zone is centered along **Avenida López Mateos.** High-rise hotels, souvenir shops, restaurants, and bars line the avenue from its beginning at the foot of the Chapultepec Hills for eight blocks south to the dry channel of the Arroyo de Ensenada. Locals shop for furniture, clothing, and other necessities a few blocks inland on (20) **Avenida Juárez** in Ensenada's downtown area.

(21) **Las Bodegas de Santo Tomás,** Baja's oldest winery, gives tours and tastings of its downtown winery and bottling plant. The restaurant in the winery is one of Baja's finest. The winery also operates **La Esquina de Bodegas,** a café, shop, and gallery in a bright blue building across Avenida Miramar. ⊠ *Av. Miramar 666,* ☎ *61/78–33–33; 619/454–7166 in the U.S.* ⊠ *$1.* ⏱ *Tours Mon.–Sat. 11 AM, 1 and 3 PM; Sun. 11 AM and 1 PM.*

(22) The city's largest cathedral, **Our Lady of Guadalupe** (⊠ Av. Floresta at Av. Juárez), is the center of processions and celebrations during religious holidays.

(23) **La Bufadora** (⊠ Hwy. 23, 31 km [19 mi] south of Ensenada) is an impressive blowhole (*la bufadora* means the buffalo snort) in the coastal cliffs at **Punta Banda,** an isolated, mountainous point jutting into the sea. The road along Punta Banda to La Bufadora is lined with stands where growers sell locally grown olives, homemade tamales, strands of chilies and garlic, and terra-cotta planters. The drive gives short-term visitors a sampling of Baja's wilderness and is well worth a half-day excursion. The blowhole is impressive, with seawater splashing up to 75 ft in the air with startling power, spraying sightseers standing nearby. Legend has it the blowhole is created by a whale or sea serpent trapped in an undersea cave; both these stories and the less romantic scientific facts are posted on a plaque at the side of the road. A fenced-in viewing platform was designed to keep people from scram-

bling on the cliffs by the blowhole. Public rest rooms are located in a small building by the platform. There is a small fee to park near the blowhole. From the lot you will file through a row of permanent vendors' stands en route to the cliff.

Beaches

The waterfront in Ensenada proper is taken up by fishing boats, boat repair yards, and commercial shipping. The best swimming beaches are south of town. **Estero Beach** is long and clean, with mild waves; the Estero Beach Hotel takes up much of the oceanfront, but the beach is public. Surfers populate the beaches off Highway 1 north and south of Ensenada, particularly **San Miguel, California, Tres Marías,** and **La Joya**; scuba divers prefer **Punta Banda**, by La Bufadora. Lifeguards are rare, so swimmers should be cautious. The tourist office in Ensenada has a map that shows safe diving and surfing beaches.

Dining and Lodging

\$\$\$　✕ **La Embotelladora Vieja.** The most elegant restaurant in Ensenada
★　is in a converted wine-aging room at the Santo Tomás winery. The decor is classic country French, with rustic brick archways and crystal goblets glistening on candlelit tables. The so-called Baja French menu includes appetizers of smoked tuna and French pâté; among the most sublime entrées are the grilled lobster in cabernet sauvignon sauce, beef Montpellier with green peppercorns, and quail with sauvignon blanc sauce. Teetotalers, note: nearly every dish is prepared with wine, though much of the alcohol is diffused during cooking. You can order some dishes without alcohol-infused sauces. All of Baja's wineries are represented on the extensive wine list. ⊠ *Av. Miramar 666,* ☎ *61/74–08–07. MC, V. Closed Tues.*

\$\$　✕ **Bronco's Steak House.** A great find near the San Nicolas Hotel, Bronco's serves exceptional steaks and Mexican specialties. Try the Boca del Rio, a New York steak stuffed with grilled onions and fiery serrano chilies. Tripe appears frequently on the menu, satisfying the cravings of local diners gathered at many of the wood tables. Brick walls, wood plank floors, and hanging spurs and chaps give the place a Wild West feel, but the mood is subdued and relaxed. ⊠ *Av. López Mateos 1525,* ☎ *61/76–19–01. MC, V.*

\$\$　✕ **Casamar.** A long-standing, dependable restaurant, Casamar is known for its wide variety of excellent seafood. Lobster and shrimp are prepared in several ways but seem freshest when grilled *con mojo y ajo* (with butter and garlic). When ordering fish, always ask about the catch of the day; you might luck out and get a thick steak of fresh yellowfin tuna. ⊠ *Blvd. Lázaro Cárdenas 987,* ☎ *61/74–04–17. MC, V.*

\$\$　✕ **El Rey Sol.** This family-owned French restaurant opened in 1947,
★　and it remains in its charming building with stained-glass windows, wrought-iron chandeliers, and heavy oak tables and chairs. Specialties include French and Mexican presentations of fresh fish, poultry, and vegetables grown at the owner's farm in the Santo Tomás Valley. Appetizers come with the meal. The excellent pastries are baked on the premises, and a side room at the front of the restaurant has been turned into a patisserie with a few small lace-covered tables and a pastry case full of delectables. It's a lovely spot for an afternoon espresso and sweets, or you can choose a few tasty items to go. ⊠ *Av. López Mateos 1000,* ☎ *61/78–17–33. AE, MC, V.*

\$　✕ **El Charro.** You can find less (and more) expensive rotisserie chicken,
★　beans, rice, and tortillas at other places in downtown, but El Charro still attracts a steady stream of locals and tourists. Hungry patrons hover over platters of *chiles rellenos* (chilies stuffed with cheese and deep-fried in batter), enchiladas, and fresh chips and guacamole at heavy wooden picnic tables under a ceiling of charred wooden beams. Plump

chickens slowly turn over a wood fire by the front window, and the aroma of grilled beef and simmering beans fills the air. Other restaurants with similar names have opened on the same block; stick with the original and you won't be disappointed. ⊠ *Av. López Mateos 475,* ☎ *61/78–38–81. MC, V.*

$ ✕ **Mariscos de Bahía de Ensenada.** Red lights flicker around the front
★ door, making this popular seafood house just off the main drag easy to spot. On weekends upstairs and downstairs dining rooms are packed at lunch and dinner; tables are easier to come by weeknights. Clams, shrimp, lobster, red snapper, squid, and other seasonal sea creatures are fried, baked, broiled, or grilled, and served with a basic iceberg lettuce salad, white rice, and tortillas made fresh at the window-front tortilleria. ⊠ *Av. Riveroll 109,* ☎ *61/78–10–15. MC, V.*

$$$ ▥ **Hotel Coral & Marina.** This ambitious 1995 project is the largest re-
★ sort on the Baja Norte coast, and unlike others in the area it appears to have been built to survive and thrive. A marina, long needed in Ensenada, has slips for 600 boats and facilities for clearing customs. The rooms in two eight-story towers are decorated in burgundy and dark green; most have waterfront balconies, seating areas, cable TV, and in-room international phone service (still a novelty in this area). Conventions, fishing and golf tournaments, and boat races fill the hotel on weekends; rates are often 30%–50% lower on winter weekdays. ⊠ *Mexico Hwy. 1 north of town, 22800,* ☎ *61/75–00–00; 800/862–9020 in the U.S.,* 𝔽𝔸𝕏 *61/75–00–05. 18 rooms, 129 suites. Restaurant, 1 indoor and 2 outdoor pools, 2 hot tubs, spa, 2 tennis courts, exercise room, dive shop, boating, fishing. MC, V.*

$$$ ▥ **Las Rosas.** This elegant pink palace just north of town is both inti-
★ mate and upscale. The atrium lobby has marble floors, mint green-and-pink upholstered couches facing the sea, and a green glass ceiling that glows at night. All rooms face the ocean and pool; some have fireplaces and hot tubs, and even the least expensive are lovely. The hotel is booked solid most weekends—make reservations far in advance. ⊠ *Mexico Hwy. 1 north of town, 22800,* ☎ *61/74–43–20; 800/522–1516 in AZ, CA, NV; 800/225–2786 elsewhere in the U.S. and Canada,* 𝔽𝔸𝕏 *61/74–45–95. 32 suites. Restaurant, bar, pool, hot tub. AE, MC, V.*

$$$ ▥ **Punta Morro.** For seclusion and the sound of crashing surf, you can't
★ beat this all-suites hotel. The three-story tan building faces the north end of the bay. The lovely restaurant sits on rock pilings above the waves; you won't find a more romantic spot than at a window seat here. Enjoy eggs Benedict or French toast in the morning, or toast the sunset with champagne while feasting on lobster, steak, or quail. All accommodations have terraces facing the ocean, kitchenettes, and seating areas; some have fireplaces. Stairs lead down to a rocky beach, but the surf is usually too rough for swimming. Rates are significantly lower on weekdays. ⊠ *Mexico Hwy. 1, 3 km (2 mi) north of town, Box 2891, 22800,* ☎ *61/78–35–07; 800/526–6676 in the U.S.,* 𝔽𝔸𝕏 *61/74–44–90. In the U.S.:* ⊠ *Box 43-4263, San Ysidro, CA 92143. 30 suites. Restaurant, bar, pool, hot tub, beach. MC, V.*

$$ ▥ **Estero Beach Resort.** Families settle in for a week or more at this long-standing resort on Ensenada's best beach. The rooms (some with kitchenettes) are housed in several mint-green buildings. The best are those right by the sand; the worst (and cheapest) are in the oldest section by the parking lot. No one expects anything fancy here, and at times it seems all the guests are attending huge wedding or birthday celebrations or family reunions. Guests spend their days swimming in the ocean or the pool, fishing, riding horses, playing volleyball, and generally hanging out with friends. Nights are spent at the casual restaurant and bar. The resort is 10 km (6 mi) south of town. Midweek winter rates are a real bargain, and the resort feels almost deserted and peaceful at this time. Nonguests can use the hotel's facilities for a low daily fee. ✉ *Mexico Hwy. 1 between Ensenada and Maneadero, 22810,* ☎ *61/76–62–35,* ℻ *61/76–69–25. In the U.S.:* ✉ *482 San Ysidro Blvd., Suite 1186, San Ysidro, CA 92173. 106 rooms, 2 suites. Restaurant, bar, kitchenettes, pool, 4 tennis courts, horseback riding, volleyball, shops, playground. MC, V.*

$$ ▣ **San Nicolás.** Hidden behind cement walls painted with Indian murals, this massive resort doesn't look like much from the street. The San Nicolás was built in the early 1970s, but much of it has been refurbished since then. The suites have bedrooms with mirrored ceilings, tiled hot tubs, and living rooms with deep-green carpeting, mauve furnishings, and beveled-glass doors. Less extravagant rooms are comfortable and decorated with folk art. A waterfall cascades into the pool, and a good restaurant overlooks the gardens. Special rates are often available on weekdays and in winter. ✉ *Av. López Mateos (also called Calle 1) and Av. Guadalupe, Box 19, 22800,* ☎ *61/76–19–01,* ℻ *61/76–49–30. In the U.S.:* ✉ *Box 43706, San Diego, CA 92143,* ☎ *619/298–4105; 800/522–1516 in AZ, CA, and NV; 800/225–2786 elsewhere in the U.S. and Canada. 140 rooms and 10 suites. 2 restaurants, bar, 1 indoor and 1 outdoor pool, hot tub, dance club. AE, MC, V.*

$ ▣ **Hotel del Valle.** Fishermen and budget travelers frequent the clean, basic rooms in this small hotel on a relatively quiet side street. Though the rooms lack air-conditioning they do have fans, phones, and televisions (with local stations only). Guests have use of a coffeemaker in the lobby and parking spaces in front of the rooms. Ask about rate discounts—those posted behind the front desk are about 40% higher than guests in the know normally pay. ✉ *Av. Riveroll 367, 22800,* ☎ *61/78–22–24,* ℻ *61/74–04–66. 20 rooms. AE, MC, V.*

$ ▣ **Joker Hotel.** A bizarre, brightly colored mishmash of styles makes it hard to miss the Joker, which is conveniently located for those traveling south of Ensenada. Spacious rooms have private balconies, satellite TV, and phones. Traffic noise from the highway and from guests leaving at the crack of dawn can be a problem; try to stay away from the road and the busiest parts of the parking lot. ✉ *Km 12.5 Mexico Hwy. 1, 22800,* ☎ ℻ *61/76–72–01. 40 rooms. Pool, hot tub. MC, V.*

Nightlife and the Arts

Ensenada is a party town for college students, surfers, and other young tourists. **Hussong's Cantina** (✉ Av. Ruíz 113, ☎ 61/74–07–20) has been an Ensenada landmark since 1892 and has changed little since then. A security guard stands by the front door to handle the often-rowdy crowd—a mix of locals and tourists of all ages over 18. The noise is usually deafening, pierced by mariachi and ranchera musicians and the whoops and hollers of the inebriated. **Papas and Beer** (✉ Av. Ruíz at López Mateos, ☎ 61/74–01–45) attracts a collegiate crowd, which hangs out the second-story windows shouting at their friends.

Outdoor Activities and Sports

FISHING

Boats leave the **Ensenada Sportfishing Pier** regularly. The best angling is from April through November, with bottom fishing good in the winter. Charter vessels and party boats are available from several outfitters along Avenida López Mateos and Boulevard Costero and off the sportfishing pier. Trips on group boats cost about $35 for a half day or $100 for a full day. Licenses are available at the tourist office or from charter companies.

Ensenada Clipper Fleet (✉ Sportfishing Pier, ☎ 61/78–21–85) has charter and group boats. **Gordo's Sportfishing** (✉ Sportfishing Pier, ☎ 61/78–35–15, ℻ 61/78–23–77), one of the oldest sportfishing companies in Ensenada, has charter boats, group boats, and a smoke-house. You can book sportfishing packages including transportation, accommodations, and fishing through **Baja California Tours** (☎ 619/454–7166 in the U.S., FAX 619/454–2703).

GOLF

The **Baja Country Club** (⊠ Hwy. 1 south of Ensenada at Maneadero, ☎ 61/73–03–03) has a secluded 18-hole course in a resort development.

KAYAKING

Estero Beach and Punta Banda (en route to La Bufadora south of Ensenada) are both good kayaking areas, though facilities are limited. **Southwest Kayaks** (☎ 619/222–3616 in San Diego, CA) offers occasional kayaking workshops at both areas.

WHALE-WATCHING

Boats leave the **Ensenada Sportfishing Pier** for whale-watching trips from December through February. The gray whales migrating from the north to bays and lagoons in southern Baja pass through Todos Santos Bay, often close to shore. Viewers from boats usually can easily see the whales spouting and breeching not far from them. There are restrictions on how close the boats can get to the whales, so you won't be able to touch them but should be able to get good photos. Binoculars and telephoto camera lenses come in handy. The trips last about three hours. Vessels and tour boats are available from several outfitters, including Gordo's (☞ Fishing, *above*), along Avenida López Mateos and Boulevard Costero and off the sportfishing pier. You can also book whale-watching packages, which include transportation, accommodations, and the boat trips, through **Baja California Tours** (☎ 619/454–7166 in the U.S., FAX 619/454–2703).

Shopping

Most of the tourist shops are located along Avenida López Mateos beside the hotels and restaurants. There are several two-story shopping arcades, many with empty shops. Dozens of curio shops line the street, all selling similar selections of pottery, woven blankets and serapes, embroidered dresses, and onyx chess sets.

Artes Don Quijote (⊠ Av. López Mateos 503, ☎ 61/76–94–76) has an impressive array of carved-wood doors, huge terra-cotta pots, and crafts from Oaxaca. **Artesanías Castillo** (⊠ Av. López Mateos 656, ☎ 61/76–11–87) and **Los Castillo** (⊠ Av. López Mateos 815, ☎ 61/76–11–87) both have extensive displays of silver jewelry from Taxco. **Girasoles** (⊠ Av. López Mateos, ☎ No phone) stocks a great selection of dolls, pine-needle baskets, and pottery made by the Tarahumara Indians from the Copper Canyon. **La Mina de Salomón** (⊠ Av. López Mateos 1000, ☎ 61/78–28–36) carries elaborate jewelry in a tiny gallery next to El Rey Sol restaurant. **Carlos Importer** (⊠ Av. López Mateos at Alvarado, ☎ 61/78–24–63) is one of the largest shops in town with high-quality pottery, tile, blown glassware, and iron furniture.

Centro Artesenal de Ensenada has a smattering of galleries and shops. The best by far is the **Galería de Pérez Meillón** (⊠ Blvd. Costera 1094–39, ☎ 61/74–03–94), with its museum-quality pottery and varied folk art by indigenous northern Mexican peoples. **La Esquina de Bodegas** (⊠ Av. Miramar at Calle 6, ☎ 61/78–35–57) is an innovative gallery, shop, and café in a century-old winery building. Baja's finest wines are sold here at reasonable prices, and an upstairs gallery sells glassware, pottery, and books. The café at the back of the building serves coffee, wine, and a small menu of soups and entrées.

Tecate

32 km (20 mi) east of Tijuana, 112 km (70 mi) northeast of Ensenada.

Tecate is a quiet border community with a population of about 100,000. So incidental is the border to local life that its gates close from 10 PM until 6 AM daily. Tecate beer, one of the most popular brands in Mexico, is brewed here. Maquiladoras and agriculture are the other main industries. Tecate is also known for the vast pottery yards on the outskirts of town that line the highways to Tijuana and Ensenada. The artisans make bricks, paving tiles, roof tiles, and all sorts of planters and fountains. One of the largest yards is at **Baja-Mex-Tile** (⊠ Blvd. Juárez 9150, Carretera Tecate a Tijuana, ☎ 665/4–02–04). Tecate's primary tourist draw is Rancho la Puerta, a fitness resort that caters to well-heeled travelers from north of the border. A bit farther south, the valleys of Guadalupe and Calafía boast some of Mexico's lushest vineyards. Olives are also grown in profusion here.

You can easily explore the town of Tecate in a few hours, lingering along the way. But you'll need a cab or car to wander the countryside and visit pottery workers, outlying ranches, and other sights. Downtown is centered around the **Parque Hidalgo.** A few cab drivers, shoe shine boys, schoolkids, and snuggling couples hang out here around the small gazebo, patches of lawn, and wrought-iron benches. On summer evenings, dance and band concerts are held in **Parque López Mateos,** on Highway 3 south of town.

Railroading fans enjoy the infrequent rail tours from Campo (on the U.S. side of the border), over a steel trestle bridge spanning the Campo Creek, and through the only international train tunnel to the United States and on into Tecate. **Baja California Tours** (⊠ 7734 Herschel Ave., Suite O, La Jolla, CA 92037, ☎ 619/454–7166, 𝔽𝔸𝕏 619/454–2703) runs occasional rail tours.

Water parks have always delighted Mexican families. Now Tecate has **Parque Lo Sahuaro** with a 200-ft-high water slide, several smaller slides, and plenty of pools. Barbecues abound on weekends as families claim tables and lawn for their multiple generations. The park is open from mid-March to mid-September. ⊠ *8 km (5 mi) east of Tecate off Hwy. 2,* ☎ *661/4–0562.* ⊡ *$3,* ☉ *Mar.–Sept. 1, daily 7 AM–8 PM.*

Dining and Lodging

$$ ✕ **El Tucan.** Fancy by local standards, this motel restaurant is the current favorite for everything from hamburgers to spicy beefsteaks. The full bar and banquet facilities are favored by maquiladora executives and local bigwigs, and everyone enjoys the lively ambience in the dining room. ⊠ *Av. Juárez 1100,* ☎ *665/4–13–33. MC, V.*

$ ✕ **Panaderia de Tecate.** Open 24 hours every day except Christmas and New Year's, this simple bakery is famed throughout the region. The kitchen whips up more than 100 types of cookies, donuts, *pan dulce* (sweet bread), crunchy *bolillos* (rolls), and cakes. (Workers have to constantly wash down the sidewalk outside to keep ants away from all the sugar passing through the door.) Snacks and burritos are served at the adjacent tiled bar. ⊠ *Av. Juárez 331,* ☎ *665/4–00–40. No credit cards.*

$ ✕ **Plaza Jardin.** The setting is plain and the food simple Mexican fare, but the café tables outside have a gratifying view of the plaza. ⊠ *Callejón Libertad 274,* ☎ *665/4–34–53. No credit cards.*

$$$$ 🏨 **Rancho la Puerta.** This peaceful, isolated health spa and resort just west of Tecate is an idyllic resort—for $1,400 to $2,500 a week. Spanish-style buildings with red-tile roofs and modern glass-and-wood structures are spread throughout the sprawling ranch. Hiking trails lead off into scrub-pine hills and Kuchuma Mountain, and a large bright-

blue pool is a central gathering spot. Guests stay in luxurious private cottages and usually check in for a week or more, taking advantage of the special diet and exercise regimen to lose weight and shape up. Transportation is available to and from San Diego airport. Weekend rates are available. ⊠ *Hwy. 2, 5 km (3 mi) west of Tecate, 21275,* ☎ *665/4–11–55; 760/744–4222 or 800/443–7565 in the U.S.,* FAX *665/4–11–08. 80 rooms. Restaurant, pool, beauty salon, massage, 4 tennis courts, 3 health clubs. AE, MC, V.*

$$ 🏨 **Hacienda Santa Veronica.** Billed as an off-road and dirt-racing country club, the Hacienda is a pretty countryside resort whose rooms are furnished with Mexican colonial beds, bureaus, and fireplaces. The off-road raceway is sufficiently far away from the rooms to keep the noise of revving engines from disturbing you; a number of trails for horseback riding traverse the property. Bullfighting lessons and practice fights take place here, as do "bloodless" fights where both the matador and bull escape unscathed. ⊠ *30 km (19 mi) east of Tecate off Hwy. 2,* ☎ *66/81–74–28 in Tijuana; 619/298–4105 or 800/522–1516 in CA, AZ, NV; 800/225–2786 elsewhere in the U.S. and Canada. 87 rooms. Restaurant, bar, pool, 2 tennis courts, horseback riding. MC, V.*

Mexicali

136 km (84 mi) east of Tijuana.

Mexicali, with a current population estimated at 850,000, shares the Imperial Valley farmland and the border crossing with Calexico, a small California city. The capital of Baja California, Mexicali sees a great deal of government activity and a steady growth of maquiladoras. Most visitors come to town on business, and the city's sights are few and far between. A tourist-oriented strip of curio shops, restaurants, and bars is located along Avenida Francisco Madero, a block south of the border. The **Museo del Estado** (State Museum), administered by the Autonomous University of Baja California (UABC), provides a comprehensive introduction to the natural and cultural history of Baja. ⊠ *Av. Reforma 1998, near Calle L,* ☎ *65/52–57–17.* 🎫 *Free.* 🕐 *Tues.–Sat. 9–6, Sun. 10–2.*

Dining and Lodging

$$ ✕🏨 **La Lucerna.** The prettiest hotel in Mexicali, the colonial-style Lucerna has plenty of palms and fountains around the pools and carved wood furnishings in the dark, somber rooms. A newer section has suites with separate seating areas and more modern furnishings. The three restaurants are pleasant, with local decor and good Mexican meals. Conventions and business meetings sometimes fill the hotel; advance reservations are advised. ⊠ *Av. Benito Juárez 2151, 21270,* ☎ *65/64–70–00; 800/582–3762 in the U.S.,* FAX *65/66–47–06. 175 rooms, 28 cabins, 4 suites. 3 restaurants, bar, 2 pools. MC, V.*

En Route **Parque Nacional San Pedro Martir.** Baja's interior mountain ranges are filled with hidden caves and mountain hideaways. This park is more accessible than most, and even a short drive or hike up its rough trails offers a whole new perspective on Baja. As long as it hasn't been raining, a regular car can handle the dirt road into the park. ⊠ *140 km (87 mi) south of Ensenada, turn off of Hwy. 1 south of Colonet and drive 98 km (61 mi) east to the park.*

San Quintín

191 km (118 mi) south of Ensenada.

Agricultural fields line the highway as you enter San Quintín, the largest producer of tomatoes in Baja. The Oaxacan migrant workers who plant and pick the fertile valley's produce live in squalid camps out of the view of travelers, many of whom are towing boats behind their Suburbans. **Bahía de San Quintín,** which fronts a few small hotels, along with **Bahía Falsa** and **Bahía Santa Maria,** is among northern Baja's best fishing grounds, and the area's few hostelries tend to cater to anglers. The weather is unpredictable. High winds can kick up at almost any time, blowing sand and scrub brush across empty fields and the highway. There's little reason to come, unless the fishing is good.

Pismo clams collected in the sand at water's edge along San Quintín's bays are considered a local delicacy. Roadside stands sell them fresh and cooked—travelers often stop here for essentials en route farther south. Sandy side roads lead to windswept coves and isolated hideaways. If you explore these, it's best to be in a four-wheel-drive vehicle, as the roads are rugged and the drives tend to be lengthy. Your best bet for a short scenic drive is to follow the signs to the Old Mill at the edge of Bahía de San Quintín or the Hotel la Pinta south of town on Playa Santa Maria.

Lodging

$ 🖼 **Old Mill.** Anglers ease their boats into the sheltered bay at this longtime favorite hideaway and set up housekeeping in a variety of rooms, some with kitchens and fireplaces. Others arrive in RVs. The lodgestyle bar with its huge fireplace is filled with locals and travelers on weekend nights, and the restaurant serves hearty meals, including thick steaks and generous Mexican combo plates. ⊠ *South of town on a dirt road leading to the bay,* ☎ 📠 *877/800-4081 or 619/271–0952 (no local phone or fax). 25 rooms, 2 suites. Restaurant, bar, camping, fishing. MC, V accepted with advance reservations; no credit cards at resort.*

San Felipe

198 km (123 mi) south of Mexicali, 244 km (151 mi) southeast of Ensenada.

San Felipe (pop. 20,000) is the quintessential dusty fishing village with one main street (two if you count the highway into town). The **malecón** runs along a broad beach facing the Sea of Cortés and San Felipe Bay, with a swimming area in the middle and public changing rooms at the north end. Taco stands, bars, and restaurants line the sidewalk across the street from the beach. The only landmark in town is the **shrine of the Cerro de la Virgen** (Virgin of Guadalupe), at the north end of the malecón on a hill overlooking the sea.

In 1948 the first paved road from Mexicali was extended into town, and at that point San Felipe became significant. Prior to that time only a few fishermen and their families lived along the coast; now there are impressive fishing and shrimping fleets. **Bahia San Felipe** has dramatic changes in its tides. They crest at 20 ft, and because the beach is so shallow, the waterline can move in and out up to 1 km (about ½ mi). Local fishermen are well aware of the peculiarities of this section of the Sea of Cortés. Many of them visit the shrine of the Virgin before setting sail.

A getaway spot for years, San Felipe used to be a place where hardy travelers in RVs and campers hid out for weeks on end. Now there are at least two dozen campgrounds and a dozen hotels in town and on the coastline both north and south of town, which fill up quickly during winter and spring holidays. At times, up to 5,000 part-time residents can be in attendance, wandering the beaches, filling the few restaurants, and enjoying the sun. On holiday weekends San Felipe can be boisterous—dune buggies, motorcycles, and off-road vehicles abound—but most of the time it's a quiet, relaxing place. The town also appeals to sportfishermen, especially in spring. Launches, bait, and supplies are readily available.

Dining and Lodging

$$ ✕ **George's.** A favorite with resident Americans, George's has comfy padded red Naugahyde booths, powerful margaritas, and very good chiles rellenos, carne asada, and seafood. ⊠ *Av. Mar de Cortés 336,* ☏ *657/7–10–57. MC, V.*

$ ✕ **El Toro.** Open for breakfast only, El Toro is renowned among locals and San Felipe regulars for its chorizo, *machaca* (marinated shredded beef), *huevos rancheros* (fried eggs served on a corn tortilla and covered with a tomato, onion, and green-pepper sauce), and American-style breakfasts. The parking lot fills with trailers hauling dune buggies and motorcycles as groups gather to fuel up before a day on the dunes. ⊠ *Hwy. 5 north of town,* ☏ *657/7–10–32. No credit cards.*

$ ✕ **Tony's Tacos.** The most popular of the many taco stands along the waterfront, Tony's is a simple spot with sidewalk picnic tables and a counter lined with condiments for the house specialty—cheap, delicious fish tacos. ⊠ *Malecón at Av. Chetumal,* ☏ *No phone. No credit cards.*

$ ✕ **Viva Mexico.** This family-run operation (formerly called Juan's Place) two blocks east of the waterfront offers consistently excellent home-style cooking at reasonable prices. The catch of the day and grilled meats come with boiled vegetables—ask for beans, rice, and the delicious homemade tortillas instead. ⊠ *Calle de Ensenada,* ☏ *No phone. No credit cards.*

$$$ ▥ **San Felipe Marina Resort.** This full-scale resort will eventually include a 100-slip marina along with resort homes and hotels, though construction has been delayed. At present, the low-slung terra-cotta building facing the sea has 60 units available as hotel rooms, time-share units, or private condos. Most rooms have kitchens, woven rugs on white-tile floors, folk art decorations, and balconies or patios with sea views. The least expensive rooms lack kitchens and ocean views. The pool sits above the beach next to a palapa bar; a second indoor pool is a delight on cold winter days. The resort is a five-minute drive south of town and has an RV campground next door. ⊠ *Km 4.5 Carretera San Felipe Aeropuerto, 21850,* ☏ *800/522–1516 or 619/298–4105 from within AZ, CA, NV,* ☏ *657/7–15–68. 60 rooms, 123 RV spaces. Restaurant, bar, 2 pools, 2 tennis courts, exercise room, shops. AE, MC, V.*

$$ ▥ **Las Misiones.** A pretty oasis of blue pools and green palms by the beach, this resort is big with group tours. It's also a good choice if you want to get away from it all—but you'll need a car or cab to get to town. A building just down the street from the hotel contains suites that have kitchens. ⊠ *Av. Misión de Loreto 148, 21850,* ☏ *657/7–12–80; 800/298–4105 in the U.S,* ☏ *657/7–12–83. 185 rooms, 32 suites. Restaurant, bar, 2 pools, 2 tennis courts. AE, MC, V.*

$ ▥ **El Cortez.** Easily the most popular hotel in San Felipe, the El Cortez has several types of accommodations, including moderately priced bungalows and modern hotel rooms with white walls, pastel bedspreads and drapes, and white-tile floors. The hotel's beachfront and second-story bars are both enduringly beloved, and the restaurant is the nicest water-view dining spot in town. The hotel is a five-minute walk from the malecón. ⊠ *Av. Mar de Cortés s/n, 21850,* ☏ *657/7–10–56,* ☏ *657/7–10–56. In the U.S.:* ⊠ *Box 1227, Calexico, CA 92232. 102 rooms. Restaurant, bar, pool. MC, V.*

Outdoor Activities and Sports

FISHING

The Sea of Cortés offers plentiful sea bass, snapper, corbina, halibut, and other game fish. Clamming is good here as well. Several companies offer sportfishing trips; among the most established are **Alex Sportfishing** (☎ 657/7–10–52), **Pelicanos** (☎ 657/7–11–88), and **San Felipe Sportfishing** (☎ 657/7–10–55). **Del Mar Cortés Charters** (✉ Box 9, San Felipe 21850, ☎ 657/7–13–03) conducts fishing trips, full- and half-day trimaran tours of the Sea of Cortés, and boat charters. It can also arrange kayak and Hobie Cat rentals through the El Dorado private community north of town.

BAJA NORTE A TO Z

Arriving and Departing

By Bus

Greyhound (☎ 619/239–1288; 800/231–2222 in the U.S.) serves Tijuana from San Diego several times daily; the Greyhound terminal in Tijuana is at Avenida Mexico at Calle 11 (☎ 66/86–06–95). **Five Star Tours/Mexicoach** (☎ 619/232–5049) runs buses from the trolley depot on the U.S. side of the border to their depot on Avenida Revolución in Tijuana. **ABC–US** (☎ 66/26–11–46) runs buses from the San Ysidro trolley stop to downtown Tijuana, Pueblo Amigo, Plaza Río Tijuana, and the Agua Caliente racetrack.

Buses connect all the towns in Baja Norte and are easy to use. Buses traveling to Rosarito no longer stop in town, but instead stop at the Rosarito exit on the toll road where taxis are waiting to transport passengers to town. There is no official bus station here; check at the hotels for bus schedule information.

Autotransportes de Baja California covers the entire Baja route and connects in Mexicali with buses to Guadalajara and Mexico City. **Elite** has first-class service to mainland Mexico. **Transportes del Pacífico** goes to Mexico City and other points on the mainland from Mexicali; **Transportes Norte de Sonora** frequents border towns in Baja and on mainland Mexico.

Bus stations are in Ensenada (✉ Av. Riveroll between Calles 10 and 11, ☎ 61/78–67–70 or 61/78–66–80), **Mexicali** (✉ Centro Cívico, Av. Independencia, ☎ 65/57–24–22), **San Felipe** (✉ Av. Mar Caribe at Av. Manzanillo, ☎ 657/7–15–16), **Tecate** (✉ Av. Benito Juárez and Calle Abelardo Rodríguez, ☎ 665/4–12–21), and **Tijuana** (✉ Calzada Lázaro Cárdenas and Blvd. Arroyo Alamar, ☎ 66/21–29–82).

By Car

From San Diego, U.S. 5 and I–805 end at the border crossing into Tijuana at San Ysidro; Highway 905 leads from I–5 and I–805 to the Tijuana border crossing at Otay Mesa, near the Tijuana airport. U.S. 94 from San Diego connects with U.S. 188 to the border at Tecate, 57 km (35 mi) east of San Diego. I–8 from San Diego connects with U.S. 111 at Calexico—203 km (126 mi) east—and the border crossing to Mexicali. San Felipe lies on the coast, 200 km (124 mi) south of Mexicali via Highway 5.

To head south into Baja from Tijuana, follow the signs for Ensenada Cuota, the toll road (also called Highway 1 and on newer signs the Scenic Highway) that runs south along the coast. There are two clearly marked exits for Rosarito, and one each for Puerto Nuevo, Bajamar, and Ensenada. The road is excellent, though it has some hair-raising curves atop the cliffs and is best driven in daylight (the stretch from Rosarito to Ensenada is one of the most scenic drives in Baja). Tollbooths accept U.S. and Mexican currency; tolls are usually about $1.60. Rest rooms are available near the booths. The alternate free road—

Highway 1D or Ensenada Libre—has been vastly improved, but it is difficult for the first-timer to navigate. Highway 1 continues south of Ensenada through San Quintín to Guerrero Negro at the border between Baja California and Baja Sur and on to the southernmost tip of Baja; it is no longer a toll road past Ensenada, however.

Mexico Highway 2 runs from Tijuana to Tecate and Mexicali. A toll road between Tijuana and Tecate opened in 1994, and another was completed between Tecate and Mexicali in 1995. The 134-km (83-mi) journey from Tecate east to Mexicali on La Rumorosa, as the road is known, is as exciting as a roller-coaster ride, with the highway twisting and turning down steep mountain grades and over flat, barren desert.

If you are traveling only as far as Ensenada or San Felipe, you do not need a tourist card, unless you stay longer than 72 hours. If you know you'll be traveling south of Ensenada, you can get the form at the **Mexican Customs Office** (⊠ Inside San Ysidro border crossing, ☎ 66/83–1405 or 66/84–77–90) . You must have Mexican auto insurance, available at agencies near the border.

Many U.S. car-rental companies do not allow their cars to be driven into Mexico (☞ Car Rental, *below*).

By Plane
Tijuana's Aeropuerto Alberado Rodriguez is located on the eastern edge of the city, near the Otay Mesa border crossing, and is served from cities in Baja and mainland Mexico by **Mexicana** (☎ 66/83–28–50), **Aeroméxico** (☎ 66/85–44–01), **AeroCalifornia** (☎ 66/84–21–00 or 66/84–28–76), and **Taesa** (☎ 66/84–84–84). **Mexicana** (☎ 65/52–93–91) and **Aeroméxico** (☎ 65/57–25–51) fly to Mexicali's international airport.

By Trolley
The **San Diego Trolley** (☎ 619/233–3004) travels from the Santa Fe Depot, at Kettner Boulevard and Broadway, to within 100 ft of the border every 15 minutes from 5 AM to midnight. The 45-minute trip costs $1.75.

Getting Around

By Bus
In **Tijuana,** the downtown station for buses within the city is at Calle 1a and Avenida Madero (☎ 66/86–95–15). Most city buses at the border will take you downtown; look for the ones marked CENTRO CAMIONERA. To catch the bus back to the border from downtown, go to Calle Benito Juárez (also called Calle 2a) between Avenidas Revolución and Constitución. **Five Star Tours/Mexicoach** (☎ 619/232–5049) runs buses from the trolley depot on the U.S. side of the border to their depot on Avenida Revolución in Tijuana. *Colectivos* (small vans usually painted white with colored stripes) cover neighborhood routes in most Baja cities and towns. The destination is usually painted on the windshield; look for them on main streets.

By Car
The best way to tour Baja Norte is by car, though the driving can be difficult and confusing at times. If you're just visiting Tijuana, Tecate, or Mexicali, it's easiest to park on the U.S. side of the border and walk across.

The combination of overpopulation, lack of infrastructure, and heavy winter rains makes many of **Tijuana**'s streets difficult to navigate by automobile. It's always best to stick to the main thoroughfares. There are parking lots along Avenida Revolución and at most major attractions. Most of **Rosarito** proper can be explored on foot, which is a good idea on weekends, when Boulevard Juárez has bumper-to-bumper traffic. To reach **Puerto Nuevo** and other points south, continue on Boulevard Juárez (also called Old Ensenada Highway and Ensenada Libre) through town. Most of **Ensenada**'s attractions are within five blocks of the waterfront; it is easy to take a long walking tour of the city. A car is necessary to reach La Bufadora and most of the beaches. When driving farther south to **San Quintín, Guerrero Negro,** and **Baja Sur,** be sure to fill up your gas tank when it's half full. Few towns appear on the highway, and you quickly have the feeling you are headed into the unknown (unless you're following a caravan of RVs). Don't drive at night, and watch your speed. You never know when a pothole or *arroyo* (riverbed) will challenge your driving skills.

Contacts and Resources

Car Rental

Avis (☎ 800/331–1212 in the U.S.) permits its cars to go from San Diego into Baja as far as 724 km (450 mi) south of the border. Cars must be returned by the renter to San Diego, and Mexican auto insurance is mandatory. **Courtesy Rentals** (✉ 2975 Pacific Hwy., San Diego, CA 92101, ☎ 619/497–4800; 800/252–9756 in the U.S.) allows its cars as far as Ensenada. **M&M Jeeps** (✉ 2200 El Cajon Blvd., San Diego, CA 92104, ☎ 619/297–1615, FAX 619/297–1617) rents two- and four-wheel-drive vehicles with packages covering tours of the entire Baja peninsula. **California Baja Rent-A-Car** (✉ 9245 Jamacha Blvd., Spring Valley, CA 91977, ☎ 619/470–8368 or 888/470–7368) rents four-wheel drive vehicles, convertibles, and sedans for use Baja-wide.

ENSENADA

Fiesta Rent-a-Car (☎ 61/76–33–44) has an office in the Hotel Corona at Boulevard Costero; **Hertz** (☎ 61/78–29–82) is on Avenida Blancarte between Calles 1 and 2.

TIJUANA

The larger U.S. rental agencies have offices at the Tijuana International Airport. Offices in town include **Avis** (✉ Av. Agua Caliente 3310, ☎ 66/86–40–04 or 66/86–37–18) and **Budget** (✉ Paseo de los Héroes 77, ☎ 66/34–33–03).

Emergencies

THROUGHOUT BAJA NORTE

Police (☎ 134), **Cruz Roja** (Red Cross, ☎ 132), and **Fire** (☎ 136).

TIJUANA

U.S. Consulate (☎ 66/81–74–00). The **Attorney General for the Protection of Tourists Hot Line** (☎ 66/88–05–55) takes calls weekdays to help with tourist complaints and problems.

Guided Tours

Baja California Tours (✉ 7734 Herschel Ave., Suite O, La Jolla, CA 92037, ☎ 619/454–7166, FAX 619/454–2703) has comfortable, informative bus trips throughout the Baja Peninsula. Seasonal day and overnight trips focus on whale-watching, fishing, shopping, wineries, sports, art and cultural events in Tijuana, Rosarito, Ensenada, and San Felipe. There are also adventure tours to Meling Ranch, a working ranch in the San Pedro Martir mountains about 240 km (150 mi) south of the border, and whale-watching trips to Baja California Sur.

Language Classes

A great way to get to know Ensenada and improve your Spanish is to attend weekend or week-long classes at the **International Spanish Institute of Ensenada** (☎ 61/76–01–09; 818/242–5263 in L.A.).

Reservation Agencies

Several companies specialize in arranging hotel reservations in Baja Norte. Contact **Baja Information** (⊠ 7860 Mission Center Ct., Suite 202, San Diego, CA 92108, ☎ 619/298–4105; 800/522–1516 in CA, NV, AZ; 800/225–2786 elsewhere in the U.S., Canada, Puerto Rico, FAX 619/294–7366); **Baja California Tours** (⊠ 7734 Herschel Ave., Suite O, La Jolla, CA 92037, ☎ 619/454–7166, FAX 619/454–2703); **Baja Lodging** (☎ 619/491–0682); **Mexico Condo Reservations** (⊠ 5801 Soledad Mountain Rd., La Jolla, CA 92037, ☎ 619/275–4500 or 800/262–4500, FAX 619/456–1350); **Mexico Resorts International** (⊠ 4126 Bonita Rd., Bonita, CA 91902, ☎ 619/422–6900 or 800/336–5454, FAX 619/472–6778).

Travel Club

Baja tours, Mexican auto insurance, a monthly newsletter, and workshops are available through **Discover Baja Travel Club** (⊠ 3089 Clairemont Dr., San Diego, CA 92117, ☎ 619/275–4225 or 800/727–2252, FAX 619/275–1836).

Visitor Information

Regional tourist offices are usually open weekdays 9–7 (though some may close in early afternoon for lunch) and weekends 9–1. **Ensenada** (⊠ Blvd. Costera 1477, ☎ 61/72–30–22 or 61/72–30–81; ⊠ Blvd. Costera at entrance to town, ☎ 61/78–24–11); **Mexicali** (⊠ Convention and Tourism Bureau, Calz. López Mateos at Calle Compresora, ☎ 65/52–23–76 or ☎ FAX 65/57–25–61; ⊠ State Secretary of Tourism Office, Calle Calafia at Calz. Independencia, ☎ 65/56–10–72 or 65/57–12–56); **Rosarito** (⊠ Blvd. Juárez, 2nd floor of Quinta Plaza shopping center, ☎ 661/2–03–96 or 661/2–30–78); **San Felipe** (⊠ Av. Mar de Cortés, ☎ 657/7–11–55 or 657/7–18–65); **Tecate** (⊠ Callejón Libertad, ☎ 665/4–10–95); **Tijuana Chamber of Commerce** (⊠ Av. Revolución and Calle 1, ☎ 66/88–16–85); and the **Tijuana Convention and Tourism Bureau** (⊠ Inside San Ysidro border crossing, ☎ 66/84–04–81 or 66/84–77–90; ⊠ Av. Revolución between Calles 3 and 4, ☎ 66/83–05–30 or 66/84–05–37).

BAJA CALIFORNIA SUR

Baja Sur was nearly inaccessible by land until the 1,708-km-long (1,059-mi-long) Transpeninsular Highway, also called Mexico Highway 1, was completed in 1973. Until then, commerce was conducted via boats from mainland Mexico, across the Sea of Cortés. After the paved, four-lane road was completed, travelers gradually found their way south, drawn by the wild terrain and the pristine beaches along the Pacific Ocean and Sea of Cortés coastlines. In 1974 Baja California Sur became Mexico's 30th state, and the population and tourism began to increase. Still, Baja Sur remains a mysterious and largely undeveloped land. Highway 1, which travels through some of the most desolate desert and mountains imaginable, could hardly be called a freeway. Most people still make their way here via plane.

Whale-watching has winter appeal in Guerrero Negro, Scammon's Lagoon, San Ignacio Lagoon, and Magdalena Bay. History buffs enjoy Loreto, where Padre Eusebio Kino established the first mission in the Californias. La Paz, today a busy governmental center and sportfishing city, was the first Spanish settlement in Baja. At the southernmost tip of the peninsula, where the Pacific Ocean and the Sea of Cortés merge, fishing aficionados, golfers, and sun worshippers gather in Los Cabos, one of Mexico's most popular and most expensive coastal resorts.

Baja California Sur

Isla Angel de la Guarda

Isla del Tiburón

Hermosillo

Mazatán

Pta. San Gabriel

San Rafael

Tecoripa

Cieneguita

Guaymas

15

El Arco

1

San Ignacio

Santa Rosalía
Mulege

Isla Lobos

Ciudad Obregón

Laguna de San Ignacio

TO GUERRERO NEGRO

Pta. Concepción

Navajoa

1

Bahía Concepción

Huatabampo

15

BAJA

Golfo de California

Loreto

La Poza

Isla Carmen

Las Grullas Márgen Derecha

Misión San Javier

Topolobampo

CALIFORNIA

SIERRA GIGANTA

TO LOS MOCHIS

Insurgentes

Constitución

Isla San José

SUR

Bahía Magdalena

Santa Rita

Isla Partida

Isla Santa Margarita

Bahía la Paz

Pichilingue

TO MAZATLÁN

1

Isla Cerralvo

La Paz

PACIFIC OCEAN

Bahía los Muertos

Punta Pescadero

El Triunfo

Los Barriles

Buenavista

La Ribera

Todos Santos

Santiago

SIERRA DE LA LAGUNA

Cabo Pulmo

9

1

San José del Cabo

Cabo San Lucas

N

KEY

—— Rail Lines

🚢 Ferry Lines

0 _____ 100 miles

0 _____ 150 km

Guerrero Negro and Scammon's Lagoon

720 km (446 mi) south of Tijuana, 771 km (478 mi) north of La Paz.

Humans aren't the only mammals to migrate below the border in winter. Every December through March, thousands of great gray whales swim 8,000 km (5,000 mi) south from the Bering Strait off Alaska to the tip of the Baja Peninsula. For those few months, people come from all over the world to Guerrero Negro and a few bays and lagoons farther south. Up to 6,000 whales stop close to the shore at several spots along the Baja coast, including Scammon's Lagoon—at the 28th parallel, just over the state line between Baja California and Baja Sur—to give birth to their calves. Far from diminutive, the newborns weigh about half a ton and drink nearly 50 gallons of milk each day. In the past, Guerrero Negro was the headquarters for whale-watching trips, and it's still the easiest place to spot the whales from shore or to arrange a boat trip amid the pods of whales in Scammon's Lagoon. But many of the whale-watching operators have moved their tours farther south to Magdalena Bay and San Ignacio Lagoon. Both are accessed from San Ignacio, Loreto, or La Paz (☞ *below*).

If it weren't for the whales and the Transpeninsular Highway, which passes near town, few would venture to **Guerrero Negro** (☞ Baja California [North] map), a town of 10,000. Those traveling south can easily bypass the town. The name Guerrero Negro, which means Black Warrior, was derived from a whaling ship that ran aground in nearby Scammon's Lagoon in 1858. Near the Desierto de Vizcaíno (Vizcaíno Desert), on the Pacific Ocean, the area is best known for its salt pans, which provide work for much of the town's population and produce one-third of the world's salt supply. Saltwater collects in some 780 square km (300 square mi) of sea-level ponds and evaporates quickly in the desert heat, leaving great blocks of salt. The town is dusty, windy, and generally unpleasant, but it happens to be a favored roosting spot for osprey, which build huge nests on power poles around town.

Scammon's Lagoon is about 27 km (17 mi) south, down a rough but passable sand road that crosses the salt flats. The lagoon got its name from U.S. explorer Charles Melville Scammon of Maine, who discovered it off the coast of Baja in the mid-1800s. On his first expedition to the lagoon, Scammon and his crew collected more than 700 barrels of valuable whale oil, and the whale rush was on. Within 10 years, nearly all the whales in the lagoon had been killed, and it took almost a century for the whale population to increase to what it had been before Scammon arrived. It wasn't until the 1940s that the U.S. and Mexican governments took measures to protect the whales and banned the whalers from the lagoon.

These days, whale-watching boats—most of them *pangas* (small skiffs)—must get permission from the Mexican government to enter Scammon's Lagoon, now a national park called **Parque Natural de Ballenas Gris** (Gray Whale Natural Park). The other major whale-watching spots (also protected by the government) are farther south at **Laguna San Ignacio** and **Bahía Magdalena,** both on the Pacific coast. If traveling on your own, you can reach Laguna San Ignacio from the town of San Ignacio (☞ *below*). Bahía Magdalena—regulars call it "Mag Bay"—is about a four-hour drive across the peninsula from La Paz. Fishermen will take you out in their boats to get closer to the whales at both places. But for a better view, and an easier stay in this rugged country, travel with an outfitter who will arrange your transportation, accommodations, and time on the water. Whales will come close to your boat, rising majestically from the water, and sometimes swim close enough to be patted on the back.

Dining and Lodging

There are several hotels in Guerrero Negro, none of which is worth visiting for its own sake. Double-occupancy rooms cost from about $25 to $70 per day; rates tend to increase during the peak whale-watching season from January through March. None of the hotels has heat, and winter nights can be downright frigid. Credit cards are not normally accepted, but the hotels do take traveler's checks. The food in the hotel restaurants recommended below is far from haute cuisine, but it's about as good as you're going to get in the area.

$ ╳ **La Espinitá.** This small restaurant and market is a good choice if you don't want to spend the night in Guerrero Negro. The restaurant serves good homestyle Mexican and American breakfasts, along with standard enchiladas, tacos, and fish for lunch and dinner. The market next door has cold drinks, purified water, and snacks. ⌧ *Hwy. 1 at 28th parallel next to La Pinta, Domicilio Conocido,* ☎ *No phone. No credit cards.*

$ ╳▥ **Malarrimo.** This trailer park and Mexican and seafood restaurant has a 10-room motel—Cabañas San Miguelito—with private baths and TV. It fills up quickly and is one of the best deals in town. The restaurant is a favorite gathering spot for caravans heading farther south. The grilled or steamed fresh fish, lobster, and clams are legendary, and the dining room walls are covered with maps and photos of Baja. Whale-watching excursions from the hotel are also immensely popular and are run by knowledgeable local guides. ⌧ *Blvd. Zapata, 23940,* ☎ *115/7–02–50,* ℻ *115/7–01–00. 10 rooms. Restaurant. No credit cards.*

$$ ▥ **La Pinta.** A few kilometers outside of town, looking like an oasis of palms in the desert, La Pinta is the largest hotel in the area. The clean, functional rooms are dependable, the setting more attractive than that of other local lodgings, and the American-Mexican restaurant decent, but the rates are high for the area. Package deals are sometimes available if you plan to use La Pinta hotels throughout the peninsula. Whale-watching excursions can be arranged here. ⌧ *La Pinta Hwy. 1 at 28th parallel, Domicilio Conocido, 23940,* ☎ *115/7–13–01 or 800/262–4500,* ℻ *115/7–13–06. 26 rooms. Restaurant. MC, V.*

Outdoor Activities and Sports

WHALE-WATCHING

The gray whales that migrate from the Bering Strait are Guerrero Negro's biggest attraction. With a sturdy vehicle you can drive the 24-km (15-mi) washboard dirt and sand road to Scammon's Lagoon and arrange a trip with the boat captains who await passengers there. Trips usually cost $15 per hour for a boat with up to four passengers. Start early to take advantage of the calmest water and best viewing conditions. Whale-watching from the shores of the lagoon can be disappointing without binoculars. But it is still an impressive sight to see the huge mammals spouting water high into the air, their 12-ft-wide tails striking the water.

Eco-Tours Malarrimo (⌧ Blvd. Zapata, 23940, ☎ 115/7–02–50, ℻ 115/7–01–00) is the best tour operator in the area. They have four-hour trips with bus transportation to and from the lagoon, three hours in small skiffs among the whales with English-speaking guides, and lunch for $37 per person. Reserve several months in advance, especially for February when whales appear in abundance.

San Ignacio

227 km (141 mi) southeast of Guerrero Negro.

This small town is set in the mountains off the highway between the two coasts, near a wide river. The **Spanish mission** on the town square is one of the best preserved on the peninsula. Some groups based in the United States use the hotels in town as a base for whale-watching trips to Laguna San Ignacio and Magdalena Bay.

Lodging

$$ 🏨 **La Pinta.** If the room rates weren't so high, this small hotel would be a wonderful Baja hideaway. White arches frame the courtyard and pool, and the rooms are decorated with folk art and wood furnishings. Both the river and town are within walking distance. The hotel staff can set up whale-watching trips with local guides. ✉ *2 km (1 mi) west of Hwy. 1 on unnamed road into town, Apdo. 37, 23943,* ☎ *115/40–300 or 800/262–4500. 28 rooms. Restaurant, bar, pool. No credit cards.*

Outdoor Activities and Sports

WHALE-WATCHING

San Ignacio is the base for trips to Laguna San Ignacio arranged through **Baja Discovery** (✉ Box 152527, San Diego, CA 92195, ☎ 619/262–0700 in San Diego or 800/829–2252 elsewhere in the U.S.). The company has a comfortable base camp at the lagoon. The tour includes round-trip transport from San Diego to San Ignacio, with an overnight at the La Pinta hotel in San Ignacio, before and after overnight camping trips at the lagoon.

Kuyima Tours in San Ignacio (☎ 115/4–00–26) offers transport between La Paz and the lagoon in San Ignacio and uses local guides as boat captains.

Santa Rosalia

77 km (48 mi) southeast of San Ignacio.

You'll find a fascinating mix of French, Mexican, and American Old West–style architecture in the dusty mining town of Santa Rosalia. It's known for its **Iglesia Santa Barbara,** a prefabricated iron church designed by Alexandre-Gustave Eiffel, creator of the Eiffel Tower. Be sure to stop by **El Boleo** (✉ Av. Obregón at Calle 4), the best-known bakery in Baja, where fresh breads bring a lineup of eager customers weekday mornings at 10.

Lodging

$$ 🏨 **El Morro.** The best hotel in town is located on the waterfront—it's not on a beach, but there is a pool. Rooms, in a series of one-story buildings connected by rock arches and tiled mosaics, are large and comfortable. Some have terraces and tiled bathrooms. The restaurant serves bountiful Mexican combo plates, imported steak, and local seafood. The bar is a popular gathering spot for tourists. ✉ *Hwy 1, 1½ km (1 mi) south of Santa Rosalia, 23900,* ☎ 🅕🅐🅧 *115/2–0414. 39 rooms. Restaurant, bar, pool. MC, V.*

$$ 🏨 **Hotel Frances.** The former glory of this 1886 French mansion shines through despite its modest furnishings. The Frances sits on a steep hill, and many of its refurbished rooms open onto a second-story porch with views of town and the sea. There's a small pool in the courtyard, but no restaurant. ✉ *Av. 11 de Julio at Calle Jean M. Cousteau, 23900,* ☎ 🅕🅐🅧 *115/2–2052. 17 rooms. Pool. No credit cards.*

Mulege

64 km (40 mi) south of Santa Rosalia.

Once a mission settlement and now a charming tropical town set beside a river flowing into the Sea of Cortés, Mulege has become a popular base for exploring the nearby mountains and for kayaking in **Bahía Concepción,** the largest protected bay in Baja. The village of some 3,500 residents swells in winter, when Americans and Canadians fleeing the cold arrive in motor homes. There are several campgrounds outside town and a few good hotels and restaurants in town and on the coast.

Lodging

$$$ ☉ **Hotel Serenidad.** A Mulege mainstay for Baja aficionados since the late 1960s, the Serenidad is owned by Don and Nancy Johnson and their family, longtime Baja residents. The hotel is a delightful escape, with simple rooms in brick and stucco buildings scattered under bougainvillea vines and fruit trees. Some rooms have fireplaces and/or air-conditioning; all have private baths. The Saturday night pig roast is a Baja tradition. ⊠ *Hwy. 1, 2½ km (1½ mi) south of Mulege, 23900,* ☎ *115/3–05–30,* FAX *115/3–03–11. 29 rooms. Restaurant, bar, pool, private airstrip. MC, V.*

$ ☉ **Hacienda.** Guests read and lounge in rocking chairs by the pool or at stools along the bar at this small, comfortable hotel. Kayak trips and tours to the cave paintings in the mountains can be arranged, and special fiestas are planned for groups. Even when other hotels in the area are nearly empty, the Hacienda is filled with Europeans attracted by the ambience and incredibly low, by Baja standards, room rates. ⊠ *Calle Madero, 23900,* ☎ FAX *115/3–00–21. 20 rooms. Restaurant, bar, pool, travel services. No credit cards.*

Outdoor Activities and Sports

KAYAKING

Baja Tropicales (⊠ Box 60, Mulege, BCS 23900, ☎ 115/3–04–09, FAX 115/3–01–90) offers kayaks, wet suits, and other gear and several types of kayaking tours, including day trips and overnighters in the area of Mulege. Whale-watching trips on the Pacific coast are also available.

Loreto

134 km (83 mi) south of Mulege.

Loreto's Sea of Cortés setting is truly spectacular. The gold and green hills of the Sierra Gigante seem to tumble into the cobalt sea. Rain is rare. According to the local promoters, the skies are clear 360 days of the year. There are few bugs to plague vacationers—the dry, desert climate is not one in which insects thrive.

Loreto was the site of the first California mission, founded in 1697 by Jesuit Father Juan María Salvatierra. Seventy-two years later, a Franciscan monk from Mallorca, Spain—Father Junípero Serra—set out from Loreto to establish a chain of missions from San Diego to San Francisco, in the land then known as Alta California. Four Indian tribes—the Kikiwa, Cochimi, Cucapa, and Kumyaii—inhabited the barren lands of Baja when Father Salvatierra arrived. It didn't take long for war and European diseases to nearly obliterate them.

Mexico won its independence in 1821, and the missions were gradually abandoned, as priests were ordered home to Spain. Then with the withering of the mission and the 1829 hurricane that virtually destroyed the settlement, the capital of the Californias was moved to La Paz. For a century the village languished. The U.S. fishermen who rediscovered

Loreto were a hardy breed who flew down in their own aircraft and went after marlin and sailfish in open launches.

In 1976, when the coffers filled up with oil revenue, the government tapped the Loreto area for development. Streets were paved in the dusty little village, and telephone service, electricity, potable water, and sewage systems were installed in both the town and the surrounding area. Even an international airport was built. A luxury hotel and championship tennis center were opened in Nopoló, about 8 km (5 mi) south of town. Then the money dried up, investors could no longer be found, and everything came to a halt.

With its population of 10,000, Loreto is a good place to escape the crowds, relax, and go fishing. The fears of sports enthusiasts that the town would be spoiled have thus far been largely unfounded, though the residential trailer parks are filling up and private homes are clustered in secluded enclaves. Loreto is much the way it was decades ago, except that now it is more accessible.

You could spend 15 minutes looking around downtown Loreto and still have time left over. The renovated **malecón**, built in 1991, has turned the waterfront into a pleasant place for a stroll. A marina shelters yachts and the panga fleet, the adjoining beach is a popular gathering spot for locals, especially on Sunday afternoons, and the beach playground has an assortment of play equipment for children.

Loreto's only historic sight is **La Misión de Nuestra Señora de Loreto,** the first of the California missions. The stone walls, beamed ceilings, gilded altar, and primitive-style portraits of its priests are worth seeing. **El Museo de los Misiones,** also called the Museum of Anthropology and History (☎ 113/5–05–41), contains religious relics, tooled leather saddles used in the 19th century, and displays of Baja's history. It's next door to the mission; hours are erratic.

Nopoló, an area being developed for luxury resorts, is about 8 km (5 mi) south of Loreto. The nine-court tennis complex and 18-hole golf course are ready for play, and private homes are appearing in the neighborhood.

In **Puerto Escondido,** 16 km (10 mi) down the road from Nopoló, the marina contains more than 100 boat slips. An RV park, Tripui, has a good restaurant, a few motel rooms, snack shop, bar, stores, showers, laundry, a pool, and tennis courts. A boat ramp has been completed at the marina; to pay the fee required to launch here, go to the port captain's offices (☎ 113/5–06–56, FAX 113/5–04–65) just south of the ramp; the offices are open weekdays 8–3.

Isla Danzante, 5 km (3 mi) southeast of Puerto Escondido, has good reefs and diving opportunities. Picnic trips to nearby **Coronado Island,** inhabited only by sea lions, may be arranged in Loreto at Nopoló or in Puerto Escondido. The snorkeling and scuba diving on the island are excellent. Danzante and other islands off Loreto are now part of the Parque Marítimo Nacional Bahía de Loreto. Commercial fishing boats are not allowed within the 60-square-km (23-square-mi) park.

A trip to **Mision San Javier,** 32 km (20 mi) southwest of Loreto, is one of the best ways to see Baja at its most picturesque. A high-clearance vehicle is essential for the three-hour drive to the mission—and don't even try getting here if the dirt and gravel road is muddy. The road climbs past small ranches, palm groves, and the steep cliffs of the Cerro de la Giganta. Unmarked trails lead off the road to caves and remnants of **Indian cave paintings.** The mission village is a remote community of some 300 residents, many of whom come outdoors when visitors arrive. The church, built in 1699, is impressive and well preserved, set amid fruit orchards. It is often locked; ask anyone hanging about to find the person with the keys and you'll be allowed to go inside to look at the stained-glass windows and ornate altar. Slip a few pesos into the contribution box as a courtesy to the village's inhabitants, who need all the help they can get to keep the church well maintained. Though you can drive to San Javier on your own, it helps to have a guide along to lead you to the caves and Indian paintings. Most hotels, or the tour companies listed below, can arrange tours.

Dining and Lodging

$$$ ✕ **El Nido.** Hungry for steak, chicken, and bodacious Mexican combo plates? Then this is your place. It's the fanciest restaurant in town, though clean shorts and T-shirts are the costume of choice. The wood and brass decor, courteous waiters, and abundance of wood make up for prices that seem outrageously high for the neighborhood. ⊠ *Calle Salvatierra s/n,* ☎ *13/50–28–54. MC, V.*

$$ ✕ **Anthony's Pizza.** Pizzas, omelets, grilled fresh fish, well-prepared burgers, and homemade brownies and muffins all keep this small restaurant packed. The owner and staff are familiar with customers' favorites—and eager to hand out samples of new concoctions. ⊠ *Calle Francisco Madero 29,* ☎ *113/5–07–33. No credit cards.*

$$ ✕ **El Super Burro.** This large, palapa-covered restaurant a half block from the waterfront is as popular with locals as tourists. Meats are grilled at the front of the dining room, where cooks juggle take-out and dine-in orders. The Mexican combination plate isn't outstanding, but it is plentiful; a better choice is the fresh fish. If you're on a budget, fill up on tacos or baked potatoes stuffed with cheese and meat. ⊠ *Paseo Hidalgo between Madero and the malecón,* ☎ *No phone. No credit cards.*

$ ✕ **Café Olé.** The best taquería in town also serves good burgers, ice-cream cones, chocolate shakes, and french fries. ⊠ *Calle Francisco Madero,* ☎ *113/5–04–96. No credit cards.*

$$ 🏨 **La Pinta.** Part of a chain of Baja California hotels, La Pinta is a collection of plain brick buildings with spacious (but unremarkable) air-conditioned rooms with satellite TVs, and a large pool. ⊠ *Blvd. Misión de Loreto, 23880,* ☎ *113/5–00–25 or 800/54–23–283; 800/522–1516 in CA, AZ, NV; 800/225–2786 elsewhere in the U.S. and Canada,* 𝕱𝕬𝕏 *113/ 5–00–26. 48 rooms. Restaurant, bar, pool, tennis court, fishing. MC, V.*

$$ 🏨 **Oasis.** One of the original fishing camps, Oasis remains a favorite with those who want to spend as much time as possible on the water. Many of the rooms, set amid an oasis of palms, have a view of the water. The hotel has its own fleet of skiffs. ⊠ *Calle de la Playa at Zaragoza, Box 17, 23880,* ☎ *113/5–01–12,* 𝕱𝕬𝕏 *113/5–07–95. 35 rooms. Pool, tennis court, boating, fishing. MC, V.*

$$ 🏨 **Plaza Loreto.** Since its opening in 1992, the Plaza Loreto has garnered a loyal following of Loreto regulars who appreciate the prime downtown location near the old mission. The two-story hotel has an upstairs bar overlooking the street. Rooms are not consistently maintained—the best of the lot have TVs, coffeemakers, and huge showers. Check a few before choosing one. Construction on the pool has stopped, and the restaurant is not always open. ⊠ *Paseo Hidalgo, 23880,* ☎ *113/5–02–80,* 𝕱𝕬𝕏 *113/5–08–55. 20 rooms. Bar. MC, V.*

$$ 🏨 **Villas de Loreto.** This is one of Loreto's nicest hideaways, just south of town. There are 10 large rooms with refrigerators and front porches, along with a large swimming pool. An RV campground is behind the hotel buildings. Bikes are available for guests' use free of charge, and horseback riding, kayaking (for experienced paddlers), and fishing tours can be arranged. Smoking is not permitted in the rooms or on the property. Continental breakfast is included in the room rate. To

get here, turn right off Salvatierra onto Madero and drive across the dry riverbed to signs for the hotel. ⊠ *Antonio Mijares at beach, 23880,* ☏ FAX *113/5–05–86. 10 rooms. Pool, laundry service. MC, V.*

Outdoor Activities and Sports

FISHING

Fishing put Loreto on the map, especially for American sports enthusiasts. Cabrillo and snapper are caught year-round; yellowtail in the spring; and dorado, marlin, and sailfish in the summer. If you plan to fish, bring tackle, as top-notch gear can be difficult to find, though some sportfishing fleets do update their equipment regularly. All Loreto-area hotels can arrange fishing, and many own skiffs. Local fishermen congregate with their small boats on the beach at the north and south ends of town. **Alfredo's Sportfishing** (⊠ Blvd. Mateos at Juárez, across from marina, ☏ 113/5–01–65, FAX 113/5–05–90) has good fishing guides. **Arturo's Fishing Fleet** (⊠ Calle Hidalgo between the plaza and the marina, ☏ 113/5–04–09, FAX 113/5–00–22) has several types of boats and fishing packages. **The Baja Big Fish Company** (⊠ Paseo Hidalgo 19 by the plaza, ☏ 113/5–00–78; 888/533–2252 in the U.S., FAX 113/5–00–78; 760/414–1855 in the U.S.) has full fishing packages from the United States, including air and hotel, as well as fishing trips if you are in Loreto. Baja Big Fish specializes in tag-and-release and in light tackle and fly-fishing.

GOLF

The 18-hole **Loreto Campo de Golf** (☏ 113/5–07–88 or 113/3–05–54) is along Nopoló Bay at the south side of the Fonatur resort. Several hotels in Loreto have golf packages and reduced or free greens fees.

KAYAKING

The islands off Loreto's shores are ideal sites for kayakers. Tours and rentals can be arranged through the Villas de Loreto (☞ Lodging, *above*), Baja Outpost (☞ Scuba Diving, *below*), and **Calafia Sea Kayaking** (⊠ Blvd. Mateos by the marina, ☏ 113/5–04–08).

TENNIS

The **Loreto Tennis Center** (☏ 113/5–07–00), 8 km (5 mi) south of town, has nine courts open to the public.

SCUBA DIVING

The **Baja Outpost** (⊠ Blvd. Mateos near the Oasis Hotel, ☏ 113/5–11–34; 800/789–5625 in the U.S., FAX 113/5–11–34; 310/306–6090 in the U.S.), has scuba certification courses, dive trips to the islands, kayaking, gear rental, and guest rooms for clients.

Shopping

There are few opportunities for shopping in Loreto. **El Alacran,** in the small complex behind the church on Calle Salvatierra, has remarkable folk art, jewelry, and sportswear. You can also find some nice silver shops in this complex. Groceries and ice are available on Calle Salvatierra at **El Pescador,** the town's only supermarket.

La Paz

354 km (220 mi) south of Loreto.

La Paz is one of those cities that makes you wish you'd been here 30 years ago. In the slowest of times, in late summer when the heat is oppressive, you can easily see how it must have been when it was a quiet place, living up to its name: "Peace." Today the city has a population of 175,000, with a large contingent of retirees from the United States and Canada. Travelers use La Paz as both a destination in itself and a stopping-off point en route to Los Cabos. Some call it the most Mexican city on the peninsula, with the feel of a mainland community that has adapted to tourism while retaining its character. And there is always excellent scuba diving and sportfishing in the gulf—La Paz is the stop-off for divers and fishermen headed for **Cerralvo, La Partida,** and the **Espíritu Santo** islands, where parrot fish, manta rays, neons, and angels blur the clear waters by the shore, and marlin, dorado, and yellowtail leap out of the deep, dark sea.

Hernán Cortés and his soldiers were drawn to La Paz in 1535 by stories of the magnificent pearls and beautiful women. In 1720 the Jesuits arrived to civilize and convert the Indians. Instead, they inadvertently decimated the local populace by introducing smallpox. Within 30 years, there was no one left to convert.

A permanent settlement was established here in 1811, when the rest of Mexico was being torn apart by revolution. La Paz became a refuge for those escaping the mainland wars. Then after a hurricane leveled Loreto in 1829, La Paz became the capital of the Californias. In 1853 a group of U.S. southerners, led by William Walker, tried to make La Paz a slave state, but Mexicans quickly banished them. Peace reigned for the next century. In 1940 disease wiped out the oyster beds, and with the pearls gone, La Paz no longer attracted prospectors and was left alone.

La Paz officially became the capital of Baja California Sur in 1974, and it is now the state's largest settlement. The city underwent considerable restoration in the late 1990s, with the main road between the airport and town enlarged to four lanes and construction of new residential areas constantly under way. It is the site of the governor's house and the state's bureaucracy, jail, and power plant, as well as the ferry port to Mazatlán.

Sights to See

㉔ The **malecón** is La Paz's seawall, tourist zone, and main drag rolled into one. As you enter town from the southwest, Paseo Alvaro Obregón turns into the malecón at a cluster of high-rise condos. A luxurious resort hotel has opened at the 500-acre **Fidepaz Marina** at the west end of town; the marina itself has been fully constructed but has yet to open.

㉖ A two-story white gazebo is the focus of the **Malecón Plaza,** a small cement square where musicians sometimes appear on weekend nights. The tourist information center sits beside the gazebo. Across the street, Calle 16 de Septiembre leads inland to the city center. Around the plaza and all along the malecón, a steady stream of teens cruise through town, red and yellow car lights twinkling around their license plates and the latest U.S. hits blaring on their radios. **Marina La Paz,** at the southwest end of the malecón, is an ever-growing development with condominium buildings, vacation homes, and a pleasant walkway lined with casual cafés.

㉗ ㉘ La Paz's downtown is the busiest in Baja Sur, with shops crammed together on narrow crowded streets. The *zócalo* (central plaza) also goes by the names **Plaza Constitución** and Jardín Velazco. **La Catedral de Nuestra Señora de La Paz** (Our Lady of La Paz Cathedral) is downtown's big attraction. It was built in 1860 near the site of La Paz's first mission, which was established in 1860 by Jesuit Jaime Bravo. You'll see it just across from the zócalo.

㉙ The **Biblioteca de las Californias,** a library specializing in the history of Baja California, has reproductions of local prehistoric cave paintings, oil paintings of the missions, and the best collection of historical documents on the peninsula. Films and lectures are sometimes presented

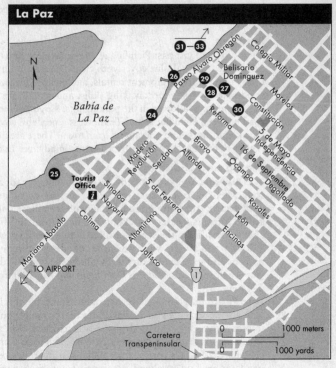

La Paz

in the evening. Check the bulletin board outside the library or ask the librarian for information. ✉ *Madero at Cinco de Mayo,* ☎ *112/2–01–62.* ☉ *Weekdays 8–6.*

③⓪ La Paz's culture and heritage is well represented at the **Museum of Anthropology,** constructed in 1983. Exhibits include re-creations of Comondo and Las Palmas Indian villages, photos of cave paintings found in Baja, and copies of Cortés's writings on first sighting La Paz. Many exhibit descriptions are written only in Spanish, but the museum's staff will help translate for you. ✉ *Altamirano and Cinco de Mayo,* ☎ *112/ 2–01–62.* ▣ *Donation.* ☉ *Weekdays 8–6, Sat. 9–2.*

Northeast of town, Paseo Alvaro Obregón, or the malecón, becomes what is commonly known as the **Pichilingue Road,** which curves northeast along the bay about 16 km (10 mi) to the terminals where the ferries from Mazatlán and Topolobampo arrive and many of the sportfishing boats depart. Just outside town the road divides, with outgoing traffic climbing up a steep cliff overlooking deserted beaches.

③① The **Government House,** surrounded by guards and gates, is a few kilometers south of the spot where the road divides. Home of the governor of Baja California Sur, the house has an impressive view of the curving **③②** bay and city lights. At the **Ferry Terminal,** south of Government House, warehouses serve as waiting rooms. Roadside stands serving oysters and grilled fish line the highway across the street.

③③ Since the time of pirate ships and Spanish invaders, **Pichilingue** was known for its preponderance of oysters bearing black pearls. In 1940 an unknown disease killed off all of them, leaving the beach deserted. Today Pichilingue is a pleasant place for sunbathing and watching sportfishing boats bringing in their hauls. Palapa-covered restaurants on the beach serve cold beer and oysters *diablo* (raw oysters steeped in a fiery-hot sauce), as well as some of the freshest and least expensive grilled fish in town.

Beaches

Off a dirt road just past Pichilingue, **Playa Tecolote and Playa Coyote** are adjacent crystal-blue coves with clean beaches. Both have restaurants, watersports equipment rentals, and palapas for shade. This is a good place to test your kayaking skills, and rentals are available on site. Camping is allowed in the parking lots. **Playa Balandra,** on a side road between Pichilingue and Tecolote, is a peaceful cove favored by kayak and snorkeling operations from town. There are no facilities or rentals at this beach. Make arrangements in advance in town.

Dining and Lodging

$$$ ✕ **El Bismark.** You've got to go a bit out of your way for a local home-
★   style Mexican restaurant. Specialties include carne asada, served with beans, guacamole, and homemade tortillas; and enormous grilled lobsters. Seafood cocktails are huge, too, and fish fillets are always fresh from the sea. You'll see families settle down for hours at long wood tables, while waitresses divide their attention between patrons and soap operas on the TV above the bar. The desultory service is a drawback. ⊠ *Santos Degollado and Av. Altamirano,* ☎ *112/2–48–54. MC, V.*

$$ ✕ **La Paz-Lapa.** The noise level here is deafening, but this is a fun place, with a wide-screen TV in the bar and waiters so jolly you expect them to break into song. The food—basic beef, chicken, fish, and Mexican selections—is tasty and plentiful. Also referred to as Carlos 'n' Charlie's, La Paz-Lapa is part of the popular Carlos Anderson chain. Live bands appear on weekend evenings on the back patio. ⊠ *Paseo Obregón at Calle 16 de Septiembre,* ☎ *112/5–92–90. MC, V.*

$$ ✕ **La Pazta.** Locals who crave international fare rave about this trattoria with sleek black-and-white decor and excellent homemade pasta. Imported cheeses and wines, fresh herbs and vegetables, and bracing espresso and cappucino are all welcome changes from the local seafood and taco fare. ⊠ *Allende 36,* ☎ *112/5–11–95. MC, V.*

$$ ✕ **Pazeño Grill.** One of the more pleasant spots for a meal with a view of the sea, this second-story eatery is located at the north end of the malecón. The ambitious Argentinian-style menu includes a good beef fillet stuffed with ham and mozzarella cheese, mussels in garlic sauce, lobster with mushrooms and spinach, and beef with Argentinian churrasco sauce. ⊠ *Paseo Obregón.* ☎ *112/3–30–33. No credit cards.*

$ ✕ **El Quinto Sol Restaurante Vegetariano.** El Quinto's bright green exterior walls are painted with Indian snake symbols and smiling suns. The back room is a natural-foods store stocked with grains, soaps, lotions, oils, and books. To readjust your travel-weary stomach try the restaurant's yogurt with bananas and wheat germ, ceviche tostadas, and a non-meat version of machaca. ⊠ *Belisario Domínguez and Independencia,* ☎ *112/2–16–92. No credit cards.*

$ ✕ **Taco Hermanos Gonzalez.** La Paz has plenty of great taco stands, but the Gonzalez brothers still corner the market with their hunks of fresh fish wrapped in corn tortillas. Bowls of condiments line the small stand, and the best fast food in town draws crowds of sidewalk munchers. ⊠ *Mutualismo and Esquerro,* ☎ *No phone. No credit cards.*

$$$ ⌑ **Club El Moro.** A vacation-ownership resort with suite rentals on a nightly and weekly basis, El Moro has a garden of lush palms and a densely landscaped pool area with one of the few hot tubs in town. You can recognize the building by its stark-white turrets and domes. Rooms are Mediterranean in style and decor, with arched windows, Mexican tiles, and private balconies. Some rooms have kitchens and can sleep up to five persons. The restaurant is elegant and excellent.

✉ *Km 2 Carretera a Pichilingue, Box 357, 23010,* ☎ 🖷 *112/2–40–84 or 112/5–28–28. 17 suites. Restaurant, bar, pool. AE, MC, V.*

$$$ 🏨 **Crowne Plaza Resort.** By far the loveliest and most modern resort in La Paz, this hacienda-style inn sits beside the Marina Fidepaz. Its suites range in size and style; the largest have two bedrooms and kitchenette. The pool flows through several levels in the courtyard, and there is a children's playground. The restaurant, with its cordial service, serene ambience, and excellent cuisine, has become a favorite among local executives. The well equipped fitness center has sauna and steam baths and a squash court. Future plans include an artificial beach, 150 more rooms, and a spa. ✉ *Lote A, Marina Fidepaz, Box 482, 23000,* ☎ *112/4–08–30 or 800/227–6963,* 🖷 *112/4–08–37. 54 suites. Restaurant, bar, pool, health club, nightclub, travel services. AE, MC, V.*

$$$ 🏨 **Mar y Sol.** If you plan to stay a week or more, you'll be delighted
★ with these lovely apartments. Each is furnished with folk art, colorful serapes, leather *equipale* (pigskin) chairs, and full kitchens. Fountains and a square swimming pool are set amid palms and flowering plants. It's a two-block walk to the beach, and the owners can arrange fishing, diving, and whale-watching tours. ✉ *Calle Insurgentes at Margaritas, Box 438, 23000,* ☎ *112/5–24–67,* 🖷 *112/2–01–80. 10 apartments. Pool. No credit cards.*

$$ 🏨 **Club Hotel Cantamar.** Fernando Aguilar, the most famous scuba diving master in the area, has expanded his operation to include this small sports lodge beside a private marina. Rooms have balconies that look out on the pool and the sea. The restaurant is in the clubhouse beside the dive boats. This is the ideal hangout for divers, who have easy access to some of the best diving in the Sea of Cortés. ✉ *Carretera Pichilingue, 14 km (9 mi) north of town; mailing address: Calle Obregón 1665, Box 782, 23000.* ☎ *112/2–18–26 or 112/2–70–10,* 🖷 *112/2–86–44. 18 rooms. Restaurant, bar, pool, dive shop, snorkeling.*

$$ 🏨 **La Concha Beach Resort.** Come to La Concha for its clean, curving
★ beach, modern rooms, complete water-sports center, and very good restaurant. Small, dark rooms have tiled floors, TVs, phones, and small refrigerators. Guests gather at the pool and the Cortez Club, a full-scale water-sports center with a bar, equipment rental, and scuba, snorkeling, kayaking, and sportfishing tours. Whale-watching trips are extremely popular in winter, the scuba operation is one of the best in La Paz, and you can arrange tours and rentals through the club even if you're not staying here. A separate building houses condos with kitchenettes, living rooms, and bedrooms ($$$), and its own pool. Another section, located in town, has 6 suites available for long-term rental. There is a shuttle to town and back. ✉ *Km 5 Carretera a Pichilingue, 23010,* ☎ *112/1–63–44 or 112/1–61–61; 800/999–2252 in the U.S.,* 🖷 *112/1–62–18; 619/294–7366 in the U.S. 107 rooms. Restaurant, 3 bars, pool, water sports, shop, travel services, car rental. AE, MC, V.*

$$ 🏨 **La Perla.** This brown low-rise hotel has a long-standing reputation as one of the best places to stay in La Paz. Rooms have white walls and light-wood furnishings; some have king-size beds. The pool is on a second-story sundeck away from main street traffic. Noise is a factor in the oceanfront rooms; the trade-off is wonderful sunset views over the malecón. ✉ *Paseo Obregón 1570, 23010,* ☎ *112/2–07–77,* 🖷 *112/5–53–63. 101 rooms. Restaurant, bar, pool, shop. MC, V.*

$$ 🏨 **Los Arcos.** Los Arcos is the only true colonial Mexican lodging in town. Resist the waterfront view and request a room in the central courtyard, where the rush of water in the fountain drowns out the music from the street and the noise from the pool area. All rooms have balconies. The self-service coffee shop opens early—so you can have breakfast and pick up a box lunch if you're going fishing—and it's a cool lunchtime escape from the midday heat. The Cabañas de Los Arcos

next door consists of several small brick cottages surrounded by gardens and a small hotel with a swimming pool. ⊠ *Paseo Obregón 498, between Rosales and Allende, 23000,* ☎ *112/2–27–44,* FAX *112/5–43–13. In the U.S.:* ⊠ *6 Jenner St., No. 120, Irvine, CA 92618,* ☎ *714/450–9000 or 800/347–2252,* FAX *714/450–9010. 180 rooms at main hotel, 30 bungalows and rooms at Cabañas. Restaurant, bar, coffee shop, 2 pools, sauna, fishing. MC, V.*

$ 🔳 **Pension California.** This run-down hacienda still has clean blue-and-white rooms with baths and draws backpackers and low-budget travelers. The courtyard has picnic tables and a TV. A laid-back camaraderie prevails. ⊠ *Av. Degollado 209, 23000,* ☎ *112/2–28–96. 25 rooms. No credit cards.*

Nightlife and the Arts
El Teatro de la Ciudad (⊠ Av. Navarro 700, ☎ 112/5–00–04) is La Paz's cultural center. The theater seats 1,500 and is used for stage shows by visiting performers as well as local ensembles. **La Terraza** (⊠ Paseo Obregón in the La Perla hotel, ☎ 112/2–07–77) is the best spot for both sunset- and people-watching along the malecón.

Outdoor Activities and Sports
BOATING AND FISHING
The considerable fleet of private boats in La Paz now has room for docking at three marinas: the **Fidepaz** at the north end of town, and the **Marina Palmira** and **Marina La Paz** south of town. Most hotels can arrange sportfishing trips. Tournaments are held in August and November. The **Dorado Velez Fleet** (⊠ Box 402, 23000, ☎ 112/2–27–44 ext. 608), operated by Jack Velez in the Los Arcos hotel, has cabin cruisers; charters start around $240 per day.

DIVING
Popular diving spots include the white coral banks off Isla Espíritu Santo, the sea-lion colony off Isla Partida, and the seamount 14 km (9 mi) farther north. **Baja Diving & Service** (⊠ Paseo Obregón, ☎ 112/2–18–26, FAX 112/2–86–44) rents equipment and operates diving, snorkeling, and tours to Espíritu Santo and the wreck of the *Salvatierra*, a sunken ferryboat. **Baja Quest** (⊠ Sonora 174, ☎ 112/3–53–20, FAX 112/3–53–21) offers day trips and live-aboard dive cruises. Two-tank dive trips run about $80. Cortez water-sports center at the **La Concha Beach Resort** (☞ Dining and Lodging, *above*) also has dive trips.

WHALE-WATCHING
La Paz has become a center for whale-watching expeditions across the peninsula to San Ignacio Lagoon and Magdalena Bay. Most tours are run by U.S.-based companies (☞ Baja Sur A to Z, *below*). You can get to Magdalena Bay from La Paz on your own by taking a bus (a three-hour ride) from La Paz to San Carlos, the small village by the bay, and hiring a boat captain there. You can also arrange a trip in La Paz through **Baja Quest** (☞ Diving, *above*), **Contactours** (⊠ In the Hotel La Perla, ☎ 112/3–22–12, FAX 112/3–50–51), or **Viajes Balandra** (⊠ Paseo Obregón at Degollado, ☎ 112/2–60–01, FAX 112/2–84–11). And **Discover Baja** (☎ 800/727–2252 in the U.S.) has guided camping tours and whale-watching trips to Bahía Magdalena.

Shopping
Shops carrying a predictable assortment of sombreros, onyx chess sets, and painted plaster curios are scattered along Avenida Obregón across from the malecón. **Artesanías la Antigua California** (⊠ Av. Obregón 220, ☎ 112/5–52–30) has the nicest selection of Mexican folk art in La Paz, including wooden masks and lacquered boxes from Guerrero, along with a good supply of English-language books on Baja.

La Tiendita (✉ Los Arcos Hotel, Av. Obregón 498, ☎ 114/2–27–44) has embroidered guayabera shirts and dresses, tin ornaments and picture frames, and some black pottery from Oaxaca. **Artesanía Cuauhtémoc** (✉ Av. Abasolo between calles Nayarit and Oaxaca, ☎ No phone) is the workshop of weaver Fortunado Silva, who creates and sells woven cotton placemats, rugs, and tapestries.

Buena Vista and the East Cape

105 km (65 mi) south of La Paz.

The Sea of Cortés coast north of Los Cabos has long been a favored hideaway for anglers and adventurers. Now it's growing with housing developments and hotels. The appeal? A curvaceous, sometimes craggy coastline with great bays for fishing, diving, kayaking, and windsurfing—and with that a sense of really getting away. A series of settlements lines the coast running south from Punta Pescadero to Los Barriles, Buena Vista, and La Ribera, all accessible from Highway 1. Sand and dirt roads lead from these communities to small bays and coves and the coral reefs and shipwrecks off Cabo Pulmo.

Windsurfers take over the East Cape in January, when stiff breezes provide ideal conditions. Water-sports equipment and boat trips are available through area hotels, though regulars tend to bring their own gear and rent cars for getting to isolated spots. The nearest airport is at San José del Cabo, about a two-hour drive from the farthest East Cape hotels; several car rental agencies have desks at the airport. Expensive shuttle service can be arranged through most hotels, and there are plenty of cabs in the area. Most hotels have meal plans—a good idea since decent restaurants are scarce.

Dining and Lodging

$$ ✕ **La Bretagne.** French-Mex cuisine is an uncommon category, but chef Jean Paul manages to add his home country's style even to chiles rellenos and tuna tacos. Better yet is homemade pâté with red onion marmalade, and imported filet mignon. The cozy restaurant and outdoor garden are considered a real treat by local expats who want a special night out. ✉ *On the main road through La Ribera,* ☎ *No phone. No credit cards.*

$$ ✕ **Otra Vez.** If you're craving pasta with fresh veggies, sandwiches with avocado and sprouts, or even prime rib and juicy burgers, you'll find yourself wanting to come back to this California-style bar and restaurant. The clientele largely consists of expat retirees and tourists who gossip freely while listening to the Beach Boys and Fleetwood Mac. ✉ *Calle 20 de Noviembre, Los Barriles,* ☎ *114/2–02–49. MC, V.*

$ ✕ **Tia Licha.** You might be able to fit a dozen friendly diners in this tiny café renowned for its homestyle chiles rellenos, huevos rancheros, and fresh fish. Locals congregate here for breakfast, which is said to be the best on the Cape. ✉ *On the road to Hotel Buena Vista Beach Resort (☞ below),* ☎ *No phone, No credit cards.*

$$$ ⊞ **Hotel Buena Vista Beach Resort.** The most pleasant surroundings on the coast are at this old-time resort built around a 1940s private mansion. The hotel has gone through several transitions, leaving it with 60 tile-roofed bungalows set along flower-lined paths next to swimming pools and lawns. Some rooms have private terraces. The fishing fleet is one of the best in the area, and there are plenty of other diversions, including scuba diving, snorkeling, kayaking, horseback riding, trips to natural springs and caves, and tours into Los Cabos and La Paz. Airport shuttle service can be arranged in advance. Room rates include meals and the shuttle service. ✉ *Buena Vista, 32 km (20 mi) north of San José,* ☎ *114/1–00–33; 619/425–1551 or 800/752–3555 in the U.S.,* FAX *114/*

1–01–33; 619/425–1832 in the U.S. 60 rooms. Restaurant, 2 pools, hot tub, massage, beach, dive shop, fishing. MC, V.

$$$ ✕ **Hotel Palmas de Cortés.** A long-standing favorite with anglers, this casual lodge is often featured at sportfishing shows. It's near the famed Cortés banks, where marlin and tuna abound. The rooms and suites are furnished to serve basic comforts and have few frills beyond powerful air conditioners and hot showers. Caged parrots and macaws hang about the gardens among hammocks. Food is hearty and abundant. ⊠ *On the beach (take the road through Los Barriles and continue to the beach), Los Barriles, ☎ 818/591–9463 in the U.S. 30 rooms, 10 suites, 10 condos. Restaurant, pool, fishing, private airstrip. MC, V.*

$$$ ✕ **Hotel Punta Pescadero.** Despite the vacation homes sprouting up in the area, this secluded resort is one of the most peaceful spots in Baja. Rooms have private waterfront terraces and are reserved far in advance by regulars (some 75% of the clientele is made up of returnees). They endure the half-hour drive along a hilly dirt road to the hotel for the sense of complete escape—miles of windswept beach, and calm coves with superb snorkeling—and the camaraderie of the staff and guests. ⊠ *Camino de los Barriles a El Cardonal, Punta Pescadero, 12 km (7 mi) north of Los Barriles, ☎ ₣₳ₓ 114/1–01–01. 21 rooms. Restaurant, refrigerators, pool, beach, snorkeling, fishing, private airstrip. MC, V.*

$$$ ⛱ **Rancho Leonero.** Diehard anglers love this casual seaside hotel. Thatch-roofed bungalows are scattered about the landscaped property. Though far from fancy, the rooms are serviceable with tiled floors, hard mattresses, and powerful showers. Meals (included in the room rate) are served family-style in the large dining room, the ambience of which depends on the guests, who can tend toward the rowdy side. In the afternoon the pool fills with sunburned boaters and their fish-story boasting. The fishing fleet, diving at nearby Cabo Pulmo's reefs, and use of kayaks are other pluses. ⊠ *Buena Vista, 32 km (20 mi) north of San José, ☎ 114/1–02–16; 800/334–2252 in the U.S., ₣₳ₓ 114/1–02–16. 27 rooms. Restaurant, pool, beach, fishing. MC, V.*

Los Cabos

195 km (121 mi) south of La Paz.

At the southern tip of the 1,625-km (1,000-mi) Baja California peninsula, the land ends in a rocky point called El Arco (The Arch), a place of stark and mysterious beauty. The warm waters of the Sea of Cortés swirl into the Pacific Ocean's rugged surf as marlin and sailfish leap above the waves. The desert ends in sandy coves, with cactus standing at their entrances like sentries under the soaring palm trees.

The conquistadores focused their attention on La Paz during expeditions from mainland Mexico in the mid-1500s, but pirates found the tip of the Baja peninsula an ideal point for spotting Spanish galleons traveling from the Philippines to Spain's empire in central Mexico. In their turn missionaries came to save the souls of the few thousand local Indians who lived off the sea. The Jesuits established the mission of **San José del Cabo** in the mid-1700s, but their settlements did not last long. The missionaries (and other Europeans) had brought syphilis and smallpox along with their preachings, and, as at La Paz, the indigenous population was nearly wiped out after a few decades.

A different sort of native brought explorers back. It was the mighty game fish that appeared to be trapped in the swirl of surf where the ocean meets the sea. When pilots flew over Baja during World War II, they spotted the swirling waters and fertile fishing grounds from the air, and word soon spread. Wealthy adventurers with private planes and boats created a demand for fishing lodges, airstrips, and other ser-

Los Cabos Coast

Los Pozos — Los Cabos International Airport — San José del Cabo ㉞–㊳ — Cabo San Lucas ㊴–㊷ — Playa de Amor — Playa Médano — Bahía San Lucas — Bahía Santa María — Bahía Chileno — Costa Azul — Bahía San José del Cabo — Playa Palmilla — PACIFIC OCEAN — Golfo de California

vices, and the region became a cult destination. By the 1960s a half-dozen exclusive resorts were thriving on the cliffs and shores amid the barren landscape.

Connected by a 32-km (20-mi) stretch of highway called the **Corridor,** the two towns of Cabo San Lucas and San José del Cabo were distinct until the late 1970s, when the Mexican government's office of tourism development (FONATUR) targeted the southern tip of Baja as a major resort and dubbed the area Los Cabos. The destination now consists of three major areas: San José del Cabo, Cabo San Lucas, and the Corridor separating the two towns.

In the process Los Cabos has become one of Mexico's most popular and most expensive coastal getaways, with deluxe hotels, championship golf courses, and some of the finest sportfishing in the world. Some of the world's finest hotel chains—Ritz Carlton, Four Seasons, and Quinta Real—are rumored to be arriving soon. The population rate is growing faster than in any other part of Mexico, and infrastructure will soon be a problem. Despite all the development that has taken place, and the steep prices that have come along with it, the area remains a mysteriously natural hideaway.

San José del Cabo

San José del Cabo is the municipal headquarters for the two Los Cabos towns and has a population of about 25,000. The hotel zone faces a long stretch of waterfront on the Sea of Cortés; a nine-hole golf course and private residential community have been established south of the town center. The downtown area with its adobe houses and jacaranda trees still maintains the languid pace of a Mexican village, though bumper-to-bumper traffic often clogs the streets during weekday business hours. Despite the development, San José remains the more peaceful of the two towns—the one to come to for a quiet escape.

❸❹ The main street in San José del Cabo is **Boulevard Mijares.** The south end of the boulevard has been designated the tourist zone, with the Los Cabos Club de Golf as its centerpiece. A few reasonably priced hotels are situated along this strip, on a beautiful long beach where the surf, unfortunately, is too dangerous for swimming.

❸❺ The **Estero de San José,** where the freshwater Río San José flows into the sea, is at the end of the tourist strip, on Paseo San José by the Presidente Inter-Continental. The estuary is now a natural preserve closed to boats. Wildlife is gradually reappearing; more than 200 species of birds can be spotted here. A building at the edge of the estuary serves as a cultural center with exhibits on Baja's indigenous people.

Within town, Boulevard Mijares is lined with restaurants and shops.
❸❻ The modest yellow **City Hall** is near Avenida Zaragoza, where Boule-

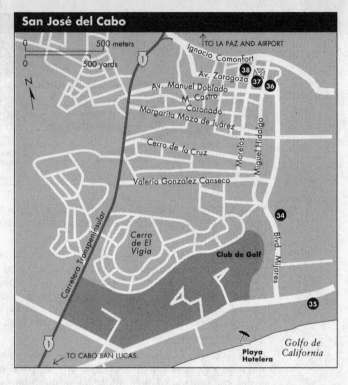

vard Mijares ends—a spot marked by a long fountain. There is a small, shaded plaza here with a few café tables in front of small restaurants.

㊲ Locals and travelers mingle at the large central **plaza,** with a white wrought-iron gazebo and green benches set in the shade. The town's
㊳ church, the **Iglesia San José,** looms above the plaza. Be sure to walk up to the front and see the tile mural of a captured priest being dragged toward a fire by Indians.

BEACHES

Playa Hotelera is the stretch of beach that most of the finer hotels use. It's beautiful, but the current is dangerously rough, and swimming is not advised. At the east end of the beach, near the Presidente Inter-Continental, there is a freshwater lagoon filled with tropical birds and plants. If you plan to spend time here, be sure to douse yourself with insect repellent. The best swimming beach near San José is **Playa Palmilla,** which is protected by a rocky point just south of town. The northern part of the beach is cluttered with boats and shacks, but if you walk south you'll reach the Hotel Palmilla beach, a long stretch of white sand and calm sea.

DINING AND LODGING

$$$ ✕ **Damiana.** For a special night out, come to this small hacienda
★ tucked beside the plaza, past the center of town. The lounge area has overstuffed couches where you can unwind before claiming your table on the patio. Fuchsia bougainvillea wraps around the tall pines shading the wrought-iron tables, and the pink adobe walls glow in the candlelight. Start with fiery oysters diablo, then move on to the tender chateaubriand, charbroiled lobster, or the restaurant's signature imperial shrimp steak, made with ground shrimp. You'll find the setting so relaxing and charming that you might want to linger well into the night. ⊠ *Blvd. Mijares 8,* ☎ *114/2–04–99. AE, MC, V.*

$$$ ✕ **Tequila Restaurante.** An old adobe home serves as the setting for the classiest restaurant in town. The lengthy tequila list gives you a chance to savor the finer brands of Mexico's national drink, and the menu challenges you to decide between excellent regional dishes and innovative Pacific Rim spring rolls, salads, and seafood with mango, ginger, and citrus sauces. Take your time and sample all you can. ⊠ *Manuel Doblado s/n,* ☎ *114/2–11–55. No credit cards. Closed Wed.*

$$ ✕ **Tropicana Bar and Grill.** Start the day with coffee and French toast at the sidewalk tables in front of this enduringly popular restaurant. Later, as the temperature rises, it's more comfortable to sit inside the large, air-conditioned bar over an ice-cold lemonade, watching sporting events and music videos on TV. In the evening the back patio quickly fills with a loyal clientele who enjoy the garden setting and decent cooking. The menu has grown over the years to include U.S. cuts of beef and imported seafood along with fajitas, chiles rellenos, and lobster, always in demand. The nightly dinner special is usually a good deal. ⊠ *Blvd. Mijares 30,* ☎ *114/2–15–80. AE, MC, V.*

$ ✕ **El Café Fiesta.** The location couldn't be better—set at the plaza at the end of Mijares, the international café has shaded outdoor tables and indoor seating, and lingering is welcome except in the busiest times. There's something on the menu for nearly every mood: fresh orange juice and an omelet on the plaza in the morning, or salads, sandwiches (served into the evening), and vegetarian specials at midday. Espresso and pastries are a good pick-me-up in early evening. ⊠ *Blvd. Mijares s/n,* ☎ *114/2–18–16. MC, V.*

$ ✕ **Las Hornillas.** Chicken roasted on a spit over an open fire is the specialty at this casual eatery, more popular with locals than tourists. The half chicken with rice, beans, and tortillas is more than sufficient for a ravenous diner, and the chicken fajitas come on a platter loaded with grilled onions, green peppers, and white meat. The hours are not consistent here, but it's usually open for late lunch and early dinner. ⊠ *Calle Manuel Doblado 610,* ☎ *114/2–23–24. No credit cards.*

$ ✕ **Restaurant La Playita.** A longtime local secret, this small, out-of-the-way restaurant has undergone several changes in owners and chefs but always draws dedicated locals and tourists. The main attraction is the seafood brought in daily by fishermen who beach their boats just a few yards away. The fish is prepared according to the whims of the cook and available ingredients; you can't go wrong if you stick with the catch of the day grilled with oil and garlic. Lunch here is a nice midday outing, especially when followed by a long walk down the largely deserted beach. ⊠ *Pueblo la Playa, 2 km (1 mi) south of San José,* ☎ *114/2–37–74. MC, V.*

$$$$ ⊞ **Presidente Inter-Continental Los Cabos.** By far the nicest—and one of the oldest—hotels in San José, the Presidente sits amid cactus gardens next to the estuary at the end of the hotel zone. The buildings curve around an enormous pool; the best rooms have shaded patios, king-size beds, and a sitting area facing the sliding glass doors. The hotel operates on an all-inclusive basis (rates include all meals and some activities). Few other restaurants are in the immediate vicinity, so you'll save on taxis by eating here. The all-inclusive rate is quite reasonable, and other promotional rates are often available. ⊠ *Paseo San José, at end of hotel zone, 23400,* ☎ *114/2–02–11; 800/327–0200 in the U.S.,* FAX *114/2–02–32. 244 rooms, 6 suites. 2 restaurants, bar, pool, 2 tennis courts, horseback riding, beach, fishing, dance club. AE, MC, V.*

$$ ⊞ **Huerta Verde.** Though far from the sea in an unlikely rural setting just north of San José, this seven-room B&B is one of the most picturesque properties in Los Cabos. A dirt road leads through mango groves, fragrant in early summer, to the property's arched entryway. Brick stairs lead through hibiscus and bougainvillea hedges to the main house and guest

rooms. Suites are in adjacent brick buildings with hand-laid, dome ceilings, gorgeous handcrafted furnishings, and comfy beds and chairs. The heated pool is surrounded by tropical gardens. Hikers enjoy the trails leading to hilltops with views of the sea. Be sure to get directions to the property, which is south of the small town of Santa Rosa between the airport and San José. Rates include breakfast; you can order other meals in advance. Credit cards are accepted only with advance reservations, which are strongly advised. ⊠ *Las Animas Altas, 2 km (1 mi) off Hwy. 1, 23400,* ☎ FAX *114/8–05–11,* ☎ *303/431–5162 in the U.S.,* FAX *303/431–4455 in the U.S. 3 rooms, 4 suites, 1 master suite. Restaurant, bar, pool.*

$$ 🏨 **La Playita.** The small community of Pueblo la Playa just outside San José has long been a favorite day-trip escape for those in the know. The small hotel on the beach is the perfect hideaway if you're not interested in shopping or bar-hopping. The rooms in the two-story building are painted stark white and have air-conditioning, tiled bathrooms, ceiling fans, and satellite TVs; phone service is available at the front desk. There are two penthouses—a two-bedroom and a one-bedroom—both with kitchenettes. The restaurant is a two-minute walk away. Rates go down about 20% in summer. ⊠ *Pueblo la Playa, 2 km (1 mi) south of San José, 23400,* ☎ FAX *114/2–41–66; 818/962–2805 in the U.S. 24 rooms, 2 penthouses. Restaurant, bar, pool, beach, fishing. MC, V.*

$$ 🏨 **Tropicana Inn.** This small hotel is a great option if you aren't desperate to be on a beach. The stucco buildings decorated with tiled murals of Diego Rivera paintings frame a pool and palapa bar in a quiet enclave behind San José's main boulevard. Rooms are air-conditioned, have satellite TV, and are maintained to look brand new. Book in advance in high season. ⊠ *Blvd. Mijares 30, 23400,* ☎ *114/2–09–07,* FAX *114/2–15–90; 510/939–2725 in the U.S. 39 rooms, 1 suite. Restaurant, bar, room service, pool. AE, MC, V.*

$ 🏨 **Posada Terranova.** San José's best budget hotel is a friendly place where guests return so frequently they're almost part of the family. The large, air-conditioned rooms are painted bright white and have two double beds and tiled bathrooms. The hotel has expanded in recent years. Even so, when guests congregate at the front patio tables or in the restaurant, it still feels like a private home. ⊠ *Calle Degollado at Zaragoza, 23400,* ☎ *114/2–05–34,* FAX *114/2–09–02. 26 rooms. Restaurant, bar. AE, MC, V.*

NIGHTLIFE AND THE ARTS

The hottest nightspot in town is **Iguana Bar** (⊠ Blvd. Mijares 24, ☎ 114/2–02–66), a local hangout with live rock and roll on weekend nights during the high season.

OUTDOOR ACTIVITIES AND SPORTS

Fishing. Most hotels in San José can arrange trips. As there is no marina in town, you'll board your boat at the marina in Cabo San Lucas—hotels will also set up transportation to the marina and prepare lunches. Pangas (smaller skiffs) depart from the sand at La Playita; you can arrange trips through hotels.

Kayaking. Kayak tours and rentals are available through **Los Lobos del Mar** (⊠ Brisas del Mar RV park on the south side of San José, ☎ 114/2–29–83). The tours paddle along the Corridor's peaceful bays and are especially fun in the winter months when gray whales pass by offshore.

Surfing. Killer Hook Surf Shop (⊠ Av. Hidalgo, ☎ 114/2–24–30) sells and rents snorkeling gear, along with surfboards and boogie boards.

SHOPPING

Shopping opportunities in San José del Cabo occur in the few streets around the main plaza and City Hall. Across from City Hall is **Almacenes**

Goncanseco (⊠ Blvd. Mijares 18, ☎ No phone), where you can get film, postcards, groceries, and liquor. **ADD** (⊠ Av. Zaragoza at Hidalgo, ☎ 114/3–20–55), an interior design shop, sells gorgeous hand-painted dishes from Guanajuato and carved-wood furniture from Michoacán. **Copal** (⊠ Plaza Mijares, ☎ 114/2–30–70) has a nice array of carved animals from Oaxaca, masks from Guerrero, and heavy wooden furnishings. For fresh produce, flowers, meat, fish, and a sampling of local life in San José, visit the **Mercado Municipal** off Calle Doblado.

The Corridor

Many of the legendary fishing lodges and exclusive resorts built before the government stepped in were located along the wild cliffs between San José del Cabo and Cabo San Lucas. Since the mid-1980s, the area has developed as a destination unto itself. It now has several private communities and large-scale resorts, and three championship golf courses. The highway along the Corridor has been widened to four lanes. The road is in good shape most of the time, but tends to flood during heavy rains, especially between August and November.

BEACHES

Costa Azul is the most popular surfing beach in Los Cabos. A few small campgrounds and casual restaurants line the beach facing the waves. **Playa Palmilla** is one of the Corridor's best swimming beaches.

Two bays, **Bahía Chileno** and **Bahía Santa María,** are terrific for diving and snorkeling (☞ Outdoor Activities and Sports, *below*).

DINING AND LODGING

$$$ ✕ **Pitahayas.** Now that Corridor resorts are firmly established, smaller businesses are cropping up to take advantage of the upscale clientele. This elegant restaurant has found its niche in a lovely spot just above the beach at Cabo del Sol. The wide-ranging menu features Pacific Rim cuisine, blending touches of Thai, Polynesian, and Chinese cooking in unusual recipes. Lobster appears in the form of gourmet hash, duckling is served with a plum tangerine sauce, and fresh organic vegetables are lightly stir-fried and served while still crisp. Soft jazz plays in the background, and the setting is decidedly romantic. ⊠ *Km 10 on Hwy. 1,* ☎ *114/3–21–57. AE, MC, V.*

$$ ✕ **Da Giorgio II.** The best sunset-watching in all of Los Cabos is at the cliffside tables outside of this restaurant. Staggered along the cliffs and poised beside a small pond with a waterfall, the tables have great views of the arch at land's end. The menu focuses on pastas and pizza, and the salad bar has an abundance of fresh veggies. ⊠ *Km 5 on Hwy. 1,* ☎ *114/3–29–88. MC, V.*

$ ✕ **Zippers.** Home of the surfing crowd and those who like a bit of sand in their burgers, this casual palapa-roofed restaurant sits on Costa Azul beach just south of San José. Burgers, ribs, and chicken are all decent, but it's the crowd that makes the place fun. ⊠ *Km 18.5 on Hwy 1,* ☎ *No phone. No credit cards.*

$$$$ ☷ **Casa Del Mar.** One of the smallest properties in the area, this hacienda-style hotel is all about luxurious privacy. An antique hand-carved wooden door leads into the courtyard-lobby with stone fountains and stairways that curve up to the rooms, spa, and library. Rooms are designed with pampering in mind—the bathrooms with whirlpool bathtubs and shower and separate toilet stalls are set a few steps above the main bedroom, where cushy beds covered in satiny soft sheets afford sea views. A series of flowing streams, fountains, and gardens leads around the pool to a wide stretch of beach where you can leave footprints in the untrammeled sand. The restaurant is excellent. ⊠ *Km 19.5 on Hwy. 1,* ☎ *114/4–00–30; 800/221-8808 in the U.S.,* ℻ *114/4–00–34, 24 rooms, 32 suites. Restaurant, pool, spa, beach. AE, MC, V.*

$$$$ 🏨 **Las Ventanas al Paraíso.** Taking the Corridor by storm in early 1997,
 ★ Las Ventanas has set the standard for luxury, privacy, and amenities
in the Los Cabos. All suites have individual hot tubs, wood-burning
fireplaces, and telescopes for viewing whales at sea and stars at night.
The service is sublime—courteous staff seem to pop out of nowhere
to offer anything from a beach towel to a cool drink. A sort-of hand-
book on contemporary seaside elegance, the hotel is filled with handcrafted lamps and doors, sculpture and painting, and the walkways were
hand laid in stone patterns. The outstanding restaurant is worth a visit
for the chef's homebaked breads and innovative recipes. Guests have
access to off-property golf and tennis facilities nearby. ⊠ *Km 19.5 Carretera Transpeninsular, Cabo San Lucas 23400,* ☎ *114/4–02–57; 888/
525–0483 in the U.S.,* 𝖥𝖠𝖷 *114/4–02–55; 310/824–1218 in the U.S. 61
suites. Restaurant, pool, spa, beach, fishing. AE, MC, V.*

$$$$ 🏨 **Meliá Cabo Real.** This Meliá sprawls over a hilltop with a crystal-
blue pool, fountains, waterfalls, white canopies shading rest areas, and
a private beach created by a small jetty jutting from the rocky hillside.
Maya carvings and bas-reliefs adorn the walls in the rooms, which all
have landscaped terraces. The Cabo Real resort development around
the hotel is ongoing, with an 18-hole golf course now open. Meliá guests
can use it for a fee. The hotel shuttle runs to its sister property in Cabo
San Lucas. ⊠ *Km 19.5 Carretera Transpeninsular, Cabo San Lucas
23400,* ☎ *114/4–00–00; 800/336–3542 in the U.S.,* 𝖥𝖠𝖷 *114/4–01–01;
305/854–0660 in the U.S. 340 rooms. 2 restaurants, café, pool, 2 tennis courts, exercise room, beach, dive shop, fishing. AE, MC, V.*

$$$$ 🏨 **Palmilla.** Just outside San José, the Palmilla is a gracious, sprawl-
 ★ ing, hacienda-style resort with a small white adobe chapel. Established
in 1956, the Palmilla underwent a $12 million renovation in 1996, re-
sulting in even more lavish accommodations set amid palm groves and
lush gardens. Tiled stairways lead up from flower-lined paths to large
apartments with hand-carved furniture, French doors opening onto private patios, tiled baths, and, for the first time in the hotel's history, TVs
and phones in all rooms. There is also a swimming pool with fountains, a swim-up bar, and plenty of space for serious swimmers. The
buildings are spread along a hillside overlooking the beach, the service is delightfully personalized, and the hotel's La Paloma restaurant
is excellent. There is a 27-hole Jack Nicklaus–designed golf course, and
construction is under way on a large-scale resort development surrounding the hotel. ⊠ *Km 1 Carretera Transpeninsular (about 8 km
[5 mi] from San José), 23400,* ☎ *114/4–50–00; 800/637–2226 in the
U.S.,* 𝖥𝖠𝖷 *114/4–51–00. In the U.S.:* ⊠ *4343 Von Karman Ave., Newport Beach, CA 92660. 78 rooms, 36 suites, 1 villa. Restaurant, bar,
pool, golf privileges, 2 tennis courts, beach. AE, MC, V.*

$$$$ 🏨 **Twin Dolphin.** Sleek and Japanese-modern, with an austere air, the
Twin Dolphin has been a hideaway for the rich and famous since
1977. Guest rooms are in low-lying casitas along a seaside cliff and
are furnished in minimalist style, without TVs and phones. The hotel
is worth a visit if only for the reproductions of Baja's cave paintings
on the lobby wall. ⊠ *Km 11.5 Carretera Transpeninsular, Cabo San
Lucas 23410,* ☎ *114/3–02–56,* 𝖥𝖠𝖷 *114/3–04–96. In the U.S.:* ⊠ *1625
W. Olympic Blvd., Suite 1005, Los Angeles, CA 90015,* ☎ *800/421–
8925,* 𝖥𝖠𝖷 *213/380–1302. 44 rooms, 6 suites. Restaurant, bar, pool, massage, 2 tennis courts, beach, fishing. MC, V.*

$$$$ 🏨 **Westin Regina Resort.** The Westin is architecturally astounding, if
intimidating in size. It's a long walk from the parking lot and lobby
to the rooms and pool, set above a man-made beach. The luxurious
rooms are among the best in Los Cabos, with satellite TVs, in-room
safes, hair dryers, bathtubs and separate walk-in showers, and both
air-conditioning and ceiling fans—a boon if you prefer open windows

and sea breezes. The Royal Beach Club Villas are decorated with gorgeous pottery and have full kitchens and whirlpool tubs facing the sea. Two of Los Cabos's best golf courses are nearby, and the hotel is designed to keep its guests happy without their ever having to leave the grounds. ⊠ *Km 22.5 Carretera Transpeninsular, Box 145, San José del Cabo 23400,* ☎ *114/2–90–00; 800/228–3000 in the U.S.,* FAX *114/ 2–90–10. 243 rooms, 60 villas. 3 restaurants, 5 pools, 2 tennis courts, exercise room, beach. AE, MC, V.*

$$$ ⌂ **Hotel Cabo San Lucas.** Looking like a mountain lodge nearly buried in palms, this long-standing Corridor hotel is a favorite of Baja devotees. The rooms are furnished with sturdy, dark-wood pieces; suites and villas are more luxurious. The hacienda-style buildings are located right above Chileno Beach, one of the best diving spots in Los Cabos. ⊠ *Km 14.5 Carretera Transpeninsular, Cabo San Lucas 23410,* ☎ *114/ 4–00–14; 800/733–2226 in the U.S.,* FAX *114/4–00–15; 213/655–3243 in the U.S. 89 rooms. Restaurant, pool, beach, dive shop, fishing. AE, MC, V.*

OUTDOOR ACTIVITIES AND SPORTS

Diving and Snorkeling. Bahía Chileno, an underwater preserve, teems with marine life and is a wonderful place for snorkeling and diving. You'll need to bring your own equipment. **Bahía Santa María,** a picture-perfect white-sand cove protected by towering brown cliffs, also has superb snorkeling, with hundreds of colorful fish swarming through chunks of white coral. There is a concession stand on the beach with snorkeling gear rental; its hours are erratic.

Fishing. Most Corridor hotels have excellent fishing fleets, with the boats anchored at the marina in Cabo San Lucas. Hotels typically can set up the trips and provide transportation to the marina and box lunches. **Victor's Aquatics** (☎ 114/2–10–92, FAX 114/2–10–93) has a fleet of pangas on the Palmilla beach. **Jig Stop Tours** (☎ 800/521–2281 in the U.S.) books fishing trips for several Los Cabos fleets.

Golf. In just the past few years, Los Cabos has become a hot spot for golf, hosting tournaments including the PGA Senior Grand Slam. The courses that have brought so much attention this way are all in the Corridor and serve as the centerpieces for megaresort developments. If you aren't staying at a hotel associated with one of the courses, reserve a tee time a week in advance. Expect to pay exorbitant greens fees—$200 on average. Among the most spectacular is the 27-hole Jack Nicklaus–designed course at the **Palmilla Golf Club** (⊠ Palmilla Resort, ☎ 114/ 4–52–50; 800/386–2465 in the U.S.). A second 18-hole Nicklaus course is at **Cabo del Sol** (☎ 114/5–82–00; 800/386–2465 in the U.S.), a resort development in the Corridor that will eventually include three 18-hole courses (a second 18-hole course is being designed by Tom Weiskopf). The Robert Trent Jones–designed **Cabo Real Golf Club** (⊠ Meliá Cabo Real Hotel, ☎ 114/2–90–00 ext. 9205) is expected to have all 36 of its holes open for play by 2000.

Cabo San Lucas

Cabo San Lucas, once an unsightly fishing town with dusty streets and smelly canneries, has become Los Cabos's center of tourism activity. The sportfishing fleet is headquartered here, and cruise ships anchored off the marina disperse passengers into town. Trendy restaurants and bars line the streets, and massive hotels have risen on every available plot of waterfront turf—alas, a five-story condo-hotel complex along the bay blocks the view from the town's older hotels. Cabo San Lucas is decidedly *in*—for its rowdy nightlife, its slew of restaurants, and its shopportunities.

Cabo San Lucas

N

Golfo de
California

Playa
de Amor

Blvd. Marina

0   500 meters

0   500 yards

PACIFIC OCEAN

39 Highway 1 leads into the center of Cabo San Lucas, ending at Kilometer 1 on the Transpeninsular Highway. The main downtown street, Avenida Lázaro Cárdenas, passes the pretty **Plaza San Lucas** with its white wrought-iron gazebo. Buildings around the plaza house galleries and restaurants. Most of the shops, services, and restaurants are located between Avenida Cárdenas and the waterfront.

40
41 Boulevard Marina has been transformed from a dusty main drag into a busy thoroughfare lined with hotels and cafés. Paved walkways now run from here to the hotels and beaches on the east end of town and west to the **Handicrafts Market** at the Cabo San Lucas marina (☞ Shopping, *below*). The sportfishing fleet is docked in the **Bahía de Cabo San Lucas,** and there are glass-bottom boats available at the water's edge.

42 The most spectacular sight in Cabo San Lucas is **El Arco.** The natural rock arch is visible from the marina and from some of the hotels but is more impressive from the water. **El Faro de Cabo Falso** (Lighthouse of the False Cape), built in 1890 and set amid sand dunes, is a little bit farther on from El Arco. You need a four-wheel-drive vehicle to reach the lighthouse by land. If you don't take at least a short boat ride out to the arch and Playa de Amor, the beach underneath, you haven't fully appreciated Cabo.

BEACHES

Playa de Amor consists of a secluded cove at the very end of the peninsula, with the Sea of Cortés on one side and the Pacific Ocean on the other. The contrast between the peaceful azure cove on the Sea of Cortés and the pounding white surf of the Pacific is dramatic. **Playa Hacienda,** in the inner harbor by the Hacienda Hotel, has the calmest waters of any beach in town and good snorkeling around the rocky point. **Playa Médano,** just north of Cabo San Lucas, is the most popular stretch in Los Cabos (and possibly in all Baja) for sunbathing and people-watching. The 3-km (2-mi) span of white sand is always crowded, especially on weekends. **Playa Solmar,** fringing the Solmar Hotel, is a beautiful wide beach at the base of the mountains leading into the Pacific, but it has dangerous surf with a swift undertow. Stick to sunbathing here.

DINING AND LODGING

$$$ ✕ **El Galeón.** Considered by some the most distinguished dining room in town, El Galeón is across from the marina. The choice seats are on the outside terraces facing the water; the inside is decorated with heavy wooden furniture. Traditional Italian, Mexican, and American dishes are prepared expertly, with an emphasis on thick, tender cuts of beef. The piano bar is a nice setting for a late-night brandy. ⊠ *Across from marina by road to Finisterra Hotel,* ☎ *114/3–04–43. AE, MC, V.*

$$$ ✕ **Mi Casa.** One of Cabo's best restaurants is in an eye-catching, cobalt-
★ blue building painted with a mural of a burro, just across the street from
the main plaza. Mexican cuisine reaches gourmet status here with fresh
tuna and dorado served with tomatillo salsa or Yucatecan achiote, or
with sophisticated dishes such as *chili en nogada* (a meat-stuffed pep-
per topped with walnut sauce and pomegranate seeds). The restaurant
quickly outgrew its small dining room and has spread into a large back
courtyard. It's especially nice at night, illuminated by candlelight and
the moon. ⊠ *Av. Cabo San Lucas,* ☎ 114/3–19–33. MC, V.

$$$ ✕ **Peacocks.** The ubiquitous fresh-fish dinner achieves gustatory em-
★ inence when prepared by Bernard Voll. His dorado is coated with a
crust of chopped pecans, and his shrimp masterfully tossed with spinach
fettuccine. This chef is known for his incredible desserts—if you miss
dinner, be sure to stop by for a cappuccino and a tequila mousse. The
candlelit two-level dining room has an open kitchen and is topped by
an enormous palapa; you can also dine on an outdoor patio. ⊠ *Paseo
Pescador near Playa Médano,* ☎ 114/3–15–58. AE, MC, V.

$$ ✕ **Edith's Café.** Calm and romantic by local standards, this small café
starts out with live jazz and blues in the background and views of the
sea. Lobster and other seafood, an excellent wine list, and good cof-
fees and desserts fill out the picture of a long, romantic dinner here.
⊠ *Paseo del Pescador near Playa Médano,* ☎ 114/3–08–01. MC, V.

$$ ✕ **El Shrimp Bucket.** This is the calmest of the three Carlos Anderson
restaurants in Cabo San Lucas. A few tables are set out on the walk-
way that runs along the marina in front of the Marina Fiesta Hotel, a
good spot to relax and watch the boats rock on the water. The indoor
dining room has the chain's typical mishmash decor and quirky adorn-
ments. The food—barbecued ribs and chicken, burgers, piles of fried
shrimp—is dependable and abundant. ⊠ *Blvd. Marina in Marina Fiesta complex,* ☎ 114/3–19–98 or 114/3–26–89. AE, MC, V.

$$ ✕ **Pancho's.** With more than 100 brands of tequila at the bar and an
expansive menu of Mexican dishes, this bright, colorful restaurant is
a sure bet for a festive evening. Vivid blue, pink, and yellow place mats
cover the tables, and drinks are served in heavy handblown glass gob-
lets. Try the mole, chiles rellenos, or carne asada. You may well want
to come back here for more. ⊠ *Hidalgo between Zapata and Serdan,*
☎ 114/3–09–73. AE, MC, V.

$ ✕ **Fish Company.** It's easy to overlook this small seafood joint surrounded
by flashier restaurants, but don't: the owner has perfected the art of
preparing flavorful meals at reasonable prices. Nine tables covered with
blue-and-white cloths sit just in from the sidewalk in the narrow din-
ing room, and the aroma of fresh grilled fish fills the air. Breakfast spe-
cialties include a great chorizo-and-cheese omelet. Among lunch and
dinner choices are shrimp with oyster sauce and fresh fish smothered
in garlic. For a low-cost feast, bring your own catch here to have it
prepared. ⊠ *Av. Guerrero between Blvd. Marina and Zapata,* ☎ 114/
3–14–05. *No credit cards.*

$ ✕ **Mariscos Mocambo.** Feast with locals on crab, shrimp, and lobster
at the most reasonable place in town. Of course, your tab will run a
bit higher if you go all the way and order shrimp ceviche and the seafood
parrillada for two, which is loaded with every imaginable type of fish.
But you can get by quite reasonably with seafood soup, shrimp em-
panadas, and the grilled fish of the day, all served in crowded, com-
fortable quarters where Spanish is as common as English. ⊠ *Vicario
at 20 de Noviembre,* ☎ 114/3–21–22. *No credit cards.*

$ ✕ **The Office.** Playa Médano is lined with cafés on the sand, some with
lounge chairs, others with more formal settings. All serve the same ba-
sics—cold beer, snacks, fish tacos, french fries–and most accompany
the meal with loud American rock. The Office, which has provided per-

fect vacation photo opportunities for over a decade, has grown like its neighbors but remains a locals' hangout. ⊠ *Playa Médano,* ☎ *No phone. No credit cards.*

$ ✕ **Señor Greenberg's Mexicatessen.** Pastrami, chopped liver, knishes, bagels, lox, cheesecake—such wonders one finds behind the glass counters at this decent Mexican incarnation of a New York deli. It's open 24 hours, which allows anglers to pick up deluxe box lunches at dawn before heading out to sea. The tables, cool air-conditioning, stacks of newspapers, and soft music all encourage frequent visits. ⊠ *Plaza Nautical on Blvd. Marina,* ☎ *114/3–56–30. AE, MC, V.*

$$$$ ⛱ **Finisterra.** One of the oldest hotels in Cabo, the Finisterra is now also one of the most modern, thanks to the two modern towers rising directly from the beach. An eight-story-high palapa covers the restaurant and bar on the beach next to two free-form swimming pools. Rooms in the new buildings, with oceanfront balconies, are by far the nicest; some have king-size beds. Longtime guests favor the less-expensive older section of the hotel, with its stone buildings that have a fishing-lodge feel. The restaurant is only fair, but the Whale Watcher bar atop a high cliff has the best view in town. ⊠ *Blvd. Marina, 23410,* ☎ *114/3–33–33,* FAX *114/3–05–90. In the U.S.:* ⊠ *6 Jenner St., No. 120, Irvine, CA 92618,* ☎ *714/450–9000 or 800/347–2252,* FAX *714/450–9010. 237 rooms. 2 restaurants, 2 bars, 3 pools, travel services. AE, MC, V.*

$$$$ ⛱ **Hotel Hacienda.** Set on the tip of a tree-filled point jutting into Bahía San Lucas, the Hacienda resembles a Spanish colonial inn with its white arches and bell towers, stone fountains, and statues of Indian gods set amid scarlet hibiscus and bougainvillea. The bar is a veritable museum of Indian artifacts. The white rooms have red-tile floors, tile baths, and folk art on the walls. The water-sports center, located on the calmest beach in town, has kayaks, Jet Skis, snorkeling equipment, and any other gear you might need. The hotel has a three-night minimum stay on weekdays, and a four-night minimum on weekends in the high season. ⊠ *Playa Médano, 23410,* ☎ *114/3–20–62 or 114/3–01–22; 800/ 733–2226 in the U.S.,* FAX *213/655–2323. 51 rooms, 12 suites, 10 town houses, 9 garden patio rooms, 30 beachfront cabañas. Restaurant, bar, pool, beach, dive shop. MC, V.*

$$$$ ⛱ **Meliá San Lucas.** From the moment you enter the Meliá and spot
 ★ El Arco framed by the lobby's arches, you know you're at a hotel where details are important. The blue walls and linens in the rooms complement the views of the aquamarine sea; the outer adobe walls of the terraced hotel buildings glow orange and gold with the changing sunlight. The Meliá has a long beach with calm waters, a spacious hot tub under the palms, and all the equipment you could need for playing on and in the water. Early reservations are essential. ⊠ *Playa Médano, 23410,* ☎ *114/3–44–44 or 114/3–44–08; 800/336–3542 in the U.S.,* FAX *114/3–04–18 or 114/3–04–20. 142 rooms, 6 suites. 3 restaurants, 2 pools, hot tub, beach. AE, MC, V.*

$$$$ ⛱ **Pueblo Bonito Rosé.** Soft pink Mediterranean-style buildings surround lush gardens populated with strolling peacocks at this Playa Médano resort. Waterfalls, fountains, and a hot tub separate the pool area into several sections so serious swimmers have room for laps while kids have their own area for splashing about. Many of the commodious suites have kitchenettes, and the restaurants are worth checking out. ⊠ *Playa Médano, 23410,* ☎ *114/3–29–00; 800/937–9567 in the U.S. 260 suites. 2 restaurants, pool, beach, snorkeling, jet skiing. MC, V.*

$$$$ ⛱ **Solmar Suites.** From afar, the Solmar looks like a space colony, set
 ★ against granite cliffs at the tip of Land's End, facing the wild Pacific. The rooms, decorated in Mexico–Santa Fe style, have separate sitting areas and tile baths; the best ones are set up against the rocks right over the beach. The adjacent time-share and condo units have kitchenettes and

a private pool area. The surf here is far too dangerous for swimming, but don't miss a stroll along the wide strip of beach. Most visitors hang out around the two additional pools and swim-up bars, joining in with the ever-present musicians. The Solmar's sportfishing fleet is first-rate. The good restaurant hosts a Saturday night Mexican fiesta and buffet dinner. ⊠ *Blvd. Marina, Box 8, 23410,* ☎ *114/3–35–35,* FAX *114/3–04– 10. In the U.S.:* ⊠ *Box 383, Pacific Palisades, CA 90272,* ☎ *310/459– 9861 or 800/344–3349,* FAX *310/454–1686. 86 rooms, 4 suites, 68 con- dos. Restaurant, bar, 3 pools, beach, dive shop, fishing. AE, MC, V.*

$$$ 🏨 **Casa Rafael's.** This intimate boutique hotel is the perfect spot if you are looking for privacy rather than recreational diversions. Rooms are individually decorated with an eclectic collection of antiques and mod- ern furnishings; all have air-conditioning and private baths. A lap pool on the terrace behind the house is surrounded by plants, and there's a small exercise room and hot tub. ⊠ *Calle Médano at Camino Pescador, 23410,* ☎ FAX *114/3–07–39,* FAX *114/3–16–79. 12 rooms. Restaurant, pool, hot tub, exercise room. AE, MC, V.*

$$ 🏨 **The Bungalows Breakfast Inn.** If solitude and a reasonable room rate are more important than being in the center of the action, this is your place, 10 blocks from the beach. Several two-story buildings frame a small, heated pool. Rooms are beautifully decorated with Mexican tex- tiles and art. Breakfast is included in the rates; smoking is not permitted. ⊠ *Calle Constitución (5 blocks from main plaza), 23410,* ☎ FAX *114/ 3–50–35. 16 suites. Pool. No credit cards.*

$ 🏨 **Las Villas Turismo Juvenil.** Cabo's youth hostel is about 10 blocks from the waterfront in a quiet neighborhood. Two dormitory rooms have bunk beds and shelves, and there are several private rooms with shared baths. In the courtyard, you can use sinks and counters to fix meals and wash clothes. ⊠ *Av. de la Juventud, 23410,* ☎ *114/3–01– 48. 2 dorms, 11 private rooms. No credit cards.*

$ 🏨 **Siesta Suites.** You'll have to forgo air-conditioning to remain in the inexpensive range, but you'll get a large, immaculate room with kitch- enette. The three-story hotel sits on a fairly quiet side street just two blocks from the marina, and the proprietors are the friendliest in town. ⊠ *Calle Zapata, Box 310, 23410,* ☎ FAX *114/3–27–73; 909/945–5940 in the U.S. 15 suites with kitchenettes, 5 rooms. Kitchenettes. No credit cards.*

NIGHTLIFE AND THE ARTS

Some travelers choose Cabo San Lucas for its nightlife, which consists mainly of noisy bars with blaring music and plenty of dancing, flirt- ing, and imbibing. Members of the rock band Van Halen own **Cabo Wabo** (⊠ Calle Guerrero, ☎ 114/3–11–98). The latest U.S. bands play over an excellent sound system, but the real highlight is the impromptu jam sessions with appearances by Sammy Hagar and his many friends in the music business. **Squid Roe** (⊠ Av. Cárdenas, ☎ 114/3–06–55) is the rowdiest spot in town, packed with young foreigners who work in the local tourist industry and know how to party. **Giggling Marlin** (⊠ Blvd. Marina, ☎ 114/3–11–82) seems to have been around for- ever as the favorite watering hole for fishermen and their girlfriends. **El Galeón** (⊠ Blvd. Marina, ☎ 114/3–04–43) is a welcome refuge for the quieter crowd, who sip brandy by the piano bar. **Edith's** (⊠ Paseo del Pescador at Playa Médano, ☎ 114/3–08–01) presents live jazz in a tasteful garden setting.

OUTDOOR ACTIVITIES AND SPORTS

Diving. El Arco is a prime diving and snorkeling area, as are several rocky points off the coast. Most hotels offer diving trips and equipment rental. The oldest and most complete dive shop in the area is **Amigos del Mar** (⊠ Near sportfishing docks at harbor, ☎ 114/3–05–05; 800/344-3349 in the U.S., FAX 114/3–08–87). **Cabo Acuadeportes** (⊠ Hotel Hacienda,

☎ 114/3–01–17), offers diving trips along with all other imaginable water sports. The **Solmar V** (☒ At Solmar Hotel and marina, ☎ 114/3–00–22; 800/344–3349 in the U.S., FAX 310/454–1686 in the U.S.), a live-aboard dive boat, takes weeklong trips to the islands of Socorro, San Benedicto, and Clarion, and the coral reefs at Cabo Pulmo. It has 12 cabins with private baths (maximum, 24 passengers).

Fishing. There are more than 800 species of fish in the waters off Los Cabos. Most hotels will arrange fishing charters, which include a captain and mate, tackle, bait, licenses, and drinks. Prices start at $250 per day for a 25-ft cruiser. Some charters provide lunch, and most can arrange to have your catch mounted, frozen, or smoked. Most of the boats leave from the sportfishing docks in the Cabo San Lucas marina. Usually there are a fair number of pangas for rent at about $30 per hour with a five-hour minimum. Dependable companies include the following: **Gaviota Fleet** (☒ At marina, ☎ 114/3–04–30; 800/521–2281 in the U.S.); **Minerva's** (☒ At marina and on Madero between Blvd. Marina and Guerrero, ☎ 114/3–12–82, FAX 114/3–04–40); **Pisces Sportfishing Fleet** (☒ At marina, ☎ 114/3–12–88); and **Solmar Fleet** (☒ At Solmar Hotel and Marina, ☎ 114/3–35–35 or 114/3–00–22; 800/344–3349 in the U.S., FAX 114/3–04–10; 310/454–1686 in the U.S.).

Horseback Riding. Cantering down an isolated beach or up a desert trail is one of the great pleasures of Baja (as long as the sun isn't beating down on your head). Horses are available for rent in a shady grove in front of the Playa Médano hotels; contact **Rancho Collins Horses** (☎ 114/3–3652). **Red Rose Riding Stables** (☒ Km 4 on Hwy. 1, ☎ 114/3–48–26) has healthy horses for all levels of riders and an impressive array of tack. The **Cuadra San Francisco Equestrian Center** (☒ On Corridor highway across from Cabo Real development, ☎ No phone, arrange at your hotel desk) is a professional center with training and trail rides.

Whale-Watching. The gray whale migration doesn't end at Baja's Pacific lagoons. Plenty of whales of all sizes make it down to the warmer waters off Los Cabos and into the Sea of Cortés. Several companies run whale-watching trips from Cabo San Lucas. Check with **Cabo Acuadeportes** (☞ Diving, *above*) or any of the fishing companies. To watch whales from shore, go to the beach at the Solmar or any Corridor hotel, or the lookout points along the Corridor highway.

SHOPPING

Some of the nicest shops in Cabo San Lucas are located in **Plaza Bonita** on the waterfront at the beginning of Boulevard Marina. **Cartes** (☒ Plaza Bonita, ☎ 114/3–17–70) is the best of Los Cabos's many interior-design stores, with an irresistible array of hand-painted pottery and tableware, pewter frames, handblown glass, and carved furniture. **Libros** (☒ Plaza Bonita, ☎ 114/3–17–70) carries a vast number of English-language novels and magazines. **Dos Lunas** (☒ Plaza Bonita, ☎ 114/3–19–69) has a trendy selection of colorful sportswear. **Francisco's Café del Mundo** (☒ Plaza Bonita, ☎ 114/3–23–66) is the place to take an espresso or cappuccino break.

Boulevard Marina and the side streets between the waterfront and the main plaza are filled with an ever-changing parade of small shops. **Necri** (☒ Blvd. Marina between Madero and Ocampo, ☎ 114/3–02–83) has an excellent selection of folk art and furnishings. **El Callejon** (☒ Guerrero between Cárdenas and Madero, ☎ 114/3–11–39) has multiple showrooms with gorgeous furniture, lamps, dishes, and pottery. **Cuca's Blanket Factory** (☒ Cárdenas at Matamoros, ☎ 114/3–19–13) sells the typical array of serapes and cotton blankets with a twist—you can design your own and have it ready the next day. **Mama Eli's** (☒ Av.

San Lucas, ☎ 114/3–16–16) is a three-story gallery with fine furnishings, ceramics, appliquéd clothing, and children's toys. **Galeria Gatemelatta** (✉ On dirt road to Hotel Hacienda, ☎ 114/3–11–66) specializes in colonial furniture and antiques.

At the **Handicrafts Market** in the marina you can pose for a photo with an iguana, plan a ride in a glass-bottom boat, or browse to your heart's content through stalls packed with blankets, sombreros, and pottery.

Todos Santos

30 km (19 mi) north of Cabo San Lucas.

The Pacific Ocean side of the tip of Baja has remained largely undeveloped. The exception is the small agricultural town of Todos Santos, which has become a haven for artists, architects, and speculators who have contributed to a rapid rise in real estate prices. The town sits a bit inland from the rugged coast and is classically charming with its 19th-century brick-and-stucco buildings and small central plaza. It's an ideal retirement haven for those who deplore the over-development of Baja's tip, since both Los Cabos and La Paz are within easy driving distance. Todos Santos also benefits from cooling breezes from the Pacific and fresh water from underground springs. New neighborhoods are rising in the outskirts of town, usually before electricity, telephone lines, and water pipes are installed. Stop lights have appeared in abundance, along with NO PARKING signs. Entrepreneurs have turned some of the plaza-front buildings into galleries and cafés with erratic hours determined by the presence of tourists; real-estate offices, on the other hand, are easily accessed.

Los Cabos regulars typically drive up the coast to Todos Santos on day trips, eyeing the latest billboards announcing housing developments and stopping to watch surfers at Playa Migrio, Playa los Cerritos, and Punta Gaspareo, where a few solitary villas and motor homes sit on idyllic, though windy, beaches. El Pescadero is the largest settlement before Todos Santos, populated by ranchers and farmers who grow herbs and vegetables for the restaurants in Los Cabos. Seasonal produce is sold at small stands by the side of the road. Dirt roads intersect the highway at several points along the way to Todos Santos, but you should attempt these roads only with four-wheel-drive vehicles—sands on the beach or in the desert will stop conventional vehicles in their tracks.

During high season, you might be surprised to find tour buses clogging the streets around the plaza in Todos Santos: it is a pit stop on tours between Cabo San Lucas and La Paz. When the buses leave, the town is a pleasant and peaceful place to wander before and after a lunch at the Cafe Santa Fe. If you drive to Todos Santos on your own be sure to head back to Cabo before dark. Highway 19 between the two towns is unlit and is prone to high winds and flooding.

Dining and Lodging

$$ ✕ **Cafe Santa Fe.** Owners Paula and Ezio Colombo can be credited with much of their town's popularity since their Italian restaurant is a destination in its own right. And many Cabo residents lunch here weekly. The setting, with tables amid herb gardens in an overgrown courtyard, is part of the appeal, but the reason you can't get a table on weekends is the food—salads and soups made from homegrown organic vegetables and herbs, homemade pastas and calzone, and fresh fish with light herbal sauces. It's tempting to linger for hours over a bottle of imported Chianti, but make sure you've got an alert designated driver to get you home. The café is closed Tuesday and for parts of September and October. ✉ *Calle Centenario,* ☎ *114/5–03–40. No credit cards.*

$ ✕ **Caffé Todos Santos.** Omelets, bagels, granola, and delicious whole-grain breads delight the breakfast crowd at this small café, where the best tables are covered with bright paintings and set in a back garden. Deli sandwiches, cobb salad, and tamales are the lunch highlights; be sure to check out the daily specials and pick up a loaf of bread for snacks. ⊠ *Calle Centenario 33,* ☎ *No phone. No credit cards.*

$$ ⊡ **Hosteria Casitas.** If the Cabos have got you feeling like turning down the volume (and the cash flow), this rustic B&B in a lush, tropical garden setting might give you the quiet you're looking for—and great breakfasts to start the day. Owner Wendy Faith's art glass studio is also on site. ⊠ *Calle Rangel at Obregon and Hidalgo, Apartado Postal 73, 23300,* ☎ 𝖥𝖠𝖷 *114/5–02–55. 3 rooms with private ½ bath and shared showers, 2 suites with bath. No credit cards.*

$$ ⊡ **Hotel California.** The biggest and most established hotel in town is the California, long falsely rumored to be the inspiration for the Eagle's song of the same name. Though the rooms lack air-conditioning, TVs, and phones, the hotel's simplicity and low rates are no less attractive as an escape. ⊠ *Calle Juárez, 23300,* ☎ *114/5–00–02,* 𝖥𝖠𝖷 *114/5–23–33. 16 rooms. Restaurant, pool, bar. No credit cards.*

$$ ⊡ **Todos Santos Inn.** The four guest rooms in this converted 19th cen-
★ tury house are unparalleled in design and comfort. Gorgeous antiques are set against stone walls under brick ceilings. Ceiling fans and the shade from garden trees keep the rooms cool and breezy. The absence of telephones and televisions makes a perfect foil for the conceits of Los Cabos. And good restaurants are within easy walking distance. The whole house can be booked by vacationing families. ⊠ *Calle Legaspi, 23300,* ☎ 𝖥𝖠𝖷 *114/5–00–40. 4 rooms. No credit cards.*

BAJA SUR A TO Z

Arriving and Departing

By Boat

Cruise lines that use Cabo San Lucas as a port of call include the following: **Carnival** (☎ 800/327–9501 in the U.S.); **Princess** (☎ 800/421–0522 in the U.S.); and **Royal Caribbean** (☎ 800/327–0271 in the U.S.).

By Bus

Autotransportes de Baja California bus line runs the length of the peninsula from Tijuana to Los Cabos, stopping at towns en route; the peninsula-long trip takes 22 hours. The **Aguila** bus line runs from Santa Rosalia to Los Cabos.

GUERRERO NEGRO

Autotransportes de Baja California (☎ 112/2–64–76) runs buses from La Paz to Guerrero Negro; the bus stops at the highway entrance to town.

LA PAZ

Autotransportes de Baja California (☎ 112/2–70–94) and **Aguila** (☎ 112/2–42–70) run along the Transpeninsular Highway to the border and to Los Cabos.

LORETO

Loreto is serviced by **Autotransportes de Baja California** and **Aguila.** The **Loreto bus terminal** (⊠ Salvatierra and Tamaral, ☎ 113/5–07–67) sits at the entrance to town.

LOS CABOS

Autotransportes de Baja California (☎ 114/2–02–00) travels from Tijuana to Los Cabos and between Cabo San Lucas and San José daily.

By Car

Mexico Highway 1, also known as the Transpeninsular Highway, runs the entire 1,600 km (1,000 mi) from Tijuana to Cabo San Lucas. The highway's condition varies depending on the weather and intervals between road repairs. Do not drive it at high speeds or at night—it is not lighted. There are exits for all the principal towns in Baja Sur.

The city of La Paz curves along the bay of La Paz and faces the sea in a northwesterly, rather than an easterly, direction. When you approach the city on Highway 1 from the north, you'll enter from the southwest.

The road between San José del Cabo and Cabo San Lucas was widened to four lanes and is in good condition, though dips and bridges become flooded in heavy rains.

By Ferry

LA PAZ

The ferry system connecting Baja to mainland Mexico has been privatized and is constantly undergoing changes in rates and schedules. Currently there are **Sematur** ferries from La Paz to Mazatlán five days a week. Tickets are available at the **ferry office** (☎ 112/2–94–85, FAX 112/5–65–88) at the dock on the road to Pichilingue and at the **Sematur downtown office** (⊠ Av. 5 de Mayo 502, ☎ 112/5–38–33, FAX 112/5–46–66). Purchase your ticket personally in advance of your trip—and expect confusion. If you plan to take a car or a motor home on the ferry to the mainland, you must obtain a vehicle permit before boarding the ferry. Tourism officials in La Paz strongly suggest that you obtain the permit when crossing the border into Baja; though permits are not needed in Baja, offices at the border are better equipped to handle the paperwork than those in La Paz. Everyone crossing to the mainland needs a tourist card, also available at the border.

SANTA ROSALIA

Ferries travel from Santa Rosalia to Guaymas on the mainland Pacific coast. They depart for the seven-hour trip to the mainland at 11 PM on Wednesday and Sunday and arrive in Santa Rosalia at 4 PM Tuesday and Sunday. Buy tickets in advance at the **Santa Rosalia ferry terminal** (☎ 115/2–00–14, FAX 115/2–00–13), just south of town on Highway 1. Schedules are often erratic.

By Plane

LA PAZ

The La Paz airport, about 16 km (10 mi) north of town, is served by **AeroCalifornia** (☎ 112/5–10–23) from Tijuana and Loreto and **Aeroméxico** (☎ 112/2–00–91) from Los Angeles, Tucson, Tijuana, Mexico City, and other cities within Mexico.

LORETO

AeroCalifornia (☎ 113/5–00–50 or 113/5–05–55) has daily flights from Los Angeles and La Paz to Loreto's airport, which is 7 km (4½ mi) southwest of town.

LOS CABOS

The **Los Cabos International Airport** (☎ 114/2–03–41) is about 11 km (7 mi) north of San José del Cabo and about 48 km (30 mi) from Cabo San Lucas. **AeroCalifornia** (☎ 114/3–37–00 or 114/2–09–42; 800/237–6225 in the U.S.) flies to Los Cabos from Los Angeles and Tijuana; **Mexicana** (☎ 114/2–06–06) from Guadalajara, Mexico City, and Los Angeles; **Aeroméxico** (☎ 114/2–03–97 or 114/2–03–98; 800/237–6639 in the U.S.) from San Diego and Mexico City; **Alaska Airlines** (☎ 114/2–10–15; 800/426–0333 in the U.S.) from Anchorage, Fairbanks, Portland, Phoenix, San Francisco, San Diego, Los Angeles, and

Seattle; **America West** (☎ 114/2–28–82 or 114/2–28–80; 800/235–9292 in the U.S.) from Phoenix; **Continental** (☎ 114/2–38–80 or 114/2–09–59; 800/525–0280 in the U.S.) from Houston. Other international airlines may have service in winter.

Getting Around

La Paz

A car isn't necessary if you plan to stay in town; taxis are readily available and inexpensive. It's also fairly easy to get around by bus in La Paz: city buses run along the malecón and into downtown. If you'd like to explore the remote beaches, *see* Car and Jeep Rental, *below*.

Loreto

Taxis are in good supply and fares are inexpensive. There are two gas stations in Loreto; be sure to fill your tank before heading out on any long jaunts.

Los Cabos

The best way to see the sights is on foot. Downtown San José and Cabo San Lucas are compact, with the plaza, church, shops, and restaurants within a few blocks of one another. Bus service runs between the towns, although buses may not stop along the Corridor. If you plan to dine at the Corridor hotels or travel frequently between the two towns, it's a good idea to rent a car for a few days. Taxi fares are steep here.

Contacts and Resources

Car and Jeep Rental

LA PAZ

Avis (⊠ At airport, ☎ 112/2–18–13 or 112/2–26–51), **Budget** (⊠ Paseo Obregón at Hidalgo, ☎ 112/2–10–97 or 112/2–76–55), **Hertz** (⊠ At airport, ☎ 112/2–09–19).

LORETO

M&M Jeeps (⊠ Madero 78, ☎ 113/5–09–71 or 113/5–09–72, ℻ 113/5–09–81; in San Diego, CA: ☎ 619/297–1615, ℻ 619/297–1617) rents two- and four-wheel-drive vehicles that you can take throughout Baja. Advance reservations are strongly recommended. Rentals are also available through **Thrifty** (⊠ Blvd. Misiones s/n, ☎ 113/3–07–00).

LOS CABOS

M&M Jeeps (☎ 113/5–09–71 or 113/5–09–72, ℻ 113/5–09–81; in San Diego, CA: ☎ 619/297–1615, ℻ 619/297–1617) rents two- and four-wheel-drive vehicles that you can take throughout Baja and drop off in Los Cabos. Advance reservations are strongly recommended. **California Baja Rent-A-Car** (⊠ 9245 Jamacha Blvd., Spring Valley, CA 91977, ☎ 619/470–8368 or 888/470–7368) rents four-wheel-drive vehicles, convertibles, and sedans for use throughout Baja; you can drop off the cars in Los Cabos.

The following car-rental agencies have desks at the airport and in one or both Cabos: **Avis** (☎ 114/3–46–07, 114/2–11–80, or 114/2–14–80); **Dollar** (☎ 114/2–01–00 or 114/3–12–50); **National** (☎ 114/2–24–22 or 114/3–14–14); and **Thrifty** (☎ 114/2–16–71 or 114/3–16–66).

M&M Jeeps (⊠ At Hotel Presidente Inter-Continental Los Cabos, ☎ 114/2–11–81; 619/297–1615 in San Diego, CA, ℻ 619/297–1617 in San Diego, CA) rents two- and four-wheel-drive vehicles and has a Baja-wide package options. Make reservations through the San Diego office; you can rent a car in Los Cabos only with an advance reservation.

Emergencies

LA PAZ

Police (☎ 112/2–66–10), **Fire** (☎ 112/2-74–74), and **Red Cross** (☎ 112/2–11–11).

LOS CABOS

Police: Cabo San Lucas (☎ 114/3–26–00) and San José del Cabo (☎ 114/2–03–61). **Hospital**: Cabo San Lucas (☎ 114/3–01–02) and San José del Cabo (☎ 114/2–10–66). **Red Cross**: Cabo San Lucas (☎ 114/3–33–00) and San José del Cabo (☎ 114/2–03–16).

Guided Tours

GUERRERO NEGRO

Eco-Tours Malarrimo (✉ Blvd. Zapata, 23940, ☎ 115/7–02–50, FAX 115/7–00–20) is the best tour operator on the top end of Baja Sur. The company runs four-hour tours ($40 per person) by bus to and from Scammons Lagoon, three hours in small skiffs among whales with English-speaking guides, and lunch. Reserve several months in advance, especially for February, when whales appear in abundance.

LA PAZ

The **Cortez Club** at the La Concha Beach Resort (☞ Dining and Lodging in La Paz, *above*) has diving, fishing, whale-watching, and cruising tours and is the most complete tour facility in La Paz.

Several U.S. companies have whale-watching and kayaking tours that begin in La Paz. **Baja Expeditions** (✉ 2625 Garnet Ave., San Diego, CA 92109, ☎ 619/581–3311; 800/843–6967 in the U.S. and Canada FAX 619/581–6542) has hotel and diving packages and live-aboard dive-boat trips to the islands, seamount, and wrecks; whale-watching trips on boats and kayaks; and trips to Mulege and Bahía Concepción, which are especially popular for paddling. **Baja California Tours** (✉ 7734 Herschel Ave., Suite O, La Jolla, CA 92037, ☎ 619/454–7166, FAX 619/454–2703) has information and makes reservations with several companies offering whale-watching tours. **Discover Baja** (✉ 3089 Clairemont Dr., San Diego, CA 92117, ☎ 619/275–4225 or 800/727–2252, FAX 619/275–1836) has whale-watching trips to San Ignacio Lagoon. **Holiday Expeditions** (✉ 544 E. 3900 S, Salt Lake City, UT 98410, ☎ 801/266–2087; 800/624–6323 outside Utah, FAX 801/266–1448) runs whale-watching and kayak excursions out of La Paz. **Special Expeditions** (✉ 720 5th Ave., New York, NY 10019, ☎ 212/765–7740, ☎ FAX 800/397–3348) runs live-aboard whale-watching trips from La Paz to Magdalena Bay.

LORETO

Picnic cruises to Isla Coronado, trips inland to Misíon San Javier and prehistoric rock paintings, as well as kayaking, sportfishing, diving, and day trips north to Mulege can be arranged through hotels and the following agencies: **Alfredo's Sportfishing** (✉ On malecón, Box 39, Loreto 23880, ☎ 113/5–01–65 or 113/5–0–32, FAX 113/5–05–90), for general local information and tours; and **Las Parras Tours** (✉ Salvatierra at Madero, ☎ 113/5–10–10, FAX 113/5–09–00).

LOS CABOS

With the water as the main attraction, most tours involve getting into a boat and diving or fishing. It's a must to take a ride to El Arco, the natural rock arches at Land's End, and Playa de Amor (Lover's Beach), where the Sea of Cortés merges with the Pacific. Nearly all hotels have frequent boat trips there; the fare depends on how far your hotel is from the point. Tour boats dock by the arts-and-crafts market in the Cabo San Lucas marina, and the sidewalk along the water is lined with salesmen offering boat rides. Check out the boat before you pay, and make sure there are life jackets on board.

Contactours (⌧ Hotel Finisterra, ☎ 114/3–33–33 or 114/3–24–39; also at several other hotels) and **TourCabos** (⌧ Plaza los Cabos, Paseo San José, ☎ 114/2–09–82, FAX 114/2–07–82) run boat trips and offer horseback riding and can provide information on water sports. **Baja Travel Adventures** (☎ 114/3–19–34 or 114/3–44–74) has trips to Todos Santos and La Paz and will individually design tours; ask at hotel tour desks if there's no answer when you phone the company's office.

Pez Gato (⌧ On marina near Plaza Las Glorias hotel, ☎ 114/3–37–97) has sailing and sunset cruises on a 46-ft catamaran, with live music ($50 per person, including drinks), as well as snorkeling and sailing tours ($30 per person). All trips depart from the marina in Cabo San Lucas; call or stop by the booth at the marina for further information.

Visitor Information

La Paz (⌧ Mariano Abasolo s/n, ☎ 112/4–01–00, FAX 112/4–07–22; ⌧ On malecón near Calle 16 de Septiembre, ☎ 112/2–59–39).

At present there are no official tourist information offices in **Los Cabos;** hotel tour desks are the best sources of information. Avoid tour stands on the streets; they are usually associated with time-share operations.

4 SONORA

Cowboys still ride the range in Mexican ranch country, but beaches have upstaged beef as this northwestern state's economic indicator. Along with relatively unspoiled and inexpensive coastal towns such as Bahía Kino and San Carlos, Sonora's lures include colonial Alamos, a sprinkling of Spanish missions, and an immaculate former silver-mining center with cobblestone streets and restored haciendas that evoke the spirit of Old Mexico.

SONORA, Mexico's second-largest, second-richest state, is a vacationland with its own band of devoted followers. Many are from Arizona, for whom the beaches of Sonora, its sister state, are closer, cheaper, and more interesting than those of southern California; and this stretch of the Mexican northwest is reminiscent of the old Wild West in the United States. *Rancheras,* ballads not unlike country-and-western songs, blare from saloons and radios. Irrigated ranch lands feed Mexico's finest beef cattle, and rivers flowing westward from the Sierra Madre are diverted by giant dams to irrigate a low rainfall area that now produces cotton, sugarcane, and vegetables. Hermosillo, Sonora's capital, bustles with agricultural commerce in the midst of the fertile lands that turn dry again toward the coast.

Updated by
Michael Oliver

Mexico Highway 15 begins at the border town of Nogales, Sonora, adjacent to the U.S. town of Nogales, Arizona. It passes south through Hermosillo and reaches the Sea of Cortés (also called the Gulf of California) at Guaymas, 418 km (259 mi) from the Arizona border. The Sonoran desert dominates the landscape through northern Sonora, as it does in southern Arizona. Long stretches of flat scrub are punctuated by brown hills and mountains, towering saguaros, and organ-pipe cacti. Highway 15 continues southward after Guaymas, as the landscape gradually takes on a more tropical aspect, and finally enters the state of Sinaloa just north of the city of Los Mochis. Except in the mountains, the entire region is uncomfortably warm between May and late September, with afternoon temperatures sometimes exceeding 120°F.

In 1540 Francisco Vázquez de Coronado, governor of the provinces to the south, became the first Spanish leader to walk the plains of Sonora. More than a century later, Father Eusebio Francisco Kino led a missionary expedition to Sonora and what is now southern Arizona—an area referred to historically as the Pimeria Alta—founding several towns and missions there. Although Alamos, in the south of Sonora, boomed with silver-mining wealth in the late 17th century, no one paid much attention to the northern part of the region for the next three centuries. It was not part of the Mexican territory ceded to the U.S. after the War of 1847. Sonora became a haven for Arizona outlaws, and international squabbles bloomed and faded over the next decades as officials argued over issues such as the right to pursue criminals across the border. During the last quarter of the 19th century, Porfirio Díaz, dictator of Mexico between 1876 and 1911, finally moved to secure the state by settling it.

For Don Porfirio, however, developing Sonora may have been a mistake: the revolutionaries who later overthrew him came from here. In fact, Mexico was ruled by the Sonora dynasty for nearly a quarter of a century and, until the tragic 1994 assassination of Sonora native son Luis Donaldo Colosio, the ruling party candidate for president, it appeared likely that a Sonoran would soon control the destiny of the country again. The Mexican Revolution brought prosperity to the state, and it continues to thrive. With irrigation from the state's dams, inhabitants have been able to grow enough wheat not only for Mexico but for export, as well.

Pleasures and Pastimes

Beaches

Lively hotels and restaurants line the shores of San Carlos, Guaymas, and Puerto Peñasco, but if you are willing to take more time for travel and forgo facilities, you'll find miles and miles of more secluded beaches that run along the Sea of Cortés. Most of Sonora's main beaches have paved access roads, but some of the best—like pristine Playa San Nicolás just south of Bahía Kino (Kino Bay)—await the adventurous at the end of rutted, washed-out dirt tracks.

Dining

Sonoran cuisine is distinguished by the excellent quality of its steaks and the freshness of its fish. Sonora is also the home of the giant flour tortilla and bean burritos. There are no five-star restaurants in the state, but shrimp lovers will find plenty to like in Sonora, especially in Guaymas. Traditional-Mexican foodies will be contented as well, with an abundance of dishes like enchiladas, tamales, and some of the best *carne asada* (grilled meat) in Mexico. Indeed, the style of Mexican cooking with which most Americans are familiar derives from this region. Casual dress (but not beachwear) is always acceptable, and reservations are rarely needed.

CATEGORY	COST*
$$$$	over $35
$$$	$25–$35
$$	$15–$25
$	under $15

per person for a three-course meal, excluding drinks, service, and tax

Lodging

In Sonora you might find yourself sleeping in a converted convent in fashionable Alamos, growing a Hemingway beard in a beach bungalow at Bahía Kino, or luxuriating in a five-star resort in San Carlos. Lodging in Sonora is no longer the bargain it once was, but prices are still lower here than for comparable accommodations in the better-known vacation spots in other parts of Mexico.

CATEGORY	COST*
$$$$	over $100
$$$	$70–$100
$$	$35–$70
$	under $35

All prices are for a standard double room, excluding tax.

Missions

Nestled among the hills and river valleys of Sonora are a handful of almost forgotten missions founded by Jesuit fathers in the 17th and early 18th centuries, and completed by the Franciscans in the late-18th and 19th centuries. Some of the churches, such as San Ignacio, still serve the small agricultural communities around them, whereas others, like Cocospera, are mostly shadows of their remarkable past.

Exploring Sonora

Sonoran landscapes are as varied as the state is vast. From the seemingly endless tracts of desert that tumble into the Sea of Cortés to the mountains of the Sierra Madre and the fields and valleys that nurture its produce and livestock, Sonora is a place of dramatic contrasts.

Mexico Highway 2 enters Sonora's far northwest from Baja California, paralleling the U.S. border. There are several crossing points, but most people entering the state from the United States do so at Nogales, south of Tucson, Arizona. It is also a point of entry for winter fruit and vegetables exported to the United States.

Numbers in the text correspond to numbers in the margin and on the Sonora map.

Great Itineraries

Because it is so diverse, the state of Sonora demands eight days or more to really do it justice. With less time, you'll have to decide whether seashore, mountains, or missions are most important.

IF YOU HAVE 3 DAYS

Take Highway 15 south from Nogales to **Magdalena** ⑤ and stop to see the plaza and church, and the bones of missionary explorer Eusebio Francisco Kino. If you're interested in churches, you might spend the night in this area—nine missions founded by Father Kino are accessible from here by car. Then continue south on the same highway to the state capital, **Hermosillo** ⑥, where you will find a variety of good hotels and restaurants. Overnight here and spend the next morning touring the city or browsing through the Centro Ecologico, which is of special interest to children. After lunch, drive west on Highway 16 to **Bahía Kino** ⑦, a perfect beach for a one- or two-night retreat. It's about six hours from Kino Bay back to the Arizona border.

An alternative three-day itinerary would be to cross the U.S. border at Lukeville-Sonoyta, explore the lunarlike regions of the **Sierra del Pinacate** ②, and then cool off on the beaches of **Puerto Peñasco** ③ for the rest of that day and the next. Then take Highway 2 about 2¾ hours to **Magdalena** ⑤ and stop for lunch and a visit to the Kino shrine before heading north on Highway 15 to **Nogales** ①. Spend an afternoon shopping there before you cross the U.S. border.

IF YOU HAVE 5 DAYS

Take Highway 15 from Nogales to **Guaymas** ⑨; the drive will take six or seven hours. Exploring the town of Guaymas and the adjacent resort area of **San Carlos** ⑩ will give you plenty to do for two days and nights. Continue south and then east for 3½ hours to charming colonial **Alamos** ⑪, in the foothills of the Sierra Madre. After one or two nights in Alamos, head back north. You might consider spending the night along the tranquil shores of **Bahía Kino** ⑦ on your way home.

IF YOU HAVE 8 DAYS

Combine the second of the three-day itineraries with the five-day itinerary, but stop off at **Hermosillo** ⑥ on the way down to **Guaymas** ⑨. If you have extra time, you might want to take a short side trip from Alamos to **Aduana** ⑫, former site of a thriving silver mine and current location of a thriving gourmet restaurant.

When to Tour

Temperatures in Sonora in summer are as high as they are in southern Arizona, so unless you are prepared to broil, plan your trip sometime between October and April.

Nogales

❶ *100 km (62 mi) south of Tucson via Highway 19, on the Arizona-Mexico border.*

Bustling Nogales can become fairly rowdy on weekend evenings, when under-age Tucsonans head south of the border to drink. It has some good restaurants, however, and visitors can find fine-quality crafts and furnishings in addition to the usual made-for-tourists souvenirs. If you're just coming for the day, it's best to park on the Arizona side of the border—you'll see many guarded lots that cost about $8 for the day—and walk across. Practically all the good shopping is within easy strolling distance of the border.

The shopping area centers mainly on **Avenida Obregón,** which begins a few blocks west of the border entrance and runs north–south; just

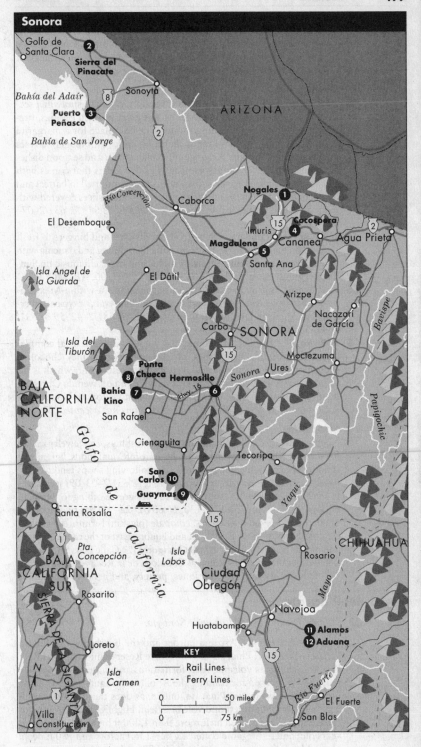

Sonora

Golfo de Santa Clara

2

Sierra del Pinacate

Bahía del Adaír

Sonoyta

8

Puerto Peñasco **3**

Bahía de San Jorge

ARIZONA

Río Concepción

Caborca

El Desemboque

Nogales **1**

Imuris

15

Cocospera **4**

Magdalena **5**

Cananea

Agua Prieta

2

Santa Ana

Isla Angel de la Guarda

El Dátil

Arizpe

Nacozari de García

Bavispe

Carbó

SONORA

Moctezuma

15

Isla del Tiburón

Punta Chueca **8**

Hermosillo **6**

Sonora

Ures

Papigochic

Bahía Kino **7**

Hwy 16

San Rafael

BAJA CALIFORNIA NORTE

Golfo

Cienaguita

Tecoripa

San Carlos **10**

de

Guaymas **9**

Santa Rosalía

California

Yaqui

CHIHUAHUA

1

Pta. Concepción

Isla Lobos

Rosario

BAJA CALIFORNIA SUR

Ciudad Obregón

Mayo

SIERRA DE LA GIGANTA

Rosarito

Navojoa

Loreto

Huatabampo

Alamos **11**

Aduana **12**

15

N

Isla Carmen

KEY

— Rail Lines
--- Ferry Lines

Río Fuerte

Villa Constitución

1

0   50 miles

0   75 km

El Fuerte

San Blas

follow the crowds. Most of the good restaurants near the border are also on Obregón. Take Obregón as far south as you like; you'll know you have entered workaday Mexico when the shops are no longer fronted by smiling, English-speaking hucksters trying to hustle you in the door ("What you need? I got the best! Cheap! Take a look!").

Dining

$$ ✕ **El Balcon de la Roca.** This elegant restaurant on the sprawling sec-
★ ond floor of a stately old stone house has great beamed ceilings, fire-
places, and a variety of dining rooms. The best place for a margarita is on the balcony overlooking a charming patio with magnolia trees and a gurgling fountain. Among the excellent meat and seafood dishes is *carne tampiqueña,* an assortment of grilled meats that comes with a *chili relleno* (chili pepper stuffed with cheese and fried in batter) and an enchilada. The *queso la Roca* (seasoned potato slices covered with melted cheese) makes a fine starter. ⊠ *Calle Elias 91,* ☎ *631/2–07–60. AE, MC, V.*

$$ ✕ **El Cid.** You'll find everything from sandwiches and burgers to fresh seafood on the menu here. There is candlelight dining and dancing with live music on Friday and Saturday nights and mariachi music on Sunday evenings. ⊠ *Av. Obregón 124,* ☎ *631/2–64–00. AE, MC, V.*

$$ ✕ **El Greco.** As its name implies, this Mediterranean-with-a-Mexican-
colonial-twist serves up Greek salads, Alaskan king crab, or typical Amer-
ican and Mexican fare. ⊠ *Av. Obregón 152,* ☎ *631/2–42–59 or 631/2–43–58. AE, MC, V.*

$ ✕ **Elvira.** The free shot of tequila that comes with each meal comple-
ments Elvira's fine fish dishes, chicken *mole* (in a spicy chocolate sauce), or chiles rellenos. This large, friendly restaurant, which is di-
vided into intimate dining areas, is at the very end of Avenida Obregón, next to the border. It is popular with frequent visitors to Nogales. ⊠ *Av. Obregón 1,* ☎ *631/2–47–73. Reservations not accepted. MC, V.*

Shopping

Nogales's wide selection of handicrafts, furnishings, and jewelry makes for some of Sonora's best shopping. At more informal shops, bargaining is not only acceptable but expected. The following shops tend to have fixed prices: **El Sarape** (⊠ Av. Obregón 161, ☎ 631/2–03–09) specializes in sterling-silver jewelry from Taxco and designer clothing for women. **Mickey** (⊠ Av. Obregón 128–130, ☎ 631/2–22–99) has two floors of handcrafted Mexican treasures, *equipale* (pigskin) furniture, Talavera ceramic dishes, pottery, glassware, and liquors. East of the railroad tracks and off the beaten tourist path, **El Changarro** (⊠ Calle Elias 93, ☎ 631/2–05–45), in the same building as El Balcon de la Roca restaurant, car-
ries high-quality furniture, antiques, pottery, and handwoven rugs.

Sierra del Pinacate

❷ *50 km (31 mi) west of Lukeville-Sonoyta.*

Midway between the Arizona border and the beach town of Puerto Peñasco, Sierra del Pinacate is a Biosphere Reserve International Park best known for its volcanic rock formations and craters so moonlike that they were used for training the Apollo astronauts. The diversity of the lava flows makes Pinacate unique, as does the striking combi-
nation of Sonoran desert and volcanic field. Highlights of the area in-
clude **Santa Clara peak,** a little more than 4,000 ft high and 2.5 million years old, and **El Elegante crater,** 1½ km (1 mi) across and 750 ft deep, created by a giant steam eruption 150,000 years ago.

There are no facilities of any kind at Pinacate. You'll need to bring your own water—take plenty of it—food, and extra gasoline, as well as a good map, which you can get in Arizona at Si Como No bookstore in Ajo or at Tucson's Map and Flag Center, or in Mexico at the Desert and Ocean Studies Center (CEDO; ☞ Puerto Peñasco, *below*). A high-clearance vehicle is strongly advised, and four-wheel drive is recommended. Camping is allowed with a permit obtainable from the Oficina Sierra del Pinacate in Sonoyta, a block south of the border crossing on the west side of the street. You must register at the park entrance.

Summer temperatures can be blistering. The best time to visit is between November and March, when daytime temperatures range between 60°F and 90°F. Tours can be arranged through the tourism office in Puerto Peñasco. An excellent naturalist-led tour in English is also available from **Ajo Stage Lines** (✉ 1041 Solana St., Ajo, AZ 85321, ☎ 520/387–6559 or 800/942–1981). As with protected wilderness areas in the United States, no animals, plants, or archaeological artifacts may be removed.

Puerto Peñasco

❸ *104 km (65 mi) south of the Arizona border at Lukeville on Mexico Highway 8.*

The real appeal of Puerto Peñasco, at the north end of the Sea of Cortés, is the miles of sandy beaches, often punctuated by stretches of black, volcanic rock that get inundated at high tide. Rocky Point has a remarkably high tide change—as much as 23 ft, depending on the season. At low tide the rocky stretches of coastline are great for poking among countless shallow tidal pools inhabited by such local marine life as octopus, shrimp, and starfish.

This coastline is rapidly changing. Construction began in 1998 on the $150 million Marina Peñasco, a complex that will eventually include a shopping center, luxury hotel, condos and villas, a yacht club, and a 200-slip marina, all designed to attract a more upscale U.S. clientele. Other developers are waiting in the wings, pending its success.

The town was established about 1927, when Mexican fishermen found abundant shrimp beds in the area and American John Stone built the first hotel; Al Capone was a frequent visitor during the Prohibition era, when he was hiding from U.S. law. Puerto Peñasco is rather faceless, but the "old town" has a number of interesting shopping stalls, fish markets, and restaurants.

Puerto Peñasco was dubbed Rocky Point by British explorers in the 18th century, and that's the name most Americans know it by today. For now it is a popular wintering spot for American RVers and retirees, and a favorite weekend getaway for beach-seeking Arizonans—especially college kids during spring break. Thanks to a program called "Sonora Only," Mexican immigration laws—as well as vehicle import laws—are relaxed for tourists crossing in this so-called free zone. Simply drive through—but don't neglect to get Mexican auto insurance, which is crucial in case of an accident.

The northern Gulf area forms a desert-coast ecosystem unmatched in the Western Hemisphere, and scientists from both the United States and Mexico conduct active research programs at the **Desert and Ocean Studies Center** (known as CEDO, its acronym in Spanish), about 3 km (2 mi) east of town on Fremont Boulevard. You can tour the facility to learn about its history and current projects, or come by to pick up a tide calendar—useful if you're planning beach activities. Don't forget to stop in at the small **CETMAR Aquarium** next door, which is an especially kid-friendly, hands-on experience. Talks are sporadically given on a wide range of topics. ⊠ *Turn east at municipal building and follow signs for Caborca Rd., where there will be signs for Las Conchas Beach and CEDO,* ☎ *638/2–01–13.* 🎫 *Free.* ☉ *Tour hrs and scheduled talks are posted on door.*

Dining and Lodging

$$$ ✕ **Puesta del Sol.** As the name ("setting of the sun") implies, this is a
★ perfect place to see the sun set, with plenty of outdoor seating on a patio overlooking the beach. Puesta del Sol serves many seafood dishes and soups, with appetizers to appeal to American tastes. The fish Mornay (with a creamy cheese sauce) is good, as is the grilled lobster—and the margaritas are to die for. ⊠ *Hotel Playa Bonita, Paseo Balboa,* ☎ *638/3–25–86. MC, V.*

$$–$$$ ✕ **Costa Brava.** In town, this small, split-level restaurant has excellent service and a great view of the Gulf. For four, try the excellent *marinera de la casa,* a combination of octopus, shrimp, sea snails, and clams. The house specialty is a dish of succulent prawns, done any way you like, and the seafood soup is also good. Hundreds of business cards on the wall testify to this place's popularity with Americans. ⊠ *Blvd. Kino and Paseo Estrella,* ☎ *638/3–31–30. MC, V.*

$$ ✕ **Friendly Dolphin.** You'll recognize this charming downtown spot by the bright blue dolphins on its doorway. Inside, the place feels like a wealthy Mexican family home, with nicely stuccoed ceilings, wood-paneled windows, and exquisite hand-painted tiles. Interesting old photographs, including some of Emiliano Zapata and Pancho Villa, line the hallways. Gaston, the owner, can often be found on the premises singing in an operatic baritone as rich and robust as the food he serves. Unique family recipes include foil-wrapped shrimp or fish prepared *estilo delfin*—steamed in orange juice, herbs, and spices. An upstairs porch overlooks the harbor. ⊠ *Av. Alcantar 44,* ☎ *638/3–26–08. MC, V.*

$$ ✕ **La Casa del Capitán.** Perched atop Rocky Point's tallest "rock," this restaurant has the best views over the bay and the town below. There's inside dining, but the long outdoor porch overlooking the sea is the place to be. A wide-ranging menu includes everything from nachos and quesadillas to flaming brandied jumbo shrimp. ⊠ *Follow Blvd. Benito Juárez to* LA CASA DEL CAPITÁN *sign and head up the steep hill,* ☎ *638/3–60–27. Reservations not accepted. AE, MC, V.*

$ ✕ **La Curva.** This friendly family restaurant with great Mexican food is easy to spot if you look for the mermaid on the sign. Turn east where the railroad tracks cross the main road into town. ⊠ *Blvd. Kino and Comonfort,* ☎ *638/3–34–70. AE, MC, V.*

$$$–$$$$ 🏨 **Plaza Las Glorias.** One of a chain of hotels in Mexico, Plaza Las Glorias is the first lodging of its kind at Puerto Peñasco. Changing the face of the town, this soaring monument to Mexico's desire to promote tourism at any cost sits like a sand-colored fortress overlooking the beach. The open, marble-floored lobby with its towering quadrangular ceiling and bamboo-covered skylights draws gasps of admiration from the busloads of tourists who have started to flock to the hotel after its inauguration in 1995. Rooms are well appointed, many of them with kitchenettes; all offer ocean views. The hotel sells condominiums and has a marina and a shopping center. ⊠ *Paseo Las Glorias, Las Explanadas 83550,* ☎ *638/3–60–10; 638/3–60–27; 01–800/ 2–6446 in Mexico; 713/448–2829 in the U.S. 210 rooms. Restaurant, bar, pool. AE, MC, V.*

$$$ 🏨 **Playa Bonita.** One of the first three hotels in Rocky Point, Playa Bonita offers clean, comfortable rooms; ask for one facing the hotel's broad, sandy beach. This place is very popular with Americans, who also enjoy the **Puesta del Sol** restaurant (☞ *above*). An RV park offers 200 hookups at $16 a day. ⊠ *Paseo Balboa 100, 83550,* ☎ *638/3–25–86;*

520/994–4475 or 602/994–4475 in the U.S. 76 rooms, 2 suites. Restaurant, bar, beach. MC, V.

$$ ⊞ **Costa Brava.** All the rooms in this small, clean, and economical downtown hotel overlook the Gulf. Right down the street are the fish markets, popular with those who like to bring the catch of the day back across the border. ⊠ *Malecón Kino and Paseo Estrella, 83550,* ☎ *638/ 3–41–00 or 638/3–41–01,* FAX *638/3–36–21. 25 rooms. Restaurant, bar. MC, V.*

Nightlife and the Arts

Nightlife tends to be spontaneous and informal in Puerto Peñasco. A favorite dance spot is the **Pitahya Bar.** All ages tend to congregate along the beaches near **Manny's Beach Club** (⊠ Av. Coahuila and Blvd. Matamoros, ☎ 638/3–36–05), where recorded music is always blaring. Manny's is the place for those who don't want to put too much distance between the water's edge and their next margarita; it's right on the beach, with signs like NO SHOES, NO SHIRT, NO PROBLEM. The food is nothing special, but as the quintessential beach hangout for all ages, Manny's is not to be missed.

Outdoor Activities and Sports

WATER SPORTS

At **Sun and Fun Dive Shop** (⊠ Av. Benito Juárez and Parque Industrial, ☎ 638/3–54–50) you can rent diving or snorkeling equipment or receive PADI and NAUI scuba instruction.

Cocospera

❹ *104 km (65 mi) southeast of Nogales, between Imuris and Cananea.*

Cocospera is one of the two dozen churches established in the state of Sonora and Arizona by Father Eusebio Francisco Kino between 1687 and 1711; the crumbling adobe mission sits on a bluff above an oak forest and farmlands in a mountain pass in the Sierra Madre Occidental. To get here, take Highway 15 Libre to Highway 2.

Magdalena

❺ *25 km (16 mi) south of Imuris, 96 km (60 mi) from Nogales.*

The grave of Father Eusebio Francisco Kino was discovered in Magdalena in 1966. His remains are in a mausoleum across the plaza from **Santa Maria Magdalena de Buquivaba,** the cathedral that stands on one of the missions he founded. A $1 million monument to the memory of this pioneer priest also stands here. A number of shops surround the plaza, selling curios, blankets, and religious artifacts; stop in at the bakery for some excellent sweet rolls and bread. Magdalena is now also known as the final resting place of its beloved native son, slain presidential candidate Luis Donaldo Colosio, whose statue also presides over the plaza.

If you're really interested in Spanish missions and in rural Mexican life as it has been lived for centuries, drive just a few kilometers north of Magdalena on a clearly marked dirt road to **San Ignacio,** another of Father Kino's churches, still in use in a tiny Mexican farming village.

Hermosillo

❻ *185 km (115 mi) south of Magdalena on Highway 15.*

Hermosillo (pop. 750,000) is the capital of Sonora, a status it has held on and off since 1831. It is the seat of the state university and benefits from that institution's cultural activities. If you know a bit of

Spanish, you might think the city's name means "little beauty." In fact, it honors José Mariá González Hermosillo, one of the leaders in Mexico's War of Independence.

Settled in 1742 by Captain Augustín de Vildosola and a contingent of 50 soldiers, Hermosillo was originally called Pitic, the Pima Indian name for "the place where two rivers meet." The city's most prestigious neighborhood—home to the governor and U.S. consul, among other prominent citizens—still bears the name Pitic. Located immediately north of the highway into town and just behind the Hotel Bugambilia, the area is worth an hour's stroll to view the creative handling of concrete, tile, and other materials in the homes of Hermosillo's affluent residents.

A business center for the state of Sonora, Hermosillo is largely modern, but some lovely plazas and parks hark back to a more graceful postcolonial past. Although Hermosillo is usually just considered a jumping-off point for Bahía Kino or Guaymas, it has a number of attractions in its own right, as well as the best accommodations and restaurants until you reach Guaymas or San Carlos.

The city's main boulevard is lined with monuments to Sonora's famous sons: Adolfo de la Huerta, Alvaro Obregón, Plutarco Elías Calles, and Abelardo Rodríguez (after whom the boulevard is named), all presidents of the country after the revolution (Rodríguez also served as governor of Sonora). At the center of town, look for the **Plaza Zaragoza** and the standout **Catedral de San Agustín** (1878), which has been regilded at great expense. Across from the cathedral is the **Palacio de Gobierno del Estado,** its graceful courtyard surrounded by somewhat disjunctive modern murals depicting Sonoran history, and between the two buildings sits an ornate Victorian gazebo. On the south edge of town, the **Plaza de los Tres Pueblos** marks the original settlement.

Overlooking the city on the Cerro la Campana (Hill of Bells), the **Museo de Sonora,** a former penitentiary, has a variety of regional history displays; you can also tour the tiny, dark prison cells. ⊠ *Calle California,* ☎ *62/13–12–34.* ⌑ *$1.50, free Sun.* ☉ *Wed.–Sat. 10–5, Sun. 9–4.*

The **Museo de la Universidad de Sonora** has interesting exhibits of pre-Columbian artifacts, including 500-year-old Pima mummies. ⊠ *Blvds. Luis Encinas and Rosales.* ☎ *No phone.* ⌑ *Free.* ☉ *Weekdays 9–1 and 4–6, Sat. 9–1.*

On the highway south of town, stop at the **Centro Ecologico,** an environmental and ecological park (read: zoo) where more than 500 species of plants and animals—both native to Sonora as well as exotic—can be found. It is modeled after the Arizona-Sonora Desert Museum in Tucson and is best visited November through March because of the heat and lack of shade the rest of the year. ⊠ *Hwy. 15, 5 km (3 mi) south of Hermosillo,* ☎ *62/50–11–37,* ⌑ *$1.00.* ☉ *Wed.–Sun. 8–6.*

Dining and Lodging

$$$ ✕ **Xochimilco.** This large and friendly place, which offers indoor and outdoor dining, is deeply shaded by large fiddle-leaf figs and yucateca trees on a narrow side street in the southern part of town (from Rosales, follow the sign near the Oxxo store). Popular with locals and regulars from across the border, Xochimilco serves well-prepared typical Sonoran dishes. ⊠ *Av. Obregón 51,* ☎ *62/50–40–89. AE, MC, V.*

$$ ✕ **Hotel Bugambilia Restaurant.** A small dining room with beamed ceilings and red-checked tablecloths and curtains, this cheerful place serves excellent tortilla soup and Mexican-style veal cutlets. For breakfast, try *chilaquiles con huevos* (chopped tortillas cooked in red chili sauce,

topped with scrambled or fried eggs), a house specialty. ⊠ *Blvd. Kino 712,* ☎ *62/14–50–50. Reservations not accepted. AE, MC, V.*

$$ ✕ **Sonora Steak.** Here in a restored old house you can enjoy the finest cuts of the famous Sonoran beef at reasonable prices. An organist plays mellow music to help digest that steak. The restaurant also serves seafood. ⊠ *Blvd. Kino 914,* ☎ *62/10–03–13. AE, MC, V.*

$$$$ 🏨 **Fiesta Americana.** Hermosillo's only five-star hotel, this full-service property is the largest in town and popular among business travelers. The decor is predictable, but some rooms have excellent views, and the beds are large and firm. ⊠ *Blvd. Kino 369, 83010,* ☎ *62/59–60–00; 800/504–5000 in the U.S.,* 📠 *62/59–60–60. 221 rooms. Restaurant, cafeteria, lobby lounge, pool, hot tub, tennis courts, dance club, travel services. AE, MC, V.*

$$$$ 🏨 **Holiday Inn Hermosillo.** Two-thirds of the attractive rooms in this contemporary Spanish-style hotel look out on extensive, well-kept gardens and a good-size pool. The staff is geared toward accommodating the many Mexican business travelers who stay here. ⊠ *Blvd. Kino and Ramón Corral, 83010,* ☎ *62/14–45–70,* 📠 *62/14–64–73. 132 rooms. Restaurant, bar, pool, airport shuttle. AE, MC, V.*

$$$ 🏨 **Hotel Bugambilia.** This green oasis on the boulevard into Hermosillo is one of the first motels in town. Here you will find a more personal atmosphere than at some of the faceless chain hotels around it. Rates include breakfast. ⊠ *Blvd. Kino 712, 83010,* ☎ *62/14–50–50,* 📠 *62/14–52–52. 104 rooms. Restaurant, pool. AE, MC, V.*

$$ 🏨 **Hotel Gandara.** One of the old traditional spots in Hermosillo, this hotel, with its palm trees, gardens, and colonnades, has the charm of Old Spain. You can stay in bungalows or in conventional-style hotel rooms; all offer cable TV and coffeemakers. ⊠ *Blvd. E. Kino 1000, 83010,* ☎ *62/14–44–14 or 62/15–64–24,* 📠 *62/14–99–26. 141 rooms, 8 suites. Restaurant, bar, coffee shop, pool. AE, DC, MC, V.*

Nightlife and the Arts

Hermosillo is home to several lively night spots, including **La Trova** (⊠ Calle Guerrero and Tamaulipas, ☎ 62/14–28–61), with live Latin-style music nightly; **Bar Freedom** (⊠ Blvd. Kino 1012, ☎ 62/15–06–40), a popular upscale bar and restaurant; and **Marco n' Charlie's** (⊠ Corner of Blvd. Rodríguez and Calle San Luis Potosí, ☎ 62/15–30–61), a crowded watering hole for young, middle-class locals.

Shopping

In the downtown markets of Hermosillo, particularly along Avenidas Serdán and Monterrey, you can buy anything from blankets and candles to wedding attire, as well as a variety of *charro* (Mexican cowboy) items; the variety of goods concentrated in this area equals what you'll find in Nogales, and the prices are better.

En Route Drive from Hermosillo through flat agricultural land and dusty vineyards to where the desert finally meets the sea and the monochrome landscape gives way to a refreshing palette of colors.

Bahía Kino

➐ *104 km (65 mi) west of Hermosillo on Highway 16.*

On the shore of the Sea of Cortés lies Bahía Kino, home to some of the prettiest beaches in northwest Mexico. For many years, Bahía Kino was undiscovered except by RV owners and other aficionados of the unspoiled. In the last decade, great change has come at the hands of North Americans who have been plopping down trailers and building condos and beach houses here. Bahía Kino itself is divided into **Kino Viejo** (Old Kino), the Mexican village; and **Kino Nuevo** (New Kino), where the beaches, condos, RV sites, and other typical tourist facilities are.

Consider taking a run across the narrow channel to **Isla del Tiburón** (Shark Island), which is being developed into one of the finest wildlife and game refuges in North America. Permission to visit Tiburón may be obtained from the Port Captain, at the end of the main street in Kino Viejo. Ask at any of the area hotels or RV parks where to find a reliable guide. Only the Seri Indians, for whom Isla del Tiburón is a traditional fishing ground, need no permit. For a crash ethnography of the Seri, poke around the hodgepodge of a collection in the **Museo de los Seris.** You can buy their fine ironwood carvings of animals, tightly woven and prized baskets, as well as other crafts in the museum's gift shop. ⊠ *Mar de Cortés at Calle Progreso.* 🎟 *30¢.* ⊙ *Wed.–Sun. 9–4.*

Note: The Seri are sensitive about having their picture taken. The polite thing to do is to ask permission before snapping.

Dining and Lodging

$$ ✕ **El Pargo Rojo.** The best-known restaurant in town has fish and fishnets decorating its two rooms (with a small bandstand for musicians). The catch of the day varies, but you can depend on consistent quality, including such classics as a brimming shrimp cocktail for starters and fresh lobster any way you want it. Fine cuts of meat are available and, depending on your luck, you'll either be serenaded by Mexican musicians or the ceaseless wailing of recorded, polka-like *norteña* music. ⊠ *Blvd. Mar de Cortés 1426, Kino Nuevo,* ☎ *624/2–02–05. MC, V.*

$ ✕ **La Palapa.** This thatch-roof restaurant, with a casual interior and a small balcony overlooking the beach, has great seafood. The shrimp brochette with green chilies is memorable, especially with a glass of some very palatable Mexican wine. ⊠ *Mar de Cortés and Wellington on the way into Kino Nuevo,* ☎ *624/2–02–10. No credit cards.*

$ ✕ **Restaurant Kino Bay.** Owned by an American, this clean, comfortable family restaurant overlooks the bay. One of the few places serving breakfast, lunch, and dinner, it's a perfect spot for coffee, morning pancakes, and pelican viewing. ⊠ *Near the end of Blvd. Mar de Cortés, Kino Nuevo,* ☎ *624/2–00–49. Reservations not accepted. No credit cards.*

$ ✕ **Restaurant Marlin.** This restaurant in Kino Viejo is only hard to find the first time; after that, you will return frequently, drawn by the clean, unpretentious atmosphere and congenial service—not to mention margaritas as big as fishbowls. After serving you superb seafood dishes such as *sopa de siete mares* (soup of the seven seas) or *jaiba a la diabla* (deviled crab), your waiter might produce a guitar and serenade you free of charge. ⊠ *Calles Tastiota and Guaymas,* ☎ *624/2–01–11. Reservations not accepted. AE, MC, V.*

$$$ 🏨 **Anchor House.** Opened in June '96, this bed-and-breakfast, the first in town, is a spacious, beachfront home away from home for travelers who want a warm American welcome. The owners have lived in Kino for years and are knowledgeable about every facet of life in this growing community. Coffee is always brewing, and the breakfasts, included in the rate, are hearty. Children and pets are not allowed, and there is a two-night minimum. ⊠ *Blvd. Mar de Cortés 3525, Kino Nuevo 83340,* ☎ *624/2–01–41. 5 rooms. No credit cards.*

$$$ 🏨 **Posada Santa Gemma.** On a beautiful strip of beach, these eclectically furnished two-story bungalows with kitchenettes, fireplaces, and spectacular views of the sea are ideal for families. Each has two bedrooms and sleeps four or five comfortably. Bring your own cooking utensils and settle in. ⊠ *Blvd. Mar de Cortés, Kino Nuevo 83340,* ☎ *624/2–00–26. 14 bungalows. Beach. AE, MC, V.*

$$ ⌖ **Kino Bay RV Park and Motel.** Your best buy for the money, this small, friendly motel across from the beach offers clean, comfortable rooms with two double beds, microwaves, refrigerators, and sinks; in addition it has 200 RV spaces with full hookups ($18). A barbecue area sits under huge rubber trees. ✉ *At end of main road, Kino Nuevo (Reservations: Box 857, Hermosillo 83000),* ☎ *624/2–00–83. 8 rooms. Grocery, 5-hole golf course. MC, V.*

$$ ⌖ **Posada del Mar.** Across the street from the beach and set back from a rambling garden with a small swimming pool and winding walkways hewn from rock, this mission-style hotel was one of the first in Kino Nuevo. Antiques and Mexican art lend the place an old-world charm. ✉ *Blvd. Mar de Cortés and Creta, Box 132, Kino Nuevo 83340,* ☎ *624/2–01–55; 62/18–12–17 in Hermosillo. 42 rooms, 2 suites, 4 bungalows. Restaurant, bar, pool. MC, V.*

Punta Chueca

❽ *27 km (17 mi) north of Bahía Kino.*

This rustic Seri fishing village perches at the end of a bumpy, winding dirt road. You'll pass exquisite vistas of the bay, distant empty beaches, and rolling mountains. The inhabitants of this community live a subsistence life-style, relying on the sea and desert much as they have for hundreds of years.

With fewer than 1,000 Seris left in existence, this tribe represents an ancient culture on the verge of extinction. The Seris' love for their natural surroundings is evident in the necklaces that they have traditionally worn and now create to sell. Pretty little shells are wound into the shape of flowers and strung with wild desert seeds and tiny bleached snake vertebrae to result in delicate necklaces. Seri women weave elaborate *canastas* (baskets) of torote grass, which have become highly prized and expensive.

As you get out of your car and head toward the only "store" in town for a soda, be prepared to encounter a growing entourage of Seri women dressed in colorful ankle-length skirts, their heads covered with scarves and their eager outstretched arms laden with necklaces for sale. The Seri are also famous for carving figures from ironwood that represent the animal world around them, including dolphins, turtles, and pelicans. Note: In recent years, many Mexican merchants have taken to machine-making large figures out of ironwood for the tourist trade, thereby seriously depleting the supply of the unique tree that grows only in the Sonoran desert. Make sure the ones you buy are made by the Seri people.

Guaymas

❾ *128 km (79 mi) south of Hermosillo.*

The buzz and bustle of Guaymas—Mexico's seventh largest port—is pleasantly backdropped by a landscape of rusty red, saguaro-speckled mountains that nudge the deep-blue waters of a sprawling bay on the Sea of Cortés.

The Spanish arrived in this "port of ports" as early as the mid-16th century. In 1701, two Jesuit priests, Father Francisco Eusebio Kino and his colleague Juan María Salvatierra, erected a mission base here intended to convert the native Guaimas, Seri, and Yaqui Indians.

Guaymas was officially declared a port in 1814 and became an important center of trade with Europe as well as within Mexico. In 1847, during the Mexican–American War, U.S. naval forces attacked and occupied the town for a year. Bumbling filibuster William Walker also managed to take Guaymas for a short time in 1853, and, in 1866, during Maximilian's brief reign, the French took control. Today, foreign invaders in Guaymas are mostly travelers passing through on their way somewhere else. Given its proximity to the beaches of San Carlos (☞ San Carlos, *below*) and Mazatlán, as well as the twice-weekly ferry that travels between Guaymas and Santa Rosalia on the Baja peninsula, modern Guaymas is more a stepping stone than a destination. That said, there is plenty to do here to put together a pleasant day in this congenial seaside town.

Downtown, take a walk on the *malecón* (boardwalk), and look out over the bay at fishing boats loaded down with heavy black nets and the giant shrimp Guaymas is famous for. The shrimp fleet is only allowed to go out to sea between September and May so that the shrimp have time to replenish their numbers. A small plaza along the port has a handsome bronze statue commemorating the local fishermen.

After pushing your way through the throngs at the *mercado,* a daily municipal market, you'll find a quieter place waiting for you in the 19th-century **Catedral de San Fernando.** Or you might relax in the typical Mexican park across the street from the church, **Plaza 13 de Julio,** with its white, Moorish-style, lacy wrought-iron bandstand and time-worn, tree-shaded benches. The **Plaza de los Tres Presidentes** is within walking distance of the Plaza 13 de Julio. In front of the 1899 **Palacio Municipal** (City Hall) loom imposing statues of the three presidents of Mexico born in Sonora: Plutarco Elías Calles, Adolfo de la Huerta, and Abelardo Rodríguez.

Dining and Lodging

$ ✕ **Los Barcos.** Across the street from the harbor, Los Barcos offers a predictable seafood-and-steak menu. The main room is large and pseudo–beach casual, with picnic tables and overhead palm fronds and nets; there are also two smaller, more traditional dining rooms. The crab tostadas are especially good. ⊠ *Malecón Malpica between Calles 21 and 22,* ☎ *622/2–76–50. Reservations not accepted. AE, MC, V.*

$ ✕ **Los Delfines.** At the end of the harbor, this spacious restaurant offers a variety of no-frills fresh seafood and a postcard-perfect view of the water. Popular with the locals, who enjoy the *ambiente familiar* (family atmosphere), Los Delfines has a festive air; on weekends, a band plays in the afternoon. ⊠ *At end of Blvd. Sanchez Taboada,* ☎ *622/ 2–92–30. Reservations not accepted. No credit cards.*

$$$ 🏨 **Playa de Cortés.** This fine, sprawling old hotel overlooking the Bacochibampo Bay is built and decorated like a Spanish colonial hacienda, with towering wooden beamed ceilings and a lavish fireplace in the reception room. With tropical landscaping and a sweeping view of the bay, this hotel evokes its genteel past before condos and time-shares. The rooms are furnished with hand-carved antiques; many have fireplaces and balconies. Some private casitas are available, each with the name of a small Sonoran town. To reach this hotel from the highway, take the turnoff for Colonia Miramar. ⊠ *Bahía Bacochibampo, San Carlos 85506,* ☎ *622/1–12–24 or 622/1–10–48,* ℻ *622/1–01–35. 120 rooms. Restaurant, bar, pool, tennis, beach. AE, DC, MC, V.*

$$ 🏨 **Hotel Armida.** Close to the shops and restaurants of downtown Guaymas, this sand-color hotel has a large, well-kept pool; a good coffee shop where locals gather for power breakfasts; and an excellent steak house, **El Oeste.** Rooms in the hotel's old section are dark, with ill-matched furnishings. The larger, brighter accommodations in the newest section, done in light wood, are worth the higher rates; many have balconies overlooking the pool. ⊠ *Carretera Internacional, Box*

296, 85420, ☎ *622/2–52–20; 800/732–0780 in the U.S.,* ⅋ᴀ̄ˣ *622/2–04–48. 80 rooms, 45 suites. 2 restaurants, bar, coffee shop, room service, pool, dance club, laundry service, airport shuttle, car rental. AE, MC, V.*

$$
★ 🖫 **Las Playitas.** The best deal in town, this combination trailer park–motel on Guaymas Bay has plain but appealing rooms—with tinwork mirrors and beamed ceilings—opening out onto a cobblestoned, bougainvillea-lined path. Even if you don't sleep here, come for the lively, eclectically decorated restaurant and bar. The food is good and inexpensive, but if you'd rather eat what you caught that day, you can get it cooked up, with trimmings added, for a small price. ⊠ *Carretera al Varadero Nacional, 85420,* ☎ *622/2–27–53. 29 bungalows with shower, 93 RV spaces. Restaurant, bar, pool. MC, V.*

Nightlife and the Arts

Gathering spots in the area include the disco **Xanadu** (⊠ Malecón Malpica, ☎ 622/2–83–88) and, for the younger set, **Charles Baby** (⊠ Av. Serdán and Malecón, ☎ No phone).

Shopping

Plaza el Vigía, a huge shopping center on the main road from the north into Guaymas, has everything from groceries, film, toiletries, and clothes to household wares. In Guaymas itself, the **Mercado Publico** is the best place for *artesanías* (crafts) such as baskets, hats, necklaces, and other trinkets. Visit the **Casa de las Conchas** (⊠ Calle 24, No. 3 across from Plaza de la Madre, ☎ 622/2–01–99) and admire beautiful seashell handicrafts, as well as 400 to 500 types of seashells; right next door is a great little ice-cream parlor.

San Carlos

🄿 *32 km (20 mi) northwest of Guaymas.*

Long considered an extension of Guaymas, this resort town—on the other side of the rocky peninsula that separates Bacochibampo Bay from San Carlos Bay—has a personality of its own. Whitewashed, red tile–roof houses snuggle together along the water where countless yachts and motorboats are docked. The town is a laid-back favorite among professional anglers, North American tourists, and the time-share crowd, as well as wealthy Mexican families from Guaymas. There is a growing assortment of hotels, motels, and condominiums, as well as a country club with an 18-hole golf course.

The overlapping of desert and tropical flora and fauna has created a fascinating diversity of species along this coast. Among marine life, more than 650 species of fish exist here; red snapper, marlin, corbina, yellowtail, sea bass, and flounder are commonly caught. Whales have been spotted in San Carlos Bay, and there is an abundance of dolphins and pelicans. The water is calm and warm enough through October for the whole family to enjoy excellent swimming. Scuba, snorkeling, fishing, and boat excursions are popular, too.

The quiet 5-km (3-mi) stretch of sandy beach at **Los Algodones,** where the Plaza San Carlos and Club Med are now, was in the 1960s a location site for the film *Catch 22.* Mexico's first man-made marina lies in the shadow of the jagged twin-peaked **Tetakawi mountain,** once a sacred site where Indian warriors gathered to gain spiritual strength. An interesting day trip can be made by boat out to the pristine **San Pedro Island,** where sea lions frolic on the rocks.

To reach San Carlos from Guaymas, take Mexico 15 north for about 8 km (5 mi) to the well-marked turnoff for San Carlos. Continue along for 24 km (15 mi) on the four-lane **Corredor Escénico** (Scenic Corridor), completed in 1995 to replace an infamously bumpy road.

Dining and Lodging

$$ ✕ **Bananas.** American food (BLTs, burgers, fries), Mexican fare—try "shrimp bananas," wrapped in bacon with barbecue sauce—and even sushi are served in a single large room with a peaked ceiling lined with palm fronds. There are a few seats in the entrance patio as well. A copy of Charlie Chaplin's 1924 marriage license hangs on the wall by the rest rooms. ⊠ *On main road through San Carlos,* ☎ *622/6–06–10. Reservations not accepted. MC, V.*

$–$$ ✕ **El Pueblito.** This is San Carlos's most sophisticated eatery, although the excessive "authentic" Mexican decor is a bit of overkill. Here in the San Carlos Plaza Hotel, you'll be treated to creative international cuisine, as well as regional favorites. The Tetakawi Prawns, stuffed with other shellfish and served in a rich and creamy *béchamel* sauce, are a heavenly indulgence. ⊠ *San Carlos Plaza Hotel, Mar Barmejo 4, Los Algodones, Box 441,* ☎ *622/6–07–77. AE, MC, V.*

$–$$ ✕ **Rosa's Cantina.** Bearing little resemblance to the saloon in M. Robins's song, "El Paso," this cozy, pink, laid-back restaurant has picnic tables that fill two large dining rooms. Come to feast on ample breakfasts of *huevos rancheros* (eggs with chorizo). The tortilla soup is great for lunch or dinner, and the homemade salsa is divine. ⊠ *Carretera San Carlos,* ☎ *622/6–10–00. Reservations not accepted. MC, V.*

$$$$ ⊡ **Club Med Sonora Bay.** Although San Carlos is expanding rapidly in its direction, this Club Med is still secluded from the main tourist area, its verdant 42-acre complex spreading fortresslike behind a large gate fronted by saguaro cacti. Accommodations are characteristically tasteful but plain, and the range of available activities is as great as one would expect from the chain. All meals, soft drinks, and tips—and many sports, such as sailing and scuba diving—are included. It's worth paying extra for the dawn horseback ride to the foothills of the nearby Sierra Madre. ⊠ *Playa de los Algodones, 85400,* ☎ *622/7–00–09; 800/258–2633 in the U.S.,* ⊞ *622/6–00–70. 375 rooms. Restaurant, bar, pool, 2 saunas, golf course, 31 tennis courts, horseback riding, beach, windsurfing, boating. AE, MC, V. Closed end of Oct.–mid-Mar.*

$$$$ ⊡ **Plaza Las Glorias.** This condo-hotel complex overlooks the San Carlos marina. It's smaller than the San Carlos Plaza but nearly as impressive. Subtle pastels set a tasteful tone in the comfortable modern rooms. Most accommodations have a tiny kitchenette; a few have private hot tubs. ⊠ *Plaza Comercial San Carlos 10, Planta Baja, 85006,* ☎ *622/6–10–21 or 622/6–10–34,* ⊞ *622/6–10–35. 87 rooms, 18 suites. Restaurant, snack bar, 3 pools, golf, baby-sitting, travel services, car rental. AE, MC, V.*

$$$$ ⊡ **San Carlos Plaza Hotel and Resort.** This huge structure, rising from San Carlos Bay en route to Club Med, is thoroughly and strikingly pink. This is the most luxurious hotel in Sonora, with a marble-floored atrium lobby that opens onto a large pool and beach. Rooms are done in an attractive contemporary style. All have safes and minibars, and rooms on the first two floors have balconies overlooking the sea. Children love the swimming-pool slide and horseback riding on the beautiful beach. ⊠ *Mar Barmejo 4, Los Algodones, Box 441, 85506,* ☎ *622/7–00–77; 800/854–2320 in the U.S.,* ⊞ *622/7–00–98. 148 rooms, 25 suites. 2 restaurants, 2 bars, snack bar, 2 pools, hot tub, 2 tennis courts, exercise room, horseback riding, volleyball, beach, travel services, car rental. AE, MC, V.*

$$ ⊡ **Fiesta San Carlos.** One of the first in San Carlos, this small hotel on the bay has a lot of charm and is clean and comfortable. Accommonuns' cells and have fireplaces, tiled baths, antique furnishings, and high-quality handicrafts on the walls. Room rates include breakfast, and there is an excellent restaurant. ⊠ *Av. Obregón 10, Box 12, 85760,* ☎ *642/8–00–10,* FAX *642/8–04–00. 14 rooms. Restaurant, bar, pool. MC, V.*

$$$ 🏨 **Casa Encantada.** Set just off the main square, this lovely B&B owned by a California couple is the converted 250-year-old mansion of one of Alamos's former Spanish mine owners. Rooms retain a colonial character, with high-beamed ceilings, fireplaces, and carved-wood furnishings; all have tiled private baths and good lighting, Andalusian-style. The copious breakfast, served on a plant-filled patio overlooking a small pool, might include frittatas, fresh fruit, and home-baked breads. ⊠ *Calle Juárez 20, 85760,* ☎ *642/8–04–82 or 800/422–5485,* FAX *642/8–02–21. 9 rooms. Pool, bicycles, meeting room. MC, V.*

$$$ 🏨 **Casa Obregón Dieciocho.** This sprawling 275-year-old casa owned by artist and chef Roberto Bloor has three suites, each with a bedroom, sitting room, fireplace, coffeemaker, bath, and private patio. Guests can sit out in a lovely, lush garden; colorful crafts and paintings abound throughout the house. Write away for reservations or (at a slightly extra expense) book through Fraser & Pratt Real Estate in Alamos (☎ 642/8–07–90 or 642/8–01–18). ⊠ *Av. Obregón 18, 85760,* ☎ *No phone. 3 suites. No credit cards.*

$$$ 🏨 **Hotel la Mansion.** With its stately rooms centered on a flowering courtyard, this pretty 17th-century mansion and well-run hotel holds the honor of having hosted several of Mexico's presidents. ⊠ *Calle Obregón 2, 85760,* ☎ *642/8–02–21. 12 rooms. Restaurant, tapas bar. No credit cards.*

Shopping

It's worth a peek into the three crowded rooms of **El Nicho Curios** (⊠ Cuatro Caminos 15, across from the church, ☎ 642/8–02–13), filled with treasures from Mexican *retablos* (religious paintings) to old jewelry and regional pottery. In addition, small stores lining the **Alameda** (northwest of the central plaza) sell Mexican sweets, fabrics, belts, and hats, among other items.

Aduana

⑫ *8 km (5 mi) west of Alamos, 3 km (2 mi) off the road from Navajoa.*

Aduana was formerly the site of one of the richest mines in the district. Today it is the unlikely location of one of Sonora's best restaurants, **Casa la Aduana.** Mexican tourists and expats living in Alamos spill from the nondescript dining room onto the patio of this gourmet eatery run by California exile Samuel Beardsley. A four-course, prix-fixe menu ($12 or $16) is served at both lunch and dinner, and entrée selections might include chicken in apple chipotle cream or grilled Norwegian salmon. Call ahead for reservations (☎ 648/2–02–60).

After the meal at Casa la Aduana, stroll across the plaza to the **Iglesia de Nuestra Señora de Balvanere.** A cactus that grows out of one of the church's walls is said to mark the spot where the Virgin appeared to the Yaqui Indians in the late 17th century, an event that is celebrated by a procession every November 21.

SONORA A TO Z

Arriving and Departing

By Bus

In Mexico, **Elite** runs a deluxe air-conditioned coach from Nogales to Hermosillo for around $10. Frequent buses travel to Hermosillo and

Guaymas from Nogales, Tijuana, and Mexicali via **Tres Estrellas de Oro** and **Transportes de Sonora.** Try the comfortable **TUFESA** buses, which travel all the way to Ciudad Obregón and Navajoa.

By Car

Many visitors to Sonora travel by car from Tucson via I–19 to the border in Nogales, Arizona, and then pick up Mexico 15, which begins in Nogales, Sonora. Highway 15 is now a divided four-lane road, making the ride much quicker and easier than it used to be. This convenience, however, doesn't come cheaply: drivers heading down to Alamos can expect to pay approximately $35 in fees. The alternative "Libre" (free) routes are much slower and often poorly maintained.

There are two points of entry into Nogales. Most drivers take U.S. I–19 all the way to the end and then follow the signs to the border crossing. This route, however, will take you through the busiest streets of Nogales. It's better to take the Mariposa exit west from I–19, which leads to the international truck crossing and joins a small periphery highway that connects with Highway 15 after skirting the worst of Nogales traffic.

The official checkpoint for entering Mexico is 21 km (13 mi) south of Nogales. It is here that you have to buy insurance and complete the paperwork to bring in your car if you haven't already done so in Tucson at either **Sanborn's Mexico Insurance** (⊠ 2900 E. Broadway, ☎ 520/327–1255) or the **Arizona Automobile Association** (⊠ 8204 E. Broadway, ☎ 520/296–7461; ⊠ 6950 N. Oracle Rd., ☎ 520/885–0694). *See* Driving *in* Smart Travel Tips A to Z, at the end of this book, regarding requirements for driving into Mexico.

As a result of the **Sonora Only** program, if you are not planning to go farther into Mexico, you do not have to leave a credit-card imprint or pay an $11 deposit (though insurance is still required). Stop at the "Sonora Only" booth at the Km 21 checkpoint.

By Ferry

Ferries from Guaymas to Santa Rosalia on the Baja coast leave on Tuesday and Friday at 8 AM and arrive (tentatively) at 3 PM. You can buy tickets the day before or the morning of the day you plan to travel unless you have a car, for which you must make reservations three weeks in advance. Fares are about $14 for a reclining seat and $30 for a cabin. Car transportation is priced by car size, with the smallest cars costing at least $150. Purchase tickets at the **Sematur ferry terminal** on Avenida Serdán, just east of the center of Guaymas (☎ 622/2–23–24). Check with the Guaymas tourist office (☞ Visitor Information, *below*) for the latest information and schedules.

By Plane

AeroCalifornia (☎ 62/60–25–55; 800/237–6225 in the U.S.) offers a daily nonstop jet service from Los Angeles and Tucson to Hermosillo. **Aeroméxico** and its subsidiary **Aero Litoral** (☎ 622/2–01–23; 01–800/021–4000; 800/237–6639 in the U.S.) has daily flights to Hermosillo and Guaymas from Tucson, and flights from Los Angeles to Hermosillo. Aeroméxico has direct flights to Hermosillo from many cities in Mexico—including Mexico City, Tijuana, Chihuahua, and Guadalajara—and from La Paz and Mexico City to Guaymas; connections to other U.S. cities can be made from these points.

Getting Around

By far the easiest way to get around is by automobile—Guaymas and San Carlos are particularly spread out. Most hotels have car-rental agencies. Buses between towns are frequent and inexpensive.

Contacts and Resources

Car Rental

In **Guaymas,** the agencies to contact are **Budget** (☎ 622/2–14–50) and **Hertz** (☎ 622/2–10–00), both on the main highway.

Rental agencies in **Hermosillo** include **Budget** (✉ Carmendia 46 and Tamaulipas, ☎ 62/14–30–33) and **Hertz** (✉ Blvds. Rodríguez and Guerrero, ☎ 62/14–85–00).

Consulate

There is a **U.S. consulate** in Hermosillo (✉ Calle Monterrey 140, in back of Hotel Calinda near downtown, ☎ 62/17–23–75).

Emergencies

Guaymas: Police (☎ 622/2–00–30), **Red Cross** (☎ 622/3–05–87), **hospital** (☎ 622/2–01–22).

Hermosillo: Police (☎ 62/13–40–46), **Red Cross** (☎ 62/14–07–69), **hospital** (☎ 62/13–25–56). The **Green Angels** (☎ 62/14–63–04) is a very helpful state-run road service for travelers.

Puerto Peñasco: Red Cross (☎ 638/3–22–66).

Guided Tours

Arizona Coach Tours (✉ 5865 E. 2nd St., Tucson, AZ 85711, ☎ 520/748–0369) runs mostly senior-citizen package tours to Alamos, San Carlos, and Puerto Peñasco. **Mexico Tours** (✉ 1800 E. Ft. Lowell, 126-144, Tucson, AZ 85719, ☎ 520/325–3284) offers package tours to San Carlos and Puerto Peñasco. **Apex Mexi Trips** offers group and individual trips to the area (✉ Box 32368, Tucson, AZ 85751, ☎ 520/806–1631).

Visitor Information

Note: In addition to the tourism offices listed below—which are better to visit than to try to reach by phone— the **Sonora Department of Tourism** (☎ 800/4SONORA) has a toll-free information number in the U.S., and they will send you mounds of information and a helpful, full-color magazine.

Alamos (✉ Main Plaza, Calle Juárez 6, ☎ 642/8–04–50); **Guaymas** (✉ Malecón Malpica between Calles 22 and 23, ☎ 622/2–17–51); **San Carlos** (✉ Corredor Escénico San Carlos, Edificio Bella Mar, ☎ 622/6–12–22); **Hermosillo** (✉ Centro de Gobierno, 3rd floor, Paseo Canal and Comonfort, ☎ 62/17–00–60 or 62/13–18–61; 800/4SONORA in the U.S.); and **Puerto Peñasco** (✉ Blvds. Juárez and V. Estrella, ☎ 638/3–41–29 or 638/3–25–55).

5 THE COPPER CANYON: FROM LOS MOCHIS TO CHIHUAHUA CITY

In the heart of the scenic, rugged Sierra Madre, the Copper Canyon—a series of gorges, some deeper than the Grand Canyon in the United States—is known for hikes that range from pleasant walks to thigh-busting descents to the canyon floor. These gorges are home to the largely reclusive Tarahumara Indians. One of North America's most spectacular train trips snakes its way through this magnificent, largely uncharted region, usually beginning or ending in the lively city of Chihuahua.

Updated by
Michael Oliver

THE MAGNIFICENT series of gorges known collectively as *Barranca del Cobre*—the Copper Canyon—is the real hidden treasure of the Sierra Madre. Inaccessible to the casual visitor until the early 1960s and still largely uncharted, the canyons may now be explored by taking one of the most breathtaking rides in North America: the *Chihuahua al Pacífico* railroad whistles down 661 km (410 mi) of track, passing through 87 tunnels and crossing 35 bridges through rugged country as rich in history and culture as in physical beauty.

The *barrancas* (canyons) of the Sierra Tarahumara, as this portion of the Sierra Madre Occidental is known, are on the eastern edge of the Pacific "Ring of Fire." Seismic and volcanic activity set the stage, in the process hurling a good quantity of the earth's buried mineral wealth to the surface. The canyons were then carved over eons by the Urique, Septentrión, Batopilas, and Chínipas rivers and further defined by wind erosion. Totaling more than 1,452 km (900 mi) in length and capable of enveloping four times the area of the Arizona Grand Canyon, the gorges are nearly a mile deep and wide in places. The average height of the peaks is 8,000 ft, and some rise to more than 12,000 ft. Four of the major barrancas—Copper, Urique, Sinforosa, and Batopilas—descend deeper than the Grand Canyon, Urique by nearly 1,500 ft.

The idea of building a rail line to cross this region was first conceived in 1872 by Albert Kinsey Owen, an idealistic American socialist. Owen met with some success initially. More than 1,500 people came from the states to join him in Topolobampo, his utopian colony on the Mexican west coast, and in 1881 he obtained a concession from Mexican president General Manuel Gonzáles to build the railroad. Construction on the flat stretches near Los Mochis and Chihuahua presented no difficulties, but eventually the huge Sierra Madre mountains got in the way of Owen's dream, along with the twin scourges of typhoid and disillusionment within the community.

After Owen abandoned the project in 1893, it was taken up in 1900 by American railroad magnate and spiritualist Edward Arthur Stilwell. One of Stilwell's contractors in western Chihuahua was Pancho Villa, who ended up tearing up his own work during the Mexican Revolution in order to impede the movement of government troops. By 1910, when the Mexican Revolution started, the Mexican government had taken charge of building the railroad line. But progress was very slow until 1940, when surveying the difficult Sierra Madre stretch finally began in earnest. Some 90 years and more than $100 million after it started, the Ferrocarril Chihuahua al Pacífico was dedicated on November 23, 1961.

The railroad no longer starts on the coast at Topolobambo but at nearby Los Mochis, and Chihuahua City, capital of the eponymous state, is at the other end of the line. It was established in 1709, after the Spanish discovered silver in the area around 1649. Chihuahua still derives its wealth from mining, as well as ranching, agriculture, and lumber.

Closely related to the Pima Indians of southern Arizona, the Tarahumara Indians once occupied the entire state of Chihuahua. They are renowned for their running ability—*Tarahumara* is a Spanish corruption of their word, *Rarámuri,* which means "running people." It is said that in earlier times they hunted deer by chasing them to the point of collapse. Like so many native groups, the Tarahumara were totally disrupted by the European arrival in the area. The Spanish made them serve in the mines, then the Mexicans and Americans put them to work on the railroads. The threat of slavery and the series of wars that began in the 1600s and continued until the 20th century forced them to retreat deeper and deeper into the canyons, where they are still subject to having their lands taken over by loggers and drug lords. Many are seminomadic, roaming the high plateaus of the Sierra Madre in summer and moving down to the warmer canyon floor in winter to live in stone cliff dwellings or hidden wooden houses. Their population, ravaged over the years by disease, drought, and poverty, is estimated at around 50,000.

Pleasures and Pastimes

Dining

Throughout the canyons you'll encounter relatively undeveloped areas where there are few eateries besides those connected with lodges. In Los Mochis and Topolobampo your best bet is seafood. At the hotels in Cerocahui, Divisadero, and Posada Barrancas, hearty meals are generally included in room rates. There are a few more dining options in Creel, where, in addition to hotel dining rooms, you'll find small cafés along the town's main street, Avenida López Mateos.

You'll have the greatest choice of restaurants in Chihuahua City. The state is a large producer of beef, so upscale steak houses and places serving *carne asada* (charbroiled strips of marinated beef) abound, but Mexican specialties and seafood flown in from the coast are also available. Many of Chihuahua's well-appointed international restaurants are in the Zona Dorada, on Calle Juárez starting at its intersection with Calle Colón.

Dress is casual everywhere except at some of Chihuahua's pricier restaurants. Unless otherwise indicated, reservations are not necessary.

CATEGORY	COST*
$$$$	over $20
$$$	$15–$20
$$	$8–$15
$	under $8

*per person for a three-course meal, excluding drinks and service, but including 15% sales tax

Hiking

Hiking in the Copper Canyon is fantastic if you take the proper precautions. *Mexico's Copper Canyon Country,* by M. John Fayhee, is a good source of information. But even the most experienced trekkers should enlist the help of local guides, who can be contacted through all the hotels in the area or through travel agents in Los Mochis and Chihuahua. Few adequate maps are available for even the so-called marked trails, and many of the better-worn routes into the canyon are made by the Tarahumara, whose prime concern is getting from one habitable area to the next rather than getting to the bottom.

Urique Canyon is most easily reached from Cerocahui (Bahuichivo stop). The Copper Canyon proper is most accessible from Divisadero. Trails range from easy rim walks to a 27-km (17-mi) descent to the bottom, which takes seven or eight hours. If you're in Creel, a gentle and rewarding hike is the 6-km (4-mi) walk from the Copper Canyon Lodge to 100-ft-high Cusárare Falls. More difficult but equally scenic are the treks down to Recohauta Hot Springs and to the base of Basaseachi Falls. Both are full-day outings. The descent into Batopilas Canyon from Creel—a not-for-the-faint-of-heart affair—requires an overnight stay.

Horseback Riding

Most hotels in the canyon area can arrange for local guides with gentle horses. Most trips are not for couch potatoes, however. The trails into the canyon are badly defined and can be rocky as well as slippery if the weather is icy or wet. At rough spots you might be asked to dismount and walk part of the way. A fairly easy and inexpensive ride is to Wicochic Falls at Cerocahui, about two hours round-trip, including a half-hour hike at the end, where the trail is too narrow for the horses. From Divisadero, the four-hour round-trip to Bacajipare, a Tarahumara village in the Copper Canyon, has stunning vistas, but it's not for the fainthearted.

Lodging

Accommodations in this area tend to fall into two categories: comfortable but characterless in the cities, and charming but rustic in the villages. In Cerocahui, Divisadero, Posada Barrancas (*posada* means "inn"), and Creel, all the hotels send buses or cars to meet the train. If you don't have a reservation, you'll have to make a quick decision and then hop on the hotel vehicle of your choice. In summer, October, and around Christmas and Easter, it's important to book in advance. Where indicated, rates for hotels include meals.

CATEGORY	COST*
$$$$	over $90
$$$	$60–$90
$$	$25–$60
$	under $25

All prices are for a standard double room, excluding 15% tax.

Nightlife

Conversing with fellow guests in your lodge or stargazing from a rooftop balcony are about the extent of nighttime activities in the heart of Sierra country, though occasionally one of the larger hotels will have performances in the evening by Tarahumara dancers or Mexican musicians. Entertainment is considerably less rural in Los Mochis, and Chihuahua is a typically bustling, late-night Mexican city.

Shopping

A main source of cash income for the Tarahumara are their crafts, including lovely handwoven baskets made from *sotol* (an agavelike plant) or pine needles, carved wooden dolls, rustic pottery, roughly carved wooden masks, brightly colored woven belts and sashes made on back-strap looms, and wooden fiddles decorated with faces, from which the men produce haunting music. The Tarahumara women, who are generally shy about talking with tourists, sell their wares throughout the Copper Canyon area. Their prices are fair, so bargaining is unnecessary. Tarahumara wares are sold at the Divisadero train station and at shops in Creel and Chihuahua. Chihuahua is known for affordable cowboy boots, and *bota* (boot) shops proliferate downtown.

Exploring the Copper Canyon

Imagine visiting the Grand Canyon in the days before it was tamed by tourist facilities, and you'll have some sense of what a trip through the Copper Canyon will be like—for better and for worse. That is, with the opportunity to encounter a relatively untouched natural site come some of the discomforts of the rustic experience. But if you are careful in your choice of time to visit and are properly prepared, the trip's myriad rewards should far outstrip any temporary inconveniences.

Numbers in the text correspond to numbers in the margin and on the Copper Canyon map.

Great Itineraries

You'll see some beautiful scenery even if you only ride the railroad—including a panoramic look into the canyons during a 15-minute stop at Divisadero—but you'll take in only a fraction of what the canyons have to offer if you don't get off the train. If possible, plan on a night in Cerocahui (Bahuichivo stop), one at Posada Barrancas or Divisadero (the train stations are five minutes apart), and one or two at Creel.

Most people make their way into the Copper Canyon via Los Mochis, which is the easiest route if you're coming from California or Arizona. On top of that, some of the best scenery is at the western end of the ride, and you're likely to miss it if you approach Los Mochis in the evening. Train delays of three hours or more are not unusual, so even during the extended daylight hours of summer, you can't count on reaching the scenic end of the route before dark. A dam finished in 1996 has added lovely mountain-reflecting "lake" views between Los Mochis and Divisadero.

Even if you drive down to either Los Mochis or Chihuahua, your itinerary will be largely dependent on the schedule of the *Chihuahua al Pacífico* train: it runs in each direction only once a day, so you must plan the time spent in each stop accordingly. The following itineraries assume you will add on a day's train ride to return to your starting point—unless you catch one of the Aerolitoral flights between Los Mochis and Chihuahua. The small turboprops fly low over the mountains and canyons, providing magnificent views.

Note: The state border of Sinaloa and Chihuahua divides two time zones: Mountain Time to the west and Central Time to the east.

IF YOU HAVE 3 DAYS

Departing from **Los Mochis** ①, take the 6 AM *Chihuahua al Pacífico* train and get off at Bahuichivo, where you can explore the mission at **Cerocahui** ③ and the overlook into Urique Canyon. The next day, continue to **Divisadero** ④, where it's practically impossible not to get a room with a view. Spend your last day exploring **Creel** ⑤ and taking a short hike to the falls near Cusárare. If you begin the trip in **Chihuahua City** ⑧, make Cerocahui your final stop.

IF YOU HAVE 5 DAYS

Starting in the west, consider spending a day in the old colonial town of **El Fuerte** ②, then catching the train through the canyons at 7:30 the next morning. Follow the three-day itinerary, above, and use the last day and night to extend your time in **Creel** ⑤, with a visit to the Tarahumara community of San Ignacio or a drive to Basaseachi Falls. If you start in the east, you might take the extra day to explore **Chihuahua City** ⑧. Don't miss Pancho Villa's home, now a museum.

IF YOU HAVE 8 OR MORE DAYS

Spend a day each in **El Fuerte** ②, **Cerocahui** ③, and **Divisadero** ④, then extend your stay in **Creel** ⑤ to include a trip down to the former silver mining town of **Batopilas** ⑥. It's six to eight hours each way by car (preferably four-wheel drive) or bus, so you'll want to spend at least two nights. You'll be ready for modern conveniences after that, so plan to enjoy the restaurants and museums of **Chihuahua City** ⑧ for an additional day. Another option would be to visit the Mennonite community near **Cuauhtémoc** ⑦ before going on to Chihuahua.

When to Tour

Unless you are planning to head deep into the barrancas, winter—December through February—is not the best time to come. Many of the hotels in the region are inadequately prepared for the cold, and the minor

Copper Canyon

rainy season in January renders some of the roads for side excursions impassable. The warm months are May through September. The rainy season, June through September, brings precipitation for a short period every day, but this shouldn't interfere with your enjoyment in any way. It's temperate in the highlands during the summer. If you're planning to hike down into the canyons, however, remember that the deeper you go, the hotter it will get. The best months to visit are October and November, when the weather is still warm and rains have brought out all the colors in the Sierra Tarahumara.

Many people come during Easter and Christmas, specifically to see the Tarahumaras' colorful take on church holidays. On these and other religious feast days, Tarahumara villages challenge one another in races that can go for days. The men run in small groups, upwards of 161 km (100 mi) or more, all the while kicking a wooden ball. It's not *just* fun and games—each village places a huge communal wager for this winner-take-all event.

Los Mochis

❶ *763 km (473 mi) south of Nogales on the Arizona-Mexico border.*

At the western end of the rail line, Los Mochis (population 331,000) is an agricultural boomtown. The rail terminus and the city's location about 19 km (12 mi) from the harbor at Topolobampo make it the export center of the state of Sinaloa, which produces many of Mexico's basic crops. You can tour Benjamin Johnston's sugar refinery, the **Ingenio Azucarero,** around which the town grew. Near Johnston's estate you can still see the American colony—the group of brick bungalows that housed his associates.

The **Museo Regional del Valle del Fuerte** rotates work by local, regional, national, and international artists, and has a didactic exhibit on the area's history. A replica of a railroad steam engine is on permanent display. Labels are in Spanish only. ⊠ *Calles Obregón and Mina,* ☎ 68/12–46–92. ⊡ *$1.* ◔ *Mon.–Sat. 11–2 and 4–7, Sun. 10–1.*

Cottonwood trees and bougainvillea line the highway from Los Mochis to **Topolobampo.** Fields en route are planted with crops ranging from sugarcane to marigolds and mangoes (36 varieties are produced here). Once the site of Albert Owen's utopian colony and the center of the railroad-building activity in the area, it is now a suburb of Los Mochis, 15 minutes away. A huge tuna-packing factory sits at the entrance to the bay, and local fisherman—90% of the population—ply the harbor in small shrimp boats. They compete for their catch with the many dolphins that cavort in the bay. **Isla El Farallón,** off the coast, is a breeding ground for the sea lions that gave the town its name: in the language of the Mayo Indians who once dominated the area, *Topolobampo* means "watering place of the sea lions."

Dining and Lodging

$$ ✕ **El Farallón.** Nautical decor and murals set the tone for the excellent fish served at this simple restaurant. Sushi and sashimi are especially good, as is the *pitalla* (cactus fruit with brightly colored flesh) ice cream. ⊠ *Obregón 593, at Angel Flores,* ☎ *68/12–14–28 or 68/12–12–73. AE, MC, V.*

$$ ✕ **La Fuente.** This unpretentious, colonial-style restaurant specializes in Sinaloan and U.S. beef cuts. Try the local favorite, *Cabreria*—a thinly cut fillet—and bear in mind that Mexicans generally like their beef well done. ⊠ *Republica de Chile 1070 Nte. (North), corner of López Mateos,* ☎ *68/12–47–70. AE, DC, MC, V.*

$$ ✕ **Restaurante España.** This slightly upscale restaurant in downtown Los Mochis is popular with the local business crowd. Good seafood, U.S. cuts of beef, and Spanish dishes are served around an indoor fountain. ⊠ *Obregón 525,* ☎ *68/12–22–21 or 68/12–23–35. AE, MC, V.*

$ ✕ **El Taquito.** In the very center of Los Mochis, this diner-style restaurant serves well-prepared and reasonably priced Mexican standards 24 hours a day, every day. For a hearty meal try the *carne tampiqueña*— a tasty steak with enchiladas, guacamole, and *frijoles* (beans) on the side. ⊠ *Calle Leyva between Hidalgo and Independencia,* ☎ *68/12–81–19. AE, MC, V.*

$$$ ✕⌷ **Hotel Plaza Inn.** This one-time 40-room motel was bought by the Balderrama family in 1986 and is now Los Mochis's only five-star hotel. Catering to businessmen and tourists, the rooms contain luxuries that you won't necessarily find elsewhere: three telephones, one in the bathroom; tubs; card keys; and locks and security safes. Furniture is sturdy but rather standard; beds are covered with floral spreads. A small club for duck hunters and fishermen was recently opened. ⊠ *Leyva and Hidalgo, Box 159, Sinaloa 81200,* ☎ *68/18–70–46; 800/896–8196 in the U.S.,* ℻ *68/12–00–46. 97 rooms, 26 suites. Restaurant, bar, nightclub, travel services. AE, DC, MC, V.*

$$$ ✕⌷ **Hotel Santa Anita.** The central reservations link of the Balderrama chain, this downtown hotel is also an informal information center for what's happening along the *Chihuahua al Pacífico* route and a place to book tours. Built in 1959, the property has medium-size rooms fitted with tasteful and comfortable modern furniture. All have cable TVs, and many have hair dryers and scalloped onyx sinks. The restaurant is one of the best in town. ⊠ *Leyva and Hidalgo, Box 159, Sinaloa 81200,* ☎ *68/18–71–89; 800/896–8196 in the U.S.,* ℻ *68/12–00–46. 133 rooms. Restaurant, bar, travel services. AE, DC, MC, V.*

$$ ⌷ **Corintios Hotel.** This modern-style four-year old dwelling with a dark-glass facade has a bit more class than the other reasonable hotels in town. Rooms have diffused lighting, with both carpeted and tile floors. The hotel has no elevator. ⊠ *Obregón 580 Pte., Sinaloa 82000,* ☎ *68/18–22–24; 800/690–3000 in the U.S.,* ℻ *68/18–22–77. 34 rooms, 1 suite, 6 junior suites. Restaurant, bar, hot tub, exercise room, travel services. AE, MC, V.*

$$ 🏨 **Villa Cahita.** Just two blocks from El Dorado, the main attraction to this rustic hotel is its expansive lobby and restaurant area with comfortable *equipale* (tree-branch-and-pigskin) chairs and high ceilings. The junior suites are a good buy, and a secure parking area is available. ⊠ *Ignacio Ramirez 400 Pte., corner of N. Leyva, Sinaloa 82000,* ☎ *68/12–11–00,* ℻ *68/12–63–35. 50 rooms, 26 junior suites. Restaurant, bar, travel services. AE, DC, MC, V.*

Nightlife

Locals kick up their heels at **Fantasy Laser Club** (⊠ Hotel Plaza Inn, Leyva and Cardenas, ☎ 68/18–70–46) and **Morocco** (⊠ Leyva and Rendon, ☎ 68/12–13–88), two downtown discos. The newer **Yesterday** (⊠ Obregón and Guerrero, ☎ 68/15–38–10) has live bands for an over-30 audience.

Shopping

If you're headed to Divisadero, Creel, or beyond, snacks and reading material can help pass the nine-hour-plus journey. **Libreria Los Mochis** (⊠ Calle Madero Pte. 402, corner of Leyva), has a few dozen English-language best-sellers and magazines and Spanish-language daily newspapers. Across the street from Hotel Santa Anita (☞ Dining and Lodging, *above*), **La Cava Deli** (⊠ Av. Leyva 425, ☎ 14/18–06–36) sells American and Mexican beers, a good selection of wines and liquors, Cuban cigars, and canned and packaged snack foods. If a celebration is in order, you can pick up piñatas for $5–$10 at the **small family business** at Callejon Guadalupe Victoria 43.

El Fuerte

❷ *80 km (50 mi) northeast of Los Mochis.*

If you're ready for old Mexico, take a bus to El Fuerte—instead of the train that leaves at the crack of dawn—stay a night there, and sleep in an hour longer before grabbing the 7:30 train to points east. A bus with comfortable seats leaves from **Mercado Independencia** (⊠ Corner of Avenidas Independencia and Degollado), every half hour from 6:30–7 in the evening for the 1½-hour trip. Fresh foods and prepared meals are available at the mercado.

The small colonial town of El Fuerte was named for the 17th-century fort built by the Spaniards to protect against attacks by the local Mayo, Sinaloa, Zuaque, and Tehueco Indians. Conquistador Don Francisco de Ibarra and a small group of soldiers founded it in 1564, and they called their town San Juan de Carapoa. Located on the central El Camino Real route, El Fuerte was at one time the frontier outpost from which the Spanish set out to explore and settle New Mexico and California. For three centuries, it was a major trading post for gold and silver miners from the nearby Sierras and the most important commercial and farming center of the area. It was chosen as Sinaloa's capital in 1824 and remained so for several years.

There are intact colonial mansions in what is now a rather sleepy town of 25,000. One of the best is the Hotel Posada Hidalgo (☞ Dining and Lodging, *below*). Most of El Fuerte's historic houses are set off the cobblestone streets leading from the central plaza. A number of them have been converted into government offices.

Dining and Lodging

$$ ✕ **El Meson del General.** Just a block off the main plaza, this is the best bet in town for good freshwater fish and crayfish caught in a nearby lake. A varied menu includes Mexican fare, *langostino caque* (local river crawfish) and *lobina* (black bass), and tasty steaks. ✉ *Benito Juárez 202,* ☎ *68/93–02–60. No credit cards.*

$$$$ ✕▥ **Hotel El Fuerte.** Long-time hunting guide Robert Brand expanded
★   his lodge in the restored 380-year-old mansion of Spanish explorer Francisco Ibarra situated on the old Camino Real—two blocks off the town square—and now offers it to canyon travelers. A flower-filled courtyard has been fitted with a waterfall and hidden Jacuzzi, and some of Mexico's best *artesanía* (folk art) adorns the rooms and common areas. ✉ *Montesclaro 37, Sin.,* ☎ *68/93–02–26. 25 rooms. Bar, dining room, air-conditioning, pool. MC, V.*

$$$ ✕▥ **Hotel Posada Hidalgo.** You'll be transported back to a more gra-
★   cious era at this restored hacienda, with its gardens and cobblestone paths, built in 1895 by Rafael Almada, the richest man in nearby Alamos. He had furniture shipped from as far as San Francisco for his lavish home, where he entertained the local elite. It's difficult to choose between the larger rooms with balconies, set off of a lobby filled with period artifacts, and those that open onto the gardens. All are decorated with rough-hewn handcrafted furniture. *Langostino* (crawfish) is a specialty of the hotel dining room. ✉ *Hidalgo 101,* ☎ *68/93–02–42; reservations:* ✉ *Hotel Santa Anita, Leyva and Hidalgo, Box 159, Los Mochis, Sin. 81200,* ☎ *68/18–71–89; 800/896–8196 in the U.S.,* 🖷 *68/12–00–46. 40 rooms. Bar, dining room, pool, dance club. AE, MC, V.*

$$ ✕▥ **Mirador de Montesclaros.** Located on the Cerro de las Pilas, the
★   highest spot in town, with a commanding view of the El Fuerte River and the town, this small, adobe-and-wood posada is owned by local guide Eleazar Gamez, who includes a Continental breakfast and a tour of El Fuerte in the room price. Rooms are rustic but very creatively decorated with family heirlooms and old antiques from friends in town, each with its own story that the owner will gladly share. ✉ *Cerro de las Pilas, Sinaloa,* ☎ *68/93–10–05. 5 rooms. Bar. No credit cards.*

En Route   As the train ascends almost 5,906 ft from El Fuerte to Bahuichivo, it passes through 87 tunnels and over 24 bridges, including the longest and highest ones of the rail system. The scenery shifts from Sinaloan thorn forest, with cactus and scrublike vegetation, to the pools, cascades, and tropical trees of the Río Septentrión canyon, to the oak and pine forest that begins to take over past Temoris, where a plaque marks the dedication of the railroad by President López Mateos in 1961. A new dam adds lakelike pools that reflect the mountains.

Cerocahui

❸ *160 km (100 mi) northeast of El Fuerte.*

The quiet mountain village of Cerocahui is a good place to get a sense of how people live in the canyon area. Next door to the Hotel Misión is a Jesuit mission, established around 1690 by Juan María de Salvatierra, who proselytized widely in the region. It is said that because the Tarahumara were the most difficult Indians to convert, he considered this mission his favorite among the many he founded. Nearby, the church operates a boarding school for Tarahumara children. From the train station at Bahuichivo, two hotels have buses that make the 45-minute ride up the bumpy, unpaved road to Cerocahui.

The prime reason to come to Cerocahui is its accessibility to **Urique Canyon.** It's a kidney-crunching ride to the **Cerro del Gallego lookout,** where amid mountains spread against the horizon you can make out the slim thread of the Urique River and the old mining town of **Urique,** a dot on the distant canyon bottom. On the way up you'll pass a Tarahumara cave where women sell baskets. Nearby, a shrine to the Virgin is strikingly set against a spring in the mountainside surrounded by tropical foliage. From Cerro del Gallego the road continues down the canyon into Urique, which has a few basic hotels and restaurants. A public bus makes the trip from Cerocahui a few times a week, but many people opt for the local hotels' round-trip, full-day tours.

One good hike from Cerocahui is to the **Cueva de las Cruces,** a native funerary cave painted with dozens of crosses. There are other hikes around the area; start at the Paraíso del Oso Lodge.

Dining and Lodging

$$$$ ╳▦ **Hotel Misión.** Part of the Balderrama chain—the Copper Canyon's equivalent of the Grand Canyon's Fred Harvey hotel empire—this is the only accommodation in Cerocahui itself. The main house, which looks like a combination ski lodge and hacienda, contains the hotel's office, small shops, and a dining room, bar, and lounge. There are two large fireplaces around which to huddle in winter: Cerocahui isn't wired for electricity, and the hotel uses its generator for only a few hours, generally from 7 to 9 in the morning and 7 to 11 in the evening. The plain rooms have beamed ceilings, Spanish colonial–style furnishings, and wood-burning stoves and kerosene lamps. ✉ *Cerocahui; reservations: Hotel Santa Anita, Leyva and Hidalgo, Box 159, Los Mochis, Sinaloa 81200,* ☎ *68/18–70–46 ext. 432; 800/896–8196 in the U.S.,* ℻ *68/12–00–46. 30 rooms. Restaurant, bar. AE, DC, MC, V.*

$$$$ ╳▦ **Paraíso del Oso Lodge.** This lodge near Cerocahui has plain rooms with simple handmade wooden furniture. You have to stoke the stove for heat at night, as there is no electricity here. A huge window-filled lobby affords excellent views of the cliffs above the lodge, and a gift shop carries local crafts as well as wares from other parts of Mexico. ✉ *5 km (3 mi) outside of Cerocahui; reservations: Box 31089, El Paso, TX 79931,* ☎ ℻ *14/21–33–72 in Chihuahua City. 16 rooms. Dining room. MC, V in U.S., no credit cards on premises.*

Divisadero

❹ *80 km (50 mi) northeast of Cerocahui.*

There's little to do in Divisadero, a postage stamp of a place on the Continental Divide, but it's impossible to be unmoved by its Copper Canyon vistas—don't miss the canyon at sunset. You can also glimpse a bit of the distant Urique and Tararecua canyons from here. A popular excursion (the Hotel Cabañas Divisadero-Barrancas has a $65 guided trip) that takes about five hours round-trip on foot or on horseback is to Bacajipare, a Tarahumara village in the canyon. The views en route are spectacular. Divisadero and Posada Barrancas offer the greatest comfort in the most spectacular setting on the route.

Dining and Lodging

$$$$ ╳▦ **Hotel Cabañas Divisadero-Barrancas.** The dining room and Rooms 1 through 10 in the old section and 35 through 52 in the newer section of this canyon-rim hotel have panoramic views. The old rooms, with dark furnishings, have decks; newer ones, lighter in decor, have balconies. Food and service get mixed reviews from the international visitors who sign the guest log, but you're not likely to notice what you're eating when you look out of the dining-room window. The Sandoval family has owned the vast tract of land surrounding the hotel since the former mayor of Batopilas, Indalecio Sandoval, bought it to escape the summer heat of that town, and later to hide himself and his

family from Pancho Villa's revolutionaries. ⊠ *Divisadero; reservations: Av. Mirador 4516, Box 661, Colonia Residencial Campestre, Chihuahua, Chihuahua 31000, ☎ 14/10–33–30, ℻ 14/15–65–75. 52 rooms with shower. Restaurant, bar. AE, MC, V.*

$$$$ ✕🖭 **Hotel Posada Barrancas Mirador.** This beautiful pink hotel—an-
★   other link in the Balderrama chain—is perched on the edge of the Copper Canyon. The dining room and all the guest rooms have spectacular
views, and balconies seem to hang right over the abyss. Accommodations are bright, with custom-made furniture, hand-loomed textiles, and
heat from fireplaces. The copious meals are good. The hotel can organize day trips to Creel and the surrounding area. ⊠ *Posada Barrancas;
reservations: Hotel Santa Anita, Leyva and Hidalgo, Box 159, Los
Mochis, Sinaloa 81200, ☎ 68/18–70–46; 800/896–8196 in the U.S.,
℻ 68/12–00–46. 32 rooms. Restaurant, bar. AE, DC, MC, V.*

$$$$ ✕🖭 **Rancho Posada Hotel.** This is a good base from which to explore
the Barranca del Cobre. The 14 remodeled rooms have ocher stucco
walls, ceramic tile floors, and colonial-style, hand-painted furniture;
all but six have cozy fireplaces. The older accommodations, also slated
for remodeling, have plain, contemporary-style furnishings of dark wood.
The redecorated lobby–dining room has a massive stone fireplace,
beamed ceiling, and new wood furniture. ⊠ *Posada Barrancas; reservations: Hotel Santa Anita, Leyva and Hidalgo, Box 159, Los Mochis,
Sinaloa 81200, ☎ 68/18–70–46; 800/896–8196 in the U.S., ℻ 68/12–
00–46. 34 rooms, 1 suite. Restaurant, bar. AE, DC, MC, V.*

$$$ ✕🖭 **Hotel Mansion Tarahumara.** It's a bit disconcerting to come across
a red-turreted, medieval-style "castle" out here in barranca country,
but somehow this whimsical fancy works. All rooms (15 in separate
cabins) have Spanish-contemporary-style light-pine furniture, plus fire-
places and individual heaters. The newest units have pine-log walls.
Older rooms have gray cobblestone walls that match the lodge's ex-
terior. The large dining hall is hard to keep warm in winter but has
wonderful views of the Sierra Madre. ⊠ *Posada Barrancas; reserva-
tions: Av. Juárez 1602–A, Colonia Centro, Chihuahua, Chihuahua
31000, ☎ 14/15–47–21, ℻ 14/16–54–44. 47 rooms. Restaurant, bar,
dance club. AE, MC, V.*

Creel

⑤ *60 km (37 mi) northeast of Divisadero.*

Nestled in pine-covered mountains, Creel is a rugged mining, ranch-
ing, and logging town that grew up around the railroad station. The
largest settlement in the area, it's also a gathering place for Tarahu-
mara Indians seeking supplies and markets for their crafts. It's easy to
imagine American frontier towns at the turn of the century looking like
Creel—without, of course, the international backpacking contingent
that makes this town its base. A cluster of small hotels and tour agen-
cies, most of them along the main street, Avenida López Mateos, of-
fers day trips to the many points of interest in the region.

It's 19 km (12 mi) from Creel to **Cusárare,** a Tarahumara village with
a 300-year-old Jesuit mission. En route you'll pass limpid-blue Lake
Arareco and the turnoff for the strange volcanic-rock formations of
the Valley of the Mushrooms. An impressive waterfall can be reached
by an easy 6-km (4-mi) hike from town through a lovely piñon forest.

If the unpaved roads are passable, consider taking the longer trips to
the **Recohuata Hot Springs,** a fairly strenuous hike down from the rim
of the Tararecua Canyon, and to **El Tejaban,** a spectacular overlook
at the Copper Canyon. Among several worthwhile day trips along the
way to the colonial town of Batopilas (☞ *below*) are **Basihuare,** where

huge vertical outcroppings of rock are crossed with wide horizontal bands of color; the **Urique Canyon overlook,** a perspective that differs from the one at Divisadero; and **La Bufa,** site of a former Spanish silver mine. Seventy-three kilometers (45 miles) northeast of Creel, along an unpaved, winding road, the 806-ft **Basaseachi Falls** are among the highest cascades in North America.

Dining and Lodging

$ ✕ **Tío Molcas.** Furnished with chunky wooden tables and chairs, this small, cheerful restaurant dishes up delicious Mexican food, especially the cheese enchiladas topped with a zesty red pepper sauce. ⊠ *Av. López Mateos 35,* ☎ *145/6–00–33. No credit cards.*

$ ✕ **Veronica's.** This clean, simple eatery on the main street is popular with locals and tourists for its variety of tasty and economic meals. *Comidas corridas*—set meals with soup, main course, and dessert—are available, or you can order à la carte. Try the *sopa de verduras* (vegetable soup), or the vegetarian tacos. The salsa is sublime. ⊠ *Av. López Mateos 34,* ☎ *No phone. No credit cards.*

$$$$ ✕⊞ **Copper Canyon Sierra Lodge.** About 24 km (15 mi) from Creel,
★ set in a peaceful piñon forest near Cusárare Falls, this hotel is a successful blend of elegant and rustic. There's no electricity, but the pine-paneled rooms with antique furnishings and tiled, hot-water baths are romantically equipped with bright kerosene lamps and blazing wood stoves. People usually book rooms here as part of an all-inclusive package deal with a sister lodge in Batopilas (☞ *below*), but walk-ins are welcome, space permitting. ⊠ *Cusárare,* ☎ *No phone; reservations in the U.S.:* ⊠ *Copper Canyon Lodges, 2741 Paldan, Auburn Hills, MI 48326,* ☎ *248/340–7230 or 800/776–3942. 14 rooms. Restaurant, bar. AE, D, MC, V.*

$$$ ⊞ **Best Western: The Lodge at Creel.** At the other end of town from the plaza, this lodge is actually several log buildings with four rooms each. The spacious, well-lighted quarters exude rustic-chic charm with their pine floors and walls, high double beds with thick coverlets, Tarahumara artifacts, and old-fashioned "woodstoves" that are really gas-log heaters controlled by wall thermostats. A few even have a porch swing. The main lodge building has a small bar/dining area with leather-and-wood furniture. A Continental breakfast is available for about $3, lunch for about $5, and dinner for about $8; arrange meals well in advance. ⊠ *Av. López Mateos 61, Creel, Chihuahua 33200,* ☎ *145/6–00–71,* FAX *145/6–00–82. 27 rooms. Restaurant, bar. AE, MC, V.*

$$ ⊞ **Margarita's Plaza Mexicana.** This pretty hotel with two floors of rooms around a private courtyard is one of the town bargains, serving up solid meals and honest hospitality at low prices. The rooms, with private baths, individual heat, and plenty of hot water, are decorated with locally crafted pine furniture and charming murals depicting Tarahumara activities. Rates include breakfast and dinner. ⊠ *Calle Chapultepec a block off López Mateos, Creel, Chihuahua 33200,* ☎ *145/6–02–45 or 145/6–00–45. 26 rooms. Restaurant, bar. AE, MC, V.*

$$ ⊞ **Motel Parador de la Montaña.** This clean, well-run motel has large, comfortable, no-frills rooms with private, hot-water baths; a secure parking area; and a cozy wood-paneled lounge where the warmth radiating from the huge stone fireplace beckons you to plop down on the funky, handmade pine furniture and relax. ⊠ *Av. López Mateo 41, Creel, 33200,* ☎ *145/6–00–77. 55 rooms. Restaurant, bar. AE, MC, V.*

$ ⊞ **Margarita's.** If a small boy at the train station offers to take you to
★ Margarita's, and the prospect of hanging with a motley neo-beatnik crowd appeals, go with him for one of the best deals in town: there's no sign on the door, and even if you follow directions (it's between the two churches facing the plaza), you may think you're walking into a

private kitchen when you enter. At this gathering spot for backpackers, you can get anything from a bunk bed in a dorm room (under $5) to a double room with two beds and a private bathroom (around $8 per person). Prices include breakfast and dinner. The rooms—with wrought-iron lamps, light-wood furnishings, and clean, modern baths—are as pleasant as anything you'll find for three times the price. ⊠ *Av. López Mateos y Parroquia 11, Creel, 33200,* ☎ *145/6–00–45 or 145/6–02–45 (☞ Margarita's Plaza Mexicana, above). 21 rooms, 15 with private bath. Restaurant. No credit cards.*

Nightlife

When the sun goes down in Creel, head to the **Motel Parador de la Montaña** (☞ Dining and Lodging, *above*) for an after-dinner drink, or to **Laylo's Lounge** next to **El Caballo Bayo** restaurant (⊠ Av. Lopez Mateos, at the west end of town, ☎ No phone).

Shopping

For Tarahumara dolls and handiwork, check out **Artesanías Misíon** or the gift shop in **Casa de las Artesanías,** an excellent museum focusing on traditional Tarahumara life, including a beautiful exhibit of black-and-white photographs. Both are on the plaza. At the west end of López Mateos, **Artesanías Victoria** sells huge Tarahumara pots and handmade wood furniture.

Batopilas

⑥ *80 km (50 mi) southeast of Creel.*

This remote village of about 600 people was once one of the wealthiest towns in Mexico because of the nearby veins of silver mined on and off from the time of the conquistadores. At one time it was the only place in the country besides Mexico City that had electricity. The hair-raising, 80-km (50-mi) ride down dusty, unpaved roads to the now-sleepy town at the bottom of Batopilas Canyon takes about 6½ hours by car from Creel (closer to eight hours on the local bus, which runs about three times a week). Sights in this lush, flower-filled oasis include the ruined **hacienda of Alexander Shepherd,** built in the late 1800s by one of the town's wealthiest mine owners; the original **aqueduct,** which still services the town (it's set along the Camino Real); and a triple-domed 17th-century **cathedral,** mysteriously isolated in the Satevo Valley on a scenic 6½ km (4-mi) hike from town. Because it takes much of a day to get down to Batopilas, you'll need to stay overnight at one of the town's modest posadas or at the quirkily opulent Copper Canyon Riverside Lodge.

Lodging

$$$$ 🖾 **Copper Canyon Riverside Lodge.** The sprawling grounds of this restored late-19th-century hacienda are filled with tucked away courtyards, secluded rooftop sun porches, and all sorts of delicious nooks and crannies to explore. Each of the high-ceilinged rooms is individually decorated—for example, one with a prayer niche, another with vintage Elizabeth Taylor posters—but all have spacious private baths and huge, soft feather duvets. Only partially wired for electricity, the accommodations have an odd mix of kerosene reading lamps and electrical outlets for hair dryers. The gourmet meals are excellent, and guests are free to raid the refrigerator and liquor cabinet. Rooms are usually booked as part of an all-inclusive package deal with a sister lodge in Cusárare (☞ Creel, *above*), but walk-ins are welcome, space permitting. ⊠ *Batopilas; reservations in the U.S.: Copper Canyon Lodges, 2741 Paldan, Auburn Hills, MI 48326,* ☎ *810/340–7230 or 800/776–3942. 14 rooms. Restaurant. AE, D, MC, V.*

Cuauhtémoc

❼ *128 km (79 mi) northeast of Creel, 105 km (65 mi) southwest of Chihuahua.*

A rather anomalous experience in Mexico is a visit to the large **Mennonite community** (Campos Menonitas) in the town of Cuauhtémoc. Approximately 20,000 Mennonites came to the San Antonio Valley in 1922 at the invitation of President Alvaro Obregón, who gave them the right to live freely and autonomously in return for farming the 247,000 acres of land.

You can set up a tour in Cuauhtémoc at the **Tarahumara Inn** (✉ Av. Allende and Calle 5A, ☎ 158/1–19–19) or Mennonite David Friesen's travel agency **Cumbres Friesen** (✉ Calle 3A No. 466, ☎ 158/2–54–57, FAX 158/2–40–60), or in Chihuahua (☞ Guided Tours *in* The Copper Canyon and Chihuahua City A to Z, *below*).

Chihuahua City

❽ *375 km (233 mi) south of the El Paso–Ciudad Juárez border, 1,440 km (893 mi) northwest of Mexico City.*

If you're arriving from the peaceful Copper Canyon, the sprawling city of Chihuahua with nearly 1 million inhabitants might come as a bit of a jolt. But, then, the city is known for its jolting nature—two of Mexico's most famous revolutionaries are closely tied to Chihuahua. The father of Mexican independence, Father Miguel Hidalgo, and his coconspirators were executed here by the Spanish in 1811. And Chihuahua was home to General Pancho Villa. His revolutionary army, the División del Norte (Army of the North), was decisive in overthrowing dictator Porfirio Díaz in 1910 and securing victory in the ensuing civil war. A half-century earlier Benito Juárez, known as the Abraham Lincoln of Mexico, made Chihuahua his base when the French invaded the country in 1865.

Whatever you do, don't miss the Museo Histórico de la Revolución en el Estado de Chihuahua, better known as **Pancho Villa's House.** Villa lived in this 1909 mansion, also called the "Quinta Luz" (*quinta* can mean "mansion"), with his second wife, Luz Corral (he had three wives, none of whom he divorced). She stayed here until her death on June 6, 1981, willing the residence to the government, which restored it as a national museum. The 50 small rooms that used to board Villa's bodyguards now house a vast array of artifacts of Chihuahua's cultural and revolutionary history, and some of the house's walls are adorned with vivid and moving murals portraying the Revolution. Parked in the museum's courtyard is the bullet-ridden 1919 Dodge in which Villa was assassinated in 1923 at the age of 45. ✉ *Calle Décima 3014,* ☎ 14/16–29–58. 🎫 *$1.* ☉ *Tues.–Sat. 9–1 and 3–7, Sun. 9–5.*

The **Catedral,** on the town's central square, is also worth a visit. Construction on this beautiful baroque structure was started by the Jesuits in 1726 and not completed until 1825 because of local Indian uprisings. The exterior is made of the pinkish limestone quarried in this region. Inside, the opulent church has Carrara marble altars, a 24-karat solid-gold ceiling, a cedar-and-brass depiction of Saints Peter and Paul, and a huge German-made organ. In the back of the cathedral, the **Museum of Sacred Art** displays the work of seven local artists of the 18th-century Mexican Baroque tradition, as well as commemorations of the 1990 visit of Pope John Paul II. ✉ *Plaza de la Constitución,* ☎ No phone. 🎫 *50¢.* ☉ *Weekdays 10–2 and 4–6.*

The **Palacio de Gobierno** (State Capitol) was built by the Jesuits as a convent in 1882. Converted into government offices in 1891, it was destroyed by a fire in the early 1940s and rebuilt in 1947. Murals around the patio by artist Pino Mora depict famous episodes from the history of the state of Chihuahua. A plaque commemorates the spot where Father Hidalgo was executed on the morning of July 30, 1811. ⊠ *Plaza Hidalgo,* ☎ *14/10–63–24.* ☒ *Free.* ⊙ *Daily 8–8.*

The **Palacio Federal** (Federal Building) houses the city's main post office and telegraph office, as well as the dungeon where Hidalgo was imprisoned before he was executed by the Spanish. His pistols, traveler's trunk, crucifix, and reproductions of his letters are on display here. ⊠ *Calle Libertad, around the corner from Plaza Hidalgo,* ☎ *14/10–35–95.* ☒ *Free.* ⊙ *Tues.–Sun. 9–7.*

The 1721 **Iglesia de San Francisco** (San Francisco Church) is the oldest church built in Chihuahua that is still standing. Father Hidalgo's decapitated body was interred in the chapel of this simple church from 1811 to 1827, when it was sent to Mexico City. His head was publicly displayed for 10 years by Spanish Royalists in Guanajuato on the Alhóndiga de Granaditas (☞ Guanajuato *in* Chapter 7). ⊠ *Av. Libertad at Calle 15,* ☎ *No phone.* ☒ *Free.* ⊙ *Daily 7–7.*

Slightly outside the center of town but well worth a visit is the Cultural Center of the University of Chihuahua, known as **Quinta Gameros.** This hybrid French Second Empire–Art Nouveau mansion, with stained-glass windows, ornate wooden staircases, rococo plaster wall panels, and lavish ironwork, was built in 1910 by Julio Latorre, a Colombian architect, for Manuel Gameros, a wealthy mining engineer. Here you'll see European art of the last two centuries as well as changing exhibitions ranging from Mennonite crafts to contemporary art. ⊠ *Calle Bolívar 401,* ☎ *14/16–66–84.* ☒ *$1.* ⊙ *Mon.–Sat. 11–7.*

Not to be confused with the University Cultural Center, the **Chihuahua Cultural Center** displays exquisite Paquimé ceramics from the pre-Columbian settlement of Casas Grandes northwest of Chihuahua. Around the turn of the century, this downtown mansion belonged to the state governor. ⊠ *Aldama and Ocampo,* ☎ *14/16–13–36.* ☒ *Free.* ⊙ *Tues.–Sun. 10–2 and 4–7.*

A restoration project has made the site of the town's original settlement, **Santa Eulalia,** particularly appealing. The 30-minute drive southeast of town, about $10 one-way by taxi (less by bus), is repaid by the colonial architecture and cobblestone streets of this village, which was founded in 1652. Tours of local silver mines can be arranged by guides in town. The religious artwork in the 18th-century cathedral is noteworthy, and the **Mesón de Santa Eulalia** restaurant, near the plaza, (☎ 14/11–14–27) has a lovely open-air courtyard, open weekends 1:30–7. People start arriving around 3.

Casas Grandes. Some 350 km (161 mi) northwest of Chihuahua, the twin towns of Nuevo Casas Grandes and Casas Grandes are the gateways to the ancient **Paquimé ruins.** Nuevo Casas Grandes, a two-horse town with wide, dusty streets and cowboys en regalia, has the hotels and most of the local restaurants. Sleepy Casas Grandes, 8 km (5 mi) away, occupies a single square block.

Near the aspen-lined Casas Grandes River, sheltered by the burnt-sienna peaks of the Sierra Madre Occidental, Paquimé was inhabited by Pima, Concho, and Tolima peoples between AD 700 and AD 1500. A key site poised between the Pueblo cultures of the now-American southwest and their Mesoamerican neighbors—with architecture borrowed from each—Paquimé was a cosmopolitan center for trade whose residents raised fowl and manufactured jewelry. Evidence of their worldliness still stands, in the form of heat-shielding walls and intricate indoor plumbing systems. The high-tech museum on site houses Paquimé artifacts and ceramics and has bilingual descriptions of local cultural, religious, and economic practices. Museum: $1; ruins: Tues.–Sat. 10–6, Sun. 11–5.

In Nuevo Casas Grandes, **Restaurante Constantino** (⊠ Juárez, across from Hotel Paquimé, ☎ 169/4–10–05) makes great enchiladas and has a full breakfast menu. In Casas Grandes, **El Pueblo** (⊠ off Juárez, ☎ 169/2–41–22; no breakfast) draws residents from all around with great food and a full bar. **Motel Piñón** (⊠ Juárez 605, Nuevo Casas Grandes, ☎ 169/4–01–66) has a swimming pool and a private collection of ancient *ollas* (clay pots) from Paquimé. **Omnibus de México** makes the 5½-hr trip from Chihuahua (☞ Copper Canyon/Chihuahua A to Z, *below*) to Nuevo Casas Grandes. To get to the ruins, hop a blue-and-gold CASAS GRANDES bus (30¢) at Constitución and 16 de Septiembre. After 15 minutes, get off at Casas Grandes' zócalo. Paquimé is a 10-minute walk from town—follow the PAQUIMÉ sign on Constitución. The last bus returns to Nuevo Casas Grandes at 9:00 PM.

Dining and Lodging

$$ ✕ **Club de Los Parados.** Almost four decades of Chihuahua's history
★ have passed through the doors of this landmark restaurant in an adobe-style house. It was started by Tony Vega, a wealthy cattle rancher who died in 1991, as a place to socialize with his fellow ranchers. The story goes that when they went out drinking, the one who sat (or fell) down first had to pick up the tab; Los Parados means "the standing ones." Excellently grilled steaks and chicken as well as tasty Mexican specialties are served in a large room with a wood-burning kiva fireplace—carne asada with guacamole is particularly good. In the bar, saddles serve as stools and metal brands line the walls. ⊠ *Av. Juárez 3901,* ☎ *14/15–35–04 or 14/10–35–59. AE, MC, V.*

$$ ✕ **La Calesa.** A large, dimly lit room with wood paneling and red table-cloths and curtains, this looks like the classic steak house it is. The onion soup and chilies with *aserdo* (a local cheese) make good appetizers. The filet mignon and rib-eye steaks from the area are particularly recommended as entrées; try the former cooked with mushrooms. The clubby bar has a good selection of wines and liquors. ⊠ *Av. Juárez 3300,* ☎ *14/10–10–38 or 14/16–02–22. AE, MC, V.*

$$ ✕ **La Casona.** Something of a hangout for young Chihuahuans, this bistro serves steaks, shrimp dishes, and Mexican finger food. ⊠ *Av. Universidad 1301,* ☎ *14/14–30–53. AE, DC, MC, V. Closed Sun.*

$$ ✕ **Rincon Mexicano.** The folks who run the Mesón de Santa Eulalia restaurant in Santa Eulalia also serve some of the best Mexican food in Chihuahua and always have mariachi musicians to serenade you. ⊠ *Av. Cuauhtémoc 224,* ☎ *14/11–14–27. AE, MC, V.*

$–$$ ✕ **La Casa de Los Milagros.** According to locals, this blue house with frilly white trim was once the favorite "Casa de Muñecas" (dollhouse) of Pancho Villa and his compañeros. Today it's the happening place for light Mexican snacks, drinks, and music after 9 PM, when the courtyard and rooms of this rambling abode start to fill with well-heeled, twentysomething Chihuahuans. ⊠ *Victoria 812, near Ocampo,* ☎ *14/37–06–93. AE, MC, V.*

$ ✕ **Ah Chiles.** If you like it hot, this is the spot. A block from Plaza Hidalgo, this Chihuahua chain serves *norteño* (northern Mexican) food and dishes out a dozen different salsas. It also has foot-long hot dogs, hot wings, stuffed baked potatoes, and shrimp burgers. Ah Chiles is next to three other worthy, modestly priced restaurants: Ricky's Tacos, 1000 Tortas, and El Burro Seguido. ⊠ *Aldama 712, corner of Guerrero,* ☎ *14/37–09–77. No credit cards.*

$$$$ 🏨 **Camino Real Chihuahua.** At the edge of town atop a rise that has magnificent views of the city and surrounding mountains, Chihuahua's first *gran turismo* (Mexico's highest quality level) hotel sparkles with fountains and marble. Designed around an atrium with a several-story waterfall cascading down one wall, the hotel is a contemporary palace of sorts in contrast to the rustic accommodations of the Copper Canyon. Rooms are plush, with richly patterned textiles, comfortable furniture, TV in a tall chest, and bath with both tub and shower. ⊠ *Barranca del Cobre 3211, Frac. Barrancas, 31125,* ☎ *14/29–29–29,* FAX *14/29–29–00. 204 rooms. 2 restaurants, bar, pool, health club, car rental. AE, DC, MC, V.*

$$$ ★ 🏨 **Holiday Inn Hotel & Suites.** This appealing property combines comfort, style, and convenience: 10 minutes from the downtown sights, Chihuahua's first all-suites hotel is decorated in contemporary style with a green or blue-and-beige color scheme. Each room has a kitchenette with stove, dishwasher, and coffeemaker, as well as a VCR. A complimentary Continental breakfast buffet is served at the Clubhouse, which also houses the hotel's indoor pool, hot tub, and exercise equipment. The English-speaking staff is friendly and helpful. ⊠ *Escudero 702, 31000,* ☎ *14/14–33–50; 01–800/0–09–99–00 toll-free in Mexico,* FAX *14/14–33–13. 74 suites. Restaurant, 2 pools, spa, basketball, exercise room. AE, DC, MC, V.*

$$$ 🏨 **Hotel San Francisco.** A favorite of Mexican business travelers, this modern five-story hotel has a prime location right next to the Catedral and Plaza de Armas. Its clean and comfortable if somewhat bland rooms are equipped with color TVs and telephones. The lobby, somewhat gloomy during the day, can be lively at night. ⊠ *Victoria 409, 31000,* ☎ *14/16–75–50; 01–800/71–41–107 toll-free in Mexico; 800/847–2546 in the U.S.,* FAX *14/15–35–38. 111 rooms, 20 suites. Restaurant, bar. AE, MC, V.*

$$$ ★ 🏨 **Palacio del Sol.** This five-star hotel, just two blocks from the cathedral, is set up for businessmen staying long term: some rooms include such luxuries as computer ports and a radio. Although convenient to downtown and very comfortable, it lacks the Mexican charm of some lesser quality hotels. ⊠ *Independencia 116,* ☎ *14/16–60–00; 01–800/1–40–07 toll-free in Mexico; 800/852–4049 in the U.S.,* FAX *14/15–99–47. 110 rooms, 70 suites. 2 restaurants, lobby bar, exercise room, billiards, coin laundry, laundry service, car rental. AE, MC, V.*

$$ 🏨 **Posada Tierra Blanca.** Across the street from the Palacio del Sol but considerably less expensive, this modern motel-style property is convenient to downtown sights. Rooms, decorated in red and black with pseudo-antique furnishings, are large and well heated in winter; all have TVs. The striking *Stages of Man* mural in the lobby was painted by Pina Mora, the same artist who decorated the courtyard of the Palacio de Gobierno. ⊠ *Niños Heroes 102,* ☎ *14/15–00–00,* FAX *14/16–00–63. 98 rooms, 5 suites. Restaurant, piano bar, pool. AE, MC, V.*

Nightlife and the Arts

Chihuahua has the most nightlife options in the Copper Canyon area. **La Reggae** (⊠ Blvd. Ortiz Mena and Bosque de la Reina, ☎ 14/15–47–55) draws a dancing crowd with its rock-and-roll bands. At **Chihuahua Charlie** (⊠ Av. Juárez 3329, ☎ 14/15–70–65), DJs spin discs nightly, and the food is as good as the music. **Taberna La Cerveceria** (⊠ Av. Juárez 3333, ☎ 14/15–83–80) is a glass-encased, neon-laced restaurant and bar in a four-story former brewery where you can play pool on the first floor or dance to a DJ on the fourth. And **La Casa de Los Milagros** (☞ Dining and Lodging, *above*) starts to groove after 9 PM.

El Leñador (⊠ Avs. Tecnologico and Pascual Orozco) is a more tranquil scene with Mexican and Cuban folksingers. The **Hotel San Francisco** (☞ Dining and Lodging, *above*) has a piano bar. The **Hotel**

Sicomoro (⊠ Blvd. Ortiz Mena 411, ☎ 14/13–54–45) has live entertainment nightly in its lobby bar.

Shopping

Mercado de Artesanías (⊠ Calle Victoria 506 and Aldama 511, ☎ 14/15–34–62), a block wide with two entrances, sells everything from jewelry, candy, and T-shirts to crafts from all over the region. Across the street from the *calabozo* (calaboose) where Padre Miguel Hidalgo was jailed, the **Casa de las Artesanías del Estado de Chihuahua** (⊠ Av. Juárez 705, ☎ 14/37–12–92) carries the best selection of Tarahumara and regional crafts in the state. In addition to selling gems and geodes from the area, the **Rock Shop** (⊠ Calle Décima, directly across from Pancho Villa's home, ☎ 14/15–28–82) carries a wide variety of crafts.

COPPER CANYON/CHIHUAHUA A TO Z

Arriving and Departing

By Boat

The Sematur **car ferry** runs daily from La Paz to Topolobampo, depending on the weather. It leaves La Paz at 11 AM and arrives in Topolobampo at approximately 8 PM. The return trip leaves at 10 PM and arrives in La Paz at 7 AM. In Los Mochis, contact the travel agency **Festival Tour** (⊠ Allende Sur 655, below Hotel Americas, Los Mochis, ☎ 68/18–39–86) for information and reservations. In Topolobampo, contact **Sematur** (☎ 68/62–01–41, ⅀ᴀⅩ 68/62–00–35).

By Bus

Chihuahua: The **Chihuahuenses** (☎ 14/29–02–42 or 14/29–02–40) and **Omnibus de México** (☎ 14/10–30–90 or 14/20–15–80) lines run clean, air-conditioned buses from Ciudad Juárez to Chihuahua. These leave approximately every 30 minutes from 7 AM to 8 PM. The cost of the 4½-hour trip is approximately $15 for first class. Buses shuttle between El Paso and Ciudad Juárez every two hours; the price is $5.

Los Mochis: The **Elite** (☎ 63/13–54–01 in Nogales; 68/12–17–57 in Los Mochis), **Transportes del Pacífico** (☎ 63/13–16–06 in Nogales; 68/12–03–41 in Los Mochis), **Transport Norte de Sonora** (☎ 63/12–54–54 in Nogales; 68/12–04–11 in Los Mochis), and **TUFESA** (☎ 63/13–38–62 in Nogales) bus lines all leave every hour from Nogales, Sonora, to Los Mochis. With luck, the $30 trip should take about 12 hours.

By Car

Most U.S. visitors drive to **Chihuahua** via Mexico Highway 45 from the El Paso–Ciudad Juárez border, a distance of 375 km (233 mi), or up from Mexico City, 1,440 km (893 mi). The drive down to **Los Mochis** from Nogales on the Arizona border via Mexico Highway 15, four lanes much of the way, is a distance of 763 km (473 mi).

Paved roads now connect Chihuahua to **Creel** and **Divisadero**: take Mexico Highway 16 west to San Pedro, then State Highway 127 south to Creel. The 300-km (186-mi) trip takes 3½ to 4 hours if the weather is good. This drive, through the pine forests of the Sierra Madre foothills, is more scenic than the railroad route via the plains area. Driving is a good option if you have a four-wheel-drive vehicle, because there are many worthwhile, if difficult, excursions into the canyons from Creel. From Divisadero to **Bahuichivo,** the road is full of potholes and especially dangerous in rain or snow, even with a four-wheel-drive vehicle.

By Plane

To Chihuahua: Aeroméxico and its feeder airline, **Aerolitoral** (⊠ Paseo Bolivar 405, next to Quinta Gameros, ☎ 91–800/9–09–99 toll-free in

Mexico), have daily flights from Los Angeles, Phoenix, and Tucson, and from San Antonio and El Paso. Within Mexico, the airlines have daily flights from Mexico City, Monterrey, Guadalajara, and Tijuana. **Aero-California** (☎ 14/37–10–22 in Chihuahua) has flights from Mexico City and Tijuana. **Lone Star Airlines** (☎ 14/20–91–54 in Chihuahua; 95–800/ 817–1932 toll-free in Mexico) flies nonstop from El Paso and Dallas.

To Los Mochis: AeroCalifornia (☎ 68/18–16–16 in Los Mochis) has daily flights from Los Angeles, Tucson, Tijuana, Mexico City, and Guadalajara. **Aeroméxico** and Aerolitoral (☎ 68/15–29–50 in Los Mochis) fly from Los Angeles, Phoenix, Tucson, San Antonio, El Paso, Mexico City, La Paz, and Chihuahua. On clear days, Aerolitoral's flights between Chihuahua and Los Mochis afford spectacular views of the Sierras and canyons.

By Train

There is no first-class service from any U.S. border city to either Los Mochis or Chihuahua. Some luxury trains go directly from the United States to the Copper Canyon (☞ Train Tours *in* Guided Tours, *below*).

Getting Around

By Taxi

In **Chihuahua** and **Los Mochis,** taxis are easy to find and can be engaged at hotels or hailed on the street. The trip from the airport into town costs about $6 in Chihuahua and $7 in Los Mochis. Always agree on a price before getting into the cab.

By Train

The **Ferrocarril Chihuahua al Pacifico line** (*Che'Pa'*, as it is affectionately called by locals) runs a first-class and a second-class train daily in each direction from Chihuahua and Los Mochis through the Copper Canyon. In January 1998 this line was sold to a consortium of private investors, but at press time, neither travel agents nor the railroad ticket office could give information on long-term reservations or prices. Your best bet is to stay in touch with one of the private train companies or tour operators (☞ Guided Tours, *below*).

The first-class train departs from Los Mochis at 6 AM (sit on the right side of the train for the best views) and arrives in Chihuahua 15 hours later. Westbound, it departs from Chihuahua at 7 AM and arrives in Los Mochis around 7 PM (most of the time, but delays of three hours or more are not unusual). You can buy tickets at the train station or at almost any hotel in Los Mochis or Chihuahua. The price is about $20 each way, plus a 15% charge for up to two stopovers en route, which you should arrange when you buy tickets. Make reservations (☎ 14/15–77–56 in Chihuahua; 68/12–08–53 in Los Mochis; FAX 14/ 10–90–59 in Chihuahua; 68/15–77–75 in Los Mochis) at least a week in advance during the busy months of July, August, and October, and around Christmas and Easter. It's best to book through a hotel, tour company, or travel agency, as the phones in the local train stations are rarely answered. Note: Once the pride of the Mexican rail system, the first-class train, called *El Nuevo Chihuahua al Pacífico,* has become run-down in recent years. It's the scenery, not the vehicle, that continues to draw passengers. Guards armed with automatic weapons often patrol the passenger cars to discourage robberies. Exercise caution by carrying passports and cash in a money belt and leaving your jewelry at home. Bring your own food and drink, as there is no guarantee that even on the first-class train there will be any for sale.

The second-class train, *El Pollero,* leaves an hour later from each terminus but makes many stops and is scheduled to arrive 3½ hours later in both directions than the first-class train. Though it is less comfortable, this train is a good way to meet local residents and their poultry. No reservations are needed; prices are approximately $9 each way.

If you're driving down to Los Mochis, you're better off leaving your car there and taking the train round-trip. If you're coming via Chihuahua, however, consider driving to Creel or Divisadero and doing a round-trip from there.

Contacts and Resources

Car Rental

CHIHUAHUA

Avis (⊠ Av. Universidad 1703, ☎ 14/14–19–99), **Budget** (⊠ Ortiz Mena 3322, ☎ 14/14–21–71), and **Hertz** (⊠ Av. Revolución 514, ☎ 14/16–64–73) all have offices at the airport.

LOS MOCHIS

Car companies at the airport and in town include **AGA** (⊠ Leyva and Callejón Municipal, ☎ 68/12–53–60), **Budget** (⊠ G. Prieto 850 Nte., ☎ 68/15–83–00, FAX 68/15–84–00), and **Hertz** (⊠ Leyva 171 Nte., ☎ 68/12–11–22, FAX 68/15–19–29).

Emergencies

CHIHUAHUA

Police (☎ 14/81–19–00), **Cruz Roja** (Red Cross; ☎ 14/11–14–84 or 14/11–22–11), and **Bomberos** (Fire Dept.; ☎ 14/10–07–70). Two facilities for handling the injured or sick are **Clínica del Parque** (⊠ Calle de la Llave and Leal Rodriguez, ☎ 14/15–74–11 or 14/15–73–39) and **Hospital del Centro del Estado** (⊠ Calle 33 and Rosales, ☎ 14/15–47–20 or 14/15–90–00).

LOS MOCHIS

Police (☎ 68/12–00–33 or 68/12–02–92), **Cruz Roja** (Red Cross; ⊠ Guillermo Prieto and Tenochtitlan, ☎ 68/15–08–08 or 68/18–64–64), and **Bomberos** (Fire Dept.; ☎ 68/12–01–00).

Guided Tours

Most large hotels in Los Mochis and Chihuahua have in-house travel agencies that arrange city tours and tours of the Copper Canyon area, as well as hiking, hunting, and fishing expeditions. In **Los Mochis,** the Santa Anita and La Colinas hotels offer city tours for about $29 per person; these take approximately 3½ to 4 hours and include a boat trip around Topolobampo Bay. In **Chihuahua,** independent travel agencies include the American Express agent **Rojo y Casavantes** (⊠ Calle Vincent Guerrero 1207, ☎ 14/15–58–58 or 14/15–74–70, FAX 14/15–53–84), and, particularly recommended, **Turismo Al Mar** (⊠ Calle Verna 2202, ☎ FAX 14/16–65–89, ☎ 14/16–59–50). Half-day city tours average $16 per person; full-day van trips into Mennonite country run about $40 per person. In Cuauhtémoc, **Cumbres Friesen** (⊠ Calle 3A, No. 466, Cuauhtémoc, ☎ 158/2–54–57, FAX 158/2–40–60), owned by Mennonite David Friesen, can arrange Mennonite tours.

From the United States, the oldest operator in the area is **Pan American Tours** (⊠ Box 9401, El Paso, TX 79984, ☎ 915/778–5395 or 800/876–3942). Prices for tailor-made tours between Los Mochis and Chihuahua range from about $300 to $700 per person, depending on length of stay and number of stops made. **Synergy Tours** (⊠ 7336 E. Shoeman La., Suite 120, Scottsdale, AZ 85251, ☎ 800/569–1797, FAX 602/994–4439) runs individual and group trips about 10 times a year, including off-the-beaten-path treks. **California Native** (⊠ 6701 W. 87th Pl., Los Angeles, CA 90045, ☎ 800/926–1140) runs a seven-day escorted trip through the Copper Canyon every month for $1,540, and also has backpacking, mountain biking, and deluxe excursions.

TRAIN TOURS

Sierra Madre Express of Tucson (⊠ Box 26381, Tucson, AZ 85726, ☎ 520/747–0346 or 800/666–0346) runs its own deluxe trains (with dome/dining and Pullman cars) to the Copper Canyon from Tucson on eight-day, seven-night trips about four times a year. Its trips combine the charm of sleeping on the train with first-class accommodations. The luxury train **South Orient Express** (⊠ 16800 Greenspoint Park Dr., Suite 245 N, Houston, TX 77060, ☎ 800/659–7602) offers all-inclusive "rail cruises"—in domed, dining/lounge, and Pullman cars—from Chihuahua and Los Mochis spring and fall (and from Fort Worth twice a year), starting at $1,549 per person for a five-day trip. The company also has individual trips year-round on its slightly less luxurious "VSP" train, ranging from transportation only ($198 one-way between Chihuahua and Los Mochis with unlimited stops) to packages with lodging, meals, and sight-seeing.

Late-Night Pharmacies

CHIHUAHUA

Chihuahua has an abundance of pharmacies with late-night service in the city center. **Farmacia Mendoza** (⊠ Calle Aldama 1901, ☎ 14/16–44–14 or 14/10–27–96) is open 24 hours a day.

LOS MOCHIS

Farmacia San Jorge (⊠ Av. Independencia and Angel Flores, ☎ 68/15–74–74; and ⊠ corner of Degollado and Juárez, ☎ 68/18–18–19) has two stores in Los Mochis that are open 24 hours.

Money Exchange

Be sure to change money before you get into real barranca country: there are no banks in Cerocahui, Divisadero, or Posada Barrancas, and no guarantee that the hotels in those places will have enough cash to accommodate you. A bank in the main plaza at Creel transacts foreign exchanges from 10:30 to noon only. In Los Mochis, most banking hours are weekdays between 8:30 and 4:30; some banks open Saturday mornings. In Chihuahua, most banks open weekdays from 9 to 1:30 and from 3:30 to 7:30, and Saturday from 9 to 1:30. **Banco Bital** downtown (⊠ Libertad 1922, ☎ 14/16–08–80) is open Monday–Saturday 8–8. The **Casa de Cambio Rachasa** (⊠ Av. Ocampo and Niños Heroes, ☎ 14/10–03–33), open Monday–Saturday 9–9, Sunday 9–2, has good exchange rates and quick service. In El Fuerte, **Bancomer** (⊠ Corner of Constitución and Juárez) is open Monday–Saturday 8:30–3. Hotels have slightly lower exchange rates but charge no commission, and you normally won't have to wait in line.

Visitor Information

CHIHUAHUA

Government Tourist Office (⊠ Av. Libertad and Calle 13, 1st floor, ☎ 14/29–34–21; 14/29–33–00 ext. 4511 or 4512) is open weekdays 9–4. **Oficina de Información** (⊠ Central patio of Palacio de Gobierno in Plaza Hidalgo, ☎ 14/29–33–00 ext. 1061; 14/10–10–77) is open Monday–Saturday 9–4. At the Oficina, Sonia Estrada, who speaks fluent English, will answer questions and help visitors (in person or over the phone) make travel arrangements all over the state.

LOS MOCHIS

Oficina de Turismo (⊠ Allende and Ordoñez, inside the Unidad Administrativa del Gobierno del Estado building, 1st floor in back, ☎ 68/12–66–40 or 68/12–76–10 ext. 131).

6 GUADALAJARA

Including Tlaquepaque, Tonalá,
and Lake Chapala

Colonial architecture that dates to the city's
heyday as center of regional commerce is
among the lures of Guadalajara, which
introduced the world to mariachis, tequila,
charreadas (rodeos), and *el jarabe tapatío*
(the Mexican hat dance). On the city's
outskirts, Tlaquepaque has some of
Mexico's finest crafts, as does Tonalá,
about 10 minutes farther away. A near-
perfect semitropical climate and proximity
to the Pacific Ocean—240 km (149 mi)
away—ensure warm, sunny days with just
a hint of humidity and cool, clear nights.

Updated by
Sean Godfrey

TRADITIONS ARE PRESERVED and customs perpetuated in Guadalajara; it's a place where the siesta is an institution and the fiesta an art form. Mexico's second-largest city, and the capital of the state of Jalisco, Guadalajara is engaged in a struggle to retain its provincial ambience and colonial charm as its population approaches 4 million. Émigrés from Mexico City after the devastating 1985 earthquake and staggering numbers of the rural poor seeking employment created a population explosion that continues to strain public services and the city's often outdated infrastructure. Visitors to the city can enjoy the tree-lined boulevards, parks, plazas, and stately churrigueresque architecture, but recent years have brought traffic jams and increasingly heavy pollution.

Guadalajara has always been one of the most socially traditional and politically conservative cities in Mexico. It has also been the seat of Christian fundamentalism and was one of the strategic areas of the *Cristeros,* a movement of right-wing Catholic zealots in western Mexico in the 1920s. *Tapatíos,* as the city's residents are called (the name comes from *tlapatiotl,* three units or purses of cacao or other commodities used as currency by the Indians of the area), even seem to take a certain amount of pride in their straight and narrow outlook.

Still, Tapatíos are historically accustomed to challenge and change. Within 10 years of its founding in 1531, the location of the city changed three times. In 1542 the City Council followed the advice of Doña Beatriz Hernández to build the city in the center of the Atemajac Valley, where it could expand. Thus Guadalajara was placed on a mile-high plain of the Sierra Madre, bounded on three sides by rugged cliffs and on the fourth by the spectacular Barranca de Oblatos (Oblatos Canyon).

Geographically remote from the rest of the republic during the nearly 300 years of Spanish rule, the city cultivated and maintained a political and cultural autonomy. By the end of the 16th century, money was flowing into Guadalajara from the rich farms and silver mines in the region, creating the first millionaires of what was then known as New Galicia. Under orders from Spain, much of the wealth was lavished on magnificent churches, residences, and monuments. Many of these reminders of the golden era still stand in downtown Guadalajara.

The suburbs of Tlaquepaque (pronounced Tla-kay-*pah*-kay) and Tonalá (pronounced Toe-na-*la*) produce some of Mexico's finest and most popular traditional crafts and folk art. Lake Chapala —Mexico's largest body of fresh water—and the nearby towns of Chapala and Ajijic have attracted retired former residents of the United States and Canada, who enjoy most of the amenities and services they were accustomed to north of the border.

Pleasures and Pastimes

Arts and Architecture

You can find all kinds of Mexican and international arts in Guadalajara—everything from the traditional Ballet Folklórico at the Teatro Degollado to rock groups at the Instituto Cultural Cabañas. Galleries and museums around town also offer the best of modern and traditional work. Numerous 16th-century colonial buildings fill the downtown area, connected by a series of large, Spanish-style plazas.

Churches

Guadalajara seems to have a church every block or two—there are 15 in the downtown area alone, all dating from the colonial era. Some have elaborately carved facades, and others conceal ornate Baroque altars and priceless colonial oil paintings behind sober stone exteriors.

Dining

The variety of Guadalajara's restaurants includes classic Mexican dishes, Continental delicacies, Argentine-style steaks, and fresh seafood. Savory regional specialties—often served in simpler places—include *birria,* a spicy stew prepared with goat, lamb, or beef in a light tomato broth; *pozole,* a thick pork and hominy soup; and *carne en su jugo,* consisting of steak bits in a clear spicy broth with bacon, beans, and cilantro, usually served with a side of tiny, grilled whole onions.

Lodging

Hotels run the gamut from older establishments in the downtown historic district—including one finely restored building that has been a hotel since 1610—to representatives of the large chains, most of which are on or near Avenida López Mateos Sur, a 16-km (10-mi) strip extending from the Minerva Fountain to the Plaza del Sol shopping center. In the mid-1990s several hotels have also gone up close to the Expo-Guadalajara convention center, which opened in 1987.

Shopping

Blown glass, hand-carved wood furniture, fine leatherwork, and hand-glazed pottery are Guadalajara traditions. Two of the most common ceramic techniques are *barro bruñido,* in which the pieces are hand-burnished to a soft sheen, and *petatillo,* in which glaze is applied to earthenware in a fine crosshatch pattern. Guadalajara is also home to a thriving shoe industry. At sprawling markets you can bargain for anything from embroidered shirts to huaraches, and sleek shopping malls have full-service department stores and trendy boutiques.

Sports

Highly stylized *charreadas,* traditional Mexican rodeos, are presented here weekly, and there are bullfights in October and November. In late August through May, soccer fans crowd Jalisco Stadium.

EXPLORING GUADALAJARA

Metropolitan Guadalajara consists of a historic city center and nearby urban districts, as well as neighboring Tlaquepaque, Tonalá, and Zapopan, and the tranquil villages on the shores of Lake Chapala.

Numbers in the text correspond to numbers in the margin and on the Downtown Guadalajara, Tlaquepaque, Tonalá, and Lake Chapala Area maps.

Great Itineraries

It's not surprising that Guadalajara has been described as *señorial y moderna* (lordly and modern). Along with the graciousness of colonial Mexico, you can take in as much as you want of the 20th century. And nearby pueblos are an eye on traditional rural life. Ten days would allow you to fully explore the city and surrounding villages, as well as take an excursion or two to points farther afield. With five days to spend here, you'll have time to see most of the city's highlights and get to know Tlaquepaque, Tonalá, and the Lake Chapala area. In three days, you can take in the historic city center and make day trips to Tlaquepaque, Tonalá, and Lake Chapala.

IF YOU HAVE 3 DAYS

Spend your first day in the historic **el centro** ①–⑩. The next day, spend the morning in **Tlaquepaque** ⑳–㉚, have lunch there, and visit **Tonalá** ㉛–㊳ in the afternoon. On your third day, head toward **Lake Chapala** ㊴–

㊺; stroll and shop, take a boat trip on the lake, and enjoy lunch or dinner in one of the area's fine restaurants.

IF YOU HAVE 5 DAYS

See **el centro** ①–⑩ on your first day, then consider your interests. If traditional crafts lure you, devote a day to **Tlaquepaque** ⑳–㉚ and the following day to **Tonalá** ㉛–㊳. Or explore the two towns in one day, leaving you a day—or two—to spend around **Lake Chapala** ㊴–㊺. Take your final day back in Guadalajara in additional museums and the **Basilica of the Virgin of Zapopan** ⑯, for which you'll need several hours, or even the Guadalajara **zoo** ⑭ and **planetarium** ⑮. Plan an afternoon strolling by the mansions built by Guadalajara's upper classes in the glorious twilight before the 1910 revolution—the best area is in a six-block radius around Avenida Vallarta west of Avenida Chapultepec. If you'd like to get your feet on the ground in more natural surroundings, hike in the nearby **Barranca de Oblatos.**

IF YOU HAVE 7 DAYS

You will be able to cover all of the **el centro** ①–⑩ plus the other city sights, and **Tlaquepaque** ⑳–㉚, **Tonalá** ㉛–㊳, and the **Lake Chapala** ㊴–㊺ area. Fill in the gaps with a visit to Tequila and a stay in the soothing thermal waters of **San Juan Cosalá** or **Río Caliente.**

Guadalajara

Beginning around 1960, 20th-century architecture started to threaten the historical integrity of this provincial state capital. In the early 1980s the city declared a 30-square-block area in the heart of downtown a cultural sanctuary, and in the late 1990s private-sector groups formed a trust to continue spiffing up el centro (city center). The 16th-century buildings here are connected by a series of large Spanish-style plazas where children chase gaily colored balloons, young lovers coo on tree-shaded park benches, and grandparents stroll hand in hand past vendors and marble fountains. At nearby **Plaza de los Mariachis,** the nostalgic songs and music of sombrero-topped troubadours fill the air.

In addition to the city center, most tourist sights and large hotels are located in three other areas: near Avenida Chapultepec, near the Minerva Fountain and Los Arcos monument, and in the Plaza del Sol shopping area (several miles southwest of downtown).

A Good Walk

Guadalajara's 17th-century **Catedral** ①, on Avenida Alcalde between Avenida Hidalgo and Calle Morelos, is the place to start exploring downtown. After you've marveled at the interior, exit through the main doors and cross Avenida Alcalde to Plaza Guadalajara, with its large fountain, outdoor café, and benches scattered beneath square-cut laurel trees. To your right (with your back toward the cathedral) across Avenida Hidalgo is the deceptive facade of the **Palacio Municipal** ②, or City Hall.

From the corner of Avenidas Alcalde and Hidalgo, head one block east to Calle Liceo, where you'll see the **Museo Regional de Guadalajara** ③. You'll pass the Rotonda de Hombres Ilustres de Jalisco, a tree-shaded square whose central colonnaded rotunda covers a mausoleum containing the remains of 17 of the state of Jalisco's favorite sons and one daughter. Statuary surrounding the square further memorializes those buried inside.

After you leave the museum, you can turn either way on Calle Liceo: three blocks to your right is the **Casa-Museo López Portillo** ④ and north and west of that, on Avenida Alcalde, the **Museo del Periodismo y de las Artes Gráficas** ⑤. Around the corner to the left of the Museo

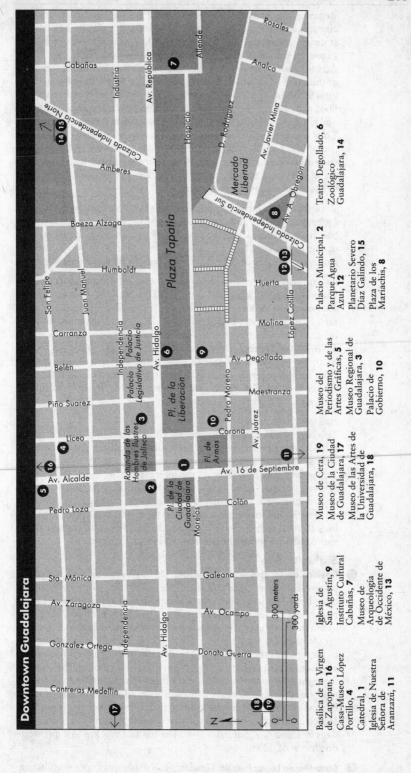

Downtown Guadalajara

Rosales
Analco
Allende
Cabañas
Industria
Av. República
Hospicio
D. Rodríguez
Av. Javier Mina
Amberes
Calzada Independencia Norte
Mercado Libertad
Av. A. Obregón
Baeza Alzaga
Calzada Independencia Sur
Plaza Tapatía
Humboldt
Huerta
San Felipe
Juan Manuel
Molina
López Cotilla
Carranza
Independencia
Palacio Legislativo de Justicia
Av. Hidalgo
Av. Degollado
Belén
Pl. de la Liberación
Maestranza
Piño Suárez
Rotunda de los Hombres Ilustres de Jalisco
Pedro Moreno
Liceo
Corona
Av. Juárez
Av. Alcalde
Pl. de Armas
Av. 16 de Septiembre
Pedro Loza
Pl. de la Ciudad de Guadalajara
Colón
Morelos
Sta. Mónica
Galeana
Av. Zaragoza
Av. Ocampo
Gonzalez Ortega
Independencia
Av. Hidalgo
Donato Guerra
Contreras Medellín

300 meters
300 yards

N

Basílica de la Virgen de Zapopan, **16**
Casa-Museo López Portillo, **4**
Catedral, **1**
Iglesia de Nuestra Señora de Aranzazú, **11**

Iglesia de San Agustín, **9**
Instituto Cultural Cabañas, **7**
Museo de Arqueología de Occidente de México, **13**

Museo de Cera, **19**
Museo de la Ciudad de Guadalajara, **17**
Museo de las Artes de la Universidad de Guadalajara, **18**

Museo del Periodismo y de las Artes Gráficas, **5**
Museo Regional de Guadalajara, **3**
Palacio de Gobierno, **10**

Palacio Municipal, **2**
Parque Agua Azul, **12**
Planetario Severo Díaz Galindo, **15**
Plaza de los Mariachis, **8**

Teatro Degollado, **6**
Zoológico Guadalajara, **14**

Regional, on Avenida Hidalgo, are the Palacio Legislativo, a former customs house, tobacco warehouse, and inn that today houses Jalisco's state legislature, and the Palacio de Justicia, which was built in 1588 as part of Guadalajara's first convent and now is the state courthouse. Across Avenida Hidalgo on your right sprawls the Plaza de la Liberación, at the east end of which rises the spectacular **Teatro Degollado** ⑥. Behind it begins the Plaza Tapatía, a five-block-long pedestrian mall lined with shops, trees, and whimsical sculpture; it is frequented by mimes and street musicians. At the end, visit the **Instituto Cultural Cabañas** ⑦. Then proceed back west to the modernistic Quetzalcóatl Fountain in the center. Turn left and walk down the stairs to the sprawling **Mercado Libertad** (☞ Shopping, *below*). Turn left again when you leave the market and cross the pedestrian bridge over Avenida Javier Mina to the **Plaza de los Mariachis** ⑧.

Return to Plaza Tapatía by heading right to the intersection of Calzada Independencia Sur and Avenida Javier Mina, in front of the Iglesia de San Juan de Dios. Continue two blocks past the church and go back up the stairs. Turn left and walk west four blocks (so you can see the stores on this side of the plaza) to the **Iglesia de San Agustín** ⑨.

As you leave the church, turn left down Calle Morelos to Avenida Corona. Turn left again and walk a half block to the main entrance of the **Palacio de Gobierno** ⑩ to see two of José Clemente Orozco's murals. Exit the palacio back onto Avenida Corona (the way you came in) and cross the street to the Plaza de Armas, where you can rest on a wrought-iron bench, imagining yourself in the *Porfiriato*—Mexico's Victorian period–when gracious *dons* and *doñas* strolled amid the trees and flower beds around the ornately sculpted kiosk, a gift from France in 1910. With the cathedral to your right, you've come full circle back to the north side of the plaza.

TIMING

You can take in most of downtown Guadalajara in a day. The sights outside of the center can easily take a half or full day each. Most museums, the zoo, and the planetarium are closed Monday. In early September Guadalajara hosts the international mariachi and tequila festival, bringing traditional troubadours from as far away as Japan and running daily train trips to Tequila, home of the fiery elixir of the same name. In October, the city puts on the Fiestas de Octubre, a month-long cultural festival that exudes a county fair–like atmosphere and is sprinkled with top-flight international entertainment.

Sights to See

⑯ **Basílica de la Virgen de Zapopan.** This vast church, with an ornate plateresque facade and *mudéjar* (Moorish) tiled dome, was consecrated in 1730. It is known throughout Mexico as the home of La Zapopanita, Our Lady of Zapopan. The 10-inch-high statue is venerated as the source of many miracles in and around Guadalajara. Every year on October 12, more than a million people crowd the streets leading to Zapopan as the Virgin is returned to the basilica after a five-month absence, during which she visits every parish church in the state. In the right side of the basilica is the **Museo Huichol** (✉ Avs. Avila Camacho and de las Américas), a small gallery and shop featuring exquisite beadwork and other handicrafts by the Huichol Indians of northern Jalisco and neighboring states Zacatecas and Nayarit. It's open weekdays 9–1 and 4–7, Saturday 9–1. The basilica is 7 km (4½ mi) west–northwest of downtown.

④ **Casa-Museo López Portillo.** Guadalajara's illustrious López Portillo family included prominent writers and politicians, such as an early 20th-century Jalisco governor and his Mexico City–born grandson, José López Portillo, president of Mexico from 1976 to 1982. As is typical of homes built by Mexico's 19th-century upper class, the plain stucco exterior belies the rich interior, where French baroque–style rooms ring a spacious interior patio. ⊠ *Liceo 177, at San Felipe,* ☎ *3/613–2411.* ☜ *Free.* ☉ *Weekdays 9–8:30, Sat. 9–1.*

★ ❶ **Catedral.** Consecrated in 1618, this focal point of downtown is an intriguing mélange of Baroque, Gothic, and other styles, the result of design and structural modifications during its 57 years of construction. Its emblematic twin towers replaced the originals, which fell in the earthquake of 1818. Ten of the silver-and-gilt altars were gifts of King Fernando VII, in appreciation of Guadalajara's financial support of Spain during the Napoleonic Wars; the 11th, of sculpted white marble, was carved in Italy in 1863. On the walls of the cathedral hang some of the world's most beautiful *retablos* (altarpieces); above the sacristy is the priceless 17th-century painting of Bartolomé Esteban Murillo, *The Assumption of the Virgin.* In a loft high above the main entrance is a magnificent late-19th-century French organ, featured in an organ festival usually held every May. ⊠ *Av. Alcalde between Av. Hidalgo and Morelos.* ☉ *Daily 8–7.*

⓫ **Iglesia de Nuestra Señora de Aranzazú.** Don't be fooled by Our Lady of Aranzazú's drab brown stone exterior: inside is a spectacular Baroque gilt altar whose 14 niches contain life-size statues of saints. The walls' and ceilings' intricate floral details are painted in bright shades of turquoise, rose, and rust. The church is on the west side of Parque San Francisco, a small green oasis that draws food vendors, families, and senior citizens. ⊠ *Av. 16 de Septiembre and Prisciliano Sánchez.* ☎ *3/614–4083.* ☉ *Daily 10–2 and 4–7.*

❾ **Iglesia de San Agustín.** The venerable St. Augustine Church is one of the oldest churches in the city. It has been remodeled many times since its consecration in 1574, but the sacristy is preserved in its original form. The building left of the church, originally an Augustinian cloister, is now the **Escuela de Música** (School of Music) of the University of Guadalajara. Free recitals and concerts are held on its patio. ⊠ *Morelos at Av. Degollado.* ☎ *3/614–5365.* ☉ *Daily 8–8.*

★ ❼ **Instituto Cultural Cabañas.** This landmark neoclassical-style cultural center was designed by the famous Spanish architect–sculptor Manuel Tolsá. Originally an orphanage founded by Bishop Juan Cruz Ruíz de Cabañas y Crespo, the building served as home for 400 orphans and indigent children until the 1970s, when the orphanage moved to a new location. The rooms, which surround 23 flower-filled patios, contain permanent and revolving art exhibits. The central dome and walls of the main chapel display a series of murals painted by José Clemente Orozco in 1938–39. *The Man of Fire,* which depicts a man enveloped in flames who is ascending toward infinity and yet not consumed by the fire, represents the spirit of humankind. It is generally considered to be his finest work. There is a permanent exhibit of Orozco's paintings, cartoons, and drawings in Room 33. Ask the attendant at the front desk for an English-speaking guide. ⊠ *Calle Cabañas 8, at Plaza Tapatía,* ☎ *3/617–4322 or 3/617–4440.* ☜ *About $1; free Sun.* ☉ *Tues.–Sat. 10:15–6, Sun. 10:15–3.*

⓭ **Museo de Arqueología de Occidente de México.** The Archaeological Museum of Western Mexico houses pottery and other artifacts used by ancient peoples of what are now the states of Colima, Jalisco, and Nayarit. It's in the street divider across from the entrance to Parque Agua Azul. ⊠ *Calzada Independencia Sur and Av. del Campesino,* ☎ *No phone.* ☜ *40¢.* ☉ *Tues.–Sun. 10–2 and 4–7.*

⟳ ⑲ **Museo de Cera.** At Guadalajara's 120-figure wax museum, now in the historic downtown area across from Plaza de la Liberación, go eye-to-eye with Madonna, Mahatma Gandhi, beloved Mexican comic Cantinflas, and a host of other Mexican and international political and artistic luminaries. Visit the underground Aztec sacrificial chamber, a hall of Mexican history, all of Mexico's presidents, world leaders, and a chamber of horrors. A wax mariachi, playing "Guadalajara Guadalajara," greets you at the door. ⊠ *Morelos 217,* ☎ *3/614–8487.* ▨ *$1.50.* ⊘ *Daily 11–8:30.*

⑰ **Museo de la Ciudad de Guadalajara.** In a series of rooms surrounding the tranquil interior patio of this spacious remodeled colonial home, you'll find informative artwork, artifacts, and reproductions of documents about the city's development from pre-Hispanic times through the 20th century. ⊠ *Calle Independencia 684, between Contreras Medellín and Mariano Bárcenas,* ☎ *3/658–2531 or 3/658–3706.* ▨ *30¢; free Sun.* ⊘ *Wed.–Sat. 10–5:30, Sun. 10–2:30.*

⑱ **Museo de las Artes de la Universidad de Guadalajara.** This impressive contemporary art museum and its exquisite early 20th-century building belong to the University of Guadalajara. It has a permanent collection of 20th-century drawings and paintings and revolving exhibits of modern Latin American, U.S., and European work. Look for the murals Orozco painted upon returning to Guadalajara at age 53. The paraninfo—a round theater in the museum's center—frequently hosts chamber music groups. There is also a charming café.

Behind the museum on Avenida Lopez Cotilla, the **Templo Expiatorio** is a striking Gothic church built at the turn of the last century and modeled after the Orvieto Cathedral in Italy. ⊠ *Av. Juárez at Av. Enrique Díaz de León,* ☎ *3/825–6114 or 3/825–7553, ext. 66.* ▨ *About $1; free Sun.* ⊘ *Tues.–Sat. 10:30–6:30, Fri. till 8, Sun. 11–6.*

⑤ **Museo del Periodismo y de las Artes Gráficas.** In 1792 Guadalajara's first printing press was set up on this site, where today you can see displays of historic newspapers, printing presses, recording equipment, and a complete television studio. The building has long been known as the Casa de los Perros because of the two wrought-iron dogs (*perros*) "guarding" the roof. ⊠ *Av. Alcalde 225,* ☎ *3/613–9286.* ▨ *About 50¢.* ⊘ *Tues.–Sat. 10–6, Sun. 10:30–3.*

★ ③ **Museo Regional de Guadalajara.** Constructed as a seminary in 1701, this distinguished building has been home to the Regional Museum (also known as the State Museum) since 1918. The first-floor galleries, which surround a garden courtyard, contain artifacts and memorabilia that trace the history of western Mexico from prehistoric times through the Spanish conquest; there are also revolving arts and crafts exhibits. On the second-floor balcony are five 19th-century carriages; the galleries offer an impressive collection of paintings by European and Mexican artists, including Bartolomé Esteban Murillo, and displays about the history of Jalisco. ⊠ *Liceo 60,* ☎ *3/614–9957.* ▨ *About $1.60; free Tues.* ⊘ *Tues.–Sat. 9–6:45, Sun. 9–3.*

⑩ **Palacio de Gobierno.** Built in 1643, this churrigueresque and neoclassical structure houses Jalisco's state government offices and two of José Clemente Orozco's most passionate murals. You'll see the first one in the stairwell to the right after you enter: a gigantic Father Miguel Hidalgo looming amid shadowy figures representing oppression and slavery. The second, in the former state legislature quarters on the upper level, depicts Juárez and other figures of the 1850s Reform era. ⊠ *Av. Corona between Morelos and Pedro Moreno.* ⊘ *Daily 9–8:45.*

② **Palacio Municipal.** Guadalajara's city hall is a clever, colonial-style fake: it was built in 1952 with an arched facade and interior patio to fit in with neighboring buildings. Inside is a colorful mural depicting the founding of the city. ⊠ *Av. Hidalgo at Av. Alcalde.* ☉ *Daily 9–8.*

⑫ **Parque Agua Azul.** Amid acres of trees and flowers, this popular park has carnival rides, tropical birds in cages, an orchid house, and a geodesic dome covering a tropical garden. Next to the park entrance, the small **Teatro Experimental** (☎ 3/619–1176) presents many Spanish-language children's plays, including English-language classics in translation. Dramas and chamber music are also performed here. The lively **Museo Infantil** (☎ No phone) on the southeast side of the park has hands-on displays on geography, outer space, and natural history for kids. ⊠ *Calzada Independencia Sur and Av. del Campesino 973,* ☎ *3/619–0328, 3/619–0332.* 🎫 *40¢.* ☉ *Tues.–Sun. 10–6:30.*

⑮ **Planetario Severo Díaz Galindo.** A modern facility with astronomy shows and aeronautical displays, the planetarium also has exhibits that allow children to test the forces and laws of nature. It's 6 km (4 mi) northeast of downtown. ⊠ *Anillo Periférico Manuel Gomez Morin 401, east of the Calzada Independencia,* ☎ *3/674–4106 or 3/674–3978.* 🎫 *Museum 20¢; astronomy show and movie 40¢.* ☉ *Tues.–Sun. 9–7.*

★ ⑧ **Plaza de los Mariachis.** Experience the most Mexican of music in this picturesque little plaza complete with cafés, where strolling mariachi groups perform. Though the action here lasts all night, it's best to visit during the day. The plaza is next to the **Iglesia de San Juan de Dios;** use the pedestrian overpass from the Mercado Libertad to avoid the heavy traffic. ⊠ *Calzada Independencia Sur between Av. Javier Mina and Alvaro Obregón.* 🎫 *Mariachi serenade about $4 a song.*

★ ⑥ **Teatro Degollado.** Inaugurated in 1866, this magnificent theater was modeled after Milan's La Scala. Above the Corinthian columns gracing the entrance way is a relief depicting Apollo and the nine Muses. Inside, the recently refurbished theater has kept its traditional red and gold color scheme, but it now has alternating seats, so that in orchestra seats you will no longer have to stare at the head of the person in front of you. The balconies ascend to a multitiered dome adorned with Gerardo Suárez's depiction of Dante's *Divine Comedy.* The theater is the permanent home for the Jalisco Philharmonic and the Ballet Folklórico of the University of Guadalajara and also hosts visiting orchestras, plays, and numerous other performances.

According to tradition, Guadalajara was founded on the site of what is now the **Plaza de los Fundadores,** which flanks the east side of the theater. A sculpted frieze on the rear wall of the Teatro Degollado depicts the historic event. ⊠ *Calle Degollado between Av. Hidalgo and Morelos,* ☎ *3/614–4773 or 3/613–1115.* ☉ *Mon.–Sat. 10–2 and during performances.*

NEED A
BREAK?

A signature pink-and-white color scheme heralds the city's most popular ice-cream chain. A stop at **Helados Bing** (on the north side of Plaza Tapatía, east of the Quetzalcóatl Fountain) provides a welcome respite from an afternoon of sight-seeing. Choose from more than 20 flavors of pasteurized ice cream and ices, and relax on a shaded bench.

⑭ **Zoológico Guadalajara.** On the edge of the jagged Barranca Huentitán (Huentitán Canyon), the impressive Guadalajara Zoo has more than 1,500 animals representing some 300 species. For 50¢ a train provides guided tours. The adjacent **Selva Mágica,** or Magic Jungle amusement park, has carnival rides and attractions for about $1.30. The complex is 6 km (nearly 4 mi) northeast of downtown, near the planetarium. ⊠ *Paseo del Zoológico 600,* ☎ *3/674–1034.* 🖂 *$1.80.* ☉ *Zoo Wed.– Sun. 9:30–6, Selva Mágica Tues.–Sun. 10–7.*

OFF THE
BEATEN PATH
BARRANCA DE OBLATOS – A spectacular 2,000-ft-deep gorge, Oblatos Canyon also has hiking trails and the narrow **Cola de Caballo** waterfall, named for its horse-tail shape. For the best view, go to the lookout area, or Parque Mirador, at the top. ⊠ *10 km (6 mi) northeast of downtown Guadalajara via Calzada Independencia Norte.*

DINING

Guadalajara eateries continue to be very affordable. Most are open throughout the evening, though seafood restaurants often close earlier. A number of places listed below have branches elsewhere in the city; our choices are either the most colorful, original locations or those most convenient to the hotel areas. Because Guadalajara is a big, business-oriented city, it is advisable to dress well for $$$ restaurants.

CATEGORY	COST*
$$$	$15–$25
$$	$10–$15
$	under $10

*per person for a three-course meal, excluding drinks, service, and 15% sales tax

$$$ ✕ **Santo Coyote.** Recently opened in the former U.S. Consul General's residence, this *nuevo* Mexican eatery is the talk of the town. Huge *palapas* hang off willow trees bedecked with hundreds of basket lanterns and surrounded by a garden full of plants from all 32 Mexican states. Murals of goddesses adorn one dining area, waterfalls flow, and candles burn at a huge shrine to Mexico's patron saint—the Virgin of Guadalupe. Look on the menu for wood-fired roast or grilled *cabrito* (goat)—a house specialty—or baby back ribs topped with a tamarind and pepper sauce, or marrow soup. Service and presentation are excellent. ⊠ *Lerdo de Tejada 2379,* ☎ *3/616–6978. AE, MC, V.*

$$ ✕ **Copenhagen 77.** Decorative tilework by Tonalá artisan Jorge Wilmot
★ covers the walls here, where the signature dish is paella. Since 1952 the Copenhagen has served up the famous dish of Valencia, Spain, as well as beef and seafood entrées, pastas, and Spanish-style tortillas, which—unlike the Mexican variety—are large omelets stuffed with potato and onion. Copenhagen is also the unofficial headquarters for Guadalajara's jazz aficionados—some of the city's best jazz musicians play everything from Brubeck to Count Basie Monday–Saturday nights after 9. ⊠ *Marcos Castellanos 136-Z,* ☎ *3/826–1787. AE.*

$$ ✕ **El Farallón de Tepic.** Set underneath a bright blue awning, this open-
★ air establishment is reminiscent of beach restaurants in the nearby state of Nayarit. Order your fresh *pescado* (fish)—usually red snapper or an equally mild fish—grilled with garlic or butter, in classic tomato sauce, breaded, or stuffed with seafood and cheese. *Pescado sarandeado* (whole barbecued fish, stuffed with vegetables) is grilled to order over a wood fire and worth every second of the 30-minute wait. Try the homemade flan for dessert. ⊠ *Av. Niño Obrero 560,* ☎ *3/121–2616 or 3/121–9616. AE, MC, V.*

$$ ✕ **Formosa Gardens.** With sister restaurants in Bejing and Taiwan it's no wonder Asian residents of Guadalajara visit Formosa Gardens for a taste of home. Peking duck is crisp and tasty, but go for the deep-fried orange beef—sweet and tangy. In this beautiful Asian-arched mansion, which opens onto a garden dining area, a fresh gerbera blos-

som floats inside a large blue margarita glass set on crisp linen at each table. Formosa Gardens is open for three meals a day. ⊠ *Av. Union 322,* ☎ *3/615–7415. AE, MC, V.*

$$ ✕ **La Destilería.** If you can't make it to the village of Tequila, here's the next best thing: a restaurant cum "Tequila Museum" that serves novelle Mexican specialties and 87 varieties of the fiery liquor. Lining the redbrick walls are antique photos of tequila distilleries, authentic implements, and bilingual plaques explaining tequila's history. ⊠ *Av. México 2916,* ☎ *3/640–3110. AE, MC, V.*

$$ ✕ **La Feria.** The first of a dozen new restaurants and bars to renovate
★ historic downtown buildings, La Feria offers up a fairlike Mexican atmosphere with spectacular entertainment by mariachis, charros, and ballet folklórico. Come for a late supper or appetizers to catch the show. The shrimp tacos are scrumptious, and meat lovers will want to share the *parillada* for two—a mixed grill including tender flank steak, roast pork leg and chicken, and spicy Mexican *chorizo* (sausage). After the show, play *lotteria* (a type of bingo) or have a parakeet choose your fortune. ⊠ *Corona 291,* ☎ *3/613–1812 or 3/613–1839. AE, MC, V.*

$$ ✕ **Parilla Argentina.** Animal hides and posters of Argentina adorn the walls of this restaurant where—as throughout Argentina—tender grilled meat reigns supreme. Choose from T-bones, ribs, flank steaks, sausages, and Argentine-style *parillada* (a mixed grill of beef, sausages, and selected organ meats). Grilled chicken is also on the menu. ⊠ *Fernando Celada 176,* ☎ *3/615–7361. AE, MC, V.*

$$ ✕ **Pierrot.** This quiet French dining room offers mouth-watering pâtés
★ followed by seafood, chicken, and beef entrées, among them trout almondine, osso buco, and chicken breast stuffed with pâté in tarragon sauce. Wall-mounted lamps with fringed velvet shades and fresh flowers on each table lend a gracious touch. ⊠ *Justo Sierra 2355,* ☎ *3/ 630–2087 or 3/615–4758. AE, MC, V. Closed Sun.*

$$ ✕ **Restaurant Nasser.** Located on the top floor of La Gran Plaza shopping mall in a huge food court, the excellently prepared Lebanese food here makes this place worth the trouble. The Sunday buffet with 30 plus items is a fantastic buy at about $7. But leave room for the *mamul* (date cake). ⊠ *Av. Vallarta 3959,* ☎ *3/122–6153. AE, MC, V.*

$ ✕ **Karne Garibaldi.** According to the *Guinness Book of World Records,* this no-nonsense *tapatío* institution has the fastest service in the world. Seconds after you arrive, grilled onions, tortillas, and refried beans mixed with corn bid you to dig in. The only dish is *carne in su jugo,* a tasty combination of finely diced beef and bacon simmered in a rich beef broth, which takes less than a minute to arrive. With a beer or a soda, this is a great down-home meal. ⊠ *Garibaldi 1306,* ☎ *3/826–1286. AE, MC, V.*

$ ✕ **La Chata.** Sombreros, gaily striped serapes, and exquisitely glazed plates adorn the white walls of this popular downtown eatery. Start off with guacamole and then savor the zesty *chiles rellenos* (stuffed peppers). Or try one of the spicy roasted meat dishes, such as *carne tampiqueña,* served with rice, beans, and enchiladas. Complement your meal with a cool, sweet *horchata,* a drink made from rice and brown sugar simmered in milk, then chilled. ⊠ *Av. Corona 126, between López Cotilla and Av. Juárez,* ☎ *3/613–0588. AE, MC, V.*

$ ✕ **La Pianola.** The entrance—through what looks like an open-air
★ kitchen where costumed women are making tortillas—may be misleading to first-timers: in back is a large restaurant and garden with an excellent, varied Mexican menu. Specialties include pozole; *chiles en nogada,* spicy stuffed chili peppers in a walnut cream sauce; and *menudo,* a spicy tripe soup. The signature player-piano music accompanies the meal. ⊠ *Av. México 3220,* ☎ *3/813–1385 or 3/813–2412. AE, MC, V.*

$ ✕ **Los Itacates.** Excellently prepared traditional Mexican dishes at
★ very reasonable prices are what draw people here. Most entrée items
can also be ordered in tacos, so you can try unfamiliar food in small
portions. Even the ambience is solidly traditional, with carved wooden
chairs and bright pottery. ⊠ *Av. Chapultepec Norte 110, between Av.
México and Justo Sierra,* ☎ *3/825–1106. MC, V.*

$ ✕ **Mondo Cafe.** Among the half dozen cafés on wide, tree-lined Avenida
Chapultepec, the alluring odor of Mondo's coffee roaster belches into
the Chapultepec air from the second floor of the shop. Foreign and
local students frequent this favorite coffee house for its large picture-
window views onto the busy avenida and for various blends of fresh-
roasted coffee. Breakfasts are hearty and the mixed fruit and vegetable
juices and flavored coffees are the perfect way to start the day. The American owner is a former manager of Starbucks in Seattle. ⊠ *Av. Cha-
pultepéc and Pedro Moreno,* ☎ *3/616–2709. No credit cards.*

$ ✕ **Restaurant Vegetariano Zanahoria.** The name of this casual dining
spot means "carrot," but that's far from the only vegetable on the all-
vegetarian menu. Choose from fresh fruit juices, fruit and vegetable
salads, soups, and "fish" dishes made from cheese, potatoes, and soy.
⊠ *Av. de las Américas 332,* ☎ *3/616–6161. AE, DC, MC, V.*

LODGING

Guadalajara has a variety of hotels in all price ranges. Call ahead if
you're apprehensive about noise levels outside your hotel room. Many
hotels are on busy intersections, and you'd be well advised to consult
the reservation clerk on the matter of a room away from the hubbub.

The rates given are based on the year-round or peak-season price; off-
peak (summer) or promotional rates may be lower. You can expect ho-
tels in the $$$ and $$$$ categories to have purified-water systems and
English-language TV channels. Many hotels have begun to install in-
room modem lines, so ask when you reserve.

CATEGORY	COST*
$$$$	over $160
$$$	$90–$160
$$	$40–$90
$	under $40

*All prices are for a standard double room, excluding 15% VAT and 2%
hotel tax.*

$$$$ ▦ **Quinta Real.** Stone and brick walls, colonial arches, and objets
★ d'art highlight all public areas of this luxury hotel on the city's west
side. Suites are plush and intimate, with select neocolonial furnishings,
including glass-topped writing tables with carved-stone pedestals and
fireplaces with marble mantelpieces. Tiled bathrooms have marble
sinks and bronze fixtures; some suites have sunken hot tubs. Deluxe
tower accommodations are more lavish, though removed from the gardens below. ⊠ *Av. México 2727, at López Mateos Sur, 44680,* ☎ *3/
615–0000 or 01–888/561–2817; 800/445–4565 in the U.S.,* FAX *3/
630–1797. 76 suites. Restaurant, no-smoking floor, pool, baby-sitting,
concierge, free parking. AE, DC, MC, V.*

$$$ ▦ **Camino Real.** A 15-minute cab ride from downtown will bring you
to this sprawling resort located 3 km (2 mi) west of the Minerva Foun-
tain. The rooms are in two-story wings surrounding manicured lawns
and tropical gardens. All rooms are large and have placid pastel color
schemes, matching bedspreads and curtains, and modern furniture. Those
in the rear face noisy Avenida Vallarta. ⊠ *Av. Vallarta 5005, 45040,*
☎ *3/121–8000 or 01–800/947–7325; 800/996–7325 in the U.S.,* FAX

3/121–8070. 195 rooms, 10 suites. Restaurant, bar, coffee shop, in-room modem lines, no-smoking rooms, 5 pools, tennis court, health club, baby-sitting, concierge, free parking. AE, DC, MC, V.

$$$ 🏨 **Crowne Plaza Guadalajara.** Those who come to Guadalajara for its eternally springlike climate will enjoy the expansive, shaded, well-tended gardens surrounding a large pool and sunbathing area. Rooms have marble baths, upholstered furniture, carpeting, and lots of natural light. Tower rooms have mountain views. ☒ *Av. López Mateos Sur 2500, 45050,* ☎ *3/634–1034 or 01–800/365–5500,* 🖷 *3/631–9393. 288 rooms, 4 suites. 3 restaurants, bar, coffee shop, in-room modem lines, no-smoking floor, pool, beauty salon, massage, miniature golf, 2 tennis courts, health club, shops, baby-sitting, concierge, airport shuttle, car rental, free parking. AE, DC, MC, V.*

$$$ 🏨 **Fiesta Americana.** The dramatic glass facade of this luxury high-rise
★ faces the Minerva Fountain, on the city's west side. Four glass-enclosed elevators ascend above the 11-story atrium lobby and adjoining lobby bar to ample pastel rooms with modern furnishings and panoramic views. The best rooms are on the upper floors, well away from the revelers down in the bar. ☒ *Aurelio Aceves 225, 44110,* ☎ *3/825–3434 or 01–800/504–5000; 800/343–7821 in the U.S.,* 🖷 *3/630–3725. 389 rooms, 25 suites. Restaurant, bar, coffee shop, in-room modem lines, no-smoking floor, pool, beauty salon, 2 tennis courts, exercise room, shops, baby-sitting, concierge, car rental, free parking. AE, DC, MC, V.*

$$$ 🏨 **Presidente Inter-Continental.** Spacious, carpeted rooms surround the plush 12-story atrium lobby of this imposing pyramidical structure. For the best city view, request a room on an upper floor facing the Plaza del Sol shopping center. There's a Tane silver shop on the premises, and guests can use nearby golf and tennis facilities. ☒ *Av. López Mateos Sur and Moctezuma, 45050,* ☎ *3/678–1234 or 01–800/904–4400; 800/447–6147 in the U.S.,* 🖷 *3/678–1222. 266 rooms, 145 suites. Restaurant, bar, coffee shop, in-room modem lines, pool, spa, health club, shops, baby-sitting, concierge, airport shuttle, car rental, free parking. AE, DC, MC, V.*

$$ 🏨 **Carlton.** This modern 20-story tower hotel on the edge of downtown offers oversize rooms with light beige walls and ceilings and matching pale turquoise curtains and bedspreads. Ivy-draped walls surround the rear gardens and fountain. Though the hotel is convenient for tourists, it caters to the business traveler. The upper floors offer a spectacular city view and a retreat from the horrendous street noise. ☒ *Av. Niños Héroes 125, at Av. 16 de Septiembre, 44100,* ☎ *3/614–7272,* 🖷 *3/614–7402. 207 rooms, 8 suites. Restaurant, 2 bars, no-smoking floor, pool, health club, free parking. AE, MC, V.*

$$ 🏨 **De Mendoza.** The convenience of this downtown hotel—on a quiet
★ side street a block from the Teatro Degollado—and charming postcolonial architecture and ambience make it an easy choice. Beamed ceilings, hand-carved furniture and doors, and wrought-iron railings decorate public areas and rooms. The staff is quite helpful. ☒ *Venustiano Carranza 16, 44100,* ☎ *3/613–4646, 3/613–2809, or 01–800/3–61–26; 800/221–6509 in the U.S.,* 🖷 *3/613–7310. 77 rooms, 27 suites. Restaurant, in-room modem lines, no-smoking rooms, pool. AE, DC, MC, V.*

$$ 🏨 **Diana.** Mexican and European tourists favor this six-story hotel two blocks from the Minerva Fountain. The white stucco lobby adjoins a small lounge and busy restaurant. Standard-size rooms have white-on-white walls and ceilings with brightly patterned curtains and bedspreads. The quietest rooms are on the upper floors in the rear; some suites have private saunas. ☒ *Circunvalacíon Agustín Yáñez 2760, 44100,* ☎ *3/615–5510, 3/615–6428, or 01–800/25–36–789,* 🖷 *3/630–3685. 110 rooms, 20 suites. Restaurant, bar, coffee shop, pool, baby-sitting, airport shuttle, free parking. AE, DC, MC, V.*

$$ ☐ **Francés.** Guadalajara's oldest hotel, dating from 1610, was de-
★   clared a national monument in 1981 following extensive restoration.
Stone columns and colonial arches surround a three-story enclosed atrium
lobby with a polished marble fountain and cut-crystal chandeliers. Week-
ends, loud live music is played at the lobby bar until midnight. Though
room sizes vary, all have colonial ambience, with white stucco walls,
polished wood floors, and high-beamed ceilings. For the best city
views (though there's a slight noise trade-off), ask for a room facing
Calle Maestranza. ☒ *Maestranza 35, 44100,* ☎ *3/613–1190 or 3/613–
0936,* ☒ *3/658–2831. 50 rooms, 10 suites. Restaurant, bar, fans,
dance club, car rental, free parking. AE, MC, V.*

$$ ☐ **Plaza Del Sol.** Location and price bring families, young adults, and
tour groups to this two-building hotel at the south end of the Plaza del
Sol shopping center. Rooms—all modern and carpeted—and public areas
are painted glossy white trimmed in aquamarine, beige, or green. Accommodations in the cylindrical tower are a bit larger and have views
of Plaza del Sol below. ☒ *Avs. López Mateos and Mariano Otero, 45050,*
☎ *3/647–8790 or 01–800/36–88–000,* ☒ *3/122–9685. 341 rooms,
16 suites. Restaurant, bar, coffee shop, pool, baby-sitting, free parking. AE, DC, MC, V.*

$$ ☐ **Posada Guadalajara.** Rooms in this colonial-style hotel open onto
airy, wrought-iron–railed hallways overlooking the small patio and its
enormous stone fountain. Accommodations are clean and comfortable
and have carved wood furniture. In addition to its loyal international
patrons, the Posada welcomes visiting sports teams, so evenings here
can seem either festive or raucous. The hotel is south of Calzada
Lázaro Cárdenas, about 1½ km (1 mi) northeast of Plaza del Sol. ☒
Av. López Mateos Sur 1280, 45040, ☎ *3/121–2022 or 3/121–2904,*
☒ *3/122–1834. 148 rooms, 22 suites. Restaurant, bar, pool, baby-sit-
ting, free parking. AE, DC, MC, V.*

$$ ☐ **Santiago de Compostela.** This cozy downtown hotel in a converted
19th-century building is across from the Parque San Francisco and of-
fers modern, carpeted accommodations with a sea-green color scheme.
Rooms overlooking the park—where you can watch worshipers file
into the two colonial churches—have tall, narrow windows with metal
grillwork. Inside rooms open onto an atrium painted in turquoise, tan,
and lavender. In contrast to many hotels, all the bathrooms here have
tubs, and the suites have Jacuzzis. The open-air pool and sunning area
on the fifth floor overlooks the park. A drawback is that there is one
small elevator to service the six floors. ☒ *Colón 272, 44100,* ☎ *3/613–
8880 or 01–800/365–5300,* ☒ *3/658–1925. 97 rooms, 8 suites. Restaurant, bar, pool, free parking. AE, DC, MC, V.*

$ ☐ **Posada San Pablo.** Inside a renovated white stucco house (look for
the large painting of Our Lady of Guadalupe above the door) are tidy,
though slightly threadbare, rooms with private or shared bath. The
friendly, eager-to-please owners have decorated the freshly painted
lobby courtyard with brightly colored photographs of Guadalajara. For
little over $1 per day, you can have kitchen privileges. ☒ *Madero 218,
between Donato Guerra and Ocampo, 44100,* ☎ *3/613–3312. 9
rooms. Coin laundry. No credit cards.*

$ ☐ **San Francisco.** Once on its quiet downtown side street, you can't
miss the attractive pale orange walls of this restored two-story colonial-style building. The lushly planted courtyard makes a pleasant sitting area, and brightly polished copper lamps lend a delightful sparkle
to the simply furnished, earth-tone rooms. San Francisco is a favorite
among American residents visiting from Puerto Vallarta. ☒ *Degollado
267, 44100,* ☎ *3/613–8954,* ☒ *3/613–3257. 74 rooms, 2 suites.
Restaurant, baby-sitting, laundry service, free parking. AE, MC, V.*

Spa

$$ 🏨 **Río Caliente.** Come to this quirky, delightfully unpretentious health resort and vegetarian, alcohol-free spa to "practice the forgotten art of resting." Steam away your tensions and body toxins in a volcanic sauna scented with eucalyptus leaves, then dip into one of four therapeutic hot mineral water–filled swimming pools. The resort has spare but comfortable accommodations, facials, mud packs, massages, hiking, horseback riding, and classes in yoga and body awareness. Rates include hot-spring baths, saunas, yoga, Tai Chi, water-exercise classes, hiking, an evening lecture/workshop, and three hearty low-fat meals a day; treatments, trips, and horseback riding are extra. Río Caliente is off Highway 15, 30 km (19 mi) northwest of the Minerva Fountain. Bookings must be prepaid to the U.S. office via personal or traveler's check. ⊠ *Apdo. 5-67, Zapopan, Jalisco 43042,* ☎ FAX *3/615–7800 (answering service in Guadalajara). For U.S. reservations:* ⊠ *Box 897, Millbrae, CA 94030,* ☎ *415/615–9543,* FAX *415/615–9543. 50 rooms. Restaurant, 4 pools, massage, spa. No credit cards.*

NIGHTLIFE AND THE ARTS

Guadalajara is an active cultural and performing arts center, offering excellent local talent and well-known artists and entertainers from abroad. The U.S. and Canadian communities have also developed a schedule of English-language cultural events. During the afternoon and evening many cafés along Avenida Chapultepec also have live music.

The Arts

DANCE

Ballet Folklórico of the University of Guadalajara. The university's internationally acclaimed troupe offers traditional Mexican folkloric dances and music in the Teatro Degollado every Sunday at 10 AM. ⊠ *Calle Degollado between Av. Hidalgo and Morelos,* ☎ *3/614–4773 or 3/616–4991.* ☞ *$2.50–$11.*

PERFORMANCE VENUES

Cine Cinematógrafo I, II, and III. Founded by two Guadalajara-area movie buffs, these theaters often present English-language and other foreign films, of the art-house variety, with Spanish subtitles. ⊠ *Av. Vallarta 1102,* ☎ *3/825–0514.* ⊠ *Av. México 2222,* ☎ *3/630–1208.* ⊠ *Av. Patria 600,* ☎ *3/629–4780.*

Ex-Convento del Carmen. Music groups of all types perform on the spacious patio of the former convent of Our Lady of Mt. Carmel. There's also a café, spacious art gallery, and bookshop. It's six and a half blocks west of Avenida 16 de Septiembre. ⊠ *Av. Juárez 638,* ☎ *3/614–7184.*

Instituto Cultural Cabañas. Large-scale theater, dance, and musical performances take place on a patio within the institute. The Tolsá Chapel hosts more intimate events, and subtitled English-language films are often shown in a movie theater. Exhibits of both Mexican and foreign art are on display, and free art classes are taught here. ⊠ *Calle Cabañas 8, at Plaza Tapatía,* ☎ *3/617–4322 or 3/617–4440.*

Plaza de Armas. The **State Band of Jalisco** plays here every Thursday and Sunday evening at 6:30. On Tuesday evening, the **Municipal Band of Guadalajara** performs at 6:30. ⊠ *Av. Corona between Morelos and Pedro Moreno, across from Palacio de Gobierno.*

Teatro Degollado. Nationally and internationally famous artists perform here year-round. The refurbished velvet seats are comfortable, the acoustics are excellent, and the central air-conditioning can be a treat. ⊠ *Calle Degollado between Av. Hidalgo and Morelos,* ☎ *3/614–4773 or 3/613–1115.*

Orquesta Filarmónica de Jalisco. Conducted by Maestro Guillermo Salvador, performances take place Sunday and Friday at the Teatro Degollado (☞ *above*). ☎ *3/658–3812.* ☎ *$2–$20.*

Nightlife

A string of Guadalajara night spots generally geared to the under-30 crowd line Avenida Vallarta and the newly renovated centro area, but there are alternatives. Recently opened **Habana** (✉ La Paz 2199, on the edge of the Zona Rosa, ☎ 3/616–00–96) offers up Cuban salsa every night except Sunday in a beautiful old house filled with island nostalgia and expensive cigar smoke. Another salsa spot is **Cubilete** (✉ General Río Seco 9, in the nine-corners area of downtown, ☎ 3/613–2096), where every Friday and Saturday Rosalia—a younger version of Celia Cruz—belts out tunes that keep you dancing between the tables. For a bit of local color stop at **La Maestranza** (✉ Maestranza 179, downtown, ☎ 3/613–5878), a recently renovated 1940s cantina chockfull of bullfighting memorabilia.

The best hotel clubs are the Fiesta Americana's sleek **Lobby Bar,** for pop and mariachi-style music, and the **Caballo Negro** dance club, with live entertainment; **La Diligencia,** a romantic spot in the Camino Real featuring tropical and other music for dancing; and Crowne Plaza's jungle-themed **Manglar,** which has a game room, large-screen TV, and Latin and mariachi music for dancing.

As at 1960s coffeehouses, patrons sit around a small stage at **Peña Cuicacalli** (✉ Av. Niños Héroes 1988, on the traffic circle, ☎ 3/825–4690) to listen nightly to folk music from Mexico, Latin America, and Spain; call for performance times. **Deseñadaro** (✉ Av. Vallarta 1110, ☎ 3/825–5853) has similar music Tuesday through Saturday at 9 PM and Sunday at 6:30 PM in an airy patio setting. Jazz combos hold court at the intimate **Copenhagen 77** (✉ Marcos Castellanos 136-Z, ☎ 3/826–1787) Monday through Saturday after 9 PM.

The newest hot spot in town is the 94th **Hard Rock Café** (✉ Av. Vallarta 2125, in the Centro Magno mall, ☎ 3/616–4560 or 3/616–4564). Live bands play from 10 PM on. You can dance most of the night to live Latin music at the multilevel **Tropigala** (✉ Av. López Mateos Sur and Iztaccíhuatl, across from Plaza del Sol shopping center, ☎ 3/122–5553 or 3/122–7903) or **Co-Co & Co-Co** (✉ Av. Corona 160, ☎ 3/614–5714) at the Fenix hotel downtown.

To dance, head to **Salón Veracruz** (✉ Manzano 486, behind the Hotel Carlton, ☎ 3/613–4422), a spartan, old-style dance hall, where a 15-piece tropical band keeps hundreds of hoofers moving to cumbias, merengue, and danzón. It's open Wednesday through Sunday, 9:30 PM–3:30 AM. Another good dance club with a live Latin beat is the **Copacabana** (✉ Av. López Mateos Sur and Las Aguilas, ☎ 3/631–4596).

Good downtown discos are **Maxim's** in the Francés (☞ Lodging, *above*), the **Factory** in the Plaza Del Sol (☞ Lodging, *above*), and the Hotel Aranzazú (✉ Av. Revolución 110, ☎ 3/613–3232).

OUTDOOR ACTIVITIES AND SPORTS

Spectator Sports

Bullfighting

Corridas (bullfights) begin at 4:30 PM at **Plaza Nuevo Progreso** on Sunday, weekly in October, November, and early December, and every other week from mid-January through March. *Novilleros* (apprentice matadors) work the cape each Sunday in April and May. You can buy tickets for either the *sol* (sunny) or *sombra* (shady) side of the bullring. Since the action begins in the late afternoon, take cheaper seats on the sunny side. You can buy tickets at the bullring (about 5 km [3 mi] northeast of downtown) or at the bullring's booth in Plaza México. ✉ *M. Pirineos 1930 and Calzada Independencia Norte, across from Estadio Jalisco,* ☎ *3/637–9982 or 3/651–8378.* 🎫 *$5–$38.*

Charreadas

Charreadas (traditional Mexican rodeos) take place at the **Lienzo Charros de Jalisco** every Sunday at noon. The *charros* (cowboys) compete in 10 events, mariachis or *bandas* (brass bands) perform during breaks, and food and alcoholic beverages are available. ✉ *Av. Dr. R. Michel 577, next to Parque Agua Azul,* ☎ *3/619–3232.* 🎫 *About $2.*

Soccer

You can see afternoon and evening professional soccer matches at **Estadio Jalisco.** Schedules vary with the team. ✉ *Siete Colinas 172 and Calzada Independencia Norte, across from bullring,* ☎ *3/637–0563, 3/637–0301, or 3/637–0299.* 🎫 *90¢–$15, depending on the team.*

Participant Sports

Fitness Clubs

The **Presidente Inter-Continental** (☎ 3/678–1234) fitness club is open to nonguests for about $7.50 per day. Celebrities visit **Gold's Gym** (✉ Av. Xóchitl 4203, near Plaza del Sol shopping center, ☎ 3/647–0420) for its unique amenities, like a climbing wall, a full basketball court, and boxing, kickboxing, and Tae Kwon Do lessons. Guest passes are available for about $6.50 per day.

Golf

Golf clubs that admit foreign travelers upon payment of a greens fee (ranging from $25 to $55) include the following: **Atlas Golf Club** (✉ Carretera Guadalajara-Chapala, across from Montenegro Park, ☎ 3/689–2620 or 3/689–2783); **Las Cañadas Country Club** (✉ Av. Bosques San Isidro 777, ☎ 3/685–0049 or 3/685–0363; Tuesday and Thursday are the least crowded); **Chula Vista Country Club** (✉ Paseo de Golf 5, near Lake Chapala, Chapala, ☎ 376/5–22–81); **Chapala Country Club** (✉ Vista del Lago 1, San Nicholás Ibarra, Chapala, ☎ 376/3–51–36; closed to visitors Tuesday); and **Club de Golf Santa Anita** (✉ Carretera a Morelia, Km 6.5, ☎ 3/686–1931).

Ice-Skating

The **Iceland Pista de Hielo** (✉ Av. México 2582, ☎ 3/615–4438 or 3/615–7876), ⏱ 9:20 AM–9:40 PM, has daily one-hour public ice-skating sessions. There's also a restaurant and ice-cream parlor.

Tennis

The **Crowne Plaza Guadalajara** (✉ López Mateos Sur 2500, ☎ 3/634–1034, ⏱ 7–7) and **Camino Real** (✉ Av. Vallarta 5005, ☎ 3/121–8000, ⏱ 7 AM–10 PM) allow nonguests to use their courts for a fee. **Club de Tenis Royal** (✉ San Ignacio 316, next to La Gran Plaza, ☎ 3/647–5348, ⏱ 7 AM–11 PM) offers lessons, and English is spoken. Municipal courts at **Parque Avila Camacho** (✉ Av. Avila Camacho, south of Plaza Patria shopping mall, ☎ No phone) cost a nominal fee.

Amusement Park

If you're with teenagers, the **Formula One** go-cart racetrack park will please them. Four different tracks are available inside a tree-lined former city park. Budding Mario Andrettis from 8 to 80 can reach speeds of up to 60 miles per hour in quality go-carts on well-designed tracks that have banked curves, trees, and landscaping. A cafeteria and amusement arcade are also on site. ⊠ *Av. Avila Camacho 2700,* ☎ *3/823–2413.* ◷ *Daily 10–10.*

SHOPPING

Guadalajara has a great variety of high-quality merchandise at low prices, although you also can find high-priced low-quality items—*caveat emptor.* Store hours tend to be Monday through Saturday 9–8, Sunday 10–2; shopping mall stores generally stay open at lunch. *Tianguis* (street markets) run every day throughout the Guadalajara area; you never know what you'll find. If you are interested in traditional arts and crafts, don't miss Tlaquepaque and Tonalá (☞ Side Trips, *below*).

Malls

In Guadalajara, as in all other major cities, shopping malls are springing up everywhere. The metropolitan area now has more than 30. **El Charro,** an excellent leather-goods store, has branches in La Gran Plaza and Plaza del Sol as well as downtown.

La Gran Plaza. A sleek three-story glass-and-steel exterior houses 334 commercial spaces and a 14-plex cinema, surrounded by a large food court and some quality restaurants. It's east of the Guadalajara Chamber of Commerce and the Camino Real hotel, on the city's far west side. ⊠ *Av. Vallarta 3959,* ☎ *3/122–3004.* ◷ *Daily 10–9:30.*

Plaza del Sol. The city's largest mall sprawls like a park, with 270 commercial spaces, outdoor patios, trees and garden areas, and parking for 2,100 cars. It's across from the Presidente Inter-Continental hotel. ⊠ *Avs. López Mateos Sur and Mariano Otero,* ☎ *3/121–5950.* ◷ *Weekdays 10–8, Sat. 10–9, Sun. 10–7.*

Plaza Galería del Calzado. The 60 stores in this west-side complex all sell shoes. Guadalajara is one of Mexico's leading shoe centers, and high-quality footwear and accessories are available here, many at lower prices than in the States. ⊠ *Av. México and Juan Palomar y Arias,* ☎ *3/647–6422.* ◷ *Mon.–Sat. 11–9, Sun. 11–8:30.*

Plaza México. There are about 120 stores in the city's second most popular shopping mall, seven blocks west of the Plaza Galería del Calzado. ⊠ *Av. México 3300,* ☎ *3/813–2488.* ◷ *Daily 10–8.*

Centro Magno. This three-story mall recently opened with great fanfare just a few blocks from the Minerva. A number of upscale boutiques and bistros, along with a Hard Rock Café, make this a trendy spot to shop and dine. A large cineplex is under construction on the top floor. ⊠ *Av. Vallarta 2125.* ◷ *Daily 10–10.*

Markets and Handicrafts

Calle Esteban Alatorre. Several blocks of shoe stores—all reasonably priced—line this street. ⊠ *East of Calzada Independencia Norte and 4 blocks north of Av. Hidalgo.*

Instituto de Artesanías Jaliscienses. Run by the state government, this store has a wide selection of the exquisite blown glass and hand-glazed pottery typical of Jalisco artisans. There are also fine crafts from other parts of Mexico. Everything is sold at fixed prices. ⊠ *Calzada González Gallo 20 and Calzada Independencia Sur, next to Parque Agua Azul.* ☎ *3/619–4664.* ◷ *Weekdays 10–6, Sat. 10–5, Sun. 10–3.*

El Baratillo. This is one of the world's largest flea markets. Thirty city blocks are lined with stalls, tents, and blankets piled high with new, used, and antique merchandise. ⊠ *On and around Calle Esteban Loera, some 15 blocks east of Mercado Libertad.* ◷ *Sun. 7–5.*

Mercado Libertad. Also known as the Mercado San Juan de Dios, the

Liberty Market is one of Latin America's largest enclosed markets. Within a three-square-block area you can browse through more than 1,000 privately owned stalls selling everything from clothing to crafts to live animals and gold watches. ⊠ *Calzada Independéncia Sur between Dionísio Rodríguez and Av. Javier Mina.* ☉ *Daily 10–8.*

Bazar Capitán. Serious art, crafts, and antique lovers may want to consult an expert if time is limited. Bazar Capitán's Robert Alvarado, who has 30 years in the art and antiques business, runs personalized buying tours for small groups. His bilingual *El Antiquario* magazine promotes local antiquities dealers. ⊠ *Argentina 73, a half block off Avenida Vallarta.* ☎ *3/827–1990.* ☉ *Weekdays noon–6.*

SIDE TRIPS FROM GUADALAJARA

No trip to Guadalajara is complete without an excursion of some kind out of the city, whether you're into shopping for Mexican crafts, taking in the freshwater breezes of Lake Chapala, or unlocking the secrets of tequila in Tequila.

Tlaquepaque and Tonalá

For inveterate shoppers, a combined visit to the crafts meccas of Tlaquepaque and Tonalá makes a perfect day trip from Guadalajara. There's at least one bed-and-breakfast in Tlaquepaque if you really want to shop until you drop, but it's easy enough to return to the wider selection of lodgings in Guadalajara.

Tlaquepaque

7 km (4½ mi) southeast of downtown Guadalajara.

Tlaquepaque is known throughout Mexico as an arts-and-crafts center. Among its offerings are intricate blown-glass miniatures; exquisite pottery; jewelry, silver, and copperware; leather and hand-carved wood furniture; and handwoven clothing. More than 300 shops line pedestrian malls and plazas in this charming town.

Distinctive decorated pottery, sold in stores throughout the town, was first fashioned by nearby Tonaltecan Indians in the mid-16th century. The small village remained virtually isolated until June 13, 1821, when local authorities met here to sign a regional proclamation of independence from Spain. Soon after, wealthy Guadalajara residents began to build palatial summer houses. Many of these magnificent buildings have been restored, and today they house shops and restaurants.

In 1870 the art of glass-blowing was introduced from Europe. As people started coming to purchase the pottery and intricate glass creations, more artisans—weavers, jewelers, and wood-carvers—arrived and built workshops. In 1973 downtown Tlaquepaque underwent a major renovation, the highlight of which was the creation of a wide pedestrian mall, Calle Independencia. More shops line Calle Juárez, a block south, as well as the many side streets. Typical store hours are Monday through Saturday 10–2 and 4–7, and Sunday 10–2; unless otherwise indicated, the stores listed here keep roughly these hours.

The following are some of the highlights you'll come across if you start walking from the west end of Calle Independencia.

20 Color seems to explode in the more than 10 rooms of **La Casa Canela,** exquisitely decorated with vivid papier-mâché flowers and finely glazed pottery. All surround a patio blooming with tropical plants. ⊠ *Independencia 258,* ☎ *3/635–3717 or 3/657–1343.* ☉ *Weekdays 10–2 and 3–7, Sat. 10–6, Sun. 11–3.*

★ ㉑ Housed in a colonial mansion, **Museo Regional de la Cerámica** (Regional Museum of Ceramics) covers the evolution of ceramic wares in the Atemajac Valley during the past century. ⊠ *Independencia 237,* ☎ *3/635–5404.* 🎟 *Free.* ☉ *Tues.–Sat. 10–6, Sun. 10–2.*

㉒ Sergio Bustamante's work is found in galleries throughout the world, but you can purchase his whimsical sculpture or silver- and gold-plated jewelry for considerably less at **Galería Sergio Bustamante.** At the back is an art gallery featuring work by Mexican artists. The flamingos under the waterfall in the rear are real. ⊠ *Independencia 236,* ☎ *3/639–5519.* ☉ *Mon.–Sat. 10–7, Sun. 11–3.*

㉓ **La Rosa de Cristal** contains a large variety of handblown glass objects and figures, including surprisingly inexpensive miniatures. Almost all of it is made in Tlaquepaque's oldest blown-glass factory, around the corner. Here you can watch glassmakers shove long tubes into a white-hot fire, retrieve a bubbling glob, and create a piece similar to what you saw in the store. ⊠ *Store: Independencia 232,* ☎ *3/639–7180.* ☉ *Mon.–Sat. 10–7, Sun. 11–2.* ⊠ *Factory: Contreras Medellín 173, corner of Donato Guerra.* ☉ *Weekdays 10–1, Sat. 10–noon.*

㉔ Step through the doors of **Agustín Parra Diseño Barroco,** and you'll swear you're back in the 18th century. Here are exquisite baroque-style statues, wood-and-gilt altarpieces, candlesticks, and other ornaments. ⊠ *Independencia 158,* ☎ *3/657–8530 or 3/657–0316.* ☉ *Weekdays 9–2 and 4–6, Sat. 9–3, Sun. 10–2 and 3–5.*

㉕ Franciscan friars founded the **Templo Parroquial de San Pedro** during the Spanish conquest, naming the parish church in honor of San Pedro de Analco. In line with the custom of naming a town after its principal church, in 1915 the town's name was officially changed to San Pedro Tlaquepaque. The altars of Our Lady of Guadalupe and the Sacred Heart of Jesus are intricately carved in silver and gilt. ⊠ *In square at Calles Guillermo Prieto and Morelos.* ⊙ *Daily 7 AM–9 PM.*

㉖ In 1959 Ken Edwards introduced more durable stoneware (which is by nature lead-free) into the Tonalá pottery vernacular—the original local earthenware is more fragile. His store, **Cerámica de Ken Edwards,** is filled with brightly colored, hand-decorated plates, cups, and vases. Ask to see the seconds, some real bargains. Edwards also has a workshop in Tonalá (☞ Tonalá, *below*). ⊠ *Francisco Madero 70,* ☎ *3/635–5456.* ⊙ *Mon.–Sat. 10:30–7, Sun. 11–6.*

㉗ At the **Plaza de Artesanías,** browse through boutiques selling high-quality leather goods, embroidered clothing, ceramics, and blown glass. Some shops close on weekends. ⊠ *Juárez 145.* ⊙ *Daily 9–7.*

㉘ Striking hand-carved furniture and antiques fill the two-story **Bazar Hecht.** The Hecht family is known throughout Mexico for its high-quality, ornately sculpted tables and chairs. ⊠ *Juárez 162,* ☎ *3/659–0205.* ⊙ *Weekdays 10–2:30 and 3:30–7, Sat. 10:30–3 and 4–7.*

㉙ Vibrantly painted hand-carved wood furniture is created at **Cerámica El Palomar.** The Velasco family has been well-known for decades for its decorative ceramics as well. Michoacán hand-sewn table linens and Tonalá blown glass are also available. ⊠ *Av. Marcelino Garcia Barragán 1905 (½ block from the arches),* ☎ *3/635–8098.* ⊙ *Weekdays 10–7, Sat. 10–2.*

㉚ When you're ready for lunch, head for **El Parián,** a 120-year-old former handicrafts market south of Independencia that now houses various restaurants and cantinas. Mariachis stroll through its open-air area in the afternoons. Although the food is only average, the margaritas slide down well after a hard day of shopping. Use the arcade shops here only to compare prices. *Shop on Calle Independencia or another main street.*

DINING

$$ ✕ **Casa Fuerte.** Dine on such gourmet Mexican dishes as chicken stuffed with *huitlacoche* (a corn fungus known as Mexico's answer to the truffle) and shrimp in tamarind sauce. For dessert, try some homemade ice cream. There are tables in the verdant patio garden or on the front sidewalk. ⊠ *Independencia 224,* ☎ *3/657–8499. AE, MC, V.*

$$ ✕ **Restaurant sin Nombre.** The "Restaurant with No Name" serves Spanish nouvelle cuisine, a combination of pre-Hispanic and modern recipes. High adobe walls surround the 17th-century colonial building and extensive gardens. Daily entertainment includes suave jazz and traditional Mexican music. ⊠ *Francisco Madero 80,* ☎ *3/635–4520 or 3/635–9677. AE, MC, V.*

$ ✕ **El Abajeño.** At this branch of the local chain that serves quality Mexican specialties, look for the *carnitas* (pork) or *filete tapado* (cheese-topped fillet of beef). ⊠ *Juárez 231,* ☎ *3/635–9019. AE, MC, V.*

Tonalá
8 km (5 mi) east of Tlaquepaque.

Tonalá is 10 minutes away but centuries removed from its commercial neighbor, Tlaquepaque. One of Mexico's oldest pueblos, Tonalá is a quiet village with dusty, cobblestone streets and adobe houses. The village was both the pre-Hispanic capital of the Atemajac Valley Indians and the capital of New Spain when Captain Juan de Oñate moved Guadalajara here in 1532. Within three years, however, unfriendly Indians and a lack of water forced the Spaniards out.

Today, municipal officials say more than 6,000 artisans live and work here. Indeed, much of the ceramics and pottery sold in Tlaquepaque (and in many other parts of the world) are made in Tonalá. In small home studios, families create the lovely pieces, cobalt-blue glassware, and playful animals with the same materials and techniques their ancestors used centuries ago. It's possible to visit many home studios by way of free tours offered by the Tonalá municipal tourist office (☞ *below*) beginning from the Casa de Artesanos with one-day advance notice.

On Thursday, much Tonalá merchandise is sold at bargain prices at one of the best tianguis in all of Mexico (avoid Sundays). Most stores are open Monday through Saturday 10–2 and 4–7, Sunday 10–2.

Below are some of the highlights of a walk north and generally east of Avenida de los Tonaltecas, a main drag lined with shops and cafés.

③¹ A virtual department store of Mexican folk art and crafts, the **Casa de los Artesanos** displays an excellent selection of works by the best of Tonalá's artisans. The work of generations is here, including items made from wood, glass, wrought iron, brass, and of course clay. More than 20 techniques of producing barro are used in the village. Prices are reasonable, and the staff here can direct you to local artisans' studios. ⊠ *Av. de los Tonaltecas Sur 140,* ☎ *3/683–0590.* ☉ *Weekdays 9–7, weekends 9–3.*

③² In the **Santuário,** or parish church, large paintings of the 14 stations of the cross fill the walls. Next door is the simple **Palacio Municipal,** or City Hall. The **Plaza Principal** is across the street. ⊠ *Juárez at Hidalgo.*

③³ One of Tonalá's largest exporters of hand-painted ceramics abroad is **Erandi.** Its new exhibition center is in founder Jorge Wilmot's former workshop. To see artisans in action, stop by their factory three blocks away. ⊠ *Morelos 86,* ☎ *3/812–1603.* ☉ *Tues.–Sat. 9–6, Sun. 9–2.* ⊠ *Factory: Lopez Cotilla 118,* ☎ *3/683–0253.*

³⁴ The Bernabe family has made exquisite petatillo ceramics for generations, as well as more simple stoneware. The sprawling workshop in back of the **Galería José Bernabe** is also open to visitors. ⊠ *Hidalgo 83, between Zapata and Constitución,* ☎ *3/683–0040.* ☉ *Weekdays 10–3 and 4–7, weekends 10–3. Workshop closed weekends.*

³⁵ Exhibits at the **Museo Nacional de la Cerámica** (National Ceramics Museum) include ceramics and pottery of several Mexican states dating from pre-Columbian times to the present. There is also a workshop and a small store. ⊠ *Constitución 104,* ☎ *3/683–0494.* 🎫 *Free.* ☉ *Tues.–Sun. 10–5, Sat. 10–3, Sun. 10–2.*

³⁶ At the **Cerámica de Ken Edwards** workshop, you can view Edwards's trademark lead-free stoneware, which revolutionized centuries-old techniques. Although Edwards has moved on to Guatemala, his quality ceramics live on. ⊠ *Morelos 184,* ☎ *3/683–0716.* ☉ *Weekdays 9–6, Sat. 9–1.*

³⁷ Tonalá native J. Cruz Coldívar, who signs his work and named his shop **El 7** ("el see-*ey*-tey") makes striking hand-painted masks, as well as decorative plates and other wall hangings. He has exhibited throughout Mexico, and also in the United States, Canada, Europe, and South America. ⊠ *Privado Obregón 28, north of town center,* ☎ *3/683–0873.* ☉ *Weekdays 9–6, Sat. 9–1.*

³⁸ In a small patio behind his home, **Salvador Vásquez Carmona** molds enormous ceramic pots and glazes them with intricate and fanciful designs. Numerous awards certificates hang in his living room. ⊠ *Av. de* los Maestros 328, *west of Av. de los Tonaltecas*, ☎ *3/683–2896.* ✆ *Weekdays; call first.*

DINING

$ ✕ **Los Geranios.** Here is a tranquil pink-and-white dining room with wooden booths and white-clothed tables. The menu focuses on traditional Mexican soups (try the avocado) and entrées. ⊠ *Hidalgo 71,* ☎ *3/683–0010. No credit cards. Closed Sat.*

$ ✕ **Restaurant Jalepeños.** Steaks are the house specialty in this small but tastefully appointed restaurant. ⊠ *Madero 23, half a block from the town hall,* ☎ *3/683–0344. No credit cards.*

$ ✕ **Restaurant Trópico de Tonalá.** This popular six-table luncheonette with counter area serves up tasty, fresh sandwiches, soups, and chicken and meat dishes. ⊠ *Madero 15,* ☎ *3/683–0398. No credit cards.*

Tlaquepaque and Tonalá A to Z

ARRIVING AND DEPARTING

By Bus. There is frequent public bus service from downtown Guadalajara and the Plaza del Sol shopping center to Tlaquepaque and Tonalá. The trips take around 30 minutes and 45 minutes, respectively.

By Car. From Guadalajara, take Avenida Revolución southeast. At the Plaza de la Bandera, jog right onto Boulevard General Marcelino García Barragán, which becomes Boulevard Tlaquepaque as it leads into town. When you reach the *glorieta* (traffic circle), follow the circle around to Avenida Niños Héroes. The first intersection is Calle Independencia, the pedestrian mall. From the Plaza del Sol area, take Calzada Lázaro Cárdenas southeast to the Alamo traffic circle. Fork off to the north onto Avenida Niños Héroes. Both routes take around 20 minutes.

To get from Tlaquepaque to Tonalá, take Avenida Río Nilo southeast directly into town, to the intersection of Avenida de los Tonaltecas.

By Taxi. The fare from downtown Guadalajara to Tlaquepaque is about $4. From downtown Guadalajara, the cab ride to Tonalá costs about $6. A cab from Tlaquepaque to Tonalá runs about $3.

VISITOR INFORMATION

The **Tlaquepaque municipal tourist office** (⊠ Pila Seca 15-16, in front of the arches, Tlaquepaque, ☎ 3/635–5756), open weekdays 9–7, is in the Centro Cultural.

The **Tonalá municipal tourist office** (⊠ Av. de los Tonaltecas 140 Sur, Tonalá, ☎ 3/683–1740), open weekdays 9–3 and Saturday 9–1, is next to the Casa de los Artesanos.

Around Lake Chapala

Could it be the area's Mexican arts and culture? Or perhaps the favorable exchange rate? Or even the springlike climate? Whatever the reason, more than 35,000 U.S. and Canadian citizens have retired in and around Guadalajara. The majority reside along the shores of Lake Chapala, Mexico's largest inland lake.

The jagged mountains that ring the lake make it seem a world away from Guadalajara. The tranquility of the area offers a welcome contrast to the bustling city. Sunsets are spectacular, and there's just enough humidity to keep the abundant bougainvillea blooming and ensure no drastic temperature fluctuations. Unfortunately, the lake is polluted and fighting an ongoing battle with *lirio* (water hyacinth), a succulent plant that threatens to cover much of the water's surface. For years the lake has been also threatened by dangerously low water levels caused by overconsumption from Guadalajara and surrounding states. But Chapala has been declared part of Mexico's national heritage, and steps are being taken to find alternate sources of water for the city and to protect the lake from further industrial dumping from Río Lerma, the river that feeds it.

Spanish settlement in the area dates from 1538, when Franciscan friar Miguel de Bolonio arrived and began to convert the Taltica Indians to Christianity. Their chief was named Chapalac, from which the name Chapala is said to have originated. Today, Chapala is the area's largest settlement. Eight km (five mi) to the west, the more tranquil village of Ajijic has been home to expatriate artists and writers since the 1920s. The towns and villages along the lake are linked by one highway with multiple names, such as Carretera Chapala-Ajijic or Carretera Ajijic-Jocotepec.

Chapala
45 km (28 mi) south of Guadalajara.

With Chapala's proximity to rapidly growing Guadalajara, as well as its comfortable climate, it is surprising that tourists did not frequent the area until the late 19th century. Then-president Porfirio Díaz heard that aristocrats had discovered this ideal place for weekend getaways, and he began spending holidays here in 1904. Soon summer homes were built, and in 1910 the Chapala Yacht Club opened. Word of the town, with its lavish lawn parties and magnificent estates, spread quickly to the United States and Europe.

Nowadays the town of Chapala has a population of some 35,000 and attracts a less influential but equally fun-loving assortment of visitors. On weekends the streets are filled with Mexican families. Throughout the week American and Canadian retirees stroll along the lakeside promenade, play golf, and relax on the verandas of downtown restaurants.

Avenida Madero, lined with pleasant restaurants, shops, and cafés, is the town's main drag. On Madero, four blocks north of the lake, the

39 **plaza,** at the corner of López Cotilla, is a relaxing spot for townspeople and tourists to sit and read the paper. Two blocks south of the plaza,

40 the **Iglesia de San Francisco** is easy to spot by the blue neon crosses on its twin steeples. The church was built in 1528 and reconstructed in

41 1580. On weekends, the tranquil lakeside **Parque la Cristianía,** on the south side of the *malecón* (boardwalk), fills with Tapatíos taking a respite from the city and browsing the ever-present souvenir booths. At the end of the park are a small handicrafts market and a number of open-air cafés featuring *pescado blanco,* the white fish native to the lake. Because of pollution, we cannot recommend that you partake of this regional delicacy, though other food is fine.

42 A visit to **Isla de los Alacranes** (Scorpion Island) is a popular excursion from the Chapala pier at the end of Avenida Madero. The view of the shore area is enchanting. From the same pier, you can also take

43 a trip to **Isla de Mezcala,** about 12 km (7½ mi) northeast of Isla de los Alacranes, and explore the ruins of a fortress that housed a band of rebels during the early 19th-century war of independence with Spain. Depending on the duration of the trip, the price ranges from about $9.35 to $60 for a launch with a capacity of eight adults.

DINING AND LODGING

$$ ✕ **Beer Garden.** The roofed terrace here has been a favorite watering hole and lunch spot since 1929. Enjoy the expansive lake view while you eat one of the tasty seafood, chicken, or beef specialties. ⊠ *Paseo Ramón Corona at northwest corner of Av. Madero,* ☎ *376/5–22–57. AE, MC, V. Closed Tues.*

$$ ✕ **Mariscos Guicho's e Hijos.** The best of the waterfront seafood joints, Guicho's serves up savory caviar tacos, frog legs, garlic shrimp, and spicy seafood soup. The audacious lime-green walls and cheery red tablecloths lend a particularly authentic Mexican charm. The second floor has a good view of the lake. ⊠ *Ramón Corona 20,* ☎ *376/5–32–32. No credit cards. Closed Tues.*

$ ✕ **El Arbol del Café** (The Coffee Tree). Local expatriates cherish this modest café for its roasted-on-the-premises specialty coffee, imported teas, and homemade cakes. Sip a decaffeinated cappuccino (which you won't often find in Mexico) and peruse the day's English-language papers. ⊠ *Av. Hidalgo 236,* ☎ *No phone. No credit cards. Closed Sun.*

$ ✕ **Restaurant Cazadores.** This grandly turreted building was once the summer home of the Braniff family, owners of the now-defunct airline. The food is nothing special—just come for a cool drink and watch the action along the malecón. ⊠ *Av. Madero and Paseo Ramón Corona, northeast corner,* ☎ *376/5–21–62. AE, MC, V. Closed Mon.*

$$$ 🏨 **Quinta Quetzalcóatl.** Behind 12-ft stone walls, the "QQ" is on the
★ grounds of the villa where D. H. Lawrence wrote *The Plumed Serpent* in the 1920s. Owners Dick and Barbi Henderson have restored and enlarged the property and furnished it with colorful antiques; guests also enjoy a living-dining room and lush tropical gardens. Rates include breakfast (except on Sunday). In high-season, seven-day packages, two gourmet dinners, and one barbecue are also included. There's a three-night minimum, and a deposit is required by check. ⊠ *Zaragoza 307 (Apdo. 286), 45900,* ☎ *376/5–36–53,* 🅵🅰🆇 *376/5–34–44. Payments to:* ⊠ *Quinta Quetzalcoatl, 9051-C Siempre Viva Rd., Suite 71, Box 208, San Diego, CA 92173-3628. 8 suites. 2 bars, pool, hot tub, library, meeting room. AE, MC, V.*

$ 🏨 **Hotel Nido.** The oldest hotel on the lake was built in the early 1900s to accommodate President Porfírio Díaz and his entourage. In the 1940s Mexican film star María Félix spent the first of her numerous

Lake Chapala Area

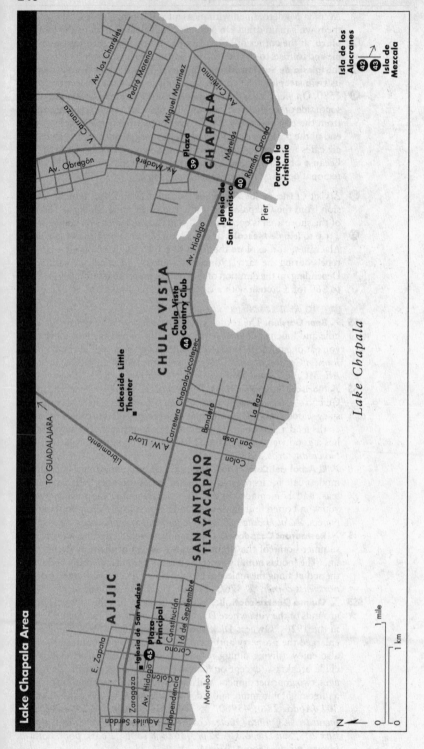

TO GUADALAJARA

Libramiento

AJIJIC

Iglesia de San Andrés

Plaza Principal

43

Aquiles Serdán
E. Zapata
Zaragoza
Av. Hidalgo
Colón
Constitución
Parroquia
16 de Septiembre
Independencia
Morelos

**SAN ANTONIO
TLAYACAPÁN**

Colón
San José
La Paz
Bandera
A.W. Lloyd
Carretera Chapala-Jocotepec

CHULA VISTA

Lakeside Little Theater

Chula Vista Country Club **44**

Av. Hidalgo

Iglesia de San Francisco

Pier

40

41 Parque la Cristianía

Ramón Corona
Morelos

CHAPALA

39 Plaza

Av. Madero
Av. Obregón
V. Carranza
Av. los Charales
Pedro Moreno
Miguel Martínez
A. Cristianía

Lake Chapala

42 Isla de los Alacranes

43 Isla de Mezcala

N

0   1 mile
0   1 km

honeymoons here, and the whitewashed high-ceiling lobby still feels like the scene of a melodrama waiting to happen. Photos of turn-of-the-last-century Chapala adorn the walls, and there's a picturesque patio and garden in the rear. However, rooms are strictly functional, and only the ones in the front have televisions. ✉ *Av. Madero 202, 45900,* ☎ *376/5–21–16. 30 rooms. Restaurant, bar, pool, laundry service, free parking. MC, V.*

$ 🏨 **Hotel Villa Montecarlo.** Look out on spacious lawns, complete with strolling peacocks, high on a hill above the lake. The comfortable rooms, in three-story contiguous units, have carved wooden furniture and light multicolored bedspreads. One of the two swimming pools is filled with natural thermal water. ✉ *Hidalgo 296, about 1 km (½ mi) west of Av. Madero, 45900,* ☎ 🖷 *376/5–22–16, 376/5–21–20, 376/5–20–20, or 376/5–33–66. 46 rooms, 2 suites. Restaurant, bar, 2 pools, 2 tennis courts, laundry service, free parking. AE, MC, V.*

$ 🏨 **Lake Chapala Inn.** In this renovated turn-of-the-last-century mansion with 18-ft ceilings, most rooms face the lake and have oversized baths and large garden terraces; all have TVs and phones. A dining room, library, and gourmet kitchen are also on site. An English-style breakfast is included in the rates. ✉ *Paseo Ramon 23, down the malecón from the Beer Garden, 45900,* ☎ 🖷 *376/5–47–86 or 376/5–48–09. 4 rooms. Pool, laundry, free parking. No credit cards.*

Chula Vista
3 km (2 mi) west of Chapala.

Chula Vista, the most American neighborhood in Mexico, lies between Chapala and Ajijic. Dozens of condos dot the hillside north of ④④ the road. The **Chula Vista Country Club** (✉ Paseo de Golf 5, ☎ 376/5–22–81) is a favorite of the local *norteamericano* community. The "billy-goat" (read: hilly) golf course here—open to nonmembers who pay the greens fee—has great views of the lake and offers a real workout, as the rugged terrain cannot be negotiated by golf cart.

DINING

$ ✗ **Chicken Lick'n.** As its name suggests, this place serves roast chicken, but you'll also find soups, salads, sandwiches, and American-style pies and cakes. You know the birds are fresh—you're right next door to Puritan Poultry. ✉ *Carretera Chapala-Ajijic 101, in Riberas del Pilar,* ☎ *376/5–43–99. No credit cards. Closed Sun.*

NIGHTLIFE AND THE ARTS

Just west of Chula Vista, above the PAL Trailer Park and next to the Oak Hill High School, is the 112-seat **Lakeside Little Theater** (☎ 376/6–09–54), which stages English-language musicals and plays throughout the year. Box office hours are 10 AM to 1 PM starting three days before performances and during the run of any show. To find out what's playing, look for *The Guadalajara Colony Reporter.*

Banana's Night Club has a live house band weekends and has become a favorite of North Americans and locals who count a beer mug with their name at the bar. There is line dancing Wednesday to country favorites, and the avocado and pork burritos are scrumptious. ✉ *Carretera Chapala-Jocotepec 159, San Antonio Tlayacapán,* ☎ *376/6–09–35. No credit cards. Closed Sun.–Tues.*

Ajijic
8 km (5 mi) west of Chapala.

Despite blocks of galleries and crafts shops, Ajijic's small-town ambience is still defined by its narrow cobblestone streets, whitewashed buildings, and gentle pace. Still, the foreign influence is unmistakable:

English is spoken almost as widely here as Spanish, and license plates run the gamut from Alaska to Texas. A recent building boom is straining the traffic capacity of the pueblo.

45 Some visitors park near the **Plaza Principal** (also called the Plaza de Armas or Jardín), the tree- and flower-filled central square at the corner of Colon and Hidalgo, although it may be easier to find space a few blocks farther on at the edge of the pier. The **Iglesia de San Andrés** (Church of St. Andrew) sits on the Jardín's north side. In late November the plaza fills for the saint's nine-day fiesta, including fireworks, parades, music, and dancing.

Walk down Calle Morelos (the continuation of Avenida Colón) toward the lake and you'll find stores and boutiques that sell everything from designer fashions to traditional arts and crafts. Turn left onto Independencia to find about a dozen art galleries and studios.

DINING AND LODGING

In addition to the establishments listed below, there are other good-quality lodgings in the area. Consult the tourist office in Chapala, the *Ojo del Lago* newspaper, or *The Guadalajara Colony Reporter*. Note that restaurants in Ajijic often seem to come and go yearly.

$$ ✕ **Ajijic Grill.** Savor Japanese specialties prepared table-side, grilled meats,
★ seafood, and fresh salads (quite safe) in an airy, partially roofed patio.
⊠ *Morelos 5,* ☎ *376/6–24–58. MC, V.*

$$ ✕ **Johanna's German Restaurant.** This small, intimate bit of Bavaria on the lake serves up a variety of excellent sausages and authentic German cuisine. ⊠ *Blvd. Ajijic 118A, in front of the La Floresta Auditorium,* ☎ *376/6–04–37. No credit cards. Closed Mon.*

$$ ✕ **La Luz de La Luna.** In the expansive gardens of La Colección Moon, high style and presentation and a Spanish influence in the menu make this a worthy stop. ⊠ *Río Zula 4,* ☎ *376/6–20–92. MC, V. Closed Mon.*

$ ✕ **La Casa del Waffle.** Stop in this bright cheery spot for breakfast and choose from 12 varieties of waffles and numerous other U.S. morning favorites. ⊠ *Carretera Chapala–Jocotepec Poniente 75, on the highway west of Ajijic,* ☎ *376/6–23–01. No credit cards. Closed Tues.*

$ ✕ **Salvador's.** An afternoon hangout for local expatriates, this restaurant has a well-kept salad bar and specialties from both south and north of the border. ⊠ *Carretera Chapala–Jocotepec 56, inside Plaza Bugambilias,* ☎ *376/6–23–01. No credit cards.*

$$ ✕🏨 **La Nueva Posada.** Luxuriant gardens framed in bougainvillea over-
★ look the lake at this charming inn, run by a gracious Canadian family. The spacious, well-lighted rooms have warm pastel color schemes and original watercolors. Chef Lorraine Rousseau's eclectic menu is delicious, and there is fine entertainment most evenings, typically an American jazz trio or tropical music. ⊠ *Donato Guerra 9, Apdo. 30, 45920,* ☎ *376/6–14–44,* ☎ FAX *376/6–13–44. 17 suites. Restaurant, bar, fans, pool, laundry service, free parking. MC, V.*

$$ 🏨 **Inn at San Andres.** This small bed and breakfast integrates hand-painted tiles and rustic furniture in each one-of-a-kind suite. Full breakfast is included in the rates. ⊠ *Galeana 22-A, 1 block off the plaza, 45920,* ☎ *376/6–12–50; in the U.S. 703/830–8398 with Denise Clark. 5 suites. Pool. No credit cards.*

$$ 🏨 **Los Artistas.** One of Ajijic's elegant walled-in homes, this friendly inn is surrounded by an acre of sumptuously landscaped gardens. Each room is uniquely decorated with colorful handwoven Mexican bedspreads and fresh-cut tropical bouquets. Rates include a breakfast buffet of local fruits, yogurt, granola, and fresh homemade breads. ⊠ *Constitución 105, 45920,* ☎ *376/6–10–27,* FAX *376/6–17–62. 6 rooms. Pool, free parking. No credit cards.*

$$ \ \boxed{\mathbb{T}}\ $$ **Real de Chapala.** Rooms here are airy and ample, and all suites have small individual swimming pools. The Sunday mariachi lunch is popular with weekend visitors from Guadalajara. ⊠ *Paseo del Prado 20, 45920,* ☎ *376/6–00–14 or 376/6–00–21,* ℻ *376/6–00–25. For reservations in Guadalajara:* ⊠ *Hoteles Real, Rubén Darío 262, Guadalajara, 44630,* ☎ *3/641–9097 or 3/641–9093,* ℻ *3/642–8878. 80 rooms, 5 suites. Restaurant, bar, fans, pool, wading pool, 2 tennis courts, volleyball, laundry service, free parking. AE, MC, V.*

NIGHTLIFE AND THE ARTS

The rambling, hacienda-style **Posada Ajijic** (⊠ Calle Morelos, facing the lake, ☎ 376/6–07–44 or 376/6–04–30) is a restaurant, bar, and popular weekend dance place with a spectacular water view. A cozy, candlelit nightclub, **Viva Maria** (⊠ Donato Guerra 20, ☎ 376/6–09–84) presents an eclectic range of live musical offerings—from jazz, rock, and classical to flamenco and even pre-Hispanic music. Dance clubs and night spots come and go quickly here; ask about the latest craze at your hotel or tourist office.

SHOPPING

The shores of Lake Chapala are teaming with artisan workshops, many of which have replaced Tonalá as the region's source of export quality crafts. Though Ajijic does not have as many boutiques and crafts shops as inhabitants, it sometimes seems that way. **Casa de las Artesanías Ajijik** (⊠ Carretera Chapala-Jocotepec, Km 6.5, ☎ 376/6–05–48; ⊘ weekdays 10–6, Sat. 10–4, Sun. 10–2) is a branch of the state-run Instituto de Artesanias Jaliscienses crafts shop (☞ Shopping *under* Guadalajara, *above*). Inside **La Colección Bárbara** (⊠ Av. Independencia 7&9A, ☎ 376/6–18–24; ⊘ Mon.–Sat. 10–5) are traditional crafts, antiques, and fine furniture. **La Colección Moon** (⊠ Río Zula 4, south of Ocampo, ☎ 376/6–10–00; ⊘ weekdays 8–1 and 4–6, weekends 9–6) carries a selection of owner Billy Moon's high-end lamps, wrought-iron furniture, and other decorative items, as well as an international-style restaurant (☎ 376/6–20–92). **Mi México** (⊠ Morelos 8, ☎ 376/6–01–33; ⊘ Mon.–Sat. 10–2 and 3–6, Sun. 11–3) boutique sells pottery, blown glass, women's clothing, and other crafts and gifts. **Opus Boutique and Galería** (⊠ Morelos 15, ☎ 376/6–17–90) sells masks, folk art, jewelry, and women's clothing. Exhibits of sculpture, paintings, prints, photography, pottery, and a number of other art mediums by local artists can be found at **Galería Americas** (⊠ Ramón Corona 11, across from the Lake Chapala Society, ☎ 376/6–12–92), **Galería Daniel Palma** (⊠ Ocampo 30, ☎ 376/6–16–88), and **Galería Di Paola** (⊠ Colón 11, ☎ 376/6–10–10).

For Cuban and Mexican cigars, go to **La Antigua Axixic Tobacco and Gift Shop** (⊠ Constitución 71A, ☎ No phone. ⊘ Tues.–Sun. 10–6).

SPORTS

Take a break with the kids—or pretend you're one again—and explore the **Tobolandia** water park. ⊠ *Carretera Chapala-Ajijic, Km 7,* ☎ *376/6–21–20.*

San Juan Cosalá

10 km (6 mi) west of Chapala.

San Juan Cosalá is known for its natural thermal-water spas on the shores of Lake Chapala, with the mountains rising to the north. The **Hotel Balneario San Juan Cosalá** (☎ 376/1–02–22) welcomes both day-trippers and overnight guests to its four large swimming pools and two wading pools. A restaurant with international fare is on the premises. The **Villas Buenaventura Cosalá** (☎ 376/1–02–02) only accepts overnight guests. Facilities here include six one-bedroom furnished suites and 11 with two bedrooms, all with kitchenettes, TVs, and thermal-water bathtubs. There are also thermal hot tubs and swimming pools. ✉ *Apdo. Postal 181, Chapala, Jalisco 45900 is reservations address for both hotels.*

Lake Chapala A to Z

ARRIVING AND DEPARTING

By Bus. There is frequent bus service to Chapala, Ajijic, and other lakeside towns from both Guadalajara's **Antigua Central Camionera** (Old Bus Station) and **La Central Camionera Nueva** for about $2. Make sure you ask for the *directo* as opposed to *clase segunda,* which stops at every little pueblo en route.

By Car. From downtown Guadalajara take Avenida Federalismo south to Calzada Lázaro Cárdenas, turn left, and continue southeast. Follow the signs as Lázaro Cárdenas converges with the Carretera a Chapala, whose route number is both 23 and 44. The trip takes 50 minutes.

ENGLISH-LANGUAGE PUBLICATIONS

The *Ojo del Lago* monthly newspaper is available free of charge throughout town. *The Guadalajara Colony Reporter* weekly newspaper (☞ Contacts and Resources *in* Guadalajara A to Z, *below*) devotes a section to lakeside news and events. **Libros de Chapala** (✷ Daily 9–2, 3–6) across from the plaza on Avenida Madero in Chapala, has an extensive range of English-language magazines, U.S. and Canadian newspapers, and a large selection of books on Mexico in English. In Ajijic, supermarkets **Super Lake** in San Antonio and **El Torito** in La Floresta carry English-language newspapers and magazines. **Portalibros** (✉ Constitución 2A, ☎ 376/6-19-98. ✷ Mon.–Sat. 9:30–5) carries a wide selection of used books in English.

VISITOR INFORMATION

The **Jalisco state tourism office** (✉ Hidalgo 407, 2nd floor, ☎ FAX 376/5-31-41) in Chapala is open weekdays 9–7, Saturday 9–1.

In Ajijic, the nonprofit **Lake Chapala Society** (✉ Av. 16 de Septiembre, No. 16A, ☎ No phone), open Monday–Saturday 10–1, provides information about the area.

Tequila

56 km (35 mi) northwest of Guadalajara.

For a close look at how Mexico's most famous liquor is made from the spiny blue agave plant that grows in the fields alongside the highway, spend part or all of a day in this tidy village. Centuries ago the Tiquilas, a small Nahuatl-speaking tribe, were said to have discovered that the heart of the agave produced a juice that could be fermented to make various intoxicating drinks. When distilled (an innovation introduced after the arrival of the Spanish in the 16th century), the fermented liquid turns into the now-famous heady liquor. You can tour the famous Sauza Distillery or one of the other modern tequila distilleries here. Follow the signs, and plan to arrive on a weekday between 10 AM and 1 PM. Frequent bus service is available from Guadalajara's Old Bus Station, and various Guadalajara tour companies offer guided excursions (☞ Guided Tours *in* Guadalajara A to Z, *below*). Each Saturday the Tequila Express leaves Guadalajara on a 10-hour trip that includes the Herradura Distillery, a sumptuous lunch, a folkloric ballet performance, serenades by mariachis, and an unlimited supply of Mexico's most famous liquor.

GUADALAJARA A TO Z

Arriving and Departing

By Bus

First-class, air-conditioned buses with rest rooms run daily to Guadalajara from most major cities on the border. **Greyhound** (☎ 01–800/712–8819) has schedule and fare information for service into Mexico, though you will have to change to a Mexican carrier at the border. Guadalajara's **Nueva Central Camionera** (New Bus Station) is 10 km (6 mi) southeast of downtown Guadalajara on the highway to Zapotlanejo. First-class bus companies that serve Guadalajara from within Mexico include **Elite** (☎ 3/679–0404); **ETN** (☎ 3/600–0605 or 3/600–0858); **Primera Plus** (☎ 3/600–0398); and **Omnibus de México** (☎ 3/600–0469).

By Car

Major routes include Highway 54, which leads south to Colima (220 km, or 136 mi) and north to Zacatecas (320 km, or 198 mi). Highway 15D goes southeast to Morelia (255 km, or 158 mi), continuing to Mexico City (209 km, or 130 mi). The Plan de Barrancas Highway 15 heads north through some of the most beautiful country in Jalisco and neighboring Nayarit state. If you have a choice between a free or toll road, remember that the latter tend to be quite expensive but are in far better condition than their free counterparts.

By Plane

The **Libertador Miguel Hidalgo International Airport** (☎ 3/688–5248 or 3/688–5127) is 16½ km (10 mi) south of Guadalajara. A new international terminal is planned in the next decade to help meet the demands of increased air service to the area.

Aeroméxico (☎ 01–800/021–4000) has nonstop service to Guadalajara from Los Angeles. **Mexicana** (☎ 3/678–7676 or 01–800/366–5400) has direct flights from Chicago, Los Angeles, San Francisco, and San José. **Taesa** (☎ 3/688–5858 or 01–800/904–6300) flies direct from Chicago and Oakland. Through Dallas, **American Airlines** (☎ 3/616–4090) provides service to Guadalajara from all cities in its system. **Continental Airlines** (☎ 3/647–4251 or 01–800/900–5000) provides the same service through Houston. **Delta Air Lines** (☎ 3/630–3530) flies direct from Los Angeles.

FROM THE AIRPORT TO DOWNTOWN

By Car. The Chapala Highway 23 (also numbered 44)—a well-paved four-lane thoroughfare—stretches north from the airport to the city. The 30-minute trip can be delayed by slow-moving caravans of trucks and weekend recreational traffic.

By Taxi or Van. Autotransportaciones Aeropuerto (☎ 3/812–4278 or 3/812–4308) is a *combi* (VW minibus) and taxi service to and from anywhere in the Guadalajara area. Fares, based on distance from the airport, range from $8 to $12 for up to three people going to the same destination. At the airport, buy a ticket from the booth outside the terminal exit. Going to the airport, a regular city taxi should charge similar fares, though they are not allowed to pick up passengers at the airport.

By Train

The Mexican train system has been privatized and all passenger service in the country has been suspended, except for two tourist trips, one to the Copper Canyon in Sonora and Chihuahua states and a recently inaugurated excursion day trip each Saturday from Guadalajara to Tequila and back. Tickets are only available from the **Camera de Comercio** (Chamber of Commerce, ☎ 3/635–4035) for $40. The trip runs from 10 AM to 8:30 PM. Some information is available from **Mexico by Train** (FAX 210/725–3659). Guadalajara's **Estación de Ferrocarriles** (train station: ☎ 3/650–0826 or 3/650–1082) is at the south end of Avenida 16 de Septiembre, past Parque Agua Azul.

Getting Around

Guadalajara's major attractions are best seen on foot. For points outside the city center, Guadalajara has an inexpensive, well-organized public transportation system.

By Bus

This is without a doubt the most economical and efficient but sometimes least comfortable means of traversing the city. Buses run every few minutes between 6 AM and 10 PM to all local attractions, including Tlaquepaque, Tonalá, and Zapopan. Fares are roughly 25¢, making buses the preferred mode of transportation for Guadalajara natives, so expect to stand during daylight hours. Various "luxury" buses—which run on some of the main routes through the city, including out to Tlaquepaque and Tonalá—cost 55¢ and are much less crowded and vastly more comfortable.

Buses to and from such nearby destinations as Chapala, Ajijic, and Tequila depart from the Antigua Central Camionera (Old Bus Station) just northeast of the Parque Agua Azul on Avenida Dr. R. Michel between Calles Los Angeles and 5 de Febrero.

By Car

Beware of heavy traffic and *topes* (speed bumps). *Glorietas* (traffic circles) are common at many busy intersections. Parking in the city center can be scarce, so take a taxi or bus if you're not staying nearby; otherwise, try the underground lots across from the Palacio Municipal (⊠ Av. Hidalgo and Calle Pedro Loza) and below the Plaza de la Liberación (⊠ Av. Hidalgo and Calle Belén, in front of the Teatro Degollado). If you park illegally, the police may tow your vehicle and you'll have to go to the municipal transit office to pay a fine as well as to one of the *correlones* (holding areas) to pay the tow charge (around $15) and retrieve your car.

By Subway

Guadalajara's underground *tren ligero* (light train) system is clean, safe, and efficient. Line 1 runs along Avenida Federalismo from the Periférico (city beltway) Sur to Periférico Norte, near the Benito Juárez Auditorium. Line 2 runs east–west along Avenida Javier Mina (which becomes Avenida Juárez at the Calzada Independencia) from Tetlán in eastern Guadalajara to Avenida Federalismo. Trains run about every 15 minutes from 6 AM to 10:30 PM; a token for one trip costs about 25¢. **Juárez Station,** where the two lines meet, serves as a public art gallery, featuring changing exhibits of Mexican artists.

By Taxi

Taxis are readily available and reasonably economical. Tell the driver where you are going and agree on a fare *before* you enter the cab. Fare schedules listing prices to downtown and all major attractions are posted in the lobby of most hotels. *Sitios* (cab stands) are near all hotels and attractions. Fares go up about 25% at night.

Contacts and Resources

Car Rental

Car rental agencies with offices at the Guadalajara airport include **Avis** (☎ 3/688–5528 or 3/688–5656)), **Budget** (☎ 3/688–5216 or 3/688–

5649; also ⊠ Av. Niños Héroes 934, at Av. 16 de Septiembre, ☎ 3/ 613–0027), **Dollar** (☎ 3/688–5659; also ⊠ Av. Federalismo Sur 540A, ☎ 3/826–7959), **Hertz** (☎ 3/688–5403; also ⊠ Hotel Quinta Real, ☎ 3/615–0000, ext. 121), **National** (☎ 3/688–5645; also ⊠ Av. Niños Héroes 961-C, ☎ 3/614–7175), and **Thrifty** (☎ 3/688–5645; also ⊠ Av. Niños Héroes 963-2, ☎ 3/614–7280).

Consulates

For information about consulates other than those listed below, call **Guadalajara's consular association** (☎ 3/616–0629), open weekdays 9–3 and 5–8.

United States. ⊠ Progreso 175, between López Cotilla and Libertad, ☎ 3/825–2700 or 3/825–2998; 3/826–5553 after-hours emergency. ☉ Weekdays 8–4:30, American Citizens Services office weekdays 8–noon.

Canada. ⊠ Fiesta Americana hotel, Aurelio Aceves 225, ☎ 3/616– 6226 or 3/616–5642; 01–800/706–2900 after-hours emergency. ☉ Weekdays 9–5.

Emergencies

Dialing 080 will connect you with a central emergency system (for all of the organizations listed below and other metro-area police stations) similar to 911 in the U.S. Ask for an English-speaking operator, available 24 hours, daily. **Guadalajara City police** (☎ 3/617–6060); **State police** (☎ 3/617–5828 or 3/617–5538); **Highway patrol** (☎ 3/629–5082 or 3/629–5085); **Fire department** (☎ 3/619–0794 or 3/619–5155); **Cruz Roja** (Red Cross, ☎ 3/613–1550, 3/614–5600, or 3/614–2707); and **Cruz Verde** (Green Cross municipal emergency medical service, ☎ 3/ 812–5143 or 3/613–1572).

DOCTORS AND DENTISTS

The U.S. Consulate (☞ Consulates, *above*) maintains a list of English-speaking doctors and dentists. All major hotels have the names of doctors who are on 24-hour call.

HOSPITALS

Hospital del Carmen (⊠ Tarascos 3435, near Plaza México mall, ☎ 3/813–0025 or 3/813–0042); **Hospital México-Americano** (⊠ Colomos 2110, ☎ 3/641–3141 or 3/642–4520); **Hospital San Javier** (⊠ Av. Pablo Casals 640, Col. Providencia, ☎ 3/669–0222); and **Hospital Santa María Chapalita** (⊠ Av. Niño Obrero 1666, in Chapalita district, ☎ 3/620–0901).

English-Language Bookstores and Publications

Sandi Bookstore (⊠ Av. Tepeyac 718, in Chapalita district, ☎ 3/121–0863) sells many newspapers, magazines, and books.

The Guadalajara Colony Reporter, a weekly newspaper sold for 70¢ at newsstands and hotels, provides news stories and excellent community and cultural listings for Guadalajara, Chapala, and Puerto Vallarta. Distributed in hotels, the monthly *Let's Enjoy/Disfrutemos Guadalajara* offers feature articles and information on attractions. Two excellent sources of information on the Lake Chapala area and other excursions in the states of Jalisco, Colima, Nayarit, and Michoacán are Tony Burton's *Western Mexico: A Traveller's Treasury* (Espadaña Press, 1993) and *Outdoors in Western Mexico* by John and Susana Pint (Editoriales Agata, 1998).

Guided Tours

Most tour operators in the city have guided city tours and excursions to Tequila, Lake Chapala, Tlaquepaque, and Tonalá.

CALANDRIAS

You can hire a horse-drawn carriage in front of the Museo Regional, the Mercado Libertad, or Parque San Francisco. The charge is about $12 for an hour-long tour for up to four passengers. Few drivers speak English.

PERSONAL GUIDES

The **Sindicato de Guías de Turistas** (☎ 3/634–1566) maintains a list of licensed bilingual guides, though you may have trouble getting an answer if you phone. These guides charge about $13.50 per hour (4-hr minimum) for guided tours on foot or in their own automobiles. Most hotels have a list of guides available on short notice.

TOUR OPERATORS

Copenhagen Tours (✉ Av. J. Manuel Clouthier 152, Col. Prados Vallarta, ☎ 3/629–7957 or 3/629–4758). **Panoramex** (✉ Av. Federalismo Sur 944, ☎ 3/810–5109 or 3/810–5005, also ✉ Av. Mariano Otero 2407-3, on the traffic circle, ☎ 3/647–0972).

Charter Club Tours (✉ Carretera Chapala–Jalisco Oriente 1, Ajijic, ☎ 376/6–17–77).

Money Exchange

The most convenient places to change dollars are *casas de cambio,* generally open weekdays from 9 until 6 (though they may close between 2 and 4) and Saturday morning. There are many of them on Calle López Cotilla downtown and in the Plaza del Sol area. Banks tend to have more limited hours, longer waits, and offer a poorer exchange rate.

Pharmacies

Farmacias Guadalajara (✉ Av. Las Americas 2, ☎ 3/615–8516; ✉ Av. Javier Mina 221, between Cabañas and Vicente Guerrero, ☎ 3/617–8555; ✉ Av. Tepeyac 646, in Chapalita district, ☎ 3/121–2581; ✉ Plaza México, ☎ 3/813–2698) has several branches that are open 24 hours.

Travel Agencies

Many of the city's 100-plus travel agencies are in the two hotel zones, el centro (downtown), and Avenida López Mateos Sur, on the city's southwest side. Near the Minerva Fountain you'll find **American Express** (✉ Av. Vallarta 2440, near Los Arcos monument, ☎ 3/818–2323 or 3/818–2325).

Visitor Information

The **Jalisco state tourist offices** have information about Guadalajara and other parts of Mexico. ✉ *Calle Morelos 102, in Plaza Tapatía,* ☎ *3/658–2222 or 01–800/363–2200,* ☉ *weekdays 9–8, Sat. 9–1.* ✉ *Palacio de Gobierno,* ☉ *weekdays 10–3 and 4–8, Sat. 9:30–1.*

Guadalajara has **tourist information booths** (☎ 3/616–3333, or 3/616–3335, ☎ FAX 3/616–3332), open daily 9–7, which are staffed by city tourist police. Locations are downtown in the **Plaza Guadalajara,** in **Los Arcos monument** on Avenida Vallarta just east of the Minerva Fountain, in **Parque San Francisco,** in front of the **Instituto Cultural Cabañas,** in front of **Mercado Libertad,** at **Vicente Guerrero 233** (open weekdays only), and at the **airport.** English-language tours can be arranged by a request in writing; fax the request to the Director General de Turismo y Promoción Económica.

7 THE HEARTLAND

Rich with the history of Mexico's revolution, the heartland is a treasury of colonial towns—Guanajuato, Zacatecas, Querétaro, Morelia, and Pátzcuaro, among others—whose residents lead quiet, largely traditional lives. Even in San Miguel de Allende, an American art colony and home to a well-known language institute, women wash their clothes and gossip at the local lavandería as they have for hundreds of years.

MEXICO'S HEARTLAND, so named for its central position in the country, is known for its well-preserved colonial architecture, fertile farmland and surrounding mountains, and its leading role in Mexican history, particularly during the War of Independence (1810–21). The Bajío (ba-*hee*-o), as it is also called, corresponds roughly to the states of Guanajuato and parts of Querétaro and Michoacán. In the hills surrounding the cities of Guanajuato, Zacatecas, Querétaro, and San Miguel de Allende, the Spanish found silver in the 1500s, leading them to colonize the area heavily.

Updated by
Gina Hyams

Three centuries later, wealthy Creoles (Mexicans of Spanish descent) in Querétaro and San Miguel took the first audacious steps toward independence from Spain. When their clandestine efforts were discovered, two of the early insurgents, Ignacio Allende and Father Miguel Hidalgo, began in earnest the War of Independence. One of the bloodiest skirmishes was fought in the Alhóndiga de Granaditas, a mammoth grain-storage facility in Guanajuato that is now a state museum.

When Allende and Hidalgo were executed in 1811, another native son, José María Morelos, picked up the independence banner. This mestizo (mixed race) mule skinner–turned–priest–turned–soldier, with his army of 9,000, came close to gaining control of the land before he was killed in 1815. Thirteen years later, the city of Valladolid was renamed Morelia in his honor.

Long after the War of Independence ended in 1821, the cities of the Bajío continued to play a prominent role in Mexico's history. Three major events took place in Querétaro alone: in 1848 the Mexican-American War ended with the signing of the Treaty of Guadalupe Hidalgo; in 1867 Austrian Maximilian of Hapsburg, crowned Emperor of Mexico by Napoleon III of France, was executed in the hills north of town; and in 1917 the Mexican Constitution was signed here.

The heartland honors the events and people that helped shape modern Mexico. In ornate cathedrals or bucolic plazas, down narrow alleyways or atop high hillsides, you'll find monuments—and remnants—of a heroic past. During numerous fiestas, you can savor the region's historic spirit. On a night filled with fireworks, off-key music, and tireless celebrants, it's hard not to be caught up in the vital expression of national pride.

Tourism is welcomed in the heartland, especially in these hard economic times, and tourists for the most part do not disrupt the normal routines of residents. Families visit parks for Sunday picnics, youngsters tussle in school courtyards, old men chat in shaded plazas, and Purépecha women in traditional garb sell their wares in crowded *mercados* (markets). Unlike areas where attractions have been specifically designed for tourism, the Bajío relies on its historic ties and the architectural integrity of its cities to appeal to travelers. Although this is an interesting area to tour by car, there is frequent inexpensive bus service from one city to the next throughout the Bajío.

Pleasures and Pastimes

Architecture

Financed largely by the region's fabulously wealthy silver mines, the cities of the heartland are architectural masterpieces full of buildings richly worked with curvaceous lines, human, animal, plant, and geometric motifs, and sculptural depth that accents the play of light and shadow. From the stately, almost European grandeur of Morelia to the

Heartland

KEY
— Rail Lines

0 ___ 20 miles
0 ___ 30 km

ZACATECAS

Ouelos de
Jalisco

Ocampo

Santa María
del Río

Villa de
Reyes

JALISCO

80

Lagos de
Moreno

León

SIERRA
DE
GUANAJUATO

Dolores
Hidalgo

San Luis
de la Paz

110

51

57

45

☆ Guanajuato

Silao

San Miguel
de Allende

XILITLA

Manuel
Doblado

GUANAJUATO

Irapuato

45
D

QUERÉ-
TARO

51

Querétaro ☆

45
D

Salamanca

Celaya

57

TO
SAN JUAN DEL RÍO,
TEQUISQUIAPAN

La Piedad
de Cabadas

15

Lago
Yuriria

Moroleón

Lerma

51

Acámbaro

43

Lago de
Cuitzeo

ZAMORA/GUADALAJARA

15

Isla Yunuen

Morelia

Ciudad
Hidalgo

TO
PARICUTÍN VOLCANO

Quiroga

Lake
Pátzcharo

Isla
Janitzio

15

51

14

Tzintzuntzan

Uruapan

Pátzcuaro

Zitacuaro

Parque
Nacional
Eduardo
Ruíz

Santa Clara
del Cobre

MICHOACAN

Tuzantla

120

Nueva
Italia

La Huacana

Nocupétaro

134

Bejucos

Presa del
Infiernillo

Huetamo

Balsas

steep, labyrinthine allure of Guanajuato and the sandstone pink splendor of Zacatecas, no two towns are alike. San Miguel de Allende's Gothic-style parish church puts a Gallic touch on an otherwise very Mexican skyline. And in Pátzcuaro and Querétaro, the ornate 16th-century colonial mansions surrounding the city squares have been converted into hotels and government offices, making their interior patios accessible to the public.

Dining

It's no surprise that culinary tastes vary widely in the heartland, which spans a large area across central Mexico. In the state of Michoacán, Purépecha Indian influences predominate. The tomato-based *sopa tarasca* (a soup with cheese, cream, and tortillas) is one of the best-known regional specialties. Because of the numerous lakes and rivers in the state, several types of freshwater fish are often served in Michoacán restaurants.

At the northern end of the heartland, in Zacatecas, the hearty, meat-eating tastes of the *norteños* (northerners) rule the dinner table. Although beef is the favored dish, other specialties include *asado de boda* (wedding barbecue), pork in a spicy but semisweet sauce. The region is also known for its cheese and wine. And because of San Miguel's expatriate community, the city has a wealth of worthy eateries.

CATEGORY	COST*
$$$$	over $15
$$$	$10–$15
$$	$5–$10
$	under $5

per person for a three-course meal, excluding drinks and service

Hiking and Walking

With its rolling farmland, lofty volcanoes, lakes, and Indian villages, Michoacán is a perfect area for day hikes. Trails near Pátzcuaro wind up to nearby hilltops for great views across town and the surrounding countryside, while in Uruapan—64 km (40 mi) away and 2,000 ft lower in elevation—you can walk along a lush, raging river valley. And no tour of the heartland would be complete without a few days of leisurely strolling on the avenues and back streets of colonial cities and towns—admiring the architecture, lingering in museums, or resting in plazas, watching the world go by.

Lodging

In many of the heartland's colonial cities, restored haciendas of the fabulously rich residents of centuries past make the best lodgings. Often near the center of town, sometimes facing directly onto plazas, some of these mansions date from the 16th century. There are also deluxe modern high-rises and functional, low-cost hotels. Except for five-star hotels, most properties in the region are not heated, and you may want to bring warm, comfortable clothes for indoor wear, or to inquire in advance if heating is important to you. In restored colonial properties, rooms often vary dramatically as to size and furnishings, so if you aren't satisfied with the one you are shown, ask to see another. High season, for the most part, is limited to specific dates surrounding Christmas, Easter, and regional festivals. Most moderate and inexpensive hotels quote prices with 15% value-added tax already included.

CATEGORY	COST*
$$$$	over $90
$$$	$50–$90
$$	$25–$50
$	under $25

All prices are for a standard double room, including 15% tax.

Exploring the Heartland

Many travelers barrel past the heartland to points north or west of Mexico City. But there are plenty of reasons to stop here—browsing in the shops of San Miguel or Guanajuato for bargains in silver and other local crafts, or heading to the state of Michoacán, renowned for its folklore and folk crafts, especially ceramics and lacquerware. Stay longer to linger over the wealth of architectural styles that each of the colonial cities has to offer.

Numbers in the text correspond to numbers in the margin and on the San Miguel de Allende, Guanajuato, Zacatecas, Querétaro, Morelia, and Pátzcuaro maps.

Great Itineraries

If you have only a couple of days to spare, stop in any of several colonial cities for a taste of life in the heartland—each one has its own particular flavor. If you happen to fall under the heartland's peaceful, friendly spell, you'll want a week to 10 days to give yourself time to drink in the atmosphere of two or three of the region's cities.

IF YOU HAVE 3 DAYS

Head to **Guanajuato** ⑫–㉒ (365 km, or 226 mi, from Mexico City), the most architecturally dramatic of the heartland cities. Make a day trip from here to the picturesque town of **San Miguel de Allende** ①–⑪, 90 minutes away by car or bus, to shop for crafts.

Another option is to go from Mexico City to the Michoacán capital of **Morelia** ㊵–㊾ (about four hours by car) and spend a day taking in its stately architecture and café-lined plaza. The next day, drive on to **Pátzcuaro** ㊿–㊾, set among volcanoes in the center of Purépecha Indian country. Spend the morning in the bustling market or strolling in the surrounding countryside before making a late-afternoon return to Mexico City.

IF YOU HAVE 5 DAYS

Make **Guanajuato** ⑫–㉒ your base and allow an extra day to see its churches and museums—perhaps even the gruesome Mummy Museum. Stop off at the town of Dolores Hidalgo, home of Mexican independence, on your way to a day of shopping in San Miguel. Overnight in San Miguel and the next morning head for **Querétaro** ㉜–㊴, 63 km (39 mi) away. This quiet colonial city is considered the capital of the Bajío. After a night in a downtown hotel, return to Mexico City (3 hours) or to the airport outside Guanajuato (2½ hours).

If you decide to spend several days in Michoacán, you can easily fill your time exploring the state's colonial towns and enjoying the lush, mountainous countryside. After three days in **Morelia** ㊵–㊾ and **Pátzcuaro** ㊿–㊾, take a day trip to explore the crater on an extinct volcano in **San Juan Parangaricútiro** or the ruins of an ancient Purépecha Indian capital, **Tzintzuntzan** (both are easy day trips from Pátzcuaro), before returning on the final day to Morelia and Mexico City.

IF YOU HAVE 7 DAYS

From your base in **Guanajuato** ⑫–㉒, consider adding to the first of the five-day itineraries a round-trip flight from Guanajuato airport to **Zacatecas** ㉓–㉛. This would give you a day and a half to explore this northern colonial mining city. Because it lies off the main tourist track, Zacatecas has a refreshingly unselfconscious mood. Another possibility for a week in the heartland would be to make a loop from Mexico City that includes both Morelia and Guanajuato. You'd have time for leisurely side trips to Pátzcuaro and **San Miguel de Allende** ①–⑪ and a stop in **Querétaro** ㉜–㊴. When in **Pátzcuaro** ㊿–㊾, be sure to take a boat out to the island town of **Janítzio** on nearby Lake Pátzcuaro, home of Mexico's most famous November Day of the Dead festival (lasting up to two days), or to the more authentic island of Yunuen, which is not as yet besieged by tourists.

When to Tour the Heartland

One of the most pleasing aspects of the heartland is its superb climate—it rarely gets overly hot, even in the middle of summer, and although winter days can get nippy, especially in northern Zacatecas, they are generally temperate. Average temperatures in the southern city of Morelia range from 20°C (68°F) in May to just under 10°C (49°F) in January. Zacatecas is more extreme, with winter temperatures as low as 0°C (32°F) and snow flurries every several years, and summer highs of 28°C–30°C (81°F–85°F). Nights are cool all year in most of the region's cities. The rainy season all across the heartland hits between June and October and is generally strongest in July and August.

Consider going to the heartland for cultural festivals or religious events—in October Guanajuato's three-week-long International Cervantes Festival, which brings actors, musicians, painters, and hundreds of thousands of visitors to town; in late November San Miguel's Jazz Festival International; and November 1–2 on the island of Janítzio, where local Purépecha (also called Tarascan) Indians hold a Day of the Dead in honor of their ancestors. Of ecological interest is the arrival of millions of monarch butterflies near Morelia between early November and early March.

SAN MIGUEL DE ALLENDE

San Miguel de Allende first began luring foreigners in the late 1930s when American Stirling Dickinson and prominent local residents founded an art school in this mountainous settlement. The school, now called the Instituto Allende, has grown in stature over the years—as has the city's reputation as a writers' and artists' colony. Walk down any cobblestone street and you're likely to see residents of a variety of national origins. Some come to study at the Instituto Allende or the Academia Hispano-Americana, some to escape the harsh northern winters, and still others to retire.

Cultural offerings in this town of about 110,000 reflect its large American and Canadian community. There are literary readings, art shows, a yearly jazz festival, psychic fairs, aerobics and past-life-regression classes, and a lending library. International influence notwithstanding, San Miguel, declared a national monument in 1926, retains its Mexican characteristics. Wandering down streets lined with 18th-century mansions, you'll also discover fountains, monuments, and churches—all reminders of the city's illustrious, and sometimes notorious, past. The onetime headquarters of the Spanish Inquisition in New Spain, for example, is located at the corner of Calles Hernández Macías and Pila Seca. The former Inquisition jail stands across the way. Independence day is celebrated with exceptional fervor in San Miguel, with fireworks, dances, and parades on September 15 and 16, and bullfights and cultural events for the remainder of the month, including the running of the bulls, Pamplona style.

Exploring San Miguel de Allende

You'll find most of San Miguel's sights in a cluster downtown, which you can visit in a couple of hours.

A Good Walk

Begin at the main plaza, otherwise known as **El Jardín** ①. After you get a feel for the square, stop into **La Parroquia** ②, the sandstone church on its south side. Three blocks northeast of La Parroquia (take Calle San Francisco, on the north side of El Jardín, to Calle Juárez) is the **Iglesia de San Francisco** ③, with a fine *churrigueresque* (heavily ornamented) facade. Take a few steps north on Calle Juárez to Calle Mesones, then east to Calle Colegio where the colorful **Mercado Ignacio Ramírez** (☞ Shopping, *below*) occupies a cavernous structure off the west side of the street. The dome of the **Oratorio de San Felipe Neri** ④ is visible just before the market.

A block west of the church on Calle Insurgentes, **La Biblioteca Pública** ⑤ is a great place to catch up on town events and replace your travel-worn paperbacks. Continue west from the library two blocks to Calle Hernández Macías, then head south to the **Bellas Artes** ⑥ cultural center at No. 75 and the ornate **Iglesia de la Concepción** ⑦ behind it. Take Hernández Macías south for a block and turn left on Umarán to reach the **Casa de Ignacio Allende** ⑧, birthplace of the Mexican national hero. You've circled back to the southwest corner of the Jardín.

After making your way around the center of town, consider a leisurely stroll to sights a bit farther afield. From the south side of the plaza (by La Parroquia), head west four blocks on Calle Umarán until you reach Calle Zacateros. Turn south on this narrow cobblestone street for some of the town's most interesting crafts shops—stocked with everything from silver jewelry to Mexican ceremonial masks.

Past the shops, Calle Zacateros becomes Ancha de San Antonio. On your left at No. 20 is the renowned **Instituto Allende** ⑨, where many of San Miguel's foreign visitors come to study. From the institute, continue south on Ancha de San Antonio until you reach Callejón del Cardo on your left. Continue past St. Paul's Episcopal Church, an expat house of worship, until you arrive at the cobblestone Calle Aldama on your left. Head downhill and walk briefly through a neighborhood of whitewashed houses before reaching the north entrance to the 5-acre Parque Benito Juárez, an oasis of evergreens, palm trees, and gardens.

From the north edge of the park, follow Calle Diezmo Viejo to the terra-cotta-color mansion known as La Huerta Santa Elena. From here turn left and walk one block uphill to the **Lavandería** ⑩, San Miguel's outdoor laundry and a favorite gathering spot for local women. Calle Recreo, above the Lavandería, heads north back toward the plaza: follow Recreo until reaching Calle Correo, turn left, and walk three blocks to return to El Jardín.

Sights to See

❻ Bellas Artes. This impressive cloister across the street from the U.S. Consulate was once the Royal Convent of the Conception. Since 1938 it has been an institute for the study of music, dance, and the visual arts. There are rotating exhibits and a cafeteria on the patio. A bulletin board at the entrance lists cultural events. ⊠ *Calle Hernández Macías 75,* ☎ *415/2-02-89.* ⌨ *Free.* ☉ *Mon.–Sat. 9–8, Sun. 10–2.*

❽ Casa de Ignacio Allende. Now housing a museum and gallery, this is the birthplace of Ignacio Allende, one of Mexico's great independence heroes. Allende was a Creole aristocrat who, along with Father Miguel Hidalgo, plotted in the early 1800s to overthrow the Spanish regime. At clandestine meetings held in San Miguel and nearby Querétaro, the two discussed strategies, organized an army, gathered weapons, and enlisted the support of clerics for the struggle ahead.

Spanish Royalists learned of their plot and began arresting conspirators in Querétaro on September 13, 1810. Allende and Hidalgo received word of these actions and hastened their plans. At dawn on September 16, they rang out the cry for independence, and the fighting began. Allende was captured and executed by the Royalists the following year. As a tribute to his brave efforts, San Miguel El Grande was renamed San Miguel de Allende in the 20th century. ⊠ *Calle Cuna de Allende 1,* ☎ *415/2-24-99.* ⌨ *$1.75.* ☉ *Tues.–Sun. 10–4.*

El Charco del Ingenio. Founded in 1991 northeast of the city center, San Miguel's botanical garden is an enjoyable place to walk, particularly in the early morning or late afternoon. Its five-odd miles of pathways wind past more than 1,500 species of cacti and succulents. ⊠ *1½ km (1 mi) northeast of El Jardín (☞ below); signs point the way off Cuesta de San Jose.* ⌨ *7 pesos.* ☉ *Sunrise–sunset.*

❶ El Jardín (the Garden). The heart of San Miguel is the plaza commonly known as El Jardín. Seated on one of its wrought-iron benches, you'll quickly get a feel for the town: old men with canes exchange tales, young lovers smooch, fruit vendors hawk their wares, and bells from the nearby La Parroquia pierce the thin mountain air at each quarter hour. At dusk thousands of grackles make a fantastic ruckus as they return to roost in the laurel trees. ⊠ *Bounded by Calle Correo on the south, Calle San Francisco on the north, Portal Allende on the west, and Portal Guadalupe on the east.* ☉ *24 hrs.*

NEED A BREAK?

On the southwest corner of the main plaza is **Café del Jardín** (⊠ Portal Allende 2, ☎ 415/2-50-06). This unassuming little café has excellent coffee, cappuccino, hot chocolate, and in the evening, pizza. Breakfasts are tasty and inexpensive. There's friendly service and, best of all—it's that American influence—free coffee refills.

⓫ **El Mirador.** Climb El Mirador (the Lookout) for a panorama of the city, mountains, and reservoir below. The vista is great at sunset, and chances are you won't be alone. Locals and tourists like to join Ignacio Allende, whose bronze image commands this spot. ⊠ *1 block before town, turn right off Calle Recreo onto Calle Hospicio. Follow Hospicio 3 blocks to Calle Pedro Vargas. Turn right and head uphill to the overlook.*

❼ **Iglesia de la Concepción.** Located just behind the Bellas Artes cultural center, this church has one of the largest domes in Mexico. The two-story dome (completed in 1891) and the elegant Corinthian columns and pilasters gracing its drum are said to have been inspired by the dome of the Hôtel des Invalides in Paris. Ceferino Gutiérrez (of La Parroquia fame) is credited with its design. ⊠ *Calle Canal between Hernández Macías and Zacateros.*

❸ **Iglesia de San Francisco.** The San Francisco Church has one of the finest churrigueresque facades in the state of Guanajuato. This term refers to José Churriguera, a 17th-century (Baroque) Spanish architect, noted for his extravagant surface decoration. Built in the late 18th century, it was financed by donations from wealthy patrons and by revenue from bullfights. Topping the elaborately carved exterior is the image of Saint Francis of Assisi. Below, along with a crucifix, are sculptures of Saint John and Our Lady of Sorrows. ⊠ *Calle Juárez between San Francisco and Mesones.*

❾ **Instituto Allende.** The school is set in the former country estate of the Count of Canal. Since its founding in 1951, thousands of students from around the world have come to learn Spanish and to take classes in social studies and the arts. Courses last from a couple of weeks to a month or longer. Lush with bougainvillea, rosebushes, and ivy vines, the grounds provide a quiet refuge for students and visitors alike. ⊠ *Ancha de San Antonio 20,* ☎ *415/2–01–90,* ⅁ᴬˣ *415/2–45–38.* ☉ *Weekdays 8–6, Sat. 9–1.*

❺ **La Biblioteca Pública.** Notices—about things like literary readings or yoga and aerobics classes—are posted on the bulletin board in the entranceway to the library. There is a lovely courtyard café inside, as well as the offices of the English-language newspaper, *Atención San Miguel,* and reading rooms with back issues of popular publications and books in English. It's a great place to take a breather from sight-seeing. On Sunday a two-hour house-and-garden tour of San Miguel leaves the library at noon. Proceeds from tickets (about $15) go to the library's computer literacy and scholarship projects benefiting the youth of San Miguel. ⊠ *Calle Insurgentes 25,* ☎ *415/2–02–93,* ⅁ᴬˣ *415/2–37–70.* ☉ *Weekdays 10–2 and 4–7, Sat. 10–2.*

❷ **La Parroquia.** This towering Gothic Revival parish church, made of local *cantera* sandstone, was designed in the late 19th century by self-trained Indian mason Ceferino Gutiérrez, who sketched his designs in the sand with a stick. Gutiérrez was purportedly inspired by postcards of European Gothic cathedrals. Since the postcards gave no hint of what the back of those cathedrals looked like, the posterior of La Parroquia was done in quintessential Mexican style.

La Parroquia still functions as a house of worship, though its interior has been changed over the years. Gilded wood altars, for example, were replaced with neoclassical stone altars. The original bell, cast in 1732, still calls parishioners to mass several times daily. ⊠ *South side of El Jardín on Calle Correo.*

⑩ **Lavandería.** At this outdoor public laundry—a collection of red cement tubs set above Juárez Park—local women gather daily to wash clothes and gossip as their predecessors have done for centuries. Though some women claim to have more-efficient washing facilities at home, the lure of the spring-fed troughs—not to mention the chance to catch up on the news—brings them daily to this shaded courtyard. ⊠ *Calle Diezmo Viejo at Calle Recreo.*

Los Pocitos. This is said to be the largest private orchid collection in Mexico, set around the home of the late Stirling Dickinson, cofounder of the Instituto Allende. Admission is free, but visitors are encouraged to make a donation to Cante, the nonprofit ecological organization that manages both this and the botanical garden. ⊠ *Santo Domingo 38.* ⚏ *Free; donations suggested.* ☉ *Mon.–Sat. 11–3.*

❹ **Oratorio de San Felipe Neri.** Built by local Indians in 1712, the original chapel can still be glimpsed in the eastern facade, made of pink stone and adorned with a figure of Our Lady of Solitude. The newer, southern front was built in an ornate Baroque style. In 1734 the wealthy Count of Canal paid for an addition to the Oratorio. His **Templo de Santa Casa de Loreto,** dedicated to the Virgin of Loreto, is just behind the Oratorio. Its main entrance, now blocked by a grille, is on the Oratorio's left rear side. Peer through the grille to see the heavily gilded altars and effigies of the count and his wife, under which they are buried. ⊠ *Calle Insurgentes and Loreto.*

Dining

For its size, San Miguel has a surprising number of international restaurants. The recent influx of Americans and Canadians has given rise to new Tex-Mex and health-food places. A European influence has contributed to variations on French, Italian, and Spanish themes.

$$$ ✕ **Bugambilia.** Founded in 1945, Mercedes Arteaga Tovar's restaurant
★ has a well-earned reputation for serving fine traditional Mexican cuisine. Try such classic specialties as *pollo en pulque* (chicken stewed in pulque—the fermented juice of the agave plant) and *tinga* (shredded pork loin, chorizo, and potatoes in a tomato, onion, and chipotle chili sauce). The candlelit, tree-filled colonial courtyard and live classical guitarist make for a romantic setting. ⊠ *Calle Hidalgo 42,* ☎ *415/2–01–27. AE, MC, V.*

$$$ ✕ **La Antigua Restaurant y Tapa Bar.** A cheerful room with fewer than a dozen tables (each with a vase of orange carnations) and a long, polished wood bar, La Antigua puts you in the mood for a large variety of tapas with its European café furniture and Spanish bolero music. Among its specialties are *queso antiguo* (baked cheese with chilies), *chisterra* (a sliced and fried Spanish-style sausage), *camarones con tocineta* (jumbo shrimp fried with bacon), and *pulpo antiguo* (octopus sautéed in garlic and herbs). ⊠ *Calle Canal 9,* ☎ *415/2–25–86. AE, MC, V.*

$$ ✕ **Fonda Mesón de San José.** On an umbrella-shaded cobblestone
★ patio inside a complex of small shops, this well-established restaurant serves German, Mexican, and vegetarian cooking. Locals wax enthusiastic about owner-chef Angela Merkel's roulade, potato pancakes, and German chocolate cake, as well as her *chile en nogada,* a mild chili stuffed with ground meat and raisins and topped with cream sauce and pomegranate seeds. The sunny patio is great for lunch, less popular for dinner. ⊠ *Mesones 38,* ☎ *415/2–38–48. MC, V.*

$$ ✕ **Mama Mia.** If you want a change from Mexican food you will enjoy Mama Mia's satisfying assortment of pastas and pizzas, as well as a decent fettuccine Bolognese and spaghetti Parmesana. Try the house special: fettuccine Alex (with white wine, ham, cream, and mush-

rooms). Folk musicians entertain on the lush outdoor patio come dusk. ⊠ *Calle Umarán 8,* ☎ *415/2–20–63. AE, MC, V.*

$$ ✕ **Rincón Español.** The soft pink walls of this pleasant Spanish restaurant are covered with reproductions of the works of famous Spanish artists—Joan Miró, Picasso, and Salvador Dalí—and its nickname, La Casa de la Paella, reveals its specialty. Not a little of Rincón's charm derives from the evening guitar music and flamenco dancing, pleasing adjuncts to dessert. ⊠ *Correo 29,* ☎ *415/2–29–84. AE, MC, V.*

$ ✕ **Café de la Parroquia.** Stop in for breakfast or lunch, both served either outside on the charming patio or indoors. Economical daily lunch menus include soup, main dish, beverage, dessert, and coffee. ⊠ *Calle Jesús 11,* ☎ *415/2–31–61. No credit cards. Closed Mon. No dinner.*

$ ✕ **La Buena Vida.** Don't miss this fabulous bakery and tiny coffee shop and its mouthwatering orange scones, chocolate chip cookies, and light breakfasts. If the few patio tables are full, take your treats to the plaza. ⊠ *Hernández Macías 72–5,* ☎ *415/2–22–11. No credit cards.*

Lodging

San Miguel has a wide selection of hotels, ranging from cozy B&Bs to elegant all-suites properties. Rooms fill up quickly during summer and winter seasons, when northern tourists migrate here in droves. Make reservations several months in advance if you plan to visit at these times or during the September Independence Day festivities.

$$$$ ✕⊡ **Casa de Sierra Nevada.** Built in 1580 as the residence of the arch-★ bishop of Guanajuato, this elegant country-style inn still attracts ambassadors, diplomats, film stars, and other luminaries; children under 16 are not admitted, however. Its complex of eight colonial buildings, all located within a few blocks of the main plaza, contains 20 individually decorated suites and 17 deluxe rooms. Lace curtains, handwoven rugs, and chandeliers adorn some rooms; fireplaces, cozy private terraces, and skylights enhance others. The international cuisine at the hotel's original restaurant is delicately prepared and beautifully presented. Jazz enlivens the formal dining room on Wednesday evenings, and classical duets play during weekend lunch. In 1997, the hotel opened **Casa de Sierra Nevada en el Parque** (⊠ Santa Elena 2), an exquisitely restored 18th-century ex-hacienda with just five guest rooms. Its restaurant serves refined versions of traditional Mexican dishes and has a wonderful view of Parque Benito Juárez. Restaurant reservations required. ⊠ *Calle Hospicio 35, 37700,* ☎ *415/2–70–40; 888/341–5995 in the U.S.,* ℻ *415/2–23–37. 17 rooms, 20 suites. 2 restaurants, bar, pool, massage, spa, horseback riding. AE, MC, V.*

$$$$ ⊡ **La Puertecita Boutique Hotel.** Set in a secluded, wooded canyon in the tony Atascadero neighborhood, this luxury no-smoking hotel has uniquely decorated rooms with rustic Mexican furnishings, domed vaulted ceilings, and in many cases private patios, fireplaces, and garden bathrooms. Customized vacation packages including room, meals, mountain biking, horseback riding, hot springs excursions, and yoga, cooking, art, or Spanish classes are available. The hotel has a membership at Club Malanquin to allow guests to use its golf and tennis facilities. ⊠ *Santo Domingo 75, 37740,* ☎ *415/2–50–11 or 415/2–22–50; 800/336–6776 in the U.S.,* ℻ *415/2–55–05. 18 rooms, 6 suites. Restaurant, bar, 2 pools, massage, spa, billiards. AE, MC, V.*

$$$$ ⊡ **Villa Jacaranda.** Near the Parque Benito Juárez, the Villa Jacaranda has a full range of amenities. Rooms, though unimaginatively decorated, have space heaters (not something to be taken for granted in these parts) and cable TVs. The hotel's Cine/Bar shows American movies daily at 7:30 PM and live sports events on a giant screen. The price of admission—roughly $3.50—includes a drink. The restaurant serves in-

ternational and Mexican cuisine in the homey dining room or a stained-glass gazebo, and there is a delicious Sunday champagne brunch for about $7.50. ⊠ *Calle Aldama 53, 37700,* ☎ *415/2–10–15 or 415/2–08–11; 800/310–9688 in the U.S.,* FAX *415/2–08–83. 5 rooms and 11 suites. Restaurant, hot tub, cinema. AE, MC, V.*

$$$ 🏨 **Casa Carmen.** Run by a friendly San Miguel family, this pension is an oasis of peace in the center of town. It is in a 200-year-old house 2 blocks from the Jardín, and it has large, clean rooms, each with desk or writing table and portable gas heater, and two small patios for relaxing with a good book. The large suite on the top floor has a great view of the city for the same price, but is often booked far in advance. Breakfast and lunch are included in the room rate. ⊠ *Correo 31, 37700,* ☎ *415/2–08–44. 12 rooms. No credit cards.*

$$$ 🏨 **Casa Luna.** In a restored 300-year-old Spanish colonial house, this
★ lovely B&B has 2-ft-thick walls, 20-ft-high ceilings, and tranquil fountain- and flower-filled patios. The luxurious rooms have romantic antiques, fireplaces, featherbeds, and bathtubs. The rooftop honor bar is spectacular at night, lighted by some 2 dozen miniature tin star lights. A three-night minimum stay is required; children are allowed only when the entire house is rented to one party. ⊠ *Pila Seca 11, 37700,* ☎ FAX *415/2–11–17. 7 rooms, 1 suite. MC, V.*

$$$ 🏨 **Villa Mirasol.** Each of this lodge's nine rooms is tastefully decorated with original prints, oil paintings, pastels, or small sculptures. Most rooms are flooded with sunlight during the day. All have either a private or shared terrace, and those facing Calle Pila Seca have beautiful views of the surrounding hills. On a quiet street about a 10-minute walk from the main plaza, the hotel was a private house until 1983, and its cozy and intimate atmosphere is a welcome alternative to larger, less personal hotels. Villa Mirasol includes in its price a rich breakfast. Children are not permitted. ⊠ *Pila Seca 35 (Apdo. 409), 37700,* ☎ *415/2–15–64,* FAX *415/2–66–85. 5 rooms, 4 suites. AE, MC, V.*

$$ 🏨 **La Mansión del Bosque.** On a quiet side street across from the Parque Benito Juárez, this cozy guest house caters to long-term guests, especially in winter. The hotel, which operates on a Modified American Plan that includes breakfast and dinner, is an attractive red-stucco building of many levels, resembling a Taos pueblo dwelling. Some rooms have motel-like furnishings and day beds, others are more pleasingly decorated. Many have working fireplaces; all have private or shared plant-filled terraces. The lounge invites mingling with other guests and has books, magazines, cable TV, and a telephone for long-distance calls. ⊠ *Calle Aldama 65, 37700,* ☎ FAX *415/2–02–77. 23 rooms. Restaurant, bar, lounge. No credit cards.*

$$ 🏨 **Posada de las Monjas.** This 19th-century inn has been operating as a hotel for more than 50 years. Rooms are simply furnished in a colonial style. Some in the old wing are uncomfortably dark and cramped. The rooftop public terrace has tables and lounge chairs and offers commanding views of mountains and city. Some rooms have fireplaces, and there's a communal television in the lobby, which looks like a formal Mexican living room, with plastic flowers in vases and stiff furniture lining the walls. ⊠ *Calle Canal 37, 37700,* ☎ *415/2–01–71,* FAX *415/2–62–27. 65 rooms. Restaurant, bar, laundry service, free parking. AE, MC, V.*

$ 🏨 **Quinta Loreto.** Clean, plain, comfortable rooms, shady and pleasantly kept grounds, and excellent *comida casera* (home cooking) make this inexpensive hotel a favorite with snowbirds and other San Miguel aficionados. Each room has a gas heater, television, and telephone. There is a dilapidated tennis court and an unheated pool, which is uninvitingly dirty. The hotel is about a 10-minute walk north of the main plaza, near the market. Many nonguests take their meals in the unpretentious dining room, especially the diet-defying *comida corrida* (fixed-menu lunch) served daily. ⊠ *Calle Loreto 15, 37700*, ☎ *415/2–00–42*, ꜰᴀх *415/2–36–16. 38 rooms, 6 suites. Restaurant, pool. AE, MC, V.*

Nightlife and the Arts

The Arts

San Miguel, long known as an artists' colony, continues to nurture that image today. Galleries, museums, and arty shops line the streets near El Jardín, and two government-run salons—at **Bellas Artes** and **Instituto Allende** (☞ Exploring San Miguel de Allende, *above*, for both)—feature the work of Mexican artists. For a sampling of both regional and international talent, visit the **Galería San Miguel** (⊠ Plaza Principal 14, ☎ 415/2–04–54 or 415/2–10–46), **Galería Atenea** (⊠ Calle Cuna de Allende 15, ☎ 415/2–07–85), **Kligerman Gallery** (⊠ San Francisco 11, ☎ 415/2–09–51), the **Galería del Pueblo** (⊠ Correo 12A, ☎ 415/2–14–48), and **Galería Duo Duo** (⊠ Pila Seca 3, ☎ 415/2–62–11). Most close weekdays between 2 and 4 PM and are open Sunday 10 or 11 AM to 2 or 3 PM.

The **Jazz Festival International,** now in its sixth year, takes place around the last week in November. There is live jazz, workshops, and after-hour jam sessions. Also, coinciding with Christmas vacation in late December, San Miguel hosts the **Winter Festival,** a feast of classical music. Tickets may be purchased individually or for the series. Contact the tourist office for dates and details.

Nightlife

On most evenings in San Miguel you can readily satisfy a whim for a literary reading, an American movie, a theatrical production, or a turn on a disco dance floor. The most up-to-date listings of events can be found in the English-language paper *Atención San Miguel*, published every Friday. The bulletin board at the public library (⊠ Calle Insurgentes 25) is also a good source of current events.

You can hear live music at **Pancho and Lefty's** (⊠ Calle Mesones 99, ☎ 415/2–19–58) from rock, jazz, or blues bands, depending on the night. **La Fragua** (⊠ Calle Cuna de Allende 3, ☎ 415/2–11–44), located just a couple of doors off the Plaza, often has traditional Mexican soloists or bands, and couples dance in the courtyard. **Mama Mia** (⊠ Calle Umarán 8, ☎ 415/2–20–63) offers everything from Peruvian folk music, classical guitar, and flamenco to salsa and rock. **San Miguelito** (⊠ Calle San Francisco 1, ☎ 415/2–33–72) bills itself as "A Place for Grown-Ups" and attracts a mixed crowd of Mexicans and foreigners, who listen to piano music in the evenings as they lounge on comfortable couches under twinkling lights and towering cactuses. Jazz and blues reign every night at **Tío Lucas** (⊠ Calle Mesones 103, ☎ 415/2–49–96), a favorite Instituto Allende art students' hangout.

Outdoor Activities and Sports

Taboada (⊠ Dolores Hidalgo Hwy., Km 8) has three outdoor geothermally heated pools, one of which is Olympic-size and good for doing laps. They are open to the public for $3.50; closed Tuesday. The nearby, more exclusive **Hotel Hacienda Taboada** (⊠ Dolores Hidalgo Hwy., Km 8, ☎ 415/2–08–88 or 415/2–08–50, ꜰᴀх 415/2–17–98) has several geothermal pools, manicured grounds, and tennis courts. It is open to the public for about $15, which includes lunch; closed Wednesday. The **Club de Golf Malanquin** (⊠ Celaya Hwy., Km 3, ☎ 415/2–05–16) has a heated pool, steam baths, tennis courts, and nine holes of golf, all of which are open to the public for a guest fee of $15 on weekdays or $20 on weekends; it is closed Monday.

Bicycle Rental

Bici-Burro (⊠ Calle Hospicio 1, esq. Barranca, ☎ 415/2–15–26) rents and services bikes for exploring San Miguel and environs. **Aventuras San Miguel** (⊠ Calle Recreo 10, ☎ FAX 415/2–64–06) rents bicycles at reasonable prices.

Horseback Riding

Aventuras San Miguel (☞ Bicycle Rental, *above*) rents horses at reasonable rates. The equestrian center of the **Casa de Sierra Nevada** (☞ Lodging, *above*) offers riding lessons, carriage rides, and horse rental at its 500-acre ranch for about $30 per hour.

Hot Air Ballooning

Gone with the Wind Balloon Adventures (⊠ Calle Recreo 68, ☎ 415/2–67–35) has hot air balloon rides over town and the surrounding countryside with licensed/certified pilots from Napa Valley, California. The one-hour flights depart at 6 or 7 AM, depending on the season. The $125 cost includes breakfast upon landing.

Spectator Sports

To witness the pageantry of a traditional Mexican bullfight, go to the **Plaza de Toros Oriente** (⊠ Off Calle Recreo), which has events several times a year. The most important contest takes place in the last week of September during *la fiesta de San Miguel*. Contact the tourist office (☞ Visitor Information *in* San Miguel de Allende A to Z, *below*) for more information.

Shopping

For centuries San Miguel's artisans have been creating crafts ranging from straw products to metalwork. Though some boutiques in town may be a bit pricey, you can find good buys on silver, brass, tin, woven-cotton goods, and folk art. Store hours tend to be erratic, but most stores open daily at around 9 AM, shut their doors for the traditional afternoon siesta (2 through 4 or 5), then reopen in the afternoon until 7 or 8 PM, and open for just a half day on Sunday. Most San Miguel shops accept MasterCard and Visa.

Markets

Mercado Ignacio Ramírez, a traditional Mexican covered market off Calle Colegio, one block north of Mesones, is a colorful jumble of fresh fruits and vegetables, flowers, bloody butchers' counters, inexpensive plastic toys, taco stands, and blaring Mexican-made cassettes. Spilling out for several blocks behind the Mercado Ignacio Ramírez, the **Mercado de Artesanías** (artisans' market) is where you'll find vendors of local work—glass, tin, and papier mâché—as well as some of the best prices on silver jewelry in town.

Specialty Shops

FOLK ART

Artes de México (⊠ Calzada Aurora 47 at Dolores Hidalgo exit, ☎ 415/2–07–64) has been producing and selling traditional crafts, including furniture, metalwork, and ceramics, for more than 40 years. Although the inventory at the **Casa Maxwell** (⊠ Calle Canal 14, ☎ 415/2–02–47) has slipped in quality, there is still a reasonable selection of folk art. **La Calaca** (⊠ Mesones 93, ☎ 415/2–39–54) also focuses on folk art from the Americas, mainly Mexico, Guatemala, and Peru. **Tonatiu Metzli** (⊠ Calle Juárez 7, ☎ 415/2–08–69) has a wonderful selection of both antique and contemporary masks from all over Mexico. **Veryka** (⊠ Zacateros 6-A, ☎ 415/2–21–14), whose emphasis is on Latin American folk art, has a particularly fine selection of *muertos* (skeleton figurines for the Day of the Dead) from Puebla. **La Guadalupana**

MÉXICO: HECHO A MANO

HANDMADE IN MEXICO: Some of the world's finest artesanías (handicrafts) come from this country. Artisanal work is varied, original, colorful, and inexpensive, and it supports millions of families who are carrying on ancient and more recent traditions. Though cheap, shoddy items masquerading as "native crafts" are certainly common, careful shoppers who take their time can come away with real works of folk art. Also keep in mind that many items are exempt from duty.

The crafts to look for are ceramics, woodwork, lacquerware, leather, weaving and textiles, silver, gold, and semiprecious stone jewelry. Each region has its specialty. Cities that are noted for the quality of their crafts are Puebla (Chapter 2); Nogales in Sonora (Chapter 4); Guadalajara, Tlaquepaque, and Tonalá in Jalisco (Chapter 6); San Miguel de Allende, Guanajuato, and Pátzcuaro in the heartland (Chapter 7); Taxco in Morelos (Chapter 9); Oaxaca City in Oaxaca (Chapter 10); San Cristóbal de las Casas in Chiapas (Chapter 11); and Mérida in Yucatán (Chapter 13).

Ceramics. Talavera-style tiles (blue majolica) and other ceramic ware are at their best in Puebla. Oaxaca state is known for its unglazed, burnished black pottery. Inventive masks and figurines come from Valle de Bravo, Pátzcuaro in the state of Michoacán, Tonalá outside of Guadalajara, Taxco, and Chiapas.

Jewelry. Silver is best in Taxco, San Miguel de Allende, and Oaxaca; be sure purchases are stamped "925," which means 92.5% pure silver. You can find gold filigree in Guanajuato and Oaxaca. Oaxaca and Chiapas are also known for their amber, but be aware that much of what is sold as amber is in fact glass or plastic. Good rules of thumb: don't buy amber off the street; and if it seems like

a great bargain, it's probably fake. For semiprecious stones, go to jewelers' shops in Puebla and Querétaro. Coral jewelry is sold in the Yucatán and other coastal areas, but because of the massive ecological damage caused by coral harvesting, the whole practice around it is environmentally unsensible.

Leather. The key places to find quality leatherwork are Guadalajara, Oaxaca (for sandals), Chiapas (for belts and purses), and the Yucatán (for bags).

Metalwork. Look for copper in Santa Clara del Cobre in Michoacán, and tin in San Miguel de Allende and Oaxaca.

Weavings and Textiles. Fabric work is quite varied: you'll find *rebozos* (shawls) and blankets around Oaxaca, Guadalajara, Jalapa, and Pátzcuaro; *huipiles* (heavily embroidered tunics worn by Indian women) and other embroidered clothing in Michoacán, Oaxaca state, Chiapas, and the Yucatán; masterfully woven rugs, some colored with natural dyes, in Oaxaca; hammocks and baskets in Oaxaca and the Yucatán; lace in the colonial cities of the heartland area; *guayaberas* (comfortable, embroidered and/or pleated men's dress shirts, now usually mass-produced) along the Gulf coast; and reed mats in Oaxaca and Valle de Bravo. The Mezquital region east of Querétaro can also be rewarding, as can shopping for Huichol Indian yarn paintings and embroidery near Puerto Vallarta.

Woodwork. Look for masks in Mexico City; *alebrijes* (painted wooden animals) in Oaxaca; furniture in Cuernavaca, Guadalajara, San Miguel de Allende, Querétaro, Tequisquiapan, and Pátzcuaro; lacquerware in Uruapan and Pátzcuaro in Michoacán, Chiapa de Corzo in Chiapas, and Puerto Vallarta for pieces from Olinalá in Guerrero state; and guitars in Paracho, Michoacán.

(⊠ Calle Codo 1B, ☎ No phone) sells all manner of items adorned with images of Mexico's beloved Virgin of Guadalupe—from temporary tattoos to coffee mugs.

HOUSEWARES

Casa Canal (⊠ Calle Canal 3, ☎ 415/2–04–79), set in a beautiful old hacienda, sells new furniture, though much of it is made in traditional styles. **Casa María Luisa** (⊠ Calle Canal 40, ☎ 415/2–01–30) has a fantastic jumble of furniture, glassware, wall hangings, and lamps, as well as an enormous selection of collectibles made of tin, iron, wood, and glass. **Casa Vieja** (⊠ Calle Mesones 83, ☎ 415/2–12–84) has tons of glassware and ceramics, decorative and functional housewares, picture frames, furniture, and more. **México Lindo** (⊠ Calle Mesones 85, ☎ 415/2–07–30) has a good selection of hand-painted tiles and ceramics from Dolores Hidalgo.

JEWELRY

Established in 1963, **Joyería David** (⊠ Calle Zacateros 53, ☎ 415/2–00–56) has an extensive selection of gold, silver, copper, and brass jewelry, all made on the premises. A number of pieces contain Mexican opals, amethysts, topaz, malachite, and turquoise. The reputable **Beckmann Joyería** (⊠ Calle Hernández Macías 105, ☎ 415/2–16–13) designs its own gold and silver pieces. **Platería Cerroblanco** (⊠ Calle Canal 17, ☎ 415/2–05–02) also creates and crafts its own silver and gold jewelry and will arrange a visit to its *taller* (workshop) on request. **Joyería Precolombina** (⊠ Calle Hidalgo 13, ☎ No phone) does quality reproductions of pre-Columbian jewelry in silver, copper, and gold.

Side Trip to Dolores Hidalgo

50 km (31 mi) north of San Miguel via Rte. 51.

Dolores Hidalgo played an important role in the fight for independence. It was here, before dawn on September 16, 1810, that Father Miguel Hidalgo—the local priest—gave an impassioned sermon to his clergy that ended with the *grito* (cry), "Viva Ferdinand VII (king of Spain at the time)! Death to bad government!" At 11 PM on September 15, politicians throughout the land repeat a revised version of the grito—"Viva Mexico! Viva Mexico! Viva Mexico!"—signaling the start of Independence Day celebrations. On September 16 (and only on this day), the bell in Hidalgo's parish church is rung.

Casa Hidalgo, the house where Father Hidalgo lived, is now a museum. It contains copies of important letters Hidalgo sent or received, and other independence memorabilia. ⊠ *Calle Morelos 1,* ☎ *418/2–01–71.* ⌨ *About $2; free Sun.* ☉ *Tues.–Sat. 10–5:45, Sun. 10–4:45.*

Dolores Hidalgo is famous for its lovely hand-glazed **Talavera-style ceramics,** most notably tiles and tableware. There are good prices at the town's many stores and factories. After shopping, head for the plaza for some of the most **exotic ice creams** you'll taste—flavors such as mole, avocado, beer, corn, and even cactus paddles with shrimp! The town is an easy one-hour bus ride from San Miguel de Allende's Central de Autobuses.

San Miguel de Allende A to Z

Arriving and Departing

BY BUS

Daily buses run direct from Mexico City's Central del Norte (North Bus Station) to the Central de Autobuses in San Miguel. Several major lines—including **ETN** (☎ 415/2–00–78 or 415/2–31–04; buy tickets through The Travel Institute of San Miguel de Allende), **Flecha Amarilla** (☎ 415/2–73–23), **Primera Plus** (☎ 415/2–50–43), **Herradura de Plata** (☎ 415/2–07-25), and **Pegasso Plus** (☎ 415/2–07–25)—have frequent service. Travel time is about four hours.

BY CAR

Driving time from Mexico City to San Miguel is roughly four hours via Route 57 (to Querétaro) then Route 111. Traveling on Route 45 from Mexico City, a road connecting to Routes 57 and 111 bypasses Querétaro, saving a half hour. Guanajuato is 100 km (62 mi), about 1½ hours, west of San Miguel.

BY PLANE

International airlines that fly into Leon's Guanajuato International Airport, which is about 1½ hours from San Miguel, include **Aeroméxico** (☎ 47/14–05–74) from Los Angeles; **American** (☎ 47/16–05–02) from Dallas–Fort Worth; **Continental** (☎ 47/14–71–10) from Houston; **Mexicana** (☎ 47/13–45–50) from Chicago; and **Taesa** (☎ 47/16–98–31) from Oakland, California.

Taxis from the Leon/Guanajuato airport to downtown San Miguel take about 1½ hours and cost about $50.

Getting Around

San Miguel de Allende is best covered on foot, keeping in mind two pieces of advice. The city is more than a mile above sea level, so you might tire quickly during your first few days here if you are not accustomed to high altitudes. Streets are paved with rugged cobblestones, and some have no sidewalks. Sturdy footwear, such as athletic or other rubber-soled walking shoes, is recommended.

BY TAXI

You can easily hail a taxi on the street or find one at taxi stands such as **Sitio Allende** in the main plaza (☎ 415/2–05–50 or 415/2–01–92), **Sitio San Francisco** on Calle Mesones (☎ No phone), or **Sitio San Felipe** on Calle Juárez (☎ No phone). Flat rates to the bus terminal, train station, and other parts of the city apply.

Contacts and Resources

BUSINESS SERVICES

La Conexión (✉ Aldama 1, ☎ FAX 415/2–16–87 or 415/2–15–99) has 24-hour answering and fax service, a Mexico address for receiving mail, lockboxes, packing and shipping, and other services. At **Unísono Net** (✉ Calle Hernández Macías 72B, upstairs, ☎ 415/2–63–31, FAX 415/2–49–58, unisono@unisono.net.mx) you can send and receive E-mail for a small fee.

CAR RENTAL

Rentacar (✉ Salida Celaya 5, ☎ 415/2–01–98) has a limited selection of manual transmission compacts available.

CONSULATE

U.S. Consulate (✉ Calle Hernández Macías 72, ☎ 415/2–23–57 during office hours; 415/2–00–68 or 415/2–06–53 emergencies); open Monday and Wednesday 9–1 and 4–7, Tuesday and Thursday 4–7.

EMERGENCIES

Police (☎ 415/2–00–22), **Traffic Police** (☎ 415/2–05–38), **Fire Department** (☎ 415/2–28–88), **Ambulance–Red Cross** (☎ 415/2–41–21 or 415/2–42–25).

Hospital. The staff at **Hospital de la Fé** (✉ Libramiento a Dolores Hidalgo 43, ☎ 415/2–22–33 or 415/2–23–20) can refer you to an English-speaking doctor.

Pharmacies. San Miguel has many pharmacies. American residents recommend **Botica Agundis** (⊠ Calle Canal 26, ☎ 415/2–11–98), where English speakers are often on hand. It's open daily 10:30–11.

ENGLISH-LANGUAGE BOOKSTORES

El Colibrí (⊠ Sollano 30, ☎ 415/2–07–51) has a good selection of paperback novels, magazines, and a few art supplies. **Libros el Tecolote** (⊠ Calle Jesús 11, ☎ FAX 415/2–73–95) has a great new and used selection of books on Mexican art, history, literature, and cooking.

MONEY EXCHANGE

A better bet for money exchange than the slow-moving bank lines is **Deal Casa de Cambio** (⊠ San Francisco 4, Correo 15, or Juárez 27, ☎ 415/2–29–32), open weekdays 9–6, Saturday 9–2.

TOUR OPERATORS

Aventuras San Miguel (⊠ Calle Recreo 10, ☎ FAX 415/2–64–06) has off-the-beaten-track mountain-bike treks, "ghost town" trips, even nighttime full-moon excursions. **Colonial México Tours** (⊠ Plaza Portal Allende 4, 2nd floor, ☎ FAX 415/2–57–94) runs historical tours to Guanajuato, Querétaro, and Dolores Hidalgo. Recommended for local tours is **The Travel Institute of San Miguel** (⊠ Cuna de Allende 11, ☎ 415/2–00–78 or 415/2–31–04, FAX 415/2–01–21).

TRAVEL AGENCY

Viajes Vértiz (⊠ Calle Hidalgo 1A, ☎ 415/2–18–56 or 415/2–16–95, FAX 415/2–04–99) is the American Express representative.

VISITOR INFORMATION

Delegación de Turismo (⊠ Southeast corner of Plaza Principal in a glassed-in office next to la Terraza restaurant, ☎ 415/2–65–65).

GUANAJUATO

100 km (62 mi) west of San Miguel de Allende, 365 km (226 mi) northwest of Mexico City.

Once Mexico's most prominent silver-mining city, Guanajuato is a colonial gem, tucked into the mountains at 6,700 ft. This provincial state capital is distinguished by twisting cobblestone alleyways, colorful houses, 15 shaded plazas, and a vast subterranean roadway where a rushing river once coursed. In the center of town is **Alhóndiga de Granaditas**, an 18th-century grain-storage facility that was the site of Mexico's first major victory in its War of Independence from Spain.

The city fills to overflowing in mid-October with the **International Cervantes Festival**, a three-week celebration of the arts. Hotels and private dwellings are completely saturated with guests, and some visitors must lodge in nearby cities. During the rest of the year, things regain a semblance of normalcy. Students rush to class with books tucked under their arms, women eye fresh produce at the Mercado Hidalgo, and old men utter greetings from behind whitewashed doorways. On weekend nights, *estudiantinas* (student minstrels dressed as medieval troubadours) serenade the public in the city squares.

Guanajuato celebrates its annual **Hot Air Balloon Festival** for a week in late November each year. Colorful balloons fill the sky, and events such as antique car parades and student art contests take place.

Exploring Guanajuato

Though Guanajuato's many plazas and labyrinthine streets may seem confusing at first, this is not a bad city in which to get lost. The center is small, and there are wonderful surprises around every corner. Remember that the top of the Alhóndiga (which you can see from many spots in town) points north, and the spires of the Basílica Colegiata Nuestra Señora de Guanajuato, at the Plaza de la Paz, point south.

A Good Walk

The tourist office, at Plaza de la Paz 14, is a good place to begin a walking tour. Turn right and walk up Avenida Juárez to reach **Jardín Unión** ⑫, Guanajuato's central square. The ornate **Teatro Juárez** ⑬ is just past the Jardín to your right on Calle Sopeña. The hardy might want to make a detour to **El Pípila** ⑭, a monument looming over the center of the city that is a half hour's climb. If you're interested bear right on Calle Sopeña just past the Teatro Juárez. A sign marked EL PÍPILA will direct you onto Callejón de Calvario, which eventually leads up to the hillside memorial.

Head back into town on Calle Cantarranas, a main street that winds down the hill and around the Jardín Unión. Just before Calle Cantarranas changes its name to Calle Pocitos, you'll see the **University of Guanajuato** ⑮. A short way down from where Calle Cantarranas becomes Calle Pocitos is **El Museo Casa Diego Rivera** ⑯, birthplace of Mexico's famous muralist. Calle Pocitos weaves past more residences and eventually becomes Calle 28 de Septiembre. On the left, just past the junction with Mendizabal, is the **Alhóndiga de Granaditas** ⑰, a former fortress converted into a state museum. Head one block south to return to Avenida Juárez and the glassed-in **Mercado Hidalgo** ⑱.

Turn right on Juárez as you leave the market and continue until the road splits near the Jardín Reforma. Bear left and cut down Calle Reforma, a short alleyway lined with shops. Keep left at the end of the street and you'll come to two pleasant courtyards: Plaza San Roque, which hosts outdoor performances during the Cervantes Festival, and Plaza San Fernando, a shady square where many book fairs are held. This short detour will return you to Avenida Juárez, where it's a slight climb up to Plaza de la Paz, a square built from 1895 to 1898 and surrounded by some of the city's finest colonial buildings, including the 18th-century **Mansión del Conde de Rul** ⑲. The bright-yellow 17th-century Baroque **Basílica Colegiata de Nuestra Señora de Guanajuato** ⑳ dominates the plaza. If you continue up Avenida Juárez about half a block past the plaza, you'll pass the tourist office again and arrive back at the Jardín Unión.

Sights to See

⑰ **Alhóndiga de Granaditas.** A massive stone structure with horizontal slit windows, this 18th-century grain-storage facility served as a jail under Emperor Maximilian and a fortress during the War of Independence, where **El Pípila** committed his courageous act (☞ El Pípila, *below*). It is now a state museum with exhibits on local history, archaeology, and crafts. The hooks on which the Spanish Royalists hung the severed heads of Father Hidalgo, Ignacio Allende, and two other independence leaders still dangle on the exterior. ⊠ *Calle 28 de Septiembre 6,* ☎ *473/2–11–12.* ⊡ *About $2; free Sun.* ☼ *Tues.–Sat. 10–1:30 and 4–5:30, Sun. 10–2:30.*

⑳ **Basílica Colegiata de Nuestra Señora de Guanajuato.** A 17th-century Baroque church painted a striking shade of yellow, the Basílica dominates the Plaza de la Paz. Inside is the oldest Christian statue in Mexico, a bejeweled 8th-century statue of the Virgin. The highly venerated figure was a gift from King Philip II of Spain in 1557. On the Friday preceding Good Friday, miners, accompanied by floats and mariachi bands, parade to the Basílica to pay homage to the Lady of Guanajuato. ⊠ *Plaza de la Paz.* ☼ *Daily 9–8.*

Guanajuato

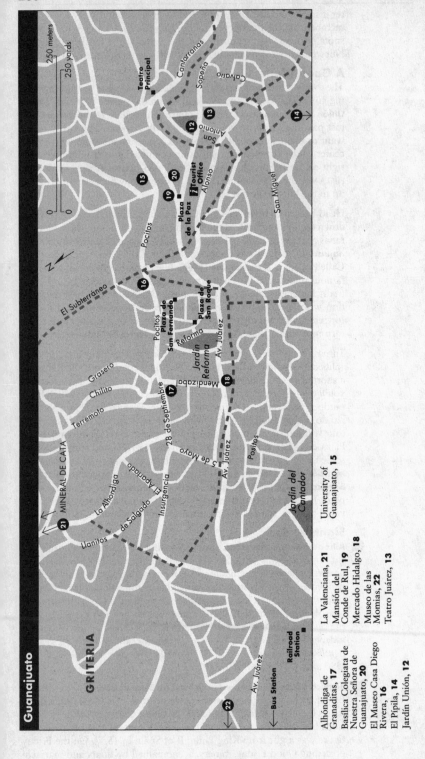

Alhóndiga de Granaditas, **17**

Basílica Colegiata de Nuestra Señora de Guanajuato, **20**

El Museo Casa Diego Rivera, **16**

El Pípila, **14**

Jardín Unión, **12**

La Valenciana, **21**

Mansión del Conde de Rul, **19**

Mercado Hidalgo, **18**

Museo de las Momias, **22**

Teatro Juárez, **13**

University of Guanajuato, **15**

⑯ El Museo Casa Diego Rivera. This museum, birthplace of Mexico's best-known muralist, Diego Rivera, contains family portraits and furniture as well as works by the master, among them his studies for the controversial mural commissioned for New York City's Rockefeller Center. Completed in 1933, the mural contained a portrait of Lenin and had a decidedly Communist bent, which caused it to be removed immediately after it was displayed. The museum's upper galleries house revolving contemporary art exhibits. ⊠ *Calle Pocitos 47,* ☎ *473/2–11–97.* ⊡ *$1.30.* ⊘ *Tues.–Sat. 10–6:30, Sun. 10–2:30.*

⑭ El Pípila. A half hour's climb from downtown is the monument to Juan José de los Reyes Martínez, a young miner and hero of the War of Independence of 1810. Nicknamed El Pípila, De los Reyes crept into the **Alhóndiga de Granaditas,** where Spanish Royalists were hiding. With a stone shield strapped to his back, he set the front door ablaze. The Spanish troops were captured by Father Hidalgo's army in this early battle, giving the independence forces their first major military victory. There's a splendid panoramic view of the city from the monument. It's easiest to take a taxi or a bus (marked PÍPILA) from the Jardín. ⊠ *Carretera Panorámica, on bluff above south side of Jardín Unión.*

⑫ Jardín Unión. This tree-lined, wedge-shape plaza is Guanajuato's central square. All three sides of the wedge are pedestrian walkways. On Tuesday, Thursday, and Sunday evenings, musical performances take place in the bandshell here; at other times, groups of musicians break into impromptu song along the plaza's shaded tile walkways.

NEED A BREAK?

For alfresco dining at the Jardín, try the terrace at the **Hotel Museo Posada Santa Fé** (⊠ Jardín Unión 12, ☎ 473/2–00–84). You can order a cappuccino and a slice of cake, or a full meal. Try the *pozole estilo Guanajuato* (hominy soup into which you spoon, or squeeze, the desired amounts of onions, radishes, lettuce, lime, and chili peppers). **Rincón del Arte** (⊠ Sopeña 10, ☎ 473/2–25–66) has both indoor and outdoor tables next to Teatro Juárez and serves good soups and sandwiches, as well as an interesting assortment of spiked specialty coffees—among them *cafe Guerrero* (coffee, Kahlúa, and pineapple juice) and *cafe diable* (coffee, rum, and lemon juice).

㉑ La Valenciana. Officially called La Iglesia de San Cayetano, this is one of the best-known colonial churches in all of Mexico. The mid- to late-18th-century pink stone facade is brilliantly ornate. Inside are three altars, each hand-carved in wood and gilded, in separate styles: plateresque, churrigueresque, and baroque. There are also fine examples of religious painting from the viceregal period. The silver mine near the church, also called La Valenciana, was discovered in 1760 and is still in operation today. Although you can't descend into the 1,650-ft-deep mine shaft, if the caretaker is around he'll usually let you take a peek down. La Valenciana is included in any guided tour of the city, and there are also frequent buses (marked LA VALENCIANA) from the center. ⊠ *Carretera Guanajuato–Dolores Hidalgo, Km 2.* ⊘ *Daily 9–6.*

⑲ Mansión del Conde de Rul. This 18th-century residence, now a government office, housed the count of Rul and Valenciana, who owned what was then the country's richest silver mine (☞ La Valenciana, *above*). The two-story structure was designed by famed Mexican architect Eduardo Tresguerras. ⊠ *Plaza de la Paz at Av. Juárez and Callejón del Estudiante.* ⊘ *Weekdays 8–3.*

⑱ Mercado Hidalgo. You can't miss this 1910 cast-iron-and-glass structure, designed by the one-and-only Gustave Eiffel. Though the balcony stalls are filled with T-shirts and cheap plastic toys, the lower level is full of authentic local wares and colorful basketry, as well as fresh produce, peanuts, and honey-drenched nut candies shaped like mummies. Vendors line the sidewalk in front of the market, hawking flowers and local crafts. ✉ *Calle Juárez near Mendizabal.* ⊙ *Daily 8–8.*

㉒ **Museo de las Momias.** For a macabre thrill, check out this unique museum located at the municipal cemetery off Calzada del Panteón, at the west end of town. In the museum, mummified human corpses— once buried in the cemetery—are on display. Until the law was amended in 1858, if a grave site had not been paid for after five years, the corpse was removed to make room for new arrivals. Because of the mineral properties of the local soil, these cadavers (the oldest is more than 130 years old) were in astonishingly good condition upon exhumation. The most gruesome are exhibited in glass cases. ✉ *Panteón Municipal,* ☎ *473/2–06–39.* 🎫 *$2.* ⊙ *Daily 9–6.*

⑬ **Teatro Juárez.** Adorned with bronze lion sculptures and a line of large Greek muses overlooking the Jardín from the roof, the theater was inaugurated by Mexican dictator Porfirio Díaz in 1903 with a performance of *Aïda.* It now serves as the principal venue of the annual International Cervantes Festival (☞ Nightlife and the Arts, *below*). A brief tour of the Art Deco interior is available. ✉ *Calle Sopeña s/n,* ☎ *473/2–01–83.* 🎫 *Tour 50¢.* ⊙ *Tues.–Sun. 9–1:45 and 5–7:45.*

⑮ **University of Guanajuato.** Founded in 1732, the university was formerly a Jesuit seminary. The original churrigueresque church, **La Compañía,** still stands next door. The facade of the university building, built in 1955, was designed to blend in with the town's architecture. If you do wander inside, check out the bulletin boards for notices of cultural events in town. (Also check bulletin boards along the pedestrian walkways of the Jardín.) ✉ *Calle Lascurain de Retana 5, ½ block north of Plaza de la Paz,* ☎ *473/2–00–06.* ⊙ *Weekdays 8–3:30.*

OFF THE
BEATEN PATH

MINERAL DE CATA – The modest church at Mineral de Cata, officially called Señor de Villaseca, is a moving testament to pure religious faith. Since its founding in 1725, silver miners and their families have come here to offer heartfelt *ex-votos* (sometimes called *retablos*)—folk paintings with text about prayer and gratitude. The church is now covered floor to ceiling with these remarkable offerings. Those near the ceiling are a couple hundred years old, painted on tin. The recent lower ones deal with contemporary issues such as immigration—Jésus drawn in glitter on a photocopy of a green card. It is best to take a taxi here and have the driver wait while you look inside. ✉ *Callejón del Quijote.*

Dining

Guanajuato's better restaurants are located in hotels near the Jardín Unión and on the highway to Dolores Hidalgo. For simpler fare, private eateries around town offer a good variety of Mexican and international dishes. Dress tends to be casual in this provincial university town.

$$$ ✕ **Casa del Conde de la Valenciana.** Come to this refurbished 18th-
★ century home across the street from La Iglesia de San Cayetano for superbly prepared traditional Mexican and international fare. Fresh gazpacho soup comes in a bowl made of ice, and the tender *lomo en salsa de ciruela pasa* (pork shoulder in prune sauce) and *pollo a la flor de calabaza* (chicken with poblano chili slices and squash blossom sauce) are delicious. ✉ *Km 5 Carretera Guanajuato–Dolores Hidalgo,* ☎ *473/ 2–25–50. MC, V. Closed Sun. No dinner.*

$$$ ✕ **El Comedor Real.** Continental cuisine served in a medieval environment
★ defines El Comedor Real. The bright whitewashed and brick-domed
restaurant in the Hotel Castillo Santa Cecilia serves such specialties as
filete pimienta (steak with peppercorns), breaded trout with tartar
sauce, and fish soup with vegetables. Troubadours perform every Fri-
day and Saturday at 10:30 PM at La Cava, the bar next door. ✉
Camino a la Valenciana s/n, Km 1, ☎ *473/2–04–85. AE, MC, V.*

$$$ ✕ **Tasca de los Santos.** This cozy restaurant, across the street from the
Basílica, specializes in Spanish and international fare. Recommended dishes
include the *sopa de mariscos* (a rich broth with shrimp, mussels, clams,
and crabs, all in their shells) and *filete parrilla* (grilled beef with baked
potatoes and spinach). *Huevos Reina* is a tasty light dish consisting of
eggs and mushrooms baked in a cheese and wine sauce. Dine inside or
out under white umbrellas on the plaza, with a view of the fountain. A
variety of music, ranging from French to Russian, enhances the cosmopolitan mood. ✉ *Plaza de la Paz 28,* ☎ *473/2–23–20. AE, MC, V.*

$$ ✕ **El Retiro.** This traditional Mexican restaurant up the street from
the Teatro Juárez is often crowded for the main midday meal. At other
times you can relax with a steaming cappuccino. Though local resi-
dents swear by El Retiro's reputation, it is hardly the "retreat" that
its name implies. The food is still good, but the waiters are often mes-
merized by televised soccer games, and pop music sometimes replaces
the classical fare that prevailed in gentler times. A full comida cor-
rida runs less than $3; or try the *mole poblano* (a complex sauce made
with poblano chilies and chocolate) with chicken, broiled steak with
mushroom sauce, or Spanish omelet. ✉ *Calle Sopeña 12,* ☎ *473/2–
06–22. AE, MC, V.*

$ ✕ **El Pingüis Cafeteria.** Cheap and plentiful food attracts the univer-
sity crowd to this spartan eatery decorated with Mexican art posters.
For about $3, a midday meal consists of soup, Mexican rice, a chicken
or beef dish, dessert, and coffee. *Consumé de verduras* (vegetable soup)
is good, as is the *café americano.* Service can be slow, but vibrant music
and a lively crowd will keep you entertained. ✉ *Jardín Unión at Al-
lende 3,* ☎ *473/2–14–14. No credit cards.*

$ ✕ **El Unicorno Azul.** If you are growing weary of heavy meat dishes,
stop by this food counter just behind Jardín Unión: it serves fruit
drinks, yogurt, and vegetarian burgers and sandwiches. The owner will
cheerfully recommend other health-food places and yoga classes. ✉
Plaza del Baratillo 2, ☎ *473/2–07–00. No credit cards. Closed Sun.*

$ ✕ **Truco 7.** Red tile floors, *equipale* (pigskin) chairs, and original art en-
★ liven this cozy coffeehouse and restaurant. In the morning, serious stu-
dents hunch over coffee and textbooks. Later in the day locals and savvy
tourists pile in for the inexpensive comida corrida, sandwiches, or grilled
chicken. The atmosphere is also lively at night, when Mexican wines are
served by the glass. ✉ *Calle Truco 7,* ☎ *473/2–83–74. No credit cards.*

Lodging

Guanajuato's less expensive hotels are along Avenida Juárez and Calle
de la Alhóndiga. Moderately priced and upscale properties are near
the Jardín Unión and on the outskirts of town. It's best to secure reser-
vations at least six months in advance if you plan to attend the Cer-
vantes Festival, which usually runs from mid- to late October.

$$$–$$$$ ▦ **La Casa de Espiritus Alegres Bed and Breakfast.** A paradise for folk
★ art lovers, this "house of good spirits" is filled with extraordinary crafts
from every state in Mexico. Owned by a California artist, the lovingly
restored hacienda (circa 1700) has thick stone walls and serene grounds
lush with bougainvillea, banana trees, and calla lilies. All rooms have
hand-glazed tile baths, fireplaces, and a private terrace, patio, or bal-

cony. Rates include a sumptuous breakfast served in a glassed-in atrium overlooking the garden. Children are not admitted. Marfil is about a 15-minute drive from the center of town—frequent bus service is available. ⊠ *La Ex-Hacienda La Trinidad 1, Marfil 36250,* ☎ FAX *473/3–10–13. 5 rooms, 3 suites. Bar, shop, free parking. No credit cards.*

$$–$$$ 🏨 **Parador San Javier.** This immaculately restored hacienda was con-
   ★   verted into a hotel in 1971. In fact, a safe from the Hacienda San Javier and old wood trunks still decorate the large, plant-filled lobby. Rooms are clean and have attractive appointments: lace curtains, crisp coverlets, and blue-and-white-tiled baths. A few of the 16 colonial-style rooms reached via a stone archway have fireplaces. Newer rooms in the adjoining high-rise have satellite TVs. A word of caution: large convention groups sometimes crowd the facility. ⊠ *Plaza Aldama 92, 36000,* ☎ *473/2–06–26,* FAX *473/2–31–14. 104 rooms, 11 suites. 2 restaurants, bar, café, pool, dance club, free parking. AE, MC, V.*

$$ 🏨 **Hosteria del Frayle.** A half block off Jardín Unión, this quiet four-story lodging was once the Casa de Moneda, where ore was taken to be refined after it was brought out of the mines. Built in 1673 and turned into a hotel in the mid-1960s, it has whitewashed plaster and wood-beamed rooms (which nonetheless are somewhat dark), arranged around a small maze of stairways, landings, and courtyards. All have telephones and TVs (local channels only), and some afford excellent views of the Pípila, Teatro Juárez, and Jardín Unión. The staff is extremely friendly and helpful. ⊠ *Calle Sopeña 3,* ☎ *473/2–11–79,* FAX *473/2–11–79, ext. 138. 32 rooms, 5 suites. Restaurant, bar. MC, V.*

$$ 🏨 **Hotel Museo Posada Santa Fé.** This colonial-style inn, at the Jardín Unión, has been in operation since 1862. Large historic paintings by local artist Don Manuel Leal hang in the wood-paneled lobby. A sweeping, if tattered, carpeted stairway leads to second-floor quarters. Each room—decorated in warm, autumnal colors—has cable TV and a telephone. Rooms facing the plaza can be noisy; quieter rooms face narrow alleyways. ⊠ *Plaza Principal at Jardín Unión 12, 36000,* ☎ *473/2–00–84,* FAX *473/2–46–53. 47 rooms, 9 suites. Restaurant, 2 bars, outdoor hot tub, airport shuttle. AE, MC, V.*

$ 🏨 **Hotel Socavón.** One of Guanajuato's newer hotels, this modest five-story property was built in 1981. Don't be put off by the gloomy, tunnel-like entrance: open-air walkways, with views of surrounding mountains, lead to guest quarters. Each small room—simply furnished with a bed, desk, and tiny television—has a wood-beamed ceiling and a modern bath. Fourth-floor corner rooms have some good views. ⊠ *Calle de la Alhóndiga 41A, 36000,* ☎ *473/2–66–66,* ☎ FAX *473/2–48–85. 40 rooms. Restaurant, bar. AE, MC, V.*

Nightlife and the Arts

Guanajuato, on most nights a somnolent provincial capital, awakens each fall for the **International Cervantes Festival.** For three weeks in October world-renowned actors, musicians, and dance troupes (which have included the Bolshoi Ballet) perform nightly at the Teatro Juárez and other venues in town. The Plaza San Roque, a small square near the Jardín Reforma, hosts a series of *Entremeses Cervantinos*—swash-buckling one-act farces by classical Spanish writers. Grandstand seats require advance tickets, but crowds often gather by the edge of the plaza and watch for free. An estimated 450,000 people attended the 1997 festivities, a fact that those who abhor crowds should take into account. If you plan to be in Guanajuato for the festival, contact the **Festival Internacional Cervantino office** (⊠ Plaza de San Francisquito 1, ☎ 473/2–57–96 or 473/2–64–87, FAX 473/2–67–75) or **Ticketmaster** (☎ 5/325–9000) at least six months in advance for top-billed events.

At other times of the year, nightlife in Guanajuato mostly consists of dramatic, dance, and musical performances at the **Teatro Juárez** (⊠ Calle de Sopeña, ☎ 473/2–01–83). Friday and Saturday at 8 PM, *callejoneadas* (mobile musical parties) begin in front of the Teatro Juárez and meander through town (don't forget to tip the musicians). The **Teatro Principal** (⊠ Calle Hidalgo, ☎ 473/2–15–23) shows American movies several times a week, and some hotels, including the Parador San Javier and the Castillo Santa Cecilia, provide evening musical entertainment. There are several nightclubs located in or near the downtown area, including **Discoteque El Pequeño Juan** (⊠ Panorámica Al Pípila at Callejón de Guadalupe, ☎ 473/2–23–08)—whose panoramic view of the city at night is stunning. Live music, poetry readings, and visits from the troubadours make **La Peña Bohemia Rincón del Beso** (⊠ Alonso 21A, ☎ No phone) the place to go to experience the romantic soul of Guanajuato. Things start hopping after midnight.

Shopping

You'll find painterly, old-style majolica ceramics at **Capelo** (⊠ Cerro de la Cruz s/n, a dirt road off the Guanajuato–Dolores Hidalgo Hwy., just past Valenciana, ☎ FAX 473/2–84–13) and at the **Gorky González Workshop** (⊠ Pastita Ex-huerta de Montenegro s/n, past the baseball stadium, ☎ FAX 473/2–43—06). Both venerable studios now use leadsafe glazes. Located next to the Casa del Conde de la Valenciana restaurant, **Fonart** (⊠ Km 5 Carretera Guanajuato–Dolores Hidalgo, ☎ 473/2–25–50) specializes in brass, tin, ceramic, and wrought-iron home decorations. There is some jewelry and regional knickknacks at the **Mercado Hidalgo** (☞ Exploring Guanajuato, *above*). **Artesanías Vázques** (⊠ Cantarranas 8, ☎ FAX 473/2–52–31) carries Talavera ceramic ware from Dolores Hidalgo. There are other shops that sell ceramic ware and woolen shawls and sweaters around the Plaza de la Paz and Jardín Unión. Silver is available from street vendors and shops clustered near La Valenciana and El Pípila.

Side Trip

León
56 km (35 mi) northwest of Guanajuato.

Best known as the shoemaking capital of Mexico, León is also an important center for industry and commerce. With more than 1 million people, it is the state's most populous urban area.

If you know footwear and have the time (and patience) to browse through the downtown shops, you might find some good buys in León. First try the **Plaza del Zapato** (☎ 47/17–29–08), a mall with 70 stores on Boulevard Adolfo López Mateos, roughly one block from the bus station. From here take a taxi west (about a 10-minute ride) to the **Zona Peatonal,** a pedestrian zone with several shoe stores. On **Calle Praxedis Guerrero** there are various artisans' stands selling leather goods.

Flecha Amarilla **buses** leave Guanajuato's Central Camionera every 15 minutes for León; the ride takes about 45 minutes and costs less than $1. **Taxis** cost about $16 one way. Pick up a map of León at the tourist office in Guanajuato.

Guanajuato A to Z

Arriving and Departing
BY BUS
Direct bus service is available between the Central del Norte (North Bus Station) in Mexico City and Guanajuato's Central Camionera (☎

473/3–13–33). **Taxis** to downtown from the Camionera cost $2–$3.
Several lines—including **Flecha Amarilla** (☎ 473/3–13–32 or 473/3–
13–33) and **Estrella Blanca** (☎ 473/3–13–44)—have hourly service.
Travel time is about five hours. Deluxe buses, including those of **ETN**
(473/3–15–79 or 473/3–02–89), **Primera Plus** (473/3–13–32 or 473/
3–13–33), and **Omnibus de México** (☎ 473/3–13–56 or 473/2–04–38),
connect Guanajuato to Mexico City, San Miguel, and Guadalajara. There
are several departures daily.

BY CAR

Guanajuato is 365 km (226 mi), about five hours, northwest of Mexico City via Route 57 (to Querétaro), then via Route 45.

BY PLANE

Leon's Guanajuato International Airport is 56 km (35 mi) north of the
city of Guanajuato. *See* By Plane *under* Arriving and Departing *in* San
Miguel de Allende A to Z, *above,* for international carriers that serve
this airport. The taxi ride from the airport to town costs about $16
and takes about 45 minutes.

Getting Around

Don't bother with a car in Guanajuato. Many of the attractions are
within strolling distance of one another and located between Avenida
Juárez and Calle Pocitos, the city's two major north–south arteries. The
twisting subterranean roadway—El Subterráneo—also has a primarily north–south orientation.

BY TAXI

You can hail nonmetered taxis on the street or find them at *sitios* (taxi
stands) near the Jardín Unión, Plaza de la Paz, and Mercado Hidalgo.

Contacts and Resources

CAR RENTAL

Both **Avis** (✉ Hotel Fiesta Americana lobby, Los Gabilanes, León, ☎
FAX 47/13–60–40) and **Hertz** (✉ Prol. Calzada de los Heroes 108, La
Martinica, León, ☎ FAX 47/14–14–98) will drop a car at your hotel in
Guanajuato.

EMERGENCIES

Note: Few people in Guanajuato have a good command of English, so
in an emergency it's best to contact your hotel manager or the tourist
office.

Police (☎ 473/2–02–66). **Ambulance–Red Cross** (☎ 473/2–04–87).
Hospital General (☎ 473/3–15–76).

GUIDED TOURS

The following tour operators have half- and full-day tours with English-speaking guides. These tours typically include the Museum of Mummies, the church and mines of Valenciana, the monument to Pípila, the
Panoramic Highway, subterranean streets, and residential neighborhoods. Night tours often begin at the Pípila Monument for a nighttime city view and end at a discotheque. Estudiantinas usually perform
during the weekend tours.

Transporte Exclusivo de Turismo (✉ Av. Juárez and Calle Cinco de Mayo,
☎ 473/2–59–68) has several tours of Guanajuato and its environs.

Transporte Turísticos de Guanajuato (✉ Plaza de la Paz 2, by Basílica
de Guanajuato, ☎ 473/2–21–34 or 473/2–28–38) also has a kiosk at
the main bus terminal (no phone).

PHARMACY
El Fénix (✉ Juárez 104, ☎ 473/2–61–40) is open Monday–Saturday 8 AM–9:45 PM, Sunday 9–9.

TRAVEL AGENCIES
Viajes Georama (✉ Plaza de la Paz 34, ☎ 473/2–59–09 or 473/2–19–54, FAX 473/2–19–54) is the local American Express representative. **Viajes Frausto** (✉ Calle González Obregón 10, ☎ 473/2–35–80, FAX 473/2–66–20) is reliable for hotel and airline reservations.

VISITOR INFORMATION
The **Guanajuato tourist office** (✉ Plaza de la Paz 14, ☎ 473/2–15–74 or 473/2–19–82, FAX 473/2–42–51) is open weekdays 8:30–4.

ZACATECAS

In colonial days Zacatecas was the largest silver-producing city in the world, sending great treasures of the precious metal to the king of Spain. Still a large silver-mining center, with factories producing silver jewelry and trade schools training apprentices in the fine art of handmade silver craft, Zacatecas is relatively undiscovered by foreigners. Although it is a state capital with a population of some 300,000, it has the feel of a much smaller place. Zacatecas is kept spotlessly clean, thanks to civic pride and a mandate by the governor of the state of Zacatecas. This city is rightly famous for its historic role as the scene of one of Pancho Villa's most spectacular battles and for its 18th-century colonial architecture.

One of the town's unique charms is the *tambora*, a musical walk up and down the streets and alleyways led by a *tamborazo*, a typical local band that shatters the evening quiet with merriment. Also known as a callejoneada (*callejón* means "alley"), the tambora is a popular free-for-all, in which everyone along the way either joins in the procession or leans from balconies and doorways to cheer the group on. During the December *feria* (festival), the tamborazos play night and day as they serenade the Virgin of Zacatecas.

Exploring Zacatecas

Most of Zacatecas's colonial sights are near the city center, making it an easy place to explore on foot—and there is rarely much traffic in town. For an overview of Zacatecas, you can walk or taxi up to the mine, catch an elevator to a nearby hilltop, take the cable car across the city, then return to your starting point below by taxi or bus.

A Good Walk

Start your tour at the Plaza de Armas, in the center of the city. Here you'll find the stunning **Catedral de Zacatecas** ㉓ and the **Palacio del Gobierno** ㉔. Across the street from the plaza are two beautiful colonial buildings worth exploring; one is known as the **Palacio de la Mala Noche** ㉕ because of a local legend. Go to the Plaza Santo Domingo, two blocks west of the cathedral, to see the art in the **Pedro Coronel Museum** ㉖ and the Baroque **Templo de Santo Domingo** ㉗ right next door. To visit the museum of the other Coronel brother—both were equally fanatical art collectors—return to the cathedral, turn left on Avenida Hidalgo, and walk about 1 km (½ mi) north of the plaza to the **Rafael Coronel Museum** ㉘.

For a longer walk, head south on Avenida Hidalgo until you come to Juárez, then go right (roughly west) up the hill, passing the several-block-long Alameda park and the Social Security Hospital to get to the **Eden Mine** ㉙. After touring the mine, you can take an elevator up to

Cerro del Grillo (Cricket Hill) and catch the **Teleférico** ㉚ cable car across
the city to **Cerro de la Bufa** ㉛, site of Pancho Villa's famous battle.

Sights to See

㉓ **Catedral de Zacatecas.** This is one of Mexico's finest interpretations
of Baroque style. Each of the facades tells a different legend. According to one of them, an anticlerical governor of the state used the cathedral's silver cross and baptismal font to mint Zacatecas's first silver
coins. ⊠ *South side of Plaza de Armas on Av. Hidalgo.*

NEED A BREAK?	The **Café y Nevería Acrópolis** (⊠ Av. Hidalgo at Plazuela Candelario Huizar, ☎ 492/2–12–84), alongside the cathedral, is a quaint diner where locals talk shop over strong Turkish coffee ($1.50). The café is open daily from 8 AM to 10 PM, selling lots of homemade pastries and cakes, as well as a variety of Mexican snacks.

㉛ **Cerro de la Bufa.** The city trademark, this rugged hill is the site of Pancho Villa's definitive battle against dictator Victoriano Huerta in June
1914. The spacious **Plaza de la Revolución,** paved with the three
shades of pink Zacatecan stone, is crowned with three huge equestrian
statues of Villa and two other heroes, Felipe Angeles and Panfilo Nat-
era. Also on the site are the **Sanctuary of the Virgin of Patrocinio,** a
chapel dedicated to the patron of the city, and the **Museo de la Toma
de Zacatecas,** which has nine rooms filled with historic objects such
as guns, newspapers, furniture, and clothing from the days of Pancho
Villa. ⊠ *If driving, follow Av. Hidalgo north from town to Av. Juan
de Tolosa; turn right and continue until you come to a fountain; take
1st immediate right off retorno (crossover) onto Calle Mexicapan,
which leads to Carretera Panorámica. Turn right to signposted Carretera La Bufa, which leads to top of hill.* ☎ *492/2–80–66 museum.*
⊠ *$1.* ⊙ *Tues.–Sun. 10–4:30.*

㉙ Eden Mine. Now a tourist attraction, La Mina Eden supplied most of Zacatecas's silver from 1586 until 1960. An open mine train runs down into the underground tunnels. The tour is in Spanish, but you'll have no trouble imagining what the life of the miners was like. Be sure to wear sturdy shoes. Remember that mines are dark; through much of the tour, your only light may be the guide's flashlight. Farther down the train track there is another stop at, of all places, a discotheque (☞ Nightlife and the Arts, *below*). There's a small gift shop at the entrance. ⊠ *Entrance on Antonio Dovali off Av. Torreon beyond Alameda García de la Cadena,* ☎ *492/2–30–02.* ☜ *$2.* ⊙ *Daily 11–6.*

㉕ Palacio de la Mala Noche. The Palace of the Bad Night is one of two beautiful 18th-century colonial buildings across from the downtown plaza. Both declared national monuments, they are built from native pink stone and have lacy ironwork balconies. One of them now houses the Continental Plaza hotel (☞ Lodging, *below*), and the other is presently a municipal building known as El Palacio de la Mala Noche. Legend has it that this was the home of a silver-mine owner who was called upon so often to help the needy that he built a hidden door from which he could enter and leave the palace undisturbed. One night a terrible storm was raging, yet a worker had the temerity to pound on the front door. He finally gained entrance with his good news: silver had been found in a mine considered exhausted. Up the hill along the side of the palace, you will find the so-called hidden door. ⊠ *Av. Hidalgo 639.* ☜ *Free.* ⊙ *Weekdays 10–2 and 4–7.*

㉔ Palacio del Gobierno. The Governor's Palace is an 18th-century mansion with flower-filled courtyards and, on the main staircase, a powerful mural painted in 1970 by António Pintor Rodríguez that depicts the history of Zacatecas. ⊠ *East side of Plaza de Armas.* ☜ *Free.* ⊙ *Weekdays 9–2 and 5–8, Sat. 9–1.*

★ **㉖ Pedro Coronel Museum.** Originally a Jesuit monastery, this building was used as a jail in the 18th century. The museum is one of a kind in Mexico and Latin America, housing the work of Zacatecan artist and sculptor Pedro Coronel and his extensive collection of work by Picasso, Dalí, Miró, Braque, and Chagall among others, as well as art from Africa, China, Japan, India, Tibet, Greece, and Egypt. ⊠ *Av. Fernando Villalpando at Plaza Santo Domingo,* ☎ *492/2–80–21.* ☜ *About $1.50.* ⊙ *Fri.–Wed. 10–5.*

★ **㉘ Rafael Coronel Museum.** The museum is in the Ex-Convento de San Francisco, northeast of the town center toward Lomas del Calvario. Its mellowed pink 18th-century facade conceals a rambling structure of open, arched corridors, all leading through garden patios to rooms that contain an amazing collection of some 4,500 *máscaras* (masks)— saints and devils, wise men and fools, animals and humans—used in regional festivals all over Mexico. There is also an outstanding display of puppets. ⊠ *Off Vergel Nuevo between Chaveño and Garcia Salinas,* ☎ *492/2–81–16.* ☜ *About $1.75.* ⊙ *Thurs.–Tues. 10–5.*

㉚ Teleférico. The only cable car in the world that crosses an entire city, the Teleférico runs from **Cerro del Grillo** (Cricket Hill) above the Eden Mine to **Cerro de la Bufa** and operates daily from 10 until dusk, except when there are high winds. True, it crosses at the narrowest point, but it presents a magnificent panoramic view of the city and its many Baroque church domes and spires. It's also well worth the cost (about 75¢ each way) to get the ride up to Cerro de la Bufa, which is quite a climb otherwise. ⊠ *Cerro del Grillo station of Teleférico is just off Paseo Díaz Ordaz, a steep walk from plaza,* ☎ *492/2–56–94.* ☜ *About $2.* ⊙ *Daily 10–6.*

㉗ **Templo de Santo Domingo.** This 18th-century Jesuit church has an ornamented facade and a rich interior that includes gold-leaf religious
paintings. The sacristy also contains an impressive collection of religious art. ⊠ *Av. Fernando Villalpando at Plaza Santo Domingo.* ☉
Daily 8–2 and 5–9.

Dining

Several of Zacatecas's better restaurants are in hotels. Another is right
in El Mercado, the boutique area on Calle Hidalgo near the cathedral.
Other popular restaurants are on Avenida Juárez, which intersects Hidalgo.

$$$ ✕ **La Cuija.** Regional food is the strength of this large restaurant,
★   whose name means "the gecko." Start off with an appetizer of three
quesadillas: one each of squash blossoms, cheese, and *huitlacocha* (a
corn fungus delicacy). Also recommended are the *sopa campera* (a cream
soup with corn and squash blossoms), and *asado de boda* (pork in a
semisweet and spicy sauce). The decor approximates a wine cellar, and
in addition to fine food, the restaurant serves wine from the owner's
Cachola Vineyards in Valle de las Arsinas. A traditional Mexican trio
plays Thursday–Sunday afternoons. ⊠ *Centro Commercial El Mer-
cado, bottom level,* ☎ *492/2–82–75. AE, MC, V.*

$$ ✕ **Cenaduría Los Dorados.** Hidden on a small square adjacent to the
Ex-Convent of San Francisco, this small, cheery restaurant is packed
with memorabilia from the War of Independence. There is a no-smoking section, and the food is tasty and wholesome, if perhaps a bit toned
down for tourists' palates. Dinner is the most popular meal here. ⊠
Plazuela de García 1314, ☎ *492/2–57–22. No credit cards.*

$ ✕ **Mesón la Mina.** Hang with local small-business men in this no-frills
restaurant near the Jardín Independencia. In seeming contradiction, waiters in crisp black and white hurry attentively to your faux-grain
Formica table, bringing tasty meals in extra-large portions on institu-
tion-style plastic plates. There are meats, burgers, sandwiches, enchiladas, and a huge fixed-price midday meal of soup, rice, main dish,
vegetable, beans, dessert, and coffee—for about $3. ⊠ *Juárez 15,* ☎
492/2–27–73. No credit cards.

$ ✕ **Rancho Viejo.** This informal ranch-style restaurant serves dishes with
a Zacatecan flavor, including *huchepos* (tamales with sweet cream) and
enchiladas covered with vegetables and a rich red chili sauce. ⊠ *Av.
Universidad 101,* ☎ *492/2–67–47. AE, MC, V.*

Lodging

Many of Zacatecas's best lodgings are in beautiful, well-preserved
18th- and 19th-century buildings.

$$$ ✕🏨 **Continental Plaza.** This beautiful old colonial building faces the
Plaza de Armas and the cathedral in the heart of the city. The pink-
stone facade dates from the 18th century; unfortunately the modern
interior is rather stark and charmless. Rooms are fitted with new but
unexceptional furniture. Those facing the plaza are within earshot of
late-night and early morning tamborazo music during festivals. That
said, you'll get a great view of the goings-on from your small balcony.
The hotel's restaurant, Candiles, is one of the best in Zacatecas. The
menu includes both Continental and regional dishes, and there is a daily
breakfast buffet. ⊠ *Av. Hidalgo 703, 98000,* ☎ *492/2–61–83 or 492/
2–61–86,* 𝔽𝔸𝕏 *492/2–62–45. 86 rooms, 13 suites. Restaurant, bar, con-
vention center. AE, MC, V.*

$$$$ · ★ 🏨 **Quinta Real.** This hotel must be one of the most unusual in the world: it is built around Mexico's oldest bullring, the second one constructed in the Western Hemisphere. The terrazzo-paved ring provides a unique view for the guest rooms, each with a balcony overlooking the *plaza de toro* (bullring) itself. Large and bright, the plush rooms are decorated in pastel fabrics that complement the dark traditional furniture. The bar occupies some of the former bull pens, and an outdoor café with bright-white umbrella tables takes up two levels of the spectator area. Fine Continental cuisine is served in the elaborate, formal restaurant, with an awesome view of the bullring and the aqueduct beyond. ⊠ *Av. Rayon 434, 98000,* ☎ *492/2–91–04 or 01–800/36–015; 800/445–4565 in the U.S.,* FAX *492/2–84–40. 36 rooms, 11 suites. Restaurant, bar, café, shop. AE, MC, V.*

$$$ 🏨 **Holiday Inn.** One of the most modern hotels in Zacatecas, this pleasant property is only three blocks from the historic town center. From the bay windows of its front rooms you can see over the rooftops of the whitewashed dome of the beautiful baroque-style Templo San José. Furnishings in rooms—all with satellite TVs, individual climate control, and marble baths—include Mexican chests painted white and lacy white ironwork headboards. ⊠ *Blvd. López Matéos y Callejón del Barro, 98000,* ☎ *492/2–33–11; 800/465–4329 in the U.S.,* FAX *492/2–34–15. 111 rooms, 15 suites. 2 restaurants, bar, coffee shop, pool, sauna, shop, nightclub, playground. AE, MC, V.*

$$$ · ★ 🏨 **Mesón de Jobito.** This early 19th-century apartment building stood for well over a hundred years before its recent conversion to a four-star hotel. The two levels of guest rooms are done in tasteful modern decor, with wall-to-wall carpet and striped drapes. All rooms have cable TVs and telephones. The restful atmosphere is enhanced by the Mesón's perfect location on a blissfully quiet little plaza a few blocks from the cathedral. ⊠ *Jardín Juárez 143, 98000,* ☎ *492/4–17–22,* FAX *492/4–35–00. 25 rooms, 6 suites. Restaurant, bar. AE, MC, V.*

$ 🏨 **Posada de la Moneda.** This very Mexican hotel in the middle of downtown is adequate if you're on a budget. Everything is highly polished, especially the lobby's marble floor. If the room furnishings are a bit threadbare, they are clean, and the carpet is relatively new. Each room has a telephone and TV (local channels only). The second-floor lounge has some impressive chartreuse Naugahyde furniture. ⊠ *Hidalgo 413, 98000,* ☎ FAX *492/2–08–81. 34 rooms, 2 suites. Restaurant, bar. AE, MC, V.*

Nightlife and the Arts

A must-see if only for its uniqueness, **El Malacate** (☎ 492/2–30–02, ☉ Thurs.–Sat. nights), the discotheque in La Mina Eden, is a stop on the Eden Mine train, more than 1,000 ft underground. It's best to make reservations at this popular place, which is both crowded and noisy. There is a $7 cover charge. Atop a mountain outside Zacatecas, **El Elefante Blanco** (⊠ Mina La Gallega 15, ☎ 492/2–71–04; ☉ Thurs.–Sat. nights) is a discotheque with a panoramic view of the city. There's live music in the lobby bar of the **Continental Plaza** (☞ Lodging, *above*), and the **Holiday Inn** has a nightclub with live entertainment (☞ Lodging, *above*).

Shopping

Don't expect to find quality crafts in Zacatecas: souvenirs are more along the line of tacky knickknacks than handicrafts. There is some decent silver jewelry, although not as much as one would expect.

Crafts

Opposite the east end of the Plaza de Armas is **La Cazzorra** (⊠ Hidalgo 713, ☎ 492/4–04–84), a collectibles shop with authentic antiques, books about Zacatecas, wood furniture, Huichol art, and ceramics. The husband-and-wife owners are a good source of information about the city.

Silver

Centro Platero Zacatecas, located downtown in **Centro Comercial El Mercado** (⊠ Calle Hidalgo, next to cathedral, ☎ 492/3–10–07), sells silver jewelry with regional designs, made in its factory in nearby Guadalupe (☞ Side Trips, *below*). **Yohuatl** is also in the Centro Comercial El Mercado (⊠ Calle Hidalgo, ☎ No phone); it has a large selection of silver jewelry and accessories for women and men.

Side Trips

Guadalupe

7 km (4½ mi) southeast of Zacatecas.

If you are interested in colonial art and architecture, don't miss seeing this small town. Its centerpiece is the **Ex-Convento de Guadalupe,** founded by Franciscan monks in 1707. It currently houses the **Museo de Arte Virreinal** (*virreinal* means "viceregal," or colonial), run by the Instituto Nacional de Antropología e Historia. The convent is itself a work of art, with its Baroque **Templo de Guadalupe** and the **Capilla de Nápoles,** but even more impressive is the stunning collection of religious art under its roof. Works by Miguel Cabrera, Nicolás Rodríguez Juárez, Cristóbal de Villalpando, and Andrés López are included, among others. ⊠ *Jardín Juárez s/n,* ☎ *492/3–23–86 or 492/3–20–89.* ⊡ *$2; free Sun.* ☉ *Daily 10–4:30.*

In the 18th-century mansion of don Ignacio de Bernárdez, the **Centro Platero Zacatecas** is a school and factory for handmade silver jewelry and other items. Stop in to watch student silversmiths master this fine tradition. (⊠ *Casco de la Ex-Hacienda Bernárdez,* ☎ *492/3–10–07.* ☉ *Weekdays 10–6.*

Zona Arqueológica La Quemada

50 km (31 mi) southwest of Zacatecas on Hwy. 54, 3 km (2 mi) off highway.

This ancient city was already a ruin before the Spaniards arrived in the 16th century. The site's original name, "Chicomostoc," means "place of the seven tribes." Although it was once believed that seven different Indian cultures built here, one community atop the other, this theory is currently under scrutiny. The remaining edifices appear to be constructed of thin slabs of stone wedged into place. The principal draw is a group of rose-color ruins containing 11 large, round columns built entirely of the same small slabs of rock seen in the rest of the ruins. There is now an impressive site museum with a scale model of the ruins and some interesting artifacts. To get here, take a bus toward Villanueva, get off at the entrance to La Quemada, and walk in 3 km (2 mi). The bus ride takes about an hour. Alternatively, take a taxi or guided tour. ☎ No phone. ⊡ $2; free Sun. ☉ Site and museum daily 10–4:30.

Zacatecas A to Z

Arriving and Departing

BY BUS

Omnibus de México (☎ 492/2–02–74) and **Turistar** and **Futura** (☎ 492/2–00–42) run several first- and second-class buses daily from Mexico City to Zacatecas. The trip takes eight to nine hours.

BY CAR

Zacatecas is 603 km (375 mi), about 7½–8 hours, northwest of Mexico City via Route 57 (to Querétaro and San Luis Potosí) and Route 49.

Mexicana (☎ 492/2-74-29, 492/2-74-70, or 492/2-32-48) has direct service to Zacatecas from Chicago, Denver, and Los Angeles. In Zacatecas, the Mexicana office is at Hidalgo 406. The airport is 29 km (18 mi) north of town. **Aerotransportes** (☎ 492/2-59-46) makes the trip for about $4; private **taxis** cost about $12.

Getting Around

You can get to most of the town-center attractions on foot, although you might want to hire a taxi if you want to tour a mine or take a ride on the Teleférico (cable car) to the top of Cerro de la Bufa. The city has an excellent and inexpensive bus system.

Contacts and Resources

EMERGENCIES

Police (☎ 492/2-01-80). **Red Cross** (☎ 492/2-30-05). **Hospital San José** (☎ 492/2-03-60 or 492/2-58-73). **Emergency Service** (☎ 06). English is not generally spoken in Zacatecas, so it's best to contact your hotel manager or the tourist office in case of an emergency.

GUIDED TOURS

Viajes Mazzoco (⊠ Calle Satima 115, ☎ 492/2-08-59, FAX 492/2-55-59), a well-established travel agency and the local American Express representative, has a four-hour tour of the city center, the Eden Mine, the Teleférico, and La Bufa for about $11 per person. There are also tours to La Quemada ruins and environs ($15).

Operadora Zacatecas (⊠ Av. Hidalgo 630, ☎ 492/4-00-50) is recommended by the tourism office, and offers much the same tours as Viajes Mazzoco (☞ *above*).

PHARMACY

Farmacia Isstezac (⊠ Tacuba 153, ☎ 492/4-06-90) is open daily 8 AM-10 PM.

VISITOR INFORMATION

The **tourist information office** (⊠ Av. Hidalgo 629, ☎ 492/4-40-47 or 492/4-05-52), open weekdays 9-8, weekends 9-7, is across the street from the town cathedral.

The state **Dirección Estatal de Turismo** (⊠ Prolongación González s/n, ☎ 492/4-05-52 or 492/4-03-93, FAX 492/2-93-29), open weekdays 9-8, is across from the train station.

QUERÉTARO

In 1810 the first plans for independence were hatched at the Querétaro home of Josefa Ortiz de Domínguez—known as La Corregidora, wife of El Corregidor, Querétaro's mayor of the time. She was a heroine of the independence movement. In 1848 the Mexican-American War was concluded in this city with the signing of the Treaty of Guadalupe Hidalgo. Emperor Maximilian made his last stand here in 1867 and was executed by firing squad on the *Cerro de las Campanas* (Hill of the Church Bells), north of town. A small memorial chapel, built by the Austrian government, marks the spot. A gigantic statue of Benito Juárez crowns a park on the crest of the hill just above it. Also, in 1917 the Mexican Constitution, which is still in force, was signed here. Now Querétaro is a state capital and an industrial center of nearly 1 million people.

Throughout Querétaro are markers, museums, churches, and monuments that commemorate the city's heroes and historic moments. A prevailing sense of civic pride is evident in the impeccably renovated mansions, the flower-draped cobblestone pedestrian walkways, and the hospitable plazas, which are softly lighted at night. On Sunday evenings couples dance to live *danzón* music in the main plaza, or simply chat and enjoy the company of their friends. The people are among the most congenial in central Mexico and are quick to share their favorite sites and tales with travelers.

Querétaro is also renowned for opals—red, green, honey, and fire stones. Caveat emptor: some street vendors sell opals so full of water that they crumble shortly after purchase. Buy from reputable dealers (☞ Shopping, *below*).

Exploring Querétaro

Though Querétaro extends for some distance, the historic district is in the heart of town. You can easily spend a day or two here visiting museums, admiring architecture, and taking in local history.

A Good Walk

Most sights are near the **Plaza de la Independencia** ㉜. The **Palacio del Gobierno del Estado** ㉝ is on the plaza's northwest corner. If you walk around the square counterclockwise, you'll come to the Palacio de Justicia, originally built as a mansion for the wealthy Domingo Iglesia and, beside it, the **Casa de Ecala** ㉞. Just past the Casa de Ecala is Avenida Libertad Oriente, one of the city's bougainvillea-draped pedestrian walkways. Turn west here and walk two blocks to reach Calle Corregidora. Bear right again, and in the middle of a long block you'll find the entrance to the **Museo Regional de Querétaro** ㉟. Cross the street to Avenida Madero, another "pedway," this one lined with shops. The city's main square, Jardín Obregón, will be on your right.

One block past Avenida Juárez on the corner of Allende Sur and Madero you'll see the former **Casa de la Marquesa** ㊱, an old estate converted into a hotel (☞ *below*). Across Allende, next to the Church of Santa Clara, is the neoclassical **Fountain of Neptune** ㊲. From the fountain, make a left on Calle Allende and walk almost a block to a fine example of Baroque architecture, the **State Museum of Art** ㊳. Retrace your steps to Calle Corregidora. Make a left and walk one block to Calle 16 de Septiembre. Across the street is the **Jardín de la Corregidora** ㊴.

Sights to See

㉞ **Casa de Ecala.** Currently housing the offices of DIF, a family services organization, this Mexican Baroque palace has its original facade. As the story goes, its 18th-century owner adorned his home elaborately in order to outdo his neighbor, starting a remodeling war in which the Casa de Ecala eventually triumphed. Visitors are welcome to walk around the courtyard when the offices are open. ⊠ *Pasteur Sur 6, Plaza de la Independencia.* ☉ *Weekdays 9–9, Sat. 9–1.*

㊱ **Casa de la Marquesa.** Today a five-star hotel (☞ Lodging, *below*), this beautifully restored 18th-century house was built by the second Marqués de la Villa del Villar del Aguila. Most of the legends about the house's construction suggest that it was built to impress a nun with whom the marquis was terribly smitten. But he didn't live to see the casa completed in 1756, and its first resident was his widow, who had a penchant for things Arabic. The interior is *mudéjar* (Moorish) style, with lovely tilework. Stop in for a drink and the so, so elegant atmosphere of Don Porfirio's Bar. ⊠ *Madero 41.*

㊲ **Fountain of Neptune.** Built in 1797 by Eduardo Tresguerras, the renowned Mexican architect and a native of the Bajío, the fountain originally stood in the orchard of the Monastery of San Antonio. According to one story, when the monks faced serious economic problems, they sold part of their land and the fountain along with it. It now stands next to the Church of Santa Clara. ✉ *Calle Allende at Madero.*

㊴ Jardín de la Corregidora. This plaza is prominently marked by a statue of the War of Independence heroine—Josefa Ortiz de Domínguez—whose moniker it bears. Behind the monument stands the **Arbol de la Amistad** (Tree of Friendship). Planted in 1977 in a mixture of soils from around the world, the tree symbolizes Querétaro's hospitality to all travelers. You may want to find a bench in the Jardín and sit for a while: this is the calmest square in town, with plenty of choices for patio dining. ✉ *Av. Corregidora and Andador 16 de Septiembre.* ✇ *Free.*

�35 Museo Regional de Querétaro. This bright yellow, 17th-century Franciscan monastery displays the works of colonial and European artists in addition to historic memorabilia, including early copies of the Mexican Constitution and the table on which the Treaty of Guadalupe Hidalgo was signed. ✉ *Calle Corregidora 3 at Cinco de Mayo,* ☎ 42/12–20–31. ✇ *About $2.50; free Sun.* ✇ *Tues.–Sun. 10–7.*

�33 Palacio del Gobierno del Estado. Also known as La Casa de la Corregidora, in 1810 this was the home of Querétaro's mayor-magistrate (El Corregidor) and his wife, Josefa Ortiz de Domínguez (La Corregidora). On many evenings, conspirators—including Ignacio Allende and Father Miguel Hidalgo—came here under the guise of participating in La Corregidora's literary salon. When El Corregidor learned that they were actually plotting the course for independence, he imprisoned his wife in her room. La Corregidora managed to whisper a warning to a coconspirator, who notified Allende and Hidalgo. A few days later, on September 16, Father Hidalgo tolled the bell of his church to signal the beginning of the fight for freedom. A replica of the bell can be seen atop the building. Now the Palacio houses municipal government offices. ✉ *Northwest corner of Plaza de la Independencia.* 🎫 *Free.* ◷ *Weekdays 9–8, Sat. 9–2.*

③ **Plaza de la Independencia.** Bordered by carefully restored colonial mansions, this immaculate square, also known as Plaza de Armas, is especially lovely at night, when the central fountain is lighted. Built in 1842, the fountain is dedicated to the Marquis de la Villa del Villar, who constructed Querétaro's elegant aqueduct and provided the city with drinking water. The old stone aqueduct with its 74 towering arches still stands at the east end of town, though it no longer brings water into the city. ✉ *Bounded by Av. Cinco de Mayo on the north, Av. Libertad on the south, Luis Pasteur on the east, and Vergara Sur on the west.*

③ **State Museum of Art.** A fine example of Baroque architecture, the museum is housed in an 18th-century Augustinian monastery. Its collection focuses on European and Mexican paintings from the 17th through 19th centuries, and there are rotating exhibits of 20th-century art. Note the elegant and fascinating Baroque patio, and ask for an explanation of the symbolism of its columns and the figures in the conch shells at the top of each arch. ✉ *Calle Allende 14 Sur,* ☎ *42/12–23–57 or 42/12–35–23.* 🎫 *About $1.50; free Tues.* ◷ *Tues.–Sun. 11–7.*

Dining

Many of Querétaro's dining spots are located near the main plaza (Jardín Obregón), along Calle Corregidora, near the Teatro de la República, and particularly in the Jardín de la Corregidora. There are more upscale restaurants in hotels on the Plaza Independencia or off Route 57, north of the city.

$$$ ✕ **Fonda del Refugio.** Situated in the Jardín de la Corregidora, this restaurant offers intimate indoor and outdoor dining. Inside, fresh flowers adorn white-clothed tables; outside, comfortable leather chairs face the surrounding gardens. Seafood and beef fillets are the specialty; order the fillet of beef cooked in red wine, lemon, mustard, and peppers, or the scallops prepared in marsala. Cocktails are served on the terrace at night, when diners are often serenaded by guitar-playing trios. ✉ *Jardín de la Corregidora 26,* ☎ *42/12–07–55. AE, MC, V.*

$$$ ✕ **Restaurante Josecho.** Bullfight aficionados and other sports fans frequent this highway road stop next to the bullring at the southwest end ★ of town as much for the lively atmosphere as for the food. Wood-paneled walls are hung with hunting trophies, including geese, elk, bears, and leopards; waiters celebrate patrons' birthdays by banging on pewter plates and blasting a red siren. The place quiets down at night, when a classical guitarist or pianist performs. House specialties include *filete Josecho* (steak with cheese and mushrooms), *filete Chemita* (steak sautéed in butter with onions), and shrimp crepes smothered in a cheese-and-tomato sauce. ✉ *Dalia 1, next to Plaza de Toros Santa María,* ☎ *42/16–02–29 or 42/16–02–01. AE, MC, V.*

$$ ✕ **El Mesón de Chucho el Roto.** Named after Querétaro's version of Robin Hood, this restaurant is located on the quiet Plaza de Armas. It has an interesting menu that highlights regional cooking, including exotic tacos of either steamed goat, shrimp with nopal cactus, or squash blossoms. The *chile en nogada* is a mild pepper stuffed with ground beef and dried fruits and covered in walnut sauce. You can enjoy a variety of breakfast foods here as well, either overlooking the plaza from the café tables outside, indoors, or on the back patio. ✉ *Plaza de Armas,* ☎ *42/12–42–95. AE, MC, V.*

$ ✕ **La Flor de Querétaro.** There should be something for everyone at the plain but pleasant downtown "flower of Querétaro." Groups of the neighborhood's small-business men seem permanently ensconced at their favorite Formica tables. There is a vintage cappuccino machine, an ancient freezer, and best of all, no television: classical music plays unobtrusively in the background. Most of the menu is à la carte: there are good chicken enchiladas *suizas* (with a mild red sauce) and *chiles rellenos* (green pepper stuffed with seasoned ground meat), and those starved for fresh veggies can order a massive side dish of sautéed carrots or greens. ✉ *Av. Juárez Nte. 5,* ☎ *42/12–01–99. No credit cards.*

$ ✕ **La Mariposa.** Celebrating more than 50 years in business, La Mariposa is easily recognized by a wrought-iron butterfly (*mariposa*) over the entrance. This is the place for coffee and cake or a light Mexican lunch: enchiladas, tacos, tamales, and *tortas* (sandwiches). It's a favorite among locals despite its very plain, cafeteria-like appearance; some visitors describe it as "sterile." ✉ *Angela Peralta 7,* ☎ *42/12–11–66 or 42/12–48–49. No credit cards.*

Lodging

Several new hotels in various price ranges have opened in Querétaro in the past 10 years. Lower-priced hotels are located near the main plaza and thus tend to be noisy; restored colonial mansions are on or near the city's many plazas in the heart of town; and deluxe properties are on the outskirts of town.

$$$$ 🏨 **Casa de la Marquesa.** This beautifully restored property, originally
★ an 18th-century private home (☞ Exploring Querétaro, *above*), is perfectly situated in the heart of Querétaro. The central courtyard of the main building is a beautifully decorated sitting room. Each large guest room is furnished differently with antique furniture, tasteful art, parquet floors, and area rugs, and each has a direct-dial telephone. Rooms in the main building are more elegant and expensive than those in La Casa Azul (children under 12 are not admitted in the main building). The property's award-winning restaurant, Comedor de la Marquesa, is elegant and a bit austere. It specializes in such regional rarities as boar, venison, and *escamole* (ant eggs) in season, as well as more traditional international cookery. ✉ *Madero 41, 76000,* ☎ *42/12–00–92,* 🖷 *42/12–00–98. 6 rooms, 19 suites. 2 restaurants, bar, room service, shop. AE, MC, V.*

$$$$ 🏨 **Hacienda Jurica.** A favorite getaway for Mexico City families, this
★ sprawling 16th-century ex-hacienda has nearly 30 acres of grassy sports fields, topiary gardens, a horse stable, and heated pool, and you can play golf at a nearby course. The grounds and courtyards are dotted with antique horse-drawn carriages, and the spacious earth-tone rooms have substantial dark wood furniture, satellite TVs, and minibars. The hacienda is in Jurica, an upscale residential neighborhood 13 km (8 mi) northwest of the city off Highway 57 and is easiest to reach by car. ✉ *Carretera Mexico–San Luis Potosí Km 229 (Box 338), 76100,* ☎ *42/18–00–22 or 01–800/40–111,* 🖷 *42/18–01–36. 176 rooms, 6 suites. Restaurant, bar, minibars, pool, 2 tennis courts, horseback riding, billiards, travel services, free parking. AE, MC, V.*

$$$ 🏨 **Holiday Inn Querétaro.** This gracious, well-run establishment has a lot more charm than others in the chain. Located 3 km (about 2 mi) west of the historic district off Highway 57, the contemporary building incorporates many colonial touches such as stone archways and domed *boveda* (vaulted) ceilings. Sunny, ample rooms are comfortably appointed with rustic Mexican furnishings, cheery pastel bedspreads, satellite TVs, and minibars. ✉ *Av. 5 de Febrero 110, 76000,* ☎ *42/ 16–02–02 or 01–800/00–999; 800/465–4329 in the U.S.,* 🖷 *42/16– 89–02. 171 rooms, 4 suites. 2 restaurants, piano bar, minibars, no-smok-*

ing rooms, pool, exercise room, baby-sitting, travel services, free parking. AE, MC, V.

$$$ ⊞ **Mesón de Santa Rosa.** Located on the quiet Plaza de la Indepen-
★ dencia, this elegant all-suites property was used almost 300 years ago
as a stopover for travelers to the north. Rooms are clustered around
a quiet courtyard, and lace-hung glass doors, warm autumn-color
decor and furnishings, and wood-beamed ceilings maintain the colo-
nial charm. Amenities such as satellite TVs, minibars, and a heated pool
make this lovely hotel comfortable as well. ⊠ *Pasteur Sur 17, 76000,*
☎ *42/24–29–93 or 42/24–26–23,* ⅎ⅍ *42/12–55–22. 21 suites. Restau-
rant, bar, minibars, pool. AE, MC, V.*

$$ ⊞ **Hotel Mirabel.** A favorite among business travelers and conventioneers,
this modern high-rise hums with activity. Its carpeted rooms are insu-
lated and quiet and have cable TVs, telephones, wooden desks, and
air-conditioning. Some double rooms have views of the Alameda Hidalgo park; some singles overlook a soccer stadium. ⊠ *Av. Constituyentes
Oriente 2, 76000,* ☎ *42/14–30–99 or 42/14–34–44,* ⅎ⅍ *42/14–35–85.
166 rooms, 5 suites. Restaurant, bar. AE, MC, V.*

$ ⊞ **Hotel Señorial.** This sprawling four-story property has plain but clean,
large, and modern rooms with telephones and cable TVs. Rooms in
front face a narrow, busy street, but traffic slows in the evening. There
are purified-water dispensers in the hallways. The restaurant serves a
Sunday buffet lunch. ⊠ *Guerrero Nte. 10-A, 76000,* ☎ *42/14–37–00,*
ⅎ⅍ *42/14–19–45. 45 rooms. Restaurant. MC, V.*

Nightlife and the Arts

Band concerts are held in the **Jardín Obregón,** Querétaro's main square,
every Sunday evening at 6. A monthly newspaper called *Tesoro Turístico,* available at the tourist office, provides information about current
festivals, concerts, and other cultural events.

Shopping

A number of stores around town sell **opals** (not milky white, like Australian opals, but beautiful nonetheless) and other locally mined gems.
If you're in the market for loose stones or opal jewelry, do some comparison shopping, as you're apt to find better prices here than in the
United States. Just off Plaza Principal, **El Rubí** (⊠ Av. Madero 3 Pte.,
☎ 42/12–09–84) is a reputable dealer. The owner, Señora Villalon, provides information on the mining, care, and value of opals. The store
is generally open all but Saturday afternoon and Sunday, but she suggests calling ahead, as family obligations sometimes keep her from opening the shop. Another trustworthy gem dealer is **Lapidaria Querétaro**
(⊠ Corregedora 149 Nte., ☎ 42/12–00–30). For high quality crafts,
visit **Fonart** (⊠ Andador 16 de Septiembre 44, ☎ 42/12–26–48), which
has a particularly nice selection of hand-blown glassware.

Side Trips from Querétaro

San Juan del Río and Tequisquiapan are both within an hour's drive
of Querétaro. The highway between Querétaro and San Juan del Río
is paved with factories, and San Juan is a bustling manufacturing center whose only real appeal is the semiprecious gems—especially opals,
topaz, and amethyst—sold here, both loose or in settings. Tequisquiapan, on the other hand, is a tranquil and pretty *pueblo* (town)
drenched in sun and bougainvilleas and flowering trees, and known
as a producer of wicker and other handicrafts. Once frequented by har-
ried Mexican urbanites who came to soak in the area's thermal waters, "Tequis" (as the locals call it) now suffers a dearth of hot water.

A car is the best means to get around. Buses serve both towns from Querétaro, but the trip is longer. If you go to both towns, shop first in San Juan del Río, then head to Tequisquiapan to look around, shop a bit, and perhaps have a meal or a snack. A taxi between the two towns costs about $4.50.

San Juan del Río
51 km (32 mi) southeast of Querétaro via Rte. 57.

Most of San Juan's gem shops are located near the main plaza downtown, and along Avenida Juárez and Calle 16 de Septiembre. **Lapidaria Guerrero** (⊠ Av. Juárez Poniente 4, ☎ 427/2–14–81) has an exceptionally large collection of opal, amethyst, turquoise, and topaz jewelry. The store is open daily 10–2 and 3–7:30.

Tequisquiapan
19 km (12 mi) east of San Juan, off Rte. 120.

This town, which has been famous for centuries for its restorative thermal waters, has in recent years lost much of its thermal flow, reportedly due to the extraordinary water consumption of a paper mill in the area. Many spas struggle on as simple swimming pools/recreation areas, but the main tourist draw has receded with the once-warm waters, and most are deserted midweek, although things liven up on hot weekends. The **tourist office** (⊠ Morelos 7, ☎ 427/3–02–95), open daily 9–7, seems unaware of these geothermal changes and will cheerfully direct you to one or more of the spas, most of which are outside of town.

After lunch or a snack, head to the shops or to the **Mercado de Artesanías** (⊠ Calzado de los Misterios s/n, ☎ No phone), where woven goods, jewelry, and locally made furniture are sold. The **Templo de Santa María de la Asunción**, on the main plaza, was begun in 1874 in the neoclassical style, but not completed until the beginning of the 20th century. Each August the city hosts a weeklong **wine and cheese festival** that includes open-air theater, expositions, and concerts.

Xilitla
Approximately 320 km (198 mi) northeast of Querétaro.

Feel the ordinary world fade away with a trip to the decidedly off-the-beaten-path **Las Pozas** (the pools), the extraordinary sculpture garden of the late, eccentric, English millionaire Edward James (1907–84). Friend of artists Dalí and Picasso and rumored to be the illegitimate son of King Edward VII, James spent 20 years building 36 surrealist concrete structures deep in the waterfall-filled Xilitla jungle. These amazing structures are half-finished fantasy castles, gradually falling to ruin as the rain forest slithers in to claim them. It's like the ultimate child's fort. The castles don't have walls—just vine-entwined pillars, secret passageways, and operatic staircases leading nowhere.

It is a six- to seven-hour thrilling but exhausting mountainous drive to Xilitla, with hairpin turns and spectacular desert, forest, and jungle vistas. Plan on staying at least two nights, as you'll want time to soak up the jungle magic. If you choose not to drive you can take a bus to Ciudad Valles (1½-hour drive from Xilitla) or fly to Tampico (3½-hour drive from Xilitla), and arrange ahead for the **Posada El Castillo** (☞ *below*) staff to pick you up. ⊠ *From Querétaro, head north on Hwy. 57 (Carretera Mexico–San Luis Potosí). Not far from the city, take the* PEÑA DE BERNAL *turnoff, marked on a bridge overpass and also on a smaller sign at the Cadareyta exit. Continue north through Bernal, after which the road will join Hwy. 120. Take 120 through Jalpan then on to Xilitla, just across the border in the state of San Luis*

*Potosí. The turnoff to Las Pozas is just beyond Xilitla on the left after
passing a small bridge.* 🏛 *$1.50.* ☉ *Daily dawn–dusk.*

LODGING

$$ 🏨 **Posada El Castillo.** When he wasn't living in his jungle hut, James
stayed in town (a 10-minute drive away) in a whimsical house that feels
like an extension of the garden structures—except that it has walls. That
house, El Castillo (the castle), is now a quirky inn run by Lenore and
Avery Danziger, who have made an award-winning documentary film
about James that they happily screen for guests. Rooms are adorned
with simple wooden furnishings and freshly cut wild orchids; the best
rooms have huge Gothic windows and panoramic mountain views. You
can arrange to have meals here; otherwise there are few dining options
in the area. ✉ *Ocampo 105, Xilitla, San Luis Potosí 79900,* ☎ *136/
5–00–38,* FAX *136/5–00–55. 7 rooms. Pool, shop. No credit cards.*

Querétaro A to Z

Arriving and Departing

BY BUS

Daily buses run direct between Mexico City's Central del Norte (North
Bus Station) and Querétaro's Central de Autobuses. Major lines—in-
cluding **Flecha Amarilla** ☎ (42/11–40–01), **Omnibus de México** ☎ (42/
29–00–29 or 42/29–03–29), **ETN** (☎ 42/29–00–78, 42/29–00–77, or
42/29–00–19), and **Futura** (☎ 42/29–00–22) —have frequent service;
travel time is about three hours. Buses also leave several times a day
for Guanajuato, San Miguel de Allende, and Morelia.

BY CAR

Querétaro is 220 km (136 mi) northwest of Mexico City, a three-hour
drive on Route 57.

Getting Around

Most of Querétaro's historic sites are within walking distance of one
another in the downtown district and can be reached by a series of walk-
ways that are closed to automobile traffic most of the day. If you want
to venture farther afield, you will find that buses and taxis run frequently
along the main streets and are inexpensive.

Contacts and Resources

CAR RENTAL

Budget (✉ Av. Constituyentes Oriente 73, ☎ 42/13–44–98, FAX 42/13–
44–38). **National** (✉ Calle 13 de Septiembre 34, ☎ 42/16–35–44, FAX
42/16–52–40).

EMERGENCIES

Police (☎ 42/20–83–83 or 42/20–85–03). **Ambulance–Red Cross** (☎
42/29–05–45 or 42/29–06–65). **Fire Department** (☎ 42/12–39–39).
Green Angels (☎ 42/13–84–24).

Hospital. Sanatorio Alcocer Pozo (✉ Calle Reforma 23, ☎ 42/12–01–
49 or 42/12–17–87).

GUIDED TOURS

The tourist office conducts hour-long trolley tours of the city's historic
landmarks at 9, 10, and 11 AM and at 4, 5, and 6 PM Tuesday–Sunday.
To arrange a city tour in English, call the office (☞ Visitor Informa-
tion, *below*)—one day in advance if possible. The cost is about $1.50.

MONEY EXCHANGE

Casa de Cambio Acueducto (✉ Av. Juárez Sur 58, ☎ 42/12–93–04) is
open weekdays 9–2 and 4–6, Saturday 9–1.

TRAVEL AGENCY
Turismo Beverly (⊠ Av. Tecnologia 118, ☎ 42/16–15–00 or 42/16–12–60, FAX 42/16–85–24).

VISITOR INFORMATION
Dirección de Turismo del Estado (⊠ Plaza de la Independencia at Pasteur 4 Nte., ☎ 42/12–14–12 or 42/12–09–07, FAX 42/12–10–04) is open Monday–Saturday 8–8, Sunday 9–8.

MORELIA

With its long, wide boulevards and earth-tone colonial mansions, Morelia is the gracious capital of the state of Michoacán. Founded in 1541 as Valladolid (after the Spanish city), it changed its name in 1828 to honor José María Morelos, the town's most famous son. The legendary mule skinner–turned–priest took up the battle for independence after its early leaders were executed in 1811.

Morelos began with an ill-equipped army of 25 but soon organized a contingent of 9,000 that nearly gained control of the country. Though he was defeated and executed in 1815, he left behind a long-standing reformist legacy that called for universal suffrage, racial equality, and the demise of the hacienda system. The city today still pays tribute to Morelos—his former home has been turned into a museum, and his birthplace is now a library.

Morelianos love music, and several festivals each year are designed to indulge them. Each year in May the city celebrates the **International Organ Festival** in the cathedral, giving voice to its outstanding 4,600-pipe organ. The last two weeks in July are given to the **Festival International de Música,** featuring baroque and chamber music, with orchestras participating from throughout Mexico.

Morelia has the delicious distinction of being the candy capital of Mexico. So strong is the sweet-eating tradition that the city has a **Mercado de Dulces**—a sweets market. Morelia is also the home of writers, artists, philosophers, and poets, as well as American retirees.

Exploring Morelia

To explore Morelia and its surrounding hillside neighborhoods thoroughly would take some time. However, if you stroll through the historic plazas and frequent the cafés (as many locals do), you will begin to feel the city's vitality. Although the vehicle and sidewalk traffic can get a little heavy at times, Morelia is a pedestrian-friendly city.

A Good Walk
Begin your walk in Morelia's tree-lined downtown **Plaza de Armas** ⑩, on the east side of which is the city's famed **Catedral** ㊶. As you leave the cathedral, cross Avenida Madero to the **Palacio de Gobierno** ㊷, a former seminary. From the palace it's four blocks east along Avenida Madero to Calle de Belisario Domínguez. Make a right and walk one block south to the Church of San Francisco. To the rear of the church, in the former convent of San Francisco, is the entrance to the **Casa de las Artesanías del Estado de Michoacán** ㊸, a virtual cornucopia of crafts from around the state.

Walk two blocks south on Calle Vasco de Quiroga, a street lined with vendors, until you come to Calle del Soto Saldaña. Head west another two blocks to Avenida Morelos Sur. The corner building on the right is the **Casa Museo de Morelos** ㊹, which displays memorabilia of the independence leader. It's one block north from the museum to Calle

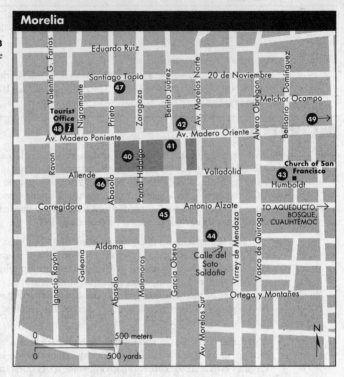

Antonio Alzate and then one block west (where the street name changes
to Calle Corregidora) to Calle García Obeso. On this corner stands
the **Museo Casa Natal de Morelos** ④⑤, Morelos's birthplace. Continue
west on Calle Corregidora until you reach Calle Abasolo. On Calle Allende, one block to the north, you'll find the **Museo Regional Michoacano** ④⑥.

After leaving the museum take Calle Abasolo back to the plaza; 2½
blocks to the north, you'll see the **Museo del Estado** ④⑦ on the right side
of the street (which changes to Calle Guillermo Prieto at Avenida
Madero). Return to Avenida Madero, and then go two blocks to the
right to the corner of the Valentín Gómez Farias, to the **Mercado de
Dulces** ④⑧.

For a longer stroll, take Avenida Madero east a dozen blocks or so to
where it forks. Stay to the right; you'll see the **Fountain of the Taras-
cans** on a traffic island to your left. Just past the fountain, Morelia's
mile-long **aqueduct** begins. This 1875 structure, which consists of 253
arches, once carried the city's main source of drinking water. It's particularly beautiful at night when its arches—some rising to 30 ft—are
illuminated. Two blocks farther along (Madero is now called Avenida
Acueducto) is the entrance to **Bosque Cuauhtémoc,** Morelia's largest
park. If you happen by during the week, you may encounter university students studying (or lounging) beneath the palms and evergreens.
On weekends, especially Sunday, families on outings take over. Two
blocks past the park entrance, you'll see the **Museo de Arte Contemporáneo** ④⑨, also on the right side of the street.

Sights to See

③ **Casa de las Artesanías del Estado de Michoacán.** In the 16th century,
Vasco de Quiroga, the bishop of Michoacán, helped the Purépecha Indians develop artistic specialties so they could be self-supporting. At

this two-story museum and store, you can see the work that the Purépechas still produce: copper goods from Santa Clara del Cobre, lacquerware from Uruapan, straw items and pottery from Pátzcuaro, guitars from Paracho, fanciful ceramic devil figures from Ocumicho. At the **Museo Michoacana de las Artesanías** in the two main floors around the courtyard, some of these items are showcased behind glass while artists demonstrate how they are made. There is a gift shop to the right of the museum entrance. ⊠ *Calle Fray Juan de San Miguel s/n,* ☎ *Museum 43/12–24–86; store 43/12–12–48.* ☞ *Free.* ☉ *Daily 9–3 and 5–7:30.*

㊹ Casa Museo de Morelos. What is now a two-story museum was acquired in 1801 by the Mexican independence leader and served as home to generations of the Morelos family until 1934. Owned by the Mexican government, it contains family portraits (including one of Morelos's mother, who, he said, "gave him constant spirit and strength"), a copy of Morelos's birth certificate, various artifacts from the independence movement (such as a camp bed used by Ignacio Allende), and the blindfold Morelos wore for his execution. The excellent free tour is in Spanish only. ⊠ *Av. Morelos Sur 323,* ☎ *43/13–26–51.* ☞ *About $1.50.* ☉ *Daily 9–3 and 5–7.*

㊸ Catedral. Morelia's cathedral is a majestic structure built between 1640 and 1744. It is known throughout Mexico for its 200-ft Baroque towers, among the tallest in the land, and for its 4,600-pipe organ, one of the finest in the world. The organ on the balcony at the back of the cathedral is the vehicle for the international organ festival held here each May. ⊠ *Av. Madero between Plaza de Armas and Av. Morelos.*

㊽ Mercado de Dulces. If you have a sweet tooth, don't miss Morelia's famous candy market, just behind the tourist office. All sorts of local sweets are for sale, such as *ate* (a candied fruit) and *cajeta* (heavenly caramel sauce made from goat's milk). ⊠ *Av. Madero Poniente and Valentín Gómez Farías.* ☉ *Daily 10–9.*

㊺ Museo Casa Natal de Morelos. Morelos's birthplace is now a library and national monument housing mostly literature and history books (as well as two murals by Moreliano Alfredo Zalce). Be sure to visit the courtyard in back: it's a tranquil square, adjacent to the Church of San Agustín, with rosebushes, evergreens, and wild poinsettias; a marker and an eternal flame honor the fallen hero. ⊠ *Calle Corregidora 113,* ☎ *43/12–27–93.* ☞ *Free.* ☉ *Weekdays 9–2 and 4–8, Sat. 9:30–2, Sun. 9–2.*

㊾ Museo de Arte Contemporáneo. The works of contemporary Mexican and international artists are on view at this well-lighted museum near the Bosque Cuauhtémoc. ⊠ *Av. Acueducto 18,* ☎ *43/12–54–04.* ☞ *Free.* ☉ *Tues.–Sun. 10–2 and 4–8.*

㊼ Museo del Estado. Just across from a small plaza with statues of Bishop Vasco de Quiroga and Spanish writer Miguel de Cervantes, this history museum is located in a stately mansion that was once the home of the wife of Augustín de Iturbide, Mexico's only native-born emperor. A highlight of the collection is a complete Morelia pharmacy dating from 1868. ⊠ *Guillermo Prieto 176,* ☎ *43/13–06–29.* ☞ *Free.* ☉ *Weekdays 9–2 and 4–8, weekends 9–2 and 4–7.*

㊻ Museo Regional Michoacano. An 18th-century former palace, the museum traces the history of Mexico from its pre-Hispanic days through the Cardenista period, which ended in 1940. President Lázaro Cárdenas, a native of Michoacán, was one of Mexico's most popular leaders because of his nationalization of the oil industry and his support of other populist reforms. The ground floor contains an art gallery, plus archaeological exhibits from Michoacán. Upstairs is an assortment of colonial objects, including furniture, weapons, and religious paintings. ⊠ *Calle Allende 305,* ☎ *43/12–04–07.* ⊠ *About $2; free Sun.* ☺ *Tues.–Sat. 9–7, Sun. 9–2.*

NEED A
BREAK? When you've finished your tour of the Museo Michoacana, walk across the street to the colonial, stone *portales* (arcades). The portales on one side of the square contain popular sidewalk cafés. For a sandwich or a fruit cocktail, or a good selection of juices, coffees, and teas, try **Café Catedral** (⊠ Portal Hidalgo 213, ☎ 43/12–32–89). No one will mind if you linger over a book or newspaper for the better part of an hour sipping an excellent café americano—in fact, you might have to wait that long just to get the bill.

㊷ **Palacio de Gobierno.** This former Tridentine seminary, built in 1770, has had such notable graduates as independence hero José María Morelos, social reformer Melchor Ocampo, and the first emperor of Mexico, Agustín de Iturbide. Striking murals decorate the stairway and second floor. Painted by local artist Alfredo Zalce in the early 1960s, they depict dramatic, often bloody scenes from Mexico's history. From the second floor you can catch a glimpse of the cathedral spires across the way. ⊠ *Av. Madero 63,* ☎ *43/12–78–72.* ⊠ *Free.* ☺ *Weekdays 9–3 and 6–9.*

㊵ **Plaza de Armas.** During the War of Independence, several rebel priests were brutally murdered on this site, and the plaza, known as Plaza de los Mártires, is named after them. Today, however, the square belies its violent past: sweethearts stroll along the tree-lined walks, vendors sell mounds of roasted peanuts, placards announce cultural events, and lively recorded music blasts from a silver-domed bandshell. ⊠ *Bounded on the north by Av. Madero, on the south by Calle Allende, on the west by Calle Abasolo, and on the east by the cathedral.*

Dining

Some of Michoacán's tastiest dishes—Lake Pátzcuaro whitefish, tomato-based Tarascan soup, corn products such as *huchepos* (sweet tamales) and *corundas* (savory triangular tamales), and game (rabbit and quail)—are served at Morelia restaurants. Traditional chicken and beef fare are also available, as well as international dishes. As a rule, more upscale restaurants are in hotels near the plaza and on the outskirts of town.

$$$ ✕ **Fonda Las Mercedes.** This delightful restaurant's arty, modern fur-
★ nishings somehow fit perfectly in the plant-filled stone patio of this restored colonial mansion. The ambience is intimate yet airy, with a lovely soft natural light during the day. The inside dining room, which is equally pleasant, may be cozier on chilly days or evenings. Offerings from the eclectic menu include lots of soups and six kinds of crepes. If you dare, try the sinfully rich pasta with pistachios and pine nuts in cream sauce. ⊠ *León Guzmán 47,* ☎ *43/12–61–13. AE, MC, V. No dinner Sun.*

$$ ✕ **Boca del Río.** Large picture windows opening onto a busy intersection provide ample light for this cheerful yet cafeteria-like restaurant, which claims to have fresh fish and seafood trucked in daily from Sinaloa and Veracruz. There are light snacks such as *coctel de camarones* (shrimp cocktail) or the hands-on sopa de mariscos, along with heartier fare, such as the *jaiba rellena* (crabs stuffed with mushrooms and cheese and liberally seasoned with garlic). Beef and chicken dishes and a vegetarian sandwich are also served. After lunch, head for dessert to the sprawling Mercado de Dulces, just across the street. ⊠ *Valentín Gómez Farías 185,* ☎ *43/12–99–74. AE, MC, V.*

$$ ✕ **Cenaduría Lupita II.** This restaurant is outside the city center in the
★ financial district near the Gigante supermarket and cinema. Although
the name labels it a dinner spot (*cena* means dinner), enormous buf-
fets are served for all three meals. The lunch buffet offers unlimited
access to salads, soup, meats, desserts, coffee, juices, and beer or
tequila. Dinner is built around *antojitos* (appetizers), but this is still a
huge amount and assortment of foods. Eating here is a great way to
try different regional specialties and find your favorites. ⊠ *Av. Cameli-
nas 3100, Col. Jardines del Rincón,* ☎ *43/24–40–67. AE, MC, V.*

$ ✕ **Taquería Pioneros.** There's a reason the tables are full at lunch at
★ this positively plain taco shop: it has absolutely delicious grilled meats,
served Michoacán style with salsas and mountains of fresh, hot tor-
tillas made on site. The *pionero* (beef, ham, bacon, onions, and cheese,
all grilled) is the only style served in a half portion, which is plenty for
most appetites. Quesadillas, *sincronizadas* (quesadillas with ham), and
beans are also served, as is beer and soda. ⊠ *A. Serdán 7 at Ocampo,*
☎ *No phone. No credit cards.*

Lodging

Morelia offers a number of pleasant colonial-style hotels both in the
downtown and outlying areas. Generally, the cheapest properties are
near the bus station, moderately priced selections are clustered around
the plaza (or on nearby side streets), and deluxe resort hotels are in or
near the Santa María hills.

$$$$ 🏨 **Villa Montaña.** French count Philippe de Reiset has fitted this villa with
★ all the trappings of a wealthy Mexican estate. High above Morelia in
the Santa María hills, its five impeccably groomed acres are dotted with
a pool, tennis court, and stone sculpture. Each individually decorated
unit has at least one piece of antique furniture, and most have a fireplace
and private patio. The hotel's renowned restaurant serves North Amer-
ican, French, and Mexican cuisine, and huge windows afford a marvelous
view of Morelia, especially at night. Children under eight are discour-
aged from dining in the restaurant, but the hotel can provide baby-sit-
ters if requested a day in advance. ⊠ *Calle Patzimba 201, 58000,* ☎ *43/
14–02–31 or 43/14–01–79; 800/525–4800 in the U.S.,* FAX *43/15–14–23.
17 rooms, 26 suites. Restaurant, piano bar, in-room safes, pool, tennis
court, shop, baby-sitting, laundry service, free parking. AE, MC, V.*

$$ 🏨 **Hotel Catedral.** Located in a restored colonial mansion, this three-
story property began operating as a hotel some 30 years ago. Its mod-
ern rooms are clustered around a skylighted courtyard; eight of them
overlook the main plaza and cathedral on Avenida Madero. Interior
quarters have less dramatic views but are less noisy. All rooms have
dark wood furnishings, telephones, and cable TVs. The rather soft beds
have dark blue flowered spreads. Rates include a complimentary Continental breakfast. ⊠ *Calle Zaragoza 37, 58000,* ☎ *43/13–07–83 or
43/13–04–67,* FAX *43/13–04–06. 43 rooms, 2 suites. Restaurant, bar,
baby-sitting, dry cleaning. AE, MC, V.*

$$ 🏨 **Hotel Mansión Acueducto.** An elaborate wood and wrought-iron stair-
case leads from the elegant lobby to more modest quarters upstairs.
Rooms have dark, colonial-style furniture, telephones, and color cable
TVs. Older rooms overlook the aqueduct and nearby park. Rooms in
the motel-like wing have views of the garden, pool, and surrounding
city. Student groups at times book the entire property. ⊠ *Av. Acueducto
25, 58000,* ☎ *43/12–33–01,* FAX *43/12–20–20. 36 rooms, 1 suite.
Restaurant, bar, pool, free parking. AE, MC, V.*

$$ 🏨 **Hotel Posada de la Soledad.** Set in a restored private mansion built
★ in the late 17th century, the Posada de la Soledad is conveniently lo-
cated one block from the Plaza de Armas. Rooms vary in size, deco-

ration, amenities, and price. The rooms in the original section surround an elegant patio with a large fountain and massive bougainvilleas, where birds twitter at dusk. Rooms in a newer section are smaller and plainly furnished but are quiet and have cable TVs. Rooms on Calle Ocampo have fuzzy local TV only, and loud traffic noise from the street. If you're not impressed with the room you are shown, ask to see another. ⊠ *Ignacio Zaragoza 90, 58000,* ☎ *43/12–18–88,* FAX *43/12–21–11. 48 rooms, 9 suites. Restaurant, bar. AE, MC, V.*

\$\$ 🏨 **Hotel Virrey de Mendoza.** Built in 1565 to house a Spanish noble-
★ man, this downtown hotel still radiates plenty of Old World atmosphere. The elegant lobby lounge is fitted with an enormous stone fireplace and cushy black leather couches. Guest rooms have dark colonial-style furnishings, lace curtains, soaring ceilings, and creaking hardwood floors, as well as cable TVs and telephones. The bathrooms have porcelain tubs and positively gleaming checkerboard-patterned black and white tile work. ⊠ *Av. Madero Pte. 310, 58000,* ☎ *43/12–06–33 or 43/12–49–40,* FAX *43/12–67–19. 48 rooms, 9 suites. Restaurant, bar, coffee shop, laundry service, free parking. AE, MC, V.*

\$ 🏨 **Hotel Valladolid.** Located right on the plaza and a sister to the slightly more impressive Hotel Catedral, the Valladolid has plain but clean rooms with brick floors and striped bedspreads. Twenty of the rooms have cable TV (none have phones), and the price includes a Continental breakfast in the hotel's restaurant, right across from the Plaza de Armas. ⊠ *Portal Hidalgo 245, 58000,* ☎ *43/12–00–27 or 43/12–46–63,* FAX *43/13–04–06. 25 rooms. Restaurant. AE, MC, V.*

Nightlife and the Arts

Morelia has two lively folk music clubs, both in beautiful colonial court-yards downtown. Named after Mexican Revolutionary hero General Emiliano Zapata's army, **Bola Suriana** (⊠ Allende 355, ☎ 43/12–41–41) presents traditional Mexican music Tuesday–Saturday from 9 PM to 1 AM. **Colibri** (⊠ Galeana 36, ☎ 43/12–22–61) has folk music from throughout Latin America every night from 9 PM to 1 AM.

Side Trip to Santuario de Mariposas el Rosario

Approximately 115 km (71 mi) east of Morelia.

Every year 100 million monarch butterflies migrate from the United States and Canada to winter in the easternmost part of Michoacán, near the border of México state. A visit to the **Santuario de Mariposas el Rosario** (El Rosario Monarch Butterfly Sanctuary) between early November and early March is an awesome sensory experience. Caked with orange and black butterflies, the pine forest looks like it's on fire. Listen closely and you'll hear the rustle of nearly a billion wings beating. The hike to the groves is a steep climb and the high altitude (10,400 ft) will require that you take it slowly.

This day trip takes about 10 hours, but it's well worth the effort. If you choose not to drive the rough roads, catch a tour with one of the travel agents in Morelia (☞ Guided Tours, *below*). ⊠ *Hwy. 15 east to Zitácuaro, then take marked but unnumbered road north to Angangueo, and on to sanctuary entrance.* 🎫 *$3 (plus tip for guide).* ☉ *Daily 10–5.*

Morelia A to Z

Arriving and Departing
BY BUS

Direct bus service is available daily between the Terminal Poniente (West Terminal, commonly referred to as the Observatorio) in Mexico City and Morelia's **Central de Autobuses** (☎ 43/12–56–04). Several bus lines have frequent service; the most direct trip ($12.50) takes four hours on either **ETN** (☎ 43/13–74–40 or 43/13–41–37) or **Herradura de Plata** (☎ 43/12–29–88). Buses leave every hour or two around the clock.

BY CAR

The drive from Mexico City to Morelia (302 km, or 187 mi) on the toll road through Toluca, Atlacamulco, Contepec, and Maravatio takes about four hours.

BY PLANE

There are daily flights between Francisco Mujica International Airport, 24 km (15 mi) north of Morelia, and Mexico City's International Airport on **Aeroméxico** (☎ 43/24–24–24). **Mexicana** (☎ 43/24–38–08 or 43/24–38–18) has direct flights to/from Los Angeles, San Francisco, and Chicago; **Taesa** (☎ 43/13–40–50 or 43/13–42–10) serves Oakland and Chicago. Flights are subject to cancellation, and flight times change often and must be confirmed one day in advance. The 45-minute taxi ride from the airport to Morelia costs about $17.

Getting Around

As in many heartland cities, Morelia's major sights are near the center of town and easy to get to on foot. Street names in Morelia change frequently, especially on either side of Avenida Madero, the city's main east–west artery. Taxis in Morelia can be hailed on the street or found near the main plaza. Buses run the length of Avenida Madero.

Contacts and Resources

CAR RENTAL

Budget. (✉ Francisco Mujica International Airport, ☎ 43/13–33–99).

EMERGENCIES

Police (☎ 43/12–22–22). **Ambulance–Red Cross** (Cruz Roja, ☎ 43/14–51–51). **Hospital de la Cruz Roja** (☎ 43/14–50–25). **Consumer Protection Office** (☎ 43/12–40–49). **Fire Department** (☎ 43/12–12–35). **Hospital Memorial** (☎ 43/15–10–47 or 43/15–10–99). **Green Angels** (☎ 43/12–77–77).

GUIDED TOURS

The following operators have tours of Morelia and the butterfly sanctuary: **Ayangupani** (✉ contact through the Villa Montaña front desk, Calle Patzimba 201, ☎ 43/11–48–88 cellular, ☎ FAX 43/15–40–45), **Explora Viajes** (✉ Av. Madero Oriente 493B, ☎ 43/12–77–66, FAX 42/12–76–60), and **Morelia Operadores de Viajes** (✉ Gómez Farías 131, ☎ 43/12–87–23 or 43/12–87–47, FAX 43/12–95–91).

MONEY EXCHANGES

Casa Cambio Valladolid (✉ Portal Matamoros 86, ☎ 43/12–85–86) is open weekdays 9–6, Saturday 9–1:30.

TRAVEL AGENCIES

Gran Turismo (✉ Edificio Ejecutivo Camelinas, Av. Camelinas 3233, Int. 102–103, ☎ 43/24–04–84, FAX 43/24–04–95) is the American Express representative. **Servicios Establecidos Para el Turismo** (✉ Portal Hidalgo 229, ☎ 43/12–90–02 or 43/13–19–02, FAX 43/12–36–64) makes typical travel arrangements.

VISITOR INFORMATION

Secretaría Estatal de Turismo (✉ Palacio Clavijero, Calle Nigromante 79, ☎ 43/13–26–54, 43/12–80–81, or 01–800/45–023, FAX 43/12–98–16) is open weekdays 8:30 AM–8 PM, weekends 9–7.

PÁTZCUARO

Pátzcuaro, the 16th-century capital of Michoacán, exists in a time warp. A bit more than an hour by car from Morelia, this beautiful lakeside community set at 7,250 ft in the Sierra Madre is home to the Purépecha Indians, who fish, farm, and ply their crafts as they have for centuries. Women wrapped tightly in their striped wool *rebozos* (shawls) hurry to market in the chilly morning air. Men in traditional straw hats wheel overburdened carts down crooked, dusty backstreets.

The architecture, too, has remained largely unchanged over the years. In the 16th century, under kindly Bishop Vasco de Quiroga, Pátzcuaro underwent a building boom. After he died in 1565, the state capital was moved to Morelia, and the town became a cultural (and architectural) backwater for hundreds of years. These days 16th-century mansions surround the downtown plazas; one-story whitewashed houses with sloping red tile roofs line the side streets and hills.

Despite the altitude, the weather in Pátzcuaro is temperate year-round. (Autumn and winter nights, however, are cold; sweaters and jackets are a must.) On November 1—the night preceding the Day of the Dead—the town is inundated with tourists en route to **Janítzio**, an island in Lake Pátzcuaro, where one of the most elaborate graveyard ceremonies in all of Mexico takes place. Go to the island of **Yunuen** for an authentic glimpse of daily island life, and you can stay overnight. At numerous small towns around the lake you can buy craft items from their makers, in the process absorbing a bit of small-town rural Mexico. These towns are just beginning to attract tourism, and many new dining and lodging venues are opening up outside of Pátzcuaro. The **Delegación de Turismo** can share suggestions for adventures outside Pátzcuaro, as can expert local tour guide **Marilyn Mayo** (☞ Guided Tours *in* Pátzcuaro A to Z, *below*).

Exploring Pátzcuaro

Most of Pátzcuaro's sights can be seen in a few hours, but the town and outlying areas deserve to be explored at a leisurely pace. There can be some traffic in the Plaza Bocanegra and on the main road coming into town, but elsewhere it is blissfully quiet.

A Good Walk

Start your stroll at the **tourist office** (Plaza Vasco de Quiroga 50A), where you can pick up maps and brochures. Walk across the large **Plaza Vasco de Quiroga** ㊿ to the east side of the square and turn right on Calle Dr. José María Coss; in less than a block you'll see a long cobblestone walkway leading to **La Casa de los 11 Patios** �51, a former convent now housing a number of crafts shops. As you leave the complex, continue up a stone walkway to Calle Lerín. To the north (past Calle Portugal) is the **Templo de la Compañia** �52, the state's first cathedral. After visiting the church, continue another half block along Calle Lerín to the **Museo de Artes Populares** �53 on your right.

Directly down Calle Lerín and across a cobblestone courtyard is **La Basílica de Nuestra Señora de la Salud** �54. Walk downhill from the basilica (take Buenavista to Libertad and turn left) to reach the **Biblioteca Pública Gertrudis Bocanegra** �55. For a nice detour from the library, continue for a half block to the large outdoor **mercado** sprawled along Calle Libertad and its side streets. At times the road is so crowded with people and their wares—fruit, vegetables, beans, rice, herbs, and other necessities of daily life—that it is difficult to walk. If you press on for about a block, you'll see an indoor market to your left, filled with more produce, large hanging slabs of meat, hot food, and a variety of cheap trinkets. When

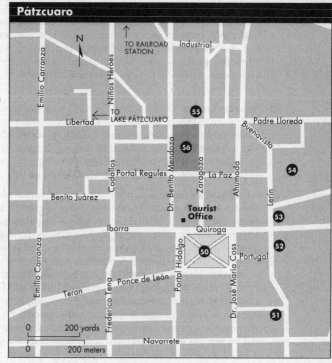

you're done with your market tour, retrace your steps down Calle Libertad. Across the street from the library, you can rest at **Plaza Bocanegra** ⑤⑥, just one block north of your starting point, Plaza Vasco de Quiroga.

Sights to See

⑤⑤ **Biblioteca Pública Gertrudis Bocanegra.** In the back of this library, a vast mural painted by Juan O'Gorman in 1942 depicts in great detail the history of the region and of the Purépecha people. Look at the bottom right of the mural to see Gertrudis Bocanegra, a local heroine who was shot in 1814 for refusing to divulge the revolutionaries' secrets to the Spaniards. ⊠ *North side of Plaza Bocanegra.* ☉ *Weekdays 9–7.*

⑤④ **La Basílica de Nuestra Señora de la Salud** (Basilica of our Lady of Health). The church was begun in 1554 by Vasco de Quiroga, and throughout the centuries others—undaunted by earthquakes and fires—took up the cause and constructed a church in honor of the Virgin of Health. Near the main altar is a statue of the Virgin made of derivatives of cornstalks and orchids. Several masses are still held here daily; the earliest begins shortly after dawn. Out front, Purépecha women sell hot tortillas, herbal mixtures for teas, and religious objects. You can glimpse Lake Pátzcuaro in the distance from here. ⊠ *Calle Lerín s/n, near Calle Cerrato.*

⑤① **La Casa de los 11 Patios.** An 18th-century convent, 11 Patios houses a number of high-quality shops featuring Purépecha handiwork. As you meander through the shops and courtyards, you'll encounter weavers producing large bolts of cloth, artists trimming black lacquerware with gold, and seamstresses embroidering blouses. If you plan to shop in Pátzcuaro, this is a good place to start. You can view the selection of regional goods and begin to compare prices. ⊠ *Calle Madrigal de las Altas Torres, s/n.* ☉ *Daily 10–2 and 4–8.*

☺ Museo de Artes Populares. Home to the Colegio de San Nicolás Obispo in the 16th century, the building today houses displays of colonial and contemporary crafts, such as ceramics, masks, lacquerware, paintings, and ex-votos in its many rooms. Behind this building is a *troje* (traditional Purépecha wooden house) braced atop a stone platform. ⊠ *Calle Lerín,* ☎ *434/2–10–29.* ☑ *About $2; free Sun.* ☉ *Tues.–Sat. 9–7, Sun. 9–2:30.*

☺ Plaza Bocanegra. The smaller of the city's two squares (it's also called Plaza Chica), this is the center of Pátzcuaro's commercial life. Bootblacks, pushcart vendors, and bus and taxi stands are all in this plaza, which is embellished by a statue of the local heroine. ⊠ *Bounded by Av. Libertad on the north, Portal Regules on the south, Dr. Benito Mendoza on the west, and Calle Zaragoza on the east.*

☺ Plaza Vasco de Quiroga. A tranquil courtyard surrounded by ash and pine trees and 16th-century mansions (since converted into hotels and shops), the larger of the two downtown plazas commemorates the bishop who restored dignity to the Purépecha people. During the Spanish conquest, Nuño de Guzmán, a lieutenant in Hernán Cortés's army, committed atrocities on the local population in his efforts to conquer western Mexico. He was eventually arrested by the Spanish authorities, and in 1537 Vasco de Quiroga was appointed bishop of Michoacán. Attempting to regain the trust of the indigenous people, he established a number of model villages in the area and promoted the development of artesanía commerce among the Purépechas. Quiroga died in 1565, and his remains were consecrated in the **Basílica de Nuestra Señora de la Salud** (☞ *above*). ⊠ *Bounded by Calle Quiroga on the north, Av. Ponce de León on the south, Portal Hidalgo on the west, and Dr. José María Coss on the east.*

<table>
<tr><td>NEED A
BREAK?</td><td>Before heading to Lake Pátzcuaro, sit in Plaza Vasco de Quiroga for a moment and enjoy a rich Michoacán ice cream for sale under the portals on the west side of the plaza. Or sip a warming Doña Paca Cappuccino spiked with rompompe (egg liqueur) at the sidewalk café in front of Mansíon Iturbe (☞ Lodging, below). Then grab a taxi or the San Bartolo–Lago bus to the embarcadero (dock).</td></tr>
</table>

☺ Templo de la Compañía. Michoacán's first cathedral was begun in 1540 by order of Vasco de Quiroga and completed in 1546. When the state capital was moved to Morelia some 20 years later, the church was taken over by the Jesuits. Today it remains much as it was in the 16th century. Moss has grown over the crumbling stone steps outside; the dank interior is planked with thick wood floors and lined with bare wood benches. ⊠ *Calle Lerín s/n, near Calle Alcantaría.*

<table>
<tr><td>OFF THE
BEATEN PATH</td><td>LAKE PÁTZCUARO – Just a 10-minute taxi ride from downtown are the tranquil shores of Lake Pátzcuaro. There are a few lakeside restaurants here that serve fresh whitefish and other local catches. Amble along the dock or peek into the waterfront crafts shops. A boat trip to Janítzio (the largest of Lake Pátzcuaro's five islands), or to tiny Yunuen, is recommended. Wooden launches, with room for 25 people, depart for Janítzio and the other islands daily from 9 to 6. Purchase round-trip tickets for $3 at a dockside office (where prices are controlled by the tourist department). The ride to Janítzio takes about 30 minutes and is particularly beautiful in late afternoon, when the sun is low in the sky. Once you're out on the lake, fishermen with butterfly nets may approach your boat. The nets are no longer used for fishing, but for a small donation these locals will let you take their picture.</td></tr>
</table>

On most days (November 1 being the exception), Janítzio is a quiet albeit touristy island inhabited by Purépecha Indians. It is crowned by a huge statue of independence hero José María Morelos, which is accessible by a cobblestone stairway. Though the road twists past many souvenir stands as it ascends, don't be discouraged. The view from the summit—of the lake, the town, and the surrounding hills—is well worth the climb. Inside the statue are some remarkable murals that spiral up from the base to the tip of the monument.

Although Janítzio has succumbed to tourism, the small island of Yunuen is just beginning to attract visitors. This tranquil town has just 21 families, and provides a more accurate picture of island life than does Janítizio. You can get a boat to here from the ferry landing, or arrange to stay overnight in simple yet clean and new cabins recently opened for visitors. The office of tourism will gladly provide information.

Dining

Many restaurants in Pátzcuaro specialize in seafood. In addition to whitefish, look for *trucha* (trout) and *charales* and *boquerones* (two small, locally caught fish served as appetizers). Purépecha dishes, such as sopa tarasca, are also common. As a rule, restaurants are located around the two plazas and in hotels. Since the large meal is served at midday, many dining establishments are shuttered by 9.

Note: Many Pátzcuaro restaurants and hotels do not accept traveler's checks, though some will take major credit cards.

$$$ ✕ **El Primer Piso.** This second-floor restaurant overlooks the plaza, and
★ on warm nights you can watch the comings and goings from a balcony table. There's plenty to look at inside, as well, for the restaurant doubles as an art gallery and its walls are covered with original prints or paintings. The eclectic menu provides a break from the rather monotonous Pátzcuaro fare: try the pear salad with goat cheese, walnuts, and watercress, or the white chocolate mousse with blackberries and melon cream. ⊠ *Plaza Vasco de Quiroga 29,* ☎ *434/2–01–22. AE. Closed Tues.*

$$ ✕ **El Patio.** Though this low-key restaurant features mouthwatering whitefish platters (including salsa, vegetables, and french fries), it's possible to duck in at midday for just a strong cappuccino or glass of Mexican wine. (There are several varieties of wine; waiters can help you choose one.) For a late-afternoon snack, a plate of quesadillas with a side order of guacamole is highly recommended, and the sopa tarasca is superb. ⊠ *Plaza Vasco de Quiroga 19,* ☎ *434/2–04–84. MC, V.*

$ ✕ **Restaurante Gran Hotel.** Though this one-room restaurant is connected to the Gran Hotel, it is independently owned and attracts a mix of locals and tourists to its midday meal. The tables outside on the sidewalk are a fun spot to take in the Plaza Chica hubbub. The food is good and wholesome. Specialties include lightly breaded whitefish, chicken with mole sauce, and Tarascan soup. ⊠ *Portal Regules 6,* ☎ *434/2–04–43. No credit cards.*

Lodging

Though Pátzcuaro has no deluxe hotels, there are an ample number of clean, moderately priced properties. Most are on or within a few blocks of the Plaza Vasco de Quiroga. Several more expensive hotels are on Avenida Lázaro Cárdenas, the road to Lake Pátzcuaro. If you're planning to be in town on or near November 1–2, the Mexican Day of the Dead, make hotel reservations at least six months in advance.

$$$ 🏨 **Hotel Posada de Don Vasco.** Located several minutes out of town on the road to Lake Pátzcuaro, this sprawling resort hotel offers a wide range of amenities, including satellite TV. Its 30 newer rooms are thickly carpeted and have either balconies or patios; the older quarters, which are oddly decorated with gold and brown patterned rugs and bright checkered bedspreads, are smaller and open onto a courtyard. The lovely, manicured grounds are relatively quiet despite the occasional rumbling of a passing bus or truck. The restaurant is decorated like a prosperous country estate, with a large fireplace that blazes on cold nights. At the Saturday buffet dinner the regional Dance of the Old Men is performed at 8:30 PM. Unfortunately, the food is uninspired. ⊠ *Av. Las Americas 450, 61600,* ☎ *434/2–39–71 or 434/2–24–90,* FAX *434/2–02–62. 99 rooms, 4 suites. Restaurant, pool, tennis court, badminton, bowling, billiards. AE, MC, V.*

$$ 🏨 **Cabañas Yunuen.** This complex was built in 1993 on the island of Yunuen in collaboration with the Department of Tourism to promote visits to some of the area's more authentic communities. There are six cabins in all: two each for 2, 4, and 16 persons; each has a kitchenette with small refrigerator, and—surprise!—satellite TV. Breakfast or dinner and round-trip transportation by boat is included in the price: about $28 for two people. ⊠ *Domicilio Conocido, Isla de Yunuen,* ☎ *434/ 2–44–73; 43/11–76–80 in Morelia. 6 cabins. Dining room, kitchenettes. No credit cards.*

$$ 🏨 **Los Escudos.** Today a cozy hotel, this property was originally a 16th-century home. Its courtyards bloom with potted plants, and some guest rooms contain small murals of Purépecha Indian scenes. Ten rooms situated in back and shielded from street noise open onto an outdoor patio. All rooms have color cable TVs and telephones; five have fireplaces. The adjoining restaurant has a varied menu, ranging from club sandwiches to multicourse midday meals. Particularly tempting is the *pollo especial Los Escudos* (chicken sautéed in tomato sauce and vegetables). ⊠ *Portal Hidalgo 73, 61600,* ☎ *434/2–01–38 or 434/2–12– 90,* FAX *434/2–06–49. 31 rooms, 2 suites. Restaurant. MC, V.*

$$ 🏨 **Mansión Iturbe.** This hotel, housed in a 17th-century mansion, still
★   retains much of its colonial charm. Both the rooms and corridors are frailly lighted, giving the impression of a true 17th-century home. Plant-filled courtyards are ringed by stone archways. Rooms, with large wood-and-glass doors, are partially carpeted and decorated with red-and-black–checked spreads and curtains. Bicycles are lent to guests for a few hours per stay, and every fourth night is free. Breakfast is included in the room rate. There are several restaurants, the most lively being El Viejo Gaucho, where pizzas, meats, and *empanadas* (meat-filled pastries) are served and live music is performed Wednesday–Sunday nights. ⊠ *Portal Morelos 59, 61600,* ☎ *434/2–03–68 or 434/2–36–28,* FAX *43/ 13–45–93 in Morelia. 10 rooms, 4 suites. 3 restaurants, bicycles, shop. AE, MC, V.*

$ 🏨 **Hotel Posada La Basílica.** This colonial-style inn, housed in a 17th-
★   century building, faces the Basílica de Nuestra Señora de la Salud, and on some mornings strains from a post-dawn mass filter softly into the hotel. The property has comfortable, individually decorated rooms, some with fireplaces. Thick wood shutters cover floor-to-ceiling windows, and walls are trimmed in hand-painted colonial designs. The restaurant has views of the mountains, the lake, and tile-roofed homes. Open for breakfast and lunch only, this dining spot offers such regional specialties as broiled trout with garlic and tamales with sweet cream. Service can be slow, as the waiter tends to hide in the kitchen. ⊠ *Calle Arciga 6, 61600,* ☎ *434/2–11–08,* FAX *434/2–06–59. 12 rooms. Restaurant. MC, V.*

$ ⚏ **Mesón del Gallo.** On a fairly quiet side street near the Casa de los 11 Patios, this two-story property is beginning to look a bit shabby. Beds have wood-and-tile headboards and magenta spreads and curtains. Suites, complete with minibars, are furnished in more subdued hues. All rooms have telephones but no TV. There is a grassy patio encircled by bougainvillea and fruit trees with a lonely umbrella table in the middle. Rates include breakfast. ⊠ *Calle Dr. Coss 20, 61600,* ☎ *434/2–14–74,* FAX *434/2–15–11. 20 rooms, 5 suites. Restaurant, bar. AE, MC, V.*

Nightlife and the Arts

The **Danza de los Viejitos** (Dance of the Little Old Men), a widely known regional dance, is performed during Saturday dinner at Hotel Posada de Don Vasco (☞ Lodging, *above*) for approximately $12 (includes dinner). The dance is also performed Saturday nights at 8 PM at the Hotel Los Escudos, on Plaza de Quiroga.

Shopping

Pátzcuaro has some of Mexico's finest folk-art shopping. **Mantas Tipicas** (⊠ Dr. Coss 5, ☎ 434/2–13–24) sells hand-loomed tablecloths and more; **Bordados Santa Cruz** (⊠ Dr. Coss 3, ☎ No phone) is a women's embroidery collective; and **Galería del Arcángel** (⊠ Arciga 30, ☎ 434/2–17–74) has high-quality ceramics, furniture, and silver jewelry. And don't miss the stands in front of the basilica and at the daily mercado west of Plaza Chica. **Galería Iturbe** (⊠ Portal Morelos 59) has a whimsical assortment of Ocumicho devil figures, copper jewelry, and the work of local painters. Ask the hotel desk clerk to open the store for you as it's often closed. Since 1898, the family-run **Chocolate Casero Joaquinita** (⊠ Enseñanza 38, ☎ 434/2–45–14) has been concocting delectable homemade cinnamon-spiced hot chocolate tablets.

Side Trips

Tzintzuntzan

17 km (10½ mi) northeast of Pátzcuaro.

When the Spanish came to colonize the region in the 16th century, some 40,000 Purépechas lived and worshiped in this lakeshore village, which they called "place of the hummingbirds." The ruins of the pyramid-shape temples, or *yacatas,* found in the ancient capital of the Purépecha kingdom still stand today and are open to the public for a small admission charge. There are also vestiges of a 16th-century Franciscan monastery where Spanish friars attempted to convert the Indians to Christianity. Though Tzintzuntzan lost some prominence when Bishop Vasco de Quiroga moved the seat of his diocese to Pátzcuaro in 1540, the village is still well known for the straw and ceramic handicrafts made by the Purépecha Indians and sold in numerous shops along the main street of town. The bus marked QUIROGA takes a half hour to get from Pátzcuaro's Central Camionera to Tzintzuntzan.

Santa Clara del Cobre

20 km (12½ mi) south of Pátzcuaro.

Since pre-Conquest times, Santa Clara del Cobre has been a center for copper arts. Now the local copper mines are empty, but the artisans still make gorgeous vessels, plates, napkin rings, and jewelry using the traditional method of pounding out each piece of metal by hand. For an introduction to quality and range of styles available, visit the **Museo del Cobre** (⊠ Calles Morelos and Pino Suárez, half a block from the plaza), open Tuesday–Sunday 10–3 and 5–7. Admission is 25¢. Then explore the 50-some little shops and factories in town. The bus to Santa Clara del Cobre from Pátzcuaro's Central Camionera takes 40 minutes.

Uruapan
64 km (40 mi) west of Pátzcuaro.

The subtropical town of Uruapan is distinctly different from its lakeside neighbor: some 2,000 ft lower than Pátzcuaro, though still at an elevation of 5,300 ft, it is a populous commercial center with a warm climate and lush vegetation. The town's name is derived from the Purépecha word *urupan,* meaning "where the flowers bloom." Uruapan celebrates Palm Sunday with a lively procession through the streets, brass bands, and a spectacular, bargain-filled crafts market in the central plaza—one of the best in all of Mexico.

You can get to Uruapan from Pátzcuaro by car, bus, or train. Route 14 and the new toll road are the most direct routes between the two cities. There is also frequent bus service on the Flecha Amarilla and other major lines; travel time is about 70 minutes. The train takes about two hours each way, passing through lovely wooded countryside.

You can see several points of interest within a few hours. The first, **La Huatápera,** is opposite the north side of Uruapan's Plaza Principal. This 16th-century hospital has been converted into the **Museo Regional de Arte Popular.** It houses a collection of crafts from the state of Michoacán, including an excellent display of lacquerware made in Uruapan. ☎ *452/4-34-34.* ⊠ *Free.* ⊙ *Tues.–Sun. 9:30–1:30 and 3:30–6.*

The **Mercado de Antojitos,** an immense, sprawling market, begins directly in back of the museum and extends quite a distance north along Calle Constitución. Along the road, Purépecha Indians sell large mounds of produce, fresh fish, beans, homemade cheese, and a variety of cheap manufactured goods. If you travel south along Calle Constitución, you'll come to a courtyard where vendors sell hot food.

★ **Parque Nacional Eduardo Ruiz** (about six long blocks from the Plaza Principal off Calle Independencia) is a gem of an urban park. Its paved paths meander through verdant tropical acreage past abundant waterfalls, fountains, and springs to the source of the River Cupatitzio. There is also a trout farm here and a popular playground.

Eleven kilometers (7 miles) south along the river is the magnificent waterfall at **Tzaráracua.** At this point the Cupatitzio plunges 150 ft off a sheer rock cliff into a riverbed below; a rainbow seems to hang perpetually over the site. Buses marked TZARÁRACUA leave sporadically from the Plaza Principal in Uruapan. You can also take a taxi for about $3, or drive there via Avenida Lázaro Cárdenas.

Farther afield, about 32 km (20 mi) north of Uruapan, lies the dormant **Paricutín volcano.** Its initial burst of lava and ashes wiped out the nearby village of San Juan Parangaricútiro in 1943. Today travelers can visit this buried site by hiring gentle mountain ponies and a Purépecha guide in the town of Angahuan. To reach Angahuan, take the Los Reyes bus from Uruapan's Central Camionera or go by car via the Uruapan–Carapan highway.

DINING
For good comida casera, try **El Rincón del Burrito** (⊠ Portal Matamorros 7, ☎ No phone) or the restaurant at **Mansión de Cupatitzio,** in the national park at the mouth of the Cupatitzio River (⊠ Parque Nacional s/n, ☎ 452/3–20–70 or 452/3–21–00).

Pátzcuaro A to Z

Arriving and Departing

BY BUS

Buses run daily between the Terminal Poniente (West Terminal, commonly referred to as the Observatorio) in Mexico City and Pátzcuaro's Central Camionera. Several lines offer frequent service; the most direct trip, which takes five hours, is on either **Herradura de Plata** or **Pegasso Plus** (☎ 434/2–10–45 for both lines) or **ETN** (☎ 434/2–10–60). Transportation coming from most heartland cities goes to Morelia; buses leave about every 15 minutes from there on the 45-minute trip to Pátzcuaro.

BY CAR

The Mexico City–Guadalajara tollway cuts driving time to Pátzcuaro to 4½ or 5 hours, and the trip on to Guadalajara to 4 hours by car. From Morelia, the excellent free road to Pátzcuaro takes just over an hour. You'll have to rent a car in Mexico City or Morelia, as there are no rental outlets in Pátzcuaro.

Getting Around

Many of Pátzcuaro's principal sights are near the Plaza Vasco de Quiroga and Plaza Bocanegra in the center of town. Taxis and buses to the lake can also be found at the latter square. If you want to visit surrounding villages, taxi drivers will drive you for a reasonable rate. Be sure to agree on a fee before setting out.

Contacts and Resources

EMERGENCIES

Police (☎ 434/2–00–04). **Traffic Police** (☎ 434/2–05–65). **Rescue** (☎ 434/2–10–91).

Hospital Civil (Romero 10, ☎ 434/2–02–85).

Pharmacy. Farmacia La Paz (⊠ La Paz and Bocanegra in Plaza Bocanegra, ☎ 434/2–08–10).

GUIDED TOURS

Marilyn Mayo (⊠ Apdo. 416, 61600, ☎ 434/2–23–01, FAX 434/2–27–56) designs custom tours based on your interests. She can take you to exuberant fiestas in tiny villages, to the home studios of master artisans, to the butterfly sanctuary, or any other place you want to go. Guide **Francisco Castilleja** (⊠ Centro Eronga, Profr. Urueta 105, ☎ 434/4–01–67) is highly knowledgable about pre-Hispanic philosophy, history, archaeology, and medicinal herbs. He speaks fluent English, German, French, and Spanish.

MONEY EXCHANGE

Banca Promex (⊠ Portal Regules 9, ☎ 434/2–24–66). **Banamex** (⊠ Portal Juárez 32, ☎ 434/2–15–50 or 434/2–10–31). **Bancomer** (⊠ Zaragoza 23, ☎ 434/2–03–34). A **Banamex Caja Permanente ATM** is located on Dr. Benito Mendoza, between the two plazas.

VISITOR INFORMATION

Delegación de Turismo (⊠ Plaza Vasco de Quiroga 50A, ☎ FAX 434/2–12–14) is the official tourism office and, although you may not find anyone here who speaks English, they will do their best to provide information regarding excursions outside Pátzcuaro. It is open Monday–Saturday 9–2 and 4–7, Sunday 9–2.

Dirección de Orientación y Fomento al Turismo (⊠ Portal Hidalgo 1 on Plaza de Quiroga, ☎ 434/2–02–15 or 434/2–02–16, FAX 343/2–09–67) offers maps and can answer basic questions about tourist facilities in Pátzcuaro.

8 PACIFIC COAST RESORTS

Hollywood introduced us to two of the Mexican Riviera's most popular towns: Ava Gardner and Richard Burton's sleepy, steamy Puerto Vallarta in *The Night of the Iguana* and the sparkling Manzanillo coast that served as the backdrop to Bo Derek— and Dudley Moore's antics—in *10*. These days both places are prime cruise-ship stops, as is Mazatlán, a bustling port that attracts sportfishing enthusiasts and surfers. Ixtapa/Zihuatanejo has two-for-one appeal, a laid-back fishing village adjoining a glitzy resort.

By Wendy Luft

ACROSS THE GULF OF CALIFORNIA from the Baja California Peninsula lies Mazatlán, Mexico's largest Pacific port and the major Mexican resort closest to the United States, some 1,200 km (745 mi) south of the Arizona border. This is the beginning of what cruise-ship operators now call the Mexican Riviera, or the Gold Coast. The coastline for the next 1,400 km (870 mi) is Mexico's tropical paradise. The Gulf of California, or the Sea of Cortés, as it is also called, ends just below the Tropic of Cancer, leaving the Pacific coastline open to fresh sea breezes. The coast's resorts—Mazatlán, Puerto Vallarta, Manzanillo, Ixtapa/Zihuatanejo, and Acapulco—are therefore less muggy than gulf towns to the north. The water is colder, too, and waves can get very rough.

The Pacific coast doesn't have the rich cultural heritage of Mexico's inland colonial villages and silver cities, and the history is sketchy at best. It's not the place to see ruins, museums, and cathedrals; it's a gathering spot for sun worshipers, sportfishing enthusiasts, surfers, and swimmers. Not far from the resort regions are jungle streams and ocean coves, but the majority of visitors never venture to these isolated sites, preferring instead to immerse themselves in the simultaneously bustling and restful resort life-style, where great dining, shopping, and sunbathing are the major draws.

Mazatlán is first and foremost a busy commercial center, thanks to an excellent port and the fertility of the surrounding countryside. More than 600,000 acres of farmland near Mazatlán produce tomatoes, melons, cantaloupes, wheat, and cotton, much of which is shipped to the United States. And nearly all the 150,000 tons of shrimp that are hauled in annually are processed and frozen for the American and Japanese markets.

Sportfishing accounts for Mazatlán's resort status. The port sits at the juncture of the Pacific and the Sea of Cortés, forming what has been called the world's greatest natural fish trap. Hunters are drawn to the quail, duck, and dove that thrive in the hillsides, and surfers find great waves on nearby beaches. Another draw is that accommodations are about half the cost of those in Cancún.

Tepic, capital of the state of Nayarit, lies between Mazatlán and Puerto Vallarta. From here, travelers coming down from the border by bus change buses to head to the coast. Budgeteers and those who shun megaresorts often head straight for **San Blas,** a small seaside village some 37 km (23 mi) northwest of Tepic through the jungle.

Some 323 km (200 mi) south of Mazatlán is **Puerto Vallarta,** by far the best-known resort on the upper Pacific coast. The late film director and sometime resident John Huston put the town on the map when he filmed Tennessee Williams's *The Night of the Iguana* on the outskirts of the village in 1963. Elizabeth Taylor came to keep Richard Burton company during the filming, and the gossip about their romance—both were married at the time, but not to each other—brought this quaint Mexican fishing village with its cobblestone lanes and whitewashed, tile-roofed houses to the public's attention. Before long, travel agents were deluged with queries about Puerto Vallarta, a place many had never heard of before.

The fabled cobblestone streets are clogged with bumper-to-bumper traffic during the holiday season, but, despite the city's resort status, parts of Puerto Vallarta are still picturesque. For a sense of the Eden that once was, travel south of town to the lush green mountains where the

TO
LA PAZ

Navolato

Culiacán

DURANGO

Lázaro
Cárdenas

El Dorado

SINALOA

Santiago
Papasquiaro

Canatlán

La Cruz

15

El-Salto

Durango

Estación
Dimas

Presidio

Tropic of Cancer

40

Mazatlán

Copala

Villa Unión

Concordia

El Caimanero

Rosario

Mezquital

Escuinapa
de Hidalgo

Golfo de California

Tecuala

*Agua
Brava*

Tuxpan

*Islas
Marías*

San Blas

NAYARIT

*Bahía
Matachén*

Tepic

Río Grande de Santiago

Rincón de
Guayabitos

Punta de
Mita

Sayulita

*Bahía de
Banderas*

Lo De Marcos

San Francisco

**Playa
Las
Ánimas**

Cruz de
Huanacaxtle

Cabo
Corrientes

**Boca de
Tomatlán**

Puerto Vallarta

Mismaloya

15

Ameca

PACIFIC OCEAN

200

N

Tomatlán

Guadalajara

Chamela

Ayotitlán

JALISCO

*Lake
Chapalá*

80

Armería

Ciudad
Guzmán

KEY

San Patricio Helaque

—— Rail Lines

Barra de Navidad

COLIMA

54

- - - Ferry Lines

Manzanillo

110

Colima

0   100 miles

0   150 km

Tecomán

Zihuatanejo
Ixtapa

Río Tomatlán tumbles over boulders into the sea, or north to Punta Mita on the northern tip of Banderas Bay in neighboring Nayarit. But get there fast, because the inauguration of the luxurious Four Seasons hotel (scheduled to open in the spring of '99) promises to ignite a building boom in this remote area.

Conquistador Hernán Cortés envisioned **Manzanillo** as a gateway to the Orient: from these shores, Spanish galleons would bring in the riches of Cathay to be trekked across the continent to Veracruz, where they would fill vessels headed for Spain. But Acapulco, not Manzanillo, became the port of call for the Manila galleons that arrived each year with riches from beyond the seas. Pirates are said to have staked out Manzanillo during the colonial era, and chests of loot are rumored to be buried beneath the sands.

With the coming of the railroads, Manzanillo became a major port of entry, albeit not a pretty one. It is now Mexico's second busiest port and the lights of freighters at anchor can be seen along the southern beaches. Forty or 50 years ago, a few seaside hotels opened up on the outskirts of town, which vacationers reached by train. The jet age, however, seemed to doom the port as a sunny vacation spot. Then Bolivian tin magnate Antenor Patiño built **Las Hadas** (The Fairies), a lavish Moorish-style resort complex inaugurated in 1974. It attracted the beautiful people, and for a while Las Hadas was better known than Manzanillo itself. The film *10* made a star of the resort as well as household names of its stars, Bo Derek and Dudley Moore.

In recent years there's been a push to turn Manzanillo and coastal villages to the north in neighboring Jalisco, such as **Barra de Navidad, Melaque, Tenacatita,** and **Costa de Careyes,** into a tourist zone. A four-lane toll road now cuts the driving time between Manzanillo and Guadalajara, Mexico's second-largest city, to three hours. Older hotels have been spruced up and all-inclusive resorts constructed. **Karmina Palace** on Santigo Peninsula, just over the hill from **Las Hadas,** is the area's newest luxury resort; it's scheduled to open in the spring of 1999. January 1997 marked the inauguration of the posh **Grand Bay hotel,** in Isla Navidad, a deluxe residential–tourist–golf complex that spreads over some 1,200 acres on a peninsula between the Pacific Ocean and the Navidad Lagoon, 20 minutes west of the Manzanillo airport.

The southernmost of the Pacific Coast resorts and the newest kid on the scene—like Cancún, it was developed by the Mexican government in the early 1970s—**Ixtapa/Zihuatanejo** lies in the northwestern part of the State of Guerrero coastline, some 500 km (300 mi) south of Manzanillo. It's unique among Mexican beach getaways in that it comprises two distinct destinations only 7 km (4½ mi) from each other. Ixtapa is the glitzier of the two, with international chain hotels lining its hotel zone, but it's far smaller and more low key than older resorts like Puerto Vallarta and newer ones such as Cancún. Its development put neighbor Zihuatanejo, a sleepy fishing village virtually unknown even among Mexicans, on the tourist map.

Pleasures and Pastimes

Beaches
Mexico's Pacific coast doubtless has some of North America's most inviting beaches, with deliciously warm waters and spectacular sunsets. There are beaches for every taste: long stretches of creamy sand, crescents of soft gold and black volcanic grains, secluded coves, and pristine shores accessible only by boat.

Dining

The emphasis in **Mazatlán** is on casual, bountiful dining, and the prices are reasonable. Shrimp, octopus, oysters and fresh fish are the highlights; be sure to have a seafood cocktail along the beach. **Puerto Vallarta** has the widest array of restaurants, some with spectacular views, others hidden in the small, romantic patios of former homes, and still others—especially those on the *malecón* (seaside walkway)—as popular for people-watching as they are for their great seafood. Several **Manzanillo** dining spots have scenic views of the jungle and water that compensate for their lack of culinary excitement. In **Ixtapa/Zihuatanejo,** restaurants range from simple beach eateries to deluxe establishments with international chefs.

Some hotel restaurants add a 10%–15% service charge to your tab.

CATEGORY	COST*
$$$$	over $35
$$$	$25–$35
$$	$15–$25
$	under $15

per person for a three-course meal including 15% sales tax, and excluding drinks and service

Fishing

Mazatlán is tops in the Mexican Pacific for billfishing. Sailfish run from March to December, blue and black marlin from May to December, and swordfish and striped marlin from December to April. Other sportfish include roosterfish, wahoo, yellowfin tuna, bonita, mahi mahi, and shark. Light-tackle fishing in the lagoons and just off the beach in *pangas* (small boats) for *huachinango* (red snapper) is also popular. Bass anglers will be pleased with the fresh waterlakes in the local foothills of the Sierra Madre mountains.

Sportfishing is good off **Puerto Vallarta** most of the year, particularly for billfish, rooster fish, mahi mahi, yellowtail, and bonito. **Manzanillo** claims to be the sailfish capital of the world; the season runs from mid-October through March. Blue marlin and dorado are also abundant. **Ixtapa/Zihuatanejo** is becoming Mexico's new sportfishing destination. Anglers revel in the profusion of sailfish, black and blue marlin, yellowfin tuna, and dorado. In **November,** Mazatlán, Puerto Vallarta, and Manzanillo host international fishing tournaments. If you're not after a memento, most operations have a catch and release option.

Horseback Riding

In most of the Pacific Coast resorts, horseback riding along the shore is popular and horses can be rented by the hour at major beaches. In **Puerto Vallarta,** several stables have sunset rides, three-hour mountain trips, and rides to colonial villages in the Sierra Madre.

Lodging

Although not known for its upscale resorts, **Mazatlán** now has its share of luxury properties, along with comfortable beachfront hotels. It also has one of the highest concentrations of trailer parks in the country. In **Puerto Vallarta,** accommodations range from tiny inns to luxury waterfront hotels and spectacular resorts tucked away on hidden coves. **Ixtapa/Zihuatanejo** runs the lodging gamut—big beachfront properties are the norm in Ixtapa; Zihuatanejo has budget hotels and two of the most exclusive small hotels in Mexico.

Most hotels raise their rates for the high season (December 15 through Easter Week); rates are lowest in May and June, the beginning of the rainy season (which lasts from late May to early October) and in

September and October when hurricanes sweep the coast. Rates rise somewhat during July and August when most Mexican families take advantage of the warm waters and swarm the beaches for their summer vacations. Price categories are based on high-season rates—expect to pay 25% less during the off-season.

CATEGORY	COST*
$$$$	over $200
$$$	$100–$200
$$	$50–$100
$	under $50

*All prices are for a standard double room, excluding 15% VAT (17% in the state of Jalisco).

Shopping

You can spend as much time shopping in **Puerto Vallarta** as you can lazing in the sun. Shops selling excellent crafts from around the country vie with upscale art galleries and clothing and jewelry boutiques for buyers' attention, especially in the downtown area. The selection of Mexican crafts in **Mazatlán** is almost as good. **Zihuatanejo** has some extremely colorful crafts markets. The unique ceramics and masks from the state of Guerrero, where the little fishing town is located, are especially plentiful.

Water Sports

Parasailing, swimming, windsurfing, sailing, kayaking, and waterskiing are popular at Pacific Coast resorts. Manzanillo and Mazatlán have some of the finest surfing in Mexico, while the best diving spots in this area are found around the islands off Puerto Vallarta, Ixtapa and Mazatlán. Puerto Vallarta hosts Mexico's annual boat show each November, as well as various sailing regattas in winter.

Exploring the Pacific Coast Resorts

Resorts on this coastal stretch are at their best in winter, with temperatures in the 70s and 80s (a bit higher in Ixtapa/Zihuatanejo, to the south). The off-season brings humidity, mosquitoes, and higher temperatures (northernmost Mazatlán remains coolest), but also emptier beaches, warmer water (well into the 70s), and less-crowded streets—plus 25% to 35% lower room rates and cheaper rental-car costs. Toward the end of the rainy season (June–September), which involves mostly brief daily showers, the countryside and the mountainous backdrop of the Sierra Madre del Sur turn brilliantly green with multicolored tree and flower blossoms.

MAZATLÁN

Mazatlán is the Aztec word for "place of the deer," and long ago its islands and shores sheltered far more deer than humans. Today it is a city of some 400,000 residents and draws about 1.5 million tourists a year. Sunning, surfing, and sailing have caught on here, and in the winter months visitors from inland Mexico, the United States, and Canada flock to Mazatlán for a break in the sun. Hotel and restaurant prices are lower than elsewhere on the coast, and the ambience is more that of a fishing town than a tourist haven.

Upscale resorts and ritzy restaurants are not part of Mazatlán's repertoire, though there is a fair dose of luxury at El Cid, Royal Villas, and Pueblo Bonito resorts. An economic downturn has slowed work under way on two adjacent marina/golf complexes on the estuary that stretches north from the El Cid golf course.

Hunting and fishing were the original draw for visitors. At one time, duck, quail, pheasant, and other wildfowl fed in the lagoons; and jaguars, mountain lions, rabbits, and coyotes roamed the surrounding hills. Hunters have to search a little harder and farther for their prey these days, but there's still plenty of wildlife near Mazatlán. The city is the base for Mexico's largest sportfishing fleet; fishermen haul the biggest catches (in size and number) on the coast. The average annual haul is 10,000 sailfish and 5,000 marlin. A record 988-pound marlin and 203-pound sailfish were pulled from these waters.

The Spanish settled in the Mazatlán region in 1531 and used the indigenous people as a labor force to create the port and village. In the ensuing centuries, the center of Mazatlán gradually moved north. The original site is now the village of Villa Union, 24 km (15 mi) southeast of the harbor.

In the early 1600s, the colonial government built a small fort and watchtowers atop the hills in the city to control the English and French pirates who used the harbor as a place from which to attack the rich Spanish galleons that plied the coast. Pirates were gone by 1800, but legends of buried treasure in the caves along the coast still circulate.

The port has a history of blockades. In 1847 during the Mexican War, U.S. forces marched down from the border through northeast Mexico and closed it. In 1864, the French bombarded the city and then controlled it for several years. The British occupied the port for a short period in 1871. Mexico's own internal warring factions took over from time to time. And after the Civil War in the United States, a group of Southerners tried to turn Mazatlán into a slave city.

Mazatlán has the country's largest shrimping fleet. Sinaloa, one of Mexico's richest states, uses the port to ship its agricultural products.

Exploring Mazatlán

Mazatlán's highlights are spread far and wide, and walking from one section of town to the other can take hours. The best way to travel is via *pulmonías* (open-air jitneys, literally "pneumonias") so you can sunbathe and take pictures as you cruise along, although you won't be able to roll up any windows to protect yourself from automobile fumes. If you choose to rent a car and drive, you can tour at your own pace. There are no traffic jams in Mazatlán, except near the market in downtown, where parking can also be a major problem. Downtown is virtually the only area of Mazatlán that can be walked; many visitors never see it, but it's worth spending a morning here.

Numbers in the text correspond to numbers in the margin and on the Mazatlán map.

A Good Tour

Start from the **Zona Dorada** ①, Mazatlán's central tourist area, which begins at Punta Camarón. If you travel north from here along the coast on Avenida Sábalo, you'll pass some of the city's most luxurious and priciest hotels. This route affords a good view of Mazatlán's three Pacific islands—Isla de los Pájaros, Isla de los Venados, and Isla de los Chivos. Just past the Camino Real resort, Avenida Camarón Sábalo becomes Avenida Sábalo Cerritos and crosses over the Estero del Sábalo, a long lagoon popular with bird-watchers. The area north of here is developing as an exclusive touring and resort area; towering condos are already being built.

South of the Zona Dorada, the main road changes names frequently. The 16-km (10-mi) malecón, Mazatlán's version of a main highway

Mazatlán

0   1000 meters

0   1000 yards

N

Playa los
Cerritos

Playa
Sábalo

Estero del
Sábalo

Av. Camarón Sábalo

Isla
de los
Pájaros

**ZONA
DORADA**

El Cid
Resort

1

Isla
de los
Venados

Isla
de los
Chivos

**Playa las
Gaviotas**

**Playa Isla
de los Venados**

Av.
Loaiza

Bullring
Boulevard Rafael Buelna

Punta
Camarón

Av. del Mar

Av. Reforma

**Teodoro Mariscal
Baseball Stadium**

15
TO AIRPORT,
ESTRELLA DEL
MAR GOLF AND
BEACH RESORT,
COPALA, AND
CONCORDIA

Av. Insurgentes

Bahía del Puerto Viejo

Los
Deportes

2

**Bus
Station**

Playa Norte

Río
Tamazula

Av. Juan Carrasco

Estero
del
Infiernillo

Punta de
Tiburón

Playa los Pinos

Playa Olas Altas

Cerro de la Nevería

*Bahía
Olas Altas*

Paseo
Claussen

5 del Mayo

Juárez

Zaragoza

Gutierrez Nájera

Av. Gabriel Leyva

Ocampo

4

M.
Escobedo

3

6 **5**

Av. M.
Aleman

Av. del Puerto

Paseo del
Centenario

Av. Cannaval

Canal de Navegación

7

Isla
de la
Piedra

Cerro del Creston

and beachfront boardwalk, begins at Punta Camarón and is here called Avenida del Mar. In a few blocks, you'll come to the city's highly recommended aquarium, **Acuario Mazatlán** ②, down Avenida de los Deportes. Avenida del Mar continues past beaches popular with residents and travelers staying at the budget hotels across the street. You're sure to notice the avenue's main landmark, the Monumento al Pescador: an enormous, voluptuous, nude woman reclines on an anchor, her hand extended toward a nude fisherman dragging his nets.

Calle Juárez and Calle Cinco de Mayo intersect with Avenida del Mar and lead to Mazatlán's real downtown, where the streets are filled with buses and people rushing to and from work and the market. The heart of the city is the **Plaza República** ③ or *zócalo*; just across the street you'll see the twin-spired **Mazatlán Catedral** ④. On the streets facing the zócalo are the City Hall, banks, post office, and telegraph office. About three blocks southeast of the zócalo, a school for the arts and the Teatro Angela Peralta, both built in 1860 and now beautifully restored, were declared historic monuments in 1990. Stop for a drink or a bite at any one of the establishments in front of the nearby Plaza Machado, where neighborhood fiestas are held on special occasions. Head three blocks west to the **Museo de Arte de Mazatlán** ⑤, as well as the simple **Instituto Nacional de Antropología y Historia** ⑥ with its exhibits on the cultural legacy of the state of Sinaloa.

Back along the waterfront, Avenida del Mar turns into Paseo Claussen as it heads south. If you continue along the malecón, you'll pass El Fuerte Carranza, an old Spanish fort built to defend the city against the French; Casa del Marino, a shelter for sailors; Playa Olas Altas (☞ Beaches, *below*); High-Divers Park, where young men climb to a white platform and plunge into the sea—spectacular at night, when the divers leap carrying flaming torches; and La Mazatleca, a bronze nymph rising from a giant wave. Across the street is a small bronze deer, Mazatlán's mascot. A recent addition to the port's statuary just south is the Monument to the Continuity of Life, a large fountain with a handsome couple on top of a large conch shell and a school of porpoises leaping from the water. Paseo Claussen leads to Olas Altas, site of Old Mazatlán, the center for tourism in the 1940s. Olas Altas ("high waves") ends at a small traffic circle. A plaque at the circle bears the state symbol of Sinaloa. Above Olas Altas is **Cerro de Vigía** ⑦.

Sights to See

🐚 ❷ **Acuario Mazatlán.** A perfect child-pleaser, Mazatlán's aquarium features tanks of sharks, sea horses, eels, lobsters, and multicolored salt-and freshwater fish. A fanciful bronze fountain and sculpture of two boys feeding a dolphin marks the aquarium's entrance, and an aviary sits amid the trees in the adjacent botanical garden. Bird and sea lion shows are performed throughout the day. ☒ *Av. de los Deportes 111,* ☎ *69/81–78–15.* ☒ *About $3.50.* ☉ *Daily 9:30–6:30.*

❼ **Cerro de Vigía** (Lookout Hill). The view from this windy hill above Olas Altas is fantastic: you can see both sides of Mazatlán, the harbor, and the Pacific. It's a steep climb up, better done by taxi than on foot. If you decide to hike it, do it early in the morning before the sun is at its hottest; and although a shop at the top frequently sells soft drinks, you should bring some water. At the top of the hill you'll see a weather station, along with a rusty cannon and the **Centenario Pérgola**, built in 1848 to celebrate the end of the U.S. invasion.

❻ **Instituto Nacional de Antropología y Historia.** The town's archaeological museum houses a small but fairly interesting collection of artifacts from the region. Particularly interesting is an exhibit of exquisite polychrome pottery with elaborate black and red designs left behind by the Totorames, an indigenous tribe that inhabited the area up until 200 years before the Spanish arrived. ✉ *Sixto Osuna 76, off Paseo Olas Altas.* 🎫 *About $2, free Sun.* ⊙ *Tues.–Sun. 10–1 and 4–7.*

NEED A BREAK? The sidewalk tables at **Copa de Leche** and **Fonda Santa Clara** (✉ Av. Olas Altas) are perfect for watching the sunset.

❹ Mazatlán Catedral. The blue-and-gold spires of the downtown cathedral are a city landmark. Built in 1890 and made a basilica in 1935, this church has a gilded and ornate triple altar, with murals of angels overhead and many small altars along the sides. A sign at the entrance requests that visitors be appropriately attired (no shorts or tank tops inside). ✉ *Calles Juárez and Plazuela República.*

❺ Museo de Arte de Mazatlán. This small museum shows the work of local, regional, and national artists. ✉ *Sixto Osuna and Venustiano Carranza,* ☎ FAX *69/85–35–02.* 🎫 *75¢.* ⊙ *Tues.–Sat. 10–2 and 5–8; Sun. 10–2.*

❸ Plaza República. This city square at the center of downtown hosts one of the most fascinating gazebos in Mexico—what looks like a '50s diner inside the lower level and a wrought-iron bandstand on top. The green-and-orange tile on the walls, ancient jukebox, and soda fountain serving shakes, burgers, and hot dogs couldn't make a more surprising sight. Sunday afternoons tourists and locals fill the plaza to hear local musicians play from the bandstand. ✉ *Bounded by 21 de Marzo to the north, Flores to the south, Benito Juárez to the east, and Nelson to the west.*

NEED A BREAK? **Nieves de Medrano** (✉ Corner of Cinco de Mayo and Angel Flores) serves traditional homemade ice cream in dozens of exotic flavors.

❶ Zona Dorada. Marking the beginning of Mazatlán's tourist zone is **Punta Camarón** (Shrimp Point), the rocky outcropping on which Valentino's Disco sits, resembling a Moorish palace perched above the sea. To the north, Avenida Camarón Sábalo forms the eastern border of the zone, whereas Avenida Loaiza runs closer to the beach. In this four-block pocket are many of the hotels, shops, and restaurants, and the majority of nonresidents intent on having a good time sunning, shopping, and partying. This is the place to souvenir-shop, hit the discos, and check out the hotel bars.

NEED A BREAK? **Owen Café** (✉ Constitución 517, in Plaza Machado, ☎ 69/82–09–55) serves good coffee and fresh blended juices along with pastries, bagels, and hefty American-style sandwiches between 9 AM and 11 PM. **No Name Café** (✉ Av. Rodolfo T. Loaiza 417, ☎ 69/13–20–31), in the Mazatlán Arts and Crafts Center, is a good spot for a beer or *agua mineral* (mineral water) and lime. Mexico's version of Baskin-Robbins, **Helados Bing** (✉ Avs. Camarón Sábalo and Gaviotas, ☎ 69/13–55–10) has good hot-fudge sundaes and ice-cream cones. At the **Panadería Panamá** (✉ Av. Camarón Sábalo across from Las Palmas hotel, ☎ 69/13–69–77), you can sit at a table and enjoy fragrant cinnamon-flavored coffee with fresh-baked pastries.

Around Mazatlán

CONCORDIA

48 km (30 mi) northeast of Mazatlán.

Concordia is known for its furniture makers (a huge wood chair marks the entrance to the small town), its 18th-century church, and its brown clay pottery. The trip, over a spectacular road, makes a nice change of pace from Mazatlán.

COPALA
25 km (15 mi) east of Concordia.

A scenic colonial mining town at the foot of the Sierra Madre Occidental, Copala features a charming zócalo, cobblestone streets, colorful facades, and beautiful ironwork balconies and windows. Stop into Daniel's restaurant on the square for a slice of delicious cream pie.

TEACAPAN
25 km (15 mi) south of Mazatlan.

A serene drive into cattle and coconut country, with a stop in the pueblo of Esquinapa to see its interesting church, is topped off with a cruise on the large estuary spanning the border of Sinaloa and Nayarit states for bird-watching—and a seaside meal of shrimp *empanadas*. Let Marlin Tours (☞ Guided Tours *in* Mazatlán A to Z, *below*) handle this one for you.

Beaches

Playa Isla de la Piedra. On weekends, local families bearing toys, rafts, and picnic lunches ride over to Stone Island (which is in fact a peninsula) on pangas (small, motor-powered skiffs) from docks near the train tracks and from the ferry docks. Sixteen kilometers (10 miles) of unspoiled beaches here allow enough room for all visitors to spread out and claim their own space. This is the place to rent a horse for a good long ride on the beach—there's nothing but sand and coconut palms. Look for the numerous sand dollars that cover the southern end of the peninsula. On Sunday, the beach looks like a small village, with lots of music and fun. Many of the small *palapas* (thatched-roof huts) set up along the north end of the beach serve a tasty smoked marlin. The palapas near the launches to Isla de la Piedra sell sugarcane sticks, which look like bamboo and are good for quenching your thirst.

Playa Isla de los Venados. Boats make frequent departures from the Zona Dorada hotels for this beach on Deer Island. It's only a 10-minute ride, but the difference in ambience is striking. The beach is pretty, uncluttered, and clean, and you can hike around the southern point of the island to small, secluded coves covered with shells. The El Cid Hotel employs a 1964 army surplus Lark-5 amphibious vehicle, affectionately known as "the shark," to take you from the beach to the island and back.

Playa Los Cerritos. The northernmost beach on the outskirts of town, which runs from Camino Real Resort to Punta Cerritos, is also the cleanest and least populated. The waves can be too rough for swimming, but they're great for surfing, and Mazatlán's local surfing club frequently uses the area to train its members for competitions throughout Mexico. A good palapa restaurant/bar on the north end of the beach is a good place to meet local surfers.

Playa Norte. This strand begins at Punta Camarón (Valentino's is a landmark) along Avenida del Mar and the malecón and runs to the Fisherman's Monument. The dark brown sand is dirty and rocky at some points, but clean at others, and is popular with those staying at hotels without beach access. It is also a favorite area for runners at dawn and dusk. Palapas selling cold drinks, tacos, and fresh fish line the beach. Be sure to try the fresh coconut milk.

Playa Olas Altas. This beach, whose name means "high waves," was the first tourist beach in Mazatlán, running south along the malecón from the Fisherman's Monument. Surfers congregate here during the summer months, when the waves are at their highest.

Playa Sábalo and Playa las Gaviotas. Mazatlán's two most popular beaches are at either end of the Zona Dorada. There are as many vendors selling blankets, pottery, lace tablecloths, and silver jewelry as there are sunbathers. Boats, windsurfers, and parasailers line the shores. The beach is protected from heavy surf by the three islands—Venados, Pájaros, and Chivos. You can safely stroll these beaches until midnight and eavesdrop on the social action in the hotels while enjoying a few solitary, romantic moments without vendors and crowds.

Dining

$$$ ✕ **Angelo's.** With its fresh flowers, cream-and-beige decor, live music
★ year-round, and soft candlelight, this is by far the most attractive restaurant in Mazatlán. The Italian and Continental cuisine is outstanding—try the veal scallopini with mushrooms or shrimp marinara on pasta—and the service impeccable. ⊠ *Pueblo Bonito hotel, Av. Camarón Sábalo 2121,* ☎ *69/14–37–00. AE, DC, MC, V. No lunch.*

$$$ ✕ **Casa Loma.** An out-of-the-way, elegant restaurant in a converted villa, Casa Loma serves international specialties such as chateaubriand, duck à l'orange, and osso buco. Lunch on the patio is less formal. Have a martini made by an expert, and save room for the luscious bananas flambée. ⊠ *Av. Gaviotas 104,* ☎ *69/13–53–98. MC, V.*

$$$ ✕ **Pedro & Lola.** Good seafood is served in this 19th-century building in the heart of the historic center, decorated with neo-Mexican art. Live music plays in the evenings. ⊠ *Carnaval and Constitución, next to Plaza Machado,* ☎ *69/82–25–89. AE, MC, V. No lunch.*

$$$ ✕ **Shrimp Factory.** This plain, open-sided restaurant, with white plas-
★ tic tables and chairs, serves no soups, desserts, or views, just top-quality shrimp and lobster, by the kilo (boiled) or the plate (virtually any style). ⊠ *Avs. de las Garzas 14 and Rodolfo T. Loaiza, across from Playa Mazatlán hotel,* ☎ *69/16–53–18. AE, MC, V.*

$$$ ✕ **Sr. Peppers.** Elegant yet unpretentious, with ceiling fans, lush foliage, and candlelit tables, Sr. Peppers serves choice steaks and lobsters cooked over a mesquite grill. Enjoy the dance floor and live music. ⊠ *Av. Camarón Sábalo across from Camino Real hotel,* ☎ *69/14–01–20. AE, MC, V. No lunch.*

$$ ✕ **El Shrimp Bucket.** In Old Mazatlán, under forest-green awnings, is an establishment that was the original Carlos 'n' Charlie's. The garden patio restaurant is much quieter than its predecessors—some would call it respectable. This is the in spot for Mazatlán businessmen and social mavens at breakfast (from 6 AM). For lunch or dinner, best bets are fried shrimp served in clay buckets and barbecued ribs. Portions are large. ⊠ *Olas Altas 11–126,* ☎ *69/81–63–50. AE, MC, V.*

$$ ✕ **La Concha.** One of the prettiest waterside dining spots, La Concha
★ is a large enclosed palapa with three levels of seating, including a spacious dance floor decked with twinkling lights and outdoor tables by the sand. Adventurous types might attempt the stingray with black butter or calamari in its ink, while the more conservative can try a thick filet mignon cooked to perfection. During the winter season there's live music. La Concha is also open for breakfast and lunch. ⊠ *El Cid Resort, Av. Camarón Sábalo,* ☎ *69/13–33–33. AE, DC, MC, V.*

$$ ✕ **La Costa Marinera.** It's always a party at this seafood restaurant with a live mariachi band. Pacific lobster is the house specialty, and their local seafood is as fresh as it gets. ⊠ *Priv. Camarón and Priv. Florida,* ☎ *69/14–19–28. No credit cards.*

$$ ✕ **Señor Frog.** Another member of the Carlos Anderson chain, Señor Frog is as noisy and entertaining as the rest. Bandidos carry tequila

bottles and shot glasses in their bandoliers, leather belts that held ammunition in the old westerns. Barbecued ribs and chicken, served with corn on the cob, and heaping portions of standard Mexican dishes are the specialty, and the drinking, dancing, and carousing go on well into the night. The tortilla soup is excellent. ⊠ *Av. del Mar,* ☎ *69/82–19–25. AE, MC, V.*

$–$$ ✕ **El Paraíso Tres Islas.** A wonderful palapa on the beach, across from
★   Sea Shell City (☞ Shopping, *below*), Tres Islas is a favorite with families who spend all Sunday afternoon feasting on fresh fish. Try smoked marlin, oysters diablo, octopus, or the seafood platter. The setting is the nicest in town, close to the water with a good view of the three islands. The waiters are friendly and eager to help. ⊠ *Av. Rodolfo T. Loaiza 404,* ☎ *69/14–28–12. MC, V.*

$ ✕ **Karnes en Su Jugo.** A small family-run café on the malecón, with
★   a few outdoor tables and a large indoor restaurant, this establishment specializes in *karnes en su jugo,* (literally, "beef in its juice"), a Mexican stew with chopped beef, onions, beans, and bacon. It's a satisfying meal, especially when eaten with a basket of homemade tortillas. ⊠ *Av. del Mar 550,* ☎ *69/82–13–22. No credit cards.*

$ ✕ **Pepe's & Joe.** This restaurant in the Fiesta Land complex (☞
★   Nightlife, *below*) is Nirvana for beer lovers—the brew is made on the premises. There are also good hamburgers, hot dogs, club sandwiches, and the like. ⊠ *Punta Camarón,* ☎ *69/84–16–66. AE, MC, V.*

$ ✕ **Pura Vida.** This health conscious eatery has a low calorie menu and fresh fruit drinks and cocktails. Vegetarian fare includes delicious salads, vegetable and fruit juices, and the very popular soy burgers and *burrotes,* very large vegetarian burritos filled with your choice of ingredients. ⊠ *Av. Las Garzas 69,* ☎ *69/85–41–42. No credit cards.*

Lodging

Most of Mazatlán's hotels are in the Zona Dorada, along the beaches. Less expensive places are in Old Mazatlán, the original tourist zone along the malecón on the south side of downtown.

$$$$ 🏨 **Hacienda Las Moras.** Ideal for riders and nonriders alike, this aban-
★   doned 19th-century tequila ranch, tucked away at the foot of the Sierra Madre mountains about 30 minutes from Mazatlán, has been renovated with the finest authentic Mexican furnishings and art. There are more than 3,000 acres to explore either by horseback, wagon, or foot. Exotic animals roam the grounds, along with horses. Accommodations are in six villa-suites or in five individual casitas. There are no TVs, clocks, or phones in the rooms, but there is a phone in the hotel's office. The rate includes three meals and transportation to and from the airport. Mailing address: ⊠ *Av. Camarón Sábalo 204–17, Mazatlán 82110,* ☎ FAX *69/16–50–45 for reservations. 11 units. Restaurant, bar, pool, 2 tennis courts, horseback riding. AE, MC, V.*

$$$ 🏨 **Camino Real.** Location is the big plus at this property, which is far from the frenzy of the Golden Zone, past a rocky point at the northernmost edge of town. The beach is a bit of a hike from the hotel rooms, through the densely landscaped grounds and down a small hill. The hotel, one of the first in Mazatlán, is still comfortable, if a bit worn. A pink color scheme now prevails. If you're more interested in relaxing in peace than in carousing, this is one of your best bets. ⊠ *Av. Camarón Sábalo, 82110,* ☎ *69/13–11–11; 800/722–6466 in the U.S.,* FAX *69/14–03–11. 169 rooms. 2 restaurants, 2 bars, pool, 2 tennis courts, beach. AE, DC, MC, V.*

$$$ 🏨 **El Cid.** The largest resort in Mazatlán, and perhaps in Mexico, El
★   Cid has 1,320 rooms that spread over 900 acres. A 100-slip marina began operating in 1994, and the Marina El Cid and Yacht Club, with

210 suites, opened in 1995. Other perks include a full-service spa and fitness center, the John Jacob's School of Golf and attendant 27-hole course, and a megatravel service with its own deep-sea fishing fleet, sightseeing and cultural tours, sailing, snorkeling, sunset cruises, bass fishing, and hunting. The spacious hotel rooms overlook the pool and beach (one of the longest and cleanest in the area), and the hotel is popular with convention groups as well as individual travelers. The glass-enclosed arcade has nice boutiques, and La Concha (☞ Dining, *above*) is one of the most romantic spots on the beach. ⊠ *Av. Camarón Sábalo, 82110,* ☎ *69/13–33–33; 800/525–1925 in the U.S.,* FAX *69/14–13–11. 720 rooms, 600 suites. 5 restaurants, 4 bars, 8 pools, 27-hole golf course, 17 tennis courts, health club, beach, shops, dance club. AE, DC, MC, V.*

$$$ ☷ **Holiday Inn Sunspree Resort.** A consistently good hotel, the Holiday Inn has been drastically improved in recent years. Tour and convention groups fill the rooms and keep the party mood going by the pool and on the beach. The Kid's Spree program provides activities that keep tots busy and parents relaxed. All of the rooms are done in whites and pastels, with large sliding doors that open to pretty views of the islands. Standard amenities now include remote-control cable TV, hair dryer, refrigerator, and coffeemaker. ⊠ *Punta del Sabalo, 82110,* ☎ *69/13–22–22,* FAX *69/14–12–87. 165 rooms. 2 restaurants, 2 bars, pool, tennis court, exercise room, volleyball, beach, children's programs (ages 6 to 15). AE, MC, V.*

$$$ ☷ **Pueblo Bonito.** By far the most beautiful property in Mazatlán, this
★ all-suites hotel and time-share resort has an enormous lobby with chandeliers, beveled-glass doors, and gleaming red-and-white tile floors. The pink terra-cotta rooms have domed ceilings. An arched doorway leads from the tile kitchen into the elegant seating area, which is furnished with pale pink and beige couches and glass tables. Pink flamingos stroll on the manicured lawns, golden koi swim in small ponds, and bronzed sunbathers repose on padded white lounge chairs by the crystal-blue pool. **Angelo's** (☞ Dining, *above*) is a dining must. This is as elegant as Mazatlán gets. ⊠ *Av. Camarón Sábalo 2121, 82110,* ☎ *69/14–37–00; 800/937–9567 in the U.S.,* FAX *69/14–17–23. 250 suites. 3 restaurants, bar, 2 pools, exercise room, beach. AE, MC, V.*

$$$ ☷ **Royal Villas Resort.** This startling 12-story structure, shaped like a
★ pyramid, is decidedly more attractive on the inside. Panoramic elevators transport you from the cool marble atrium lobby to the upper floors. The large guest rooms with tile floors are decorated in cool colors; all have remote-control TVs, balconies, and kitchenettes. Access to the inviting pool is by a bridge that crosses over a tropical fish–filled pond. ⊠ *Av. Camarón Sábalo 500, 82110,* ☎ *69/16–61–61; 800/898–3564 in the U.S.,* FAX *69/14–07–77. 125 rooms. 2 restaurants, bar, pool, hot tub, exercise room, beach. AE, MC, V.*

$$ ☷ **Casa Contenta.** A small surprise on the beach one block north of
★ Las Flores, this property has seven one-bedroom apartments in a colonial-style building as well as a large beachfront house with three bedrooms, three baths, living and dining room, and even servants' quarters; the house accommodates eight people. All units have equipped kitchens, but there are no TVs or phones in the rooms. Casa Contenta has many longtime repeat clients who book years in advance. ⊠ *Av. Rodolfo T. Loaiza 224, 82110,* ☎ *69/13–49–76,* FAX *69/13–99–86. 8 units. Kitchenettes, pool. MC, V.*

$$ ☷ **El Quijote Inn.** On the beach, in the midst of the hotel zone, the five-story El Quijote Inn is a tranquil alternative to some of the more frenzied facilities. Accommodations include studios and one- or two-bedroom suites (the suites have full kitchens). All units have tile floors, rattan furnishings, satellite TV, and patios or balconies. ⊠ *Avs. Camarón Sábalo* *and Tiburón, 82110,* ☎ *69/14–11–34,* FAX *69/14–33–44. 67 suites. Restaurant, bar, pool, hot tub. AE, MC, V.*

$$ ⌧ **Fiesta Inn.** One of Mazatlán's newest hotels, the Fiesta Inn is operated by Posadas, a large Mexican hotel chain. The sleek nine-story tower is on the beach between the Holiday Inn and the Doubletree hotels. All the guest rooms are nicely decorated with marble floors, light-wood furniture, and pleasing pastels. ⌧ *Av. Camarón Sábalo 1927, 82110,* ☎ *69/89–01–00 or 01–800/504–5000; 800/343–7821 in the U.S.,* FAX *69/89–01–30. 117 rooms. 2 restaurants, bar, pool. AE, DC, MC, V.*

$$ ⌧ **Hotel Plaza Marina.** This is Mazatlán's newest hotel, located near the Fisherman's Monument downtown. All suites have ocean views. Rooms face the pool and have pastel color schemes. For kids, the hotel pool has a 12-ft underwater tunnel. Don't be frightened by the lifelike, 4-ft-tall wooden cobra in the lobby. ⌧ *Av. del Mar 73, 82110,* ☎ *69/82–36–22 or 01–800/711–9465,* FAX *69/82–34–99. 56 rooms, 43 suites. 2 restaurants, 2 bars, pool, exercise room, travel services. MC, V.*

$$ ⌧ **Los Sábalos.** A white high-rise in the center of the Zona Dorada, Los Sábalos has a great location, a long clean beach, and lots of action. You feel as though you're a part of things, amid the flight attendants who lay over here, and it's the home of Joe's Oyster Bar, one of the most popular discos in town. ⌧ *Av. Rodolfo T. Loaiza 100, 82110,* ☎ *69/83–53–33; 800/528–8760 in the U.S.,* FAX *69/83–81–56. 185 rooms. 3 restaurants, 2 bars, pool, 2 tennis courts, health club, beach, dance club. AE, DC, MC, V.*

$$ ⌧ **Playa Mazatlán.** Palapas are set up on the patios by the rooms in
★ this casual hotel, which is popular with Mexican families and laid-back singles more concerned with comfort than style. The bright, sunny rooms have tiled headboards over the beds and tiled tables by the windows. There's a volleyball net on the beach, and two small stands sell good, inexpensive snacks. Don't miss their Mexican Fiesta Night, without a doubt the best in town. ⌧ *Av. Rodolfo T. Loaiza 202, 82110,* ☎ *69/89–05–55; 800/762–5816 in the U.S.,* FAX *69/14–03–66. 425 rooms. 2 restaurants, bar, 3 pools, beach. AE, MC, V.*

$ ⌧ **Azteca Inn.** This hotel across the street from the Playa Mazatlán hotel is a great find for budget travelers who like to be in the center of things. The brown-and-white exterior color scheme isn't carried over into the rooms, which are decorated in reds and yellows. Most of the accommodations have two double beds, and all have cable TV. The staff couldn't be friendlier. ⌧ *Av. Loaiza 307, 82110,* ☎ *69/13–44–77,* FAX *69/13–74–76. 74 rooms. Restaurant, bar, pool, hot tub. AE, DC, MC, V.*

$ ⌧ **Hotel Siesta.** This traditional, unpretentious budget hotel in the downtown area has cable TV, air-conditioning, and immaculate rooms. Built in the 1940s, the three-story building has a large lobby aquarium filled with local fish. Interior facing rooms line a balcony, which looks into the courtyard and the Shrimp Bucket restaurant, where live music is played nightly in winter until 11 PM. ⌧ *Olas Altas 11 Sur, 82110,* ☎ *69/81–26–40, 800/697–7000,* FAX *69/13–74–76. 67 rooms. No credit cards.*

$ ⌧ **Plaza Gaviotas.** Most of the salmon-color rooms in this clean, colonial-style budget hotel, located across the street from Playa Mazatlán, have balconies, and all have showers. ⌧ *Av. Rodolfo T. Loaiza and Bugambilias 100, 82110,* ☎ *69/13–43–22,* FAX *69/13–66–85. 67 rooms. Restaurant, bar, pool. AE, DC, MC, V.*

Nightlife

Valentino's, Bora Bora, Pepe's & Joe, and Sheik are all part of the complex known as **Fiesta Land** (☎ 69/84–17–22, 69/84–16–66, or 69/84–17–77). Valentino's, with its stark white towers rising on Punta Camarón at the beginning of the Zona Dorada, still draws a glitzy crowd. Enjoy easy listening or romantic music here. Other options include karaoke, or rocking around the clock on the dance floor. **Bora Bora** is a casual palapa bar on the beach that stays alive with music and dancing from 9 PM to 4 AM. **El Caracol Disco Club** at El Cid has been revamped and has disco, live band, billiards, board and arcade games, and different theme nights throughout the week. A hefty $20 cover charge includes all drinks and games. **Pepe's & Joe** (☞ Dining, *above*) is a microbrew-beer factory with good eats, and **Sheik** is a restaurant extravaganza complete with waterfalls, ocean views, Moorish-inspired stained-glass windows, marble floors, and a central domed skylight; this place shouldn't be missed, at least for an early evening drink. **Joe's Oyster Bar** (⊠ Los Sábalos hotel, ☎ 69/83–53–33) is a popular beachfront spot where the dancing starts at noon and lasts til 2 AM. **Copa Habana** (⊠ Olas Altas 1220-B South, ☎ 69/82–41–94) serves up live Cuban salsa music for dancing Thursday–Saturday 9:30 PM–4 AM and Sunday until 2 AM for a $2 cover charge.

The **Mexican Fiesta,** held Tuesday, Thursday, and Saturday from 7 to 10:30 PM, at the **Playa Mazatlán** (☞ Lodging, *above*), is a good entertainment bet. The $20 fee includes a lavish Mexican buffet, open bar, folk dances, a cockfight, and live music for dancing. Almost all hotel travel desks can provide you with information on days and times.

Outdoor Activities and Sports

Participant Sports

ECOTOURS

The **Mazatleco Sport Center** (⊠ Rodolfo T. Loaiza 408-1B, ☎ 69/16–53–62) in the Golden Zone has mangrove kayaking, snorkeling, birdwatching, mountain biking, and sailing tours and equipment rentals.

FISHING

More than a dozen sportfishing fleets operate from the docks south of the lighthouse. Hotels can arrange charters, or you can contact the companies directly. Charters include a full day of fishing, bait, and tackle. Prices range from $70 to $80 per person on a party boat, to $200 to $300 to charter an entire boat. Charter companies to contact include **Bill Heimpel's Star Fleet** (☎ 69/82–26–65), **Flota Faro** (☎ 69/81–28–24), **Flota Bibi** (☎ 69/81–36–40), and **De Oro** (☎ 69/82–31–30).

GOLF

Arthur Martori and Merv Griffin are two of the investors in the new **Estrella del Mar and Beach Resort Complex** (☎ 69/82–33–00, FAX 69/82–33–69) south of Mazatlán proper, off the airport highway on the road to Isla de la Piedra. Here you'll find a championship 18-hole Robert Trent Jones golf course open to the public. The spectacular 27-hole course at **El Cid** (☎ 69/13–33–33), designed by Robert Trent Jones and Lee Trevino, is reserved for members of the resort, hotel guests, and their guests from November 1 through April 14; it's open to the general public the rest of the year.

HORSEBACK RIDING

You don't have to stay at **Hacienda Las Moras** (☞ Lodging, *above*) to mount one of their steeds. Day-trippers are welcome at this huge, converted tequila ranch. You can also rent horses on **Isla de la Piedra** for about $3 per hour, guide included, unless you ask to go it alone.

TENNIS

Many of the hotels have courts, some of which are open to the public, and there are a few public courts not connected to the hotels. Call in advance for reservations at **El Cid Resort** (☎ 69/13–33–33), 17 courts; the **Racket Club** (☎ 69/13–59–39), 6 courts; **Costa de Oro** (☎ 69/13–53–44), 3 courts; and **Camino Real** (☎ 69/13–11–11), 2 courts.

WATER SPORTS

Jet skis, Hobie Cats, and windsurfers are available for rent at most hotels, and parasailing is very popular along the Zona Dorada. Scuba diving and snorkeling are catching on, but there are no really great diving spots. The best is around Isla de los Venados. For rentals and trips, contact the following operators: **Doubletree** (⊠ Av. Camarón Sábalo, ☎ 69/13–02–00), **El Cid Resort Aqua Sport Center** (⊠ Av. Camarón Sábalo, ☎ 69/13–33–33), **Los Sábalos** (⊠ Av. Camarón Sábalo, ☎ 69/83–53–33), and **Camino Real Sports Center** (☎ 69/13–11–11).

Parque Acuático Mazaguas (⊠ Av. Sábalo Cerritos and Entronque Habal Cerritos, ☎ 69/88–00–41) has water slides, wading pools, and a pool with man-made waves—a total of 20 water activities on four acres.

Spectator Sports

BASEBALL

The people of Mazatlán loyally support their team, **Los Venados** (☎ 69/83–79–33), a Pacific League Triple A team. Games are played at the **Teodoro Mariscal Baseball Stadium** (⊠ Blvd. Justo Sierra) from October through April.

BULLFIGHTS AND CHARREADAS

Bullfights are held most Sunday afternoons between December and May at the bullring on Calzada Rafael Buelna. Charreadas take place year-round. Tickets (about $20) are available at the bullring (☎ 69/86–91–55, 69/86–86–33), through most hotels and travel agencies, and from **Valentino's.**

Shopping

Zona Dorada

In the Zona Dorada, particularly along Avenidas Camarón Sábalo and Rodolfo T. Loaiza, you can buy everything from piñatas to designer clothing. Leather shops are clustered along the southern end of the Zona Dorada.

CLOTHING

For sportswear, visit **Aca Joe** (⊠ Avs. Camarón Sábalo and Gaviotas, ☎ 69/13–33–00), whose line of well-designed casual clothes for men is popular throughout Mexico and the United States.

Designer's Bazaar (⊠ Av. Rodolfo T. Loaiza 217, ☎ 69/83–60–39), a two-story shop near Los Sábalos Hotel, has a nice selection of folk art and hand-embroidered clothing.

Señor Frog's Official Store (⊠ Av. del Mar, ☎ 69/82–19–25), attached to the popular restaurant of the same name (☞ Dining, *above*) carries its own fun line of souvenirs, sports, and beachwear.

CRAFTS

The best place for browsing is the **Mazatlán Arts and Crafts Center** (⊠ Av. Rodolfo T. Loaiza 417, ☎ 69/13–50–22), originally designed as a place to view artisans at work and buy their wares. The center has a good sampling of the city's souvenir selection—onyx chess sets, straw sombreros, leather jackets, sandals, coconut masks, and Mickey Mouse piñatas. The shops are open 9–6. Wednesday at 11 AM and Thursday at 11 AM and 2:30 PM there's a show for cruise-ship passengers (other spectators are welcome, but should check in first with the public relations office) featuring the *voladores de Papantla* (a traditional Indian ritual dance performed atop a tall pole) and folk dancing.

Madonna (⊠ Av. Las Garzas, ☎ 69/14–23–89) displays an extensive collection of silver and gold jewelry as well as masks and handicrafts.

Dealers Ron and Teresa Tammekand represent a number of top artists at **Mazatlán Art Gallery** (⊠ Plaza Balboa on Av. Camarón Sábalo 4480, ☎ 69/14–36–12) and hold one-person shows in winter.

La Carreta (⊠ Playa Mazatlán, ☎ 69/13–83–20) has the finest selection of high-quality Mexican folk art in town.

Sea Shell City (⊠ Av. Rodolfo T. Loaiza 407, ☎ 69/13–13–01) is a must-see. It has two floors packed with shells from around the world that have been glued, strung, and molded into every imaginable shape from lamps to necklaces. Check out the enormous fountain upstairs, covered with thousands of shells.

JEWELRY

Rubio Jewelers (⊠ Costa de Oro hotel, ☎ 69/14–31–67) carries fine gold and silver jewelry, as well as ceramics. They're also Mazatlán's exclusive distributors of Sergio Bustamante's whimsical sculptures in papier-mâché.

Downtown

The **Mercado Central,** between Calles Juárez and Serdán, is a gigantic place filled with produce, meat, fish, and handicrafts that are sold at the lowest prices in town. It takes more searching to find good-quality handicrafts, but that's part of the fun. Browse through the stalls along the street outside the market for the best crafts. At **Nidart** gallery and workshop (⊠ Libertad and Carnaval, ☎ 69/81–00–02) handcrafted leather masks and figures and other Mexican arts and crafts are displayed in a beautiful setting.

Mazatlán A to Z

Arriving and Departing

BY BUS

Transportes Norte de Sonora, Estrella Blanca, Elite, and Trans-Pacífico (☎ 69/81–36–84 or 69/81–53–08) have service to Mazatlán from Nogales, Sonora, and connect the coast with inland Mexico. The bus terminal is on Carretera Internacional 1203, three blocks behind the Sands Hotel.

BY CAR

Mazatlán is 1,212 km (751 mi) from the border city of Nogales, Arizona, via Mexico Route 15, either on the excellent, but quite expensive, toll road or on the federal highway. An overnight stop is recommended, as driving at night in Mexico can be hazardous.

BY FERRY

Ferry service between La Paz and Mazatlán was privatized a few years back and the service is now fairly reliable. The **ferry** (☎ 69/81–70–20) departs daily from Mazatlán's Playa Sur terminal at 3 PM and takes about 18 hours to reach La Paz. The one-way fare is about $20 for regular passage and $60 per person for a private cabin for two with bed and bath.

BY PLANE

Airport and Airlines. Mazatlán's **Rafael Buelna International Airport** (☎ 69/82–21–77) is serviced by several airlines. **Aeroméxico** (☎ 69/14–11–11 or 01–800/362–0200) has flights from Tucson and several cities in Mexico. **Alaska Airlines** (☎ 69/85–27–30) flies in from San Francisco and Los Angeles. **AeroCalifornia** (☎ 69/13–20–42) has flights from Los Angeles, and **Mexicana** (☎ 69/82–77–22) flies in from

Denver, Los Angeles, and several Mexican cities. **America West** (☎ 800/235–9292 in the U.S.; no local phone) links Mazatlán with Phoenix.

Between the Airport and Hotels. The airport is a good 40-minute drive from town. **Autotransportes Aeropuerto** (☎ 69/82–70–08) provides shuttles using Volkswagen vans. The cost is $6 per person for *colectivo* service, $22 for a private car.

BY SHIP

Carnival Cruise Line, Celebrity Cruises, Cunard, Holland America Line, and **Krystal P&O,** among other cruise lines, include Mazatlán on their winter itineraries.

BY TRAIN

The railroads were privatized in January of 1998 and the previously subsidized passenger service along Mexico's Pacific corridor (and elsewhere in the country) has been suspended.

Getting Around
BY BUS

There are several bus lines, which run frequently along all major avenues. Routes are clearly marked. Fares start at about 30¢ and increase slightly depending on the destination.

BY CAR

A car is not necessary in town since public transportation is good, but you might want one for a self-guided tour of the area. Rentals usually include free mileage. A Volkswagen Beetle costs about $50 per day with insurance; a sedan with air-conditioning and automatic transmission is about $90 per day.

BY TAXI AND JITNEY

Most tourist hotels are located in the Zona Dorada, about 3 km (2 mi) north of downtown, but taxis cruise the strip regularly. Fares start at $1.50. A fun way to get around is on the pulmonías. The fare, for up to three passengers, starts at about $1 and increases according to the length of the trip. Complaints have been registered, however, about one's susceptibility to fumes from other vehicles.

CITY BUS

Mazatlán's minibuses will take you from the downtown market area all the way to the Golden Zone for 25¢.

Contacts and Resources
CAR RENTAL

The following rental firms have desks at the airport: **Hertz** (⊠ Av. Camarón Sábalo 314, ☎ 69/13–60–60), **Budget** (⊠ Av. Camarón Sábalo 402, ☎ 69/13–20–00), and **National** (⊠ Av. Camarón Sábalo in Plaza el Camarón, ☎ 69/13–60–00).

EMBASSIES AND CONSULATES

United States (⊠ Av. Rodolfo T. Loaiza 202, ☎ 69/16–58–89), **Canada** (⊠ Av. Rodolfo T. Loaiza 202, ☎ 69/13–44–55).

EMERGENCIES

The **Public Tourism Ministry** (☎ 69/14–32–22) is an agency of the police department instituted specifically for tourists. **Cruz Roja** (Red Cross, ☎ 69/81–36–90); **Sharp Hospital** (☎ 69/86–56–76).

GUIDED TOURS

Marlin Tours and **Viajes el Sábalo** (☞ Travel Agencies, *below*) have a full range of tours with pickup service. Note: Formerly ubiquitous sidewalk stands staffed by persuasive hawkers of free tours of the area along with free drinks and meals—whose true goal is to sell time-shares and condos—have been limited to areas in front of these properties.

The three-hour **city tour,** which should cost around $12, is a good way to get the lay of the land, particularly downtown, which can be a bit confusing.

Cruises aboard the **Yate Fiesta** (☎ 69/85–22–37) cost about $10 and navigate the bay and the harbor, past the islands and sportfishing fleet. A day tour on the square rigger **Chemainus** (☎ 69/87–07–89) includes boom netting. They also run a sunset tour. These and other harbor cruises generally last about three hours and feature music and dancing. Viajes El Sábalo runs a five-hour tour to see the seals at Isla de la Piedra (Stone Island), with time for lunch and a swim. The cost is about $23.

Also available are all-day **country tours,** which go to Concordia and Copala (about $35). Marlin Tours runs a trip to **Teacapan,** an ecological reserve. The nine-hour excursion costs $45 and includes Continental breakfast served on the bus, a stop at Rosario, and a seafood lunch at the almost deserted La Tambora beach. The tour companies also have **individual guided tours** and **sportfishing outings.**

TRAVEL AGENCIES
American Express (⊠ Plaza Balboa, Locale 4/16, ☎ 69/13–06–00), **Marlin Tours** (⊠ Calle Laguna 300, ☎ 69/13–53–01), **Viajes el Sábalo** (⊠ Los Sábalos shopping center, ☎ 69/83–19–33, also at the Camino Real hotel [☞ Lodging, *above*]). Agencies are open weekdays 10–2 and 4–7, Saturday 10–2.

VISITOR INFORMATION
City Tourism Bureau (⊠ Av. Camarón Sábalo, Banrural Bldg., 4th floor, ☎ 69/16–51–60 to 67) is open weekdays 8:30–2 and 5–7:30.

PUERTO VALLARTA

On the edge of the Sierra Madre range sits one of the most popular vacation spots in Mexico. When Puerto Vallarta first entered the public's consciousness, with John Huston's 1964 movie *The Night of the Iguana,* it seemed an almost mythical tropical paradise. At the time it was a quiet fishing and farming community in an exquisite setting.

Puerto Vallarta's Bahía de Banderas (Bay of Flags) attracted pirates and explorers as early as the 1500s; it was used as a stopover on long sailings as a place for the crew to relax (or maybe plunder and pillage). Sir Francis Drake apparently stopped here. In the mid-1850s Don Guadalupe Sánchez Carrillo developed the bay as a port for the silver mines by the Río Cuale. Then it was known as Puerto de Peñas and had about 1,500 inhabitants. It remained a village until 1918, when it was made a municipality by the state of Jalisco and named after Ignacio L. Vallarta, a governor of Jalisco.

In the 1950s Puerto Vallarta was essentially a pretty hideaway for those in the know—the wealthy and some hardy escapists. After the publicity brought on by *The Night of the Iguana,* tourism began to boom. PV—as the former fishing village is called these days—is now a city with more than 300,000 residents. Airports, hotels, and highways have supplanted palm groves and fishing shacks. About 1.5 million tourists visit each year, and from November through April cobblestone streets are clogged with pedestrians and cars. There are now more than 9,000 hotel rooms in Puerto Vallarta.

Despite the transformation, every attempt has been made to keep the town's character and image intact. Even the parking lot at the local

Gigante supermarket is cobblestone, and by law any house built in town must be painted white. When you visit, you'll still see houses with red-tile roofs on palm-covered hills overlooking glistening blue water. Pack mules clop down the steep cobblestone streets. Within 16 km (10 mi) of town are peaceful coves, rivers rushing to the sea, and steep mountain roads that curve and twist through jungles of pines and palms.

Exploring Puerto Vallarta

Central Puerto Vallarta has three major components: the northern hotel and resort region, the downtown area (also called Old Town), and the area encompassing the Río Cuale—where you'll find a sliver of an island that's home to a language-and-arts school, the Anthropology Museum, restaurants, and shops—and Playa de los Muertos, the region's most popular beach. A rental car or cab is necessary to explore the hotel zone, which is basically a long stretch of shopping centers, restaurants, and hotels, but you don't want to have a car downtown and in the Río Cuale area. Most of the interesting sights can be covered on foot—just be sure you wear comfortable shoes for the cobblestone streets.

Numbers in the text correspond to numbers in the margin and on the Puerto Vallarta map.

A Good Walk

When you start seeing cobblestone streets, you're in the downtown area also known as **Old Town.** This is the heart of PV, a vestige of old Puerto Vallarta. Start your walk at the northern end of the delightful **malecón** ⑧, which runs parallel to Díaz Ordáz beginning at 31 de Octubre. Two and a half blocks south on Díaz Ordáz, where it merges with Morelos at the old lighthouse tower, is the town's main zócalo, Plaza de Armas. On the northern side of the busy tree-shaded plaza you'll see the **City Hall** ⑨, uninteresting but for a charming Manuel Lepe mural depicting his vision of life in Puerto Vallarta. Dominating the square from a block east is **La Iglesia de Nuestra Señora de Guadalupe** ⑩, which is topped by a distinctive crown. Los Arcos Amphitheater, across the street from the plaza on the malecon, is host to a number of concerts and other performances. Local artists show their wares here in the evenings.

Head south a few blocks and you'll come to the bustling **Mercado Municipal** (☞ Shopping, *below*); it's at the foot of the upper bridge over the Río Cuale, which runs into the bay just past Plaza Serdán. The steep hillside above, dotted with charming villas, is called **Gringo Gulch** ⑪. Reach it by climbing the steps on Zaragoza street. In the middle of the Río Cuale lies the **Isla Río Cuale** ⑫, an inviting place for dining and browsing, reachable via steps leading under the two bridges.

Sights to See

❾ **City Hall.** The late Manuel Lepe's 1981 mural depicting Puerto Vallarta as a fanciful seaside fishing and farming village hangs above the stairs on city hall's second floor. Lepe, known for his blissful, primitive-style scenes of the city, filled with smiling angels, is Puerto Vallarta's most famous—and most copied—artist. The tourism office is on the first floor. ✉ *Av. Juárez by zócalo.* ☉ *Mon.–Sat.*

⓫ **Gringo Gulch.** Named after the hundreds of expatriates from the United States who settled here in the 1950s, this neighborhood's most famous attraction is Elizabeth Taylor's former home, **Casa Kimberly,** which now includes Richard Burton's former home across the street, connected by the "love bridge" he had constructed. The house has been converted into a B&B (☞ Lodging, *below*), but you needn't despair if you're not staying there. Tours of the 23,000–square ft *casa,* which include the

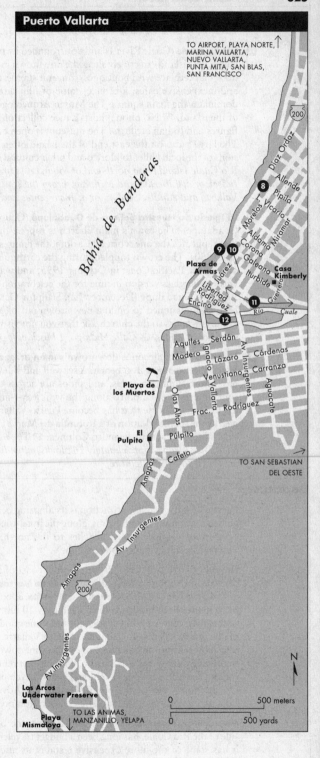

Puerto Vallarta

TO AIRPORT, PLAYA NORTE,
MARINA VALLARTA,
NUEVO VALLARTA,
PUNTA MITA, SAN BLAS,
SAN FRANCISCO

Bahía de Banderas

Díaz Ordaz
Allende
8
Pípila
Vicario
Morelos
Aldama Miramar
Corona
Galeana
9 **10** Juárez
Iturbide
Plaza de
Armas
Libertad
Rodríguez
Encino
11
Río Cuale
12

Casa
Kimberly

Guerrero

Aquiles Serdán
Madero
Ignacio Vallarta
Lázaro Cárdenas
Venustiano Carranza
Av. Insurgentes
Aguacate
Rodríguez

Playa de
los Muertos

Olas Altas
Frac.

El
Pulpito

Pulpito

Cafeto

TO SAN SEBASTIAN
DEL OESTE

Amapas

Av. Insurgentes

Amapas

200

N

Las Arcos
Underwater Preserve

Playa
Mismaloya

TO LAS ANIMAS,
MANZANILLO, YELAPA

0   500 meters

0   500 yards

200

Liz and Dick museum, run daily 9–6 in season and Monday–Saturday 10–2 off-season. ✉ *Calle Zaragoza 445,* ☎ ℻ 322/2–13–36.

⑫ **Isla Río Cuale** (Cuale River Island). Surrounded by two arms of the Río Cuale, this island effectively slices the downtown in two. It has an outdoor marketplace with boutiques, souvenir stands, trendy restaurants, and inexpensive cafés; a bronze statue of film director John Huston dominates the main square. The **Museo Arqueológico** (✉ Western tip of the island, ☎ No phone) hosts a nice collection of pre-Columbian figures and Indian artifacts. The museum is open daily 10–2 and 4–6. The large patio on the east end of the island often hosts practice sessions of the local ballet folklorico and other cultural events. ✉ *To reach Río Cuale Island from north end of town, cross bridge at Encino and Juárez or at Libertad and Miramar. From the south, cross at Ignacio Vallarta and Aquiles Serdán, or at Insurgentes and Aquiles Serdán.*

⑩ **La Iglesia de Nuestra Señora de Guadalupe** (Church of Our Lady of Guadalupe). The town's main church is topped by an ornate crown that replicates the one worn by Carlota, the empress of Mexico in the late 1860s. The crown toppled during the earthquake that shook this area of the Pacific Coast in October 1995, and was quickly replaced with a fiberglass version in time for the celebration of the Feast of the Virgin of Guadalupe (December 12). Sculptor Octavio Gonzalez has been commissioned to build a new crown out of brass. Signs posted at the entrances to the church ask that you not visit wearing shorts or sleeveless T-shirts. ✉ *Calle Hidalgo, 1 block east of zócalo.*

⑧ **Malecón.** The malecón is downtown's main drag, a nice place to rest on a white wrought-iron bench. A seawall and sidewalk run along the bay, and restaurants, cafés, and shops are across the street. There is some interesting sculpture along the walkway—among other pieces, the bronze sea horse that has become Puerto Vallarta's trademark, as well as the recent addition of a **Rotunda del Mar,** a collection of whimsical statues by artist Alejandro Colunga. ✉ *The malecón runs parallel to Díaz Ordáz approximately 16 blocks, extending from Río Cuale northeast to 31 de Octubre.*

Beaches

Puerto Vallarta's stellar attraction is its amazing beaches: crescents of golden sand, fringed with palms, along the hotel zone; endless stretches of gloriously unpopulated beaches to the north; and soft creamy beaches on craggy coves to the south.

Nayarit. North of Puerto Vallarta on the coast of Nayarit is a string of beautiful, unpopulated beach areas. **Lo de Marcos,** about 40 km (25 mi) away, is one of the most attractive. **Sayulita,** about 45 minutes away, has a great beach hidden behind a hill only 10 minutes on foot north of the town center, excellent surfing, and some good eating spots. People have described it as being like Puerto Vallarta 40 years ago. Fifteen minutes beyond Sayulita is the interesting town of **San Francisco,** unofficially known as San Pancho, with modest rental bungalows and eateries and a 1½-km-long (1-mi-long), barely developed stretch of beach. On the north end of the beach, **Costa Azul Adventure Resort** (☞ Lodging, *below*) sponsors a turtle-conservation program.

Playa de los Muertos. Playa de los Muertos, the beach on the south side of the Río Cuale, has long been a budget traveler's domain, though it has some of the more expensive restaurants and shops; it's by far the most popular and most crowded beach in Puerto Vallarta. Long ago, the beach was the site of a battle between pirates and Indians. The town's boosters tried for years to change the name Playa de los Muertos (Beach of the Dead) to Playa del Sol (Beach of the Sun), but they weren't successful. The area around the beach is now promoted as the Zona Romantica, but locals still call it Los Muertos. Strolling vendors selling lace tablecloths, wooden statues, kites, and jewelry are almost as abundant as sunbathers. Beach toys for rent include everything from rubber inner tubes to windsurfers. **Plaza Lázaro Cárdenas** is a pretty spot at the north end of the beach; to the south, Playa de los Muertos ends at a rocky point called **El Púlpito**.

<table>
<tr><td>

NEED A
BREAK?

</td><td>

Eating grilled fish on a stick at Playa de los Muertos is like having a hot dog at Coney Island. Buy it from one of the stands at the south end of the beach, then stroll along and watch the show. For a sit-down break, try the dorado-style fish, broiled with a thick layer of melted cheese at **El Dorado** (✉ Amapas and Púlpito, ☎ 322/2–15–11), on the north end of the beach.

</td></tr>
</table>

Playa Las Ánimas and Yelapa. Playa Las Ánimas and Yelapa are secluded fishing villages accessible only by boat. The former is about 25 minutes southeast of Puerto Vallarta, the latter approximately an hour away in the same direction. Both villages have small communities of hardy isolationists; of late, Yelapa has attracted more and more foreigners who settle in permanently. At Yelapa, take a 20-minute hike from the beach into the jungle to see the waterfalls. At Quimixto (another beautiful beach with calm, clear waters to the south of Mismaloya) mount a horse for a 15-minute ride up to a spectacular large clear pool under a waterfall for swimming and a light seafood lunch. Tour groups arriving on cruise ships visit the beaches daily, and motor launches leave from Tomatlán (☞ *below*) and the pier at Los Muertos for Las Ánimas, Quimixto, and Yelapa; the cost is from $10 to $20 per person.

Playa Mismaloya and Boca de Tomatlán. A visit to Puerto Vallarta without a side trip to Playa Mismaloya is nearly unthinkable, since this is where "the movie" was made. The 13-km (8-mi) drive south from the center of town on Highway 200 passes by spectacular houses, some of PV's oldest and quietest resorts, and a slew of condo and time-sharing developments. A pretty cove, somewhat spoiled by La Jolla de Mismaloya—a huge hotel complex built on its shores—Mismaloya is backed by rugged, rocky hills and affords a good view of **Los Arcos,** a rock formation in the water. Catamaran cruises, which can be booked through **Vallarta Adventures** (☎ 322/1–06–57), leave the Cruise Ship Terminal nightly at 6 for dinner and dancing on the terraces of John Huston's former home, set at the edge of the jungle on a private bay in Las Caletas, southeast of Mismaloya Beach (and accessible only by boat). Or hoist the skull and crossbones and depart on the *Marigalante* (☎ 322/ 31–03–09 or 322/3–16–62), a replica of a 15th century caravel that sails to the Marietas Islands during the day and passes Los Arcos on a sunset cruise that includes fireworks and a BBQ dinner.

Boca de Tomatlán is a small village at the mouth of the Tomatlán River, about 4 km (2½ mi) south of Mismaloya and 17 km (10½ mi) south of Puerto Vallarta. It's a beautiful spot away from the crowds and popular with the locals. Just before you reach the dirt road to the beach, there are several large palapa restaurants. Chee Chee's, a massive restaurant, shopping, and swimming-pool complex, spreads down a steep hillside like a small village. Farther along the main road, through Boca, is Chico's Paradise (☞ Dining, *below*). Just a bit farther on is Las Orquidias, a riverfront restaurant half a mile down a dirt road, where you can swim in clear river pools and delight in the orchids blooming there in the summer. Tour boats leave from Boca to Los Arcos and the more secluded beaches of Playa Las Ánimas and Yelapa (☞ *above*).

Playa Norte. Also known as Playa de Oro, this is Puerto Vallarta's north-ernmost beach, stretching from the marina and cruise-ship terminal to downtown. The beach changes a bit with the character of each hotel it fronts, but it is particularly nice by the Fiesta Americana and the Krys-tal hotels.

Punta de Mita. Twelve kilometers (7 miles) north of Nuevo Vallarta, on yet another beautiful beach, is the town of Bucerias. From here, you fol-low the bend of Banderas Bay past several small and pristine beaches—including Cruz de Huanacaxtle and Anclote—to Punta de Mita, on the northern tip of the Bahía de Banderas. A four-lane highway is under con-struction to link it to the Puerto Vallarta airport now that this area has become the site of new developments, including the posh Four Seasons Resort, slated to open by May '99. Punta de Mita has blue bay water that's perfect for swimming, and around the bend there are waves for surfing. Here, the views of the bay and of the Sierra Madre mountains are fantastic. This is a prime spot to view a sunset and, during the win-ter months, the whales that come here to mate in the warm waters of the Mexican Pacific. Scuba divers like the fairly clear waters and abundance of tropical fish and coral on the bay side of the **Isla Marietas,** offshore.

Dining

$$$$ ✕ **Café des Artistes.** Quite breathtaking and exquisitely romantic, this is Puerto Vallarta's most sophisticated dining spot. Owner/chef Thierry Blouet combines Mexican ingredients with European techniques to pro-duce such interesting combinations as cream of prawn and pumpkin soup, marinated mussels in white wine with cream and herbs, and roast duck with tamarind and honey. A piano/flute duo provides the musi-cal accompaniment. ✉ *Guadalupe Sánchez 740,* ☎ *322/2–32–28. Reservations essential. AE, DC, MC, V. No lunch.*

$$$$ ✕ **Cuiza.** This spacious and beautiful riverside restaurant is enchant-ing in its evening lights. Don't miss the sautéed crabcakes St. Moritz in a papaya-basil salsa, or the scallops mandarin with a fine ginger un-dertone, for appetizers. Jazz singer and guitarist Beverly and Willow perform from 8:30 on. ✉ *Isla Río Cuale No. 3,* ☎ *322/2–56–46. AE, DC, MC, V.*

$$$ ✕ **Adobe Café.** Shades of white and earth tones, stark trees, fresh flowers, and an interesting menu make for a delightful dining experi-ence. Specialties include cream of coriander soup, pork tenderloin with peach chutney, and one of the best desserts in town, a sinfully rich chocolate mousse between two layers of chocolate cake and chocolate icing. ✉ *Basilio Badillo 252,* ☎ *322/2–67–20. AE, MC, V. No lunch.*

$$$ ✕ **Bombo's.** This place is elegant and romantic, with a serene orchid-and-white decor, flickering candles, and a sweeping view of Puerto Val-larta. An exceptionally creative international menu includes smoked salmon mousse, kiwi margaritas, and cream of artichoke soup with pis-tachio nuts. ✉ *Corona 327, at Matamoros,* ☎ *322/2–51–64. AE, MC, V. No lunch.*

$$$ ✕ **Café Maximilian.** Efficient and fluid service accompanied by gen-uine smiles from both diners and staff make this a top spot to eat out in Los Muertos. Viennese-German entrées dominate the menu, in-cluding braised baby lamb strips with rosemary and an excellent pork loin escallop with homemade noodles. A separate espresso and dessert bar share the dozen sidewalk tables. ✉ *Olas Altas 380,* ☎ *322/3–07–60. AE, MC, V.*

$$$ ✕ **Chef Roger.** The cozy patio of a typical Puerto Vallarta house is the
★ unpretentious setting for one of the best restaurants in town. Roger Dreier, the Swiss owner and chef, combines his European training with Mexican ingredients, and the results are superb. Don't leave town

without trying the coconut breaded shrimp with pineapple sauce, and for dessert, the fried apples with vanilla sauce. Upstairs you'll find a bar and atrium. ⊠ *Augustín Rodríguez 267,* ☎ *322/2–59–00. Reservations essential. AE, DC, MC, V. No lunch.*

$$$ ✗ **Daiquiri Dick's.** The beachside patio dining room of this long-time *vallartense* favorite for Sunday brunch frames one of the best views of the bay. The Caesar salad explodes with flavor. The medallions of beef tenderloin demi-glacé are superb. Finish off with a hazelnut daiquiri. ⊠ *Olas Altas 314,* ☎ *322/2–05–66. MC, V.*

$$$ ✗ **Trio.** Two young German chefs, Bernhard Guth and Peter Lodes, have become the favorites of local diners with their avant-garde creations— like Lebanese beet salad with goat cheese, or chili-roasted grilled red snapper fillet with a vegetable ratatouille and lemon cilantro sauce. The service at this downtown garden restaurant is top notch, the wine list large enough to please most tastes. Italian jazzman Lello Scassa plays saxophone weekends. ⊠ *Guerrero 264,* ☎ *322/2–21–96. AE, MC, V.*

$$ ✗ **Don Pedro's.** Everything is a treat at this giant beachfront palapa
★ in Sayulita, half an hour north of the airport, where European-trained chef and co-owner Nicholas Parrillo serves an array of fish, seafood, and poultry sprinkled with herbs and grilled over mesquite. Everything is fresh as can be and made on the premises, from the crusty herbed breads and pizzas to the rich mango ice cream. ⊠ *Calle Marlin 2, midway along Sayulita town beach, 35 km (22 mi) north of Puerto Vallarta airport,* ☎ *327/5–02–29. MC, V. Closed July–Oct.*

$$ ✗ **Felipe's.** Sitting high on a hill, Felipe Palacio's gracious family home has the charm of old Vallarta mixed with spectacular views of the bay and town from its multilevel terraces. Grilled seafood and steaks are superbly prepared. ⊠ *Insurgentes 466,* ☎ *322/2–38–20. AE, MC, V.*

$$ ✗ **Flaming Sombrero.** Unique: grill your own marinated beef, lamb, chicken, pork, marlin, or prawns on a huge searing brass sombrero at the table with vegetables sizzling on the rim. Also served are English fish and chips, prawns, and lobster. The drink of the house is a Nicholashka: chew a slice of lime with ground coffee and sugar and take shot of tequila. ⊠ *31 de Octubre 380,* ☎ *322/2–55–95. MC, V.*

$$ ✗ **Las Palomas.** Better known as a prime spot for people-watching than for its cuisine, this malecón café has become a hangout for Puerto Vallarta regulars. You'll probably even run into a few of the characters depicted in the café's wall mural. ⊠ *Díaz Ordáz at Aldama,* ☎ *322/ 2–36–75. Reservations not accepted. AE, MC, V.*

$–$$ ✗ **Chico's Paradise.** It's easy to while away hours—or even the day—
★ under the huge palapa, enjoying the sound of the waterfall, taking a dip in the river, or watching tortillas being made by hand. Two parrots will keep you occupied with their antics. Seafood, including fresh jumbo shrimp or stuffed crab, is a specialty, but *chiles rellenos* (stuffed chili peppers) and chicken burritos are also popular. Or just come for some of the huge tropical drinks—take the bus marked MISMALOYA (they run about every 15 minutes from the corner of Insurgentes and Basilio Badillo to Boca de Tomatlán and back). ⊠ *Carretera a Manzanillo, Km 20,* ☎ *322/2–07–47. No credit cards.*

$ ✗ **Andale.** A Playa de los Muertos hangout and a good spot for an afternoon beer with locals, this restaurant serves giant shrimp, great herb garlic bread, and delicious black bean soup. ⊠ *Paseo de Velasco 425,* ☎ *322/2–10–54. DC, MC, V.*

$ ✗ **Graffiti Resto Bar.** This pleasant neighborhood eatery is worth the hike up the steep painted stairs that lead to Liz Taylor's former home. French chef Jean Talbot serves up frittatas and good toasted bagels for breakfast. New England clam chowder and the veal scallopini with a very mild marsala sauce are recommended at dinner. ⊠ *Miramar 271, in Gringo Gulch,* ☎ *322/3–10–02. DC, MC, V.*

$ ✕ **Really Rosie's.** This is where to go if you want a taste of home. With a menu listing homemade corned beef hash, biscuits and gravy, and cheese blintzes for breakfast—and meat loaf and country-fried steak and mashed potatoes among other dinner favorites—Rosie Sorrenson's food will soothe you if you're wearying of the exotic. And the place delivers. ✉ *31 de Octubre 149,* ☎ *322/2–44–77. DC, MC, V.*

$ ✕ **Rito's Baci.** This popular deli and pizza parlor delivers to homes and hotels. All the pastas are made on the premises. The crispy-crusted pizza is excellent, and 24 types of pasta are fresh and flavorful. Try the sausage sandwich as well. Owner Rito Calzada is the host and chef. ✉ *Calle Ortiz de Domínguez 181,* ☎ *322/2–64–48. MC, V.*

Lodging

Most of PV's deluxe resorts are located to the north of downtown. Many are concentrated in the Marina Vallarta complex, practically a town unto itself with a marina, hundreds of condominiums, shopping centers, an 18-hole golf course, and the Royal Pacific Yacht Club. Farther north is Nuevo Vallarta, just over the Jalisco state line in Nayarit, at the mouth of the Río Ameca. This beautiful community with beachfront houses and condos on canals with direct access to the bay is home to several all-inclusive resorts, among them the Sierra Puerto Vallarta and two Diamond Resort hotels. South of downtown and the Río Cuale, in the Playa de los Muertos and Olas Altas areas, the rates are lower. If you head farther south still, the prices go up again: some spectacular properties are tucked away on hidden coves on the road to Manzanillo.

Rates at most hotels usually go down 25% to 30% just after Easter week through December 15, although they rebound during July and August when most nationals take a two-week vacation. Reservations are a must at Christmas, the New Year, Easter, and in July and August. Hotels in the state of Jalisco charge a 2% room tax in addition to the 15% VAT.

$$$$ 🏨 **Four Seasons Resort.** This secluded, private resort community at Punta
★ Mita, a 40-minute drive northwest of the Puerto Vallarta International Airport, is scheduled for a May 1999 opening. The 79 rooms and 21 suites are housed in quaint red-tile-roofed Mexican-style casitas of one, two, and three stories. The unusually spacious rooms, furnished like a luxurious Mexican home and fitted with the traditional Four Seasons amenities, feature a private terrace or balcony, a coffeemaker, and views of the beach and sea. Each of the suites has a private plunge pool as well as a fax machine. Sports facilities include a Jack Nicklaus–designed 18-hole championship golf course. In winter, Punta Mita is a prime whale-watching spot. ✉ *Punta Mita, Nayarit 63732,* ☎ *322/1–24–81; 800/322–3442 in the U.S.,* 𝖥𝖠𝖷 *322/1–24–88. 79 rooms, 21 suites. Restaurant, bar, pool, hot tub, spa, 18-hole golf course, 2 tennis courts. AE, DC, MC, V.*

$$$$ 🏨 **La Jolla de Mismaloya.** Despite the fact that the overpowering de-
★ sign of this hotel has ruined the view of beautiful Mismaloya Bay, the lucky guests here literally have half of the bay to themselves, as well as a fabulous view of Puerto Vallarta's famous arches (rock formations jutting out of the sea). The southern half of the bay is crowded with beachfront restaurants and motor launches that go to even more remote beaches. The hotel's huge one- and two-bedroom suites have terraces, and the many activities for kids makes it an ideal family getaway. This hotel consistently gets high marks from guests. ✉ *Off Hwy. 200 at Mismaloya Bay, 48300,* ☎ *322/8–06–60; 800/322–2344 in the U.S.,* 𝖥𝖠𝖷 *322/8–05–00. 303 suites. 5 restaurants, bar, 4 pools, 2 tennis courts, exercise room, beach. AE, DC, MC, V.*

$$$$ ▣ **Marriott Casa Magna.** Located in Marina Vallarta, with El Salado beach to the front and the Marina's 18-hole, Joe Finger–designed golf course to the rear, the Marriott Casa Magna is one of Vallarta's newest, largest, and most glamorous hotels. The vast, plant-filled marble lobbies that open onto the huge pool area are hung with chandeliers. The rooms are decorated with light woods and cream colors. All have at least a partial view of the bay. And if the water sports, tennis, restaurants, nightclubs, kids' club, and other amenities of the hotel aren't enough, you also have access to the facilities of the Marina Vallarta complex, including a huge shopping center, a yacht club, and yet more restaurants. Rates include a gigantic buffet breakfast. ⊠ *Marina Vallarta, 48354,* ☎ *322/1–00–04; 800/223–6388,* 𝔽𝔸𝕏 *322/1–07–60. 433 rooms, 29 suites. 4 restaurants, 3 bars, pool, 3 tennis courts, exercise room, beach, dance club. AE, DC, MC, V.*

$$$$
★ ▣ **Meliá Puerto Vallarta.** On the beach in Marina Vallarta, this Sol Meliá hotel is a top-of-the-line all-inclusive resort only three blocks from the marina's 18-hole golf course. The exterior is an off-putting institutional style, but the lobby is a delicious blend of textures and colors, with marble and tile floors contrasting with colorful Mexican crafts and cozy wicker furniture. The large rooms are decorated in soft natural tones of cream and sand, with colorful accents. Amenities include hair dryers and in-room safes, the largest pool in the area—shaped like Picasso's *The Dove*—the Mini Club, an outdoor theater, and nightly shows. Two children under the age of seven can stay free of charge (including meals and activities) if they share a room with their parents. ⊠ *Paseo de la Marina Sur, 48354,* ☎ *322/1–02–00; 800/336–3542 in the U.S.,* 𝔽𝔸𝕏 *322/1–01–18. 370 rooms and suites. 3 restaurants, 3 bars, pool, 2 tennis courts, archery, exercise room, beach, shops, video games, children's program (ages 4–12), meeting rooms. AE, DC, MC, V.*

$$$$ ▣ **Paradise Village.** Built like an Aztec pyramid, this Nuevo Vallarta hotel has its own marina and zoo (with a pair of tigers, a crocodile, deer, and various birds). All suites have a bone color scheme with tile floors and balconies with either marina or ocean views. Sofa-beds and a full kitchen—including stove, microwave, refrigerator, and good cookware—are de rigueur. Locals come by to use the spa, which is noted for its massages and facials and has weights, aerobic machines, a steam room, and sauna. ⊠ *Paseo de los Cocoteros 18, Nuevo Vallarta, 63732,* ☎ *322/6–67–07,* 𝔽𝔸𝕏 *329/6–67–13. 480 suites. 2 restaurants, 2 bars, 2 snack bars, 3 pools, 4 tennis courts, aerobics, volleyball, beach, windsurfing, jet skiing, travel services, car rental. AE, DC, MC, V.*

$$$$ ▣ **Sierra Hotel Nuevo Vallarta.** Situated on a long, wide expanse of creamy sand beach in Nuevo Vallarta, the Sierra is another deluxe all-inclusive property. The rooms are light and airy, with tile floors, light-wood and wicker furniture, and the ubiquitous pastel bedspreads. Activities are nonstop: There are cookouts, beach parties, Mexican fiestas, disco blasts, theme nights, musicals, karaoke, restaurants, and bars. Daytime activities include aerobics, beach and pool volleyball, tennis, minigolf, windsurfing, kayaking, and water biking, as well as jungle and city tours. A golf course is minutes away. ⊠ *Paseo de los Cocoteros 19, Nuevo Vallarta, 63732,* ☎ *329/7–13–00; 281/448–2829,* 𝔽𝔸𝕏 *329/7–08–00. 350 rooms and suites. 3 restaurants, 3 bars, 3 pools, tennis court, aerobics, volleyball, beach, windsurfing. AE, DC, MC, V.*

$$$$ ▣ **Westin Regina.** This attractive hotel is situated on a choice 21-acre site in Marina Vallarta. In addition to four pools, a long stretch of beach, and a full range of facilities and activities (including an excellent kids' club), the Westin has spacious balconied rooms with brightly colored, handwoven spreads and drapes. Thirteen of the suites have Jacuzzis; the presidential suite is decorated with sculpture by Sergio Bustamante. Each room has at least a partial view of the bay. The hotel also has a turtle nursery, which allows you to help release baby turtles back to the sea. ⊠ *Paseo de la Marina Sur 205, 48321,* ☎ *322/1–11–00; 800/228–3000 in the U.S.,* ℻ *322/1–11–41. 280 rooms, 14 suites. 2 restaurants, 3 bars, 4 pools, 3 tennis courts, exercise room, beach, video games. AE, DC, MC, V.*

$$$–$$$$ 🏨 **Krystal Vallarta.** A full-service resort that sprawls over acreage equiv-
★ alent to that of a small town, the Krystal has hotel rooms and villas with private pools. Many of the accommodations exude Mexican character, with tiled floors and Spanish colonial–style furnishings. There are five restaurants, including Tango, which serves Argentine *churrasco* (thick rib steaks); Kamakura, which serves Japanese food; and Bogart's, the signature restaurant of the Krystal chain, with a Casablanca theme. Not all rooms are by the ocean, but the secluded beach can accommodate all sunseekers. ⊠ *Carretera Aeropuerto, 48300,* ☎ *322/ 4–01–11; 800/231–9860 in the U.S.,* ℻ *322/4–02–22. 421 rooms, 33 villas. 5 restaurants, 3 bars, 4 pools, 2 tennis courts, beach, dance club, travel services. AE, DC, MC, V.*

$$$ 🏨 **Camino Real.** One of PV's first hotels, this property sits on a lovely
★ small bay south of town. The rooms have cool marble floors with white furniture and bright pink, yellow, and purple highlights against stark white walls. The hotel has all the five-star touches—from plush robes in the rooms and the feel of an established, comfortable resort to the palapas on the beach and the fragrant white jasmine blooming along the natural waterfall. La Brisa restaurant, on the northern end of the beach, serves superb seafood lunches. A newer 11-story tower houses the Camino Real Club, which also has a convention-banquet center. The club's upper floors have whirlpool baths. ⊠ *Playa Las Estacas, 48300,* ☎ *322/1–50–00; 800/722–6466 in the U.S.,* ℻ *322/1–60–00. 337 rooms. 5 restaurants, 3 bars, 2 pools, wading pool, 2 tennis courts, exercise room, health club, beach. AE, DC, MC, V.*

$$$ 🏨 **Continental Plaza Puerto Vallarta.** Ideal for tennis lovers, this Mexican colonial complex has a tennis club with eight courts and daily tennis clinics. The resort has a shopping plaza, several restaurants and bars, a large swimming pool, and a nice beach. ⊠ *Carretera Aeropuerto, Km 0.5, Zona Hotelera Las Glorias, 48300,* ☎ *322/4–01–23; 800/882– 6684 in the U.S.,* ℻ *322/4–52–36. 309 rooms, 113 suites. 3 restaurants, 2 bars, pool, 8 tennis courts, beach. AE, DC, MC, V.*

$$$ 🏨 **Fiesta Americana.** A seven-story palapa covers the lobby and a large round bar. The dramatically designed terra-cotta building rises above a deep blue pool that flows under bridges, palm oases, and palapa restaurants set on platforms over the water. The rooms have a modern pink and terra-cotta color scheme; each has white marble floors, tiled bath with powerful shower, and balcony. The beach bustles with activity—parasailing, windsurfing, boat touring, snorkeling, and, of course, sunbathing. The restaurants are excellent, especially the breakfast buffet by the pool. ⊠ *Blvd. Francisco M. Ascencío, Km 2.5, 48300,* ☎ *322/4–20–10 or 01–800/504–5000; 800/345—5094 in the U.S.,* ℻ *322/4–21–08. 255 rooms, 36 suites. 3 restaurants, 5 bars, room service, pool, beauty salon, excercise room, beach, dance club, travel services. AE, DC, MC, V.*

$$–$$$ 🏨 **Buenaventura.** This hotel's location is ideal, on the edge of down-
★ town, within walking distance (10 blocks or so) of the Río Cuale and, in the opposite direction, of the shops, hotels, and restaurants on the airport highway. From the street it looks rather austere, but just inside the door is an enormous five-story open lobby and bar. The bright, cheerful rooms, decorated in white and green, have beamed ceilings and palewood furnishings and all have a view of the ocean. A new seven-story luxury tower has opened with six different styles of suites, most with at least one Jacuzzi. ⊠ *Av. México 1301, 48350,* ☎ *322/2–37–37,* ℻

322/2–35–46. *220 rooms, 90 suites. 2 restaurants, 2 bars, 2 pools, hot tub, exercise room, beach. AE, DC, MC, V.*

$$–$$$ ☆ ★ 🏨 **Casa Kimberly.** The former homes of Elizabeth Taylor and Richard Burton, located on opposite sides of the street but joined by a footbridge (in a part of town now called Gringo Gulch), have been converted into a B&B. Both houses are surprisingly unpretentious; only Liz's had a pool. The current owner, naturally enough, exploits the Liz and Dick legend and has added on a museum devoted to them. Lavender (supposedly Elizabeth's favorite color, at least during her Puerto Vallarta days) prevails, and tables and walls are adorned with photos of the famous lovers. Rates include a full breakfast. ⊠ *Calle Zaragoza 445, 48300,* ☎ 🗏 *322/2–13–36. 8 suites. Pool. No credit cards.*

$$–$$$ ★ 🏨 **Costa Azul Adventure Resort.** This environment-friendly resort, some 48 km (30 mi) north of Puerto Vallarta, was designed by a group of southern Californians, and predictably, surfing is big here. But that's not all: the adventure trips, led by enthusiastic and knowledgeable guides, range from kayaking and snorkeling to deep-sea fishing and whale-watching. Cultural trips as well as horseback riding and mountain biking through an ecological preserve are also available. The sweeping, palmfringed beach is as yet unspoiled. Rooms in this intimate, friendly place are simply but attractively decorated, and the adventure package, including all meals and most activities, is very reasonably priced. There is a minimum two-night stay. ⊠ *Km 188 Carretera Tepic–Puerto Vallarta, San Francisco, Nayarit 63732,* ☎ 🗏 *327/5–00–99,* ☎ *800/ 365–7613 in the U.S. 28 units. Restaurant, bar, pool, horseback riding, snorkeling, surfing, boating. MC, V.*

$$–$$$ ★ 🏨 **Dulce Vida.** This rambling group of six suites of various sizes—four blocks off the bustling malecón—is decorated with Mexican art and comfortable furniture. All overlook a beautiful red-tile pool, and all have kitchens; the largest has a dining room table and service for eight. Located in a Mexican neighborhood with all the charm of crowing roosters and burros plodding down the cobblestone road, this friendly spot is booked for a few dozen wedding parties each year due to its beautiful gardens and large patios overlooking the bay. It's also a quiet spot for couples looking for romance. ⊠ *Calle Aldama 291, 48300,* ☎ 🗏 *322/2–10–08. 6 suites. Pool. AE, MC, V.*

$$–$$$ 🏨 **Villa Amor.** Tarzan never had it so good. What began as a home on top of a hill migrated into luxury palapa suites among the trees, with more outdoor than indoor living and beautiful views of Sayulita's coast. The larger suites have plunge pools on their terraces—but leave the younger children at home, as they are definitely not childproof. A good restaurant on the premises has live music on weekends. A beautiful beach is just a two-minute walk away. ⊠ *Playa Sayulita, Nayarit,* ☎ 🗏 *327/5–01–96; 800/225–4885 in the U.S. 10 villas. Restaurant, snorkeling, surfing. No credit cards.*

$$ 🏨 **Majahuitas Resort.** With a third of a mile of beach on its own bay, this intimate resort is as close to your own island as you can get on Banderas Bay. There are no roads to these unique beach houses, which are only 20 minutes from Boca de Tomatlán by boat. Rates include breakfast and dinner. ⊠ *Playa Majahuitas, El Tuito,* ☎ 🗏 *322/1–58– 04. Pool. No credit cards.*

$$ 🏨 **Playa Los Arcos.** By far the most popular hotel on the beach by the Río Cuale, Los Arcos has a pretty central courtyard and pool and a friendly air. A glass elevator rises by the pool to the rooms, which are fitted with light-wood and pastel furnishings and have small balconies. ⊠ *Olas Altas 380, 48380,* ☎ *322/2–05–83,* 🗏 *322/2–24–18. 180 rooms. Restaurant, bar, pool, beach. AE, DC, MC, V.*

$ ★ 🏨 **Hotel Rosita.** The city's first official hotel opened its doors in 1948. Since then, this family-run business has served many repeat guests. On the northern edge of the malecón, it's a great spot for budget travelers who want to be close to the action. All rooms have air-conditioning. ⊠ *Paseo Díaz Ordaz 901, 48380,* ☎ *322/2–10–33,* 𝔽𝔸𝕏 *322/1–21–71. 112 rooms. Restaurant, pool. AE, MC, V.*

$ ⌑ **Posada de Roger.** One of PV's least expensive hotels, the Posada
★ de Roger is in many ways the most enjoyable, if you like the company of Europeans and Canadians who are savvy about budget traveling. The rooms have telephones, TVs, and air-conditioning; the showers are hot, the beds comfortable, and the pool is an international meeting spot. You can have your mail held here, and the desk clerks are knowledgeable about other budget hotels and restaurants. ⊠ *Basilio Badillo 237, 48380,* ☎ *322/2–08–36,* 𝔽𝔸𝕏 *322/3–04–82. 50 rooms. Restaurant, bar, pool. AE, MC, V.*

En Route to Manzanillo

The coastline south of Puerto Vallarta is sprinkled with some of the Mexican Riviera's most exclusive and secluded one-of-a-kind resorts. But you'll never see them from Highway 200 as you head south—it's a rugged, twisting road a short distance from the coast that runs through a tropical forest of pines and palms. Most resorts are on unpaved roads. To get down here, fly to Puerto Vallarta or Manzanillo (one hour south) and take a taxi or hotel van to your resort. Once in situ, you're likely to stay put for a week or more, leaving only for the requisite shopping spree in PV. South of PV, the best resorts are in Cihuatlán, Careyes, and San Patricio Melaque.

Lodging

$$$$ ⌑ **Bel-Air Costa Careyes.** Resembling an idyllic village nestled on a peaceful bay, this exquisitely understated luxury resort is situated on Mexico's "Turtle Coast," 98 km (60 mi) north of Manzanillo airport and 172 km (107 mi) south of Puerto Vallarta. There are 51 recently renovated intimate rooms and suites decorated in warm Mediterranean colors (some with private plunge pools), pool, tennis, golf nearby at El Tamarindo, and a full-service spa featuring European beauty and body treatments. There's also a full range of water sports and excursions to nearby lagoons, tropical forests, and Teapa Beach to see turtles breeding between July and October. ⊠ *Barra de Navidad Hwy., Km 53.5, Cihuatlán, Jalisco 48970,* ☎ *335/1–00–00,* 𝔽𝔸𝕏 *335/1–10–00. 51 rooms and suites. Restaurant, bar, pool, spa, 2 tennis courts, beach, snorkeling, boating, fishing. AE, DC, MC, V.*

$$$$ ⌑ **El Tamarindo.** This exclusive resort, nestled in tropical palm groves
★ and surrounded by more than 2,000 acres of ecological reserve and jungle, lies on 16 km (10 mi) of private coast. The 14 villas, all with private plunge pools, have been designed of natural regional materials and textures, and blended with soft colors. Meals are served under an awning on the beach in a casual rustic setting. Highlights include an 18-hole golf course, a tennis club, three secluded beaches, and gracious service. ⊠ *Melaque–Puerto Vallarta Hwy., Km 7.5, Cihuatlán, Jalisco 48970,* ☎ *335/1–50–31,* 𝔽𝔸𝕏 *335/1–50–32. 14 villas. Restaurant, bar, pool, 18-hole golf course, 2 tennis courts, beach, dive shop, snorkeling, boating. AE, DC, MC, V.*

$$$$ ⌑ **Las Alamandas.** One of Mexico's most exclusive—and expensive—
★ resorts, Las Alamandas is low key rather than glitzy. Surrounded by a natural preserve with abundant wildlife, the property's villas and one casita are decorated with folk art and traditional Mexican furnishings (some also have TVs and VCRs). Among the outdoor activities are horseback riding, fishing, hot-air balloon rides, and boat rides along the San Nicolás River. Many guests fly into the hotel's private helipad; others take the hotel's limo from either the Puerto Vallarta (1¾ hours) or Man-

zanillo (1½ hours) airport. There's a two-night-stay minimum; meal packages are available. ⊠ *Apdo. Postal 201, San Patricio Melaque, Jalisco 48980,* ☎ *328/5–55–00,* FAX *328/5–50–27. Reservations in the U.S.:* ⊠ *3525 Sage Rd., Houston, TX 77056,* ☎ *713/961–3117 or 800/ 223–6510,* FAX *713/961–3411. Casita, 4 villas. Restaurant, in-room VCRs, pool, tennis court, croquet, exercise room, Ping-Pong, volley-ball, 5 beaches, mountain bikes. AE, MC, V.*

$$$ 🏨 **Playa Blanca.** This Club Med has all the services the pioneer all-inclusive chain is known for—diving, fishing, pool bars, horseback riding, and even a trapeze and circus school. The food, usually served buffet style, is ample and good, and there's a dinner-only restaurant where you can be served by waiters. The resort doesn't exactly feel isolated: with 300 rooms, a disco, and aerobics classes, the ambience is more celebratory than somnolent. Guests here tend to be earthy, active couples and singles in their late 20s to early 40s. Playa Blanca has a rock-climbing wall and offers mountain biking. The staff comes from around the world. ⊠ *Off Hwy. 200, Playa Blanca, Costa Careyes 48980,* ☎ *335/1–00–01 or 335/1–00–02; 800/258–2633 in the U.S.,* FAX *335/1–00–04. 300 rooms. 2 restaurants, bar, dining rooms, pool, tennis court, horseback riding, beach. AE, DC, MC, V.*

Nightlife and the Arts

Puerto Vallarta is a party town, where the discos open at 10 PM and stay open until 3 or 4 AM. A minimum $20 cover charge is common in the popular discos, many of which are at hotels. The Krystal has **Christine's,** which features a spectacular light show set to music from disco to classic rock nightly at 11:30. **Champions Sports Bar,** at the Marriott, has music for almost all ages, and **Friday López,** at the Fiesta Americana, has karaoke and dancing. **The Zoo** (⊠ Díaz Ordaz 630, ☎ 322/2–49–45) and **Cactus Club** (⊠ Ignacio Vallarta 399, ☎ 322/2–60–37) attract a young crowd. Motorcycle fans can let loose at **The American Legend** (⊠ Ignacio L. Vallarta 237, ☎ 322/2–24–00), where live rock mixes with Harley Davidsons. Harley rentals and clothing are available.

Everything its name implies and more, **Collage** (☎ 322/1–05–05), on the highway at the Marina Vallarta complex, hosts several restaurants, a bowling alley, a large-screen video-golf game, billiards, two bars, shuffleboard, a video arcade, and a disco. The **Kit Kat** (⊠ Pulpita 120 ☎ 322/3–03–93), somewhere between Art Deco and a Santa Monica fern bar, has the best martinis in town. **Cuiza** (⊠ Isla Río Cuale 3, ☎ 322/2–56–46) has the best live jazz in the hands of Beverly and Willow, and an excellent bar and cigar shop. **El Faro** (the lighthouse) (⊠ Royal Pacific Yacht Club, Marina Vallarta, ☎ 322/1–05–41) is a romantic spot to watch a lightning storm roll into the bay at night in hurricane season, or just to see a good piece of the bay and marina from on high.

Mexican **fiestas** are popular at the hotels and can be lavish affairs with buffet dinners, folk dances, and fireworks. Reservations may be made with the hotels or travel agencies. Some of the more spectacular shows are at **La Iguana Tourist Center** (☎ 322/2–01–05), the Krystal, and the Sheraton.

Outdoor Activities and Sports

Swimming, sailing, windsurfing, and parasailing are popular sports at the beachfront hotels, which have stands on the beach offering boat trips and equipment. You needn't be a guest to buy these services.

Biking

Bike Mexico (✉ Guerrero 361, ☎ 322/3–16–80) provides the gear (21-speed mountain bikes, helmets, lunch, and refreshments) for four- to six-hour bike tours to rivers, mountains and jungles; these jaunts are tailored to each rider's experience and fitness level.

B-B-Bobby's Bikes (✉ Miramar 399, ☎ 322/3–00–08) rents all types of bikes and equipment by the day or week and has tours.

Fishing

The Progreso Fishermen's Cooperative has a shack on the north end of the malecón and has a variety of fishing trips; most hotels can arrange your reservations. Large group boats cost about $60 per person for a day's fishing. Other cruisers may be chartered for prices ranging from $150 to $350 a day, depending on the size of the boat and the length of the trip. Charters include a skipper, license, bait, and tackle; some also include lunch. Canadian Candice Shaw runs a bilingual-crewed boat, **Fishing with Carolina,** with three chairs (☎ 322/4–72–50 329/ 2–29–53) that runs $300 for an all-day trip.

Golf

There is a Joe Finger–designed, 18-hole course at the **Marina Vallarta** complex (☎ 322/1–01–73). The 18-hole course at **Los Flamingos Country Club** (✉ 12 km [8 mi] north of airport, ☎ 329/8–02–80) was designed by Percy Clifford. Reservations should be made through your hotel a day in advance. Two new courses in nearby Nayarit state are expected to be open by 2000.

Horseback Riding

Horseback riding along the shore is popular, and horses can be rented by the hour at major beaches. Several stables, including **Rancho Charro** (✉ Francisco Villa 895, ☎ 322/4–01–14) and **Rancho El Ojo de Agua** (✉ Cerrada de Cardenal 227, ☎ 322/4–82–40), run three-hour trips into the mountains, sunset rides, and longer excursions to charming colonial villages in the Sierra Madre. Time is allotted for lunch and a swim in a mountain stream or lake.

Swim with the Dolphins

A magical experience awaits those at **Dolfin Adventure park** where you can touch, feel, talk to, and even kiss one of five Pacific dolphins. The center has a program for children with special needs. Reservations are a must. (✉ Marina Nueva Vallarta, ☎ 322/1–06–57 or 329/7–07–07).

Ultra-Light Planes

See and photograph Vallarta from a bird's-eye view while certified pilots from **Wings Air Tours** (✉ Francisco Medina Ascencío 2333, ☎ 322/ 4–96–40) take you on any number of tours for up to an hour.

Tennis

Most of the larger hotels have tennis courts. Nonmembers can also play at the **Continental Plaza Tennis Club** (☎ 322/4–01–23) and the **Iguana Tennis Club** (☎ 322/1–06–83).

Water Sports

Snorkeling and diving are best at Los Arcos, a natural underwater preserve on the way to Mismaloya. Punta Mita, about 80 km (50 mi) north of Puerto Vallarta, has some good diving spots, as does Quimixto Bay, about 32 km (20 mi) south and accessible only by boat. Experienced divers prefer Las Marietas, a group of three islands off the coast.

Some hotels have snorkeling and diving equipment for rent and have short courses on diving at their pools. For dive trips and rentals, contact **Chico's Dive Shop** (✉ Díaz Ordaz 772, ☎ 322/2–18–95) or **Pacific Scuba** (✉ Juárez 722, ☎ 322/2–47–41).

Shopping

Puerto Vallarta has been described as one huge shopping mall interspersed with hotels and beaches. This is an exaggeration, but PV can definitely get into a shopper's blood. There are dozens of excellent shops stocked with some of the best crafts from all around Mexico, as well as several fine art galleries. Prices in the shops are fixed, and American dollars and credit cards are accepted. Bargaining is expected in the markets and by the vendors on the beach, who also freely accept American money. Most stores are open 10–8. A few close for siesta at 1 or 2, then reopen at 4.

Art

The late Manuel Lepe is perhaps Puerto Vallarta's most famous artist. His primitive style can be seen in the prints and posters that are still available at several of the galleries and shops around town. Sergio Bustamante, the creator of life-size brass, copper, and papier-mâché animals, has his own galleries: **Sergio Bustamante** (✉ Av. Juárez 275, ☎ 322/2–11–29; ✉ Paseo Díaz Ordaz 716, ☎ 322/3–14–07; ✉ Paseo Díaz Ordaz 542, ☎ 322/2–54–80). Many collectors of Mexican art come to Vallarta to find a good buy. Gallery cocktail showings in the evenings are frequent in winter. **Galería Uno** (✉ Morelos 561, ☎ 322/2–09–08) specializes in art from all over Mexico, but owners Jan Lavender and Martina Goldberg are especially enthusiastic about promoting local talent. Contemporary art and sculpture are displayed in one of Mexico's finest galleries, **Galería Pacífico** (✉ Aldama 174, ☎ 322/2–19–82). **Galería Rosas Blancas** (✉ Juárez 523, ☎ 322/2–11–68) combines a gallery featuring local and other Mexican artists with an artist's store. The very well-run **Galería Arte Latinoamericano** (✉ Josefa Ortiz Dominguez 155, ☎ 322/2–44–06) is the area's newest gallery. On the promenade in Marina Vallarta, **Arte de las Américas** (✉ Marina las Palmas II–16, ☎ 322/1–19–85) displays the work of celebrated and emerging contemporary artists.

Clothing

Most of the brand-name sportswear shops are located along the malecón and down its side streets. Many of these stores also have branches in the shopping centers or along Carretera Aeropuerto. **Aca Joe** (✉ Díaz Ordaz 588, ☎ 322/3–04–24) sells excellent quality pants, T-shirts, shorts, jackets, and sweats in smashing colors, all neatly displayed. **Express–Guess** (✉ Paseo Díaz Ordaz 660, ☎ 322/2–64–70) carries its own line of well-designed quality sportswear.

More elegant, dressier clothes, made of soft flowing fabrics in tropical prints, can be found at **Sucesos Boutique** (✉ Libertad and Hidalgo, ☎ 322/2–10–02), which features hand-painted fabrics and fashionable gauze resortwear. **La Bohemia** (✉ Juárez 479, ☎ 322/2–63–76; ✉ Marina Las Iguanas H–7, ☎ 322/1–21–60) displays contemporary resortwear, original designer artwear, unique jewelry, and accessories. **Gueros** (✉ Zaragoza 160, ☎ 322/2–06–33) carries outfits with a Mexican accent, designed by Alejandro Julián and hand-embroidered with Huichol Indian motifs.

Lina (✉ Zaragoza and Morelos, ☎ 322/2–47–85) carries handmade and embroidered clothes from Chiapas. **María de Guadalajara** (✉ Puesta del Sol condominiums in Marina Vallarta, ☎ 322/1–02–62 ext. 1015; ✉ Morelos 550, ☎ 322/2–23–87; ✉ Plaza Malecón and Paseo Díaz Ordaz, ☎ 322/2–47–35) carries easy-to-wear clothing for women in gauzy cotton fabrics dyed in luscious colors. **Nina & June** (✉ Hidalgo 227–8, ☎ 322/2–30–99) specializes in Nina's handwoven originally designed fashions, fanciful accessories, and June's silver jewelry.

Folk Art

Few cities in Mexico have a collection of the country's fine folk art that is as representative as the one in Puerto Vallarta. Masks, pottery, lacquerware, clothing, mirrors, glass dishes, windows and lamps, carved-wood animals and doors, antiques and modern art, hand-dyed woven rugs, and embroidered clothing are all available in the markets and from vendors. **Alfarería Tlaquepaque** (✉ Av. México 1100, ☎ 322/3–21–21) stocks a varied selection of baked earthenware suns, carved-wood figures, blown glass, baskets, ceramics, and painted animals from all over Mexico. **Talavera Etc.** (✉ Ignacio L. Vallarta 266, ☎ 322/2–41–00) has fine, handcrafted majolica ceramics and antique Mexican jewelry. **Mundo de Azulejos** (✉ Carranza 374, ☎ 322/2–26–75) sells a line of Talavera tiles and will create tile replicas of your favorite scene or work of art in 24 to 48 hours. **Puerco Azul** (✉ Marina Las Palmas II promenade, ☎ 322/1–19–85) carries one-of-a-kind items for the home, including furniture, ceramics, antiques, glassware, and whimsical pigs and other animals. **Olinalá** (✉ Lázaro Cárdenas 274, ☎ 322/2–49–95) is a two-story gallery and shop filled with masks from all over Mexico, as well as colonial-inspired carvings, lacquered boxes, and trays from Michoacán. **Galería de Ollas** (✉ Morelos 101, ☎ 322/3–10–45) has the wondrous pottery of Mata Ortiz exclusively. Original hand-loomed rugs, fabrics, and hand-painted furniture are on display at **Tamacani** (✉ Plaza Marina D-2, ☎ 322/1–09–82). **Mundo de Cristal** (✉ Insurgentes and Basilio Badillo, ☎ 322/2–41–57) is a glass factory where glassblowers create both avant-garde and classic designs.

Jewelry

There is a good selection of Mexican silver in Puerto Vallarta, but watch out for fake silver made with alloys, which is known as *chapa*. Real silver carries the 925 silver stamp required by the government. It is best to visit a reputable jeweler, such as **Pladi** (✉ Hidalgo 163, ☎ 322/2–56–06), which displays the creative silver jewelry designs of Rocio Guardia and Martha García. At **Ric Taxco** (✉ Pueblo Viejo shopping center, ☎ 322/3–01–43; ✉ Villa Vallarta shopping center, ☎ 322/4–45–98) much of the sterling silver and gold jewelry was inspired by pre-Hispanic designs. **Joyas Finas Suneson** (✉ Morelos 593, ☎ 322/2–57–15) specializes in fine silver jewelry and objets d'art by some of Mexico's finest designers.

Markets

The **Mercado Municipal,** at Avenida Miramar and Libertad, is a typical market plopped down in the busiest part of town. Flowers, piñatas, produce, and plastics are all shoved together in indoor and outdoor stands that cover a full city block. The strip of **shops along Río Cuale Island** is an outdoor market of sorts, with souvenir stands and exclusive boutiques interspersed with restaurants and cafés. Bargaining at the stalls in the market and on the island is expected.

Shopping Centers

The highway on the north side of town is lined with small arcades and large shopping centers that are occupied by handicrafts and sportswear shops. The best selections are at **Plaza Malecón,** at the beginning of Díaz Ordaz; **Plaza Marina,** on the highway at Marina Vallarta; the **Gigante Plaza,** by the Fiesta Americana hotel; and **Villa Vallarta,** by the Plaza las Glorias hotel.

Puerto Vallarta A to Z

Arriving and Departing

BY BUS

A kilometer (half mile) north of the airport is PV's new **Central Camionero** (central bus station) (⊠ Puerto Vallarta–Tepic Hwy., Km 9, ☎ 322/1–07–39). **ETN** (☎ 322/1–05–50) has the most luxurious service to Guadalajara and Mexico City, with reclining seats that rival first-class airline seats in their roominess. Two other major bus lines, **Transportes del Pacifico** (☎ 322/1–08–69) and **Elite** (☎ 322/1–08–48), are located here. Elite, which incorporates three lines (Estrella Blanca, Tres Estrellas de Oro, and Norte de Sonora), has excellent first-class service (reclining seats, air-conditioning, refreshment service, functioning bathroom) to Guadalajara, Aguascalientes, and Mexico City.

BY CAR

Puerto Vallarta is about 1,900 km (1,200 mi) south of Nogales, Arizona, at the United States–Mexico border, 354 km (220 mi) from Guadalajara, and 167 km (104 mi) from Tepic. Driving to Puerto Vallarta is not difficult, but driving in the city can be horrid. From December through April—peak tourist season—traffic clogs the small cobblestone streets. During the rainy season, from July through October, the streets become flooded and the hills are muddy and slippery.

BY PLANE

Airport and Airlines. Puerto Vallarta's **Gustavo Díaz Ordaz International Airport** (☎ 322/1–12–98) is 6½ km (4 mi) north of town, not far from the major resorts. The Mexican airlines have daily flights from Mexico City, Guadalajara, Monterrey, Manzanillo, Tampico, and Tepic. **Mexicana** (☎ 322/4–89–00) has direct service from Chicago, Los Angeles, and Denver via Mazatlán. **Aeroméxico** (☎ 322/4–27–77) flies from Los Angeles, New York, Dallas, and San Diego. Several American carriers also serve Puerto Vallarta, including **Alaska Airlines** (☎ 322/1–13–53), **American** (☎ 322/1–17–99), and **Continental** (☎ 322/1–10–25). **America West** (☎ 800/235–9292; no local phone) flies in from Phoenix.

Between the Airport and Hotels. Volkswagen vans provide economical transportation from the airport to hotels, and all the car-rental agencies have desks in the airport.

BY SHIP

Several cruise lines, including **Carnival, Celebrity, Crystal P&O, Cunard, Holland America Line, Krystal, Princess Cruises, Royal Caribbean Cruises,** and **Royal Cruise Line,** sail to Puerto Vallarta from Los Angeles during the winter months.

Getting Around

BY BUS

City buses serve downtown, the northern hotel zone, and the southern beaches. Bus stops—marked by blue-and-white signs—are located every two or three blocks along the highway (Carretera Aeropuerto) and in town. *Combis* (Volkswagen vans) are used as shared economical taxis in Nayarit and will drop off passengers in Puerto Vallarta along the main road as far south as the malecón.

BY RENTAL CAR

There are several agencies in Puerto Vallarta that rent Jeeps, open-air Volkswagen Beetles, and automatic-transmission sedans (☞ Car Rental, *below*). During the high season, rentals start at $60 per day, including insurance and mileage; off-season, they start at $45 per day. Be certain to ask about special promotions, even during the high season. All the car-rental agencies below have desks at the airport; some have offices along the highway, but they are spread out, so compare prices at the airport or call from your hotel.

BY TAXI

Many hotels post fares to common destinations; be sure to agree on a fare before the cab takes off. The ride from the north-side hotels to downtown costs about $2.50, plus 50¢ to cross the bridge.

Contacts and Resources

CAR RENTAL

Agencies to contact include **Avis** (⊠ Airport, ☎ 322/1–11–12), **Budget** (⊠ Carretera Aeropuerto, Km 7.5, ☎ 322/1–18–88), **Dollar** (⊠ Paseo de las Palmas 1728, ☎ 322/3–13–54), **Hertz** (⊠ Paseo de las Palmas 1602, ☎ 322/2–00–24), and **National** (⊠ Carretera Aeropuerto, Km 1.5, ☎ 322/2–11–07).

CONSULATES

U.S. Consul (⊠ Calle Zaragoza 160, ☎ 322/2–00–69); **Canadian Consul** (⊠ Calle Zaragoza 160, ☎ 322/2–53–98).

EMERGENCIES

Police (⊠ City Hall on Calles Morelos and Iturbide, ☎ 322/2–01–23); **Fire Department** *Bomberos* (☎ 322/4–77–01); **Red Cross** (⊠ Río de la Plata and Río Balsas, ☎ 322/2–15–33); **Hospital** (⊠ Plaza Neptuno, Marina Vallarta, ☎ 322/1–00–23).

GUIDED TOURS

The three-hour **city tour** is a good way to get the lay of the land, from Gringo Gulch and the Río Cuale to Mismaloya Beach. Almost everyone goes on at least one daytime or sunset cruise around the bay, sighting scenic isolated coves and barren beaches from the deck of a sailboat or yacht. A full-day excursion to Yelapa or Las Ánimas, seaside communities that can be reached only by boat, gives you a feeling of what life is like in a secluded tropical paradise.

Tropical tours visit mango and banana plantations in Nayarit and include stops in Nayarit's capital, Tepic, and the small seaside town of San Blas for a boat ride on the Río Tovara, through jungle thick with tropical plants and birds, with a stop for a refreshing swim in a natural spring. Other trips head south to Boca de Tomatlán, the mouth of the river that flows from the mountains into the sea.

Daytime cruises take passengers to Los Arcos, Yelapa, Quimixto, and Playa Las Ánimas, and to Isla Marietas for whale-watching (during winter months), snorkeling, swimming, and lunch. Intermar has a dinner cruise to movie director John Huston's former home, on a private bay south of the city, with dancing on the return trip. Charter **airline tours** fly to San Sebastián del Oeste, an interesting old mining town in the Sierra Madre, 62 km (38 mi) from Puerto Vallarta.

Tours may be arranged through your hotel or one of the many tour operators with offices at hotels and in town. City tours run about $16; tours to Yelapa run about $30; and tours to Las Ánimas and Quimixto cost approximately $40. It's worth the few extra dollars to go on a private tour (small groups) in a van rather than with a large group on a tour bus.

TRAVEL AGENCIES

American Express (⊠ Morelos 660, ☎ 322/3–29–55). **Intermar Vallarta** (⊠ Paseo de la Marina s/n, Condominio Via Golf, ☎ 322/1–07–34).

VISITOR INFORMATION

State Tourism Office (⊠ Blvd. Francisco Medina Ascencío 1712, ☎ 322/3–07–44) is open weekdays 9–7, Saturday 9–1. Dial ☎ 01–800/492–9832 for the toll-free tourist information help line.

MANZANILLO

Nature is undoubtedly Manzanillo's best attraction. Its twin *bahías* (bays), Manzanillo and Santiago, where crystal blue waters lap the black and gold volcanic sand, have caught outsiders' eyes since Cortés conquered Mexico. In the July–September rainy season, rivers and lagoons swell, forming waterfalls and ponds. White herons and pink flamingos flock to the fertile waters, and white butterflies flutter above the flowers in the chamomile fields—*manzanillo* is Spanish for chamomile.

Santiago Peninsula, which divides Bahía Santiago and Bahía Manzanillo, is the site of **Las Hadas** resort. From the water or points above the beach, the resort seems a mirage, a sea of white domes and peaks that radiate in the midday heat. When Bolivian tin magnate Antenor Patiño conceived of this white palace in the early 1960s, Manzanillo was easier to reach by sea than land, a rugged, primitive port that attracted the hardy who didn't mind creating their own tropical paradise. In 1974 when Señor Patiño's retreat was complete, the international social set began to visit Manzanillo, thus putting the city in magazines and on television screens around the world. Even then, Manzanillo remained essentially a port city with only a few tourist attractions.

The October 1995 earthquake did considerable damage to the area. It leveled one of the hotels as well as the headquarters of the state attorney general and caused a great deal of damage to the golf courses. With typical Mexican resilience in the face of adversity, however, most everything was back in shape by the start of the winter season.

Manzanillo is still relatively undeveloped, a sleeper compared with other Pacific Coast resorts. Investors have plenty of land to divvy up for their financially rewarding havens, and existing resorts are spread out. The latest of these, **Isla Navidad,** is on 1,230 acres on a peninsula about 20 minutes north of the Manzanillo airport. Robert Von Hagge designed the 27-hole golf course, and other amenities include a full-service marina. Many shops and hotel desks close for afternoon siesta, and on Sunday most businesses (including restaurants) shut down and everyone heads for the beach.

Exploring Manzanillo

A vacation in Manzanillo is not spent shopping and sightseeing. You stay put, relax on the beach, and maybe take a few hours' break from the sun and sand to survey the local scene casually.

A Good Tour
The **Santiago** area, on Santiago Bay between the Santiago and Juluapan peninsulas, is tourist-oriented, with clusters of shops and restaurants by the beach. The next area to the east, **Salahua,** is residential, with a baseball field and restaurants. Farther southeast on Manzanillo Bay, past the traffic circle and Avenida Morelos, you'll see **Las Brisas** beach, where some of the more reasonably priced hotels are located.

Downtown is busy and jam-packed, but of little tourist interest, except for the bustling seaport and, just north of downtown, the **Archeological Museum,** which is at the San Pedrito campus of the University of Colima. This happy surprise in this otherwise culturally bereft region, the museum displays 5,000 of its more than 18,000 collected artifacts, which come from the immediate region, the state of Colima, and Mesoamerica. ⊠ *San Pedrito traffic circle,* ☎ *333/2–22–56.* ✉ *$1.* ⊙ *Tues.–Sat. 10–2 and 5–8, Sun. 10–1.*

Manzanillo

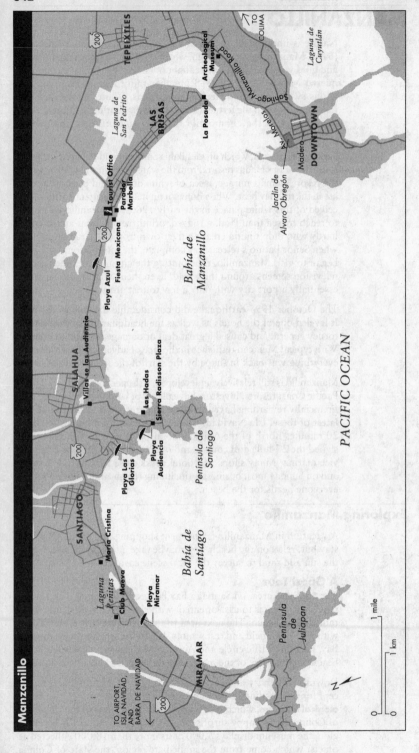

TO COLIMA

Laguna de Cuyutlán

TEPEIXTLES

200

Archeological Museum

Santiago-Manzanillo Road

LAS BRISAS

La Posada

Laguna de San Pedrito

AV. MORELOS

DOWNTOWN

Madero

Jardín de Alvaro Obregón

Tourist Office

Parador Marbella

200

Fiesta Mexicana

Playa Azul

Bahía de Manzanillo

SALAHUA

Villas se las Audiencia

Las Hadas

Sierra Radisson Plaza

200

Playa Las Glorias

Playa Audiencia

Península de Santiago

SANTIAGO

María Cristina

Laguna Peñitas

Club Maeva

Playa Miramar

Bahía de Santiago

MIRAMAR

200

TO AIRPORT, ISLA NAVIDAD, AND BARRA DE NAVIDAD

Península de Juliapan

PACIFIC OCEAN

N

0 — 1 mile
0 — 1 km

At the beginning of the harbor, Highway 200 jogs around downtown and intersects with Highway 110 to Colima. Avenida Morelos leads past the shipyards and into town. Just before you reach the port, stop at **Laguna de San Pedrito,** where graceful white herons and vivid pink flamingos assemble at sunset. The zócalo, or **Jardín de Obregón,** is right on the main road by the waterfront. It's a small square, quite lively in the evening.

Beaches

Manzanillo's biggest attraction is its beaches. Every day is a beach day, and Sundays are downright festive, with half the town gathered to play onshore. The volcanic sand is a mix of black, white, and brown, with the southernmost beaches the blackest. Most beaches post warning flags if the conditions are dangerous or jellyfish have been sighted.

Playa Miramar, at the north end of Santiago Bay, is populated by windsurfers and boogie-boarders. The beach in front of Club Santiago, once the favored hangout for locals, is now accessible only by walking north along the beach from the highway or by passing the guards at the club gates. The main stretch of beach is across the highway from Club Maeva. Manzanillo's best beach is probably **Playa Audiencia,** in a cove along the north side of Santiago Peninsula. The local Indians supposedly granted Cortés an audience here—thus the name. Located between two rock outcroppings, it's a good spot for snorkeling. The Sierra hotel is located in the middle of the beach, making public access limited. **Playa Azul,** also called Playa Santiago, is a long strand that runs from Santiago Peninsula along Manzanillo Bay to Playa Las Brisas. The surf gets rough along the north end; swimming is better toward Las Brisas. South of town is **Playa Cuyutlán,** a black-sand beach on the open sea. Legend has it that the great *ola verde* (green wave) rises some 30 ft each spring during the full moon. In reality, the surf is high in spring but not quite as big as the original ola verde, which took the tiny town of Cuyutlán by surprise in 1959.

Barra de Navidad and **San Patricio Melaque,** to the north, have popular beaches that are good for surfing in the fall months. Palapa restaurants along the beach serve fresh fish. In Barra there are panga trips to a small island just offshore, where unbroken seashells are abundant. When the tide is low, it is possible to walk along the beach from Barra to Melaque, a distance of about 6 km (almost 4 mi).

Dining

$$$ ✕ **Legazpi.** This international restaurant is at Las Hadas, and it is beau-
★ tiful. The service is white-glove perfection, but friendly rather than pretentious, and the food is decidedly elegant. The emphasis is on Continental cuisine with a Mexican touch, including Tulum salad (lettuce with crabmeat, avocado, and quail eggs) and grilled salmon with Jamaica sauce. ⊠ *Las Hadas,* ☎ *333/4–00–00. AE, DC, MC, V. Closed Wed., Fri., Sun. No lunch.*

$$–$$$ ✕ **L' Recif.** With a huge palapa set on a cliff with waves crashing on
★ the rocks below, and a pool/bar to one side, this is undoubtedly the best dinner-with-a-view in the area. If you see a whale in the bay and tell the waiters, they will charge you a 15% "whale tax." Seafood is the specialty, but all the food is gourmet quality. ⊠ *Cerro del Cenicero s/n, El Naranjo, Condominio Vida del Mar.,* ☎ *333/5–59–00. MC, V. Closed Sept.–Oct.; Mon. May–Aug.*

$$–$$$ ✕ **Willy's.** Some people have been known to dine at Willy's every
★ night of their stay in Manzanillo, although locals say the waiters can be a bit overbearing. The French-inspired food is that good, and the

owner, Jean François, is that personable and gracious. Michelle, Jean's wife, prepares delicious onion soup, a sublime bordelaise sauce, and decadent desserts. A guitarist enlivens the informal beachfront setting. ⊠ *Crucero Las Brisas,* ☎ *333/3–17–94. MC, V. No lunch.*

$$ ✕ **El Bigotes.** Great seafood is served in this chain's two separate restaurants at a very leisurely pace, under an incredible palapa on the beach (at the Miguel de la Madrid location, noon–6 PM) and on the highway (at the Puesta del Sol location, 6–11 PM). The house specialty is a spicy *pescado sarandeado* (whole fish marinated and grilled over hot coals). The flan *napolitano* is a good choice for dessert. ⊠ *Blvd. Miguel de la Madrid 3157,* ☎ *333/4–08–31;* ⊠ *Puesta del Sol 3,* ☎ *333/3–12–36. No credit cards.*

$$ ✕ **El Meson Español.** Paella, roast leg of lamb, and a superb Caesar salad prepared tableside are just a few of the specialties at this new family-run restaurant. Don't pass up the gazpacho Andaluz. ⊠ *Santiago–Manzanillo Rd. s/n,* ☎ *No phone. AE, MC, V.*

$$ ✕ **El Vaquero Campestre.** *Vaquero* means "cowboy," so it's no surprise to find a setting reminiscent of a ranchers' saloon and a menu emphasizing beef. The selections are prepared either marinated and seasoned as *carne asada* or grilled as good old American steaks. Some steaks are served and priced by weight to satisfy the biggest appetite. ⊠ *Av. la Audiencia,* ☎ *333/4–15–48. MC, V.*

$$ ✕ **Los Tibores.** One of Manzanillo's special-occasion romantic spots,
★ this place is popular with locals and vacationers. The menu doesn't try to be inventive, offering standard international and Mexican fare. The food is well prepared and beautifully presented, and the seafood dishes are truly outstanding. Theme menus (Italian, Mexican, Hawiian, etc.) are frequent. ⊠ *Av. de la Audiencia 1, Sierra,* ☎ *333/3–20–00. Reservations essential (1 day in advance). AE, DC, MC, V. No lunch.*

$$ ✕ **Porto Fino's.** If local food is starting to weigh you down, come here for the city's best all around Italian menu and wood-fired pizzas—or have them deliver to your hotel. ⊠ *Blvd. Costero M. de la Madrid, Km 10,* ☎ *333/3–13–33. MC, V.*

$ ✕ **Juanito's.** This gringo hangout is owned by an American who married a local girl and settled in Manzanillo 23 years ago. It specializes in great burgers, malts, and fries, American breakfasts, barbecued ribs, and fried chicken. Juanito's is the spot to watch U.S. football in good company. It is also Manzanillo's only cybercafé, in case you need a 'net fix. Expect good service and good coffee. ⊠ *Blvd. Costero M. de la Madrid, Km 14,* ☎ *333/3–13–88. Reservations not accepted. AE, MC, V.*

$ ✕ **La Posada.** Breakfast here is an integral part of any Manzanillo experience. Pancakes, French toast, fried eggs, and bacon are made to order and served in the large *sala* (living room) facing the sea. The mood is casual. Sandwiches, hamburgers, fish, and drinks are offered in the afternoon, but breakfast is your best bet for only $5. ⊠ *La Posada, Las Brisas,* ☎ *333/3–18–99. AE, MC, V.*

$ ✕ **Rosalba's.** Tasty *huevos rancheros* (fried eggs with salsa), American-style breakfasts, seafood, steaks, and tacos served under a palapa have made this place popular with residents and tourists alike. ⊠ *Blvd. Miguel de la Madrid 29, next to gas station in Santiago,* ☎ *333/3–04–88. MC, V.*

Lodging

Lodging in Manzanillo was at one time a bargain, and although the $10 room is a thing of the past, there are still several decent places where you can lay your head for less than $40. Travelers on a tighter budget usually head to the towns of Barra de Navidad and Melaque. As with the rest of the Pacific Coast, Manzanillo is undergoing a building boom, mainly condominiums, to accommodate the growing number of people from Guadalajara buying vacation homes here. The resorts are spread out along the Santiago–Manzanillo Road.

$$$$ ▦ **Grand Bay.** Set on a 1,320-acre residential–golf–tourism development on a peninsula between the Pacific and the Navidad lagoon, about 35 minutes from Manzanillo airport, this no-holds-barred resort cascades down a hill to a delightful stretch of private beach. Rooms in this traditionally Mexican-style hotel, with Spanish arches, balconies, fountains, shady patios, and lush gardens, have mountain or sea views, marble baths, hand-carved wooden walls and hand-painted Mexican tile floors—as well as deluxe amenities like bathrobes. Perched at the top of a hill, the Governor's and Presidential suites share a private pool. ⊠ *Isla Navidad, Jalisco 48987,* ☎ *335/5–63–90; 888/ 804–7263 in the U.S.,* ℻ *335/5–60–70. 158 rooms, 33 suites. 3 restaurants, 3 bars, 2 pools, 27-hole golf course, 3 tennis courts, health club, volleyball, beach, dive shop, snorkeling, jet skiing, waterskiing, fishing. AE, DC, MC, V.*

$$$$ ▦ **Karmina Palace.** Manzanillo's newest hotel is just across the hill from Las Hadas (☞ *below*). This Aztec temple–looking behemoth sat dormant for some four years before opening in February 1999 as an all-inclusive hotel. All luxury suites face either the ocean or Las Hadas's golf course. In fact, the 18th hole is on Karmina's spacious lawns, which have cascades, fountains, a multi-tiered lagoon-pool and a beautiful palapa restaurant on the edge of the ocean. Junior suites include two TVs and a VCR, marble floors, a refrigerator, air-conditioning and fans, a balcony or terrace, and large tubs with separate shower facilities and double vanities in the bathrooms. Complementary soda, water, and upscale beauty products come in all rooms. The resort has 24-hour conceirge service and a well-equipped business center. ⊠ *Av. Vista Hermosa 13, Fracc. Peninsula de Santiago, Santiago, Colima 28200,* ☎ *333/4– 13–13,* ℻ *333/4–19–15. 323 suites. 3 restaurants, 2 pools, 10 tennis courts, 18-hole golf course, health club, beach, video games, baby sitting. AE, V.*

$$$$ ▦ **Las Hadas.** A member of the Leading Hotels of the World, Las Hadas
★ was for many years Manzanillo's premier resort, the kind of place where guests were content to check in and stay put. The setting and grounds are still beautiful, and service is outstanding, making a stay at Las Hadas a very special experience. ⊠ *Av. Vista Hermosa and de los Riscos, 28200,* ☎ *333/4–00–00; 800/722–6466 in the U.S.,* ℻ *333/4–13–70. 184 rooms, 36 suites. 4 restaurants, 3 bars, 2 pools, beauty salon, massage, 18-hole golf course, 10 tennis courts, beach, shops, dance club, babysitting, laundry service, travel services. AE, DC, MC, V.*

$$$$ ▦ **Sierra.** This 19-story white stucco giant is popular with families (up to two children under six years of age stay free in their parents' room) and conventioneers. Most of the 317 inviting rooms and suites have private balconies and a view of the bay. A large free-form pool, four tennis courts, and several bars and restaurants round out the property. Light wood and pastel colors dominate the pleasant decor. Three buffet meals, snacks, dinners at a gourmet restaurant, all drinks, and tennis are included in the price. ⊠ *Av. de la Audiencia 1, 28200,* ☎ *333/ 3–20–00. 317 rooms and suites. 3 restaurants, 4 bars, pool, 4 tennis courts, beach, children's programs (ages 4 to 12). AE, DC, MC, V.*

$$$ ▦ **Marina Puerto Dorado.** There are excellent views of the bay and har-
★ bor from this recently remodeled six-year-old family hotel. With 30 suites and 10 penthouse suites with Jacuzzi and a wet bar on top-floor patios, this is a good bet for large families. ⊠ *Av. Lázaro Cárdenas 101, Fracc. Las Brisas Playa Azul, 28200,* ☎ *333/4–14–80,* ℻ *3/ 647–98–50. 40 suites. Restaurant, 2 bars, pool, beach. AE, MC, V.*

$$ ▥ **La Posada.** This "passionate pink" hotel has been a favorite for North
★ Americans since 1957. With only 24 rooms, most guests get to know
each other well, mingling in the sala, a large living-dining room with
a communal coffeepot. Rooms are comfortable and simple; old iron
keys work the antique locks. The room rate includes a complete break-
fast. The beer and soft drink service is on an honor system. ⊠ *Las Brisas,
28200,* ☎ *333/3–18–99,* ℻ *333/3–18–99. 24 rooms. Bar, snack bar,
pool, beach. AE, MC, V.*

$$ ▥ **Villas la Audiencia.** Well located—it's a block from the Las Hadas
turnoff and about 1 km (½ mi) from the beach—this small white-and-
red hotel and villa complex overlooks the Mantarraya golf course. Everything is spotless, and the air-conditioned rooms and villas (the villas
have kitchenettes) are pleasantly decorated and quite comfortable. ⊠
*Av. de la Audiencia and Las Palmas, off Santiago–Manzanillo Rd.,
28860,* ☎ *333/3–08–61,* ℻ *333/3–26–53. 20 rooms, 26 villas. Restaurant, pool. AE, MC, V.*

$ ▥ **María Cristina.** This super-clean two-story motel is located in the San-
tiago area, five blocks from the beach. All the rooms have TVs, but only
three of them—they call them "suites"—are air-conditioned; they're well
worth the small difference in price. ⊠ *Calle 28 de Agosto 36, 28860,*
☎ *333/3–09–66,* ℻ *333/4–14–30. 21 rooms. Pool. MC, V.*

$ ▥ **Parador Marbella.** This hotel is one of the few reasonably priced
places on the beach. The best rooms are on the ocean; each has a tiny
balcony under the palms. The accommodations are color-coordinated
and have air-conditioning and TV. The Parador has a good seafood–
Spanish restaurant, El Marinero. ⊠ *Santiago–Manzanillo Rd., Km 9.5,
28869,* ☎ *333/3–11–03,* ℻ *333/3–12–22. 92 rooms. Restaurant, bar,
pool. AE, MC, V.*

Nightlife and the Arts

For a rowdy drinking and dancing scene, head for **Colima Bay Café**
(⊠ Santiago–Manzanillo Rd. 921, ☎ 333/3–11–50). **VOG**(⊠ Km 9.2
on Santiago–Manzanillo Rd., ☎ 333/3–18–75), **Le Cartouche** (⊠ At
Las Hadas, ☎ 333/4–00–00), and **Boom Boom** (⊠ At Club Maeva, ☎
333/5–05–93) are popular places to boogie. **Olas** (⊠ Blvd. Costero
Miguel de la Madrid, Km 7.5, ☎ 333/4–03–83) is a good spot for pool
and oldies rock and roll. The **Lobby** (⊠ At Las Hadas, ☎ 333/4–00–
00) piano bar is a relaxing, romantic spot for a nightcap.

Outdoor Activities and Sports

Fishing
Sportfishing charters ($50–$500) are available at major hotels and tour
agencies.

Golf
La Mantarraya (☎ 333/4–00–00), the 18-hole golf course at Las
Hadas, designed by Roy Dye, has been rated among the world's 100
best courses by *Golf Digest.* **Club Santiago** (☎ 333/5–04–10) has a nine-
hole course designed by Larry Hughes. Robert Von Hagge created the
27-hole course at **Isla Navidad** (☎ 333/5–63–90).

Water Sports
Windsurfing has become quite popular on Manzanillo's beaches, and
Jet Skis roar about, but there isn't much in the way of parasailing. The
rocky points off Manzanillo's peninsulas and coves make good spots
for snorkeling and scuba diving. Pangas can be rented on some beaches
so you can reach the better spots.

Shopping

Most of the hotels offer a small selection of folk art and beachwear, but, in general, shops selling items that might interest tourists don't fare well in Manzanillo, probably because most visitors are more interested in activities involving the sun and sea. There are some fairly uninteresting shops around Manzanillo's main square, hardly worth the trip downtown, and there are some shops at Plaza Manzanillo, a shopping center at Km 7.5 on the Santiago–Manzanillo Road. Most of the shops are closed from 2 to 4; many are open Sunday from 10 to 2. **Centro Artesenal Las Primaveras** (⊠ Juárez 40, Santiago, ☎ 333/3–16–99) is about the best bet for handcrafted folk art.

Side Trip

Colima

311 km (192 mi) northeast of Manzanillo.

Colima, the state capital, is less than two hours from Manzanillo via an excellent toll road that continues on to Guadalajara. An easygoing provincial city, with well-maintained colonial buildings, Colima is most famous for the pre-Hispanic "Colima Dog" figurines, which originated in this state and which are on display, along with other archaeological pieces, at the **Museo de las Culturas del Occidente** (Museum of Western Cultures) (⊠ Casa de la Cultura, Calzada Galván, and Av. Ejército Nacional, ☎ 331/2–31–55). The **Museo de Artes Populares María Teresa Pomar** (María Teresa Pomar Handicrafts Museum; ⊠ Calle Gabino Barreda and Manuel Gallardo, ☎ 331/2–68–69) displays a large collection of pre-Hispanic and contemporary Indian costumes, masks, instruments, and other artifacts.

The town of **Comala,** a 15-minute ride north of Colima, is noted for hand-painted colonial furniture and ironwork. The imposing twin peaks of Colima's volcanoes rise up from the **Volcán de Colima National Park,** about 30 km (18 mi) north of Comala.

Manzanillo A to Z

Arriving and Departing

BY BUS

Elite and **Estrella Blanca** (☎ 333/2–04–32 for both), and **Primera Plus** (☎ 333/2–14–31) have first-class service (lavatory, TV, and air-conditioning) to Puerto Vallarta, Guadalajara, Tijuana, Acapulco, and Mexico City. Service is also available to coastal towns. Many of the area's resorts are 1–2 km (½–1 mi) from the bus stop on the highway. **ETN** (Blvd. Costero Miguel de la Madrid, Km 13.5, ☎ 333/4–10–50) has by far the most comfortable buses, with wide, almost totally reclining seats, to Guadalajara and Mexico City.

BY CAR

The trip south from the Arizona border to Manzanillo is about 2,419 km (1,500 mi); from Guadalajara, it is 332 km (200 mi) over mostly well-kept highways; from Puerto Vallarta, 242 km (150 mi) over windy mountain roads. Highway 200 runs along the coast from Tepic, Nayarit, to Manzanillo. The road is quite narrow but well maintained. However, drivers should constantly be on the alert for an unexpected cow, burro, dog—or drunk—on the road. Detours are frequent, especially during the rainy season. If you are stopped by federal police or army soldiers at periodic check stations, you have nothing to fear unless you are carrying weapons or drugs. They generally wave tourists on without going through their belongings.

BY PLANE

Airport and Airlines. Manzanillo's **Aeropuerto Internacional Playa de Oro** (☎ 333/3–25–25) is 32 km (20 mi) north of town, on the way to Barra de Navidad. **Aeroméxico** (☎ 91–800/3–62–02) and **Mexicana** (☎ 333/3–23–23) serve most major cities via Mexico City. **America West** (☎ 800/235–9292; no local phone) flies in from Phoenix, with a stop in Puerto Vallarta, and **Aero California** (☎ 333/4–14–14) flies in from Los Angeles daily.

From the Airport. Volkswagen vans transport passengers from the airport to major resorts; these shuttles are less expensive than taxis.

Getting Around

A car is almost essential for exploring the area on your own. The highway from Santiago to Manzanillo is commonly called Carretera Santiago–Manzanillo, Manzanillo–Aeropuerto, Salahua–Santiago, or any number of things depending on the closest landmark. It's called the Santiago–Manzanillo Road throughout this chapter to lessen confusion. Highway 200 runs north along the coast past Manzanillo and Santiago bays to Barra de Navidad and Melaque; Highway 110 goes east to Colima.

Avenida Morelos, the main drag in town, runs from Manzanillo Bay past the port and shipyards to the plaza. If you plan to explore the downtown, park along the waterfront across from the plaza and walk—all the shops and hotels are within a few blocks. Rates vary depending on where you rent your car, but rentals are fairly costly ($50 per day for a standard shift without air-conditioning, to $70 for a model with automatic transmission and air-conditioning). Most offer 200 km (120 mi) free, which should give you enough roaming for one day.

Street addresses are not often used in Manzanillo; instead, locations are designated by neighborhood—the Las Brisas area, Santiago Peninsula (also known as the Las Hadas Road), and so on. Maps with actual street names are rare (or inaccurate).

Contacts and Resources

CAR RENTAL

Dollar (Paseo de las Palmas, ☎ 333/3–14–32) and **National** (Blvd. Costero Miguel de la Madrid 1070, ☎ 333/3–06–11 or 333/3–11–40) have offices in the airport, and most large hotels have at least one company represented.

EMERGENCIES

Police (☎ 333/2–10–06), **Hospital** (☎ 333/6–72–72).

GUIDED TOURS

Manzanillo is so spread out that if you want to get the lay of the land, it's best to go on a guided tour. More appealing, though, than the city tours are the sportfishing trips, sunset cruises, horseback outings, and excursions to Colima, Comala, and the volcanoes that can be arranged through a travel agency.

TRAVEL AGENCIES

Most hotels offer at least one agency's services. Agencies include **Avitesa** (⊠ Av. Costero Miguel de la Madrid, Km 11.5, ☎ 333/3–29–99), **Bahías Gemelas Agencia de Viajes** (⊠ Blvd. Costero Miguel de la Madrid 1506, ☎ 333/3–10–00), **Aeroviajes Manzanillo** (⊠ Av. México 69, ☎ 333/4–24–24), and **Viajes Héctur** (⊠ Av. Costero Miguel de la Madrid 3147, ☎ 333/3–17–07).

VISITOR INFORMATION

The **State Tourism Office** (⊠ Blvd. Costero Miguel de la Madrid, Km 9.5, ☎ 333/3–22–77) is open weekdays 9–3 and 5–7:30, Saturdays 9–2.

IXTAPA/ZIHUATANEJO

One of the most appealing of the Pacific Coast destinations, Ixtapa/Zihuatanejo is a taste of Mexico present and past. Ixtapa (pronounced eeks-*tah*-pa), where most Americans stay—probably because they can't pronounce Zihuatanejo (see-wa-ta-*nay*-ho)—is young and glitzy. Exclusively a vacation resort, it was created in the early 1970s by Fonatur, Mexico's National Fund for Tourism Development, which also brought us Cancún, Huatulco, and San José del Cabo. World-class hotels cluster in the hotel zone around Palmar Bay, where conditions are ideal for swimming and water sports; across the road are clusters of shopping plazas. The hotels are well spaced; there's always plenty of room on the beach, which is lighted for strolling at night; and the pace is leisurely. One thing you won't see is a Pacific sunset. The coastline here faces south, not west.

Zihuatanejo, only 7 km (4 mi) down the coast (southeast) from Ixtapa, is an old fishing village on a picturesque sheltered bay. Until the advent of Ixtapa, it was hardly known even among Mexicans. But long before Columbus sailed to America, Zihuatanejo was a sanctuary for indigenous nobility. Figurines, ceramics, stone carvings, and stelae still being found in the area verify the presence of civilizations dating as far back as the Olmecs (3000 BC). The original name, Cihuatlán, means "place of women" in the Náhuatl language. Weaving was likely the dominant industry in this matriarchal society, as evidenced by pre-Hispanic figurines, bobbins, and other related artifacts found in the area.

In 1527, Spanish conquistadors launched a trade route from Zihuatanejo Bay to the Orient. Galleons returned with silks, spices, and, according to some historians, the first coconut palms to arrive in the Americas, brought from the Philippines. But the Spaniards did little colonizing here. A scout sent by Hernán Cortés reported back to the conquistador that the place was nothing great, tagging the name Cihuatlán with the demeaning Spanish suffix "nejo"—hence "Zihuatanejo."

With the advent of Ixtapa, Zihuatanejo began to grow and the little dirt streets were paved with decorative brick. The place has managed to retain its charm, but it's also the area's municipal center, and its malecón and narrow streets are lined with hotels, restaurants, and boutiques.

Exploring Ixtapa/Zihuatanejo

Ixtapa and Zihuatanejo have few sights per se, but they're both pleasant places to stroll—the former especially if you enjoy a modern beach ambience and shops, the latter if you like local color.

A Good Tour

The entire **hotel zone** in **Ixtapa** extends along a 3-km (2-mi) strip of wide sandy beach called Playa del Palmar, on the open Pacific. It's fun to walk along the beach to check out the various hotel scenes and watersports activities. Alternatively, you can stroll the length of the zone on Boulevard Ixtapa, a nicely landscaped and immaculate thoroughfare; a series of Mexican village–style shopping malls line the boulevard across the street from the hotels. At one end of the hotel zone (when you enter from Zihuatanejo) is the 18-hole Ixtapa Golf Club, while on the other (generally described as being "up the coast," but actually lying to the northwest) you'll come to the Marina Ixtapa development, which includes a 600-slip yacht marina, a promenade with restaurants and shops, and the 18-hole Marina Golf Course. If you want to venture out of this compact resort area, take a taxi 15 minutes up the coast to **Playa**

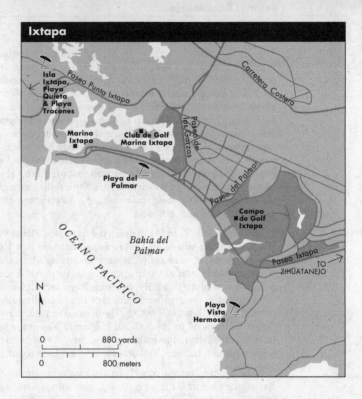

Ixtapa

Linda. It's a 10-minute boat ride from here to **Ixtapa Island** (☞ Beaches, *below*, for both), where you can spend the day eating, sunning, and swimming.

Zihuatanejo flanks a charming enclosed bay with calm beaches. A simple way to tour the town is to take a taxi to the **municipal pier** (*muelle*), from which skiffs continually depart for the 10-minute ride to **Playa las Gatas** (☞ Beaches, *below*), accessible only by water. The sportfishing boats depart from this pier, too, and it's the beginning of the **Paseo del Pescador** (Fisherman's Walk) or malecón, which runs along the municipal beach, the most picturesque part of town. The brick-paved seaside path, only ½ km (⅓ mi) long, is lined with small restaurants and overflowing shops; you'll pass a basketball court that doubles as the town square. The malecón ends at the **Museo Arquélogico** (⊠ East end of Paseo del Pescador, ☎ 755/3–25–52), where close to a thousand pre-Hispanic pieces as well as murals and maps are on permanent display; it's open Tuesday–Sunday 10–6. If you continue beyond the museum, you can take a footpath cut into the rocks to **Playa la Madera** (☞ Beaches, *below*).

Beaches

Ixtapa

Ixtapa Island. The most popular beach on Ixtapa Island is Playa Cuachalalate, named for a local tree whose bark has been used as a remedy for kidney ailments since ancient times. This beach is lined with good seafood eateries. A short walk across to the other side of the island takes you to the gorgeous sandy Varadero beach, a wonderful spot for sunset viewing. It is also lined with small restaurants, and there are water-sports facilities. Just behind the restaurants is Playa Coral, with crystal-clear water that's ideal for snorkeling. Playa Carey, toward the south end of the island, is small and isolated. Pangas run between the

Zihuatanejo

boat landings at both Cuachalalate and Varadero beaches and Playa Linda on the mainland.

Playa del Palmar. Ixtapa's main beach, this 3-km-long (2-mi-long) broad sandy stretch runs along the hotel zone. Water-sports facilities are available all along the shore. Since this is essentially open sea, the surf can be quite strong.

Playa Linda. About 10 minutes beyond the Ixtapa hotel zone, the long, pristine Playa Linda has a handicraft mart at its edge, as well as a rock jetty from which covered pangas make the 10-minute trip to Ixtapa Island (☞ *above*). Boats run continuously from early morning until 5 PM. A round-trip costs about $3 (hold onto your ticket stub for the return).

Zihuatanejo

Playa la Madera. Across Zihuatanejo Bay from Playa Municipal, Playa la Madera may be reached via a seaside footpath cut into the rocks. Also accessible by car, this pancake-flat beach has a sprinkling of small hotels and restaurants. It was named madera, or "wood," beach because it was a Spanish port for shipping oak, pine, cedar, and mahogany cut from the nearby Sierra Madre Sur.

Playa la Ropa. On the other side of a rocky point, Playa la Ropa is the most beautiful beach in the area; it's a five-minute taxi ride from town. Along this 1-km (½-mi) stretch of soft sand are water-sports facilities, open-air restaurants, and a few hotels. It got its name ("clothes beach") when a Spanish galleon returning from the Orient ran aground here, strewing its cargo of silks and clothing.

Playa las Gatas. Named for the *gatas* (docile nurse sharks) that used to linger here, this beach has a mysterious long row of hewn rocks just offshore that serves as a breakwater. Legend has it that a Tarascan king built it to shelter his royal daughter's private beach. It is now lined with simple seafood eateries that also have lounge chairs for sunning. Las Gatas is accessible only by boat, and pangas run continuously to and from the municipal pier until 5 PM. Purchase your round-trip ticket (about $2) at the Cooperativa office at the beginning of the pier. Keep the ticket stub for your return trip.

Playa Municipal. At the edge of town, the town's picturesque main beach is rimmed by the Paseo del Pescador. Here local fishermen keep their skiffs and gear, used for nightly fishing journeys out to sea. They return here in the morning to sell their catch to the local townspeople and to restaurateurs.

Dining

Ixtapa

$$$$ ✕ **Villa de la Selva.** These multilevel cliff-top terraces have views of the sunset, the stars, and the night-lit surf breaking on the rocks below. Excellent international dishes include grilled steaks, seafood, and Mexican specialties. ⊠ *Beyond Westin Brisas on Paseo la Roca,* ☎ *755/ 3-03-62. Reservations essential. AE, DC, MC, V. No lunch.*

$$$–$$$$ ✕ **Bogart's.** Play it again: the setting is strikingly Moroccan, à la *Casablanca,* and anyone who's been to any of the links in the Krystal hotel chain is familiar with this exotic (and expensive) eatery. A Moorish fountain and piano music add to the movie-theme atmosphere. The largely international menu includes Suprema Casablanca (breaded chicken breasts stuffed with lobster). ⊠ *Hotel Krystal, Blvd. Ixtapa,* ☎ *755/3-03-03. Reservations essential. AE, DC, MC, V.*

$$$ ✕ **Beccofino.** Part of the promenade along Marina Ixtapa, this restaurant serves excellent northern Italian cuisine—the seafood pasta is an excellent choice—in a serene Mediterranean-style atmosphere. There's alfresco seating on a canopied deck that sits on the water. ⊠ *Plaza Marina Ixtapa,* ☎ *755/3-17-70. AE, MC, V.*

$$$ ✕ **El Galeón.** Seafood lovers and people-watchers like to settle in at Marina Ixtapa's nautical-decor bar and outdoor terrace; there's additional seating on a simulated galleon right on the water. The fresh tuna steak is outstanding, as are the pastas, and upscale Mexican fare is also available. ⊠ *Plaza Marina Ixtapa,* ☎ *755/3-21-50. AE, MC, V.*

$$ ✕ **El Infierno y la Gloria.** "Hell and Glory" is a Mexican cantina-bar and restaurant, serving an array of typical dishes. The food is good, and you'll enjoy looking at the walls, hand-painted with Mexican scenes and allegories. ⊠ *La Puerta Shopping Center,* ☎ *755/3-03-04. AE, MC, V.*

$$ ✕ **El Marlin.** This is a great place to settle in for some lunch, swimming, and sun. Simple, wholesome, and delicious seafood dishes include (naturally) marlin: try it steamed with vegetables in aluminum foil. El Marlin closes at 5 PM, when the last boats leave for the mainland. ⊠ *Varadero Beach, Ixtapa Island,* ☎ *No phone. No credit cards.*

$$ ✕ **La Valentina.** This recent addition to Ixtapa's dining scene is part
★   of a relatively new—and highly successful—group of restaurants that have opened in Mexico City. The team of PR whizzes who are behind these ventures have access to some of the finest Mexican gourmet recipes, many from celebrities such as artist Martha Chapa. Truly memorable is the *pollo en mole de tamarindo* (chicken in a spicy sauce flavored with tamarind and chocolate). The decor is as Mexican as the menu. Also on the premises is a video bar and disco. ⊠ *Blvd. Ixtapa, next to Doubletree hotel,* ☎ *755/3-11-90. AE, MC, V. No lunch.*

$–$$ ✕ **Mamma Norma y J. J. Cuisine.** You can dine indoors or alfresco at this casual Italian eatery, which has the best pizzas in town as well as tasty grilled tuna steaks, shrimp, lobster, and wholesome salads. ⊠ *La Puerta Shopping Center,* ☎ *755/3-02-74. AE, MC, V. No lunch.*

$ ✕ **Nueva Zelanda.** From breakfast through dinner everybody drops in to this sparkling little coffee shop–style eatery, which serves tortas and an array of fresh tropical fruit juices and fruit salads. ⊠ *Los Patios Shopping Center, behind bandstand,* ☎ *755/3–08–38;* ⊠ *Calle Cuauhtémoc 23, Zihuatanejo,* ☎ *755/4–23–40. Reservations not accepted. No credit cards.*

Zihuatanejo

$$–$$$ ✕ **Coconuts.** Chef Patricia Cummings prepares shrimp tacos, Mexican bean soup, coconut shrimp, an irresistible pasta Ciprion, served with a shrimp, basil, anchovy, and wine sauce, and creamy flan, in the oldest building in Zihuatanejo, originally a weigh-in station for a coconut plantation. ⊠ *5 de Mayo across from handicraft market,* ☎ *755/4–25–18. AE, DC, MC, V. Closed late May–early Oct.*

$$ ✕ **Casa Elvira.** Opened in 1956, this Zihuatanejo institution near the town pier has a pleasant dining room and serves a wide variety of seafood and Mexican dishes. Lobster is the house specialty. It gets crowded during high season. ⊠ *Paseo del Pescador 8,* ☎ *755/4–20–61. MC, V.*

$$ ✕ **El Patio.** Seafood and authentic Mexican dishes are served in a delightful hacienda-style garden. There's live music during high season. ⊠ *5 de Mayo 3, next to church,* ☎ *755/4–30–19. AE, MC, V.*

$$ ✕ **Kau-Kan.** Opened in the mid-1990s, this restaurant immediately became a local favorite. Owner-chef Ricardo Rodriguez, previously the chef at the nearby Casa que Canta and, before then, at Mexico City's Champs-Elysées restaurant, serves imaginative, exquisitely prepared seafood, from fillet of sea bass to potato stuffed with shrimp and lobster in a basil and garlic sauce. Although the restaurant is right on Madera Beach, the service and setting are elegant. ⊠ *Playa Madera,* ☎ *755/4–84–46. AE, MC, V.*

$–$$ ✕ **La Sirena Gorda.** Oil paintings and a bronze statue depict the namesake "fat mermaid," and a small boutique sells logo T-shirts and memorabilia. Specialties at this friendly restaurant near the pier include seafood tacos and octopus kebab. The setting is casual, with an outdoor patio. ⊠ *Paseo del Pescador 20,* ☎ *755/4–26–87. Reservations not accepted. MC, V. Closed Wed.*

$–$$ ✕ **Rossy.** A local favorite for dining on the roof terrace or right on the beach, Rossy's features seafood, including a tempting shrimp-and-pineapple brochette. Musicians usually serenade diners on weekends. ⊠ *South end of Playa la Ropa,* ☎ *755/4–40–04. MC, V.*

$ ✕ **Casa Puntarenas.** Talk about homey restaurants: Casa Puntarenas is not only family-owned and -operated, but it's run out of the family residence. You'll select from a menu of seafood specialties and write your order on a piece of paper, which later becomes your check. To get here, cross the footbridge over the lagoon at the west end of town near the pier (or take a taxi). ⊠ *Noria 12,* ☎ *755/4–21–09. Reservations not accepted. No credit cards. Closed mid-Mar.–mid-Dec.*

$ ✕ **La Mordida.** Join the throngs at this simple, very popular eatery for pizza and tasty charcoal-broiled burgers. ⊠ *Paseo de la Boquita 20,* ☎ *755/4–82–16. No credit cards. No lunch.*

$ ✕ **La Perla.** Eat indoors if you want video sports-bar action, or outdoors on La Ropa Beach. Among the seafood specialties, *filete "La Perla"* (baked with cheese in aluminum foil) is a favorite. ⊠ *Playa la Ropa,* ☎ *755/4–27–00. AE, MC, V.*

Dining and Lodging

Zihuatanejo

$$$$ ✕🏨 **La Casa Que Canta.** Resembling a thatched-roof pueblo village, ★ "The House That Sings" is perched on a cliffside high above Zihuatanejo Bay. The multilevel palapa-topped lobby is adorned with folk-art fur-

nishings, including handpainted chairs with Frida Kahlo motifs. The individually designed rooms, named for Mexican songs, also feature beautiful handcrafted pieces and have modern amenities such as air-conditioning and hair dryers. Because of the stepped architecture, the main swimming pool seems to be airborne. Below, overlooking the sea, a saltwater pool features a therapeutic whirlpool. Seven extraspacious suites have their own pools. The multilevel restaurant serves fine Continental and Mexican fare as well as stupendous views (reservations required). Children under 16 are not accepted at either the restaurant or the hotel and there's a minimum five-night stay January–February. ⊠ *Camino Escénico a Playa la Ropa, 40880,* ☎ *755/4–27–22; 888/ 523–5050 in the U.S.,* ℻ *755/4–20–06. 24 rooms and suites. Restaurant, 2 pools, exercise room. AE, DC, MC, V.*

$$$$ ✕⊡ **Villa del Sol.** This is the ultimate in luxurious beach living. One-
★ and two-story suites in a series of casitas nestle amid coconut palms, lush tropical gardens, fountains, and meandering paths leading to Playa la Ropa, one of the loveliest beaches on the Pacific Coast. Guest rooms and baths are artistically designed, with canopied king-size beds, colorful folk-art furnishings, and terraces or balconies with hammocks; all have satellite TVs, minibars, and hair dryers, and some boast private outdoor hot tubs. You can sit under a palapa on the beach and order snacks, lunch, or drinks from a casual menu. In the evening the European and Mexican chefs prepare fine international and local dishes—try resisting Chef Fabrice's apple-and-cinnamon tacos—using the freshest of ingredients. Even if you're not staying here, don't miss the elaborate "Mexican Fiesta" buffet on Friday nights. Children under 14 are not accepted during high season. The rate includes breakfast and lunch or dinner. ⊠ *Playa la Ropa, Box 84, 40880,* ☎ *755/4–22–39; 888/389–2645 in the U.S.,* ℻ *755/4–27–58. 72 1- and 2-bedroom suites. Restaurant, 3 pools, 2 tennis courts, beach. AE, MC, V.*

Troncones

$$ ✕⊡ **Casa Ki.** These bungalows, overseen by Ed and Ellen Weston, are a homey haven in the wilds of Troncones. A fully equipped kitchen and BBQ are available to guests, and breakfast is included in the rates. ⊠ *Troncones Beach, Apdo. 405, Zihuatanejo, Guerrero 40880,* ☎ *755/ 7–09–92,* ℻ *755/3–42–17. 3 bungalows, 1 house. Beach. No credit cards.*

$$ ✕⊡ **El Burro Borracho.** For out-of-the-way seclusion, you can venture some 30 minutes northwest up the coast to 5-km-long (3-mi-long) Troncones Beach, near the tiny village of the same name. Six comfortable stone cottages and a congenial restaurant-bar sit right on the beach. The menu ranges from cheeseburgers to fresh lobster. Lie in a hammock or go beachcombing, boogie-boarding, hiking, or cave exploring. Owners Dewey and Carolyn are also known for their Casa de la Tortuga B&B, just up the beach. Trailer spaces are also available. ⊠ *Troncones Beach, Apdo. 277, Zihuatanejo, Guerrero 40880,* ☎ ℻ *755/ 7–32–96. 6 bungalows. Restaurant, hiking, beach. No credit cards.*

Lodging

There is a wide range of hotel accommodations in Ixtapa and in Zihuatanejo. Pricier Ixtapa has almost exclusively deluxe, beachfront properties, and almost all are located along the Zona Hoteleria, a 3-km (2-mi) stretch of Palmar Beach. They do not always match the other members of international chains whose names they bear in quality, however. Most of the budget accommodations are in Zihuatanejo, where the best hotels are on or overlooking La Madera or La Ropa beach, and the least expensive are downtown.

Elizabeth Williams (⊠ Box 169, Zihuatanejo, Guerrero, ☎ 755/4–26–06, FAX 755/4–47–62) specializes in apartment, home, and villa rentals and sales. She is also the U.S. Consular Agent in the area with an office in Ixtapa (☎ 775/3–11–08).

Ixtapa

$$$$ 🏨 **Presidente Inter-Continental Ixtapa.** This all-inclusive property is a member of the Inter-Continental hotel chain. Rooms are attractively decorated in cool creams and whites. The room rates include all meals, 24-hour beverage service, and 17 hours of recreational activities, including snorkel and scuba-diving clinics. If you want tranquillity, request a room near the east pool, away from where the action is. ⊠ *Blvd. Ixtapa, 40880,* ☎ *755/3–00–18; 800/327–0200 in the U.S.,* FAX *755/3–23–12. 400 rooms and suites. 3 restaurants, bar, 2 pools, wading pool, sauna, steam room, 2 tennis courts, exercise room. AE, DC, MC, V.*

$$$–$$$$ 🏨 **Krystal Ixtapa.** This beachfront hotel, shaped like a boat with its bow pointing to the sea, is part of a Mexican chain known for quality and service. All rooms are standard contemporary style with a view to the ocean, and there is a no-smoking floor. The Club Krystalito provides recreational activities for children, and because of its meeting facilities, the hotel is often filled with conventioneers. The Krystal is home to **Christine,** Ixtapa's most popular disco, and **Bogart's** (☞ Dining, *above*). ⊠ *Blvd. Ixtapa, 40880,* ☎ *755/3–03–33; 800/231–9860 in the U.S.,* FAX *755/3–02–16. 254 rooms and suites. 4 restaurants, coffee shop, pool, beauty salon, massage, sauna, 2 tennis courts, racquetball, dance club, laundry service, travel services, car rental. AE, DC, MC, V.*

$$$–$$$$ 🏨 **Westin Brisas Ixtapa.** This immense, pyramid-shape architectural ★ wonder slopes down a hillside to its own secluded cove and beach, Playa Vista Hermosa. The grounds are luxuriant with jungle vegetation; fresh flowers on the bed welcome you to your room. Every vibrantly colorful unit has a private balcony with a hammock, ocean view, and a table for room-service dining; spacious junior suites have larger balconies with hot tubs. Guests and nonguests enjoy the hotel's excellent **Portofino** and **El Mexicano** restaurants. ⊠ *Playa Vista Hermosa (Box 97), 40880,* ☎ *755/3–21–21; 800/228–3000 in the U.S.,* FAX *755/3–07–51. 447 rooms and suites. 4 restaurants, 2 bars, 3 pools, wading pool, beauty salon, 4 tennis courts, laundry service, travel services, car rental. AE, DC, MC, V.*

$$$ 🏨 **Dorado Pacífico.** This privately owned beachfront hotel is known for its fine food and good service. The huge pool, with two water slides, makes it a favorite with youngsters. The furnishings are fairly nondescript, but the ocean-view rooms have private balconies. Glass elevators look out on the dramatic atrium lobby. Try the beachside **Cebolla Roja** restaurant for dinner. ⊠ *Blvd. Ixtapa, 40880,* ☎ *755/3–20–25; 800/448–8355 in the U.S.,* FAX *755/3–01–26. 285 rooms and suites. 3 restaurants, bar, pool, 2 tennis courts. AE, DC, MC, V.*

$$$ 🏨 **Posada Real.** Smaller and more intimate than most of the other Ixtapa hotels, this member of the Best Western chain sits on Palmar Beach, has lots of charm, and is a good value. ⊠ *Blvd. Ixtapa, 40880,* ☎ *755/3–16–85; 800/528–1234 in the U.S.,* FAX *755/3–18–05. 110 rooms. Restaurant, bar, 2 pools, wading pool. AE, DC, MC, V.*

$$$ 🏨 **Villa del Lago.** This B&B in a modern colonial-style house, totally remodeled in 1997, is the only listed Ixtapa property that is not on the beach. It is, however, a golfer's dream, facing the sixth hole tee-off of the Campo de Golf Ixtapa (designed by Robert Trent Jones Jr.). The two-level master suite, terrace, and swimming pool have views of the lush green course and the mountains beyond. Golf packages are available for this course as well as for the Robert Von Hagge–designed 18-hole course at Marina Ixtapa, and the hotel provides free transportation

to any place in Ixtapa. The master and junior suites have plunge pools, and all rooms have phones but no TVs. Rates include breakfast. ⊠ *Retorno Alondras 244, 40880,* ☎ *755/3–14–82,* FAX *755/3–14–22; 619/575–1766 in the U.S. 7 suites. Restaurant, pool, library. AE, DC, MC, V.*

Zihuatanejo

$$$$　🖭 **Puerto Mío.** On a rocky peninsula just inside the mouth of Zihuatanejo Bay, this small hotel, now under management of the Villa del Sol group, has a seaside level with a pool, terrace bar, dining room, guest rooms, and a marina where the Zihuatanejo Scuba Center is based. A hilltop "mansion" level features another pool and additional suites with sweeping bay views. Locals as well as guests enjoy the seafood, Continental cuisine, and romantic setting of the hotel's Moro Viejo restaurant. Children under 14 are not accepted during the high season. ⊠ *Playa del Almacén, 40880,* ☎ *01–800/711–2080; 888/369–2645 in the U.S.,* ☎ FAX *755/4–33–44. 31 rooms and suites. Restaurant, bar, 2 pools, dive shop. AE, MC, V.*

$$–$$$　🖭 **Irma.** One of Zihuatanejo's originals, this simple and clean colonial-style hotel sits on a bluff overlooking Madera Beach (accessible by a stairway). ⊠ *Playa la Madera, Box 4, 40880,* ☎ *755/4–21–05,* FAX *755/4–37–38. 73 rooms. Restaurant, bar, pool. AE, DC, MC, V.*

$$　🖭 **Bungalows Pacificos.** Terraced down a cliffside above Madera Beach, each of the spacious bungalows has its own large veranda with a sweeping view of Zihuatanejo Bay as well as a fully equipped kitchen. The owner speaks Spanish, English, and German. ⊠ *Cerro de la Madera, Box 12, 40880,* ☎ FAX *755/4–21–12. 6 units. No credit cards.*

$$　🖭 **Catalina-Sotavento.** Really two hotels in one, this multilevel oldie-but-goodie sits on a cliff overlooking the bay. Below, accessible by extensive stairs, are Playa la Ropa and the hotel's beach bar and lounge chairs. Rooms are large and well maintained, with ceiling fans and ample terraces sporting hammocks and a chaise longue in each room. ⊠ *Playa la Ropa, Box 2, 40880,* ☎ *755/4–20–32,* FAX *755/4–29–75. 109 units. 2 restaurants, 2 bars, beach. AE, DC, MC, V.*

$$　🖭 **Solimar Inn.** Near the town center, this comfortable hotel features large, air-conditioned rooms with cable TV, kitchenettes, and ceiling fans. Guests tend to stay for weeks or more. ⊠ *Plazas los Faroles, 40880,* ☎ FAX *755/4–36–92. 12 rooms. Bar, pool. MC, V.*

$$　🖭 **Villas Miramar.** This pleasant colonial-style hotel is in two sections (divided by a small street). The front section overlooks and has access to Madera Beach. The rooms are nicely decorated and have balconies, tiled showers, air-conditioning, and ceiling fans. ⊠ *Playa la Madera, Box 211, 40880,* ☎ *755/4–21–06,* FAX *755/4–21–49. 17 rooms, 1 suite. Restaurant, bar. AE, MC, V.*

$　🖭 **Ávila.** In the center of town facing the beachside Paseo del Pescador, the Ávila has large clean rooms (all are air-conditioned), TVs, and ceiling fans. ⊠ *Calle Juan N. Álvarez 8, 40880,* ☎ *755/4–20–10,* FAX *755/4–32–99. 27 rooms. AE, MC, V.*

$　🖭 **Las Urracas.** Each of the casita-style units has a porch in a shaded garden, a kitchen, and a stove. Located on La Ropa Beach, it is a great bargain—which lots of people know about, so reserve far in advance. ⊠ *Playa la Ropa, Box 141, 40880,* ☎ *755/4–20–53. 16 bungalows. No credit cards.*

Nightlife

A good way to start an evening is a happy hour at one of Ixtapa's hotels. Sunset is an important daily event, and plans should be made accordingly. Tops for sunset viewing (with live music) is the lobby bar at the **Westin Brisas.** To follow sunset viewing by dancing to tropical music until about 2 AM, take the elevator up to the **Faro Bar** nightclub atop the 85-ft-high faux-lighthouse tower in **Marina Ixtapa** (755/3–20–90). **Christine,** at the Krystal in Ixtapa, is the town's liveliest high-tech disco. Or head over to **Señor Frog's** (⊠ Opposite the Hotel Presidente, ☎ 755/3–02–72) for "sky" dancing.

Carlos 'n' Charlie's (⊠ Blvd. Ixtapa, next to the Best Western Posada Real, ☎ 755/3–00-85) has a party atmosphere, with late-night dancing on a raised platform by the beach. There's a new desert-inspired disco, complete with blue sky and cactus, at **La Valentina** restaurant–video bar–disco complex (⊠ Blvd. Ixtapa, next to Doubletree hotel, ☎ 755/3–11–90). Some discos have dress codes, so shorts, sandals, and tennis shoes should be left in the closet.

A number of hotels feature **Mexican Fiesta Nights** with buffets, handicraft bazaars, and live folkloric music and dance performances. In high season you'll find Mexican Fiesta Nights on Mondays at the Krystal, Tuesdays at the Dorado Pacífico, and Wednesdays at the Sheraton.

Outdoor Activities and Sports

Fishing

Bookings and information about sportfishing can be obtained through **Ixtapa Sportfishing Charters** (⊠ 33 Olde Mill Run, Stroudsburg, PA 18360, ☎ 717/424–8323, FAX 717/424–1016) or **Zihuatanejo** (⊠ Paseo del Pescador 6, ☎ 755/4–41–62). You can also arrange trips at the **Cooperativo de Pescadores**(☎ 755/4–20–56) at the Zihuatanejo municipal pier.

Golf

There are two 18-hole championship courses in Ixtapa. Each has its own clubhouse with a restaurant and tennis courts. The **Club de Golf Ixtapa** (☎ 755/3–10–62), designed by Robert Trent Jones Jr., is on a wildlife preserve that runs from a coconut plantation to the beach. A round costs $45, cart and/or caddie extra. Part of the Marina Ixtapa complex, the challenging **Club de Golf Marina Ixtapa** (☎ 755/3–14–10) was designed by Robert Von Hagge. Greens fees are $85 (include caddie or cart).

Horseback Riding

You can rent horses with guides at **Rancho Playa Linda** (☎ 755/4–30–85) just up the coast from Ixtapa, or at La Manzanillo Ranch, near Playa la Ropa in Zihuatanejo.

Scuba Diving

Some 30 dive sites in the area range from deep canyons to shallow reefs. The waters here are teeming with sea life, and visibility is excellent. At the north end of Playa Cuachalalate on Ixtapa Island, **Nacho's Dive Shop** (☎ No phone) provides rental equipment, instruction, and guided dives. The **Zihuatanejo Scuba Center** (⊠ Calle Cuauhtémoc 3, ☎ FAX 755/4–21–47; ⊠ At marina of Hotel Puerto Mío), owned and operated by master diver and marine biologist Juan Barnard and his partner Ed Clark, runs one- and two-tank dives as well as an intensive five-day certification course. This authorized NAUI (National Association of Underwater Instructors) Pro Facility has an enthusiastic and knowledgeable staff, including some expatriate Americans.

Tennis

All major Ixtapa hotels have lighted tennis courts, as do the **Club de Golf Ixtapa** (☎ 755/3–10–62 or 755/3–11–63) and the **Club de Golf Marina Ixtapa** (☎ 755/3–14–10). Fees are $10–$12, and equipment rentals are available. In Zihuatanejo, **Hotel Villa del Sol** (☎ 755/4–22–39) also has courts.

Water Sports

You'll find a variety of water sports along Playa del Palmar in Ixtapa. Parasailing costs about $20 for an eight-minute ride; waterskiing runs about $20 per half hour; banana boat rides are about $2.50 per person for a 20-minute trip. On La Ropa Beach, next to La Perla restaurant, Hobie Cats rent for $20 per hour, and classes cost $25 per half hour. Windsurfers rent for $20 per hour; classes, which include six hours over four days, cost $40.

Shopping

Ixtapa

As you enter Ixtapa from the airport or from Zihuatanejo, you'll see a large handicrafts market, **Mercado de Artesanía Turístico,** on the right side of Boulevard Ixtapa. The result of a state law that banned vendors from the beach, this market hosts some 150 stands, selling handicrafts, T-shirts, folk apparel, and souvenirs.

Across the street from the hotel zone, the shopping area is loosely divided into *centros comerciales,* or malls. These clusters of pleasant colonial-style buildings feature patios containing boutiques, restaurants, cafés, and grocery minimarkets. The first one you'll come to is **Los Patios,** where La Fuente (☎ 755/3–08–12) sells locally designed clothes, art, crafts, and home furnishings. Behind Los Patios, in a terra-cotta–color building, is **Plaza Ixpamar,** host to El Amanecer (☎ 755/3–19–02) and its nice array of folk art. After Plaza Ixpamar comes **Las Fuentes,** where you'll find **Nautica** (☎ 755/3–12–72); **Bye-Bye** (☎ 755/3–09–79 ext. 13) beach and casual wear; the ubiquitous sportswear emporium **Aca Joe** (☎ 755/3–03–02); and the handy **Supermercado Scruples** (☎ 755/3–21–28). The last mall in the hotel zone strip is **La Puerta,** which includes **Ferrioni Collection** (☎ 755/3–23–43) with colorful Scottish terrier–logo casual wear, and **Mic-Mac** (☎ 755/3–17–33) with crafts and Mexican regional art and clothing.

Zihuatanejo

Downtown Zihuatanejo has a colorful **municipal market** with a labyrinth of small stands on the east side of the town center, on Calle Benito Juárez at Antonio Nava. On the west edge of town, along Calle 5 de Mayo, is the **Mercado de Artesanía Turístico,** similar to the craft and souvenir market in Ixtapa, but larger, with 255 stands. Good purchases include local hand-painted Guerrero wooden masks and ceramics, huaraches, and silver jewelry.

Near the mercado, across from the Aeroméxico office and facing the waterfront, **Casa Marina** (⊠ Paseo del Pescador 9, ☎ 755/4–23–73) is a two-story building containing several boutiques, all belonging to the same family. **El Embarcadero** has an extensive selection of folk art from all over Mexico; **Manos** sells handicrafts; **La Zapoteca** features hammocks and hand-loomed rugs; and **El Jumil** has an array of Guerrero ceremonial masks. You might want to poke around here first to check prices, and then head for the market, where you'll often pay less for the same wares if you have a good eye and are willing to bargain.

There are a number of interesting shops in the tiny three-block nucleus of central Zihuatanejo. **Galería Maya** (⊠ Calle Nicolás Bravo 31, ☎ 755/4–46–06) is very browseable for its folk art and leather goods. **Lupita's** (⊠ Juan N. Álvarez 5, ☎ 755/4–22–38) and **Botique de Xochil** (⊠ Calle Ejido at Cuauhtémoc, ☎ 755/4–21–31) both have good selections of colorful handmade tropical-chic women's apparel from Oaxaca and Chiapas. **Alberto's** (⊠ Calle Cuauhtémoc 12 and 15, ☎ 755/4–21–61) and **Ruby's** (⊠ Calle Cuauhtémoc 7) are two of the best places to find authentic silver jewelry. **Coco Cabaña** (⊠ Agustín Ramírez 1, ☎ 755/4–25–18) is a fascinating folk-art shop. Over at Playa la Ropa, **Gala Art** (⊠ Hotel Villa del Sol, ☎ 755/4–22–39) exhibits and sells paintings and sculptures by prominent local artists.

Arte Mexicano Nopal (⊠ Álvarez 13-B, across street from Hotel Avila, ☎ 755/4–75–30) stocks quality handmade furniture.

Ixtapa/Zihuatanejo A to Z

Arriving and Departing

BY BUS

Various bus companies run from the **Central de Autobuses** (⊠ Paseo Zihuatanejo at Paseo La Boquita). **Estrella de Oro** (☎ 755/4–21–75) has deluxe service (with air-conditioning, video, bathrooms, and soft drinks) between Acapulco and Zihuatanejo. The trip takes less than four hours and costs about $12. The trip from Mexico City takes about five hours, bypassing Acapulco.

BY CAR

The trip from Acapulco is a 3½-hour drive over a good two-lane road that passes through small towns and coconut groves and has some spectacular ocean views for the last third of the way. The drive from Manzanillo is eight hours with a meal stop, and should only be done during daylight, due to reports of car jackings around Playa Azul. Military and police patrols have been increased on Highway 200 in the last year, and the number of incidents has dramatically decreased.

BY PLANE

Mexicana (☎ 755/3–22–08) has direct daily flights from Los Angeles, and **Aeroméxico** (☎ 755/4-20-18) flies direct from Los Angeles, and has one-stop service from Atlanta, Dallas, and Houston. Both airlines operate several daily nonstops (35 minutes) between Mexico City and Zihuatanejo. **Continental** (☎ 01–800/900–5000) flies nonstop from Houston. **Northwest** (☎ 5/785–1693 or 01–800/907–4700) departs from Minneapolis/St. Paul and Detroit Saturdays December–March.

BY SHIP

Several cruise lines, including **Cunard, Holland America Lines, Krystal Cruises, Princess Cruises, Royal Caribbean Cruises,** and **Royal Cruise Lines,** sail to Ixtapa/Zihuatanejo from Los Angeles in winter.

Getting Around

Unless you plan to travel great distances or visit remote beaches, taxis and buses are by far the best way to get around. Taxis are plentiful, clean, and reliable, and fares are reasonable and fixed. The fare from the Ixtapa hotel zone to Zihuatanejo is about $2. Taxis are usually lined up in front of hotels. Two radio taxi companies are **APAAZ** (☎ 755/4–36–80) and **UTAAZ** (☎ 755/4–33–11). Minibuses run every 10 to 15 minutes between the Ixtapa hotels and between the Ixtapa hotel zone and downtown Zihuatanejo; fare is about 30¢.

Contacts and Resources

CAR RENTAL

Hertz (☎ 755/4–25–90) and **Dollar** (☎ 755/4–23–14) have locations at the airport and in Ixtapa and/or Zihuatanejo. A good local agency is **Quick Rent-A-Car** (⊠ Across from Doubletree hotel, ☎ 755/3–18–30). Jeeps are available.

EMERGENCIES

Police (☎ 755/4–38–37); **Public Safety** (Seguridad Publica; ☎ 755/4–71–71); **Red Cross** (☎ 755/4–20–09).

GUIDED TOURS

Most major hotels have lobby tour desks or travel agencies that have a selection of sight-seeing tours of Ixtapa, Zihuatanejo, and surrounding areas. Another option is a 6½-hour cruise on the 100-passenger trimaran *Tri-Star*, which sets sail from Zihuatanejo Bay. For $60, you'll get ground transportation, an open bar (domestic drinks), and a fresh-fish lunch at Ixtapa Island. You can also book a three-hour sunset cruise of Zihuatanejo Bay, $40 including open bar and hors d'oeuvres, or a four-hour cruise to Playa Manzanillo, just outside the mouth of the bay, for great snorkeling, swimming, and spinnaker flying (like parasailing). This trip ($52) includes lunch on board and an open bar. For details about all of these cruises, contact **Yates del Sol** (☎ 755/4–26–94 or 755/4–82–70).

You can hire a fisherman's boat from the municipal pier to go to **Los Moros de Potosí,** large white rocks in the ocean where rare web-footed brown boobies congregate with cormorants, egrets, frigates, pelicans, and long-tailed white terns. To see pink flamingos and other birds, take a taxi to **Barra de Potosí** (15 minutes past the airport), where a beautiful *laguna* (lake) is an unofficial bird sanctuary. You can arrange a cruise with the small fishing launches in front of the palapa restaurants there, but the fishermen probably don't speak English.

TRAVEL AGENCY

American Express (✉ Arcade of Krystal Hotel, Ixtapa, ☎ 755/3–08–53, ℻ 755/3–12–06) is open Monday–Saturday 9–6.

VISITOR INFORMATION

Municipal Tourism Office (✉ Zihuatanejo City Hall, ☎ 755/4–20–01, ext. 120) is open weekdays 9–8. **Guerrero State Tourism Office** (✉ La Puerta Shopping Center, across from Presidente Intercontinental Hotel, Ixtapa, ☎ 755/3–19–68) is open weekdays 9–7, Saturday 10–2.

9 ACAPULCO

If Acapulco no longer tops the glitterati top-10 list, it remains both a sentimental favorite and a party-hearty resort town, with miles of beaches and some of the glitziest discos this side of the Pacific. A delightful three-hour drive from Acapulco is Taxco, a colonial treasure, where the Baroque towers of Santa Prisca church overlook cobblestone streets lined with silversmiths.

Updated by
Patricia Alisau

ACAPULCO IS A VIBRANT PORT CITY with one of the most beautiful bays in the world. This, no doubt, is what attracted the Hollywood celebrities of the 1950s who built homes and hotels as hideaways and places for entertaining their friends. The celebrity status continued. This is where John and Jackie Kennedy spent their honeymoon. Likewise, Bill and Hillary Clinton. And it's where Liz Taylor and Michael Todd ventured after tying the knot. In fact, Acapulco still ranks as one of the top honeymoon spots worldwide. Entertainers such as Placido Domingo come to give yearly benefit concerts and singers like Julio Iglesias and a host of others maintain residences here, carrying on the Hollywood tradition that started long ago.

Acapulco has managed to age gracefully over the years even as it's grown into a town of several million inhabitants. Care is especially lavished on its upkeep. The city fathers initiated a multimillion-dollar beautification program some time ago, which is renewed annually to keep the bay, beaches, and streets landscaped and clean.

Of course, anyone who ventures to this stretch of the Pacific, 433 km (268 mi) south of Mexico City, does so to relax. Translate that as swimming, shopping, and enjoying the nightlife. Everything takes place against a staggeringly beautiful backdrop. The natural harbor of Acapulco Bay is the city's centerpiece. By day the water looks temptingly deep blue; at night it flashes and sparkles with the city lights.

The weather is Acapulco's major draw—warm waters, almost constant sunshine, and year-round temperatures in the 80s F. It comes as no surprise, then, that most people plan their day around laying their towel on some part of Acapulco's many kilometers of beach. Both tame and wild water sports are available—everything from waterskiing to snorkeling, diving, and parasailing. Less strenuous possibilities are motorboat rides and fishing trips. Championship golf courses, tennis courts, and the food and crafts markets also lure some visitors away from the beach, but not out of the sun.

Most people rise from their hammocks, deck chairs, or towels only when impelled by hunger, and eating is one of Acapulco's great pleasures. In addition to the glitzy places, there are plenty of good no-frills, down-home Mexican restaurants. Eating at one of these joints takes you to the real Mexico: office workers breaking for lunch, groups of men socializing over cups of coffee.

At night Acapulco rouses itself from the day's torpor and prepares for the long hours ahead. Even though Acapulco's heyday is past, its nightlife is legendary, and the constant opening of new and ever more spectacular dance clubs is proof positive that this remains the disco capital of the world. Perpetually crowded, the discos are grouped in twos and threes, and most people go to several places in one night.

The name of the late Teddy Stauffer, a Swiss entrepreneur, is practically synonymous with that of modern Acapulco. He hired the first cliff divers at La Quebrada in Old Acapulco and founded the Boom Boom Room, the town's first dance hall, and Tequila A Go-Go, its first discotheque. The Hotel Mirador at La Quebrada and the area stretching from Caleta to Hornos beaches, near today's Old Acapulco, were the center of activity in the 1950s, when Acapulco was a town of 20,000 with an economy based largely on fishing.

Since the late 1940s, Acapulco has expanded eastward so that today it is one of Mexico's largest cities, with a population of approximately

2 million. Former president Miguel Alemán Valdés bought up miles of the coast just before the road and airport were built—as his namesake Avenida Costera Miguel Alemán testifies. Currently under development is a 3,000-acre expanse known as Acapulco Diamante, which encompasses the areas known as Punta Diamante and Playa Diamante and some of the city's most sparkling hotels and residential developments.

Pleasures and Pastimes

Beaches
The lure of sun and sand in Acapulco is legendary. Every sport is available, and you can eat in a beach restaurant, dance, and sleep in a *hamaca* (hammock) without leaving the water's edge. If you want to avoid the crowds, there are also plenty of quiet and even isolated beaches within reach.

Dining
Dining in Acapulco is more than just eating out—it is the most popular leisure activity in town. Every night the restaurants fill up, and every night the adventurous diner can sample a different cuisine: Italian, Belgian, Japanese, American, Tex-Mex, and, of course, plain old Mex. The variety of styles matches the range of cuisines: from greasy spoons that serve regional favorites to gourmet restaurants with gorgeous views of Acapulco Bay. Most restaurants fall somewhere in the middle, and on the Costera are dozens of beachside restaurants with *palapa* (palm frond) roofs, as well as wildly decorated rib and hamburger joints popular with visitors under 30—not necessarily in age, but definitely in spirit.

Another plus for Acapulco dining is that the food is garden fresh. Each morning the Mercado Municipal is abuzz with restaurant managers and locals buying up the fish, poultry, and vegetables that will appear on plates that evening. Although some top-quality beef is produced in the states of Sonora and Chihuahua, many of the more expensive restaurants claim that they import their beef from the States. In either case, the beef is excellent in most places. Establishments that cater to tourists purify their drinking water and use it to cook vegetables.

Lodging
Accommodations in Acapulco run the gamut from sprawling, big-name complexes with nonstop amenities to small, family-run inns where hot water is a luxury. Wherever you stay, however, prices will be reasonable compared with those in the United States, and service is generally good, as Acapulqueños have been catering to tourists for half a century.

Nightlife
Acapulco has always been famous for its nightlife, and justifiably so. For many visitors the discos and restaurants are just as important as the sun and the sand. The minute the sun slips over the horizon, the Costera comes alive with people milling around window-shopping, deciding where to dine, and generally biding their time till the disco hour. The legendary Acapulco discos are open 365 days a year from about 10:30 PM until they empty out, often not until 4 or 5 AM. Obviously you aren't going to find great culture here; theater efforts are few and far between, and except for an occasional benefit concert by Placido Domingo, there is no classical music. But disco-hopping is a high art in Acapulco, and for those who care to watch, there are live shows and folk-dance performances.

Shopping
The abundance of air-conditioned shopping malls and boutiques makes picking up gifts and souvenirs one of the highlights of a visit to Aca-

pulco. The malls are filled with clothing shops, and many others are strung along the Costera. There are also more and more high-fashion boutiques that carry custom-designed clothes. Malls in Acapulco range from the shopping arcades at several of the more lavish hotels to the huge completely enclosed and air-conditioned Plaza Bahía.

There are several good shops specializing in Mexican crafts, and the Mercado Municipal, whose aisles are piled high with fruits, vegetables, poultry, fish, and meats, is also is a good source of local handicrafts. Flea markets abound, carrying what seems to be an inexhaustible supply of inexpensive collectibles and souvenirs.

The State of Guerrero is especially known for hand-painted ceramics, items made from *palo de rosa* wood, primitive bark paintings depicting scenes of village life, local flora and fauna, and embroidered textiles. Silver is a real bargain in Mexico. Taxco, three hours away by car (four by bus), is one of the silver capitals of the world.

Sports and the Outdoors

Acapulco has lots for sports lovers to enjoy. Most hotels have pools, and many have private tennis clubs as well as courts. Many of the hotels have gyms, too. Acapulco's waters are teeming with sailfish, marlin, shark, and mahi mahi, and although the waters aren't as clear as in the Caribbean, scuba diving is popular, as are waterskiing, windsurfing, kayaking, and bronco riding (an activity done in one-person motorboats). Parasailing looks terrifying and can be dangerous, but most people who do it love the view and go back again and again. Golfers can tee off at the nine-hole municipal course, in town, or at one of the five 18-hole championship courses (three are open to the public) in the Acapulco Diamante area.

EXPLORING

It's possible to get a feel for Acapulco during a short stay if you take in some downtown sights along with your beach activities. Those who have a longer time to spend can really soak up the ambience of the place and can enjoy excursions to some isolated beaches as well as to Taxco.

Numbers in the text correspond to numbers in the margin and on the Acapulco and Taxco Exploring maps.

Great Itineraries

IF YOU HAVE 3 DAYS

Spend the first day enjoying your favorite beach activity, be it parasailing, waterskiing, or simply sunning. That evening, to get the lay of the land, take a sunset cruise that includes a ringside view of Acapulco's daredevil *clavadistas* (divers) at **La Quebrada** ⑧. The following day, experience Acapulco at its most authentic, paying an early visit to the **Mercado Municipal** ④, the **waterfront** ⑥, and the **zócalo** ⑦. After some late afternoon shopping in the boutiques and handicrafts markets along the Costera Miguel Alemán, "shake off the dust" (as they say in Mexico) at one of the city's glitzy discos. The next day you'll want to try to land a sailfish, take in the Mexican Fiesta at the **Acapulco International Center** (drinks and show only), and bid farewell to Acapulco with a late candlelit dinner at one of the city's romantic dining spots.

IF YOU HAVE 5 DAYS

Add on to the three-day itinerary a visit to **El Fuerte de San Diego** ⑤, built in the 18th century to protect Acapulco from pirates, and today home of the Anthropology Museum. For a taste of the 1950s Acapulco of John Wayne and Johnny Weissmuller, hire a taxi to take you up into the hills above Caleta and Caletilla and make it a point to drop into Los Flamingos Hotel, which Weissmuller once owned with others from the Hollywood gang. Head out to Pie de la Cuesta for a late lunch and boat ride or waterskiing on Coyuca Lagoon, and then cross the road and park your body under a palm-frond umbrella for a spectacular sunset on the beach. Save one morning for the thrilling **Shotover Jet** boat ride on the Papagayo river (☞ Water Sports *in* Participant Sports, *below*). Especially if you're traveling with kids, devote a few hours to **Mágico Mundo Marino** ⑨ and the glass-bottom boat trip to Roqueta Island.

IF YOU HAVE 7 DAYS

For a complete change of pace, you'll want to rent a car or arrange for a tour to **Taxco,** a colonial treasure of twisting cobblestone streets and some 1,000 silver shops, about a three-hour drive from Acapulco; plan to spend the night. For a change from shopping for silver, visit the **Church of San Sebastián and Santa Prisca** ⑩, Taxco's most important landmark, on Plaza Borda, and the **Casa Humboldt** ⑫, which now houses a museum of viceregal art. Try to get a front-row seat at one of the bars or restaurants on the square and spend an hour watching the constant activity: weddings, communions, funerals, baptisms, and vendors selling baskets and painted animals. The following day, before the return trip to Acapulco, tour the **Caves of Cacahuamilpa** ⑭, an amazing expanse of subterranean chambers.

Acapulco

Acapulco is a city that is easily understood, easily explored. During the day the focus for most visitors is the beach and the myriad activities that happen on and off it. At night the attention shifts to the restaurants and discos. The **Costera Miguel Alemán,** the wide boulevard that hugs Acapulco Bay from the Scenic Highway to Caleta Beach (about 8 km, or 5 mi), is central to both day and night diversions. All the major beaches, shopping malls, and big hotels—minus the more exclusive Acapulco Diamante properties—are off the Costera. Hence most of the shopping, dining, and clubbing takes place within a few blocks of this main drag, and many an address is listed only as "Costera Miguel Alemán." Although the Costera runs completely across Acapulco, most of the action is between the naval base, La Base, next to the Hyatt (which anchors the eastern terminus of the Costera) and Papagayo Park. Because street addresses are not often used and streets have no logical pattern, directions are usually given from a major landmark, such as CiCi (a theme park) or the *zócalo* (town square).

Old Acapulco, the only area of Acapulco that can easily be visited on foot, is where the Mexicans go to run their errands: mail letters at the post office, buy supplies at the Mercado Municipal, and pay their taxes. Also known as El Centro, it's where you'll find the zócalo, the church, and Fort San Diego. Just up the hill from Old Acapulco is La Quebrada.

The peninsula south of Old Acapulco contains remnants of the first version of Acapulco. This primarily residential area was prey to dilapidation and abandonment for many years, but efforts were made to revitalize it—such as reopening the Caleta Hotel and opening the aquarium on Caleta Beach and the zoo on Roqueta Island. Although its prime is definitely past, it is now a popular area for budget travelers, especially Mexican and European. The **Plaza de Toros,** where bullfights are held on Sundays from Christmas to Easter, is in the center of the peninsula.

If you arrived by plane, you've already had a royal introduction to Acapulco Bay. **Acapulco Diamante** is the area stretching east of Acapulco

366

Acapulco

Av. Adolfo Ruíz Cortines

Av. Constituyentes

Av. Durango

E. Elcano

Av. Cuauhtémoc

Calz. A. Ordaneta

Costera Miguel Alemán

Playa Hornos

Av. Ejido

Pro. D. H. de Mendoza

Av. Cuauhtémoc

Av. 5 de Mayo

Calz. Pie de la Cuesta

Av. V. Guerrero

Morelos

Av. la Quebrada

Tte. Azueta

Malecón

Av. L. Mateos

Cptn. M. Alemán

Av. Pozo

← TO PIE DE
LA CUESTA

Av. Adolfo López Mateos

Av. L. Mateos

Gran Vía T.

Playa Caletilla

Isla la Roqueta

PACIFIC OCEAN

proper from Las Brisas to Barra Vieja beach. You'll need a car or a taxi to explore this area, where you'll find most of Acapulco's poshest hotels—Las Brisas, the Acapulco Sheraton, Camino Real, the Princess and Pierre Marqués, and Vidafel Mayan Palace—and residential developments, as well as several exclusive private clubs, pounding surf, and beautiful beaches.

A Good Tour

If you want to get the lay of the land, you might take a drive or taxi ride along the Costera Miguel Alemán, starting on its eastern edge at **La Base,** the Mexican naval base south of Playa Icacos. When you come to Playa Icacos, you'll see the **Casa de la Cultura** ① cultural complex on the beach side (just past the Hyatt Regency hotel); a little farther down is **CiCi** ②, a children's amusement park. About 1 km (½ mi) past CiCi, on the right side of the Costera, lies the **Acapulco International Center** (often called the Convention Center); you might return here in the evening to attend a Mexican fiesta. Continue along through the commercial heart of the Costera until you reach **Papagayo Park** ③, one of the top municipal parks in the country. When you arrive at the intersection of the Costera with Diego H. de Mendoza, detour a few blocks inland to find Old Acapulco and the sprawling **Mercado Municipal** ④. You'll want to take the bus marked "Mercado" or have your taxi drop you off; it's best to navigate this area by foot. A few blocks west and closer to the water, **El Fuerte de San Diego** ⑤ sits on the hill overlooking the harbor next to the army barracks. You'll next see the **waterfront** ⑥ (locally known as the *malecón*) with its series of docks and, adjoining it, the **zócalo** ⑦, the center of Old Acapulco. A 15-minute walk up the hill from the zócalo brings you to **La Quebrada** ⑧, where the famous cliff divers perform their daredevil stunt daily.

Sights to See

❶ **Casa de la Cultura.** This cultural complex includes a small archaeological museum, an exhibit of Mexican and international crafts, and the Ixcateopan art gallery, with changing exhibits. ⊠ *Costera Miguel Alemán 4834,* ☎ *74/84–38–14.* ☒ *Free.* ⊙ *Weekdays 9–2 and 5–8, Sat. 9–2.*

❷ **CiCi** (Centro Internacional para Convivencia Infantil). A water-oriented theme park for children, CiCi has dolphin and seal shows, a freshwater pool with wave-making apparatus, a water slide, miniaquarium, and other attractions. ⊠ *Costera Miguel Alemán, across from Hard Rock Cafe,* ☎ *74/84–82–10.* ☒ *$4; $70 to swim with dolphins.* ⊙ *Daily 10–6.*

❺ **El Fuerte de San Diego.** Acapulco was originally an important port for the Spanish—who used it to trade with Asian countries—and they erected this fortress in the 18th century to protect the city from pirates. Their original fort, destroyed in an earthquake, was built in 1616.

The fort now houses the **Museo Historico de Acapulco.** The exhibits on display in 12 salons portray the city from prehistoric times through Mexico's independence from Spain in 1821. Especially noteworthy are the displays touching on the Christian missionaries sent from Mexico to the Far East and the cultural interchange that resulted. ⊠ *Calle Hornitos and Morelos,* ☎ *74/82–38–28.* ☒ *$2, free Sun.* ⊙ *Tues.–Sun. 10–6:30.*

❽ **La Quebrada.** High on a hill above downtown Acapulco, La Quebrada (literally "gorge"; in this case cliffs) is home to the Mirador Hotel, *the* place for tourists in the 1940s; it still retains mementos from its glory days. But these days most visitors eventually make the trip here because this is where the famous cliff divers jump from a height of 130 ft daily at 1 PM and evenings at 7:30, 8:30, 9:30, and 10:30. The dives are thrilling, so be sure to arrive early. Before they take the plunge, the brave divers say a prayer at a small shrine near the jumping-off point. Sometimes they dive in pairs; often they carry torches. The hotel's La Perla supper club is the traditional and most comfortable viewing spot, but you will be obligated to buy a drinks-show-tips ($10.50) or buffet-show-tips package ($20). The tequila, rum, and brandy drinks are watered down and only domestic so be forewarned. By all means, don't let this dissuade you from seeing the show. The divers can also be seen from a general observation deck next to the hotel (about $1.50). When you exit, some of the divers may also be waiting to greet you—and to ask for tips. (For information about viewing the divers on sunset cruises, *see* Guided Tours *in* Acapulco A to Z, *below.*)

⑨ Mágico Mundo Marino. In addition to an aquarium, the Magic Marine World has a sea-lion show, swimming pools, a toboggan, scuba diving, and (for rent) Jet Skis, inner tubes, bananas (inflatable rubber tubes pulled along the beach by motorboats), and kayaks—not to mention clean rest rooms. From **Caleta Beach**, you can take the glass-bottom boat to **Roqueta Island** (about 10 minutes each way) for a visit to the small zoo. ⊠ *Caleta Beach,* ☎ *74/83–12–15.* ▨ *Aquarium $3; round-trip ferry service to Roqueta Island, including zoo, $3.* ☉ *Mágico Mundo daily 9–7, zoo daily 9–5.*

④ Mercado Municipal. It's not for everyone, but the sprawling municipal market is Acapulco as the locals experience it. They come to purchase their everyday needs, from fresh vegetables and candles to plastic buckets and love potions. The stalls within the mercado are densely packed together, but things stay relatively cool despite the lack of air-conditioning. There are baskets, pottery, hammocks, even a stand offering charms, amulets, and talismans (☞ Shopping, *below).* It's best to come as early as possible to avoid the crowds. ⊠ *Diego Hurtado de Mendoza and Constituyentes, few blocks west of Costera.*

③ Papagayo Park. Named for the hotel that formerly occupied the grounds, the park sits on 52 acres of prime real estate on the Costera, just after the underpass that begins at Hornos beach. Youngsters enjoy the life-size model of a Spanish galleon, made to look like the ones that sailed into Acapulco when it was Mexico's capital of trade with the Orient. There is an aviary, a roller-skating rink, a racetrack with mite-size race cars, a replica of the space shuttle *Columbia,* bumper boats in a lagoon, and other rides. At press time, the rides section was being relocated to the back of the park from the streetside, which will be replanted with grass. Rides are still available while the renovation is under way. ⊠ *Costera Miguel Alemán,* ☎ *74/85–96–23.* ▨ *No entrance fee, rides 25¢–$1.50.* ☉ *Daily 10–8; rides section open 4–11 nightly.*

⑥ Waterfront. A stroll by the docks will remind you that Acapulco is still a lively commercial port and fishing center. The cruise ships anchor here, and at night Mexicans bring their children to play on the small tree-lined promenade. Farther west, by the zócalo, are the docks for the sightseeing yachts and smaller fishing boats. It's a good spot to join the Mexicans in people-watching. ⊠ *Costera Miguel Alemán, between Calle Escudero on the west and the San Diego Fort on the east.*

⑦ Zócalo. You'll find the hub of downtown and Old Acapulco at this shaded plaza, overgrown with dense trees. All day it's filled with vendors, shoe-shine men, and people lining up to use the pay phones. After siesta, they drift here to meet and greet. On Sunday evenings there's often music in the bandstand. There are several cafés and newsagents selling the English-language Mexico City *News* and the Mexico City *Times,* so tourists lodging in the area are drawn here, too. The flea market and Sanborns (☞ Shopping, *below)* are nearby. The zócalo fronts **Nues-**

tra Señora de la Soledad, the town's modern but unusual church, with its stark-white exterior and bulb-shape blue and yellow spires. ✉ *Bounded by Calle Felipe Valle on the north, Costera Miguel Alemán on the south, Calle J. Azueta on the west, and Calle J. Carranza on the east.*

NEED A BREAK? Just off the zócalo, **Sanborns** attracts locals and tourists alike; many linger for hours over a newspaper and a cup of coffee. **Cafetería Astoria** is a little outdoor café on the zócalo where businessmen stop in for breakfast before work or meet midmorning for a cappuccino and a sweet roll.

Beaches

Some beaches, such as Revolcadero and Pie de la Cuesta, have very strong undertows and surf, so swimming is not advised. Despite an enticing appearance and claims that officials are cleaning up the bay, it remains polluted. In addition, although vending on the beach has been officially outlawed, you'll still find yourself approached by souvenir hawkers. A new corps of tourist beach police dressed in blue shorts and white shirts, however, have been somewhat successful in shooing away the vendors. Of course, you can always follow the lead of the Mexican cognoscenti and enjoy the waters at your hotel pool when you're in the mood for a swim.

Beaches in Mexico are public, even those that seem to belong to a big hotel.

Barra Vieja
About 27 km (17 mi) east of Acapulco, between Laguna de Tres Palos and the Pacific, this long stretch of uncrowded beach is somewhat more inviting than Pie de la Cuesta (☞ *below*) because the drive out is much more pleasant. Most people make the trip out here for the solitude and to feast on *pescado a la talla* (fish marinated in spices and grilled over hot coals).

Caleta and Caletilla
On the peninsula in Old Acapulco, these two beaches once rivaled La Quebrada as the main tourist area in Acapulco's heyday. Now they attract families. Motorboats to Roqueta Island (☞ Mágico Mundo Marino *in* Exploring, *above*) leave from here.

Condesa
Facing the middle of Acapulco Bay, this stretch of sand has more than its share of tourists, especially singles, and the beachside restaurants are convenient for bites between parasailing flights.

Hornos and Hornitos
Running from the Plaza las Glorias Paraíso to Las Hamacas hotel, these beaches are packed shoulder to shoulder on the weekends with locals and Mexican tourists who know a good thing: graceful palms shade the sand, and there are scads of casual eateries within walking distance.

Icacos
Stretching from the naval base to El Presidente hotel, this beach is less populated than others on the Costera, and the morning waves are especially calm.

Pie de la Cuesta
You'll need a car or cab to reach this relatively unpopulated spot, about a 25-minute drive west of Acapulco, through one of the least picturesque parts of town. A four-lane highway, scheduled for comple-

tion by the year 2000, should cut down on driving time and make this experience more pleasant. A string of rustic restaurants border the wide beach, and straw palapas provide shade. What attracts people to Pie de la Cuesta, besides the long expanse of beach and spectacular sunsets, is beautiful **Coyuca Lagoon,** a favorite spot for waterskiing, freshwater fishing, and boat rides. The boats will ferry you to La Laguna restaurant, where, some people claim, the *pescado* (fish) *a la talla* (marinated in chilies and spices and then charcoal broiled) is even better than at Barra Vieja.

Puerto Marqués
Tucked below the airport highway, this strand is popular with Mexican tourists, so it tends to get crowded on weekends.

Revolcadero
A wide, sprawling beach next to the Vidafel Mayan Palace, Pierre Marqués, and Princess hotels, its water is shallow and its waves are fairly rough. People come here to surf and ride horses.

DINING

The top restaurants in Acapulco can be fun for a splurge and provide very good value. Even at the best places in town, dinner rarely exceeds $35 per person, and the atmosphere and views are fantastic. Ties and jackets are out of place, but so are shorts or jeans. Unless stated otherwise, all restaurants are open daily for lunch and then again for dinner from 6:30 or 7 until the last diner leaves. Several restaurants have two seatings: 6:30 for the gringos and 9 for the Mexican crowd, who wisely head directly to the discos after dinner to dance off the calories.

Note: Loud music blares from many restaurants along the Costera, and proprietors will aggressively try to hustle you inside with offers of drink specials. If you're looking for a hassle-free evening, it's best either to avoid this area or decide in advance precisely where you want to dine.

CATEGORY	COST*
$$$$	over $35
$$$	$25–$35
$$	$15–$25
$	under $15

*per person for a three-course meal, excluding drinks, service, and 15% sales tax

American

$$–$$$ ✕ **Hard Rock Cafe.** This link in the international Hard Rock chain is one of the most popular spots in Acapulco, and with good reason. The famous hamburgers and brownies plus southern-style food—fried chicken, ribs—are well prepared, and the portions are more than ample. The taped rock music begins at noon, and a live group starts playing at 11 PM (except Tuesday). There's always a line at the small boutique on the premises, where you can buy sports clothes and accessories bearing the Hard Rock label. ⊠ *Costera Miguel Alemán 37,* ☎ *74/84–66–80. Reservations not accepted. AE, MC, V.*

$$ ✕ **Carlos 'n' Charlie's.** An Acapulco landmark, this is still one of the most popular restaurants in town. Part of the Anderson group (with restaurants in the United States and Spain as well as Mexico), Carlos 'n' Charlie's cultivates an atmosphere of controlled craziness. Prankster waiters, a jokester menu, and eclectic decor add to the chaos. The crowd is mostly young and relaxed, seemingly oblivious to the rush-hour traffic noise that filters up to the covered balcony where people dine. The menu straddles the border, with ribs, stuffed shrimp, and oysters among the best offerings. The restaurant now opens for lunch and has a popular $6 buffet on Sundays. ⊠ *Costera Miguel Alemán 112,* ☎ *74/84–12–85 or 74/84–00–39. Reservations not accepted. AE, DC, MC, V.*

Belgian

$$ ✕ **La Petite Belgique.** Mexican-born Yolanda Brassart, who spent
★ years in Europe studying the culinary arts, reigns in the kitchen of this small bistro. Guy, her Belgian husband, makes certain that the customers are happy. Diners are greeted by the enticing aromas of goose-liver pâté, home-baked breads, and apple strudel. The menu changes every four months but usually includes boned duck stuffed with almonds and mushrooms and served with a white wine and mushroom sauce. ⊠ *Plaza Marbella,* ☎ *74/84–77–25. AE, DC, MC, V.*

French

$$$ ✕ **Le Jardin des Artistes.** A parking lot has been transformed into a chic garden hideaway that bears little resemblance to its former life. Tables laid with fresh flowers and Tiffany lamps grace an alfresco dining area while discreet waiters deliver platters of French dishes deliciously rich with classic cream and butter sauces. Swiss chef Richard already has a local following for his escargots in garlic butter, red snapper fillet with savory mustard sauce, and smoked trout soufflé. Traditional Gallic crêpes suzette, cherries jubilee, and chocolate mousse headline the dessert list, and the wine cellar holds vintages from France, Italy, Germany, Chile, and Mexico. After dinner, stroll through the snazzy art gallery adjoining the garden. ⊠ *Vicente Yanez Pinzón No. 11,* ☎ *74/84–83–44. Reservations essential. AE, DC, MC, V.* ◷ *No lunch.*

Health Food

$ ✕ **100% Natural.** Along the Costera Miguel Alemán there are several of these 24-hour restaurants specializing in light, healthful food—yogurt shakes, fruit salads, and sandwiches made with whole-wheat bread. The service is quick and the food is a refreshing alternative to tacos. You can recognize them by the green signs with white lettering. The original—and best—is across from the Acapulco Plaza hotel. ⊠ *Costera Miguel Alemán 200, near Acapulco Plaza,* ☎ *74/85–39–82;* ⊠ *Next to Oceanic 2000,* ☎ *74/84–84–40. MC, V.*

International

$$$ ✕ **Coyuca 22.** This is Acapulco's most beautiful restaurant, and more
★ celebrities have eaten here than you can shake a stick at. Its romantic setting has also been used for filming segments of the "Love Boat" TV series. On hilltop terraces that overlook the bay from Old Acapulco, the understated decor consists of Doric pillars and statuary, and diners gaze down on an enormous illuminated obelisk and a small pool. It's like eating in a partially restored Greek ruin without the dust. Diners can choose from two fixed menus or order à la carte. Seafood and prime ribs are house specialties. ⊠ *Av. Coyuca 22 (10-min taxi ride from zócalo),* ☎ *74/82–34–68 or 74/83–50–30. Reservations essential. AE, DC, MC, V. Closed Apr. 30–Nov. 1.*

$$$ ✕ **Madeiras.** A local favorite, Madeiras is very difficult to get into, es-
★ pecially on weekends and during the Christmas and Easter holidays. The bar-reception area is decorated with dramatic coffee tables whose glass tops rest startlingly upon carved-wooden animals, the dishes and flatware were created by silversmiths in nearby Taxco, and all tables afford views back across the bay toward Acapulco, whose lights glit-

ter brilliantly in the evening. Dinner is served from a four-course, prix-fixe menu and costs about $30 without wine. Specialties include a delicious red snapper baked in sea salt (a Spanish specialty), tasty chilled soups, and a choice of steaks and other seafood, as well as the *crepas de huitlacoche* (huitlacoche, also called *cuitlacoche,* is a corn fungus the Aztecs considered a delicacy). Seatings are every 30 minutes from 7 to 10:30 PM. ⊠ *Scenic Hwy. 33-B, just past La Vista shopping center,* ☎ *74/84–69–21. Reservations essential. AE, DC, MC, V.*

$$–$$$ ✕ **Bella Vista.** This alfresco restaurant in the exclusive Las Brisas area has fantastic sunset views of Acapulco. Its large menu includes items that range from Asian appetizers to Italian and seafood entrées. Try the delicious (and spicy!) Thai shrimp, sautéed in sesame oil, ginger, Thai chili, and hoisin sauce; or the red snapper étouffée, cooked in chardonnay, tomato, herbs, basil, and oyster sauce. Part of the restaurant has been enclosed and air-conditioned for those who like it cool. ⊠ *Carretera Escéncia 5255,* ☎ *74/84–15–80 ext. 500. Reservations essential. AE, DC, MC, V.*

$$–$$$ ✕ **Costa Constanza.** Mediterranean cuisine can't get much better than ★ it is at this pretty, fresh-looking new restaurant, which shares a beach with local fishermen who save the best of the day's catch for the kitchen. Italian-trained Loreli Fernandez assembles creative combinations of Italian, French, and Spanish fish and meat dishes. Tables are set up on a cozy pier at water's edge and in a glass-wrapped, air-conditioned dining room filled with attractive hand-decorated dishware from Michoacán. Consider starting with creamed oyster soup, then moving on to a grilled salmon steak flavored with yogurt-dill sauce and served with lime rice and sautéed vegetables. And there's always bouillabaisse (25 minutes to prepare). ⊠ *Costera Miguel Alemán No. 239, across from Las Hamacas hotel,* ☎ *74/82–28–61. AE, MC, V.*

$$–$$$ ✕ **El Olvido.** The view, the foliage, the Mediterranean decor, and the nueva cocina make this one of Acapulco's most popular dining spots, especially for the locals who have made it their social center. A terraced, open-air dining area provides a panoramic vista of the bay for all tables. French chef Daniel Janny created the dishes blending recipes from many lands with Mexican ingredients, which results in creations such as salmon roll with mango vinaigrette and quail in a honey, pineapple, and *pasilla* chili sauce. For dessert, try the unusual but tasty *guanábana* (soursop sherbet) with black *zapote* fruit sauce. ⊠ *Plaza Marbella,* ☎ *74/81–02–14. AE, DC, MC, V.*

$$–$$$ ✕ **Spicey.** In addition to another spectacular view of Acapulco's diamond-studded bay from the air-conditioned dining room or the terrace, this relative newcomer has an innovative menu of dishes that blend international techniques and spices. The results are delicious, as well as a delight to the eye: spring rolls filled with smoked salmon, cream cheese, and vegetables served with a Chinese plum sauce, and whole red snapper flavored with star anise and rosemary, glacéed with honey. ⊠ *Scenic Hwy., Fracc. Marina Las Brisas,* ☎ *74/81–13–80. Reservations essential. AE, MC, V.*

Italian

$$–$$$ ✕ **Casa Nova.** Another ultraromantic spot created by Arturo Cordova, ★ the man behind Coyuca 22 (☞ *above*), Casa Nova is carved out of a cliff that rises up from Acapulco Bay. The views, both from the terrace and the air-conditioned dining room, are spectacular, the service impeccable, and the Italian cuisine divine. Diners can choose the fixed-price menu (called *menu turístico*) or order à la carte. Favorites include antipasto, fresh pastas, a delightful *cotolette de vittello* (veal chops with mushrooms), lobster tail, and *linguini alle vongole* (linguine with

Acapulco Dining and Lodging

Dining
Bella Vista, **32**
Beto's, **21**
Carlos 'n'
Charlie's, **20**
Casa Nova, **33**
Costa Constanza, **11**
Coyuca 22, **4**
El Cabrito, **28**
El Olvido, **19**
Hard Rock Cafe, **26**
La Cabaña, **5**
La Casa de Tere, **9**

La Petite Belgique, **20**
La Vela, **36**
Le Jardin des
Artistes, **17**
Madeiras, **32**
100% Natural, **13**
Pípo's, **28**
Spicey, **35**
Suntory, **30**
Villa Fiore, **25**
Zapata, Villa y Cia, **30**
Zorrito's, **12**

Lodging
Acapulco Princess, **39**
Camino Real
Acapulco
Diamante, **37**
Continental Plaza, **18**
Costa Club, **16**
Elcano, **26**
Fiesta Americana
Condesa
Acapulco, **23**
Hotel Misión, **8**

Howard Johnson
Maralisa, **14**
Hyatt Regency
Acapulco, **31**
Las Hamacas, **10**
Los Flamingos, **3**
Majestic, **7**
Parador del Sol, **1**
Park Hotel & Tennis
Center, **15**
Pierre Marqués, **38**
Plaza las Glorias
El Mirador, **2**

N

| 0 | 880 yards |
| 0 | 800 meters |

Paseo del Farallon

Diana
Glorieta

Playa
Condesa

Golf
Course

Centro
International

Robo Solitario

Av. Almirante

Almirante
Cristóbal Colón

Magallanes

Horacio Nelson

Costera Miguel

Alemán

Playa
Icacos

Bahía de
Acapulco

La Base

Punta
Guitarrón

Escénica

Carretera

TO AIRPORT →

Quinta Real, **41**
Suites Alba, **6**
Vidafel Mayan
Palace, **40**
Villa Vera, **24**
Westin Las Brisas, **33**

clams, tomato, and garlic). ⊠ *Scenic Hwy. 5256, just past Madeiras,* ☎ *74/84–68–19. Reservations essential. AE, DC, MC, V.*

$$–$$$ ✕ **Villa Fiore.** Here, the owners of Madeiras (☞ *above*) bring you fine Italian dining in the candlelit garden of what looks like an 18th-century Venetian villa. Diners can choose from two fixed menus that include appetizer, soup, main course (chicken, fish, meat, or pasta), dessert, and coffee. Opt for the calamari *fritti* (fried in marinara sauce) as a starter, and one of the veal dishes or fillet of stuffed sea bass with artichoke sauce for an entrée. Service is excellent. ⊠ *Av. del Prado 6,* ☎ *74/84–20–40. AE, DC, MC, V. Closed Wed.*

Japanese

$$$ ✕ **Suntory.** At this traditional Japanese restaurant you can dine either in a blessedly air-conditioned interior room or in the delightful Asian-style garden. It's one of the few Japanese restaurants in Acapulco and also one of the only deluxe restaurants that are open for lunch. Specialties are the sushi and the teppanyaki, prepared at your table by skilled chefs. ⊠ *Costera Miguel Alemán 36, across from La Palapa hotel,* ☎ *74/84–80-88. AE, DC, MC, V.*

Mexican

$$ ✕ **Zapata, Villa y Cia.** This is the Mexican version of a Hard Rock Cafe, where the music and excellent food are strictly local and the memorabilia recalls the Mexican Revolution, with guns, hats, and photographs of Pancho Villa. The highlight of an evening here is a visit from a sombrero-wearing burro, so be sure to bring your camera. ⊠ *Hyatt Regency Acapulco,* ☎ *74/69–12–34. AE, DC, MC, V.*

$ ✕ **El Cabrito.** This is a local favorite for true Mexican cuisine and ambience. The name of the restaurant—"The Goat"—is also its specialty. In addition, you can choose among *mole*; jerky with egg, fish, and seafood; and other Mexican dishes. ⊠ *Costera Miguel Alemán, between CiCi and Centro Internacional,* ☎ *74/84–77–11. Reservations not accepted. AE, MC, V.*

$ ✕ **La Casa de Tere.** Hidden in a commercial district downtown (signs point the way), La Casa de Tere is in a league of its own—expect beer-hall tables and chairs, colorful Mexican decorations, and photos of Acapulco of yore. But that's part of the mix at this spotlessly clean, open-air establishment. And so is its small but varied menu that includes an outstanding *sopa de tortilla* (tortilla soup), chicken mole, and flan. Powerful overhead fans make up for the lack of air-conditioning. ⊠ *Alonso Martín 1721, 2 blocks from Costera Miguel Alemán,* ☎ *74/85–77–35. No credit cards. Closed Mon.*

$ ✕ **Zorrito's.** When Julio Iglesias is in town, this is where he heads in the wee hours of the morning, after the discos close. He's been known to sing along with the band that plays evenings from 10 PM on. The menu of this open-air streetside eatery, which stays open 22 hours of the day, includes a host of steak and beef dishes, Acapulco's famous green-and-white *pozole* (pork and hominy soup), and the special, *filete tampiqueña* (a strip of tender grilled beef), which comes with tacos, enchiladas, guacamole, and beans. ⊠ *Costera Miguel Alemán and Anton de Alaminos, next to Banamex,* ☎ *74/85–37–35. Reservations not accepted. AE, MC, V. Closed 7 AM–9 AM and Tues. 7 AM–2 PM.*

Seafood

$$–$$$ ✕ **La Vela.** Set on a wharf that juts out into Pichilingue Bay, this open-
★ air dining spot is protected by a dramatic roof that simulates a huge white sail. It's very atmospheric after dark, when a stillness hangs over

the bay and the lights of Puerto Marqués flicker in the distance. There are a variety of fish and shellfish dishes on the menu, but the specialty of the house is the red snapper *à la talla* (basted with chili and other spices and broiled over hot coals). ⊠ *Camino Real Acapulco Diamante, Carretera Escénica, Km 14,* ☎ *74/66–10–10. AE, DC, MC, V.*

$$ ✕ **Beto's.** By day you can eat right on the beach and enjoy live music; by night this palapa-roofed restaurant is transformed into a dim and romantic dining area lighted by candles and paper lanterns. Whole red snapper, lobster, and ceviche are recommended. There is a second branch next door and a third at Barra Vieja Beach—where the specialty is pescado à la talla. ⊠ *Beto's, Costera Miguel Alemán at Condesa Beach,* ☎ *74/84–04–73;* ⊠ *Beto's Safari, Costera Miguel Alemán, next to Beto's,* ☎ *74/84–47–62;* ⊠ *Beto's Barra Vieja, Barra Vieja Beach,* ☎ *No phone. AE, MC, V.*

$$ ✕ **La Cabaña.** This humble seaside restaurant run by the Alvarez family attracted the likes of Mexican songwriter Agustin Lara and his lady love Maria Feliz in the 1950s—and other notables craving good seafood ever since. You can see their photo over the bar and sample the same dishes that made the place famous then, such as baby shark tamales, oyster mousse, or seafood crepes made with a variety of denizens of the sea. For heartier appetites, there's steaming seafood casserole or shrimp prepared with sea salt, curry, or garlic. The restaurant is smack in the middle of Caleta beach and has free lockers if you've dropped in for breakfast, lunch, or dinner. ⊠ *Playa Caleta Lado Oriente, s/n, Fraccionamiento Las Playas (a 5-min taxi ride east of the town square),* ☎ *74/82–50–07. AE, DC, MC, V.*

$$ ✕ **Pipo's.** Situated on a rather quiet part of the Costera, this family-
★ run seafood restaurant doesn't have an especially interesting view, but diners come here for the fresh fish, good service, and reasonable prices. *Huachinango veracruzano* (red snapper baked with tomatoes, peppers, onion, and olives) and fillet of fish in *mojo de ajo* (garlic butter) are about as sophisticated as the food preparation gets. The ceviche is an Acapulco tradition, as is *vuelve à la vida,* an immense seafood cocktail that, as the name implies, is guaranteed to bring you "back to life." ⊠ *Costera Miguel Alemán and Nao Victoria, across from Acapulco International Center,* ☎ *74/84–01–65;* ⊠ *Almirante Bretón 3, downtown,* ☎ *74/82–22–37. Reservations not accepted. AE, MC, V.*

LODGING

Although Acapulco has been an important port since colonial times, it lacks the converted monasteries and old mansions found in Mexico City. But the Costera is chockablock with new luxury high-rises and local franchises of such major U.S. hotel chains as Hyatt and Howard Johnson. As these hotels tend to be characterless, your choice will depend on location and what facilities are available. All major hotels can make water-sports arrangements.

In Acapulco geography is price, so where you stay determines what you pay. The most exclusive area is the Acapulco Diamante, home to some of the most luxurious hotels in Mexico—so lush and well equipped that most guests don't budge from the minute they arrive. The minuses: Revolcadero Beach is too rough for swimming (though great for surfing), and this area is a 15- to 25-minute (expensive) taxi ride from the heart of Acapulco. The atmosphere of Acapulco Diamante is refined and revolves around a game of golf or tennis, dining at some of Acapulco's better restaurants, and dancing at the glamorous Extravaganzza, Palladium, and Fantasy discos.

There is much more activity on Costera Miguel Alemán, where the majority of large hotels, discos, American-style restaurants, and airline offices may be found, along with Acapulco's most popular beaches. All the Costera hotels have freshwater pools and sun decks, and most have restaurants and/or bars overlooking the beach, if not on the sand itself. Hotels across the street are almost always less expensive than those directly on the beach; because there are no private beaches in Acapulco, all you have to do is cross the road to enjoy the sand.

Moving west along the Costera leads you to downtown Acapulco. The beaches and restaurants here are popular with Mexican vacationers, and the dozens of hotels attract Canadian and European bargain hunters.

You can assume that accommodations that cost more than $50 (double) will be air-conditioned (though you can find air-conditioned hotels for less) and will include a telephone, TV, and a view of the bay. There is usually a range of in-house restaurants and bars, as well as a pool. Exceptions exist, such as Las Brisas, which, in the name of peace and quiet, has banned TVs from all rooms. So if such extras are important to you, be sure to ask ahead. If you can't afford air-conditioning, don't panic. Even the cheapest hotels have cooling ceiling fans.

Note: Most hotels are booked solid Christmas and Easter week, so if you plan to visit then, it's wise to make reservations months in advance.

CATEGORY	COST*
$$$$	over $200
$$$	$100–$200
$$	$50–$100
$	under $50

*All prices are for a standard double room, excluding 15% sales (called IVA) tax.

Acapulco Diamante

$$$$ ★ 🏨 **Acapulco Princess.** Recently taken over by the Canadian Pacific hotel company, the Princess is one of those megahotels that is always holding at least three conventions. But more rooms equal more facilities (several of the restaurants and bars close during the low season, May–October), including tennis, golf, and shopping in a cool arcade. The pool near the reception desk is sensational—fantastic tropical ponds with little waterfalls and a slatted bridge leading into a swimming-sunning area. Rooms are light and airy, with cane furniture and rugs and curtains in colorful tropical prints. In winter, guests can also use the facilities of the hotel's smaller sibling, the Pierre Marqués. The Modified American Plan (breakfast and dinner) is obligatory from mid-December through mid-April. ✉ Box 1351, Playa Revolcadero, 39300, ☎ 74/69–10–00; 800/223–1818, ℻ 74/69–10–16. 927 rooms, 92 suites. 7 restaurants, 7 bars, 5 pools, 18-hole golf course, 7 tennis courts, basketball, exercise room. AE, DC, MC, V.

$$$$ ★ 🏨 **Camino Real Acapulco Diamante.** This stunning hotel is set at the foot of a lush tropical hillside on exclusive Pichilingue Beach, far from the madding crowd. All rooms are done in luscious pastels, with tiled floors, balcony or terrace, luxurious baths, ceiling fans, and air-conditioning. Each has a view of peaceful Puerto Marqués bay. Rates include a buffet breakfast. A health club was added in 1998. ✉ Carretera Escénica, Km 14, Calle Baja Catita, 39867, ☎ 74/66–10–10; 800/722–6466 in the U.S., ℻ 74/66–11–11. 145 rooms, 11 suites. 2 restaurants, 2 bars, 3 pools, tennis court, health club. AE, DC, MC, V.

$$$$ ★ ⊞ **Pierre Marqués.** This hotel is especially blessed because guests have access to all the Princess's facilities without the crowds. In addition, it has an 18-hole golf course, three pools, and five tennis courts. Rooms are furnished identically to those at the Princess (no TVs here, however), but villas and duplex bungalows with private patios are available. The price of a room includes breakfast (breakfast and dinner during Christmas week). Now that Canadian Pacific is running the hotel, it is open year-round, instead of just seasonally as before. ⊠ *Box 1351, Playa Revolcadero, 39907,* ☎ *74/66–10–00; 800/223–1818 in the U.S.,* FAX *74/66–10–46. 274 rooms, 70 suites. 2 restaurants, bar, 3 pools, 18-hole golf course, 5 tennis courts. AE, DC, MC, V.*

$$$$ ⊞ **Quinta Real.** In summer 1998 one of Mexico's most prestigious hotel chains inaugurated this exclusive low-slung resort in the posh Punta Diamante section, about a 10-minute drive from downtown Acapulco. The 74 suites built on a hillside overlooking the sea are decorated with Mexican-made hardwood furniture and earth-tone drapes, rugs, and bedcovers. All have balconies, climate control, satellite TVs, marble floors, and door handles on the closets shaped like iguanas, the hotel's signature motif. Guests take advantage of the large freshwater pools and the endless stretch of lovely beach. ⊠ *Paseo de la Quinta, Lote 6, Desarrollo Turmstico Real Diamante, 39907 Guerrero,* ☎ *74/69–15–00; 800/457–4000 in the U.S.,* FAX *74/69–15–15. 74 suites. Restaurant, bar, 4 pools. AE, DC, MC, V.*

$$$$ ⊞ **Vidafel Mayan Palace.** This all-suites resort will knock your socks off. Guests are welcomed in a 100,000-square-ft lobby that's sheltered under 75-ft palapa roofs. The rooms, on the other hand, are surprisingly subdued. Airy and spacious, they are beautifully appointed with marble floors, light-wood furniture, sand-color walls, original paintings, and luxurious baths; they range from a studio with hot tub (Crown Suite) to a one-bedroom with kitchenette and sitting areas (Acapulco Suite). Canoes and paddleboats are available to paddle around the man-made, fish-filled canal, and you can swim in the 850-yard pool. By the end of 1999 the new waterpark should be completed. ⊠ *Playa Revolcadero, 39000,* ☎ FAX *74/69–02–01; 800/843–2335 in the U.S.. 366 suites. 4 restaurants, 3 bars, 18-hole golf course, 12 tennis courts. AE, DC, MC, V.*

$$$$ ★ ⊞ **Westin Las Brisas.** Set high on a hillside, Las Brisas remains distinct in Acapulco for the secluded haven it provides its guests. This self-contained luxury complex, which celebrated its 40th anniversary in 1997, has accommodations that range from one-bedroom units to deluxe private casitas, complete with private pools that are small yet swimmable. All have beautiful bay views. Attention to detail is Las Brisas's claim to fame: fresh hibiscus blossoms are set afloat in the pools each day. Transportation is by white-and-pink Jeep. You can rent one for about $70 a day; or, if you don't mind a wait, the staff will do the driving. And transport is necessary—it is a good 15-minute walk to the beach restaurant, and all the facilities are far from the rooms. Tipping is not allowed, but a service charge of $20 a day is added to the bill. The rate includes Continental breakfast stylishly delivered to your room each morning. ⊠ *Carretera Escénica 5255, 39868,* ☎ *74/84–15–80; 800/228–3000 in the U.S.,* FAX *74/84–22–69. 300 rooms. 3 restaurants, 2 bars, 3 pools (2 saltwater), hot tub, sauna, 5 tennis courts. AE, DC, MC, V.*

The Costera

$$$ ⊞ **Continental Plaza.** Built by former president Miguel Alemán during Acapulco's heyday, this landmark hotel—right in the center of everything—is still quite popular, especially with groups from all over the world who keep the lobby abuzz day and night. The 390 large and airy rooms (including 12 suites) have terraces overlooking the bay. There are several good eating spots, including a **Tony Roma's,** an excellent beach, shopping center, and meeting and banquet facilities. Most spectacular is the large and lavish pool that winds around an "island" and through lush, palm-shaded gardens. ⊠ *Costera Miguel Alemán, 39580,* ☏ *74/69–05–05; 800/882–6684 in the U.S.,* FAX *74/84–21–20. 378 rooms, 12 suites. 3 restaurants, 3 bars, pool, 2 tennis courts, exercise room. AE, DC, MC, V.*

$$$
★ 🏨 **Elcano.** One of Acapulco's traditional favorites has been completely remodeled, while still (thankfully) maintaining its '50s flavor. The A+ rooms are snappily done in nautical white and navy blue, with white tiled floors and beautiful modern bathrooms. There's a delightful beachside restaurant with an outstanding breakfast buffet, a more elegant indoor one, and a gorgeous pool that seems to float above the bay, with whirlpools built into its corners. Maintenance is excellent throughout the hotel. ⊠ *Costera Miguel Alemán 75, 39690,* ☏ *74/ 84–19–50,* FAX *74/84–22–30. 163 rooms, 17 suites. 2 restaurants, bar, pool. AE, DC, MC, V.*

$$$ 🏨 **Hyatt Regency Acapulco.** A megahotel that you never have to leave, this property is popular with business travelers and conventioneers. The decor is striking, with strong Caribbean colors adding spice to rooms and common areas—in fact the glamorous setting of the hotel has appeared in many a Mexican soap opera. Tennis courts, four eateries (a beachside seafood place, a popular Mexican dining spot, a snack bar, and a kosher restaurant), three bars, and a lavish shopping area are among the reasons for staying put. The Hyatt is also the only hotel in Latin America with an on-site synagogue (and a *mikvah tevila*) supervised by the orthodox rabbinate of Mexico City. The Hyatt is a little out of the way, a plus for those who seek quiet. To avoid the noise of the maneuvers at the neighboring naval base, ask for a room on the west side of the hotel. ⊠ *Costera Miguel Alemán 1, 39869,* ☏ *74/69–12–34; 800/233–1234 in the U.S.,* FAX *74/84–30–87. 607 rooms, 17 suites. 3 restaurants, 3 bars, snack bar, 2 pools, massage, 5 tennis courts, shops, parking (fee). AE, DC, MC, V.*

$$$ 🏨 **Villa Vera.** A five-minute drive north of the Costera leads to what was once one of Acapulco's most exclusive hotels. Some of the villas, which were once private homes, have their own pools. Standard rooms have been converted into suites. The main pool, with its swim-up bar, is the hotel's hub. By night, guests dine at the terraced restaurant, with its stunning view of the bay. There's an exercise facility, and two championship tennis courts host the Veterans tennis tournament. Children under 16 are not allowed. ⊠ *Box 560, Lomas del Mar 35, 39690,* ☏ *74/84–03–33,* FAX *74/84–74–79. 20 rooms, 40 suites. Restaurant, piano bar, 15 pools, beauty salon, massage, sauna, 2 tennis courts, exercise room. AE, MC, V.*

$$ 🏨 **Costa Club.** This resort hotel (the former Acapulco Plaza) still has more facilities than many Mexican towns: four bars and as many restaurants, tennis, a sauna, three pools, and a location next door to the Plaza Bahía, Acapulco's largest shopping mall. The **La Jaula** bar, at the mezzanine level, is most extraordinary—a wooden hut, suspended by a cable from the roof, reached by a gangplank and overlooking a garden full of exotic birds. Guest rooms now have tile floors and pastel and blond-wood decor, and guests continue to be content with the facilities and service. There's a new all-inclusive option for $74 a person. ⊠ *Costera Miguel Alemán 123, 39670,* ☏ *74/85–90–50; 800/343–7821 in the U.S.,* FAX *74/85–54–93. 506 rooms. 4 restaurants, 4 bars, 3 pools, sauna, 3 tennis courts, health club. AE, DC, MC, V.*

$$ 🏨 **Fiesta Americana Condesa Acapulco.** The Condesa, as everyone calls it, is right in the thick of the main shopping and restaurant district, and it is ever popular with tour operators. And no wonder—it's right on one of the best beaches in town. Newly renovated guest rooms have shed their former gaudy colors and settled on soothing creams and pastels instead. ⊠ *Costera Miguel Alemán 97, 39690,* ☎ *74/84-28-28; 800/343-7821 in the U.S.,* FAX *74/84-18-28. 492 rooms, 8 suites. 2 restaurants, bar, 2 pools. AE, DC, MC, V.*

$$ 🖭 **Howard Johnson Maralisa.** Formerly the sister hotel of the Villa Vera
★   (☞ *above*), this property, on the beach side of the Costera, is now part of the Howard Johnson chain. The rooms are light, decorated in whites and pastels. This is a small, friendly place; all rooms have TVs, some have balconies, and the price is right. ⊠ *Box 721, Calle Alemania, 39670,* ☎ *74/85-66-77; 800/446-4656 in the U.S.,* FAX *74/85-92-28. 85 rooms, 5 suites. Restaurant, bar, 2 pools, beach. AE, DC, MC, V.*

$$ 🖭 **Las Hamacas.** At the low end of its price range, Las Hamacas is a friendly, old-fashioned Acapulco hotel built in the 1950s with rooms surrounding a large inner courtyard. Across the street from the beach, it has a lovely garden of coconut palms from its former days as a plantation, as well as two pools and a large parking lot. Tile floors, new bathrooms, and air-conditioners are in all of the spacious, light-filled cream and white guest rooms. Junior suites can sleep two adults and two children, which makes the hotel appealing to Mexican families. Twenty second-story rooms have bay views, but also lie above the busy Costera; rooms facing the leafy courtyard are the quietest. The hotel is about a three-minute ride from downtown. ⊠ *Costera Miguel Alemán, 39670,* ☎ *74/83-70-06,* FAX *74/83-05-75. 100 rooms, 20 suites. Restaurant, bar, 2 pools, beauty salon, beach, parking (fee). MC, V.*

$$ 🖭 **Park Hotel & Tennis Center.** A helpful staff and prime location make this hotel an appealing, intimate, and cordial place. In the recent past, rooms were uninspired; now colonial-style wood furniture has been refinished, walls were painted, and quiet, individually controlled air-conditioning units were installed. Rooms are well-situated around a garden with a good-size pool. Other assets include refrigerators, TVs, plenty of hot water, kitchenettes in some for a small fee, and balconies in some, and all are spotlessly clean and well priced. The Park has excellent tennis facilities, and it's only a block to the beach. Although the restaurant has been closed, there are plenty of others close at hand. Since the hotel is right on the Costera, ask for a room overlooking the tennis courts in the back, if you'd prefer quiet. ⊠ *Box 269, Costera Miguel Alemán 127, 39670,* ☎ *74/85-59-92,* FAX *74/85-54-89. 88 rooms. Bar, pool, 3 tennis courts, beach. MC, V.*

Old Acapulco

$$–$$$ 🖭 **Plaza las Glorias El Mirador.** The old El Mirador has been taken over by the Plaza las Glorias chain, which is part of the Sidek conglomerate responsible for marina and golf developments all over Mexico. Very Mexican in style—white with red tiles—Plaza las Glorias is set high on a hill with a spectacular view of Acapulco and of the cliff divers performing at La Quebrada. ⊠ *Quebrada 74, 39300,* ☎ *74/83-11-55; 800/342-2644 in the U.S.,* FAX *74/82-45-64. 72 rooms, 58 suites. 2 restaurants, 3 pools. AE, DC, MC, V.*

$$ 🖭 **Majestic.** This dowager hotel once upon a time served as a Club Med.
★   The stunning decor of the spacious rooms—tile floors, cool colors, and good lighting—is completely unexpected in a hotel in this price category. Entrance is through the seventh-floor lobby, and the rest of the hotel is terraced down a rocky cliff. Many of the rooms in the main building have private terraces and each has a double bed and two studio couches; the villa rooms are smaller. There is no beach at the hotel, but free transportation is provided to the hotel's beach club, which is located next to the Club de Yates (Yacht Club). An all-inclusive plan

is also available from $45 a person; regular double rooms run $60. ⊠ *Av. Pozo del Rey 73, 39390,* ☎ *74/83–27–13,* FAX *74/84–20–32. 72 rooms, 58 suites. 2 restaurants, 2 bars, 2 pools, tennis court, dance club, parking (fee). AE, DC, MC, V.*

$–$$ 🖭 **Los Flamingos.** Almost a historical monument, this hot pink hotel was the favored hangout of John Wayne, Johnny ("Tarzan") Weissmuller, Errol Flynn, and the rest of the "Hollywood gang" back in the '50s, and their photographs adorn the walls of the lobby. The hotel is strung out along a cliff that has some of the finest views in Acapulco— from Pie de la Cuesta all across Acapulco Bay. Los Flamingos also attracts plenty of Europeans who come to bask in the ambience of Old Hollywood and toss down the *coco locos,* which barman Esteban Castañeda will tell you were invented here in the 1960s. In 1997 the rooms were spruced up with bright pink walls and flowered print spreads. Baths are spartan (shower only), but adequate. The circular two-bedroom master suite, set apart on a small rise, was once Johnny Weissmuller's digs. It goes for $180 per night. The hotel offers free transportation to the beach and downtown. ⊠ *Av. López Mateos,* ☎ *74/ 82–06–90,* FAX *74/83–98–06. 234 rooms, 2 suites. Restaurant, bar, pool. MC, V.*

$ 🖭 **Hotel Misión.** Two minutes from the zócalo, this charming, colonial-style hotel surrounds a greenery-rich courtyard with an outdoor dining area that functions only on Thursday. Ask for the green-and-white pozole. The rooms are small and by no means fancy, with wrought-iron beds, tile floors, painted brick walls, and ceiling fans. Every room has a shower, and there's plenty of hot water. The Misión appears in several European guidebooks, so expect a Continental clientele. The best rooms are on the second and third floors; the top-floor room is large but hot in the daytime. ⊠ *Calle Felipe Valle 12, 39300,* ☎ *74/ 82–36–43,* FAX *74/82–20–76. 20 rooms. No credit cards.*

$ 🖭 **Suites Alba.** On a quiet hillside in *Acapulco Tradicional,* the Alba is a resort-style hotel with bargain prices. All suites sleep four and have a kitchenette, private bath, and terrace. There is no extra charge for up to two children under 12 sharing a room with relatives, which makes it especially popular with families. A cable car takes guests to the hotel's beach club on the bay, next door to the Club de Yates, with a 330-ft-long toboggan. During the high season (mid-December–mid-April) there's free transportation from the hotel to Caleta beach and downtown. ⊠ *Grand Via Tropical 35, 39390,* ☎ *74/83–00–73,* FAX *74/83– 83–78. 244 suites. 3 restaurants, bar, grocery, 3 pools, tennis court, beach, free parking. AE, DC, MC, V.*

Pie de la Cuesta

$$$ 🖭 **Parador del Sol.** If you want to get away from it all, this is the per-
★ fect place. Traversing both the lagoon and the Pacific Ocean sides of the Pie de la Cuesta road, this all-inclusive property gives the impression that it was designed as a luxury resort. The 150 rooms are distributed among pink villas that are scattered over some 1,100 square ft of gardens. Spacious, with tile floors and baths, each room is air-conditioned and equipped with color TV, phone, and a fan-cooled terrace complete with hammocks. The rate includes all meals and refreshments, domestic drinks, tennis, and nonmotorized water sports. ⊠ *Carretera Pie de la Cuesta–Barra de Coyuca, Km 5, Box 1070, 39300,* ☎ *74/60–20–03,* FAX *74/60–16–49. 150 rooms. Restaurant, 2 bars, 2 pools, miniature golf, 4 tennis courts, exercise room, dance club. AE, DC, MC, V. FAP.*

NIGHTLIFE AND THE ARTS

The companies listed in the Orientation Tours section of Acapulco A to Z (☞ *below*) can organize evening jaunts to most of the dance and music places listed below. And don't forget the nightly entertainment at most hotels. The big resorts have live music to accompany the early evening happy hour, and some feature big-name bands from the United States for less than you would pay at home. Many hotels sponsor theme parties—Italian Night, Beach Party Night, and similar festivities.

Cultural Shows

Acapulco International Center (✉ Costera Miguel Alemán, ☎ 74/84–32–18), also known as the Convention Center, has a Mexican fiesta Wednesday and Friday, where you can take in mariachi bands, singers, and the *voladores* (flyers) from Papantla. The show with open bar and buffet costs about $35; entrance to the show alone is $20. The performance starts at 8. On Friday at El Mexicano restaurant in **Las Brisas** hotel, the Mexican Fiesta starts off with a *tianguis* (marketplace) of handicrafts and ends with a spectacular display of fireworks.

Dance

Salon Q (✉ Costera Miguel Alemán 23, ☎ 74/84–32–052) is a combination dance hall and disco where the bands play salsas, merengues, and other Latin rhythms. There's a live show weekends—mostly impersonations of Mexican entertainers—as well as dance contests.

Discos

Reservations are advisable for a big group, and late afternoon or after 9 PM are the best times to call. New Year's Eve requires advance planning.

Except for Palladium, Fantasy, and Enigma, all the discos are clustered on the Costera.

Alebrije (formerly News) is enormous, with seating for 1,200 people in love seats and booths. The most popular night is Friday, when everyone is bathed in foam, with a kind of wet-T-shirt effect. From 10:30 (opening time) to 11:30, the music is slow and romantic; then the disco music and the light show begin, and they go on till dawn. ✉ *Costera Miguel Alemán 3308, across from Hyatt Regency,* ☎ 74/84–59–02.

Andromeda, which opened in July 1996, is proof that Acapulco remains the disco capital of the world. Quite spectacular, even for a city known for its splendiferous discos, this one will impress even the most jaded discoers. Entrance to the Queen of the Sea's "castle" is over a torchlit moat; once inside, the impression is of being in a submarine, with a window to the sea. There are supposedly two dance floors, but the 18-to-25 crowd dances everywhere to the latest techno and techno-pop sounds. ✉ *Costera Miguel Alemán 15, at Fragata Yucatán,* ☎ 74/84–88–15.

Baby O is a private club that is known to accept a few select nonmembers. Eschewing the glitz and mirrors of Acapulco's older discos, Baby O resembles a cave in a tropical jungle. The crowd is 25 to 35, mostly well-dressed, wealthy Mexicans. When the pandemonium gets to you, retreat to the little snack bar downstairs. ✉ *Costera Miguel Alemán 22,* ☎ 74/84–74–74.

Discobeach is Acapulco's only alfresco disco and its most informal one. The under-30 crowd sometimes even turns up in shorts. The waiters are young and friendly—some people find them overly so. (In fact, this is one of Acapulco's legendary pickup spots.) One night they're all in togas carrying bunches of grapes; the next they're in pajamas. Every Wednesday, ladies' night, all the women receive flowers. "Sex on the Beach"—rum, vodka, Cointreau, fruit juice, and grenadine (don't say you weren't warned!)—is the house specialty, in all senses of the words. ⊠ *On Condesa Beach,* ☎ 74/84–70–64.

★ **Enigma** (formerly called Extravaganzza) claims to have the ultimate in light and sound and is Acapulco's answer to the Luxor hotel in Las Vegas with its lavish, New Egyptian–theme premises that include murals painted by a well-known Cuban artist. It accommodates 700 at a central bar and in comfortable booths, and a glass wall provides an unbelievable view of Acapulco Bay, which includes fireworks on weekends. No food is served, but there are several restaurants nearby. The music (which is for all ages) starts at 10:30. ⊠ *On Scenic Hwy. to Las Brisas,* ☎ 74/84–71–64.

★ **Fantasy** attracts a 25–50 crowd—mainly couples—and is one of the few discos where people really dress up, with the men in well-cut pants and shirts and the women in racy outfits and cocktail dresses. Singles gravitate toward the two bars in the back. Fantasy is quite snug, to put it nicely, and people tend to come here earlier than they do to other places. By midnight the dance floor is so packed that people dance on the wide windowsills that look out over the bay. At 2 AM there is a fireworks display. A glassed-in elevator provides an interesting overview of the scene and leads upstairs to a little shop that stocks T-shirts and lingerie. ⊠ *On Scenic Hwy. to Las Brisas,* ☎ 74/84–67–27.

Hard Rock Cafe, filled with rock memorabilia, is part bar, part restaurant, part dance hall, and part boutique (☞ Dining, *above*). **Planet Hollywood** is basically more of the same, but with Hollywood memorabilia and California-style cuisine. ⊠ *Costera Miguel Alemán 2917, next to CiCi,* ☎ 74/84–42–84.

Palladium is another spectacular production of Tony Rullán, creator of Enigma (☞ *above*). A waterfall that cascades down the hill from the dance-floor level makes this place hard to miss. As at Enigma, the dance floor is nearly surrounded by 50-ft-high windows, giving dancers a wraparound view of all Acapulco. ⊠ *On Scenic Hwy. to Las Brisas,* ☎ 74/81–03–30.

OUTDOOR ACTIVITIES AND SPORTS

Participant Sports

Fishing

Fishing trips can be arranged through your hotel, downtown at the Pesca Deportiva near the *muelle* (dock) across from the zócalo, or through travel agents. At the docks near the zócalo you can hire a boat for $30 a day (two lines). It is safer to stick with one of the reliable companies whose boats and equipment are in good condition. Boats accommodating 4 to 10 people cost $200–$500 a day, $45–$60 by chair. Excursions usually leave about 7 AM and return at 1 or 2 PM. You are required to get a fishing license ($8–$10, depending on the season) from the Secretaría de Pesca; you'll find their representative at the dock. Don't show up during siesta, between 2 and 4 in the afternoon.

For deep-sea fishing, **Divers de México** (☞ Scuba Diving, *below*) has well-maintained boats for 4 to 10 passengers for $200 to $800. It also has private yacht charters. Small boats for freshwater fishing can be rented at **Cadena's** and **Tres Marías** at Coyuca Lagoon.

In case you want to see the world.

At American Express, we're here to make your journey a smooth one. So we have over 1,700 travel service locations in over 130 countries ready to help. What else would you expect from the world's largest travel agency?

do more

Travel

Call 1 800 AXP-3429 or visit
www.americanexpress.com/travel

In case you want to be welcomed there.

We're here to see that you're always welcomed at establishments everywhere. That's why millions of people carry the American Express® Card – for peace of mind, confidence, and security, around the world or just around the corner.

do more **AMERICAN EXPRESS**

Cards

In case you're running low.

We're here to help with more than 190,000 Express Cash locations around the world. In order to enroll, just call American Express at 1 800 CASH-NOW before you start your vacation.

do more

AMERICAN EXPRESS

Express Cash

Fitness and Swimming

Most of the time, Acapulco weather is like August in the warmest parts of the United States. This means that you should cut back on your workouts and maintain proper hydration by drinking plenty of water.

Acapulco Princess Hotel has the best hotel fitness facilities, including a gym with stationary bikes, Universal machines, and free weights. Because the Princess is about 15 km (9 mi) from the city center and the pollution of Acapulco, you can even swim in the ocean here if you beware of the strong undertow.

Villa Vera Spa and Fitness Center (⊠ Lomas del Mar 35, ☎ 74/84–03–33) has a modern spa and fitness center and is equipped with exercise machines (including step machines), free weights, and benches. Masseuses and cosmetologists give facials and massages inside or by the pool, as you wish. Both the beauty center and the gym are open to nonguests.

Westin Las Brisas is where you should stay if you like to swim but don't like company or competition. Individual casitas come with private or semiprivate pools; the beach club has two saltwater pools (☞ Lodging, *above*). Most of the major hotels in town along the Costera Miguel Alemán also have pools.

Golf

Two 18-hole championship golf courses are shared by the **Princess and Pierre Marqués** hotels. Reservations should be made in advance (☎ 74/69–10–00). Greens fees are $65 for guests and $85 for nonguests. A round at the 18-hole **Vidafel Mayan Palace** (☎ 74/66–18–79) course is $54 for guests and $79 for nonguests. There is also a public golf course at the **Club de Golf** (☎ 74/84–07–81) on the Costera across from the Acapulco Malibú hotel. Greens fees are $42 for nine holes, $52 for 18. If you're staying at Las Brisas, you can play on the links at Tres Vidas. Otherwise Tres Vidas and Diamante Country Club are reserved for members and their guests.

Jogging

If you don't like beach jogging, the only real venue for running in the downtown area is along the sidewalk next to the Costera Miguel Alemán at the seafront, but you'll have to go very early, before traffic fumes set in. Away from the city center, the best area for running is out at the Acapulco Princess Hotel, on the airport road. A 2-km (1-mi) loop is laid out along a lightly traveled road, and in the early morning you can also run along the asphalt trails on the golf course.

Rollerblading

For a change of pace from sand and sea activities, come to **Roller Gran Prix** (⊠ Brisamar, east of Costera Miguel Alemán, just before Los Rancheros restaurant, ☎ 74/84–93–13) for rollerblading to disco music and racing formula one–style go-carts. The $2.50 fee includes blades, and instruction is available. Go-karts cost $1.50 for five minutes.

Scuba Diving

Arnold Brothers (⊠ Costera Miguel Alemán 205, ☎ 74/82–18–77) runs daily scuba-diving excursions and snorkeling trips. The scuba trips cost $30 and last for 2 to 2½ hours; snorkeling costs $15.

Tennis

Court fees range from about $8 to $25 an hour during the day and are 15% more in the evening. At the hotel courts, nonguests pay about $5 more per hour. Lessons with English-speaking instructors start at about $10 an hour; ball boys get a $2 tip.

Places in town to play tennis include **Acapulco Plaza** (☎ 74/85–90–50), three hard-surface courts, two lighted; **Acapulco Princess** (☎ 74/69–10–00), two air-conditioned indoor courts, five outdoor; **Hyatt Regency** (☎ 74/84–12–25), three lighted courts at the Municipal Golf Club; **Park Hotel & Tennis Courts** (☎ 74/85–59–92), three lighted courts; **Pierre Marqués** (☎ 74/66–10–00), five courts; **Tiffany's Racquet Club** (⊠ Av. Villa Vera 120, ☎ 74/84–79–49), five courts; **Vidafel Mayan Palace** (☎ 74/69–18–79), 12 lighted courts; and **Villa Vera Hotel** (☎ 74/84–03–33), two outdoor lighted clay courts.

Water Sports

Waterskiing, broncos (one-person motorboats), and parasailing can all be arranged on the beach. Parasailing is an Acapulco highlight; a five-minute trip costs $15. Waterskiing is about $30 an hour; broncos cost $30–$85 for a half hour, depending on the size. Windsurfing can be arranged at Caleta and most of beaches along the Costera but is especially good at Puerto Marqués. The main surfing beach is Revolcadero.

Acapulco's latest attraction, the **Shotover Jet,** is an import from the rivers around Queenstown, New Zealand. For $45, you're driven via air-conditioned coach from the outfit's Acapulco offices to a site near the town of Tierra Colorado (35 minutes each way). There you climb aboard the 12-passenger craft for an exciting 30-minute boat ride on the Papagayo River, complete with several thrilling 360-degree turns—one of the Shotover Jet's trademarks—and vistas of local flora and fauna (cacti, bats, and iguanas). After the ride, you can return directly to Acapulco or take a later shuttle bus and linger at the riverside property, which has a restaurant, souvenir shop, and an iguana nursery. ⊠ *Hotel Continental Plaza, Locale 3,* ☎ *74/84–11–54.*

Spectator Sports

Bullfights

The season runs from about Christmas to Easter, and *corridas* are held on Sunday at 5:30. Tickets are available through your hotel or at the **Plaza de Toros** ticket window (⊠ Av. Circunvalación, across from Caleta Beach, ☎ 74/82–11–81) Monday–Saturday 10–2 and Sunday 10:30–5. Tickets in the shade (sombra)—the only way to go—cost about $16. Preceding the fight are performances of Spanish dances and music by the Chili Frito band.

Jai Alai

The **Jai Alai Acapulco Race & Sports Book** (⊠ Costera Miguel Alemán 498, ☎ 74/84–31–95) has two restaurants and a bar, and capacity for 1,500 spectators. The fast-paced games take place Thursday through Sunday at 9 PM, mid-December through January 6, Easter week, and throughout July and August. Entrance is $4.

In addition to bets on jai alai, wagers are taken on all major sports events—basketball, football, baseball, boxing, horse and greyhound racing—that are transmitted directly via satellite.

SHOPPING

The main shopping strip is on Costera Miguel Alemán from the Acapulco Plaza to the El Presidente Hotel. Here you can find **Guess, Peer, Aca Joe, Amarras, Polo Ralph Lauren,** and other fashionable sportswear boutiques. Downtown (Old) Acapulco doesn't have many name shops, but this is where you'll find the inexpensive tailors patronized by the Mexicans, lots of little souvenir shops, and a vast flea market with crafts.

Also downtown is **Sanborns.** Most shops are open from 10 to 7 Monday through Saturday and closed on Sunday.

Department Stores and Supermarkets

Except for the waitresses' uniforms, the food, and a good handicrafts selection, **Sanborns** is very un-Mexican. Still, it is an institution throughout Mexico. It sells English-language newspapers, magazines, and books, as well as a line of high-priced souvenirs. This is a useful place to come for postcards, cosmetics, and medicines. Sanborns' restaurants are popular for their enchiladas *suizas* (prepared with lots of cream and cheese), *molletes* (toasted rolls spread with refried beans and cheese), and their seven-fruit drink. The Calinda branch (⊠ Costera Miguel Alemán 1226, ☎ 74/84–44–13), the Oceanic 2000 branch (⊠ Costera Miguel Alemán 3111, ☎ 74/84–20–25), and the downtown branch (⊠ Costera Miguel Alemán 209, ☎ 74/82–61–67) are open from 7 AM to midnight during the high season and from 7:30 AM to 11 PM the rest of the year.

Branches of **Aurrerá, Gigante, Price Club, Sam's, Walmart** (in case you don't get enough of them back home), and **Comercial Mexicana** are all on the Costera and sell everything from liquor and fresh and frozen food to light bulbs, clothing, garden furniture, and sports equipment.

Malls

Malls in Acapulco range from the delightful air-conditioned shopping arcade at the Princess hotel to rather gloomy collections of shops that sell cheap jewelry and embroidered dresses. Malls are listed below from east to west.

The multilevel **Marbella Mall,** at the Diana Glorieta, is home to **Martí,** a well-stocked sporting-goods store; a health center (drugstore, clinic, and lab); the Canadian Embassy; and **Bing's Ice Cream,** as well as several restaurants. **Aca Mall,** which is next door, is all white and marble; here you'll find **Tommy Hilfiger, Peer,** and **Aca Joe.**

Plaza Bahía, next to the Acapulco Plaza hotel, is a place for serious shopping. It is a huge, completely enclosed and air-conditioned mall where you could easily spend an entire day. Stores include **Dockers, Mossimo, Nautica,** and **Ferrioni,** for chic casual wear for men and women; **Ragazza,** which carries an exquisite line of fine lingerie; **Aspasia,** which sells locally designed, glitzy evening dresses and chunky diamanté jewelry; a large **Martí** for sporting goods; restaurants and snack bars; and a bowling alley, go-carts, and video-game arcade.

Markets

In addition to fresh fruits and vegetables, meat, fowl, fish, and flowers, the **Mercado Municipal** is also stocked with serapes, piñatas, leather goods, baskets, hammocks, and framed paintings done on velvet of the Virgin of Guadalupe, as well as traditional Mexican cooking utensils. There are even stands offering charms, amulets and talismans, bones, herbs, fish eyes, sharks' teeth, lotions, candles, incense, and soaps said to help one find or keep a mate, increase virility or fertility, bring peace to the home, or ward off the evil eye (☞ Exploring, *above*).

El Mercado de Artesanías El Parazal, a conglomeration of every souvenir in town, is a 15-minute walk from Sanborns. You'll find fake ceremonial masks, the ever-present onyx chessboards, $15 hand-embroidered dresses, imitation silver, hammocks, ceramics, and even skin cream made from turtles (don't buy it, because turtles are endangered and you won't get it through U.S. Customs). ⊠ *From San-borns downtown head away from the Costera to Vázquez de León and turn right 1 block.* ⊙ *Daily 9–9.*

In an effort to get the itinerant vendors off the beaches and streets, the local government set up a series of **flea markets** along the Costera, mostly uninviting dark tunnels of stalls that carry what seems to be an inex-haustible supply of inexpensive collectibles and souvenirs, including serapes, ceramics, straw hats, shell sculptures, carved walking canes, and wooden toys. The selections of archaeological-artifact replicas, bam-boo wind chimes, painted wooden birds (from $5 to $30 each), shell earrings, and embroidered clothes begin to look identical. Prices at the flea markets are often quite low, but it's a good idea to compare prices of items you're interested in with prices in the shops, and bargaining is essential. It's best to buy articles described as being made from semi-precious stones or silver in reputable establishments. If you don't, you may find that the beautiful jade or lapis lazuli that was such a bargain was really cleverly painted paste, or that the silver was simply a fac-simile called *alpaca.*

Specialty Shops

Art

Edith Matison's Art Gallery (⊠ Costera Miguel Alemán 2010, across from Club de Golf, ☎ 74/84–30–84) shows the works of renowned international and Mexican artists, including Calder, Dalí, Siqueiros, and Tamayo, and a large line of Mexican crafts. **Galería Rudic** (⊠ Yañez Pinzón 9, across from Continental Plaza and adjoining the Jardin des Artistes restaurant, ☎ 74/84–10–04) is one of the best galleries in town, with a good collection of top contemporary Mexican artists, includ-ing Armando Amaya, Leonardo Nierman, Gastón Cabrera, Trinidad Osorio, and Casiano García.

Look for the work of contemporary Mexican artists, including Patri-cia Strembler and Ranulfo González at **S'tilo** (⊠ Hyatt Regency, ☎ 74/69–12–34 ext. 8195), and along the walls of the hotel lobby. **Pal Kepenyes** (⊠ Guitarrón 140, ☎ 74/84–37–38) continues to receive good press for his sculpture and jewelry, on display in his workshop. The whimsical, painted papier-mâché and giant ceramic sculpture of **Sergio Bustamente** (⊠ Costera Miguel Alemán 120-9, across from Fi-esta American Condesa hotel, ☎ 74/84–49–92) can be seen at his gallery.

Boutiques

KOS (⊠ Costera Miguel Alemán, outside entrance to Fiesta Americana Condesa del Mar hotel, ☎ 74/81–24–34; ⊠ Acapulco Plaza Hotel, ☎ 74/85–25–15) carries a sensational line of swimsuits for equally sen-sational bodies. **Nautica** (⊠ Plaza Bahía, ☎ 74/85–75–11; smaller shop at ⊠ Las Brisas hotel, ☎ 74/84–16–50) is a boutique stocked with stylish casual clothing for men. **Armando's** (⊠ Costera Miguel Alemán 127, ☎ 74/85–34–86; ⊠ Costera Miguel Alemán 1252-7, in La Torre de Acapulco, ☎ 74/84–51–11) carries its own line of women's dresses, jackets, and vests with a Mexican flavor, as well as some interesting Luisa Conti accessories. **Pit** (⊠ Princess arcade, ☎ 74/69–10–00) has a smashing line of beach cover-ups and hand-painted straw hats, as well as bathing suits and light dresses.

Custom-Designed Clothes

Benny (⊠ Costera Miguel Alemán 98, across from Hotel El Presidente, ☎ 74/84–15–47; ⊠ Downtown at Ignacio de la Llave 2, Local 10, ☎ 74/82–22–28), known for years for his custom-designed resort wear for men, now caters to women as well.

Esteban's (⌧ Costera Miguel Alemán 2010, across from Club de Golf, ☎ 74/84–30–84) is the most glamorous shop in Acapulco, boasting a clientele of international celebrities and many of the important local families. Estaban's made-to-order clothes are formal and fashionable; his opulent evening dresses range from $200 to $3,000, though daytime dresses average $100. Recently a men's clothing section was added on the second floor. If you scour the sale racks, you can find some items marked down as much as 80%. For a refreshing pick-me-up after trying on these luscious creations, try the store's café, which serves coffee and pastries.

Handicrafts

AFA (⌧ Horacio Nelson and James Cook, near Hyatt Regency, ☎ 74/84–80–39) is a huge shop offering a vast selection of jewelry, handicrafts, clothing, and leather goods from all over Mexico. **Alebrijes & Caracoles** (⌧ Plaza Bahía, ☎ 74/85–04–90) comprises two shops designed to look like flea-market stalls. Top-quality merchandise is on display, including papier-mâché fruits and vegetables, Christmas ornaments, wind chimes, and brightly painted wooden animals from Oaxaca. **Marielena**(⌧ Hyatt Regency, ☎ 74/69–12–34, ext. 8986) has attractive hand-crafted candles, dressy women's cocktail jackets, and sculptures of the human form by Mexican Imelda Bravo.

Silver and Jewelry

Antoinette (⌧ Acapulco Princess shopping arcade, ☎ 74/69–10–00) has gold jewelry of impeccable design, set with precious and semiprecious stones, that you wouldn't be surprised to find on Fifth Avenue. Also on display is Emilia Castillo's line of brightly colored porcelain ware, inlaid with silver fish, stars, and birds. It's worth going to window-shop, even if you know you won't buy anything.

Suzett's (⌧ Hyatt Regency hotel, ☎ 74/69–12–34), a tony shop that's been around for years, has a very laudable selection of gold jewelry.

Tane (⌧ Hyatt Regency hotel, ☎ 74/84–63–48; ⌧ Las Brisas hotel, ☎ 74/81–08–16) carries small selections of the exquisite flatware, jewelry, and objets d'art created by one of Mexico's most prestigious (and expensive) silversmiths.

SIDE TRIP TO TAXCO, THE SILVER CITY

275 km (170 mi) north of Acapulco.

This is Mexico's most medieval-looking city—marvelously preserved colonial buildings nuzzle cobblestone streets that wind up and down the foothills of the Sierra Madre in the state of Guerrero. You could say that its white stucco buildings, red-tile roofs, and quaint inns and cafés make it a centuries-old Mexican town at its best—which is why the government declared the city a national monument in 1928. The city Taxco (pronounced *tahss*-ko) is a living work of art. For centuries its silver mines drew foreign mining companies here. Now its charm, mild temperatures, abundant sunshine, flowers, and silversmiths make Taxco a popular getaway.

Hernán Cortés discovered Taxco's mines in 1522. The silver rush lasted until the next century, when excitement tapered off. Then in the 1700s a Frenchman, who Mexicanized his name to José de la Borda, discovered a rich lode that revitalized the town's silver industry and made him exceedingly wealthy. After Borda, however, Taxco's importance faded, until the 1930s and the arrival of William G. Spratling, a writer-architect from New Orleans. Enchanted by Taxco and convinced of its potential as a silver center, Spratling set up an apprentice shop, where his artistic talent and his fascination with pre-Columbian design combined to produce silver jewelry and other artifacts that soon earned Taxco its worldwide reputation as the Silver City. Spratling's inspiration lives on in his students and their descendants, many of whom are the city's current silversmiths.

⑩ The **Church of San Sebastián and Santa Prisca** has dominated Plaza Borda—one of the busiest and most colorful town squares in all Mexico—since the 18th century. (A government directive of 1999 is pouring funds into restoring the buildings surrounding the square; the project should be finished by year's end). Usually just called Santa Prisca, it was built by French silver magnate José de la Borda in thanks to the Almighty for his having literally stumbled upon a rich silver vein. The style of the church—sort of Spanish Baroque meets rococo—is known as churrigueresque, and its pale pink exterior is a stunning surprise. This is one of Mexico's most beautiful colonial churches and Taxco's most important landmark. ⊠ *Southwest side of Plaza Borda.*

NEED A BREAK?
Around Plaza Borda are several *neverías* (ice cream stands) where you can treat yourself to an ice cream in exotic flavors such as tequila, corn, avocado, or coconut. **Bar Paco,** directly across the street from Santa Prisca, is a Taxco institution; its terrace is the perfect vantage point for watching the comings and goings on the zócalo while sipping a margarita or a beer.

⑪ The former home of William G. Spratling houses the **Spratling Museum.** This small gallery explains the working of colonial mines and displays Spratling's collection of pre-Columbian artifacts. ⊠ *Porfírio Delgado 1,* ☎ *762/2–16–60.* ☞ *$1.50.* ☉ *Tues.–Sat. 10–5, Sun. 9–3.*

⑫ **Casa Humboldt** was named for the German adventurer Alexander von Humboldt, who stayed here in 1803. The Moorish-style 18th-century house has a finely detailed facade. It now houses a wonderful little museum of colonial art. ⊠ *Calle Juan Ruíz Alarcón 6,* ☎ *762/2–55–01.* ☞ *$1.* ☉ *Tues.–Sat. 10–5, Sun. 10–3.*

⑬ If you want to experience a typical Mexican market, with everything from peanuts to electrical appliances, the **Mercado Municipal** is worth a visit. On Saturday and Sunday mornings, when locals from surrounding towns come with their produce and crafts, the market spills out onto the surrounding streets. You'll find it directly down the hill from Santa Prisca.

⑭ The largest caverns in Mexico, the **Grutas de Cacahuamilpa** (Caves of Cacahuamilpa) are about 15 minutes northeast of Taxco. These 15 large chambers comprise 12 km (7½ mi) of geological formations. All the caves are illuminated, and a tour takes around two hours. ☞ *$2 (includes tour).*

Dining and Lodging

Gastronomes can find everything from tagliatelle to iguana in Taxco restaurants, and meals are much less expensive than in Acapulco. Dress is casual, but less so than at Acapulco resorts. There are several categories of hotel to choose from within Taxco's two types: the small inns nestled on the hills skirting the zócalo and the larger, more modern hotels on the outskirts of town.

$$–$$$ ✕ **El Mural.** This is one of the nicest restaurants in town, with seating
★ indoors or on a poolside terrace, where there's a view not only of a Juan O'Gorman mural but of the stunning Santa Prisca church. The chef prepares classic international favorites—filet mignon and surf and turf—and some delicious Mexican specialties, including cilantro

Taxco Exploring

soup, and huitlacoche crepes. ⊠ *Posada de la Misión, Cerro de la Misión 32,* ☎ *762/2–21–98. AE, DC, MC, V.*

$$–$$$ ✕ **Pagaduría del Rey.** This restaurant has a long-standing reputation
★   for international fare served in comfortable surroundings. ⊠ *Calle H. Colegio Militar 8 (Col. Cerro de la Bermeja, south of town),* ☎ *762/ 2–34–67. MC, V.*

$$–$$$ ✕ **Toni's.** Prime rib and lobster are the specialties. There's also a great view and a romantic setting. ⊠ *Monte Taxco Hotel,* ☎ *762/2–13–00. AE, DC, MC, V.*

$$ ✕ **Señor Costilla.** That's right, the name of this whimsical restaurant translates as "Mr. Ribs." The Taxco outpost of the zany Anderson chain serves barbecued ribs and chops in a restaurant with great balcony seating. ⊠ *Plaza Borda 1,* ☎ *762/2–32–15. MC, V.*

$–$$ ✕ **Cielito Lindo.** This charming restaurant has a Mexican-international menu. Give the Mexican specialties a try—for example, *pollo en pipian verde* (chicken simmered in a mild, pumpkin seed–based sauce). ⊠ *Plaza Borda 14,* ☎ *762/2–06–03. MC, V.*

$ ✕ **Hostería el Adobe.** The lack of view (there are only two window
★   tables) is more than made up for by the original decor—for example, hanging lamps made of a cluster of masks—and the excellent food. Favorites include garlic-and-egg soup and the *queso adobe* (fried cheese on a bed of potato skins, covered with a green tomatillo sauce). ⊠ *Plazuela de San Juan 13,* ☎ *762/2–14–16. MC, V.*

$ ✕ **Pizza Pazza.** All nine varieties of pizza served here are tasty, but for
★   a real treat order the *pozole norteño,* a spicy pork and hominy soup that comes with pork cracklings, chopped onion, lemon, and avocado. This cozy place, with scotch-plaid tablecloths and flowering plants, overlooks Plaza Borda. ⊠ *Calle del Arco 1,* ☎ *762/2–55–00. Reservations not accepted. MC, V.*

$ ✕ **Santa Fe.** Mexican family-type cooking at its best is served in this simple place. Puebla-style *mole* (spicy chocolate-chili sauce), Cornish hen in garlic butter, and enchiladas in green or red chili sauce are among the tasty offerings. ⊠ *Hidalgo 2,* ☎ *762/2–11–70. AE, MC, V.*

$$ 🏨 **Monte Taxco.** A colonial style predominates at this hotel, which has a knockout view, a funicular, three restaurants, a disco, and nightly entertainment. It *is* a few miles from town, so plan to take taxis to get back and forth. ⊠ *Box 84, Lomas de Taxco, 40210,* ☎ *762/2–13–00,* 𝔽𝔸𝕏 *762/2–14–28. 153 rooms, 6 suites, 32 villas. 3 restaurants, 9-hole golf course, 3 tennis courts, horseback riding, dance club. AE, DC, MC, V.*

$$ 🏨 **Posada de la Misión.** Laid out like a colonial-style village, this hotel
★ is within walking distance of town. Rooms range from standard doubles to two-bedroom suites with kitchenettes, fireplaces, and terraces. The pool area is adorned with murals by the noted Mexican artist Juan O'Gorman. ⊠ *Box 88, Cerro de la Misión 32, 40230,* ☎ *762/2–00–63,* 𝔽𝔸𝕏 *762/2–21–98. 120 rooms, 30 suites. Restaurant, bar, pool, golf privileges, tennis court, dance club. AE, DC, MC, V.*

$–$$ 🏨 **De la Borda.** Long a Taxco favorite, De la Borda is a bit worn, but the rooms are large and comfortable and the staff couldn't be more hospitable. Ask for a room overlooking town. There's a restaurant, and many bus tours en route from Mexico City to Acapulco stay here overnight. ⊠ *Box 6, Cerro del Pedregal 2, 40200,* ☎ *762/2–00–25,* 𝔽𝔸𝕏 *762/2–06–17. 98 rooms, 12 suites. Restaurant, bar, pool. AE, MC, V.*

$ 🏨 **Agua Escondida.** Popular with some regular visitors to Taxco, this small hotel has simple rooms decorated with Mexican-style furnishings. ⊠ *Guillermo Spratling 4, 40200,* ☎ *762/2–11–66,* 𝔽𝔸𝕏 *762/2–13–06. 50 rooms. Restaurant, bar, café, pool, free parking. MC, V.*

$ 🏨 **Los Arcos.** If you're looking for an affordable place to stay in central Taxco, Los Arcos has basic rooms that surround a pleasant patio. ⊠ *Calle Juan Ruíz de Alarcón 4, 40200,* ☎ *762/2–18–36,* 𝔽𝔸𝕏 *762/2–79–82. 21 rooms. No credit cards.*

$ 🏨 **Posada de los Castillo.** This in-town inn is straightforward, clean, and good for the price. The Emilia Castillo silver shop is off the lobby. ⊠ *Juan Ruíz de Alarcón 7, 40200,* ☎ *762/2–13–96. 14 rooms. MC, V.*

$ 🏨 **Posada de San Javier.** This sprawling, very private establishment
★ is set somewhat haphazardly around a garden with a pool and a wishing well. In addition to the rooms, there are seven one-bedroom apartments with living rooms and kitchenettes (generally monopolized by wholesale silver buyers). ⊠ *Estacas 32 or Exrastro 6, 40200,* ☎ *762/2–31–77,* 𝔽𝔸𝕏 *762/2–23–51. 18 rooms, 7 apartments. Pool. No credit cards.*

$ 🏨 **Rancho Taxco-Victoria.** This in-town hotel is under the same management as the De la Borda (☞ *above*). Like the De la Borda, it is past its prime but exudes a certain charm. The rooms are always freshly painted, and the Mexican decor is simple but attractive. There's also the requisite splendid view. ⊠ *Box 83, Carlos J. Nibbi 5, 40200,* ☎ *762/2–02–10,* 𝔽𝔸𝕏 *762/2–00–10. 60 rooms, 4 suites. Restaurant, bar, pool. AE, MC, V.*

$ 🏨 **Santa Prisca.** The patio with fountains is a plus at this colonial-style hotel. ⊠ *Cena Obscuras 1, 40200,* ☎ *762/2–00–80,* 𝔽𝔸𝕏 *762/2–29–38. 30 rooms, 2 suites. Restaurant, bar. AE, MC, V.*

Nightlife and the Arts

FESTIVALS

Taxco's biggest single cultural event is the Jornadas Alarconianos—which honors one of Mexico's greatest dramatists with theater, dance, and concerts (dates change every year). But it is also known for its abundance of fiestas, which are an integral part of the town's character. These fiestas provide an opportunity to honor almost every saint in heaven with music, dancing, marvelous fireworks (Taxco is Mexico's fireworks capital), and lots of fun. The people of Taxco demonstrate their pyrotechnic skills with set pieces—wondrous blazing "castles" made of bamboo. (Note: Expect high occupancy at local hotels and inns during fiestas.)

January 18–20, the feast of Santa Prisca and San Sebastián, the town's patron saints, is celebrated with music and fireworks.

Holy Week, from Palm Sunday to Easter Sunday, brings processions and events that blend Christian and Indian traditions; the dramas involve hundreds of participants, images of Christ, and, for one particular procession, black-hooded penitents who flagellate themselves with boughs of thorns following a colonial custom. Most events are centered on Plaza Borda and the Santa Prisca Church. You must also reserve a hotel months in advance for Easter week.

September 29, Saint Michael's Day (Dia de San Miguel), is celebrated with regional dances and pilgrimages to the Chapel of Saint Michael the Archangel.

In **early November,** on the Monday following the Day of the Dead celebrations on November 1 and 2, the entire town takes off to a nearby hill for the Fiesta de los Jumil. The *jumil* is a crawling insect, said to taste strongly of iodine, that is considered a great delicacy. Purists eat them alive, but others prefer them stewed, fried, or combined with chili in a hot sauce.

In **late November or early December,** the National Silver Fair (Feria Nacional de la Plata) draws hundreds of artisans from around the world for a variety of displays, concerts, exhibitions, and contests held around the city.

NIGHTLIFE

You should satisfy your appetite for fun after dark in Acapulco. Taxco has a few discos, a couple of bars, and some entertainment, but the range is limited.

Still, you might enjoy spending an evening perched on a chair on a balcony or in one of the cafés surrounding the Plaza Borda. Two traditional favorites are the **Bar Paco** (⊠ Plaza Borda 12, ☎ 762/2–00–64) and **Bertha's** (⊠ Plaza Borda 9, ☎ 762/2–01–72), Taxco's oldest bar, where a tequila, lime, and club-soda concoction called a Bertha is the house specialty. It is supposedly the forerunner of today's margarita cocktail. In addition, some of the town's best restaurants have music on weekends.

Or immerse yourself in the thick of things, especially on Sunday evening, by settling in on a wrought-iron bench on the zócalo to watch children, lovers, and fellow people-watchers.

There are a few discos, including **La Barra** (⊠ Av. de los Plateros 12, ☎ No phone). Much of Taxco's nighttime activity is at the Monte Taxco hotel's **Windows** discotheque on weekends. Or, on Saturday nights, the hotel has a buffet and a terrific fireworks display. The **La Pachanga** discotheque at the Hotel Posada de la Misión is open nightly and is popular with townsfolk and tourists.

Outdoor Activities and Sports

You can play golf or tennis, swim, and ride horses at a few hotels around Taxco. Call to see if the facilities are open to nonguests, because the policy seems to change from time to time. Bullfights are occasionally held in the small town of Acmixtla, 6 km (4 mi) from Taxco. Ask at your hotel about the schedule.

Shopping

CRAFTS

Lacquered gourds and boxes from the town of Olinalá and masks, bowls, straw baskets, bark paintings, and many other handcrafted items native to the state of Guerrero are available from strolling vendors and are displayed on the cobblestones at "sidewalk boutiques."

Arnoldo (⊠ Palma 2, ☎ 762/2–12–72) has an interesting collection of ceremonial masks; originals come with a certificate of authenticity as well as a written description of origin and use. For $100 per person, Arnoldo will take you on a tour of the villages where the dances using the masks are performed on Feb. 2, Dec. 12, and May 15.

D'Elsa (⊠ Plazuela de San Juan 13, ☎ 762/2–16–83), owned by Elsa Ruíz de Figueroa, carries a selection of native-inspired clothing for women, and a wide and well-chosen selection of arts and handicrafts.

Sunday is market day, which means that artisans from surrounding villages descend on the town, as do visitors from Mexico City. It can get crowded, but if you find a seat on a bench in **Plaza Borda,** you're set to watch the show and peruse the merchandise that will inevitably be brought to you.

SILVER

Most of the people who visit Taxco come with silver in mind. Many of the more than 1,000 silver shops carry almost identical merchandise, although a few are noted for their creativity. Three types are available: sterling, which is always stamped .925 (925 parts in 1,000) and is the most expensive (and desirable); plated silver; and the inexpensive alpaca, which is also known as German silver or nickel silver. Sterling pieces are usually priced by weight according to world silver prices; of course, fine workmanship will add to the cost. Work is also done with semiprecious stones; you'll find garnets, topazes, amethysts, and opals.

Bangles start at $3, and bracelets range from $10 to $250. William Spratling, Andrés Mejía, and Emilia Castillo, daughter of renowned silversmith Antonio Castillo, are some of the more famous design names. Designs range from traditional bulky necklaces (often inlaid with turquoise) to streamlined bangles and chunky earrings.

Alvaro Cuevas (⊠ Plaza Borda 1, ☎ 762/2–18–78) has fine workmanship to match its fine designs.

The stunning pieces at **Galería de Arte en Plata Andrés** (⊠ Av. John F. Kennedy 28, ☎ 762/2–37–78) are created by the talented Andrés Mejía.

Emilia Castillo (⊠ Juan Ruíz de Alarcón 7, ☎ 762/2–34–71) is the most famous and decidedly one of the most exciting silver shops; it's especially renowned for innovative designs and for combining silver with porcelain (Neiman Marcus sells the wares in its U.S. stores).

Talleres de los Ballesteros (⊠ Florida 14, ☎ 762/2–10–76) and their branch, **Joyería San Agustín** (⊠ Cuauhtémoc 4, ☎ 762/2–34–16), carry a large collection of well-crafted silver jewelry and serving pieces. They have three additional branches in Mexico City and one in San Antonio, Texas.

Spratling Ranch (⊠ South of town on Hwy. 95, ☎ 762/2–61–08) is where the heirs of William Spratling turn out designs using his original nal molds.

Taxco A to Z

ARRIVING AND DEPARTING

By Bus. First-class **Estrella de Oro** buses leave Acapulco several times a day from the Terminal Central de Autobuses de Primera Clase (Av. Cuauhtémoc 158, ☎ 74/85–87–05). The cost for the approximately 5½-hour ride is about $12 one-way for deluxe service. The Taxco terminal is at Avenida John F. Kennedy 126 (☎ 762/2–06–48). **Sistema Estrella Blanca** buses depart Acapulco several times a day from the Terminal de Autobuses (Ejido 47, ☎ 74/69–20–29). Purchase your tickets at least one day in advance at the terminal. The one-way ticket is about $10 for first-class service. Buses depart from Taxco at Avenida John F. Kennedy 104 (☎ 762/2–01–31).

By Car. It takes about three hours to make the drive to Taxco from Acapulco, using the expensive (about $20) toll road. It is common practice to take an overnight tour. Check with your hotel for references and prices.

GETTING AROUND

Because of the byways, alleys, and tiny streets, maneuvering anything bigger than your two feet through Taxco will be difficult. Fortunately, almost everything of interest is within walking distance of the zócalo. Wear sensible shoes for negotiating the hilly streets. Minibuses travel along preset routes and charge only a few cents, and Volkswagen "bugs" provide inexpensive (average $1) taxi transportation. Taxco's altitude is 5,800 ft, so if you have come from sea level, take it easy on your first day.

VISITOR INFORMATION

Tourism Office (Av. de los Plateros 1, ☎ 762/2–66–16) is open weekdays 9–2 and 5–8.

ACAPULCO A TO Z

Arriving and Departing

By Bus

Bus service from Mexico City to Acapulco is excellent. First-class buses, which leave every hour on the hour from the Tasqueña station, are comfortable and in good condition. The trip takes 5½ hours, and a one-way ticket costs about $22. There is also deluxe service, called *Servicio Diamante,* with airplanelike reclining seats, refreshments, rest rooms, air-conditioning, movies, and hostess service. The deluxe buses leave four times a day, also from the Tasqueña station, and cost about $29. *Futura* service (regular reclining seats, air-conditioning, and a rest room) costs $25.

By Car

The trip to Acapulco from Mexico City on the old road takes about six hours. A privately built and run four-lane toll road connecting Mexico City with Acapulco is expensive (about $50 one-way) but well maintained, and it cuts driving time between the two cities from 6 to 3½ hours. Many people opt for going via Taxco, which can be reached from either road.

By Plane

The **Juan N. Alvarez International Airport** (☎ 74/66–94–34) is located about 20 minutes east of the city. From the United States, **American** (☎ 74/81–01–61) has nonstop flights from Dallas, with connecting service from Chicago and New York. **Continental** (☎ 91–800–90–050) has nonstop service from Houston. **Delta's** (☎ 74/66–90–32) direct flights are from Los Angeles and Atlanta. **Mexicana's** (☎ 74/84–12–15) flights from Chicago and Los Angeles stop in Mexico City before continuing on to Acapulco. **Aeroméxico's** (☎ 74/85–16–00) flight from New York to Acapulco stops in Mexico City. The carrier also has one-stop or connecting service from Atlanta, Chicago, Houston, Los Angeles, New York, Miami, and Orlando.

From New York via Dallas, flying time is 4½ hours; from Chicago, 4¼ hours; from Los Angeles, 3½ hours.

BETWEEN THE AIRPORT AND CITY CENTER

Private taxis are not permitted to carry passengers from the airport to town, so most people rely on **Transportes Aeropuerto** (☎ 74/62–10–95), a special airport taxi service. The system looks confusing, but there are dozens of helpful English-speaking staff members to help you figure out which taxi to take.

Look for the name of your hotel and the number of its zone on the overhead sign on the walkway in front of the terminal. Then go to the desk designated with that zone number and buy a ticket for an airport taxi. The ride from the airport to the hotel zone on the strip costs about $3.50 per person for the *colectivo* (shared minivan) and starts at $17 for a nonshared cab, depending on your destination. The drivers are usually helpful and will often take you to hotels that aren't on their list. Tips are optional. The journey into town takes 20 to 30 minutes.

By Ship

Many cruises include Acapulco as part of their itinerary. Most originate from Los Angeles. Cruise operators include **Celebrity Cruises** (☎ 800/437–3111), **Crystal P&O** (☎ 310/785–9300), **Cunard Line** (☎ 800/528–6273), **Krystal Cruises** (☎ 800/446–6640), **Princess Cruises** (☎ 800/421–0522), and **Royal Caribbean Cruises** (☎ 800/327–6700). Bookings are generally handled through a travel agent.

By Train

There is no train service to Acapulco from anywhere in the United States or Canada, nor is there service from Mexico City.

Getting Around

Getting around in Acapulco is quite simple. You can walk to many places, and the bus costs less than 50¢. Taxis cost less than they do in the United States, so most tourists quickly become avid taxi takers.

By Bus

The buses tourists use the most are those that go from Puerto Marqués to Caleta and stop at the fairly conspicuous metal bus stops along the way. New yellow air-conditioned tourist buses, marked ACAPULCO, now run about every 30 minutes along this route. If you want to go from the zócalo to the Costera, catch the bus that says LA BASE (the naval base near the Hyatt Regency). This bus detours through Old Acapulco and returns to the Costera just east of the Ritz Hotel. If you want to follow the Costera for the entire route, take the bus marked HORNOS. Buses to Pie de la Cuesta or Puerto Marqués say so on the front. The Puerto Marqués bus runs about every 10 minutes and is always crowded.

By Car

If you plan to visit some of the more remote beaches or decide to visit Taxco on your own, renting a car is convenient but fairly expensive. Prices start at about $56 a day for a Volkswagen sedan without air-conditioning. Don't expect a full tank; your car will have just about enough gas to get you to the nearest Pemex station.

By Horse and Carriage

Buggy rides up and down the Costera are available evenings. There are two routes: from Papagayo Park to the zócalo and from Condesa Beach to the Naval base. Each costs about $10 (be sure to agree on the price beforehand).

By Taxi

How much you pay depends on what type of taxi you get. The most expensive are hotel taxis. A price list that all drivers adhere to is posted in hotel lobbies. Fares in town are usually about $2 to $6; to go from downtown to the Princess Hotel is about $11; to go from the hotel zone to Caleta Beach is about $6. Hotel taxis are by far the roomiest and are kept in the best condition.

Cabs that cruise the streets usually charge by zone. There is a minimum charge of $1.50; the fare should still be less than it would be at a hotel. Some taxis that cruise have hotel or restaurant names stenciled on the side but are not affiliated with an establishment. Before you go anywhere by cab, find out what the price should be and agree with the driver on a price.

A normal—i.e., Mexican-priced—fare is about $2 to go from the zócalo to the International Center. Rates are about 50% higher at night, and though tipping is not expected, Mexicans usually leave small change.

You can also hire a taxi by the hour or the day. Prices vary from about $10 an hour for a hotel taxi to $8 an hour for a street taxi. Never let a taxi driver decide where you should eat or shop, since many get kickbacks from some of the smaller stores and restaurants.

Contacts and Resources

Car Rental

Local car-rental agencies include **Hertz** (☎ 74/85–89–47), **Avis** (☎ 74/62–00–85), **Dollar** (☎ 74/66–94–93), **Quick** (☎ 74/86–34–20), and **Saad** (☎ 74/84–34–45). All have offices at the airport.

Consulates

United States (✉ Continental Plaza Hotel, Costera Miguel Alemán 121–14, ☎ 74/84–03–00); **Canada** (✉ Marbella Mall, Suite 23, ☎ 74/84–13–05).

Doctors and Dentists

Your hotel can locate an English-speaking doctor, but they don't come cheap—house calls are about $100. The U.S. consular representative has a list of doctors and dentists, but it's against their policy to recommend anyone in particular.

Emergencies

Police (☎ 74/85–06–50). **Red Cross** (☎ 74/85–41–00). Two reliable hospitals are **Hospital Privado Magallanes** (✉ Wilfrido Massiue 2, ☎ 74/85–65–44) and **Hospital del Pacífico** (✉ Fraile y Nao 4, ☎ 74/87–71–80).

English-Language Bookstores

English-language books and periodicals can be found at **Sanborns,** a reputable American-style department-store chain, and at the newsstands in some of the larger hotels. Many small newsstands carry the Mexico City *News* and the Mexico City *Times*.

Guided Tours

ORIENTATION TOURS

There are organized tours everywhere in Acapulco, from the red-light district to the lagoon. Tours to Mexican fiestas in the evenings or the markets in the daytime are easy to arrange. Tour operators have offices around town and desks in many of the large hotels.

If your hotel can't arrange a tour, contact **Mexico Travel Advisors** at the Torre de Acapulco (⊠ Costera Miguel Alemán 1252, ☎ 74/84–74–00) or **Viajes Acuario** (⊠ Costera Miguel Alemán 186–3, ☎ 74/85–61–00).

SUNSET CRUISES

The famous cliff divers at La Quebrada (☞ Exploring, *above*) give one performance in the afternoon and four performances every night. For about $30, **Divers de México** organizes sunset champagne cruises that provide a fantastic view of the spectacle from the water. For reservations, call ☎ 74/82–13–98 or stop by the office downtown near the *Fiesta* and *Bonanza* yachts. The *Fiesta* (☎ 74/82–49–47) runs cruises at 7 PM on Tuesday, Thursday, and Saturday for about $50. The *Bonanza*'s (☎ 74/82–49–47) sunset cruise, with open bar (domestic drinks) and live and disco music, costs about $10. All boats leave from downtown near the zócalo. Many hotels and shops sell tickets, as do the ticket sellers on the waterfront.

Travel Agencies

American Express (⊠ La Gran Plaza shopping center, Costera Miguel Alemán 1628, Suites 7, 8, and 9, ☎ 74/69–11–66 to 25); **Viajes Wagon-Lits** (⊠ Las Brisas Hotel, Scenic Hwy. 5255, ☎ 74/84–16–50 ext. 392).

Visitor Information

State of Guerrero Department of Tourism/Acapulco International Center (SEFOTUR: ⊠ Costera Miguel Alemán, ☎ 74/84–24–23) is open weekdays 9–2 and 4–7.

10 OAXACA

The geographic, ethnic, and culinary diversity
of Oaxaca has made the state a favorite of
Mexico aficionados. The majority of residents
are descendants of native Zapotec and
Mixtec peoples, who centuries ago built the
Monte Albán and Mitla complexes near
Oaxaca City. Their contemporary crafts and
festivals are extremely colorful. Though less
exotic than Oaxaca City, the state's coastal
developments of Puerto Escondido and
Bahías de Huatulco are beloved by surfers
and beach bums.

Updated by
Jane Onstott
and Gina
Hyams

OAXACA (pronounced woh-*hah*-kah) is both a pre-Columbian and a colonial treasure. The state has a vast geographic and ethnic diversity. Together with neighboring Chiapas, Oaxaca has the largest Indian population in the country, which explains its richness and variety in handicrafts, folklore, culture, and gastronomy. Two out of three Oaxaqueños descend from Zapotec or Mixtec Indians, whose villages dot the valleys, mountainsides, and coastal lowlands. They come from one of 16 distinct linguistic groups and speak 52 dialects—each very different from the other. If they speak Spanish—which many now do—it is a second language to them.

Indigenous tribes flourished in the area thousands of years ago, and the archaeological ruins of Monte Albán, Mitla, and Yagul are among the vivid remnants of their cultures. Located within a 40-km (25-mi) radius of the city of Oaxaca, the ruins bear witness to highly religious, artistic, and advanced civilizations whose members were master engineers and geometers.

The Zapotec and Mixtec civilizations were conquered by the irrepressible Aztecs, who in the 15th century gave Oaxaca its name: *Huaxyaca*. In the Nahuatl language it probably means "by the acacia grove," referring to the location of the Aztec military base. Then came the Spanish conquest in 1528. The Spanish monarch Charles V gave Cortés the title of *Marqués del Valle de Oaxaca* as a reward for his conquest of Mexico. Cortés preferred to live elsewhere, so an estate was never built on the lands conferred with the title, but Cortés's descendants kept the property until Mexico's bloody 1910 Revolution.

Oaxaca's legacy to Mexican politics has been two presidents: Benito Juárez, the first full-blooded Indian to become chief of state, and Porfirio Díaz, a military dictator who declared himself president-for-life. Juárez, a Zapotec, was a sheepherder from San Pablo Guelatao, a settlement about 64 km (40 mi) north of Oaxaca. As a child he spoke only his native Zapotec tongue. Often referred to as Mexico's Abraham Lincoln, Juárez was trained for the clergy but later studied law and entered politics. He was elected governor of the state (1847), chief justice of the Supreme Court of Mexico (1857), and then president (1858–72), defeating a French effort in 1867 to install Hapsburg Archduke Ferdinand Maximilian of Austria as emperor. Porfirio Díaz, one of Juárez's generals, seized the presidency in his 1877 coup and held office until he was kicked out in 1911.

Oaxaca sits on the vast, fertile, 1½-km- (1-mi-) high plateau of the Oaxaca Valley, encircled by the majestic Sierra Madre del Sur mountain range. Mexico's fifth largest state, it lies in the southwest, bordered by the states of Chiapas to the east, Veracruz and Puebla to the north, and Guerrero—whose touristic claims to fame are Acapulco and Ixtapa—to the west. The south of Oaxaca State spans 509 km (316 mi) of lush tropical Pacific coastline with magnificent beaches. Until recently, these beaches had been relatively unknown and unexploited, except for the long-established small fishing town and seaside hideaway of Puerto Escondido and the even smaller town of Puerto Angel. But now Bahías de Huatulco, 125 km (77 mi) west of Puerto Escondido, is on the map—thanks to the government working to turn it into a world-class resort.

Note: Assaults and highway banditry have increased throughout Mexico, as the continuing economic crisis exacerbates long-standing poverty. First-class buses are sometimes the target of highway robbery, especially the route between Juchitan, on the Oaxaca coast, and San

Cristóbal de las Casas in Chiapas. Night buses are most vulnerable. Although this is indeed cause for concern, occurrences are infrequent.

Pleasures and Pastimes

Dining

One highlight of Oaxaca is its traditional cookery, one of the finest and most elaborate in all Mexico. Oaxaca is known as "the land of seven moles" because of its seven distinct kinds of multispiced mole sauces. One of them, *mole negro,* rivals that of neighboring Puebla in thickness and flavor because of the outstanding local chocolate from which it is made. Tamales, either sweet or stuffed with chicken, are another treat. The home- and factory-made mezcal, the alcoholic drink derived of the blue agave cactus, differs in flavor with each maker and can be as high as 80 proof. The cream variety, thick and sweet, is flavored with orange, lime, or other fruits or nuts.

Oaxacan cuisine—the cheeses, mole sauces, and meats that make dining in the capital memorable—is sadly in short supply along the coast, where seafood is your best bet. Huatulco's restaurants are getting better, and some of the places in Puerto Escondido are very good. With a few exceptions, cooking in Puerto Angel is mediocre. Dress is casual and reservations are unnecessary at all restaurants unless otherwise noted. Prices are quite inexpensive throughout the state, with the exception of the Huatulco resort.

CATEGORY	COST*
$$$$	over $15
$$$	$10–$15
$$	$5–$10
$	under $5

per person for a three-course meal, excluding drinks and tip

Lodging

Oaxaca City has no luxury resorts, but it does have some magnificently restored properties, including a 16th-century convent and dozens of smaller, moderately priced accommodations, most in downtown locations. These smaller hotels are very popular around December and January and require six months to a year advance booking. Day of the Dead celebrations (October 31–November 2) and Holy Week are also times of high occupancy, so plan accordingly.

Hotel rates vary considerably in the coastal area. In Puerto Escondido and Puerto Angel, most of the accommodations fall into the $$ or $ price range. Those in Huatulco, where you'll find luxury compounds, are considerably pricier, with the exclusive Quinta Real topping the scale. The high season along the coast runs from mid-December through Holy Week; rates increase by 20% or more during this time. Budget accommodations are scarce in Huatulco, although more moderately priced rooms are becoming available, especially in La Crucecita.

CATEGORY	COST*
$$$$	over $120
$$$	$70–$120
$$	$30–$70
$	under $30

All prices are for a standard double room, including 17% tax.

Shopping

Oaxaca City is a magnet for both *mestizos* (people of mixed European and Indian descent) and indigenous people who live in the valley and nearby mountains. They come to town to buy and sell, especially on

Saturday. The market might not be as colorful as it was in D. H. Lawrence's *Mornings in Mexico,* but it is an authentic, exotic spectacle. El Central de Abastos is the largest Indian market in all Mexico, and only Michoacán and Chiapas have Oaxaca's variety and quality of crafts. Expect hectic activity and bright colors. At markets, listen for the singsong, tonal Zapotec and Mixtec languages, in which changes in the pitch of the voice change the meanings of words. In town, galleries exhibit the pottery, textiles, and fanciful wooden animals called *alebrijes* that have drawn international attention to Oaxaca's artisans.

Surfing

Oaxaca's Puerto Escondido is a household name for serious surfers who migrate to this sunny port for all-out surfing championships each year. These challenging waves have been attracting surfers from all parts of the globe since word first got out in the 1960s.

Exploring Oaxaca

Travelers tend to gravitate toward two parts of Oaxaca—Oaxaca City, the state capital, spread over a valley in the Sierra Madre mountains; and the Pacific Coast area due south of the capital.

Numbers in the text correspond to numbers in the margin and on the Oaxaca City and Oaxaca Coast maps.

Great Itineraries

If you only have three days to spend in the state, choose between Oaxaca City and the coast. Go to Puerto Escondido for unspoiled beaches and wildlife, or if you'd rather spoil yourself, think about the million-dollar resorts of Huatulco. Oaxaca City is food for the soul for history and folk-art aficionados, with its magnificent colonial buildings, world-famous crafts, and the ancient temples just outside the city. For a culture-beach combination, plan at least seven days—Oaxaca City and the coast merit three days apiece.

IF YOU HAVE 3 DAYS IN OAXACA CITY

Explore downtown to see the stunning colonial monuments that have been declared World Heritage structures by the United Nations. The first day, take in the **Catedral Metropolitana** ④, the **Museo de Arte Contemporáneo** ⑤, the **Iglesia y Ex-Convento de Santo Domingo** ⑦, and the adjoining **Museo Regional** ⑧. On Day 2, beat the crowds by catching a tour or bus right after breakfast for **Monte Albán,** the ruins of an ancient, mountaintop Zapotec capital. After returning to the city and a late lunch, enjoy coffee at the 16th-century **Ex-Convento de Santa Catalina** ⑥, now the Camino Real hotel, and take in the patio garden with the stone tub where the nuns washed clothes. Visit the **Museo de Arte Prehispánico Rufino Tamayo** ⑩ on Day 3, then shop for regional arts and crafts at the **Mercado de Abastos** and the **Mercado de Artesanías.** Watch the sun set over Oaxaca from the terrace bar of the **Hotel Victoria,** just above the city proper.

IF YOU HAVE 5 DAYS IN OAXACA CITY

Follow the three-day itinerary and, on Day 4, add a visit to the Mixtec ruins at **Mitla,** stopping on the way or back to see the 2,000-year-old *ahuehuete* cypress in Tule (or, on a Sunday, to experience a country market day in **Tlacolula**); then spend the rest of the afternoon back in Oaxaca City people-watching and dining at the *zócalo* ①, or town square. Day 5, head to the villages near Oaxaca City, where beautiful handicrafts are made before your eyes. Back again in Oaxaca City, visit the **Basílica de Nuestra Señora de la Soledad** ⑪ and the boutiques full of high-quality crafts on **Calle Macedonio Acalá.**

Using **Bahías de Huatulco** ⑭–⑯ as your base, take a boat tour of the bays on the first day, followed by a spell at the beach for a blazing sunset finale. Day 2, tour the small beaches and hidden bays between Huatulco and **Puerto Escondido** ⑫. On Day 3, laze on the beach or rent water toys and, in late afternoon, taxi to **La Crucecita** ⑰ for some strolling, followed by dining at one of the small restaurants on the main square.

Follow the three-day itinerary, then sign up for bird-watching on the **Manialtepec Lagoon** on Day 4. Day 5, head inland for a special lunch on the **Coffee Plantation tour.** If you choose laid-back **Puerto Escondido** ⑫ as your base, you might spend Day 4 touring the **Lagoon of Chacahua,** and Day 5 riding horses on the beach in the morning, and relaxing with a soothing Temescal steam bath (a pre-Hispanic–style sauna) and massage in the afternoon.

You can immerse yourself in the cultural treasures of **Oaxaca City** ①–⑪ and **Monte Albán,** then kick back with some sea and sun. You could spend Days 1–4 at the sights outlined in the first four days of the city itinerary. On Day 5, fly to **Bahías de Huatulco** ⑭–⑯ and, on arrival, sign up for a boat tour of the bays. Take Days 6 and 7 on the beach, or bird-watching and exploring **La Crucecita** ⑰. If you're staying longer, don't miss the Museum of the Sea Turtle tour.

When to Tour Oaxaca

Oaxaca celebrates Mexican holidays and its own state's fiestas with an intensity of color, tradition, and talent that attracts hordes. **El Día de Muertos** (Day of the Dead) begins with graveyard celebrations in the city and nearby villages on October 31 and ends in the cemeteries on November 2, when families partake of the favorite food of those they are honoring. The most frequently visited village is Xoxo, but many others, including Atzompa and Xochimilco, also have colorful festivities. In festival time the city is abuzz with activity, and everywhere you'll see altars honoring the deceased. On December 23, **Noche de Rábanos** (Night of the Radishes), the zócalo is packed with growers and artists displaying their hybrid radishes carved and arranged in tableaux that depict everything from Nativity scenes to space travel. Prizes are awarded for the biggest and the best, and competition is fierce. Other arrangements are made with *flores inmortales* ("eternal flowers;" small dried flowers) or *totomoxtl* (corn husks, pronounced to-to-*mosh*-tl). Bring plenty of film.

Oaxaca's other major celebration is the **Guelaguetza** (Zapotec for "offering" or "gift"), usually held on the last two Mondays in July. Dancers from all the mountain and coastal communities converge on the city bearing tropical fruits, coffee, and other regional products. They perform elaborate dances in authentic costumes from early morning until early afternoon at the Guelaguetza Auditorium, an open-air amphitheater in the hills just northwest of the city's center.

Keep in mind that if you plan to come for these celebrations, you'll need to book far in advance.

OAXACA CITY

Oaxaca City is traditionally Indian, and although cosmopolitan touches are everywhere, women and children still peddle everything from gardenias to chili-seasoned grasshoppers, men and boys offer shoe shines around the city's many parks, and destitute families play accordions along the city streets in the hopes of acquiring spare change.

The city is officially called Oaxaca de Juárez, and it is decidedly the state's major attraction, with a population of about 800,000 and more than a million visitors a year.

Exploring Oaxaca City

The colonial heart of Oaxaca is laid out in a simple grid, with all major attractions within walking distance of one another. Most of the streets in the city's core change names once they pass the zócalo.

A Good Walk

Begin your exploration of Oaxaca at the shady **zócalo** ①, the heart of the city and its pedestrian-only main square. On the south side of the square visit the **Palacio de Gobierno** ②—step inside and check out the mural stretching from the first to the second floor. Upon leaving the government palace, go to the northwest corner of the zócalo and you will reach **El Alameda** ③, a second square that abuts the zócalo. On the east side of the Alameda, you can't miss the **Catedral Metropolitana de Oaxaca** ④. After visiting the cathedral, turn right on Avenida Independencia and left at the next corner. This puts you on the pedestrian mall on Calle Macedonio Alcalá, where you'll see restored colonial mansions in a palate of pastels, and some of Oaxaca's best galleries, shops, museums, and restaurants. It is also lively and well lighted at night, and there are frequent outdoor arts-and-crafts exhibits. After a short 1½ blocks you'll see the **Museo de Arte Contemporáneo de Oaxaca** ⑤ on your right. Continue north on Alcalá, turn right on Calle Murguía, and left on the first street, Avenida 5 de Mayo. Taking up the entire block on the east side of the street is the **Ex-Convento de Santa Catalina** ⑥, now the Hotel Camino Real. Catercorner from the Camino Real is Parque Labastida, where ingenuous artists sell their wares, and musicians sometimes entertain. Continue north until Avenida 5 de Mayo ends at Calle Gurrión and the fabulous **Iglesia y Ex-Convento de Santo Domingo** ⑦. You can enter the church from its southern entrance, and leave via the front door onto Calle Alcalá. Adjacent to the church is the **Museo Regional de Oaxaca** ⑧, which contains priceless artifacts taken from Tomb 7 of Monte Albán, as well as an interesting ethnographic exhibit.

Continue north on Calle Alcalá a half block and walk up the steps of La Plazuela del Carmen Alto, where Triqui women in colorful red, beribboned *huipiles* sell embroidered blouses, dresses, and other handicrafts. Take a right on Calle García Vigil, and just half a block up, on the left side of the street, you'll find the **Museo Casa de Benito Juárez** ⑨, a museum honoring Oaxaca's most revered statesman. Upon leaving, return south on García Vigil 4½ blocks and turn right on Avenida Morelos. One and a half blocks up on the right, in a beautifully restored colonial mansion, is the **Museo de Arte Prehispánico Rufino Tamayo** ⑩. After seeing the museum, continue west on Morelos 2½ blocks. Descend the steps and cross the large plaza, past the vendors of interesting religious trinkets, to the massive **Basílica de Nuestra Señora de la Soledad** ⑪. On the left side of the church is a small museum housing items related to Oaxaca's patron saint. Go east on Avenida Independencia past the telegraph office and you'll be back at El Alameda, where you can stop and watch the daily parade of Oaxaqueños.

Sights to See

⑪ **Basílica de Nuestra Señora de la Soledad.** The Baroque basilica houses the statue of Our Lady of Solitude, Oaxaca's patron saint. According

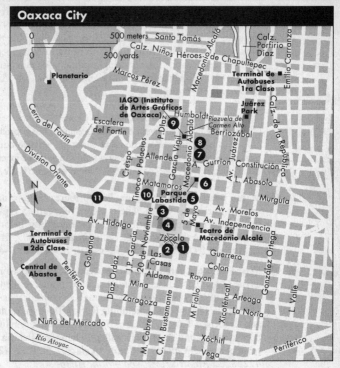

Oaxaca City

to legend, this statue was found in the pack of a mule that had mysteriously joined a mule train bound for Guatemala; when the mule perished at the site of the present church and the statue was discovered in its pack, the event was construed as a miracle, and the church was built in 1682 to commemorate it. The Virgin, who is believed to have supernatural healing powers, remains the object of fervent piety for the devout populace. She now stands in a gilded shrine and wears a magnificent robe of jewel-studded black velvet. A small museum at the side of the church displays devotional items left by the faithful over the years. ⊠ *Av. Independencia 107 at Galeana,* ☎ *No phone.* 🖾 *Donation.* ☉ *Daily 7–7.*

④ Catedral Metropolitana de Oaxaca. Begun in 1544, the cathedral was destroyed by earthquakes and not finished until 1733. The king of Spain gave the city the wooden-cogged clock that you can see in the facade. ⊠ *Av. Independencia 700,* ☎ *9/51–64401.* ☉ *Daily 8 AM–9 PM.*

③ El Alameda. This shady square is home to the cathedral and the post office. Vendors here sell Che Guevara T-shirts, huge balloons, cassette tapes, snacks, and, during festivals, myriad souvenirs and crafts.

⑥ Ex-Convento de Santa Catalina. This building is now the Hotel Camino Real and, like everything in downtown Oaxaca, is a National Heritage Site. It's worthwhile to explore the hotel's three courtyards; a large stone basin where the nuns did the convent's laundry 400 years ago still stands in the center of one of the patios. ⊠ *Cinco de Mayo 300.*

★ **⑦ Iglesia y Ex-Convento de Santo Domingo.** The most brilliantly decorated church of the city, this 16th-century wonder has an ornately carved facade that stands between two high bell towers. The interior is a profusion of white and gold—yes, that's real gold leaf—typical of the energy with which Mexico seized on the Baroque style and made of it something unique. The entire complex of the Ex-Convento is all the more splendid because of the two-year (1997–1999) renovation, for which the Oaxaca government, Banamex bank, and INAH (National Institute of Anthropology and History) picked up the tab. There are now botanical gardens in addition to a beautifully augmented museum. The café and school for restoring antique books are still being completed. ⊠ *Calle Macedonio Alcalá and Av. Gurrión,* ☎ *9/51–63720.* ⊙ *Daily 7 AM–8 PM.*

NEED A BREAK? **El IAGO** (Instituto de Artes Gráficos de Oaxaca), just across the street and north of the Ex-Convent of Santo Domingo, has a pretty outdoor café in its back patio. You can relax under the massive bougainvillea over coffee or ice cream, or enjoy a light snack or full lunch. ⊠ *Macedonio Alcalá 507,* ☎ *9/51–66980. No credit cards. Closed Tues.*

⑨ Museo Casa de Benito Juárez. Benito Juárez lived in this house as a servant during his youth. The museum re-creates a typical 19th-century house; none of the furnishings or memorabilia belonged to Juárez or his employer/benefactor. ⊠ *Calle García Vigil 609,* ☎ *9/51–61860.* 🎫 *About $1.40, free Sun.* ⊙ *Tues.–Sat. 10–7, Sun 10–5.*

★ **⑤ Museo de Arte Contemporáneo de Oaxaca.** This museum, also known as the MACO, is housed in an attractive colonial residence. It exhibits works in a variety of media; the permanent collection has that of some of Oaxaca's native sons, including Rufino Tamayo, Rodolfo Morales, and Francisco Toledo. Be sure to check out what remains of the frescoes in the second-floor front gallery. There's a cafeteria on one of the front patios. ⊠ *Calle Macedonio Alcalá 202,* ☎ *9/51–42818 or 9/51–42228.* 🎫 *About $1.* ⊙ *Wed.–Mon. 10:30–8.*

★ **⑩ Museo de Arte Prehispánico Rufino Tamayo.** This carefully restored colonial mansion contains a small but excellent collection of pre-Hispanic pottery and sculpture. It was originally the private collection of the late painter-muralist Rufino Tamayo, who presented it to his hometown in 1979. There are exhibits from all over the country, arranged geographically and chronologically. ⊠ *Av. Morelos 503,* ☎ *9/51–64750.* 🎫 *About $1.40.* ⊙ *Mon. and Wed.–Sat. 10–2 and 4–7.*

★ **⑧ Museo Regional de Oaxaca.** Laid out in a series of galleries around the cloister of the **Ex-Convento de Santo Domingo** (☞ *above*), this museum, along with the entire ex-convent, has been totally refurbished. The ground floor now contains temporary galleries, a gift shop, and administrative offices. On the second floor you'll find 14 excellent thematic rooms, including those dedicated to Oaxacan music, medicine, indigenous languages, pottery, and more. Another gallery is dedicated to the treasure taken from the tombs at **Monte Albán** (☞ Side Trips, *below*), just outside the city. The stunning gold jewelry from Tomb 7 was one of the greatest archaeological finds of all time. Tours of the new botanical gardens are available in English Tues.–Sat. at 1 PM for no additional cost. ⊠ *Plaza Santa Domingo,* ☎ *9/51–62991.* 🎫 *$2, free Sun. and national holidays.* ⊙ *Tues.–Sun. 10–8.*

② Palacio de Gobierno. The splendid 19th-century neoclassical state capitol building sits on the south side of the zócalo. The fascinating murals inside depict the history and cultures of Oaxaca (but it's often closed whenever there's a peaceful protest in the zócalo, which is quite often). ☎ *9/51–44016.* ⊙ *Daily 9–3 and 6–8.*

★ **① Zócalo.** During the day, everyone comes to Oaxaca's shady main plaza, with its green wrought-iron benches and matching bandstand. At night, mariachi and marimba bands play under colonial archways or in the bandstand, filling the air with music. ⊠ *Bounded by Portal de*

Clavería on the north, Portal del Palacio on the south, Portal de Flores on the west, and Portal de Mercaderes on the east.

Dining

The open-air cafés surrounding the zócalo are good for drinks, snacks, and people-watching, with the scene changing from peaceful serenity over early morning coffee to throngs of people watching parades with brass bands, floats, and *monos* (giant papier-mâché dolls) on holiday evenings. Most serve the economical *comida corrida* (midday set menu) after 1:30 PM. But you won't be very much out of pocket wherever you choose to dine: the devaluation of the peso has put even most higher-quality restaurants into the $$ price range.

$$$ ✕ **El Asador Vasco.** Basque (*vasco*) cuisine is served in this prizewinning restaurant, along with an outstanding Oaxacan version of mole sauce—sweet and mildly spicy, and marvelous on chicken or turkey—and a sumptuous gratiné of oysters in *chipotle* chili sauce. The tables overlooking the zócalo are in great demand. From 8 to 9 PM, serenading by *tuna* (traditionally dressed student minstrels) evokes medieval Spain. Later, marimba music floats up from the restaurant below. ⊠ *West side of zócalo, upstairs, Portal de Flores 11,* ☎ *9/51–44755. AE, DC, MC, V.*

$$ ✕ **Catedral.** This elegant yet accessible local favorite has recently expanded to encompass the entire original colonial house. Favorite dishes include mushroom soup flavored with a local herb, *epazote,* and chicken in squash blossom sauce, served with rice and a squash blossom stuffed with cheese. You can feast at the lavish Sunday lunch buffet, served 2–7 PM, ending up with some of Catedral's great strong coffee. There's dancing in the patio bar Friday and Saturday nights after 9:30. ⊠ *1 block north of cathedral, Calle García Vigil 105 at Av. Morelos,* ☎ *9/51–63285 or 9/51–63988. AE, MC, V. Closed Tues.*

$$ ✕ **El Colibrí.** If you want a restaurant that is quiet and air-conditioned but not expensive, with romantic background music, free refills of super hot coffee, and fresh rolls and butter on the table, try this one—favored by upscale Mexican families and beeper-toting businesspeople. The menu is large: in addition to a full menu of Oaxaca specialties, there are 10 different salads and five spaghetti dishes, plenty of appetizers, and burgers with fries. You can order half portions of some items. ⊠ *Calz. Heroes de Chapultepec 903,* ☎ *9/51–58087. AE, MC, V.*

$$ ✕ **El Naranjo.** Melodic music in the background and the work of local artists on the walls lend atmosphere to this large, covered interior patio. Each of Oaxaca's seven moles is featured once a week, and there are many delicious variations of *chiles rellenos* (stuffed peppers)—from mild to hot—to choose from. Unusual dishes such as a cream soup of smoky chipotle chili and nuts, and a spinach salad (with a lovely light dressing over fresh spinach leaves, jicama, bacon, and red hibiscus flowers) make this newish restaurant a breath of fresh air for Oaxacan cuisine. ⊠ *Trujano 203,* ☎ *9/51–41878. AE, MC, V.*

$$ ✕ **La Olla.** The name of this friendly restaurant, one block south of Santo Domingo church, means "the pot." It doubles as a gallery, and local artists' work hangs on Olla's peach-color walls. The menu is varied—its strengths are the large, delicious, and healthy salads and regional dishes that the owner creates herself. A new second-floor dining room doubles the restaurant space, and although the rustic rooftop terrace, complete with hammocks, is meant mainly for the adjoining hotel's guests, you can also take a drink up there for a good view of the city. Service tends to be slow. ⊠ *Reforma 402,* ☎ *9/51–66668. No credit cards. Closed Sun.*

$$ ✗ **Nuu-Luu.** The name in Mixtec, "picturesque place," couldn't be more appropriate. In a pretty suburb in the northern part of town, this open-air restaurant has been a favorite for 28 years. Come for Oaxacan specialties, which start off with a free *botana* (appetizer) and a small *donají,* a drink with juice and mescal. Popular dishes include *sopa de guias,* a soup of young squash blossoms, squash, corn, and cornmeal, and the entrée *pescado a la yerba santa,* fish topped with a sauce of green tomatoes, herbs, onion, and garlic and steamed in fresh banana leaves. The open dining room overlooks a tree-garden. Private transportation is provided for groups of four or more. ✉ *Iturbide 100, San Felipe del Agua,* ☎ *9/51–53187. AE. No dinner.*

$$ ✗ **Restaurant Asunción.** This elegant, rather formal restaurant in the Hostal de la Noria has starched, white tablecloths with lilac accents and purple napkins. Among the house favorites are a delicious chicken mole, and foil-wrapped fish fillets steamed in a mescal sauce. Even more subtle is *pollo a la poblana* (chicken breast stuffed with mild chilies, manchego cheese, and squash blossoms topped with a tomato-chile sauce and melted cheese). ✉ *918 Hidalgo,* ☎ *9/51–47844. AE, MC, V.*

$$ ✗ **Terranova.** For delicious mole tamales and a good *caldo tlalpeño* (chicken-based soup with rice, avocado, chili, and tomato), make your way to the east side of the plaza. The daily tourist menu is served after 2 PM, and one or more musicians are usually on hand 8:30–10:30 PM for some contemporary electric latino sounds. ✉ *Portal B. Juárez 116,* ☎ *9/51–40533. AE, MC, V.*

$ ✗ **El Mesón.** Mesón's inviting, inexpensive buffet is right off the zócalo. Stop by for a snack or full meal from the paper menu, where you check off your items of choice. Tortillas are made fresh on site, and there are 13 types of tacos, as well as *pozole* (hominy soup), *cochinita píbil* (spicy Yucatecan-style pork), and other Mexican dishes. For an intense sugar fix, have a cup of rich Oaxacan chocolate and a slice of nut or cheese pie. ✉ *Av. Hidalgo 805, at Valdivieso,* ☎ *9/51–62729. AE.*

Coffeehouses

✗ **Coffee Beans.** This is a great place for coffee, and there is a small selection of cakes and quiches. Different types and roasts of Mexican coffee beans are also on sale. ✉ *Calle 5 de Mayo 400,* ☎ *No phone. No credit cards.*

✗ **El Gecko.** The mustard-color courtyard of this tranquil coffeehouse is drenched in purple flowering vines. There is a variety of coffee drinks—including a fabulous iced cappuccino with whipped cream and chocolate sprinkles—as well as light food and snacks. You can use the Internet services at Milenio, in the same plaza, as you sip your java. ✉ *Calle 5 de Mayo 412, in Plaza Gonzalo Lucero,* ☎ *9/51–48024. No credit cards. Closed Sun.*

Lodging

$$$$ 🏨 **Hotel Camino Real Oaxaca.** A monastic air lingers in the breezy pa-
★ tios and enclosed gardens of this beautifully restored former convent (1576), and Gregorian chants float softly through the hotel in the morning hours. The rooms themselves are far from austere, but there is nonetheless a touch of the divine in the hotel's atmosphere. El Refectorio restaurant is open for breakfast, lunch, and dinner. The most popular meals are the massive buffets: the Saturday night spread, accompanied by mariachi music; the elaborate Sunday *comida* (late lunch); and the breakfast buffet. ✉ *Cinco de Mayo 300, 68000,* ☎ *9/51–60611; 800/722–6466 in the U.S.,* 🖷 *9/51–60621. 91 rooms. Restaurant, 2 bars, pool, travel services. AE, DC, MC, V.*

$$$ ★ ☎ **Hotel Victoria.** Surrounded by terraced grounds and well-kept gardens, this sprawling salmon-color complex is perched on a hill overlooking the city. Draw back your curtains at dawn and catch your breath at the view: Oaxaca awakening under the Sierra Madre. The hotel has a good restaurant, tennis court, and heated pool. Rooms, bungalows, and suites are available; be sure to request one with a view. You can take a shuttle bus on the half hour to the city center, 10 minutes away. El Tule, the veranda dining room that overlooks the hotel gardens and the valley below, serves international fare in addition to Oaxacan specialties. ⊠ *Lomas del Fortín 1, 68070,* ☎ *9/51–52633,* FAX *9/51–52411. 59 rooms, 57 suites, 34 bungalows. Restaurant, bar, pool, tennis court, travel services. AE, MC, V.*

$$$ ☎ **Misión de los Angeles.** Though this resort-style hotel is a long way from the zócalo, its peaceful gardens and relaxed ambience make it a good choice. It is much closer to El Llano, a city park frequented more by locals than by tourists. The hotel's commodious dining room is popular with tour groups. ⊠ *Calzada Porfirio Díaz 102, 68050,* ☎ *9/51–51500,* FAX *9/51–51680. 152 rooms, 18 junior suites, 3 suites. 2 restaurants, 2 bars, pool, tennis court, jogging, recreation room, free parking. AE, MC, V.*

$$ ☎ **Hotel Rivera del Angel.** This large, plain-looking hotel, formerly called the Mesón de Angel, is a favorite with Mexican families, groups, and traveling salesmen. Southwest of the zócalo near the markets, it has a huge garden pool. The attractive rooms have wide terraces, orthopedic mattresses, desk fans, and telephones. Tourist buses to Monte Albán leave from here on the half hour until 3:30 PM. ⊠ *F. J. Mina 518, 68000,* ☎ *9/51–66666,* FAX *9/51–45405. 62 rooms. Restaurant, room service, pool, free parking. No credit cards.*

$$ ☎ **Hotel Señorial.** This is a good choice if you want a relatively inexpensive hotel right on the zócalo; the seven rooms that overlook the square have tiny balconies. Uncarpeted rooms have TVs and telephones, and the beds are fairly comfortable, although far from firm. The clean bathrooms are tiled in cheerful light blue tiles. ⊠ *Portal de Flores 6, 68000,* ☎ *9/51–63933,* FAX *9/51–63668. 128 rooms. Restaurant, café, pool, free parking. No credit cards.*

$$ ☎ **Suites Colibrí.** The 21 suites in this business-oriented hotel are a good value at about $66. Large rooms have firm beds, cable TV, and telephones. The three newest units have tile floors and painterly frescoes on the walls. All rooms have bathtubs and hair dryers. ⊠ *Privada de las Flores 109, off Calz. Heroes de Chapultepec, 68050,* ☎ *9/51–36211,* FAX *9/51–36433. 21 suites. Restaurant, bar, room service, free parking. AE, MC, V.*

$–$$ ☎ **Villa María.** Popular with foreigners, this compound of one-, two-, and three-bedroom furnished apartments overlooks a spacious patio. Friendly, bilingual hostess María García makes her guests feel at home. Linens and dishes come with the units (which have suitable touches of Mexican decor), but phones, cable TVs, and maid service are extra. It's a 15-minute walk to the main square from here, but taxis and buses run frequently. Rentals are by the week or month, with rates starting at $175 a week for a one-bedroom apartment, although the two bedroom units are much homier. Monthly rates are discounted by about 50%. Advance reservations and deposits—up to a year prior to arrival depending on the season—are required. ⊠ *Arteaga 410, 68000,* ☎ *9/51–65056,* FAX *9/51–42562. 14 apartments. No credit cards.*

$ ☎ **Hotel Cazomalli.** Even the baked-earth floor tiles shine in this lovable new hostelry, 15 minutes from downtown Oaxaca in the sleepy, cobblestoned barrio of Jalatlaco. The hotel lives up to its name, which in Nahuatl means "house of tranquility." Clean, bright, quiet rooms have blond pine furnishings and hand-woven spreads and curtains.

Rooms have no TVs—there *is* one in a small second-floor salon—but there are telephones. Owner Marina Flores and her family make the ambience friendly, and serve breakfast 8–10 AM in either the restaurant or central courtyard, where geraniums bloom en masse. Head up to the roof to jump into the small whirlpool or to wash your own clothes. ⊠ *El Salto 104, at Aldama, Jalatlaco, 68080,* ☎ *9/51–38605* 𝖥𝖠𝖷 *9/51–33513. 15 rooms. Restaurant, bar, hot tub. AE, MC, V.*

$ 🖭 **Las Golondrinas.** This intimate hotel is tastefully ablaze with color,
★   from the profusion of flowering plants to the walls—painted pink, blue, mustard, and rust. Guests read books or lounge around the blissfully tranquil patios. Plain but cheerful rooms have red-tile floors and comfortable beds; none has TV or telephone, but there is a TV in the common sitting room. Breakfast (not included in room rates) is served 8–10 AM. ⊠ *Tinoco y Palacios 411, 68000,* ☎ *9/51–43298 or 9/51–42126. 24 rooms. Laundry service. No credit cards.*

Nightlife and the Arts

Oaxaca has plenty of entertainment in evening hours. On almost any night you'll find live marimba, Andean music, or nouveau flamenco in the open-air cafés surrounding the zócalo. There are plenty of discotheques playing salsa or rock, and Sunday at 12:30 PM the **Oaxaca State Band** sets up under the Indian laurel trees in the main square. The **Teatro Macedonio Alcalá** has orchestral and theatrical performances sporadically—even the occasional opera. See the monthly *Guía Cultural* (on sale in bookstores for about 70¢) for information on these and other events.

El Sol y La Luna is *the* place to listen to live music, often jazz or jazzy Mexican and American ballads. You can sit over drinks or order dinner on the outside patio or inside at the latest residence-turned-restaurant, directly across from the Oaxaca Institute of Culture. A cover is charged ($2–$4 depending on the band) when the music begins at 9–9:30 PM. Off-season, there is usually music Thursday–Saturday only. ⊠ *Reforma 502, at Constitución,* ☎ *9/51–48069.*

Candela hums after 10 PM with live salsa, *cumbia* (a Latin dance of Cuban origin), and other styles of Latin music as foreigners and locals crowd the tiny dance floor. ⊠ *Murguía 413,* ☎ *9/51–42010.* 📼 *$3 cover. Closed Mon.*

Every Friday night—and Wednesday in busier seasons—the Hotel Camino Real hosts the **Guelaguetza** (☎ 9/51–60611), a smaller version of the pre-Hispanic Oaxacan dance fête displaying regional dances from throughout the state. The $25 price includes buffet dinner (beginning at 7 PM) and show (8:30 PM) in the former convent's 16th-century chapel. Drinks are not included in the price. Reservations recommended. If you want to see a less-expensive Guelaguetza show, check with the tourist office for recommendations.

Shopping

Prospective folk-art buyers in Oaxaca City and surrounding villages should heed one major caveat, or risk being saddled with more than they expected. It is not too difficult to ship your purchases home from many of the city's shops and shipping services, provided you have a receipt showing that you paid the 15% sales tax on all items purchased. Many artisans have begun giving out official government tax receipts, but if you buy from one who does not, you may have a hard time finding someone to ship your wares for you. Ask for receipts and for referrals to shipping agents if you plan to buy more than you can carry home. Also, check out the displays at the shops in town and learn about quality and design before you start spending lots of pesos.

Markets

The Saturday market is held at the functionally named **Central de Abastos** (Supply Center) on the southern edge of the town center. By noon on Saturday the enormous covered market is swarming with thousands of sellers and shoppers—both from Oaxaca and the surrounding villages—and the experience can be quite overwhelming. Don't burden yourself with a lot of camera equipment or purses and bags— you'll have a hard enough time keeping track of companions in the jostling, bumping crowd. If you see something you really like, purchase it on the spot—you might never find your way back. The market is active during the rest of the week, too. If you go then, you can check out the mounds of multicolored chilies and herbs, the piles of tropical fruit, and the aisles of baskets, rugs, and fragile green or black pottery. But it's on Saturday that you see the best handicrafts: *huipiles* (embroidered tunics) that vary with the village of origin; *rebozos* (shawls) of cotton and silk; distinctive pottery from many villages; colorful woven baskets; wooden and tin toys. Bargaining is not unexpected, although some sellers quote the actual price these days.

Several other markets in Oaxaca are active daily. **Mercado Benito Juárez** is south of the zócalo between Calles 20 de Noviembre and Miguel Cabrera at Colón. Here there are handicrafts as well as cheese, mole, chocolate, fruits, and much more. **Mercado 20 de Noviembre** is directly south of the Juárez market; here locals, budget travelers, and other adventurers eat regional food at tiny stalls. Two blocks farther south is **Mercado de Artesanías,** on Calle J. P. García near Ignacio Zaragoza, which sells mostly textiles. While they tend their stands, Trique Indian women and children weave wall hangings with simple back-strap looms.

Each neighborhood has its own market day in a nearby square or structure, although these do not generally sell handicrafts. If you're interested in seeing neighborhood markets, check out **Mercado de Conzatti** on Friday until 4 PM (✉ Calle Reforma at Humboldt) or the **Mercado de Merced** (✉ Calzada de la República at Morelos) on Sunday.

For information on the colorful markets in the Indian villages outside Oaxaca, *see* Side Trips, *below.*

Shops and Galleries

Besides having a mother lode of markets, Oaxaca has some spectacular shops and galleries—some are closed Sunday and others close at midday—so plan your shopping days accordingly.

FINE ARTS

La Mano Mágica (✉ Macedonio Alcalá 203, ☎ 9/51–64275) is an upscale crafts and fine arts gallery with a large inventory and high price tags. **Galería Quetzalli** (✉ Constitución 104, ☎ 9/51–42606) features both established and up-and-coming Oaxacan artists—prices are high, but the work is excellent. **Galería Arte Mexicano** (✉ Plaza Santo Domingo, M. Alcalá 407–15, ☎ 9/51–43816) displays local artists' work, and in adjoining stores, folk art, antiques, and silver jewelry.

HANDICRAFTS

ARIPO (✉ García Vigil 809, ☎ 9/51–44030) is a government-run artist cooperative with competitive prices and much exclusively Oaxacan work. It's one of the few craft stores open on Sunday. The **FONART** store (✉ Crespo 114, ☎ 9/51–65764) has a representative selection of quality arts and crafts from elsewhere in Mexico. You can support the women-artists' co-op (also open daily) by shopping at the huge warren of shops that makes up **Mujeres Artesanas de las Regiones de Oaxaca** (⊠ Av. 5 de Mayo 204, ☎ 9/51–60670). Selection and quality are good, and prices are reasonable. **Artesanías Chimalli** (⊠ García Vigil 513–A, ☎ 9/51–42101) has an excellent selection of *alebrijes*—brightly painted copal-wood animals with comical expressions and fantasy shapes. There is also a large assortment of quality crafts from throughout Mexico. Chimalli will cheerfully ship what you buy there, or what you've bought elsewhere. **Artesanías de El Patrón** (5 de Mayo 210, at Murguía, ☎ 9/51–62108) specializes in tableware from Michoacán, woven goods, nativities, and elegant stylized statues that reinvent black pottery from San Bartolo Coyotepec. The two-story **Corazón del Pueblo** (⊠ M. Alcalá 307–9, ☎ 9/51–30547) has beaded Huichol Indian masks, mystical tapestries from Nayarit state, *papel picado* (colorful cutout paper flags), and a good selection of English-language books on Mexican art and history; the furniture is also for sale.

JEWELRY

Oro de Monte Albán (⊠ Macedonio Alcalá 403 at Allende, ☎ 9/51–43813) is one of several branches of this store that sells gold and silver reproductions of pre-Columbian jewelry found in the tombs of royalty at Monte Albán (there's also a shop at the archaeological site). There are plenty of other fine shops that sell jewelry in both traditional and modern styles, many of them along the length of Macedonio Alcalá and adjacent streets, as well as the streets west of Mercado 20 de Noviembre (☞ *above*).

Side Trips from Oaxaca City

A trip to the colonial city of Oaxaca isn't complete without heading out to see the area's ancient past and the local village life that connects it with the present. The dramatic settings of the Zapotec and Mixtec ruins of Monte Albán, Mitla, and Yagul date back some 2,600 years. And the nearby towns that produce the wares sold in the Oaxaca City market give a taste of traditional regional lifestyles. All of these places are easily reached by public transportation, taxi, or on a tour. Recently, SEDETUR, the state tourism board, has developed the Tourist Yu'u project, which provides opportunities to experience life outside the city. The project makes available basic, comfortable, clean accommodations in artisan villages and near natural phenomena such as the cold-water springs and fossilized waterfalls at Hierve el Agua. Contact the tourism department (☞ Visitor Information *in* Oaxaca City A to Z, *below*) for details and reservations.

Monte Albán

 9 km (5½ mi) southwest of Oaxaca.

The onetime holy city of more than 30,000 Zapotecs, Monte Albán is arguably the most interesting and well-preserved ruin in the state. Experts estimate that a mere 10% of the site is uncovered—excavations are constantly taking place to unearth more knowledge about the fascinating culture of the Zapotec people who lived here.

Monte Albán overlooks the Oaxaca Valley from a flattened mountaintop 1,300 ft high. Either Zapotecs or their predecessors leveled the site around 600 BC. The Zapotecs did construct the existing buildings along a north–south axis, with the exception of one structure thought to have been an observatory, which is more closely aligned with the stars than with the earth's poles. And the varying heights of the site follow the contours of distant mountain ranges. The oldest of the four temples is the **Gallery of the Dazantes** (dancers), so named for the elaborately carved stone figures that once covered the building—the originals are now in the site museum. Experts are unsure whether the figures, mostly male nudes, represent captives, medical cases, or warriors; the theory that they were dancers has been discarded.

Another major point of interest is the **ball court,** where one or more ball games were played. Hips, shoulders, knees, and elbows were probably used to hit a wooden or rubber ball. Some insist the captain of the winning team was sacrificed as an honor, others condemn the losers—the exact outcome of these games is unknown. There is some speculation that the games were a means of solving disputes among factions or villages within the domain.

No one knows for sure if the Zapotecs abandoned the site gradually or suddenly, but by AD 1000 they had vacated it. Until then, they had expanded the city and taken on Mayan influences in buildings and stelae, as had other cultures in the region. The Mixtecs, who took over the site years after the Zapotec departure, used Monte Albán as a lofty necropolis, a massive cemetery of lavish tombs. More than 200 tombs and 300 burial sites have been explored to date; in 1932 **Tomb 7** yielded a treasure unequaled in North America. Inside were more than 500 priceless Mixtec objects, including gold breastplates, jade, pearl, ivory, and gold jewelry, and fans, masks, and belt buckles of precious stones and metals. Many of these treasures are now on view at the Museo Regional de Oaxaca (☞ Exploring Oaxaca City, *above*). What you'll find here is a small **site museum** with information in Spanish only and an excellent **bookstore/gift shop** (☎ 9/51–61215). The restaurant is not half bad, and has an excellent view of the valley of Oaxaca.

Special buses go to Monte Albán from the Hotel Rivera del Angel (☞ *above*) every half hour from 8:30 to 3:30; the last bus back is at 6 PM. The fare is about $1.50 round-trip (to stay longer than two hours you must pay a 75¢ surcharge). A taxi from the zócalo runs about $5. 🖃 *$2, free Sun. and holidays.* ☉ *Daily 8–6.*

Mitla

 40 km (25 mi) southeast of Oaxaca.

Mitla, like Monte Albán, is a complex of structures started by the Zapotecs and later taken over by the Mixtecs. In fact, the site of these palaces grew even as Monte Albán declined. Mitla's architecture is striking—and unique in the area—for the elegance of its geometric patterns and the brilliance of its stone. Unlike other ancient buildings in North America, there are no human figures or mythological events represented—only abstract designs. The name, from the Aztec word *mictlan,* means "place of the dead." 🖃 *$1.50, free Sun. and holidays.* ☉ *Archaeological zone daily 8–5.*

Yagul

 36 km (22 mi) southeast of Oaxaca.

Although the palace ruins at Yagul are not nearly as elaborate as those at Monte Albán or Mitla, they stand handsomely atop a hill and are certainly worth a visit, especially if Oaxaca's ancient cultures are of interest. This city was predominantly a fortress set slightly above a group of palaces and temples; it includes a ball court and more than 30 uncovered underground tombs. 🖃 *$1, free Sun. and holidays.* ☉ *Archaeological zone daily 8–5.*

Indian Villages

Many of the dozen or more villages around Oaxaca City are known for the skills of their artisans, who use both ancient and modern techniques to create their folk-art pieces; they often live among generations

414

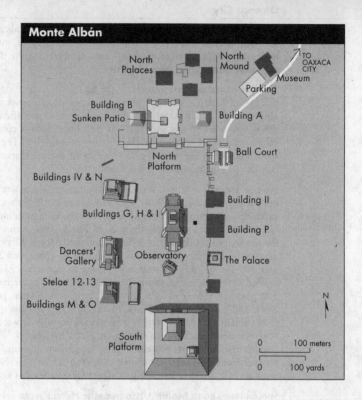

Monte Albán

North Palaces

North Mound

TO OAXACA CITY

Museum

Parking

Building B
Sunken Patio

Building A

North Platform

Ball Court

Buildings IV & N

Building II

Buildings G, H & I

Building P

Dancers' Gallery

Observatory

The Palace

Stelae 12-13

Buildings M & O

South Platform

N

0   100 meters

0   100 yards

of families who have their own special designs for pottery, woven rugs, and wood carvings.

A west-to-south counterclockwise route from the city takes in **Atzompa,** where Dolores Porras, the descendants of Teodora Blanco, and many others in town create fanciful clay pots and sculptures. Other potters make the region's traditional green-glazed plates, bowls, and cups. The Tuesday market day has shrunk in recent months, however, and some of the town's best wares are found in downtown Oaxaca shops. In **Arrazola,** artists carve alebrijes. On Thursday, **Zaachila** has the most authentic livestock and food market in the area. The southern route goes to **San Bartolo Coyotepec,** the center for glossy, unglazed black pottery sold in people's homes and from a multistall cooperative next to the town square. In **Santo Tomás Jalietza,** women sell belts and table runners from pastel cotton made on small, back-strap looms. San Martín Tilcajete, south of Santo Tomás Jalietza on the road to Ocotlán, also has a town full of painted wooden animals. Friday's colorful market in **Ocotlán** is known for its handicrafts, especially handcrafted machetes and knives, famous throughout Mexico. Some of the impressive knives are inscribed with colorful local sayings.

An eastward route includes **Teotitlán del Valle,** where giant rug looms sit in the front rooms of many houses. One of the town's most respected rug makers is Isaac Vásquez. The small Museo Comunitario (closed Monday) on the main square focuses on the anthropology, crafts, and culture of the area. In **Santa Ana del Valle,** Lucio Aquino is the most famous rug maker, although there are many skilled artisans in town. In nearby **Tlacolula,** the Sunday market spreads for blocks around the Baroque 16th-century chapel. On Sunday it seems that all of Oaxaca takes this route, starting at the Tule Tree (☞ *below*), moving to the ruins of Mitla, and then on to the crafts centers and market.

North of the city center, off the road to Mexico City, is **Etla**; its Wednesday market is famous for cheeses, mole, bread, and chocolates.

The markets on other routes are held on special days throughout the week, and you can easily fill a week with tours and never see the same sight twice. If you have to budget your time, use tour guides for these trips so you don't miss out on the fascinating details.

The Tule Tree
14 km (8½ mi) east of Oaxaca.

In the town of Santa María del Tule stands a huge ahuehuete cypress estimated to be more than 2,000 years old. One of the largest in the world, it is some 140 ft high, with roots buried more than 60 ft in the earth. It takes 35 adults with their arms outstretched to embrace it. The tree is the traditional center of the town of Santa María and is larger than the church behind it.

OAXACA CITY A TO Z

Arriving and Departing

By Bus
Deluxe buses make the six-hour nonstop run from Mexico City to Oaxaca for about $19. The first-class terminal is called the **ADO** (✉ Calzada Niños Héroes de Chapultepec 1036, at Emilio Carranza), from which the **ADO** (☎ 9/51–51703) and **Cristóbal Colón** (☎ 9/51–51214) bus lines provide service. The second-class bus station, **Central de Autobuses** (✉ Prolongación de Trujano at the Periférico, ☎ 9/51–65326) serves intermediate towns within the state. Other lines serving the surrounding states have desks at one or both terminals.

By Car
From Mexico City, you can take Mexico 190 (Pan American Highway) south and east through Puebla and Izúcar de Matamoros to Oaxaca City—a distance of 546 km (338 mi) along a rather curvy road. This route takes six to seven hours. The toll road, which connects Mexico City to Oaxaca City via Tehuacan, is better. It cuts down on curves and on driving time by about an hour.

By Plane
Mexicana (☎ 9/51–68414 or 9/51–67352) flies from various U.S. cities (including Chicago, Los Angeles, San Francisco, Miami, and New York) to Oaxaca City with a stop in Mexico City. You will have to change planes in Mexico City on other flights from the United States for **Aeroméxico** (☎ 9/51–61066) or **Mexicana** to get to to Oaxaca City's **Benito Juárez Airport,** about 8 km (5 mi) south of town. There is also service for triangle flight itineraries, including the Oaxacan coastal resorts of Bahías de Huatulco or Puerto Escondido.

Domestic service to Oaxaca includes **Aviacsa** (☎ 9/51–31809) from Tuxtla Gutiérrez; **Aero Vega** (☎ 9/51–62777) for charters to and from Puerto Escondido; **Aeromorelos** (☎ 9/51–15100) from Puerto Escondido and Huatulco; and **Aerocaribe** (☎ 9/51–60266 or 9/51–60229) to and from Acapulco and Huatulco.

BETWEEN THE AIRPORT AND DOWNTOWN
Transportes Aeropuerto (✉ Alameda de León, ☎ 9/51–44350) will trundle you into the soonest available van and drop you off at your hotel for $1.50. There are usually no taxis in sight. From town, buy a ticket ahead of time for inexpensive airport transportation.

Getting Around

By Car

You won't need a car in Oaxaca City, which is fairly compact. Even outlying sights are easily accessible by taxi or on a tour. That said, a car is a great way for adventurous souls to see the countryside.

By Taxi

Taxis are plentiful, clearly marked, and reasonably priced. You can usually find them at any hour of the day cruising on downtown streets. There are also taxi stands on Independencia at G. Vigil, on one side of Alameda Park, and on Calles Abasolo and Cinco de Mayo, near the Hotel Camino Real. Cabs are not metered. Determine the fare ahead of time (in town, usually $1.50–$2); for outlying destinations, ask the driver to show you the tariff card.

Contacts and Resources

Car Rental

Cars are for rent at the airport, in town, and through travel agencies at various hotels. **Hertz** is conveniently located on the zócalo in the Hotel Marqués del Valle (⊠ Portal de Clavería s/n, Local 7, ☎ 9/51–62434, FAX 9/51–60009) and at the airport (☎ 9/51–15478).

Consulate

U.S. Consulate (⊠ Macedonio Alcalá 201, Int. 204, ☎ FAX 9/51–43054) is open weekdays 10–3. **Canadian Consulate** (⊠ Pino Suarez 700, Local 11-B, ☎ 9/51–33777) is open weekdays 11–2.

Emergencies

Dial 06 locally for all emergencies, including police and hospital. **Police** (☎ 9/51–60455 or 9/51–60400). **Hospital–Red Cross** (☎ 9/51–64455).

Guided Tours

Unless you're on a strict budget, take advantage of the many tour companies that offer guided trips to the archaeological sites, colonial churches and monasteries, outlying towns (some of which have weekly market days), and folk-art centers. Prices start at $10. Licensed guides are available as well through the tourism office and travel agencies for up to $5 per hour for a minimum of three persons. **Viajes Turísticos Mitla** (⊠ F. J. Mina 518, in the Hotel Rivera de Angel, ☎ 9/51–66175 or FAX 9/51–43152) and **Agencia Marqués del Valle** (⊠ Portal de Clavería s/n, ☎ 9/51–46970 or 9/51–46962, FAX 9/51–69961) are among the most established agencies.

Visitor Information

The **Oficina de Turismo** (⊠ Independencia, at García Vigil, ☎ 9/51–64828) is open daily 9–8.

THE OAXACA COAST

Oaxaca's 520-km (322-mi) coastline is mainland Mexico's last Pacific frontier. Huatulco, a Fonatur (Mexican government's tourism developers) project, was launched in the early 1980s. Bahías de Huatulco, as the entire area is called, covers 51,900 acres of mountain lowlands and coastal stretches, 40,000 acres of which is supposed to remain a nature reserve. The focal point of the master-planned development is a string of nine sheltered bays (*bahías*) with golden sands that stretches across 35 km (22 mi) of some of the Pacific's prettiest coastline.

Huatulco's beauty is arguably best seen from a boat (☞ Guided Tours *in* Oaxaca Coast A to Z, *below*), even though some of the bays are ac-

Finally, a travel companion that doesn't snore on the plane or eat all your peanuts.

MCI WORLDCOM WorldPhone®

123 456 7891 2345
J.D. SMITH

When traveling, your MCI WorldCom Card is the best way to keep in touch. Our operators speak your language, so they'll be able to connect you back home—no matter where your travels take you. Plus, your MCI WorldCom Card is easy to use, and even earns you frequent flyer miles every time you use it. When you add in our great rates, you get something even more valuable: peace-of-mind. So go ahead. Travel the world. MCI WorldCom just brought it a whole lot closer.

You can even sign up today at www.mci.com/worldphone or ask your operator to make a collect call to 1-410-314-2938.

EASY TO CALL WORLDWIDE

1 Just dial the WorldPhone access number of the country you're calling from.
2 Dial or give the operator your MCI WorldCom Card number.
3 Dial or give the number you're calling.

Argentina	
To call using Telefonica	0-800-222-6249
To call using Telecom	0-800-555-1002
Brazil	**000-8012**
Mexico	
Avantel	01-800-021-8000
Telmex ▲	001-800-674-7000
Collect access in Spanish	980-9-16-1000
Morocco	**00-211-0012**

For your complete WorldPhone calling guide, dial the WorldPhone access number for the country you're in and ask the operator for Customer Service. In the U.S. call 1-800-431-5402.

▲ When calling from public phones, use phones marked LADATEL.

EARN FREQUENT FLYER MILES

AmericanAirlines
A'Advantage®

Continental Airlines
OnePass

▲ **Delta Air Lines**
SkyMiles®

▬ **MILEAGE PLUS®**
United Airlines

U·S AIRWAYS
DIVIDEND MILES

MCI WorldCom, its logo and the names of the products referred to herein are proprietary marks of MCI WorldCom, Inc. All airline names and logos are proprietary marks of the respective airlines. All airline program rules and conditions apply.

MCI WORLDCOM

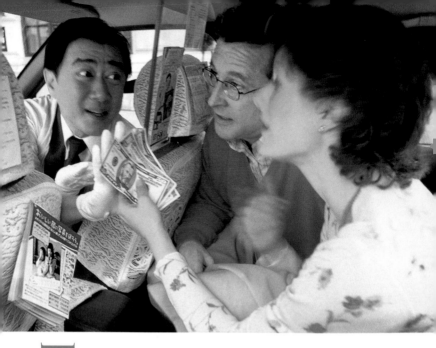

The first thing you need overseas is the one thing you forget to pack.

FOREIGN CURRENCY DELIVERED OVERNIGHT

Chase Currency To Go® delivers foreign currency to your home by the next business day*

It's easy–before you travel, call 1-888-CHASE84 for delivery of any of 75 currencies

Delivery is free with orders of $500 or more

Competitive rates– without exchange fees

You don't have to be a Chase customer–you can pay by Visa® or MasterCard®

CHASE

THE RIGHT RELATIONSHIP IS EVERYTHING.®

1•888•CHASE84
www.chase.com

cessible by road. Bahía Tangolunda is the site of the area's most exclusive hotels, whereas Bahía Santa Cruz has middle-range hotels, a marina, and a small plaza. Bahía Chahué has been developed in the last few years, with some moderately priced hotels; a parking lot makes the beach here quite accessible. The town of La Crucecita, originally built to house the construction crews and workers building Huatulco, has come along nicely: it has a pretty plaza and a newly frescoed church, as well as some budget hotels and plenty of restaurants.

Puerto Escondido has long been prime territory for international surfers. The town has the coast's first airport (not international) and has grown up to tourism in a much more natural, and to some minds, pleasant, way than Huatulco. Although the four-block pedestrian walkway—crowded with open-air seafood restaurants, shops, and café bars—is lively, the "real" town above the strip, with its busy market and stores, provides a look at local life and a dazzling view of the coast. The tiny port town of Puerto Angel, midway between the two airports, was hard hit by Hurricane Pauline in September 1997. The town is slowly pulling itself back together, but it will take time to regain its services. There are a limited selection of hotels and bungalows spread into the hills.

Puerto Escondido

12 *310 km (192 mi) south of Oaxaca City.*

A coffee-shipping port in the 1920s, Puerto Escondido is the first tourist town on the Oaxaca coast, southeast of Acapulco on Highway 200. The town market, **Mercado Benito Juárez,** is a long walk (but a short cab or bus ride) from most hotels, and it's worth checking out, especially on market days: Saturday and Wednesday. If you want a bit of pampering, cleanse body and soul according to ancient traditions at the **Temazcalli** (⊠ Av. Infraganti, esq. Calle Temazcalli, ☎ 958/2–10–23), which "combines the energy of wood, fire, rock, and medicinal herbs." Massages are also offered, and afterward you can watch the sunset from the cliffs above the ocean. Back in town, at the north end of the main beach, you can hire a driver from among the *panga* (small boat) fleet for bay tours or fishing trips. **La Playa Principal** (main beach) and the **Laguna Agua Dulce** are at the south end of the tourist strip, followed by **Marinero Beach,** then a sharp outcropping of rocks, and, finally, the most famous beach of all, **Zicatela** (☞ *below*).

The main intersection in Puerto Escondido is at Highway 200 (also called the *carretera costera,* or coast highway) and Avenida Alfonso Pérez Gasga, which meanders south into the tourist zone. On the north side of the highway this street is called Avenida Oaxaca. Traveling down a steep hill, Avenue Gasga passes many of the tourist hotels; at the bottom, traffic is prohibited and the street becomes a four-block-long pedestrian mall lined with shops, restaurants, and lodgings that spread to the sands of the main beach.

The airport is on the northern edge of town, as are the hotels favored by charter groups. **Playa Bacocho,** just south of the airport, is an upscale housing-and-hotel development; some inviting bars, discos, and restaurants have opened in this area, although most of the action still centers around the tourist zone to the south.

Beaches

One of the top 10 surfing beaches in the world, **Zicatela** is a long stretch of cream-color sand battered by the Mexican Pipeline, as this stretch of mighty surf is called. In November international surfing championships are held here, and the town fills with sun-bleached aficionados of both

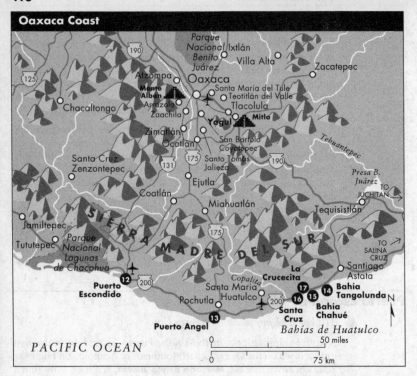

Oaxaca Coast

PACIFIC OCEAN

sexes intent on serious surfing and hard partying. Do not swim in these waters unless you can withstand deadly undertows and rip currents. Instead, watch the surfers at sunset from the *palapa* (thatched-roof) restaurant at the Arco Iris Hotel.

The safest swimming and snorkeling beaches in Puerto Escondido are **Puerto Angelito** and **Carrizalillo**; both can be reached on foot, but more easily by cab or by boat from the town beach. Transportation is available from the many fishermen who park their pangas on the sand near town and use them as water taxis. The ride should cost about $5.

Dining and Lodging

Understandably, coastal cuisine centers around fresh seafood dishes, although some savvy townspeople are introducing Italian and vegetarian food for variety. For such a small town, Puerto Escondido has more than its share of good restaurants, most in the moderate or inexpensive categories.

$$ ✕ **La Perla.** Because it's in the "real" town uphill from the tourist zone, this excellent seafood restaurant has some of the best prices in town. *Pulpo* (octopus) is wonderfully tender. An excellent ceviche comes in a spicy cocktail sauce. It's a bit of a walk but a short, cheap cab ride. ⊠ *3a Poniente s/n, Sector Juárez,* ☎ *958/2–04–61. No credit cards.*

$$ ✕ **La Posada del Tiburón.** What's not to like about this place: the waiters are friendly, the food is scrumptious, and you can wiggle your toes in the sand at the tables closest to the beach. Opera music floats over lilac and light blue woven tablecloths as waves straggle up the sand along the main beach. Seafood is the specialty here: try a Lyon-style fish fillet in creamy lemon sauce, or the house fillet, topped with fine herbs and slivered almonds. There are also tasty chicken and meat dishes served with baked potato, rice, and steamed vegetables. ⊠ *Av. Gasca s/n at Playa Principal,* ☎ *958/2–07–86. AE, MC, V.*

$$ ✕ **Mario's Pizzaland.** The proprietor is a courtly, generous Italian who produces in short order pizzas with all sorts of exotic toppings, including seafood. Also on the abbreviated menu are vegetarian and meat lasagna, enormous salads, and *bistec alla pizzaiola* (steak smothered in melted cheese and pizza sauce). ⊠ *Av. Gasga just east of tourist zone,* ☎ *958/2-05-70. No credit cards.*

$$ ✕ **Perla Flameante.** Fresh dorado, shark, tuna, and pompano come with teriyaki, Cajun, or garlic seasonings at this second-story bamboo restaurant overlooking the beach. The deep-fried onion rings and zucchini are terrific. Perla is open for breakfast every day except Sunday. ⊠ *Av. Gasga near end of tourist strip,* ☎ *958/2-01-67. MC, V.*

$ ✕ **Art 'n' Harry's.** This surfer hangout overlooking the Pipeline is the place to relax with a drink and watch videos or zone out on heavy-metal CDs. The menu offers all types of stir-fries, salad, spaghetti dishes, and seafood. ⊠ *South end of Zicatela Beach,* ☎ *No phone. No credit cards. No breakfast.*

$ ✕ **Carmen's Bakery** (a.k.a. La Patisserie). This tiny green oasis of
★ soothing classical music and great coffee and pastries stands alongside the hot dusty road to Playa Marinero. A breakfast of fruit salad with yogurt and granola is sublime. The same owner runs Cafecito, a happening surfers' hangout at Zicatela beach and equally worthy of exploration. ⊠ *Entrada Playa Marinero s/n; and Calle del Morro s/n, Zicatela beach,* ☎ *No phone. No credit cards. No dinner.*

$ ✕ **La Gota de Vida.** This small vegetarian café and health-food store on Zicatela beach has all sorts of delicious salads, vegetable soups, tofu and tempeh dishes, and *licuados* (milk shakes) made with yogurt, papaya, and mango, as well as fresh vegetable and fruit juices—at very reasonable prices. It's quite often packed with surfers and health-conscious travelers. ⊠ *Calle del Morro s/n,* ☎ *No phone. No credit cards.*

$$$ ✕🛏 **Hotel Santa Fe.** This pretty hotel, framed by exuberant tropical plants at the north end of Zicatela beach, has colonial furnishings and curtains and spreads of woven Mexican cloth. Some rooms have balconies overlooking the pools and patios or the beach. The hotel also manages the eight one-bedroom Bungalows Santa Cruz next door, which have well-stocked kitchenettes, cozy furnishings, and wide verandas. By all means treat yourself to at least one meal at the hotel restaurant—whether or not you are a guest. The menu is divided between seafood, vegetarian, and traditional Mexican dishes, and tables overlooking the surf are wonderful at dawn and sunset. ⊠ *Calle del Morro s/n, Col. Marinero,* ☎ *958/2-01-70,* ℻ *958/2-02-60. 59 rooms, 2 suites, 8 bungalows. Restaurant, bar, 2 pools, wading pool, shop, laundry service. AE, MC, V.*

$$ ✕🛏 **Flor de María.** Hand-painted birds, flowers, and tropical scenes
★ illuminate this bright, attractive hotel half a block up from Playa Marinero. Crisp sheets cover firm beds, and rooms are bright and immaculate—with powerful ceiling fans, but no TV or telephone. On the roof, you can swing in a row of hammocks, or cool off in the small pool or at the rooftop bar. Like all Zicatela beach hotels, Flor de María is a short but very dark walk from the tourist esplanade. In the outstanding restaurant, efficient, Italian-born owner Maria combines New World ingredients with old-world recipes to create delicious pastas, chicken, and steaks in addition to Mexican specialties. Each day a different homemade dessert is served. ⊠ *Entrance Playa Marinero s/n,* ☎ ℻ *958/2-05-36. 24 rooms. Restaurant, bar, pool, laundry service. AE, MC, V.*

$$$ 🛏 **Hotel Aldea del Bazar.** This sparkling white hotel sits on a bluff overlooking the beach at Playa Bacocho, just south of the airport. The restaurant and some of the rooms have a view of the beach below, which can be reached by way of a ramp—a long walk back up the hill. All the tastefully decorated rooms have small separate living rooms and color TVs. One of the hotel's best features is the pre-Hispanic–style eucalyptus sauna; however, the massages are mediocre. ⊠ *Av. Benito Juárez 7, Fracc. Bacocho, 71980,* ☎ ℻ *958/2–05–08. 47 rooms. Restaurant, bar, pool, massage, spa, dance club, meeting rooms, travel services. MC, V.*

$$–$$$ ⊞ **Paraíso Escondido.** Hidden halfway up the steps of Calle Union, this colonial-style hotel has the charm of the house of a wealthy, eccentric, and somewhat dotty relative. No two rooms are alike, and all are furnished with a folkloric mixture of wood dressers, tin mirrors, and brightly colored curtains and spreads. At press time, they were building five new third-floor suites with kitchenettes and private, ocean-view terraces. ⊠ *Calle Union 10, 71980,* ☎ *958/2–04–44. 20 rooms, 5 suites. Restaurant, bar, pool. No credit cards.*

$$ ⊞ **Studios Tabachín del Puerto.** Special touches such as clocks, vases, and bookshelves with books give these wonderfully furnished studio apartments a homey feel. Especially wonderful is the fourth-floor "penthouse," with its awesome view of the coast. Each of the six studios, behind the Hotel Santa Fe near Zicatela beach, has a kitchenette stocked with necessities. Owner don Pablo also manages a small country inn, Posada Nopala, about two hours north of town, which is open October 31 to April 30. It sits in the pine forests of the Oaxaca mountains, amid coffee plantations and crystal-clear rivers. If you have a self-sufficient streak, this comfortable yet rustic lodge is perfect for experiencing life in rural Mexico. Or for a day-trip to Nopala, $25 per person includes lunch. ⊠ *Calle de Morro by Zicatela Beach, Apdo. 210, 71890,* ☎ ℻ *958/2–11–79. 6 apartments. Restaurant. MC, V.*

$–$$ ⊞ **Cabañas de Playa Acali.** A variety of sizes and styles of accommodations are available at this cluster of cabañas and bungalows on Zicatela beach. Guests mingle around the large central pool. The least expensive rooms are in small, rustic cabañas without air-conditioning; the most expensive, though still a bargain, are eight bungalows with terraces, kitchens, air-conditioning, and dining areas. This is a good choice for groups of four or six surfers sharing expenses and preparing their own meals. ⊠ *Calle del Morro s/n, 71980,* ☎ *958/2–07–54. 8 cabañas, 8 bungalows. Kitchenettes, pool. No credit cards.*

$ ⊞ **Hotel Arco Iris.** This sprawling, three-story hotel on Zicatela beach
★ resembles a gracefully aging, old-fashioned guest house. The rooms are simple yet clean, with firm beds and worn but comfortable furnishings. Some rooms have kitchenettes; most have wide verandas (bring a hammock to hook up), which overlook the surfing beach just beyond. There is a large pool, a third-story video salon, and a second-story restaurant with a wonderful ocean breeze. ⊠ *Calle del Morro s/n, Col. Marinero, Box 105, 71980,* ☎ ℻ *958/2–04–32 or 958/2–14–94. 26 rooms. Restaurant, bar, pool. MC, V.*

Outdoor Activities and Sports

RIVER TRIPS

Behind El Cafecito restaurant on Calle del Morro at Zicatela Beach, **Big Jim's River Trips** (☎ 958/2–10–26) organizes 2½-hour trips down the Colotepec River. A half-hour truck ride takes clients to the drop-off point, and a kayak-paddling guide will accompany you downriver as you float idyllically in a truck inner tube. A minimum of two clients is required, and life jackets are provided. Excursions usually depart at 9:30 AM and 2:30 PM and cost about $25.

WATER SPORTS

You can rent boogie boards and surfboards at **Las Olas** (⊠ Calle del Morro s/n, ☎ No phone) for about $6.50 per day. You must pay a deposit of about $80, which will be refunded at the end of the day unless the equipment is damaged.

Puerto Angel

⑬ *81 km (50 mi) southeast of Puerto Escondido.*

The leading seaport of the state 100 years ago, Puerto Angel today is a dusty village on a beautiful bay that, unfortunately, suffered greatly the devastating wind and rain brought by Hurricane Pauline in the autumn of 1997. Puerto Angel lost 80% of its roofs in the storm, and many trees. There are now plenty of new palapa (palm frond) roofs, but the trees and vegetation will take longer to rejuvenate. Since Puerto Angel has always been rather laid-back and basic, most of what we recommend is functioning at near-previous levels. Wooden structures destroyed by the storm are by and large being redone in concrete.

The central town beach has been taken over by the navy, and the most popular swimming-and-sunning territory is at **Playa Panteón,** just past the oceanfront cemetery (*panteón* means "cemetery"). Other good (and less populated) swimming and snorkeling beaches are nearby. Six kilometers (4 miles) west of town is **Zipolite,** a bay known for its nude sunbathing. It's a favorite with surfers, aging hippies, and travelers content with a hammock on the beach and little else in the way of creature comforts. The undertow is extremely dangerous here—*zipolite* means killer, and more than a few foolishly brave swimmers die in these waters every year.

The **Museum of the Sea Turtle** in Mazunte makes an interesting side trip from Puerto Angel. The popularity of turtle hunting once put the sea creatures, who come to this coastal area to lay eggs each year, in danger of extinction. Mazunte even had its own slaughterhouse for their meat. A 1990 government ban on turtle hunting has for the most part stopped the carnage, and Mazunte is now devoted to protecting the species. A dozen aquariums are filled with turtle specimens that once again flourish in the nearby ocean. From Puerto Angel, take Highway 200 toward San Pedro Pochutla; about 15 km (9 mi) past town, follow the turnoff marked SAN AGUSTÍN. A few kilometers later at the sign for PLAYA MAZUNTE, ask for directions to the "museo," which is on the beach. ⊠ *Playa Mazunte,* ☎ *958/4–30–55,* FAX *959/4–30–63.* ▭ *$2.* ☉ *Tues.–Sat. 10–4:30, Sun. 10–2:30.*

Dining and Lodging

$–$$ ✕▥ **Posada Cañon Devata.** California comes to Puerto Angel in this ecological hideaway carved into a wooded canyon. Simple bungalows on the hill offer private quarters; other rooms and buildings are scattered on the hillsides. At the top, the bar El Cielo (Heaven) is a good gathering place to take in the sunset. Windows have screens, and the only drawback to this tranquil space is that there's no hot water. Boat trips and occasional hatha yoga retreats are available. The cool, palapa-covered restaurant below, open to nonguests (you must reserve ahead for the 7 PM dinner, about $8), is a find for vegetarians. Meals are healthy and creative, and portions are very generous. ⊠ *Past the cemetery, off Blvd. Virgilio Uribe, Apdo. 10, 70902,* ☎ FAX *958/4–30–48. 16 rooms, 6 bungalows. Restaurant, bar. No credit cards. Closed May–June.*

$ ✕▥ **La Buena Vista.** Among its clean, simple accommodations, some have balconies, some have hammocks just outside, but none have hot water. The third-floor restaurant has one of the most dependable kitchens in town, and rooms at the top level of the hotel have a great view as well as the best breeze. There are a lot of steps to negotiate here, and no elevator. ⊠ *Apdo. 48, 70902,* ☎ FAX *958/4–31–04. 21 rooms. No credit cards.*

$ ▥ **La Cabaña de Puerto Angel.** This plain but adequate hotel is the closest to Playa Panteón, ideal if you want to roll right out of bed in the morning and walk on the beach, or have coffee overlooking the sand. Rooms have louvered windows with screens and ceiling fans; some have small, shadeless balconies, but none have closets. It's worth the extra $4 per night to rent the one triple room, which has a fantastic ocean view. There is also a small library of paperback novels and maps of Mexico. ⊠ *Across from Playa Panteón at Calle Pedro Sainz de Barranda s/n, 70902,* ☎ *958/4–31–05 or 958/4–00–26. 23 rooms. No credit cards.*

Bahías de Huatulco

277 km (172 mi) south of Oaxaca City, 111 km (69 mi) east of Puerto Escondido, 48 km (30 mi) east of Puerto Angel

Bahías de Huatulco, whose burgeoning development suffered major setbacks because of the 1994 peso devaluation, is still marching forward toward its completion date sometime after the millennium. Three of its nine bays have been developed to date, a fourth (which was originally designated as an ecological zone) is in the planning stages. There are a total of 36 tropical beaches contained by Huatulco's pristine bays. Because of the fits and starts of its construction, Huatulco has an unfinished look, and this lack of polish makes the area less popular than places like Cancún and Ixtapa. If you have a car at your disposal, you can drive to several bays that so far have not been developed and play Robinson Crusoe to your heart's content.

Another popular option is to tour the bays by boat. Standard four- to eight-hour trips—depending on how many bays you visit—might include a lunch of freshly caught fish (which costs extra). Fishing, diving, and snorkeling tours visit the beaches or reefs most suitable for those activities.

⑭ The Huatulco of the future is most evident at **Bahía Tangolunda,** where the most luxurious hotels are in full swing, and parasailers glide over fleets of sightseeing boats. The site was chosen by developers because of its five beautiful beaches. There is a challenging 18-hole golf course here as well, the Campo de Golf Tangolunda (☎ 958/1–00–59, FAX 958/1–00–37). A small shopping-restaurant center is across from the entrance to the Sheraton, but most of the shopping and dining takes place in the towns of Santa Cruz and La Crucecita, each about 10 minutes from the hotels by taxi, or, for the economy-minded, by buses or cooperative taxis.

⑮ **Bahía Chahué** is the most recently developed bay, and a pleasant place to spend a relaxing beach day. The new beach parking lot makes it accessible, and there are now several moderately priced hotels and restaurants along the beach.

⑯ **Santa Cruz** is on the bay of the same name. Arrange a glass-bottom boat or sightseeing tour, or a fishing trip from the marina here, or spend the day at **Tipsy's** beach club (⊠ Beach at Paseo Mitla, ☎ FAX 958/7–05–76), where you can rent water toys, take waterskiing lessons, or play volleyball. A central zócalo with a wrought-iron gazebo has been built nearby, and tourists and locals mingle in the little plaza, where you can sip a cool drink or cappuccino in the new café.

⑰ **La Crucecita,** just off Highway 200, is the only place in Huatulco that resembles a real Mexican town, with its central plaza and a recently constructed church covered inside with frescoes. Modern buildings with arches and balconies are going up along the streets by the park, and this is becoming *the* place for hanging out at sidewalk cafés and shopping in boutiques. The bus station, tourism office, Bing's ice-cream shop, and long-distance telephone office are here, along with a smattering of smaller, cheaper, and more intimate hotels.

Dining and Lodging

$$$ ✕ **Don Porfirio.** You can dine inside or out on the covered patio in this Tangolunda restaurant. There is a good variety of seafood and international dishes: try the combination shish kebab sautéed in tequila, served on a bed of rice with steamed veggies and potato. Fajitas are served with rice, beans, guacamole, and tortillas. There is no air-conditioning, and the outdoor patio is loud with street noise, but the food and service are good. ⊠ *Zona Hotelera Tangolunda, across from Hotel Maeva, Bahía Tangolunda,* ☎ *958/1–00–01. AE, MC, V.*

$$ ✕ **Restaurant de Doña Celia.** Although the official name of this long-★ time favorite beachfront restaurant is Avalos, everyone knows it by the owner's name: Doña Celia. Even Presidente Zedillo has stopped by for a seafood feast. Make your selection from the large menu, and prepare for large portions as well. Tables face the sand and sea at Santa Cruz Bay, just beyond the marina. ⊠ *Bahía Santa Cruz,* ☎ *958/7–01–28. No credit cards.*

$$ ✕ **Restaurante María Sabina.** Strangely named for a Oaxaca medicine woman immortalized for her use of "magic" (hallucinogenic) mushrooms, this is a great place from which to watch locals and tourists mingle in La Crucecita's pretty plaza. Grill orders are prepared on the outdoor *parrilla* (grill) and served with grilled onion, baked potato, and sour cream. A favorite plate is *Reboso María Sabina* (steak with melted cheese, guacamole, and fresh salsa). There are also five spaghetti dishes. ⊠ *Calle Flamboyan, west side of plaza, La Crucecita,* ☎ *958/7–02–19. MC, V. No breakfast.*

$$$$ ✕🖭 **Sheraton.** Now offering all-inclusive as well as standard room rates, ★ the Sheraton is the most user-friendly of the upscale hotels on Bahía Tangolunda. The rooms have bathtubs—a real luxury in these parts. Water sports and equipment—including kayaks, windsurfers, sailboats, and catamarans (all-inclusive guests have free use of these)— are considered top notch, and dive masters are on hand with dive equipment (☞ Outdoor Activities and Sports, *below*). The Casa Real restaurant, which is closed off season, still has the most glamorous dining in Huatulco. The menu emphasizes northern Italian dishes and there are elaborate floral arrangements and flickering candles set out at night. ⊠ *Bahía Tangolunda, Blvd. Benito Juárez, Bahías de Huatulco 70989,* ☎ *958/1–00–55; 800/325–3535 in the U.S.,* 🅵🅰🆇 *958/1–01–13. 347 rooms, 8 suites. 3 restaurants, 3 bars, 2 pools, wading pool, massage, sauna, 4 tennis courts, exercise room, beach, boating, shops, travel services. AE, DC, MC, V.*

$$$$ 🖭 **Camino Real Zaashila.** Previously of the Omni chain, this contemporary stucco Mexican-cum-Mediterranean palace overlooks a secluded lagoon with its own private beach. The resort has 27 landscaped acres of gardens, fountains, and waterfalls. Ten luxurious suites and 41 rooms have small private pools. The rates are high, and unlike those at most of the other high-end properties, they aren't all-inclusive. ⊠ *Blvd. Benito Juárez 5, Bahía Tangolunda, Bahías de Huatulco 70989,* ☎ *958/1–04–60,* 🅵🅰🆇 *958/1–04–61. 120 rooms, 10 suites. 3 restaurants, 2 bars, in-room safes, minibars, 2 pools, wading pool, tennis court, exercise room, baby-sitting, travel services. AE, MC, V.*

$$$$ 🖭 **Quinta Real.** Opened in 1997, this hilltop resort takes Huatulco lux-★ ury to new and exclusive heights. A combination of Moorish domes and thatched palapas, the property's 27 tranquil suites are airy and plush, each with creamy white leather furnishings, exquisite Guatemalan tapestries, a Jacuzzi, terrace, and spectacular ocean views. Nine suites have private pools, and a few are equipped with telescopes for dolphin-

and star-gazing. ⊠ *Bahía Tangolunda, Blvd. Benito Juárez 2, Bahías de Huatulco 70989,* ☎ *958/1–04–28,* FAX *958/1–04–29. 27 suites. 2 restaurants, bar, in-room safes, minibars, 2 pools, wading pool, tennis court, beach, baby-sitting, laundry service. AE, DC, MC, V.*

$$$–$$$$ 🏨 **Club Med.** This club's nearly 500 rooms cut a pastel swath on a hillside overlooking Bahía Tangolunda. There are three beaches, and an endless list of amenities. Weeklong fitness programs are particularly popular. Although some guests are content to never leave the grounds, coastal excursions and tours to Oaxaca City are offered. Packages with airfare included are usually available. This is one of the area's least expensive all-inclusives. Advance booking is mandatory. ⊠ *Bahía Tangolunda, 70900,* ☎ *958/1–00–33; 800/258–2633 in the U.S.,* FAX *958/ 1–01–01 or 958/1–01–56. Reservations:* ⊠ *40 W. 57th St., New York, NY 10019. 483 rooms. 4 restaurants, 3 bars, in-room safes, 4 pools, 11 tennis courts, exercise room, beach, dance club, children's programs (ages 4–17), playground. AE, MC, V.*

$$$–$$$$ 🏨 **Royal Maeva.** This all-inclusive resort caters to charter groups and Mexican families as well as lone travelers. The emphasis is on fun, fun, fun—and if you're not a fan of loud music, stay in a room that's away from the pool area. The rooms are spacious, colorful, and adorned with heavy pastel fabrics and light wooden furniture. Considering that the price per person includes all food, drinks, and access to most water and gym sports, this is a good deal if you want to do more than just work on your tan. ⊠ *Bahía Tangolunda, Blvd. Benito Juárez 227, Bahías de Huatulco 70989,* ☎ *958/1–00–00; 800/466–2382 in the U.S.,* FAX *958/1–02–20. 178 rooms, 12 suites. 4 restaurants, 7 bars, in-room safes, 4 pools, 3 tennis courts, exercise room, beach, dance club, baby-sitting, children's programs (ages 4–15), car rental. AE, DC, MC, V.*

$$–$$$ 🏨 **Posada Flamboyant.** This is the classiest option if you want to stay in the town of La Crucecita, about a five-minute cab ride from Bahía Tangolunda. The ivy-covered, four-story edifice has a vaguely European feel. All rooms have firm beds, cable TVs, and telephones, and both the pool and surrounding area are large and inviting. Four comfortable two-bedroom, two-bath suites with well-furnished living rooms and kitchens are available for $100–$200 (depending on the season) for up to six people. ⊠ *Calle Gardenia esq. Tamarindo, Bahías de Huatulco 70989,* ☎ *958/7-01-13 or 958/7–01–05,* FAX *958/7-01-21. 66 rooms, 4 suites. Restaurant, bar, coffee shop, pool, wading pool, baby-sitting, playground, travel services. AE, MC, V.*

$$ 🏨 **Marina Resort Huatulco.** This all-suites resort overlooks the marina on Santa Cruz Bay, has plenty of amenities, and is close to rental boats and the marina. Each comfortable suite's ample living area contains a small dining table, cable TV, and kitchenette. Upper-floor rooms have the best bay views; all rooms have bathtubs. There's also a disco and a beach club with water sports and a playground. ⊠ *Calle Tehunatepec 112, Santa Cruz Bay, Huatulco 70989,* ☎ *958/7–09–63,* FAX *958/ 7–08–30. 47 suites. Restaurant, 2 bars, kitchenettes, 2 pools, wading pool, dance club, playground. AE, MC, V.*

$ 🏨 **Hotel Begonias.** Catercorner from the plaza in La Crucecita, this sweet, simple hotel has colonial-style furnishings, ceiling fans, comfortable beds, and color TVs. The hotel's popular ground floor restaurant, Oasis, serves an extensive menu of Oaxacan and Japanese dishes. ⊠ *Calle Bugambilia 503, La Crucecita 70989,* ☎ *958/7-00-18,* FAX *958/ 7–13–90. 9 rooms, 3 suites. Restaurant, bar. AE, MC, V.*

$ 🏨 **Hotel Las Palmas.** Plain but acceptable furnishings and rock-bottom prices (for Huatulco) are what you'll find at this small second-story hotel just a block from the plaza in La Crucecita. The cramped rooms have TVs, hot water, and both fans and air-conditioning; the hotel is currently being enlarged. ⊠ *Calle Guamuchil 206, La Crucecita*

70989, ☎ 958/7–00–60, FAX 958/7–00–57. *8 rooms. Restaurant, bar. AE, MC, V.*

Outdoor Activities and Sports

BICYCLING

You can rent mountain bikes from **Motor Tours Huatulco** (☞ Guided Tours *in* Oaxaca Coast A to Z, *below*) or **Rent-a-Bike**(✉ Calle Flamboyant esq. Bugambilias, La Crucecita, ☎ 958/7–06–69) for guided or unguided tours.

FISHING

Sportfishing for sailfish, tuna, dorado, and other fish can be arranged through **Sociedad Cooperative Tangolunda,** the boat-owners cooperative at the marina on Santa Cruz Bay (☎ 958/7–00–81), **Hotel Begonias** (☞ Dining and Lodging, *above*), or **Cantera Tours,** at the Sheraton Hotel in Tangolunda(☎ FAX 958/1–00–30).

WATER SPORTS

The PADI-certified dive masters at **Action Sports Marina** at the Sheraton are among the most reliable in Huatulco. Certification courses are offered, as are dive trips ($50 for one tank, $70 for two) and 1½-hour snorkeling trips ($20). ✉ *Paseo Benito Juárez s/n, at Sheraton Hotel,* ☎ *958/1–00–55 ext. 842,* FAX *958/1–01–13.*

Shopping

Although Huatulco isn't exactly a shopper's paradise, there are several places worth mentioning. In La Crucecita, **Paradise** boutique (✉ Calle Gardenia esq. Guarumbo, ☎ 958/7–02–68), open seven days a week, has an excellent selection of casual yet stylish beach and resort wear, much of which comes from Bali and India. The batik and hand-painted T-shirts make great gifts, as do the Mexican crafts, including silver jewelry, coconut masks from Guerrero, and black pottery.

The **Museo de Artesanías Oaxaqueñas** (✉ Calle Flamboyan 216, La Crucecita, ☎ 958/7–15–13) is really a store, not a museum, but the artisans who create the fanciful wooden alebrijes, the woven tablecloths, typical pottery, painted tinware, and rugs from throughout the state are on hand to demonstrate how they make their traditional crafts. It's every day; avoid going at lunchtime, when the artisans take a break. Another fun place to shop is La Crucecita's **Mercado Municipal** (municipal market; ✉ Calle Guanacaste con Bugambilias, ☎ No phone), where in addition to leather sandals, postcards, and other tourist items, you'll see mountains of fresh fruits and vegetables.

OAXACA COAST A TO Z

Arriving and Departing

By Bus

Cristóbal Colón (✉ Booking office: Calle 20 de Noviembre 204A, ☎ 9/51–46655) has three first-class buses per day leaving from Oaxaca's first-class bus terminal, frequently referred to as the **ADO** (✉ Calzada Niños Héroes 1036, ☎ 9/51–51703), to Huatulco (7½ hours; $14). The same bus continues on to Puerto Escondido (9 hours; $16). There are several first-class buses each day to Pochutla (6½ hours; $15), where you can connect to Puerto Angel, but none is direct. Buses return to Oaxaca City from the **Huatulco bus station** (✉ Calle Gardenias esq. Ocotillo, La Crucecita, ☎ 958/7–02–61) and the **Puerto Escondido bus station** (✉ Calle Primera Nte. 201, ☎ 958/2–10–73).

Estrella del Valle's first-class buses run at night; daytime *ordinario* buses make many stops and are not recommended. Buses leave from the second-class station (✉ Corner of Trujano and the Periférico, ☎ 9/51–45700 or 9/51–65429) for Huatulco and Puerto Escondido ($8). The **Huatulco station** is in La Crucecita (✉ Calle Jazmin s/n, behind Corona beer warehouse, ☎ 958/7–01–93). There is also a **Puerto Escondido station** (✉ Avenida Hidalgo at Calle 3a Oriente, ☎ 958/2–00–50 or 958/2–09–53).

Direct service between Oaxaca City and Puerto Escondido is available on **Autotransportes Turísticos.** Buses leave from Oaxaca City (✉ Calle Armenta y López 721, ☎ 9/51–40806) and Puerto Escondido (✉ Av. Hidalgo between 16 de Septiembre and 4a Nte., ☎ 958/2–09–53 or 958/2–00–50) twice a day.

By Car

The drive from Oaxaca City to the isthmus on Highway 190 is challenging, with plenty of curves and hairpin turns. Highway 175 is another twisting mountain road. The recently inaugurated Highway 131, to Puerto Escondidovia Sola de Vega, is an obstacle course of potholes. Do not attempt these roads at night. Plan on taking about eight hours, and leave early enough to arrive before dark. At the coast, Highway 200 links Huatulco, Puerto Angel, and Puerto Escondido. If you want to tool around the various beaches, a car is useful.

By Plane

Aero Vega (☎ 958/2–01–51) has daily service to **Puerto Escondido** from Oaxaca's International Airport. Mexicana subsidiary **AeroCaribe** (☎ 958/2–20–24 Puerto Escondido; 958/7–12–20 Huatulco) connects **Puerto Escondido** and Oaxaca City five times a week, with daily connections to **Huatulco. Mexicana** (☎ 958/7–02–43 or 958/7–02–23 in Huatulco) flies to **Huatulco** from Mexico City, Guadalajara, Cancún, Monterrey, and several other Mexican and U.S. gateways, all with connections in Mexico City.

FROM THE AIRPORT TO TOWN
Aeropuerto Puerto Escondido (✉ Km 3 Carretera Costera, or Coast Hwy., ☎ 958/2–04–92 or 958/2–04–91) is a 10-minute taxi ride from town on Highway 200. **Aeropuerto Bahías de Huatulco** (☎ 958/1–90–08) is about 16 km (10 mi) from town on Highway 200.

Getting Around

By Bus

Frequent, inexpensive second-class buses connect Puerto Escondido, Puerto Angel, and Huatulco, but you must stop at Pochutla, just off the highway near Puerto Angel. These buses roar down the highway every 15 minutes or so, and each costs about $1.25. If you are going to Huatulco, be sure to specify that your final destination is the bus terminal in La Crucecita, which is closest to the bays.

By Car

Highway 200 from Puerto Escondido to Huatulco should be relatively hassle-free, if potholed. Having a car allows you to turn off the main road onto unmarked dirt roads leading to secluded beaches.

Contacts and Resources

Car Rental

Cars can be rented at the Huatulco airport, in Puerto Escondido, and in the Huatulco Bays area. International firms include **Budget** (☎ 958/2–03–12) in Puerto Escondido, **National** (✉ Hotel Club Plaza Huatulco, ☎ 958/1-02-93) in Tangolunda, and **Dollar** (✉ Sheraton Hotel, ☎ 958/1–00–55 ext. 787, in Huatulco; ☎ 958/1–90–04, airport).

Rental cars are expensive, starting at $45 per day for a Volkswagen Beetle, for example, and there is an additional drop-off fee if you don't return the car where you picked it up. Nonaffiliated local firms often quote lower rates, but their vehicles may be in questionable condition.

Emergencies

For all **emergencies** including police and hospital, dial ☎ 06 locally.

Guided Tours

In Puerto Escondido the most exciting tours are run by ornithologist Michael Malone, who offers dawn and sunset excursions (December–April) into the Manialtepec Lagoon, a prime bird-watching area. Arrange tours (about $35 per person) through your hotel or through **Turismo Rodimar** (⊠ Av. Gasga 905–B, ☎ 958/2–07–34, ℻ 958/2–07–37), the most reliable and comprehensive agency in town.

Bahías Plus, with offices in La Crucecita (⊠ Calle Carrizal at Calle Guanacastel, ☎ 958/7–02–16 or 958/7–09–32), is one of the most comprehensive travel agencies in Huatulco and has tours to Puerto Angel and Puerto Escondido (van tours start at a bit less than $20 per person in a group of six), as well as plane tours to Oaxaca ($337 per person). Most major hotels also have travel agencies.

Daylong tours into the Sierra Madre are available with the bilingual guides of **Motor Tours Huatulco.** One of their tours includes a visit to a working coffee plantation, with elaborate lunch. The cost is approximately $110 to be divided between one to three people. This agency also does horse, ATV, and mountain-bike treks. ⊠ *Av. Juárez s/n, Local 9, across from the Sheraton,* ☎ *958/1–03–23.*

Cantera Tours (⊠ Sheraton Hotel, ☎ ℻ 958/1–00–30) has all-day bay cruises for $22–$30 a person, excluding food. They also have four-hour horse or ATV tours, beginning inland and ending at the beach, for about $38 per person. You can also arrange bay trips through the **Sociedad Cooperative Tangolunda,** a boat-owners' cooperative at the marina on Santa Cruz Bay (☎ 958/7–00–81).

Visitor Information

Puerto Escondido tourism office (⊠ Blvd. Benito Juárez, about a block from Aldea del Bazar Hotel at Playa Bacocho development, ☎ 958/2–01–75 or 958/2–05–37) is open weekdays 9–3, Saturday 10–2. The small **information desk** (☎ No phone) at the north end of the pedestrian walkway is even more helpful than the main tourism office. It's usually open weekdays 10–3, Saturday 10–1.

Oficina Estatal de Turismo (Huatulco state tourism office; ⊠ Plaza San Miguel, Blvd. Santa Cruz at Calle Monte Albán, Bahía Tangolunda, ☎ 958/7–15–42, ℻ 958/7–15–41) is open weekdays 9–3.

11 CHIAPAS AND TABASCO

The state of Chiapas is considered by many to be the most fascinating in Mexico. It is a study in contrasts, with the luxuriant tropical lowlands around Palenque—one of the country's most brilliant Maya ruins—giving way to gorgeous valleys and finally the highlands, home to many of Mexico's most traditional indigenous peoples.

K **NOWN TO MANY** foreigners only for the ruins of Palenque and the colonial town of San Cristóbal de las Casas, Chiapas and Tabasco have typically drawn trekkers and travelers rather than tourists. World attention was drawn to Chiapas in early 1994 because of indigenous uprisings, but as peace negotiations slowly progress (some would say "stall"), it is once again receding in public consciousness. If you're looking for an outstanding travel experience, a well-planned trip to this area can be very satisfying, particularly if you come during a local festival. Unlike the country's popular beach resorts, Chiapas and Tabasco aren't an easy flight a few hours from major U.S. cities. Substantial ground transportation, either by bus or car, is usually required, although Tuxtla Gutiérrez and Villahermosa have international airports, and Palenque and San Cristóbal de las Casas have national airports with limited routes. Tourist information can be more difficult to obtain in Tabasco than in Chiapas.

Updated by
Jane Onstott

A bloody past of exploitation by and fierce confrontation with outsiders remains vividly present, as already impoverished indigenous communities in Chiapas are forced to compete for their lands with developers and new settlers. Because of its isolation, Chiapas has been at the margin of the nation's development. It is one of the poorest states in Mexico, with appallingly high rates of alcoholism, violence, illiteracy, and death due to unhygienic conditions. Land distribution, too, is skewed: 1% of landowners hold 15% of the territory—about 50% of the arable land—keeping the colonial system nearly intact, and repression is rampant. It was the indifference of the Mexican government to their plight that helped bring the anger of the indigenous people to a boil in early 1994, leading the group calling themselves the Zapatista National Liberation Army (EZLN is the Spanish acronym) to an armed uprising. The purported willingness of the government to negotiate with the rebels—and international interest in their plight—bodes well for the possibility of change in the region. The pipe-smoking Zapatista spokesman, Subcomandante Marcos, has become a cult figure in Mexico, his ski-masked image appearing on everything from magazine covers to children's toys, and he puts his poetic communiqués on the Internet for worldwide consumption.

Nominally enriched half a century ago with the discovery of oil in the Gulf of Mexico on its northern border, Tabasco also has a bloody past. During the 1920s and 1930s, Tomás Garrido Canabal, a vehemently anticlerical governor, outlawed priests and had all the churches either torn down or converted to other uses. Riots, deportations, and property confiscations were common. When British writer Graham Greene visited Tabasco in 1938, he called it "the Godless state"; his novel *The Power and the Glory* grew out of his experience. All of that said, you won't find much evidence of Tabasco's turbulent past today. A wholly different spirit prevails here than in Chiapas,

Although the Mexican economic crisis will delay some plans for building more tourism infrastructure, Chiapas is getting an extra boost from a government promotion program. It is an important segment of the Mundo Maya travel circuit created by the Mexican government in the early 1990s to showcase its splendid Maya ruins and colonial cities in the name of regional development and ecotourism. Development in the past has been a two-edged sword. The Lacandon jungle is already disappearing, its Maya inhabitants being driven to live in a smaller portion of their ancestral lands. Massive erosion and deforestation are taking their toll as new settlers burn the forest and exhaust the soil by raising cattle.

For the present, however, when you set out along tortuous mountain roads—full of dramatic hairpin turns along the edges of mist-filled ravines—you will still find remote clusters of huts and cornfields planted on near-vertical hillsides. You will pass Indian women wrapped in deep blue shawls and coarsely woven wool skirts, and Indian children selling fruit and flowers by the roadside. Chiapas has nine distinct linguistic groups, primarily the highland-dwelling Tzotzils and the Tzeltals, who live in both highland and lowland areas. In more isolated regions, many villagers speak only their native language, or a rudimentary Spanish necessary for interaction with the outside world.

Business travelers make up the majority of those who visit Villahermosa, Tabasco's capital, but the city also has a superb museum of pre-Columbian archaeology at the CICOM complex and a collection of massive Olmec heads and altars at Parque Museo La Venta. Both provide a good introduction to the Indian heritage of Tabasco and Chiapas. Palenque, with its incredible Maya ruins, is culturally and geographically linked with the lowlands in Tabasco. If you want to get into the great outdoors, there are lakes, lagoons, caves, and wild rivers surging through the jungle.

Note: Although travel in the area is reasonably safe, at press time there exists a U.S. State Department traveler's advisory for Chiapas because of recent confrontations between Zapatistas and government troops. Although these skirmishes are not near the main tourist destinations, and may have been resolved by the time you visit, contact the State Department or any of the Mexican Government Tourist Offices in the United States before you go for the current status. Carry your visa and passport even on day trips throughout the region, as there are numerous military checkpoints along both main and secondary roads.

Pleasures and Pastimes

Archaeological Sites
Ruins of Maya cities in mysterious, overgrown jungles are a big draw in this area. Unparalleled Palenque has the most appeal, and the lesser known sites of Toniná, Bonampak, and Yaxchilán (pronounced yash-chee-*lan*) are attracting more attention than ever.

Dining
Chiapas has regional specialties but borrows heavily from Yucatán and Oaxaca. Culinary adventurers should try *atole* (a cornmeal drink), tamales, locally smoked ham, candied fruit, and any dishes that contain the tasty Mexican herbs *chipilín* and *yerba santa* (or *mumu,* as locals call it). San Cristóbal's restaurants have an ample choice of Mexican and international cuisines, and lately most of them have added vegetarian dishes to their menus. Although they can be rated the best in the state, they're not outstanding compared to those in other regions of Mexico.

Prices, however, are quite reasonable: a filling dinner (helped out by tortillas in one of their myriad forms) with beer rarely costs more than $10 per person. There is no dress code to speak of in this part of Mexico, and no reservations are necessary. San Cristóbal closes down early, so unlike in other parts of Mexico, it is a fairly common practice to eat dinner before 8 PM. As is the case throughout Mexico, lunch is the main meal of the day, served between 1 and 4 PM.

Tabasco saves some of its export beef for the Villahermosa restaurants, which also serve lots of fresh fish from the Gulf and freshwater lakes and rivers. Local specialties—or oddities, if you wish—include *peje-lagarto,* an ancient fish with the head of an alligator and a strong, sweet flavor. Also try *puchero,* beef stew with vegetables and plantains; river shrimp; *tostones* (fried plantain chips); baked bananas with cream; banana liqueur; and the region's fresh, white cheese.

Generally speaking, the food served in Palenque town is modest in both quality and price. Many restaurants are open-air, which is where you want to be in this hot, humid part of Mexico. You'll spend more in the higher priced hotels; most moderate and inexpensive restaurants do not bother to charge sales tax.

CATEGORY	COST*
$$$$	over $15
$$$	$10–$15
$$	$5–$10
$	under $5

per person for a three-course meal, excluding drinks, service, and 15% sales tax

Lodging

Almost all the hotels in **San Cristóbal** are within walking distance of the major attractions. Most of those listed are colonial—historically and architecturally—in keeping with the rest of the town. All rooms, unless otherwise stated, have showers; air-conditioning is not necessary at this high altitude and, in fact, fireplaces are welcome.

Tuxtla Gutiérrez lodgings tend to be more functional than frilly—this town is the no-nonsense business and transportation hub of Chiapas. An exception to the rule is the Camino Real, which resembles a small palace perched on a hilltop.

Palenque is no longer the jungle outpost that it used to be, fit only for souls who considered rustic amenities colorful or liked "going native." This is a growing tropical town with modern, comfortable hotels. The best and newest are strung along the Palenque–Pakalná highway that goes to the Palenque ruins just outside town. Geared for groups as well as individuals, these hotels have lush gardens, inviting pools, and air-conditioning or ceiling fans. Quite a few new posadas have sprung up downtown in the last couple of years, and there are a couple of agreeable hotels and restaurants in the quiet neighborhood of La Cañada, between the downtown area and the highway.

Villahermosa hotels are relatively expensive, especially when compared with those in San Cristóbal. Fancy four- and five-star hotels geared to business travelers tend to be away from the city center, near Tabasco 2000 and Parque La Venta, but there are comfortable and economical hotels downtown, near the Grijalva river, or in the nearby, pedestrian-friendly Zona Luz (Light Zone), or Zona Remodelada (Remodeled Zone).

Many hotels (especially budget and moderate lodgings) quote prices that already include the hefty 15%–17% tax, which varies from county to county; others do not. Make sure to inquire about this when comparing hotel prices.

CATEGORY	COST*
$$$$	over $90
$$$	$60–$90
$$	$27–$60
$	under $27

All prices are for a standard double room, excluding tax (15%–17%).

Shopping

The artisans of Chiapas, especially in and around San Cristóbal, produce some of the most striking indigenous folk art of Mexico. Best are the embroidered blouses, *huipiles* (tunics), bedspreads, and table-cloths—finely woven or stitched with native designs—and leather goods, such as belts and purses. Lacandon bows and arrows and the beribboned ceremonial hats worn by local officials also make good souvenirs.

Chiapas is one of the few places in the world that has amber mines, so finely crafted jewelry made from this prehistoric resin is easy to find in San Cristóbal—as are plastic imitations sold by street vendors (stores usually sell amber and street vendors commonly have the fakes, although there is some crossover). San Cristóbal is also known for the quality wrought-iron crosses that bless its rooftops. Although many of the iron-working shops have closed, you can still find the crosses in crafts stores.

Tuxtla Gutiérrez and Palenque, although not known for handicrafts, have a few shops selling quality crafts from throughout the state.

Exploring Chiapas and Tabasco

Where Tabasco is lush, green, and pastoral, the abode of the ancient Olmecs who gave Mexico its mother culture, Chiapas is for the most part mountainous, its Maya ruins and villages isolated from modern Mexico by sinuous roads and footpaths. The colonial city of San Cristóbal once dominated both regions when the Spanish conquistadores held sway over the country. Modern Villahermosa now is the economic force in the two regions because of the petroleum industry. Tropical Palenque has more in common geographically and culturally with Tabasco than with the mountainous regions in Chiapas state, to which it belongs.

The highlights of a trip to Chiapas and Tabasco are still the ruins of Palenque and the colonial town of San Cristóbal de las Casas. These and all other major sights are accessible by road from either Tuxtla Gutiérrez or Villahermosa, the only cities with international airports. The once isolated ruins of Yaxchilán and Bonampak are now more accessible—by paved roads or via bush planes that fly from the two internationally connected cities as well as from Palenque, Ocosingo, and Comitán. Both Palenque and San Cristóbal de las Casas have small new airports that land small-bodied jets on a limited basis. If you're a first-time visitor, and especially if you don't speak Spanish, it's faster, more efficient, and more comfortable to take tours to the area's major attractions. But if you prefer to rent a car, driving directions are included in our listings of sights.

Numbers in the text correspond to numbers in the margin and on the Chiapas and Tabasco and San Cristóbal de las Casas maps.

Great Itineraries

The farther you wander into the region, the more you'll be fascinated with its natural diversity and its remnants of Maya and Spanish colonial cultures. A three-day trip gives only a superficial glance at what the region has to offer, but it will afford you the opportunity to visit Palenque and San Cristóbal de las Casas, two of Mexico's outstanding attractions. Stays of five to eight or more days will allow you to cover greater distances and get to the lesser-known wonders of Chiapas and Tabasco.

IF YOU HAVE 3 DAYS

Spend the first day and night at the Maya ruins at **Palenque** ㉒, and consider going the proverbial extra mile on a side trip to the lovely jungle waterfalls at **Misol-Há** ㉑ and **Agua Azul** ⑳. Tours from Palenque are the best way to pack it all into one day. The next day drive south

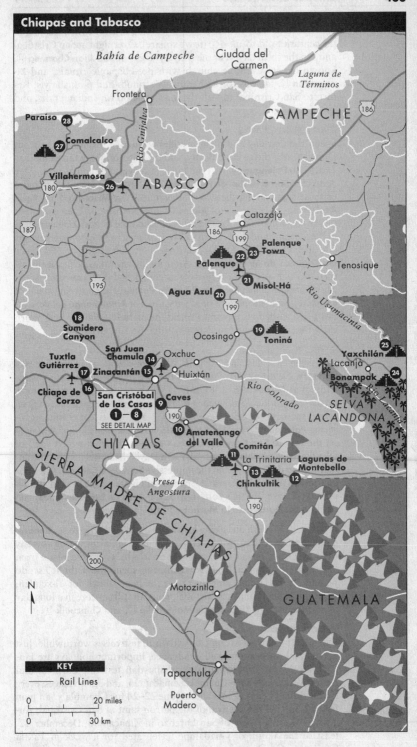

Chiapas and Tabasco

to colonial **San Cristóbal de las Casas** ①–⑧, the oldest city in Chiapas. Spend at least two hours on a walking tour of town, starting at the centuries-old *zócalo*d ① (town square). Overnight at San Cristóbal and, on the third day, visit the Maya villages of **San Juan Chamula** ⑭, known for its Catholic church with pre-Hispanic rituals, and **Zinacantán** ⑮, famous for its handwoven tunics and pink shawls. Return to San Cristóbal to visit the market, shop for Indian crafts, and spend the night.

IF YOU HAVE 5 DAYS

Spend the first day and night in **Villahermosa** ㉖, exploring the giant Olmec heads, the river walkway, and the anthropology museum. Day 2, drive to **Palenque** ㉒, visit the ruins, and overnight in Palenque. Day 3, drive to **San Cristóbal de Las Casas** ①–⑧, stopping off at two or more of these sights along the way: the waterfalls at **Misol-Há** ㉑ or **Agua Azul** ⑳, or the Maya site of **Toniná** ⑲, near Ocosingo. Then overnight in San Cristóbal. Day 4, see **San Juan Chamula** ⑭ and **Zinacantán** ⑮ in the morning and then return to San Cristóbal to shop for native crafts and spend the night. On Day 5, drive south on Highway 190 to see **Las Lagunas de Montebello** ⑫. After seeing the lakes, visit on the return trip as many of the following as your schedule permits: the small Maya sites of **Chincultik** ⑬ and **Tenam Puente**; the charming town of **Comitán** ⑪; and the pottery-producing town of **Amatenango del Valle** ⑩. For a less rushed visit, plan to spend the night in Comitán and return early the next morning for San Cristóbal or Tuxtla.

IF YOU HAVE 8 DAYS

Spend the first day and night in **Villahermosa** ㉖, as in the five-day itinerary. Next day, drive north of the city to visit the unusual Maya temples at **Comalcalco** ㉗. Return to Villahermosa for a dinner cruise on the *Capítan Buelo* along the Grijalva River and overnight here again. Spend the next four days as on Days 2–5 of the five-day itinerary—seeing **Palenque** ㉒, and then **Misol-Há** ㉑, **Agua Azul** ⑳, and **Toniná** ⑲ on the way to **San Cristóbal de Las Casas** ①–⑧, from which you can take day trips north and southeast. On Day 7, head west, touring colonial **Chiapa de Corzo** ⑯ and the impressive **Sumidero Canyon** ⑱ by boat en route to **Tuxtla Gutiérrez** ⑰. Spend that night and the next in Tuxtla. On Day 8, visit Tuxtla's zoo, shop at the **Casa de las Artesanías,** and stroll in the **Parque de la Marimba** in the late afternoon.

If you want to go all out seeing Maya sites, add a day trip to see **Bonampak** ㉔ and **Yaxchilán** ㉕—which you can take in during a long one-day road trip from Palenque or a six-hour trip by chartered plane from Palenque or Comitán. You can arrange to spend the night at Escudo Jaguar, on the Usamacinta river near the boat launch for Yaxchilán, or in Palenque. From San Cristóbal, you can still squeeze in a long day trip to **Comitán** ⑪, **Lagunas de Montebello** ⑫, and **Chincultik** ⑬.

When to Tour

Scheduling your visit to coincide with local festivals is worthwhile. Just make hotel reservations well in advance. Important holidays are January 20–22 for Zinacantán's San Sebastian festival; Carnival and Easter Week in San Juan Chamula, Zinacantán, and other villages; every Friday during Lent in Zinacantán; June 22–24 for Chamula's San Juan festival; July 24–25, festival of the patron saint of San Cristóbal; August 9–10, celebration of San Lorenzo in Zinacantán; December 12, feast of the Virgin of Guadalupe (celebrated for a week in Tuxtla Gutiérrez). On December 31 in several indigenous highland villages, there are celebrations to install new civil officials. Remember that it's beastly hot in the lowlands most of the year, but especially just prior to the rainy season, February–April.

SAN CRISTÓBAL DE LAS CASAS

San Cristóbal, the most touristic city of the Chiapas highlands, is a pretty town of about 150,000 in a valley of pine forests interspersed with maize fields and orchards. At an altitude of 6,888 ft above sea level, indigenous women with babies tied tightly in colorful shawls share the plaza with backpackers wearing Day-Glo day packs. More Europeans than Americans visit San Cristóbal—perhaps they are less put off by headlines about government troops and the EZLN (Zapatista National Liberation Army), or more intrigued by the political ramifications. In truth, the rival sides are more likely to snipe at each other during their rare trips to the negotiating table, or via newspaper editorials or the Internet, than in hostile confrontations.

San Cristóbal is beautiful and inexpensive, and it makes the perfect hub for exploring some of the region's lakes, villages, and archaeological sites. Small enough to take in on foot in the course of a day, the town is also captivating enough to invite a stay of three days, a week, or even longer. In addition to viewing colonial monuments, consider planning an early morning visit to see local Indians gather at the *mercado* (market) and browse for crafts, or explore one of the indigenous villages in the vicinity. Sunday is the best day for visiting village markets. Just soaking up the ambience in one of San Cristóbal's little cafés or unpretentious restaurants is a pleasure.

San Cristóbal is among the finest colonial towns in Mexico, and its cool climate is a refreshing change from the sweltering heat of the lower altitudes. On chilly evenings, smoke from chimney fires curls lazily over the red-tile roofs of small, brightly painted stucco houses and elegant colonial mansions. The haunting atmosphere of the place is intensified by the remarkable quality of the early morning and late-afternoon light.

In 1524 the Spaniards under Diego de Mazariegos decisively defeated the Chiapan Indians at a battle outside town. Mazariegos founded the city, which was called Villareal de Chiapa de los Españoles, in 1528. For most of the viceroyalty, or colonial era, Chiapas, with its capital at San Cristóbal, was a province of Guatemala. Lacking the gold and silver of the north, it was of greater strategic than economic importance to the Spaniards. Under Spanish rule the region's agricultural resources became entrenched in the *encomienda* system, in which wealthy Spanish landowners forced natives to work as slaves. "In this life all men suffer," lamented a Spanish friar in 1691, "but the Indians suffer most of all."

The situation improved only slightly through the efforts of Bartolomé de las Casas, the bishop of San Cristóbal who in the mid-1500s protested the torture and massacre of the Indians. The Indians protested in another way, murdering priests and other *ladinos* (whites) in infamous uprisings.

Mexico, Guatemala, and the rest of New Spain declared independence in 1821. For just two years, Chiapas remained part of Guatemala, electing by plebescite to join Mexico on September 14, 1824—the date is still celebrated in San Cristóbal and all over Chiapas as the *día dè la mexicanidad* (Dày of Mexicanization) of Chiapas. In 1892, because of San Cristóbal's allegiance to the Royalists during the War of Independence, the capital was moved to Tuxtla Gutiérrez. With that went all hope that the town would keep pace with the rest of Mexico. It was not until the 1950s that the roads into town were paved and the first automobiles arrived. Modern times came late to San Cristóbal, for which many locals and visitors are thankful.

Because of the altitude, it gets quite cold here at night, and can be chilly during the day as well: pack a warm sweater and plan to layer your clothing. When the sun does appear, it can get quite hot, but most restaurants keep doors open even during cold weather, and hotels are for the most part unheated. The cobblestone and flagstone streets are also best suited to wearing tennis shoes, hiking boots, or other flat-heeled sports shoes.

Exploring San Cristóbal de las Casas

San Cristóbal is laid out in a grid pattern centered on the **zócalo,** with street names changing on either side of the square. For example, Calle Francisco Madero to the east of the square becomes Diego de Mazariegos to the west.

The town was originally divided into several **barrios** (neighborhoods), which now blend together into a city center that is easily negotiated. In colonial times, Indian allies of the triumphant Spaniards were moved onto lands on the outskirts of the nascent city. Each barrio was dedicated to a different occupation. There were Mexican weavers, Tlaxcala fireworks manufacturers, and pig butchers from Cuxtitali. Although these divisions no longer exist, other customs have been kept alive. For example, each Saturday certain houses downtown will put out red lamps to indicate that fresh homemade tamales are for sale.

A Good Walk

Head for the heart of downtown, the Plaza 31 de Marzo, or **zócalo** ① and take in the colonial buildings around the square, many of them homes of the Spanish conquistadores. Note the 16th-century **Casa de Diego de Mazariegos** ② on its southeast corner (now the Hotel Santa Clara). Continue in a northwesterly direction around the square to the neoclassical **Palacio Municipal** ③—which gets painted a different color according to the whim of each new governor—with its numerous arcades. **La Catedral** ④ (cathedral), on the north side of the zócalo, has a fascinating facade painted ochre with details in rust, black, and white. Continue north five blocks along Avenida General Utrilla to the 16th-century **Templo de Santo Domingo** ⑤ with its ornamental baroque facade; walk around the complex to its museum and famous textiles cooperative amid the Indian families selling goods in the large exterior courtyard. Head for Avenida General Utrilla again and walk north three blocks to the **mercado** ⑥ to visit the stalls filled with fruits, vegetables, candles, and other necessities. Nine blocks east of Avenida General Utrilla on Comitán, the **Museo Na Bolom** ⑦ is a great local repository of Indian artifacts, but as you can only see it by taking a tour, you'll need to time your arrival at Na Bolom accordingly.

Sights to See

❷ **Casa de Diego de Mazariegos.** One of the most accessible pieces of colonial architecture in San Cristóbal is now the **Hotel Santa Clara** (☞ Lodging, *below*). The stone mermaid and lions outside it are typical of the period's plateresque style—as ornate and busy as the work of a silversmith. ✉ *Insurgentes 1.*

NEED A
BREAK?

The cozy and relaxing **Los Amorosos (The Lovers) Café** (✉ Calle Dr. José Flores 12A, corner of Av. Juárez, ☎ 967/8–49–28) is the favorite haunt of local intellectuals and poets, who drink their way through seven different kinds of cappuccino until midnight. Appetizers and hard liquor are also served.

---

❹ **La Catedral.** Dedicated to San Cristóbal Mártir (St. Christopher the Martyr), it was built in 1528, then demolished and rebuilt in 1693, with additions during the 18th and 19th centuries. The baroque facade, re-

San Cristóbal de las Casas

437

cently repainted in ochre with Indian red, black, and white accents, is unforgettable. Inside, don't miss the painting *Nuestra Señora de Dolores* (Our Lady of Sorrows) to the left of the altar, the gold-plated *retablo de los reyes* (altarpiece), the Chapel of Guadalupe, and the gold-washed pulpit. ⊠ *Guadalupe Victoria between 20 de Noviembre and Av. Gen. Utrilla.* ⊙ *Daily 10:30–2 and 4–8.*

⑥ Mercado. This municipal market occupies an eight-block area. Best visited early in the morning—especially on the busiest day, Saturday—the market is the social and commercial center for the Indians from surrounding villages. Stalls overflow with local produce, turkeys, medicinal herbs, flowers, firewood, and wool, as well as huaraches (sandals), grinding stones, candles, and candied fruit. Be discreet about taking photographs. ⊠ *Between Gral. Utrilla, Nicaragua, Honduras, and Belisario Domínguez.*

⑦ Museo Na Bolom. If you are interested in the culture and history of the Maya, particularly that of the Lacandon, set aside an afternoon to tour this institute, a handsome 22-room neoclassical building built as a Christian seminary in 1891. Na Bolom (House of the Jaguar) was purchased by Franz and Gertrude "Trudi" Blom in 1950—Trudi was a social activist born in the Swiss Alps and Franz was a Danish archaeologist. They set it up as an institute dedicated to ethnological and ecological advocacy; this work is still carried on today. The facilities can be used by groups as a base for special events or workshops, combining any permutation of accommodations, meals, and organized tours as they wish. Na Bolom's staff is well connected within San Cristóbal and can arrange tours to artisans' co-ops, villages, and nature reserves that are a bit off the beaten path.

Na Bolom showcases the Bloms' small collection of religious treasures that had been hoarded in attics during the anticlerical 1920s and

1930s. A museum houses Franz Blom's findings from the Classic Maya site of Moxviquil (pronounced mosh-vee-*keel*), found on the outskirts of San Cristóbal, and his personal effects, like his Remington typewriter, eyeglasses, and bottle of mescal liquor (he died of cirrhosis of the liver in 1963). Trudi's bedroom contains a case full of silver jewelry, along with her shawls, canes, collection of indigenous handicrafts, and wondrous wardrobe of 95 embroidered dresses. Also on the premises is a room full of objects from the daily life of the Lacandon, a tribe descended from the ancient Maya in the Yucatán; the Bloms documented their traditions and helped ensure their survival. A library holds more than 5,000 volumes on Chiapas and the Maya. Na Bolom is also a guest house, and revenues from guests, tours, and the gift shop go to support the work of the institute (☞ Lodging, *below*). Arrange for a meal at Na Bolom, even if you do not stay here (☞ Dining, *below*).

Na Bolom is dedicated to reforestation of the surrounding area, planting thousands of trees each year. Its own extensive nursery/garden is filled with firs, fruit trees, vegetables, and other flowering plants. Trudi Blom, who was born in 1901, received the United Nations' 500 Global Roll of Honor award in 1991 for her lifelong work on the preservation of the environment. She died in 1993, but the private, nonprofit institute is being run by a carefully selected board of directors. ☒ *Av. Vicente Guerrero 31, between Comitán and Chiapa de Corzo,* ☎ *967/ 8–14–18.* ☜ *Museum about $2; tours about $2.* ☉ *Library weekdays 10–2 and 4–9; store Tues.–Sun. 10–2 and 4–7; tours Tues.–Sun. at 11:30 in Spanish, 4:30 in English.*

❽ Museo Sergio Castro. Those interested in regional ethnic apparel might consider a visit to this private gallery. Sergio Castro has spent more than 20 years working with the Indians; many of the ceremonial costumes are collector's items. There are around 800 pieces in the collection, including textiles, weavings, and carved wooden saints, musical instruments, and toys. You must call ahead for an appointment. ☒ *Calle Guadalupe Victoria 61,* ☎ *967/8–42–89.* ☜ *Donation expected.*

❸ Palacio Municipal (Municipal Palace). Perhaps the most famous mansion in San Cristóbal is this building, with wide colonial arches and tiled patio, which was the seat of the state government until 1892, when Tuxtla Gutiérrez became the capital. It now houses municipal government offices. ☒ *Av. Hidalgo between Diego de Mazariegos and Guadalupe Victoria.* ☜ *Free.* ☉ *Daily 8–2 and 5–8.*

❺ Templo de Santo Domingo. This three-block-long complex houses a church, former convent, regional history museum, and Templo de la Caridad (Temple of the Sisters of Charity). A two-headed eagle—emblem of the Hapsburg dynasty that once ruled Spain and its American dominions—broods over the pediment of the church, which was built between 1547 and 1569. The pink stone facade (which needs a good cleaning) is carved in an intensely ornamental style known as Baroque Solomonic: saints' figures, angels, and grooved columns overlaid with vegetation motifs abound. The interior is dominated by lavish altarpieces; an exquisitely fashioned pulpit; a sculpture of the Holy Trinity; and wall panels of gilded, carved cedar, one of the precious woods of Chiapas that centuries later lured the woodsmen of Tabasco to the obscure highlands surrounding San Cristóbal. At the southeast corner of the church park lies the tiny **Templo de la Caridad,** built in 1711 to honor the Immaculate Conception. Its highlight is the finely carved altarpiece.

The Ex-Convento de Santo Domingo, immediately adjacent to the Santo Domingo church, now houses **Sna Jolobil,** an Indian cooperative selling an excellent selection of rather expensive local weavings,

embroidered clothing, and colorful postcards. The shop is open Tues.–
Sat. 9–2 and 4–7; the small **regional history museum** (☎ 967/8–16–
09. 🖾 About $1.50; free Sun.), also part of the complex, is open daily
10–5. 🖾 *20 de Noviembre s/n near Real de Mexicanos.*

❶ Zócalo. This main square around which the colonial city is built has
in its center the gazebo used by musicians on festive occasions. You
can have a coffee on the top or middle floor of the gazebo: be prepared
for little kids and women to hawk their wares doggedly. Surrounding
the square are a number of 16th-century buildings, many former mansions of the conquistadores, with wood-beamed ceilings and plant-filled
central patios. Don't be afraid to go into buildings whose doors are
open. 🖾 *Between Gen. Utrilla, Diego de Mazariegos, 16 de Septiembre, and Guadalupe Victoria.*

Outside San Cristóbal. Surrounding San Cristóbal are many small and
seldom-visited Indian villages that are celebrated for the exquisite colors and embroidery work of their inhabitants' costumes. Huixtán
(hweesh-*tan*) and Oxchuc (osh-*chuc*) are about 28 km and 43 km (17
mi and 26 mi), respectively, on the road to Ocosingo. Neither is known
for its market, although they are visited during their town festivals; Huixtán venerates San Miguel (Saint Michael) on September 29, and Oxchuc celebrates patron Saint Thomas on July 3. The Thursday market
in Tenejapa, 27 km (17 mi) northeast of San Cristóbal, is worth seeing.

Dining

$$ ✕ La Langosta. This simply furnished restaurant with hot pink walls
is San Cristóbal's best-kept secret for authentic regional cuisine. Try
the *tamales coletas,* stuffed one each with pork and chicken, in addi-
tion to chopped prunes, almonds, mole, and bell pepper; *tascalate,* a
cold cornmeal drink made with sugar and the mild *achiote* mix of spices;
and beef and chicken dishes. Although La Langosta means lobster, lob-
ster isn't served here; however, there are several seafood soups, bro-
chettes, and fish dishes. 🖾 *Madero 9,* ☎ 967/8–22–38. *AE, MC, V.*

$$ ✕ La Parrilla. A fireplace warms this horsey restaurant, where saddles
form bar stools and ranch antiques crowd wall shelves. Latino tunes
play discreetly in the background as waiters bring a variety of free appetizers: quesadillas, guacamole, fresh salsa, cheese, and crisp tostadas.
Choose the pizza or a baked potato with three toppings of your choice.
Grilled meat dishes are served with onions wrapped in foil and baked
until carmelized. Both the excellent sangria and the *frijoles charro*—
bean soup with bits of bacon and ham—are faves of locals. 🖾 *Av. Belisario Domínguez 32,* ☎ 967/8–22–20. *No credit cards. Closed Mon.*

$$ ✕ Restaurant Paraíso. Local expats rave about the steaks at this small,
★ charming chalet-style restaurant within the Hotel El Paraíso. It has sturdy
sienna-brown walls trimmed in blue, eight cozy dining tables, piped-
in classical music, and pleasant service. The margaritas are the biggest
in San Cristóbal. Swiss delights include classic raclette—melted cheese
and potato—and beef fondue for two. Homemade lime or raspberry
pie make a perfect finish to a meal. The wine list has an appropriate
selection of Italian, Spanish, Chilean, and Mexican labels. Because most
people come at night, it seems rather lonely here during the day. 🖾 *Av.
5 de Febrero 19,* ☎ 967/8–00–85. *AE, MC, V.*

$$ ✕ Restaurante el Teatro. Sunshine streams in the second-story windows
★ during the day, warming yellow walls decorated with European and
local artwork. At night, candlelight presides over a softer mood. The
French owner, Jacky, keeps the atmosphere unhurried and makes most
everything himself, including the fresh pasta and chocolate mousse. The
menu features primarily French and Italian dishes—including

chateaubriand, crepes, and watercress salad with crisp bacon, hard-boiled eggs, and homemade croutons. The wood-fire pizzas and shish kebab are also delicious; a few Mexican dishes are served. ⊠ *Av. 1 de Marzo 8,* ☎ *967/8–31–49. MC, V. Closed Mon.*

$ ✕ **La Casa del Pan.** Organically grown fruits, vegetables, and coffee
★   get top billing at this laid-back vegetarian restaurant—a bit too mellow at times, as service tends to be unreasonably slow. Still, the tasty *tamales chiapanecos* with a spicy cheese filling, hot bean soup, and the best salads in town draw return visits despite the service. The four-course special of the day, which includes variations on traditional Mexican cooking, really shines. Top it off with chocolate brownies or cheese-fruit pie. The bakery sells homemade breads, bagels, coffee, cookies, and fruit preserves. Musical groups with repertoires from jazz to pop perform 8–10 PM most weekends. ⊠ *Av. Belisario Domínguez and Dr. Navarro,* ☎ *967/8–04–68. No credit cards. Closed Mon.*

$ ✕ **La Selva Café.** Mexico's answer to Starbucks, this coffee shop has more than a dozen different kinds of organic javas and assorted coffee-flavored concoctions. The odd menu features no egg dishes, but mostly sandwiches and cold dishes, with exceptions such as codfish pie, chopped meat pie, and Chiapas tamales. There's a separate no-smoking section, and a few tables are in the lush garden out back. ⊠ *Cresencio Rosas 9, at corner of Cuauhtémoc,* ☎ *967/8–72–44. No credit cards.*

$ ✕ **Los Anafres.** Don't be put off by the white plastic tables in the courtyard—inside, the dining room of this former colonial home is warmer and more inviting. The service here is super: at breakfast, for example, waiters rush over with fresh orange juice and toast as you enter. There's a large, inexpensive set lunch with five choices of entrée, and a vegetarian meal. The *Anafre Especial* is a variety of meats brought on a small stove right to your table. The coffee is a bit weak, but you can get hot milk and refills upon request. ⊠ *Calle Flavio A. Paniagua 2,* ☎ *967/8–06–70. MC, V.*

$ ✕ **Na Bolom.** Doña Bety, the late Trudi Blom's adoptive daughter, heads the kitchen at this famous ethnological/ecological museum. Home-cooked meals emphasizing vegetarian and chicken dishes are the norm here—with foods like roast chicken, coleslaw, avocado strips, and Mexican *chayote* (a mild green squash). The communal dining table is shared by international volunteers, Lacandon Indians, resident scholars, travelers, and artists in residence. The congenial setting stimulates lively and light conversation. Breakfast is served 7:30–10, lunch at 1:30, and dinner at 7. If you are not lodging at the institute (☞ *below*), call at least two hours ahead for a lunch or dinner reservation. ⊠ *Av. Vicente Guerrero 33,* ☎ *967/8–14–18. MC, V.*

Lodging

$$$$ 🛏 **El Jacarandal.** The four guest rooms in this beautiful private estate with a great view of town are by far the most expensive in San Cristóbal, at $180 per person double occupancy, but the perfect choice if you want a special stay. American owners Nancy and Percy Wood, who restored the 19th-century mansion and gardens to their original magnificence, offer guests the run of the house, which includes the libraries, sitting rooms, terraces, and garden nooks; it's like one big house party. All rooms have bathtubs as well as Mexican and European folk-art furnishings. Meals, horseback riding, and excursions are included. The kitchen is headed by Doña Fidelia, of Mexico City, who is equally talented in Continental, American, Mexican, and European cuisines. Transportation to and from the Tuxtla Gutiérrez airport is available at extra cost. There is a three-day minimum stay. ⊠ *Comitán 7, 29220,* ☎ *967/8–10–65. 4 rooms. Dining room. No credit cards.*

$$ ▣ **Casavieja.** Three blocks east of the zócalo, this spectacular hotel maintains the architectural style of the original colonial house, built in 1740. Each plain, comfortable, clean-smelling room is charmingly decorated in Mexican furnishings and has large windows looking out onto one of the three interior courtyards. In addition to having the telephones and TVs with English channels found in all rooms, suites have hot tubs. The Espinosa family, who run and own the hotel, are warm and knowledgeable hosts. ⊠ *Ma. Adelina Flores 27, 29230,* ☎ *967/ 8–03–85,* ☎ FAX *967/8–52–23. 36 rooms, 2 suites. Restaurant, bar, free parking. AE, MC, V.*

$$ ▣ **Hotel Casa Mexicana.** This beautifully designed hotel in a restored colonial mansion is colorful, clean, bright, and friendly. Good beds, beamed ceilings, and attractive artwork all help make this an outstanding hostelry. All rooms have telephones and satellite TV, and the suites have hot tubs. The restaurant, which surrounds a lovely, plant-filled courtyard with bubbling fountain in the middle, serves international dishes such as chicken in pistachio sauce and eggplant Parmesan. ⊠ *28 de Agosto 1, 29200,* ☎ *967/8–06–98, 967/8–06–83, or 967/8–13–48,* FAX *967/8– 26–27. 49 rooms, 2 junior suites, 1 master suite. Restaurant, bar, room service, massage, sauna, baby-sitting, free parking. AE, MC, V.*

$$ ▣ **Hotel Posada El Paraíso.** This charming colonial home has 13 guest rooms with beamed ceilings: some have lofts and carpeting; eight rooms have phones. Comfortable leather-backed chairs in the guest lounge overlook a sunny, plant-filled, indoor/outdoor patio area with tables for breakfasting. The bar-restaurant offers the personal attention of owners Daniel Suter and his Mexican wife, Teresa, who met as students in Switzerland. Choose a room away from the street and lounge for more solitude. ⊠ *Av. 5 de Febrero 19, 29200,* ☎ *967/8– 00–85,* FAX *967/8–51–68. 13 rooms. Restaurant, bar. AE, MC, V.*

$$ ▣ **Hotel Santa Clara.** In the historic Casa de Diego Mazariegos, this rambling 16th-century mansion is now a hotel overlooking the action in the main plaza. It has a tangible air of past grandeur: beamed ceilings, antique furnishings (including, sadly, the mattresses in some rooms), and time-worn hardwood floors. Five of the 10 extra-roomy units with balconies overlook the pretty zócalo. There is a tiny round pool in the courtyard. For entertainment, the Cocodrilo Bar has live Latin rock and pop most nights. ⊠ *Insurgentes 1, 29200,* ☎ *967/8– 08–71 or 967/8–11–40,* FAX *967/8–10–41. 40 rooms. Restaurant, bar, coffee shop, pool, travel services, free parking. MC, V.*

$$ ▣ **La Catedral.** Reconstructed from a colonial inn and movie house, this four-story hotel has beamed ceilings, terrazzo floors, replicas of handmade wood furniture from the colonial era, and a San Cristóbal first—solar energy for heating bathwater and the swimming pool. Guest rooms surround a three-story atrium topped with a stained-glass image of San Cristóbal's cathedral. Outdoor dining is awkwardly placed in this central patio. All rooms have central heating (a rarity in town), remote-control satellite TV, piped-in music, and tiled baths with tubs, phones and hair dryers; suites have hot tubs. Rooms in the back above the pool have no central heating or tubs but cost almost half the standard rate. ⊠ *Guadalupe Victoria 21, 29200,* ☎ FAX *967/ 8–13–63. 75 rooms, 10 suites. Restaurant, bar, pool, beauty salon, business services, travel services, free parking. AE, MC, V.*

$$ ▣ **Mansión del Valle.** A few blocks from the zócalo, this 19th-century property has been converted into a modest yet comfortable hotel with tasteful Spanish colonial design details. There is a rather plain sitting room for card-playing or socializing in the large inner atrium. Rooms on the first floor are dark; nicer are the seven second-story rooms with patios overlooking La Merced park, across the street. ⊠ *Calle Diego de Mazariegos 39, 29240,* ☎ *967/8–25–82 or 967/8–25–83,* FAX *967/*

8–25–81. 40 rooms. Restaurant, bar, coffee shop, meeting room, free parking. AE, MC, V.

$$ 🔯 **Na Bolom.** Each of the rustic but cozy rooms available at this cen-
★   ter for the study and preservation of the Lacandon Indians and the rain
forest is decorated with the accoutrements of a specific indigenous com-
munity—including crafts, photographs, and books. About half the
rooms have bathtubs; all have fireplaces. Guests staying at Na Bolom
receive a free tour of the house (including a documentary presentation)
and access to the library. Book well in advance; ask for a garden view.
You can share the dining room with staff and volunteers at a separate
charge (☞ *Dining, above*). Groups are welcome and staff will make
travel and tour arrangements for a small fee. ⊠ *Av. Vicente Guerrero
33, 29200,* ☎ *967/8–14–18. 12 rooms. Restaurant. MC, V.*

$$ 🔯 **Rincón del Arco.** Near Na Bolom, this hotel has charming touches,
especially each room's freestanding fireplace. Room number 11 is se-
cluded and has a pretty view of the garden. Rooms on the top floor
share a wide balcony from which you can sit and enjoy the cityscape:
a view of the Church of Guadalupe and ancient houses with red tiled
roofs. Ask to see several rooms until you find the one you like best.
There is a warming fireplace in the cheerful dining room, which has
wrought-iron wagon-wheel chandeliers and other regional touches. ⊠
Calle Ejército Nacional 66, 29200, ☎ *967/8–13–13,* ℻ *967/8–15–68.
36 rooms. Restaurant, bar, free parking. MC, V.*

$ 🔯 **Hotel Posada San Cristóbal.** This fine budget hotel close to the
plaza is often full, so reserve a room well in advance. Large, high-ceilinged
rooms on two floors surround a lovely courtyard with colorful walls
inset with Talavera tiles. Inside, dark plank floors and antique furniture contrast nicely with clean white walls, and heavy doors block out
noise. Newly remodeled bathrooms and wide, covered balconies are
another plus. It's a steal for just $20 for a double. ⊠ *Insurgentes 3,
two blocks south of zócalo,* ☎ *967/8–68–81. 10 rooms. No credit cards.*

$ 🔯 **Posada Jovel.** Students as well as professionals on a budget choose
this converted three-story home, four blocks from the main square, for
its simple but clean rooms. Nine rooms have private baths and nine share
baths. Breakfast is available each morning between 8 and 10 AM. ⊠ *Flavio
A. Paniagua 28, 29200,* ☎ *967/8–17–34. 18 rooms. No credit cards.*

Nightlife and the Arts

San Cristóbal is acquiring more cultural events than before. Ask at the
tourist office, La Pared book shop, and El Puente coffee house and cultural center (☞ *below*) about upcoming lectures or concerts.

Museo Na Bolom (☞ *above*) occasionally sponsors talks and audiovi-
sual presentations. The elegant **Teatro Hermanos Domínguez** (⊠ Diagonal Hermanos Paniagua s/n, just outside the city limits, ☎ 967/8–
36–37) reopened in 1996 after an extensive remodeling; it features such
programs as the National Ballet of Cuba. **El Puente** (⊠ Real de
Guadalupe 55, ☎ 967/8–22–50), a casual, hip restaurant-cum-social-
center that serves breakfast all day, has videos most nights, and occasional art expositions. It's a good place to hear what's happening
around town.

Although nightlife has not traditionally been one of San Cristóbal's main
draws, there are now several good clubs with live music. One of these
is **Latinos** (⊠ Diego de Mazariegos 19, ☎ No phone), which serves up
live jazz, blues, rock, or tropical music after 9 PM Monday through Saturday. Another fun place to listen to music is **Restaurant Bar Margarita**
(⊠ Real de Guadalupe 34 near B. Domínguez, ☎ No phone). Both
double as restaurants. **Las Velas** (⊠ Madero 14, ☎ No phone) has live

reggae, tropical music, and jazz and dancing most nights after 8 PM; **Bar Cocodrilos,** part of the Hotel Santa Clara (☞ *above*), on the zócalo, also has live music most nights, mainly Latin, rock, and pop.

Outdoor Activities and Sports

A horseback ride into the neighboring indigenous villages is good exercise for mind and body. Most hotels can arrange for rentals of horses. Guides working through the tourist office and travel agencies can also hire horses and will accompany tourists. Five or six hours are needed to visit area villages or the nature reserve at Huitepec. Novices should be aware, however, that several hours on a horse can be quite—well— a pain. Many outfitters do *not* take experience into account when assigning mounts.

Los Pinguinos (⊠ 5 de Mayo 10–B, ☎ 967/8–02–02) runs guided mountain biking tours to neighboring towns ($13–$20) and has bike rentals ($1.50 per hour; $6.50 all day).

Shopping

There are no department stores in San Cristóbal. The market, although picturesque, sells more produce than handicrafts. The shops on Calle General Utrilla, south of the market, have a large selection of goods from Guatemala, and not always those of the highest quality. Guatemalan textiles sometimes sell for less in Chiapas than they do in Guatemala, and the Mexican government is considering barring their import because of unfair competition with local producers. For the time being, make sure to bargain for these textiles to get a good price. Most Guatemalan cloth is dark blue cotton with multicolor cotton needlepoint or trim.

Shops in town are generally open 9–2 and 4–8. Indian women and children often accost visitors on the streets with their wares, mostly fake amber, woven bracelets, and small dolls, but their selections are not as varied as those in the shops, and prices will not necessarily be any better. You can be assured, though, that the proceeds go directly to the craftspeople themselves.

Among its excellent selection of wares, **Sna Jolobil** (⊠ Ex-Convento de Santo Domingo, Claz. Lázaro Cárdenas 42, ☎ 967/8–71–78), the regional crafts cooperative, sells hand-dyed woolen sweaters and men's and women's tunics, embroidered pillow covers, and pre-Hispanic-design wall hangings. It is closed Sunday and at lunchtime.

Among the smart shops clustered along Real de Guadalupe are two subsidiaries of **El Arbol de la Vida,** one block apart (⊠ Real de Guadalupe 27 and 28-A, ☎ 967/8–40–85 and 967/8–50–50), which specialize in attractive designer amber jewelry mixed with silver and gold. **La Galería del Ambar** (⊠ Crescencio Rosas 4A, ☎ 967/8–79–25) also has a large selection of amber jewelry.

Artesanías Chiapanecas (⊠ Calle Real de Guadalupe 46C, ☎ No phone) has an excellent selection of embroidered blouses, huipiles, tablecloths, and bags. The government-run **Casa de las Artesanías** (⊠ Calle Niños Héroes and Av. Hidalgo, ☎ FAX 967/8–18–80; closed Mon.) has wooden toys, ceramics, embroidered blouses, bags, and handwoven textiles from throughout the state, and a tiny ethnographic museum in back. **Textiles Soriano** (⊠ Rincón del Arco Hotel, Calle Ejército Nacional 66, ☎ 967/8–13–13) specializes in handwoven bedspreads and other cloth, which can be made to order in a few days (open 7:30–3 Mon.–Sat.).

An unusual co-op in an old colonial home, **Taller Leñateros** (⊠ Flavio A. Paniagua 54, ☎ 967/8–51–74) sells handmade books, boxes, postcards, and writing paper fashioned on the premises out of recycled flower petals, plants, and bark. Handsome business cards on handmade paper can be made in as little as one day. Expat Ambar Past directs the project, where about two dozen Maya work. Ask to see if the staff can take you on an informal (free) tour of the workshop, or if there are any papermaking classes scheduled during your visit.

SOUTH AND EAST OF SAN CRISTÓBAL

Southeast of San Cristóbal lies one of the least explored and most exotic regions of Chiapas: the Selva Lacandona, said to be the second-largest rain forest in the western hemisphere. Incursions of developers, land-hungry settlers, and refugees from neighboring Guatemala are transforming Mexico's last frontier, which for centuries has been the homeland of the Lacandon, a small tribe descended from the Maya of Yucatán. Some of their people still maintain their ancient customs, living in huts and wearing long, plain tunics. However, their custom of not marrying outside the tribe is causing serious problems, and their numbers, while never large, have been reduced to about 350. The fabulous Caves of San Cristóbal (also known as Las Grutas de Rancho Nuevo) are in this region.

The Caves of San Cristóbal

9   *13 km (8 mi) southeast of San Cristóbal off Route 190.*

The spectacular limestone stalactites and stalagmites are illuminated along a 750-meter cement walkway inside these labyrinthine caves, which were discovered in 1960 and were fully explored only a few years ago, prompting the creation of the **San Cristóbal Recreational Park**. The Spanish-speaking gatekeeper (or his kids) is usually available to guide visitors for a small fee. The caves may be closed in inclement weather; if in doubt, check with the San Cristóbal tourist office first. Horses can be rented ($4 per hour) for a ride around the surrounding pine forest, and there is a picnic area on the site. To get here, catch a Teopisca-bound microbus at Boulevard Juan Sabines Gutiérrez, across from the San Diego church. Make sure to tell the driver to let you off at the "grutas." Get off at the signed entrance, and walk in about 1 km (½ mi) along the dirt road. Alternatively, catch a taxi from town for about $3. For about twice that price, you can ask him to wait while you explore the caves.

☎ *No phone.* ⌑ *30¢.* ◷ *9–5.*

Amatenango del Valle

10   *41 km (25 mi) south of San Cristóbal.*

Amatenango del Valle is a Tzeltal village known for the handsome, primitive pottery made principally by the town's women, whose distinctive red and yellow huipiles (tunics) are also much remarked upon. On the road to Comitán, the village currently has no signage; watch closely for the ocher, black, and natural clay flowerpots and animal figurines sitting by the side of the road. You can stop at any of these roadside houses, or turn into the town—almost every household has wares to sell. If you go during the dry season, you might get to see some of the pots being fired, as they are done outside and only when rain is not a threat. Spanish is definitely a second language here, and women negotiate without a lot of chitchat, or use younger children as interpreters.

En Route   The rugged foothills and pine groves surrounding San Cristóbal subside into a low plain along the next stretch of the road. The mountains appear to have been sliced in two, revealing their rust-red innards, sad evidence of the erosion caused by the clearing of the forests.

Comitán

⓫   *55 km (34 mi) southeast of Amatenango del Valle.*

Comitán, whose Maya name, *Balún-Canán*, means "nine stars" or "guardians," is a pleasant commercial center and agricultural town of about 120,000 souls. It is also the base from which many visitors tour the **Lagunas de Montebello** (☞ *below*) and the small archaeological sites nearby. Built by the Spaniards, the city flourished early on as a major center linking the lowland temperate plains to the edge of the Maya empire on the Pacific. Even today, it serves as the principal trading point for the Tzeltal Indians and such Guatemalan goods as sugarcane liquor and orchids. One of the "Hundred Colonial Cities" now being renovated by a federal government grant, its pretty plaza and surrounding streets and buildings are being refurbished in colonial style. Chiapas's governor, Roberto Albores Guillen, elected in 1998, is from Comitán, and you'll see his portrait hanging in many public buildings.

Two notable churches are **Santo Domingo de Guzmán**, whose architecture shows a Moorish influence, and **San Caralampio**, whose Spanish Baroque style shows the influence of Guatemalan artisans. From the kiosk in the zócalo there are fine views of the hills.

The **Casa-Museo Dr. Belisario Domínguez,** the lovely former home of a martyr of the revolution, opened as a museum in 1985. It houses a fascinating collection of medical instruments, pharmaceuticals, and turn-of-the-century furnishings, as well as photographs, documents, and letters from the Mexican revolution, during which the doctor was assassinated for his outspoken criticism of President Victoriano Huerta. ⊠ *Av. Dr. Belisario Domínguez Sur 35.* 🎫 *About 50¢.* ⊙ *Tues.–Sat. 9–6:45; Sun. 9–12:45.*

Museo de Arte Hermila Castellanos. This centrally located museum shows work by modern Mexican artists, including master painters Rufino Tamayo and Francisco Toledo, both from Oaxaca. In fact many of the painters represented are Oaxaqueños, and the subject matter deals largely with mestizo and indigenous people, most often in stylized, contemporary depictions. ⊠ *Av. Central Belisario Domínguez Sur 51,* 📞 *962/2–20–82.* 🎫 *20¢.* ⊙ *Mon.–Sat. 10–5:45, Sun. 10-1.*

⚒   On the outskirts of town, 15 km (9 mi) from Comitán, the small **Maya site** of **Tenam Puente** was discovered by archaeologists Franz Blom and Oliver LeFarge. Built around the same time as Chincultik (☞ *below*), restoration of this primarily ceremonial center was begun in 1993, and a royal tomb was discovered in 1996. There are three ball courts, apparently one each for the lower-, middle-, and upper-classes.

Lagunas de Montebello

⓬   *64 km (40 mi) southeast of Comitán.*

The 58 lakes and surrounding pine forest of las Lagunas de Montebello (Lakes of the Beautiful Mountain) constitute a 2,437-acre international park that is shared with Guatemala. A different color permeates each lake, whose waters glow with vivid emerald, turquoise, amethyst, azure, and steel-gray tints, caused by various oxides. The setting is serene and majestic, with clusters of oak, pine, and sweet gum. Practically the only denizens of the more accessible part of the forest are the clamorous goldfinch and mockingbirds. To the east roam puma, jaguar, deer, bear, and the rare quetzal bird.

At the park entrance, the paved road forks. The left leads to the Lagunas Coloradas (Colored Lakes). At Laguna Bosque Azul, the last lake along that road, there is a humble sit-down café in addition to the food and beverage stalls that crop up near every lake with a parking lot. Small boys will approach and offer a 45-minute horse-riding expedition to a cave and two cenotes within the forest. You can also tour the lake in a rowboat for $4 (up to 4 people). Back at the park entrance, the right fork road leads past various signed groupings of lakes to Tziscao Lake (the last) and, just outside the park boundaries, a village of the same name. The only lakes the tourist board recommends for swimming are Tziscao and Montebello. The Tziscao Lodge has been closed for more than a year for remodeling; its reinauguration is planned for September 1999. Check with the tourist board if you'd like to stay within the park; Tziscao Lodge is the only accommodation.

You can pick up a helpful map of the lakes at the tourist office in Comitán. **La Angostura** (☎ 963/2–60–00) and **Transportes Cuxtepeque** (☎ 963/2–17–28) buses leave about every half hour from Comitán (✉ 2da Av. Poniente Sur 17–B, between 2a and 3a Calles Sur Poniente) to both Laguna Bosque Azul and Tziscao. If you're riding the bus, you'll have to walk or catch the same bus between various lakes; check the map and time your forays to catch the bus on the half-hour. To get to Tziscao from Laguna Bosque Azul you must go to the fork in the road and catch the Bosque Azul bus to the next fork in the road and then board a Tziscao bus.

Chincultik

 ⑬ *56 km (35 mi) southeast of Comitán.*

The small, Late Classic Maya site of Chincultik makes a lovely stop on the way to or from las Lagunas de Montebello. It is a steep hike of about 10 or 15 minutes to the top of a restored pyramid (as well as a 5-km [3-mi] walk from the highway if you don't come by car). From the top you are rewarded with a fabulous 360-degree view of the Montebello Lakes and the surrounding countryside. You can swim in *Cenote Agua Azul,* the large sinkhole on the site (ask the guard to point you in the right direction, as signage is poor). The ruins, which are only partially restored, also include a ball court and stelae. ⊠ *About $1.50.* ☉ *Daily 8–4.*

To get to Chincultik from Comitán, continue south 15 km (9 mi) on Route 190, and turn left at the sign LAGUNAS DE MONTEBELLO outside of La Trinitaria. After 39 km (24 mi), there's a road on the left leading to the ruins, which are 5 km (3 mi) off the highway.

Dining and Lodging

$$ ✗▥ **Museo Parador Santa María.** Built around the remains of a hacienda from the 1830s, this lodging has an excellent restaurant and six well-appointed rooms. Each room is decorated with a different period of antiques, including plateresque, Chiapas, and French; some have lovely sunken tile bathtubs, a few have fireplaces. This is an excellent place to stop for a special meal after visiting the lakes. All dishes are à la carte, and a meal with wine can easily come to $20 per person, but the regional food is remarked upon by people throughout the state. Reservations are suggested for groups of more than three. ⊠ *Km 22 on the road to Lagunas de Montebello,* ☎ ℻ *963/2–51–16. 8 rooms. No credit cards.*

NORTH AND WEST OF SAN CRISTÓBAL

San Juan Chamula and Zinacantán are traditional villages in the scenic western outskirts of San Cristóbal. The small colonial town of Chiapa de Corzo will be the first major town you come to when you drive west from San Cristóbal along Route 190. Tuxtla Gutiérrez, the modern state capital, is about 15 km (9 mi) beyond Chiapa de Corzo. Sumidero Canyon is north of Tuxtla; the farthest lookout point is 22 km (14 mi) away from the capital.

San Juan Chamula

⑭ *12 km (7½ mi) northwest of San Cristóbal de las Casas.*

The spiritual and administrative center of the Chamula Indians is justly celebrated, as much for its rich past as for its turbulent present. The Chamula are a Tzotzil-speaking Maya group of nearly 52,000 individuals (out of a total of 300,000 Tzotzils) who live in hamlets scattered throughout the highlands; several thousand of them live in San Juan Chamula.

The Chamula are fiercely religious, a trait that has played an important role in their history. The Chamula uprising of 1869 started when some tribesmen were imprisoned for crucifying a boy in the belief that they should have their own Christ. Some 13,000 Chamula then rose up to demand their leaders' release and massacred scores of ladino villagers in the process. More recently, the infiltration of Protestant evangelists into the community led to the expulsion of the Indian converts by Chamula authorities. In the last 20 years, more than 30,000 have been forced to abandon their ancestral lands and now live on the outskirts of San Cristóbal de las Casas, dressing in conventional clothing and often found selling handicrafts in San Cristóbal's street markets. The Human Rights Commission is trying to mediate their return to the Chamula community.

Physically and spiritually, life in San Juan Chamula revolves around the church, a white-stucco building whose doorway is decorated with a motif of flowers in red, green, blue, and yellow. To get permission to enter the church, pay a token fee (about 40¢) at the tourist office on the main square. A pamphlet gives guidelines about how to conduct yourself in the church and the village.

Extreme discretion must be exercised inside the church. Taking photographs and videos is absolutely prohibited and strictly enforced. There are no pews, and the floor is strewn with fragrant pine needles. The Chamula sit praying silently or chanting while facing colorfully attired saints' statues. For the most part, worshipers appear oblivious to intruders, continuing with their rituals: they burn candles of various colors, drink soft drinks, and may have a live chicken or eggs with them for healing the sick. They "pass" the illness to the chicken or egg, which then gets disposed of outside the church. The church is named after Saint John the Baptist, the main god of the universe, according to Chamulan belief—Jesus Christ is revered as his younger brother.

Outside the church there is no taboo against photography, although adults prefer not to be photographed. Flocks of children will pester you to buy small trinkets and will allow you to photograph them in exchange for a small fee (about 30¢ a shot). The best time to visit San Juan Chamula is on Sunday, when the market is in full swing and more formal religious rites are performed.

To get here from San Cristóbal, head west on Guadalupe Victoria, which forks to the right onto Ramón Larrainzar. Continue 4 km (2½ mi) until you reach the entrance to the village. Most of these roads are paved, and they are far more interesting than the alternative route, which is to take the main road to Tuxtla 8 km (5 mi) and then turn right when you see signs. It is recommended that you not walk between San Cristóbal and San Juan Chamula and Zinacantán because of the threat of robbery.

Zinacantán

⑮ *4 km (2½ mi) west of San Juan Chamula.*

The village of Zinacantán (Place of the Bats) is even smaller than San Juan Chamula (☞ *above*) and is reached by taking a paved road west just outside San Juan Chamula (from San Cristóbal, take the Tuxtla road about 8 km [5 mi] and look for the signed turnoff on your right). Here photography is totally forbidden, except for the row of village weavers on view along the main street. It is the scenery en route to Zinacantán—terraced hillsides with cornfields and orchards—that draws visitors. There isn't much to see in the village except on Sundays, when people gather from the surrounding parishes, or during religious festivals. The men wear bright pink tunics embroidered with flowers; the women cover themselves with bright pink *rebozos* (shawls). If you take a tour you'll visit the homes of backstrap loom weavers. Watch for the plethora of crosses around the springs and mountains on the way to Zinacantán: they mark a Chamula cemetery of Christian origin.

The **Museo Ik'al Ojov,** on the *calle principal* (main street) behind the church, shows off Zinacantán costumes through the ages. ☎ *No phone.* ✉ *Donation encouraged.* ☉ *Tues.–Sun. 9–5.*

Chiapa de Corzo

⑯ *70 km (43 mi) northwest of San Cristóbal; 15 km (9 mi) east of Tuxtla Gutiérrez.*

Chiapa de Corzo was founded in 1528 by Diego de Mazariegos, who one month later fled the mosquitoes and transported all the settlers to San Cristóbal (then called Chiapa de los Españoles, to distinguish it from Chiapa de los Indios, as Chiapa de Corzo was originally known). The mosquitoes are still here.

Life in this small town on the banks of the Grijalva revolves, inevitably, around the **zócalo,** lorded over by *la pila,* a bizarre 16th-century Mozarabic fountain modeled after Queen Isabella's crown. The interior is decorated with stories of the Indians. Several handicraft shops line the square, selling huaraches, ceramics, lacquerware, the famous Parachico masks, and regional costumes.

Chiapa's **lacquerware museum,** facing the plaza, contains a modest collection of delicately carved and painted *jícaras* (gourds)—"The sky is no more than an immense blue jícara, the beloved firmament in the form of a cosmic jícara," explains the *Popul Vuh,* a 16th-century chronicle of the Quiché Maya. The lacquerware on display is both local and imported, coming from Michoacán, Guerrero, Chiapas, Guatemala, and Asia. A workshop behind the museum is open during the week and generally keeps the same hours as the museum. ⊠ *Plaza Angel Albino Corzo No. 35,* ☎ *No phone.* ✉ *Free.* ☉ *Tues.–Sat. 9–2 and 4–6, Sun. 9–1.*

Just outside of town, behind the Nestlé plant, are some nearly unnoticeable **Maya-Olmec ruins** dating from 1450 BC.

TAKE PICTURES. FURTHER.™

© Eastman Kodak Company, 1999. Kodak, Max and Take Pictures. Further. are trademarks.

Ever see someone

waiting for the sun to come out

while trying to photograph

a charging rhino?

New!
Kodak Max film:

Now with better color, Kodak's maximum versatility film gives you great pictures in sunlight, low light, action or still.

It's all you need to know about film.

www.kodak.com

Distinctive guides packed with up-to-date expert advice
and smart choices for every type of traveler.

Fodor's. For the world of ways you travel.

Dining

$ ✕ **Jardines de Chiapa.** In this lovely patio setting, sample an excellent and inexpensive variety of regional cuisines. Try the *tasajo* (sun-dried beef served with pumpkin-seed sauce) and the *chipilín con bolita* soup, made with balls of ground corn paste cooked in a creamy herbal sauce and topped with Chiapas's famous cheese. A marimba band sometimes enlivens the afternoon meal. ☒ *Av. Fco. I. Madero No. 395 at Benito Juárez,* ☏ *968/6–01–98. No credit cards.*

Tuxtla Gutiérrez

⑰ *289 km (179 mi) southwest of Villahermosa, 15 km (9 mi) northwest of Chiapa de Corzo, 85 km (53 mi) northwest of San Cristóbal.*

Tuxtla Gutiérrez is the thriving capital city of the state of Chiapas. In 1939 Graham Greene characterized it as "not a place for foreigners—the new ugly capital of Chiapas, without attractions. . . . It is like an unnecessary postscript to Chiapas, which should be all wild mountain and old churches and swallowed ruins and the Indians plodding by." That bleak description is slowly changing, as new luxury buildings like the Camino Real Hotel add sparkle to the city. Nonetheless, Tuxtla Gutiérrez is a city through which most visitors to Chiapas will pass unnoticing, even if it is of vital economic and political importance. It is the state's transportation hub, and it has what is probably the most exciting zoo in Mexico. It is also convenient for its proximity to Chiapa de Corzo and the Sumidero Canyon, where there is little in the way of accommodations.

Tuxtla's first name derives from the Nahuatl word *tochtlan,* meaning "abundance of rabbits." Its second name, Gutiérrez, honors Joaquín Miguel Gutiérrez, who fought for the state's independence and incorporation into Mexico.

The highway into town is endless. Tuxtla (population 525,000), the state capital since 1892, does not have many conveniences for tourists, but you can get your bearings best by staying on the main drag, which will run you smack into the zócalo, known locally as the **parque central,** which is fronted by huge government buildings.

🐾 Only the most obstinate animal-hater would fail to be captivated by **Miguel Alvarez del Toro Zoo** (a.k.a. ZooMAT)—where all the species are native Chiapans, and the more docile creatures roam free. The 100-plus species on display include jaguars, marsupials, iguanas, quetzal birds, boa constrictors and other snakes, tapirs, eagles, and monkeys. Nature videos are often presented Saturday at 11 AM, and you can visit the tiny museum and the well-stocked gift shop. ☒ *Calzada Cerro Hueco s/n, southeast of town off Libramiento Sur,* ☏ *961/2–37–54 or 961/2–99–43.* 🎟 *Free but donation appreciated.* ☉ *Tues.–Sun. 8:30–5:30.*

Amateur archaeologists and botanists should head for **Parque Madero,** which includes the **Botanical Garden,** the **Botanical Museum,** and the **Regional Museum of Chiapas.** One price gets you into the three separate museums: the excellent history museum, the ethnological museum, and a salon for revolving cultural exhibits. The botanical museum in unimpressive, but the garden is pleasant and has labels showing the native plant species. ☒ *Northeast of downtown, between Av. Nte. 5a and Calle Oriente 11a,* ☏ *961/3–44–79.* 🎟 *All Parque Madero sights $2, free Sun. and holidays.* ☉ *Garden Tues.–Sun. 9–6; orchid house Tues.–Sun. 10–1; museum Tues.–Sun. 9–4.*

A fine small museum of indigenous Indian cultures throughout Chiapas opened in 1993 at the government-run **Casa de Artesanías,** which also has a good selection of regional handicrafts for sale. Amber from Chiapas fashioned into necklaces, earrings, and pendants, as well as hand-embroidered and brocaded table mats, blouses, and huipiles, leather bags, gold filigree jewelry, and lacquerware, are among the local specialties. ⊠ *Blvd. Dr. Belisario Domínguez No. 2035,* ☎ *961/2–22–75.* 🖀 *Free.* ☉ *Mon.–Sat. 10–8.*

As its name suggests, **Parque de las Marimbas** (⊠ Av. Central and 8 Pte.) hosts marimba bands, which play old-fashioned dancing music—you can grab a partner and join in—Thursday through Sunday for 1½ hours before dusk.

Dining and Lodging

$$$$ ✕ **Montebello.** Prime rib and Mexican specialties headline the menu at
★   this classy restaurant at the Camino Real Hotel—where every roll, cake, dessert, and tortilla is made on the premises. Intimate Montebello is most romantic at night, when the city lights shimmer into view. The elegance of the earth-tone decor is set off by an unusual white mural of the Sumidero cliffs sculpted into a wall. Live, unobtrusive violin and piano music accompanies diners from 2 PM until closing. ⊠ *Blvd. Dr. Belisario Domínguez 1195,* ☎ *961/7–77–77. AE, DC, MC, V. Closed Sun.*

$$ ✕ **Las Pichanchas.** This restaurant, open for lunch and dinner, offers
★   an outstanding variety of regional dishes, as well as live marimba music in the afternoon and evening, and folkloric dances 9–10 PM. ⊠ *Central Oriente 837,* ☎ *961/2–53–51. AE, MC, V.*

$ ✕ **La Selva.** Specialties from Chiapas such as a mixed *Chiapaneco* platter with mole, rice, beans, and beefsteak top a menu full of national dishes as well as grilled meats and chicken. The atmosphere—that of a festive tropical roadhouse—improves with the live marimba music performed noon–6 PM daily; duos or trios play Wednesday–Saturday 9–11:30 PM. The restaurant, directly across from Hotel Camino Real, is open from 8 AM to 1 AM; on Sundays a giant buffet is served between 1 and 5 PM. ⊠ *Blvd. Dr. Belisario Domínguez 1360,* ☎ *961/5–07–18. MC, V.*

$$$$ 🛏 **Camino Real.** This hilltop oasis of luxury sets a standard for accom-
★   modations in Chiapas. Rooms surround a huge open-air pool and bar area with exotic vegetation. A concierge floor, business center with computer rentals, and meeting facilities draw many business travelers, who entertain clients in the Azulejos restaurant, enclosed in a sky-blue glass dome (the delicious daily breakfast and lunch buffets are well worth the price), or at the upscale Montebello (☞ *above*). All rooms have a view of the mountains, satellite TVs, room safes, minibars, phones, and full bathroom amenities. At a little more than $100 per night, this member of the Camino Real chain offers more services and amenities than others charging twice as much. ⊠ *Blvd. Dr. Belisario Domínguez 1195, 29060,* ☎ *961/7–77–77; 800/722–6466 in the U.S.,* 🖷 *961/7–77–99, tgz@caminoreal.com. 194 rooms, 26 suites. 2 restaurants, bar, pool, sauna, 2 tennis courts, health club, travel services, car rental. AE, DC, MC, V.*

$$$ 🛏 **Hotel Flamboyant.** For a restful atmosphere and Moorish touches, try one of the rooms in this luxury hotel. Accommodations are set off with long hallways and wide archways; all are air-conditioned and have TVs with some channels in English. Twenty-four rooms face the large garden, while a dozen are located off a smaller, extremely tranquil inner garden. Capacious is the byword here: the pool is huge, and so are the public areas. The restaurant is light and airy, and the food is tasty, but the service is poor; the bar down the hall is dark and tacky. A disadvantage is the location—a 10-minute drive west of the town center—but there's a pretty shopping mall next door. ⊠ *Blvd. Dr. Belisario Domínguez Km 1081, 29000,* ☎ *961/5–08–88 or 961/5–09–99,* 🖷 *961/5–00–87. 117 rooms, 2 suites. Restaurant, coffee shop, bar, pool, tennis court, travel services. AE, MC, V.*

$$ 🏨 **Bonampak.** This four-story hotel has small rooms with firm mattresses, color cable TV, and air-conditioning. It has a pool, but the lush gardens have been whittled down to make way for a shopping mall next door. The lobby and public spaces are airy and clean, with shiny marble floors. Both cafeteria and restaurant have a well-deserved reputation for good regional cooking, especially their steaks and soups. ✉ *Blvd. Dr. Belisario Domínguez 180, 29030,* ☎ *961/3–20–50 or 961/ 3–20–48,* FAX *961/2–77–37. 70 rooms. 2 restaurants, bar, cafeteria, pool, beauty salon, travel services, car rental, free parking. AE, MC, V.*

$$ 🏨 **Hotel Maria Eugenia.** Although a touch sterile, this air-conditioned downtown hotel has clean rooms with floral spreads and a floral scent as well. There is cable TV and white wrought-iron furniture around a nice pool. ✉ *4ta Av. Central Oriente 507, 29000,* ☎ *961/3–37–67 or 961/3–37–70,* FAX *961/1–01–85. 83 rooms. 2 restaurants, bar, pool, meeting room, travel services, free parking. AE, MC, V.*

Sumidero Canyon

⑱ *22 km (14 mi) northeast of Tuxtla.*

Sumidero Canyon came into its own about 12 million years ago, with the help of the Grijalva River, which flows north along the canyon's floor. The fissure meanders for some 15 km (9 mi); its near-vertical walls, in part obscured by vegetation, rise 3,500 ft at the highest point. You can admire it from above, as there are five lookout points along the highway; one of them, La Atalaya, has a restaurant.

Transportes Cañón del Sumidero (✉ *1a Norte Oriente 1121, Tuxtla Gutiérrez,* ☎ *961/2–06–49*) has a two-hour minivan trip for about $7 per person. As you visit the canyon, consider the fate of the Chiapa Indians, who jumped into it rather than face slavery at the hands of the Spaniards. Boat trips to the hydroelectric dam in Chicoasen and back depart daily between 7 AM and 4 PM from the tiny island of Cahuaré and the dock at Chiapa de Corzo; they take approximately two hours and cost about $6 per person (there's a four-person minimum). From the boat you can admire the canyon's steep, striated walls, some odd rock formations, and the animals—including ducks, pelicans, herons, raccoons, iguanas, and butterflies—that live inconspicuously at its base.

THE ROAD TO PALENQUE AND BEYOND

The road from San Cristóbal to Palenque veers slightly east on Highway 190 upon leaving town, then links up to Highway 199, which heads north to Palenque. You'll pass Ocosingo and the turnoff to Toniná along the first half of the journey, then Agua Azul and Misol-Há before reaching the ruins. It's hilly sierra country most of the way until the mild valleys around Ocosingo; the climate will get progressively hotter and more humid as you approach Palenque. The vegetation will also change from mountain pine to thick, green tropical foliage. To get to Villahermosa from Palenque, head north for 56 km (35 mi) on Highway 199, and then turn left onto Highway 186 at Catazajá for a leisurely drive on a fairly straight road.

Toniná

⑲ *98 km (61 mi) northeast of San Cristóbal; 118 km (73 mi) south and east of Palenque.*

Between San Cristóbal and Palenque, on a newly paved road running along the Jataté River in the mild Ocosingo Valley, is the archaeological site of **Toniná.** The name means "house of stone" in Tzeltal. Excavations indicate that the vanquished rulers of Palenque and Yaxchilán were brought here as prisoners for execution. To date, several ball courts and the main pyramid platform (taller than those of Tikal and Teotihuacán) have been uncovered; a small, on-site museum is under construction. Thought to be the last major ceremonial centers to flourish in this area, Toniná, with its monumental architecture and noteworthy sculptures, is rapidly adding to our knowledge of Maya civilization. To get to the site, follow the road from Ocosingo, off Route 199. ⊠ *$1.50.* ☉ *Daily 8–4.*

Lodging

$ 🏠 **Rancho Esmeralda.** This rustic guest house, with no electricity or phones, is just a 10-minute walk from the ruins. Located on a blossoming macadamia nut farm, it has five comfortable wooden cabins. There are clean latrines and a common bathhouse from which you can savor the view as you soak in the extra-long clawfoot bathtub. The help is friendly, and you could spend an afternoon just conversing with the young barman in the thatch-roof, communal dining area. Delicious, filling meals (especially breakfast and dinner, which are served buffet style) are served at extra cost; the coffee is grown, roasted, and ground on the premises. Congenial hosts Glen and Ellen can help arrange an air excursion to the ruins of Bonampak and Yaxchilán (about $125) or a three- to four-hour horseback excursion ($15) through the beautiful Ocosingo valley. Tent camping is also permitted. ⊠ *Turnoff about 8 km (5 mi) along road to Toniná ruins, Apartado 68, Ocosingo, Chiapas,* ☎ *No phone,* ℻ *967/3–07–11. 5 cabins. No credit cards.*

Agua Azul

❷⓿ *68 km (42 mi) northwest of Toniná, 64 km (40 mi) southwest of Palenque.*

The series of waterfalls and crystalline blue pools at Agua Azul are breathtaking to behold, especially well into the dry season, from about March through May. The site has lost its sense of isolation since the road was paved in the 1980s, when food shacks and tent camping facilities sprang up, marring somewhat the natural beauty. Still, it is a breathtaking spot, and you can swim in a series of interconnected pools. The cataracts are surrounded by giant palm fronds and tropical flowers; monkeys and toucans frolic in the vicinity. Six-hour day trips (booked from most any travel agency in Palenque and including a visit to Misol-Há) cost just about $10 per person and include the entrance fees. For about $7 per person you can ride with **Sociedad Cooperative Chambalum** (Calle Allende at Av. Juárez s/n, ☎ No phone) to both sites. Their service is every 10 minutes between 6 AM and 6 PM.

Misol-Há

❷❶ *46 km (29 mi) northeast of Agua Azul, 18 km (11 mi) southwest of Palenque.*

If the single cascade at Misol-Há is smaller than those at Agua Azul (☞ *above*), the area surrounding it is also less peopled with vendors and littered with trash. One can swim in the pool formed by the 100-ft cascade, or explore behind the falls, where a cave leads to another, subterranean pool. Surrounded by oversize tropical vegetation, the site has rustic rest rooms, restaurants, and campgrounds. *See* Agua Azul, *above,* for how to get there.

Palenque

 ★ ⚲ ㉒ *191 km (118 mi) northeast of San Cristóbal de las Casas, 150 km (93 mi) southeast of Villahermosa.*

Of all Maya ruins, none is more sublime than Palenque—only Tikal in Guatemala is its equal. Teotihuácan might be more monumental and Chichén Itzá more expansive, but Palenque possesses a mesmerizing quality, in part because of the intimacy that the surrounding jungle creates. In early morning or late afternoon, sunlight illuminates the structures in a hazy, iridescent glow. Birds call shrilly and eerily, and the local descendants of the Maya wander about collecting banana leaves, oranges, and avocados.

Antonio de Solis, a Spanish priest, accidently dug into a buried wall here in 1740 while he was trying to plant crops. In 1805 a royal Spanish expedition ventured here to follow up on the discovery. In 1832 an eccentric German count, Jean-Frederic Maximilien de Waldeck, set up house with his mistress for a year in a building known today as the Templo del Conde (Temple of the Count). Explorers John Lloyd Stephens and Frederick Catherwood lived briefly in the palace during their 1840 expedition. In 1923 serious excavations began under the direction of Franz Blom, cofounder of the Na Bolom foundation in San Cristóbal. Work continued intermittently until 1952, when Alberto Ruz Lhuillier, a Mexican archaeologist, uncovered the tomb of the 7th-century ruler Pacal beneath the Temple of the Inscriptions. Since the early 1970s, groundbreaking work has been done on the Maya by archaeologists, linguists, and astronomers.

Palenque's elegance makes it clear why archaeologist Sylvanus Morley honored the Maya as the "Greeks of the New World"—not only for their remarkable buildings, but for the supple naturalism of the culture's art. The masters at work here shaped stone, stucco, and ceramics into ornate, lyrical designs. Artisans also took liberties here: relief sculpture of great expressiveness replaces the freestanding stelae of other Maya cities.

The most important buildings of the site date from the Mid- to Late Classic period (AD 6th–9th centuries), although Palenque was inhabited as early as 1500 BC. At its zenith, the city dominated the greater part of Tabasco and Chiapas. The site was abandoned around AD 800, making it one of the earliest Maya sites to be deserted in what was a west-to-east pattern of abandonment. The reasons for the inhabitants' departure are still in debate.

Palenque's graceful tower—one of the site's signature structures—sets it apart from other Maya settlements. The Temple of the Inscriptions, a 75-ft pyramid, is another. It was dedicated to Pacal—the "Mesoamerican Charlemagne"—who took Palenque to its most glorious heights during his 28- to 38-year reign. He died around AD 692, having become the ruler at age 12 and living into his forties.

The ruling priest-kings communicated life at Palenque in elaborate glyphs and reliefs on the temples. The deciphering of a good portion of Palenque's hieroglyphics in 1988 has revolutionized scholars' understanding of both the Maya and the bloody history of Palenque. Only 800 out of thousands of glyphs have been deciphered so far, but they have already revealed the complex history of the Palenque dynasties. Exciting finds by archaeologists from the University of Texas in 1998 have introduced a new character, Uc-Pakal-Kinich, into the lineage of Palenque rulers. Other clues recently unearthed at Temple 19 point to a probable liaison between rulers of Palenque and of Copán, in what is now Honduras.

Palenque

In its heyday, Palenque encompassed an astonishing 128-plus square km (49 square mi). Artificial terraces were built to support the temples, which surrounded plazas, a ball court, altars, and burial grounds. The temples themselves had a complex array of corridors, narrow subterranean stairways, and galleries. And they served as fortresses in time of war. Only about 25% of the site has been excavated. Since late 1994, a huge portion of the ruins around the Temple of the Inscriptions has been reconstructed and is open. Explanations in Spanish, English, and Tzotzil have been placed at all major buildings.

As you enter the site, the first temple on your right is the reconstructed **Temple of the Skull,** which the Maya had painted red and blue in their time. A skull-shaped stucco relief, presumed to be that of a rabbit, was found at the small entrance to the temple. It is up the stairway.

The **Temple of the Inscriptions** is just past Temple 13—its nine tiers correspond to the nine-level Maya underworld. Atop this temple and the smaller ones around it, there are vestiges of roof combs—delicate vertical extensions that are among the features of southern Maya cities. This is the best view of Palenque, and it provides an excellent orientation to the other buildings. Reaching the tomb inside involves a relatively easy, if slow, climb. Once at the summit, turn and take a long look back toward the once-mighty palace on the right. From the top of the Temple of Inscriptions, climb down the steep, damp flight of stairs 80 ft into the **tomb of Pacal,** one of the first crypts found inside a Mexican pyramid. (This is not for claustrophobes.) Pacal's remains along with his diadem and majestic jade, shell, and obsidian mask are in Mexico City's Museum of Anthropology. The intricately carved sarcophagus lid, weighing some 5 tons and measuring 10 by 7 ft, however, remains. A psychoduct—a hollow stone tube in the shape of a snake through which Pacal's soul was thought to have passed to the nether-

THE ROUTE OF THE MAYA: A MESOAMERICAN GIZA

THE MAYA WERE outstanding architects, without compare in the Americas. They erected immense palaces and towering pyramids in less than hospitable climates without the aid of metal tools, the wheel, or beasts of burden. Their ancient cities still resound with the magnificence of their cultures, even though the civilizations have faded.

Río Usumacinta. Builders of pyramids of this style typically gave them additional height by placing them on hillsides or crests—as you'll see at the otherworldly Palenque—and the principal structures were covered with exquisite bas-reliefs carved in stone. The small one-story pyramid-top temples characteristically had vestibules and rooms adorned with vaulted ceilings. The wide, spacious chambers inside the pyramids had smaller, attached rooms filled with bas-relief carvings of important events that occurred during the reign of the ruler who built the pyramid. Río Usumacinta friezes slope inward, rather than standing perpendicular under the large roof combs. Finest examples: Palenque, Yaxchilán.

Río Bec. Influenced by Guatemala's Petén style, the pitch of these pyramids is rather steep, and the foundations elaborately decorated. The stairways on the outside of some pyramids were built for aesthetic rather than practical purposes, and were "false" (unclimbable). The principal structures were long, one-story affairs containing two or sometimes three tall towers. Each was capped by a large roof comb emboldened with a dramatic stucco facade. Río Bec is found only in what is now the state of Campeche. Finest examples: Calakmul, Xpuhil, Río Bec.

Chenes. Found mainly in Campeche, this style likewise had long, single-story structures. In this case they were divided into three distinct sections, each with its own doorway charmingly surrounded by a face of the rain god, Chaac, whose mouth is the entrance. Facades were smothered in serpent-like embellishments. Finest examples: Hochob, Chicanná.

Puuc. Uxmal is the most striking illustration of the beautifully proportioned Puuc style. Commonly found in the state of Yucatán, it of all styles looks like the "pure" Maya style. The buildings were designed in a low-slung, quadrangle shape and had many, many rooms. Exterior walls were probably kept plain in order to show off the friezes above, which were lavishly embellished with stone mosaic deities surrounded by geometric and serpentine motifs. The corners of buildings were characteristically lined with the curl-nosed Chaac. Pyramids here did not have roof combs. Finest examples: Uxmal, Labná, Kabah, Sayil.

Northeast Plains. The fusion of two Maya groups—the early Chichén Maya and later Itzá Maya—produced this Late Classic (AD 600–900) style famously exemplified by Chichén Itzá. Here new forms like columns and grand colonnades were introduced. Palaces with row upon row of columns carved in the form of serpents looked over private patios, platforms were dedicated to the planet Venus, and pyramids were offered to Kúkulcan, the plumed serpent god borrowed from the Toltecs, who called him Quezalcóatl. Chichén Itzá is also famous for its temple-top, reclining, carved stone chacmool (a reclining figure with an offering tray carved in its middle)—another Itzá addition. Finest examples: Chichén Itzá, Mayapán.

Quintana Roo Coast. Although somewhat influenced by the Itzá Maya, a style entirely different eventually evolved here. The large, squat-looking, one-story buildings have interior columns, wooden-beam-supported ceilings, and numerous figures of the descending or Upside Down god which began appearing in the Post-Classic era (900–1530). Friezes were distinctively decorated with small niches. Finest examples: Tulum, El Rey, San Gervasio.

— Patricia Alisau

world—leads up to the temple. It can be difficult to make out the carvings on the slab, but they depict the ruler, prostrate beneath a sacred ceiba tree, who is still revered by the Maya today. The lords of the nine underworlds are carved into stucco reliefs on the walls around him. ☉ *Tomb daily 10:30–4.*

In 1994, the small and unassuming **Temple 13,** attached to the Temple of the Inscriptions, revealed a royal tomb hidden in its depths. The tomb, which probably belonged to Pacal's mother or grandmother, is under investigation and is currently not open to the public.

The patios, galleries, and other buildings that make up the **Palace** are set on a 30-ft-high plinth. Stucco work adorns the pillars of the galleries and the inner courtyards. There are numerous friezes and masks inside, most of them depicting Pacal and his dynasty. Steam baths in the Southwestern Patio suggest that priests once dwelled in the adjoining cellars. The palace's iconic tower was built on three levels, representing the three levels of the universe as well as the movement of the stars.

To the right of the palace you'll cross the tiny Otulum River, which in ancient times was roofed over to form a 9-ft-high vaulted aqueduct. It leads to the reconstructed **Plaza of the Cross,** which contains the Temple of the Exfoliated Cross, Temple of the Sun, Temple 14, and the Temple of the Cross, the largest of the group. Inside Temple 14, there's an underworld scene in stucco relief, done 260 days after Pacal died. The most exquisite roof combs are found on these buildings, which are thankfully open to the public.

To reach the cluster called the **Northern Group,** walk north along the river, passing the palace and then the unexcavated ball court on your left. There are five buildings here in various states of disrepair; the largest and best preserved is the **Temple of the Count.**

A short hike northwest of the Northern Group lies **Grupo C,** an area containing remains of the homes of Maya nobles and a few small temples completely shrouded in jungle. In order to maintain the natural setting in which the ruins were found, minimal restoration is being done. Human burials, funeral offerings of Jaina figurines, ceramics, and kitchen utensils have been found here as well as in **Grupo B,** near a small waterfall called El Baño de la Reina (The Queen's Bath). Early explorers cut pathways through the area, which can still be followed down through two meandering creeks with footbridges.

The on-site **museum** has a remarkable collection of finely preserved heads of Maya deities in elaborate zoomorphic headdresses, discovered in front of the Temple of the Foliated Cross. The group includes 13 figures of the sun god Kinich Ahau. Also noteworthy are the handsome stucco faces of Maya men. Art historians compare their naturalistic execution with that of ancient Greek sculpture. Displays are labeled in English, Spanish, and Tzotzil. There's also a snack bar and a handicrafts store with good weavings, hand-embroidered fabrics, leather, ceramics, amber jewelry, hand-painted wooden crosses, and children's toys. The museum is about 1 km (½ mi) before the parking lot entrance to the ruins along the highway.

You can stop in the museum before entering the archaeological site or get there by walking through the Grupo C and B sections of the ruins, which end at the highway. From there, the museum is about 100 yards away. When seeing the ruins, you can hire one of Palenque's multilingual guides at the ticket booth. ⌦ *Ruins and museum $2.* ☉ *Ruins daily 9–5; museum Tues.–Sun. 9–4:15.*

Palenque Town

㉓ *8 km (5 mi) north of the ruins.*

Whereas cool highlander San Cristóbal has a polite but reserved exterior, Palenque Town wraps you in a warm tropical embrace. Its days as a sleepy cattle town are far behind, as the city swells with newcomers and longtime residents rush to turn family homes into rent-paying *posadas,* or guesthouses. In only the last few years, thanks to tourism, upgraded services like E-mail servers have arrived (although the phone company lacks digital phone service and fiber-optic wiring); likewise ATMs and 24-hour long-distance phone service. The main street is being carved up to accommodate a wider sidewalk. Women and kids from San Juan Chamula, in the mountains, hawk crafts and souvenirs in front of strings of restaurants and pharmacies along the principal downtown streets.

The principal landmark in Palenque town is the chalk white "cabeza Maya," a giant sculpture of the head of a Maya chieftain that graces the town's one traffic circle. La Cañada is a quiet neighborhood west of downtown.

Dining and Lodging

$$ ✕ **La Selva.** Although a stop on the tour-group route, this spacious palapa-roofed restaurant is still popular with locals. The setting, surrounded by luxuriant jungle gardens, is superb and so is the food. There is a scrumptious Sunday brunch buffet after 12:30 PM for about $8. Otherwise the menu has regional specialties in addition to international fare: soups, salads, and seafood. ✉ *Carr. Ruinas Km 5,* ☏ *934/5–03–63. MC, V.*

$$ ✕ **The Maya Cañada.** This new restaurant in the quiet La Cañada neigh-
★ borhood is the comely baby sister to the aging but still popular Maya downtown. Sixties rock enlivens the atmosphere in the round, thatch-roofed restaurant. Earth red walls are trimmed in cobalt blue; cane furniture and red tile floors complete the open but cozy ambience. Try the $3.50 set lunch menu, consisting of soup, main dish, and dessert, or choose something from the extensive appetizer menu, including tacos and tostadas. Mexican wines are served, and there is a full bar. ✉ *Calle Merle Green s/n, La Cañada,* ☏ *934/5–02–16. No credit cards. Downtown branch:* ✉ *Corner of Hidalgo and Independencia, across from town plaza,* ☏ *934/5–00–42. No credit cards.*

$ ✕ **El Arbolito.** Located on the main road to the ruins, this fun and funky restaurant is full of souvenirs of old ranch life. There's a wall full of hats, each inscribed with a different Mexican proverb. Other wood-paneled walls have mounted animal heads and pelts. It's no surprise that the house specialty is meat. Favorites include the spicy *consomé de borrego especial,* a broth with barbecued sheep, onions, and fresh cilantro. Beef tips in smoky chile chipotle or other mild chile sauces are served with beans, rice, garnish, and piping hot tortillas. ✉ *Carretera Palenque–Pakalná Km 1.5, across from Days Inn,* ☏ *934/5–09–00. MC, V.*

$ ✕ **Las Tinajas.** Bargain-hunters will return again and again to this plain eatery several streets southwest of the plaza. Portions are gargantuan, and the staff is used to wrapping up leftovers to go. What the restaurant lacks in ambience is made up for by the presentation of the individual plates, each adorned with tomato "roses" holding a sprig of fresh basil. Locals come for the monster breaded chicken fillet, served with french fries, or the bean empanadas (called *tlacoyos*) or chicken tostadas. Service can be slow, but the food is worth waiting for. ✉ *Calle 20 de Noviembre at Abasolo,* ☏ *No phone. No credit cards.*

$$$$ ▥ **Misión Palenque.** Four blocks from the zócalo in the downtown area, this hotel is fronted by a huge green lawn and pretty grounds but has plain, motel-like rooms. All of them are air-conditioned and have cable TV and phones; the tiny patios lack furniture. The terraced restaurant glows nightly with candlelight. Located off Route 199, it has a free shuttle bus to the ruins. Tour groups, which constitute a large percentage of the clientele, rotate in and out daily. Note that you'll be quoted a higher price if you call the 800 number in the U.S. ⊠ *Rancho San Martín de Porres, 29960,* ☎ *934/5–02–41; 800/448-8355 in the U.S.,* FAX *934/5–02–48. 256 rooms, 2 suites. Restaurant, bar, pool, 2 tennis courts, shop, travel services, free parking. AE, DC, MC, V.*

$$ ⊞ **Chan Kah.** Four kilometers (2½ miles) from the ruins in a paradisi-
★ acal jungle setting that is also a forest reserve, Chan Kah should not be confused with the sister hotel in downtown Palenque. There is a stone-lined, lagoon-style pool, aromatic jasmine bushes, and a stream flowing around the back. The restaurant is overpriced, and meals are accompanied by Muzak, but the very comfortable bungalows have wide terraces with comfy chairs, mahogany furnishings, and ceiling fans and/or air-conditioning. Bungalows 6 through 10 have views of the pool and stream. The emphasis here is on tranquility: there is no TV, and only a few rooms have phones. ⊠ *Carr. Ruinas Km 3.5, 29960,* ☎ *934/5–11–00, 934/5–07–62, 934/5–08–26, or 934/5–09–74,* FAX *934/5–08–20. 72 bungalows. Restaurant, bar, pool, free parking. AE, MC, V.*

$$ ⊞ **Days Inn Tulijá.** You can't beat the price or location of this cheer-ful little hotel, which is about a 10-minute walk from downtown. It has the basics for a comfortable stay: color cable TV, air-conditioning, and firm beds in the smallish rooms. The 25-meter-long pool is a great boon for swimmers; the tequila bar boasts over 35 brands of the dis-tilled agave liquor. ⊠ *Apdo. 57, Carr. Ruinas Km 27.5, 29960,* ☎ *934/5–01–04 or 934/5–01–65; 800/329–7466 in the U.S.,* FAX *934/5–01–63. 48 rooms. Restaurant, bar, pool, billiards. AE, MC, V.*

$$ ⊞ **Hotel Maya Tulipanes.** Located in the tranquil La Cañada neigh-borhood, this fine hotel has both air-conditioning and fans, remote-control cable TV, and screened windows. The pleasant restaurant spills outdoors around the small pool. Room 209 is a junior suite which goes for the same price as standard rooms; the management aims to please. The Maya oratory is a replica of the Temple of the Foliated Cross at Palenque. ⊠ *Calle Cañada 6, 29960,* ☎ *934/5–02–01 or 934/5–02–58,* FAX *934/5–10–04. 47 rooms, 1 jr. suite. Restaurant, bar, pool, bas-ketball court, free parking. AE, MC, V.*

$$ ⊞ **Quality Resorts Palenque Nututún.** This property, a member of the Choice Hotels International chain, has plain, ample rooms with tile floors. There is a $7 difference between rooms with a small, furnitureless terrace and TV and those without. The real draw is the large natural pool formed from a bend in the Nututún river, which runs through the grounds. Camping is permitted near the river for about $4.50 per per-son. ⊠ *Carretera Palenque–Ocosingo Km 3.5, Apdo. 74, 29960,* ☎ *934/5–01–00 or 934/5–01–61; 800/221–2222 in the U.S.,* FAX *934/5–06–20. 40 suites, 12 rooms. Restaurant, bar, pool, camping, play-ground, free parking. AE, MC, V.*

$ ⊞ **El Shalom.** A budget hotel in the heart of downtown, the Shalom's Maya arches are painted bright lilac; otherwise the decoration is quite simple. The clean-smelling rooms are ample, and some on the third floor have a great view of the mountains. Although the sheets are a bit thread-bare, the price of $10 for a double with fan and TV is hard to beat. ⊠ *Av. Juárez s/n, above Restaurant el Paisano,* ☎ *No phone. 17 rooms. No credit cards.*

Bonampak

⚠ ㉔ *183 km (113 mi) southeast of Palenque.*

Bonampak is renowned for its courtly murals of ancient Maya life. The settlement was built on the banks of the Lacanjá River during the 7th and 8th centuries and remained undiscovered until 1946. Explorer Jacques Soustelle called it "a pictorial encyclopedia of a Mayan city." In remarkable ochre and faience colors, the scenes portrayed in the three rooms of the **Templo de las Pinturas** graphically recall subjects such as life at court and the prelude and aftermath of battle. It's open daily 8–5; admission is free, but there is a $5.50 charge for the service of a Lacandon guide, who will join you near the park entrance. Segments of the paintings are constantly deteriorating because the high humidity in the area eats away at the colors, and thick white deposits of calcium from dripping water have covered some of them completely. In 1984 Mexican experts devised a technique for cleaning and restoring the murals, and with the help of the National Geographic Society—and computerized, digital amplification techniques—remarkable details and color have come to light. It stands to reason that the reproductions at the archaeological museums in Mexico City and Villahermosa are more legible than the on-site specimens.

Until recently, only the most devoted fans of the Maya attempted the trip to the ruins of Bonampak and Yaxchilán (☞ *below*). However, you can now take Highway 198 south from Palenque and travel the last 12 km (7½ mi) on a packed dirt road to get here. Tours will take you all the way in to Bonampak, or let you hike the last challenging three hours to the site, as was done before the road was completed. (If you decide to hike in, consider having the van pick you up at the site to avoid the long walk back.) Small-plane charter service to Bonampak and Yaxchilán flies out of Palenque, Ocosingo, or Comitán. In these towns, contact **Servicios Aereos San Cristóbal** (in Ocosingo ☎ 967/3–01–88; in Comitán ☎ 967/2–46–62), or in Palenque **Transporte Aereos Jataté** (☎ 934/5–00–21). Be sure to wear sturdy shoes, and bring insect repellent, good sunglasses, and a hat to protect yourself from mosquitoes, ticks, sand flies, undergrowth, and the jungle sun.

Yaxchilán

★ ⚒ ㉕ *50 km (31 mi) northeast of Bonampak, 190 km (118 mi) southeast of Palenque.*

Excavations at Yaxchilán (yash-chee-*lan*), on the banks of the Usumacinta River, have uncovered stunning temples and delicate carvings in an isolated jungle setting. Spider monkeys and toucans are, at this point, more prolific than tourists, and howler monkeys growl like lions from the towering *chico zapote* and hundred-year-old ceiba trees. Yaxchilán, which means "place of green stones," reached its cultural peak during the Late Classic period, from about AD 680–770. It is dominated by two acropolises containing a palace, temples with finely carved lintels, and great staircases. Until recently, the Lacandon, who live in the vicinity, made pilgrimages to this site in the heart of the jungle, leaving behind "god pots" (incense-filled ceramic bowls) in honor of ancient deities. They were particularly awed by the headless sculpture of Yaxachtun (ya-sha-*tun*) at the entrance to the temple (called Structure 33) and believed that the world would end when its head was replaced on its torso.

Yaxchilán was situated on the trade route between Palenque and Tikal, and the existence of a **600-ft bridge** crossing the Usumacinta River to connect Yaxchilán to Guatemalan territory has been discovered. The engineering know-how of the people of Yaxchilán is still being deciphered by modern-day engineers. The site has been threatened with destruction by a huge dam to be built by Mexico and Guatemala. Thankfully, plans have been put on hold indefinitely due to lack of funds. Most people arrive by a combination of land and river boat (a long day trip from Palenque) or air tour. ☒ *$2.* ☉ *Daily 9–5.*

Lodging

$ ⌂ **Escudo Jaguar.** This ecotourism project 144 km (89 mi) south of Palenque is run by the local Tzeltal people and designed to bring people closer to the Maya ruins of Bonampak and Yaxchilán. There are four comfortable wooden cabins painted pink with blue shutters. Each has a wide cement verandah with two large, colorful hammocks for lounging. Inside, the thatch-roofed cabins have screened windows, mosquito nets, and fans. Four more cabins are under construction, and should be ready by press time. The restaurant serves sandwiches and shakes in addition to full lunches and dinners. It is best to book trips to Bonampak and Yaxchitlán ahead of time, mentioning that you want to stay overnight at Escudo Jaguar. ✉ *Frontera Corozal, Ocosingo,* ☎ *015/201–6440 for reservations,* ☎ FAX *015/201–6441. 4 cabins. Restaurant, free parking. No credit cards.*

VILLAHERMOSA AND TABASCO

Graham Greene's succinct summation of Tabasco as a "tropical state of river and swamp and banana grove" captures its essence. Though the state played an important role in the early history of Mexico, its past is rarely on view. Instead, it is Tabasco's modern-day status as a supplier of oil that defines it. Set on a humid coastal plain and criss-crossed by 1,930 km (1,197 mi) of rivers, low hills, and unexplored jungles, the land is still rich in banana and cacao plantations. Shanty-towns and refineries are for the most part invisible to the visitor, who on bus trips passes small ranches with pastures of tall, green grass feeding horses and beef cattle. The capital city of Villahermosa epitomizes the mercurial development of Tabasco (the airplane was here before the automobile). Thanks to oil and urban renewal, the cramped and ugly neighborhoods in the mosquito-ridden town of the 1970s have been replaced by spacious boulevards, lush green parks, and cultural centers. Sandwiched between the Grijalva River and the historic downtown, the Zona Luz has been redone as a brick-paved pedestrian zone housing galleries and museums in addition to restaurants, ice cream shops, and a Howard Johnson Hotel.

This is not to say that the rest of Tabasco has nothing to offer. There are beaches, lagoons, caves, and nature reserves, but the tourism infra-structure is minimal. The fired-brick Maya ruins of Comalcalco attest to the influence of Palenque. Probably the most interesting region is the one to the south and east of Villahermosa, where rivers and canyons are home to jaguars, deer, and alligators. This was where the English pirate Sir Francis Drake hid from the Spanish navy.

Tabasco—specifically the mouth of the River Grijalva—lay along the route of the Spanish explorations of Mexico in 1518–19. At that time, the state's rivers and waterways, along which the Maya lived, served as a trade route between the peoples of the north and those of the south. When the Spaniards came to Tabasco, they had to bridge 50 rivers and contend with swarms of mosquitoes, beetles, and ants—as well as the almost unbearable heat. At the same time, the region was so lush that one early chronicler termed it a Garden of Eden.

The Spanish conquest was made easier by the extreme antipathy and tribal warfare between the Tabascans and their Aztec overlords. Among the 20 slave women turned over to the Spaniards upon their arrival in the Aztec capital was a Chiapan named Malintzín (or Malinche), who was singled out by the Spaniards for her ability to speak both the Maya and the Nahuatl languages. Called Doña Marina by the Spaniards, she learned Spanish and became not only Cortés's mistress and the mother of his illegitimate son but also an interpreter of Indian customs. Marina's cooperation helped the conquistador vanquish both Moctezuma and Cuauhtémoc, the last Aztec rulers. Even today, "La Malinche" is synonymous with "traitor" throughout Mexico.

Until the early 20th century Tabasco slumbered. It did not become a state until 1924. After the American Civil War, traders from the southern United States began operating in the region and on its rivers, hauling the precious mahogany trees upstream from Chiapas and shipping them north from the small port of Frontera. This was Tabasco's most prosperous era until the discovery of oil 50 years ago and the oil boom of the 1980s. Although PEMEX (the government-run oil monopoly) was plagued with workers' strikes throughout 1995 in Villahermosa, the oil company plans to relocate its research offices there.

Villahermosa

㉖ *821 km (509 mi) southeast of Mexico City, 632 km (392 mi) southwest of Mérida.*

There are a good many ways to spend your time in Tabasco's capital. The *zona luz,* or light district (a.k.a. *zona remodelada,* or remodeled district) is a grid of pedestrian-only streets with restored colonial buildings, sidewalk cafés, galleries, and museums of popular culture and history. Most people, however, make a beeline for the **Carlos Pellicer Museo de Antropología** (Museum of Anthropology). Named after the man who donated many of the artifacts and whom the locals call the "poet laureate of Latin America" (1897–1978), the museum is on the right bank of the Grijalva and is part of the huge CICOM cultural complex dedicated to research on the Olmec and Maya (which is what the Spanish acronym CICOM stands for). It provides one of the last tranquil vistas of Villahermosa as it might have looked 50 years ago. Although all the explanations are in Spanish, that should not detract from the visual pleasure of the displays.

Much of the collection is devoted to Tabasco and the Olmec, or "inhabitants of the land of rubber," who flourished in Tabasco as early as 1200 to 1300 BC and disappeared about AD 800. The Olmecs have long been honored as inventors of the numerical and calendrical systems that spread throughout the region. The pyramid is also attributed to them. Some of the most interesting artifacts of the Olmec, apart from the remarkable stone sculptures and giant stone heads on view at Parque Museo La Venta (☞ *below*), are the remnants of their jaguar cult displayed here. The jaguar symbolized the earth fertilized by rain (i.e., procreation), and many Olmec sculptures portray half-human, half-jaguar figures, and jaguar babies. Other sculptures portray human heads emerging from the mouth of a jaguar, bat gods, bird-headed humans, and female fertility figurines.

Many of Mexico's ancient cultures are represented on the upper two floors, from the red-clay dogs of Colima and the nose rings of the Huichol Indians of Nayarit to the huge burial urns of the Chontal Maya, who built Comalcalco. The CICOM building complex also houses a theater, restaurant, public library, and handicrafts shop. ⊠ *Carlos Pellicer 511, an extension of the malecón,* ☎ 93/12–63–44. 🎫 *About $1.50.* ⊙ *Tues.–Sun. 9–7:30.*

The giant stone heads and other figures carved by the Olmec were salvaged from the oil fields of La Venta, on the western edge of Tabasco near the state of Veracruz. They are on display in the 8-hectare **Parque Museo La Venta,** in a tropical garden on the beautiful Lago de las Ilusiones (Lake of Illusions), founded also by Carlos Pellicer. The 6-ft-tall, bold-featured carved stone heads, wearing what look like helmets and weighing up to 20 tons, have sparked endless scholarly debate. It has been theorized that they depict ancient Phoenician slaves or space invaders. The latest and least outlandish (or offensive) theory is that the faces on the sculptures—very similar to today's Tabasco Maya—are actual portraits of successful Olmec athletes, war heroes, and other public figures. La Venta contains 33 sculptures, including jaguars, priests, monsters, stelae, and stone altars. Within the park is a **zoo** with creatures such as Tabascan river crocodiles, deer, jaguars, coatimundi, monkeys, and wild parrots. There is also a gift shop and several outdoor stands selling embroidered blouses, T-shirts, and souvenirs. ⊠ *Blvd. Ruíz Cortines near Paseo Tabasco,* ☎ *93/14–16–52.* ☞ *$1.50.* ☉ *Daily 8–5 (ticket booth closes at 4); zoo closed Mon.*

The small **Museo de la Historia Natural** (natural history museum) is just outside the entrance to the park. Of most interest are the displays of Tabasco's native plants and animals, many of which are now under government protection. Other rooms are dedicated to geology, evolution, and the solar system. ⊠ *Blvd. Ruíz Cortines near Paseo Tabasco,* ☎ *No phone.* ☞ *$1.* ☉ *Tues.–Sun. 9–5.*

One of Villahermosa's newest attractions is **Yumká,** a nature reserve spread over 250 acres of jungle, savannah, and wetlands. Half-hour guided walking tours take you over a hanging bridge and past free-roaming endangered or threatened species like spider monkeys, red macaws, toucans, crocodiles, turtles, and native *tepezcuintles* (a giant rodent). Next comes a longer aerial tram ride past Asian and African species such as elephant and zebra. Optional boat tours, which have a small additional price, glide past birds wading or taking flight. ⊠ *16 km (10 mi) from downtown past the airport at Poblado Dos Montes,* ☎ *93/56–01–19 or 93/56–01–15.* ☞ *$2.* ☉ *Daily 9–5 (ticket window closes at 3:30).*

Dining and Lodging

$$$ ✕ **Los Tulipanes.** Tucked between the Esperanza Iris Theater and the
★ Carlos Pellicer Museum of Anthropology in the CICOM complex, spacious Los Tulipanes specializes in seafood and has a soothing view of the river. Try the regional appetizers, including stuffed tortillas and *empanadas* (turnovers stuffed with crab or shrimp), or the Tabasco specialty, *pejelagarto* (a small, alligatorlike fish), a succulent treat. The same owners run the $$$ **Capitán Beulo,** a small cruiser that runs 1½-hour dining trips on the Grijalva River twice daily ($5 minimum consumption). Board on the *malecón* (boardwalk) at the foot of Lerdo de Tejada, or call Los Tulipanes for reservations. Daily (except Monday) at 3:30 and 9:30 PM; Sunday 1:30 and 3:30. ⊠ *Carlos Pellicer 511,* ☎ *93/12–92–09 or 93/12–92–17. AE, MC, V.*

$$ ✕ **El Mesón del Duende.** This restaurant, which translates as the House of the Elf, adds a regional accent to standard meat and fish dishes. Try the house favorites, *filete en salsa de espinaca y queso* (beef fillet in a cheese and spinach sauce) and *la posta de robalo* (grilled snook). The modest decor is in keeping with the family-style atmosphere. ⊠ *Gregorio Méndez 1703,* ☎ *93/15–13–24. AE, MC, V.*

$ ✕ **Acuarius.** Vegetarians will delight in finding this healthful eatery in the heart of the Zona Luz. What it lacks in ambience—walls are unadorned and the radio sometimes blares music—it makes up for in a wide variety of fruit and vegetable juices, soy burgers, and other meatless fare. There are extensive breakfast and lunch buffets for $3.50 and $4, respectively. Keep your eyes open for their other locations throughout the city. ⊠ *Zaragoza 513,* ☎ *93/12–05–79. No credit cards.* ☉ *Closed Sun.*

$ ✕ **Leo.** This popular spot for tasty beef and pork tacos—with a meaty menu and a spacious, clean, no-frills dining area—is frequently packed with Mexican families. Loud music, whirling fans, and downtown traffic drown out the noise of kids cavorting at the front of the restaurant on bright plastic play equipment—it isn't exactly the place for a tête-à-tête. Service is quite efficient, however. It's a carnivore's heaven for $5 during the Sunday buffet, 10–6. ✉ *Paseo Tabasco 429, Col. Mayito,* ☎ *93/12–44–63. MC, V.*

$$$$ ⊞ **Hotel Camino Real.** This inviting nine-story resort property at the fringe of the Tabasco 2000 shopping complex has air-conditioned rooms with blue carpet, bathtubs, and clock radios in addition to amenities such as cable TV and minibars. The rambling lobby, with rattan furniture in attractive niches, eventually leads to the Tabasco 2000 shopping mall, which has the largest number of upscale stores in Villahermosa. Shaded by bamboo curtains, the restaurant's floor-to-ceiling windows overlook a lovely garden. There's live entertainment in the lobby lounge nightly except Sunday. Continental breakfast and an appetizer hour are offered for those staying in more capacious rooms on the executive floor. ✉ *Paseo Tabasco 1407, 86030,* ☎ *93/16–44–00; 800/722–6466 in the U.S.,* FAX *93/16–44–00. 190 rooms, 9 suites. Restaurant, bar, coffee shop, room service, pool, beauty salon, exercise room, travel services, car rental, free parking. AE, DC, MC, V.*

$$$$ ⊞ **Hyatt Regency Villahermosa.** This American-style luxury hotel built in 1983 offers the amenities of the worldwide Hyatt chain: air-conditioned rooms with cable TV, voice mail, and minibars, and two executive floors with concierge service. Rooms have marble floors and polished wood furnishings with accents in forest green and burgundy. The La Ceiba Café has pleasing tropical decor and a superb daily breakfast buffet ($10) to which local families flock on Sundays. In the lobby, El Plataforma video bar is decked out like the inside of an offshore oil platform with photos of oilmen at work; there is live music nightly at 8. ✉ *Av. Juárez 106, Zona Hotelera, 86050,* ☎ *93/13–44–44 or 93/15–12–34; 800/228–9000 in the U.S.,* FAX *93/15–58–08 or 93/15–12–35. 262 rooms, 8 suites. 2 restaurants, 3 bars, pool, 2 tennis courts, travel services, car rental. AE, DC, MC, V.*

$$$ ⊞ **Calinda Viva Villahermosa.** The common areas of this five-story member of the Choice Hotels International chain are more inviting than the ordinary rooms. The enormous square pool is surrounded by plenty of lounge chairs and umbrella-shaded tables, and peacocks strut about the grounds or roost on ground-level balconies. All rooms have air-conditioning, FM stereos, color satellite TV, and small balconies. The restaurant serves many regional dishes, with a daily breakfast and lunch buffet. ✉ *Av. Ruíz Cortines at Paseo Tabasco s/n, Col. Linda Vista, 86050,* ☎ *93/15–00–00; 800/221–2222 in the U.S.,* FAX *93/15–30–73. 249 rooms, 1 suite. Restaurant, 2 bars, pool, massage, sauna, steam room, exercise room. AE, DC, MC, V.*

$$$ ⊞ **Maya Tabasco Best Western.** A few blocks from the first-class (ADO) bus station, the Maya Tabasco has rooms with air-conditioning, cable TV, and phones; a rather plain lobby; and an energetic staff. This hotel is outclassed by others of similar price range; however it will do if your first choices are booked. You can check out open-mike night in the new Belle Epoque Trova Bar Café, smack in the middle of the swimming pool. ✉ *Ruíz Cortines 907, 86000,* ☎ *93/14–44–66 or 93/14–03–60; 800/528–1234 in the U.S.,* FAX *93/12–10–97. 150 rooms, 2 suites. 2 restaurants, bar, café, pool, dance club, travel services, car rental. AE, DC, MC, V.*

$$–$$$ ⊞ **Cencali.** This two-story hotel, just across from La Venta museum and park, sits on a lagoon and is surrounded by lush greenery; it has the best view in town. Most of the small, cheerfully decorated rooms

have lots of light; 30 of the best also have balconies overlooking the lagoon, which is fringed with coconut palms, mango, and cacao trees. All rooms have bathtubs, air-conditioning, and cable TV. Don't miss the fabulous lobby mural of pre-Columbian indigenous life (inspired by the Maya document *Popol Vuh*) by Tabascan master Daniel Ponce Montúy (1925–). The airy La Isla coffee shop, overlooking the pool and the lagoon, has a daily breakfast buffet ($7) and lunch specials. ✉ *Av. Juárez and Paseo Tabasco, 86040,* ☎ *93/15–19–19,* FAX *93/15– 66–00. 116 rooms, 3 suites. Restaurant, bar, coffee shop, pool. AE, DC, MC, V.*

$$ 🏨 **Howard Johnson.** This five-story hotel is conveniently located in the pedestrian-only Zona Luz area, not far from the historic downtown and the malecón. Just four years old, it has lots of conveniences for its price range, including cable TV, complimentary newspaper, room service, and an Internet café on the premises. Weekend rates offer a substantial discount (as do most business-oriented hotels here). The coffee shop's attentive waiters serve mugs of hot coffee with real cream and refills. ✉ *Av. Aldama 404, 86000,* ☎ FAX *93/14–46–45,* ☎ *800/446– 4656 in the U.S. 88 rooms, 6 suites. Coffee shop, room service, free parking. AE, MC, V.*

$$ 🏨 **Plaza Independencia.** Sandwiched between the Grijalva River and the Plaza de Armas, this attractive hotel has a lot to recommend it besides an excellent location. Common areas are overwashed in Mexican pink, sky blue, and sunny yellow paint, and there is a medium-size pool in the back patio. Some of the rooms have wacky decorations, with mint green and orange furnishings clashing with cotton bedspreads in other bright colors. Others rooms are more subdued. All have room safes, closets, cable TV, and air-conditioning. Ask for a room with a balcony overlooking the river. ✉ *Av. Independencia 123, 86000,* ☎ *93/12–12–99,* FAX *93/14–47–24. 89 rooms, 1 suite. Restaurant, bar, pool, free parking. AE, DC, MC, V.*

Comalcalco

🔺 ㉗ *60 km (37 mi) northwest of Villahermosa off Rte. 187.*

Comalcalco, which means "place of the clay griddles (bricks)" in Nahuatl, is the most important Maya site in Tabasco. The abundant cacao trees in the region provided food and livelihood for a booming population during the Late Classic period (AD 600–900); it was founded approximately in the 1st century BC. The site marks the westernmost reach of the Maya, and descendants of its builders, the Chontal, still live in the vicinity. This site is unique among Maya cities for its use of fired brick (made of sand, seashells, and clay), as the Tabasco swamplands lacked the stone for building that was found elsewhere in the empire. The bricks were inscribed and painted with figures of reptiles and birds, geometric figures, and drawings of hands and feet before being covered with stucco. The major pyramid, **Temple IV,** on the Great Eastern Acropolis, is decorated with large stucco masks of the sun god Kinich Ahau and carvings, and the **museum** houses many of the artifacts that were uncovered there. 🎫 *About $2.* ⊙ *Daily 9–4:30.*

Paraíso

㉘ *19 km (12 mi) north of Comalcalco.*

If not seeing the Gulf of Mexico will leave you feeling deprived, you can continue on from Comalcalco to the coast and Paraíso, where you'll get a glimpse of small town life and a pretty coast. Take a boat ride through mangrove-lined channels or climb nearby **Teodomiro Hill** for a spectacular view of Las Flores lagoon and coconut plantations. Small seafood restaurants and several small hotels dot the shore here; others are a few kilometers inland, in town.

CHIAPAS AND TABASCO A TO Z

Arriving and Departing

By Bus

PALENQUE

First- and second-class service is available to Villahermosa (2 hrs), Ocosingo (3 hrs), San Cristóbal (4½ hrs), Mexico City (18 hrs), Cancún (12 hrs), Mérida (8 hrs), Campeche (6 hrs), and Tuxtla Gutiérrez (7 hrs) on **ADO** and **Cristóbal Colón**. Buses leave from the **ADO bus terminal** at Avenida Juárez, near Avenida de la Vega (☎ 934/5–13–44). Many of the same destinations can be reached on **Omnibus de Chiapas** (☎ 934/5–16–56) and **Express Plus** (☎ 934/5–10–12), both a few doors down.

SAN CRISTÓBAL

Cristóbal Colón (✉ Av. Insurgentes and Blvd. Juan Sabines Gutiérrez s/n, ☎ 967/8–02–91) has first- and second-class buses to major destinations in Chiapas and beyond. The green vans of **Corazón de María** (☎ No phone) leave right next door to the Cristóbal Colon terminal for Tuxtla Gutiérrez as soon as they fill up (about every 20 minutes) from 5 AM to 10 PM and cost less than $2. Second-class service on **Transportes Tuxtla Express Plus** (☎ 967/8–48–69) to Tuxtla, Palenque, and Guatemala departs from the terminal at Allende, ½ block up from Boulevard Juan Sabines Gutiérrez, about four blocks to the west.

TUXTLA GUTIÉRREZ

Cristóbal Colón (✉ Av. 2 Nte. at 2 Pte. 268, ☎ 961/2–16–39 or 961/2–26–24) offers deluxe and first- and second-class bus service between Tuxtla and Oaxaca, Palenque, Villahermosa, Tapachula, Mérida, Mexico City, San Cristóbal, Cancún, and Playa del Carmen. First- and second-class transportation within the state is available on **Sociedad de Transportes Dr. Rodulfo Figueroa** (✉ 4a Poniente Sur 1060, ☎ 961/3–65–92).

VILLAHERMOSA

There is frequent second-class service to Campeche, Chetumal, Mérida, Mexico City, Palenque, San Cristóbal, Tapachula, Tuxtla Gutiérrez, Veracruz, and elsewhere. Buses arrive and depart from **Central Camionera de 2a Clase** (✉ Av. Ruíz Cortines s/n, ☎ 93/12–29–77 or 93/12–10–91). Deluxe and first-class service is available to the above cities at the **ADO** bus terminal (✉ Calle F. J. Mina 297), which is served by ADO (☎ 93/12–76–27 or 93/12–76–92), **UNO** (☎ 93/14–58–18 or 93/14–20–54), **G. L.** (☎ 93/12–76–27), and **Cristóbal Colón** (☎ 93/12–29–37 or 93/12–89–00).

By Car

From Tuxtla Gutiérrez, Highway 190 goes east through Chiapa de Corzo to San Cristóbal before continuing southeast to Comitán and the Guatemala border. Highway 199 to Highway 186 (the turnoff is at Catazajá) is the preferred route from San Cristóbal to Villahermosa; it'll take you via Toniná, Agua Azul, and Palenque. The drive from San Cristóbal to Palenque takes about five hours along a winding paved road, and it's another two hours from Palenque to Villahermosa along a fairly straight road.

On the map, Highway 195 may look like the most direct way to travel between San Cristóbal and Villahermosa, but it entails hours of hairpin curves—it's only for the stalwart and absolutely not to be traveled at night because of seasonal fog as well as a lack of reflectors, illumination, and other cars to help in case of emergency.

To get to Villahermosa from Coatzacoalcos and Veracruz, take Highway 180. In all cases, exercise caution during the rainy season (June through October), when roads are slick. Though expensive, car rentals are available at the Tuxtla and Villahermosa airports as well as in San Cristóbal (☞ Car Rental, *below*).

By Plane

BONAMPAK AND YAXCHILÁN

For charter flights to the ruins of Bonampak and Yaxchilán, contact the following air charters: in Tuxtla Gutiérrez, **Montes Azules** (☎ 961/ 3–22–56 or 961/3–29–93); in Comitán, **Servicio Aéreo San Cristóbal** (☎ 963/2–03–09).

PALENQUE

Aerocaribe flies to Palenque from Flores, Guatemala (near the Tikal ruins), and Tuxtla Gutiérrez (with connections to Oaxaca and Mexico City). You can charter a small plane to Bonampak, Yaxchilán, or elsewhere with **Transporte Aereas Jataté** (☎ 934/5–00–21).

SAN CRISTÓBAL

The **San Cristóbal airport** (✉ Corazón de María Km 17) opened in October 1997. It serves Mexico City, Palenque, and Tuxtla Gutiérrez on a limited basis via **Aerocaribe** (☎ 961/8–68–63). The closest major airport is in Tuxtla Gutiérrez (☞ *below*), 85 km (53 mi) to the west. You can get from Tuxtla to San Cristóbal by first-class bus, which leaves several times each day (two hours; about $2.50), or by taxi (1½ hours; $13 for one to four persons). Many travel agencies in both cities provide private taxi service. You can also catch a *colectivo* (shared minivan) to San Cristóbal at either of the two airports in Tuxtla Gutiérrez: From the Llano San Juan airport, it costs about $5 per person; from the Terán airport, $3.

TUXTLA GUTIÉRREZ

Two airports serve Tuxtla: **Llano San Juan airport** (☎ 961/2–17–72), which is in the town of Ocozocoautla, 22 km (14 mi) west of the city, and **Terán Airport** (☎ 961/5–15–30), 8 km (5 mi) southwest of the city center. Flights are routed to one of these two airports depending on meteorological conditions, as fog is frequently a problem. **Aerocaribe** (☎ 961/2–17–72 or 961/2–00–20) flies nonstop to Mexico City, Oaxaca, Villahermosa; the latter continues on to Palenque. **Aviacsa** (☎ 961/ 2–49–88 or 961/2–88–84) also has direct flights from Mexico City, Oaxaca, and Tapacula; from Cancún, Guadalajara, and other cities you have to connect through Mexico City. You can catch a colectivo taxi from San Cristóbal to Tuxtla at the corner of Boulevard Juan Sabines Gutiérrez and Allende, across from the second-class bus station. The taxi ($5 per person) will leave when it has four passengers.

VILLAHERMOSA

Aeroméxico (☎ 93/12–15–28 or 93/12–95–54) has two to three daily nonstop flights from Mexico City and twice a week from Houston, Texas. **Mexicana** (☎ 93/16–31–32 to 35 or 12–15–28) has two to three daily nonstop flights to Mexico City also, and both airlines have connecting flights to other Mexican cities. **Aviasca** (☎ 93/16–57–33) flies nonstop to Mexico City and Mérida. **Aerocaribe,** Mexicana's regional line (☎ 93/16–50–46), serves southwest Mexico, Mexico City, and Havana, Cuba.

Getting Around

Palenque

A car or a tour arranged through a local travel agency is the easiest way to reach Palenque's surrounding attractions, although the ruins themselves can easily be reached via private taxi or inexpensive colectivo service from downtown (corner of Hidalgo and Allende) or from the ADO bus station. The local *sitio* (**taxi stand**) is at the town park (☎ 934/5–01–12 or 934/8–23–53). The downtown itself is small enough to traverse on foot.

San Cristóbal

As with many other colonial towns, the most enjoyable and thorough way to explore San Cristóbal is on foot. If you do come to town with a car, leave it in the hotel garage until you're ready to take an excursion outside San Cristóbal. Taxis cruise the streets and can also be found at the **sitio** across from the cathedral (☎ 967/8–03–96); there is colectivo service to outlying villages, departing from and returning to the market.

Villahermosa

Of the three rivers surrounding it, Villahermosa is oriented toward the River Grijalva to the east, which is bordered by a malecón. The city is huge, and driving can be tricky. The main road through town, Boulevard Adolfo Ruíz Cortines, is almost a highway; exit ramps are about 1 km (½ mi) apart, and tourist destinations are not clearly marked. There is both *special* (individual) and collective taxi service, so you can flag down taxis even if they have other passengers and see if they are going near your destination. Call 93/15–83–33 for a radio taxi. Information about city buses can be difficult to find.

Contacts and Resources

Car Rental

SAN CRISTÓBAL
Budget (⊠ Calle Diego de Mazariegos 36, ☎ FAX 967/8–18–71 or 967/8–31–00) is the only car rental agency in town.

TUXTLA GUTIÉRREZ
Budget (☎ 961/5–13–82 or 961/5–06–72) and **Alamo** (☎ 961/2–52–61 or 961/2–89–32) are represented at both Tuxtla airports.

VILLAHERMOSA
Internationally known companies with offices at the airport and downtown Villahermosa include **Advantage** (☎ 93/56–00–76 or 93/51–32–18), **Dollar** (☎ 93/15–48–30 or 93/56–02–11), **Hertz** (☎ 93/16–44–00 or 93/56–02–00), and **National** (☎ 93/15–12–34, ext. 3710 or 93/56–03–93).

Emergencies

In larger cities such as Tuxtla Gutiérrez and Villahermosa, dial **06** for fire, theft, and medical emergencies. If you don't speak Spanish, it might be better to call hotel personnel or the tourist office (during open hours) and ask for an English-speaking representative.

PALENQUE
For tourist-related problems contact the **Agencia del Ministerio Público** at the tourist office (☞ Visitor Information, *below*). Visit the **Centro de Salud** (⊠ Prolongación Juárez s/n, ☎ No phone), weekdays 7 AM– 8 PM for medical consultation. In an emergency, the **Hospital General** (☎ 934/5–07–33), next door, is open 24 hours a day, as is **Farmacia Lastra** (⊠ Av. Juárez s/n at Abasolo, downtown, ☎ 934/5–11–19).

Municipal police (⊠ Blvd. Juan Sabines Gutiérrez, s/n, near la Unidad Deportiva, ☎ 967/8–05–54); **Federal Highway Police** (⊠ Blvd. Juan Sabines Gutiérrez, s/n, ☎ 967/8–64–66); **Cruz Roja** (Red Cross, ⊠ Prolongación Ignacio Allende 55, ☎ 967/8–07–72 or 967/8–65–65); **Hospital General** (⊠ Insurgentes 24, ☎ 967/8–07–70 or 967/8–38–34). **Farmacio Regina** (⊠ Crescencio Rosas at Diego de Mazariegos ☎ 967/8–02–41), is a 24-hour pharmacy.

Fire (☎ 961/2–11–15); **Police** (☎ 961/2–05–30); **Red Cross hospital and ambulance service** (⊠ 5ta Nte. Pte. 1480, ☎ 961/2–00–96). **Farmacia del Ahorro** (⊠ Av. Central Poniente No. 874 at 8va Oriente Norte, ☎ 961/3–88–18) is a 24-hour pharmacy with delivery.

Red Cross Hospital (⊠ Av. Sandino, s/n, Col. Primero de Mayo, ☎ 93/15–55–55 or 93/13–35–93); **Seguridad Para Turista** (☎ 91–800/903–9200, toll-free number for legal and medical advice); **Fire** (☎ 06). **Farmacia Unión** (⊠ Av. 27 de Febrero 1205, ☎ 93/15–47–17) is a 24-hour pharmacy.

English-Language Bookstores

In San Cristóbal, **Chilam Balam** (2 locations: ⊠ Casa Utrilla at Av. Gen. Utrilla No. 33 and Dr. Navarro; Insurgentes 18, ☎ 967/8–04–86) has the latest editions of travel, archeology, and art books along with posters and maps of Mexico. **La Pared** (⊠ Hidalgo 2, ☎ FAX 967/8–63–67) is an informal information center for foreigners. In addition to buying or trading books, you can send or receive phone calls, faxes, and E-mail. **La Mercantil** (⊠ Diego de Mazariegos 21) has the best selection of English- and Spanish-language periodicals.

Guided Tours

From the town of Palenque, most tour operators offer half-day guided tours of Palenque ruins for about $6, which includes guide, entrance to the ruins, hotel pick-up, and lunch. Also offered are six-hour tours to the waterfalls at Misol-Há and Agua Azul, at about $10 per person, which is a good deal as it includes entrance to both sites and transportation. Longer trips to San Cristóbal, Toniná, and the Sumidero Canyon are also available. Reliable, recommended tour operators include **Intertravel** (⊠ Av. Juárez 48, ☎ 934/5–15–66) and **Kukulcán** (⊠ Av. Juárez s/n at Allende, ☎ 934/5–15–06). Both have one- and two-day trips to Bonampak and Yaxchilán by land or by plane. A one-day trip costs $50–$60 via land and boat, including transportation, Spanish-speaking guide, and lunch. You can visit one or both sites via small plane for about $175 (with four passengers). Two-day trips overnight in tents at the Lacandon village of Lacanjá and cost about $60, including five meals, transportation, and guide services. Both companies can arrange air or river trips to the Maya ruins at Tikal, in Guatemala, as well as day trips to Misol-Há and Agua Azul waterfalls near Palenque. **Ceiba Adventures** (⊠ Box 2274, Flagstaff, AZ 86003, ☎ 520/527–0171, FAX 520/527–8127) has guided adventure tours throughout the Ruta Maya, including excursions to Palenque, Bonampak, Yaxchilán, and Tikal. Available are cave explorations and river rafting along several Chiapan waterways sunk deep in the jungle. **Sacred Earth Adventures** (⊠ 368 Village St., Suite A7, Millis, MA, 02054, ☎ 888/479–1320) leads journeys to sacred Maya sites, integrating hatha yoga, breathing, and meditation with visits to important Maya sites and lectures about the Maya world. Groups are small and vegetarian food is available.

Orientation Tours. Full-day city bus tours also cover the village of San Juan Chamula and the San Cristóbal Caves. Five-hour horseback tours to the caves or San Juan Chamula can also be arranged.

Guides. Pepe Santiago and his partner lead tours ($8) seven days a week to San Juan Chamula and Zinacantán, leaving from Na Bolom (see Lodging, above) at 10 AM and returning about 3:30. Mercedes Hernández leaves from the zócalo at approximately 9 AM; look for her colorful umbrella. Raul and Alex meet near the giant cross in front of the cathedral at 9:30 AM; look for the blue van. The latter two charge $6 per person. All of these guides speak English and are recommended by the tourist department, which can also recommend personal, English-speaking guides.

Regional Tours. A. T. C. (⊠ Av. 16 de Septiembre No. 16, ☎ 967/8–25–57, 🖷 967/8–31–45); **Viajes Pakal** (⊠ Calle Cuauhtémoc, No. 6A, ☎ 967/8–28–18 or 967/8–42–93, 🖷 967/8–28–19, pakal@mundo-maya.com.mx); and **Viajes Pedrero** (⊠ Calle Insurgentes Sur, No. 1, in the Hotel Santa Clara, ☎ 967/8–69–83 or 967/8–11–40, 🖷 967/8–10–41) have local tours as well as Bonampak, Yaxchilán, Palenque, Agua Azul, Lagunas de Montebello, Amatenango, Chincultik, Comitán, Sumidero Canyon, and Tuxtla Gutiérrez; some arrange transportation to Guatemala, the Yucatán, and Belize. The seven-hour round-trip tour aboard Cessna planes to Bonampak and Yaxchilán flies out of Comitán and costs about $120 per person (minimum four people); it includes only airfare and transportation to Comitán. **Pronatura** (⊠ Av. Juárez 11–B, ☎ 967/8–50–00) offers day trips to the tropical cloud forests of **Reserva Huitepec** Tuesday, Thursday, and Saturday at 9, or by appointment; profits go to Chiapas conservation and reforestation programs. Most tour operators transport passengers in minibuses and can arrange hotel pickup. **DANA** (⊠ Dr. Navarro 10, ☎ 967/8–04–68, 🖷 967/8–43–07) offers low-impact four-day guided hiking tours to Laguna Miramar, the largest natural lake in southwestern Mexico, in the Lacandon rain forest. Here you'll experience lakeside camping, swimming, snorkeling, fishing, hiking, horseback riding, and visits to small area ruins and indigenous communities. A three-night stay (minimum stay) costs about $180 if you go by land, $280 by air. Longer visits can also be arranged.

Viajes Lido (⊠ Av. Central Poniente No. 861–A, ☎ 961/5–56–56; 🖷 961/2–11–30) and **Viajes Miramar** (⊠ Hotel Camino Real, Local 2, ☎ 961/7–77–77 ext. 7230; 🖷 961/5–59–25), run by the Fernandez sisters, offer city tours of Tuxtla Gutiérrez, plus excursions to Chiapa de Corzo and Sumidero Canyon for $25.

Agencia de Viajes Tabasco (⊠ Hyatt Regency Hotel, ☎ 93/15–12–34 or 93/15–57–90); also at ⊠ Galeria Tabasco 2000, Local 173, ☎ 93/16–40–88, 🖷 93/16–40–90 or 93/16–43–37) has city tours as well as trips to Comalcalco, Palenque, and San Cristóbal.

Visitor Information

The state of Chiapas has a toll-free tourist information number, which can be dialed from anywhere in Mexico (☎ 91–800/2–80–3), but which is not always answered.

Tourist office (⊠ Ground floor of Municipal Palace, facing zócalo, ☎ 963/2–40–47), open weekdays 9–3 and 6–9, Saturday 9–2.

Tourist information (✉ Av. Juárez and Abasolo at the Plaza de Artesanías, ☎ 934/5–03–56), open Monday–Saturday 8:30–9, Sunday 8:30–1:30.

The people at the **Municipal tourist office** (✉ Palacio Municipal [City Hall], ground floor, on zócalo, ☎ 967/8–06–65 or 967/8–01–35) have some information about San Cristóbal proper, although they are less than attentive. The people at the **State tourist office** (✉ Miguel Hidalgo 2, ½ block from zócalo, ☎ FAX 967/8–65–70) are very knowledgable and helpful and have information about attractions throughout the state. Both open Monday–Saturday 9–9, Sunday 9–2.

Tourist office (✉ Edificio Plaza de las Instituciones, ground floor, Blvd. Dr. Belisario Domínguez 950, ☎ 961/3–44–99 or 961/3–93–96), open weekdays 9–9, Saturday 9–7, Sunday 9–3.

Tourist office (✉ Paseo Tabasco 1504, ☎ 93/16–36–33 or 93/16–28–89), open weekdays 9–3 and 6–9; Saturday 9–1. The auxiliary office at Parque Museo La Venta is open daily 9–4; the airport information booth is supposed to be open daily 8–8.

12 VERACRUZ AND THE NORTHEAST

The superb but little-explored pyramids of El Tajín and the raffish charm of Veracruz, the first European city established on the North American mainland, are among Mexico's indisputable highlights. Many Texans get their first taste of Mexico in the northeastern border towns of Nuevo Laredo, Reynosa, and Matamoros. Texan or otherwise, if you venture farther down to Monterrey, you'll find far more sophisticated dining, shopping, and cultural attractions in the country's third largest city.

Updated by
Gina Hyams

THERE ARE PLENTY of reasons to make your way down into the state of Veracruz, not least of which are its culture and history. You can explore El Tajín—its Temple of the Niches is one of the most enchanting pre-Columbian buildings in Mexico. Or wander the venerable port of Veracruz, where the Spanish first landed in 1519; witness the fascinating aerial ritual of the *voladores* (fliers) of Papantla; and enjoy an archaeological museum second only to the one in Mexico City. You can also stroll the plazas of quaint mountain villages, laze on sandy beaches, and dine on some of the best seafood in Mexico, prepared in the famous Veracruz style.

If the northeasternmost Mexican states of Nuevo León and Tamaulipas are not, for the most part, the Mexico touted in glossy magazines—which is one reason they are unique—they are by no means bereft of appeal. A hybrid of Mexican and U.S. culture, the three border cities of Nuevo Laredo, Reynosa, and Matamoros are good places to pick up handicrafts and sample authentic Mexican dishes at relatively low prices. Improved roads have also led more people to take advantage of the opportunity to visit Monterrey, Mexico's third-largest city. With its cultural attractions, five-star hotels and restaurants, and, of course, shops, it is a highlight of the region. In Monterrey, you can arrange horseback rides, mountain biking excursions, and treks into the pine forests of the nearby Sierra Madre mountains. And in southern Tamaulipas state, the port of Tampico prides itself on its fine river fishing.

Pleasures and Pastimes

Dining

The state of **Veracruz** is famous for its signature dish, known as *huachinango a la veracruzana* (red snapper covered in tomatoes, onions, olives, and herbs). Leaving Veracruz without sampling this would be both a shame and a bit of a feat, as every chef has his own special version, which he will insist you try.

In Veracruz, as befits a hot, breezy port town, the emphasis is on simple, fresh food, mostly *pescado* (fish) and *mariscos* (shellfish). Whether at night or during the day, a stop at one of the town's cafés is de rigueur—the 18th-century Café de la Portal is known internationally for its atmosphere and its fantastic coffee. **Jalapa** probably has the best restaurants in the state; the cookery is just as creative as the town's arts and music scene. It's not uncommon to hear the pat-pat of tortillas being hand-formed as you eat, and beans, rice, and cheese, and occasionally chilies (this is, after all, the hometown of the jalapeño) are cleverly integrated into main dishes of meat and river fish such as trout. You can eat cheaply and heartily in **Papantla,** but with little variation. Just as **Tuxpán**'s best attractions are its pretty river and nearby beaches, some of the best places to eat here are the small, family-run seafood *palapas* (thatch-roofed huts) lining the beach as well as the river, as it makes its way to the Gulf at Playa Tuxpán. If you ask for the *platillo del día* (daily dish), most likely you'll be treated to a cold shrimp, calamari, or crab cocktail, or a plate of fried fish or shrimp with Mexican rice and tortillas.

Although **the northeast** isn't especially renowned for its cuisine, you'll find a nice variety of dishes from around the country. Among the regional specialties are *cabrito* (roast kid), *carne asada* (grilled fillet of beef), and *café de olla* (a delicious blend of coffee, cinnamon, and brown sugar brewed in a clay pot).

Very little in the state of Veracruz or the northeast is truly formal. Even in the cities of Veracruz and Monterrey reservations are almost never necessary, and a jacket and tie would look out of place almost anywhere (unless we note otherwise). In a town like Papantla, to say that dress is casual would be an understatement: shorts and a T-shirt won't get you a second glance even in the town's fanciest dining room.

CATEGORY	COST*
$$$$	over $20
$$$	$15–$20
$$	$8–$15
$	under $8

*per person for a three-course meal, excluding drinks, service, and tax

Fishing

Northeastern Mexico is a popular place for American anglers. **Lake Vicente Guerrero,** near Ciudad Victoria, has some of the best bass fishing in Mexico. You're likely to hook something at **La Pesca**—its name means "the fish"—on the Tamaulipas coast between Matamoros and Tampico east of Ciudad Victoria and Soto La Marina.

Lodging

The state of **Veracruz** is just starting to get world-class hotels like the super-deluxe Fiesta Americana in Veracruz. The port city also has a number of inexpensive hotels with plenty of atmosphere, and the moderately priced and more expensive places offer good value for your money, especially in comparison with their counterparts in areas of Mexico that see more foreign tourists.

Although there are plenty of clean, comfortable, and inexpensive options in downtown **Jalapa,** more upscale choices are limited. The two nicest hotels, the Fiesta Inn and Posada de Coatepec, are a bit out of town, which can be inconvenient if you don't have a car, because local bus service is infrequent and Jalapa's many cultural offerings are concentrated in the *zona centro.* Many people choose to see **El Tajín** as a day trip from the more developed city of Tuxpán, only briefly passing through Papantla. If you decide to spend a night or two here, your options are limited. **Papantla** has few hotels, and none are exceptional, though the Premier is well equipped. Fortunately, they are concentrated in a five-block radius and almost never fill up, so you can simply walk around town once you arrive and decide which suits you best. **Tuxpán** also has a five-star hotel, a fancy place—for Tuxpán—called Hotel May Palace. Otherwise, there are plenty of safe and comfortable budget rooms in town. Tuxpán sees few foreigners, and aside from during Semana Santa (Easter week) and July and August, when middle-class Mexicans head en masse for the beach, its hotels are usually empty.

Catering mostly to business travelers and short-term tourists, the hotels in the **border towns** are what you'd expect—not luxurious but reasonably priced and mostly well kept. **Monterrey** affords more choices in all price ranges, and new hotels keep popping up to keep pace with the increase in corporate travelers. The posh Quinta Real typifies the new breed of lodgings.

CATEGORY	COST*
$$$$	over $110
$$$	$70–$110
$$	$40–$70
$	under $40

*All prices are for a standard double room, excluding tax.

Exploring Veracruz and the Northeast

The lively port city of Veracruz was of vital importance in the history of the Spanish conquest of Mexico. The lush coastal state of Veracruz also has its share of colonial history, as well as native ruins and newly established adventure-tourism routes.

Northeastern Mexico consists of a string of border towns across from the United States, the city of Monterrey, and some surrounding natural wonders. Although the border towns are worth a visit to sample Mexican cuisine and buy handicrafts at cheaper prices than in the United States, their charm is limited. You might want to linger longer in Monterrey, a major city with some worthwhile restaurants and sights.

Numbers in the text correspond to numbers in the margin and on the Veracruz and East Central Mexico, Veracruz, The Northeast, and Monterrey maps.

Great Itineraries

The state of Veracruz and Northeast Mexico are separate regions, which is how most travelers approach them when planning a trip. Veracruz is closer to Mexico City and more appealing. Northeast Mexico is closer to Texas and is more often frequented by Texans hopping across the border than by people using Mexico City as a gateway. Our approach to the northeast is therefore from Texas. The drive up the coast from Veracruz is possible, but considering that it is 502 km (311 mi) Veracruz–Tampico and 1,005 km (623 mi) Veracruz–Monterrey, the distances look a bit daunting from behind the wheel.

IF YOU HAVE 3 DAYS

If you are flying, head straight for the port of **Veracruz** ①–⑤, the most Caribbean of the Gulf of Mexico cities. You'll have no problem occupying two days here: in addition to the excellent aquarium or the museums, there are some of the best cafés, music, and seafood restaurants in the country. The last day, take a day trip to the state capital, **Jalapa** ⑧, and its magnificent Museum of Anthropology; stop on the way at **Antigua** to see the ruins of Cortés's house, and at the archaeological site of **Cempoala** ⑦, a major Totonac religious and military city.

If you are driving down from Texas and have limited time, you could simply explore the area around **Monterrey** ⑮–㉒, the cultural and industrial giant of the northeast, to get a feeling for Mexico. Spend the first day walking around the Gran Plaza area, where the modern art and history museums are outstanding, and then drive to the **Cuauhté-moc Brewery** ⑳ on the outskirts of town. Devote the next two days to enjoying some of the region's natural attractions, including the **Barranca de la Huasteca** ㉓, an impressive gorge; the ancient **Grutas de García** ㉔; and the **Parque Nacional Cumbres de Monterrey** ㉕, with its spectacular waterfall. For some colonial color, visit downtown **Saltillo** ㉖, where Mexican tiles are made. If you get hooked on its charm, spend one night here instead of driving back to Monterrey.

IF YOU HAVE 5 DAYS

Start in **Veracruz,** ①–⑤. On the second day make your way out of the city to the cool hill towns of **Los Tuxtlas** ⑥, where you can consult a *curandero* (healer) for whatever ails you. Then on day three make your way to the city of **Jalapa** ⑧ for its renowned Museum of Anthropology. Plan your last days at **El Tajín** ⑨, overnighting in the nearby town of **Papantla de Olarte** ⑩. Make your way back down the coast to Veracruz, and consider stopping on the way at **Antigua** and **Cempoala** ⑦.

For five days in **the northeast,** add an excursion to **Tampico** ㉘, on the Gulf of Mexico, to the three-day jaunt. On the first day, check out sculptures of Tlazoltéotl, the pre-Hispanic Huastecan Goddess of Love, at the **Museo de la Cultura Huasteca,** or kick back with picnicking Mexican families at Playa Miramar. Spend the second bass fishing at Lake Vicente Guererro.

IF YOU HAVE 7 DAYS

Follow the five-day itinerary above, but extend the trip to include time in **Jalapa** ⑧ by overnighting in the picturesque colonial town of Coatepec, only about 10 km (6 mi) away. The next day, go river rafting on the Río Pescados southeast of Jalapa. If you drive, consider adding a visit to **Los Tuxtlas** ⑥; if you don't have a car, spend a leisurely extra day enjoying the beaches and seafood restaurants of **Boca del Río,** a small fishing village that is turning into a suburb of Veracruz, or visiting more of the sights you missed in the port's downtown.

When to Tour

In Veracruz, the weather is balmy between November and April. The famous *nortes*—gusty, chilly winds that blow in off the Gulf of Mexico—usually appear between October and February, and especially in December. Pack a sweater and light coat or jacket if you plan to travel during these months. In summer, both the temperature and humidity soar, but the frequent rains afford a respite from the heat.

A great time to visit Veracruz is the week before Ash Wednesday for *Carnaval,* Mexico's version of Mardi Gras. It's wild and merry but has a small-town ambience that makes it saner and safer than the better-known celebrations in Río or New Orleans. The biggest problem at such times is finding a room (reserve one well in advance), but the local tourist office can usually come up with acceptable accommodations. The same is true during Christmas and Easter week, when all of Mexico goes on vacation and heads for the beach.

The hottest months in the northeast are April through June. The cooling rains arrive in July and last through August. There are never any crowds at the border towns or in Monterrey except during major U.S. holidays, when Americans head south for a day or weekend.

THE STATE OF VERACRUZ

A long, skinny crescent of land bordering the Gulf of Mexico, the state of Veracruz is often ignored by travelers, many of whom do no more than glimpse the state through the window of a bus barreling toward the Yucatán Peninsula. Although Veracruz's ruins and beaches don't quite compare with those on the Yucatán, the state is popular with vacationing Mexicans, drawn to the cool hill towns of the Sierra de Los Tuxtlas and the liveliness of Veracruz city.

Descending from the volcanic Sierra, the Veracruz coast consists of flat lowlands that have their share of terrible heat and swamps and are pockmarked by noisome oil refineries. As you head inland a ways—Veracruz is only 140 km (87 mi) across at its widest point—the land rises to meet the Sierra Madre Oriental range, with its 6,100-ft Pico de Orizaba (also called Citlaltépetl), Mexico's highest mountain. In the foothills of this range, you'll find the university town and state capital of Jalapa, where students share the colonial streets with local farmers who have come to town to market their crops. Jalapa is a favored place for foreigners to study Spanish, and the nearby town of Jalcomulco is a base for river-rafting explorations on the Río Pescados. The state does have some good beaches along the coast, particularly around the northern city of Tuxpán, but the real reasons to come are the atmosphere, the history, and the people. All these are at their best in the city of Veracruz, a working port with so many marimba bands in the *zócalo* (main square) on weekend evenings that they have to compete to be heard.

Olmec civilization thrived in Veracruz long before the rise of the Maya. The state's best-preserved ruins, at El Tajín near Papantla, are thought to have been the work of yet another civilization, which had its heyday later, between AD 550 and 1100. By the time Hernán Cortés landed in Veracruz in 1519, the Aztecs held sway, but within a very short time the Indian population was decimated by war and European diseases.

The state of Veracruz played a pivotal role in Cortés's march to Tenochtitlan. A circuit, sponsored by the Mexican government called the *Ruta de Cortés* (Route of Cortez), traces the Spanish conquistador's footsteps, beginning with his Veracruz landing through to his arrival in Mexico City, where he defeated the Aztec rulers. It's a mélange of soft adventure excursions like river rafting combined with visits to colonial cities, old haciendas, and archaeological zones that were instrumental in the Spanish Conquest.

In modern times, the discovery of oil in Veracruz caused a population explosion that saw the number of *veracruzanos* go from about 1 million at the beginning of the century to more than 7 million today. For most foreign travelers, the occasional sulfurous stench of a coastal oil refinery is an unpleasant intrusion on their tropical reverie, but for many of the state's residents, it's their bread and butter.

Veracruz

502 km (311 mi) south of Tampico, 345 km (214 mi) west of Mexico City.

Veracruz was the first European city established on the North American mainland. In 1519 Hernán Cortés landed about 25 km (16 mi) to the northwest in La Antigua, a tiny slip of a place, but Veracruz became the major gateway for Spanish settlement of Mexico. Its name, which appears throughout Latin America, means "true cross."

To meet their labor needs, the Spanish brought a large number of Africans to Veracruz as slaves. Later, Cuban immigrants flooded the port. This mix in modern days has created an open-minded city, where tourists of all cultural extractions are generously welcomed.

But perhaps the most profound influence of Veracruz's mixed population can be seen in its music and dance. Veracruz is the hometown of "La Bamba," a song that dates back to the 17th century. In addition to its most famous song, the city has a special brand of music, played by lively trios outfitted in white and slapping away at tiny guitars and portable harps. In the evening, mariachis entertain outside the sidewalk cafés around the main plaza. Whether at night or during the day, a stop at one of these coffeehouses is de rigueur.

The *danzón*, a languorous two-person dance with lots of subtle hip movement, was brought to the city by penniless refugees fleeing Cuba in 1879 following its War of Independence. Most ended up living outside the city walls (only Veracruz aristocrats were allowed to live inside), but the sons of the elite, who sneaked into the poor neighborhoods at night, eventually introduced the danzón to high society. Sensuous compared to the stiff and formal dance that had been the norm until this time, the danzón was at first considered scandalous, but it soon won the hearts of even its detractors and became the most popular dance in the city. It later spread throughout the country.

Veracruz and East Central Mexico

Veracruz was Mexico's premier seaside resort and the port of entry for most foreign visitors until a few decades ago; travelers arrived by ship, then boarded a train to Mexico City, often looking wistfully back. Today relatively few foreigners find their way to Veracruz's beaches, but domestic vacationers are lured into the fun-loving town by prices far lower than those found in Acapulco, Puerto Vallarta, or Cancún.

① If this is your first visit to the port of Veracruz, a good place to get oriented is the **Museo de la Ciudad.** The region's history is narrated through artifacts and displays, and scale models of the city help you get the lay of the land. Also exhibited are copies of pre-Columbian statues and contemporary indigenous art. A $1 donation pays for a guided tour by a bilingual student. ⊠ *Zaragoza at Morelos,* ☎ *29/31–84–10.* 🏛 *Free.* ☉ *Tues.–Sun. 10–4.*

② During the Viceregal era, Veracruz was the only east-coast port permitted to operate in New Spain. As a result, it was frequently attacked by pirates. The great **Fort of San Juan de Ulúa,** built shortly after the conquest and the last territory in Mexico to be held by the Spanish Royalists, is a monument to that swashbuckling era. A miniature city in itself, the island fort is a maze of moats, ramparts, and drawbridges smack in the middle of the busy port area (it's now connected to the mainland by a causeway). Fortification of the island began in 1535 under the direction of Antonio de Mendoza, the first viceroy of New Spain. Ground coral, sand, and oyster shells were used for the original walls. A few centuries later, the fort was used as a prison, housing such figures as Benito Juárez, who was held prisoner here by conservative dictator Santa Anna before being exiled to Louisiana in 1853. After Independence, it was used in unsuccessful attempts to fight off first the invading French, the Americans, then the French again and, in 1914, the Americans again. ⊠ *Reached via causeway from downtown Veracruz,* ☎ *No phone.* 🏛 *$2; free Sun.* ☉ *Tues.–Sun. 10–4:30.*

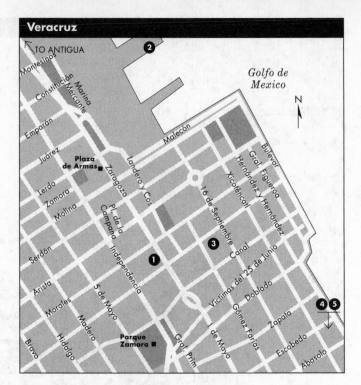

❸ The **Baluarte de Santiago,** a fortress and museum, is all that's left of the old city walls; like the Fort of San Juan de Ulúa, the colonial bulwark was built as a defense against pirates (but some 100 years later, in 1635). The structure is impressively solid from the outside and romantically lighted at night. Inside is a small museum that has an exquisite permanent exhibit of gold pre-Columbian jewelry—definitely Spanish plunder—which was accidentally discovered by a fisherman 25 years ago and has been on display since 1991. ✉ *Canal at 16 de Septiembre,* ☎ *No phone.* ✆ *$1.75; free Sun.* ☉ *Tues.–Sun. 10–4:30.*

❹ Since 1993, Veracruz has been the home of the state-of-the-art **Acuario de Veracruz,** one of the three most important aquariums in the world. In addition to its public displays, the complex also houses a marine research center. The main exhibits include a tank full of 3,000 species of marine life native to the Gulf of Mexico, including nurse sharks, manta rays, barracudas, sea turtles, and the pre-Hispanic *pejelagartos,* which look like a combination of crocodile and fish. Smaller display cases host swimming sea horses and the lethal but beautiful scorpion fish, with its long, porcupinelike quills. Check out the 18-ft-long outline on the far wall, above the caption THIS IS THE ACTUAL SIZE OF A GREAT WHITE SHARK CAUGHT OFF THE COAST OF TUXPÁN, VERACRUZ. ✉ *Plaza Acuario, Blvd. Manuel Avila Camacho s/n,* ☎ *29/34–79–84 or 29/32–79–84.* ✆ *$2.* ☉ *Daily 10–7.*

❺ Don't miss the **Casita Blanca** (White House), the museum-home of Agustín Lara, one of Mexico's most beloved songwriters and singers. Lara's occupations included playing the piano in a house of ill repute and being a bullfighter; he is also famous for marrying seven women, including Mexican screen goddess María Félix. He died in 1970 at the age of 73 after spending the last years of his life writing and recording music at La Casita Blanca. Among his most famous songs, piped in via cassette, are "Maria Bonita," which he dedicated to Félix, and "Granada." Newspaper clippings, caricatures, and a replica of the radio station where Lara went on the air nightly with "La Hora Azul" (The Blue Hour) help plunge you into a life that was constantly in the public eye. ⊠ *Blvd. Adolpho Ruíz Cortines s/n, Boca del Río,* ☎ *29/37–02–09.* ☜ *$2.* ⊙ *Tues.–Sun. 10–2 and 4–8.*

OFF THE
BEATEN PATH

LA ANTIGUA – This town, which was given its name by the Spaniards after they abandoned it, was the site of the first European landing in the New World and the conquistadors' capital for 75 years. Cortés's home, which once had 22 rooms surrounding a huge courtyard, lies abandoned on the northern edge of the village. It's worth seeing if only for its crumbling, roofless masonry, taken over by clinging vines and massive tree roots. Antigua also hosts the first church of New Spain, a little white stucco structure in remarkably good condition. Here, where Cortés and his soldiers prayed and the first converted Indian was baptized, masses are still said today. La Antigua is 25 km (16 mi) north of Veracruz, off Highway 180 (toward Poza Rica). The turnoff is just past the toll booth.

Beaches

Veracruz City's beaches are much less inviting than you might expect: most are somewhat dirty, and the water is polluted. Good beaches begin south of town in **Mocambo,** about 7 km (4½ mi) from downtown, and get better even farther down: about 4 km (2½ mi) south of Playa Mocambo, **Boca del Río** is a small fishing village at the mouth of the Río Jamapa that is quickly getting sucked into Veracruz's orbit.

Dining and Lodging

In addition to the restaurants in Veracruz, you'll want to try one in the fishing village of **Boca del Río,** where the little Jamapa river meets the sea about 10 km (6 mi) south of downtown. Many of them—they seem to turn up between every other house—are modest but serve some of the finest seafood in Mexico. Boca del Río holds a spot in *The Guinness Book of Records* for the largest fish fillet stuffed with shellfish— it was prepared at Pardiño's restaurant.

$$$ ✕ **La Mansion.** This elegant restaurant is part of a nationwide chain that specializes in grilled meats. The Veracruz branch, on the boulevard east of downtown in Boca del Río, has attractive southwestern decor and brisk, efficient service. A few soups and salads are served, but the menu is dominated by thick cuts of steak. The extensive wine selection consists almost exclusively of domestic, Spanish, and French reds. A jacket and tie would not be out of place here. ⊠ *Blvd. Adolpho Ruíz Cortines s/n next to Agustín Lara Museum, Boca del Río,* ☎ *29/37–13–63 or 29/37–13–30. AE, MC, V.*

$$$ ✕ **Mariscos Villa Rica Mocambo.** This casual, seafront palapa restau-
★ rant is worth the small effort to find it. Hidden on a small street that runs parallel to Playa Mocambo, the Villa Rica is a favorite with locals in the know but sees almost no casual tourists. The menu consists entirely of seafood. Specialties include mussels, shark, grouper, and octopus prepared as you wish. There are a few meat dishes available for carnivores. The wine list is small and the wine is reasonable, but the beverage of choice among loyal patrons is cold Sol (beer) with lime. Live music is performed Thursday–Sunday from 3 to 7 PM. ⊠ *Calzada Mocambo 527, near Hotel Mocambo, Boca del Río,* ☎ *29/22–21–13 or 29/22–37–43. AE, MC, V.*

$$$ ✕ **Villa Marina Shrimp and Steak House.** This casual eatery sits just off the *malecón* (boardwalk), suspended on stilts above the water. Waiters bring glistening platters of the day's catch to the table for you to choose from—fresh lobster, shrimp, clams, and sea bass. Then you get to pon-

der the 18 different *al gusto* ways to cook your selection—breaded, grilled, sautéed in garlic, with cheese sauce, and so on. The menu also lists prime rib, rib eye, and T-bone steaks, as well as a number of pasta dishes. A modest selection of mostly Mexican wines complements the food. ⊠ *Blvd. M. Avila Camacho, s/n,* ☎ *29/35–10–34. AE, MC, V.*

$$ ✕ **El Gaucho Restaurante.** Since 1984, this cavernous family-friendly ranch-style restaurant has been packed morning, noon, and night with meat lovers. The epic menu lists nearly 100 dishes—from spicy *chorizo* sausage and Veracruz-style tongue to Hereford steaks and chicken *fajitas.* The house specialty drink, *jarra de clericot* (red wine mixed with chewy bits of watermelon, pineapple, and cantaloupe), is delicious. ⊠ *Bernal Diaz del Castillo No. 187 at Colon,* ☎ *29/35–04–11. AE, MC, V. Closed Mon.*

$$ ✕ **La Fragata.** If you do not stay at the old-fashioned Hotel Mocambo, visit its restaurant for an evening meal and see the place at its best—when night breezes off the water blow and the terraced gardens are illuminated. For the full effect, request an outdoor table. Dinner offerings range from filet mignon to *huachinango* (red snapper) stuffed with shrimp and calamari, but there's nothing in the way of lighter fare beyond a few disappointing salads. The restaurant is rarely crowded, and service is casual and very friendly. ⊠ *Ruíz Cortines 4000 on Playa Mocambo, Boca del Río,* ☎ *29/22–02–05. AE, DC, MC, V.*

$$ ✕ **Pardiño's.** This modest eatery is a star among Boca del Río's many
★ seafood restaurants and a local favorite. Its fame has even spread abroad—it's not unusual for the chef to be invited to gastronomic festivals in France. Plain tables in a storefront on the village's main square belie the elegant preparation of such dishes as crabs *salpicón* (finely chopped with cilantro, onion, and lime), grilled sea bass, and, of course, huachinango à la veracruzana, here served with *plátanos fritos* (fried plantains). Also delicious are the simple, fresh appetizers, such as shrimp cocktail with generous chunks of ripe avocado. Owner Rafael Pardiño, who comes from many generations of restaurateurs, has added some of his own creations to the menu—coconut stuffed with succulent seafood plus mouthwatering breaded crab claws. Pardiño's has another, much smaller, location in downtown Veracruz in a restored colonial building. The Boca del Río location is the only one in the area with air-conditioning. ⊠ *Zamora 40, Boca del Río,* ☎ *29/86–01–35;* ⊠ *Landero y Coss 146 at malecón (boardwalk), Veracruz,* ☎ *29/32–37–11. AE, DC, MC, V.*

$$ ✕ **Restaurant Albatros.** This unlikely establishment, tucked away in a residential neighborhood a few blocks from the waterfront, has the feel of a semiexclusive men's club, an effect enhanced by dark-wood furnishings. The menu includes some unusual dishes, such as *filete de res Banderas* (steak with three different sauces—tomato, creamy mushroom, and avocado—representing the red, green, and white colors of the Mexican flag). The real appeal, however, is the fresh seafood, which the accommodating chef will prepare to your specifications. ⊠ *16 de Septiembre 1480, at Azueta,* ☎ *29/31–25–85. AE, MC, V. Closed Sun.*

$ ✕ **Gran Café de la Parroquia.** Don't be confused if someone tells you this is the wrong Gran Café de la Parroquia: the coffeehouse that long held that name is now called Gran Café del Portal (☞ *below*). Meanwhile, this malecón eatery is run by a black-sheep faction of the Fernandez family, kicked out of del Portal in 1995 after the settlement of a 20-year lawsuit. The story makes for a good soap opera. The menu and music are practically the same at both places and both tend to draw lots of local families. La Parroquia now has two locations, on either end of the same block on the malecón. ⊠ *Insurgentes Veracruzanos, at the corner of Gómez Farías and of 16 de Septiembre,* ☎ *29/32–25–84. No credit cards.*

$ ✕ **Gran Café del Portal.** Opened by a Spanish immigrant in 1835 in a former monastery, this most famous of Veracruz's sidewalk cafés eventually grew to cover an entire city block. For a long time it was called the Gran Café de la Parroquia, but after a family feud that ousted the cousins who had been running the place, it resumed its original name, Gran Café del Portal, in 1995. An indispensable stop for a *café lechero* (coffee with hot milk)—every Mexican president since Benito Juárez has been here—it's lively from dawn to dusk with the animated babble of customers, the tapping of spoons against glasses to summon waiters, and live marimba music played by the best musicians in town. The menu has a wide selection of egg dishes, as well as soups, sandwiches, a traditional version of huachinango à la veracruzana, and hearty steak and chicken entrées, but the coffee—the formula for which is a well-guarded family secret—is the real draw. ⊠ *Independencia 105 across from cathedral,* ☎ *29/31–27–59. No credit cards.*

$$$$ 🏨 **Fiesta Americana.** This splashy hotel on Playa Costa de Oro, inaugurated by the Mexican president in 1996, has the best business facilities in the state of Veracruz. It has seven floors and miles of marble corridors, all of which seem to lead to the giant serpentine pool and lush gardens facing the ocean. Rooms have terraces, voice mail, closet safes, and luxurious bathrooms with tubs, phones, audio systems, and hair dryers. Fiesta Club floors have a business center, concierge service, and a bilingual staff. Guests have access to a nine-hole golf course, 20 minutes away. No-smoking rooms and wheelchair-accessible units are available. ⊠ *Blvd. Manuel Avila Camacho at Bacalao, Fraccionamiento Costa de Oro, Veracruz 94299,* ☎ *29/89–89–89; 800/343–7821 in the U.S.,* 𝖥𝖠𝖷 *29/89–89–04. 211 rooms, 22 suites. 2 restaurants, 3 bars, in-room safes, no-smoking rooms, pool, 3 hot tubs, massage, tennis court, dive shop, baby-sitting, children's programs (age 4+), car rental, free parking. AE, DC, MC, V.*

$$$ 🏨 **Hotel Lois.** For those with a sense of humor, this swanky Boca del Río hotel is an over-the-top Postmodern mishmash of Art Deco, 50s kitsch, and riotous neon tropical colors. The coffee shop alone has sparkling ceilings, lavender Naugahyde chairs, etched glass windows, several random Roman columns, and lots of gleaming chrome. Guest rooms are more conventionally appointed with rattan furniture and cable color TVs and have a subdued pastel palette. ⊠ *Calz. A. Ruiz Cortínes No. 10, Boca del Río 94260,* ☎ *29/37–82–90 or 29/37–75–98; 01–800/29–136 in Mexico,* 𝖥𝖠𝖷 *29/37–80–89. 107 rooms, 9 suites. Restaurant, 2 bars, coffee shop, in-room safes, minibars, pool, sauna, tennis court, squash, billiards, baby-sitting, children's programs (ages 3–9), car rental, free parking. AE, MC, V.*

$$$ 🏨 **Torremar.** This deluxe high-rise resort on Playa Mocambo is somewhat excessively decorated in pastels, but you'll find all the amenities here. Suites have small balconies with fantastic views of the Gulf of Mexico. An executive floor, with special concierge service and complimentary breakfast, is also available. Kids will like the cascading poolside fountain and the organized activities in the children's play area. ⊠ *Av. Adolpho Ruíz Cortines 4300, Boca del Río 94260,* ☎ *29/21–34–35, 29/21–34–43, 29/21–34–75, or 01–800/2–99–00 in Mexico;* 𝖥𝖠𝖷 *29/21–02–91. 231 rooms, 18 suites. 2 restaurants, 2 bars, 2 pools, exercise room, baby-sitting, children's programs (ages 3–11), laundry service, concierge floor, car rental, free parking. AE, DC, MC, V.*

$$ 🏨 **Hotel Emporio.** The lobby of this large, elegant hostelry on the
★ malecón is a dramatic sweep of marble and potted palms. Some of the immaculate, light-filled rooms have sea views, all have marbled bathrooms with bathtubs (those in the suites are hot tubs), satellite color TVs, and air-conditioning. Dine in the popular restaurant, decorated in neoclassical French style, or in the shade of an umbrella at any of the hotel's three pools (one is equipped with a waterfall, slides, and a miniature ship structure nearby for kids to play on). ⊠ *Insurgentes Ve-*

racruzanos 210, Veracruz 91700, ☎ 29/32–00–20, ℻ 29/31–22–61. 181 rooms, 22 suites. Restaurant, bar, coffee shop, 3 pools, sauna, exercise room, children's programs (ages 5–8), car rental, free parking. AE, MC, V.

$$ ☆ ⊞ **Hotel Hawaii.** This little jewel of a hotel with a prime location on the malecón is one of the best deals in town, offering comfort, class, and personalized service at a reasonable price. All the impeccably maintained rooms come with a pair of queen-size beds, air-conditioning, phone, color cable TV, and marble bathrooms. The staff is eager to please, and there's always a bowl of fresh flowers at the check-in desk. You can have all the free coffee you want at the snug ground-floor coffee shop, and maps are available for the asking. The management also sees to it that each guest gets a bag of fine Veracruz coffee to take home. ⊠ Insurgentes Veracruzanos 458, Veracruz 91700, ☎ 29/31–04–27, ℻ 29/32–55–24. 30 rooms. Coffee shop, room service, laundry service, free parking. AE, MC, V.

$$ ⊞ **Hotel Mocambo.** When the Mocambo was built in 1934, it was Mexico's only Gulf Coast resort. But what used to be the loveliest and most romantic hotel in the area has lost some of its luster. The spacious, red tile-floored guest rooms have faded floral bedspreads and only modestly effective air-conditioning. The hotel's sprawling, terraced gardens make for a five-level trek to the beaches and pools at palm-lined Playa Mocambo. Dark-wood fixtures and Art Deco touches—such as stained-glass windows in the lobby and flowerlike pillars around the indoor pool—are charming remnants from the Mocambo's more glamorous days. ⊠ Calz. Adolpho Ruíz Cortines 4000 on Playa Mocambo, Boca del Río 94260, ☎ 29/22–02–05 or 01–800/290–0100 in Mexico, ℻ 29/22–02–12. 116 rooms, 4 suites. Restaurant, 2 bars, coffee shop, 3 pools, massage, tennis court, exercise room, baby-sitting, playground, laundry service, car rental, free parking. AE, DC, MC, V.

$$ ⊞ **Villa del Mar.** This unassuming hotel, just across from one of the nicer sections of the downtown beach, is an ideal place to bring kids. The standard, motel-style rooms are spacious and comfortable and surround a large, pretty garden with a tennis court, pool, and small playground. All accommodations have color TVs, telephones, and air-conditioning. The staff is very helpful, and some English is spoken at the reception desk. A number of bungalows (accommodating up to five people) are also available: they aren't air-conditioned and are a bit gloomy, but some have kitchenettes. ⊠ Blvd. Avila Camacho 2707 at Bartolomé de las Casas, Veracruz 91700, ☎ 29/31–33–66, ℻ 29/32–71–35. 91 rooms, 14 bungalows. Restaurant, bar, pool, hot tub, tennis court, playground, laundry service, free parking. AE, MC, V.

$ ⊞ **Hotel Concha Dorada.** The basically characterless Concha Dorada has the cheapest accommodations on the zócalo. Rooms are cramped but clean, and some have color TVs (local stations only), telephones, and air-conditioning. The downstairs restaurant–sidewalk café serves simple fare and is especially popular (read noisy) at lunchtime and on weekend nights. ⊠ Miguel Lerdo 77 near Zaragoza, Veracruz 91700, ☎ 29/31–29–96, ℻ 29/31–32–46. 46 rooms, 2 suites. Restaurant, bar, room service, laundry service. AE, MC, V.

$ ⊞ **Hotel Ruiz Milan.** This multistory waterfront hotel is a good value for the price. Guest rooms, though on the small side, are clean, comfortable, and modern. All have color TVs (local stations only), telephones, balconies, ample closet space, and sizable bathrooms; about half have air-conditioning. The invitingly cool, creamy yellow-walled and marble-floored lobby is usually crowded with Mexican businesspeople, and the hotel itself has the amenities of a more expensive establishment, including an indoor pool, a pleasant restaurant, and free covered parking. ⊠ Paseo del Malecón 432, Veracruz 91700, ☎ 29/

32–27–72, ⌧ 29/32–37–77 ext. 106. *69 rooms, 19 suites. Restaurant, room service, pool, free parking. AE, MC, V.*

$ ⌧ **Hotel Villa Florencia.** This comfortable, quiet hotel is tucked away on an affluent residential street paralleling one of the prettier stretches of Playa Mocambo. Large, standard motel-style rooms are brightened by splashes of tilework. All have two beds and color TVs, most with peaceful private terraces overlooking the attractive pool area. No rooms have phones. ⌧ *Calzada Mocambo 207, Boca del Río 94260,* ☎ *29/21–02–44. 22 rooms, 3 suites. Restaurant (breakfast only), laundry service, free parking. AE, MC, V.*

Nightlife and the Arts

Every Tuesday, Friday, and Saturday night after 8, at the **Plaza de Armas** (zócalo), a local troupe dressed in white performs danzón on stage, then hits the street to join the townsfolk in this traditional Veracruz dance, accompanied by live marimba music. Sunday nights, the dancing moves to **Parque Zamora** from 6 to 9 PM. The **Instituto Veracruzo de Cultura** (Veracruz Cultural Institute) (⌧ Calles Canal and Zaragoza, ☎ 29/31–69–67) offers danzón classes for a minimal fee three times a week.

For authentic Cuban music, head for the unpretentious **El Rincón de la Trova** (⌧ Callejon de Lagunilla 59, ☎ No phone), where people of all ages gather to dance to a famous tropical band until the wee hours; the floors are cement and the ambience is fun and strictly local.

Discos and video bars are plentiful along the malecón. Both **Ocean** (⌧ Av. Adolfo Ruíz Cortines 8, at Avila Camacho, ☎ 29/35–23–90), a flashy, modern discotheque, and **Blue Ocean** (⌧ Avila Camacho 9, ☎ 29/22–03–66), a video bar with a light show, are packed on Friday and Saturday nights with a young, largely local crowd.

Outdoor Activities and Sports

Deep-sea fishing is popular in Veracruz, and you'll find places to windsurf in the coastal areas a few miles beyond Boca del Río. An annual regatta from the Port of Galveston in Texas to the Port of Veracruz takes place at the end of May. Check with the **Mexican Government Tourist Office** in Houston for details (☎ 713/780–3740).

Shopping

Stands lining the **malecón** sell a variety of ocean-related items: seashells and beauty creams and powders derived from them, black coral jewelry, ships-in-a-bottle, key rings with miniature sea-life inside, and more. You'll also find Coatepec coffee, T-shirts, bloody crucifixes, and tacky stuffed frogs, iguanas, and armadillos. The **Plaza Artesanía** market on the malecón purveys slightly higher-quality goods, including leather and jewelry, with higher prices to match.

For an authentic slice of Mexican daily life, head for the wildly vibrant and chaotic **Mercado Hidalgo** (⌧ between Calles Cortés and Soto, Madero and Hidalgo), where you'll find artful displays of strawberries and chilies beside heaps of mysterious medicinal herbs and platters of cow eyeballs and chicken feet.

One of the most unusual shops in town is in the aquarium: **Fiora** (⌧ Plaza Acuario, ☎ 29/31–90–29) sells beautiful jewelry designed from miniature flowers grown in Veracruz.

Los Tuxtlas

❻ *140 km (87 mi) south of Veracruz.*

A small volcanic mountain range, the Sierra de Los Tuxtlas, meets the sea at Los Tuxtlas. This area has lakes, waterfalls, rivers, mineral springs, and access to beaches, making it a popular stopover for travelers heading east from Mexico City to the Yucatán. The region's three principal towns—**Santiago Tuxtla, San Andrés Tuxtla,** and **Catemaco**—are carved into the mountainsides some 600 ft above sea level, lending them a coolness even in summer that's the envy of the perspiring masses on the coastal plain. The Tuxtlas gain an air of mystery from the cool, gray fog that slips over the mountains and lakes and the whisperings among the townspeople about the *brujos* (witches), also called *curanderos* (healers), who read tarot cards, prescribe herbal remedies, and cast spells here. Today, the economic life of Los Tuxtlas depends on cigar manufacturing (the town of San Andrés Tuxtla is famous for its hand-rolled variety, which comes in several sizes) and tourism. Tours can be arranged by just showing up at several factories, including **Te-Amo** (✉ Blvd. 5 de Febrero 10), just outside of town on the highway to Catemaco and Santa Clara, on the bypass road. All have stores open to the public.

Although much of the architecture here is of the 1960s school of looming cement, all three towns are laid out in the colonial style around a main plaza and a church, and all have a certain amount of charm. Santiago Tuxtla has managed to retain more of its colonial character than the other two Tuxtla towns. The region was also a center of Olmec culture, and Olmec artifacts and small ruins abound. A huge stone Olmec head dominates the zócalo at Santiago Tuxtla, and 21 km (13 mi) east are the ruins of **Tres Zapotes,** now decidedly unspectacular but once an important Olmec ceremonial center believed to have been occupied as early as AD 100. The town also has an informative museum, where you can learn about the region's indigenous heritage and contemporary local cultures.

The largest of the three towns, and the only one with an ATM, is San Andrés, but **Catemaco** is by far the most picturesque and relaxing place to stay. Many of Catemaco's lodgings are on the lake shore, while others are grouped around the small square. Catemaco is popular among Mexicans as a summer and Christmas resort and is also the place to go for a *consulta* (consultation) with a brujo or curandero, should you have any problems or questions that require some spiritual clarity or supernatural intervention. Tours of Lake Catemaco, which was formed from the crater of a volcano and which harbors a colorful colony of fish-eating baboons, can be arranged through most local hotels. Beyond Catemaco a paved road continues over the hills and down to a lovely stretch of undeveloped coastline. Twenty kilometers (12½ miles) from Catemaco is the village of **Sontecomapan,** where you can take a *lancha* (launch) across the lagoon to a desolate beach. A bumpy dirt road follows the coast 19 km (12 mi) north of Sontecomapan to the sleepy fishing village of **Montepío**, which has a wide beach and a couple of inexpensive, basic hotels.

Cempoala

 ❼ *42 km (26 mi) north of Veracruz.*

Cempoala (often spelled Zempoala) was the capital of the Totonac nation, whose influence spread throughout Veracruz in pre-Hispanic times. The name means "Place of 20 Waters," after the sophisticated irrigation system the Totonacs used. The site gains its role in history as the place where, in 1519, conquistador Hernán Cortés formed his first alliance with a native chief. At the time, the population of Cempoala was estimated at around 20,000. The alliance with the Totonacs enlarged Cortés's paltry army of 200 men and encouraged the Spaniard to push on to Mexico City and fight the Aztecs. In his turn, the leader of the Totonacs—dubbed "Fat Chief" by his own people because of his enormous girth—was an avowed enemy of the powerful Aztecs, who forced his people to perform human sacrifices to their war god and put military garrisons on Totonac land.

Cempoala was rediscovered by Francisco del Paso y Troncoso in 1891. Seven out of the 60 to 90 structures at Cempoala have been excavated and can be visited. All are built of river stones, shells, sand, and "glue" made from the whites of turtle and bird eggs. As the story goes, when Cortés first sighted Cempoala at night, the buildings glowed white under a full moon. Greedy Cortés thought he had discovered a city of silver.

Upon entering the ruins, you come upon **Circulo de los Gladiadores,** a small circle of waist-high walls to the right of center. This was the site of contests between captured prisoners of war and Totonac warriors: each prisoner was required to fight two armed warriors. One such prisoner, the son of a king from Tlaxcala, won the unfair match and became a national hero. His statue stands in a place of honor in Tlaxcala. Another small structure to the left of the circle marks the spot where an eternal flame was kept lighted during the sacred 52-year cycle of the Totonacs.

The **Templo Mayor,** the main pyramid, is the largest structure on the site. Follow the dirt path that lies straight ahead when you enter. Cortés, after gaining the allegiance of the Fat Chief, placed a Christian cross atop this temple—the first gesture of this sort in New Spain—and had mass said by a Spanish priest in his company.

At the smaller **Templo de la Luna** (Temple of the Moon), to the far left of Templo Mayor, outstanding warriors were honored with the title "Eagle Knight" or "Tiger Knight" and awarded an obsidian nose ring to wear as a mark of their status. Just to the left of the Moon Temple is the **Templo del Sol** (Temple of the Sun), where the hearts and blood of sacrificial victims were placed.

Back toward the dirt road and across from it is the **Templo de la Diosa de la Muerte** (Temple of the Goddess of Death), where a statue of the pre-Hispanic deity was found along with 1,700 small idols.

A small on-site **museum** opened in 1997. The voladores of Papantla usually give a performance on weekends. Well-trained guides are available but tours are mainly in Spanish. ☎ *No phone.* ▦ *$2; free Sun.* ☾ *Tues.–Sun. 10–5.*

Jalapa

❽ *90 km (56 mi) northwest of Veracruz.*

Jalapa, which was a Totonac ceremonial center when Cortés arrived, is perched on the side of a mountain, between the coastal lowlands of Veracruz and the high central plateau. More than 4,000 ft above sea level, the city has a bizarre climate—sun, rain, and fog are all likely to show themselves in the course of a day. However, for perspiration-soaked escapees from the coast, it's an enviable change. The capital and cultural hub of the state of Veracruz, Jalapa is a university town with a diverse population; you are as likely to see long-haired young people sitting around in cafés as you are wizened campesinos walking to work. The town is also home to a symphony orchestra, a ballet company, and a state theater that attracts big-name performers. Jalapa is filled with pretty parks and lakes, and since the grit has been removed from their surfaces, the government buildings downtown are showing off their stateliness once more. The hills here pose intriguing engineering problems—in some places you'll find the twisting, cobblestone streets bordered by 6-ft-high sidewalks built to compensate for sudden, sharp inclines. (Note: You'll often see the name of the city spelled Xalapa. Jalapa is the Hispanicized version of the original Nahuatl word.)

The town's prime cultural attraction is the **Museo de Antropología de Jalapa.** With 3,000 out of 29,000 pieces on display, it is second only to Mexico City's archaeological museum and is a treasure trove of artifacts from the three main pre-Hispanic cultures of Veracruz: Huastec, Totonac, and, most important, Olmec. Its three sections are filled with magnificent stone Olmec heads, carved stelae and offering bowls, terra-cotta jaguars and cross-eyed gods, cremation urns in the forms of bats and monkeys, lovely Totonac murals, and, most touching of all, life-size sculptures of women who died in childbirth (the ancients elevated them to the status of goddesses). At a burial site, you can see ancient bones, ritually deformed skulls, and ceremonial figurines. Guided tours by English-speaking students are available daily 11 AM–4 PM, but it is best to call in advance and make an appointment, as the tour schedule is unpredictable. ✉ *Av. Jalapa s/n,* ☎ *28/15–09–20 and 28/15–07–08.* ☜ *$1.25, $10 for tour in English.* ☉ *Daily 9–5.*

Dining and Lodging

$$ ✕ **La Casa de Mama.** This extremely popular restaurant is on a busy
★   thoroughfare just east of the center of town. The dark, antique furnishings and lazy ceiling fan almost succeed in giving this place the feel of a northern Mexican hacienda, but the incessant street noise reminds you that you're in a busy capital city. Never mind; you'll be focusing on the generous portions of charcoal-broiled steaks and the succulent shrimp and fish dishes, served with *charro* beans (black beans cooked in a spicy sauce) or Mexican rice. The place is especially well known for its desserts, which include smooth lemon tarts, bananas flambéed in brandy, and vanilla ice cream topped with Kahlúa. ✉ *Avila Camacho 113,* ☎ *28/17–31–44. AE, MC, V. No dinner Mon.*

$$ ✕ **La Estancia de los Tecajetes.** For fine regional dishes with a dash of
★   creativity, try this rustic, lodgelike restaurant overlooking the lushly tropical Parque Los Tecajetes. It's cozy and relaxing, always buzzing with diners feasting on *cecina* (paper-thin fillet of beef) with enchiladas, beans, and avocado; *pollo à la Ribera* (boned chicken breast, grilled and bathed in salsa and mushrooms); or *crepa consentida* (crepes filled with chicken and smothered in poblano chilies and local cheese). Corn tortillas are made on the premises, and the walls are filled with charming sepia-tone photos of Jalapa past. ✉ *Avila Camacho 90–12, Plaza Tecajetes,* ☎ *28/18–07–32. AE, MC, V.*

$$ ✕ **La Pérgola.** Designed in the early 1960s by Enrique Murillo, the attractive Pérgola is a relaxing place for an afternoon or evening meal. The menu concentrates on steaks and shrimp, painstakingly prepared and imaginatively presented. For dessert, try the *plátanos flameados con brandy* (plantains flambéed in brandy) or an order of crêpes suzette. Umbrella-shaded tables on the patio have a view of the leafy entrance to the Universidad Veracruzana and its enormous sports stadium. ✉ *Av. Universidad at Calle Pérgola, Lomas del Estadio,* ☎ *28/17–47–14. AE, MC, V. No dinner Sun.*

$ ✕ **El Balcón de la Agora.** This small café, part of the Agora de la Ciudad cultural center in Parque Juárez, is popular with students who come to study over a strong cup of coffee or an inexpensive sandwich. Open-air balcony seating provides an excellent view of the green city below and, in the distance, the Pico de Orizaba mountain. Order at the cash register as you enter, and then present your receipt at the counter as you repeat your order. ✉ *Bajos del Parque Juárez,* ☎ *28/18–57–30 or 28/18–53–00, ext. 16. No credit cards.*

$ ✕ **La Fonda.** The entrance to this charming, traditional, breakfast-and-lunch-only restaurant is hidden on a small pedestrian walkway off busy Calle Enríquez, a block from Parque Juárez. Brightly colored streamers, baskets, flowers, and a mural of Mount Orizaba adorn the walls and ceiling, and the warm corn tortillas served with every meal are made before your eyes. The food is hearty northern Veracruzan fare: beef or chicken and beans, *nopales* (cactus strips), and/or chili are essential elements of almost every dish. ⊠ *Antonio M. de Rivera 1 (also known as Callejon del Diamante) at Enríquez,* ☎ *28/18–72–82. No credit cards. Closed Sun. No dinner.*

$ ✕ **La Sopa.** Modest as it may look, this 20-table restaurant draws foodies from all walks of life—local politicians, students, and blue-collar workers—who make a beeline for the bargain *comida corrida* (fixed price) lunch. One of the best-kept secrets in town, La Sopa's four-course attraction might include carrot-and-potato soup, chicken with rice accompanied by fresh corn tortillas, and vanilla pudding served with coffee or tea. The menu features light Mexican *antojitos* (appetizers) in the evening, including *chiles rellenos* (green chili peppers stuffed with meat or cheese and fried in egg batter), and tamales. Live music fills the air every Thursday (Huastec folk music), Friday (danzón), and Saturday (a harpist), from about 1 in the afternoon until 11 at night. ⊠ *Antonio M. de Rivera 3-A (also known as Callejón del Diamante),* ☎ *28/17–80–69. No credit cards. Closed Sun.*

$ ✕ **1-2-3.** This midsize restaurant, located on a busy thoroughfare in the northern part of the city, looks unpromising from the street, but the interior is a pleasant surprise—dining-room walls are lined with the work of local artists, and modern sculpture is scattered about the room. And the food is more than reasonably priced. Mexican entrées include sirloin tips with chipotle chilies and *crepas de huitlacoche* (crepes filled with a delicacy, corn fungus, and bathed in cream sauce). International choices such as Waldorf salad, curried chicken, and steak tartare are knowledgeably prepared. A quiet, casual bar off the dining rooms opens onto a simple courtyard. ⊠ *Av. Adolfo Ruíz Cortines 857,* ☎ *28/14–71–22. AE, MC, V. No dinner Sun.*

$$$ ▦ **Fiesta Inn Xalapa.** This attractive chain hotel has the fresh look of a beach property in tropical climes—perhaps to offset the rather gloomy weather typical of Jalapa—and it has the most upscale amenities. It's a bit out of the way—in a primarily residential neighborhood 10 minutes by car from the center of town—but a good bet if you are looking for a comfortable, quiet, secure, and well-equipped base. The modern guest rooms in the two-story, colonial-style structure are decorated in cool blues and grays and have satellite-programmed color TVs, telephones, air-conditioning, bathtubs, and plenty of morning sunlight. Airport transfers from the port of Veracruz are available for a fee. ⊠ *Km 2.5 Carretera Xalapa–Veracruz, Fracc. Las Animas 91000,* ☎ *28/12–79–20; 01–800/5–04–50 in Mexico,* ⅨⅩ *28/12–79–46. 119 rooms, 4 suites. Restaurant, bar, coffee shop, in-room modem lines, pool, exercise room, dance club, free parking. AE, DC, MC, V.*

$$$ ▦ **Posada Coatepec.** When actor Harrison Ford was filming *Clear and*
★ *Present Danger* in the area, he stayed at this member of the prestigious Small Grand Hotels of Mexico group, a 15-minute drive from Jalapa. Specializing in fine food (but slow service) and catering to French and German travel groups, the Posada (built in 1890) is the former villa of a coffee baron. It has homey guest rooms, each with original decorative tile floors, satellite-programmed color TV, and a heater for Coatepec's chilly, rainy winters. Ask for one away from the murmur of street noise. The lobby and inner courtyard are splendidly decorated with a fine collection of antiques; a bar framed by lead crystal windows is cozy and clubby. The hotel can arrange tours to nearby coffee plantations.

⊠ *Hidalgo 9, Coatepec 91500,* ☎ *28/16–05–44,* ℻ *28/16–00–40. 7 rooms, 16 suites. Restaurant, bar, pool, laundry service. AE, MC, V.*

$$ 🖬 **Hotel Xalapa Finca Real.** The Hotel Xalapa is the most well-equipped downtown hotel, with many of the amenities of a more expensive establishment: air-conditioning, telephones, color TVs, and bathtubs; free covered parking for guests; and a disco. The building itself—another 1960s institutional behemoth—is not particularly attractive, but the rooms are large, sunny, and quiet. The hotel staff is well meaning, if not particularly competent, and the hot water supply can be dicey. ⊠ *Victoria at Bustamante, Zona Centro 91000,* ☎ *28/18–22–22 or 28/17–70–64,* ℻ *28/18–94–24. 170 rooms, 30 suites. 2 restaurants, bar, pool, dance club, playground, free parking. AE, DC, MC, V.*

$ 🖬 **Hotel Salmones.** Vestiges of the onetime glory of the Salmones remain: its high ceilings, dark-wood fixtures, and large beautiful windows have been untouched by time. The clean rooms (which start at $11) lack air-conditioning but have televisions (local stations only) and telephones; some have small balconies. Ask for one of the renovated rooms, which have peach-colored walls, smoky blue carpets, and marble sinks. Rooms in the *antigua* (old) section have threadbare cranberry red carpets and yellowing walls. ⊠ *Zaragoza 24, 91000,* ☎ *28/17–54–31,* ℻ *28/18–27–14. 65 rooms. Restaurant, bar. AE, MC, V.*

$ 🖬 **Mesón del Alférez.** A royal lieutenant of the Spanish Viceroy lived
★ in this colonial house some 200 years ago. Now it's a reasonably priced gem of a hotel, the building restored with traditional materials like earthenware tiles, rustic wood, and lime pigment washes on the walls in such luminous hues as lilac, sky blue, and magenta. Rooms surround three small bougainvillea-drenched courtyards and have lovely hand-carved wood headboards, Talavera lamps, and hand-loomed bedspreads, as well as phones and color TVs (local channels only). ⊠ *Sebastián Camacho, No. 2, at Zaragoza 91000,* ☎ *28/18–63–51 or 28/18–01–13,* ℻ *28/12–47–03. 14 rooms, 6 suites. Restaurant, room service, laundry service, free parking. AE, MC, V.*

Nightlife and the Arts

The **Agora** (⊠ Parque Juárez, ☎ 28/18–57–30) cultural center has art exhibits and the occasional folk-music performance and shows classic and avant-garde films in its cinema club. Stop by during the day to see what's planned. The **Teatro del Estado** (⊠ Ignacio de la Llave s/n, ☎ 28/17–31–10) is the big, modern state theater of Veracruz. The Orquesta Sinfónica de Jalapa performs here, often giving free concerts during the off-season (early June–mid-August). Check *El Diario de Jalapa* (the Jalapa city newspaper in Spanish, available at newsstands) for dates and times of performances, or stop by the Agora. You might find someone who speaks English here if you are lucky.

Other nightlife in this student town tends to be youth oriented. **La 7a Estacion** (⊠ 20 de Noviembre near Central Camionera, ☎ 28/17–31–55) is packed with salsa dancers on Wednesday nights; Thursday–Saturday you'll find rock and alternative music. The **Bar Lovento** (⊠ 20 de Noviembre Ote. 641, ☎ 28/17–83–34) heats up with a salsa beat for dancing Wednesday–Saturday nights. A more artsy, off-beat crowd patronizes **El Taller** (⊠ Ruiz Cortines 1812, ☎ No phone) to dance or watch performances. Across the street from the bus station is the popular **Disco La Mulada** (⊠ Calzada de Tejas, ☎ 28/17–55–23).

Outdoor Activities and Sports

RIVER RAFTING

River rafting along the Río Pescados is gaining in popularity. Most of the operators who run these trips are trained in Canada and are highly professional. Base camps with tents, rafting equipment, and dining facilities are near the river at Jalcomulco, 42 km (26 mi) southeast of Jalapa. (☞ Guided Tours *in* Mexico City A to Z *in* Chapter 1.)

Shopping

Mexico's finest export coffee is grown in this region, specifically in the highlands around the picturesque colonial towns of Coatepec and Xico, less than 10 km (6 mi) from Jalapa. Shops selling the prized *café de altura* (coffee) abound in the main squares of both places.

El Tajín

★ ▲ **◑** *13 km (8 mi) west of Papantla.*

The extensive ruins of El Tajín—the Totonac word means "thunder"—express the highest degree of artistry of any ancient city in the coastal area. The city remained hidden until 1785, when a Spanish engineer came upon it. Early theories attributed the complex—believed to be a religious center—to a settlement of Maya-related Huastecs, one of the most important cultures of the Veracruz area. Because of its immense size and unique architecture, however, scholars now believe it may have been built by a distinct El Tajín cultural group related to the Maya. Although much of the site has been restored, many structures are still hidden under thick jungle growth. Some archaeologists speculate that hundreds of buildings remain to be excavated.

El Tajín is thought to have reached its peak from between AD 600 and 1200. During this time, hundreds of structures of native sandstone were built here, including temples, double-storied palaces, ball courts, large retaining walls, and hundreds of houses. But El Tajín was already an important religious and administrative center during the first three centuries AD. Its influence is in part attributed to the fact that it had large reserves of cacao beans, used as money in pre-Hispanic times.

Evidence suggests that the southern half of the uncovered ruins—the area around the lower plaza—was reserved for ceremonial purposes. Its centerpiece is the 60-ft-high **Pyramid of the Niches,** surely one of the finest pre-Columbian buildings in Mexico. The finely wrought seven-level structure has 365 coffers built-in around its seven friezes—one for each day of the solar year. The reliefs on the pyramid depict the ruler, 13-Rabbit—all the rulers' names were associated with sacred animals—and allude also to El Tajín's main god, the benign Quetzalcóatl. One panel on the pyramid tells the tale of heroic human sacrifice and of the soul's imminent descent to the underworld, where it is rewarded with the gift of sacred *pulque,* a milky alcoholic beverage made from cactus, from the gods.

Just south of the pyramid are a series of 10 I-shaped **ball courts**—more than any other site in Mesoamerica—where the sacred pre-Columbian ball game was played. The walls are covered with relief sculpture. Note that the crosslike glyphs on the facades are related to the planet Venus. This game, played throughout Mesoamerica, is similar in some ways to soccer—players used a hard rubber ball that could not be touched with the hands, and suited up in knee pads and body protectors—but far more deadly. Intricate carvings at this and other complexes indicate that the games ended with human sacrifice. It's still a subject of debate whether the winner or loser of the match was the sacrificial victim. It is surmised that the players may have even been high-standing members of the priest or warrior classes.

El Tajín Chico, to the north, is thought to have been the secular part of the city, administrative and residential. It was likely the location of the elite's living quarters. Floors and roofing were made out of a pre-

Columbian cement of volcanic rock and limestone. The most important structure here is the Complejo de los Columnos (Complex of the Columns). The columns once held up the cement ceilings, but early settlers in Papantla removed the ceiling stones to construct houses.

Guided tours of El Tajín are not available: the plaque at the entrance tells some of what little is known about the site in Spanish, English, and French, but the rest is up to your imagination. The entrance is lined with *fondas* (covered stalls) that sell inexpensive meals and mountains of tacky souvenirs, and there's a large, cafeteria-style restaurant at the site. If you're prepared to work your way through the thick jungle, you can see some more recent finds along the dirt paths that lead over the nearby ridges. ☎ $2.50; free Sun. ☉ Daily 9–5.

Papantla de Olarte

⑩ *250 km (155 mi) northwest of Veracruz.*

Papantla de Olarte sits amid tropical hills, the center of a vanilla-producing region. A distinctive mix of Spanish colonial and indigenous influence can be seen here: Totonac men in flowing white pants lead their donkeys through the crowded streets, and palm trees shade the traditional, tiled zócalo. The town is best known for its *voladores* (fliers), who twirl off an 82-ft pole next to Papantla's ornate cathedral. This ritual was originally performed as a tribute to the god of sun and rain. The four fliers begin the dance on a platform at the top of the ceremonial pole, each facing one of the cardinal directions. They start their descent from the side of the platform facing east—where the sun rises and the world awakes—twisting left for 13 full rotations each. Between them, the four fliers circle the pole 52 times, representing the sacred 52-year cycle of the Totonacs (the Maya calendar had the same 52-year cycle). A fifth man, the prayer giver, sits atop the pole, playing a small flute while keeping rhythm on a drum as the fliers descend. Originally, the ceremony was held on the vernal equinox, but now the voladores fly for the crowds every Saturday and Sunday at 12:45 PM and give special shows during Corpus Christi.

Dining and Lodging

$ ✕ **Restaurante Sorrento.** The Sorrento is the most popular restaurant
★ in Papantla, crowded at mealtimes with locals who come to enjoy the cheap regional seafood and to catch a few minutes of the *telenovela* (soap opera) on the corner set. The lavender dining room is lined with tilework. ✉ *Enríquez 104,* ☎ *No phone. No credit cards.*

$ ✕ **Restaurant Tajín.** The Hotel Tajín's sunny restaurant is comparatively elegant and hardly more expensive than the storefront eateries near the second-class bus station. House specialties include a fillet of fish stuffed with shellfish, *jaibas rellenas* (stuffed crab), rabbit marinated in chili, and Yucatecan *pollo píbil* (chicken in a mild orange *achiote* sauce). Don't be alarmed by the misleading bilingual menu—the *tasajo cerdo* is not, in fact, "steak porpoise" but marinated pork. ✉ *Hotel Tajín, Nuñez y Domínguez 104,* ☎ *784/2–06–44. MC, V.*

$ 🏨 **Hotel Premier.** Right on Papantla's pretty, lively zócalo, the Premier is the town's swankiest hotel and a real bargain at its tariff of $36 for a double. The lobby is lined with mirrors and furnished with small purple chairs that were once dedicated to the no-longer-functional bar. The rooms themselves are spotless and good-size and have tiny balconies overlooking the square. Amenities include tiled bathrooms, air-conditioning, telephones, and satellite-programmed color TVs. However, if you want to dine or drink, you'll have to frequent one of the restaurants or bars around the square. ✉ *Enríquez 103, 93400,* ☎ *784/2–16–45,* ℻ *784/2–10–62. 16 rooms, 4 suites. Free parking. MC, V.*

$ 🏨 **Hotel Tajín.** Under the same management as the Hotel Premier, the Tajín has more amenities and is less expensive than its slightly more central cousin. Some televisions are black and white, some rooms have ceiling fans instead of air-conditioning, and telephones don't always work, but all in all this is a good deal. The hillside perch makes for nice views, and rooms, although fairly small, are spotless and comfortable. Hotel services are in an annex adjoining the main building; there's usually an English-speaking staff member at the reception desk. With one week's notice, the hotel can arrange horseback-riding tours for 6–10 people for $26 per person, to the ruins at El Tajín. ⊠ *Nuñez y Domínguez 104, 93400,* ☎ *784/2-01-21,* 𝔽𝔸𝕏 *784/2-10-62. 59 rooms. Restaurant, bar, beauty salon, free parking. MC, V.*

Tuxpán

⑪ *193 km (120 mi) south of Tampico, 309 km (192 mi) north of Veracruz, 133 km (82 mi) northeast of Papantla.*

Tuxpán is a peaceful riverside town with graceful winding streets—and the Río Tuxpán is even clean enough to swim in. **Juárez,** the main street, running parallel to the river, is lined with diners, hotels, and shops. The **Parque Reforma** is the center of social activity in town, with more than a hundred tables set around a hub of cafés and fruit stands. It has a memorial to Fausto Vega Santander, a member of the 201st Squadron of the Mexican Air Force and the first Mexican to be killed in combat during World War II. *Lanchas* (flat-bottom boats) shuttle passengers across the river to the **Casa de Fidel Castro,** where Castro lived for a time while planning the overthrow of Fulgencio Batista. A replica of the *Granma,* the ship that carried Fidel's men from Tuxpán to Cuba, molders outside. Inside, the casa is bare save some black-and-white photos of Fidel and Mexican president Lázaro Cárdenas.

Beaches

Tuxpán's main appeal is the untouristed miles of beaches that begin just 7 km (4½ mi) east of the town. The first, and most accessible, is **Playa Tuxpán.** The surf here isn't huge, but there's enough action to warrant breaking out your surf or Boogie board. Of the palapas on Playa Tuxpán, the most established is **Restaurant Miramar,** which has an extensive menu and also provides umbrellaed beach chairs for customers. Farther down, try **El Tigre Costeño,** run by a friendly family whose men moonlight weaving palm-frond beach hats.

Dining and Lodging

$$ ✕ **Antonio's.** Next to the Hotel Reforma on Juárez and serving as its restaurant, Antonio's is a quiet, comparatively elegant eatery with a varied menu. The *cazuela de mariscos* (shellfish stew) is excellent, as are the prawns, served grilled or in garlic sauce. A number of beef dishes and sandwiches are also available, as well as cocktails from the full bar. ⊠ *Av. Juárez 25 at Garizurieta,* ☎ *783/4-16-02. MC, V.*

$$ ✕ **El Gabiopa Azul.** The restaurant in the Hotel Tajín (☞ *below*), across the river from central Tuxpán, is bright and airy, with a semicircular wall of windows overlooking the Río Tuxpán. Corn chips and fresh salsa with plenty of cilantro arrive at your table as soon as you order. Dishes run the gamut from local favorites such as *camarones al mojo de ajo* (shrimp in garlic sauce) and pescado à la veracruzana to American-style offerings such as T-bone steaks and hamburgers. It's nothing to make a special trip for, but come if you happen to be on this side of the river visiting the Casa de Fidel Castro (still a taxi ride away from here, however) or just want an excuse to make the pleasant skiff crossing. ⊠ *Hotel Tajín, Km 2.5 Carretera a Cobos,* ☎ *783/4-22-60. AE, MC, V.*

$ ⊞ **Hotel Florida.** Don't be deceived by the dark lobby or the cramped
★ elevator: the Hotel Florida is the best hotel deal in downtown Tuxpán.
The rooms are decorated in bright pastels and have ample light and
space, as well as large, immaculate bathrooms. Basic rooms have telephones and vigorous ceiling fans. Slightly more expensive rooms add
TVs (local stations only) and air-conditioning. Terraces on each floor
enjoy views of the cathedral and waterfront. ⊠ *Av. Juárez 23, across
from cathedral, 92800,* ☎ *783/4–02–22 or 783/4–06–02. 75 rooms.
Restaurant, bar. MC, V.*

$ ⊞ **Hotel May Palace.** The most luxurious lodgings in Tuxpán can be
secured at this five-star hotel in the center of town. The modern five-
story property is geared to a business clientele. The rooms are swathed
in pastels and set off by unique rattan furniture custom designed for
the hotel. All units have phones, satellite-programmed TVs, and air-
conditioning. Guest services include a small video bar, a restaurant specializing in seafood and regional dishes, a rooftop pool, and meeting
salons. ⊠ *Av. Juárez 44, facing Parque Reforma, 92800,* ☎ FAX *783/
4–88–82 or 783/4–44–61. 68 rooms, 2 suites. Restaurant, bar, room
service, pool, 2 meeting rooms, free parking. AE, DC.*

$ ⊞ **Hotel Reforma.** The Reforma is a lovely building a block from the
waterfront in the heart of downtown. It lacks a lobby but has a central courtyard with a number of skylights, a fountain, and a few
wrought-iron tables where guests often congregate in the afternoon.
Rooms are carpeted and have phones, cable color TVs, and good-size
bathrooms. Street noise can be a problem on the first floor. ⊠ *Av. Juárez
25, 92800,* ☎ *783/4–02–10,* FAX *783/4–06–25. 88 rooms, 10 suites.
Restaurant, bar, room service, free parking. AE.*

$ ⊞ **Hotel Tajín.** This place looks like a first-class resort from the out-
side, but once you enter, you'll be reminded of nothing so much as a
college dorm: long beige hallways with faded blue carpets lead past
scores of identical, bland rooms with almost no decorative touches.
However, the Tajín's location on the banks of the river, across from
the city center, means that almost every room overlooks the water and
green Tuxpán. It also means that traffic noise is replaced by the sounds
of river birds at night. The hotel is easy to reach by car (cross the bridge
and drive east for five minutes), but there is no bus service. Without a
car, you must take a longish taxi ride from the center or catch a beach-
bound bus to the Paso de Esquifes La Peñita, where a skiff will shuttle you across the river. The hotel is a three-minute (often muddy) walk
from the landing. ⊠ *Km 2.5 Carretera a Cobos, 92800,* ☎ *783/4–22–
60 or 783/4–25–72,* FAX *783/4–25–19. 110 rooms, 10 suites. Restaurant, bar, pool, dock, dance club. AE, MC, V.*

Outdoor Activities and Sports

WATER SPORTS

There are some nice places to submerge in the Tuxpán area. For scuba
diving, head to **Tamiaula,** a small village just north of Tuxpán, where
you can hire a fishing boat for the 45-minute journey to the prime diving around **Isla Lobos** (Wolf Island), a protected eco-reserve that shares
its space with a military outpost and a lighthouse. In the shallow water
offshore you'll find a few shipwrecks and colorful reefs that are home
to a large variety of sea life, including puffer fish, parrot fish, dam-
selfish, and barracuda. **Aquasport** (☎ 783/7–02–59), just before Playa
Tuxpán, arranges scuba-diving trips to Isla Lobos and also has deep-
sea fishing excursions. Other outfits run trips to the island that include
permits, scuba gear, lunch, and transportation.

VERACRUZ A TO Z

Arriving and Departing

By Car

The city of Veracruz can be reached within about eight hours by traveling south from Tampico via Mexico 180, or within six hours from Mexico City via Mexico 150. The roads throughout the state, paved and kept up with oil money, are generally very good.

By Plane

Both **Mexicana** (☎ 29/32–22–42 or 29/32–86–99) and **Aeroméxico** (☎ 29/35–08–33 or 29/35–02–83) provide nonstop service from Mexico City to the port of Veracruz.

BETWEEN THE AIRPORT AND DOWNTOWN

A cab to the city center costs $7. No city bus serves the airport. An air-conditioned minivan ($9) runs between the airport and the downtown office of **Transavion** (⊠ Hidalgo 826 between Canal and Morales, ☎ 29/37–87–19 or 29/37–89–78).

Getting Around

By Bus

Veracruz's main **bus terminal** (⊠ Díaz Mirón 1698, ☎ 29/37–57–44) is about 4 km (2½ mi) south of the zócalo. The main bus company is **ADO** (☎ 29/37–29–22 or 29/35–07–83), with daily service to Jalapa every 20 minutes from 6 AM to midnight and round-the-clock departures for Mexico City. ADO also offers first- and second-class service to Reynosa, on the Texas border. If you are headed north and east, the deluxe bus line **UNO** (☎ 29/35–07–83 or 29/37–29–22) goes to Jalapa, Puebla, and Mexico City. **Cuenca** (☎ 29/35–54–05) goes south to Oaxaca. **Cristóbal Colón** (☎ 29/37–57–44) runs from another station on the same block and offers frequent first- and second-class service to Los Tuxtlas.

Contacts and Resources

Car Rental

Jalapa. Renta de Autos Sánchez (⊠ Ignacio de la Llave 14, ☎ 28/17–70–46) is the only rental agency in town.

Veracruz. Avis (⊠ Airport, ☎ 29/34–96–23), **Dollar** (⊠ Víctimas del 5 y 6 de Julio 883, ☎ 29/35–52–31 or 29/35–33–77), **Hertz** (⊠ Hotel Costa Verde, Avila Camacho 3797, Boca del Río, ☎ 29/37–41–00), and **National** (⊠ Díaz Mirón 1036, ☎ 29/31–17–56 or 29/31–33–12) are represented.

Currency Exchange

Jalapa. One block from Parque Juárez, **Casa de Cambio Jalapa** (⊠ Zamora 36, ☎ 28/18–68–60) has good rates; it's open 9–2 and 4–6:30 weekdays. You can also change money in the mornings at several banks on Parque Juárez.

Papantla. Banamex (⊠ Enríquez 102, past Andy's Cadillac Bar) changes both cash and traveler's checks weekdays 9–noon and has an ATM that accepts Cirrus, Plus, Visa, and MasterCard.

Tuxpán. Bancomer (⊠ Av. Juárez at Escuela Médico Militar, ☎ 783/4–00–09) changes cash and traveler's checks weekdays 8:30–2:30.

Veracruz. The best rates in town are at **Bancomer** (⊠ Av. Juárez at Independencia, ☎ 29/31–00–95), but money-changing hours are limited to weekdays 9 AM–11:30 AM, so you'll have to arrive early to make it through the lines. For later hours, try **Casa de Cambio Puebla** (⊠ Av. Juárez 112, ☎ 29/31–24–50), open weekdays 9–6, or use the ATM at **Banamex** (⊠ Av. Juárez at Independencia, ☎ 29/32–68–93) that accepts Cirrus, Plus, Visa, and MasterCard.

Emergencies

Jalapa. Police (☎ 28/18–74–90 or 28/18–71–99); for an ambulance, call the **Cruz Roja** (Red Cross; ☎ 28/17–34–31 or 28/17–81–58).

Papantla. Police (☎ 784/2–00–75), **Cruz Roja** (☎ 784/2–01–26).

Tuxpán. Police (☎ 783/4–02–52), **Cruz Roja** (☎ 783/4–01–58).

Veracruz. Dial **06** for medical, fire, and theft emergencies. **Oficinas Para La Seguridad del Turista** (☎ 01–800/9–03–92) has a country-wide 24-hour toll-free hot line to provide legal and medical help for tourists. **Police** (⊠ Playa Linda 222, ☎ 29/38–06–64 or 29/38–06–93); **Hospital Regional de Veracruz** (⊠ 20 de Noviembre s/n, ☎ 29/37–15–93 or 29/37–08–04); **Cruz Roja** (☎ 29/37–55–00).

Pharmacies

Jalapa. Calle Enríquez is lined with pharmacies. For 24-hour service, the **Farmacia Plus** (⊠ Revolución 173 at Sagayo, ☎ 28/17–27–77 or 28/17–27–97) is your best option.

Papantla. Farmacia Médico (⊠ Gutiérrez Zamora 103, ☎ 784/2–19–41), open daily 7:30 AM–10 PM, is the largest pharmacy in town.

Veracruz. Benavides (⊠ Independencia 1291, at Serdán, ☎ 29/31–89–29) is a big, convenient drugstore downtown; it closes at 10 PM daily. For 24-hour service, try **Farmacia Mercado Bravo** (⊠ Independencia 1197, ☎ 29/31–08–83).

Guided Tours

Jalapa. Bike Shuttle/Expediciones en Bicicleta de Montaña (⊠ Iglesia No. 7, Lomas Quebradas, San Jeronimo, Mexico, D.F. 10200, ☎ Pager 5/447–1111 No. 549–3030, FAX 5/681–1831) hosts four-day mountain biking tours that trace the Cortés Route from Pico de Orizaba to Jalapa through glaciers, pine forests, subtropical vegetation, and coffee plantations.

Expediciones Mexico Verde (⊠ Homero 526, Int. 801, Colonia Polanco, Mexico, D.F. 11560, ☎ 5/255–44–00 or 01/800–362–8800 in Mexico, ☎ FAX 5/255–4465) has river rafting for individuals or groups along the Río Pescados near Jalapa. One-day or overnight excursions are available. All equipment, including life jackets, helmets, and oars, is provided. The outfit also runs 7- or 10-day trips on the Cortés Route, which includes Veracruz City, Antigua, Cempoala, Jalapa, and Coatepec in the state of Veracruz and continues on to conquistador-related sites in the states of Tlaxcala, Puebla, and Mexico. English is spoken.

The Jalapa tourist office also recommends the following two bilingual river-rafting outfits: **Veraventuras** (⊠ Santos Degollado No. 81, Int. 8, Jalapa 91000, ☎ 28/18–97–79 or 01–800/2–65–72 in Mexico, FAX 28/18–96–80) and **Iguana Expediciones** (⊠ Cotaxtla Sur 16, Colonia Petrolera, Boca del Río 91889, ☎ FAX 29/21–15–50).

Veracruz. Boat tours of the bay depart from the malecón daily 7–7. Boats leave whenever they're full, and the $2.50 half-hour ride includes a (Spanish-language) talk on Veracruz history. Longer trips to nearby **Isla Verde** (Green Island) and **Isla de Enmedio** (Middle Island) leave daily from the shack marked PASEO EN LANCHITA near the Plaza Acuario.

Again, boats wait until they're full to set off, so it's best to be in a group. The cost should be about $3–$5 per person, but feel free to bargain.

Martin Sandoval Tours (✉ Balboa 327, between Washington and Martí, ☎ 29/30–40–23 or ☎ FAX 29/35–31–72) has city tours as well as trips to Tajín and Papantla, Los Tuxtlas, and Jalapa. Diving and fishing trips are available, too. There are also travel desks at the Torremar, Emporio, Continental Plaza, and Fiesta Americana hotels.

Visitor Information

The **Jalapa tourist office** (✉ Blvd. Cristóbal Colón 5, Jardines de las Animas, ☎ 28/12–85–00, ext. 130, FAX 28/12–59–36) is in the large office building on the way out of town toward Veracruz (known as Torre Animas) and is open weekdays 9–9. There is also a **Jalapa tourist information booth** (✉ Calle Enrique No. 14 in front of the Palacio Municipal) open daily 9–9.

The **Tuxpán tourist office** (✉ Av. Juárez 26, ☎ 783/4–01–77) is open daily 8–3 and 4–8.

The **Veracruz Dirección Municipal de Turismo** (✉ Palacio Municipal on zócalo, ☎ 29/32–19–99, FAX 29/32–75–93) is open Monday–Saturday 9–9, Sunday 10–1.

THE NORTHEAST

Few travelers go out of their way to visit northeastern Mexico, an arid area that's becoming increasingly industrial as more and more multinational companies establish *maquiladoras* (foreign-owned factories in duty-free zones) along the border and create more and more air pollution. But day- and weekend-trippers from Texas enjoy the foreign color and cuisine of border towns like Nuevo Laredo, Matamoros, and Reynosa. And only about three hours from the border is Monterrey, a fast-paced city that's home to Mexico's major brewery, some good museums, and one of Latin America's finest universities.

Nature lovers can enjoy the Parque Nacional Cumbres de Monterrey, northwest of the city, with its impressive Cola de Caballo waterfall. Also near Monterrey is the dramatic cut of the Barranca de la Huasteca, as well as the Grutas de García, caves with an underground lake and a stalactite and stalagmite forest. Anglers and hunters are lured farther into the area by the magnificent fish and game at Lake Vincente Guerrero, not far from Ciudad Victoria. And **Tampico** is known both for its seaside appeal and its interesting architectural sights.

Nuevo Laredo

⓬ *1½ km (1 mi) south of Laredo, Texas.*

Of all the eastern border towns, Nuevo Laredo receives the largest onslaught of American souvenir seekers. Shopping is the primary pursuit here, and you'll find a warren of stalls and shops as well as a large crafts market concentrated on Avenida Guerrero in a seven-block stretch that extends from the International Bridge to the main plaza. In addition to the standard border-town curios, Nuevo Laredo shops stock a good selection of high-quality handicrafts from all over Mexico, at somewhat inflated prices. Wander a few blocks off the main drag in any direction for better prices and smaller crowds.

Nuevo Laredo was founded after the Treaty of Guadalupe Hidalgo in 1848, which ended the Mexican-American War. The treaty established the Río Bravo (or Rio Grande) as the border between the two countries and forced Mexico to give up a substantial amount of territory.

Northeastern Mexico

Sabinas
Nuevo Laredo ⑫ Laredo
85

TEXAS

Sabinas Hidalgo
Parque Nacional Cumbres de Monterrey ㉕
Monterrey ⑮—㉒ 54
SEE DETAIL MAP
Rio Grande McAllen
Grutas de García ㉔
Reynosa ⑬ Brownsville
Barranca de la Huasteca ㉓ ★
40 Matamoros ⑭
97
㉖ Saltillo
85 180

Padre Island

Laguna Madre

Laguna Madre

Boca Jesús Maria

Golfo de Mexico

Linares
57

Matehuala
Ciudad Victoria
101 85
101 180
Lake Vicente ㉗ Guerrero
Tampico ㉘
57

0 — 50 miles
0 — 75 km
N

Many of Laredo's Mexican residents, who suddenly found themselves living in the United States, crossed the river and founded Nuevo Laredo on what had been the outskirts of town. Today, Nuevo Laredo's economy depends greatly on gringos who head south for a few days of drunken revelry, returning home with a bottle of tequila, suitcases full of souvenirs, and a mean hangover.

Dining and Lodging

$$$ ✕ **Winery (La Vinteria).** This Mexican version of a Continental wine
★ bar serves such regional specialties as *carne tampiqueña* (grilled steak) and *queso fundido* (melted cheese), often served in a bowl with *chorizo* (spicy sausage) to be spread on tortillas. It has the best selection of Mexican wines in town. ⊠ *Matamoros 308, at Victoria,* ☎ *87/12–08–95. AE, DC, MC, V.*

$$ ✕ **El Dorado.** Dating from the Prohibition era, this spot is a favorite with the Texas crowd—a hangout better known for its atmosphere than for its cuisine. Try the combination plate of grilled meat, which includes two selections of either goat, quail, or frogs' legs. ⊠ *Ocampo at Belden,* ☎ *87/12–00–15. AE, MC, V.*

$$ ✕ **México Típico.** This establishment, gaily decorated in bright Mexican colors, offers both indoor and outdoor patio dining, with mariachis coming in from the street to entertain. The patio, partially covered, features a waterfall. Specialties are carne asada and cabrito. True to its name, México Típico serves the typical Mexican plate of beef or chicken enchiladas with rice and refried beans. ⊠ *Guerrero 934,* ☎ *87/12–15–25. MC, V.*

$$ 🏨 **El Río.** A modern redbrick structure spread out on large landscaped grounds, this motel has a spacious lobby and large guest rooms with dark Spanish colonial-style furniture. All units have a shower, color TV, and telephone. ⊠ *5 km (3 mi) south on Hwy. 85, Nuevo Laredo,*

Tamps. 88280, ☎ *87/14–36–66,* FAX *87/15–12–32. 126 rooms, 4 suites. Restaurant, bar, 2 pools, free parking. AE, MC, V.*

$ ⛨ **Hotel Posada Mina.** This is a good bet if you're looking for budget accommodations, not luxury, in a quiet location. A remodeled old yellow-brick building about six blocks west of the bridge, the Mina has very small rooms, but they are clean with decent beds, individual air-conditioning and heat, color TVs, and private baths. ✉ *Mina 3521, Nuevo Laredo, Tamps. 88000,* ☎ *87/13–14–73,* FAX *87/12–30–70. 4 rooms, 2 suites. Coffee shop, free parking. No credit cards.*

$ ⛨ **Hotel Reforma.** An older hotel just a half block south of Plaza Hidalgo, Reforma has a restaurant, marble lobby, and secure parking a block away. Rooms in the older section, although somewhat small and rather nondescript, are comfortable; the junior suites in the newer section are slightly bigger and have fresh carpets and curtains, although the hallways smell musty. All units come with shower, cable color TV, and telephone. ✉ *Guerrero 822, Nuevo Laredo, Tamps. 88000,* ☎ *87/12–62–50,* FAX *87/12–67–14. 45 rooms, 11 suites. Restaurant, bar, free parking. MC, V.*

Nightlife and the Arts

Victoria's, three blocks from Bridge 1, is a noisy favorite; the **Winery** and **El Dorado** are somewhat more sedate; and **Quintana Rock** and the new **Plaza San Miguel** are the local discos. All of the above are on Avenida Guerrero in the heart of the shopping district.

Shopping

On the stretch where International Bridge 1 leads into Avenida Guerrero you'll find most of Nuevo Laredo's shops—classy and junky alike. **Granada** (✉ Guerrero 504, ☎ 87/12–86–44) has better-quality items than many of the other vendors, including lead crystal and serapes. Artisan shops selling lots of leather goods and ceramics are in the **Nuevo Mercado de la Reforma** market, three blocks south of the bridge at Avenida Guerrero and Calle Belden. The **Ma Cristina** mall, one-half block north of the square at Avenida Guerrero 631, houses about three dozen curio outlets. Most stores remain open until 8 PM.

Reynosa

⑬ *16 km (10 mi) south of McAllen, Texas.*

Because of its manageable size and mellow attitude, Reynosa is one of the most pleasant points of entry into Mexico. It is also a convenient starting point if you're bound for Mexico City, Monterrey, or Veracruz. That said, Reynosa is still an industrial border town of limited charm, driven economically by the petrochemical industry, agriculture, and the ever-present tourist trade. As you enter town, you'll see the **Zona Rosa** (Pink Zone) tourist district, with a few curio shops and a couple of bars and restaurants. The heart of the city, around **Plaza Principal,** is about five blocks from the International Bridge. It's being made even more presentable with an urban renewal project started in 1996 that is enlarging sidewalks and putting in park benches, cobblestone streets, and new street signs. After leaving downtown, the rest of Reynosa is a jumble of tacky border-town urban sprawl.

Plaza Principal is in many ways a typical Mexican town center, but its original colonial church has been joined like a Siamese twin to an ultramodern newer addition with arches and stained-glass windows. **Hidalgo Street,** a colorful pedestrian mall of shops and street vendors, leads off from the plaza. Many Texans save money by having their teeth fixed south of the Rio Grande—which explains the many dental offices you'll see in this area.

Dining and Lodging

$$ ✕ La Majada. Like all good cabrito restaurants, this one is simple and to the point: Roast kid, guacamole, and quesadillas are pretty much what you'll find. Don't come for the atmosphere but for local specialties at their best. ⊠ *Av. Miguel Alemán (½ block from bridge),* ☎ *89/22–88–18. Reservations not accepted. MC, V.*

$$ ✕ Sam's. Wild game like quail and dove served in season (November–January) and seafood are the reasons to come here. Desserts are limited to flan and cheesecake. In winter, Sam's is frequented by Americans from the Rio Grande Valley and snowbirds from Minnesota. ⊠ *Allende 1100,* ☎ *89/22–00–34 or 89/22–34–34. AE, MC, V.*

$$ ▦ Astromundo. Downtown and handy to the market and the few good local restaurants, this popular hotel gets a lot of traffic from weekending Texans. ⊠ *Juárez 675, Reynosa, Tamps. 88500,* ☎ *89/22–56–25,* ◪ *89/22–98–88. 88 rooms, 6 suites. Restaurant, bar, free parking. AE, MC, V.*

$$ ▦ Hacienda. Located along the highway to Monterrey about 16 km (10 mi) from the U.S. border, this sparkling new hotel is luxurious by Reynosa standards. Its tiled lobby is decorated with colonial-style furniture and handicrafts, which carry over into the light-filled, cheerful rooms; all have color cable TVs, air-conditioning, and direct-dial phones. ⊠ *Blvd. Hidalgo 2013, Reynosa, Tamps. 88650,* ☎ *89/24–60–10,* ◪ *89/23–59–62. 20 rooms, 13 suites. Restaurant, bar, meeting room, travel services, car rental, free parking. AE, MC, V.*

$ ▦ San Carlos. This five-story hotel on the square has air-conditioned rooms with colonial-style furniture and satellite TVs. Business travelers and tourists appreciate its central location, close to the square and shopping center, and the friendly staff, which aims to please. ⊠ *Hidalgo 970, Reynosa, Tamps. 88500,* ☎ *89/22–12–80,* ◪ *89/22–26–20. 72 rooms. Restaurant. MC, V.*

Nightlife and the Arts

The **Imperial** offers quiet, slow-dance music with a combo or strolling trio, depending on the night; the older clientele is well dressed. The Zona Rosa has several discos and **Trevino's** (⊠ Av. Virreyes 1075, ☎ 89/22–14–44), which has a piano bar.

Shopping

Trevino's (☞ *above*) has a good selection of Mexican arts and crafts, sculpture, papier-mâché, perfumes, liquors, and clothing, with a cocktail lounge in the rear.

Matamoros

⓮ *1 km (about ½ mi) south of Brownsville, Texas.*

Matamoros, across from Brownsville, Texas (the southernmost point in the continental United States), is the most historic of the border towns, dating from the 18th century. It is named H. Matamoros, or Heroic Matamoros, for one of the many rebellious priests who were executed by the Spanish during the War of Independence (1810–21). The first major battle of the Mexican-American War was fought here when guns in Matamoros began shelling Fort Brown on the north side of the Rio Grande. Shortly afterward, troops of Zachary Taylor occupied Matamoros and began their march south.

Today Matamoros is the commercial center of a rich agricultural area and a manufacturing center for Mexico's in-bond industry. Some 20 years ago, **Avenida Alvaro Obregón,** which leads from the main bridge, was spruced up to "dignify" the Mexican side of the border, and of the three border towns it makes the prettiest entryway. This is where you'll find the town's best shops, restaurants, and accommodations. Also of interest is the **Casa Mata Museum** in the remains of Fort Mata, built in 1845 to defend the city against American invasion. The fortress wasn't completed in time, and Zachary Taylor's troops were able to capture Matamoros easily. Casa Mata now displays photos and artifacts, mostly from the Mexican Revolution. ⊠ *Guatemala and Santos Degollado,* ☎ *88/13–59–29.* ☒ *Free.* ☉ *Mon.–Sat. 9:30–5, Sun. 9:30–3.*

Beach

Playa Bagdad is about 30 km (18 mi) from downtown Matamoros. It's worth a visit only if you hanker for the Gulf of Mexico. It's the site of the Confederacy's only open harbor during the U.S. Civil War. Freighters skirting the Union naval blockade unloaded their war supplies and loaded up with Confederate cotton destined for Europe. Today, there's an air of decrepit charm about the place: about 100 palapas are lined up in neat rows along the gritty shore waiting for visitors, accompanied by a couple of seafood restaurants that seem to be barely surviving. On the weekends, hordes of Mexican middle-class families pour into the place. The entrance fee is about $1.50 per vehicle.

Dining and Lodging

$$ ✕ **Garcia's.** Rebuilt and redecorated over its own parking garage, this
★ is a romantic place for dancing and dining on lobster or steak and your choice of a dozen fine tequilas. An elevator from the garage leads up to a gift shop with wares from all over Mexico as well as to the restaurant and a bar. ⊠ *Calle Alvaro Obregón 82,* ☎ *88/12–39–29 or 88/13–18–33. AE, DC, MC, V.*

$ ✕ **Los Nortenos.** A goat slow-roasting over hot coals in the window is the not-so-subtle advertisement for the best cabrito in town. A dozen plain tables with plastic tablecloths are the setting for an equally spare menu—goat, guacamole, and quesadillas. ⊠ *Calle Matamoros entre 8 y 9,* ☎ *88/13–00–37. No credit cards.*

$$$ ☷ **Gran Hotel Residencial.** The best hotel in the city, this pleasant low-
★ rise built along Spanish colonial lines is the center of activity for much of Matamoros. All rooms have terraces, two queen-size beds, and color cable TVs. There's also a large pool and a play area for children in the lush garden. ⊠ *Alvaro Obregón 249, at Amapolas, 6 blocks from bridge, Matamoros, Tamps. 87330,* ☎ *88/13–94–40,* ⅢX *88/13–27–77. 109 rooms, 5 suites. Restaurant, bar, pool. AE, MC, V.*

Nightlife and the Arts

Garcia's and the **Gran Hotel Residencial** (☞ Dining and Lodging, *above*) are good places for a relaxed drink. If you're looking for some dance action, head out Alvaro Obregón toward the international bridge, where you'll find several discos, including **Tequila's, Crazy Lazy,** and **Mr. Lee's.**

Shopping

The most appealing shops are on Calle Alvaro Obregón, which leads from the border bridge to the center of town. The salmon-color building that houses **Garcia's** restaurant (☞ Dining and Lodging, *above*) also contains a huge gift shop, where you can buy everything from tacky souvenirs and big sombreros to quality tequila, silver, Oaxaca wedding dresses, and leather jackets. Across from Garcia's, the shacklike **Azteca Gift Shop** (⊠ Alvaro Obregón 77, ☎ 88/12–88–19) has run-of-the-mill woolen rugs and crafts at discount prices. **Barbara** (⊠ Alvaro Obregón 37, ☎ 88/16–54–56) sells attractive craft items, home furnishings, and good costume jewelry and imported cosmetics. The covered, block-long **Matamoros Market** downtown is the place to haggle for bargains; you get what you pay for.

Monterrey

235 km (146 mi) southwest of Nuevo Laredo, 225 km (140 mi) west of Reynosa, 325 km (201 mi) west of Matamoros.

Monterrey is a favorite with weekenders and "winter Texans" from the Rio Grande valley who find the city so near—a three-hour drive from the border or a short flight from Dallas, Houston, or San Antonio—and yet so foreign. The top hotels are clustered downtown in the Zona Rosa (Pink Zone) or Barrio Antiguo (Old Quarter), and several streets, including Avenida Morelos—the main drag—are now pedestrian malls.

Monterrey celebrated the 400th anniversary of its founding in 1996. It is Mexico's third-largest city and the capital of the state of Nuevo León. This industrial center is a brewer of beer and forger of steel, with nothing in the way of a laid-back lifestyle. It is where some of the country's most powerful captains of industry hold sway—a fact that earned the city its nickname, the Sultan of the North. Monterrey also has the country's most sophisticated convention center—a high-tech facility called Cintermex—and is building a gigantic sports arena to host international events. The Dallas Cowboys and San Diego Padres have started playing exhibition games there in the summer.

The impressive **Gran Plaza**—at 100 acres one of the country's largest squares—was completed in 1985 as part of an urban renewal project that also includes the first stages of a San Antonio–style riverwalk with cafés and shops. The plaza is within walking distance of the downtown hotels. Better known as Macroplaza, it extends from the modernistic Palacio Municipal (City Hall) several blocks past the newly painted cathedral, the old City Hall, and the Legislative Palace to the Palacio de Gobierno (State House).

⑮ Towering above the neoclassical **Palacio de Gobierno** is a concrete slab topped by the Lighthouse of Commerce, a laser beam that flashes from 8 to 11 nightly. It was designed by Luis Barragán to commemorate the 100th anniversary of the founding of the city's Chamber of Commerce. Handsome Saddle Mountain and the craggy Sierra Madre provide a majestic backdrop to this austere modern monument. ⊠ *Between Av. Constitución, Av. Cuauhtémoc, Calz. Francisco Madero, and Av. Felix Gomez.*

★ ⑯ The opulent **Museo de Arte Contemporaneo (MARCO)** (Museum of Contemporary Art) is the principal sight on the Gran Plaza. Designed in the style of a Moorish palace by renowned Mexican architect Ricardo Legorretta, it has 14 galleries that display the cutting-edge art of Mexico and Latin America and, at times, of other parts of the world. There's an outstanding collection of art books for sale at the gift shop. You can listen to live music alongside a reflecting pool on the beautiful marble patio on Wednesday afternoons (4:30–8) and watch the candlelit tables fill up with culture vultures sipping coffee and nibbling on pieces of pie. ⊠ *Gran Plaza at Zuazua and Ocampo,* ☎ *8/342–4820.* 🎫 *About $1.50; free Wed.* ☉ *Tues. and Thurs.–Sat. 11–7, Wed. and Sun. 11–9.*

⑰ The **Museo de Historia Mexicana** (Mexican History Museum) has a mini riverwalk with cafés and a boat ride on its grounds. It displays the country's most complete history of its 1910–20 Revolution. Battles, marches, and political protagonists come to life in the newsreels of the period, part of a sophisticated multimedia show held inside a railroad car that served as a troop carrier for the insurgents. Life-size plaster-of-paris casts of the *Villistas* (soldiers under the command of Pancho Villa) sit shotgun on the roof of a car that we are led to believe has just been "liberated" from the Mexican army. Other exhibits

Monterrey

KEY

— Rail Lines

Cathedral, **18**
Centro Cultural
Alfa, **21**
Cuauhtémoc
Brewery, **20**
Museo de Arte
Contemporaneo
(MARCO), **16**

Museo de Historia
Mexicana, **17**
Obispado, **19**
Palacio de
Gobierno, **15**
Parque Plaza
Sesamo, **22**

include the first bottle-capping machine used by Coca-Cola, a depiction of café society in Mexico circa 1910, and Precolumbian Huastec artifacts. ⊠ *Dr. Coss 445 Sur,* ☎ *8/345–9898.* ⊠ *$1.25; guided tours in English free (call ahead to confirm that an English-speaking guide is available).* ⊙ *Tues.–Thurs. 11–6, Fri.–Sun. 11–8.*

⑱ Monterrey's Spanish history began in 1596, and for its first couple of centuries it was little more than an outpost. Construction of the **cathedral** began in 1600 but took some 250 years to finish. As a result a baroque facade is set off by neoclassical columns and two huge ornate plateresque medallions on the main door. Murals by local artists frame the main altar. ⊠ *Gran Plaza and Ocampo and Dr. Coss.*

⑲ The **Obispado** (Bishop's House) is the only landmark to be completed in the colonial era (1788). Built on a hilltop as a home for retired prelates, the Obispado was used as a fort during the Mexican-American War (1847), the French Intervention (1862), and again during the Mexican Revolution (1915). Today it houses the **Museo Regional de Nuevo León El Obispado,** with exhibits that focus on the history of the entire area. The museum's major appeal, however, is its splendid view of Monterrey. Currently closed for renovation, the museum may open by 2000. ⊠ *Far west end of Av. Padre Mier at Rafael José Berger,* ☎ *8/ 346–0404.* ⊠ *$1.25.* ⊙ *Tues.–Sun. 10–5.*

⑳ The explosion of the popularity of Mexican beer in recent years owes much to the **Cuauhtémoc Brewery,** which opened a century ago. Named after a famous Aztec chief, the brewery is the heart of an industrial empire producing Carta Blanca and Tecate beer. Today the brewery complex includes the Mexican Baseball Hall of Fame, a sports museum, the Museo de Monterrey Electronic Arts Gallery, and a beer garden with free beer—obviously the big draw. ⊠ *Av. Alfonso Reyes 2202 Nte.,* ☎ *8/328–5746.* ⊠ *Free.* ⊙ *Tues.–Sun. 11–8. Brewery tours by request, weekdays 9–1 and 3–6; call 8/375–2200 to book.*

㉑ The Cuauhtémoc Brewery spawned a glass factory for bottles, a steel mill for caps, a carton factory, and, eventually, several industrial conglomerates. One of the last, Alfa, gave Monterrey the **Centro Cultural Alfa** (Alfa Cultural Center), probably the best museum of science and technology in the country. The museum has many hands-on exhibits and an IMAX theater. Free buses to the museum run from the downtown *alameda* (main square) every hour from 3 to 8 daily. ⊠ *Roberto Garza Sada 1000,* ☎ *8/303–0002.* ⊠ *$3.50.* ⊙ *Tues.–Fri. 3–9, Sat. 2–9, Sun. noon–9.*

㉒ The newest recreational/educational play area for children is the cleverly designed **Parque Plaza Sesamo** (Sesame Plaza Park), a sprawling theme park built on the grounds of Parque Fundidora that also houses the city's Cintermex convention complex. There are three main areas. One has a world of water sports with 17 water toboggans, pint-size pools, interactive games, and minirivers. A second area has a computer center where kids can plug into the Internet and play nonviolent video games. The last section is taken up by restaurants and theaters where the park's own personalities put on musical shows. Families can easily spend an entire day here. ⊠ *Calle Agricola 3700–1 Oriente, Col. Agricola in Parque Fundidora,* ☎ *8/354–5400.* ⊠ *$10.* ⊙ *June–Aug. daily 11–9:30; Sept.–May daily 3–3.*

Dining and Lodging

$$$$ ✕ **Luisiana.** Perhaps the most elegant dining room downtown, this is
★ a taste of how New Orleans is imagined in Mexico. There are no Cajun specialties on the menu, but the deepwater crawfish are divine. Wonderfully prepared steak and seafood dishes make this one of the best

restaurants in the country. The waiters wear tuxedos, and there's always soft piano music playing at dinnertime. ⊠ *Hidalgo Ote. 530,* ☎ *8/340–2185 or 8/343–1561. AE, DC, MC, V.*

$$$ ✕ **Residence.** A clubby meeting place for Monterrey's high-powered ★ industrialists and executives, Residence has a menu featuring both Mexican specialties and Continental dishes like prime rib cooked slowly in its juice. ⊠ *Degollado 605 Sur at Matamoros,* ☎ *8/342–7230, 8/345–5040, or 8/345–5478. AE, DC, MC, V.*

$$ ✕ **El Rey de Cabrito.** The restaurant's name ("King of Cabrito") is no lie: this is *the* place to try what is probably the best roast kid you'll ever eat. (The owner keeps his own goat herds.) The hunting lodge–theme restaurant covers half a city block and has become so well known that it's constantly filling out-of-town orders. You can fill up on steaks and fried blood, as well as the famous cabrito. ⊠ *817 Constitución,* ☎ *8/345–3232. MC, V.*

$ ✕ **Sanborns.** Part of a national chain that is a Mexican institution, this is the place for hamburgers and malts as well as tacos and enchiladas. ⊠ *Escobedo Sur 920 off Plaza Hidalgo,* ☎ *8/343–1834. AE, MC, V.*

$$$$ ⊞ **Fiesta Americana Centro Monterrey.** In the center of the Zona Rosa is a spiffy-looking pink sandstone building with a striking atrium lobby that is abuzz with business travelers. The light-filled units (all of them two-room suites) include an office with a hookup for a personal computer, modem, and fax; they're tastefully decorated ar.d have burgundy carpets and pastel bedspreads. Rooms facing the plaza have fabulous mountain views. ⊠ *Av. Corrigidora Ote. 519, Zona Rosa, 64000,* ☎ *8/319–0900; 01–800/504–5000 in Mexico,* ⅎAX *8/319–0980. 207 suites. Restaurant, bar, minibars, no-smoking rooms, pool, exercise room, baby-sitting, laundry service, concierge, free parking. AE, DC, MC, V.*

$$$$ ⊞ **Quinta Real.** This elegant all-suites business hotel holds sway in Mon-★ terrey's financial district and exudes the aura of a prosperous hacienda of bygone days. The high-domed lobby is set with French furnishings in soothing colors, huge bowls of fresh flowers, and carvings of classic Mexican handicrafts, many of them one-of-a-kind works. A collection of finely executed indigenous weavings and embroideries lines the long lobby corridors. The suites, which are decorated in earth tones and rich floral prints, come in 16 varieties. They have either two double beds or one king, robes, color TVs, and luxury bathroom soaps and lotions. The hotel's restaurant serves excellent French and Mexican cuisine and has built up quite a local following. ⊠ *Av. Diego Rivera 500, Fracc. Valle Oriente, San Pedro Garza García, Nvo. León 66260,* ☎ *8/368–1000; 800/445–4565 in the U.S.,* ⅎAX *8/368–1070. 125 suites. Restaurant, bar, minibars, no-smoking rooms, sauna, exercise room, baby-sitting, laundry service, concierge, travel services, car rental, free parking. AE, DC, MC, V.*

$$$$ ⊞ **Radisson Plaza Gran Hotel Ancira.** Built in 1912, this hotel is remi-★ niscent of the grand hotels of Europe: an elegant spiral staircase dominates an expansive Art Deco lobby accented by a black-and-white tile floor and crystal chandeliers. Legend has it that Pancho Villa, taken with the place, settled in and stabled his horse in the lobby. Card-key rooms are conservatively decorated with tasteful pastel walls and matching furnishings. All have minibars, cable TVs, and large marble baths. The Plaza Club business-floor suites have exercise bicycles and impeccable concierge service. ⊠ *Hidalgo at Escobedo, 64000,* ☎ *8/345–7575; 800/333–3333 in the U.S.,* ⅎAX *8/344–5226. 223 rooms, 23 suites. Restaurant, 2 bars, coffee shop, minibars, no-smoking rooms, pool, beauty salon, outdoor hot tub, sauna, exercise room, baby-sitting, laundry service, concierge floor, travel services, car rental, free parking. AE, DC, MC, V.*

$$$$ ⊞ **Sheraton Ambassador.** One of the best hotels in this part of Mex-★ ico, this downtown landmark has spacious rooms and a newly remodeled

executive floor that has rooms with modem ports, work areas, and complimentary Continental breakfast in the executive lounge. There's also a concierge with secretarial and fax service. A health club, an upscale Mediterranean restaurant, and a piano bar with an old-fashioned stained-glass ceiling are among the Ambassador's other amenities. ⊠ *Hidalgo 310 Ote., at Emilio Carranza, 64000,* ☎ *8/340–7000; 800/ 325–3535 in the U.S.* ℻ *8/345–1984. 223 rooms, 16 suites. 2 restaurants, bar, minibars, no-smoking rooms, pool, massage, tennis court, health club, racquetball, laundry service, concierge floor, travel services, free parking. AE, DC, MC, V.*

$$$ 🏨 **Hotel Chipinque.** This hilltop resort overlooking the city on 700 acres of forest land is a tranquil choice if you have a car. The view from the restaurant is extraordinary, especially at night. All rooms have either a king or two queen-size beds, satellite TVs, and phones; some have fireplaces. ⊠ *Meseta de Chipinque No. 1000, San Pedro Garza García, Nvo. León 66297,* ☎ *8/378–1100 or 8/378–6600; 888/237–3316 in the U.S.,* ℻ *8/378–1338. 58 rooms, 13 suites. Restaurant, bar, airconditioning, pool, outdoor hot tub, tennis court, racquetball, billiards, 6 meeting rooms, free parking. AE, MC, V.*

$$ 🏨 **Royalty.** You get your money's worth at this downtown hotel, where prices are lower than usual for this expensive city. The interior, including the lobby and terrace restaurant, is dominated by a cheerful pink-and-white color scheme. Extras include a tiny outdoor pool, video bar, cable TVs, happy hour every afternoon between 6 and 8, and a complimentary American-style breakfast Monday–Saturday. ⊠ *Hidalgo Oriente 402, 64000,* ☎ *8/340–2800,* ℻ *8/340–5812. 57 rooms, 5 suites. Restaurant, bar, pool, health club (for men only), free parking. AE, DC, MC, V.*

$ 🏨 **Colonial.** This no-frills hotel—the oldest in Monterrey—has an ideal central downtown location and budget-price rooms. The small lobby, furnished in colonial style, has one of the last remaining manually operated elevators in the city—it's more than 100 years old. Rooms have cable TVs, carpeting, and air-conditioning units. At night, rooms facing the street get an earful from the noisy men's club next door. ⊠ *Hidalgo 475 Oriente, 64000,* ☎ *8/343–6791,* ☎ ℻ *8/342–1169. 100 rooms. Air-conditioning, laundry service and dry cleaning, free parking. AE, DC, MC, V.*

Nightlife and the Arts

Fashionable folk, residents, and visitors flock to downtown hotels for after-dark action. The pianist at the **Sheraton Ambassador** (Hidalgo 310 Ote., at Emilio Carranza, ☎ 8/340–7000) is rather reserved, as is the lobby bar jazz combo at the **Fiesta Americana Centro Monterrey** (⊠ Av. Corregidora Ote. 519, ☎ 8/319–0900). At the Gran Ancira Radisson Plaza, the classic but upscale Mexican cantina, **Bar 1900** (⊠ Hidalgo at Escobedo, ☎ 8/345–7575), presents an eclectic mix of live music—from rock to romantic Mexican ballads—Tuesday–Saturday nights. The **Far West Rodeo** (⊠ Av. Los Angeles and Universidad, ☎ 8/351–3030) has line dancing to Tex-Mex country music Thursday to Sunday. **Vat–Kru,** (⊠ Blvd. Constitución 3050 Pte., ☎ 8/333–5241), bizarre name and all, is one of the hottest discos in town.

Shopping

Top-quality shops center on Plaza Hidalgo, near the major hotels. Leather and cowboy boots are the local specialties. Owner Porfirio Sosa has handpicked all of the items he sells at the upscale **Carápan** (⊠ Hidalgo 305 Ote., ☎ 8/345–4422) and loves to tell you about them. His array of Mexican antiques, hand-loomed rugs, shawls, clay figures from Michoacán, metal sculptures, and hand-blown glassware rivals that of stores anywhere in the country. **Sanborns** (⊠ Escobedo 920, off Plaza

Hidalgo, ☎ 8/343–1834) offers a standard selection of silver, onyx, and other Mexican craft items. **Plaza Fiesta San Agustín** (⊠ Ave. Real de San Agustín at Lázaro Cárdenas, San Pedro Garza García) is an enormous upscale mall where Monterrey socialites shop for evening gowns, precious gems, and imported perfumes. The **Mercado Indio** (⊠ Bolivar Nte. 1150) is a typical Mexican market with dozens of stalls, although the selections are a little monotonous.

Sports

GOLF

Hotels can arrange temporary memberships in one of **Monterrey**'s three golf courses.

ICE SKATING

☉ **Pista de Hielo San Pedro** (⊠ Plaza San Pedro Local 10, ☎ 8/356–7293) is a popular ice-skating rink. ☉ It is open weekdays 10–3 and 4:30–8, weekends 10–8.

Barranca de la Huasteca (Huastec Canyon)

🖑 ㉓ *23 km (14 mi) southeast of Monterrey.*

The Barranca de la Huasteca, with its 1,000-ft-deep gorge, is spectacular for the striated grooves etched into its walls, making it resemble a giant piece of Lalique glassware. A play area for children has a miniature train ride, two pools, and rest rooms. ⊠ *From Monterrey, 20 km (12 mi) east on Hwy. 40 to Santa Catarina, then 3 km (2 mi) south on marked road to canyon,* ☎ *No phone.* ☞ *$1 per car, 10¢ per person.* ☉ *Daily 9–6.*

Grutas de García (Garcia Caves)

㉔ *49 km (30 mi) southwest of Monterrey.*

The Grutas García are an estimated 50 to 60 million years old and at one time were submerged by an ocean. You can see petrified sea animals in some of its walls. You can hike the steep 1 km (½ mi) from the entrance to the caves or hop on a swaying funicular. Guides lead the way through a strenuous mile of underground grottoes and caverns. This site is far less commercialized than similar places north of the border. ⊠ *From Monterrey, Hwy. 40 west for 40 km (25 mi) to Saltillo, then 9 km (5½ mi) on marked road to caves,* ☎ *No phone.* ☞ *$2 without funicular, $3.50 to ride funicular.* ☉ *Daily 9–5.*

Parque Nacional Cumbres de Monterrey

㉕ *90 km (56 mi) northwest of Monterrey.*

One of the highlights of a trip to the Parque Nacional Cumbres de Monterrey, tucked into the Sierra Madre mountains, is a view of **La Cascada Cola de Caballo** (Horsetail Falls), a dramatic 75-ft-high waterfall that tumbles down from the pine-forested heights. The waterfall is about 1 km (½ mi) from the park's entrance, up a cobblestone road. You can rent a docile horse or burro for about $3 per hour from the local kids who hang out by the ticket booth, or hop on a horse-pulled carriage for $2. ⊠ *From Monterrey, Hwy. 85 90 km (56 mi) northwest to falls,* ☎ *No phone.* ☞ *$1.50.* ☉ *Daily 9–7.*

Saltillo

㉖ *40 km (25 mi) southwest of Monterrey.*

Spanish captain Alberto de Canto founded Saltillo in 1577. Occupying a strategic position along the Camino Real, the main artery from

Mexico City north into what is now Texas, the city was a crucial colonial outpost in its heyday. It was the capital of the Texas territory from 1835 to 1847, when Mexico lost it to the United States.

Saltillo is perhaps best known these days for the unglazed terra-cotta tiles it produces. Knockoffs of these plain but attractive tiles line patios and floors throughout Mexico and the southwest United States. This prosperous city has a great deal of industrial sprawl, but city fathers have preserved the historic **main plaza**, which is surrounded by buildings dating back to the colonial period. Much smaller than Monterrey, Saltillo nonetheless has its own convention center and some outstanding hotels and restaurants.

Lake Vicente Guerrero

㉗ *316 km (196 mi) southwest of Matamoros, 304 km (188 mi) southeast of Monterrey.*

The man-made Lake Vicente Guerrero is a favorite with American bass fishermen year-round and, in winter, an excellent place to hunt duck and white-wing dove. Several camps in the area, such as El Tejon and El Sargento lodges, cater to Americans. ⊠ *From Monterrey, 288 km (181 mi) south on Hwy. 85 to Ciudad Victoria, then 16 km (10 mi) northeast on Hwy. 101 to lake.*

Tampico

㉘ *504 km (312 mi) south of Matamoros, 583 km (361 mi) southeast of Monterrey.*

Tampico is a picturesque port adjoining Ciudad Madero, an oil-refining center. Usually a low-profile place, Tampico made big news in 1995 when it was discovered to be the hometown of the elusive subcomandante Marcos, spokesman of the Zapatista rebels in Chiapas.

Shortly after the Spanish conquest, the Franciscans established a mission in the area near a Huastec fishing village, but the settlement was constantly battered by hurricanes and pirate attacks. In 1828 the Spaniards attempted to reconquer then-independent Mexico by landing troops at Tampico, but they were soundly defeated. After later invasions by the Americans and the French, the port languished until oil was discovered in the region a century ago. The British and Americans developed the industry until it was nationalized in 1938. Petroleum helped Tampico prosper, but it isn't the kind of thing to enhance tourism. Río Pánuco is so polluted that it no longer attracts tarpon fishermen, although the big ocean freighters are an impressive sight.

Still, because of its relative proximity to the border, Tampico gets a smattering of U.S. visitors. And it is a fascinating place to wander around for a spell—the old part of town has something of the feel of a rundown New Orleans French Quarter. **Plaza Libertad**, near the harbor, is shaggy and unkempt—very much the tropical waterfront. A block away is the regal **Plaza de Armas**, with its majestic City Hall guarded by towering palms. The **cathedral** here, started in 1823, was completed with funds donated by Edward L. Doheny, an oil magnate implicated in the Teapot Dome scandal of the 1920s.

In nearby Ciudad Madero, the small but impressive **Museo de la Cultura Huasteca** (Museum of Huastec Culture) houses an exquisite collection of pre-Hispanic ceramics, shellwork and costumes, and some pots dating as far back as 1100 BC. ⊠ *1 de Mayo at Sor Juana Inés de la Cruz, Instituto Tecnológico,* ☏ *12/10–22–17.* 🖼 *Donations appreciated.* ⊙ *Weekdays 10–5, Sat. 10–3.*

Beaches

Playa Miramar, about 5 km (3 mi) from town, is a favorite with locals. Lounge chairs, towels, and showers are available for rent from the hotels and restaurants along the beach. Public transportation is available from Tampico for about 35¢.

Dining and Lodging

$ ✕ **Café y Nevería Elite.** This is a popular gathering spot for breakfast, coffee, and ice-cream treats. Don't be put off by the noise and the rather worn Formica tables; it's all part of the local color. ⊠ *Av. Díaz Mirón 211 Ote.,* ☎ *12/12–03–64. MC, V.*

$$$ ⊡ **Camino Real.** Attractively decorated, this low-rise property 20 minutes from the city center is a resort hotel—the best you'll find in Tampico (in spite of the name, it's not part of the Camino Real chain). Its rooms and bungalows surround a huge garden filled to overflowing with tropical trees and flowers. Rooms contain Chippendale-style furniture, minibars, cable color TVs, and direct-dial telephones. Fishing excursions can be booked through the hotel's travel agency. ⊠ *Hidalgo 2000, Tampico, Tamps. 89140,* ☎ *12/13–88–11,* FAX *12/13–92–26. 100 rooms, 3 suites. Restaurant, bar, pool, tennis court, travel service, car rental. AE, DC, MC, V.*

$ ⊡ **Plaza.** This centrally located budget hotel is clean and comfortable, if a little drab. Rooms are small but air-conditioned, and all have phones and cable color TVs. ⊠ *Madero 204, Tampico, Tamps. 89000,* ☎ *12/14–17–84. 60 rooms. No credit cards.*

Nightlife and the Arts

Eclipse (⊠ Universidad 2004, ☎ No phone) has dancing on Thursday only; the rest of the week, it's a video bar. **Byblos** (⊠ Byblos 1, ☎ 12/13–08–27) is another popular disco. The bar at the **Camino Real Hotel** (⊠ Hidalgo 2000, ☎ 12/13–88–11) has music and dancing Thursday to Saturday evenings.

Outdoor Activities and Sports

FISHING

Although the river is polluted, tarpon and snapper fishing is still popular at **Chairel Lagoon,** with boats and equipment available for rent (just don't plan to eat what you hook). You can also arrange for a boat, guide, and equipment through the Camino Real Hotel in Tampico.

GOLF

Lagunas de Miralta Country Club (☎ 12/24–00–03) sells day passes at Centro Commercial Tres Arcos on Hidalgo for its golf course at Km 26.1 on the Carretera Tampico–Altamira. Ask at your hotel about passes or special discounts at other local clubs.

THE NORTHEAST A TO Z

Arriving and Departing

By Car

With unleaded gasoline now more widely available, an increasing number of American motorists are exploring Mexican highways. A car trip is not without its red tape, however.

For details about driving into Mexico, *see* Driving *in* Smart Travel Tips A to Z *in* Chapter 14. It's essential to have all your documents in order. **Sanborn's Mexican Insurance** (⊠ 2009 S. 10th St., McAllen, TX 78503, ☎ 800/222–0158, FAX 956/686–0732) can help you complete the paperwork in advance—for free if you buy insurance there, otherwise for a fee.

Distances are deceiving in this part of Mexico because of mountainous driving in the Sierra Madre Oriente. It generally takes three hours to drive from the border to Monterrey. From Monterrey to Ciudad Victoria, it's another four hours.

BORDER TOWNS

Downtown Nuevo Laredo is reached by two bridges: International Bridge 1 in town, and the Columbia–Laredo Bridge (42 km, or 26 mi, northwest of Laredo). Both have facilities for clearing you for travel to the interior of Mexico. (When parking your vehicle in Nuevo Laredo, use only parking lots with attendants on duty—there have been a number of reports of theft of luggage and car stereos.)

The New Bridge is the best route from downtown Brownsville to downtown Matamoros. U.S. 281 leads down to Hidalgo, Texas, and the bridge crossing into Reynosa. For brief excursions across the border, consider leaving your car in Texas and walking over. This eliminates the long wait—often a half hour or more—to bring a car back into the United States.

From Matamoros, Mexico 180 runs down the Gulf coast to Tampico, Veracruz, and beyond. A turnoff on Mexico 101 leads to the hunting and fishing camps at Lake Vicente Guerrero. Mexico 97 leads from Reynosa into Mexico 101/180, which meet up for a bit. From Reynosa, you can drive the free routes Mexico 40 to Mexico 35 to Linares; here Mexico 58 will lead you across to San Roberto (and Mexico 57) via a spectacular road with a most unusual mural by Frederico Cantú chiseled out of the side of a mountain.

MONTERREY

From Laredo, the old Pan-American Highway, Mexico 85 Libre (free), and the four-lane Mexico 85 Cuota (toll) both lead to Monterrey, some 242 km (150 mi) south. The latter road, which ends in Monterrey, is a much better one, although the toll is expensive (about $15). It's around the same price to take the toll road Mexico 40 to Monterrey from Reynosa. Although the Laredo route is more scenic, traversing some nice mountains, Laredo itself is more congested to get through than Reynosa. The Reynosa road, although flat and dull, is more convenient to downtown Monterrey.

TAMPICO

The port is roughly a seven-hour drive from Matamoros on Mexico 180, or eight hours from Monterrey via Mexico 85, which connects with Mexico 80.

By Plane

BORDER CITIES

From Mexico City, **Aeroméxico** has service to Matamoros (☎ 88/12–24–60) and Reynosa (☎ 89/22–11–15). **Mexicana** flies to Nuevo Laredo (☎ 87/12–20–52).

MONTERREY

Mexicana (☎ 8/356–3050) has flights from Chicago, San Antonio, San Francisco, Los Angeles, and Denver to Monterrey, via Mexico City. **Aeroméxico** (☎ 8/343–5560) has direct service to Houston and Los Angeles and flights to New York via Mexico City. **Continental** (☎ 8/348–4282) flies from Chicago, Las Vegas, Los Angeles, Miami, and New York, via Houston. **American** (☎ 8/340–3031) has six flights a day to Monterrey from Dallas. **Aerolitoral** (☎ 8/386–2070) has service from McAllen and San Antonio, Texas. **Taesa** (☎ 8/369–0847) flies from Mexico City.

Monterrey's **Aeropuerto Internacional Mariano Escobedo** (☎ 8/345–4432), equipped with luggage storage ($4 per day) and a money-exchange booth, is 6 km (4 mi) northeast of downtown. The only way to get here is by taxi, which will cost about $8.

TAMPICO

Aerolitoral (☎ 12/28–05–55) has nonstop flights to Tampico from Mexico City. Both **Aeroméxico** (☎ 12/27–03–01) and **Mexicana** ☎ 12/13–96–00) have flights between Tampico and Mexico City.

By Train

Currently, there is no first-class train service from the border to Monterrey or Tampico. For up-to-date information about schedules and prices, contact **Mexico by Train** in Laredo (☎ FAX 210/725–3659 or 800/321–1699).

Getting Around

By Bus

Northeastern Mexico is well connected by buses, which are becoming downright luxurious while fares remain low. Information on Mexican bus service is available from **Transportes del Norte** in Laredo (Valley Transit, ☎ 956/723–4324), McAllen (Valley Transit, ☎ 956/686–5479), and Brownsville (Valley Transit, ☎ 956/546–7171). **Transportes del Norte** (☎ 8/372–4965), in conjunction with **Greyhound,** goes from San Antonio, Dallas, and Houston to Monterrey.

By Subway

The Monterrey metro, which runs along elevated tracks across the city, is modern and efficient. There are only two lines. Magnetic cards are used to enter the station. Buy them from station vending machines in units of one, three, or five rides. Each ride costs less than 30¢. The metro runs every day from 6 AM to midnight.

By Taxi

Taxis are pretty scarce and expensive in border towns but plentiful and moderately priced in Monterrey. They usually cruise the streets on a 24-hour basis. In Monterrey, **Metrotaxi** (8/342–2069) provides reliable on-call service.

Contacts and Resources

Consulates

Matamoros. United States (⊠ Calle 1, 2002 and Azaleas, ☎ 88/12–44–02).

Monterrey. Canada (⊠ Edificio Kalos, Calle Mariano Escobedo and Av. Constitución, Suite 108, ☎ 8/344–3200 or 8/344–2753). **United States** (⊠ Av. Constitución 411 Poniente, ☎ 8/343–7124 or 8/345–2120).

Emergencies

Matamoros. Police (⊠ Pedro Cardenas and Soledad, ☎ 88/17–01–35). **Cruz Roja Hospital**(⊠ García and L. Caballero, ☎ 88/12–00–44).

Monterrey. Police (⊠ Gonzalitos and Lincoln, ☎ 8/338–2695 or 8/338–0933). **Cruz Roja** (⊠ Av. Alfonso Reyes No. 2503, ☎ 8/375–1212).

Nuevo Laredo. Police (⊠ Maclovio Herréra and Ocampo, ☎ 87/12–21–46 or 87/12–30–25). **Cruz Roja** (⊠ Independencia 1619 and San Antonio, ☎ 87/12–09–49 or 87/12–09–89).

Reynosa. Police (✉ Morales between Veracruz and Nayarit, ☎ 89/22–00–08 or 89/22–07–90). **Hospital Santander** (✉ Fco. y Madero and Ortiz Rubyo, ☎ 89/22–96–22).

Tampico. Police (✉ Sor Juana Inés de la Cruz and Tamaulipas, ☎ 12/12–10–32). **Cruz Roja Hospital** (✉ Tamaulipas and Colegio Militar, Zona Centro, ☎ 12/12–13–33).

English-Language Bookstore

In Monterrey, the **American Bookstore** (✉ Av. del Estado 124-A, ☎ 8/387–0838 or 8/358–0677) has a great selection of books in English.

Guided Tours

Sanborn's Viva Tours (✉ 2015 S. 10th St., McAllen, TX 78503, ☎ 956/682–9872 or 800/395–8482) runs shopping and sightseeing tours to the border towns and coach excursions into the interior, including to El Tajín (☞ The State of Veracruz, *above*). **Osetur Tours** (✉ Calles San Francisco and Loma Larga, Monterrey, ☎ 8/347–1599 or 8/347–1614) has sight-seeing trips in the area, as does **Tours Gray Line** (✉ Av. Eugenio Garza Sada No. 2256, Monterrey, ☎ 8/369–6472 or 8/369–6473).

Visitor Information

In the U.S. The best information about this part of Mexico is found in Texas border towns, especially at places that sell the (mandatory) Mexican automobile insurance. These include **Sanborn's Viva Tours** (✉ 2015 S. 10th St., McAllen, TX 78503, ☎ 956/682–9872 or 800/395–8482), **Sanborn's Mexican Insurance** (✉ 2009 S. 10th St., McAllen, TX 78503, ☎ 800/222–0158, FAX 956/686–0732), **Bravo Insurance** (✉ 2212 Santa Ursula, Laredo, TX, ☎ 956/723–3657, FAX 956/723–0000), and **Johnny Ginn's Travel** (✉ 1845 Expressway 77, Brownsville, TX, ☎ 956/542–5457, FAX 956/504–2919). The **Brownsville Chamber of Commerce** (✉ 1600 E. Elizabeth, 1 block from International Bridge into Matamoros, ☎ 956/542–4341) is open daily 9–5.

In Mexico. Matamoros Tours-Transport (✉ Tamaulipas and Alvaro Obregón, a few blocks from International Bridge, ☎ 88/12–21–18) is open daily 8–6. **Nuevo Laredo** (✉ Calles Herrera and Juárez, ☎ 87/12–01–04) is open daily 8–8. **Reynosa** (✉ Puente Internacional, ☎ 89/2–11–89 or 89/2–24–49) is open weekdays 7:30 AM–8 PM. **Monterrey Infotour** (✉ Calle Hidalgo 477, Col. Centro, ☎ 8/345–0870, 8/345–0902, or 01–800/83–222 in Mexico; 800/235–2438 in the U.S.) is open Tuesday–Sunday 10–5. **Tampico** (✉ Olmos 101, at Carranza, ☎ 12/12–26–78) is open weekdays 9–7.

13 THE YUCATÁN PENINSULA

The Yucatán Peninsula is Mexico's perennial favorite for more reasons than you can count—the high-profile sparkle of Cancún, the laid-back beachcombing of Isla Mujeres, the spectacular seas around Cozumel, the fascinating Spanish-Maya mix of Mérida, and the evocative Maya ruins of Tulum, Chichén Itzá, and Uxmal. And if the heart of nature moves your blood, there are two huge coastal eco-zones: Sian Ka'an Biosphere Reserve and Parque Natural Río Lagartos, migration stopovers for thousands of flamingos and other birds.

Updated by
Shelagh
McNally and
Jane Onstott

FOR MOST PEOPLE, Mexico's great appeal is its beaches and its ancient ruins. Cancún and the Yucatán have the best of both. Cancún is Mexico's most popular tourist mecca, and it rises against a backdrop of Maya culture—both ancient ruins and modern villages. Although much of the Yucatán peninsula is vast, scrubby desert with a smattering of jungles and hills, its eastern coastline on the clear, turquoise waters of the Caribbean has superb natural features. In addition to a semitropical climate, the Caribbean coast has unbroken stretches of beach and the world's second-longest barrier reef, starting off the coast of Cancún and extending in its entirety down into South America. Isla Mujeres (Isle of Women) and Cozumel are also part of the Yucatán. And on the west side of the peninsula, Mérida, one of Mesoamerica's first Spanish cities, has colonial atmosphere rare in this part of Mexico.

In its entirety, the 113,000-square-km (43,600–square–mi) peninsula encompasses the Mexican states of Yucatán, Campeche, and Quintana Roo, as well as Belize and part of Guatemala. Within its bounds there is tremendous bird-watching, water sports, archaeology, handicrafts, and savory Yucatecan cuisine. Above all, there are the *Yucatecos* themselves—short and dark like their Maya ancestors, with prominent cheekbones and aquiline noses. Veteran travelers to Mexico often remark on the openness and friendliness of these people.

As many activities as there are on the Yucatán, there is an equal range of accommodations, from the never-leave-the-site resorts of Cancún to more modest properties near the ruins and humble but adequate beach shacks. That means that you'll see a broad range of travelers: package tour-groups, backpackers, people tripping around in rental cars. International airports at Cancún and Cozumel provide nonstop service from several North American cities. The Mérida airport handles primarily domestic flights. Cruise ships call at Cozumel and Playa del Carmen, and other harbor facilities are being developed at Progreso on the north coast off the Gulf of Mexico.

Pleasures and Pastimes

Beaches

Cancún and the rest of the Yucatán have a wonderful variety of beaches: Those who thrive on the resort atmosphere will probably enjoy Playa **Chacmool** and **Playa Tortugas** on the bay side of Cancún, which is calmer, if less beautiful, than the windward side. On the north end of Isla Mujeres, **Playa Norte** (or Playa Cocoteros) offers handsome sunset vistas. Beaches on the relatively sheltered leeward side of Cozumel are wide and sandy. The Caribbean Coast abounds with hidden and not-so-hidden beaches—at Puerto Morelos, Playa del Secreto, Paamul, Chemuyil, Xcacel, Punta Bete, and along the Xcalak peninsula. There are also long stretches of white sand, usually filled with sunbathers, at Playa del Carmen, Akumal, and Tulum. Around Campeche and Progreso, the waters of the Gulf of Mexico are deep green, shallow, and tranquil.

Bird-Watching

The Yucatán Peninsula is one of the finest areas for birding in Mexico. Habitats range from wildlife and bird sanctuaries to unmarked lagoons, estuaries, and mangrove swamps. Frigates, tanagers, warblers, and macaws inhabit Isla Contoy (off Isla Mujeres) and the Laguna Colombia on Cozumel. There is an even greater variety of species in the Sian Ka'an Biosphere Reserve on the Boca Paila peninsula south of Tulum. Along the north and west coasts of Yucatán—at Río Lagartos, Laguna Rosada, and Celestún—flamingos, herons, ibis, cormorants, pelicans, and peregrine falcons thrive.

Dining

The mystique of Yucatecan cooking has a lot to do with generous doses of local spices and herbs, although generally the spices aren't too fiery hot. Among the specialties are *cochinita píbil* and *pollo píbil* (succulent pork or chicken baked in banana leaves with a spicy, pumpkin-seed-and-chili sauce), *poc chuc* (Yucatecan pork marinated in sour-orange sauce with pickled onions), *tikinchic* (fried fish prepared with sour orange), *panuchos* (fried tortillas filled with black beans and topped with turkey, chicken, or pork, pickled onions, and avocado), *papadzules* (tortillas stuffed with hard-boiled eggs and drenched in a sauce of pumpkin seed and fried tomato), and *codzitos* (rolled tortillas in pumpkin-seed sauce). *Achiote* (annatto), cilantro (coriander), and the fiery *chile habanero* are heavily favored condiments.

The following price categories apply everywhere outside of Cancún and Cozumel, which are more expensive than the rest of the Yucatán, and for which we have included separate price charts in the relevant sections of this chapter.

CATEGORY	COST*
$$$$	over $20
$$$	$15–$20
$$	$8–$15
$	under $8

per person for a three-course meal, excluding drinks and service

Fishing

The rich waters of the Caribbean and the Gulf of Mexico support hundreds of species of tropical fish, making the Yucatán coastline and the outlying islands a paradise for deep-sea fishing, fly-fishing, and bone-fishing. Particularly between April and July, the waters off Cancún, Cozumel, and Isla Mujeres teem with sailfish, marlin, red snapper, tuna, barracuda, and wahoo. Bill fishing is so rich around Cozumel, Isla Mujeres, Puerto Morelos, and Puerto Aventuras that each holds its own annual tournament.

Farther south, along the Boca Paila peninsula, banana fish, bonefish, mojarra, shad, permit, and sea bass provide great sport for flat fishing and fly-fishing, while oysters, shrimp, and conch lie on the bottom of the Gulf of Mexico near Campeche and Isla del Carmen. At Progreso, on the north coast, sportfishing for grouper, dogfish, and pompano is quite popular.

Lodging

Accommodations in the Yucatán range from the ultra glitzy mega resorts of Cancún to the charming colonial mansions in Mérida and the rustic but character-filled lodgings near the ruins. The following price categories apply everywhere outside of Cancún and Cozumel, which are more expensive than the rest of the destinations in the Yucatán and for which we have included separate price charts.

CATEGORY	COST*
$$$$	over $90
$$$	$60–$90
$$	$25–$60
$	under $25

All prices are for a standard double room in the high season, excluding service charges and 17% tax.

Ruins

Amateur archaeologists will find heaven in the Yucatán. Pick your period and your preference, whether for well-excavated sites or overgrown, out-of-the-way ruins barely touched by scholars' shovels. The major Maya sites are Cobá and Tulum on the Caribbean Coast and Chichén Itzá and Uxmal in the state of Yucatán, but smaller ruins scattered throughout the peninsula are often equally fascinating.

Scuba Diving and Snorkeling

The clear turquoise waters of Cozumel, Akumal, Puerto Morelos, Isla Mujeres, and other parts of Mexico's Caribbean Coast are filled with exquisitely colored fish swimming in the brilliant coral formations. Currents allow for drift diving, and there are both reefs and offshore wrecks to dive, many of which are safe enough for neophytes. The peninsula's cenotes (natural sinkholes) also provide unusual dive experiences.

Water Sports

Along the Yucatán's coasts, you can do it all—jet skiing, catamaran sailing, sailboarding, waterskiing, sailing, sea kayaking, parasailing— you name it.

Exploring the Yucatán Peninsula

Numbers in the text correspond to numbers in the margin and on the Cancún, Isla Mujeres, Cozumel, Caribbean Coast, Campeche City, Mérida, and State of Yucatán maps.

Great Itineraries

If you go to the major beach-resorts of Cancún and Cozumel, you are likely to settle in for the entire stay, perhaps taking side trips to the ruins of Tulum or Chichén Itzá or the city of Mérida. As for beach experiences, Cancún has a higher profile and is more expensive, Isla Mujeres tends to be more relaxed. The following itineraries are designed to keep you on the move from a base either in one of the Caribbean Coast towns or in Mérida. The former is ideal for water sports, the latter for steeping yourself in Maya civilization.

IF YOU HAVE 3 DAYS

If you want to base yourself on the Caribbean Coast, get a room in **Playa del Carmen** ㉒, and start out by visiting the cliffside ruins of the Maya city of **Tulum** ㉛. Afterward, climb down to the small beach alongside it for a dip in the ocean. Day 2, head out to **Xel-Há** ㉙, where you can snorkel, swim, sunbathe, and see some more modest ruins back on land. Day 3, head for **Akumal** ㉖ for a diving or deep-sea fishing excursion, snorkeling, or swimming. Later in the day visit the tiny lagoon of **Yalkú** ㉗, which was around during the time of the Maya traders.

An alternative is to spend two days in **Mérida** ㉞–㊾, savoring the city's unique character as you make your way among its historic churches and mansions, and enjoy its parks and restaurants. You can easily devote a full day to exploring the heart of downtown, including the **zócalo** and its surrounding buildings, the **Casa de Montejo, Palacio Municipal,** and the **catedral.** Take a second, more leisurely day to visit the Museum of Anthropology and History in the **Palacio Cantón** and, perhaps, the **Museo de Arte Popular** or the **El Centenario Zoo.** On the third day, drive or take a tour to one of Yucatán's most famous Maya ruins—either **Chichén Itzá** ㊶ or **Uxmal** ㊻. Each is within about two hours of Mérida.

IF YOU HAVE 7 DAYS

Again basing yourself in **Playa del Carmen** ㉒, visit **Tulum** ㉛ on the first day, and then spend Day 2 touring **Xcaret** ㉓, a Disney-like ecological theme park where you can swim with dolphins or take in a Mexican rodeo show. Day 3, start the morning at the Maya ruins of **Cobá** ③② and spend the afternoon at **Xel-Há** ②⑨, cooling off in the water. Day 4, head for **Akumal** ②⑥ and its water sports. Day 5, sign up for a tour of the **Sian Ka'an Biosphere Reserve** ③③. On Days 6 and 7, head west for the colonial city of **Mérida** ③④–④⑨. Spend one day in the city and the next out at **Chichén Itzá** ⑤① or **Uxmal** ⑤⑥.

On a week-long trip in and around Mérida, take in the city's sights first, then take two separate overnight excursions. First, head for Uxmal and overnight at one of the nearby archaeological hotels. The next day explore the Ruta Puuc, the series of lost cities south of Uxmal that includes **Kabah, Sayil,** and **Labná,** as well as the fascinating **Loltún Caves.** On the second excursion, to Chichén Itzá, allow as much as a full day en route to explore some of the present-day Maya villages along the way, especially **Izamal** ⑤⓪. After seeing the Chichén Itzá ruins, beat the afternoon heat in the **Cave of Balamkanchén** ⑤③ or on a swim in one of the cool subterranean cenotes nearby. An alternate side trip—go north of **Valladolid** ⑤④ to see the flamingo nesting grounds at **Parque Natural Río Lagartos** ⑤⑤.

IF YOU HAVE 10 DAYS

With even more time, consider continuing from **Mérida** ③④–④⑨ to **Campeche City** ⑤⑦–⑦④. After spending a day seeing the city's sights—almost all those of interest are within the compact historic district—head inland the next morning to visit **Edzná,** a magnificently restored ceremonial center an hour's drive from the city. Return to your Campeche City hotel—accommodations are crude or nonexistent in the area—and set out the next day to the **Hopelchén** region, beyond Edzná, where you can explore the little-known Maya temples at **Hochob** and **Dzibilnocac,** as well as **Las Grutas de Xtacumbilxunaan** near **Bolonchén de Rejón,** one of the large cave systems on the peninsula.

When to Tour the Yucatán Peninsula

Thousands of people swarm to Chichén Itzá for the vernal equinox on March 21st (the first day of spring) to see the astronomical phenomenon that makes a shadow resembling a snake—which represented the plumed serpent god Kukulcán—appear on the side of the main pyramid. The phenomenon also occurs on the first day of fall, but the rainy autumnal weather tends to discourage visitors. Both the capital and outlying villages of Campeche state, with their predominantly Maya population, celebrate the Day of the Dead (November 1 and 2) with special fervor because it corresponds to a similar observance in ancient Maya tradition.

High season in the states of Yucatán and Campeche generally corresponds to high season in the rest of Mexico: Christmas time, Easter week, and the months of July and August. Rainfall is heaviest and—humidity most uncomfortable—between May and October or November. On the Caribbean Coast, including Cancún, Cozumel, and Isla Mujeres, the peak tourist times are mid-December through late March. In less visited towns, levels of service differ drastically between the high and low seasons (when staff and activities may be cut back), so be prepared for the trade-off. The rainy season isn't a bad time to visit if you don't mind the afternoon showers and the sometimes reduced tourist attentions. Visitors are fewer, and prices tend to be lower. On the coast, hurricane season is September–October.

CANCÚN

Updated by
Shelagh
McNally

If you want dazzle for your dollar, Cancún is the place with beachside high-rise hotels, glitzy discos, air-conditioned malls, and miles and miles of sand. For a glimpse of a more "real" Mexico, head downtown to the markets and restaurants for a taste of authentic Yucatecan specialties.

Flying into Cancún, you see nothing but green treetops for miles and miles. This is a resort that was literally carved out of the jungle. When development began here in 1974, the beaches were deserted except for the birds and iguanas. Now, luxury hotels, shopping malls and restaurants line Cancún's ocean front. Nearly 2 million visitors come here for the white-sand beaches, crystalline turquoise waters, sizzling night life, excellent restaurants, and the close proximity of Maya ruins throughout the Yucatán. Although some consider the resort too glitzy and tourist-oriented, it continues to draw thousands of repeat visitors.

Cancún City is on the mainland, and the hotel zone is on a 22½-km (14-mi) barrier island off the Yucatán peninsula. The resort is designed to please average American tastes—most people speak English, and devotees of cable TV and Pizza Hut will not be disappointed. Shopping, eating, and lounging in the sun are the main activities here. Beach lovers can bask in Cancún's year-round tropical warmth and sunny skies. The sun shines an average of 240 days a year, reputedly more than at almost any other Caribbean spot. Temperatures linger appealingly around 80°F. At night you can get into nightlife that ranges from knocking back tequila slammers at any number of bars or listening to great music at clubs to watching folkloric dance performances or sampling Yucatecan food.

Of course, there can be more to the resort than plopping down under a *palapa* (thatched roof). The reefs off Cancún, Isla Mujeres, and nearby Cozumel are among the best in the world. And you can use Cancún as a home base for side trips to the stupendous ruins of Chichén Itzá, Tulum, and Cobá—remnants of the Yucatán's Maya legacy—as well as the coast and its lagoons.

The most important buildings in Cancún, however, are the modern hotels. The resort has gone through the life cycle typical of any tourist destination, first attracting the jet set and gradually welcoming less affluent tourists. Today there are large numbers of package-tour takers and college students, particularly during spring break when hordes of flawless, tanned young bodies fill the beaches and restaurants.

As for the island's history, not much was written about it before its birth as a resort. It doesn't even appear on early navigators' maps, and little is known about the Maya who lived here; apparently Cancún's marshy terrain discouraged settlement. It is recorded that Maya settled the area during the Preclassic era, around AD 200, and remained until about the 14th or 15th century. In the mid-19th century minor Maya ruins were sighted, but they went unstudied archaeologically until the 1950s. In 1967, the Mexican government, headed by Luis Echeverría, commissioned a study to pinpoint the ideal place for an international Caribbean resort. Cancún was the winner. At that time its only residents were the three caretakers of a local coconut plantation. In 1972 work began on the first hotel, and the island grew from there. Today there are more than 25,000 hotel rooms in the *Zona Hotelera* alone.

Success has come with a price. Cancún's natural environment has suffered. Its lagoons and mangrove swamps have become polluted, and a number of species, like conch and lobster, are dwindling. Parts of the coral reef are dead—because of excessive human contact. Although the beaches still appear pristine for the most part, an increased effort will have to be made in order to preserve the physical beauty that is the resort's prime appeal.

Exploring

Cancún is divided into two parts: the hotel zone, *Zona Hotelera,* a numeral 7–shaped island; and Cancún City or downtown Cancún, known as *el centro,* 4 km (2½ mi) west of the hotel zone on the mainland.

Paseo Kukulcán is the main drag in the hotel zone, and since the island is less than 1 km (½ mi) wide, you can see both the Caribbean and the lagoons from either side of it. The hotel zone consists entirely of hotels, restaurants and shopping complexes, marinas, and time-share condominiums, with few residential areas. It's not the sort of place you can get to know by walking, although there is now a bicycle/walking path that starts at the Convention Center, ending downtown.

A Good Tour

Cancún's scenery consists mostly of beautiful beaches and crystal-clear waters, but there are a few intriguing historical sites tucked away among the modern hotels. In addition to what is listed below, two modest vestiges of ancient Maya civilization are worth a visit if you love archaeology. Neither is identified by name. One is on the 12th hole of Pok-Ta-Pok golf course (⊠ Paseo Kukulkán, between Km 6 and Km 7), whose Maya name means "ball game"—there is a ruin consisting of two platforms and the remains of other buildings. The other is the ruin of a tiny Maya shrine, cleverly incorporated into the architecture of the Hotel Camino Real (on the beach at Punta Cancún).

You don't need a car in Cancún, but if you've rented one to make extended trips, it might be worth starting in the southern hotel zone at **Ruinas del Rey** ① and **San Miguelito** ②, driving north to **Yamil Lu'um** ③ and then stopping in at the **convention center** ④ before heading west to **downtown** ⑤.

Sights to See

❹ **Cancún Convention Center.** This strikingly modern venue for cultural events is the jumping-off point for a 1-km-long (½-mi-long) string of shopping malls that extends west to the Hotel Presidente. In the convention center complex itself, **Inter Plaza** contains 15 restaurants, 21 boutiques, a bank, and several airline offices. ⊠ *Paseo Kukulcán, Km 9,* ☎ *98/83–01–99.*

The **National Institute of Anthropology and History,** the small museum on the ground floor of the convention center, traces Maya culture by showcasing a fascinating collection of 1,000- to 1,500-year-old artifacts collected throughout Quintana Roo. ☎ *98/83–03–05.* ⊡ *About $3, free Sun.* ☉ *Tues.–Sun. 9–7. Guided tours available in English, French, German, and Spanish.*

❺ **El Centro** (Downtown Cancún). This is Cancún's window onto a more provincial Mexico that has markets instead of malls. The main street, **Avenida Tulum,** is easily recognizable for the huge sea-shell sculpture in the roundabout, which adds drama to the city when lighted up at night. Many restaurants and shops are located along this street, in particular **Ki Huic,** the largest crafts market in Cancún. If you're looking for bargains, prices are better on the parallel **Avenida Yaxchilán,** particularly in **Mercado Veinteocho (Market 28).** Located just off Avenida Yaxchilán and Sunyaxchen, this market is the hub of downtown, filled with shops and restaurants frequented by locals.

❶ **Ruinas del Rey.** Located on the lagoon side at Cancún Island, roughly opposite El Pueblito and Playa de Oro, these small ruins have been incorporated into the Caesar Park Resort complex. Large signs point out the site. Del Rey may not be particularly impressive when compared with major archaeological sites such as Tulum or Chichén Itzá, but it

Cancún

is the largest ruin in Cancún and definitely worth a look. Skeletons found buried both at the apex and at the base indicate that the site might have been a royal burial ground. ☒ *Paseo Kukulcán, Km 17,* ☏ *No phone.* 🎫 *About $3, free Sun.* ☉ *Daily 8–5.*

② **San Miguelito.** On the east side of Paseo Kukulcán is a very small stone Maya building (about the size of a shack) with a number of columns about 4 ft high. ☒ *Paseo Kukulcán, Km 16.5,* ☏ *No phone.*

③ **Yamil Lu'um.** A small sign at the Sheraton will direct you to the dirt path leading to this site, which stands on the highest point on Cancún, adjoining the hotel—the words "Yamil Lu'um" mean hilly land. Although it consists of two structures—one probably a temple, the other probably a lighthouse—this is the smallest of Cancún's ruins. Discovered in 1842 by John Lloyd Stephens, the remains date from the late-13th or early 14th century. ☒ *Paseo Kukulcán, Km 12,* ☏ *No phone.*

Dining

With more than 1,200 restaurants in Cancún, finding the right one isn't easy. Some pitfalls to avoid: Avenida Tulum restaurants often have tables spilling onto sidewalks choked with gas fumes and hordes of people, which detracts from the outdoor-café romance. At the same time, many hotel-zone restaurants cater to what they assume is a tourist preference for bland, not-too-foreign-tasting food.

One key is to find local haunts—mostly in the downtown area. Just off Avenida Tulum, **Parque de las Palapas** is where locals go for expertly prepared Yucatecan-style food (☞ La Habichuela, El Pescador, and Rosa Mexicano, *below*). Further into the city center you can find the freshest seafood and other traditional Mexican fare at **Mercado 28** (☞ El Cejas, *below*), where dozens of small restaurants serve great food at reasonable prices.

A cheap and filling trend in Cancún's dining scene is the array of sumptuous buffet breakfasts offered by an increasing number of restaurants and hotels on the island. Another hint: many $$$$ and $$$ restaurants have floor shows during peak months—mid-December–late March. Usually there are two seatings nightly, each including entertainment and dinner. Reservations are advised, since the shows draw crowds.

Generally speaking, dress is casual here, but many restaurants will not allow bare feet, short shorts, or no shirts. At more upscale restaurants, wear pants or a skirt or dress instead of shorts for dinner.

CATEGORY	COST*
$$$$	over $40
$$$	$25–$40
$$	$15–$25
$	under $15

per person, excluding drinks and service

Hotel Zone

Hotel-zone restaurants are located on the Cancún Hotel Zone Dining and Lodging map.

$$$$ ★ ✕ **Club Grill.** The intimate dining rooms of Cancún's Ritz-Carlton (☞ Lodging, *below*) are the hands-down favorite for exceptional food and romantic dining. In the Club Grill, everything is quietly elegant: rich wood trimmings, fresh flowers, tall windows overlooking a courtyard fountain. European grill is the house specialty, and the rich sauces add a distinctly Mexican flavor to the grilled chops, steaks, chicken, and seafood. Try the *chipotle* (a smoked pepper) duck in honey tequila sauce. A cigar dinner includes peppered rack of venison with wild mushrooms and foie gras, along with Cuba's best for after-dinner smoking. ⊠ *Paseo Kukulcán, Retorno del Rey 36,* ☎ *98/85–08–08. AE, DC, MC, V.*

$$$$ ★ ✕ **La Dolce Vita.** At this Cancún grande dame, the kitchen uses the finest ingredients in creative ways to produce appealing turns with classic Italian cuisine. With candlelit tables, lace tablecloths, soft live music, and pretty furniture it has a romantic, casual elegance. The whole atmosphere is enhanced by the incredible view of Laguna Nichupté, especially on a full moon night. Favorites from the excellent Northern Italian and Continental menu include *boquinete* dolce vita (snapper in puffed pastry) or green *tagliolini* (pasta with lobster and shrimp in a white wine sauce). ⊠ *Paseo Kukulcán, Km 14.5, across from Marriott Hotel,* ☎ *98/85–01–50 or 98/85–01–61. AE, MC, V.*

$$$ ✕ **Lorenzillos.** Named after a 17th-century pirate, this is one of the handsomest waterfront restaurants in the hotel zone. Built right on the water with an outdoor terrace overlooking the lagoon, it's the perfect spot

to watch the sun set. The chairs made from native hardwood are especially comfortable. It has its own lobster farm, so the delicacy is offered year-round (you can pick your own). The soft shell crab and whole fish Veracruz style are also great. Look for the gigantic palapa roof. ⊠ *Paseo Kukulcán, Km 10.5,* ☎ *98/83–12–54. MC, V.*

$$$ ✕ **Maria Bonita.** Here is the authentic Mexico in food, music, and atmo-
★ sphere, and a fine place to learn more about Mexico and its cuisines.
This charming restaurant overlooking the water is divided into sections named after three states of Mexico—Jalisco, Michoacán, and Oaxaca—whose specialties are the mainstays of the menu. *La Doña* is a *poblano* (from Puebla) pepper stuffed with lobster and mushrooms in a cream sauce. Also worth trying are the various *mole* dishes. ⊠ *Hotel Camino Real, Punta Cancún,* ☎ *98/83–17–30. MC, V.*

$$$ ✕ **The Rosato.** The secret at the restaurant of the Fiesta Americana Con-
★ desa (☞ *below*) is attention to details and confidence that simplicity
is sometimes the best approach. Sophisticated and free of gimmicks, Rosato is basic yet elegant, with white tablecloths, comfortable chairs, crystal, and soft lighting. Straightforward Italian fare is transformed into masterpieces—try the superb risotto, the clean and fresh ricotta gnocchi served with lobster stew, or veal escallops with Gorgonzola sauce. *Paseo Kukulcán, Km 15.5,* ☎ *98/85–08–08. AE, DC, MC, V.*

$$ ✕ **The Cove.** Both waterfront locations serve vast, inexpensive break-
fast buffets under palapa roofs. The decor is decidedly nautical, with rigging draped on the walls and chandeliers in the shape of ships' steering wheels. The restaurant near the Casa Maya Hotel overlooks the Caribbean toward Isla Mujeres; the other is beside the Nichupté Lagoon. Both have lunch and dinner menus filled with seafood dishes and charbroiled steak and chicken. Parents appreciate the lower-priced children's menu, an unusual feature in Cancún. ⊠ *Paseo Kukulcán, Km 16.5, lagoon-side across from Royal Mayan Hotel,* ☎ *98/85–00–16;* ⊠ *Beachside next to Casa Maya Hotel,* ☎ *98/83–06–69. Reservations not accepted. No credit cards.*

$$ ✕ **Farandula.** Oh the glamour and stars of Mexico's Golden Age of
★ Cinema! (You'll be amazed at how many there are.) Farandula's walls
are decorated with movie memorabilia, and while you eat, favorite screen characters come to life in look-alike actors who perform at your table; waiters are dressed in period costumes. Consider trying *gorditas* (small tortillas filled with cheese and fried) and *pescado Veracruzana* (fish cooked with tomatoes, onions, and olives). ⊠ *Paseo Kukulcán Blvd. and Calle Cenzontle,* ☎ *98/83–01–60. AE, MC, V.*

$ ✕ **100% Natural.** Looking for something healthy? Head to one of the
three locations of this cheery open-air restaurant serving a broad array of soups, salads, and fresh fruit drinks. Egg dishes, sandwiches, grilled chicken and fish, and Mexican and Italian fare are available as well. ⊠ *Paseo Kukulcán at Kukulcán Plaza,* ☎ *98/85–29–04;* ⊠ *Plaza Terramar,* ☎ *98/83–11–80;* ⊠ *Av. Sunyaxchen 62,* ☎ *98/84–36–17. Reservations not accepted. AE, MC, V.*

$ ✕ **Studebaker Bar & Grill.** The Fonz would be right at home in this
1950–60s theme diner centered around the golden era of the Studebaker. Stop in to satisfy those north-of-the-tropics burger and shake cravings. ⊠ *Paseo Kukulcán (Hotel Baccará), Km 11.5,* ☎ *98/83–20–77. AE, MC, V.*

Downtown

Downtown restaurants are located on the Downtown Cancún Dining and Lodging map.

$$$ ✕ **La Habichuela.** This Cancún landmark, once an elegant home, is a
★ romantic and charming garden restaurant, decorated with the precious
hardwood of the region and Maya sculpture. Don't miss the *crema de*

Dining
Club Grill, **11**
The Cove, **2, 15**
Farandula, **3**
La Dolce Vita, **12**
Lorenzillos, **9**
Maria Bonita, **6**
100% Natural, **5, 10**
The Rosato, **14**
Studebaker Bar &
Grill, **8**

Lodging
Baccará, **8**
Caesar Park Beach &
Golf Resort, **16**
Calinda Viva
Cancún, **4**
Club Las Velas, **1**
El Pueblito Beach
Hotel, **17**
Fiesta Americana
Condesa, **14**
Hyatt Regency
Cancún, **7**
Meliá Cancún, **13**
Ritz-Carlton
Cancún, **11**
Westin Regina Resort
Cancún, **18**

Cancún Hotel Zone Dining & Lodging

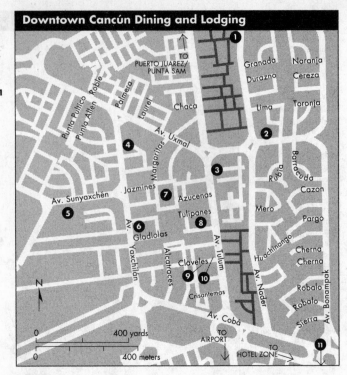

Downtown Cancún Dining and Lodging

habichuela (a rich, cream-based seafood soup) or the *cocobichuela* (lobster and shrimp in a light Indian sauce served on rice inside a coconut)—both are house specialties. Grilled seafood and steaks are also tasty. Finish off your meal with *Xtabentun* (Maya coffee). ⊠ *Margaritas 25,* ☎ *98/84–31–58. AE, MC, V. No lunch during low season.*

$$ ✕ **El Pescador.** The lines are long, but the wait for seafood here is worth it. This rustic, Mexican-style restaurant is popular with both locals and tourists, especially the open-air patio. Heavy hitters on the menu include red snapper broiled with garlic, charcoal-broiled lobster, Creóle-style shrimp, and stone-crabs. For dessert consider sharing ice cream–filled cake covered with peaches and strawberry marmalade. ⊠ *Tulipanes 28,* ☎ *98/84–26–73. Reservations not accepted. AE, MC, V.*

$$ ✕ **La Parrilla.** This is the place to come and meet locals young and old. Classic by Cancún standards (it opened in 1975), everything here—from the food to the bougainvillea and the palapa roof—is authentic. Popular dishes include grilled beef with garlic sauce, and tacos *al pastor* (with pork, pineapple, coriander, onion, and salsa). ⊠ *Av. Yaxchilán 51,* ☎ *98/84–53–98. Reservations not accepted. AE, MC, V.*

$$ ✕ **Rosa Mexicano.** At one of Cancún's prettiest Mexican colonial–style
★ restaurants, colorful paper banners and piñatas hang from the ceiling, and waiters dress as *charros* (Mexican cowboys). For extra romance make a reservation for the candlelit patio. Savory appetizers include *nopalitos*—cactus strips sautéed with corn, cilantro, and cheese. Specialties are *filete* Rosa (beef and onions in a tequila-orange sauce) and *camarones al ajillo* (shrimp sautéed in olive oil and garlic, with chili peppers). ⊠ *Calle Claveles 4,* ☎ *98/84–63–13. AE, MC, V. No lunch.*

$ ✕ **El Cejas.** Located in the heart of the bustling, lively Mercado 28, this
★ is a neighborhood restaurant with an international reputation. The seafood is fresh, wonderful, and half the price as elsewhere. Their cocktail *Vuelva la vida* (Return to life) really does have restorative powers.

⊠ Mercado 28, Av. Sunyaxchen, ☎ No phone. Reservations not accepted. No credit cards.

$ ✕ **Los Almendros.** On this restaurant's totally Yucatecan menu, illustrations take some of the guesswork out of ordering. Specialties include lime soup and poc chuc. You'll find it opposite the bullring. Avs. Bonampak and Sayil, ☎ 98/87–13–32. Reservations not accepted. MC, V.

Lodging

Cancún has a bewildering variety of hotels to choose from. For the most part, the amenities of downtown hotels don't approach the luxury of the hotel-zone properties. They do, however, allow you to stay in a popular resort without paying resort prices, and many have free shuttle service to the beach. Expect minibars, satellite TV, laundry and room service, private safes (ask in advance about extra charges for using safes), and bathroom hair dryers in $$$$ hotels.

Almost every major hotel has suites, rooms for people with disabilities, no-smoking rooms, an in-house travel agency and/or a car-rental concession, guest parking, water-sports facilities, beauty salon and spa, fully equipped gymnasium, and a daily schedule of planned games and activities for guests. Unless otherwise noted, all hotels have air-conditioning and private baths. All Cancún hotels are within the 77500 postal code.

CATEGORY	COST*
$$$$	OVER $200
$$$	$120–$200
$$	$50–$120
$	under $50

*All prices are for a standard double room, excluding 12% tax.

Hotel Zone

Hotels in this section appear on the Cancún Hotel Zone Dining and Lodging map.

$$$$ 🏨 **Baccará.** This hotel was recently rescued from neglect by new own-
★ ers who spent more than $1 million renovating it. The results are outstanding. Beautiful blue and yellow rooms are furnished individually with authentic Mexican pieces and art. Living and dining rooms overlook the ocean, and all guest rooms have fully equipped kitchens. The lobby is intimate and informally elegant, with a beautiful bar that leads out to the artfully designed pool area. The care of the staff only adds to the warmth that Baccará exudes. ⊠ Paseo Kukulcán, Km 11.5, across from Planet Hollywood, ☎ 98/83–21–73 or 888/784–2801, 𝖥𝖠𝖷 98/83–21–73. 34 rooms. 3 restaurants, 3 bars, pool, car rental. AE, DC, MC, V.

$$$$ 🏨 **Caesar Park Beach & Golf Resort.** At this elegant resort on 250 acres of prime beach-front property, the lobby is airy and light, filled with plants that cascade down from the top floors to create a dramatic waterfall of green. Seven lavish interconnecting pools wind through palm-dotted lawns; a terraced fountain brings the dancing water into the hotel's interior. The rooms themselves are large and decorated with a simple elegance in pastel furnishings and rugs. All rooms have sea views; some look onto both the lagoon and the ocean. The Royal Beach Club section comprises 80 luxurious oceanfront villas with extra-spacious rooms. ⊠ Paseo Kukulcán, Km 17, Box 1810, ☎ 98/81–80–00; 800/228–3000 in the U.S., 𝖥𝖠𝖷 98/81–80–80. 426 rooms, 4 suites. 3 restaurants, 3 bars, lobby lounge, 7 pools, beauty salon, 2 hot tubs, 2 saunas, 18-hole golf course, 2 tennis courts, aerobics, exercise room, shops, children's programs. AE, DC, MC, V.

$$$$ 🏨 **Fiesta Americana Condesa.** This sprawling, friendly hotel has the same casual elegance and luxurious amenities as its older sister, the Fiesta Americana Cancún. The Condesa is easily recognized by its 120-ft-tall palapa room—the highest in Mexico—leading to an incredible lobby decorated with stylized marble, stained-glass awnings, jewel-tone fabrics, and lots of greenery. Three seven-story towers overlook an inner courtyard with hanging plants and falling water. Swimming pools are joined by arched bridges. The tranquil rooms have dusty-pink stucco walls and Mexican tile floors. Each three standard rooms share one balcony; pricier rooms have their own. Oceanfront suites have a private hot tub on the terrace. ⊠ *Paseo Kukulcán, Km 16.5, Box 5478,* ☎ *98/85–10–00; 800/343–7821 in the U.S.,* 🖷 *98/85–16–50. 502 rooms, 26 suites. 5 restaurants, 2 bars, pool, beauty salon, 3 tennis courts, health club, shops. AE, DC, MC, V.*

$$$$ 🏨 **Meliá Cancún.** This boldly modern version of a Maya temple is fronted by a sheer black marble wall and a sleek waterfall. The ultrachic atrium has lush tropical flora dappled with sunlight flooding in from corner windows and the pyramid skylight overhead. Ivory, dusty-pink, and light-blue hues softly brighten rooms (all with private balconies or terraces), and ivory-lacquered furniture and wall-to-wall carpeting create a luxurious ambience. The upscale spa has an array of pampering and rejuvenating body treatments. The hotel strictly enforces a policy against bringing in outside food or beverages (except bottled water). The Meliá Turquesa (☎ 98/81–25–00, 🖷 98/81–25–02), a 408-room sister property across the street from Flamingo Plaza, is not as glitzy, and has a more intimate, friendlier atmosphere. ⊠ *Paseo Kukulcán, Km 16,* ☎ *98/8–51–14; 800/336–3542 in the U.S.,* 🖷 *98/85–12–63. 450 rooms. 5 restaurants, 3 bars, 2 pools, spa, 18-hole golf course, 3 tennis courts, health club, paddle tennis, shops. AE, DC, MC, V.*

$$$$ 🏨 **Ritz-Carlton Cancún.** Ultraposh, ornate, and sumptuous, the Ritz here
★ radiates an old-world elegance with a lobby richly appointed with thick carpets, plush furniture, and fine European and American antiques and oil paintings. Rooms are done with a sophisticated flair: comfortable shades of teal, beige, and rose offset wall-to-wall carpeting; large balconies overlook the Caribbean. Travertine marble bathrooms have telephones and separate tubs and showers. The hotel's elegant restaurants, especially the Club Grill (☞ Dining, *above*) and the recently opened northern Italian Fantino, are standouts. ⊠ *Paseo Kukulcán, Retorno del Rey 36,* ☎ *98/85–08–08; 800/241–3333 in the U.S.,* 🖷 *98/85–10–15. 365 rooms, 40 suites. 3 restaurants, 2 bars, 3 pools, beauty salon, hot tub, spa, 3 tennis courts, health club, pro shop, shops. AE, DC, MC, V.*

$$$$ 🏨 **Westin Regina Resort Cancún.** A location on the southern end of the hotel zone on Punta Nizuc gives this luxury resort more seclusion than other places. The low-rise, postmodern-style hotel was designed by one of Latin America's leading architects, Ricardo Legorreta. From the lobby you can look down on a stylish restaurant with stunning ocean views. The rooms are even more elegant, with oak tables and chairs standing out against white walls and pale marble floors. For even more exclusive and private rooms try staying in the six-story tower. ⊠ *Paseo Kukulcán, Km 20, Box 1808,* ☎ *98/85–00–86 or 98/85–05–37; 800/228–3000 in the U.S.,* 🖷 *98/85–00–74. 293 rooms, 24 suites. 4 restaurants, 3 bars, 5 pools, hot tub, 5 outdoor hot tubs, 2 tennis courts, exercise room, children's programs. AE, DC, MC, V.*

$$$ 🏨 **El Pueblito Beach Hotel.** El Pueblito, which means "little town," is
★ a sweet name and a perfect description for this all-inclusive property, built on a hill above the sea with clusters of guest rooms in tri-level units that evoke Old Mexico. Interconnecting pathways lined with tropical foliage lead to intriguing terrace pools with waterfalls and stone

archways; there's also a long, separate water slide for kids. Rooms, which are large for the price, have marble floors and simple rattan furnishings; a few have kitchenettes. ⊠ *Paseo Kukulcán, Km 17.5,* ☎ *98/85–04–22,* FAX *98/85–07–31. 239 rooms. 3 restaurants, bar, 5 pools, tennis court, shops, travel services. AE, MC, V.*

$$$ 🏨 **Hyatt Regency Cancún.** A cylindrical 14-story tower with the Hyatt trademark—a striking central atrium filled with tropical greenery and topped by a sky-lighted dome—affords a 360° view of the sea and the lagoon. Rooms are clean, comfortable, and functional, if bland, with all the usual amenities. This hotel, much larger and livelier than its sister property—the Hyatt Cancún Caribe Villas & Resort, farther south in the zone—has an enormous two-level pool with a waterfall. Cilantro, the hotel's pretty waterfront dining room, offers a good breakfast buffet. It's close to the Convention Center and several shopping malls. ⊠ *Paseo Kukulcán, Box 1201,* ☎ *98/83–09–66 or 98/83–12–34; 800/233–1234 in the U.S.,* FAX *98/83–14–38. 300 rooms. 2 restaurants, 3 bars, pool, health club, recreation room. AE, MC, V.*

$$ 🏨 **Calinda Viva Cancún.** This eight-story blockhouse is the "plain Jane" hotel in the zone. But it makes a reliable standby and actually has quite a handsome patio garden and a decent Mexican restaurant. The real standout is the great beach, safe for swimming, and its walking-distance proximity to all shops and restaurants. Rooms have standard pastel coloring and marble floors, and are moderately sized and functional. Half have private balconies and ocean views, one quarter have kitchenettes. ⊠ *Paseo Kukulcán, Km 8.5, Box 673,* ☎ *98/83–08–00; 800/228–5151 in the U.S.. 216 rooms. Restaurant, bar, pool, 2 tennis courts, dock, shops. AE, DC, MC, V.*

$$ 🏨 **Club Las Velas.** Delightfully private, Las Velas is a replica of a Mex-
★ ican village, complete with central plaza, fountains, and lush gardens. Winding stone pathways connect the Mexican colonial–style attached villas and four five-story towers with the Laguna Nichupté beachfront, palapa restaurant, and pools. Rooms have white stucco walls, tropical-print bedspreads, and rattan furniture. Tower rooms from the second floor up all have balconies. The duplex villas are especially suited to families—their adjoining bedrooms can easily form two- or three-bedroom suites. ⊠ *Paseo Kukulcán and Galeon,* ☎ *98/83–22–22; 800/707–8815 in the U.S.,* FAX *98/83–21–18. 226 rooms, 59 villas. 2 restaurants, 2 bars, snack bar, 2 pools, 2 tennis courts, aerobics, exercise room, shops, children's programs. AE, MC, V.*

Downtown

Downtown hotels appear on the Downtown Cancún Dining and Lodging map.

$$$ 🏨 **Holiday Inn Centro Cancún.** The place to stay if you want to be down-
★ town and have all the amenities, this is the newest (1990) and most upscale hotel in the area. It's less expensive than similar properties in the hotel zone, and it provides free transportation to the beach of the Crown Princess Club. The attractive pink four-story structure with a Spanish-tile roof affords easy access to restaurants and shops. Although rooms are generic motel modern, with mauve and blue color schemes, they have appealing Mexican touches. Its twin-sister hotel, Hotel Margaritas off Avenida Yaxchilán, is slightly cheaper and has the same amenities. ⊠ *Av. Nader 1, SM 2,* ☎ *98/8–44–55; 800/465–4329 in the U.S.,* FAX *98/84–79–54. 246 rooms. 2 restaurants, 2 bars, pool, beauty salon, tennis court, exercise room, nightclub, coin laundry, travel services, car rental. AE, DC, MC, V.*

$$ 🏨 **Antillano.** Right on the main strip, this pleasant hotel is beautifully
★ maintained and stands out from the others in its league. Each room is fitted with wood furnishings, one or two double beds, a sink area sep-

arate from the bath, red-tile floors, and a small television. There is a cozy little lobby bar and decent-size pool. The quietest rooms face the interior—avoid the noisier rooms that face Avenida Tulum. ⊠ *Av. Tulum at Calle Claveles,* ☎ *98/84–15–32,* FAX *98/84–18–78. 48 rooms. Pool, shops, baby-sitting, travel services. AE, DC, MC, V.*

$$ ⊡ **Hotel el Rey del Caribe.** A marvel in downtown Cancún, el Rey del
★ Caribe has been designed to have zero impact on the environment, in part by using solar energy for electricity, a water-recycling water plan, and special composting toilets. And its luxuriant garden, which blocks the heat and noise of downtown, makes it an oasis. Hammocks hang poolside, and wrought-iron tables and chairs are placed throughout the grounds. Rooms are on the small size, but all have kitchenettes. The hotel is within walking distance of all shops and restaurants. ⊠ *Corner of Uxmal and Nader,* ☎ *98/84–20–28,* FAX *98/84–98–57. 26 rooms. Pool, hot tub. AE, MC, V.*

$$ ⊡ **Mex Hotel.** This three-story Spanish colonial–style hotel has a small shopping plaza that fronts the busy street. Rooms are in back, decorated with pleasant Mexican touches: tile floors, terra-cotta pottery, and textiles in tasteful earth tones. The Mex is within walking distance of restaurants, shops, and open-air concerts. ⊠ *Av. Yaxchilán 31,* ☎ *98/84–30–78; 800/221–6509 in the U.S.,* FAX *98/34–78–81. 81 rooms. Restaurant, bar, pool. AE, DC, MC, V.*

$ ⊡ **Hotel Parador.** At this perfectly located heart-of-the-city hotel, rooms are strung along two long narrow courtyards that lead back to a pool, grassy sunning area, and palapa bar. Functional and modern inside, rooms have two double beds, showers, cable television, and bottled water in the hallways. ⊠ *Av. Tulum, No. 26,* ☎ *98/84–10–43 or 98/84–13–10,* FAX *98/84–97–12. 66 rooms. Bar, pool, baby-sitting. AE, MC, V.*

Nightlife and the Arts

The Arts
The **Casa de Cultura** (⊠ Prol. Av. Yaxchilán, SM 21, ☎ 98/84–83–64) hosts local cultural events, such as art exhibits, throughout the year.

FESTIVALS
Cancún's **Jazz Festival** is an annual weeklong event in late May that draws a huge international crowd from the States, South America, and Europe. The **Cancún Hotel Association** (⊠ Av. Ign. García de la Torre, SM 1, Lote 6, Cancún, QR, 77500, ☎ 98/84–70–83) can provide information about this popular gathering.

Each November the state of Quintana Roo hosts the **Caribbean Culture Festival.** Cancún and other regional cities present a series of events that range from Caribbean music to readings by Mexican poets and exhibits by Latin American painters and sculptors. The real draw, however, is the variety of salsa music. Salsa groups from countries throughout the Caribbean come to Cancún to perform the best of the genre. Consult your hotel's concierge for event schedules.

FILM
In the hotel zone, **Cinemas Kukulcán** (⊠ Plaza Kukulcán, ☎ 98/85–30–21) and **Forum by the Sea** (☎ 98/87–57–17) show American movies. Downtown, American and Mexican movies run at **Plaza Las Americas** (⊠ Av. Tulum, SM 4 and 9, ☎ 98/87–58–93) and **Tulum Plus** (⊠ Av. Tulum, SM 2, ☎ 98/84–34–51).

PERFORMANCES
The **Ballet Folklórico de Cancún** performs nightly at the **Convention Center.** This is a popular ballet folklórico dinner show with upbeat music and dances from across Mexico (⊠ Paseo Kukulcán, Km 9, ☎ 98/83–

01–99 ext. 193 and 194). Cocktails are at 6:30; dinner, a typical Mexican buffet, is at 7; and the dance production goes on at 8. Tickets start at around $35.00

Nightlife

Nightlife happens all over Cancún in a variety of places. Numerous restaurants do double duty as party centers, discos offer music (sometimes taped, sometimes live) and have light shows, and nightclubs feature live music and dancing. Lines between the three can get blurred.

DINNER CRUISES

AquaWorld's *Cancún Queen* (⊠ AquaWorld Marina, Paseo Kukulcán, Km 15.2, ☎ 98/85–22–88) paddlewheeler (the only one in Mexico), which departs from the AquaWorld Marina, has a full lobster or steak spread with an open bar and dancing for $65. The 62-ft galleon *Columbus's* lobster dinner cruise (⊠ Royal Yacht Club, Paseo Kukulcán, Km 16.5, ☎ 98/83–32–83 or 98/83–14–88) goes on sunset cruises at 5 PM or star cruises at 8 PM, for $54.50. **Pirates Night** (⊠ Playa Langosta dock at the Casa Maya hotel, Paseo Kukulcán, Km 5.5, ☎ 98/83–14–88) has a three-course buffet dinner with trips to Treasure Island on Tuesday and Thursday, leaving at 6:30 PM and returning at 11:30. The modern sailboat is decked out like a pirate ship, the crew like pirates.

RESTAURANT PARTY CENTERS

Althogh the food at the following restaurants is usually quite good, the real draw is the nightly parties that usually have live music, which keeps the places hopping until dawn. At **Carlos 'n' Charlies** (⊠ Paseo Kukulcán, Km 5.5, ☎ 98/83–08–46) zany waiters perform on stage with live rock bands. **Pat O'Briens** (⊠ Paseo Kukulcán, Km 11.5, ☎ 98/83–04–18) brings the New Orleans party scene to the zone with live rock bands and its famous cocktails. For low-key partying right on the beach, check out the **Baccara Beach Bar** (⊠ Paseo Kukulcán, Km 11.5, ☎ 98/83–20–77).

Discos

Cancún wouldn't be Cancún without its glittering discos, which generally start jumping about 10:30. **Christine** (⊠ Krystal Cancún Hotel, ☎ 98/83–11–33) is the grande dame of the disco scene and puts on an incredible light show. **Dady'O** (⊠ Paseo Kukulcán, Km 9.5, ☎ 98/83–31–34) has been around for a while but is still a very in place, especially with the younger set. The wild, wild **Coco Bongo** (⊠ Paseo Kukulcán, Km 9.5, across the street from Dady'O, ☎ 98/83–44–28) has no chairs, and everyone dances on the spot or on top of their tables. **La Boom** (⊠ Paseo Kukulcán, Km 3.5, ☎ 98/83–11–52) is always the last to close; it has a video bar with a light show and regular weekly events.

Music

Azucar (⊠ Hotel Camino Real, ☎ 98/84–48–14) is a beautiful night club that showcases the very best of Latin American bands; proper dress is required. **Batacha** (⊠ Hotel Miramar Misión, ☎ 98/83–17–55) is down-to-earth, a great spot for Latin American and Mexican music. For Caribbean-beat dance music (marimba, reggae, etc.), head to **Jalapeños** (⊠ Paseo Kukulcán, Km 7, ☎ 98/83–28–96) nightly from 8. **Cat's Reggae Bar** (⊠ Paseo Kukulcán, Km 9, ☎ 98/83–19–00) imports the hottest reggae bands from the United States and from Jamaica and other Caribbean islands. The downtown **Roots Bar** (⊠ Tulipanes Av. 26, near Parque de las Palapas, ☎ No phone) is the place for jazz, flamenco, blues, and modern Brazilian music.

Outdoor Activities and Sports

Bullfights

The Cancún **bullring,** a block south of the Pemex station, hosts year-round bullfights. A matador, charros, a mariachi band, and flamenco dancers entertain during the hour preceding the bullfight (from 2:30 PM). ⊠ *Paseo Kukulcán at Av. Bonampak,* ☎ *98/84–54–65 or 98/84–82–48.* 🎫 *About $40.* ☉ *Fights Wed. at 3:30.*

Golf

The main course is at **Pok-Ta-Pok** (⊠ Paseo Kukulcán between Km 6 and Km 7, ☎ 98/83–08–71), a club with fine views of both sea and lagoon, whose 18 holes were designed by Robert Trent Jones Sr. The **Caesar Park Cancún** (⊠ Paseo Kukulcán, Km 17, ☎ 98/81–80–00) has an 18-hole championship course. The 18-hole executive course (par 53) at the **Hotel Melia Cancún** (⊠ Paseo Kukulcán, Km 12, ☎ 98/85–11–60) circles half the property and shares its beautiful ocean views. Greens fees for all are about $20.

Water Sports

There are myriad ways to get your adrenaline going while getting wet in Cancún. The most popular are detailed below. You'll be able to go parasailing (about $35 for eight minutes), waterskiing ($70 per hour), or jet skiing ($70 per hour, or $60 for Wave Runners, double-seated jet skis). Paddle boats, kayaks, catamarans, and banana boats are also available.

Aqua Tours (⊠ Paseo Kukulcán, Km 6.25, ☎ 98/83–02–27, FAX 98/83–04–03) and **AquaWorld** (⊠ Paseo Kukulcán, Km 15.2, ☎ 98/85–22–88, FAX 98/85–22–99) maintain large fleets of water toys. **Wet 'n' Wild** (⊠ Paseo Kukulcán, Km 25, ☎ 98/85–18–55, 🎫 $25), Cancún's newest water theme park, has swimming pools with waves, seven different water slides, and the "Montana Swinger," which takes you as high as 180 ft and descends at speeds of up to 60 mph.

FISHING

Some 500 species of tropical fish, including sailfish, bluefin, marlin, barracuda, and red snapper, live in the waters adjacent to Cancún. Deep-sea fishing boats and gear may be chartered from outfitters for about $350 for four hours, $450 for six hours, and $550 for eight hours. Charters generally include a captain, a first mate, gear, bait, and beverages.

The **Royal Yacht Club** (⊠ Paseo Kukulcán, Km 16.5, ☎ 98/85–29–30) has charter boats for deep-sea fishing. **Barracuda Marina** (⊠ Paseo Kukulcán, Km 14.0, ☎ 98/85–24–44) has deep-sea fishing for sailfish, wahoo, and other large game fish for $70 per hour for four lines, $100 for six lines (about $17 per person per hour). Trips last from four to eight hours. Prices include soft drinks, bait, and fishing gear.

SAILBOARDING AND KAYAKING

Sailboarding is not as popular in Cancún as it once was—it's been eclipsed by the fast and noisy Wave Runner. But some die-hards remain, promoting this sport. The **International Windsurfer Sailing School** (☎ 98/84–20–23) rents windsurfing equipment at the Club International Beach for $40 per day and has two-hour lessons for $25. Kayaking is gaining popularity. Many of the hotels now have their own kayaks for guests, free of charge.

SNORKELING AND SCUBA DIVING

Snorkeling is best at Punta Nizuc, Punta Cancún, and Playa Tortugas, although you should be especially careful of the strong currents at the last. You can generally rent gear for $10 per day from many of the scuba diving places, and most hotels and resorts have their own gear for rent.

If you've brought your own snorkeling gear and want to save money, just take a city bus down to Club Med and walk along the resort's beach for less than 1 km (½ mi) until you get to Punta Nizuc.

Barracuda Marina (⊠ Paseo Kukulcán, Km 14.0, ☎ 98/85–24–44) has a two-hour Wave Runner–jungle tour through the mangroves, which ends with snorkeling at the Punta Nizuc coral reef. The $38.50 fee includes snorkeling equipment, life jackets, and refreshments.

Scuba diving has gained in popularity in Cancún. A word of caution about one-hour "resort" courses offered as a freebie by the resorts: this does not prepare you to dive in the ocean, no matter what high-pressure concessions will tell you. A one-hour lesson in a controlled environment like a pool differs vastly from the open ocean. If you have caught the scuba bug, invest in a few more lessons and prepare yourself properly so you can enjoy the experience. Remember that scuba diving accidents can be fatal.

The secret of a good scuba company is personal attention. Ask to meet the dive master and check out the company's equipment and certifications thoroughly. **Scuba Cancún** (☎ 98/83–10–11) specializes in diving trips and offers NAUI, CMAS, and PADI instruction. It's operated by Luis Hurtado who has more than 35 years of experience. **Blue Peace Diving** (⊠ Paseo Kukulcán, Km 16.2, ☎ 98/85–14–47) has two-tank dives for $85 with NAUI, SSI, and PADI instruction. The outfit goes to Cozumel, Akumal, Xpu-ha, and Isla Mujeres.

Shopping

Resort wear and handicrafts are the most popular purchases in Cancún, but prices are high and the selection standard. If you're traveling elsewhere in Mexico, postpone your shopping spree until you get to another town. Bargaining is expected in the markets; stores usually have fixed prices. If you can do without plastic, you may get the 12% sales tax lopped off at shops that don't want to pay high commissions to credit-card companies.

Shopping hours are generally weekdays 10–1 and 4–7, although more and more stores are staying open throughout the day rather than closing for siesta between 1 and 4 PM. Many shops keep Saturday morning hours, and some are now open on Sunday until 1 PM. Shops in malls tend to be open weekdays from 9 or 10 AM to 8 or 10 PM.

Downtown

The variety of shops along Avenida Tulum (between Avenidas Cobá and Uxmal) includes **Fama** (⊠ Av. Tulum 105, ☎ 98/84–65–86), a department store with English magazines, clothing, and *latería* (crafts made of tin), among other things. Also on Tulum is the oldest and largest of Cancún's crafts markets, **Ki Huic** (⊠ Av. Tulum 17, between Bancomer and Bital, ☎ 98/84–33–47), which is open daily from 9 AM to 10 PM and houses about 100 vendors. Another good spot for souvenirs is **Mercado Veinteocho** (Market 28), just off Avenidas Yaxchilán and Sunyaxchen. This popular market is filled with shops selling many of the same souvenir items found in the hotel zone at half the price. **Plaza las Americas** (⊠ Av. Tulum SM 4 and 9, ☎ 98/87–58–93) is the newest shopping center downtown. Its 50-plus stores, 3 restaurants, 8 movie theaters, video arcade for kids, fast food, and 3 large department stores will make you think you're back home.

Hotel Zone

Fully air-conditioned malls—*centros comerciales*—are as streamlined and well kept as any in the United States or Canada.

There's only one open-air market in the hotel zone. Next to the **Convention Center**, **Coral Negro** is a collection of about 50 stalls selling craft items. It's open daily until late evening.

Kukulcán Plaza (✉ Paseo Kukulcán, Km 13) is a mall that never seems to end, with around 130 shops (including Benetton and Harley Davidson), 12 restaurants, a bar, a liquor store, a bank, a three-screen cinema, bowling lanes, and a video arcade.

Flamingo Plaza (✉ Paseo Kukulcán, Km 11.5, across from the Hotel Flamingo) is a small, high-tech plaza beautifully decorated with marble. Its biggest drawing card is the Planet Hollywood boutique. There are a few designer emporiums, duty-free shops, an exchange booth, sportswear shops, and two boutiques selling Guatemalan imports.

Forum Plaza (✉ Paseo Kukulcán, Km 9.5) is the sparkling new entertainment/shopping plaza in the zone, with the biggest selection of popular brand-name stores and chain restaurants in a circuslike atmosphere. There is also a five-plex cinema.

The largest and most contemporary of the malls, **Plaza Caracol** (✉ Paseo Kukulcán, Km 8.5) is north of the Convention Center. It houses about 200 shops and boutiques, including two pharmacies, art galleries, a currency exchange, and folk art and jewelry shops, as well as cafés and restaurants. Boutiques include Benetton, Bally, Gucci, and Ralph Lauren, with prices lower than in their U.S. counterparts.

Plaza Mayafair (Paseo Kukulcán, Km 9) has a large open-air center filled with restaurants, bars, and shops. Adjacent is an indoor shopping mall decorated to resemble a rain forest, complete with replicas of Maya stelae. The mall has more than 30 specialty shops and offers a free nightly show of Maya dance and music.

Specialty Shops

GALLERIES

Orbe (✉ Plaza Caracol, ☎ 98/83–15–71) sells sculpture and paintings by contemporary Mexican artists. **Mordo's** (✉ Plaza Mayafair, ☎ 98/83–08–38) is the local outlet for a small Mexico City chain that sells handcrafted leather goods. **The Renato Dorfman Gallery** (✉ Avs. Sunyaxchen and Yaxchilán 63, SM 25, ☎ 98/87–46–15) carries Dorfman's original pieces as well as his hand-carved replicas of Maya art and stelae. The **Huichol Collection** (✉ Plaza Kukulcán and Plaza Caracol, ☎ 98/83–33–79) sells handcrafted beadwork and embroidery made by the Huichol Indians of the West Coast.

Grocery Stores

Major supermarkets include **Comercial Méxicana** (✉ Avs. Tulum and Uxmal; and Av. Kabah, farther north, ☎ 98/87–13–03).

Cancún A to Z

Arriving and Departing

BY BUS

The downtown **bus terminal** (✉ Avs. Tulum and Uxmal, ☎ 98/84–13–78 or 98/84–39–48) serves first-class buses making the trip from Mexico City and first- and second-class buses coming from Puerto Morelos, Playa del Carmen, Tulum, Chetumal, Cobá, Valladolid, Chichén Itzá, and Mérida. Public buses (Route 8) run to Puerto Juárez and Punta Sam for the ferries to Isla Mujeres, and taxis will take you from the bus station to Puerto Juárez for about $2.

BY CAR

Cancún spells the end of **Highway 180,** which passes from Matamoros on the Texas border through Valladolid, Campeche, and Mérida. The trip from Texas can take up to three days. **Highway 307** runs south from Cancún through Puerto Morelos, Tulum, and Chetumal, then into Belize. There are few gas stations on these roads, so try to keep your tank full. Highway 307 has a Pemex station between Cancún and Playa Del Carmen. Construction is ongoing to turn the two lanes into four.

BY PLANE

Cancún International Airport is 16 km (10 mi) southwest of the heart of Cancún City, 10 km (6 mi) from the southernmost point of the hotel zone. **Aeroméxico** (☎ 98/84–10–97 or 98/84–35–71) flies nonstop from Houston, Miami, and New York. **American** (☎ 98/86–00–86) has nonstop service from Dallas and Miami. **Continental** (☎ 98/86–00–40) has daily service from Houston. **Mexicana** (☎ 98/87–44–44 or 98/83–48–81) nonstops depart from Los Angeles, Miami, and New York. In Cancún, Mexicana subsidiaries **Aerocaribe** (☎ 98/84–20–00 downtown; 98/86–00–83 airport) and **Aerocozumel** (☎ 98/84–20–00 downtown; 98/86–01–62 airport) fly to Cozumel, the ruins at Chichén Itzá, Mérida, and other Mexican destinations.

Between the Airport and Hotels. There are currently no buses allowed into the airport. The options are taxis or *colectivos* (vans). A counter at the airport exit sells colectivo and taxi tickets; prices range from $15 to $40, depending on the destination. Arriving at the airport is cheaper than leaving: on the way out rates range from $10 to $22 for taxis. Hotels post the most current rates. Be sure to agree on a price before getting into the taxi.

Getting Around

Motorized transport of some sort is necessary, as sights are somewhat spread out. Public buses are good, taxis relatively inexpensive.

BY BUS

Public buses run between the hotel zone and downtown from 6 AM to midnight; the cost is about 3 pesos. There are designated bus stops, and you can flag down drivers along Paseo Kukulcán. The service is quite reliable. Buses run frequently and can save you considerable money on taxis, especially if you're staying at the southern end of the hotel zone. Buses from the zone do not go downtown but will drop you off at Avenida Tulum, where you can catch a connecting bus.

BY CAR AND MOPED

Mopeds are extremely dangerous—essentially, you're risking your life using one either in the zone or downtown. **Renting a car** in Cancún is an unnecessary expense that entails tips for valet parking, gasoline, and rather high rental rates. Driving is harrowing with the many one-way streets, *glorietas* (traffic circles), poor traffic lights, ill-placed *topes* (speed bumps), lots of pedestrians, and large potholes. Be sure to observe all speed limits in the zone and downtown, because the traffic police are vigilant. If you do plan to explore beyond Cancún, using it as a base, roads are excellent within a 100-km (62-mi) radius.

BY SHIP

North of Cancún City, boats leave Puerto Juárez and Punta Sam for Isla Mujeres every half hour or so (☞ Isla Mujeres A to Z, *below*).

BY TAXI

Taxi rides within the hotel zone cost $5–$7; between the hotel zone and downtown, $8 and up; and to the ferries at Punta Sam or Puerto Juárez, $15–$20 or more. Prices depend on distance, your negotiating skills, and whether you pick up the taxi in front of a hotel or go onto the avenue to hail one more cheaply (look for green city cabs). Most hotels list rates at the door; confirm the price with your driver *before* you set out. If you lose something in a taxi or have questions or a complaint, call the **Sindicato de Taxistas** (☎ 98/88–69–85).

Contacts and Resources

ADDRESSES

SM in Cancún addresses stands for Super Manzana. All neighborhoods are labeled with a SM number (SM 23, SM 25, etc.) with the various main streets running around them. Each SM has its own park or square and the area streets are fashioned around the park.

BANKS

Banks in Cancún are generally open weekdays 9–5, with money-exchange desks open 9–1:30. Go early to avoid hours of waiting in long lines. Downtown locations are along Avenida Tulum; some larger banks have locations scattered along the hotel zone. **Banamex** (⊠ Av. Tulum 19, next to City Hall, ☎ 98/84–31–15), **Bital** (⊠ Av. Tulum 15, ☎ 98/84–10–95), and **Bancomer** (⊠ Av. Tulum 20, ☎ 98/87–00–00).

CAR AND MOPED RENTAL

Rental cars are available at the airport and in town. Most are standard-shift subcompacts and Jeeps. For air-conditioned cars with automatic transmission, reserve well in advance. Rental agencies include **Avis** (☎ 98/86–02–22 airport; 98/83–08–03 Plaza Mayafair); **National** (☎ 98/86–01–53 airport); **Localiza Rent a Car** (☎ 98/83–19–17 Dos Playas; ☎ 98/8–50–89 El Pueblito Hotel); **Hertz** (☎ 98/86–01–50 airport; 98/87–66–44 Reno 35); and **Zipp Rental Cars** (☎ 98/83–20–77 Baccara Hotel). The **Car Rental Association** (☎ 98/84–20–39) can help arrange rentals as well. Rates average $45 per day.

Mopeds and scooters are available on the island. They are fun, but the accident rate is high, especially downtown, and no insurance is available for driver or vehicle. Rates start around $25 per day.

CONSULATES

U.S. Consulate (⊠ Plaza Caracol, 3rd floor, HZ, ☎ 98/83–02–72) is open weekdays 9–1.

Canadian Consulate (⊠ Plaza Caracol 11, third floor, Local 330, ☎ 98/84–37–16 or 800/706–2900, ℻ 98/83–32–32) is open daily 11 AM– 1 PM. For emergencies outside office hours, call the **Canadian Embassy** in Mexico City (☎ 015/724–7900).

DOCTORS AND DENTISTS

Hospital Americano (⊠ Calle Viento 15, ☎ 98/84–61–33) and **Total Assist** (⊠ Claveles 5, ☎ 98/84–37–16 or 98/84–81–16), both with English-speakers on staff, provide emergency medical care.

EMERGENCIES

To report an emergency dial **06,** the equivalent to 911 in North America. **Municipal Police** (☎ 98/84–19–13). **Traffic Police** (☎ 98/84–07– 10). **Highway Police** (☎ 98/84–24–45). **Immigration Office** (☎ 98/84– 17–49). **Red Cross** (⊠ Av. Xcaret and Labná, SM 21, ☎ 98/84–16– 16). **Fire Department** (☎ 98/84–12–02).

GUIDED TOURS

Air Tours. Aerolatino (⊠ Plaza México, Av. Tulum 200, ☎ 98/87–13– 53 or 98/84–39–38), a small Guatemalan carrier, flies to Guatemala City and on to Flores and the ruins at Tikal for $290 round-trip.

Trans Caribe (☎ 98/87–15–99 or 98/87–16–92) seaplanes offer panoramic tours of Cancún that depart daily from Laguna Nichupté.

Prices start around $35 for 20 minutes. Trans Caribe also flies to Isla Mujeres, Cozumel, Tulum, and Chichén Itzá.

Day Cruises. Day trips to Isla Mujeres—where you can snorkel in El Garrafón, shop downtown, have open-bar buffet lunches, hear music, or lounge at Playa Norte—are popular. Although plenty of tour groups have day trips to Isla, it's just as simple and far cheaper to plan your own trip. Just catch one of the ferries that leaves every half hour or so from Puerto Juárez and Punta Sam—both north of Cancún City—for Isla Mujeres (☞ *below*).

If you do want someone else to do the planning and don't mind spending the money, **Aqua Tours Adventures** (✉ Paseo Kukulcán, Km 6.25, ☎ 98/83–02–27) has an "Isla Mujeres Adventure." It departs at 10 AM from the pier in front of Fat Tuesday's, returns at 5 PM, and costs about $55.

Dolphin Discovery (✉ Playa Langosta, ☎ 98/83–07–79 or 98/83–07–80) sails daily from Playa Langosta and Playa Tortugas to the company's dock on Isla Mujeres. The $134 (per person) program includes an instruction video, a 30-minute swim session in a pool with the dolphins, and time to explore the island.

Reserva Ecológica El Eden (✉ Apdo. Postal 308, Postal 770, Cancún, Quintana Roo 77500, ☎ FAX 98/80–50–32) runs "eco-science" tours on their 500,000-acre reserve 2½ hours northwest of Cancún. It is a good opportunity to experience the landscape and animals of the region first hand. Prices start at $235 and include transportation to and from Cancún, lodging, all meals, cocktails, and guided nature walks.

Submarine Cruises. *Nautibus* (☎ 98/83–35–52 or 98/83–21–19), or the "floating submarine," has a 1½-hour Caribbean-reef cruise. *Nautibus* currently departs at 9:30, 11:30, 1, and 3, but times often change, so double-check in advance. The $30 price includes music and drinks. Submarine trips that actually go underwater (the others float on the surface and have window seats below) are aboard the **Atlantis** (✉ Marina Aqua Tours, Blvd. Kukulcan, Km 6.25, ☎ 98/83–30–21), depart every hour from 10 to 3, and include an hour-long cruise to Playa Indios on Isla Mujeres, a 45-minute reef tour, food and drink at the Atlantis Bar & Grill, towels, and locker service for $69.

LATE-NIGHT PHARMACIES
Farmacia Turística (✉ Plaza Caracol, ☎ 98/83–18–94) and **Farmacia Extra** (✉ Plaza Caracol, ☎ 98/83–28–27) deliver to hotels 9 AM–10 PM. **Farmacia Canto** (✉ Avs. Yaxchilán at Sunyaxchen, ☎ 98/84–40–83) is open 24 hours.

TRAVEL AGENCIES AND TOUR OPERATORS
Mayaland Tours (✉ Hotel America, Av. Tulum, ☎ 98/87–54–11) and **Turismo Aviomar** (✉ Calle Venado 30, ☎ 98/84–64–33) offer day-trips.

VISITOR INFORMATION
Cancún Tips (✉ Av. Tulum 29, Suites 1–5, ☎ 98/84–14–58), open daily 9–9, twice a year publishes a free pocket-size guide to hotels, restaurants, shopping, and recreation with excellent maps and discount coupons.

The Mexican Ministry of Tourism has established a 24-hour English-language **help line** (☎ 01–800/9–03–92) for tourists, and **Informatel** (☎ 98/81–23–45) has a general information number with an English-speaking staff.

There are also the **State Tourism Office—Quintana Roo (SECTUR)** (✉ Government Palace, Av. Tulum, ☎ 98/84–32–38) and the **State Tourism Information Center** (✉ Av. Tulum No. 26, ☎ 98/84–80–73).

ISLA MUJERES

Updated by
Shelagh
McNally

Isla Mujeres (*ees*-lah moo-*hair*-ayce) has a magic all its own that defies change. This tiny, fish-shape island 8 km (5 mi) off Cancún is a tranquil alternative to its bustling western neighbor. Only about 8 km (5 mi) long by 1 km (½ mi) wide, Isla has flat sandy beaches on its northern end and steep rocky bluffs to the south.

No one remembers who gave the isle its name, which means "Island of Women." Many believe it was the ancient Maya who used the island as a religious center for worshiping *Ixchel* (ee-*shell*), the Maya goddess of rainbows, fertility, and childbirth. Another popular legend has the Spanish conquistador, Hernández de Córdoba, naming the island when he landed in 1517, blown off course from Cuba. When he and his crew came on shore they saw only women (the men were out fishing) and found hundreds of female-shape clay idols dedicated to Ixchel and her daughters. Still others claim the name is a legacy from pirate days when, like many other Caribbean islands in the 17th century, Isla was a haven for buccaneers and smugglers. These pirates would stash their women on Isla before heading out to rob ships at sea.

After its popularity waned with pirates and smugglers, Isla settled into life as a quiet fishing village. In the late '70s, day-trippers came over from Cancún, bringing Isla's hotel, restaurant, and shop owners more business than ever. Isla has withstood the onslaught, managing to keep its character and remain a peaceful island retreat with a rich history and culture centered on the sea.

Exploring

For orientation purposes, think of Isla Mujeres as an elongated fish, the southern tip the head, the northern prong the tail. The island's only town, known simply as *el pueblo,* extends the full width of Isla's north end. The village is sandwiched between sand and sea to the north, south, and east; no high-rises block the view.

A Good Tour

To explore most of the island you will need to hire a taxi or rent either a moped or golf-cart. You can walk to Isla's historic **cemetery** ⑥ by going north on Avenida Lopez Mateos. Then head south along Avenida Rueda Medina, past the piers to reach the Mexican naval base. It's off-limits to tourists, and the Mexican navy doesn't like anyone photographing the crew, base, or ships. But you can see the flag ceremonies from the road at sunrise and sunset. Continue south and you'll see the **Laguna Makax** ⑦ on your right.

At the end of the lagoon, a dirt road to the left leads to the remains of the **Hacienda Mundaca** ⑧. About a block southeast of the hacienda, turn right off the main road at the sign that says SAC BAJO to a smaller, unmarked side road, which loops back north. Approximately ½ km (⅓ mi) farther on the left is the entrance to the **Tortuga Marina Turtle Farm** ⑨. When you return to the main Avenida Rueda Medina and go south past Playa Lancheros, you'll soon see **El Garrafón National Park** ⑩. Slightly more than ½ km (⅓ mi) along the same road, on the windward side of the tip of Isla Mujeres, is the site of a small **Maya ruin** ⑪, which stood for centuries until Hurricane Gilbert destroyed it in 1988. Follow the paved eastern perimeter road north back into town; it's a beau-

Isla Mujeres

TO ISLA
CONTOY

Punta Norte

Playa Norte

6

Cemetery

Piers
Mexican Naval Base

Main Square

TO
PUNTA SAM

TO
PUERTO JUAREZ

Caribbean Sea

Airport

Av. Rueda Medina

Hidalgo

Juárez

Marina

7

Laguna Makax

Dolphin Discovery

Bahía de Mujeres

Salina Grande

Perimeter Rd.

Tortuga Marina Turtle Farm **9**

8

Hacienda Mundaca

Playa Paraíso

Playa Lancheros

KEY

Ferry

0   1 mile

0   1 km

El Garrafón National Park **10**

Maya Ruin **11**

Punta Sur

tiful, scenic drive with a few pull-off areas along the way, perfect for a secluded picnic.

Sights to See

6 **Cemetery.** You'll find Isla's unnamed cemetery, with its 100-year-old gravestones, on Lopez Mateos, the road that parallels Playa Norte. It is filled with carved angels and flowers, and its most beautifully decorated tombs are those in memory of children. Hidden among them is the tomb of the notorious Fermín Mundaca (☞ Hacienda Mundaca, *below*). This 19th-century slave trader (often billed more glamorously as a pirate) carved his own tombstone with a skull and crossbones and the menacing epitaph AS YOU ARE, I ONCE WAS; AS I AM, SO SHALL YOU BE. Mundaca's grave is empty, however; his remains lie in Mérida where he died. The monument is not easy to find—ask a local to point out the unidentified marker.

10 **El Garrafón National Park.** Recently bought by the owners of Xcaret (☞ *below*), the park is undergoing a major revamping in an attempt to restore the coral reef. As a snorkeling mecca for day-trippers from Cancún, the reef has suffered at the hands and fins of eager visitors as well as from the anchors cast from the fleet of boats arriving at the park. Still, nearly 25,000 visitors each year have been impressed by the scenery—parrot fish, angelfish, and the rich blue-green water. The new owners have plans to turn it into a well advertised "ecological" tourist spot, so expect to pay higher prices and share the park with lots of other tourists when it reopens after renovations. ⊠ *Av. Rueda Medina, 2½ km (1½ mi) south of Playa Lancheros,* ☎ *To be announced (TBA).* 🖭 *TBA.* ☉ *Hours TBA.*

8 **Hacienda Mundaca.** A dirt drive and stone archway mark the entrance to the remains of the mansion built by Fermín Mundaca de Marechaja, the 19th-century slave trader–cum–pirate. When the British navy began cracking down on slavers, Mundaca settled on the island. He fell in love with a local beauty, nicknamed "La Trigueña" (the brunette). In order to woo her, Mundaca built a sprawling estate with verdant tropical gardens. His courtship, however, failed—La Trigueña chose a young islander instead. Mundaca went slowly mad waiting for her to change her mind, watching as she bore the other man's children and settled into a happy family life. He finally died in a brothel in Mérida.

There is little to see of the actual hacienda. It has mysteriously vanished; locals say the government tore down the mansion, or at least neglected its upkeep. All that remains are a small crumbling guardhouse, a rusted cannon, an arch, and a well. You must push your way through the jungle and ferocious mosquitoes to reach the ruined stone archway and triangular pediment, carved with the following inscription: *Huerta de la Hacienda de Vista Alegre MDCCCLXXVI* (Orchard of the Happy View Hacienda, 1876). In contrast, the gardens have remained lovely and serene. To get here continue south from town along the main road until you come to the "S" curve at the end of Laguna Makax (☞ *below*). You'll see the dirt road to your left. ⊠ *East off Av. Rueda Meina,* ☎ *No phone.* 🖭 *Free.*

Isla Contoy. About 30 km (19 mi) north of Isla Mujeres, Isla Contoy (Isle of Birds) is a national wildlife park and bird sanctuary. Birders, snorkelers, and nature lovers come here to enjoy the unspoiled beauty of the island. In order to safeguard the flora and fauna, the island enjoys protected sanctuary status, and the number of visitors is carefully regulated. Contoy is only 6½ km (4 mi) long and less than 1 km (about ½ mi) wide. It is officially open from 9 to 5:30; overnight visits are not allowed. For information on diving around and getting to the island, *see* Snorkeling and Scuba Diving *under* Outdoor Activities and Sports *and* Guided Tours *under* Isla Mujeres A to Z, *below.*

❼ Laguna Makax. Heading south from town along Avenida Rueda Medina, you'll pass a Mexican naval base and see some *salinas* (salt marshes) on your left. Across the road is this lagoon, where pirates are said to have anchored their ships as they lay in wait for the hapless vessels plying the Spanish Main (the geographical area in which Spanish treasure ships trafficked).

⓫ Maya Ruin. The sad vestiges of a temple once dedicated to Ixchel, the goddess of fertility, are about 1 km (½ mi) below El Garrafón National Park, at the southern tip of Isla. Though Hurricane Gilbert walloped the ruin and succeeded in blowing most of it away, restoration efforts are under way. The adjacent **lighthouse** still stands, and the keeper sometimes allows visitors to ascend it. This is an incredible lookout spot to the open ocean on one side and Mujeres Bay on the other.

❾ Tortuga Marina Turtle Farm. Run by an outfit called Eco Caribe, this facility is devoted to the study and preservation of sea turtles. During working hours you can examine outdoor tanks that contain hundreds of hatchlings and young turtles of various species. The farm's budget is small, but because the turtle population along the Mexican Caribbean is dwindling, these ecologists have devoted themselves to the care of the hatchlings.

The staff feeds the turtles at the farm until they are large enough to be let out to sea. During hatching season from May through September, upwards of 6,000 infant turtles are released. There is also a small but interesting museum explaining the various stages of the turtles as well as different parts of the coral reef. ⊠ *Follow main road to fork, about a block southeast of Hacienda Mundaca; bear right onto smaller road that loops back north. Entrance to turtle farm is about ½ km (⅓ mi) on left.* ☎ *987/7–05–95.* 🎫 *$2.* ☉ *Daily 9–5.*

NEED A BREAK? Walk north from the Turtle Farm along the lovely beach past the Cristalmar Hotel to **Hacienda Gomar** (☎ 987/7–05–41), a good Mexican restaurant with a buffet lunch and marimba music. If you'd rather not put your shoes back on, try the excellent barbecued grouper, snapper, or barracuda at the restaurants along **Playa Lancheros.** Also in the area, you'll find handicraft and souvenir shops, a beach bar, and small palapas for shade.

Beaches

The island's finest and most popular beach is on the northwest end of the island. **Playa Norte** (also called Playa Cocoteros) is simple to find: go north on any of the north–south streets in town. At the beach the blue sea is as calm as a lake, and you can wade out for 40 yards and still be only waist deep. Playa Norte is famous for its congenial atmosphere. There are quite a few palapa bars where you can sit and enjoy a drink or snack. A fun place is **Las Palapas de Chimbo,** which serves fresh seafood and has cold beer. It's popular with locals and tourists who gather to chat or play dice. Also along the beach are stands where you can rent snorkel gear, jet skis, floats, and sailboards, and there is sometimes parasailing. Playa Norte is a great place to meet the isleños and share the beauty of the place.

On the west side of Isla you'll find **Playa Paraíso,** a good spot for lunch or for shopping at the small stands that sell local handicrafts, souvenirs, and T-shirts. Another good beach with vendors is **Playa Lancheros,** which has a sea pen in which some pet sea turtles and harmless *tiburones gatos* (nurse sharks) reside. On the ocean side live the carnivorous *tintorera* (female sharks), which have seven rows of teeth and weigh as much as 500 kilograms (1,100 pounds).

Playa Indios is near Playas Paraíso and Lancheros. Although lovely, it is the drop-off and pick-up point for tours to the Atlantis submarine. So it's busy with lots of people milling about while arrivals and departures are announced over a booming public address system.

Dining

As in the rest of Mexico, locals eat their main meal during siesta hours, between 1 and 4, and have a light dinner in the evening. Unless otherwise stated, restaurants are open daily for lunch and dinner.

CATEGORY	COST*
$$$	over $15
$$	$10–$15
$	under $10

per person, excluding drinks and service

$$$ ✕ **Chez Magaly.** This pleasant poolside restaurant is on the grounds of the shocking pink Nautibeach Condo-Hotel on Playa Norte. Inside the decor is more subdued: wood floors, hanging plants, white and blue tables, and a palapa roof. It's the perfect spot in which to move from a beach day to a romantic dinner, watching the sunset. French cuisine is administered with a Caribbean twist in specialties that include tender steaks and succulent lobster. ⊠ *Av. Rueda Medina, Playa Norte,* ☎ 987/7–02–59 or 987/7–04–36. *MC, V. Closed Mon. and 2 wks in June.*

$$$ ✕ **Zazil-Ha.** This fine restaurant, on the grounds of the Hotel Na
★ Balam at Playa Norte (☞ Lodging, *below*), serves delicious vegetarian dishes, homemade bread, and well-prepared regional specialties. The indoor eating area is a cozy palapa dining room decorated with light-wood furniture, tile floors, and Mexican pottery. Outside there is a lovely shaded terrace with wooden tables. Look for daily seafood specials, *chaya* (Maya spinach) with pasta, or *caracol Caribe,* a Caribbean seashell stuffed with seafood. The breakfast menu includes homemade bread, tropical fruits, a variety of egg dishes, and good coffee. ⊠ *Hotel Na Balam,* ☎ 987/7–02–79. *AE, MC, V.*

$$ ✕ **Bucanero.** This large outdoor café has a great menu of seafood and Yucatecan specialties for breakfast, lunch, and dinner. Try *huevos motuleños* (fried eggs served on a corn tortilla heaped with beans, ham, cheese, peas, and marinated red onions covered in tomato sauce) or a classic American breakfast, which costs around $3.50. Lunch and dinner specialties include avocado stuffed with shrimp and *mar y cielo* (fish fillet and chicken breast with french fries and onions). ⊠ *Av. Hidalgo 11,* ☎ 987/7–02–10. *Reservations not accepted. MC, V.*

$$ ✕ **Café Cito.** This is one of the prettiest cafés on the island, decorated in
★ shades of pink and blue, with stained-glass windows and mobiles. Glass-tops on tables cover arrangements of sand and shells. Drink great cappuccino and espresso with a breakfast of fresh waffles, fruit-filled crepes, fruit plates, or egg dishes. For dinner, the chef whips up different daily specials. For the brave and curious, the owner, Sabrina, will read your tarot cards. ⊠ *Avs. Juárez and Matamoros,* ☎ 987/7–04–38. *Reservations not accepted. No credit cards. No lunch, closed Thurs. and Sun.*

$ ✕ **La Casita.** The emphasis here is fresh-baked pastries, breads, cakes, and hearty sandwiches. Coffee and cappuccino are among the best on the island. ⊠ *Av. Madero 10, between Avs. Hidalgo and Guerrero,* ☎ *No phone. Reservations not accepted. No credit cards.*

$ ✕ **Lonchería La Lomita.** The word here is home-style—the bright aqua
★ home-style decor isn't much to look at, but the home-style servings of
chicken, steak, and seafood cooked to order (grilled, fried, or sautéed)
are hearty and filling. The octopus sautéed in butter and garlic is particularly tasty. Breakfasts are amazingly low-priced. At lunch and dinner, set menus include beans, rice, and tortillas or bread. ⊠ *Av. Juárez
25-B, past Av. Allende,* ☏ *No phone. Reservations not accepted. No
credit cards.*

$ ✕ **Red Eye Café.** The logo says it all: a bloodshot eye looking for cof-
fee. This is the place to come and get your morning caffeine fix. Gus
and Inga know their coffee and serve it with hearty American-style breakfasts with a German flair. Fresh sausage, made by a German sausage
maker in Cancún, accompanies the egg dishes. ⊠ *Av. Hidalgo,* ☏ *No
phone. No credit cards. Closed Tues.*

$ ✕ **Velazquez.** This family-owned palapa-style restaurant on the beach
★ serves the freshest seafood on the island. Be sure to try the Yucatecan
specialty dish *tikinchic* (fried fish marinated in a sour orange sauce with
the achiote herb and cooked over an open flame). You haven't eaten
Yucatecan until you've had tikinchic. Watch your head before entering the place. ⊠ *Av. Rueda Medina,* ☏ *No phone. No credit cards.*

$ ✕ **Villa del Mar.** Locals love this tiny place—and its lack of decor seems
to make its fresh-as-it-gets seafood taste that much better. Located steps
from the docks, it's a great place to sit and watch the ferries come and
go or see fishermen come to shore with their catch of the day—which
usually ends up on your plate. The ceviche and fried fish are phenomenal,
and the cook is an expert at Yucatecan dishes. ⊠ *Av. Rueda Medina,*
☏ *No phone. No credit cards.*

Lodging

With 31 hotels and 831 rooms, there is no shortage of accommodations on Isla. Generally the older, more modest places are right in
town, and the newer, more costly properties tend to have beachfront
locations around Punta Norte or on the peninsula near the lagoon. Most
hotels have ceiling fans; some have air-conditioning; few have TVs or
phones. Luxurious, self-contained time-share condominiums are another option, which you can learn more about from local travel agencies. All hotels share the 77400 postal code.

CATEGORY	COST*
$$$$	over $100
$$$	$60 –$100
$$	$25–$60
$	under $25

All prices are for a standard double room, excluding 12% tax.

$$$$ ▥ **La Casa de los Sueños.** Tucked away at Isla's south end, this resi-
★ dence turned (no-smoking) bed-and-breakfast is the perfect place for
a honeymoon. You enter through a large interior courtyard, which leads
to an open-air sunken living room decorated in sunset colors. Beyond,
an outdoor terrace has a two-tiered swimming pool on a cliff that overlooks the ocean. Off to the left, a glassed-in dining room has a staircase that leads down to a private beach. All nine rooms are individually
decorated and have ocean-view balconies or terraces. Included in the
price is a full American breakfast, use of bicycles, kayaks, and snorkeling equipment, and scuba lessons in the pool. ⊠ *Carretera el Garrafon,* ☏ *987/7–06–51; 800/551–2558 in the U.S.,* 🖷 *987/7–07–08. 9
rooms. Pool, beach, dock, snorkeling, boating. AE, MC, V.*

$$$$ ▥ **Na Balam.** This intimate hotel on Playa Norte will fulfill all your
★ tropical-paradise fantasies. The building faces the ocean, and the three

corner suites have outstanding views of the sea and sunsets. Rooms have palapa roofs, sitting areas, dining tables, and patios or balconies that face the beach. Furnished with carved furniture and Mexican photos and folk art, the rooms are simple yet elegant. Landscaped trails lead to the beach and restaurant. Eight more rooms, a swimming pool, and meeting room are across the street. Off season the hotel has courses in massage, Maya medicine, and other holistic workshops (there is also a meditation room on site). Breakfast at the Zazil-Ha restaurant (☞ Dining, *above*) is a delightful way to kick off the day. ✉ *Calle Zazil Ha 118,* ☎ *987/7–02–79; 800/552–4550 in the U.S.,* ⅻ *987/7–04–46. 31 rooms. Restaurant, bar, air-conditioning, pool, beach. AE, MC, V.*

$$$ 🏨 **Cabañas Maria del Mar.** This eclectic mix of rooms has three dif-
★   ferent sections: bungalows, the tower, and the castle. All rooms have a plenty of character, which is part of the unique Mexican atmosphere here overall. Tower rooms have ocean-view balconies with large beds and a refrigerator. Bungalow rooms are farther from the beach and furnished sparingly (they are also much cheaper). The castle section is across the street and has hand-carved wood furnishings by local artisans in a combination of Spanish and Maya styles, folk art, tiled baths, and hand-painted sinks. All rooms have refrigerators, and all have terraces that overlook Playa Norte. Rates include a Continental breakfast. ✉ *Av. Carlos Lazo 1,* ☎ *987/7–01–79; 800/223–5695 in the U.S.,* ⅻ *987/ 7–02–13. 42 rooms, 14 cabañas. Restaurant, bar, pool, motorbikes, travel services. MC, V.*

$$ 🏨 **Hotel Frances Arlene.** This small peach-colored hotel is a real deal:
★   budget prices with five-star standards. The Magaña family operates the hotel behind the family home and takes great care with its upkeep, and with maintaining a relaxed, casual ambience. All rooms are centered around a pleasant courtyard and are fitted with double beds, bamboo furniture, and refrigerators. Kitchenettes are available in some. From its central location, the beach and downtown are a short stroll away. ✉ *Av. Guerrero, No. 7,* ☎ *987/7–04–30,* ⅻ *987/7–04–29. 11 rooms. AE, MC, V.*

$ 🏨 **Hotel Osorio.** This heart-of-town hotel is one of the cheapest on the island. Rooms are basic, each with a small bathroom, each opening onto a courtyard. ✉ *Corner of Juárez and Madero,* ☎ *No phone. Ceiling fans. No credit cards.*

Nightlife and the Arts

The Arts

The island celebrates many religious holidays and festivals in the main square, usually with live entertainment at the outdoor stage. Carnival is in February and is spectacular fun. Other popular events are the springtime regattas. The **Isla Mujeres International Music Festival** takes place the second week in October. The island is filled with music and dancers from everywhere.

Casa de la Cultura, near the youth hostel, offers folkloric dance classes year-round and runs a small public library and book exchange. ✉ *Av. Guerrero,* ☎ *987/7–06–39.* ☉ *Mon.–Sat. 9–1 and 4–8.*

Nightlife

In keeping with the life-style of Isla, nightlife on the island is laid back. Most restaurant bars have a happy hour with two drinks for the price of one from 5 to 7; the palapa bars at Playa Norte are an excellent place to watch the sun go down. The current hot spot is **YaYa's** (✉ Av. Rueda Medina 42, near the lighthouse and Playa Norte, ☎ No phone), which serves up huge Texas steaks, chili dogs, and shrimp étouffée along with live jazz, rock, and reggae jam sessions until 2 or 3 AM. **Buho's,** the bar/restaurant at Cabañas María del Mar (✉ Av. Carlos Lazo 1, ☎

987/7–14–79) is a good choice for a relaxing drink at sunset or later at night. They have a great outdoor bar with swings. Another "swing-up" bar is the **Posada del Mar** (⊠ Av. Rueda Medina 15A, ☎ 987/7–03–00), which is hopping in high season. **Daniels Bar & Grill** (⊠ Av. Hidalgo, 2 doors down from park), ☎ No phone) is a fun bar with friendly staff, funky decor, great Mexican food, live music, and more than 100 different kinds of tequila to try.

Outdoor Activities and Sports

For water sports, beaches on the north and west sides are the calmest.

Fishing

Bahía Dive Shop (⊠ Av. Rueda Medina 166, across from pier, ☎ FAX 987/7–03–40) has hourly rates ($20) for offshore fishing (barracuda, snapper, and smaller fish) and day rates ($200–$250) for deep-sea fishing and casting (tarpon, snook, and bonefish). To join the springtime **Red Cross Billfish Tournament,** contact Michael Creamer (⊠ A.P. 54 Isla Mujeres, Q. Roo 77400, ☎ FAX 987/7–04–43).

Snorkeling and Scuba Diving

There is good snorkeling near **Playa Norte** on the north end of the island. Beneath the waters near *el farolito* (the lighthouse) is a partially buried but still visible statue of the Virgin. There's excellent diving and snorkeling at **Xlaches** (pronounced *ees*-lah-chays) reef, due north on the way to Isla Contoy. One of Contoy's most alluring dives is the **Cave of the Sleeping Sharks,** east of the northern tip. At the south end of the island, **Los Manchones** reef makes a good dive site. On the windward side of the islet north of Mujeres is an unnamed site complete with two shipwrecked galleons. Dive shops will be able to direct you to this spot and others.

Bahía Dive Shop (⊠ Av. Rueda Medina 166, across from pier, ☎ FAX 987/7–03–40) rents snorkeling and scuba equipment and runs three-hour boat and dive trips to the reefs and to Isla Contoy's Cave of the Sleeping Sharks. Snorkel gear goes for $5 a day; tanks, $45–$60, depending on the length of the dive. **Mexico Divers** (⊠ Avs. Rueda Medina and Medaro, 1 block from ferry, ☎ 987/7–01–31), also called Buzos de México, runs three-hour snorkeling tours for $15; two-tank scuba trips start at $55 for a reef dive and $75 for the shark-cave dive. Rental gear is available. Dive master Carlos Gutiérrez also gives a resort course for $80 and open-water PADI certification for $350 (his prices are generally negotiable). **Coral Scuba Dive Center** (⊠ Av. Matamoros 13-A, ☎ 987/7–03–71) offers manta ray dives in May, June, and July for $80, which include a two-tank dive. The company also has five different shipwreck dives ranging from $50 to $125.

Swimming with Dolphins

To get yourself in the water with the likes of Flipper, **Dolphin Discovery** (☎ 987/7–07–42) will give you the chance to play with them in a small, supervised group. There are four swims daily, at 9 and 11 AM and 1 and 3 PM. Each session lasts an hour—a half-hour instruction video, then 30 minutes in the water. The cost is $134 if arriving by boat, which includes an all-you-can-eat Mexican buffet.

Shopping

Shopping hours are generally 10–1 and 4–7 daily, although quite a few stores now stay open through siesta. Many shops close all day Sunday.

La Loma (⊠ Av. Guerrero, ☎ No phone) has some carved wooden masks and animals from Oaxaca, beautiful boxes and clothes from Guatemala, and a large display of handcrafted jewelry. **Casa del Arte Mexica** (⊠ Av. Hidalgo 6, ☎ 987/7–04–59) has a good choice of fine limestone carvings along with silver jewelry, batiks, rubbings, wood carvings, leather, and hammocks. **Tienda Paulita** (⊠ Avs. Morelos and Hidalgo, ☎ 987/7–00–14) has a standard selection of folk art and handmade clothing in a fairly large space.

Body Map (⊠ Av. Morelos by police station, ☎ 987/7–07–62) sells exclusive casual beachwear by Mexican designers.

Isla Mujeres A to Z

Arriving and Departing
BY BOAT
Speedboats and slow passenger ferries shuttle between the main dock on Isla and Puerto Juárez on the mainland. Always check the times posted as the schedule is subject to seasonal change. You can reach the ferry office at ☎ 987/7–00–65.

Passenger ferries: On the *Sultana del Mar* or *Blanca Beatriz,* a one-way ticket is $1 and the trip takes about 45 minutes. Delays and crowding aren't unknown, but often there is live music on board, which starts an instant party. Ferries to Isla leave every hour on the half hour between 7:30 AM and 8:30 PM. Ferries leaving Isla depart at 5 AM, 6, 6:30, 7:30, 8:15, 8:45, 9:30, 10:30, 11:30, 12:30 PM, 1:30, 2:30, 3:30, 4:30, 5, 5:30, 6:30, and 9.

Speedboats: *Caribbean Lady* and *Miss Valentina* (☎ 987/7–02–54 or 987/7–02–53) are air-conditioned cruisers with bar service. A one-way ticket costs $3 and the crossing takes about 20 minutes. **Coming to Isla,** they depart Puerto Juárez from 6:30 AM to 8 PM at approximately 20-minute intervals. **Leaving Isla** they depart every half hour between 7 AM and 8 PM.

For party-goers, there now is one ferry leaving Puerto Juárez for Isla Mujeres at 11:30 PM.

A faster but more expensive service is the **Shuttle** (⊠ Cancún, ☎ 98/8–34–48, $15 round-trip), which runs directly from the Playa Tortugas dock in Cancún's hotel zone at least four times a day.

Cars are unnecessary on Isla, but there are **municipal ferries** that bring cars over as well as passengers. The ride takes about 45 minutes and the fare is just under $2 per person and about $11 per vehicle. **Coming to Isla,** the ferry leaves from Punta Sam on the mainland at 8 AM, 11, 1:30 PM, 4:45, 6:45, and 9:15. **Departing Isla** it leaves at 6:30 AM, 9:30, 12:15 PM, 3, 5:30, and 8:15. Again, check the schedule, which is subject to changes. If you have a sensitive stomach, this ferry offers the easiest ride of all three options, especially when the sea is rough.

Getting Around
BY BICYCLE
Bicycles are available for hardy cyclists, but don't underestimate the hot sun and the tricky road conditions. Watch for the many speed bumps, which can give you an unexpected jolt. And don't ride at night. Many roads have no street lights. **Rent Me Sport Bike** (⊠ Avs. Juárez and Morelos, 1 block from main pier, ☎ No phone) rents five-speed cycles from less than $3 per hour; a full day costs about $7. You can leave your driver's license in lieu of a deposit; the place is open daily 8–6.

BY BUS
Municipal buses (☎ 987/7–05–29 or 987/7–41–73) run at 20- to 30-minute intervals daily between 6 AM and 10 PM, generally following

the ferry schedule, from the Posada del Mar hotel on Avenida Rueda Medina out to Colonia Salinas on the windward side. As you might expect, service is slow because the buses make frequent stops.

BY CAR

There is little reason to bring a car to Isla Mujeres, because there are plenty of other forms of transportation that cost far less than renting and transporting a private vehicle.

BY GOLF CART

Yes, you can get around Isla by golf cart. **P'pe's Rentadora** (⊠ Av. Hidalgo 19, ☎ 987/7–00–19) and almost all of the moped rental shops listed below, as well as some hotels, rent them for $10 an hour. Be prepared to move to the side of the road to let other motorists pass.

BY MOPED

Compared with riding a moped in Cancún, riding one on Isla is a relatively safe proposition, and the island is full of moped rental shops. To beat the standard price of a moped rental try haggling (a moped rented is better than a moped not rented). To ensure a safe ride, wear a helmet, get off the road if it rains, be on the lookout for car doors opening suddenly, and use the rear brake as your main brake.

Motorent Kankin (⊠ Av. Abasolo 15, ☎ No phone) will provide a two-seat, three-speed Honda for about $5 per hour or $20 per day ($40 for 24 hours); a $20 deposit—or a credit card or passport left behind—is required. **Richa's Mopeds** (⊠ Av. Abasolo 13, ☎ 987/5–35–66) has mopeds at good prices, and the cheapest laundromat is next door.

BY TAXI

If your time is limited you can hire a **taxi** (⊠ Av. Rueda Medina, ☎ 987/7–00–66) for a private island tour at about $15 an hour. Fares run $1–$2 from the ferry or downtown to the hotels at Playa Norte.

Contacts and Resources

BANKS

Bital (⊠ Av. Rueda Medina 3, ☎ 987/7–01–04 or 987/7–00–05), the only bank on the island, exchanges money 10–noon.

EMERGENCIES

Police (☎ 987/7–00–82). **Port Captain** (☎ 987/7–00–95). The **Centro de Salud** ⊠ Av. Guerrero 5 on the plaza, ☎ 987/7–02–17) provides 24-hour emergency service and accepts regular visits between 8 AM and 8 PM. Your hotel can also help you find an English-speaking doctor. The **Red Cross Clinic** (⊠ Colonia La Gloria, south side of island, ☎ 987/7–02–80) is run by a British doctor, Dr. Greta Shorey. Payment is by donation—they operate on a shoestring budget.

GUIDED TOURS

Boat Tours. Cooperativa Lanchera (⊠ Waterfront near dock, ☎ No phone) has four-hour trips to the Virgin, the lighthouse, the turtles at Playa Lancheros, the coral reefs at Los Manchones, and El Garrafón, for about $25 including lunch. **Cooperativa Isla Mujeres** (⊠ Av. Rueda Medina, ☎ 987/7–02–74), next to Mexico Divers, rents boats for a maximum of four hours and six people ($120). An island tour with lunch (minimum six people) costs $15 per person.

Among the boating cooperatives that go to the Isla Contoy national wildlife park and bird sanctuary, **Sociedad Cooperativa "Isla Mujeres"** (☎ 987/7–02–74 pier) and **La Isleña** (⊠ ½ block from pier, corner of Avs. Morelos and Juárez, ☎ 987/7–00–36) launch boats daily at 8:30 AM, returning at 4 PM. The trip takes about 45 minutes, depending on the size of the boat, and costs $30 to $40.

Farmacia Lily (✉ Avs. Madero and Hidalgo, ☎ 987/7–01–64) is open Monday–Saturday 8:30 AM–9:30 PM and Sunday 8:30–3. **Jarumi** (✉ Carretera al Garrafon, Colonia Canotal, ☎ 987/7–00–16) is open 24 hours.

VISITOR INFORMATION

Mundaca Travel (✉ Av. Hidalgo, ☎ 987/7–00–25 or 7–00–26, FAX 987/7–00–76) is a state-of-the-art agency that sells plane and bus tickets and tours, has house rentals, and acts as a FedEx agent.

COZUMEL

Updated by
Shelagh
McNally

The 490-square-km (189-square-mi) island of Cozumel hangs 19 km (12 mi) off the tip of the Yucatán Peninsula. Calm waters wash the white sandy beaches on its leeward side, which is fringed by a spectacular reef system. On the windward Caribbean side, powerful surf and rocky strands are broken at intervals by calm bays and hidden coves. Aside from the 3% of the island that has been developed, Cozumel is made up of expanses of sandy or rocky beaches, quiet little coves, palm groves, scrubby jungle, lagoons and swamps, and a few low hills (the maximum elevation is 45 ft). A few Maya ruins provide what limited sightseeing there is aside from the island's glorious natural attractions.

The island's name comes from the Maya word *Ah-Cuzamil-Peten,* which means "land of the swallows." For the Maya, Cozumel was the sacred site of the fertility goddess Ixchel, as well as a key center of trade and navigation. For the Spanish, it was useful as a naval base in the late 16th century. For pirates, its safe harbors and the catacombs and tunnels the Maya dug were ideal for their treasure-gathering and -storing needs. After cycles of settlement and abandonment that included an economic boom based on the island's abundant supply of *zapote* trees, which produce *chicle,* a chewing-gum industry staple, Jacques Cousteau discovered its incredible reefs and diving opportunities in 1961, and the trajectory of its current life was set.

Despite the inevitable effects of cruise ships that dock here, the island's earthy charm remains largely intact, and the relaxing atmosphere remains typically Mexican—friendly and unpretentious. A mainstay of Cozumel's mood is the isleños, descendents of the Maya who have inhabited the island for centuries.

Exploring

Cozumel is about 53 km (33 mi) long and 15 km (9 mi) wide. Only a small percentage of its roads—primarily those in the southern half—are paved. To take on the dirt roads, use a four-wheel-drive vehicle.

A Good Tour

It's worth renting a Jeep to explore Cozumel, which has more sights than either Cancún or Isla Mujeres. If you go south from Cozumel's principal town, **San Miguel** ⑫, in about 10 minutes you'll come to **Chankanaab Nature Park** ⑬. Continue past Chankanaab and past Playa Corona, Playa San Francisco, and Playa del Sol; at Km 17.5 a turnoff leads about 3 km (2 mi) inland to the village and ruins of **El Cedral** ⑭ (take this detour only if you have four-wheel-drive). Backtrack to the coast and go south past Playa de Palancar—the famous reef lies offshore—to the island's southern tip, where a dirt trail to **La-guna Colombia** ⑮ leads from the Paradise Café.

If you continue on the paved road, you'll come to the eastern Caribbean coast. Directly to your right is another dirt road (in very poor condi-

Cozumel

TO PUERTO MORELOS

Punta Molas

Punta Molas Faro 18

Castillo Real 17

Sea

Punta Norte

Isla de Pasión

San Gervasio 19

Playa Santa Pilar

Playa San Juan

Airport

Cross Island Rd.

Av. Benito Juárez

Playa Oriente

San Miguel 12

La plaza

Av. Rafael Melgar

TO PLAYA DEL CARMEN

Caribbean

Sea

Caribbean

Punta Morena

Playa de San Martín

La Ceiba

Playa Bonita

Chankanaab Nature Park 13

Punta Chiqueros

Throne

Playa Corona

Playa San Francisco

Playa del Sol

El Cedral 14

Buena Vista

El Mirador

Cinco Puertas

R E E F S

N

Playa del Palancar

Playa Paradiso

Tumba del Caracol

Laguna Colombia 15

Punta Celerain Faro 16

KEY

⛴ Ferry

🚢 Cruise Ship

0   6 miles
0   9 km

tion) that leads south for 4 km (2½ mi) to **Punta Celerain Faro** ⑯. When you return to the paved road and head north, you will first pass the Tumba del Caracol, another Maya ruin that may have served as a lighthouse; a bit farther on are the minuscule ruins of El Mirador and the Throne. Beyond Punta Chiqueros, Playa Bonita, and Playa Chen Río you'll see Punta Morena, where **Avenida Benito Juárez** meets the east coast. You can take the cross-island road west toward town or continue north.

The road north is quite rough and at time treacherous. The payoff is a marvelously deserted beach where you can camp. Heading north from the beach, you'll come to **Castillo Real** ⑰, another Maya site. A number of other minor ruins are spread across the northern tip of Cozumel, which terminates at the **Punta Molas Faro** ⑱. At this point the road dead-ends, and you will have to turn around. Expect to see lots of boa constrictors, crocodiles, iguanas, and other jungle animals who like to sunbathe on the road.

If you turn west on Avenida Benito Juárez, you'll come to the turnoff for the ruins of **San Gervasio** ⑲ just past the army airfield. Follow this road for 7 km (4½ mi)—it is quite well maintained. On the grounds to the ruins is a 9-mi dirt road, navigable (just barely) by foot, that leads back to the unpaved coast road up to Castillo Real.

Sights to See

⚓ ⑰ **Castillo Real.** A Maya site on the eastern coast, near the northern tip of the island, the *castillo* (castle) comprises a lookout tower, the base of a pyramid, and a temple with two chambers capped by a false arch. The waters here harbor several shipwrecks, remnants from the days when buccaneers lay in wait for the rich cargo in galleons en route to Europe. It's a fine spot for snorkeling because there are few visitors to disturb the fish—in part because it's a difficult spot to get to.

🌿 ⑬ **Chankanaab Nature Park.** Chankanaab ("small sea"), a 10-minute drive south of San Miguel, is a lovely saltwater lagoon that the government has made into a wildlife sanctuary, botanical garden, and archaeological park. The treasures from the Cozumel Archaeological Park—full-size replicas of Toltec, Mexican, and Maya statues and stone carvings—also have their home here. Underwater caves, offshore reefs, a protected bay—which hides crusty old cannons and anchors as well as a statue of the Maya water god Chacmool and Christ statues—and a sunken ship attract droves of snorkelers and scuba divers. An interactive educational museum, four dive shops, two restaurants, two gift shops, a snack stand, and a dressing room with lockers and showers are on the premises. ⊠ *Carretera Sur, Km 9,* ☎ *No phone.* 🎟 *$7.* ☉ *Daily 6–5:30.*

⚓ ⑭ **El Cedral.** The tiny village and ruins here once were the largest Maya site on Cozumel. This was the temple sighted by the original Spanish explorers in 1518, and the first mass in Mexico was reportedly celebrated here. Unfortunately the ruins have suffered at the hand of the conquistadors, and then much later the U.S. Army Corps of Engineers, so there is little archaeological evidence of El Cedral's past. All that remains is a small structure capped by jungle growth. Its Maya arch, best viewed from inside, is covered by faint traces of paint and stucco. After exploring the ruins, you can sit for a spell nearby in a small green-and-white cinder-block church, which houses a number of crosses shrouded in embroidered lace that's typical of rural Mexico. ⊠ *Turnoff at Km 17.5 of main island road, then 3 km (2 mi) inland to site,* ☎ *No phone.*

Isla de Pasión. Beyond Punta Norte, this tiny island in the middle of Abrigo Bay is now part of a state reserve. Accessible only by boat, its beaches are extremely secluded. Fishing is permitted, but there are no facilities on the island, and since so few people go, no scheduled tours. You'll have to bargain with a local boat owner for transportation if you want to visit.

⑮ Laguna Colombia. A prime site for jungle aficionados, this lagoon lies at the island's southern tip and is most commonly reached by boat, although there is also a rugged footpath. Fish migrate here to lay their eggs, and barracuda, baby fish, and birds show up in great numbers in season. There are popular diving and snorkeling spots offshore in the reefs of Tunich, Colombia, and Maracaibo.

⑯ Punta Celerain Faro (Celerain Point Lighthouse). Located on the southernmost tip of the island, the lighthouse is surrounded by sand dunes at the narrowest point of land. It affords a misty, bewitching view of pounding waves, swamps, and scraggly jungle. Crocodiles were once hunted nearby; nowadays you may spot a soldier or two from the adjacent army post catching an iguana. The point comes to life on Sunday when the lighthouse keeper serves fried fish and beer to locals and tourists. The lighthouse is at the end of a 4-km-long (2½-mi-long) dirt road—you'll need a four-wheel-drive vehicle if you plan to visit.

⑱ Punta Molas Faro (Molas Point Lighthouse). This northernmost beach is an excellent spot for sunbathing, birding, and camping. Although this entire area is accessible only by four-wheel-drive vehicles or by boat, the jagged shoreline and the open sea offer magnificent views, making it well worth the trip. If you plan to head up here, allow plenty of time and rent a reliable four-wheel-drive vehicle: the pothole-ridden road is the preferred sunbathing spot of boa constrictors, crocodiles, and other legendary creatures of the jungle.

⑲ San Gervasio. The largest existing Maya and Toltec site on Cozumel, San Gervasio was once the island's capital and probably its ceremonial center, dedicated to the fertility goddess Ixchel. The Classic- and Post-Classic–style site was continuously occupied from AD 300 to AD 1500. Typical architectural features from the era include limestone plazas and masonry superstructures atop stepped platforms, as well as stelae, bas-reliefs, and frescoes. What remains today are several small mounds scattered around a plaza and several broken columns and lintels that were once part of the main building or observatory. There are a snack bar and some gift shops at the entrance. To get here, take the cross-island road (Avenida Juárez) to the San Gervasio access road; follow this road north for 7 km (4½ mi). The ruin usually closes in October. ☞ *$1 access to road, $3.50 access to ruins.* ☉ *Daily 8–5.*

⑫ San Miguel. Cozumel's only town has kept some of the flavor of a Mexican village, although its streets are dotted with shops and restaurants trying to draw tourist crowds. Take a walk along the *malecón* (waterfront boulevard) and enjoy the ocean breeze. The main square is where people hang out, particularly on Sunday nights when mariachi bands join the nightly assortment of food and souvenir vendors.

Museo de la Isla de Cozumel (Museum of the Island of Cozumel) is housed on two floors of what was once the island's first luxury hotel. The first floor is dedicated to natural history, with exhibits about the origins of the island, endangered species, present-day topography, and an explanation of coral reef ecology. Upstairs covers the history of Cozumel during colonial times with displays of cannons, swords, and maritime artifacts. There is also is a charming reproduction of a Maya house. The library and bookstore on the first floor is excellent; a café with great waterfront views is on the second floor. The museum also has guided tours and workshops. ⊠ *Av. Rafael Melgar between Calles 4 and 6 Norte,* ☎ *987/2–14–75.* ☞ *$3.* ☉ *Daily 10–6.*

Beaches

Cozumel's beaches vary from long, treeless, sandy stretches to isolated coves and rocky shores. Most development is on the leeward (west) side, where the coast is relatively sheltered by the proximity of the mainland 19 km (12 mi) to the west. The best sand beaches lie along the southern half of Cozumel's leeward side, some 5 km (3 mi) long—from **Playa Corona** south to **Punta Celerain**. In between them, **Playa San Francisco** and **Playa del Sol** tend to get cruise ship crowds. **Playa del Palancar** is often less crowded than those two.

Getting to the east coast requires transportation, but the succession of mostly deserted rocky coves and narrow, powdery beaches—sadly garbage-strewn in spots—poised dramatically against the turquoise water is worth the trip. **Playa Oriente** has pounding surf; there is also a café for light meals and drinks. **Punta Chiqeros** is a moon-shaped cove sheltered by an offshore reef; the cove is part of Playa Bonita, which also has a café. Swimming on parts of the east coast can be treacherous if you go too far out or if a southwest wind is blowing—in some parts a deadly undertow can sweep you out to sea in a matter of minutes—but the beaches are still great for solitary sunbathing.

Dining

Dining options on Cozumel reflect the nature of the place as a whole, breezy, relaxed, and natural with some harmless pretension at times. More than 80 restaurants in the downtown area alone offer a broad choice, from air-conditioned fast-food outlets to places serving Continental fare and seafood in semiformal "nautical" settings to simple outdoor eateries that specialize in fish. Most restaurants accept credit cards, although many less formal places accept only cash. Resort hotels' buffet breakfasts and dinners are a good value for bottomless appetites. A dining tip: don't be influenced by your cab driver's dining suggestion—usually they are paid to recommend restaurants.

CATEGORY	COST*
$$$	over $25
$$	$15–$25
$	under $15

*per person for a three-course meal, excluding drinks and service

$$$ ✕ **Arrecife.** A well-trained staff, impeccably prepared seafood, and
★ Mediterranean fare put this casually elegant hotel restaurant in a class by itself. Tall windows providing excellent views of the sea complement the stylish decor of potted palms, white wicker furniture, and pink walls. Live music further enhances the romantic mood. ⊠ *Presidente Inter-Continental Cozumel,* ☎ *987/2–03–22. AE, DC, MC, V. Closed Sept. and Oct.*

$$$ ✕ **La Cabaña del Pescador Lobster House.** Walk the gangplank to this palapa restaurant with seashells and nets hanging from the walls—yes, it's kitsch and cute but worth it if you're looking for the freshest lobster on the island. The crustaceans are sold by weight, and the rest is on the house. Its sister establishment next door, El Guacamayo King Crab House, serves the less-expensive king crab. ⊠ *Carretera San Juan, Km 4, across from Playa Azul Hotel,* ☎ *987/2–39–17. Reservations not accepted. AE, MC, V. No lunch.*

$$ ✕ **El Capi Navegante.** When the captain's motto is "The fish we serve today slept in the sea last night," you know the fish will be fresh. Blue-and-white decor accented by life preservers on the wall is the look at this popular restaurant. Specialties such as whole red snapper and stuffed squid are skillfully prepared and sometimes flambéed at your

table for effect. Highly recommended dishes include conch ceviche and deep-fried whole fish. ⊠ *Av. 10a Sur 312, at Calle 3,* ☎ *987/2–17–30. MC, V.*

$$ ✕ **La Choza.** With its white stucco walls, open kitchen, and thatched ★ roof, this family-run restaurant resembles a large Maya home. Doña Elisa Espinosa is assisted by her daughter, and together they create culinary magic. Be sure to try the chilies stuffed with shrimp or the *pollo en relleno negro* (chicken in a blackened sauce). Equally outstanding are the mole dishes. To finish, you might try the frozen avocado pie—original, cool, and refreshing. ⊠ *Calle Rosada Salas 198, at Av. 10a Sur,* ☎ *987/2–09–58. AE, MC, V.*

$$ ✕ **La Veranda.** This charming Caribbean restaurant feels like you're dining in someone's home. Start with shrimp scampi, then move on to Caribbean fish fillet in mango sauce. Another local favorite is the Caribbean delight, seafood in a teriyaki sauce. Desserts are made daily. With comfortable rattan chairs, a lush tropical courtyard, and soft classical music in the background, this is an obvious choice for romance. ⊠ *Calle Norte 4 140, between 5 Av. Norte and 10 Av. Norte,* ☎ *987/2–41–32. AE, MC, V. No lunch.*

$$ ✕ **Prima.** Located on a breezy second-floor terrace, this is the best Ital-★ ian restaurant on the island. Everything is fresh, and the vegetables come from the owner's garden. The daily menu can include such delights as angel hair pasta with lobster and sun-dried tomatoes or crab ravioli with cream sauce. The bottom level is a store where you can find Mexico's finest wines and pricey Cuban cigars. Next door is the Prima Deli, which serves delicious sandwiches and deli food. ⊠ *Av. Rosado Salas 109 A,* ☎ *987/2–42–42 or 987/2–24–77. AE, MC, V. No lunch.*

$$ ✕ **Tony Rome's.** If the prospect of great Texas-style barbecued ribs doesn't bring you running, then come to hear Tony sing nightly in Spanish and English. You'll also find homemade pasta, chicken, lobster, Kansas City steaks, and great happy-hour specials. ⊠ *Av. 5 Sur 21, between Av. Rosado Salas and Calle 3 Sur,* ☎ *987/2–01–31. MC, V.*

$ ✕ **Coconuts Bar & Grill.** This hilltop restaurant on the east coast be-★ tween Punta Morena and Chien Río has mesmerizing views. Tables and chairs are scattered throughout the trees and bushes, which makes you feel like you can soak up the surroundings in solitude. (There is also a palapa restaurant.) The menu is simple: fresh fish, chicken, and hamburgers with a variety of Mexican snacks. Lunch food is served until sunset. ⊠ *East coast, south of Punta Morena,* ☎ *No phone. No credit cards.*

$ ✕ **El Foco.** A taquería serving soft tacos stuffed with pork, chorizo (spicy Mexican sausage), and cheese, this eatery also does ribs and steak. Graffitied walls and plain wood tables make it a casual, fun spot for a bite and a *cerveza* (beer). ⊠ *Av. 5 S 13-B, between Calle Rosado Salas and Calle 3,* ☎ *No phone. No credit cards.*

$ ✕ **El Moro.** The ghastly decor here becomes unimportant once you taste the food—delicious and hearty, which is why it's so popular with divers. The filling *pollo Ticulenío* is a layered medley of tomato sauce, mashed potatoes, crispy baked tortillas, and batter-fried chicken topped with shredded cheese. Take a taxi—El Moro is too far to walk to and too difficult to find. ⊠ *Calle 75 Norte between Calles 2 and 4,* ☎ *987/2–30–29. MC, V. Closed Thurs.*

$ ✕ **Jeanie's Waffle House.** This place is usually packed—and the wait is worth it. Jeanie De Lille is the island's premier pastry chef, and she creates amazingly light fluffy waffles served any way you want them. Breakfast is served all day alongside lunch and dinner menus that include fried fish, tamales, and several pasta dishes. Jeanie's is open daily 6 AM–1 PM and 6–10 PM. ⊠ *Av. Rafael Melgar in the Vista del Mar hotel,* ☎ *987/2–05–45. AE, MC, V.*

Lodging

Cozumel's hotels are on the island's west side, north or south of, or directly in, the town of San Miguel. Because of the proximity of the reefs, divers and snorkelers tend to congregate at the southern properties. Sailors and anglers, on the other hand, prefer the hotels to the north, where beaches are better. Most budget hotels are in town. All hotels have air-conditioning unless otherwise noted, and all share the 77600 postal code.

CATEGORY	COST*
$$$$	over $160
$$$	$90–$160
$$	$40–$90
$	under $40

All prices are for a standard double room in the high season, excluding service charges and 10% tax.

North Hotel Zone

$$$$ 🏨 **Meliá Mayan Peradisus.** Lush tropical foliage and modern architecture and amenities—not to mention spectacular sunsets over the beach—make this property a memorable place to stay. Standard rooms, some with small patios opening out onto the lawn, are attractively decorated with colorful tropical-print bedspreads and light-wood furniture. On the premises is a disco, kids program and playground, horseback trails, health club, and an array of non-motorized watersports equipment. Downtown is a 15-minute taxi ride away. ⊠ *Zona Hotelera Norte, Box 9, Carretera a Sta. Pilar 6,* ☎ *987/2–04–11; 800/341–5993 in the U.S.,* FAX *987/2–15–99. 200 rooms. 3 restaurants, 5 bars, 2 pools, hot tub, 2 tennis courts, health club, horseback riding, bicycles, shops, dance club, children's programs. AE, MC, V.*

$$$ 🏨 **Playa Azul Hotel.** At this quiet, comfortable hotel bright, airy rooms have either great ocean views or face beautiful tropical gardens. The beach is lined with small palapas with comfortable chairs, and for activity on and under the sea, snorkeling, scuba diving, and fishing trips depart daily from the hotel dock. The Palma Azul restaurant serves delicious seafood. ⊠ *Zona Hotelera Norte, Carretera a San Juan, Km 4, Box 31,* ☎ *987/2–01–99 or 987/2–00–43,* FAX *987/2–01–10. 31 rooms. Restaurant, 2 bars, pool, massage, dock, snorkeling, billiards, car rental. AE, MC, V.*

South Hotel Zone

$$$$ 🏨 **Presidente Inter-Continental Cozumel.** Luxury, comfort, and privacy
★   are hallmarks of the Presidente. Rooms are done in bright, contemporary colors with white cedar furnishings; deluxe rooms have their own private terraces fronting the beach or gardens. This hotel has one of the largest beaches on the island. Another attraction is the incredible snorkeling here—barracuda, angelfish, and octopus all swim in the waters a few feet off the beach. There is also a professional dive and water-sports center. Its restaurant, Arrecife (☞ *Dining, above*), is one of the best on the island. ⊠ *Carretera a Chankanaab, Km 6.5,* ☎ *987/2–03–22; 800/327–0200 in the U.S.,* FAX *987/2–13–60. 253 rooms. 2 restaurants, 3 bars, coffee shop, pool, hot tub, 2 tennis courts, dive shop, motorbikes, shops, children's program, car rental. AE, DC, MC, V.*

$$$ 🏨 **Fiesta Americana Cozumel Reef.** One of the most popular hotels on the island is across the road from the water: a pedestrian walkway provides easy access to the beach, pool, restaurant, dive shop, and boat dock. Standard rooms are large, with sea-green headboards and light-wood furnishings; all have balconies looking out on the ocean. There is also a semicircular cluster of villas with 56 rooms facing the hotel's main entrance. The hotel is priced reasonably within its range, and the location is superb. ⊠ *Carretera a Chankanaab, Km 7.5,* ☎ *987/2–26–*

22; 800/343–7821 in the U.S., FAX 987/2–26–66. 228 rooms. 3 restaurants, 3 bars, 2 pools, 2 tennis courts, dive shop, dock, motorbikes, travel services, car rental. AE, MC, V.

$$ ★ ⊞ **Casa del Mar.** South of town near several boutiques, sports shops, and restaurants, this three-story hotel is frequented by divers. An unpretentious but tasteful lobby overlooks a small garden. Cheerful rooms are fitted with yellow-tiled headboards, nightstands, and Mexican artwork, and they have small balconies with views of the pool or the sea across the road. The bi-level cabañas, which sleep three or four, are a very good buy at $115. ⊠ Box 129, Carretera a Chankanaab, Km 4, ☎ 987/2–19–44; 800/437–9609 in the U.S., FAX 987/2–18–55. 98 rooms, 8 cabañas. 2 restaurants, 2 bars, pool, hot tub, dive shop, travel services, car rental. AE, MC, V.

Downtown Hotels

$$$ ⊞ **Galápago Inn.** This pretty white stucco hotel just south of town is for divers. Simple, comfortable, and functional rooms are rented as part of a dive package (3, 5, or 7 nights) that includes all meals. Some rooms have balconies, all have ocean views. There is a charming central garden with tiled benches and small fountain, plenty of hammocks, and a great restaurant. Be sure to take full advantage of the expert diving staff, which offers advanced diving certification. For diving packages, book through a travel agent or the 800 number. ⊠ Carretera a Chankanaab, Km 1.5, ☎ 987/2–06–63; 800/847–5708 in the U.S. 58 rooms. 2 restaurants, bar, pool. MC, V.

$$ ⊞ **Tamarindo Bed & Breakfast.** The owners of this five-room charmer have created a place that combines the flavor of Mexico with the elegance of France. Rooms are gracefully decorated with individual touches. Breakfasts consist of fresh breads, fruits in season, homemade yogurt, and French-dripped coffee. The staff will arrange diving expeditions, and there is a rinse tank and gear storage facility on site. ⊠ Calle 4 Norte 421, between Av. 20 and Av. 25, ☎ FAX 987/2–36–14. Massage, bicycles, shops, baby-sitting, laundry service. MC, V.

$$ ★ ⊞ **Villas Las Anclas.** Conveniently located parallel to the malecón, these villas are furnished apartments for rent by the day, week, or month. The duplexes have a downstairs sitting room, dining area, and fully equipped kitchenettes; spiral staircases lead up to small bedrooms overlooking a quiet courtyard garden. ⊠ Box 25, Av. 5a Sur 325, between Calles 3 and 5 Sur, ☎ 987/2–14–03, FAX 987/2–54–76. 7 units. Kitchenettes, refrigerators. No credit cards.

$ ★ ⊞ **Charrito's.** This delightful B&B is seven blocks from the plaza in a typical neighborhood, which gives you a chance to experience a slice of Mexico you won't find at other hotels. Rooms have been individually and comfortably decorated and have private baths and ceiling fans. Sandy and Marcos will treat you like one of the family, showing you the best restaurants and beaches or arranging dive trips. The full-course Mexican breakfast is huge and delicious. ⊠ Calle 21 Sur between Felipe Angeles and Av. 40, ☎ FAX 987/2–47–60. 5 rooms. Fans. No credit cards.

Nightlife and the Arts

For a slice of the island's heritage check out the the Fiesta nights at the **Fiesta Americana** (☎ 987/2–26–22) every Thursday. Carnival on Cozumel takes place in February just before Lent. The whole island explodes with music, costumes, dancing, parades, and parties.

Bars

For a quiet drink and good people-watching, try **Video Bar Aladino** at the Mesón San Miguel, at the north end of the plaza. For an evening of beer and darts check out **Scruffy Murphy's Irish Pub** (⊠ Av. 10a and Adolfo Rosada Salas, ☎ 987/2–11–54). Serious bar-hoppers like **Carlos 'n' Charlie's** (⊠ Av. Rafael Melgar 11, between Calles 2 and 4 Norte, ☎ 987/2–01–91) for hang-off-the-rafters, raucous fun; don't come here if you're the retiring type. People are always spilling out over the outdoor patio (sometimes literally) at **Sharkey's** (⊠ Av. Rafael Melgar near Av. Benito Juárez, ☎ 987/2–18–32), where a papier-mâché Marilyn Monroe in a *Some Like It Hot* pose surveys a rowdy crowd. You and your friends provide the entertainment at the sing-along **Laser-Karaoke Bar** (⊠ Fiesta Inn, ☎ 987/2–28–11). Sports fiends can play video games or check football scores at the **Sports Page Video Bar and Restaurant** (⊠ Corner 5 Av. Norte and Calle 2 Norte, ☎ 987/2–11–99).

Live Music

Sunday evenings, 8–10 PM, locals head for the **zócalo** (plaza) to hear mariachis and island musicians playing tropical tunes. For romantic piano or guitar serenades, try the dining room of **Arrecife** (⊠ Presidente Inter-Continental Cozumel, ☎ 987/2–03–22; low season only). **Hog's Breath** (⊠ Av. Rafael Milgar, ☎ No phone) has live music every night. If Frank Sinatra–style entertainment turns you on, check out **Tony Rome's** (⊠ Av. 5 Sur 21, between Av. Rosado Salas and Calle 3 Sur, ☎ 987/2–01–31), where the owner holds forth at the microphone. In addition to tasty lobster dishes, **Joe's Lobster House** (⊠ Av. 10 Sur 229, between Calle Rosada Salas and Calle 3 Sur, ☎ 987/2–32–75) serves up lively reggae and salsa every night at 10:30; this is *the* hot spot for live entertainment.

Outdoor Activities and Sports

Most people come to Cozumel to take advantage of the island's water-related sports—scuba diving, snorkeling, and fishing are particularly big, but jet skiing, sailboarding, waterskiing, and sailing remain popular as well. You will find services and rentals throughout the island, especially through major hotels and water-sports centers such as **Aqua Safari** (⊠ Av. Rafael Melgar 429, between Calles 5 and 10 Sur, ☎ 987/2–01–01). For small group or individual lessons try **Eagle Ray Dive School** (⊠ Ave. Chichen and Pamuul, ☎ 987/2–57–35).

Fishing

Local regulations forbid commercial fishing, sportfishing, spear fishing, and the collection of any marine life between the shore and El Cantil Reef, and between the cruise-ship dock and Punta Celerain.

The annual **International Billfish Tournament** (⊠ Box 442, Cozumel 77600, ☎ 800/253–2701 in the U.S., ℻ 987/2–09–99), held the last week in April or the first week in May, draws anglers from around the world.

You can charter high-speed fishing boats for $300 for a half day or $350 for a full day, for a maximum of six people, from the **Club Náutico de Cozumel** (⊠ Puerto de Abrigo, Av. Rafael Melgar, Box 341, ☎ 987/2–01–18; 800/253–2701 in the U.S., ℻ 987/2–11–35), the island's headquarters for game fishing. Daily charters are easily arranged from the dock or at your hotel, but you might also try **Aquarius Fishing and Tours** (⊠ Calle 3 S, ☎ 987/2–10–92) or **Dive Cozumel** (⊠ Av. Rosado Salas 85, between Avs. Rafael Melgar and 5 S, ☎ 987/2–41–10, ☎ ℻ 987/2–18–42). All rates vary with the season.

Scuba Diving

With more than 30 charted reefs whose average depths range from 50 to 80 ft and a water temperature that hits about 75°F–80°F during peak diving season (June–August, when the hotel rates are coincidentally at their lowest), Cozumel is far and away Mexico's number one diving destination. Diverse diving options include deep dives, drift dives, shore dives, wall dives, and night dives, as well as theme dives focusing on ecology, archaeology, sunken ships, and photography. Look for places that focus on smaller groups and offer individual attention without the "move them in, move them out" approach.

Next to your equipment, your dive master is one of the most important parts of your trip—particularly if you are new to the sport. Make sure your instructor has PADI certification (or FMAS, the Mexican equivalent) and is affiliated with the **SSS recompression chamber** (⊠ Calle 5 S 21B, between Avs. Rafael Melgar and 5a S, next to Discover Cozumel, ☎ 987/2–23–87 or 987/2–18–48) or the recompression chamber at the **Hospital Civil** (⊠ Av. 11 S, between Calles 10 and 15, ☎ 987/2–01–40 or 987/2–05–25). Also consider getting DAN (Divers Alert Network) insurance, which covers dive accidents.

DIVE SHOPS AND TOUR OPERATORS

You can choose from a variety of two-tank boat trips and specialty dives ranging from $45 to $60; two-hour resort courses cost about $50–$60, and 1½-hour night dives, $30–$35. Basic certification courses, such as PADI's Discover Scuba or NAUI's introductory course, are available for about $350, whereas advanced certification courses cost as much as $700. Equipment rental is relatively inexpensive, ranging from $6 for tanks or a lamp to about $8–$10 for a regulator and B.C. vest. Underwater camera rentals can cost as much as $35, video-camera rentals run about $75, and professionally shot and edited videos of your own dive are priced at about $160.

In addition to the dive shops in town, many hotels have their own operations and offer dive and hotel packages starting at about $350 for three nights, double occupancy, and two days of diving. You can also pick up a copy of the *Chart of the Reefs of Cozumel* in any dive shop or the diving newspaper, *Insider's Guide to Cozumel Diving & Snorkeling,* which is loaded with helpful tips and information. Before choosing a shop, check credentials, look over the boats and equipment, and consult experienced divers who are familiar with local operators. The following list should get you started on your search.

Aqua Safari (⊠ Av. Rafael Melgar 429, between Calles 5 and 10 Sur, ☎ 987/2–01–01); **Blue Angel** (⊠ Av. Rafael Melgar, next to Hotel Villablanca, ☎ 987/2–16–31) for PADI certification; **Blue Bubble** (⊠ Av. 5a Sur at Calle 3 Sur, ☎ 987/2–18–65) for PADI instruction; **Dive Cozumel** (⊠ Av. Rosado Salas 72, at Av. 5 Sur, ☎ 987/2–41–10, FAX 987/2–18–42); **Eagle Ray Dive School** (⊠ Avs. Chichen and Pamuul, ☎ 987/2–57–35); **Michelle's Dive Shop** (⊠ Av. 5 Sur 201, at Calle Adolfo Rosado Salas, ☎ 987/2–09–47); **Ramone Zapata Divers** (⊠ Chankanaab Nature Park, ☎ 987/2–05–02); **Scuba Du** (⊠ Presidente Inter-Continental Cozumel hotel, ☎ 987/2–03–22 or 987/2–13–79, FAX 987/2–41–30); **Studio Blue** (⊠ Calle Rosado Salas 121, between Calles 5 and 10, ☎ FAX 987/2–43–30); **Tico's Dive Center** (⊠ Av. 5 Norte 121, between Calles 2 and 4, FAX 987/2–02–76).

Snorkeling

Snorkeling equipment is available at the Hotel Presidente Inter-Continental, La Ceiba, Chankanaab Bay, Playa San Francisco, Club Cozumel Caribe, and directly off the beach near the Fiesta Americana Cozumel Reef and Playa Corona for less than $10 a day.

Snorkeling tours run from $25 to $50, depending on the length, and take in the shallow reefs off Palancar, Colombia, and Yucab. Contact **Eagle Ray Dive School** (⊠ Avs. Chichen and Pamuul, ☎ 987/2–57–

35), which specializes in combined diving and snorkeling trips for families in which only one member dives. **Caribe Tours** (⊠ Av. Rafael Melgar at Calle 5 Sur, ☎ 987/2–31–00 or 987/2–31–54) and **Fiesta Cozumel** (⊠ Calle 11 Sur 598, between Avs. 25 and 30, ☎ 987/2–07–25, FAX 987/2–13–89) both run snorkeling tours from the 45-ft catamaran *El Zorro* and the 60-ft catamaran *Fury*.

Shopping

Cozumel has three main shopping areas: **downtown** along the waterfront, on Avenida Rafael Melgar, and on some of the side streets around the plaza (there are more than 150 shops in this area alone); at the **crafts market** (⊠ Calle 1 S, behind plaza) in town, which sells a respectable assortment of Mexican wares ; and at the cruise-ship **passenger terminal** south of town, near the Casa Del Mar, La Ceiba, and Sol Caribe hotels. There are also small clusters of shops at **Plaza del Sol** (on the east side of the main plaza), **Villa Mar** (on the north side of the main plaza), the **Plaza Confetti** (on the south side of the main plaza), and **Plaza Maya** (across from the Sol Caribe). As a rule, newer, trendier shops line the waterfront, whereas the area around Avenida 5a houses better crafts shops. The **town market** (⊠ Calle Rosada Salas between Avs. 20a and 25a) sells fresh produce and other essentials.

Department Stores

Smaller and more like variety stores than department stores, the following carry a relatively wide array of items. **Chachy Plaza** (⊠ Av. Benito Juárez 5, near church at back of plaza, ☎ 987/2–01–30) sells everything from liquor and perfume to snorkeling gear and snack food. **Pama** (⊠ Av. Rafael Melgar S 9, ☎ 987/2–00–90), near the pier, features imported foods, luggage, snorkeling gear, jewelry, and crystal. **Prococo** (⊠ Av. Rafael Melgar N 99, ☎ 987/2–18–75 or 987/2–19–64) has a good selection of liquor, jewelry, and gift items.

Specialty Stores

CLOTHING

Several trendy sportswear stores line Avenida Rafael Melgar between Calles 2 and 6. **Miro** (⊠ Av. Rafael Melgar, 1 block from town pier, ☎ 987/2–02–60) has a wide variety of Mexican resortwear with the latest designs and styles. **Explora** (⊠ Av. Rafael Melgar 49, ☎ 987/2–03–16) offers a casual line of modish cotton sports clothing. **Poco Loco** (⊠ Rafael Melgar, No. 18, and Juárez, No. 2-A, ☎ 987/2–54–99) sells casual wear and beach bags. **Bikinis do Brasil** (⊠ Calle 1 Sur between Avs. 10 and 15, ☎ 987/2–02–60) sells a collection of Brazilian swimwear and sundresses.

JEWELRY

Jewelry on Cozumel is pricey, but it tends to be of higher quality than the jewelry you'll find in many other Yucatán towns. **Diamond Creations** (⊠ Av. Rafael Melgar Sur 131, ☎ 987/2–53–30; 800/322–6476 in the U.S., FAX 987/2–53–34) lets you custom design a piece of jewelry from its collection of loose diamonds, emeralds, rubies, sapphires, or tanzanite. You'll find silver, gold, and coral jewelry—bracelets and earrings especially—at **Joyería Palancar** (⊠ Av. Rafael Melgar N 15, ☎ 987/2–14–68). Quality gemstones and striking designs are the strong point at **Rachat & Romero** (⊠ Av. Rafael Melgar 101, ☎ 987/2–05–71). You can find some bargains at **Cozumel Silver & Gold Exchange** (⊠ 5 Ave Sur, 201-A, ☎ FAX 987/2–67–42).

MEXICAN CRAFTS

Bugambilias (⊠ Ave. 10 Sur between Avs. Rosado Salas and 1a, ☎ 987/2–62–82) sells handmade Mexican linens; **Los Cinco Soles** (⊠ Av.

Rafael Melgar Norte 27, ☎ 987/2–01–32 or 987/2–20–40) is your best bet for one-stop shopping. The nearly block-long store stocks an excellent variety of Mexican wares; **Talavera** (⌂ Av. 5a Sur 349, ☎ 987/2–01–71) carries beautiful ceramics from all over Mexico.

Cozumel A to Z

Arriving and Departing

BY CRUISE SHIP

At least a dozen cruise lines call at Cozumel and/or Playa del Carmen, including (all phone numbers in the U.S.), from Fort Lauderdale, **Chandris/Celebrity** (☎ 800/437–3111), **Cunard/Crown** (☎ 800/221–4770), and **Princess** (☎ 800/568–3262); from Miami, **Carnival** (☎ 800/327–9501), **Costa** (☎ 800/327–2537), **Dolphin/Majesty** (☎ 800/222–1003), **Norwegian** (☎ 800/327–7030), and **Royal Caribbean** (☎ 800/327–6700); from New Orleans, **Commodore** (☎ 800/327–5617); and from Tampa, **Holland America** (☎ 800/426–0327).

BY FERRY

Passenger-only ferries depart from the dock at **Playa del Carmen** (☎ No phone; ☞ *below*) for the 40-minute trip to the main pier in Cozumel. They leave approximately every hour on the hour 5 AM–11 PM, with no ferries at noon, 2, 8, and 10 PM. Return service to Playa runs every hour on the hour from 4 AM–10 PM, with no ferries at 1, 7, and 9 PM. Verify the regularly changing schedule at ☎ 987/2–15–08. The car ferry from **Puerto Morelos** (☎ 987/2–17–22), on the mainland to the north of Playa del Carmen, is not recommended unless you *must* bring a car.

BY JETFOIL

A water-jet catamaran and two large speed boats make the trip between Cozumel (downtown pier, at the zócalo) and Playa del Carmen. This service, operated by **Aviomar** (⌂ Av. 5a between Calles 2 and 4, ☎ 987/2–05–88 or 987/2–04–77), costs the same as the ferry and takes almost as long, but the vessel is considerably more comfortable and has on-board refreshments. The boats make at least 10 crossings a day, leaving Playa del Carmen every one to two hours between 5:15 AM and 8:45 PM and returning from Cozumel between 4 AM and 8 PM. Buy tickets at the piers in both ports one hour before departure; call to confirm the schedule as it tends to be erratic.

BY PLANE

The **Cozumel Airport** (☎ 987/2–09–28) is 3 km (2 mi) north of town. **Continental** (☎ 987/2–04–87) flies nonstop from Houston. **Mexicana** (☎ 987/2–01–57) flies nonstop from Miami and San Francisco. **Aerocaribe** (☎ 987/2–05–03) and **Aerocozumel** (☎ 987/2–09–28), both Mexicana subsidiaries, fly to Cancún and elsewhere in Mexico, including Chichén Itzá, Mérida, and Playa del Carmen. The airport departure tax is $16.

Between the Airport and Hotels. Because of an agreement between the taxi and bus drivers' unions, there is no taxi service from the airport. You can take a taxi *to* the airport, however, for about $8 from the hotel zones, $5 from downtown. On the way in, you'll get to your hotel on a colectivo van with a maximum capacity of eight. Buy a ticket at the airport exit: the charge is $5 per passenger to the hotel zones, a little under $3 into town. If you want to get to your hotel without waiting for the van to fill and for other passengers to be dropped off, you can hire an *especial*—an individual van costing a little less than $20 to the hotel zones, about $8 to the city.

Getting Around
BY BICYCLE, MOPED, AND MOTORCYCLE
Mopeds and motorcycles are very popular here but also extremely dangerous because of heavy traffic, potholes, and hidden stop signs—accidents happen all too frequently. Mexican law requires all passengers to wear helmets; it's a $25 fine if you don't. Drive slowly, check for oncoming traffic and don't drive a moped when it's raining. Moped rentals at **Auto Rent** (⊠ Carretera Costera S, ☎ 987/2–08–44 ext. 712), **Rentadora Caribe** (⊠ Calle Rosada Salas 3, ☎ 987/2–09–55 or 987/2–09–61), or **Rentadora Cozumel** (⊠ Calle Rosada Salas 3 B, ☎ 987/2–15–03; ⊠ Av. 10a S at Calle 1, ☎ 987/2–11–20) cost about $25 per day, insurance included.

BY BUS
Local bus service runs mainly within the town of San Miguel, although there is a route from town to the airport. Service is irregular but inexpensive (less than 20¢).

BY CAR
Open-air Jeeps and other rental cars, especially those with four-wheel drive, are a good way of getting down dirt roads leading to secluded beaches and small Maya ruins—but rental insurance policies don't always cover these jaunts. Cozumel's *one* gas station is at Avenidas Juárez and 30a, and is open daily 7 AM–midnight.

BY TAXI
Taxis are available 24 hours a day at the main location (⊠ Calle 2 N, ☎ 987/2–00–41 or 987/2–02–36) or at the malecón at the main pier in town. A 25% surcharge applies from midnight to 6 AM. You can also hail taxis on the street, and taxis wait at all the major hotels. Fixed rates of about $3 are charged to go between town and either hotel zone, about $8 from most hotels to the airport, and about $6–$12 from the northern hotels or town to Chankanaab park or San Francisco beach.

Contacts and Resources
CAR RENTAL
The following firms handle two- and four-wheel-drive vehicles (all major hotels have rental offices): **Budget** (⊠ Av. 5a at Calle 2 N, ☎ 987/2–09–03; 987/2–17–32 cruise-ship terminal; 987/2–17–42 airport), **Hertz** (☎ 987/2–38–88 airport), **National Interrent** (⊠ Av. Juárez, Lote 10, near Calle 10, ☎ 987/2–32–63 or 987/2–41–01), and **Rentadora Aguilla** (⊠ Av. Rafael Melgar 685, ☎ 987/2–07–29). Rates start at $50 a day.

DOCTORS AND DENTISTS
The **Centro de Salud clinic** (⊠ Av. 20 at Calle 11, ☎ 987/2–01–40) provides 24-hour emergency care, and the **Medical Specialties Center** (⊠ Av. 20 N 425, ☎ 987/2–14–19 or 987/2–29–19) offers 24-hour air ambulance service and a 24-hour pharmacy. **Cozumel Chiropractic** (⊠ Av. 5 Sur 24-A, between Calles 3 and 5, ☎ 987/2–50–99) offers bargain-priced therapeutic massage.

EMERGENCIES
Police (⊠ Anexo del Palacio Municipal, ☎ 987/2–04–09). **Cruz Roja** (Red Cross; ⊠ Av. Rosada Salas at Av. 20a S, ☎ 987/2–10–58). **Air Ambulance** (☎ 987/2–40–70). **Recompression Chamber** (⊠ Calle 5 S 21-B, between Avs. Rafael Melgar and 5a S, ☎ 987/2–14–30).

GUIDED TOURS
See Travel Agencies and Tour Operators, *below,* for addresses and telephone numbers of the companies mentioned here.

Air Tours. Caribe Tours has a plane trip to **Chichén Itzá**; the $145 price includes the flight, transfers to the ruins, buffet lunch, and a guide. The company also flies to the **Sian Ka'an Biosphere Reserve.** In addition to lunch, this $160 plane trip includes a boat ride through the biosphere's mangroves for a closer look at the flora and fauna of the region.

Horseback Tours. Rancho Buenavista (☎ 987/2–15–37) runs four-hour guided horseback tours ($60) that visit three Maya ruins tucked away in Cozumel's tropical forest. The tour departs from **Restaurant Acuario** (⊠ Av. Rafael Melgar at Calle 11).

Specialty Tours. Glass-bottom-boat trips are provided by **Turismo Aviomar.** The air-conditioned semisubmarine *Mermaid* glides over a number of reefs and their dazzling arrays of fish. The daily tour costs about $30, lasts one hour and 45 minutes, and includes soft drinks. **Fiesta Cozumel** has a similar trip aboard the *Nautilus IV.*

Turismo Aviomar and **Caribe Tours'** off-island trips to **Tulum** and **Xel-Há** cost about $75 and include the 30-minute ferry to Playa del Carmen, the 45-minute bus to Tulum, 1½–2 hours at the ruins, entrance fees, guides, lunch, and a snorkeling stop at Xel-Há lagoon.

Day trips to the eco-archaeological theme park of **Xcaret,** about halfway between Playa del Carmen and Tulum, are offered by Fiesta Cozumel. The $50 price includes round-trip ferry to Playa del Carmen, entrance to the park, and a bilingual guide.

LATE-NIGHT PHARMACY

The island's largest drugstore is **Farmacia Dori** (⊠ Adolfo Salas between Avs. 15 and 25, ☎ 987/2–05–59), open daily 7 AM–midnight. **Farmacia Joaquín** (⊠ North side of the plaza, ☎ 987/2–25–20) is open Monday–Saturday 8 AM–10 PM and Sunday 9–1 and 5–9. **Farmacias Canto** (☎ 987/2–53–77) is open 24 hours and delivers to hotels.

TRAVEL AGENCIES AND TOUR OPERATORS

Caribe Tours (⊠ Av. Rafael Melgar at Calle 5 S, ☎ FAX 987/2–31–00 or 987/2–31–54); **Fiesta Cozumel Holidays/American Express** (in all major hotel lobbies; ⊠ Calle 11 S 598, between Avs. 25 and 30, ☎ 987/2–07–25); **Turismo Aviomar** (in several hotel lobbies, including El Presidente; ⊠ Av. 5 N 8, between Calles 2 and 4, ☎ 987/2–05–88).

VISITOR INFORMATION

State tourism office (⊠ Upstairs in Plaza del Sol mall, at east end of main square, ☎ 987/2–09–72) is open weekdays 9–2:30. A good source of information on lodgings (and many other things) is the **Cozumel Island Hotel Association** (⊠ Calle 2 N at Av. 15a, ☎ 987/2–31–32, FAX 987/2–28–09), open weekdays 8–2 and 4–7.

THE NORTH CARIBBEAN COAST

Updated by
Shelagh
McNally

South of Cancún, the coast of the Yucatán Peninsula runs the gamut of tropical possibilities. Whereas Puerto Morelos retains the relaxed atmosphere of a Mexican fishing village, the once-laid-back town of Playa del Carmen now has resorts as glitzy as those in Cancún and Cozumel. The beaches, from Punta Bete to Tulum, are beloved by scuba divers, snorkelers, birders, and beachcombers, and there are accommodations to suit every budget, from campsites and bungalows to condos and luxury hotels. Rustic but comfortable fishing and scuba diving lodges on the even more secluded Boca Paila in the Sian Ka'an Biosphere Reserve and on the Xcalak peninsula have a well-deserved reputation for excellent bone fishing and superb diving on virgin reefs. At the same time this coast is one of the most threatened by development, and concerned environmentalists are supporting the rise of ecotourism programs such as the ones at Xcacel that get visitors involved in helping to save the threatened sea-turtle population.

Against this backdrop is the Maya culture. The modern Maya live in the cities and villages along the coast; the legacy of the ancient, at the ruins. The dramatic remains of Tulum stand on a bluff overlooking the Caribbean, welcoming the sunrise each morning. A short distance inland, at Cobá, there are towering jungle-shrouded pyramids, a testament to the site's importance as a leading center of commerce in the ancient Maya world.

The coast is divided into two areas: Puerto Morelos to Tulum, which has the most ancient sites and places to lodge; and Tulum to Chetumal, where civilization thins out quite a bit. We detail the coast as far as the Sian Ka'an Biosphere Reserve just south of Tulum. If you want to venture farther, you'll be rewarded with remote beaches, coves, inlets, lagoons, and tropical landscapes.

Puerto Morelos

20 *36 km (22 mi) south of Cancún.*

For years, Puerto Morelos was known as the small coastal town where the car ferry left for Cozumel. This lack of regard has actually been its saving grace; it has escaped the hysteria of development engulfing other communities, retaining the authentic and relaxed atmosphere of a Mexican fishing village. More and more people are discovering that Morelos makes a great base for exploring the region, because it is exactly halfway between Cancún and Playa del Carmen.

In ancient times this was the point of departure for Maya women making pilgrimages by canoe to Cozumel, the sacred isle of the fertility goddess, Ixchel. Now Puerto Morelos's landmark is the leaning lighthouse. Without a doubt, its biggest attraction is the superb coral reef only 1,800 ft offshore, which provides excellent snorkeling and scuba diving. Dive sites include a fully intact Spanish galleon with coral-crusted cannons and the caves of the sleeping sharks (of documentary movie fame) 8 km (5 mi) east of town. The close proximity of the reef makes for an exceptionally calm and safe beach. It has recently been declared a national park, which should help to protect its fragile ecosystem.

Dining and Lodging

$$ ✕ **Pizza Palapa.** This favorite hangout serves delicious pizza, salads, and Mexican snacks under a giant palapa. It also hosts the only St. Patrick's Day party on the coast with authentic Irish music. Try the chaya pizza for something unique and delicious. ⊠ *Av. Tulum across from main square,* ☎ *987/1–00–39. No credit cards.*

$$$ ⊞ **Rancho Libertad.** Serene, secluded, and relaxing, this retreat has com-
★ fortable rooms in first- or second-floor cabañas with palapa roofs, hanging beds, hammocks, ceiling fans, and small terraces overlooking the grounds and the ocean. ⊠ *South of ferry dock,* ☎ *987/1–01–82,* FAX *987/1–01–81. 12 rooms. Massage, beach, snorkeling. No credit cards.*

$$ ⊞ **Hostel Valsa.** These cozy, clean, and cheerful efficiencies decorated with Mexican blankets and handicrafts come with fully equipped kitchenettes, eating areas, and bathrooms. Located by the mangroves, they are a five-minute walk to the beach and town. The owner will negotiate for weekly and monthly rates. ⊠ *Av. Niños Heroes, 1 block west of town,* ☎ FAX *987/1–02–33. 8 units. Kitchenettes. No credit cards.*

Outdoor Activities and Sports

For snorkeling and fishing trips, contact **Almost Heaven Adventures** (☎ *987/1–02–30*), and at **El Faro Trips** (☎ *987/1–02–75*), both on the

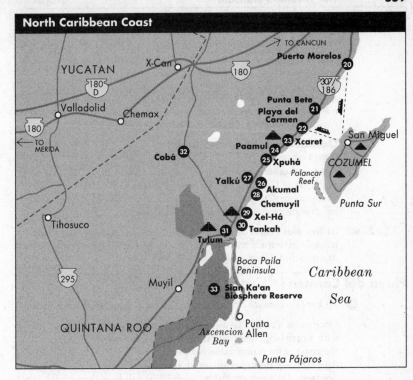

North Caribbean Coast

town's main square. For scuba lessons and excursions, contact **Sub-Aqua Explorers** (☎ 987/1–00–18) or divemaster **David Sanchez** (☎ 987/1–00–06). Deep-sea fishing expeditions can be arranged with **Secret Reef** (☎ 987/1–02–44).

Shopping

Alma Libre Libros is the only English language bookstore on the coast, with more than 16,000 books in stock. You can trade in your books for 25% of their cover prices and replenish your holiday reading. ⊠ *Av. Tulum on the main plaza,* ☎ 987/10264. ⊗ *Sept.–April, Tues.–Sat. 10–1 and 6–9.*

Punta Bete

㉑ *22 km (13½ mi) south of Puerto Morelos.*

The roads into Punta Bete may be paved with good intentions, but they aren't paved with anything resembling asphalt. But the 2⅓ km (1½ mi) of rock 'n' roll through the jungle *will* get you to a 6½-km-long (4-mi-long) isolated beach dotted with bungalow-style hotels and thatched-roof restaurants. If you want to spare yourself some grit, go for the more comfortable accommodations up the road at the Posada del Capitán Lafitte (☞ *below*).

Lodging

$$$$ **Posada del Capitán Lafitte.** Set on an invitingly long stretch of
★ beach just 10 km (6 mi) north of Playa del Carmen at Punta Bete, this posada is known for its genuinely chummy atmosphere. The three-unit cabañas are clustered around various parts of a point, each with its own private bath and ceiling fan; 31 units have air-conditioning. Four duplexes at the south end of the property have two-bedroom, two-bath units, ideal for families. If you have a choice, opt for the newer cabañas on the north end of the beach, furnished Mexican-style as opposed to

late-'80s Miami-style. Breakfast, dinner, tax, and tips are included in room rates, so you rarely need to carry money. Group activities include snorkeling trips, scuba certification and dives, horseback riding, fishing, and birding. All reservations must be prepaid. ⊠ *On dirt road (follow signs), about 3 km (2 mi) off Rte. 307, Km 62,* ☎ *987/3–02–14,* FAX *987/3–02–12. Reservations:* ⊠ *Turquoise Reef Group, Box 2664, Evergreen, CO 80439,* ☎ *303/674–9615 or 800/538–6802,* FAX *303/ 674–8735. 62 rooms. Restaurant, bar, pool, beach, dive shop, shops, video games, airport shuttle, car rental. AE, MC, V.*

Outdoor Activities and Sports

WATER SPORTS

Treasure Hunters (⊠ Posada del Capitán Lafitte, Hwy. 307 just north of Playa del Carmen, ☎ 987/3–02–14; 800/538–6802 in the U.S.) is a full-service dive shop with PADI certification courses, diving, snorkeling, fishing excursions, and specialty courses.

En Route At **Tres Ríos** (Three Rivers), you can canoe the waterways or take on miles of bike trails through the jungle. ⊠ *Hwy. 307 between Puerto Morelos and Playa del Carmen,* ☎ *98/87–49–77.*

Playa del Carmen

㉒ *10 km (6 mi) south of Punta Bete, 68 km (42 mi) south of Cancún.*

Once upon a time, Playa del Carmen was an innocent fishing village with a ravishing, deserted beach. Now it's the fastest growing city on the coast, with a population of more than 30,000. The beach is still delightful—alabaster-white sand, turquoise-blue waters—it's just not deserted. The most consistent sound you will hear throughout Playa del Carmen is that of the jackhammer. For the last few years a construction boom has been going on that regularly transforms the city every few months. Hotels, restaurants, and shops are multiplying faster than you can say *Kukulcán.*

The busiest parts of town are down by the **ferry pier,** along the commercial strip **Avenida Juárez,** and along the pedestrian walkway **Avenida 5.** Take a stroll north from the pier along the beach and you'll find a more peaceful part of town—simple restaurants roofed with palm fronds, where people sit around drinking beer for hours; overgrown tropical foliage; and a few campgrounds. On the south side of the pier the massive **Playacar** resort begins. In the middle of the development, there is an excellent open-air aviary—the best on the coast. Though peace and quiet may not be the operative words in most of Playa, the place is a fun introduction to the Caribbean coast. It is no longer a budget destination—prices, particularly in the hotels, are steadily increasing.

Dining and Lodging

There are hundreds of hotels in Playa, and more keep opening each day. The more luxurious rooms are to be found at the Playacar, more modest rooms are available in town. Most will ask for a deposit (usually the price of one night) before taking your reservation.

$$ ✕ **Da Gabi.** If you can tolerate the slightly pretentious air, you'll be rewarded with high-quality Italian fare, and people flock here to get it, under a romantic candlelit palapa. Enjoy the Maya chef's homemade fettuccine, spinach ravioli, angel hair pasta with fresh tomatoes, or oven-baked pizza. And you can't go wrong with daily specials like salmon antipasto. Top your meal off with an espresso or cappuccino. ⊠ *Av. 1 and Calle 12, Da Gabi Hotel,* ☎ *987/3–00–48. No credit cards. No lunch.*

$$ ✗ **Máscaras.** The wood-burning brick oven at this perennial local fa-
★   vorite—named for the masks that hang on its walls—produces ex-
ceptionally good thin-crust pizza and bread, and the homemade pasta
is very tasty. Fresh-squeezed sweetened lime juice, margaritas, wine,
and beer help wash down the rich Italian fare. Try smoked salmon pizza,
or calamari in garlic. ✉ *Av. Juárez across from plaza,* ☎ *987/3–10–
53. MC, V. No lunch.*

$$ ✗ **Media Luna.** This casual place with five-star food is decorated with
textiles from Guatemala. Everything that comes from the kitchen is sim-
ply scrumptious: spinach and mushroom breakfast crepes, Greek salads, fresh grilled fish, black bean quesadillas. Other entrées include
Indian, Italian, Mexican, and Chinese specialties. ✉ *Av. 5, Corner of
Calle 8,* ☎ *No phone. No credit cards.*

$$ ✗ **Yaxche.** At this celebration of Maya culture, the chef creates deli-
★   cious dishes such as papadzules (tortillas piled high with hard-boiled
eggs, drenched in pumpkin seed sauce and tomato) or pollo píbil (suc-
culent chicken baked in banana leaves). It's a refreshing change from
the pizza, pasta, and burgers in town. ✉ *Calle 8 at Avs. 5a and 10a,*
☎ *No phone. No credit cards.*

$ ✗ **El Tacolote.** Meat, margaritas, and mariachi music define this two-
story eatery enlivened with bold primary colors and Christmas lights.
Street bands playing a variety of Mexican music entertain while you
feast on platters of grilled meats, fajitas, or tacos with all sorts of fill-
ings. You can eat cheaply or splurge on a multicourse meal while
watching the action on the plaza from an outdoor table.✉ *Av. Juárez
across from plaza,* ☎ *987/3–13–63. MC, V.*

$ ✗ **The Coffee Press.** This relaxed café serves excellent coffee and fan-
tastic baked goods. The chocolate cake is delicious, as are the cinna-
mon buns and brownies. The small library of books and magazines
for sale add to the temptation to linger. ✉ *Av. 2 off Av. 5,* ☎ *987/3–
17–87. No credit cards.*

THE PLAYACAR RESORT

$$$$ ▦ **Continental Plaza Playacar.** This blush-color palace faces the
ocean on the south side of the ferry pier and possesses all the ameni-
ties of its competitors at the larger resort towns. The tropical-style
rooms have ocean views and balconies. A shopping–dining–banking
complex links the hotel to downtown Playa. The beach is one of the
nicest in Playa del Carmen—far less crowded than those to the north.
Mexican and international dishes are served at a restaurant in the
main building and at a palapa by the pool. For recreation, there is a
full-scale scuba and water-sports facility and an 18-hole championship
golf course. ✉ *Fraccionamiento Playacar at north end of the devel-
opment,* ☎ *987/3–01–00; 800/882–6684 in the U.S. and Canada,* FAX
*987/3–01–05. 188 rooms, 16 suites. 2 restaurants, bar, pool, 18-hole
golf course, tennis court, beach, dive shop, shops, travel services, car
rental. AE, MC, V.*

$$$$ ▦ **Iberostar Tucan and Quetzal.** A unique, luxurious, all-inclusive re-
★   sort has two distinct halves, with their own themes: the Quetzal has
paintings and furniture from colonial times, and the Tucan has repro-
ductions of carvings from famous Maya ruins. The hotel has worked
hard at preserving the natural surroundings, and there are plenty of
trees and animals on the premises. Spacious rooms have all the ameni-
ties, along with cheerful Caribbean colors and ocean- or jungle-view
private balconies. There is a fully equipped water-sports center and health
club to keep you busy. Playa del Carmen is a 20-minute walk, or a $4
cab ride, north. ✉ *Fraccionamiento Playacar,* ☎ *987/3–02–00; 888/
923–2722 in the U.S.,* FAX *987/3–04–24; 770/923–2734 in the U.S. 700
rooms. 3 restaurants, 2 bars, 4 pools, spa, 2 tennis courts, basketball,*

health club, dive shop, shops, nightclub, children's program (ages 4–12). AE, MC, V.

$$$$ 🏨 **Royal Maeva Playacar.** This all-inclusive Mexican club looks like a small, salmon-colored Mexican village. Several pools surround a thatched pavilion restaurant in the middle of the tropical garden, beyond which a powder-sand beach stretches several miles north to town. The friendly staff, called "Maeva Amigos," are fluent in several languages. Free room service, in-room minibars, scuba diving (additional cost), and snorkeling trips keep the Maeva in step with its all-inclusive neighbors down the beach. ⊠ *Fraccionamiento Playacar,* ☎ *987/3-11-50,* 🅵🅰🆇 *987/3–11–69. 286 rooms. 4 restaurants, 4 bars, 4 pools, 4 tennis courts, basketball, exercise room, volleyball, beach, snorkeling, theater, children's program (ages 5–10), convention center, meeting rooms, travel services, car rental, free parking. AE, DC, MC, V.*

HOTELS IN TOWN

$$$$ 🏨 **Baal Nah Kah.** The name means "home hidden among the gum trees"
★ in Maya, and the place is just a block from the beach, tucked along a sandy street just off the main drag. Guests can use the big kitchen, sitting room, and barbecue pit. There are five bedrooms and one studio on various levels, affording complete privacy. Two rooms have spacious balconies with a panoramic view of the ocean; all come with tile baths, two fans or air-conditioning, double or king-size beds, and Mexican decor. A small café serving breakfast, snacks, and light meals is next door. ⊠ *Calle 12 between Av. 5 and Av. 1,* ☎ *987/3–01–10,* 🅵🅰🆇 *987/3–00–50. Reservations:* ⊠ *Turquoise Reef Group, Box 2664, Evergreen, CO 80439,* ☎ *303/674–9615 or 800/538–6802,* 🅵🅰🆇 *303/674–8735. 5 rooms, 1 apartment. No credit cards.*

$$$ 🏨 **El Tucan Condotel Villas and Beach Club.** This lodging in the residen-
★ tial north end of town looks like a very exclusive and expensive hotel; in fact it's the best deal for the money in Playa. Catering to an eclectic European crowd, it is set around a huge jungle garden with a pool, winding flagstone paths, and even a cenote, and offers the ultimate in tranquility well away from the noise of downtown Avenida 5; however, it's a mere 10-minute walk to get there. All rooms and suites in the slate-colored buildings are fairly well separated from one another and have attractive accents such as burnished tile floors and painted wood furniture. Each has a private terrace, overhead fan, and tiny kitchenette; groceries can be purchased at a small store on the premises. A buffet breakfast is included at the Tukan Maya restaurant across the street, which also offers lunch and dinner à la carte. ⊠ *Av. 5 between Calles 14 and 16, Q. Roo 77710,* ☎ *987/3–04–17,* 🅵🅰🆇 *987/3–06–68. 56 rooms, 55 suites. Restaurant, bar, grocery, pool, beach, bicycles. MC, V.*

$$$ 🏨 **Las Palapas.** At this ideal get-away-from-it-all hideaway, white
★ cabañas are trimmed in blue, and duplexes have balconies or porches and hammocks. The thatch roofs and hexagonal shape of the buildings enhance the ocean breezes, making air-conditioning unnecessary. German tour groups keep the hotel's occupancy up to 80% year-round; make reservations early. Room rates include tasty breakfasts and dinners. ⊠ *Hwy. 307, Km 292, Box 116, Q. Roo 77710,* ☎ *987/3–05–82; 800/433–0885 in the U.S.,* 🅵🅰🆇 *987/3–0458. 75 cabañas. 2 restaurants, 2 bars, in-room safes, pool, beach, shops. AE, MC, V.*

$$ 🏨 **Alejari.** This two-story complex set amid flower-filled gardens is one of the most pleasant accommodations on Playa's north beach, and still a good deal. It's not as tranquil as it once was, thanks to the late-night revelers at bars close by. Some rooms have kitchenettes; all have fans or air-conditioning. A hearty breakfast is included in the rates, and the Mexican family that owns the hotel is extremely friendly and accommodating. ⊠ *Calle 6 N on the beach, Box 166, Q. Roo 77710,* ☎ *987/*

3–03–72, FAX *987/3–00–05. 29 rooms. Restaurant, kitchenettes. AE, MC, V.*

$$ ⊡ **Delfín.** Though not on the beach, the Delfín is a good choice for its bright, airy rooms—decorated with colorful mosaics—that are cooled by sea breezes and fans or air-conditioning. Safety-deposit boxes are available inside each room, and everything you need or want in Playa is within immediate walking distance. The management is exceptionally helpful. ⊠ *Av. 5 at Calle 6, Q. Roo 77710,* ☎ FAX *987/3–01–76. 14 rooms. MC, V.*

$$ ⊡ **Mom's Hotel.** A classic, Mom's was one of the first hotels in Playa. Though far from the beach, it remains a popular place, especially for longer stays, which are discounted. This is the place to meet unusual people, pick up rides to places, and exchange information. The large, sunny rooms face the interior courtyard and have tile floors and one or two double beds. There's a small pool and upstairs bar (with great coffee) and nightly entertainment. Downstairs there's a Chinese restaurant. Book early, because this hotel fills up fast. ⊠ *Av. 30 at Calle 4, Q. Roo 77710,* ☎ FAX *987/3–03–15. 12 rooms. Restaurant, bar, pool. No credit cards.*

$ ⊡ **Elefante.** Three blocks from the beach, this three-story, family-run hotel is well kept—and the best deal around for the price. The only sore spot is the unkempt field you pass on the way to the rooms. All the bare-bones units overlook a small plant-filled walkway and have tile floors and bathrooms, two double beds, and fans; some have kitchenettes. There's a restaurant down the street. ⊠ *Av. 12 and Calle 10,* ☎ *987/9–19–87. 38 rooms. No credit cards.*

Outdoor Activities and Sports

The oldest shop in town, **Tank Ha** (⊠ Maya-Bric and Albatros Royale hotels, ☎ FAX 987/3–13–55), with PADI-certified teachers, arranges diving and snorkeling trips to the reefs and caverns. Other dive shops are at the Iberostar, Las Palapas, El Tucan Condotel, and Continental Plaza Playacar hotels.

Shopping

Avenida 5 between Calles 4 and 10 is definitely the best place to shop in Playa, if not along the whole coast. Pretty shops and boutiques have sophisticated offerings from all of Mexico and hand-painted batiks from Indonesia. The shops listed below are open from about 10 in the morning to 9 or 10 at night.

El Vuelo de los Niños Pajaros (⊠ Rincón del Sol, Av. 5 at Calle 8, ☎ 987/3–04–45) has a great selection of regional music on CD and tape, along with handcrafted paper, cards, incense, and beaded baskets. **Amber Museum Shop** (⊠ Av. 5 between Calles 4 and 6, FAX 987/3–04–46) has simple but elegantly crafted amber jewelry by a German designer who also keeps a shop in Chiapas near the mines that provide the raw material. **La Calaca** (⊠ Av. 5 between Calles 6 and 8 and Av. 5 and Calle 4, ☎ 987/3–01–77 for both locations) carries an eclectic collection of wooden masks and other carvings—playful devils and angels are notable. **Manas Huellas** (⊠ Av. 5A Norte between Calles 10 and 12, ☎ No phone) is a small store that carries wonderful textiles and handicrafts from Oaxaca and Chiapas.

Off Avenida 5, try **Telart** (⊠ West side of main plaza next to Restaurant El Tacolote, ☎ 987/3–00–66), a small store stocked with attractive and original indigenous blankets, place mats, and wall hangings from the states of Chiapas, Michoacán, and Oaxaca. **Promoshow** (⊠ Calle 6 between Avs. 5 and 10, ☎ 987/3–12–02) sells pre-Hispanic musical instruments such as tambours, flutes, ocarinas, rain sticks, and bamboo teponaztles, as well as famous handmade guitars from Paracho, Michoacán. **El Do-**

rado (⊠ Calle 1 between Av. 5 and the ferry pier in the Las Molcas Hotel shopping arcade, ☏ No phone) has replicas of pre-Hispanic Inca and Maya jewelry fashioned in gold-dipped silver.

Xcaret

 ㉓ *10 km (6 mi) south of Playa del Carmen and 72 km (45 mi) south of Cancún.*

Six and a half miles south of Playa del Carmen is where Disney meets the Maya. Xcaret, once a sacred Maya city and port, is a 250-acre ecological theme park on a gorgeous stretch of coastline. You can't escape it since it's the most heavily advertised park on the coast, with its own buses, magazines, and stores. Billed as "nature's sacred paradise," it's expensive, contrived, and crowded. If you're a Walt Disney World fan, you will love Xcaret.

Highlights of the park include an aviary, butterfly pavilion, botanical gardens, riding stables, a tropical aquarium with a sea turtle nursery, an artificially created beach for snorkeling and swimming, a dive center with myriad sporting activities, a replica of a Maya village, a small zoo, some Maya ruins, and an underground river ride where you don life jackets and snorkel through a series of caves. There is even a Dolphinarium, where you can attend a dolphin workshop and even swim with the dolphins for a hefty fee (book early, only 36 people a day are allowed).

Evenings, there are folkloric extravaganzas that begin with candlelit walks through Xcaret's interpretation of a Maya village and end with a performance by the famed *Voladores de Papantla* (Fliers of Papantla) from the indigenous tribes of Veracruz. Plan to spend the day and to spend plenty of money. The $39 (per person) entrance fee just covers getting into the grounds and the exhibits. Other costs: snorkel mask and fins $8, swimming with dolphins for 15 minutes $50, horseback riding per hour $50, hotdog and coke $7, baby strollers per day $15, towel rental $2, locker rental $2, bottle of water (which sells for 75¢ everywhere else) $2.50. You can buy tickets from any travel agency or major hotel along the coast. ☏ 987/1–40–00. ⊠ *Theme park (including show) Mon.–Sat. $39, Sun. (no show) $30.* ⊙ *Apr.–Oct., daily 8:30– 10; Nov.–March, daily 8:30–9.*

Paamul

㉔ *10 km (6 mi) south of Xcaret.*

Beachcombers and snorkelers are fond of Paamul, a crescent-shape lagoon with clear, placid waters sheltered by a coral reef at the lagoon's mouth. Shells, sand dollars, and even glass beads—some from the sunken pirate ship at Akumal—wash onto the sandy parts of the beach. Trailer camps, cabañas, and tent camps are scattered along the shore; a restaurant sells cold beer and fresh fish; and in June and July you can see one of Paamul's chief attractions: sea turtle hatchlings on the beach. You can also take the jungle path to the north, which leads to a lagoon four times the size of the first and even more private.

Dining and Lodging

$$ **Cabañas Paamul.** If you're looking for seclusion and comfort, you'll be thrilled with this small hostelry on a perfect white sand beach. Seven bungalows painted white and peach face the sea. All have two double beds, ceiling fans, and hot-water showers. A large palapa houses the restaurant, and there is a small market just off the main highway at the road to the hotel. The property includes 140 full-service

hook-ups (gas, water, and drainage) for motor homes and tents, and a full-service dive shop. ✉ *Hwy. 307, Km 85, Box 83, Playa del Carmen, Q. Roo 77710,* ☎ *987/6–26–91,* ℻ *987/25–69–13. 10 rooms. Restaurant, dive shop. No credit cards.*

Xpuhá

㉕ *15 km (9 mi) south of Paamul.*

This used to be a tranquil little beach until it was snatched up by developers who immediately made it an all-inclusive "eco-park" where you can snorkel, swim in the cenote, and dive for $60 per person—all of which you used to be able to do for free. Thankfully, not all of the beach has been fenced off. Follow a narrow sandy road off Highway 307 where the sign reads VILLAS XPUHÁ to where you can fish, snorkel, drink beer on the beach, and relax. A cluster of pastel-color hotel buildings have inexpensive rooms available on a first-come, first-served basis, and there is a restaurant that serves simple but delicious meals.

Akumal

㉖ *37 km (23 mi) south of Playa del Carmen, 102 km (63 mi) south of Cancún.*

The Maya name means "Place of the Turtle," and for hundreds of years, this beach has been a nesting ground for turtles. The place first attracted international attention in 1926, when explorers discovered the *Mantanceros,* a Spanish galleon that sank in 1741. In 1958, Pablo Bush Romero, a wealthy businessman who loved diving these pristine waters, created the first resort, which became the headquarters for the club he formed—the Mexican Underwater Explorers Club (CEDAM). Akumal soon became a gathering spot for wealthy underwater adventurers who flew in on private planes and searched the waters for sunken treasures. Hotel rooms are at a premium during the high season, December 15 to April 30—reserve well in advance.

Akumal consists of three distinct areas. **Half Moon Bay** to the north is lined with private homes, hotels, and condominiums. It has some of the prettiest beaches and best snorkeling in the area. **Akumal Proper** consists of a large resort with a market, grocery stores, laundry facilities, and pharmacy. And farther up the highway there is a small Maya community. There's also a nature center next to the dive shop with a staff of ecologists. More condos and homes and an all-inclusive resort are at **Akumal Aventuras** to the south. The biggest attraction, of course, is diving.

For great snorkeling, check out the blessedly undeveloped lagoon of **㉗** **Yalkú,** a couple of miles north of Akumal along an unmarked dirt road. It's a series of lagoons that eventually meet the sea, and it's home to schools of parrot fish in superbly clear water with visibility to 160 ft. It has recently been given "eco-park" status so there is now a toilet, small parking lot, and entrance fee of about $6. Enjoy it while it lasts, because it, too, is scheduled for the kind of development that is exploding up and down the coast.

Dining and Lodging

$$$ ✕ **Lol Ha.** The excellent food served here in a romantic, tropical setting on the beach includes homemade sweet rolls, delicious Yucatecan specialties, fantastically prepared fresh fish, and grilled steaks. The staff is delightful, and at night there is a Yucatán folk dancing show. Next door is a place to grab a quick and delectable pizza. ✉ *Club Akumal Caribe, follow signs off Hwy. 307,* ☎ *987/59–01–12. AE, MC, V.*

$$ ✕ **La Lunita.** Located in Half Moon Bay, this converted one-bedroom condo has a breakfast and dinner menu that changes daily. The cuisine is eclectic and delicious—look for fresh fish served with a lime and cilantro sauce. The atmosphere is friendly and inclusive; you'll be sure to pick up some tips on local events. ✉ *Hacienda de la Tortuga; go through entranceway at Club Akumal Caribe, then turn left (north) at dirt road to Half Moon Bay,* ☎ *987/2–24–21 for condo office. No credit cards.*

$$$$ 🏨 **Club Oasis Akumal.** An all-inclusive luxury hotel managed by the Spanish hotel group Oasis used to be the private preserve of millionaire Pablo Bush Romero, a friend of the late Jacques Cousteau. Today, the beach—protected by an offshore reef—and the pier are used as the starting point for canoeing, snorkeling, diving, fishing, and windsurfing expeditions. The U-shape building, with nautical decor, has handsome mahogany furniture and sunken blue-tile showers between Moorish arches. Apartments have full kitchens and dining areas. All rooms have balconies (you can choose a sea view or a garden view) and air-conditioning or ceiling fans (same price). ✉ *South of Akumal off Hwy. 307,* ☎ *987/5–90–00 to reach guests,* FAX *987/5–90–09 to reach guests. Reservations in the U.S.: Travamérica,* ☎ *770/448–7700,* FAX *770/448–6911. 120 rooms, 4 apartments. Restaurant, 2 bars, 2 pools, tennis court, beach, dive shop, bicycles, shops, recreation room, travel services, car rental. AE, MC, V.*

$$$ 🏨 **Club Akumal Caribe & Villas Maya.** Accommodations at this resort on the edge of a cove overlooking a small harbor range from rustic but comfortable bungalows with red tile roofs and garden views (Villas Maya) to beachfront rooms in a modern three-story hotel building (Club Akumal). Both have cheerful rattan furniture and attractive tile floors, air-conditioning, ceiling fans, and refrigerators. Also available are the more secluded one-, two-, and three-bedroom condominiums called the Villas Flamingo, on Half Moon Bay with their own beach and pools (definite bargains). By the hotel are two dive shops offering PADI certification and cenote or cave diving. An optional meal plan includes breakfast and dinner. ✉ *Hwy. 307, Km 104,* ☎ *987/5–90–12. Reservations:* ✉ *Akutrame, Box 13326, El Paso, TX 79913,* ☎ *800/351–1622; 800/343–1440 in Canada. 21 rooms, 40 bungalows, 4 villas, 5 condos. 3 restaurants, bar, grocery, ice cream parlor, pizzeria, snack bar, pool, beach, 2 dive shops, shops, children's program (ages 5–14). AE, MC, V.*

Outdoor Activities and Sports

Akumal Dive Center rents equipment, runs dive trips, and has certification programs. For dive packages, including accommodations, contact **Akutrame Inc.** (✉ Box 13326, El Paso, TX 79913, ☎ 915/584–3552; 800/351–1622; 800/343–1440 in Canada). Mike Madden's dive shop is at **Aventuras Akumal** (☎ 987/2–28–28).

Chemuyil and Xcacel

28 *7 km (4½ mi) south of Akumal.*

Chemuyil is one of the few remaining beaches along this coast that has not been built up. It's popular with campers, backpackers, and tour bus operators who come for the fine powdery beach, calm turquoise waters, and shady coconut palms. The beach restaurant makes mouthwatering pizza.

Its sister beach, Xcacel, is the scene of an international environmental dispute that has become the symbol of what has gone wrong along the coast. In 1998 the government of Mario Villanueva sold this most important breeding grounds for Atlantic green and loggerhead turtles (both endangered species) to a Spanish conglomerate. The company immediately started plans to build a complex on the beach. Local environmentalists alerted the world to what was happening, and the fight to save the beach began. Enjoy the clear, calm waters and nearby pristine cenote and visit the turtle-farm while you can. In spite of what the hotel company claims, it may soon be gone, along with the turtles.

Xel-Há

㉙ *2 km (about 1 mi) south of Laguna de Xcacel.*

Brought to you by the people who manage Xcaret (☞ *above*), Xel-Há (pronounced shel-hah) is a natural aquarium made from coves, inlets, and lagoons cut out of the limestone shoreline. The name means "where the water is born," and the river here forms natural springs that flow out to meet the saltwater creating the perfect habitat for tropical marine life. There seem to be fewer and fewer fish each year, but there are still enough to impress the novice snorkeler.

Low wooden bridges over the lagoons allow for leisurely walks around the park. Along the trails are spots to rest or swim. Also on the grounds are a huge but overpriced souvenir shop, food stands, and a small museum housing artifacts from pre-Hispanic days. Bring your own towel and snorkel gear—they're not included in the entrance fee. Sunscreen is forbidden (it kills the fish).

Food and drink are outrageously overpriced, but there is an all-inclusive package that is a bargain if you're a big eater. It's best to arrive early in the morning before the tour buses dump literally hundreds of people. ☎ *987/5–40–70 or 987/5–40–71.* ✉ *$15, all inclusive $36.* ☉ *Daily 8–8.*

If you're sick of tour buses, head across the road to the little-visited **⚑ Jaguar House.** A small site composed of squat structures, it was thought to be inhabited from the Late Preclassic until the Late Post-Classic period. The most interesting sights are on the north end of the ruins, where remains of a Maya *sacbe* (road) and mural paintings in the Jaguar House sit near a tranquil, deep cenote. ✉ *$1.50, free Sun. and holidays.* ☉ *Daily 8–5.*

Tankah

㉚ *9½ km (6 mi) south of Xel-Há.*

South of Xel-Há and north of Tulum, Tankah is no longer the secluded beach it once was, but it is still surprisingly tranquil and has great swimming, snorkeling, diving, and fishing.

Dining and Lodging

$$$ ✕▨ **Tankah Inn.** A friendly East Texas family runs this exquisite guest
★ house—the kind of place you never want to leave—located on a sunny strip of beach. The inn is popular with divers, who come in small groups to take advantage of the nearby reefs, top-notch equipment, and full-service, personal attention. The five spacious rooms have their own balconies or terraces, some with incredible ocean views. Carved wooden furniture, tile floors, and large bathrooms add to the feeling of luxury. Upstairs is a large airy restaurant with a terrace that catches the sea breeze. The menu includes Yucatecan cuisine, but the kitchen will prepare whatever will make you happy. Group rates include all three meals. ✉ *Tankah Bay 16, Q. Roo 77780,* ☎ *987/4–2–188,* 🖷 *987/ 1–20–92. Reservations:* ✉ *Box 5, Tulum, Q. Roo,* ☎ *409/636–7721 in the U.S.,* 🖷 *409/636–7111 in the U.S.. 5 rooms. Restaurant. No credit cards.*

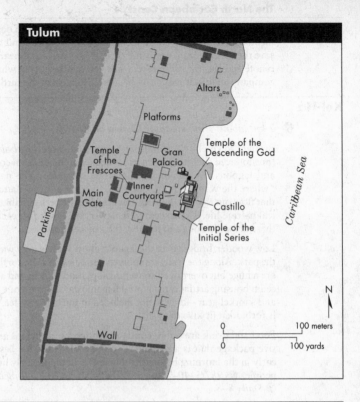

Tulum

🔺 ㉛ *2 km (about 1 mi) south of Tankah, 130 km (80 mi) south of Cancún.*

The spectacle of Tulum's limestone temples against the blue-green Caribbean waters is nothing less than riveting. This is the largest coastal city that the Maya built, and the only Maya city known to have been inhabited when the conquistadors arrived. Unfortunately, you'll share the site with roughly half of the tourist population of Quintana Roo on any given day, even if you arrive early. And no longer can you climb or enter Tulum's most impressive buildings (only three, described below, really merit close inspection), which means that you can see the ruins in two hours. You might, however, want to allow extra time for a swim or a stroll on the beach, where no doubt the ancient Maya beached their canoes.

The first significant structure you'll see is the two-story **Temple of the Frescoes,** to the left of the entrance. The temple's vaulted roof and corbeled (triangular) arch are examples of classic Maya architecture. Faint traces of blue-green frescoes outlined in black on the inner and outer walls refer to ancient Maya beliefs. One scene portrays the rain god seated on a four-legged animal—probably a reference to the Spaniards on their horses.

The largest and most famous building, the **Castillo,** looms at the edge of a 40-ft limestone cliff just past the Temple of the Frescoes. Atop the castle, at the end of a broad stairway, sits a temple with stucco ornamentation on the outside and traces of fine frescoes inside the two chambers. The regal structure overlooks the rest of Tulum and an expanse of dense jungle to the west. Researchers think the Castillo may have functioned as a watchtower to monitor enemy approaches by sea. To

CENOTES, MANGROVES, REEFS

NOWHERE is nature's divine clockwork more delicately calibrated than in the Yucatán's interchange of cenotes (sinkholes), mangroves, and coral reefs. This triad forms a unified ecosystem that supports an astonishing variety of life forms. The reef alone, the second largest in the world, is home to 500 species of fish. Mangroves are the nesting sites of more than 53 bird species, and the tangled mangrove roots provide the perfect breeding ground for marine life. At some of the larger cenotes, hidden in mangroves, you can spot manatees, sea turtles, sharks, and crocodiles. Species of fish, crabs, and other aquatic marvels swim back from the coral reef into the safe harbors of the lagoons and cenotes where the mangroves' nutrient-rich soil feeds their young and their roots offer protection.

The peninsula has no aboveground rivers or lakes. Freshwater flows from a vast subterranean system that rests under a limestone shelf. Cenotes form when this shelf erodes and crumbles, exposing clear pools of water, deep and cavernous like a giant well, or wide and shallow, turning into lagoons where the ground water runs like a river into the ocean. Cenotes are vitally important—they provide the only source of fresh water for plant and animal life in the area, and they constantly replenish the ocean.

Coral reefs themselves still have their mysteries, but scientists have come to understand that a reef is not a single entity, but the end result of a more complex system. A reef's crest is the most exposed area, where the sea batters against the coral, stimulating it to grow. This is the most visibly dramatic part—where huge formations grow and dazzling fish play.

The far less glamorous lagoon-end of the reef has shallow, calm waters where seagrass and other vegetation grow and feed small animals, such as turtles.

The mangroves are wedged between cenotes and reefs. Here, the water is mostly still, and full of trees and sediment. Mangroves are the least glamorous of the three environments, and they seem downright boring—until you look at their key role in the system. To economize their need for water, mangroves close off the pores of their leaves during photosynthesis and turn the leaves away from the noonday sun to reduce evaporation. They grow two sets of roots. Aboveground roots, *pneumatophores,* are filled with spongy tissue and covered with bark dotted with minuscule holes that allow oxygen to travel to the below-ground roots, which act as a support in the soft, muddy soil. Over time they trap nutrient-rich silt and create firmer, drier land. Nutrients gathered in the silt gradually make their way out to the ocean where they fed the coral reef. When rain falls in the mangroves, the water is filtered first through the aboveground roots and then the gathered soil. Pollutants, which would make their way into the cenotes and coral reef, are filtered out. This system of dense roots also holds dead leaves and other organic matter underwater so that carbon dioxide, a greenhouse gas, is not released into the atmosphere. The mangroves, in effect, are the kidneys of the whole ecosystem. This relationship between cenotes, mangroves, and coral reefs is only beginning to be understood. It is one aspect of the local ecology that makes the Yucatán so unique, and so much in need of protection.

— Shelagh McNally

the left of the Castillo is the **Temple of the Descending God**—so called for the carving of a winged god plummeting to earth over the doorway.

At the old turnoff to the ruins, called the *crucero* (it no longer provides access), there are a gas station and some hotels. A few yards south is the new entrance to the ruins clearly marked with overhead signs. Still farther south is the turnoff for the Boca Paila Peninsula and Sian Ka'an preserve. Most of the local beaches and restaurants are along this coastal route. Back on the highway about 4 km (2½ mi) south of the ruins is the present-day village of Tulum. As Tulum's importance as a commercial center increases, markets, restaurants, shops, services, and auto-repair shops continue to spring up along the road. There are some remarkably fine restaurants.

Dining and Lodging

$$$ ✕🏨 **Cabañas Ana y José.** Several two-story buildings face the beach at this small, well-loved hotel south of the ruins. All rooms have fans, tile floors, and hot-water showers. Those on the second floor are cooler, thanks to sea breezes. Unfortunately, the generator from the hotel next door is noisy until late at night. The restaurant, complete with an aviary full of parrots and parakeets, serves unique Mexican cuisine in a sandy palapa. Mountain bikes are available for rent, and tours to the Sian Ka'an Biosphere Reserve leave from here. Staff members can arrange diving trips. ✉ *Dirt road off Hwy. 307 between ruins entrance and Tulum pueblo, 4 mi south of ruins; reservations c/o Ms. Judith Ivarra,* ✉ *9501-C Siempre Viva Rd., No. 8-135, San Diego, CA 92173-3528,* ☎ *98/80–60–22,* 𝔽𝔸𝕏 *98/80–60–21. 16 rooms. Restaurant. MC, V.*

$$ 🏨 **Cabañas Tulum.** This property, idyllically set in a coconut grove on the beach beside Cabañas Ana y José (*above*), is 7 km (4½ mi) down the road to Sian Ka'an. Beachfront palapa bungalows with private bathrooms, and an indoor-outdoor restaurant, bar, and game room, make a good package. The mattresses are on the thin side, so you may be more comfortable sleeping in a hammock. Breakfast is the best meal of the day. The dinner menu is reliable, if not inspired. ✉ *Box 10, Tulum, Q. Roo 77780,* ☎ *98/25–82–95. 18 cabañas. Restaurant, bar, beach, recreation room. No credit cards.*

Cobá

 ⳟ 😉 *49 km (30½ mi) northwest of Tulum and 167 km (104 mi) southwest of Cancún.*

Cobá—the Maya word means "water stirred by the wind"—flourished from AD 800 to 1100, with a population of as many as 55,000 inhabitants. Now, the jungle having reclaimed many of its buildings, Cobá stands in a solitude pierced by the occasional shriek of a spider monkey or the call of a bird. Archaeologists estimate that some 6,500 structures are present in the area, but only 5% have been uncovered, and it will take decades before the work is completed. Discovered by Teobert Maler in 1891, Cobá was subsequently explored in 1926 by the Carnegie Institute but not excavated until 1972. At present there is no restoration work under way.

Sited on five lakes between coastal watchtowers and inland cities, Cobá exercised economic control over the region through a network of at least 16 *sacbeob* (white stone roads), one of which measures 100 km (62 mi), the longest in the Maya world. The city once covered 70 square km (27 square mi), which makes it a noteworthy sister nation to Tikal in northern Guatemala, to which it had close cultural and commercial ties. It's noted for its massive, soaring temple-pyramids, one of which stands 138 ft tall, the largest and highest in northern Yucatán.

Because it is easy to get lost here, stay on the main road and don't be tempted by the narrow paths leading into the jungle—unless you have a qualified guide with you.

The first major grouping, off a path to your right as you enter the ruins, is the **Cobá Group,** whose pyramids are built around a sunken patio. At the near end of the group, facing a large plaza, you'll see the 79-ft-high Iglesia (church), where some Indians still place offerings and light candles in hopes of improving their harvests. Farther along the main path to your left is the **Chumuc Mul Group,** little of which has been excavated. The principal pyramid here is covered with the stucco remains of vibrantly painted motifs (*chumuc mul* means "stucco pyramid"). A kilometer (½ mile) past the Chumuc Mul Group is the **Nohoch Mul Group** (Large Hill Group), the highlight of which is the pyramid of the same name. It is the tallest at Cobá, its uppermost chamber evocatively perched at treetop height. The pyramid, which has 120 steps—equivalent to 12 stories—shares a plaza with Temple 10. The Descending God (also seen at Tulum) is depicted on a facade of the temple atop Nohoch Mul, from which the view is excellent. The unrestored **Crossroad Pyramid** opposite Nohoch Mul was the meeting point for three sacbeob.

Beyond the Nohoch Mul Group is the **Castillo.** Its nine chambers are reached by a stairway. To the south are the remains of a ball court, including the stone ring through which the ball was hurled. From the main route follow the sign to **Las Pinturas Group,** named for the still discernible polychromatic friezes on the inner and outer walls of its large, patioed pyramid. Take the minor path for 1 km (½ mi) to the **Macanxoc Group,** not far from the lake of the same name. The main pyramid at Macanxoc is accessible by a stairway. Many of the stelae here are intricately carved with Maya dates (their time-keeping methods were incomparable) and other symbols of the history of Cobá.

Cobá is a 35-minute drive northwest of Tulum, down a well-marked and well-paved road that leads straight through the jungle. You can comfortably see Cobá in a half day. Spending the night is highly advised as you'll be able to visit the ruins in solitude when they open at 8 AM. Even on a day trip, consider taking time out for lunch to escape from the intense heat and mosquito-thick humidity of the ruins. Buses depart Cobá for Playa del Carmen and Valladolid twice daily. Check with your hotel and clerk at the ruins for times, which may not be exact. ✆ *$1.75, free Sun. and holidays.* ☉ *Daily 8–5.*

Dining and Lodging

$$ ✕▦ **Villa Arqueológica Cobá.** A 10-minute walk from the ruins, this Club Med property overlooks one of the region's vast lakes, where turtles swim to the hotel dock for a breakfast of bread and rolls. Tastefully done in white stucco and red paint, the hotel has a clean, airy feel. The air-conditioned rooms themselves are quite small. There is a decent library with a good collection of books on the Maya, along with a large-screen TV (with VCR) and a pool table. The restaurant food, alas, is mediocre but very expensive, and it is not included in the room rates. Equally disappointing, the staff is exceptionally unhelpful and unfriendly. Book early as the hotel fills up quickly with tour groups. *Reservations: ☎ 5/254–7077, ℻ 5/255–3164. 40 rooms, 3 suites. Restaurant, bar, pool, tennis court, shops. AE, MC, V.*

$ ✕▦ **El Bocadito.** Though not as lavish as the Villa Arqueológica (☞ *above*), El Bocadito is much more congenial. It's a satisfactory budget alternative, only a five-minute walk from the ruins. The simple, tiled rooms have two double beds, ceiling fan, wash basin separate from the toilet, and cold-water showers. Rooms here fill up quickly also—if you're thinking of spending the night, stop here before visiting the ruins. The restaurant next door is decent and clean and serves up delicious, simple meals. It's quite popular with tour groups. The camaraderie of the clientele and staff make up for the lack of luxury. ⊠ *On road to ruins,* ☎ *987/4–20–87. 10 rooms. AE, V.*

Sian Ka'an and the Boca Paila Peninsula

③ *15 km (9½ mi) south of Tulum to Boca Paila turnoff, located within Sian Ka'an; 137 km (85 mi) south of Cancún.*

Sian Ka'an ("where the sky is born") was first settled by the Maya in the 5th century AD. In 1986 the Mexican Government established the 1.3-million-acre **Sian Ka'an Biosphere Reserve** as an internationally protected area. The next year, it was named a World Heritage Site by the United Nations Educational, Scientific, and Cultural Organization (UNESCO). In 1996 the reserve was extended by 200,000 acres.

The reserve constitutes 10% of the land in Quintana Roo and covers 100 km (62 mi) of coast. Freshwater and coastal lagoons, mangrove swamps, watery cays, savannas, tropical forests, a barrier reef, hundreds of species of local and migratory birds, fish, other animals and plants, and fewer than 1,000 local residents (primarily Maya) share this area. Many species of the once-flourishing wildlife have fallen into the endangered category, but the waters here still teem with rooster fish, bonefish, mojarra, snapper, shad, permit, sea bass, and crocodiles. Fishing the flats for the wily bonefish and fly-fishing are especially popular, and the peninsula's few lodges run deep-sea fishing trips. The beaches are wide and white, and although many of the palms have succumbed to the yellowing palm disease imported from Florida, the beautiful vegetation is growing back.

It's recommended that you see the reserve via guided tour, which you can arrange through the private, nonprofit **Xlapak** organization (⊠ Plaza América, Av. Cobá 5, Suites 48–50, Cancún, Q. Roo 77500, ☎ 98/84–95–83, ℻ 98/87–30–80). You'll get an excellent, informed tour. Highlights include visiting the Maya ruins of **Xlapak** and jumping off the boat into one of the channels to float downstream in the current. The three-hour tour leaves from Cabañas Ana y José (☞ Dining and Lodging *in* Tulum, *above*), Monday to Thursday and Saturday mornings and includes a bilingual guide and binoculars.

If you are exploring on your own, you will be confined to swimming, snorkeling, and camping on the beaches, as there are no trails into the surrounding jungle. Deserted fishing lodges, palapas, and copra farms lend an eerie feel to the area. The narrow, extremely rough dirt road down the peninsula is filled with monstrous potholes, and during the rainy season it is completely impassable. Most fishing lodges along the way close for the rainy season in August and September, and accommodations are hard to come by. The road ends at **Punta Allen,** a fishing village whose main catch is spiny lobster, which was becoming scarce until ecologists taught the local fishing cooperative how to build and lay special traps to conserve the species. There are several small guest houses. If you haven't booked ahead, start out early in the morning so you can get back to civilization before dark.

Lodging

$$$$ 🏠 **Caphé-Ha.** Built as a private home by an American architect, this ★ small guest house—between a lagoon and the ocean—is a perfect place to stay if you're interested in bonefishing or bird-watching. A two-bedroom house with a kitchen, bath, and living room, and a two-unit bungalow (with shared baths) are your choices. Neither has fans or electricity, but all the windows have screens and catch the ocean breeze.

A caretaker-chef from Mérida cooks meals that are served in the solar-powered community palapa. Room rates include breakfast and dinner; advance reservations must be accompanied by a 50% deposit, and a three-day or longer stay is required in high season. ⊠ *30 km (19 mi) south of Tulum, on road to Sian Ka'an, 5 km (3 mi) past bridge at Boca Paila and around next rocky point,* FAX *610/912–9392 in the U.S. 1 villa, 1 bungalow. Restaurant, fishing. No credit cards.*

$$$$ 🏨 **Casa Blanca Lodge.** Punta Pájaros, to which this remote fishing re-
★ sort provides unique access, is reputed to be one of the best places in the world for light-tackle saltwater fishing. The American-managed, all-inclusive lodge—just 100 ft from the ocean—is set on a rocky outcrop covered with palm trees. Bonefish swarm in the mangrove swamps, flats, and shallow waters. The lodge's nine large, modern guest rooms, painted white with turquoise trim, and featuring slatted windows and tile and mahogany bathrooms, provide a pleasant tropical respite at dusk. An open-air thatched bar and a large living and dining area welcome anglers with drinks, fresh fish dishes, fruit, and vegetables at the start and end of the day. Rates are highest from March through June, lowest from January through March; during the high season Saturday to Saturday (weeklong) stays are required. Rates include a charter flight from Cancún to the lodge, all meals, a boat, and a guide. A 50% prepayment is required in high season. ⊠ *Reservations: Frontiers, Box 959, Wexford, PA 15090,* ☎ *412/935–1577 or 800/245–1950,* FAX *412/935–5388. 10 rooms. Restaurant, bar, fishing. MC, V.*

The North Caribbean Coast A to Z

Arriving and Departing

BY BUS

There is first-class and deluxe service on the **ADO** line (⊠ Av. Juárez at Av. 5, ☎ 987/3–01–09) between Playa del Carmen and Cancún, Valladolid, Chichén Itzá, Chetumal, Tulum, Xel-Há, Mexico City, and Mérida daily. **Mayab** (⊠ Av. Juárez, ☎ No phone) runs second-class buses to the above destinations, and deluxe express buses to Chetumal. **Autotransportes Oriente** (⊠ Av. Juárez, ☎ No phone) has express service from Playa to Mérida eight times daily, and one bus daily to Cobá. **TRP**(⊠ Av. Juárez at Av. 5, ☎ No phone) offers first–class service about every 15 minutes from Playa to Cancún.

BY FERRY

Ferries and jet foils—which can be picked up at the dock—run between Playa del Carmen and Cozumel about every hour (more frequently in the early morning and evening). **Water Jet Service** (⊠ Near the ferry dock, ☎ 987/21–08) makes the 35- to 40-minute trip for about $5.

Getting Around

BY CAR

The entire coast, from Punta Sam near Cancún to the main border crossing to Belize at Chetumal, is traversable on Highway 307. This straight road is entirely paved and has been widened into four lanes south to Tulum. Work has begun on the remaining highway south to Chetumal. Drive with caution on this road, as many locals remembering the rutted roads of yesterday like to speed on the new highway. Gas stations are increasing in number, but it's still a good idea to fill up your tank whenever you can. There are gas stations in Cancún, Puerto Morelos, Playa del Carmen, Tulum, Felipe Carrillo Puerto, and Chetumal.

BY PLANE

The airstrip in **Playa del Carmen** is near the Continental Plaza Hotel, and there is occasional shuttle service to Cozumel. A small airline called **Aero Saab** (✉ Playa del Carmen airstrip, ☎ 987/3–05–01) has daily scheduled trips to Tulum, Uxmal, and Chichén Itzá if enough passengers turn up to fill the four- and five-seat Cessnas. The company also flies to Cozumel, Mérida, Belize, and Guatemala.

BY TAXI

You can hire a taxi in Cancún to go as far as Playa del Carmen, Tulum, or Akumal, but the price is steep unless you have many passengers. Fares run about $55 or more to Playa alone; between Playa and Tulum or Akumal, expect to pay at least $25. It's much cheaper from Playa to Cancún—about $30. Negotiate before you hop into the cab. Taxis wait eagerly for passengers by the bus station in Playa, and there's a taxi stand at the entrance to Akumal.

Contacts and Resources

CAR RENTAL

In **Playa del Carmen,** car rental agencies proliferate around the ferry pier and Avenida Juárez. Agencies include **Budget** (✉ Hotel Continental Plaza Playacar, ☎ 987/3–01–00); **Hertz** (✉ White Sands Travel, ☎ 987/3–11–30 or 987/3–07–03; ✉ Hotel Continental Plaza Playacar, ☎ 987/3–00–33); and **National** (✉ Hotel Molcas, ☎ 987/3–03–60 or 987/3–08–83). If you want air-conditioning, reserve your car at least a day in advance.

EMERGENCIES

Playa del Carmen. Police (✉ Av. Juárez, between Avs. 15a and 20a, next to post office, ☎ 987/3–02–91). **Cruz Roja** (Red Cross; ✉ Av. Juárez at Av. 25, ☎ 987/3–12–33).

GUIDED TOURS

Although some guided tours are available in this area, the roads are quite good for the most part, so renting a car is an efficient and enjoyable alternative: most of the sights you'll see along this stretch are natural, and you can hire a guide at the ruins sites.

Maya Ruins. Mayaland Gray Line Tours (✉ Hotel America, Av. Tulum at Calle Brisa, Cancún, ☎ 98/87–24–50; 800/235–4079 in the U.S.đ, FAX 98/87–24–38; ✉ Las Molcas Hotel, Calle 1 Sur between Av. 5 and the ferry pier, Playa del Carmen, ☎ 987/3–11–06; 800/235–4079 in the U.S.) goes to Chichén Itzá from hotels around Punta Bete, Playa del Carmen, and Akumal. In Playa del Carmen, **Aero Fénico** Airlines (☎ 987/3–06–36) has day and half-day tours to Uxmal, Chichén Itzá, Palenque, Mérida, and Tikal in Guatemala. Entrance fees, tour guide, and lunch are included.

MEDICAL CLINICS

Playa del Carmen: Centro de Salud (✉ Av. Juárez at Av. 15a, ☎ 987/2–12–30 ext. 147) or **Dr. Victor Macias** (✉ Calle 2 Norte and Av. 35, ☎ 987/3–04–93), a bilingual physician.

TRAVEL AGENCIES

There are more major travel agencies and tour operators up and down the coast than before, and first-class hotels in Playa del Carmen, Puerto Aventuras, and Akumal usually have their own in-house travel services.

VACATION RENTALS

Puerto Morelos. Vicki Sharp (☎ 987/1–01–12), a local real-estate agent and longtime resident of Puerto Morelos, can arrange long-term rentals of houses and apartments.

VISITOR INFORMATION

In **Playa del Carmen** (✉ Av. 5, 1 block from beach, ☎ No phone), you might have to cool your heels for a while until someone actually shows up to run the information booth, which is supposedly open 8–1 and 5–8.

THE STATE OF YUCATÁN

Updated by
Jane Onstott

Almost five centuries after the conquest, Yucatán state remains one of the last great strongholds of Mexico's indigenous population. To this day, in fact, many Maya do not even speak Spanish, primarily because of the peninsula's geographic and, hence, cultural isolation from the rest of the country.

Physically, too, Yucatán differs from the rest of the country. Its geography and wildlife have more in common with Florida and Cuba—with which it was probably once connected—than with the central Mexican plateau and mountains. A mostly flat limestone slab possessing almost no bodies of water, it is rife with underground cenotes, caves with stalactites, small hills, and intense jungle.

The celebrated Maya ruins at Chichén Itzá and Uxmal are the stars of Yucatán, but small towns such as Valladolid have their own unpretentious charm. Mérida, the capital, has excellent restaurants and markets and a unique mix of Maya, Spanish, and French architectural styles.

Mérida

There is a marvelous eccentricity about Mérida. Fully urban, with maddeningly slow-moving traffic, it has a self-sufficient, self-contented air that would suggest a small town, more than a state capital of some 1.5 million inhabitants. Gaily pretentious turn-of-the-century buildings have an Iberian-Moorish flair for the ornate, but most of the architecture is low-lying, and although the city sprawls, it is not imposing. Grandiose colonial facades adorned with iron grillwork, carved wooden doors, and archways conceal marble tiles and lush gardens that hark back to the city's heyday as the wealthiest capital in Mexico.

Mérida is a city of subtle contrasts, from its opulent facades to its residents, very European yet very Maya. The Indian presence is unmistakable: people are short and dark-skinned, with sculpted bones and almond-shaped eyes. Women pad about in *huipiles* (hand-embroidered, sack-like white dresses), and craftsmen and vendors from outlying villages come to town in their huaraches.

Mérida is the cultural and intellectual center of the peninsula, with museums, schools, and attractions that provide great insight into the history and character of Yucatán. Consider making it one of the first stops in your travels, and make sure you come on a Sunday, when traffic is light, the city seems to revert to a more gracious era, and admission to archaeological sites is free.

㉞ The **zócalo** (main square), which Méridanos also call by its traditional names—the **Plaza Principal** and **Plaza de la Independencia**—was laid out in 1542 on the ruins of T'hó, the Maya city demolished to make way for Mérida. It is still the focal point around which the most important public buildings cluster. The plaza is bordered east and west by Calles 60 and 62, north and south by Calles 61 and 63.

㉟ Francisco Montejo—father and son—conquered the peninsula and founded Mérida in 1542. They built the stately **Casa de Montejo** (⊠ Calle 63 on the south side of the zócalo) 10 years later. The palace remained with the family until the late 1970s, when it was restored and converted into a bank. Built in the French style during Mérida's heyday as the world's henequen capital, it now represents the city's finest—

State of Yucatán

Mérida

and oldest—example of elaborately decorated, colonial plateresque architecture. Step into the building weekdays between 9 and 5 for a glimpse of the lushly foliated inner patio.

36 The west side of the main square is occupied by the 18th-century **Palacio Municipal**—the city hall—which is painted yellow and trimmed with white arcades, balustrades, and the national coat of arms. ⊠ *Calle 62 between Calles 61 and 63.* ☉ *Weekdays 8–7, Sat. 8–2.*

37 On the northeast corner of the zócalo, the **Palacio del Gobierno** (State Government Palace) was built in 1885 on the site of the Casa Real (Royal House). The upper floor of the palace contains Fernando Castro Pacheco's vivid murals of the bloody history of the conquest of Yucatán, painted in 1978. ⊠ *Calle 61 between Calles 60 and 62.* ☉ *Daily 8 AM–11 PM.*

38 The second-oldest **catedral** on the North American mainland (and oldest in Mexico) stands catercorner from the Palacio del Gobierno. Begun in 1561, it took several hundred Maya laborers, working with stones from the pyramids of the ravaged Maya city, 36 years to complete. Its somber Renaissance-style facade is stark and unadorned. Inside, the black **Cristo de las Ampollas** (Christ of the Blisters), on a side altar to the left of the main one, is a replica of the original, which was destroyed during the Revolution. According to legend, the Christ figure burned all night. It appeared the next morning covered only with blisters—hence its name.

39 **Museo de Arte Contemporáneo** (Museum of Contemporary Art). Originally designed as an art school but used until recently as a convent, this enormous two-story building is full of light, just perfect for an art museum. The excellent exhibits of international artists in the second-floor galleries make up for the half-hearted reproductions of some of the world's masterpieces in the World History of Art room below. There's also a bookstore (closed Sunday). ⊠ *Pasaje de la Revolución 1907, between Calles 58 and 60 on the main plaza,* ☎ *99/28–32–58 or 99/28–32–36.* ⊡ *$2, free Sun.* ⊘ *Wed.–Mon. 10–5:30.*

㊵ Two picturesque 19th-century edifices house the main post office and telegraph buildings. Behind them sprawls the pungent, labyrinthine **Mercado Municipal,** filled with local color, where almost every patch of ground is occupied by Indian women selling chilies, herbs, fruit, and essential plasticware. On the second floor of the main building is the **Bazar de Artesanías Municipales,** the principal handicrafts market, where you can buy jewelry (gold or gold-dipped filigree earrings), pottery, embroidered clothes, hammocks, and straw bags. Only about one-fifth of the stalls are open on Sunday. ⊠ *Calle 65 between Calles 56 and 58.* ⊘ *Weekdays 8–7, Sat. 8–5, Sun. 8–1.*

㊶ Only half a block north of the main plaza is the cozy **Parque Hidalgo,** or Cepeda Peraza, as it is officially known. Renovated mansions-turned-hotels and sidewalk cafés stand at two corners of the park, which comes alive at night with marimba bands and street vendors. ⊠ *Calles 60 and 59.*

㊷ The **Iglesia de Jesús,** facing Parque Hidalgo on the north side, is one of Mérida's oldest buildings and the first Jesuit church in the Yucatán. The church was built in 1618 of limestone from a Maya temple that had previously stood on the site. The former convent rooms in the rear of the building now host a pair of small art museums—the **Juan Gamboa Guzmán Painting Museum** and the adjoining **Gottdeiner Museum.** You might pass on the former, which contains oil paintings of past governors and other public figures but rarely identifies them. The latter, on the other hand, displays striking bronze sculptures of the Yucatán's indigenous people by its most celebrated 20th-century sculptor, Enrique Gottdeiner. The museums' hours are sporadic, and they often do not keep to their published schedule. ⊠ *Calle 59 between Calles 60 and 58,* ☎ *99/24–79–12.* ⊡ *Free.* ⊘ *Tues.–Sun. 8–8.*

㊸ The Italianate **Teatro Peón Contreras,** north of Parque Hidalgo on Calle 60, was designed in 1908 along the lines of the grand European turn-of-the-century theaters and opera houses. Today, in addition to performing arts, the theater also houses temporary art exhibits and the main **Centro de Información Turistica** (☎ 99/24–91–22), to the right of the lobby. A café spills out to a patio from inside the theater.

㊹ The arabesque **Universidad Autonoma de Yucatán** plays a major role in the city's cultural and intellectual life. The folkloric ballet performs on the patio of the main building Fridays at 9 PM. Photographic and other art or cultural exhibits are often hosted in its various salons, and the library has an interesting collection of regional heroes painted in frescoes on the walls. The 1711 building itself has crownlike Moorish-style upper reaches and uncloistered archways. ⊠ *Calle 60 between Calles 57 and 59,* ☎ *99/24–80–00.*

㊺ The rather plain **Parque de Santa Lucía,** draws crowds to the Thursday-night serenades of local musicians and folk dancers. The small 1575 church opposite the park was built as a place of worship for the African and Caribbean slaves who lived here. The churchyard functioned as the cemetery until 1821. ⊠ *Calle 60 at Calle 55.*

㊻ North of downtown, the 10-block-long street known as the **Paseo de Montejo** exemplifies the Parisian airs the city took on in the late 19th century, when wealthy plantation owners built opulent, impressive mansions. The broad boulevard, lined with tamarinds and laurels, is sometimes wistfully referred to as Mérida's Champs Elysées. Although the once-stunning mansions fell into disrepair a few years ago, their stateliness is being restored by a citywide beautification program. This part of town is where posh new hotels are opening.

④ The most compelling of the Paseo de Montejo mansions, the pale peach **Palacio Cantón** presently houses the **Museum of Anthropology and History**, dedicated to Maya culture and history. Although it's not that impressive compared with its counterparts in other Mexican cities, it serves as an opener to visiting nearby archaeological sites. Bilingual legends accompany the displays, but lengthier explanations are in Spanish only. Private guides are available for hire, and there's a bookstore on site. ⊠ *Calle 43 at Paseo de Montejo,* ☎ *99/23–05–57.* 🎫 *$2, free Sun.* 🕐 *Museum and bookstore Tues.–Sat. 8–8, Sun. 8–2; bookstore closed Sun.*

④ Several blocks east of the main plaza is the **Museo de Arte Popular** (Handicraft Museum), housed in a fine old mansion. The ground floor is devoted to Yucatecan arts and crafts, and the second floor focuses on the popular arts of the rest of Mexico. ⊠ *441 Calle 59, at Calle 50,* ☎ *No phone.* 🎫 *Free.* 🕐 *Tues.–Sat. 9–8, Sun. 8–2.*

④ At the south end of the city, about nine blocks below the square, stands the 1748 **Ermita de Santa Isabel,** part of a Jesuit monastery also known as the Hermitage of the Good Trip. A resting place in colonial days for travelers heading to Campeche, the restored chapel is an enchanting spot to visit at sunset. Next door is a huge garden with a waterfall and footpaths bordered with bricks and colored stones. The church hours are irregular, but the garden is almost always open during the day. ⊠ *Calles 66 and 77.*

🧒 **El Centenario Zoological Park,** Mérida's great children's attraction, is a large, somewhat tacky amusement complex consisting of playgrounds, rides (including ponies and a small train), a roller-skating rink, snack bars, and cages with more than 300 marvelous native monkeys, birds, reptiles, and other animals. There are also pleasant wooded paths, picnic areas, and a small lake where you can rent rowboats. On Sunday mornings special events, such as puppet shows, are hosted for kids. ⊠ *Av. Itzaes between Calles 59 and 65 (entrances on Calles 59 and 65).* 🎫 *Free.* 🕐 *Daily 9–6.*

Dining and Lodging

$$ ✕ **Alberto's Continental Patio.** The setting—an early 18th-century
★ building adorned with mosaic floors from Cuba—is romantic; an inner patio surrounded by rubber trees is ideal for starlit dining. Most of the guests are tourists, but that need not detract from the surroundings or the excellent cuisine. If you order Lebanese food, your plate will be heaped with servings of shish kebab, fried kibbe, cabbage rolls, hummus, eggplant, and tabbouleh. Black bean soup, enchiladas, fried bananas, and caramel custard make up the Mexican dinner. There is a Yucatecan dinner, as well as à la carte appetizers and entrées. ⊠ *Calle 64, No. 482, at Calle 57,* ☎ *99/28–53–67. AE, MC, V.*

$$ ✕ **Amaro.** Amaro is no longer strictly vegetarian, but its menu is heavy on health drinks, made mostly with local vegetables, fruit, and herbs. Recommended dishes include eggplant curry and soup made with *chaya,* a local vegetable that looks like spinach; you can also order mashed potatoes, apple salad, or guacamole à la carte. The terrace of this old historic home, alight with candles at night, provides a quiet dining atmosphere beneath a large tree. ⊠ *Calle 59, No. 507, between Calles 60 and 62,* ☎ *99/28–24–51. No credit cards. Closed Sun.*

$$ ✕ **La Casona.** This pretty mansion turned restaurant near Parque de Santa Ana has an inner patio, arcade, and swirling ceiling fans. Its bar features live, romantic music nightly. The accent is Yucatecan, with poc chuc, pollo píbil, and *huachinango* (red snapper baked in a banana leaf) among the recommended dishes. There are Italian dishes as well, many of which are made with homemade pasta. ⊠ *434 Calle 60, at Calle 39,* ☎ *99/23–83–48 or 99/23–99–96. AE, MC, V. Closed Sun.*

$$ ✕ **Los Almendros.** A Mérida classic, this restaurant credits itself with the invention of poc chuc—although others dispute the claim. The restaurant provides a good introduction to a variety of Yucatecan cuisine, including papadzules and *pollo ticuleño* (boneless, breaded chicken in tomato sauce filled with fried beans, peas, red peppers, ham, and cheese). Plan to come for live music daily between 2 and 5 PM, or the regional show Fridays at 8 PM. ⊠ *Calle 50-A, No. 493, between Calles 57 and 59,* ☎ *99/23–81–35 or 99/28–54–59. AE, MC, V.*

$$ ✕ **Pórtico del Peregrino.** A red-tile floor, iron grillwork, and lots of plants
★ set the tone in both the indoor and outdoor patio sections of this old colonial home. The menu features lime soup, baked eggplant with chicken, mole enchiladas, and seafood stew. For dessert, try coconut ice cream with Kahlúa. There is a no-smoking room. ⊠ *Calle 57, No. 501, between Calles 60 and 62,* ☎ *99/28–61–63. MC, V.*

$ ✕ **Cafetería Pop.** Across the street from the university and a favorite with students and the intelligencia, this smoke-filled joint always seems to be crowded. The busiest time is 8 AM–noon, but you can order breakfast all day (if you ask nicely). They serve sandwiches, hamburgers, spaghetti, chicken, fish, beef, and tacos. Beer, sangria, and wine are served only with food orders. ⊠ *Calle 57, No. 501, between Calles 60 and 62,* ☎ *99/28–61–63. No credit cards.*

$ ✕ **Dante's.** Lovers and families crowd this modern, bustling coffee house on the second floor of one of Mérida's largest book shops. The house specialty is crepes: you'll find 18 varieties with either sweet or savory fillings. Along with cappuccino and specialty coffees, you can order beer and wine. ⊠ *Prolongación Paseo de Montejo 138-B, near Holiday Inn and Fiesta Americana,* ☎ *99/27–74–41. No credit cards.*

$ ✕ **Nicte-Ha.** Under an arcade on the main square, this modest eatery is a fine place for people-watching. A good selection of Yucatecan fare includes *panuchos,* fried tortillas with a slender bean filling and a topping of shredded cabbage and hard cheese. Also recommended is the daily lunch special of soup, rice, and a main dish for about $3. ⊠ *Calle 61, No. 500, at Calle 60,* ☎ *99/23–07–84. No credit cards.*

$$$$ ✕🏨 **Hacienda Katanchel.** This rambling 17th-century henequen ha-
★ cienda on 650 acres was brought back to life by Anibal Gonzalez and his wife, Monica Hernandez. The guest rooms are set in small pavilions built along a garden walkway. Floors are made of local hardwoods, the roofs of red Marseille tile, and there are overhead fans, hammocks, and double beds that look like pieces of modern sculpture. The former Casa de Máquina (Machine Shop) is now a contemporary Mexican restaurant serving such dishes as puff pastry stuffed with *huitlacoche* (corn fungus) and tarragon sauce, or cold avocado cream soup with prawns and goat cheese. ⊠ *25 km (15½ mi) east of Mérida on Hwy. 180 (toward Izamal),* ☎ *99/23–40–20 or 01–800/849–3773; 888/882–9470 in the U.S.,* 🖷 *99/23–40–00. 30 suites. Restaurant, bar, fans, pool, mineral baths. Reservations essential. AE, MC, V.*

$$$$ 🏨 **Fiesta Americana Mérida.** This posh hotel is a favorite of locals who
★ come to see and be seen, and it caters to business travelers and conventions. Its lovely pink facade mirrors the architecture of Paseo de Montejo mansions on an epic scale. This classic grandeur carries into the spacious upper lobby with its massive columns, gleaming marble and brass work, and its stained-glass atrium. Floral prints, painted-wood furnishings, and slightly larger-than-life proportions maintain the theme of bygone elegance in rooms, which have plenty of modern con-

veniences, including modem ports, three phones, and remote-control TVs concealed in armoires. There are 12 concierges, and guests on the fifth floor can access the Fiesta Room for morning breakfast and afternoon appetizers. ⊠ *Av. Colón, No. 451, at Paseo Montejo,* ☎ 99/20–21–94; 800/343–7821 in U.S., ℻ 99/20–21–98. *350 rooms and suites. 2 restaurants, 2 bars, no-smoking rooms, health club, shops, travel services, car rental, free parking. AE, DC, MC, V.*

$$$–$$$$ 🏨 **Hyatt Regency Mérida.** The first of the deluxe hotels to open on Paseo de Montejo (in 1994), the 18-story Hyatt brought a new level of service to Mérida. Rooms are regally decorated with russet-hue bed quilts and rugs set off by modern blond-wood furniture and cream-color walls. Satellite TVs and minibars have been artfully integrated into each unit. Amenities not commonly found in Mérida include bathtubs and hair dryers, as well as a state-of-the-art business center and the city's only tapas bar. ⊠ *Av. Colón, No. 344, at Calle 60,* ☎ 99/42–02–02 or 99/42–12–34; 800/233–1234 in the U.S., ℻ 99/25–70–02. *296 rooms, 4 suites. 2 restaurants, 2 bars, no-smoking rooms, pool, tennis court, exercise room, travel services, car rental, free parking. AE, DC, MC, V.*

$$$ 🏨 **Casa del Balam.** This very pleasant hotel on well-heeled Calle 60
★ has a lovely, peaceful courtyard ornamented with a fountain, arcades, ironwork, and a black-and-white tile floor; cocktails and light meals are served in the recently remodeled restaurant. Rooms are capacious and well maintained and fitted with mosaic-tiled or painted sinks, wrought-iron accessories, and refrigerator/minibars. Guests have access to golf and tennis at a country club 15 minutes from the city center. ⊠ *Calle 60, No. 488, Box 988,* ☎ 99/24–88–44 or 99/24–21–50; 800/624–8451 in the U.S., ℻ 99/24–50–11. *51 rooms, 3 suites. Restaurant, 2 bars, lobby lounge, no-smoking rooms, pool, baby-sitting, travel services, car rental, free parking. AE, DC, MC, V.*

$$ 🏨 **Caribe.** An old Mérida standard, the Caribe is done in typical colonial style, including tile floors, dark-wood furniture, and a large inner courtyard with arcades. It is on Parque Hidalgo, but most of its rooms (38 of them with air-conditioning) overlook the inner courtyard, as do the open balconies, which are lined with comfortable chairs. The unshaded rooftop sundeck and swimming pool have a great view of the cathedral. The hotel's outdoor café, El Mesón, is one of the better restaurants in Parque Hidalgo. ⊠ *Calle 59, No. 500,* ☎ 99/24–90–22; 800/826–6842 in the U.S., ℻ 99/24–87–33. *56 rooms. Restaurant, café, pool, travel services, free parking. AE, DC, MC, V.*

$$ 🏨 **Casa Mexilio.** This choice B&B, run by partners Jorge and Roger, has wonderfully eclectic decor. There are Middle Eastern wall hangings, French tapestries, colorful tile floors, tile sinks, and folk-art furniture. Casa Mexilio lacks the amenities of the larger hotels (only five rooms have air-conditioning), but if you enjoy a casual ambience and the feeling of staying in a private home, you'll be happy here. Reservations are required Christmas week, the month of February, and Easter Week. ⊠ *Calle 68, No. 495, between Calles 57 and 59,* ☎ ℻ 99/28–25–05; ☎ 303/674–9615 or 800/538–6802 in the U.S., ℻ 303/674–8735 in the U.S.. *8 rooms. Breakfast room, pool. MC, V.*

$$ 🏨 **Gran Hotel.** Cozily situated on Parque Hidalgo, this legendary 1901
★ hotel is the oldest in the city. The three-story French neoclassical building exudes charm. Its centerpiece is an art nouveau courtyard. High-ceilinged rooms are furnished in antique cedar pieces. Thirteen units have balconies—most of the others have no windows at all. The rooms on the second floor in the back are the quietest. Porfirio Díaz and Fidel Castro stayed in sumptuous Room 17 (not together, of course). ⊠ *Calle 60, No. 496,* ☎ 99/24–77–30 or 99/23–69–63, ℻ 99/24–76–22. *25 rooms, 6 suites. Restaurant, bar, free parking. MC, V.*

$$ ⊞ **Mérida Misión Park Inn Plaza.** Part of the city's landscape for decades (in its earlier incarnation it was the Hotel Mérida), the Misión has two major assets: an excellent location in the heart of downtown and a genuine colonial ambience, with chandeliers, wood beams, archways, patios, and fountains in public areas. A modern addition has fine views from the upper floors. Forty-five units in the old colonial section are set around a pretty courtyard. ⊠ *Calle 60, No. 491,* ☎ *99/23–95–00; 888/224–8837 in the U.S.,* ℻ *99/23–76–65. 137 rooms, 8 suites. Restaurant, bar, snack bar, no-smoking rooms, pool, shop, travel services, car rental, free parking. AE, DC, MC, V.*

$ ⊞ **San Juan.** This new two-story downtown property has doors and furnishings of carved mahogany, tile floors, and a long garden filled with plants and wrought-iron benches. The rooms are clean and neat, albeit plain, with telephones and TVs. There is a small pool in the back patio. All rooms have both air-conditioning and fans. ⊠ *Calle 55, No. 497-A, between Calles 58 and 60,* ☎ *99/24–17–42 or 24–16–88. 39 rooms. MC, V with 5% surcharge.*

Nightlife and the Arts

Mérida enjoys an unusually active and diverse cultural life, including free government-sponsored music and dance performances nightly plus sidewalk art shows in four local parks. For information on these and other performances, consult the tourist office, the local newspapers, or the billboards and posters at the **Teatro Peón Contreras** (⊠ Calle 60 at Calle 57) or **Café Pop** (⊠ Calle 57 between Calles 60 and 62).

DANCING

A number of restaurants have live music and dancing. **El Establo** (⊠ Calle 60, No. 482, between Calles 55 and 57, ☎ 99/24–22–89) is a university crowd favorite. **Pancho's** (⊠ Calle 59 between Calles 60 and 62, ☎ 99/23–09–42) attracts locals and foreigners for a mix of live salsa and Western music.

FOLKLORIC SHOWS

Among a variety of performances presented at the **Teatro Peón Contreras** (⊠ Universidad Autónoma de Yucatán, Calle 60 at Calle 57), "The Roots of Today's Yucatán" is a combination of music, dance, and theater presented by the Folkloric Ballet of the University of Yucatán on Wednesday at 9 PM; Friday at 9 PM catch the "University Serenade," a festival of music, dance, and poetry featuring artists from throughout Mexico. Regional folkloric dance is performed Monday at 8 PM at the Palacio Municipal, on the zócalo.

Outdoor Activities and Sports

BULLFIGHTS

Bullfights are most often held October through May at the **Plaza de Toros** (⊠ Calle 72, near Calle 25, Col. Garcia Gineres). Contact the travel desk at your hotel or one of the tourist information centers.

GOLF

There is an 18-hole championship golf course (and restaurant, bar, and clubhouse) at **Club de Golf La Ceiba** (⊠ Carr. Mérida–Progreso, Km 14.5, ☎ 99/22–00–53 or 99/22–00–54), 16 km (10 mi) north of Mérida on the road to Progreso.

Shopping

CRAFT MARKETS AND STORES

On the second floor of the **Mercado Municipal** (⊠ Between Calles 65 and 67 and Calles 54 and 56) you'll find crafts, food, flowers, and live birds, among other items. The **Mercado de Artesanías "García Rejón"** (⊠ Calles 65 and 62) has neat rows of indoor stalls with leather items, palm hats, and handmade guitars, among other things. On Sunday in

Mérida, you will find an array of wares at the **Handicraft Bazaar** (⊠ In front of Municipal Palace across from main square), filled with lovely embroidered and lace blouses, dresses, huipiles, and hats. Local artisans sell their wares at the Saturday evening **Fiesta Mexicana,** at the base of Paseo Monetejo, and at a **Sunday bazaar** at Parque Santa Lucia. The streets north of the main square, especially **Calle 60,** are lined with crafts and jewelry stores.

Casa de Artesanías (⊠ Calle 63, No. 503, between Calles 64 and 66, ☎ 99/23–53–92) has a good selection of (and fixed prices on) folk art from throughout Mexico—hand-painted wooden animals from Oaxaca, beeswax candles, leather bags from Mérida, and hand-embroidered vests, shawls, blouses, and place mats from Chiapas. The best place for hammocks is **Hamacas El Aguacate** (⊠ Calle 58, No. 604, at Calle 73, ☎ 99/28–64–29), a family-run shop selling a wide variety of sizes and designs.

SPECIALTY STORES

Clothing. Tastefully designed batik dresses and pillow covers with Maya motifs, along with a nice selection of silver jewelry, can be found at **El Paso** (⊠ Calle 60, No. 501, at Calle 61, ☎ 99/28–54–52). You might not wear a guayabera to a business meeting as some men in Mexico do, but the shirts are cool, comfortable, and attractive. For a good selection, try **Camisería Canul** (⊠ Calle 62, No. 484, between Calles 57 and 59, ☎ 99/23–01–58). Pick up a *jipi* (straw hat made only in the Yucatán) at **El Becaleño** (⊠ Calle 65, No. 483, between Calles 56A and 58, ☎ 99/85–05–81), where you'll find the famous hats that the González family makes at Becal, Campeche.

Galleries. Contemporary paintings and photography are showcased in the **Teatro Peón Contreras** (⊠ Calle 60 between Calles 59 and 57), **Galería Casa Colón** (⊠ Av. Colón, No. 507, ☎ 99/25–79–52 or 99/25–82–53), and the **Palacio del Gobierno,** (⊠ Calle 61 between Calles 60 and 62, Col. Georgia Charulas).

Jewelry. La Perla Maya (⊠ Calle 60, Nos. 485–487, between Calles 59 and 61, ☎ 99/28–58–86) is one of the few jewelry shops selling difficult-to-find, old-fashioned Yucatecan filigree earrings and bracelets. **Tane** at the Hyatt Regency Hotel (⊠ Calle 60, No. 344, and Av. Colón, ☎ 99/42–02–02) is an outlet for exquisite silver earrings, necklaces, and bracelets, some with ancient Maya designs.

The Scenic Route to Chichén Itzá

Although it's possible to reach Chichén Itzá (120 km, or 74 mi, east of Mérida) along the shorter Highway 180, it's far more scenic to follow Highway 80 until it ends at Tekantó, then head south to Citilcúm, east to Dzitas, and south again to Pisté. These roads have no signs but are the only paved roads going in these directions. Ask directions frequently.

Izamal

 50 *72 km (44 mi) southeast of Mérida.*

Izamal is nicknamed Ciudad Amarillo (Yellow City) because its buildings are painted earth-tone yellow, according to city ordinance in colonial times. In the center of town stands the enormous 16th-century **Convento de San Antonio de Padua,** perched on—and built from—the remains of a pyramid devoted to Itamná, god of the heavens, day, night, and the dew. The monastery's church, which Pope John Paul II visited in 1993, has a gigantic columned portico (claimed to be second only to that of the Vatican in size) and, in the entranceway next to the gift shop, newly discovered frescoes of saints and of Christ. The Virgin of the Immaculate Conception, to whom the church is dedicated, is the patron saint of the Yucatán. Miracles are ascribed to her, and a yearly pilgrimage takes place in her honor. Another pyramid, called **Kinich Kakmó** (macaw of fire), is all that remains of a royal Maya city that flourished here hundreds of years ago.

A daylong excursion to Izamal departs Mérida Sunday at 8 AM (returning by 5:30) using a special car attached to the regular train. The train arrives at Izamal around 10, after which you are taken on a tour of the Franciscan convent, the town itself, and the ruins of the Maya pyramid Kinich Kakmó. You then have an hour around town before meeting for lunch, during which a regional dance is performed. The cost is $18 per person; make arrangements through Mérida travel agents (☞ The State of Yucatán A to Z, *below*).

Chichén Itzá

   116 km (72 mi) from Mérida.

One of the four best-known Maya ruins, Chichén Itzá (chee-*chen* eet-*zah*) was probably the most important city in Yucatán from the 10th to the 12th century. An architectural mélange, Chichén was altered by each successive wave of inhabitants. Evidence suggests that the site was first settled in AD 432, abandoned for an unknown period of time, then rediscovered in 964 by the Maya-speaking Itzá people, who are believed to have come from the Petén rain forest around Tikal, in what is now northern Guatemala. The building style is very similar to what's found in the southern Maya empire—an area extending from the Petén south to Honduras. The name itself, *Chichén Itzá*, means "the mouth of the well of the Itzás." By 1224, after some 260 years, the Itzás had deserted the site.

The majesty and enormity of this site are unforgettable. Chichén Itzá encompasses approximately 6 square km (2 square mi), though only 20 to 30 buildings of the several hundred at the site have been fully explored. It's divided into two parts, called Old and New, although architectural motifs from the Classic period are found in both sections. A more convenient distinction is topographical, since there are two major complexes of buildings separated by a dirt path.

The iconic 98-ft-tall pyramid called **El Castillo** (the castle), which dominates the site, represents a marriage of styles: the martial, imperial architecture of the Itzá, and the more cerebral design genius and astronomical expertise of the earlier Maya. Atop the castle is a temple dedicated to Kukulcán—the Maya name for Quetzalcóatl, that legendary priest-king from Tula in the Valley of Mexico who was incarnated by the plumed serpent. The structure was constructed so that twice a year, at the spring and fall equinoxes, the play of light and shadow would create an image of the god Kukulcán snaking his way down the sides of the pyramid. A more ancient temple inside the Castillo is open to the public for only a few hours in the morning and again in the afternoon. Claustrophobes should think twice before entering: the stairs are narrow, dark, and winding. A sound-and-light show in the evening highlights the architectural details in the Castillo and other buildings with a clarity the eye doesn't see in daylight; its narrative, however, has inaccuracies.

The temple rests on a massive trapezoidal square, on the west side of which is Chichén Itzá's largest **ball court,** one of seven on the site. The game played here was something like soccer (no hands were used), but

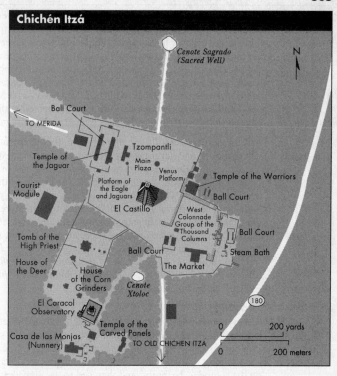

Chichén Itzá

it had a strictly religious significance. Bas-relief carvings at the court depict a player being decapitated, the blood spurting from his severed neck fertilizing the earth. Other bas-reliefs once believed to depict the Toltecs playing against the Maya are actually the Itzá playing against a Maya enemy.

Between the ball court and El Castillo stands a **Tzompantli** (stone platform) carved with rows of human skulls. In ancient times it was actually covered with stakes on which the heads of enemies were impaled. In the **Sacred Well,** a cenote 65 yards in diameter that sits 1 km (½ mi) north of El Castillo at the end of a 900-ft-long *sacbe* ("white road" in Maya), skeletons of about 50 people were found. Thousands of artifacts made of gold, jade, and other precious materials, most of them not of local provenance, have been recovered from the brackish depths of the cenote. The well's excavation by Mexican diver/businessman Pablo Bush Romero launched the field of underwater archaeology, later honed by Jacques Cousteau.

Returning to the causeway, you will see on your left the **Group of the Thousand Columns** with the famous **Temple of the Warriors,** a masterful example of the Itzá influence here. Scientists have shown that this temple was used as an official meeting place for members of the council of Lords of Chichén. Murals of everyday village life and scenes of war can be viewed here, and you can see an artistic representation of the defeat of the Maya on the interior murals of the adjacent **Temple of the Jaguar.**

To get to the less visited cluster of structures at "New" Chichén Itzá—often confused with "Old" Chichén Itzá—take the main road south from the Temple of the Jaguar past El Castillo and turn right onto a small path opposite the ball court on your left. Archaeologists are currently restoring several buildings, including the **Tomb of the High Priest,** where several tombs with skeletons and jade offerings were found, and the northern part of the site, which was used by the military. The most impressive structure in this area is the astronomical observatory, called **El Caracol.** The name, meaning "snail," refers to the spiral staircase at the building's core. Although definitely used for observing the heavens, it also served a religious function. After leaving El Caracol, continue south several hundred yards to the beautiful **Casa de las Monjas** (Nunnery) and its annex, which have long panels carved with flowers and animals, latticework, hieroglyphic-covered lintels, and masks.

At Old Chichén Itzá, "pure Maya" style—with playful latticework, Chaac masks, and gargoyle-like serpents on the cornices—dominates. Highlights include the **Date Group** (so named because of the complete series of hieroglyphic date inscriptions), the **House of the Phalli,** and the **Temple of the Three Lintels.** Maya guides will lead you down the path by an old narrow-gauge railroad track to even more ruins, barely unearthed, if you ask. A fairly good restaurant and great ice-cream stand are in the entrance building, and there are refreshment stands by the cenote and on the pathway near El Caracol. ◙ *Site and museum $4, free Sun.; sound-and-light show $3 in Spanish, $5 in English; parking $1; use of video camera $8.* ☉ *Daily 8–5. Sound-and-light show (Spanish) at 7 PM and (English) at 8 PM.*

Lodging

$$$$ ▥ **Mayaland.** This charming 1920s lodging, on a 100-acre site, is the
★ closest hotel to the ruins: it has its own entrance to the site. Colonial-style rooms in the main building have decorative tiles, ceiling fans, air-conditioning, and cable TV. The cheerful bungalows all have hammocks on the verandas, bathtubs, and thatched roofs. Bungalows 8 and 6 are right next to one of three swimming pools. Tour buses fill the road in front of the hotel, so choose a room at the back. Light meals served poolside and at tables overlooking the garden are far better than the fixed-price meals served in the dining room. ⊠ *Carretera Mérida–Puerto Juárez, Km 120,* ☎ *985/1–01–28 or 985/1–00–71. Reservations:* ⊠ *Mayaland Tours, Av. Colón 502, Mérida, Yucatán 97000,* ☎ *99/25–06–21; 800/ 235–4079 in the U.S.,* ℻ *99/25–00–87. 73 rooms, 28 bungalows, 4 suites. 3 restaurants, bar, 3 pools, free parking. AE, DC, MC, V.*

$$$ ▥ **Hacienda Chichén.** A converted 16th-century hacienda, this hotel
★ once served as the home of U.S. Consul General Edward S. Thompson and later as the headquarters for the Carnegie expedition. The rustic cottages have been modernized, and all rooms, which have comfortable, classy, furnishings of colonial Yucatecan style, have private baths, verandas, dehumidifiers, and air-conditioning, but no phones or TVs. There's a color satellite TV and VCR in the library. An enormous old pool sits in the midst of the landscaped gardens. Fairly good meals are served on the patio overlooking the grounds: stick with the Yucatecan specialties. ⊠ *Carretera Mérida–Puerto Juárez, Km 120, Yucatán 97000,* ☎ *985/1–00–45 or 99/24–88–44; 800/624–8451 in the U.S.,* ℻ *99/24–50–11. 18 rooms, 3 suites. Restaurant, bar, pool, free parking. AE, DC, MC, V.*

Pisté

🔁 *1 km (½ mi) west of Chichén Itzá on Hwy. 180.*

The town of Pisté serves mainly as a base camp for travelers to Chichén Itzá, and its hotels, campgrounds, and handicrafts shops tend to be cheaper than those south of the ruins. At the west end of town is a Pemex station, but there are no banks, so change money before you arrive (the Visitor Center at the ruins changes money). On the outskirts of Pisté, a short walk from the ruins, **Pueblo Maya,** a pseudo-Maya village, provides a shopping and dining center for tour groups. The restaurant serves a bountiful buffet at lunch ($10). Most other restaurants in town are only fair, and are overpriced as a result. Try one of the palapa-covered cafés along the main road or the small markets and produce stands, which can provide the makings for a modest picnic.

Lodging

$$ 🏨 **Pirámide Inn Resort.** The clean, open rooms in this two-story, 50s-style, American-owned motel were repainted and refurbished in 1997, but some of the mattresses are still on the thin side and lumpy. Rooms have neither phones nor TVs, and not all are air-conditioned. The garden contains a small Maya pyramid, a swimming pool, and a tennis court, and the restaurant is one of the best in Pisté. ✉ *Reservations: Box 433, Mérida,* ☎ *985/1–01–15.* 𝖥𝖠𝖷 *985/1–01–14. 35 rooms. Restaurant, pool, tennis court, travel services. MC, V.*

$ 🏨 **Dolores Alba.** The best low-budget choice near the ruins is this family-run hotel, a longtime favorite in the country south of Pisté. The rooms are simple, clean, and comfortable; some have air-conditioning. Hammocks hang by the small pool, and breakfast and dinner are served family-style in the main building. Free transportation to the ruins is provided. ✉ *Km 122 Carretera Mérida–Cancún (1½ km [1 mi] south of Chichén Itzá). Reservations:* ✉ *Calle 63, No. 464, Mérida,* ☎ *99/28–56–50,* 𝖥𝖠𝖷 *99/28–31–63. 28 rooms. Dining room, pool. AE.*

Cave of Balamkanchén

🏔 ㊾ *5 km (3 mi) northeast of Chichén Itzá.*

The Cave of Balamkanchén, a shrine whose Maya name translates as "hidden throne," remained virtually undisturbed from the time of the Conquest until its discovery in 1959. Three of the seven chambers are open to the public. Inside is a large collection of artifacts—mostly vases, jars, and incense burners. An underground lake is filled with blindfish (small fish with functionless eyes), and an altar to the rain god rises above it. In order to explore the shrine you must take one of the tours, which are broadcast throughout the caves over loudspeakers. There is also a sound-and-light show that fancifully recounts Maya history at the site. You can catch a bus or taxi to the caves from Chichén Itzá. 🎟 *Caves (including tour) $3, free Sun.; show $3.* ☉ *English tour at noon, 2 and 4 PM; Spanish at 9, 1, and 3; French at 10.*

Valladolid

㊿ *44 km (27 mi) east of Chichén Itzá.*

The second-largest city in the State of Yucatán, Valladolid (pronounced va-*ya*-do-leed) is growing in popularity among travelers en route to or from Chichén Itzá or Río Lagartos. Montejo founded Valladolid in 1543 on the site of the Maya town of Sisal. The city suffered during the Caste War, when virtually the entire Spanish population was killed by the rebellious Maya, and again during the Mexican Revolution.

Today, however, placidity reigns in this agricultural market town (population 70,000). The center is mostly colonial, although it has many 19th-century structures. The main sights are the colonial churches, principally the large **cathedral** on the central square and the 16th-century **San Bernardino Church and Convent** three blocks southwest. A briny, muddy **cenote** near the center of town draws only the most resolute swimmers. Instead, visit the adjacent **ethnographic museum**. Outside town, for $1, you can swim in the mysterious yet earthy **Cenote Xkeken** (a.k.a. Dzitnup), in a large underground cave. A natural skylight reveals stalactites as well as swarms of bats and schools of small catfish.

Valladolid is renowned for its cuisine, particularly its sausages. Try one of the restaurants within a block of the square. You can find good buys on sandals, baskets, and the local liqueur, Xtabentún, flavored with honey and anise.

Lodging

$$ 🏨 **El Mesón del Marqués.** This building, on the north side of the main square, is a well-preserved, very old hacienda built around a lovely courtyard. All rooms have air-conditioning and are attractively furnished with rustic and colonial touches; suites have unusually large bathrooms with bathtubs and bidets. The restaurant, with splashing fountain and gnarled old trees, is a lovely spot to have a reasonably good meal. ⊠ *Plaza Principal, Calle 39, No. 203, 97780,* ☎ *985/6–20–73,* 𝔽𝔸𝕏 *985/6–22–80. 54 rooms, 25 junior suites. Restaurant, bar, pool, shop. AE.*

$ 🏨 **María del Luz.** Another choice by the main plaza, this three-story hotel is built around a shallow, kidney-shape swimming pool surrounded by banana trees. Plain rooms have contemporary furnishings, including firm beds, air-conditioning, and color cable TVs. The attractive streetside restaurant offers predictable and inexpensive Mexican dishes. ⊠ *Plaza Principal, Calle 42, No. 193, 97780,* ☎ *985/6–20–71. 51 rooms. Restaurant, bar, pool, free parking. MC, V.*

Parque Natural Río Lagartos

❺❺ *101 km (63 mi) north of Valladolid; 150 km (93 mi) northeast of Mérida.*

If you're a flamingo fan, don't miss Parque Natural Río Lagartos, especially between June and March, when you'll see the largest number of flamingos. Spanning a long estuary, the 116,000-acre park was developed with ecotourism in mind—even though the alligators for which it and the village were named were hunted to near extinction years ago. In addition to sighting flamingos, look for egrets, herons, ibis, cormorants, pelicans, and even peregrine falcons flying over these murky waters. Fishing is good, too, and endangered hawksbill and green turtles lay their eggs on the beach at night.

San Felipe's **Hotel San Felipe** (☎ 986/3–37–38), one of five hotels in the area, has boat tours, as does **Restaurant Isla Contoy** (☎ 986/2–00–00). Or you can hire a boat from the docks near the hotel. You can also hire a bilingual guide by the hour with three days' advance notice through the **reserve office** (☎ 986/3–28–54) if you want to go birdwatching in the park. There are trails among the mangroves, which you can access by calling the reserve administrators (☎ 986/3–43–90; 𝔽𝔸𝕏 986/3–28–54). Guides can take you to the best birding sites.

Uxmal, the Puuc Route, and the Coast

Passing through the large Maya town of Umán on Mérida's southern outskirts, you enter one of the least populated areas of the Yucatán. The highway to Uxmal and Kabah is a fairly traffic-free route through uncultivated woodlands. The forest seems to become more dense beyond Uxmal, which was connected to a number of smaller ceremonial centers in ancient times by *caminos blancos* (white roads). Several of these satellite sites, including **Kabah,** with its 250 Chaac masks; **Sayil,** with its majestic, three-story palace; and **Labná,** with its iconic, vaulted *Puerta* (gateway), are open to the public along a side road known as the Ruta Puuc, which winds its way eastward and eventually joins busy Highway 184, a major highway. Along this route you'll also find the **Loltún Caves,** the largest known cave system in the Yucatán, containing wall paintings and stone artifacts from Maya and pre-Maya times. You can make a loop to all of these sites, ending the loop in the little town of **Ticul,** which produces much of the pottery you'll see around the peninsula. Ticul is a convenient alternative to spending the night at the hotels just outside the Uxmal ruins, and the reasonable **Plaza** hotel (☎ 997/2–04–84), just a block from the town square, is a suitable place to stay.

Uxmal

★ ⚲ ⑤ *78 km (48 mi) south of Mérida on Hwy. 261.*

If Chichén Itzá is the most monumental Maya ruin in Yucatán, Uxmal is arguably the most graceful. Where the former has a dramatic grandeur, the latter seems more understated and elegant—pure Maya, as people often say. The architecture reflects the Late Classic renaissance of the 7th to 9th centuries and is contemporary with that of the exquisite Palenque and Tikal, among other great Maya metropolises of the southern highlands.

The site is considered the finest and largest example of Puuc architecture (puuc means "low hill" in Maya), which embraces such details as ornate stone mosaics and friezes on the upper walls, intricate cornices with curled noses, rows of columns, and soaring vaulted arches. Lines are clean and uncluttered, with the horizontal—especially the parallelogram—preferred to the vertical.

Although most of Uxmal remains unrestored, three buildings in particular merit attention. The most prominent, the **Pyramid of the Magician,** is, at 125 ft, the tallest structure at the site. Unlike most other Maya pyramids, which are stepped and angular, it has a strangely elliptical design. Built five times, each time over the previous structure, the pyramid has a stairway on its western side that leads through a giant mask of Chaac, with its mouth wide open, to two temples at the summit.

West of the pyramid lies the **Nunnery,** or Quadrangle of the Nuns, considered by some to be the architectural jewel of Uxmal. You can enter the four buildings. Each comprises a series of low, gracefully repetitive chambers that look onto a central patio. Elaborate decoration blankets the upper facades. The name of the building was given to it by the Spaniards because it reminded them of a convent building in old Spain. However, recent findings say it was the palace and living quarters of the high lord of Uxmal, named Chaan Chak, which means "abundance of rain."

Continue walking south, and you'll pass the ball court before reaching the **Palace of the Governor,** which archaeologist Victor von Hagen considered the most magnificent building ever erected in the Americas. Interestingly, the palace faces east whereas the rest of Uxmal faces west. Archaeologists believe this is because the palace was used to sight the planet Venus. Covering five acres and rising over an immense acropolis, the palace lies at the heart of what must have been Uxmal's administrative center. Intricate friezes decorating the facade consist of some 20,000 individually cut stones.

First excavated in 1929 by the Danish explorer Franz Blom, the site served in 1841 as home to John Lloyd Stephens. Today a sound-and-light show recounts Maya legends, including the kidnapping of an Uxmal princess by a king of Chichén Itzá, and focuses on the people's dependence on rain—thus the cult of Chaac. The show is performed nightly in English and is one of the best of such productions. ☒ *Site and museum $4, free Sun.; sound-and-light show in Spanish $3, in English $5; parking $1; use of video camera $8.* ☉ *Daily 8–5; sound-and-light show (Spanish) at 8 PM, (English) at 9 PM.*

Dining and Lodging

$ ✕ **Las Palapas.** A great alternative to the hotel dining rooms at Uxmal, this family-run restaurant specializes in delicious Yucatecan dishes served with homemade tortillas. When tour groups request it in advance, the owners prepare a traditional feast, roasting the chicken or pork píbil style in a pit in the ground. If you see a tour bus in the parking lot, stop in—you might chance upon a memorable fiesta. ⊠ *Hwy. 261, 5 km (3 mi) north of ruins,* ☎ *No phone. No credit cards.*

$$$$ ☷ **Hacienda Uxmal.** The oldest hotel at the Maya site, built in 1955 and still owned and operated by the Barbachano family, this pleasant colonial-style building has lovely floor tiles, ceramics, and iron grillwork. The rooms—all with ceiling fans, color TV, and air-conditioning—are tiled and decorated with worn but comfortable furniture. Ask about packages that include free or low-cost car rentals for the nights you spend at Uxmal and at the Mayaland hotel in Chichén Itzá. ⊠ *Within walking distance of ruins,* ☎ FAX *99/49–47–54. Reservations:* ⊠ *Mayaland Tours, Av. Colón 502, Mérida,* ☎ *99/25–06–21; 800/235–4079 in the U.S.,* FAX *99/25–00–87. 78 rooms, 2 suites. 2 restaurants, bar, room service, 2 pools, shop, billiards, recreation room. AE, MC, V.*

$$ ☷ **Villas Arqueológicas Uxmal.** This two-story Club Med property, located directly across from the ruins, is made intimate by congenial hosts Patrick and Pamela Sellier. The French–American couple is happy to share their extensive knowledge of area restaurants and tours off the beaten path. The small, functional rooms have garden views, cozy niches for the beds, and powerful but quiet air-conditioners. If you're weary of Mexican cuisine, the restaurant highlights French and Continental food. The price, near the low end of the $$ category, is extremely reasonable considering its location and the hosts' first-rate attention. ⊠ *Carrerera Uxmal, Km 76, Box 449k, Mérida, Yucatán 97000, within walking distance of ruins,* ☎ FAX *985/28–06–44,* ☎ *800/258–2633 in the U.S.. 40 rooms, 3 suites. Restaurant, bar, pool, tennis court, shop, billiards, library. AE, MC, V.*

Celestún

57 *90 km (56 mi) west of Mérida on Routes 180 and 281.*

This tranquil fishing village, with its air of unpretentiousness, sits at the end of a spit of land separating the Celestún estuary from the gulf on the western hump of the Yucatán. It is the only point of entry to the **Parque Natural Ría Celestún,** a 100,000-acre wildlife reserve with extensive mangrove forests and salt flats and one of the largest colonies of flamingos in North America. June through March, clouds of pink wings soar over the pale blue backdrop of the estuary, up to 18,000 at a time. It also has over 200 other species of birds and a large sea turtle population. Rocks, islets, and white-sand beaches enhance the park's lovely setting. There is good fishing in both the river and the gulf, and if you're lucky you can see deer and armadillo roaming the surrounding land. Bring a bathing suit for a dip in one of the cenotes.

Celestún Expeditions (⊠ Calle 10 No. 97, ☎ 991/6–20–49) is a small company run by two natives of Celestún, David and Feliciano. In addition to the standard flamingo tours, they have three-hour guided bike tours and jungle walks (day or night) for $15 per person.

Dining and Lodging

$–$$ ✕ **La Palapa.** A facade made entirely of conch shells leads you to the best seafood place in town, famous for its *camarones a la palapa*— fried shrimp in a garlic and cream sauce. ⊠ *Calle 12 No. 105,* ☎ *991/ 6–20–63. MC, V.*

$$$$ ▨ **Hotel Eco Paraíso Xixim.** On an old coconut plantation in a nature reserve outside town, Xixim has attractive thatched-roof bungalows, with porches and hammocks, that stand right on the 5-km- (3-mi-) long beach. Bring strong insect repellent, as mosquitoes can be vicious, especially in rainy season. Room rates include ample breakfasts and dinners. Flamingo, cycling, kayaking, and other tours cost extra. ✉ *Camino Viejo a Sisal, Km 10, Celestún 97367,* ☎ *991/6–21–00; 888/ 264–5792 in the U.S.,* ℻ *991/6–21–11. 15 cabañas. Restaurant, bar, fans, in-room safes, pool, beach, billiards, library. AE, MC, V.*

$ ▨ **Hotel Sol y Mar.** Half a block from the town beach, this is the best hotel of this category around. Rooms are spare but clean, with two double beds, small table and chairs, tiled bathrooms, and either air-conditioning (in three rooms) or overhead fans. ✉ *Calle 12 No. 104, Celestún 97367,* ☎ *No phone. 8 rooms. No credit cards.*

The State of Yucatán A to Z

Arriving and Departing

BY BUS

Mérida's first-class buses, including **ADO** (☎ 99/24–83–91 or 99/24–92–63) and **UNO** (☎ 99/24–78–68), serve Akumal, Cancún, Chichén Itzá, Playa del Carmen, Tulum, Uxmal, and Valladolid, and other major Mexican cities from the **CAME Station** (✉ Calle 70, between Calles 69 and 71, ☎ 99/24–83–91 or 99/20–08–30). ADO has a branch at the Fiesta Americana Hotel on Paseo Montejo (☎ 99/25–09–10). Several other first-class lines have stations near CAME, including **Autotransportes del Oriente** (✉ Calle 69, No. 554, at Calle 70, ☎ 99/23–22–87), which serves Playa del Carmen; and the nearby **Super Expreso** (☎ 99/24–83–91), which has direct buses to Cancún.

You can also access major destinations within the Yucatán Peninsula via older, frequent-stopping second-class buses from the **second-class bus station** (✉ Calle 69, No. 544, between Calles 68 and 70, ☎ 99/24–78–68), which also go to small and intermediate towns.

BY CAR

Highway 180, the main road along the Gulf coast from the Texas border to Cancún, runs into Mérida. Mexico City is 1,550 km (960 mi) to the west; Cancún, 320 km (198 mi) due east. The *autopista,* a four-lane toll highway between Cancún and Mérida, runs somewhat parallel to Highway 180 and cuts driving time between Cancún and Mérida—formerly around 4½ hours—by about 1 hour.

BY PLANE

The following airlines serve Mérida: **Aeroméxico** (☎ 99/26–12–60, 99/46–4–00, or 99/20–12–93) from Miami with a stop (but no plane change) in Cancún; **Mexicana** (☎ 99/46–13–32 or 99/46–13–92) from Newark via Cancún and from other U.S. cities via Mexico City; **Aerocaribe** (☎ 99/46–3–66 or 99/46–13–61), a subsidiary of Mexicana, from Cancún, Chetumal, Cozumel, Oaxaca, Tuxtla Gutiérrez, and Villahermosa; **Aviateca** (☎ 99/46–12–96 or 99/25–80–59), a Guatemalan carrier, from Houston and Guatemala City; **Taesa** (☎ 99/23–64–10 or 99/23–65–53) from Mexico City; and **Bonanza** (☎ 99/27–79–99) from Palenque, Chetumal, and Belize City.

Between the Airport and City Center. Mérida's Manuel Crescencio Rejón International Airport is 7 km (4½ mi) west of the city's central square, about a 20-minute ride. A private taxi costs about $7; collective service (usually a Volkswagen minibus), about $3. For both, pay the taxi-ticket vendor at the airport, not the driver. The inexpensive (30¢) Bus 79 goes from the airport to downtown.

Getting Around

BY BUS

Mérida's municipal buses run daily from 5 or 6 AM (depending on the route) to 11 PM, but service is somewhat confusing until you master the system. In the downtown area, buses go east on Calle 59 and west on Calle 61, north on Calle 60 and south on Calle 62. You can get on a colectivo minivan to Progreso on Calle 60 between Calles 65 and 67. Unfortunately, there is no bus service from the hotels around the plaza to the long-distance bus station.

BY CAR

Driving in Mérida can be frustrating because of one-way streets (many of which end up being one-lane because of parked cars) and because traffic is dense. But having your own wheels is the best way to take excursions from the city. There are lots of car rental companies, from international companies with toll-free numbers in the United States to local companies that offer competitive prices. Try haggling, especially in low season.

BY CARRIAGE

Horse-drawn *calesas* (carriages) that drive along the streets of Mérida can be hailed along Calle 60. A ride to the Paseo de Montejo and back will cost about $7 to $9, and you can bargain. Some of the horses are heartbreakingly saddle sore, but it is doubtful if boycotting the carriages will improve their lot.

BY TAXI

Taxis are available at 13 taxi stands around the city (although empty cabs will pick up a fare), or from the taxi office (☎ 99/23–49–62). Taxis wait in front of larger hotels, but they're more expensive. Individual cabs cost $1.50 minimum.

Contacts and Resources

CAR RENTAL

There are almost 20 car-rental agencies in town, including **Budget** (⊠ Hyatt Regency, Calle 60, No. 344, at Av. Colón, ☎ 99/25–54–53; 99/46–13–80 airport), **Dollar** (⊠ Hotel Mérida Misión, ☎ 99/28–67–59; 99/46–13–23 airport), and **National** (⊠ Fiesta Americana, ☎ 99/25–75–24; 99/46–13–94 airport). A local company with helpful advice about routes and driving tips is **Mexico Rent a Car** (⊠ Callejón del Congreso, Dept. 12 on Parque de la Maternidad, ☎ 99/27–49–16; closed Sun.).

CONSULATES

United States (⊠ Paseo de Montejo 453, ☎ 99/25–50–11, 99/25–86–77, or 99/25–54–09), open weekdays 7:30–4. **United Kingdom** (⊠ Calle 58, No. 450, at Calle 53, ☎ 99/28–61–52).

EMERGENCIES

Mérida. Police (☎ 99/25–25–55). **Tourist Police** (☎ 99/24–98–18). **Cruz Roja** (Red Cross; ⊠ Calle 68, No. 583, at Calle 65, ☎ 99/24–98–13). **Fire** (☎ 99/24–92–42); **general emergency** (☎ 06). **Hospital O'Horan** (⊠ Avs. Jacinto Canek and Itzaes, ☎ 99/24–41–11 or 99/28–55–07).

GUIDED TOURS

There are more than 50 tour operators in Mérida, and they generally cover the same locales. What differs is how you go—in a private car, a van, or a bus—and whether the vehicle is air-conditioned. A day trip to Chichén Itzá, with guide, entrance fee, and lunch, runs approximately $28–$40. For about the same price you can see the ruins of Uxmal and Kabah in the Puuc region, and for a few more dollars you can add on the neighboring sites of Sayil, Labná, and the Loltún Caves. Afternoon departures to Uxmal allow you to take in the sound-and-light show at the ruins and return by 11 PM, for $50–$60 (including dinner). Another option is to tour Chichén Itzá and get dropped off in Cancún for about $60. Most tour operators take credit cards.

Special-Interest Tours. Several of the tour operators in Mérida run overnight excursions to archaeological sites farther afield, notably Cobá, Tulum, Edzná, and Palenque. Tours of the Ruta Maya, including sites in Mexico, Guatemala, and Belize, are available from **VN Travel** (⌧ Calle 58, No. 488, ☎ 99/23–90–61 or 99/24–59–96) and **Mayaland Tours** (⌧ Av. Colón 502, Mérida, Yucatán 97000, ☎ 99/25–06–21; 800/235–4079 in the U.S., FAX 99/25–00–87), which also has self-guided tours with economical rental-car rates.

Ecoturismo Yucatán (⌧ Calle 3, No. 235, between Calles 22A and 34, at Pensiones, ☎ 99/20–27–72, FAX 99/25–90–47) specializes in nature tours (especially birding), natural history, anthropology, and the Mundo Maya. **Emerald Planet** (⌧ 4076 Crystal Ct., Boulder, CO 80304, ☎ 303/541–9688 or 800/883–3260, FAX 303/449–7805) has bird-watching tours and other trips into Yucatán wildlife reserves.

TRAVEL AGENCIES AND TOUR OPERATORS
Mérida's local agencies and operators include **American Express** (⌧ Calle 56-A, No. 494, between Calles 43 and 45, ☎ 99/42–82–00 or 99/24–43–26, FAX 99/28–43–73), **Felguere's Tours** (⌧ Holiday Inn, Av. Coló, No. 498, and Calle 60, ☎ 99/20–44–77, FAX 99/25–63–89), **Intermar Caribe** (⌧ Calle 30, No. 74, at Prolongación Paseo de Montejo, ☎ 99/26–34–65 or 99/44–52–22, FAX 99/44–52–59), **Turismo Aviomar** (⌧ Calle 58A, 500-C, Glorieta San Fernando, ☎ 99/20–04–44 or 99/20–04–45, FAX 99/25–50–64), **Carmen Travel Service** (⌧ Calle 61, Local 61 between Calles 60 and 62, ☎ 99/28–30–60 or 28–30–61, FAX 99/23–92–90), and **Yucatán Trails** (⌧ Calle 62, No. 482, at Calle 57, ☎ 99/28–59–13 or 99/28–25–82, FAX 99/24–19–28).

24-HOUR PHARMACIES
Farmacia Yza Centro (⌧ Calle 63, No. 502-A, between Calles 60 and 62, ☎ 99/24–95–10 or call 99/26–66–66 for delivery).

VISITOR INFORMATION
Mérida. Tourist Information Center (⌧ Teatro Peón Contreras, Calle 60 between Calles 59 and 57, ☎ 99/24–92–90), open daily 8–8. The **City Tourist Office** (⌧ Calle 59, No. 514, between Calles 62 and 64, ☎ 99/28–65–47) is open weekdays 8–2 and 5–7.

THE STATE OF CAMPECHE

Updated by
Jane Onstott

Campeche is the most underrated and least-visited part of the Yucatán. If you are adventurous, there is plenty of charm here, and a sense of discovery not possible in the peninsula's more touristy centers. Beautification projects are restoring the colonial mansions of Campeche city—once entirely walled to fend off marauding pirates—recapturing an era of elegance. One- and two-story colonial structures are being repainted dill and olive greens, butter yellow, blue gray, sandstone, and salmon hues, with trimwork in tasteful cream. Beyond the city, ancient pyramids and ornate Maya temples are tucked in tropical forests, more accessible than ever but scarcely visited by foreign tourists.

Most of the State of Campeche is flat—never higher than 1,000 ft above sea level—but more than 60% of its territory is covered by jungle, where precious mahogany and cedar abound. Campeche's economy is based on agriculture, fishing, logging, salt, tourism, and—since the 1970s—hydrocarbons, of which it is the largest producer in Mexico. Most of the oil industry is concentrated at the southern end of the state, near Ciudad del Carmen.

Campeche City

The city of Campeche has a lovely, time-weathered air: no self-conscious, ultramodern tourist glitz here, just a friendly city by the sea, population 642,000, that is proud of its heritage and welcomes all to share in it. That good-humored, open-minded attitude is enshrined in the Spanish adjective *campechano*, meaning easygoing and cheerful.

Because it has been walled since 1686, most of the historic downtown is neatly contained in an area measuring five by nine blocks. The old city, or "Viejo Campeche," looks fresh with newly painted and remodeled historic buildings from the 16th through 19th centuries and signs guiding tourists to attractions along the streets. Seven *baluartes* (bastions) in various stages of disrepair or reconstruction are strategically placed around the perimeter of the old city. These were once connected by a 3-km (2-mi) wall in a hexagonal fortification that was built to safeguard the city against the pirates who kept ransacking it—and it was not until 1771, when Fuerte San Miguel was built on a hilltop on the outskirts of town, that pirates finally ceased their attacks. Only short stretches of the wall exist, and two stone archways—one facing the sea, the other the land—are all that remain of the four gates that provided the only means of access to Campeche.

58 Avenida Ruíz Cortines is Campeche's waterfront boulevard, currently being widened to six lanes, with a broad pedestrian walkway called the **malecón.** The sidewalk runs the length of the waterfront, from the Ramada Inn south to the outskirts of town, and is popular with joggers and strollers enjoying the cool sea breezes and view at sunset.

59 A modernistic building resembling a flying saucer (and called that, or "the sandwich," by locals) houses the **Congreso del Estado** (State Congress building), where the state legislature holds session. One block inland from the malecón, on Avenida 16 de Septiembre, the Congreso **60** del Estado shares a broad plaza with the much taller **Palacio del Gobierno** (State Government Palace), which locals have dubbed "El Tocadiscos" (the jukebox) because of its elaborate facade.

61 The **Baluarte San Carlos,** the bastion where Avenida 16 de Septiembre curves around and becomes Circuito Baluartes, houses the Sala de las Fortificaciones (Chamber of the Fortifications), containing scale models of the original defense system and the **Museo Gráfico de la Ciudad** (Graphics Museum), with photographs of the city as it developed. Don't miss the dungeon inside the bastion, where captured pirates were jailed, and the rooftop view, especially at sunset.

62 The **Ex-Templo de San José,** built by the Jesuits in 1756, occupies the full city block between Calles 10 and 12 and Calles 63 and 65. Its portal is completely covered with blue and yellow Talavera tiles and crowned by seven narrow stone finials that resemble the roof combs on many Maya temples. Campeche's first lighthouse, built in 1864, sits atop the right-hand tower. ☉ *The Ex-Templo is officially closed; ask a guard at the Instituto Campechano, next door, to show you the interior.*

63 The **Iglesia de San Román** became central to the lives of the Indians when an ebony image of Christ, the "Black Christ," was brought in about 1565. The legend goes that a ship that refused to carry the statue was wrecked, whereas the ship that did take it on board reached Campeche in record time. To this day, the Feast of San Román—when the icon is carried through the streets as part of a procession, on Au-

Campeche City

gust 31—is the biggest such celebration in Campeche. ⊠ *Calle 10 at Calle Bravo,* ☉ *Daily 7–1 and 3–8.*

64 On **Calle 59,** between Calles 8 and 18, stand some of Campeche's finest homes, some of which have been partially or totally converted for other uses. Geometric motifs decorate the cornices, and the windows are gaily adorned with iron latticework. The richest inhabitants built as close to the sea as possible, in case escape became necessary. Since 1987, a citywide beautification project has restored more than 1,600 facades of buildings on this and many adjoining streets.

65 Just east of Calle 12 (at Calle 59), the architecture and ambience of the tiny **Iglesia de San Francisquito** do justice to historic Calle 59's old-fashioned beauty. ⊠ *Calle 59 at Calle 12.* ☉ *Daily 8:30–noon and 5–7.*

66 Old Campeche ends at the **Puerta de Tierra** (land gate), the only one of the four original (and two remaining) city gates with its basic structure intact. ⊠ *Calle 18 at Calle 59.* 🎟 *$1.50.* ☉ *Sound-and-light show Tues., Fri., and Sat. 8:30 PM, more often in high season; Dec. 20–Jan. 4 daily, excluding Dec. 24 and 31 (with English translation).*

67 To take in the heart of a true Mexican inner city, stroll through the **Mercado Municipal** (municipal market), where locals congregate en masse to shop for seafood, produce, and housewares daily from dawn to dusk. ⊠ *Av. Circuito Baluartes Este at Calle 53.*

68 The unpretentious **Parque Principal** (main square) or **Plaza de la Independencia** (Independence Plaza), dating from 1540 or 1541, occupies the heart of the old city. Its southern side is lined with several modest cafés and hotels. Band concerts are held here on Sunday evenings at dusk. ⊠ *Bounded by Calles 10 (east), 8 (west), 55 (north), and 57 (south).*

★ **69** On the south side of Parque Principal, the **Baluarte de la Soledad** (Bastion of Our Lady of Solitude) was built between 1690 and 1692. It houses the disappointing **Museo de los Estela**, which houses 20 Maya stelae and a few other pieces, but has no plaques, in English or any other language. The largest of the bastions, this one has relatively complete parapets and embrasures that offer a view of the cathedral, the municipal buildings, and a sliver of sea. ⊠ *Calle 8 at Calle 57,* ☎ *No phone.* 🎟 *50¢.* 🕙 *Tues.–Sat. 8–8, Sun. 8–1.*

An exception to the generally somber architecture of colonial Campeche, ❼⓿ the **catedral** combines neoclassical and Renaissance elements. The present cathedral—which took two centuries (from 1650 to 1850) to build—occupies the site of Montejo's original church, which went up in 1540. Inside, the pièce de résistance is the magnificent ebony Holy Sepulcher, decorated with stamped silver and an army of angels. ⊠ *Calle 55, between Calles 8 and 10.* 🕙 *Daily 6–noon and 5:30–8.*

Built in the early 20th century by one of the wealthiest plantation own-❼❶ ers in Yucatán, the opulent, eclectic **Mansión Carvajal** did time as the Hotel Señorial before arriving at its present role as an office for the Family Institute, run by the governor's wife and her staff. ⊠ *Calle 10 584, between Calles 51 and 53,* ☎ *981/6–76–44.* 🎟 *Free.* 🕙 *Week-days 8–2.*

❼❷ The **Baluarte Santiago,** the last of the bastions to be built (1704), is now a tiny botanical garden with plants and trees labeled in Latin and sometimes Maya. The original bastion was demolished at the turn of the century, then rebuilt in the 1950s. ⊠ *Calle 8 at Calle 49,* ☎ *981/6–68–29.* 🎟 *Free.* 🕙 *Daily 9–2 and 5–8.*

Away from the city center, in a residential neighborhood, stands the ❼❸ beautifully restored **Iglesia de San Francisco,** the oldest church site (1546) in Campeche, constructed on the base of a Maya temple. Some con-tend it marks the spot where the first mass on the North American con-tinent was said, in 1517 (the same claim has been made for Veracruz and Cozumel). One of Cortés's grandsons was baptized here, and the baptismal font still stands. ⊠ *Av. Miguel Alemán near Av. Francisco I. Madero,* 🕙 *Daily 8–noon and 5–8.*

❼❹ The lofty **Fuerte San José,** at the northern boundary of the old city, is home to a new museum—the **Museo de Armas y Barcos,** which is half of the exhibit that used to be in the Museo Regional. The display fo-cuses on the 18th-century weapons of siege and defense in the many wars fought against the pirates. You'll also find scale ships-in-a-bot-tle, manuscripts, and a few religious paintings. The view is terrific from atop the ramparts, which were used for spotting the ships of the in-vaders. ⊠ *North of downtown on Av. Francisco Morazán s/n,* ☎ *No phone.* 🎟 *50¢.* 🕙 *Tues.–Sun. 8–8.*

★ ❼❺ At the opposite end of town from Fuerte San José is **Fuerte de San Miguel.** A well-marked scenic drive turns off Avenida Ruíz Cortines near the south end of the city and winds its way to a hilltop, where the fortress commands one of the grandest views in the Yucatán, overlooking the city and the Gulf of Mexico. Built in 1771, Fuerte de San Miguel was positioned to bombard enemy ships with cannonballs before they could get close enough to attack Campeche. As soon as it was com-pleted, pirates stopped attacking the city—fulfilling its purpose, if an-ticlimactically. The fort now houses the excellent **Museo Cultura Maya,** for which you should allow at least two hours. The collection of Campeche Maya artifacts—with explanations in English—is not to be missed. The six exquisite jade funeral masks found in tombs at Calak-mul alone are worth a visit. ⊠ *South of downtown on Av. Resurgimiento s/n,* ☎ *No phone.* 🎟 *$1.* 🕙 *Tues.–Sun. 8–8.*

Dining and Lodging

$$$ ✕ **La Pigua.** A favorite with locals lingering over long lunches, La Pigua
★ is perhaps the best seafood restaurant in town, with the most pleasant
ambience. Trees and plants are housed, terrarium-style, on both sides
of the long dining room. Soups and salads are à la carte, but light eaters
can enjoy a satisfying meal (and spend less). Huge seafood salads
could easily feed two. Try the *pescado relleno,* a fish fillet stuffed with
finely diced shellfish, with coconut cake for dessert. La Pigua is within
walking distance from the city center, a few blocks west of where Calle
8 becomes Avenida Miguel Alemán. ⊠ *Av. Miguel Alemán 197-A,* ☎
981/1–33–65. MC, V. No dinner.

$ ✕ **Centro Manik.** This health-food restaurant doubles as a new-age cen-
ter, offering yoga and meditation classes and occasional seminars. That
said, the tables have ashtrays and you can order a beer instead of an herbal
tea. The vegetarian cuisine is just fair, but there are tasty homemade breads
and you can order a meatless burger or a fresh carrot and orange juice.
There are two indoor dining rooms, but most pleasant is the plant-filled
back patio, especially at night, when candlelight draws diners out under
the starry sky. It's closed between 2 and 6 PM. ⊠ *Calle 59, No. 22, be-
tween Calles 12 and 14,* ☎ *981/6–24–48. Closed Sun. No credit cards.*

$ ✕ **Marganzo.** Just a half block south of the plaza, this popular tourist
★ spot (which is not to its detriment) has colorful decor: hanging Moor-
ish arches are painted cobalt blue, walls are mustard yellow and white.
Waitresses dress in regional costume, and the food also highlights
campechano specialties, including *pan de casón*—tortillas layered with
black beans and shredded shark and covered in a mild tomato sauce.
⊠ *Calle 8, No. 267,* ☎ *981/1–38–98. AE, MC, V.*

$ ✕ **Miramar.** This restaurant across from Hotel Castelmar offers fab-
ulous *huevos motuleños* (fried eggs blanketed in tomato sauce and gar-
nished with peas, chopped ham, and shredded cheese), red snapper,
shellfish, soups, and meat dishes. The heavy wooden tables and chairs
and the paintings of coats-of-arms give Miramar a colonial feel. Friendly
and efficient waiters bring one or more free appetizers with your beer.
⊠ *Calle 8, No. 293 A,* ☎ *981/6–28–83. No credit cards.*

$$ 🏨 **Alhambra.** Despite its average, motel-like appearance, the Alhambra is recommended for its good-size swimming pool and the fact that
rooms have bathtubs, small refrigerators, and satellite TVs (not always
working). Beds are a bit on the soft side; some rooms have carpet, others
do not. It's located near the university and the waterfront. ⊠ *Av.
Resurgimiento 85, between Avs. Universidad and Augustín Melgar,* ☎
981/6–68–22, ℻ *981/6–68–43. 96 rooms, 2 suites. Restaurant, bar,
pool, free parking. AE, MC, V.*

$$ 🏨 **Debliz.** If you come to Campeche by car, consider this modern hotel
in a residential area north of the city. Rooms at the four-story, eleva-
tor-equipped property have satellite TVs and small tables and chairs.
Visiting Yucatecos recommend the elegant yet somewhat sterile restau-
rant—with gleaming wood paneling and little other decoration—for
breaded shrimp and other seafood dishes. The Debliz can seem deserted
and lonely—until the tour buses that frequent the place pull into the
parking lot. ⊠ *Av. Las Palmas 55, off Av. Pedro Sainz de Baranda,
near baseball stadium,* ☎ *981/5–22–22,* ℻ *981/5–22–77. 114 rooms,
6 suites. Restaurant, bar, coffee shop, pool, free parking. AE, MC, V.*

$$ 🏨 **Del Paseo.** Located in the quiet San Román neighborhood, a block
from the ocean and walking distance from the town center, this hotel
is cheerful and well lighted. Rose-colored rooms have tasteful modern
furniture, small balconies, cable TVs, and air-conditioning. A glass-roofed
atrium next to the lobby is lovely, with park benches and plants. ⊠
Calle 8, No. 215, ☎ *981/1–00–84 or 981/1–01–00,* ℻ *981/1–00–97.
48 rooms, 2 suites. Restaurant, bar, shop, car rental. AE, MC, V.*

$$ 🏨 **Hotel Ramada.** This Ramada, which is luxurious by Campeche
★ standards, is independently owned, but it retains the Ramada moniker
(without the "Inn"). Fairly large rooms have bright floral bedspreads
and rattan furnishings; balconies overlook the pool or the bay. The lobby
restaurant, El Poquito, is extremely popular with locals at breakfast
and before the disco Atlantis opens at night. ⊠ *Av. Ruíz Cortines 51,
along waterfront,* ☎ *981/6–22–33; 800/228–9898 in the U.S.,* 🖷 *981/
1–16–18. 138 rooms, 11 suites. Restaurant, coffee shop, pool, exer-
cise room, shop, dance club, free parking. AE, MC, V.*

$ 🏨 **Colonial.** This former home of a high-ranking army lieutenant dates
★ from 1812. In the 1940s it was made over as a hotel, and its wonder-
fully mismatched tiles were added. As befits a colonial mansion, all rooms
are delightfully different in shape. They're all pastel-colored and spa-
cious, with ceiling fans (only four have air-conditioning), cool cotton
bedding, good mattresses, tile bathrooms, and window screens. Rooms
16, 18, 27, and 28 have lots of windows with ambient light and won-
derful views of the cathedral and city at night. Well-kept public areas
include two leafy patios, a small roof deck, and a sitting room on the
second floor for reading. ⊠ *Calle 14, No. 122, between Calles 55 and
57,* ☎ *981/6–22–22 or 981/6–26–30. 30 rooms. No credit cards.*

$ 🏨 **El Regis.** This seven-room hotel two blocks from the plaza is a great
deal, especially for those more concerned with form than function. The
Regis is a lovely two-story colonial house with a humongous wooden
front door, a wrought-iron staircase, high ceilings, balconies, and an
airy inner atrium. Rooms are spic-and-span with black-and-white tile
floors, two double beds, and cupboard closets. On the down side, bath-
rooms are tiny and there is poor lighting and somewhat lackluster air-
conditioning, which is supplemented by overhead fans. TVs have local
programming only. The front doors close at 11 PM, but the night
watchman opens up if you come in later. ⊠ *Calle 12, No. 148, between
Calles 55 and 57,* ☎ *981/6–31–75. 7 rooms. No credit cards.*

$ 🏨 **Lopez.** This cheerful little three-story hotel, with balconies in an un-
dulating design conjuring up Gaudi-designed apartment houses in
Cataluña, is a pleasant place if you're on a budget. Smallish standard
rooms (lighted by fluorescent lights) have tiny closets, armoires, lug-
gage stands, and easy chairs. Bathrooms are small but clean. Ancient
ceiling fans, however, have only two speeds: "off" and "gale-force
winds." Other units have equally loud but less blustery air-condition-
ing. The hotel doesn't have a parking garage. ⊠ *Calle 12, No. 189,
between Calles 61 and 63,* ☎ *981/6–33–44 or 981/6–24–88,* 🖷 *981/
6–30–21. 39 rooms. Laundry service. No credit cards.*

Nightlife and the Arts

If you're in the mood to dance, try one of Campeche's few discos. Most
often mentioned are the **Atlantis** (⊠ Ramada Inn, ☎ 981/6–22–33),
the only chic club in town, where politicians go to party, and the stu-
dent-oriented **El Dragon** (⊠ Sajuge complex on Av. Resurgimiento No.
87, ½ block from Alhambra Hotel, ☎ 981/1–18–10 or 981/6–42–89).
Both are open Thursday through Saturday nights only.

Three of Campeche's most conveniently located **movie theaters** are **Cine
Estelar** (⊠ Av. Miguel Alemán and Calle 49-B, ☎ 981/6–51–57), sis-
ter theater **Cine Hollywood** (directly behind the Estelar, same phone),
and **Cine Selem** (⊠ Calle 12 at Calle 57, ☎ 981/6–24–14). They usu-
ally show English-language films with Spanish subtitles.

For a fun, free evening, mix with the locals at the *Sabadito Alegre* (Fes-
tive Saturday) cultural fair, held each Saturday 7–10 PM in the Plaza
de la República, featuring folkloric and popular music and dance, co-
medians, and food and handicraft vendors. Sunday evenings you can

listen to the Campeche symphony orchestra in the main plaza between 8 and 9 PM. Confirm days and times with the tourist office.

Outdoor Activities and Sports

Hunting, fishing, and birding are popular throughout Campeche State. Contact **Don José Sansores** (or his son Fernando) at his Hotel Castel-mar office (⊠ Calle 61, No. 2, ☎ FAX 981/1–06–24) in Campeche or at the Snook Inn in Champotón (☎ FAX 982/8–00–18) for bookings and for information regarding the regulations and best areas for each sport. Sansores also has photographic wildlife safaris.

Shopping

Because Campeche is a seaport, ships-in-a-bottle, tacky statues made of seashells, and mother-of-pearl and black coral jewelry are everywhere. (Buying black coral isn't a good idea, as slow-growing coral popula-tions are becoming decimated throughout the world.) You can also find a limited selection of basketry, straw hats, leather goods, embroidered cloth, and clay trinkets. For the most part shopping is slim pickings, and even the shops listed below sell mainly souvenirs.

Visit the **Mercado Municipal** (Municipal Market; ⊠ Circuito Baluartes at Calle 53), at the eastern end of the city, for crafts and food. The new **Casa de Artesanía Tukulna** (⊠ Calle 10, No. 333, between Calles 59 and 61, ☎ 981/6–90–88, ◷ Mon.–Sat. 9–8, Sun. 10–2) is in a lovely old mansion worth a visit if only for its elegant colonial interior. You'll find well-made embroidered dresses and blouses, hammocks, hats, stucco reproductions of Maya motifs, CDs of ancient Maya songs, posters, and more. **Veleros** (⊠ Ah-Kin-Pech shopping center, ☎ 981/1–24–46, ◷ Mon.–Sat. 10–2 and 6–9) is owned by craftsman David Pérez and stocks his miniature ships, shell jewelry, furniture with nau-tical motifs, and jewelry fashioned from sanded and polished bulls' horns (a replacement for items made of the shells of endangered sea turtles).

From Campeche City to Mérida on Highway 261

This is by far the longer—and more interesting—way to reach the Yu-catán capital. The highway takes you past low-growing jungle beyond which cornfields and citrus orchards grow. Dairy and beef cows graze on the wide, open pasturelands, and you'll skirt—and sometimes pass through—villages of traditional round adobe huts with thatched roofs and tiny, weathered wooden doors. If you're driving you can take short detours to see underground caves, Maya ruins, and colonial churches and to get a feel for how people live outside the relative moder-nity of Mérida and Campeche City.

Edzná

 55 km (34 mi) southeast of Campeche City.

Archaeologists consider Edzná one of the peninsula's most important ruins because of the crucial transitional role it played among several architectural styles. It was occupied from 300 BC to AD 1450, reach-ing its pinnacle between AD 600 and 900. It was rediscovered in 1927. Although restoration work is going ahead now, there was little fund-ing for it after its initial excavation in 1943. There are information plaques in Spanish, English, and Maya in front of all of the structures, and a tourist facility on site has a snack shop, rest rooms, and a small book and souvenir store.

The 6-square-km (2-square-mi) expanse of savanna lies in a broad val-ley that is prone to flooding. Surrounding the site are vast networks of irrigation canals, the remnants of a highly sophisticated hydraulic system that channeled rainwater and water from the Champotón River into human-made *chultunes,* or wells. Commanding center stage in the **Gran Acrópolis** (Great Acropolis complex) is the **Pirámide de los Cinco Pisos** (Five-Story Pyramid), which rises 102 ft. The temple was so constructed that, in spring (May 1–3) and summer (August 7–9), the setting sun would illuminate the mask of the sun god located inside one of the pyramid's rooms. Carved into the Gran Acrópolis's **Building 414**— also called Temple of the Stone Masks—are various images of the sun deity. On the east side are portrayals of the dawn sun; those of the afternoon sun are logically found on the west side of the temple. Perhaps the most compelling image, however, is the anthropomorphic head with its huge and sinister protruding eye sockets. Local lore holds that Edzná, which means "House of the Gestures" (or "Grimaces"), may have been named for these images. More recent theories say the name comes from "Home of the Echo," as there is an acoustic effect between the main buildings; or that it means "Home of the Itzás," a Maya group native to southwest Campeche.

If you're not driving, consider taking one of the inexpensive day trips offered by most travel agencies in Campeche—this is far easier than trying to get to Edzná by bus. One such service is **Servicios Turísticos Picazh** (Calle 16 No. 348, between Calles 57 and 59, ☎ 981/6–44–26). Cost is about $15 for one person, $10 for two or more. For about $6 more you can get a guide as well. Buses leave daily from the Puerta de Tierra (Calle 59 at Av. Gobernadores), or you can arrange to be picked up at your hotel. If you do go by bus, be forewarned that you must walk about 1 km (½ mi) from the main road to the ruins. Check and double check with the driver about return buses—they are few and far between, and many tourists have been stranded until the next day. ⊠ *From Campeche City, take Hwy. 261 east for 44 km (27 mi) to Cayal, then Hwy. 188 southeast for 18 km (11 mi).* 🎟 *$2.* ☉ *Daily 8–5.*

Hopelchén
41 km (25 mi) east of the Edzná turnoff on Hwy. 261.

Hopelchén—the name means Place of the Five Wells—is a traditional Maya town noted for the lovely Franciscan church built in honor of St. Francis of Padua in 1667. Corn, beans, squash, tobacco, fruit, and henequen are cultivated in this rich agricultural center. There's also a community of blond-haired, blue-eyed Mennonites living here who make a living tilling the soil and selling homemade cheese of questionable hygienic standards.

Bolonchén de Rejón
34 km (21 mi) north of Hopelchén.

Just short of the Yucatán state line is the **Las Grutas de Xtacumbilxunaan** (Cave of the Nine Wells), named for caverns where legend says a Maya girl went for water and never returned. The caves are just a few kilometers south of Bolonchén de Rejón. (In Maya, Bolón means nine, chen means well. Rejón is the name of a famous Yucatecan politician.) In ancient times, cenotes deep in the extensive cave system provided an emergency water source during droughts. You can admire the delicate limestone formations in the upper part of the cave on an easy two-hour guided tour booked through a travel agency in Campeche City, or make arrangements at the state tourism office. There are no guides at the site, although for a small tip the caretaker will usually show you around. The rock surfaces inside are very slippery; wear good walking shoes and bring a flashlight in case the interior lights fail. 🎟 *$2.* ☉ *Daily 8–5.*

Hochob

 14 km (9 mi) south of Dzibalchén; 55 km (34 mi) south of Hopelchén.

The small Maya ruin of Hochob is an excellent example of the Chenes architectural style, which flowered in the Classic period from about AD 200 to 900. Found throughout central and southern Campeche, Chenes-style temples are easily recognized by their elaborate stucco facades forming giant masks of jaguars, birds, or other creatures, with doorways representing the beasts' open jaws. Since work began at Hochob in the early 1980s, three temples and palaces have been excavated at the site, including two that have been restored to nearly their original grandeur. ⊠ *South of Hopelchén on Dzibalchén–Chenko road,* ☎ *No phone.* ☐ *Free.* ☉ *Daily 8–5.*

Dzilibnocac

 18 km (11 mi) northeast of Dzibalchen; 30 km (19 mi) northeast of Hochob.

Although the road here was paved in 1998, few visitors make the trip to the intimate ruins at Dzilibnocac. (It is so low-key that the caretaker sometimes leaves the gate on the latch when he goes home for lunch.) Only a few structures have been excavated, but the setting—a small dale surrounded by low, tree-covered hills presided over by an ancient ceiba tree—is lovely.

A fair-size ceremonial center between AD 250 and 900, Dzilibnocac combines elements of the Puuc and Chenes architectural styles. To date only one building has been totally resuscitated, the Palacio Principal (main palace): an unusual round-cornered pyramid, a sort-of smaller version of the one at Uxmal. A square, one-room chamber at the top level is beautifully executed with dozens of Chaac curled noses carved into the outside walls. Each wall has its own open doorway. ⊠ *Northeast of Dzibalchen in the town of Iturbide. Turn right at far end of square onto dirt road; park by last houses when road becomes rutted, and walk about 150 yards,* ☎ *No phone.* ☐ *Free.* ☉ *Daily 8–5.*

The State of Campeche A to Z

Arriving and Departing

BY BUS

Assaults on **first-class buses** have been reported along Highway 261 near Escarcéga, 140 km (88 mi) south of Campeche City, during the day and night; the government has reportedly stepped up surveillance. **ADO** (⊠ Av. Gobernadores 289 at Calle 45, along Hwy. 261 to Mérida, ☎ 981/6–28–02), a first-class line, runs buses to Campeche from Mérida about every half hour, and has other daily departures throughout southern Mexico and as far north as Mexico City. The deluxe **Clase Elite** (☎ 981/1–02–61), half a block from the ADO station, also runs between Campeche, Mérida, Villahermosa, Veracruz, Jalapa, Puebla, Mexico City, and Cancún.

Head for the **second-class bus station,** directly behind the ADO station in Campeche, for destinations such as Bécal, Calkini, and Dzitbalchen on **TRP** and **Autobuses del Sur.** You can also get to Chetumal, Ciudad del Carmen, Escárcega, Mérida, and points throughout the Yucatán Peninsula on these two lines, although they make more stops.

BY CAR

Campeche is about 1½ hours from Mérida along the 160-km (99-mi) *via corta* (short route, Highway 180). The 250-km (155-mi) alternative, the *via larga* (long route, Highway 261), takes at least three hours but crosses the major Maya ruins of Uxmal, Kabah, and Sayil. There's a new four-lane toll highway ($3 one way) from Campeche City to Champotón that shaves 20 km (12 mi) off the 68-km (42-mi) trip.

BY PLANE

Aeroméxico (☎ 981/6–56–78) has one flight daily from Mexico City to Campeche City.

Getting Around

BY BUS

The municipal bus system covers all of Campeche City, but you can easily visit the major sights on foot. Public buses run along Avenida Ruíz Cortines and cost about 20¢.

There are several **free or inexpensive** ways to see the city and its cultural traditions. Guided 1½-hour walking tours depart daily at 6 PM from the municipal tourist office, next to the cathedral on the zócalo. One-hour tram tours of the city ($1) depart daily from the zócalo, on Calle 10, at 9:30 AM, 6 PM, and 8 PM—and at 7 PM weekends. A second tram route, to the forts on hills outside the city, is being planned.

BY TAXI

You can hail taxis on the street in Campeche City—or more reliably hire them from the main taxi stand (⊠ Calle 8 between Calles 55 and 53), at stands by the bus stations and market, or by calling ☎ 981/5–30–36. Taxis are scarce, so it's common to share them with people headed in the same direction as you. Don't be surprised to see an occupied cab slow down for you if the driver thinks he can pick up another fare. Shared cabs cost less than $1; private $1.50–$3.

Contacts and Resources

CAR RENTAL

VIASETUR (⊠ Ramada Inn, ☎ 981/6–22–33); **Auto Rent** (⊠ Hotel del Paseo, ☎ 981/1–01–00); and a new agency, **Rent A Car,** at the Torres de Cristal building (⊠ Av. Ruíz Cortines 112, ☎ 981/1–21–06) all rent economy Chevys and Suburbans. The lack of competition makes car rental more expensive here, and reservations more important.

EMERGENCIES

Throughout the state, call **06** locally in case of emergency.

Campeche City. Police (⊠ Av. Resurgimiento, No. 77, Col. Lazareto, ☎ 981/6–23–29). **Cruz Roja** (Red Cross; ⊠ Av. Las Palmas at Av. Ah Kim Pech, s/n, ☎ 981/5–24–11). The **Hospital General** (⊠ Av. Central at Circuito Baluartes, ☎ 981/6–09–20 or 981/6–42–33) and **Social Security Clinic** (⊠ Av. Lopez Mateos s/n, at Calle Talamantes, ☎ 981/6–56–12 or 981/6–52–02) are open 24 hours for emergencies.

TRAVEL AGENCIES AND TOUR OPERATORS

Campeche City. American Express/VIPs (⊠ Prolongación Calle 59, Edificio Belmar, Depto. 5, ☎ 981/1–10–10 or 981/1–10–00, FAX 981/6–83–33); **Viajes Campeche** (⊠ Calle 10, No. 339, ☎ 981/6–52–33, FAX 981/6–28–44); and **Destino Maya** (⊠ Av. Miguel Aleman, No. 162, Locale 106, ☎ 981/1–37–26 or 981/1–09–34; 713/440–0291 or 713/440–0253 in the U.S., FAX 981/1–09–34).

VISITOR INFORMATION

Campeche City. The **State Tourist Office** (⊠ Av. Ruiz Cortines s/n, across the street from Palacio de Gobierno, ☎ FAX 981/6–67–67, or ☎ 981/6–68–29) is open daily 9–3 and 5–8. The **City Tourism Office** (☎ 981/1–39–89 or 981/1–39–90), just south of the cathedral on the plaza principal, has general information (although little English is spoken) and takes reservations for the tram tour of Campeche. There is another module at the ADO bus station.

14 BACKGROUND AND ESSENTIALS

Portrait of Mexico

Chronology

Smart Travel Tips A to Z

LIFE BEHIND THE HEADLINES

As Mexico approaches the millennium, the country is where East Berlin found itself circa 1989. In this case there is no brick wall to tear down, but rather a slow crumbling of 70-year rule by one party, the Institutional Revolutionary Party (PRI). The party, not coincidentally, shares the colors of the Mexican flag. Instead of barbed wire to keep its citizens in, Mexico has a porous 2,000-mi border with the United States that serves as a pressure valve during hard times. But demand for change is growing from within. There is greater competition from the ballot box to the board room every day. From the scathing editorials in the growing free press to the customer service hot lines at once indifferent monopolies, Mexico is going through a political and economic transition all the more dramatic in part because it doesn't always make the nightly news.

Mexico, for all its ancient history, is a young country. About 40% of the population is between 14 and 29 years old. Many were raised on economic and political turmoil. Mexicans today are tired of seeing themselves as downtrodden. Many prefer to look for inspiration to actress Salma Hayek—a Veracruz native—or to the successful young Harvard Business School entrepreneur, Miguel Angel Davila, who started the new movie chain Cinemex. Signs of modern Mexico are everywhere: cash machines even in some small towns, *People en Español,* and forgery-proofed voter I.D. cards. But as ever, modernity does not come all at once. In much of Mexico, a brand new VW Beetle may share the road with a burro. Mexico's struggle with progress is like a Latin dance: two steps forward, one step back.

As the country has opened economically over the last two decades, a slow push for political opening has followed. Those growing up now are often dubbed the NAFTA generation, after the free trade agreement: they are more outward looking, more free enterprise savvy, and more cynical about the old one-party system. That old system failed them when the bottom fell out of the economy in 1994: the memory of what Mexicans simply call *la crisis* is very much alive. People are still shy of bank accounts, credit cards, and home loans, which are practically nonexistent since the peso crashed. Wages remain below what they were before the crisis, full-time jobs are always in short supply, and the government keeps tightening the belt. Much of Mexico, however, is booming. Exports—driven by the free trade agreement with the U.S.—are thriving. Investors are back, betting on the perennial comeback. The economy is still vulnerable to global recession, but it is much more stable than it was before la crisis.

It's the political system that is still broken. Everyone hopes it will be on the mend for 2000, when Mexicans will vote in the most competitive presidential elections in their history and test their fledgling democracy, which, so far, is proving to be pretty messy. On the agenda for 1999, the three main political parties—the PRI, the liberal Democratic Revolutionary Party (PRD), and the conservative National Action Party (PAN)—are sorting out how to nominate their candidates. Nowhere is there more confusion than in the PRI itself, which is searching for a new image and direction in the face of losing power. Election primaries have been test-run with mixed success. And debate still flares over concepts as rudimentary as reelection. Mexicans are no longer voting with only their feet; they are making their voice heard on ballots. Recent elections have voted out PRI governors in eight states and given opposition parties real power in Congress for the first time in modern history. Congressmen used to be called *levantadedos* (fingerlifters) because all they did was vote the president's bidding. Today, there is competition—even the occasional fistfight—on the House floor. And the once all-powerful presidency is within the opposition's grasp.

One likely candidate is Cuauhtémoc Cárdenas, who lost his race for president to Carlos Salinas in a 1988 election suspected of fraud. In 1997, he won the daunting job of mayor of Mexico City. If he survives the smog, traffic, and protest marches, he'll be a strong contender for president again in 2000 for his leftist PRD. Presidential campaigning began earlier than ever, unleashing self-proclaimed candidates in a confusing dogfight among the three main parties. The right-wing PAN has a swashbuckling Norteño (northern) governor named Vicente Fox who stumped so much in 1998 he earned the nickname *Ausente* (absent) Fox in his home state. The PRI candidacy is wide open.

One thing's for sure: the monarchical Mexican presidency has come to an end. No one used to look the Mexican president in the eye. Such was his power. Today, some political commentators use the informal *tu* (you) when addressing President Ernesto Zedillo. He's pilloried regularly in political cartoons. Satirists have even dubbed him "presidente lite." In fact, Zedillo was an accidental candidate, stepping in for Luis Donaldo Colosio, who was assasinated in 1994—a tragedy from which Mexico has never fully recovered. But during his *sexenio* (six-year term) Zedillo has proven himself more of an accidental reformer. By not playing the role of iron-clad president, he has opened the door to the opposition. He's expanded political funding for all parties, returned some power and money to the country's 31 states, and vowed not to handpick his successor. This tradition of handpicking, called the *dedazo,* literally "the finger-point-

ing," has existed ever since the PRI took power in 1929.

Many have predicted the demise of the PRI. But like Cuba's Fidel Castro, it keeps hanging on. Considering that the PRI machine makes Chicago's ward politics look like amateur hour, it's no wonder. Mexico is hardly free of the old dirty dealings, like vote buying and bullying from party bosses, but these days electoral fraud is much less common, especially in cities. Ballot boxes are transparent, and there is a national voter registry.

The PRI's grip on power—for now—has more to do with the opposition's immaturity, the party's ability to learn from its mistakes, and the longing many older Mexicans feel for the security the party once provided. The PRI has never been an ideological party, and it has managed to change to suit the national mood. The party is already making a comeback in state elections, in part, by moving away from its technocrats—the term refers to the cocky young reformers epitomized by former president Salinas. The "Harvard-trained economist," as he was invariably described, brought Mexico free trade, privatization, and all the promises of neoliberalism.

Salinas also brought discredit on his party and his country. Not only did his dream of First World membership die with the peso crisis, but his administration is now considered one of the most corrupt in Mexican history. Salinas lives in self-imposed exile in Dublin, Ireland, but he is still called Mexico's favorite villain. Street vendors sell masks of his face with his inimitable big ears. Bankers who cashed in under Salinas's privatizations have gone on the lam. And Salinas's older brother, Raúl, has been sentenced to 50 years for allegedly masterminding the murder of a former PRI leader. (The decision is under appeal). Meanwhile, Swiss investigators seized $114 million from Raúl's Swiss bank accounts in 1998 claiming that the money was proceeds from protecting drug traffickers. Now Mexico is investigating drug ties in the Salinas administration.

There has been a kind of don't-ask, don't-tell attitude about drug-trafficking in Mexico for years. Since Mexico became the main transportation route for Colombian cocaine growers in the 1980s, drug cartels have insinuated themselves into Mexican life, and Mexican cartels are now every bit as powerful as their Colombian counterparts. Drug use is up, and drug culture, touching everything from clothing to music, is spreading. People wink and nudge each other about the gaudy hotels and new shopping complexes, especially along the U.S. border, that they assume were built with drug money. But they shrug it off. And although both the Mexican and U.S. governments are working together to fight traffickers, it may be too little too late. Drug violence hasn't hurt the average citizen enough for Mexicans to get really angry about it. But increased crime—driven by corruption, and not poverty—has. Most Mexicans biggest concern, they'll tell you, is public safety. Although crime is still no worse than in many big U.S. cities, poor policing and weak courts make it seem that way.

As in much of Latin America, hard-liners are making a comeback. Some Mexicans are beginning to clamor for the death penalty, something almost unheard of in Catholic countries. The army has been called in to help fight street crime, drugs and guerillas. And the human rights situation, especially in states considered guerilla-friendly, is bleak. In December 1997, paramilitary forces massacred 45 peasants thought sympathetic to the Zapatista rebels in Acteal in the southern state of Chiapas. Peace talks with the Zapatistas, who sprang up in 1995, are stalled even though the ceasefire holds. The Zapatistas, or EZLN, are only the most publicity-savvy of a few small guerilla groups. They—with their charismatic spokesman Subcomandante Marcos—are still a leftist cause célèbre. At first, Mexicans had a brief romance with the pipe-smoking Marcos because he seemed to speak for the downtrodden. Now, they say they are mostly weary of the violence.

How can Mexico become a truly modern democracy? It's an ongoing debate on the editorial pages. Some claim it simply can't happen as long as the PRI has a stranglehold on the presidency. Although even the opposition supports most of the country's liberal economic changes, just what role the state will play in the future is fuzzy. Many Mexicans still believe that the government should provide, whereas the NAFTA generation wants to be free of the state's shackles. For most Mexicans, democracy remains a buzzword. But every day Mexicans have more choices and opportunities, and greater freedom.

— Martha Brandt

As bureau chief for *Newsweek* in Mexico, **Martha Brant** looked for insight into the country everywhere from Acapulco to Zacatecas. Her reporting took her to a druglord's wake, a male strip club, and immigrant ghost towns.

MEXICO AT A GLANCE

Precolumbian Mexico

ca. 50,000 BC Asian nomads cross land bridge over the Bering Strait to North America, gradually migrate south

ca. 5000 –2000 BC Archaic period, which marked the beginnings of agriculture and village life

ca. 2000– 200 BC Formative or pre-Classic period: development of pottery, incipient political structures

ca. 1500– 900 BC The powerful and sophisticated Olmec civilization develops along the Gulf of Mexico in the present-day states of Veracruz and Tabasco. Olmec culture, the "mother culture" of Mexico, flourishes along Gulf coast.

ca. 200 BC –AD 900 Classic period: height of pre-Columbian culture. Three centers at Teotihuacán (near Mexico City), Monte Albán (Oaxaca), and Maya civilization in the Yucatán. Priest-run city-states produce impressive art and architecture.

650–900 Decline of Classic cultures: fall of Teotihuacán ca. 650 leads to competition among other city-states, exacerbated by migrations of northern tribes

ca. 900–1521 Post-Classic period: rule passes to military; war and war gods gain prominence

ca. 900–1150 Toltecs, a northern tribe, establish a flourishing culture at their capital of Tula under the legendary monarch Topiltzin-Quetzalcóatl

ca. 1200 Rise of Mixtec culture at Zapotec sites of Monte Albán and Mitla; notable for production of picture codices, which include historical narratives

ca. 1000 –1450 Maya culture, declining in south, emerges in the Yucatán; under Toltec rule, Chichén Itzá dominates the peninsula

1111 Aztecs migrate to mainland from island home off the Nayarit coast. They are not welcomed by the peoples of central Mexico.

1150–1350 Following the fall of Tula, first the Chichimecs, then the Tepanecs assert hegemony over central Mexico. The Tepanec tyrant Tezozómoc (1320–1426), like his contemporaries in Renaissance Italy, establishes his power with murder and treachery.

1376 Tezozómoc grants autonomy to the Aztec city of Tenochtitlán, built in the middle of Lake Texcoco

1420–1500 Aztecs extend their rule to much of central and southern Mexico. A warrior society, they build a great city at Tenochtitlán

1502 Moctezuma II (1466–1520) assumes throne at the height of Aztec culture and political power

1517 Spanish expedition under Francisco Hernandez de Córdoba (1475–1526) lands on Yucatán coast

1519 Hernán Cortés (1485–1547) lands in Cozumel, founds Veracruz, and determines to conquer. Steel weapons, horses, and smallpox, combined with a belief that Cortés was the resurrected Topiltzin-Quetzalcóatl, minimize Aztec resistance. Cortés enters Tenochtitlán and captures Moctezuma.

The Colonial Period

1520–21 Moctezuma is killed; Tenochtitlán falls to Cortés. The last Aztec emperor, Cuauhtemoc, is executed

1528 Juan de Zumarraga (1468–1548) arrives as bishop of Mexico City, gains title "Protector of the Indians"; native conversion to Catholicism begun

1535 First Spanish viceroy arrives in Mexico

1537 Pope Paul III issues a bull declaring that native Mexicans are indeed human and not beasts. First printing press arrives in Mexico City

1546–48 Silver deposits discovered at Zacatecas

1547 Spanish conquest of Aztec Empire—now known as "New Spain"—completed, at enormous cost to native peoples

1553 Royal and Pontifical University of Mexico, first university in the New World, opens

1571 The Spanish Inquisition established in New Spain; it is not abolished until 1820

1609 Northern capital of New Spain established at Santa Fe (New Mexico)

1651 Birth of Sor (Sister) Juana Inés de la Cruz, greatest poet of colonial Mexico (d. 1695)

1718 Franciscan missionaries settle in Texas, which becomes part of New Spain

1765 Charles III of Spain (1716–88) sends José de Galvez to tour New Spain and propose reforms

1769 Franciscan Junipero Serra establishes missions in California, extending Spanish hegemony

1788 Death of Charles III; his reforms improved administration, but also raised social and political expectations among the colonial population, which were not fulfilled

1808 Napoléon invades Spain, leaving a power vacuum in New Spain

The War of Independence

1810 September 16: Father Miguel Hidalgo y Costilla (1753–1811) preaches his *Grito de Dolores*, sparking rebellion

1811 Hidalgo is captured and executed; leadership of the movement passes to Father José Maria Morelos y Pavón (1765–1815)

1813 Morelos calls a congress at Chilpancingo, which drafts a Declaration of Independence

1815 Morelos is captured and executed

The Early National Period

1821 Vicente Guerrero, a rebel leader, and Agustín de Iturbide (1783–1824), a Spanish colonel converted to the rebel cause, rejuvenate the Independence movement. Spain recognizes Mexican independence with the Treaty of Córdoba.

1822 Iturbide is named Emperor of Mexico, which stretches from California through Central America

1823 After 10 months in office, Emperor Agustín is turned out

1824 A new constitution creates a federal republic, the Estados Unidos Mexicanos; modeled on the U.S. Constitution, the Mexican version retains the privileges of the Catholic Church and gives the president extraordinary "emergency" powers

1829 President Vicente Guerrero abolishes slavery. A Spanish attempt at reconquest is halted by General Antonio López de Santa Anna (1794–1876), already a hero for his role in the overthrow of Emperor Agustín

1833 Santa Anna is elected president by a huge majority; he holds the office for 11 of its 36 changes of hands by 1855

1836 Although voted in as a liberal, Santa Anna abolishes the 1824 constitution. Already dismayed at the abolition of slavery, Texas—whose population is largely American—declares its independence. Santa Anna successfully besieges the Texans at the Alamo. But a month later he is captured by Sam Houston following the Battle of San Jacinto. Texas gains its independence as the Lone Star Republic.

1846 The U.S. decision to annex Texas leads to war

1848 The treaty of Guadalupe Hidalgo reduces Mexico's territory by half, ceding present-day Texas, New Mexico, Arizona, California, Nevada, Utah, and part of Colorado to the U.S.

1853 Santa Anna agrees to the Gadsden Purchase, ceding a further 48,000 square km (30,000 square mi) to the United States

The Reform and French Intervention

1855 The Revolution of Ayutla topples Santa Anna and leads to the period of The Reform

1857 The liberal Constitution of 1857 disestablishes the Catholic Church, among other measures

1858–61 The civil War of the Reform ends in liberal victory. Benito Juárez (1806–72) is elected president. France, Spain, and Britain agree jointly to occupy the customs house at Veracruz to force payment of Mexico's huge foreign debt.

1862 Spain and Britain withdraw their forces; the French, seeking empire, march inland. On May 5, General Porfirio Díaz repulses the French at Puebla.

1863 Strengthened with reinforcements, the French occupy Mexico City. Napoléon III of France appoints Archduke Ferdinand Maximilian of Austria (1832–1867) as Emperor of Mexico.

1864 Maximilian and his empress Charlotte, known as Carlotta, land at Veracruz

1867 With U.S. assistance, Juárez overthrows Mexico's second empire. Maximilian is executed; Carlotta, pleading his case in France, goes mad

1872 Juárez dies in office. The Mexico City–Veracruz railway is completed, symbol of the new progressivist mood.

The Porfiriato

1876 Porfirio Díaz (1830–1915) comes to power in the Revolution of Tuxtepec; he holds office nearly continuously until 1911. With his advisors, the *cientificos*, he forces modernization and balances the budget for the first time in Mexican history. But the social cost is high.

1886 Birth of Diego Rivera (died 1957)

1890 José Schneider, who is of German ancestry, founds the Cerveceria Cuauhtémoc, brewer of Carta Blanca

1900 Jesús, Enrique, and Ricardo Flores Magón publish the anti-Díaz newspaper *La Regeneración*. Suppressed, the brothers move their campaign to the United States, first to San Antonio, then to St. Louis

1906 The Flores Magón group publish their Liberal Plan, a proposal for reform. Industrial unrest spreads.

The Second Revolution

1907 Birth of Frida Kahlo (died 1954)

1910 On the centennial of the Revolution, Díaz wins yet another rigged election. Revolt breaks out.

1911 Rebels under Pascual Orozco and Francisco (Pancho) Villa (1878–1923) capture Ciudad Juárez; Díaz resigns. Francisco Madero is elected president; calling for land reform, Emiliano Zapata (1879–1919) rejects the new regime. Violence continues.

1913 Military coup: Madero is deposed and murdered. In one day Mexico has three presidents, the last being General Victoriano Huerta (1854–1916). Civil war rages.

1914 American intervention leads to dictator Huerta's overthrow. Villa and Zapata briefly join forces at the Convention of Aguascalientes, but the Revolution goes on. Birth of poet-critic Octavio Paz

1916 Villa's border raids lead to an American punitive expedition under Pershing. Villa eludes capture

1917 Under a new constitution, Venuziano Carranza, head of the Constitutionalist Army, is elected president. Zapata continues his rebellion, which is brutally suppressed

1918 CROM, the national labor union, is founded

1919 On order of Carranza, Zapata is assassinated

1920 Carranza is assassinated; Alvaro Obregón (1880–1928), who helped overthrow dictator Huerta in 1914, is elected president, beginning a period of reform and reconstruction. Schools are built and land is redistributed. In the next two decades, revolutionary culture finds expression in the art of Diego Rivera and José Clemente Orozco (1883–1949), the novels of Martin Luis Guzmán and Gregorio Lopez y Fuentes, and the music of Carlos Chavez (1899–1978)

1923 Pancho Villa is assassinated. The United States finally recognizes the Obregón regime

1926–28 Catholics react to government anticlericalism in the Cristero Rebellion

1934–40 The presidency of Lázaro Cárdenas (1895–1970) leads to the fullest implementation of revolutionary reforms

1938 Cárdenas nationalizes the oil companies, removing them from foreign control

1940 On August 20, exiled former Soviet leader Leon Trotsky murdered in his Mexico City home

Post-Revolutionary Mexico

1951 Mexico's segment of the Pan-American Highway is completed, confirming the industrial growth and prosperity of post-war Mexico. Culture is increasingly Americanized; writers such as Octavio Paz and Carlos Fuentes express disillusionment with the post-revolution world

1968 The Summer Olympics in Mexico City showcase Mexican prosperity, but massive demonstrations indicate underlying social unrest

1981–82 Recession and a drop in oil prices severely damage Mexico's economy. The peso is devalued

1985 Thousands die in the Mexico City earthquake

1988 American-educated economist Carlos Salinas de Gortari is elected president; for the first time since 1940, support for the PRI, the national political party, seems to be slipping

1993 North American Free Trade Agreement (NAFTA) is signed with United States and Canada

1994 Uprising by the indigenous peoples of Chiapas, led by the Zapatistas and their charismatic ski-masked leader, Subcomandante Marcos; election reforms promised as a result

Popular PRI presidential candidate Luis Donaldo Colosio assassinated while campaigning in Tijuana. Ernesto Zedillo, generally thought to be more of a technocrat and "old boy"-style PRI politician, replaces him and wins the election

Zedillo, blaming the economic policies of his predecessor, devalues the peso in December

1995 Recession sets in as a result of the peso devaluation. The former administration is rocked by scandals surrounding the assassinations of Colosio and another high-ranking government official; ex-President Carlos Salinas de Gortari moves to the United States

1996 Mexico's economy, bolstered by a $28 billion bailout program led by the United States, turns upward, but the recovery is fragile. The opposition National Action Party (PAN), which is committed to conservative economic policies, gains strength. New details of scandals of the former administration continue to emerge.

1997 Mexico's top anti-drug official is arrested on bribery charges. Nonetheless, the United States recertifies Mexico as a partner in the war on drugs. The Zedillo administration faces midterm party elections.

1998 Death of Octavio Paz

1999 Raúl Salinas, brother of the former president Carlos Salinas de Gortari (in exile in Ireland), sentenced for the alleged murder of a PRI leader

ESSENTIAL INFORMATION

ADDRESSES

The Mexican method of naming streets can be exasperatingly arbitrary, so **be patient when searching for street addresses.** Streets in the centers of many colonial cities (those built by the Spanish) are laid out in a grid surrounding *zócalo* (main square) and often change names on different sides of the square. Other streets simply acquire a new name after a certain number of blocks. As in the United States, numbered streets are usually designated *norte/sur* (north/south) or *oriente/poniente* (east/west) on either side of a central avenue. (Three of these are abbreviated: Nte., Ote., and Pte. Sur is spelled out.)

In many cities, streets that have proper names like Avenida Benito Juárez change names to Calle Francisco Madero, for example, when they cross some other street—and only a map will show where one begins and the other ends.

Blocks are often labeled numerically, according to distance from a chosen starting point, as in "la Calle de Pachuca," "2a Calle de Pachuca," etc.

Many Mexican addresses have "s/n" for *sin número* (no number) after the street name. This is common in small towns where there aren't many buildings on a block. Similarly, many hotels give their address as "Km 30 Carr. a Querétaro," which indicates that the property is at the 30th kilometer on the *carretera* (main highway) to Querétaro.

As in Europe, addresses in Mexico are written with the street name first, followed by the street number. A five-digit *código postal* (postal code) precedes, rather than follows, the name of the city. Apdo. (*apartado*) Postal, or A.P., means post office box number. Here is a sample address: *Hacienda Paraíso, Calle Allende 211, 68000 Oaxaca, Oax.*

AIR TRAVEL

BOOKING YOUR FLIGHT

When you book **look for nonstop flights** and **remember that "direct" flights stop at least once.** Try to avoid connecting flights, which require a change of plane.

CARRIERS

➤ MAJOR AIRLINES: **American** (☎ 800/433–7300) to Mexico City, Cancún, Acapulco, Monterrey, Guadalajara, Los Cabos, Puerto Vallarta, León/El Bajío. **Continental** (☎ 800/231–0856) to Mexico City, Cancún, Cozumel, Guadalajara, Ixtapa/Zihuatanejo, Los Cabos, Mazatlán, Monterrey, Puerto Vallarta, Veracruz, Mérida, Leon/El Bajio (the Heartland), Tampico. **Delta** (☎ 800/241–4141) to Mexico City, Cancún, Mérida, Guadalajara, Puerto Vallarta, León/El Bajío, Ixtapa/Zihuatanejo, and Acapulco. **Northwest** (☎ 800/447–4747) to Mexico City, and Cancún. **United** (☎ 800/241–6522) to Mexico City . **US Airways** (☎ 800/428–4322) to Cancún.

➤ SMALLER AIRLINES: **Aero California** (☎ 800/237–6225) to Mexico City, Manzanillo, Mazatlán, Guadalajara, Monterrey, Tijuana, Puebla, La Paz, Loreto, Los Cabos. **Aeroméxico** (☎ 800/237–6639) to Mexico City, Cancún, Guadalajara, Ixtapa/Zihuatanejo, Acapulco, León/El Bajío, Los Cabos, Guaymas/San Carlos, Cozumel, Mérida, Monterrey. **America West** (☎ 800/235–9292) to Mexico City, Ixtapa/Zihuatanejo, Los Cabos, Puerto Vallarta, Acapulco, and Manzanillo. **Mexicana** (☎ 800/531–7921) to Mexico City, Cancún, Acapulco, Ixtapa/Zihuatanejo, Guadalajara, Morelia, León/El Bajío, Los Cabos, Puerto Vallarta, Zacatecas, Mazatlán, Mérida.

➤ FROM THE U.K.: **British Airways** (☎ 0345/222111) has a nonstop flight from the United Kingdom to Mexico City. Other airlines flying to Mexico, with brief stops en route, include **Continental** (☎ 01293/776464), from Gatwick via Houston, from Birmingham and Manchester via Newark; **American** (☎ 0345/789789), via Chicago, Dallas, or Miami; **KLM** (☎ 0181/750–9820), via Amsterdam; **Air France** (☎ 0181/742–6600), via Paris; **Delta** (☎ 0800/414767), via Atlanta; **United** (☎ 0181/990–9900), via Chicago or Washington, Dulles; **Lufthansa** (☎ 0181/750–3535), via Frankfurt; and **Iberia** (☎ 0171/830–0011), via Madrid.

➤ DOMESTIC AIRLINES: **Aerocaribe** (reserve through Mexicana) serves the Yucatán and the Southeast. **Aeromar** (reserve through Mexicana or Aeroméxico) serves central Mexico. **Aerolitoral** (reserve through Aeroméxico or Mexicana) serves northeastern Mexico. **Aviacsa** (☎ 961/2–80–81 in Chiapas; 5/448–8900 in Mexico City) serves Cancún, Chetumal, and Mérida. **AeroCalifornia** (☎ 800/237–6225) serves , Guadalajara, Loreto, Puebla, Tepic, Tijuana, and several other gateways. **Taesa** (☎ 800/904–6300) serves Acapulco, Tijuana, Zacatecas, Puerto Vallarta, Morelia and Mexico City.

CHECK-IN & BOARDING

Assuming that not everyone with a ticket will show up, airlines routinely overbook planes. When that happens, airlines ask for volunteers to give up their seats. In return these volunteers usually get a certificate for a free flight and are rebooked on the next flight out. If there are not enough volunteers, the airline must choose who will be denied boarding. The first to get bumped are passengers who checked in late and those flying on discounted tickets, so **get to the gate and check in as early as possible,** especially during peak periods.

When checking in, be prepared to present your passport.

CUTTING COSTS

The least-expensive airfares to Mexico must usually be purchased in advance and are non-refundable. It's smart to **call a number of airlines, and when you are quoted a good price,** **book it on the spot**—the same fare may not be available the next day. Always **check different routings** and look into using different airports. Travel agents, especially low-fare specialists (☞ Discounts & Deals, *below*), are helpful.

Consolidators are another good source. They buy tickets for scheduled international flights at reduced rates from the airlines, then sell them at prices that beat the best fare available directly from the airlines, usually without restrictions. Sometimes you can even get your money back if you need to return the ticket. Carefully read the fine print detailing penalties for changes and cancellations, and **confirm your consolidator reservation with the airline.**

➤ CONSOLIDATORS: **Cheap Tickets** (☎ 800/377–1000). **Discount Airline Ticket Service** (☎ 800/576–1600). **Unitravel** (☎ 800/325–2222). **Up & Away Travel** (☎ 212/889–2345). **World Travel Network** (☎ 800/409–6753).

ENJOYING THE FLIGHT

For more legroom **request an emergency-aisle seat.** Don't sit in the row in front of the emergency aisle or in front of a bulkhead, where seats may not recline. If you have dietary concerns, **ask for special meals when booking.** These can be vegetarian, low-cholesterol, or kosher, for example. On long flights, try to maintain a normal routine, to help fight jet lag. At night **get some sleep.** By day **eat light meals, drink water** (not alcohol), and **move around the cabin** to stretch your legs.

FLYING TIMES

Mexico City is 4½ hours from New York, 4 hours from Chicago, and 3½ hours from Los Angeles. Cancún is 3½ hours from New York and from Chicago, 4½ hours from Los Angeles. Acapulco is 6 hours from New York, 4 hours from Chicago, and 3½ hours from Los Angeles.

From London, Mexico City is a 12½-hour flight, Cancún 11¾ hours.

HOW TO COMPLAIN

If your baggage goes astray or your flight goes awry, complain right away.

Most carriers require that you **file a claim immediately.**

➤ AIRLINE COMPLAINTS: U.S. Department of Transportation **Aviation Consumer Protection Division** (✉ C-75, Room 4107, Washington, DC 20590, ☎ 202/366–2220). **Federal Aviation Administration Consumer Hotline** (☎ 800/322–7873).

AIRPORTS

The major airports are **Acapulco** (General Juan Alvarez airport, ☎ 748/4–08–87). **Cancún** (Cancún airport, ☎ 98/860–049). **Cozumel** (Cozumel airport, ☎ 987/2–04–85). **Guadalajara** (Ramón F. Quintanilla García airport, ☎ 3/688–51–20). **Ixtapa** (Manuel Zúrita Gallegos airport, ☎ 755/42–070). **Mazatlán** (Juan Buelna airport, ☎ 69/82–23–99). **Mérida** (Hector José Navarrete Muñoz airport, ☎ 99/43–13–40). **Mexico City** (Benito Juarez airport, ☎ 5/571–3600). **Puerto Vallarta** (Gustavo Díaz Ordaz airport ☎ 322/1–12–98). **Los Cabos** (Lic. Alberto de la Mora airport ☎ 114/2–03–41). **Manzanillo** (Playa de Oro airport), ☎ 333/32–525.

BIKE TRAVEL

Bike travel in Mexico is a rough-and-ready proposition. Some roads have never seen a bicycle, and drivers are not accustomed to cyclists. In addition, most Mexican roads lack shoulders and are often pitted. Despite these drawbacks, cycling in Mexico can be fun if you plan ahead, and bikes are especially useful for travel to places where there are only dirt roads or tracks, or where public transportation is scant. In the Yucatán, for example, bikes are a primary form of transportation for locals, and bike-repair shops are common even in smaller towns. When planning your trip, consult an up-to-date AAA, Pemex, or Guía Roji map. Be sure to carry plenty of water and everything you might need to repair your bike. Pack extra patch kits, as shards of glass often litter the roads. If you can take your bike apart and fold it up, buses will allow you to store it in the cargo space; likewise on trains in the Copper Canyon.

Bicycling Mexico (Hunter Publishing Inc.), by Ericka Weisbroth and Eric Ellman, is the bible of bicyclists, complete with maps, color photos, historical information, and a kilometer-by-kilometer breakdown of every route possible. For a list of companies that run organized bike tours of Mexico, ☞ Theme Trips, *below.*

BIKES IN FLIGHT

Most airlines accommodate bikes as luggage, provided they are dismantled and boxed. For bike boxes, often free at bike shops, you'll pay about $5 from airlines. International travelers can sometimes substitute a bike for a piece of checked luggage at no charge; otherwise, the cost is about $100. Domestic and Canadian airlines charge $25–$50.

BUS TRAVEL

Getting to Mexico by bus is no longer for just the adventurous or budget-conscious. In the past, bus travelers were required to change to Mexican vehicles at the border, and vice versa. Now, however, in an effort to bring more American visitors and their tourist dollars to off-the-beaten-track markets and attractions, the Mexican government has removed this obstacle, and a growing number of transborder bus tours are available.

Gateway cities like El Paso, Del Rio, Laredo, McAllen, Brownsville, and San Antonio, Texas, along with Tijuana, are served by several small private bus lines as well as by **Greyhound Lines** ☎ (800/231–2222). If you'll be leaving Mexico by bus, you can buy tickets for the U.S. leg of your trip from the Greyhound representative in Mexico City (✉ Paseo de la Reforma 35, ☎ 5592–3766).

For travel within Mexico, buses run the gamut from comfortable air-conditioned coaches with bathrooms, video movies, and hostess service (premier, deluxe, or first class) to dilapidated "vintage" buses (second and third class) on which pigs and chickens travel and stops are made in the middle of nowhere. A lower-class bus ride can be interesting if you are not in a hurry and want to see the sights and experience the local culture—and the fares generally are up to 30% cheaper than those in the premium categories. But for comfort's sake alone, if you are planning a long-distance haul, **buy tickets for first class or better when traveling by bus within Mexico.** Unlike tickets for the other classes, these can be reserved in advance.

The Mexican bus network is extensive, far more so than that of the railroads. Buses go where trains do not, service is more frequent, tickets can be purchased on the spot (except during holidays and on long weekends, when advance purchase is crucial), and first-class buses are faster and much more comfortable than trains. On all overnight bus rides, **bring something to eat** in case you don't like the restaurant where the bus stops, and **carry toilet tissue**, as rest rooms might not have any. Smoking is prohibited on a growing number of Mexican buses, though the rule is occasionally ignored.

In large cities, bus stations are a good distance from the center of town. Though there's a trend toward consolidation, some towns have different stations for each bus line. Bus service in Mexico City is well organized, operating out of four terminals.

CLASSES

First-class bus lines include the following: **ADO** (☎ 5785–9659) serves Yucatán, Cancún, Villahermosa, and Veracruz from the Eastern Bus Terminal (known by its Spanish acronym, TAPO), and Oaxaca and Tampico from the Northern Bus Terminal (*Terminal Central Autobuses del Norte*) (☎ 5567–6247). **ADO GL** (☎ 5785–9659) leaves from the same terminals and offers deluxe service to the same destinations. **Cristóbal Colón** (☎ 5756–9926) goes to Chiapas, Oaxaca, Puebla, and the Guatemala border from the Eastern Bus Terminal. **Estrella Blanca** (☎ 5729–0707) goes to Manzanillo, Mazatlán, Monterrey, and Nuevo Laredo from the Western Bus Terminal (*Terminal Central Poniente*). **ETN** (☎ 5273–0251) goes to Toluca and Morelia from the Western Bus Terminal and to Manzanillo and Puerto Vallarta from the Northern Bus Terminal (☎ 5567–9466). **Estrella de Oro** (☎ 5549–8520) goes to Acapulco, Cuernavaca, Taxco, and Ixtapa

from the Southern Bus Terminal. **Estrella Blanca**(☎ 5729–0707) has first-class and deluxe service to all states but Yucatán, Quintana Roo, and Chiapas.

BUSINESS HOURS

BANKS & OFFICES

Banks are generally open weekdays 9 to 3. In larger cities, most are open until 5 or 7. Many of the larger banks keep a few branches open Saturday 9 to 2:30 and Sunday 10 to 1:30; however, the extended hours are often for deposits or check cashing only. Banks will give you cash advances in pesos (for a fee) if you have a major credit card. **Government offices** are usually open to the public 8 to 3; along with banks and most private offices, they are closed on national holidays.

MUSEUMS & SIGHTS

Along with **theaters** and most **archaeological sights, museums** close Mondays, with few exceptions. **Sundays,** museums across the country have free admission.

SHOPS

Stores are generally open weekdays and Saturday from 9 or 10 AM to 7 or 8 PM; in resort areas, shops may also be open on Sunday. Business hours are 9 to 7, with a two-hour lunch break from about 2 to 4.

CAMERAS & PHOTOGRAPHY

Always **keep your film and tape out of the sun.** Carry an extra supply of batteries, and **be prepared to turn on your camera or camcorder** to prove to security personnel that the device is real. Always **ask for hand inspection of film,** which becomes clouded after successive exposures to airport X-ray machines, and **keep videotapes away from metal detectors.**

CAR RENTAL

When you think about renting a car, bear in mind that you may be sharing the road with bad local drivers—sometimes acquiring a driver's license in Mexico is more a question of paying someone off than of having tested skill. In addition, the highway system is very uneven from state to state: in some regions, modern, well-paved superhighways prevail; in others—particularly the mountains—potholes, untethered livestock, and dangerous, unrailed curves are the rule. Check on local road conditions before you rent. ☞ Car Travel, *below,* for further information on driving in Mexico.

Rates in Mexico City and Acapulco begin at $56 a day and $350 a week for an economy car with air-conditioning, a manual transmission, and unlimited mileage. This does not include tax on car rentals, which is 15%, or insurance, which runs about $100 a week. ☞ Insurance *in* Car Travel, *below.*

➤ MAJOR AGENCIES: **Alamo** (☎ 800/522–9696; 0181/759–6200 in the U.K.). **Avis** (☎ 800/331–1084; 800/879–2847 in Canada; 02/9353–9000 in Australia; 09/525–1982 in New Zealand). **Budget** (☎ 800/527–0700; 0144/227–6266 in the U.K.). **Dollar** (☎ 800/800–6000; 0181/897–0811 in the U.K., where it is known as Eurodollar; 02/9223–1444 in Australia). **Hertz** (☎ 800/654–3001; 800/263–0600 in Canada; 0181/897–2072 in the U.K.; 02/9669–2444 in Australia; 03/358–6777 in New Zealand). **National InterRent** (☎ 800/227–3876; 0345/222525 in the U.K., where it is known as Europcar InterRent).

CUTTING COSTS

To get the best deal **book through a travel agent who will shop around.**

Do **look into wholesalers,** companies that do not own fleets but rent in bulk from those that do and often offer better rates than traditional car-rental operations. Payment must be made before you leave home.

➤ WHOLESALERS: **Auto Europe** (☎ 207/842–2000 or 800/223–5555, FAX 800–235–6321). **Kemwel Holiday Autos** (☎ 914/835–3000 or 800/678–0678, FAX 914/835–5126).

INSURANCE

When driving a rented car you are generally responsible for any damage to or loss of the vehicle. You also are liable for any property damage or personal injury that you may cause while driving. In Mexico it is impera-tive to have Mexican auto insurance (☞ Car Travel, *below,* for more information.

REQUIREMENTS & RESTRICTIONS

In Mexico your own driver's license is acceptable. An International Driver's Permit is a good idea; it's available from the American or Canadian automobile association, and, in the United Kingdom, from the Automobile Association or Royal Automobile Club. These international permits are universally recognized, and having one in your wallet may save you a problem with the local authorities.

SURCHARGES

Before you pick up a car in one city and leave it in another **ask about drop-off charges or one-way service fees,** which can be substantial. Note, too, that some rental agencies charge extra if you return the car before the time specified in your contract. To avoid a hefty refueling fee **fill the tank just before you turn in the car,** but be aware that gas stations near the rental outlet may overcharge.

CAR TRAVEL

There are two absolutely essential points to remember about driving in Mexico. First and foremost is to **carry Mexican auto insurance.** (☞ Insurance, *below.*)

Point number two: **if you enter Mexico with a car, you must leave with it.** In recent years, the high rate of U.S. vehicles being sold illegally in Mexico has caused the Mexican government to enact stringent regulations for bringing a car into the country—at great inconvenience to motoring American tourists. **In order to drive into the country, you must cross the border with the following documents:** title or registration for your vehicle; a birth certificate or passport; a credit card (AE, DC, MC, or V); a valid driver's license with a photo. The title holder, driver, and credit card owner must be one and the same—that is, if your spouse's name is on the title of the car and yours isn't, you cannot be the one to bring the car into the country. **For financed cars, leased cars, rental cars, or company cars,** a notarized letter of permission from the bank, lien holder, rental agency, or company is required.

When you submit your paperwork at the border and pay a $12 charge on your credit card, you will receive a tourist visa, a car permit, and a sticker to put on your vehicle, all valid for up to six months. Be sure to turn in the permit and the sticker at the border prior to their expiration date; otherwise you could incur high fines.

One alternative to going through this hassle when you cross is to **have your paperwork done in advance** at a branch of Sanborn's Mexican Insurance; look in the Yellow Pages for an office in almost every town on the U.S.–Mexico border. You'll still have to go through some of the procedures at the border, but all your paperwork will be in order, and Sanborn's express window will ensure that you get through relatively quickly. There is a $10 charge for this service. The fact that you drove in with a car is stamped on your tourist card, which you must give to immigration authorities at departure. If an emergency arises and you must fly home, there are complicated customs procedures to face.

For day trips and local sightseeing, **engaging a car and driver** (who often acts as a guide) for a day can be a hassle-free, more economical way to travel than renting a car and driving yourself. Hotel desks will know which taxi companies to call, and you can negotiate a price with the driver.

AUTO CLUBS

➤ IN AUSTRALIA: Australian Automobile Association (☎ 02/6247–7311).

➤ IN CANADA: Canadian Automobile Association (CAA, ☎ 613/247–0117).

➤ IN NEW ZEALAND: New Zealand Automobile Association (☎ 09/377–4660).

➤ IN THE U.K.: Automobile Association (AA, ☎ 0990/500600). Royal Automobile Club (RAC, ☎ 0990/722722 for membership; 0345/121345 for insurance).

➤ IN THE U.S.: American Automobile Association (☎ 800/564–6222).

EMERGENCIES

To help motorists on major highways, the Mexican Tourism Ministry operates a fleet of more than 350 pickup trucks, known as the *Angeles Verdes,* or Green Angels. The bilingual drivers provide mechanical help, first aid, radio-telephone communication, basic supplies and small parts, towing, tourist information, and protection. Services are free, and spare parts, fuel, and lubricants are provided at cost. Tips are always appreciated (figure $5 to $10 for big jobs, $2 to $3 for minor repairs). The Green Angels patrol fixed sections of the major highways twice daily from 8 AM to 8 PM (later on holiday weekends). If you break down, **pull off the road as far as possible,** lift the hood of your car, hail a passing vehicle, and ask the driver to **notify the patrol.** Most bus and truck drivers will be quite helpful. If you witness an accident, do not stop to help—inform the nearest official.

➤ CONTACTS: Green Angels, Mexico City, (☎ 5/250–8221).

GASOLINE

PEMEX franchises all gas stations in Mexico. Stations are located at most road junctions and in cities and towns. They generally do not accept U.S. credit cards or dollars. Fuel prices are the same at all stations (except near the U.S. border, where they are a bit lower) and run slightly higher than in the United States. Premium unleaded gas—called Magna Premio—and regular unleaded gas—called Magna Sin—is now available nationwide, but it's still a good idea to fill up whenever you can. Fuel quality is generally lower than that in the United States and Europe. Vehicles with fuel-injected engines are likely to have problems after driving extended distances.

At gas stations, keep a close eye on the gas meter to make sure the attendant is starting it at "0" and that you pay the price that is shown afterward. Even though standards of cleanliness have improved considerably in most gas stations in cities and on the major highways, especially *franquicia* (franchised) stations, there are still some that are leave a lot to be desired.

INSURANCE

You must carry Mexican auto insurance, which you can purchase near border crossings on either the U.S. or Mexican side. If you injure anyone in an accident, you could well be jailed—whether it was your fault or not—unless you have insurance. Guilty until proven innocent is part of the country's Code Napoléon. Purchase enough Mexican automobile insurance at the border to cover your estimated trip. It's sold by the day, and if your trip is shorter than your original estimate, some companies might issue a pro-rated refund for the unused time upon application after you exit the country.

➤ CONTACTS: **Sanborn's Mexican Insurance** (✉ 2009 S. 10th St., McAllen, TX 78505, ☎ 210/686–0711). **Oscar Padilla** (✉ 4330 La Jolla Village Dr., San Diego, CA 92122, ☎ 800/258–8600). **Instant Mexico Auto Insurance** (✉ 223 Via de San Ysidro, San Ysidro, CA 92173, ☎ 619/428–3583).

ROAD CONDITIONS

There are several well-kept toll roads in Mexico—most of them two lanes wide. The trick is that these *carreteras* (major highways) don't go too far out of the capital into the countryside. (*Cuota* means toll road; *libre* means no toll, and such roads are usually not as smooth.) Some excellent new roads have opened in the past five years, making car travel safer and faster. These include highways connecting Acapulco and Mexico City; Cancún and Mérida; Nogales and Mazatlán; León and Aguascalientes; Guadalajara and Tepic; Mexico City, Morelia, and Guadalajara; Mexico City, Puebla, Teotihuacán, and Oaxaca; and Nuevo Laredo and Monterrey. However, tolls as high as $40 one-way can make using these thoroughfares prohibitively expensive. Approaches to most of the large cities are also in good condition, and the government-sponsored Northern Border Program has encouraged the border states to keep their roads in good repair.

In rural areas, roads are quite poor: **use caution, especially during the rainy season,** when rock slides and potholes are a problem. Driving in Mexico's central highlands may also necessitate adjustments to your carburetor. Generally, driving times are longer than for comparable distances in the United States. *Topes* (speed bumps) are also common; it's best to slow down when approaching a village.

Driving at night is not recommended and should be avoided especially in remote and rural areas because of free-roaming livestock, the difficulty of getting assistance, and the risk of banditry. The last can occur anywhere, and it is best to use toll roads whenever possible. Although costly, they are much safer.

Common sense goes a long way: if you have a long distance to cover, **start early and fill up on gas**; don't let your tank get below half-full. Allow extra time for unforeseen occurrences as well as for the trucks that seem to be everywhere. By day, **be alert to animals,** especially cattle and dogs. (The number of dead dogs lying beside—and in the middle of—Mexican highways is appalling.)

Traffic can be horrendous in cities, particularly in Mexico City. As you would in metropolitan areas anywhere, **avoid rush hour** (7–9 AM and 6–8PM) and when schools let out(2–3 PM). Signage is not always adequate in Mexico, so if you are not sure where you are going, **travel with a companion and a good map.** Always lock your car, and never leave valuable items in the body of the car (the trunk will suffice for daytime outings).

The Mexican Tourism Ministry distributes free road maps from its tourism offices outside the country. *Guía Roji* and PEMEX (the government petroleum monopoly) publish current city, regional, and national road maps, which are available in bookstores; gas stations generally do not carry maps.

RULES OF THE ROAD

When you sign up for Mexican car insurance, you should receive a booklet on Mexican rules of the road. Read this booklet in order to avoid breaking laws that differ from those of your native country.

Illegally parked cars are either towed or wheel blocks are placed on the tires, which can require a trip to the traffic police headquarters for payment of a fine. When in doubt, **park in a lot instead of on the street**; your car will probably be safer there, anyway.

If an oncoming vehicle flicks its lights at you in daytime, slow down: it could mean trouble ahead. When approaching a narrow bridge, the first vehicle to flash its lights has right of way. One-way streets are common. One-way traffic is indicated by an arrow; two-way, by a two-pointed arrow. A circle with a diagonal line superimposed on the letter *E* (for *estacionamiento*) means "no parking." Other road signs follow the now widespread system of international symbols, a copy of which will usually be provided when you rent a car in Mexico.

In Mexico City, **watch out for** *"Hoy no Circula"* **notices.** Because of pollution, all cars in the city are prohibited from driving one day a week. Posted signs show certain letters or numbers paired with each day of the week, indicating that vehicles with those letters or numbers in their license plates are not allowed to drive on the corresponding day. Foreigners are not exempt.

Mileage and speed limits are given in kilometers: 100 kph and 80 kph (62 and 50 mph, respectively) are the most common maximums. A few of the newer toll roads allow 110 kph (68.4 mph). In cities and small towns, **observe the posted speed limits,** which can be as low as 20 kph (12 mph).

SAFETY ON THE ROAD

First of all, **never drive at night** in Mexico. *Banditos* are one concern, but so are potholes, cows straying into the road, and road-hogging trucks. Plan driving times ahead, and if night is falling, find a nearby hotel.

Some of the biggest hassles on the road might be from police who pull you over for breaking the law, or for being a good prospect for a small scam. Remember to **be polite**—displays of anger will only make matters worse—and be aware that a police officer might be pulling you over for something that you didn't do. Corruption is a fact of life in Mexico, and the $5 that it costs to get your license back might be supplementary income for the officer who pulled you over.

If you are stopped for speeding, the officer is supposed to take your license and hold it until you pay the fine at the local police station. But the officer will always prefer a "mordita" to wasting his time at the police station. If you decide to dispute a charge that seems preposterous, do so with a smile, and tell the officer that you would like to talk to the police captain when you get to the station. The officer will always let you go rather than go to the station.

If you are **driving from Manzanillo to Ixtapa/Zihuatanejo**—about 8 hours with a meal stop—make the trip only during daylight hours, due to reports of car jackings around the area of Playa Azul. Military and police patrols have been increased on Highway 200 in the last year and the number of incidents has dramatically decreased; still, exercise caution.

CHILDREN IN MEXICO

All children, including infants, must have proof of citizenship for travel to Mexico. Children up to age 18 and including infants traveling with a single parent must also have a notarized letter from the other parent stating that the child has his or her permission to leave their home country. In addition, parents must now fill out a tourist card for each child over the age of 10 traveling with them.

If you are renting a car don't forget to **arrange for a car seat** when you reserve.

FLYING

If your children are two or older **ask about children's airfares.** As a general rule, infants under two not occupying a seat fly at greatly reduced fares or even for free. When booking **confirm carry-on allowances** if you're traveling with infants. In general, for babies charged 10% of the adult fare, you are allowed one carry-on bag and a collapsible stroller; if the flight is full the stroller may have to be checked or you may be limited to less.

Experts agree that it's a good idea to use safety seats aloft for children weighing less than 40 pounds. Airlines set their own policies: U.S. carriers usually require that the child be ticketed, even if he or she is young enough to ride free, since the seats must be strapped into regular seats. Do **check your airline's policy about using safety seats during takeoff and landing.** And since safety seats are not allowed just everywhere in the plane, get your seat assignments early.

LODGING

Most hotels in Mexico allow children under a certain age to stay in their parents' room at no extra charge, but others charge for them as extra adults; be sure to **find out the cutoff age for children's discounts.**

SIGHTS & ATTRACTIONS

Places that are especially good for children are indicated by a rubber duckie icon in the margin.

COMPUTERS ON THE ROAD

Internet cafés have sprung up all over Mexico, making email by far the easiest way to get in touch with people back home—or anywhere for that matter. If you have a Toshiba laptop, bear in mind that having it serviced might be hopeless. Parts for these machines are hard to come by in Mexico.

CONSUMER PROTECTION

Whenever shopping or buying travel services in Mexico, **pay with a major credit card** so you can cancel payment or get reimbursed if there's a problem. If you're doing business with a particular company for the first time, **contact your local Better Business Bureau and the attorney general's offices** in your state and the company's home state, as well. Have any complaints been filed? Finally, if you're buying a package or tour, always **consider travel insurance** that includes default coverage (☞ Insurance, *below*).

➤ LOCAL BBBs: **Council of Better Business Bureaus** (✉ 4200 Wilson Blvd., Suite 800, Arlington, VA 22203, ☎ 703/276–0100, FAX 703/525–8277).

CUSTOMS & DUTIES

When shopping, **keep receipts** for all purchases. Upon reentering the country, **be ready to show customs officials what you've bought.** If you feel a duty is incorrect or object to the way your clearance was handled, note the inspector's badge number and ask to see a supervisor. If the problem isn't resolved, write to the appropriate authorities, beginning with the port director at your point of entry.

IN AUSTRALIA

Australia residents who are 18 or older may bring home $A400 worth of souvenirs and gifts (including jewelry), 250 cigarettes or 250 grams of tobacco, and 1,125 ml of alcohol (including wine, beer, and spirits). Residents under 18 may bring back $A200 worth of goods. Prohibited items include meat products. Seeds, plants, and fruits need to be declared upon arrival.

➤ INFORMATION: **Australian Customs Service** (Regional Director, ✉ Box 8, Sydney, NSW 2001, ☎ 02/9213–2000, FAX 02/9213–4000).

IN CANADA

Canadian residents who have been out of Canada for at least 7 days may bring home C$500 worth of goods duty-free. If you've been away less than 7 days but more than 48 hours, the duty-free allowance drops to C$200; if your trip lasts 24–48 hours, the allowance is C$50. You may not pool allowances with family members. Goods claimed under the C$500 exemption may follow you by mail; those claimed under the lesser exemptions must accompany you. Alcohol and tobacco products may be included in the 7-day and 48-hour exemptions but not in the 24-hour exemption. If you meet the age requirements of the province or territory through which you reenter Canada, you may bring in, duty-free, 1.14 liters (40 imperial ounces) of wine or liquor *or* 24 12-ounce cans or bottles of beer or ale. If you are 16 or older you may bring in, duty-free, 200 cigarettes and 50 cigars. Check ahead of time with Revenue Canada or the Department of Agriculture for policies regarding meat products, seeds, plants, and fruits.

You may send an unlimited number of gifts worth up to C$60 each duty-free to Canada. Label the package UNSOLICITED GIFT—VALUE UNDER $60. Alcohol and tobacco are excluded.

➤ INFORMATION: **Revenue Canada** (✉ 2265 St. Laurent Blvd. S, Ottawa, Ontario K1G 4K3, ☎ 613/993–0534; 800/461–9999 in Canada).

IN MEXICO

Upon entering Mexico, you will be given a baggage declaration form and asked to itemize what you're bringing into the country. You are allowed to bring in 2 liters of spirits or wine for personal use; 400 cigarettes, 50 cigars, or 250 grams of tobacco; a reasonable amount of perfume for personal use; one movie camera and one regular camera and 12 rolls of film for each; and gift items not to exceed a total of $300. You are not allowed to bring meat, vegetables, plants, fruit, or flowers into the country.

IN NEW ZEALAND

Homeward-bound residents 17 or older may bring back $700 worth of souvenirs and gifts. Your duty-free allowance also includes 4.5 liters of wine or beer; one 1,125-ml bottle of spirits; and either 200 cigarettes, 250 grams of tobacco, 50 cigars, or a combination of the three up to 250 grams. Prohibited items include meat products, seeds, plants, and fruits.

➤ INFORMATION: **New Zealand Customs** (Custom House, ✉ 50 Anzac Ave., Box 29, Auckland, New Zealand, ☎ 09/359–6655, FAX 09/359–6732).

IN THE U.K.

If you are a U.K. resident and your journey was wholly within the European Union (EU), you won't have to pass through customs when you return to the United Kingdom. If you plan to bring back large quantities of alcohol or tobacco, check EU limits beforehand. From countries outside the EU, including Mexico, you may bring home, duty-free, 200 cigarettes or 50 cigars; 1 liter of spirits or 2 liters of fortified or sparkling wine or liqueurs; 2 liters of still table wine; 60 milliliters of perfume; 250 milliliters of toilet water; plus £136 worth of other goods, including gifts and souvenirs. If returning from outside the EU, prohibited items include meat products, seeds, plants, and fruits.

➤ INFORMATION: **HM Customs and Excise** (✉ Dorset House, Stamford St., Bromley Kent BR1 1XX, ☎ 0171/202–4227).

IN THE U.S.

U.S. residents who have been out of the country for at least 48 hours (and who have not used the $400 allowance or any part of it in the past 30 days)may bring home $400 worth of foreign goods duty-free. U.S. residents 21 and older may bring back 1 liter of alcohol duty-free. In addition, regardless of your age, you are allowed 200 cigarettes and 100 non-Cuban cigars. Antiques, which the U.S. Customs Service defines as objects more than 100 years old, enter duty-free, as do original works of art done entirely by hand, including paintings, drawings, and sculptures.

You may also send packages home duty-free: up to $200 worth of goods for personal use, with a limit of one parcel per addressee per day (and no alcohol or tobacco products or perfume worth more than $5); label the package PERSONAL USE and attach a list of its contents and their retail value. Do not label the package UNSOLICITED GIFT or your duty-free exemption will drop to $100. Mailed items do not affect your duty-free allowance on your return.

➤ INFORMATION: **U.S. Customs Service** (inquiries, ✉ 1300 Pennsylvania Ave. NW, Washington, DC 20229, ☎ 202/927–6724; complaints, ✉ Office of Regulations and Rulings, 1300 Pennsylvania Ave. NW, Washington, DC 20229; registration of equipment, ✉ Resource Management, 1300 Pennsylvania Ave. NW, Washington, DC 20229, ☎ 202/927–0540).

DINING

Mexican restaurants run the gamut from humble hole-in-the-wall shacks, street stands, *taquerías,* and American-style fast-food joints to internationally acclaimed gourmet restaurants. Prices, naturally, follow suit. To save money, **look for the fixed-menu lunch** known as *comida corrida* or *menú del día,* which is served between 1 and 4 PM almost everywhere in Mexico.

The restaurants we list are the cream of the crop in each price category. For more information on local foods throughout Mexico, *see* the Cocina Mexicana box in Mexico City (Chapter 1) and the Dining sections that appear under Pleasures and Pastimes at the beginning of each chapter.

MEALTIMES

In Mexico, lunch is the big meal; dinner is rarely served before 8 PM.

PAYING

Credit cards—especially American Express, MasterCard, and Visa—are widely accepted at pricier restaurants. Bargains are usually cash only.

RESERVATIONS & DRESS

Reservations are always a good idea: we mention them only when they're essential or are not accepted. Book as far ahead as you can, and reconfirm as soon as you arrive. We mention dress only when men are required to wear a jacket or a jacket and tie.

DISABILITIES & ACCESSIBILITY

Mexico is poorly equipped for travelers with disabilities. There are no special discounts or passes for disabled travelers in Mexico, nor is public transportation, including the Mexico City Metro, wheelchair accessible—an exception is Veracruz city, where street corners have ramps in the downtown area. Roads and sidewalks are most often crowded and without ramps—in colonial cities cobblestone sidewalks and streets are unnavigable—and people on the street will not usually assist you unless expressly asked. Renting or bringing a car or van is your best bet for exploring comfortably.

Most hotels and restaurants have at least a few steps, and while rooms considered "wheelchair accessible" by hotel owners are usually on the ground floor, the doorways and

bathroom may not be maneuverable. It's a good idea to call ahead to find out what a hotel or restaurant can offer. Despite these barriers, Mexicans with disabilities manage to negotiate places that most travelers outside Mexico would not consider accessible. The best choice of accessible lodging is found in major resort towns like Acapulco and Mazatlán.

LODGING

When discussing accessibility with an operator or reservations agent **ask hard questions.** Are there any stairs, inside *or* out? Are there grab bars next to the toilet *and* in the shower/tub? How wide is the doorway to the room? To the bathroom? For the most extensive facilities meeting the latest legal specifications **opt for newer accommodations.**

TRAVEL AGENCIES

In the United States, although the Americans with Disabilities Act requires that travel firms serve the needs of all travelers, some agencies specialize in working with people with disabilities.

➤ TRAVELERS WITH MOBILITY PROBLEMS: **Access Adventures** (⊠ 206 Chestnut Ridge Rd., Rochester, NY 14624, ☎ 716/889–9096), run by a former physical-rehabilitation counselor. **Accessible Vans of the Rockies, Activity and Travel Agency** (⊠ 2040 W. Hamilton Pl., Sheridan, CO 80110, ☎ 303/806–5047 or 888/837–0065, FAX 303/781–2329). **Care-Vacations** (⊠ 5-5110 50th Ave., Leduc, Alberta T9E 6V4, ☎ 780/986–6404 or 780/986–8332) has group tours and is especially helpful with cruise vacations. **Flying Wheels Travel** (⊠ 143 W. Bridge St., Box 382, Owatonna, MN 55060, ☎ 507/451–5005 or 800/535–6790, FAX 507/451–1685). **Hinsdale Travel Service** (⊠ 201 E. Ogden Ave., Suite 100, Hinsdale, IL 60521, ☎ 630/325–1335). Travelers with Developmental Disabilities**New Directions** (⊠ 5276 Hollister Ave., Suite 207, Santa Barbara, CA 93111, ☎ 805/967–2841 or 888/967–2841, FAX 805/964–7344). **Sprout** (⊠ 893 Amsterdam Ave., New York, NY 10025, ☎ 212/222–9575 or 888/222–9575, FAX 212/222–9768).

DISCOUNTS & DEALS

Be a smart shopper and **compare all your options** before making decisions. A plane ticket bought with a promotional coupon from travel clubs, coupon books, and direct-mail offers may not be cheaper than the least expensive fare from a discount ticket agency. And always keep in mind that what you get is just as important as what you save.

DISCOUNT RESERVATIONS

To save money **look into discount-reservations services** with toll-free numbers, which use their buying power to get a better price on hotels, airline tickets, even car rentals. When booking a room, always **call the hotel's local toll-free number** (if one is available) rather than the central reservations number—you'll often get a better price. Always ask about special packages or corporate rates.

➤ AIRLINE TICKETS: ☎ 800/FLY–4–LESS. ☎ 800/FLY–ASAP.

➤ HOTEL ROOMS: **Players Express Vacations** (☎ 800/458–6161). **Steigenberger Reservation Service** (☎ 800/223–5652).

PACKAGE DEALS

Don't confuse packages and guided tours. When you buy a package, you travel on your own, just as though you had planned the trip yourself. Fly/drive packages, which combine airfare and car rental, are often a good deal.

ELECTRICITY

Electrical converters are not necessary because Mexico operates on the 60-cycle, 120-volt system; however, many Mexican outlets have not been updated to accommodate three-prong and polarized plugs (those with one larger prong), so **you might need an adapter.**

If your appliances are dual-voltage you'll need only an adapter. Don't use 110-volt outlets, marked FOR SHAVERS ONLY, for high-wattage appliances such as blow-dryers. Most laptops operate equally well on 110 and 220 volts and so require only an adapter.

EMBASSIES

For information on Embassies and Consulates, ☞ Consulates and Embassies *in* Mexico City, Chapter 1.

GAY & LESBIAN TRAVEL

Mexican same-sex couples keep a low profile, and it's a good idea for foreign same-sex couples to do the same. Two people of the same gender can often have a hard time getting a *cama matrimonial* (double bed), especially in smaller hotels. This could be attributed to the influence of the Catholic Church—Mexico is a devoutly Catholic country and the Church has historically exerted a powerful influence on both Mexican politics and the mores and attitudes of the Mexican people. However, the same rule that applies all over the world holds in Mexico as well: alternative lifestyles (whether they be homosexuality or any other bending of conventional roles) are more easily accepted in more cosmopolitan places, like Acapulco, Cancún, Puerto Vallarta, San Miguel de Allende, Ajijic, Cuernavaca, Guadalajara, Veracruz City, and Mexico City.

➤ GAY- AND LESBIAN-FRIENDLY TRAVEL AGENCIES: **Different Roads Travel** (✉ 8383 Wilshire Blvd., Suite 902, Beverly Hills, CA 90211, ☎ 323/651–5557 or 800/429–8747, FAX 323/651–3678). **Kennedy Travel** (✉ 314 Jericho Turnpike, Floral Park, NY 11001, ☎ 516/352–4888 or 800/237–7433, FAX 516/354–8849). **Now Voyager** (✉ 4406 18th St., San Francisco, CA 94114, ☎ 415/626–1169 or 800/255–6951, FAX 415/626–8626). **Yellowbrick Road** (✉ 1500 W. Balmoral Ave., Chicago, IL 60640, ☎ 773/561–1800 or 800/642–2488, FAX 773/561–4497). **Skylink Travel and Tour** (✉ 1006 Mendocino Ave., Santa Rosa, CA 95401, ☎ 707/546–9888 or 800/225–5759, FAX 707/546–9891), serving lesbian travelers.

HEALTH

AIR POLLUTION

Air pollution in Mexico City can pose a health risk. The sheer number of cars and industries in the capital, thermal inversions, and the inability to process sewage have all contributed to the high levels of lead, carbon monoxide, and other pollutants in the atmosphere in Mexico City. Though the long-term effects are not known, children, the elderly, and those with respiratory problems are advised to avoid jogging, participating in outdoor sports, and being outdoors more than necessary on days of high smog alerts.

DIVERS' ALERT

Do not fly within 24 hours of scuba diving.

FOOD & DRINK

In Mexico the major health risk is Montezuma's Revenge, or traveler's diarrhea, caused by eating contaminated fruit or vegetables or drinking contaminated water. So **watch what you eat.** Stay away from ice, uncooked food, and unpasteurized milk and milk products, and **drink only bottled water** or water that has been boiled for at least 20 minutes, even when you're brushing your teeth. Mild cases may respond to Imodium (known generically as loperamide or Lomotil) or Pepto-Bismol (not as strong), both of which can be purchased over the counter. Drink plenty of purified water or tea—chamomile is a good folk remedy. In severe cases, rehydrate yourself with Gatorade or a salt-sugar solution (½ teaspoon salt ([give word in local language]) and 4 tablespoons sugar ([give word in local language]) per quart of water).

When ordering cold drinks at untouristed establishments, **skip the ice:** *sin hielo.* (You can usually identify ice made commercially from purified water by its uniform shape and the hole in the center.) Hotels with water purification systems will post signs to that effect in the rooms. *Tacos al pastor*—thin pork slices grilled on a spit and garnished with the usual cilantro, onions, and chili peppers—are delicious but dangerous. It's also a good idea to pass up *ceviche,* raw fish cured in lemon juice—a favorite appetizer, especially at seaside resorts. The Mexican Department of Health warns that marinating in lemon juice does not constitute the "cooking" that would make the shellfish safe to eat. Also, be wary of hamburgers sold from street stands, because you can never be certain what meat they are made with (horse meat is common).

MEDICAL PLANS

No one plans to get sick while traveling, but it happens, so **consider signing up with a medical-assistance company.** Members get doctor referrals, emergency evacuation or repatriation, hot lines for medical consultation, cash for emergencies, and other assistance.

➤ MEDICAL-ASSISTANCE COMPANIES: **International SOS Assistance** (✉ 8 Neshaminy Interplex, Suite 207, Trevose, PA 19053, ☎ 215/245–4707 or 800/523–6586, FAX 215/244–9617; ✉ 12 Chemin Riantbosson, 1217 Meyrin 1, Geneva, Switzerland, ☎ 4122/785–6464, FAX 4122/785–6424; ✉ 331 N. Bridge Rd., 17-00, Odeon Towers, Singapore 188720, ☎ 65/338–7800, FAX 65/338–7611).

OTHER HAZARDS

Caution is advised when venturing out in the Mexican sun. Sunbathers lulled by a slightly overcast sky or the sea breezes can be burned badly in just 20 minutes. To avoid overexposure, **use strong sunscreens and avoid the peak sun hours** of noon to 2 PM.

SHOTS & MEDICATIONS

According to the U.S. government's National Centers for Disease Control (CDC) there is a limited risk of malaria and dengue fever in certain rural areas of Mexico. In most urban or easily accessible areas you need not worry. However, if you plan to visit remote regions or stay for more than six weeks, **check with the CDC's International Travelers Hotline.** In areas where malaria and dengue, both of which are carried by mosquitoes, are prevalent, use mosquito nets, wear clothing that covers the body, apply repellent containing DEET, and use spray for flying insects in living and sleeping areas. Also **consider taking antimalarial pills** if you are doing serious adventure activities in subtropical areas. There is no vaccine to combat dengue, which if you are reasonably healthy is usually not serious (only dengue hemmorrhagic fever is potentially fatal).

➤ HEALTH WARNINGS: **National Centers for Disease Control (CDC,**

National Center for Infectious Diseases, Division of Quarantine, Traveler's Health Section, ✉ 1600 Clifton Rd. NE, M/S E-03, Atlanta, GA 30333, ☎ 888/232–3228, FAX 888/232–3299).

HOLIDAYS

The month of January is full of long, regional festivals. Notable are the celebrations of the **Fiesta de la Inmaculada Concepción** (Feast of the Immaculate Conception), which transforms the city of Morelia into a sea of lights and flowers for much of the month; and a series of folkloric dances held in Chiapa de Corzo, Chiapas, that culminate in the **Feast of San Sebastian,** the third week in January.

WINTER

➤ JAN. 1: **New Year's Day** is a major celebration throughout the country. Agricultural and livestock fairs are held in the provinces; in Oaxaca, women display traditional *tehuana* costumes.

➤ JAN. 6: **Feast of Epiphany** is the day the Three Kings bring gifts to Mexican children.

➤ JAN. 17: **Feast of San Antonio Abad** honors animals all over Mexico. Pets and livestock are decked out with flowers and ribbons and taken to church for a blessing.

➤ FEB. 2: **Día de la Candelaria,** or Candlemas Day, means fiestas, parades, bullfights, and lantern-decorated streets. Festivities include a running of the bulls through the streets of Tlacotalpan, Veracruz.

➤ FEB.–MAR.: **Carnaval** is celebrated throughout Mexico—most notably in Mazatlán and Veracruz with parades with floats and bands.

SPRING

➤ MAR. 21: **Benito Juárez's Birthday,** a national holiday, is most popular in Guelatao, Oaxaca, where Juárez, the beloved 19th-century president of Mexico and champion of the people, was born. This is also the day that Cuernavaca's Fiesta de la Primavera marks the beginning of spring.

➤ MAR.–APR.: **Semana Santa** (Holy Week) is observed with parades and passion plays in the week leading to Easter Sunday.

➤ APR.–MAY: **San Marcos National Fair,** held in Aguascalientes, is one of the country's best fairs. It features Indian *matachnes* (dances performed by grotesque figures), mariachi bands, and bullfights. Also during this time, the 10-day **Festival de las Artes** (Arts Festival) brings music, theater, and dance troupes from all over Latin America to San Luis Potosí.

➤ MAY 1: **Labor Day** is a day for workers to parade through the streets.

➤ MAY 5: **Cinco de Mayo** marks the anniversary of the French defeat by Mexican troops in Puebla in 1862 with great fanfare countrywide.

➤ MAY 15: **Feast of San Isidro Labrador** is noted nationwide by the blessing of new seeds and animals. In Cuernavaca, a parade of oxen wreathed in flowers is followed by street parties and feasting.

SUMMER

➤ JUNE 1: **Navy Day** is commemorated in all Mexican seaports and is especially colorful in Acapulco, Mazatlán, and Veracruz. The **Feast of Corpus Christi** is celebrated in different ways. In Mexico City, children are dressed in native costumes and taken to the cathedral on the zócalo for a blessing. In Papantla, Veracruz, the Dance of the Flying Birdmen, a pre-Hispanic ritual to the sun, is held throughout the day.

➤ JUNE 24: **Saint John the Baptist Day,** a popular national holiday, sees many Mexicans observing a tradition of tossing a "blessing" of water on most anyone within reach.

➤ EARLY JULY: The **Feria Nacional** (National Fair) in Durango runs from the Day of Our Lady of Refuge (July 4) to the anniversary of the founding of Durango in 1563 (July 22). The old-time agricultural fair has taken on national renown for its carnival rides, livestock shows, and music.

➤ JULY 16: **Our Lady of Mt. Carmel Day** is celebrated with fairs, bullfights, fireworks, even a major fishing tournament.

➤ LATE JULY: **Guelaguetza Dance Festival,** a pre-Columbian Oaxacan affair, usually falls on the two Mondays after July 16.

The **Feast of Santiago,** a national holiday, features *charreadas,* Mexican-style rodeos.

➤ AUG.: The **Festival de San Agustín** brings a month of music, dance, and fireworks to Puebla. On August 26 (Saint Augustine's feast day) it is customary to prepare the famous *chiles en nogada.*

➤ AUG. 15: **Feast of the Assumption of the Blessed Virgin Mary** is celebrated nationwide with religious processions. In Huamantla, Tlaxcala, the festivities include a running of the bulls down flower-strewn streets.

➤ AUG. 25: **San Luis Potosí Patron Saint Fiesta** is the day the town honors its patron, San Luis Rey, with traditional dance, music, and foods.

AUTUMN

➤ SEPT. 15–16: **Independence Day** is marked throughout Mexico with fireworks and parties that outblast those on New Year's Eve. The biggest celebrations are in Mexico City.

➤ SEPT. 29: **San Miguel Day** honors St. Michael, the patron saint of all towns with San Miguel in their names—especially San Miguel de Allende—with bullfights, folk dances, concerts, and fireworks.

➤ OCT.: **October Festival** means a month of cultural and sporting events in Guadalajara.

➤ OCT. 4: **Feast of St. Francis of Assisi** is a day for processions dedicated to St. Francis in parts of the country.

➤ OCT. 12: **Columbus Day** is a national holiday in Mexico.

➤ OCT.–NOV.: **International Cervantes Festival,** in Guanajuato, is a top cultural event that attracts dancers, singers, and actors from a number of different countries.

➤ OCT. 31–NOV. 2: On **All Souls' and All Saints' Day,** or **Day of the Dead,** families welcome back the spirits of departed relatives to elaborate altars and refurbished gravesites. Especially

intriguing are the celebrations in Pátzcuaro and Oaxaca.

➤ NOV. 20: **Anniversary of the Mexican Revolution** is a national holiday.

➤ NOV.–DEC.: **National Silver Fair,** an annual Taxco event, is an occasion for even more silver selling than usual, the crowning of a Silver Queen and jewelry and silver exhibitions.

➤ DEC. 12: On **Feast Day of the Virgin of Guadalupe,** Mexico's patron saint is feted with processions and native folk dances, particularly at her shrine in Mexico City.

➤ DEC. 16–25: **The Posadas and Christmas** are candlelight processions that lead to Christmas parties and to piñatas (suspended paper animals or figurines) that are broken open to yield gifts. Mexico City is brightly decorated, but don't expect any snow.

➤ DEC. 23: **Night of the Radishes,** a pre-Christmas tradition in Oaxaca, is one of the most colorful in Mexico: participants carve giant radishes into amusing shapes and display them in the city's main plaza, while celebrants devour fritterlike *buñuelos* and smash their ceramic plates in the streets for luck.

INSURANCE

The most useful travel insurance plan is a comprehensive policy that includes coverage for trip cancellation and interruption, default, trip delay, and medical expenses (with a waiver for preexisting conditions).

Without insurance you will lose all or most of your money if you cancel your trip, regardless of the reason. Default insurance covers you if your tour operator, airline, or cruise line goes out of business. Trip-delay covers expenses that arise because of bad weather or mechanical delays. Study the fine print when comparing policies.

If you're traveling internationally, a key component of travel insurance is coverage for medical bills incurred if you get sick on the road. Such expenses are not generally covered by Medicare and by some private policies. U.K. residents can buy a travel-insurance policy valid for most vacations taken during the year in which it's purchased (but check pre-existing-condition coverage). British and Australian citizens need extra medical coverage overseas.

Always **buy travel policies directly from the insurance company**; if you buy it from a cruise line, airline, or tour operator that goes out of business you probably will not be covered for the agency or operator's default, a major risk. Before you make any purchase **review your existing health and home-owner's policies** to find what they cover away from home.

➤ TRAVEL INSURERS: In the U.S. **Access America** (✉ 6600 W. Broad St., Richmond, VA 23230, ☎ 804/285–3300 or 800/284–8300), **Travel Guard International** (✉ 1145 Clark St., Stevens Point, WI 54481, ☎ 715/345–0505 or 800/826–1300). In Canada **Voyager Insurance** (✉ 44 Peel Center Dr., Brampton, Ontario L6T 4M8, ☎ 905/791–8700; 800/668–4342 in Canada).

➤ INSURANCE INFORMATION: In the U.K. the **Association of British Insurers** (✉ 51–55 Gresham St., London EC2V 7HQ, ☎ 0171/600–3333, FAX 0171/696–8999). In Australia the **Insurance Council of Australia** (☎ 03/9614–1077, FAX 03/9614–7924).

LANGUAGE

Spanish is the official language of Mexico, although Indian languages are spoken by approximately 20% of the population, many of whom speak no Spanish at all. Basic English is widely understood by most people employed in tourism, less so in the less developed areas. At the very least, shopkeepers will know the numbers for bargaining purposes.

As in most other foreign countries, knowing the mother tongue has a way of opening doors, so **learn some Spanish words and phrases.** Mexicans are not scornful of visitors' mispronunciations and grammatical errors; on the contrary, they welcome even the most halting attempts to use the language.

Castilian Spanish—which is different from Latin American Spanish not only in pronunciation and grammar

but also in vocabulary—is most widely taught outside Mexico. Words or phrases that are harmless or every-day in one country can offend in another. Unless you are lucky enough to be briefed on these nuances by a native coach, the only way to learn is by trial and error.

LANGUAGE-STUDY PROGRAMS

Attending a language institute is an ideal way not only to learn Mexican Spanish but also to acquaint yourself with the customs and the people of the country. For total immersion, most language schools offer boarding with a Mexican family, but your choice of lodgings and of length of stay is generally flexible.

➤ LANGUAGE INSTITUTES: Recommended places to learn Spanish and live with a Mexican family include **Cetlalic** (Apdo. 1-201 Cuernavaca, Morelos, CP 62000, ☎ 73/13–35–79), with an emphasis on social justice as well as language acquisition; the **SLI– Spanish Language Institute** (Apdo. Postal 2–3, Cuernavaca, Morelos 62191, ☎ FAX 73/17–52–94; in the U.S., contact **Language Link Inc.,** Box 3006, Peoria, IL 61612, ☎ 800/552–2051, FAX 309/692–2926); **Centro Internacional de Estudios para Estranjeros** (Tomás V. Gómez 125, Guadalajara, Jalisco 44600, ☎ 3/616–4399; (Libertad 42, Local 1, Puerto Vallarta, Jalisco 48360, ☎ FAX 322/2–00–76); **Instituto Allende** (Apdo. Postal 85-A, San Miguel de Allende, Guanajuato 37700, ☎ 465/2–01–90, FAX 465/2–45–38); **National Autonomous University of Mexico (UNAM) School for Foreign Students** (Apdo. Postal 70, Taxco, Gro. 40200, ☎ FAX 762/2–01–24); **Centro de Idiomas de la Universidad Autónoma Benito Juárez** (Burgoa, at Bustamante, Oaxaca 68000, ☎ FAX 951/4–04–49), which offers classes in Mixtec and Zapotec as well as in Spanish; and **Instituto Jovel, A.C.** (Apdo. Postal 62, Ma. Adelina Flores 21, San Cristóbal de las Casas, Chiapas 29200, ☎ FAX 967/8–40–69).

AmeriSpan Unlimited (Box 40513, Philadelphia, PA 19106, ☎ 800/879–6640, FAX 215/985–4524) can arrange for language study and homestays.

➤ PHRASE BOOKS & LANGUAGE-TAPE SETS: *Fodor's Spanish for Travelers* (☎ 800/733–3000 in the U.S.; 800/668–4247 in Canada; $7 for phrasebook, $16.95 for audio set).

LODGING

The price and quality of accommodations in Mexico vary about as much as the country's restaurants, from superluxurious, international-class hotels and all-inclusive resorts to modest budget properties, seedy places with shared bathrooms, *casas de huéspedes* (guest houses), youth hostels, and *cabañas* (beach huts). You may find appealing bargains while you're on the road, but if your comfort threshold is high, **look for an English-speaking staff, guaranteed dollar rates, and toll-free reservation numbers in the United States.**

The lodgings we list are the cream of the crop in each price category. We always list the facilities that are available—but we don't specify whether they cost extra: when pricing accommodations, always ask what's included and what costs extra. Properties indicated by an ✕▥ are lodging establishments whose restaurant warrants a special trip.

Hotel rates are subject to the 15% value-added tax (the tax in the states of Quintana Roo, Baja California, and Baja California Sur is 10%), and many states are charging a 2% hotel tax, the revenues from which are being used for tourism promotion. Service charges and meals are generally not included. The Mexican government categorizes hotels, based on qualitative evaluations, into *gran turismo* (superdeluxe hotels, of which there are only about 50 nationwide); five-star down to one-star; and economy class. Keep in mind that many hotels that might otherwise be rated higher have opted for a lower category to avoid higher interest rates on loans and financing.

High- versus low-season rates can vary significantly (☞ When to Go, *below*). Hotels in this guide have air-conditioning and private bathrooms with showers, unless stated otherwise, but bathtubs are not common in inexpensive hotels and properties in smaller towns.

It's essential to **reserve in advance** if you are traveling during high season or holiday periods. Overbooking is a common practice in some parts of Mexico, such as Cancún and Acapulco. Travelers to remote areas will encounter little difficulty in obtaining rooms on a "walk-in" basis.

One last note of advice: If you are particularly sensitive to noise, you should **call ahead to learn if your hotel of choice is located on a busy street.** Many of the most engaging accommodations in Mexico are on downtown intersections that experience heavy automobile and pedestrian traffic. And large hotels are known to have lobby bars with live music in the middle of an open-air atrium leading directly to rooms. When you book, **request a room far from the bar.**

APARTMENT & VILLA RENTALS

If you want a home base that's roomy enough for a family and comes with cooking facilities **consider a furnished rental.** These can save you money, especially if you're traveling with a group. Home-exchange directories sometimes list rentals as well as exchanges.

➤ INTERNATIONAL AGENTS: **At Home Abroad** (✉ 405 E. 56th St., Suite 6H, New York, NY 10022, ☎ 212/421–9165, FAX 212/752–1591). **El Sol** (✉ P.O. Box 329, Wayne, PA 19087, ☎ 610/353–2335, FAX 610/353–7756). **Europa-Let/Tropical Inn-Let** (✉ 92 N. Main St., Ashland, OR 97520, ☎ 541/482–5806 or 800/462–4486, FAX 541/482–0660). **Rent-a-Home International** (✉ 7200 34th Ave. NW, Seattle, WA 98117, ☎ 206/789–9377, FAX 206/789–9379). **Vacation Home Rentals Worldwide** (✉ 235 Kensington Ave., Norwood, NJ 07648, ☎ 201/767–9393 or 800/633–3284, FAX 201/767–5510). **Villas and Apartments Abroad** (✉ 420 Madison Ave., Suite 1003, New York, NY 10017, ☎ 212/759–1025 or 800/433–3020, FAX 212/755–8316). **Villas International** (✉ 950 Northgate Dr., Suite 206, San Rafael, CA 94903, ☎ 415/499–9490 or 800/221–2260, FAX 415/499–9491).

B & B S

The B&B craze hasn't missed Mexico, and the same delights that you find elsewhere in the world apply here, too—personable service, interesting local furnishings and decorative talent, and tasty morning meals. San Miguel de Allende and other Heartland cities have their share of charming places. Mexico City and parts of the Yucatán do as well.

➤ RESERVATION SERVICES: If you arrive in Mexico City without a reservation, the **Mexico City Hotel and Motel Association** (☎ 5/571–3268 or 5/571–3262) operates a booth at the airport that will assist you.

CAMPING

A host of camping opportunities exist in Mexico, but don't expect the typical U.S.-style campground. Mexico's are usually trailer parks with running water, cooking areas, and room to pitch tents; sites can cost $1–$8. To enjoy more rustic surroundings, you can set up camp off the road or on the beach in relative safety, and save loads of money. Usually, you can camp at an *ejido* (farming community) or on someone's land for free as long as you ask permission first; ask locals about the safest and best spots. **Be alert and don't camp alone;** the beaches at night aren't as safe as they once were. And don't camp at archaeological sites.

Camping supplies are scarce in Mexico. Before you begin packing loads of camping gear, however, consider how much camping you will actually do versus how much trouble it will be to haul around your tent, sleeping bag, stove, and accoutrements. Finding a place to store your gear can be difficult—lockers tend to be small.

In many towns along the Pacific and Caribbean coasts, beachside *palapas* (thatched huts) are an excellent alternative to tent camping. All you'll need for a night in a palapa is a hammock (which you can purchase cheaply in Mexico), some mosquito netting, and a padlock for stashing your belongings in a locker.

HOME EXCHANGES

If you would like to exchange your home for someone else's **join a home-exchange organization,** which will send you its updated listings of available exchanges for a year and will include your own listing in at least one of them. It's up to you to make specific arrangements.

➤ EXCHANGE CLUBS: **HomeLink International** (✉ Box 650, Key West, FL 33041, ☎ 305/294–7766 or 800/638–3841, ℻ 305/294–1448; $88 per year). **Intervac U.S.** (✉ Box 590504, San Francisco, CA 94159, ☎ 800/756–4663, ℻ 415/435–7440; $83 per year).

HOSTELS

No matter what your age you can **save on lodging costs by staying at hostels.** In some 5,000 locations in more than 70 countries around the world, Hostelling International (HI), the umbrella group for a number of national youth-hostel associations, offers single-sex, dorm-style beds and, at many hostels, couples rooms and family accommodations. Membership in any HI national hostel association, open to travelers of all ages, allows you to stay in HI-affiliated hostels at member rates (one-year membership is about $25 for adults; hostels run about $10–$25 per night). Members also have priority if the hostel is full; they're eligible for discounts around the world, even on rail and bus travel in some countries.

➤ ORGANIZATIONS: **Hostelling International—American Youth Hostels** (✉ 733 15th St. NW, Suite 840, Washington, DC 20005, ☎ 202/783–6161, ℻ 202/783–6171). **Hostelling International—Canada** (✉ 400–205 Catherine St., Ottawa, Ontario K2P 1C3, ☎ 613/237–7884, ℻ 613/237–7868). **Youth Hostel Association of England and Wales** (✉ Trevelyan House, 8 St. Stephen's Hill, St. Albans, Hertfordshire AL1 2DY, ☎ 01727/855215 or 01727/845047, ℻ 01727/844126). **Australian Youth Hostel Association** (✉ 10 Mallett St., Camperdown, NSW 2050, ☎ 02/9565–1699, ℻ 02/9565–1325). **Youth Hostels Association of New Zealand** (✉ Box 436, Christchurch, New Zealand, ☎ 03/379–9970, ℻ 03/365–4476). Membership in the U.S. $25, in Canada C$26.75, in the U.K. £9.30, in Australia $44, in New Zealand $24.

HOTELS

After choosing a hotel, it's best to **reserve ahead,** especially for the high season (December–second week after Easter Week). Rooms in hotels listed have private baths unless otherwise noted.

MAIL & SHIPPING

The Mexican postal system is notoriously slow and unreliable; **never send packages** or expect to receive them, as they may be stolen (for emergencies, use a courier service or the new express-mail service, with insurance). If you are an American Express cardholder, your best bet is to send a package to the AmEx office nearest the address you're sending to.

There are post offices (*oficinas de correos*) even in the smallest villages and numerous branches in the larger cities. International postal service is all airmail, but even so your letter will take anywhere from 10 days to three weeks to arrive. Service within Mexico can be equally slow.

POSTAL ABBREVIATIONS

Mexican states have three- (or more-) letter postal abbreviations. If you plan to send mail to Mexico, here is a shortlist of Mexican state postal codes: **Baja California**: B.C.; **Baja California Sur**: B.C.S.; **Campeche**: Camp.; **Chiapas**: Chis.; **Chihuahua**: Chih.; **Distrito Federal (Mexico City)**: D.F.; **Guanajuato**: Gto.; **Guerrero**: Gro.; **Jalisco**: Jal.; **Estado de Mexico**: Edo. de Mex.; **Michoacán**: Mich.; **Morelos**: Mor.; **Nuevo Leon**: N.l.; **Oaxaca**: Oax.; **Querétaro**: Qro.; **Quintana Roo**: Q. Roo; **Sinaloa**: Sin.; **Sonora**: Son.; **Tabasco**: Tab.; **Veracruz**: Ver.; **Yucatán**: Yuc.; **Zacatecas**: Zac.

POSTAL RATES

It costs $3.50 pesos to send a postcard or letter weighing under 20 grams to the United States or Canada, and $4.40 pesos to Great Britain.

RECEIVING MAIL

To receive mail in Mexico, you can have it sent to your hotel or use *poste restante* at the post office. In the latter case, include the words "a/c Lista de Correos" (general delivery), followed by the city, state, postal code, and country. To use this service, you must first register with the local post office in which you wish to receive your mail. A list of names for whom mail has been received is posted and updated daily by the post office. American Express card- or traveler's-check holders can have mail sent to them at the local American Express office. For a list of the offices worldwide, write for the *Traveler's Companion* from **American Express** (⌧ Box 678, Canal Street Station, New York, NY 10013).

MONEY MATTERS

Prices in this book are quoted most often in U.S. dollars. We would prefer to list costs in pesos, but because the value of the currency fluctuates considerably, what costs 90 pesos today might cost 120 in six months, while the U.S. dollar value remains at $10. So instead of quoting prices in pesos and having them turn out to be quite inaccurate, we have decided to follow the unsavory practice of quoting in U.S. dollars.

Mexico has a reputation for being inexpensive, particularly compared with other North American vacation spots, like the Caribbean; the devaluation of the peso, started in late 1994, has made this particularly true, though prices of the large chain hotels, calculated in dollars, have not gone down, and some restaurant owners and merchants have raised their prices to compensate for the devaluation. In general, costs will vary with the when, where, and how of your travel in Mexico. "When" is discussed in When to Go, *below*. As to "how," if you are looking for a place as much as possible like home, travel only by air or package tour, stay at international hotel-chain properties, eat at restaurants catering to tourists, and shop at fixed-price tourist-oriented malls, you might not find Mexico such a bargain. If you want a closer look at the country and are not wedded to standardized creature comforts, you can spend as little as $25 a day on room, board, and local transportation. Speaking Spanish is also helpful in bargaining situations and when asking for dining recommendations. **As a rule, region by region, costs decrease as the amount of English that people speak decreases.**

Cancún, Puerto Vallarta, Mexico City, Monterrey, Acapulco, Ixtapa, Los Cabos, Manzanillo, and to a lesser extent Mazatlán and Huatulco are the most expensive places to visit in Mexico. All the beach towns, however, offer budget accommodations, and the smaller, less accessible ones are often more moderately priced, examples being the Gulf coast and northern Yucatán, parts of Quintana Roo, some of the less developed spots north and south of Puerto Vallarta in the states of Jalisco and Nayarit, Puerto Escondido, and the smaller Oaxacan coastal towns as well as those of Chiapas.

Average costs in major cities vary, although less than in the past because of the increase in business travelers. A stay in one of Mexico City's top hotels can cost more than $200 (as much or more than at the coastal resorts), but you can get away with a tab of $45 for two at what was once an expensive restaurant.

Probably the best value for your travel dollar is in smaller inland towns, such as San Cristóbal de las Casas, Mérida, Morelia, Guanajuato, and Oaxaca, where tourism is less developed. Although Oaxaca lodging can run more than $150 a night, simple colonial-style hotels with adequate accommodations for under $40 can be found, and tasty, filling meals are rarely more than $15.

Prices throughout this guide are given for adults. Substantially reduced fees are almost always available for children, students, and senior citizens. For information on taxes, *see* Taxes, *below.*

ATMS

ATMs are becoming commonplace in more and more Mexican towns and cities.

Before you leave home, **ask what the transaction fee will be** for taking out money in Mexico. Also **ask if you need to have a four-digit PIN** (Personal Identification Number) in order to take out money from Mexico. You might need to change that six-digit PIN before you leave home.

See Safety, *below,* on avoiding ATM robberies.

CREDIT CARDS

Traveler's checks and all major U.S. credit cards are accepted in most tourist areas of Mexico. Most smaller, less expensive restaurants and shops, however, will only take cash. Credit cards are generally not accepted in small towns and villages, except in tourist-oriented hotels. When shopping, you can usually get better prices if you **pay with cash.**

At the same time, when traveling internationally, you will **receive wholesale exchange rates** when you make purchases with credit cards. These exchange rates are usually better than rates that banks will give you for changing money. In Mexico the decision to pay cash or use a credit card might depend on whether or not the establishment in which you are making a purchase finds bargaining for prices acceptable.

To avoid fraud, it's wise to **make sure that "pesos" is clearly marked on all credit-card receipts.**

Throughout this guide, the following abbreviations are used: **AE,** American Express; **DC,** Diner's Club; **MC,** Master Card; and **V,** Visa.

➤ REPORTING LOST CARDS: Before you leave for Mexico, **be sure to find out your credit card companies' toll-free card replacement numbers**—they could be impossible to find out once you get to Mexico, and the calls you place to cancel your cards can be long ones. **Carry these numbers separately from your wallet** to be sure to have the numbers to call to report lost cards.

CURRENCY

At press time, the peso was still "floating" after the devaluation enacted by the Zedillo administration in late 1994. While exchange rates were as favorable as one U.S. dollar to $10.5 Mexican pesos, one Canadian dollar to $5.5 pesos, and a pound sterling to $13 pesos, the market and prices will continue to adjust. **Check with your bank or the financial pages of your local newspaper for current exchange rates.**

Mexican currency comes in denominations of 10-, 20-, 50-, 100-, 200-, 500-, and 1000-peso bills. Coins come in denominations of 20, 10, and 5 pesos and 50, 20, 10, and 5 centavos. Many of the coins and bills are very similar, so check carefully.

Dollar bills but not coins are widely accepted in many parts of the Yucatán, particularly in Cancún and Cozumel. However, you'll get your change in pesos. Many tourist shops and market vendors, as well as virtually all hotel service personnel, take them, too.

CURRENCY EXCHANGE

ATM transaction fees may be higher abroad than at home, but ATM rates are the best of all because they are based on wholesale rates offered only by major banks. And if you take out a fair amount of cash per withdrawl, the transaction fee becomes less of a strike against the exchange rate. Banks and *casas de cambio* (literally "money exchange houses") have the second-best exchange rates. The difference from one place to another is usually only a few centavos. You won't do as well at exchange booths in airports or rail and bus stations, in hotels, in restaurants, or in stores. To avoid airport exchange booths, **get a bit of local currency before leaving home.**

TRAVELER'S CHECKS

Do you need traveler's checks? It depends on where you're headed. If you're going to rural areas and small towns, go with cash; traveler's checks are best used in cities. Lost or stolen checks can usually be replaced within 24 hours. To ensure a speedy refund, buy your own traveler's checks— don't let someone else pay for them: irregularities like this can cause delays. The person who bought the checks should make the call to request a refund.

PACKING

When traveling internationally, it's always a good idea to pack a change of clothes in your carry-on bag in case your other luggage is lost. Take at least a change of underwear, essential toiletries, and a shirt—add to that a bathing suit if you're heading to a beach resort.

For resorts, bring lightweight sports clothes, bathing suits, and cover-ups for the beach. Bathing suits and immodest clothing are inappropriate for shopping and sightseeing, both in cities and beach resorts. Mexico City is a bit more formal than the resorts and, because of its high elevation, cooler. Men will want to bring lightweight suits or slacks and blazers for fancier restaurants; and women should pack tailored dresses or pants suits. Many restaurants require jacket and tie. Jeans are acceptable for shopping and sightseeing, but shorts are frowned upon for men and women. You'll need a lightweight topcoat for winter and an all-weather coat and umbrella in case of sudden summer rainstorms.

Resorts, such as Cancún and Acapulco, are both casual and elegant; you'll see high-style sportswear, cotton slacks and walking shorts, and plenty of colorful sundresses. The sun can be fierce; **bring a sun hat (or buy one locally) and sunscreen** for the beach and for sightseeing. You'll need a sweater or jacket to cope with hotel and restaurant air-conditioning, which can be glacial, and for occasional cool spells. Few restaurants require a jacket and tie.

In your carry-on luggage **bring an extra pair of eyeglasses or contact lenses** and **enough of any medication you take** to last the entire trip. You may also want your doctor to write a spare prescription using the drug's generic name, since brand names may vary from country to country. In luggage to be checked, **never pack prescription drugs or valuables.** To avoid customs delays, carry medications in their original packaging. And don't forget to copy down and carry addresses of offices that handle refunds of lost traveler's checks.

CHECKING LUGGAGE

International baggage allowances may be determined not by piece but by weight—generally 88 pounds (40 kilograms) in first class, 66 pounds (30 kilograms) in business class, and 44 pounds (20 kilograms) in economy.

Airline liability for baggage is limited to $1,250 per person on flights within the United States. On international flights it amounts to $9.07 per pound or $20 per kilogram for checked baggage (roughly $640 per 70-pound bag) and $400 per passenger for unchecked baggage. You can buy additional coverage at check-in for about $10 per $1,000 of coverage, but it excludes a rather extensive list of items, shown on your airline ticket.

Before departure **itemize your bags' contents** and their worth, and label the bags with your name, address, and phone number. (If you use your home address, cover it so that potential thieves can't see it readily.) Inside each bag **pack a copy of your itinerary.** At check-in **make sure that each bag is correctly tagged** with the destination airport's three-letter code. If your bags arrive damaged or fail to arrive at all, file a written report with the airline before leaving the airport.

PASSPORTS & VISAS

You'll need a passport to get to Mexico; **make two photocopies of the data page** before you go (one for someone at home and another for you, carried separately from your passport). If you lose your passport promptly call the nearest embassy or consulate and the local police.

ENTERING MEXICO

For stays of up to 180 days, **Americans must prove citizenship through either a valid passport, certified copy of a birth certificate or voter registration card (the last two must be accompanied by a government-issue photo ID).** Minors traveling with one parent need notarized permission from the absent parent. For stays of more than 180 days, all U.S. citizens, even infants, need a valid passport to enter Mexico. Minors also need parental permission.

Canadians need only proof of citizenship to enter Mexico for stays of up to six months.

Citizens of the United Kingdom need only a valid passport to enter Mexico for stays of up to three months.

PASSPORT OFFICES

The best time to apply for a passport or to renew is during the fall and winter. Before any trip, check your passport's expiration date, and, if necessary, renew it immediately.

➤ AUSTRALIAN CITIZENS: **Australian Passport Office** (☎ 131–232).
➤ CANADIAN CITIZENS: **Passport Office** (☎ 819/994–3500 or 800/567–6868).
➤ NEW ZEALAND CITIZENS: **New Zealand Passport Office** (☎ 04/494–0700 for information on how to apply; 04/474–8000 or 0800/225050 in New Zealand for information on applications already submitted).
➤ U.K. CITIZENS: **London Passport Office** (☎ 0990/210410) for fees and documentation requirements and to request an emergency passport.
➤ U.S. CITIZENS: **National Passport Information Center** (☎ 900/225–5674; calls are 35¢ per minute for automated service, $1.05 per minute for operator service).

SAFETY

The U.S. State Department has warned of "critical levels" of crime against tourists in Mexico, noting an increase in the level of violence of the crimes committed and what appeared to be a significant incidence of sexual assaults against women. Reports indicated that uniformed police officers were on occasion perpetrating the nonviolent crimes, sometimes stopping cars and seeking money (☞ Safety on the Road *in* Car Travel, *above*).

The largest increase in crime has taken place in Mexico City, where the age-old problem of pickpocketing has been overshadowed by robberies at gunpoint. Another development has been abductions and robberies in taxicabs hailed from the street (as opposed to hired from a hotel stand).

Many Americans are aware of Mexico's reputation for corruption. The patronage system is a well-entrenched part of Mexican politics and industry, and workers in the public sector—notably policemen and customs officials—are notoriously underpaid. Everyone has heard some horror story about highway assaults, pickpocketing, bribes, or foreigners languishing in Mexican jails.

It is important to note that these reports of crimes apply in large part to Mexico City and more remote areas of Oaxaca and Chiapas. So far, crime is not such a problem in the Heartland (cities like San Miguel de Allende), Puerto Vallarta, Cancún, and much of the rest of the country. Pickpocketing is usually the biggest concern.

Use common sense everywhere, but **exercise particular caution in Mexico City.** In addition, **it is best to avoid remote, less-traveled areas of Oaxaca and Chiapas** as crime in these areas can be more life-threatening. Do not pick up hitchhikers or hitchhike yourself. Also, try to use luxury buses (rather than second- or third-class vehicles), which use the safer toll roads—and it's best to travel only during the day. For the time being, **women should not venture alone onto uncrowded beaches,** and everyone should **avoid urges to get away from it all on your own (even as a couple) to go hiking in remote national parks.**

In Mexico City, **do not wear any valuables, including watches,** and try not to look too much like a tourist. Wear a money belt, put valuables in hotel safes, avoid driving on untraveled streets and roads at night, and carry your own baggage whenever possible, unless in a luxury hotel. Also, you won't need your passport in the city, so leave it in the hotel safe—replacing it would be more trouble than you need.

Country-wide, **take only registered hotel taxis or have a hotel concierge call a *sitio* (stationed cab)—do not hail taxis on the street under any circumstances.** Also, if you must use a ATM machine, do so during the day and in big, enclosed commercial areas. Avoid the glass-enclosed street variety of banks where you may be more vulnerable to thieves who force you to withdraw money for them; abduction is also possible. This cannot be stressed strongly enough.

Bear in mind that reporting a crime to the police is often a frustrating experience unless you speak excellent Spanish and have a great deal of patience. If you are the victim of an assault, contact your local consular agent or the consular section of your country's embassy in Mexico City, especially if you need medical attention (☞ Mexico City A to Z *in* Chapter 2).

WOMEN IN MEXICO

Women traveling alone are likely to be subjected to *piropos* (catcalls). To avoid this, try not to wear tight clothes or provocative miniskirts or enter street bars or cantinas alone. Your best strategy is always to try and ignore the offender and go on about your business. If the situation seems to be getting out of hand, do not hesitate to ask someone for help. Piropos are one thing, but outright harassment of women is not considered acceptable behavior. If you express outrage, you should find no shortage of willing defenders.

SENIOR-CITIZEN TRAVEL

To qualify for age-related discounts **mention your senior-citizen status up front** when booking hotel reservations (not when checking out) and before you're seated in restaurants (not when paying the bill). When renting a car ask about promotional car-rental discounts, which can be cheaper than senior-citizen rates.

➤ EDUCATIONAL PROGRAMS: **Elderhostel** (✉ 75 Federal St., 3rd fl., Boston, MA 02110, ☎ 877/426–8056, FAX 877/426–2166). **Interhostel** (✉ University of New Hampshire, 6 Garrison Ave., Durham, NH 03824, ☎ 603/862–1147 or 800/733–9753, FAX 603/862–1113).

SHOPPING

At least three varieties of outlets sell Mexican crafts: indoor and outdoor municipal markets, shops run by Fonart (a government agency to promote Mexican crafts), and tourist boutiques in towns, shopping malls, and hotels. If you buy in the municipal shops or markets, you can avoid the VAT and you'll be able to pay in pesos or dollars. Be sure to **take your time and inspect merchandise closely:** you'll find bargains, but quality can be inconsistent. Fonart shops are a good reference for quality and price (the latter are fixed), and they accept credit cards. Boutiques also accept credit cards if not dollars; although their prices may be higher, they are convenient, and sometimes carry one-of-a-kind items you won't find anywhere else. (You may be asked to pay up to 7% more on credit-card purchases; savvy shoppers with cash have greater bargaining clout.) The 15% tax (I.V.A.; 10% in the states of Quintana Roo, Baja California, and Baja California Sur) is charged on most purchases but is often included in the price or disregarded by eager or desperate vendors.

It is not always true that the closer you are to the source of an article, the better the selection and price are likely to be. Mexico City, Guadalajara, Páztcuaro, San Miguel de Allende, Puerto Vallarta, Oaxaca, San Cristóbal de las Casas, and Mérida have some of the best selections of crafts—and bargains as well. Prices are usually higher and selections more touristy at beach resorts.

Bargaining is widely accepted in markets, but you should understand that not all vendors will start out with outrageous prices. If you feel the price quoted is too high, start off by offering no more than half the asking price and then slowly go up, usually to about 70% of the original price. Always **shop around.** In major shopping areas like San Miguel, shops will wrap and send purchases back to the United States via a package delivery company. In some areas you will be able to have items such as huaraches (leather sandals), clothing, and blankets tailor-made. If you buy woolens or wooden items, it's wise to freeze or microwave them when you return to destroy possible insect infestation. Items made from tortoiseshell and black coral are not allowed into the United States.

STUDENTS IN MEXICO

➤ STUDENT I.D.s & SERVICES: **Council on International Educational Exchange** (CIEE, ✉ 205 E. 42nd St., 14th fl., New York, NY 10017, ☎ 212/822–2600 or 888/268–6245, FAX 212/822–2699) for mail orders only, in the U.S. **Travel Cuts** (✉ 187 College St., Toronto, Ontario M5T 1P7, ☎ 416/979–2406 or 800/667–2887) in Canada.

TAXES

Mexico charges an airport departure tax of US$18 or the peso equivalent for international and domestic flights. This tax is usually included in the price of your ticket, but check to be certain. Traveler's checks and credit cards are not accepted at the airport as payment for this.

Many states are charging a 2% tax on accommodations, the funds from which are being used for tourism promotion.

VALUE-ADDED TAX (V.A.T.)

Mexico has a value-added tax of 15% (10% in the states of Quintana Roo, Baja California, and Baja California Sur) called I.V.A. (*impuesto de valor agregado*), which is occasionally (and illegally) waived for cash purchases. Other taxes and charges apply for phone calls, dining, and lodging.

TAXIS

Government-certified taxis have a license with a photo of the driver and a taxi number prominently displayed, as well as a meter. However, in many cities, taxis charge by zones. In this case, be sure to agree on a fare before setting off. For reasons of security, especially in Mexico City, it is always best to call a *sitio* cab rather than to flag one on the street. Tipping is not necessary unless the driver helps you with your bags, in which case a few pesos are appropriate.

AT THE AIRPORT

From the airport, **take the authorized taxi service.** Purchase the taxi vouchers sold at stands inside or just outside the terminal, which ensure that your fare is established beforehand. However, before you purchase your ticket, it's wise to locate the taxi originating and destination zones on a map and make sure your ticket is properly zoned; if you only need a ticket to zone three, don't pay for a ticket to zone four or five. Don't leave your luggage unattended while making transportation arrangements.

IN CITIES & BEACH RESORTS

In Mexican cities, **take a taxi rather than public transportation,** which, though inexpensive, is frequently slow and sometimes patrolled by pickpockets. Always **establish the fare beforehand,** and **always count your change.** In most of the beach resorts, there are inexpensive fixed-route fares, but if you don't ask, or your Spanish isn't great, you may get taken. In cities, especially the capital, be certain that the meter is running before getting in, and remember that there is usually an extra charge after 10 PM. For out-of-town and hourly services, negotiate a rate in advance; many drivers will start by asking how much you want to pay to get a sense of how street-smart you are. In all cases, if you are unsure of what a fare should be, ask your hotel's front desk personnel or bell captain.

Hire taxis only from hotels and taxi stands (sitios), or use those that you have summoned by phone. Street taxis might be the cheapest, but an alarming increase in abductions and violent crime involves street cabs—for safety's sake, under no circumstances should you take one. And never leave luggage unattended in a taxi.

In addition to private taxis, many cities have bargain-price collective taxi services using VW minibuses (called *combis*) and sedans. The service is called *colectivo* or, in Mexico City, *pesero*. Peseros run along fixed routes, and you hail them on the street and tell the driver where you are going. The fare—which you pay before you get out—is based on distance traveled. We recommend that you take only the *colectivos* (special airport taxis) that transport passengers from—and sometimes to—airports. In places like Cozumel you'll find that collectivos only—not taxis—are permitted to take passengers from airport terminals into town.

(For information on taxis in Mexico City, *see* Chapter 2.)

TELEPHONES

Thanks to its 1991 privatization, *Teléfonos de México* (Mexico's phone service)—which was for so long exasperatingly inefficient—is gradually being overhauled. And as of January 1997, Teléfonos de México's monopoly ended, enabling competition from several long-distance services,

including MCI and AT&T. Many phones, especially in the better city hotels, have Touch-Tone (digital) circuitry. If you think you'll need to access an automated phone system or voice mail in the United States and you don't know what phone service will be available, it's a good idea to take along a Touch-Tone simulator (you can buy them for about $17 at most electronics stores). With the increased installation of new phone and fax lines in major Mexican cities, many phone numbers are in the process of being changed; a recording may offer the new number, so it's useful to learn the Spanish words for numbers 1 through 9 (☞ Spanish Vocabulary, which follows Chapter 14, Portraits).

CALLING HOME

To make a call to the United States or Canada, **dial 001 before the area code and number;** to call Europe, Latin America, or Japan, **dial 00** before the country and city codes. When calling home, the country code for the **U.S. and Canada** is 1, the **U.K.** 44, **Australia** 61, **New Zealand** 64, and **South Africa** 27.

AT&T, MCI, and Sprint international access codes make calling the United States relatively convenient, but you may find the local access number blocked in many hotel rooms. First ask the hotel operator to connect you. If the hotel operator balks, ask for an international operator, or dial the international operator yourself. One way to improve your odds of getting connected to your long-distance carrier is to travel with more than one company's calling card (a hotel may block Sprint, for example, but not MCI). If all else fails, call from a pay phone in the hotel lobby.

➤ ACCESS CODES: **AT&T Direct** (☎ 001–800/462–4240 in Mexico). **MCI WorldPhone** (☎ 001–800/674–7000 in Mexico). **Sprint International Access** (001–800/877–8000 in Mexico).

COUNTRY CODE

The country code for Mexico is 52.

LONG-DISTANCE CALLS

For local or long-distance calls, one option is to find a **caseta de larga**

distancia, a telephone service usually operated out of a store such as a papelería (stationery store), pharmacy, restaurant, or other small business; look for the phone symbol on the door. Casetas may cost more to use than pay phones, but you have a better chance of immediate success. To make a direct long-distance call, tell the person on duty the number you'd like to call, and he or she will give you a rate and dial for you. Rates seem to vary widely, so shop around. Sometimes you can make collect calls from casetas, and sometimes you cannot, depending on the individual operator and possibly your degree of visible desperation. Casetas will generally charge 50¢–$1.50 to place a collect call (some charge by the minute); it's usually better to call *por cobrar* (collect) from a pay phone.

PHONE CARDS

In some areas, pay phones accept prepaid cards, called Ladatel cards, sold in 30-, or 50-peso denominations (approximately $3 and $5) at newsstands or pharmacies. Many pay phones in Mexico only accept these cards; coin-only pay phones are usually broken. Still other phones have two unmarked slots, one for a Ladatel (a Spanish acronym for "long-distance direct dialing") card and the other for a credit card. These are primarily for Mexican bank cards, but some accept U.S. Visa or Master-Card, though *not* U.S. telephone credit cards.

To use a Ladatel card, simply insert it in the appropriate slot, dial 001 (for calls to the States) or 01 (for calls in Mexico), and the area code and number you're trying to reach. Credit is deleted from the card as you use it, and your balance is displayed on a small screen on the phone.

PUBLIC PHONES

The variety of public phones that exist in the country can be confusing at best. Occasionally you'll see traditional black, square phones with push buttons or dials; although they have a coin slot on top, you may make local calls on them for free. Other new phones have an unmarked slot for Ladatel cards (☞ *above*).

TOLL-FREE NUMBERS

Toll-free numbers in Mexico start with an 800 prefix. To reach them, you need to dial 01 before the number. In this guide, Mexico-only toll-free numbers appear as follows: 01–800/12–345 (numbers can also have six or seven digits). Some 800 numbers work in the U.S., Canada, *and* Mexico. They are listed simply: 800/123–4567. Toll-free numbers that work only in the U.S. and/or Canada are labeled accordingly.

TIPPING

When tipping in Mexico, remember that the minimum wage is the equivalent of $3 a day and that the vast majority of workers in the tourist industry live barely above the poverty line. However, there are Mexicans who think in dollars and know, for example, that in the United States porters are tipped about $1 a bag; many of them expect the peso equivalent from foreigners but are happy to accept 5 pesos a bag from Mexicans. They will complain either verbally or with a facial expression if they feel they deserve more—you and your conscience must decide. Following are some general guidelines. Naturally, larger tips are always welcome.

Porters and bellboys at airports and at moderate and inexpensive hotels: $2 per bag.
Porters at expensive hotels: $2 per person.
Tour Guides and drivers: at least $1 per half day, minimum.
Maids: $1 per night (all hotels).
Waiters: 10%–15% of the bill, depending on service (make sure a 10%–15% service charge has not already been added to the bill, although this practice is more common in resorts.
Taxi drivers: Tipping necessary only if the driver helps with your bags—5 to 10 pesos should be sufficient, depending on the extent of the help.
Gas station attendants: 3–5 pesos.
Parking attendants and theater ushers: 5–10 pesos. Some restaurants and theaters charge for "valet parking" service; it's still customary to tip the attendant at least 10 pesos.

TOURS & PACKAGES

BOOKING WITH AN AGENT

Travel agents are excellent resources. But it's a good idea to collect brochures from several agencies because some agents' suggestions may be influenced by relationships with tour and package firms that reward them for volume sales. If you have a special interest **find an agent with expertise in that area**; ASTA (☞ Travel Agencies, *below*) has a database of specialists worldwide.

Make sure your travel agent knows the accommodations and other services of the place they're recommending. Ask about the hotel's location, room size, beds, and whether it has a pool, room service, or programs for children, if you care about these. Has your agent been there in person or sent others whom you can contact?

Do some homework on your own, too: Local tourism boards can provide information about lesser-known and small-niche operators, some of which may sell only direct.

BUYER BEWARE

Each year consumers are stranded or lose their money when tour operators—even large ones with excellent reputations—go out of business. So **check out the operator.** Ask several travel agents about its reputation, and try to **book with a company that has a consumer-protection program.** (Look for information in the company's brochure.) In the United States, members of the National Tour Association and United States Tour Operators Association are required to set aside funds to cover your payments and travel arrangements in case the company defaults. It's also a good idea to choose a company that participates in the American Society of Travel Agent's Tour Operator Program (TOP).

Make sure you know exactly what your trip includes, and **beware of hidden costs.** Are taxes, tips, and transfers included? Entertainment and excursions? These can add up.

➤ TOUR-OPERATOR RECOMMENDATIONS: **American Society of Travel Agents** (☞ Travel Agencies, *below*).

National Tour Association (NTA, ✉ 546 E. Main St., Lexington, KY 40508, ☎ 606/226–4444 or 800/682–8886). **United States Tour Operators Association** (USTOA, ✉ 342 Madison Ave., Suite 1522, New York, NY 10173, ☎ 212/599–6599 or 800/468–7862, FAX 212/599–6744).

THEME TRIPS

➤ ART & ARCHAEOLOGY: **Archaeological Conservancy** (✉ 5301 Central Ave. NE, #1218, Albuquerque, NM 87108-1517, ☎ 505/266–1540). **Crow Canyon Archaeological Center** (✉ 2339 Road K, Cortez CO 81321, ☎ 970/565–8975 or 800/422–8975, FAX 970/565–4859). **Far Horizons Archaeological & Cultural Trips** (✉ Box 91900, Albuquerque, NM 87199-1900, ☎ 505/343–9400 or 800/552–4575, FAX 505/343–8076). **Smithsonian Study Tours and Seminars** (☞ Copper Canyon, *above*).

➤ BIRDING: **Field Guides** (✉ Box 160723, Austin, TX 78716-0723, ☎ 512/327–4953 or 800/728–4953, FAX 512/327–9231). **Victor Emanuel Nature Tours** (✉ 2525 Wallingwood Rd., Bldg. 10, Austin, TX 78746, ☎ 512/328–5221 or 800/328–8368, FAX 512/328–2919); **Wings** (✉ 1643 N. Alvernon Way, Suite 105, Tucson, AZ 85712, ☎ 520/320–9868, FAX 520/320–9373).

➤ BICYCLING: **Backroads** (✉ 801 Cedar St., Berkeley, CA 94710-1800, ☎ 510/527–1555 or 800/462–2848, FAX 510/527–1444). **Edelweiss Bike Travel** (✉ 129 Hillside Ave., Williston Park, NY 11596, ☎ 516/746–6761 or 800/877–2784, FAX 516/746–6690). **Imagine Tours** (✉ Box 123, Davis, CA 95617, ☎ 530/758–8782 or 888/592–8687, FAX 530/758–8778).

➤ BUTTERFLY SANCTUARIES: **Natural Habitat Adventures** (✉ 2945 Center Green Ct., Boulder, CO 80301, ☎ 303/449–3711 or 800/543–8917, FAX 303/449–3712); **Remarkable Journeys** (✉ Box 31855, Houston, TX 77231-1855, ☎ 713/721–2517 or 800/856–1993, FAX 713/728–8334).

➤ HORSEBACK RIDING: **Equitour FITS Equestrian** (✉ Box 807, Dubois, WY 82513, ☎ 307/455–3363 or 800/545–0019, FAX 307/455–2354).

➤ WALKING: **Backroads** (☞ *Bicycling, above*). **Butterfield & Robinson** (✉ 70 Bond St., Toronto, Ontario, Canada M5B 1X3, ☎ 416/864–1354 or 800/678–1147, FAX 416/864–0541).

➤ WHALE-WATCHING: **American Cetacean Society** (✉ 801 Stanley Ave., Long Beach, CA 90804, ☎ 562/438–8960, FAX 310/548–6950). **Planet Expeditions** (✉ 2549 Center Green Ct. S., Suite H, Boulder, CO 80301, ☎ 800/233–2433, FAX 303/349–3712).

TRAIN TRAVEL

By late 1997 private companies operating the Mexican railroads decided that passenger service was not profitable enough. Private rooms and berths were taken out, and only general first-class service, *Clase única primera* remained, entitling passengers to a reserved reclining seat. As first-class bus service proliferates throughout the country, first-class rail cars and schedules are being cut, often with little or no advance notice.

As a result, rail travel in Mexico is not recommended, excepting the spectacular train ride through the Copper Canyon (☞ Chapter 5), which you can do either on Mexican trains or privately run trains that originate in the United States.

➤ TRAIN INFORMATION: **Ferrocarriles Nacionales de México** (Mexican National Railways, ☎ 5/547–1097) has information on trains throughout Mexico. From the United States, you can get information on trains and rail-hotel packages by contacting **Mexico by Train** (☎ FAX 956/725–3659 or 800/321–1699).

TRAVEL AGENCIES

A good travel agent puts your needs first. Look for an agency that has been in business at least five years, emphasizes customer service, and has someone on staff who specializes in your destination. In addition **make sure the agency belongs to a professional trade organization.** The American Society of Travel Agents (ASTA), with 27,000 agents in some 170 countries, is the largest and most influential in the field. Operating under the motto "Integrity in Travel," it maintains and enforces a strict code of ethics and will step in to help

mediate any agent-client disputes if necessary. ASTA also maintains a Web site that includes a directory of agents. If a travel agency is also acting as your tour operator *see* Buyer Beware *in* Tours & Packages, *above*.

➤ LOCAL AGENT REFERRALS: **American Society of Travel Agents** (ASTA, ☎ 800/965–2782 24-hr hot line, FAX 703/684–8319, www.astanet.com). **Association of British Travel Agents** (✉ 55–57 Newman St., London W1P 4AH, ☎ 0171/637–2444, FAX 0171/637–0713). **Association of Canadian Travel Agents** (✉ 1729 Bank St., Suite 201, Ottawa, Ontario K1V 7Z5, ☎ 613/521–0474, FAX 613/521–0805). **Australian Federation of Travel Agents** (✉ Level 3, 309 Pitt St., Sydney 2000, ☎ 02/9264–3299, FAX 02/9264–1085). **Travel Agents' Association of New Zealand** (✉ Box 1888, Wellington 10033, ☎ 04/499–0104, FAX 04/499–0786).

VISITOR INFORMATION

➤ TOURIST INFORMATION Mexican Government Tourist Offices (MGO):**United States:** (☎ 800/446–3942 nationwide; 31 East 63rd St.; 3rd fl., New York, NY 10021, ☎ 212/821–0314, FAX 212/821–0367; 300 North Michigan Ave., 4th fl. Chicago, IL 60601, ☎ 312/606–9273, FAX 312/606–9015; 2401 West 6th St., 5th fl. Los Angeles, CA 90057, ☎ 213/351–2069, FAX 213/351–2074; 10440 West Office Drive Houston, TX 77042, ☎ 713/780–3740, FAX 713/780–8367; 691 Bricknell Key Drive Miami, FL 33131, ☎ 305/381–6996, FAX 305/381–8982).

Canada: (1 Place Ville Marie, Suite 1510, Montréal, Québec H3B 2B5, ☎ 514/871–1052, FAX 514/871–3825; 2 Bloor St. W, Suite 1502, Toronto, Ontario M4W 3E2, ☎ 416/925–0704, FAX 416/925–6061; 999 W. Hastings St., Suite 1610, Vancouver, British Columbia V6C 2WC, ☎ 604/669–2845, FAX 604/669–3498).

United Kingdom: (60 Trafalgar Sq., London WC2N 5DS, ☎ 0171/734–1058, FAX 0171/930–9202).

Mexico: Ministry of Tourism Presidente Masaryk 172, Mexico, D.F. 11550, ☎ 5/250–0123).

➤ U.S. GOVERNMENT ADVISORIES: **U.S. Department of State** (✉ Overseas Citizens Services Office, Room 4811 N.S., 2201 C St. NW, Washington, DC 20520; ☎ 202/647–5225 for interactive hot line; 301/946–4400 for computer bulletin board; FAX 202/647–3000 for interactive hot line); enclose a self-addressed, stamped, business-size envelope.

WHEN TO GO

Mexico is sufficiently large and geographically diverse enough that you can find a place to visit any time of year. October through May are generally the driest months; during the peak of the rainy season (June–September), it may rain for a few hours every day. But the sun often shines for the rest of the day, and the reduced off-season rates may well compensate for the reduced tanning time.

From December through the second week after Easter Week, the Mexican resorts—where the vast majority of tourists go—are the most crowded and therefore the most expensive. To avoid the masses, the highest prices, and the worst rains, **consider visiting Mexico during October, November, April, or May.** Hotel rates at the beach resorts can be cut by as much as 30% in the shoulder season, 50% in the off-season.

Mexicans travel during traditional holiday periods—Christmas through Jan.6, Three Kings Day, *Semana Santa* (Holy Week, the week before and after Easter), and school vacations in the summertime—as well as over extended national holiday weekends, called *puentes* (bridges). Festivals play a big role in Mexican national life. If you plan to travel during a major national event, reserve both lodgings and transportation well in advance.

CLIMATE

The variations in Mexico's climate are not surprising considering the size of the country. The coasts and low-lying sections of the interior are often very hot if not actually tropical, with temperatures ranging from 17°C to 31°C (63°F to 88°F) in winter and well above 32°C (90°F) in summer. A more temperate area ranging from 16°C to 21°C (60°F to 70°F) is found at altitudes of 1,220–1,830 meters (4,000–6,000 feet). In general, the high central plateau on which Mexico City, Guadalajara, and many of the country's colonial cities are located is springlike year-round.

➤ FORECASTS: **Weather Channel Connection** (☎ 900/932–8437), 95¢ per minute from a Touch-Tone phone.

ACAPULCO (PACIFIC COAST)

Jan.	88F	31C	May	90F	32C	Sept.	90F	32C
	72	22		75	24		75	24
Feb.	88F	31C	June	90F	32C	Oct.	90F	32C
	72	22		77	25		75	24
Mar.	88F	31C	July	90F	32C	Nov.	90F	32C
	72	22		77	25		73	23
Apr.	90F	32C	Aug.	91F	33C	Dec.	88F	31C
	73	23		77	25		71	22

COZUMEL (CARIBBEAN COAST)

Jan.	84F	29C	May	91F	33C	Sept.	89F	32C
	66	19		73	23		75	24
Feb.	84F	29C	June	89F	32C	Oct.	87F	31C
	66	19		75	24		73	23
Mar.	88F	31C	July	91F	33C	Nov.	86F	30C
	69	21		73	23		71	22
Apr.	89F	32C	Aug.	91F	33C	Dec.	84F	29C
	71	22		73	23		68	20

ENSENADA (BAJA CALIFORNIA)

Jan.	66F	19C	May	70F	21C	Sept.	79F	26C
	45	7		52	11		59	15
Feb.	68F	20C	June	73F	23C	Oct.	75F	24C
	45	7		54	12		54	12
Mar.	68F	20C	July	77F	25C	Nov.	72F	22C
	46	8		61	16		48	9
Apr.	69F	21C	Aug.	79F	26C	Dec.	68F	20C
	48	9		61	16		45	7

LA PAZ (BAJA CALIFORNIA SUR)

Jan.	73F	23C	May	91F	33C	Sept.	95F	35C
	54	12		59	15		73	23
Feb.	77F	25C	June	95F	35C	Oct.	91F	33C
	54	12		64	18		66	19
Mar.	80F	27C	July	97F	36C	Nov.	84F	29C
	54	12		71	22		661	16
Apr.	86F	30C	Aug.	97F	36C	Dec.	77F	25C
	55	13		73	23		54	12

MEXICO CITY (CENTRAL MEXICO)

Jan.	70F	21C	May	79F	26C	Sept.	72F	22C
	44	6		54	12		52	11
Feb.	73F	23C	June	77F	25C	Oct.	72F	22C
	45	7		54	12		50	10
Mar.	79F	26C	July	73F	23C	Nov.	72F	22C
	48	9		52	11		46	8
Apr.	81F	27C	Aug.	73F	23C	Dec.	70F	21C
	50	10		54	12		45	7

MONTERREY (NORTHEAST MEXICO)

Jan.	68F	20C	May	88F	31C	Sept.	88F	31C
	48	9		68	20		70	21
Feb.	73F	23F	June	91F	33C	Oct.	81F	27C
	52	11		72	22		63	17
Mar.	79F	26C	July	91F	34C	Nov.	73F	23C
	57	14		72	22		55	13
Apr.	86F	30C	Aug.	93F	34C	Dec.	70F	21C
	64	18		72	22		50	10

SAN MIGUEL DE ALLENDE (HEARTLAND)

Jan.	75F	24C	May	88F	31C	Sept.	79F	26C
	45	9	59	15		59	15	
Feb.	79F	26C	June	88F	30C	Oct.	79F	26C
	48	9	59	15		54	12	
Mar.	86F	30C	July	82F	28C	Nov.	75F	24C
	54	12	59	15		50	10	
Apr.	88F	31C	Aug.	82F	28C	Dec.	75F	24C
	57	14	59	15		46	8	

INDEX

L@@king © FOR A great place to go?

We know just the place. In fact, it attracts more than 125,000 visitors a day, making it one of the world's most popular travel destinations. It's previewtravel.com, the Web's comprehensive resource for travelers. It gives you access to over 500 airlines, 25,000 hotels, rental cars, cruises, vacation packages and support from travel experts 24 hours a day. Plus great information from Fodor's travel guides and travelers just like you. All of which makes previewtravel.com quite a find.

Preview Travel has everything you need to plan & book your next trip.

air, car & hotel reservations

vacation packages & cruises

destination planning & travel tips

24-hour customer service

previewtravel.com

aol keyword: previewtravel
www.previewtravel.com

FODOR'S MEXICO 2000

EDITOR: Stephen Wolf

Editorial Contributors: Patricia Alisau, Sean Godfrey, Gina Hyams, Shelagh McNally, Maribeth Mellin, Michael Oliver, Jane Onstott

Editorial Production: Nicole Revere

Maps: David Lindroth, *cartographer*; Steven Amsterdam, *map editor*

Design: Fabrizio La Rocca, *creative director*; Guido Caroti, *art director*

Cover Design: Pentagram

Production/Manufacturing: Rebecca Zeiler

Picture Editor: Jolie Novak

Photo Researcher: Melanie Marin

Cover Photo: Joan Iaconetti

ISBN 0–679–00319-3

ISSN 0196-5999

SPECIAL SALES

Fodor's Travel Publications are available at special discounts for bulk purchases for sales promotions or premiums. Special editions, including personalized covers, excerpts of existing guides, and corporate imprints, can be created in large quantities for special needs. For more information, contact your local bookseller or write to Special Markets, Fodor's Travel Publications, 201 East 50th Street, New York, NY 10022. Inquiries from Canada should be directed to your local Canadian bookseller or sent to Random House of Canada, Ltd., Marketing Department, 2775 Matheson Boulevard East, Mississauga, Ontario L4W 4P7. Inquiries from the United Kingdom should be sent to Fodor's Travel Publications, 20 Vauxhall Bridge Road, London SW1V 2SA, England.

PRINTED IN THE UNITED STATES OF AMERICA

10 9 8 7 6 5 4 3 2 1

IMPORTANT TIP

Although all prices, opening times, and other details in this book are based on information supplied to us at press time, changes occur all the time in the travel world, and Fodor's cannot accept responsibility for facts that become outdated or for inadvertent errors or omissions. So **always confirm information when it matters,** especially if you're making a detour to visit a specific place.

PHOTOGRAPHY

Joan Iaconetti, *cover (Cancún).*

Baja California Tours, *8 top, 9 bottom, 19C.*

Corbis, *1, 2 top left, 2 top right, 2 bottom left, 2 bottom center, 2 bottom right, 3 top left, 3 top right, 3 bottom left, 3 bottom right, 6C, 13C, 30E.*

Pablo Garber, *6A, 7F, 19 bottom left, 19D.*

Peter Guttman, *8A.*

Hotel Chan-Kah, *30J.*

The Image Bank: *Carolyn Brown, 15E. Luis Catañeda, 21C, 24G, 29 top. Angelo Cavalli, 22A, 23D, 24H, 25I. Steve Dunwell, 16A, 16C. Tom Owen Edmunds, 7E, 11A, 21B. Grant V. Faint, 23C, 25 bottom. Andre Gallant, 15C. Cyril Isy-Schwart, 20A, 20C. Gill C. Kenny, 10A. Don Klumpp, 12A. Mahaux Photography, 17B, 22B. Michael Melford, 8B. Andrea Pistolesi, 24F. Anne Rippy, 13B, 28, 30H. Guido Alberto Rossi, 4-5, 7D, 9C, 14B, 20B. Harald Sund, 6B. Roberto Valladares, 16B, 32. Luis Veiga, 23E, 29 bottom.*

La Casa de Espiritus Alegres, *30F.*

Las Ventanas al Paraíso, *30B.*

Marcella Martinez Associates, Inc., *26, 30C.*

Museo de Arte Contemporaneo de Monterrey (MARCO), *30I.*

Christie Parker, *14 top.*

Ashlesha Patel, *30D.*

PhotoDisc, *15D, 17A, 18A, 18B, 21A.*

Querétaro Tourism, *27 top.*

Quinta Real, *30G.*

SNA Jolobil, S.C., *27 bottom, 30A.*

Westin Brisas Resort, *17C.*

Nik Wheeler, *9D, 10B, 10C, 11B, 11C, 13D, 14A.*

ABOUT OUR WRITERS

Every Y2K trip is a significant trip. So if there was ever a time you needed travel information, it's now. Acutely aware of that fact, we've pulled out all stops in preparing *Fodor's Mexico 2000*. To help you zero in on what to see in Mexico, we've gathered some great color photos of the key sights in every state. To show you how to pull it all together, we've created great itineraries and neighborhood walks. And to direct you to the places that are truly worth your time and money, we've rallied the team of know-it-alls we're pleased to call our writers. If you knew them, you'd poll them for tips yourself.

A psychologist-turned-journalist and archaeology buff, **Patricia Alisau** was so drawn to the surrealism of Mexico City that she turned a one-week vacation into a 20-year Mexican sojourn. She was restaurant-and-nightclub columnist for the *News*, Mexico's English-language daily, and has written for Mexico's *Vogue* magazine. This year, she updated our Acapulco and Smart Travel Tips chapters.

Paige Bierma, who updated the Mexico City and Side Trips chapters, covers political and social issues for major U.S. newspapers and magazines. After working as a reporter for several years in her native Iowa and in California, she headed south of the border five years ago to bring Mexican news to the breakfast tables of the north-of-the-border public.

After crisscrossing the U.S. for 16 years as a restaurateur and recreational worker, Guadalajara and Pacific Coast Resorts updater **Sean Godfrey** came to Mexico for some Spanish lessons and never left. He is co-publisher of the *Guadalajara Colony Reporter,* a weekly newspaper for North Americans living in Jalisco.

In 1997, **Gina Hyams** and her husband and toddler daughter traded in their San Francisco yuppie lifestyle for the good life in Mexico. She is at work on a travel/parenting memoir about their experience, currently titled *Escape Artists,* excerpts of which appeared on-line in *Salon* magazine. They live in San Miguel de Allende.

Intrepid, discerning Yucatán updater **Shelagh McNally** braved the slings and arrows of contentious hotel owners to separate the wheat from the chaff on the Caribbean coast from Cancún to Chetumal. Her reporter's persistence and objectivity—along with her knowledge of Yucatán ecosystems—have refreshed our perspective on this popular corner of Mexico.

Maribeth Mellin, recent recipient of the prestigious *Pluma de Plata* award for writing on Mexico, writes in an office filled with photos and artifacts from Mexico's two isolated peninsulas, including a snapshot of the 140-pound marlin she caught in the Sea of Cortés. She refused to marry her husband until he rambled through her beloved Yucatán with her in a rented VW bug. She also covers Mexico for *San Diego Magazine*.

Despite the traumas inflicted by his first-trip-to-Mexico horrors in a Tijuana jail—at a rather tender age—Sonora and Copper Canyon updater **Michael Oliver** somehow managed to get himself hooked on Mexico. Since then he has crossed the border countless times to kayak, surf, fish, and explore jungle and beaches countrywide—and write about it for the San Francisco *Chronicle, Adventure Journal,* and *Sierra*.

An inveterate traveler, **Jane Onstott** has trekked extensively in Mexico and Latin America. She has survived a near plunge into a gorge in the highlands of Mexico, a knife-wielding robber in Madrid, and a financial shipwreck on one of the more remote Galápagos islands. Having written and edited guidebooks to Mexico, Ecuador, and Southern California, Jane lives in San Diego.

We'd also like to acknowledge Aeroméxico for their considerable assistance with travel arrangements.

Don't Forget to Write

We love feedback—positive and negative—and follow up on all suggestions. So contact the Mexico editor at editors@fodors.com or c/o Fodor's, 201 E. 50th Street, New York, New York 10022. Have a wonderful trip!

Karen Cure
Editorial Director